# Georgia's Roster of the Revolution

Containing a List of the State's Defenders; Officers
and Men; Soldiers and Sailors; Partisans and
Regulars; Whether Enlisted from Georgia
or Settled in Georgia After the
Close of Hostilities

Compiled under Authority of
**THE LEGISLATURE**
From Various Sources, Including Official Documets,
Both State and Federal, Certificates of Service,
Land Grants, Pension Rolls,
and Other Records

*Lucian Lamar Knight, LL. D., F. R. S.*
State Historian and Director of the Department
of Archives and History

HERITAGE BOOKS
2008

## HERITAGE BOOKS
*AN IMPRINT OF HERITAGE BOOKS, INC.*

**Books, CDs, and more—Worldwide**

For our listing of thousands of titles see our website
at
www.HeritageBooks.com

A Facsimile Reprint
Published 2008 by
HERITAGE BOOKS, INC.
Publishing Division
100 Railroad Ave. #104
Westminster, Maryland 21157

Originally published 1920
Atlanta, Georgia

— Publisher's Notice —
In reprints such as this, it is often not possible to remove blemishes from the original. We feel the contents of this book warrant its reissue despite these blemishes and hope you will agree and read it with pleasure.

International Standard Book Number: 978-0-7884-2004-7

# Table of Contents

Compiler's Preface, ............................................................................. 5
Letter from Secretary Knox, of the U. S. War Department, showing the number of Georgia troops enlisted, State and Continental, ............ 7
Officers of the Georgia Battalion, Feb. 16, 1776, ........................... 9
Letter from Col. McIntosh to Gen. Washington, Feb. 16, 1776, ........ 11
Letter from Col. McIntosh to Gen. Washington, April 28, 1776, ........ 13
Names of Officers in the Continental Line of the Georgia Brigade during the Revolutionary War, including Infantry, Dragoons, Legionary Corps and General Staff, ................................................................. 15
Names of Officers and Soldiers who made Application for Land, under Act of Feb. 17, 1783, .................................................................... 17
Certificates of Service in the American Revolution, on file in the Office of Secretary of State, .................................................................... 20
Explanatory: Head-Rights and Land-Lottery Grants to Revolutionary Soldiers ........................................................................................ 193
Bounty Surveys (i. e., Head-Rights) recorded by the Surveyor-General in the Office of Secretary of State, ............................................. 198
Land Lottery Grants: ........................................................................ 313
   Irwin County Lottery List, ........................................................... 314
   Jefferson County Lottery List, ..................................................... 315
   Elbert County Lottery List, .......................................................... 317
   Jackson County Lottery List, ....................................................... 319
   Franklin County Lottery List, ...................................................... 322
   Wilkes County Lottery List, ......................................................... 325
   Cherokee Land Lottery List, 1838, ............................................... 342
Certified List of Georgia Troops, compiled by Capt. B. F. Johnson, .... 405
The Harvey List, compiled by Mrs. Margaret B. Harvey, .................... 436
Revolutionary Pensioners, ................................................................. 459
Revolutionary Graves: Marked or Well Identified, ............................ 467
Index, ................................................................................................

## COMPILER'S PREFACE.

After the lapse of more than a century, the difficulty of compiling a Roster of Georgia troops in the Revolution can be readily imagined. Much of the information which an earlier period might have furnished is now unhappily beyond our reach. Many important records have been lost. To compile an exhaustive roster, therefore, is humanly impossible. The utmost at which we can aim is an approximate degree of accuracy, within the limits of meager details; and to place before the public all the data which, at this late hour, can be obtained from official sources.

Georgia did not furnish a large body of troops to the Revolutionary struggle. She was the youngest of the English colonies, and, with only a scant population, was situated on the remote southern frontier. Nevertheless, the Georgia contingent gave a good account of itself, whether in the Continental Army or in the Home Guard, whether in overthrowing Toryism or in expelling British Regulars.

At the close of hostilities with England, she rewarded her brave defenders with substantial grants of land. To encourage the rapid settlement of her territory, by the best class of immigrants, she offered handsome inducements to the veterans of independence; and thousands, availing themselves of this offer, took the mountain trails which led to Georgia. Two large counties—Franklin and Washington—carved out of lands, then recently acquired from the Indians, were subdivided among the new comers, a large percentage of whom were soldiers from other States—compatriots and comrades-in-arms of the great Washington. The grants made to these soldiers were called bounties. Thus it came to pass that, while the contributions of Georgia to the army of independence were numerically small, she acquired a vast body of veterans who here found permanent homes; and today there is hardly a State in the Union whose soil is richer in Revolutionary dust.

The earlier land grants were in the nature of Head-Rights. These in time were superceded by grants made under the old Lottery System. Elsewhere, in an article written by the late Secretary of State, Hon. Philip Cook, the differences between the two methods of distributing land, are fully explained. Records still exist in the Capitol showing, in many instances at least, to whom these lands were deeded. Certificates from superior officers attesting the fidelity of men under them are still preserved; and from sources of information like these the roster has been obtained. Other helpful sources have been the Pension Rolls of the United States Government, the records of the Federal War Department, and the reports of the Smithsonian Institution. It is the aim of this roster to include within its survey not only all Georgians who enlisted in the struggle for independence, during the seven years of its continuance, but also all soldiers from other States who settled in Georgia subsequent thereto.

Too much credit, in the preparation of this work, cannot be given to help received from others. The Compiler, in this public way and at the very forefront of this volume, wishes to acknowledge his indebtedness to Miss Helen M. Prescott, of Atlanta, official genealogist for the Joseph Habersham chapter, Daughters of the American Revolution. The researches made by Miss Prescott, in this particular field of investigation, have been of priceless value, especially since the materials gathered by her, at great personal labor and expense, have been placed freely at the disposal of the State; and she is entitled, therefore, to the gratitude of all Georgians. Scarcely less, either in value or amount, has been the service to history rendered by Mr. Wm. L. Le Conte, of Atlanta, in digesting for convenient reference the voluminous records of the State Department. With this preliminary statement, we present the Roster. Errors there must be; but many of these, if not all, will be corrected in subsequent editions.

Atlanta, Ga., July 4, 1918.

LUCIAN LAMAR KNIGHT.

# LETTER FROM SECRETARY KNOX, OF THE UNITED STATES WAR DEPARTMENT, SHOWING THE NUMBER OF GEORGIA TROOPS ENLISTED, STATE AND CONTINENTAL.

Extract from "American State Papers, Military Affairs, 1st Congress, 2d Session"; Vol. I, pp. 14 to 19:

"War Office of the United States, May 10, 1790.

"In obedience to the order of the House of Representatives, the Secretary of War submits the statement hereunto annexed, of the troops and militia furnished, from time to time, by the several States, toward the support of the late war. The numbers of the Regular Troops having been stated from the official returns, deposited in the War Office, may be depended on; and in all cases where the numbers of militia are stated from the returns, the same confidence may be observed.

"But, in some years of the greatest exertions of the Southern States, there are no returns whatever of the militia employed. In this case, recourse has been had to the letters of the commanding officer, and to well-informed individuals, in order to form a proper estimate of the numbers of the militia in service, and although the accuracy of the estimate can not be relied on, yet it is the best information which the Secretary of War can at present obtain.

"(Signed) H. KNOX, Sec. of War."

A statement of the number of non-commissioned officers and privates of the Regular Troops and militia furnished by the several States from time to time, for the support of the late war:

Georgia. From actual army returns.

| Year | Regular | Conjectural estimate of militia employed in addition to preceding. |
|---|---|---|
| 1775. | 00 | 1,000 militia, to serve 9 months. |
| 1776. | 351 in Continental pay. | 750 militia. / 1,200 State troops. |
| 1777. | *1423 Continentals. | 750 men. |
| 1778. | 673 Continental troops. | 2,000 militia, to serve 6 months. / 1,200 State troops. |
| 1779. | 87 men. | 750 militia. |
| 1780. | 00 | 750 militia. |
| 1781. | 00 | 750 militia. |
| 1782. | 00 | 750 militia. |
| 1783. | 145 Continentals. | ............ |

*By the resolve of the 15th of July, 1776, Georgia was authorized to raise in Virginia, North and South Carolina, two regiments of infantry, and also two companies of artillery, of fifty men each. These troops were chiefly enlisted for one year, and the time expired in 1777.

The army in the Northern Department was discharged November 5, 1783, and in the Southern States on November 15, 1783.

(Signed) H. KNOX, Sec. of War.

Copied J. N. LeConte, 1911.

## OFFICERS OF THE GEORGIA BATTALION.
### FEB. 16, 1776.

(White's Historical Collections of Georgia, p. 94.)

In Provincial Congress, Savannah,
Feb. 10, 1776.

Province of Georgia:

Whereas a battalion upon the Continental establishment is now raising in this Province; and whereas doubts may arise how far the same is subject to the control of the Provincial civil power: Now, therefore, be it known, and we, the several subscribers, officers bearing commissions in the same battalion, do hereby declare that we hold ourselves and the non-commissioned officers and privates, also others belonging to the said battalion, subject and subservient to such supreme and civil power of this Province as are or shall be erected for the purpose of defending our rights and liberties.

And further, we bound ourselves upon the words of soldiers and men of honour, at all times to obey and carry into effect, as far as in us lies, the orders and commands of the present or any future Congress or Council of Safety of this Province as the same shall, from time to time, be issued by us.

Provided, nevertheless, That the same do not contradict or interfere with the orders or directions of the General Congress, or a committee thereof, or any General or other officer by them appointed over us.

In witness whereof, we have hereunto set our names, together with the rank and date of our commissions opposite thereto.

A RETURN OF THE OFFICERS chosen for the Battalion, ordered to be raised for the protection and defence of the Colony of Georgia, Feb. 16, 1776:

Colonel—Lachlan McIntosh.
Lieut.-Colonel—Samuel Elbert.
Major—Joseph Habersham.

### FIRST COMPANY.
Captain—Francis Henry Harris.
First Lieut.—John Habersham.
Second Lieut.—John Jenkins.
Ensign—John Rae.

### SECOND COMPANY.
Captain—Oliver Bowen.
First Lieut.—George Henley.
Second Lieut.—John Berrien.
Ensign— ——————.

### THIRD COMPANY.
Captain—John McIntosh.
First Lieut.—Lachlan McIntosh.
Second Lieut.—Francis Arthur.
Ensign—John Morrison.

### FOURTH COMPANY.
Captain—Arthur Carney.
First Lieut.—Benjamin Odinsell.
Second Lieut.—John Eman.
Ensign—Delaplaine.
John Nilton.

### FIFTH COMPANY.
Captain—Thomas Chisholm.
First Lieut.—Caleb Howell.

Second Lieut.—Daniel Cuthbert.
Ensign—William McIntosh.

### SIXTH COMPANY.
Captain—John Green.
First Lieut.—Ignatius Few.
Second Lieut.— ─────────

### SEVENTH COMPANY
Captain—Chesley Bostick.

First Lieut.—John Martin.
Second Lieut.— ─────────

### EIGHTH OR RIFLE COMPANY.
Capt—Colson.
First Lieut.—Shadrach Wright.
Second Lieut.—George Walton.
Ensign— ─────────.
Chaplain—John Holmes.

## LETTER FROM COLONEL LACHLAN McINTOSH TO GENERAL WASHINGTON.

(White's Historical Collections of Georgia, pp. 92-93.)

Savannah, in Georgia, Feb. 16, 1776.

Sir,—My country having honoured me with the command of the Continental Battalion ordered to be raised by the General Congress for the protection and defence of this Colony (though I fear too partial to my poor abilities,) it becomes my duty to inform your Excellency of the state of our Province, as far as it concerns the service, as well as of the troops to be immediately under my command.

Our Province has a front along the sea-coast of above one hundred miles, covered by a range of islands, divided from each other by eight rivers from the mainland, which make as many good inlets and harbours, most of them capable of receiving any frigate, and, as some say, much larger ships. Our settlements extend back to the northwest above two hundred miles, in other parts to the southward not above ten, and very thinly inhabited; indeed, this large space of land, altogether, has not more than three thousand men, chiefly in the back country, and many disaffected and doubtful in our cause, especially the men of the greatest property among us. Our slaves will be above fifteen thousand souls, mostly within twenty miles of the sea-coast, and make above thirty-five thousand tierces of rice annually, besides many other articles of provision, which, with our fine harbours, make the security of this colony, though weak itself, of the utmost consequence to the whole continent of America; and we have every reason to think our enemies intend to make it a place of general rendezvous and supplies.

We are bounded south by the garrisoned Province of East Florida, who have now, as I am well informed, five hundred regulars in St. Augustine, and one thousand more expected there daily from Europe. On the west of us is the Province of West Florida, the numerous nations of the Creek, Choctaw, and Cherokee Indians, besides lesser tribes, supposed to have at least ten thousand gunmen, brave, intrepid, and eager for war, whom we will have the utmost difficulty to keep at peace with us, as we want every article of their usual supply, and now furnish them in great plenty from the two Floridas. Our metropolis is situated in the south corner of the Province, upon a bluff, or sand-hill, thirty feet high or more above the water, and fifteen miles up the river Savannah, from the inlet of Tybee, where five ships of war, the Syren, the Scarborough, the Raven, the Tamar, and Cherokee, besides tenders, are now lying, and two large transports, having it is said, above three hundred men on board, and expecting more in daily, with what design, whether for this Colony or Carolina, or both together, we are not yet informed. Our Province has declared itself in a state of alarm, and resolved not to supply the men of war with provisions, and ordered a draft of half the militia to the town of Savannah to oppose the landing of troops.

Our Provincial Congress having accepted the battalion ordered for their protection and defence, chose the officers the 29th and 30th ultimo, (a return of whom shall accompany this,) and made them sign the enclosed test before their commissions were delivered; and I have this day issued general orders for recruiting, which has been hitherto prevented by many obstacles in providing money for that and other necessary service, and I fear will yet be attended with some difficulty. We expect very few in our own Province; that of South Carolina is said to be already drained of such people as will enlist, by their Provincial regiments, besides their bounty, subsistence, &c., are so much better than ours.

Therefore, I expect we must have recourse, distant as it is, to North Carolina, with this additional disadvantage, that our currency passes in no other colony than our own, and we have received very little Continental money as yet.

I have received no kind of orders or instructions from the General Congress or your Excellency; nor have I yet been able to obtain even a copy of the American articles of war, which makes me at a loss how to act in many cases; therefore I shall wish any orders or directions your Excellency will please to send me, to be as full and frequent as possible; also to be informed how far we are under the control of the Provincial Congress, &c., of this or any other Province where we are upon duty, and what rank we hold when acting with militia or Provincial troops.

I shall take the liberty of appointing surgeons to the battalion, which are so indispensably necessary, that I suppose the neglect of not naming any must be owing to our delegates; and also to make Capt. Colson's a rifle company, when raised, which I think will be useful, and hope will meet with your Excellency's approbation; and I doubt not but we will be obliged to arm more with such guns, for want of others, which are very scarce.

I have the honour to be your Excellency's

Most obedient and most humble servant,

LACHLAN McINTOSH.

To his Excellency, George Washington, Esq.,
    Commander-in-Chief of the American Forces.

## LETTER FROM COLONEL LACHLAN McINTOSH TO GENERAL WASHINGTON.

(White's Historical Collections of Georgia, pp. 95-96.)

Savannah, in Georgia, April 28, 1776.

Sir:—I wrote to your Excellency the 16th of February and 8th of March, to which please to be referred; and now enclose you a report of our battalion made to me this day; which I deferred sending to you before, in expectation of our officers coming in with all their recruits, but the distance they were obliged to go rendered it impossible. I am informed that Captain Colson is on his way, with his Company, nearly complete; and with the other recruiting officers, may make above 70 or 80 men more than the report; and is altogether above half the complement of the battalion, which is more than the oldest battalion in South Carolina can boast of yet, though near twelve months standing, and their encouragements so much greater, their bounty being 25 pounds South Carolina currency, with the like sum for clothes, besides their rations and pay, which are also better than ours. And if the ease in which the poorest people generally live in the Southern Colonies, and the prejudice they have to any regular service on account of the restraint that any thing of a strict discipline requires, are considered, I flatter myself your Excellency will think we have not been idle. The chief of the men are enlisted for 12 months; some for 18; and a few who would not engage for more than 6 months, whom I have admitted, as I had not directions about the time, and I could not tell how soon we might have occasion for them. Our Province allows six dollars per man, enlisting money; and upon application have raised it now to eight dollars, which is still too little for the bounty of the men and expense of the officers, whose pay is so small, that they can barely afford to live in an extravagant country like this, where there are no kinds of manufactures, and the small remains of goods advanced to two or three hundred per cent. Indeed, I fear we shall be at the greatest loss to make out clothing of any kind for them, or what is far worse, proper arms. The officers who are not recruiting employ all their time in training themselves and the battalion; on which spectators are pleased to pay high compliments for the proficiency they had already made, and the appearance of the men. The Raven and the Cherokee are the only two ships of war which remains now stationed at Tybee in the mouth of the Savannah River, with whom we have no kind of communication.

Several armed vessels infest our other inlets to the southward, and have made several captures, which we cannot prevent, as we have not a single vessel of any force; but they have already been driven off the shore when they attempted to get a supply of provisions. We are informed there are 2,000 men now in St. Augustine lately arrived, and that they expect more daily; but this wants confirmation, as I think, in that poor starved colony, they must be much pinched for provisions. This Province is now raising a troop of sixty horse to prevent their getting any cattle from our Southern boundary, and another troop of a like number, to protect our Western settlements from the insults of Indians, who are like to be troublesome; all things considered, I certainly think this Colony should have a considerable force to defend and secure it, as its safety is of the utmost consequence to the great cause of the Continent. The troops of our neighbouring Province are all upon Provincial establishment, and at a distance; therefore their assistance may depend upon many circumstances.

I have the honour to be
Your Excellency's most obedient and humble servant,
LACHLAN McINTOSH.

To His Excellency, George Washington, Esqr.,
General and Commander-in-Chief.

### Return of the Strength of the Georgia Battalion, April 28, 1776.

| Companies. | Capt. | Lieut. | Ensign. | Serg. | Corp. | Drum. | Fifer. | Sentinels. |
|---|---|---|---|---|---|---|---|---|
| Capt. Francis Harris | 1 | 1 | 1 | 1 | 2 | 1 | 1 | 24 |
| Capt. Oliver Bowen | 1 | 2 | 0 | 3 | 1 | 1 | 1 | 20 |
| Capt. John McIntosh | 1 | 2 | 1 | 4 | 2 | 1 | 0 | 19 |
| Capt. Arthur Carney | 1 | 2 | 1 | 4 | 4 | 0 | 0 | 48 |
| Capt. Thomas Chisholm's | 1 | 2 | 1 | 4 | 4 | 0 | 0 | 47 |
| Capt. John Green | 1 | 2 | 0 | 4 | 4 | 0 | 0 | 39 |
| Capt. Chesley Bostick's | 1 | 2 | 0 | 2 | 0 | 1 | 0 | 29 |
| Capt. Jacob Colson's | 1 | 2 | 0 | 2 | 0 | 1 | 0 | 10 |
| Total | 8 | 15 | 4 | 24 | 17 | 5 | 2 | 236 |

### Return of the Present State of the Georgia Battalion, April 28, 1776.

| | Capt. | Lieut. | Ensign. | Serg. | Corp. | Drum. | Fifer. | Sentinels. |
|---|---|---|---|---|---|---|---|---|
| On guard | 0 | 1 | 0 | 1 | 2 | 1 | 1 | 30 |
| For guard | 0 | 1 | 0 | 1 | 2 | 1 | 1 | 30 |
| On furlough | 1 | 0 | 1 | 0 | 1 | 0 | 0 | 11 |
| Recruiting | 6 | 4 | 1 | 3 | 1 | 0 | 0 | 1 |
| Sick | 0 | 1 | 0 | 0 | 1 | 1 | 0 | 10 |
| Attending sick | 0 | 0 | 0 | 1 | 0 | 0 | 0 | 2 |
| Armourers | 0 | 0 | 0 | 0 | 0 | 0 | 0 | 1 |
| Prisoners | 0 | 0 | 0 | 0 | 1 | 1 | 0 | 5 |
| Officer's servants | 0 | 0 | 0 | 0 | 0 | 0 | 0 | 10 |
| Off duty | 0 | 8 | 3 | 18 | 10 | 1 | 1 | 136 |
| Total | 7 | 15 | 5 | 24 | 18 | 5 | 3 | 236 |

24 Sergeants, 18 corporals, 5 drummers, 3 fifers, 236 rank and file—286 enrolled.

By the information I have, I suppose our recruiting officers may have about 70 or 80 men more, who are not come in yet.

LACHLAN McINTOSH, Colonel.
Savannah, in Georgia, April 28, 1776.

## NAMES OF OFFICERS IN THE CONTINENTAL LINE OF THE GEORGIA BRIGADE DURING THE REVOLUTIONARY WAR, INCLUDING INFANTRY, DRAGOONS, LEGIONARY CORPS, AND GENERAL STAFF.

(White's Historical Collections of Georgia, pp. 113-114.)

**Brigade Generals**—Lachlan McIntosh, Samuel Elbert.

**Colonels**—James Screven, John White, Robert Rae.

**Lieut.-Colonels**—Joseph Habersham, Joseph Lane, Thomas Chisholm, Francis Moore, Philip Lowe, George Handley, Benjamin Porter; John S. Eustace, Adjutant-General; Lachlan McIntosh, Junior Brigade Inspector; John Berrien, Brigade Major; John Milton, A. D. C.; George Melven, B. Q. M.

**Captains**—John Bennis, Gideon Booker, Chestley Bostwick, Celerine Brosard, John Bard, Charles Budd, Isham Cook, Arthur Carney, Ranes Cook, Jacob Colson, John Cunningham, Alexander D. Cuthbert, Joseph Day, Daniel Duval, Peter Debosh, John Dooly, Thomas Dooly, Ignatius Few, John Greene, John Hancock, William Hornby, —— Jaret, Evans Lewis, John Lucas, William Matthews, William McIntosh, Thomas Morris, Elisha Millar, John Mosely, Charles Middleton, Littleberry Mosely, Clement Nash, Patrick Fitzpatrick, James Powell, Thomas Scott, Andrew Templeton, Thomas Threadgill, Jesse Winfrey, Shadrach Wright.

**Lieutenants**—Francis Arthur, Thomas Brown, James Bryan, John Caldwell, Cornelius Collins, Edward Cowen, Walter Dixon, George Dooly, Thomas Glascock, Caleb Howell, Arthur Hayes, Christopher Hillery, Robert Howe, Nathaniel Hughes, William Johnson, William Jordan, William Lowne, Josiah Maxwell, John Manley, John Mitchell, Thomas Mitchell, John Martin, William McDonald, Thomas Netherland, John Newdigate, Benjamin Odingsell, Thomas Payne, Nathaniel Pierre, Robert Porter, Thomas Porter, William Roach, John Rae, Abraham Seixas, Robert Simpson, E. Shick, David Sarzedas, Randolph Smith, —— Steadman, Francis Tennell, David Turner, J. P. Wagnon, George Walton, Jesse Walton, Robert Ward.

**General Staff**—Richard Wyley, Q. M. G.; Joseph Clay, P. M. G.; Mordecai Sheftall, C. G.; Sheftall Sheftall, D. C. G.; David Rees, Judge Advocate; Moses Allen, Chaplain.

**Hospital Department—Surgeons**—David Bradie, —— McKinne.

**Surgeon's Mates**—Adam Alexander, Nathan Brownson, James Houstoun, Thomas Davenport, Frederick Ridgley, —— Wood.

**Legionary Corps**—James Jackson, Colonel; Thomas Washington, Major. **Captains**—Henry Alison, Sherwood Bugg, John Morrison, James Stallings, John Lyons.

**Lieutenants**—Thomas Hamilton, Ezekiel Stallings, Benjamin Hawkins, Stephen Blount, Benjamin Harvey, Nicholas Millar.

**Artillery**—Major, Roman de Lisle.

**Captains**—Edward Young, John Fraser.

**Colonels**—Samuel Jack, John Stewart.

**Lieut.-Colonels**—Elijah Clark.

# NAMES OF OFFICERS AND SOLDIERS WHO MADE APPLICATION FOR LAND.

(White's Historical Collections of Georgia, pp. 111-113.)

---

The following is a list of the names of such officers and soldiers only who made application to the Governor and Council of the State of Georgia, in pursuance of the second section of an act of the Assembly, passed on the 17th day of February, 1783, entitled, "An Act for opening a Land Office, and for other purposes therein mentioned," for procuring a certificate in pursuance of the section above referred to, and a resolution of Congress, of the 16th of September, 1776, of the bounty of land due them respectively for their services during the last war with Great Britain, in what was called the Georgia Continental Establishment:

Anderson, Charles, soldier.
Andrews, George, soldier.
Andrew, Francis, soldier.
Allen, Moses.
Allison, Henry, Capt.

Banks, Reuben, soldier.
Barber, Chester, soldier.
Bell, Hugh, soldier.
Bennis, John, Capt.
Berrien, John, Major.
Berry, John, soldier.
Berry, Wm., soldier.
Bishop, William, soldier.
Blount, Jacob, Capt.
Booker, Gideon, Capt.
Braddock, John, Capt.
Braddock, David, soldier.
Bradley, Abram, soldier.
Bradley, Richard, soldier.
Berk, James, soldier.
Burnett, John, soldier.
Burton, Richard, soldier.
Butry, Z., soldier.
Brown, Francis, soldier.
Brown, John, soldier.
Brownson, Nathan, Hosp. Surg.
Baxter, Wm.
Bradley, M.
Brown, Jacob.

Barker, C.
Bresard, C.
Childers, Thomas.
Connelly, James.
Conway, Thomas.
Corbin, Wm.
Croker, Wm.
Chisholm, John.
Collins, Stephen.
Campbell, John.
Collins, John.
Camp, Samuel.
Childers, David.
Collins, John.
Childers, D.
Cook, Isham.
Cuthbert, A.
Corven, Edward, Lieut.
Collins, C.
Connolly, W. J.
Corney, M.

Dean, Wm.
Davenport, Stephen.
Davis, Merideth.
Davidson, Wm.
Dempier, ———, Sergeant.
Davenport, Thomas.
Dollar, John.
Ducin, John, Capt.

Devereaux, Peter.
Day, Joseph, Capt.
Davis, C., Sergeant.
Day, Robert, soldier.
Debosk, Peter, Capt.
De Laplaign, Emanuel P., Capt.
Deveaux, Peter, Aid to General Gates.
Dooly, George, 2nd Lieut.
Dooly, John, Capt.
Dooly, Thomas, Capt.
Dowman, R., Capt.
Ducoin, John, Capt.

Evans, John.
Eacholls, E.
Evans, N.
Ellis, Robert.
Evans, B.
Eimbeck, Geo., Barrack Master.
Eustace, J.
Elliott, Daniel, soldier.
Elbert, Samuel, Brig. Gen.

Frazer, John.
Fredconer, C.

Glascock, Thomas.
Gravat, O.
Gibbs, Wm.

Harsaw, Thomas.
Harris, G. L.
Hillary, C.
Haynes, Arthur, Lieut.
Hicks, J., Capt.
Hughs, N., Lieut.
Houstoun, James, Doctor.
Hendley, George, Capt.
Hancock, George, Capt.
Habersham, John, Major.

Johnston, Wm.
Jordan, Wm.

King, John, soldier.
Kneil, Patrick, soldier.

Lancaster, Rowland, soldier.
Lancaster, Wm., soldier.
Lane, James, soldier.
Lane, Joseph, Major.
Lankford, Josiah, soldier.
Lankford, Moses, soldier.
Lazarus, N., soldier.
Lester, Thos., soldier.
Low, P., Major.
Lucas, J., Capt.
Linson, J.
Lintch, J.
Lynn, C.
Lynn, J.
Lambuck, Wm.

McVickers, D.
Mabry, Ralph.
McHancy, Terry.
Mitchell, Wm.
McBride, Edward.
Mase, Joseph.
Mastein, Wm.
McIntosh, L., Brig.-Gen.
McCall, Richard.
Moore, Francis.
McIntosh, John, Col.
Marbury, L., Col.
Matthews, Geo., Brig.-Gen.
Moseley, Robert.
McIntosh, L.
Meanly, J.
Morrison, J., Capt.
Moseley, L.
Matthews, Wm., Capt.
McDowell, James.
McIntosh, Wm.
Milton, J.
Melvin, Geo.
Millar, E.
Mitchell, J.
Maxwell, Josiah.
McGilton, Vance.
McGilton, James.

Newdigate, John, Capt.
Nash, Clement.
Nugard, Michael.

## OFFICERS' AND SOLDIERS' APPLICATIONS FOR LAND.

Newnan, John.
Nix, George.
Nugan, M.

Oakman, W., Fife Major.
O'Bryan, James, soldier.
Ornsby, Daniel, Fife Major.

Pounds, R.
Parnell, Lieut.-Col.
Parham, Richard, soldier.
Paxton, Wm.
Payne, Thos., Lieut.
Pearrie, N.
Petillo, John, soldier.
Phiney, L.
Porter, B., Major.
Porter, R., Lieut.
Porter, T., Lieut.
Powell, J., Lieut.
Pray, Job, Capt.
Plaigue, D. E. L., Capt.

Reyfield, J.
Rae, Robert, Col.
Reynolds, A.
Robinson, A.
Read, Wm., Doctor.

Stiff, Wm.
Sessums, Wm.
Sampson, Samuel.
Saulberry, Thos.
Sutton, R.
Screven, James, Gen.
Smith, R.
Sick, F.
Scott, Wm.
Sheftall, M.
Sheftall, S.
Sharp, B. J.

Shields, Andrew.
Studman, James.

Tennell, S.
Thomas, B.
Threadgill, T.
Templeton, A., Capt.
Threadgill, Wm.
Tucker, P.
Turner, C.
Turner, G.
Twidall, J.
Turner, B.
Tennill, T., Capt.
Turner, D.

Vickers, Solomon.

Walton, Nathaniel, Lieut.
Webb, John.
Webster, B.
Williams, C.
White, John.
Wells, M.
Willaby, W.
Whitmore, J.
Webster, Thos.
Wash, Wm.
Winfrey, J., Capt.
Warden, J.
Wagnon, P. J.
Walton, Jesse.
White, John, Col.
Wash, Patrick, Major.
Wood, J.
Williamson, L.
Wright, S., Capt.
Wood, James.
Wash, E.
Wagnon, T.
Walton, George.

This list is taken from a book in the Executive Office at Milledgeville, prepared by the late Major A. B. Fannin.

## EXPLANATORY.

### SAMPLE OF CERTIFICATES FROM WHICH SOME OF THESE RECORDS ARE COMPILED.

BOOK: "Bonds, Bills of Sale, and Deeds of Gift," pg. 129.

I certify that John Rivers, Lewis Holloway, John Jordan, Littleton Williamson, Joshua Moss, John Rivers, Hardy Bass, and Thos. Bass, private soldiers, served their times in the second regt. of Continental Troops for the State of Georgia as good and faithful soldiers, and that Brittain Brantley, Timothy Simpson, William Vaughn, Lott Boyce, and Charles Clifton, some now killed, and others of them died in the service in the said regiment, and that Moredeth Tanner, served also as a faithful soldier in that regt., until by bodily infirmity he was rendered incapable of serving his country at which time he was discharged. Given under my hand at Augusta, this 18th of August, 1785.

S. ELBERT, late Brig.-Gen. Continental Army.

Recorded, January 20th, 1794.

## CERTIFICATES OF SERVICE IN THE AMERICAN REVOLUTION.

On File in the Office of Secretary of State, in the State Capitol.

### A.

**APPLING, DANIEL.** This is to certify that Daniel Appling was an inhabitant of this State prior to the Reduction thereof by the British arms, and was a refugee from the same, during which time he cheerfully did his duty as a soldier and friend to this and the United States. 20th day of February, 1784. Ben Few, Commdt.

**APPLING, DANIEL.** Granted 250 acres of land 28th of February, 1784, by J. Houston. Refugee soldier.

**AYCOCK, RICHARD.** On certificate of Elijah Clark, Col., granted 250 acres of land, 25th day of March, 1784.

**AMMONS, WILLIAM.** Certificate of Col. Elijah Clark that he served in a battalion of Minute Men raised for the defense of the State in 1777, though not at the time an inhabitant of the State, and was in service at the time said battalion was reduced in March, 1778. Certificate dated 2nd February, 1785.

**ANDERSON, ALEXANDER.** Certificate of Col. E. Clark, that he served in the 1st Battalion of Minute Men, was not at time of enlistment inhabitant of State. Certificate dated 6th of April, 1784.

**AYRES, THOMAS.** On certificate of Col. Greenbury Lee, granted 250 acres of land as bounty for service. 20th February, 1784.

**ANGLIN, DAVID.** Certificate of Col. E. Clark, that he served in the Battalion of Minute Men, was not at time of enlistment inhabitant of State. Certificate dated 1st April, 1784. Granted 250 acres in Washington Co.

**ADAMS, JOHN.** Certificate of Capt. Littlebury Mosby, Paymaster 2nd Ga. Batt., and Col. J. Pannill, that he was a soldier in the 2nd Ga. Batt., enlisted for three years and served his time faithfully, 9th May, 1785, prays a warrant for bounty in the name of Mrs. Daniel Young. Granted by court of Wilkes Co.

**ANDERSON, JOHN.** Private Batt. Minute Men. Certificate Col. Samuel Jack, 13th March, 1784. Prays 250 acres.

**ASHWORTH, BENJ.** Refugee soldier. Certificate of Col. E. Clark, 25th of March, 1784. Entitled to 250 acres.

**ALEXANDER, SAMUEL, SR.** Refugee soldier. Certificate of Col. E. Clark, 6th September, 1784. Prays 287½ acres in Washington Co.

**ALEXANDER, SAMUEL.** Refugee; served as a captain. Certificate of Col. E. Clark, 2nd February, 1784. Entitled to 500 acres.

**ANDERSON, ELISHA.** Refugee soldier. Certificate of Brig. John Twiggs, 14th April, 1784. Prays for bounty land in Washington Co.

**ALDREDGE, JAMES.** Certificate of Col. James McNiel, 24th February, 1784. Prays for 287½ acres in Washington Co.

**AUSTIN, RICHARD.** Captain in Minute Batt. Certificate Col. E. Clark, 8th September, 1784.

**ALEXANDER, ASA.** Refugee soldier. Certificate of Col. E. Clark, 6th September, 1784. Prays for 287½ acres in Washington Co.

**ANGLIN, WILLIAM.** Minute man. Certificate Col. E. Clark, 1st day of April, 1784. Prays land in Washington Co.

**AKINS, JOHN.** Minute man. Certificate Col. E. Clark, 16th December, 1784.

**AUTERY, JOHN (AUTRY).** Refugee; captain. Certificate Col. E. Clark, 25th February, 1784. Entitled to 750 acres.

**ADAMS, ROBT.** Refugee soldier. Certificate Brig. Gen. John Twiggs, 17th April, 1784. Prays 575 acres Washington Co. Signed Joseph Inman, for heirs of Robt. Adams.

**ANDREW, BENJ., JR.** Refugee soldier. Prays for 287½ acres in Washington Co. Certificate J. Houston.

**ALLISON, JAMES.** Refugee soldier. Certificate Col. E. Clark, 2nd February, 1784.

**AWTRY, JOHN (see Autery).**

**AWTREY, ALEXANDER, JR.** Refugee captain. Certificate of Col. E. Clark, 25th March, 1784. Entitled to 500 acres.

**ALEXANDER, JAMES.** Refugee soldier. Certificate Col. E. Clark, 25th March, 1784. Entitled to 250 acres land.

**ACREDGE, WILLIAM.** Refugee soldier. Certificate E. Clark, 5th September, 1784. Prays 250 acres in Washington Co.

**ANDERSON, ALEXANDER.** Minute man. Petition of Reuben Coleman, for 287½ acres in the right of Alexander Anderson in Franklin Co.

**ABBOTT, JOHN.** Refugee soldier. Certificate Col. Benj. Few, 28th February, 1784. Prays 250 acres in Washington Co.

**ABBET, JOHN.** Refugee soldier. Certificate Col. E. Clark, 25th March, 1784. Entitled to bounty and 250 acres.

**ANDERSON, HENRY.** Minute man. Certificate Col. E. Clark, 14th April, 1784. Prays 287½ acres Franklin Co.

**AYRES, ABM.** (deceased) "who fell in refugeeship." Certificate of Col. William Candler, 20th February, 1784. Heirs pray for 500 acres in Washington Co. Granted 16 April, 1784. Fell in battle of Longcain in December, 1780.

ADAMSON, CHARLES. Private soldier 2nd Ga. Continental Batt. Served three years. Certificate Lt. Col. J. Pannill, 17th September, 1784. Prays for land reserved for Continental troop in the fork of the Oconee River, 230 acres.

ALEXANDER, HUGH. Lieut. of Minute Men in the Florida Expedition, 1777. Certificate of Col. Samuel Jack.

AYRES, DANIEL. Lieut. of Minute Men. Certificate of Col. E. Clark, 6th April 1784. Prays for bounty in Washington Co.

ADAMS, HUGH. Minute man, 1777. Certificate Col. E. Clark, 1st December, 1784.

ANDERSON, JAMES. Lieut. Minute Men, 1777. Certificate Col. E. Clark, 18 May, 1784. Prays for 200 acres of land in Franklin Co. Granted 24th May, 1784.

AMMONS, ROBT. Minute man. Certificate Col. E. Clark, 1st April, 1784. Entitled to bounty of 250 acres.

ASHWORTH, ADAM. Minute man, 1777. Certificate E. Clark, 2nd February, 1785.

AVERA, ISAAC. Refugee soldier. Certificate Col. E. Clark, 7th April, 1784. Prays bounty of lands in Franklin Co.

ANDERSON, BARTLETT. Refugee soldier 1st Batt. Richmond Militia. Certificate Col. James McNiel, 22nd March, 1784.

ASHWORTH, ARTHUR. Minute man. Certificate Col. E. Clark, 10th October, 1784.

ALEXANDER, ROBERT. Minute man, 1777. Certificate Col. Samuel Jack, 13th April, 1784.

ANDERSON, WILLIAM. Minute man, 1777. Certificate Col. E. Clark, 7th April, 1784. Prays 250 acres land in Washington Co.

ALDRIDGE, JAMES. Soldier. Certificate Col. James McNiel, 9th February, 1784. Entitled to bounty of 250 acres of land. Said James Aldridge gives power of attorney to James Aldridge to call on Governor for certificate of bounty.

ALLISON, HENRY. Lieut. of the line of this State to the end of the war. Certificate of John Habersham, Major Late Ga. Line, 20th April, 1784. Prays for bounty land.

AYRES, WILLIAM. Captain Minute Men, 1777. Certificate Col. E. Clark, 25th February, 1784. Prays bounty land in Washington Co.

APPLING, JOHN. Refugee soldier. Certificate Col. Benj. Few, 20th February, 1784. Entitled to 250 acres land.

**ANDERSON, JOHN.** Minute man. Entitled to 250 acres as bounty. Bailey Anderson and wife, Sara, of Ninety-sixth Dist., S. C., appoint Henry Liles, of said State and District, attorney to receive bounty land coming to his father, John Anderson, deceased, and to his brother, Scarlet Anderson also, for being in the service of Georgia, this 17th January, 1784.

## B.

**BRASWELL, JAMES.** Certificate of Col. E. Clark, 10th December, 1784, entitled to a bounty of 250 acres of land, and prays for same in Washington Co.

**BREWER, GEORGE.** Certificate of Col. E. Clark, 24th April, 1784, entitled to a bounty, and prays for 250 acres in Franklin Co.

**BLOUNT, STEPHEN.** Certificate of Gen. Elbert, and Col. Jackson, 20th February, 1784. Entitled to a bounty, and prays for 575 acres in Washington Co.

**BARNARD, JESSE.** Certificate of Col. Jas. McNeil, 2nd February, 1784. Entitled to bounty of 250 acres of land, and prays for same in Franklin Co.

**BRUNSON, WILLIAM.** Sells his rights of bounty land to Mackkeen Green, and empowers said Green to apply for the certificate.

**BOWEN, RICHARD.** Certificate of Col. E. Clark, 6th April, 1784. Served in Batt. of Minute Men raised for the defense of this State, though not at the time an inhabitant. Entitled to a bounty of land. Prays for 250 acres in Washington Co.

**BAILEY, ROBT.** Certificate of Col. John Baker, 3rd April, 1785. Refugee soldier.

**BECK, SIMON.** Certificate of Col. G. Lee, 12th April, 1784. Entitled to a bounty. Appoints Rhesa Howard, attorney, to take out his warrant, on the 1st of March, 1784, in Franklin Co.

**BROWNSON, NATHAN, DR., ESQR.** Deputy Purveyor-General, Southern hospitals. On certificate of Gen. Lachlan McIntosh, 28th February, 1784, entitled to bounty, and prays for 1,150 acres of land.

**BURNSIDES, JOHN, SR.** Certificate of Gen. John Twiggs, and Capt. John Fenn. Entitled to bounty, and prays for same in Washington Co.

**BURCH, EDWARD.** Certificate of Gen. John Twiggs, 6th February, 1784. Refugee soldier. Entitled to a bounty of 500 acres.

**BEAL, ARCHIBALD.** Certificate of Col. Wm. Candler, that he was a refugee and served as adjutant to the regt. of refugees under his command in the years 1780 and 1781.

**BRUNSON, WILLIAM.** Certificate of Col. Clayborne Hinson, 29th January, 1784. Entitled to bounty of 250 acres, and prays for same in Washington Co.

## CERTIFICATES OF SERVICE IN AMERICAN REVOLUTION.

**BENDER, JOHN.** Certificate of Col. Wm. Candler. 15th July, 1784. Refugee soldier. Entitled to a bounty, and prays for same in Franklin Co.

**BRASWELL, FREDERICK.** Certificate of Col. Jas. Jackson, 19th July, 1784, entitled to a bounty of 250 acres. Prays for same in Franklin Co.

**BLAKEY, BENJ.** Petitions for 345 acres of land as a bounty for his services, in the county of Washington. Granted 24th May, 1784.

**BRANAM, SAMUEL.** Petition of Reuben Coleman in the right of Samuel Branam, a soldier in the Minute service, for bounty of 287½ acres in Washington Co.

**BRACK, ELEAZER.** Certificate of Gen. John Twiggs, 14th April, 1784. Entitled to a bounty, and prays for same in Washington Co. Appoints Mr. Elijah Anderson receiver of same.

**BERRIHILL, ANDREW.** Refugee soldier. Certificate Brig.-Gen. John Twiggs, 8th March, 1784. Prays for bounty in Washington Co.

**BURNEY, JOHN JR.** Private. Certificate of Col. E. Clark, 21st April, 1784. Prays for 250 acres land in Washington Co.

**BUCKHALTER, MICAJAH (MIKEL).** Certificate of Col. E. Clark, 25th March, 1784. Entitled to 250 acres bounty. Granted in Washington Co.

**BOLBOTH, JAMES** (deceased). Certificate of Col. E. Clark, 9th April, 1784. Entitled to 250 acres of land, which was granted to Hannah Bolboth, 16th April, 1784, in Washington Co.

**BEARFIELD, RICHARD.** Certificate of Col. E. Clark, 7th April, 1784. Entitled to bounty of 250 acres.

**BROOKS, JOHN.** Certificate of Col. E. Clark, 26th March, 1784. Prays for 287½ acres bounty in Washington Co.

**BACON, JONATHAN.** Refugee soldier. Certificate of Col. John Baker, Lt. Col. of Militia. Given at Sunbury, 10th May, 1784.

**BEALE, ARCH.** Empowers Gen. John Twiggs to receive a bounty land warrant, 28th December, 1783.

**BELL, HUGH.** Certificate of Maj. Gen. Lachlan McIntosh, 8th March, 1784. Entitled to a bounty of land for services in the Ga. Line.

**BALL, JOHN.** Of Camden Dist., S. C. Certificate of Col. Samuel Jack, 9th April, 1784. Served as a soldier in a Georgia regiment.

**BAGBY, GEORGE.** Certificate of Col. E. Clark, 26th March, 1784. Entitled to 287½ acres of land and prays for bounty in Washington Co.

**BECKHAM, SIMON.** Certificate of Col. Greenbury Lee, 25th February, 1784. Entitled to 287½ acres. Prays for same in Washington Co.

**BRUNSON, DAVID.** Certificate Brig. Gen. John Twiggs, 25th April, 1784. Entitled to bounty of 250 acres, and prays for same in Washington Co.

**BARBER, CHESTER.** Soldier of Continental line. Entitled to 230 acres in the reserve for Continental soldiers. Granted to Francis Tennill for Chester Barber.

**BOWIE, JAMES.** Certificate of Col. Greenbury Lee, 12th March, 1784. Entitled to a bounty of 250 acres of land, and prays for same in Washington Co.

**BURNS, JOHN.** Certificate of Col. E. Clark, 25th March, 1784. Entitled to bounty of 250 acres.

**BRAWNER, CHARLES.** Certificate of Lt. Col. James Jackson, July 30, 1784, that he served in the Ga. State Legion Infantry, from the reduction of Augusta, to the evacuation of the State by the British forces. Prays for 287½ acres land in Washington Co.

**BOYD, EDWARD.** Refugee soldier. Entitled to 287½ acres of land, per petition of James Stallings. Granted in Washington Co., April 6, 1784, on certificate of Col. James McNiel, February, 1784.

**BRUNSON, EBENEZER.** Entitled to 500 acres of bounty land. Prays for same in Washington Co.

**BACON, JOHN.** Certificate of Col. Jas. Martin, 24th April 1784. Entitled to 287½ acres, and prays for same in Washington Co.

**BARNETT, DANIEL.** Entitled to 250 acres of bounty land for his services. Prays for same in Franklin Co.

**BOYKIN, FRANCIS.** Refugee soldier of Burke Co., Ga., appoints Jonathan Kemp, Esq., planter of said county, to obtain his bounty of land on the 28th of January, 1784. Sworn to before David Emanuel.

**BURNET, JOHN.** Refugee captain. Certificate of Col. E. Clark, 9th April, 1784. Entitled to 500 acres of bounty. Prays for same in Washington Co. Granted 16th April, 1784.

**BOYD, JOHN.** Certificate of Col. James McNiel, 24th February, 1784. Entitled to 287½ acres. Prays for same in Washington Co., and appoints his brother, Robt. Boyd, to receive the warrant.

**BEASLEY, JOSEPH.** Certificate of Col. Greenbury Lee, 25th February, 1784. Entitled to 287½ acres of land bounty and prays for same in Washington Co.

**BURKS, JOSEPH.** Certificate Col. E. Clark, 25th March, 1784. Entitled to a bounty of 250 acres.

**BRIANT, HENRY.** Appoints James Cottenhead attorney to apply to the Governor of Georgia for his warrant for bounty land, 16th May, 1784. Witness, James Evans.

## CERTIFICATES OF SERVICE IN AMERICAN REVOLUTION. 27

**BERRY, GILSON.** Certificate of Col. Greenbury Lee, 28th February, 1784. Entitled to a bounty of 250 acres of land. Prays for same in Washington Co. On another certificate from Col. G. Lee, 26th April, 1784, he prays for 250 acres of land in Franklin Co.

**BROOKS, JOAB.** Certificate Col. E. Clark, 23d June, 1784. Entitled to 250 acres of land. Prays for same in Franklin Co., and appoints his friend, John Rutherford, Esqr., attorney to receive the same.

**BARNETT, JOHN.** Certificate Col. E. Clark, 7th April, 1784. Entitled to 550 acres of land, and prays for same in Franklin Co.

**BURKS, CHARLES.** Certificate of Col. E. Clark, 25th March, 1784. Entitled to 287½ acres of bounty land. Prays for same in Washington Co.

**BARRON, SAMUEL** (deceased). Certificate of Asa Emanuel, Col. Burke Co. Militia, 15th April, 1784. Entitled to a bounty of land. The petition of Ann Barron, relict of the late Samuel Barron, deceased, in behalf of her son, Samuel Barron, the only son and heir, humbly prays for a warrant unto the said Samuel Barron, her son, in trust for him to John Crozier, to be run in the county of Washington, Ga.

**BICKHAM, ABNER.** Certificate of Gen. John Twiggs, 4th March, 1784. Entitled to a bounty of 287½ acres, and prays for same in Washington Co.

**BEASELEY, JAMES.** Certificate Col. E. Clark, 25th March, 1784. Entitled to bounty of 250 acres.

**BREWER, MOSES.** Certificate of Col. E. Clark, 17th September, 1784. Entiled to a bounty of 250 acres.

**BROWN, FREDERICK.** Certificate of Col. James Jackson, 30th July, 1784. Served in Georgia State Legion, Infantry. Entitled to 287½ acres bounty. Prays for same in Washington Co.

**BROWN, WILLIAM.** Certificate of Col. Greenbury Lee, 11th March, 1784. Entitled to 287½ acres of land. Prays for same in Washington Co.

**BROWN, THOMAS.** Certificate of Col. E. Clark, 25th March, 1784. Entitled to 250 acres bounty land.

**BARBER, GEORGE.** Lieut. Certificate of Col. E. Clark, 25th March, 1784. Prays for 250 or 287 acres for citizen's bounty, and 350 or 402 acres for refugee bounty in the county of Franklin.

**BEESLY, JAMES.** Certificate Col. G. Lee, 26th April, 1784. Entitled to 250 acres bounty land, and prays for same in Washington county.

**BUTLER, FORD.** Certificate Col. E. Clark, 25th March, 1784. Entitled to 250 acres bounty land, and prays for same in Washington Co. Also a petition for 250 acres in Franklin Co.

**BLANCHARD, WILLIAM.** Certificate of Gen. John Twiggs, 13th April, 1784. Entitled to a bounty of land. Prays for same in Washington Co.

**BRASWELL, GEORGE.** Certificate Col. E. Clark, 10th December, 1784. Entitled to bounty of 250 acres. Prays for same in Washington Co.

**BAILEY, WILLIAM.** Certificate Col. E. Clark, 25th March, 1784. Entitled to bounty of 250 acres, and prays for same in Washington Co.

**BURNEY, RANDOL.** Certificate Col. E. Clark, 21st April, 1784. Entitled to 250 acres of land bounty, and prays for same in Washington Co.

**BLACK, HENRY.** Certificate Col. E. Clark, 2nd February, 1784. Entitled to 575 acres bounty, and prays for same in Franklin Co.

**BARNETT, NATHANIEL.** Certificate of Col. James McNiel, 17th February, 1784. Entitled to bounty of 287½ acres, and prays for same in Washington Co., and on certificate of Col. E. Clark, 7th August, 1784, prays for 575 acres in Franklin Co.

**BRADLEY, ABRAHAM.** Certificate of Elijah Clark, 24th April, 1784. Entitled to 250 acres bounty land. Prays for same in Franklin Co.

**BRITT, CHARLES.** Appoints George Lumpkin attorney to receive his warrant for land due as a bounty for services in the State of Georgia, 22nd April, 1784, and desires to take up said land in the county of Franklin.

**BROWN, THOS.** Certificate Col. E. Clark, 20th April, 1784. Entitled to 250 acres of bounty land, and prays for same in Franklin Co. Granted 24th May, 1784.

**BOWEN, OLIVER.** Commodore. Certificate James Habersham and Thos. Stone, at Savannah, October 28, 1783, is entitled to 1,150 acres in the reserve.

**BOYAKIN, JESSE.** Certificate of Brig. Gen. John Twiggs, 2nd April, 1784. Entitled to a bounty of 287½ acres of land. Empowers Mr. James Lambert attorney to receive same in Washington Co.

**BRYANT, JAMES.** Certificate of Col. Benj. Few, as per certificate of Capt. James Danely, 20th July, 1784. Entitled to a bounty of 287½ acres.

**BRASWELL, SAMPSON.** Minute man, 1777. Certificate of Col. E. Clark, 1st April, 1784. Prays for 287½ acres in Washington Co.

**BOYD, NICODEMUS.** Certificate of Col. James McNiel, 15th March, 1784. Entitled to bounty of 287½ acres.

**BRADDOCK, DAVID.** Served on board the gallies. Certificate of J. Houston, 2nd April, 1784. Prays 230 acres of land through Nathan Brownson, April 12th, 1784.

**BASSETT, GEORGE.** Certificate of Col. James Jackson, 30th July, 1784. Entitled to 287½ acres. Prays for same in Washington Co.

**BOYKIN, FRANCIS.** Certificate of Gen. John Twiggs, 6th April, 1784. Prays for bounty of 287½ acres in Washington Co., through John Morrison.

## CERTIFICATES OF SERVICE IN AMERICAN REVOLUTION.

**BEAL, JEREMIAH.** Captain; killed in action. Entitled to bounty as refugee, per certificate of Gen. John Twiggs, 22nd March, 1784. (Petition of James Beal, an infant, heir to Jeremiah Beal, deceased, by Zephaniah Beal, his father and natural guardian, for 575 acres.)

**BEAL, ZEPHANIAH.** Certificate of Gen. John Twiggs, 6th February, 1784. Entitled to 250 acres bounty. Prays for same in Washington Co., and appoints Hugh Magie to receive same on 15th January, 1784.

**BEAL, HEZEKIAH.** Certificate of Gen. J. Twiggs, 3rd March, 1784. Entitled to bounty of 250 acres, and prays for same in Washington Co.

**BOGS, JOSEPH.** Certificate of Col. G. Lee, 23rd February, 1784. Entitled to bounty of 250 acres, and prays for same in Washington Co.

**BRIGGS, SAMUEL.** Petitions for bounty, and prays for same in Washington Co. Granted 287½ acres.

**BECKEM, SHERWOOD.** Certificate Col. G. Lee, 12th April 1784. Entitled to bounty 250 acres. Prays for same in Franklin Co.

**BROWNSON, NATHAN.** Certificate of John Habersham, Maj. Late Ga. Line, April 12th, 1784. Entitled to bounty of 287½ acres, and prays for same in Washington Co.

**BRYANT, WILLIAM.** Certificate of Col. J. McNiel, 20th February, 1784. Entitled to bounty of 250 acres land, and prays for same in Washington Co.

**BURLAMON, BENJ.** Certificate of Gen. John Twiggs, 3rd April, 1784. Entitled to bounty of 250 acres. Prays for same in Washington Co.

**BROWN, THOMAS, JR.** Certificate of Col. Benj. Few, 17th April, 1784. Refugeed to the State of Virginia. Entitled to 287½ acres. Prays for same in Washington Co., Ga.

**BROWN, WILLIAM.** Burke Co. Certificate of Gen. John Twiggs, 28th April, 1784. Entitled to bounty. Prays for 287½ acres in Washington Co.

**BIRD, MICHAL.** Certificate Col. E. Clark, 4th November, 1784, that he was a Minute man in the Ga. Batt.

**BENTLEY, JOHN.** Certificate of Col. E. Clark, 2nd February, 1784. Entitled to bounty, and appoints Rev. Sanders Walker to receive the same, 24th January, 1784.

**BRYANT, JOHN.** Certificate Gen. John Twiggs, 12th April, 1784. Entitled to a bounty of land, and prays for same in Washington Co.

**BERRY, WILLIAM.** Certificate Col. E. Clark, 25th March, 1784. Entitled to a bounty of 250 acres, and prays for same in Washington Co.

**BELL, HUGH.** Soldier in Ga. Line. Certificate of Maj. Gen. Lachlan McIntosh. Entitled to 230 acres of land. Granted 17th April, 1784.

**BELL, ROBERT.** Refugee soldier. Certificate Col. John Baker, 5th November, 1784, at Sunbury.

**BICKHAM, JOHN.** Entitled to bounty, and prays for 287½ acres in Washington Co.

**BRASIL, JOHN.** Certificate Col. E. Clark, 7th April, 1784. Entitled to a bounty. Appoints George Matthews, of Wilkes Co., attorney to receive same. Prays for same in Washington Co.

**BRIGGS, SAMUEL.** Refugee soldier. Certificate Gen. J. Twiggs, 3rd March, 1784. Entitled to a bounty of land.

**BADULY, WILLIAM.** Certificate of Gen. John Twiggs, 19th March, 1784. Entitled to bounty, and prays for 287½ acres in Washington Co.

**BEAL, NATHANIEL.** Certificate of Gen. J. Twiggs, 6th February, 1784. Entitled to a bounty. Prays for 250 acres of land in Washington Co.

**BEASELEY, RICHARD.** Certificate Col. E. Clark, 25th March, 1784, and certificate Col. G. Lee, 23rd February, 1784, is entitled to bounty, and prays for 287½ acres in Washington Co., and appoints Joshua Perry, attorney to receive same on 3rd April, 1784.

**BURK, WILLIAM.** Certificate Jas. Jackson, 7th April, 1784. Entitled to a bounty of 250 acres.

**BARROW, REUBIN.** Minute man. Certificate Col. John Stewart, 15th December, 1784, and certificate of Col. E. Clark, 3rd January, 1785.

**BOSTICK, LITTLEBURY.** Refugee soldier. Certificate J. Houston, 24th January, 1784. Entitled to 575 acres of land, and prays for same in Washington Co.

**BRADY, WILLIAM.** Refugee soldier. Certificate Col. E. Clark, 8th September, 1784. Entitled to bounty, and prays for 287½ acres in Washington Co.

**BROSSARD, CELERIN.** Certificate of Gen. Lachlan McIntosh, that he was a captain in the Fourth Ga. Regiment, commanded by Col. John White, 26th June, 1777; served until 1782.

**BOYD, ROBERT.** Certificate of Col. Jas. McNiel, 24th February, 1784. Entitled to bounty, and prays for 287½ acres in Washington Co.

**BLACK, HENRY.** Refugee soldier. Certificate of Col. E. Clark, 25th March, 1784. Entitled to bounty, 250 acres.

**BOND, GEORGE.** Certificate E. Clark, Col., 24th April, 1784. Entitled to a bounty of land. Prays for 250 acres in Franklin Co.

**BREWER, WILLIAM.** Certificate of Col. Wm. Candler. Entitled to a bounty of land as a refugee soldier. Prays for same in Washington Co.

**BAKER, ARTEMUS.** Certificate of Col. J. Baker, 18th March, 1784, that he was a refugee soldier.

## CERTIFICATES OF SERVICE IN AMERICAN REVOLUTION.

**BARFIELD, SOLOMON.** Certificate Col. G. Lee, 26th March, 1784, that he was a refugee soldier. Entitled to bounty of land, and prays for 250 acres in Washington Co.

**BARTON, WILLOBY.** Refugee captain. Certificate of Gen. Twiggs, and Col. E. Clark, 6th February, 1784. Entitled to 500 acres of land.

**BENTLEY, WILLIAM.** Certificate Col. E. Clark, 19th August, 1784. Entitled to a bounty, and prays for 287½ acres in Washington Co.

**BLACK, JOHN.** Certificate Col. E. Clark, 2nd February, 1784, that he was a refugee soldier. Entitled to a bounty, and prays for 250 acres in Washington Co.

**BRUNSON, DAVID.** Refugee soldier. Certificate of Col. Jas. McKay, 20th February, 1784. Entitled to bounty of 250 acres.

**BENSON, JOHN.** Certificate Gen. John Twiggs, 26th April, 1784. Entitled to a bounty; prays for 287½ acres in Washington Co.

**BAKER, THOMAS.** Certificate of Col. John Baker, 13th April, 1784, that he was a refugee soldier.

**BEAIRD, GEORGE.** Certificate Col. John Baker, 25th November, 1784, that he was a refugee soldier.

**BURNLEY, SAMUEL.** Certificate of Col. John Baker, 26th May, 1784, that he was a refugee soldier. Granted bounty.

**BOWLING, ROBERT.** Certificate Col. J. Twiggs, 4th March, 1784, that he was a refugee soldier. Entitled to bounty land.

**BRAZEL, SAMUEL.** Certificate Col. E. Clark, 21st April, 1784, that he was a refugee soldier. Entitled to 500 acres, and prays for same in Washington Co.

**BOWENS, JOEL.** Certificate of Col. E. Clark, 25th March, 1784. Entitled to bounty of land. Prays for 287½ acres in Washington Co.

**BRASWELL, ALLEN.** Certificate Col. E. Clark, 25th January, 1785, that he was a soldier in the Minute Batt. in Ga.

**BODIMAS, GEORGE.** Certificate of Col. Samuel Jack, 6th April, 1784, that he was a Minute man. Entitled to bounty. Prays for same in Washington Co.

**BEASON, PETER.** Certificate of Gen. John Twiggs, 27th February, 1784. Entitled to a bounty of land. Prays for same in Washington Co.

**BURTON, THOMAS.** Certificate of Col. Francis Pugh, 23d April, 1784, that he was a refugee soldier, and served in another State.

**BRADLEY, RICHARD.** Certificate O. Bowen, Commodore, Savannah, February 13, 1784, that he served on board the gallies three years, and was entitled to land as a private.

ROSTER OF THE REVOLUTION.

**BARTON, WILLOBY.** Certificate of Col. S. Jack, 27th April, 1784, that he enlisted as sergeant in Batt. of Minute Men, 1777. Entitled to bounty, and prays for same in Washington Co.

**BAILEY, WILLIAM.** Refugee lieut. Certificate of Col. E. Clark, 25th March, 1784. Entitled to bounty of 350 acres, and prays for same in Franklin Co.

**BERIHILL, ALEXANDER.** Certificate of Gen. J. Twiggs, 2nd March, 1784, that he was a refugee soldier, and entitled to bounty. Prays for 250 acres in Washington Co.

**BERIHILL, SAMUEL.** Certificate Gen. J. Twiggs, 2nd March, 1784. Entitled to bounty, and prays for 287½ acres in Washington Co.

**BEALL, ARCHIBALD.** Certificate of Gen. J. Twiggs, and Col. Wm. Candler. Entitled to a bounty of land, and prays for it in Washington Co.

**BURK, JAMES.** Private soldier of the Ga. Line, deceased. Certificate of Brig. Gen. Samuel Elbert, 7th May, 1784, that his heirs are entitled to a bounty of 100 acres. Granted to Mary Burk for the heirs, 25th May, 1784.

**BARRY, JOHN.** Petitions for bounty in Washington Co. Mary Barry of 96th Dist., S. C., appoints Richard Henderson attorney to secure land she is entitled to on 10th April, 1784, and Richard Henderson endorses her power of attorney over to William Denton.

**BEALL, GARRETT.** Certificate Col. E. Clark, 24th December, 1784. Entitled to bounty, 250 acres.

**BEALL, HENRY.** Minute Man, 1777. Certificate Col. E. Clark, 25th January, 1785.

**BELLEMY, RICHARD.** Certificate of Col. E. Clark, 25th March, 1784. Entitled to bounty. Prays for 250 acres in Franklin Co.

**BACON, THOMAS.** Refugee soldier. Certificate Col. John Baker, 4th April, 1785.

**BEVILL, PAUL.** Petition for bounty of 575 acres in Washington Co., May 25th, 1784, for services.

**BEVILL, JAMES.** Petition for 575 acres as a bounty for his services, May 25, 1784.

**BACON, JONATHAN.** Petitions for 287½ acres in Franklin Co., as bounty for services.

**BOLOUGH, LEWIS.** Petition for 287½ acres in Washington Co., as bounty for services.

**BLAIR, SIBBIAH.** Petition for 250 acres in Washington Co., as bounty for services.

**BARKELOE, RICHARD.** Petition for 287½ acres in Franklin Co., as bounty for his services.

## CERTIFICATES OF SERVICE IN AMERICAN REVOLUTION.

**BAKER, THOMAS.** Petition for 287½ acres in Franklin Co., as bounty for his services.

**GREEN, JAMES.** Petition of Francis Boykin, showing that the warrants Nos. 1918 and 555 issued as bounty to James Green have been lost, and he prays for duplicates, 26th May, 1784.

**GRAVES, THOMAS.** Petition of Francis Boykin, showing that the warrant No. 220, issued as bounty to Thomas Graves, has been lost, and he prays for duplicate. 26th May, 1784.

**GRAVES, RICHARD.** Petition of Francis Boykin, showing that warrant No. 1695, issued to Richard Graves, also of Washington Co., has been lost, and he prays for duplicate of same, 26th May, 1784.

**HAMPTON, JOHN.** Petition of Francis Boykin, showing that the warrant No. 389, issued as bounty to John Hampton, of Franklin Co., has been lost, and he prays for duplicate of same, 26th May, 1784.

**NAIL, JOSEPH.** Petition of Francis Boykin, showing that the warrant No. 248, issued as bounty to Joseph Nail, of Franklin Co., has been lost and also Certificate No. 58, issued to Julian Nail, of Franklin Co., and prays for duplicates of same. 26th May, 1784.

**BUGG, SHERWOOD.** Certificate of Col. J. McNiel, 5th April, 1784, that he served in the Richmond Co. Militia, and bore the rank of captain. Entitled to bounty, and prays for 575 acres in Washington Co.

**BUGG, EDMUND.** Refugee soldier. Certificate of Col. James McNiel, 22nd March, 1784. Entitled to a bounty of land, and prays for same in Franklin Co.

**BUGG, NICHOLAS.** Certificate of Col. Jas. Martin, 17th April, 1784. Entitled to a bounty of 250 acres. Prays for same in Washington Co.

**BUGG, SAMUEL.** Certificate of Col. James McNiel, 15th March, 1784. Prays for 575 acres in Washington Co.

**BUGG, JACOB.** Certificate of Col. Jas. McNiel, 19th March, 1784. Entitled to bounty. Prays for 287½ acres in Washington Co.

**BUGG, JEREMIAH.** Certificate Col. James McNiel, 15th March, 1784. Entitled to bounty. Prays for 250 acres in Washington Co.

**BUGG, JEREMIAH.** Certificate of Gen. John Twiggs, that he is entitled to a bounty as Lt. Col. and prays for same in Washington Co., 3rd April, 1784.

**BUTLER, DANIEL.** Certificate of Col. E. Clark, 2nd February, 1784. Refugee soldier. Entitled to bounty and prays for same in Washington Co.

**BOWEN, OLIVER.** Commodore. Entitled to 1,000 acres land. Granted by John Houston, 27th January, 1784.

**BROWN, ANDREW.** Certificate of Col. E. Clark, 24th April, 1784. Refugee soldier. Entitled to 250 acres of land, and prays for same in Franklin Co.

**BRADY, WILLIAM, JR.** Certificate Col. E. Clark, 25th February, 1784, was soldier in the Batt. of Minute Men, raised in defense of this State, and was not at the time an inhabitant of this State. Received bounty of land in Washington Co.

**BLAKEY, BENJ.** On certificate of Col. E. Clark, 3rd April, 1784, served as sergeant in Batt. of Minute Men, and not an inhabitant of this State at time of enlistment.

**BURKS, EDWARD.** Certificate of Col. Jas. McNeil, 20th February, 1784. Entitled to bounty, and prays for same in Washington Co.

**BOYKIN, BAOS.** Certificate of Gen, John Twiggs, 1st January, 1784. Refugee soldier.

**BRASWELL, SAMUEL, JR.** Certificate of Col. E. Clark, 24th June, 1784. Entitled to a bounty of land. Prays for 287½ acres in Franklin Co.

**BOBBETS, JACOB.** Certificate of Col. E. Clark, 20th April, 1784. Entitled to a bounty. Prays for same in Franklin Co.

**BUSSY, HEZEKIAH.** Certificate of Col. E. Clark, 25th February, 1784. Entitled to a bounty of 250 acres of land, and prays for same in Washington Co.

**BURKS, DAVID.** Certificate of Col. E. Clark, 22nd April, 1784. Entitled to a bounty of 250 acres, and prays for same in Washington Co.

**BUSSEY, THOMAS.** Certificate of E. Clark, 19th April, 1784. Entitled to 250 acres of land. Prays for same in the county of Washington.

**BRITTAIN, HENRY.** Sergeant. Certificate of Col. E. Clark, that he was a sergeant in the Batt. of Minute Men, though not an inhabitant of this State at the time of enlistment. Prays for bounty.

**BARBER, WILLIAM.** Certificate of Col. E. Clark, 23d May, 1784. Entitled to a bounty, and prays for same in Franklin Co.

**BENNIS, JOHN.** Captain. Certificate of John Habersham, major of the late Ga. Line, that his commission as captain was dated 1st of March, 1777, and that the said captain died in the service.

**BRONSON, JOHN, SR.** Certificate of Col. Caleb Howell, January 5th, 1784, that he was refugee soldier. Entitled to bounty of 250 acres, and prays for same in Washington Co.

**BRASWELL, FREDERICK.** Certificate of Col. E. Clark, 1st April, 1784. Enlisted in Batt. Minute Men for the defense of this State, though not an inhabitant at the time. Entitled to bounty, and prays for same in Washington Co.

## CERTIFICATES OF SERVICE IN AMERICAN REVOLUTION.

**BLAIR, SAMUEL.** Certificate of Gen. John Twiggs, 6th April, 1784, that he was a refugee soldier. Entitled to bounty, and prays for same in Franklin Co.

**BANKSTON, ELIJAH.** Certificate of Col. E. Clark, 26th March, 1784. Entitled to a bounty, 250 acres, and prays for same in Washington Co.

**BARBER, GEORGE.** Certificate of Col. E. Clark, 25th March, 1784, that he was a refugee lieut. Entitled to bounty, and prays for 402 acres of land in Franklin Co.

**BARNETT, MIAL.** On certificate of Col. E. Clark, 25th March, 1784, that he was a refugee soldier. Entitled to a bounty of 250 acres of land.

**BROOKS, JAS.** Certificate of Col. Jas. McNiel, 20th February, 1784. Entitled to bounty, and prays for 287½ acres in Washington Co.

**BANKSTON, DANIEL.** Certificate of Col. E. Clark, 19th April, 1784. Entitled to bounty, and prays for 287½ acres in Washington Co.

**BECKHAM, ABNER.** Certificate of Gen. John Twiggs, 4th March, 1784, that he was a refugee soldier. Entitled to bounty.

**BURTON, RICHARD.** Certificate of Capt. Isaac Hicks, captain in the 3rd Ga. Continental Batt., 28th May, 1780; that he enlisted as a soldier 7th October, 1776, from Mechlenburg Co., Va.

**BURDEYSHAW, PETER.** Certificate of Col. E. Clark, 7th December, 1784. Entitled to a bounty, and prays for same in Washington Co.

**BALDWIN, DAVID.** Heirs of, granted 575 acres of land in Washington Co., through John Moon, May 25th, 1784.

**BURLAMON, BENJ.** Certificate of Gen. John Twiggs, 3rd April, 1784, as a refugee soldier. Entitled to bounty.

**BROOKS, ROGER.** Certificate of Col. E. Clark, 7th April, 1784. Refugee soldier, and served in Batt. Minute Men. Entitled to bounty and prays for same in Washington Co.

**BARROW, REUBEEN.** Certificate of Gen. John Twiggs, 3rd February, 1785. Entitled to a bounty of 250 acres of land.

**BRYANT, JOHN.** Certificate of Col. E. Clark, 1st of April, 1784, that he was a lieutenant in the Batt. of Minute Men, raised for the defense of this State, though was not at the time an inhabitant of the State, and prays for bounty in Washington Co.

**BAKER, WILLIAM, MAJOR.** Heirs of, on certificate of Col. John Baker, 19th March, 1784, entitled to a bounty of land.

**BLACK, JOHN.** Certificate of Col. E. Clark, 26th March, 1784. Is entitled to a bounty of land; prays for 575 acres in Franklin Co.

**BRITT, CHARLES.** Certificate of Col. E. Clark, 25th February, 1784. Served as soldier in Batt. Minute Men, and was not at the time of enlistment an inhabitant of the State.

**BRASWELL, SAMPSON.** Certificate of Col. James Jackson, 19th July, 1784. Entitled to bounty of 250 acres of land.

**BURGESS, JOSEPH.** Certificate of Col. E. Clark, December 10th, 1784. Entitled to a bounty of 250 acres of land.

**BEVIL, JAMES.** Certificate of Col. Jenkins Davis, 20th February, 1784. Refugee soldier.

**BONNELL, JOHN.** Certificate of Col. Jenkins Davis, 15th March, 1784. Refugee soldier.

**BURNETT, JOHN.** Certificate of Col. Jas. McNiel, 22nd March, 1784, served in 1st Batt. Richmond Co. Militia, and was a refugee soldier. Entitled to bounty, and prays for same in Franklin Co.

**BEDDINGFIELD, NATHANIEL.** Certificate of Col. E. Clark, 2nd February, 1784. Refugee soldier. Entitled to bounty of 250 acres of land.

**BEDDINGFIELD, CHARLES.** Certificate of Col. E. Clark, 26th March, 1784. Entitled to a bounty of land, and prays for same in Franklin Co.

**BATES, JOHN.** Certificate of Col. Greenbury Lee, 23rd February, 1784. Entitled to a bounty, and prays for same in Washington Co.

**BRADLEY, JOSHUA.** Certificate of Col. Elijah Clark, 24th April, 1784. Entitled to bounty. Prays for same in Franklin Co.

**BRADLEY, WILLIAM, SR.** Certificate Col. Elijah Clark, 25th February, 1784, that he was commissioned as a lieutenant of Minute Men, raised for the defense of this State, June 3rd, 1777, and was not at time an inhabitant of the State.

**BRADLEY, RICHARD.** Certificate of Commodore Oliver Bowen, February 17th, 1784, that he was a private on board one of the Ga. State galleys, and is entitled to 100 acres of land as bounty. Another certificate from Col. John Baker, 27th March, 1784, that he was a refugee soldier entitled to bounty. Prays for 287½ acres in Washington Co.

**BAKER, JOHN.** Col. of Liberty Co. Certificate of Nathan Brownson at Augusta, 14th April, 1784, that he was a refugee colonel.

**BRADLEY, MICHAEL.** Certificate of Lieut. Christopher Hillary, 4th Ga. Regt. that he enlisted in the 4th Ga. Regt. July, 1777, and died in the service at Savannah, and he left an only son named Abram, now in this State, about ten years old. October 1st, 1783.

**BEATY, SAMUEL.** Of Burke Co., appoints Hugh Lawson, of said county, attorney to receive warrant for land for service in the Minute Battalion, 16th May, 1784.

CERTIFICATES OF SERVICE IN AMERICAN REVOLUTION. 37

**BARKLOW, RICHARD.** Heirs of, are granted through Perry Wilson, 287½ acres of land in Franklin Co., by John Habersham, 17th May, 1784.

**BARKSDALE, ALEN.** Certificate of Col. E. Clark, 8th September, 1784, that Allen Barksdale is entitled to a bounty, and prays for 287½ acres in Franklin Co.

**BEAN, REUBIN.** Certificate of Col. E. Clark, 2nd February, 1785, was a soldier in the Batt. of Minute Men, but was not an inhabitant of the State at the time.

**BLACK, WILLIAM.** Certificate of Col. E. Clark, 25th March, 1784. Served as lieutenant, and was entitled to bounty, and prays for 575 acres in Franklin Co.

**BOOTH, ABRAM.** Certificate of Col. E. Clark, 25th March, 1784. Entitled to bounty, and prays for 287½ acres in Franklin Co.

**BARNETT, THOMAS.** Certificate of Jas. McNiell, 17th May, 1784, that he was an invalid in the 1st Batt. Richmond Co. militia. Entitled to bounty, and prays for same in Washington Co.

**BEARD, JOHN.** Certificate of Col. E. Clark, 3rd April, 1784. Served as a sergeant in Batt. of Minute Men, though not an inhabitant of this State, and is entitled to bounty, and prays for same in Washington Co.

**BARKER, WILLOBY.** On certificate of Col. Jas. Martin, that he served as a refugee captain, and was entitled to 500 acres of land, and was granted same in Washington Co., 25th May, 1784.

**BURKS, ROLAND.** On certificate of Col. E. Clark, 27th May, 1784, is entitled to a bounty, and prays for 287½ acres in Washington Co.

**BARNHART, GEORGE, JR.** Certificate of Col. E. Clark, 6th April, 1784. Entitled to a bounty of 250 acres, and prays for same in Washington Co.

**BROWNSON, NATHAN.** Certificate of John Habersham, major late Ga. line. Entitled to a bounty, and prays for 287½ acres in Washington Co.

**BRASIL, FERDINAND.** Certificate of Col. E. Clark, 25th May, 1784, that he was in the Batt. of Minute Men, raised for the defense of this State, though not at time an inhabitant. Prays for bounty in Washington Co.

**BAKER, ARTEMUS.** Granted 287½ acres.

**BOBOUGH, LEWIS.** Certificate of James Jackson, July 30, 1784, that he served in the Ga. State Legion Inf.

**BLANCHARD, REUBEN.** Appoints Capt. Thomas Bush attorney to take a bounty warrant out of the land office, and sign his name to a receipt of the same, 19th May, 1784. On certificate of Col. G. Lee, 11th March, 1784, he was granted 250 acres of land in Washington Co.

**BURT, MOODY.** Certificate of Col. Jas. McNiel, 7th April, 1784, is entitled to a bounty of 250 acres of land. Prays for same in Washington Co. He appointed Capt. Jesse Sanders to receive same.

**BERRY, JOHN.** Certificate of E. Clark, and G. Lee, 24th April, 1784, was granted bounties in Franklin and Washington counties, and appointed William Roussau to receive his warrant for same. 25th April, 1784.

**BERRY, RICHARD.** Certificate of Col. E. Clark, 7th April, 1784. Entitled to a bounty of 250 acres of land. Prays for same in the county of Washington. Signed William Berry for Richard Berry.

**BANKSTON, JACOB.** Certificate of Col. E. Clark, 26th March, 1784. Entitled to a bounty. Prays for 287½ acres in Washington Co.

**BLOUNT, JACOB.** Petition of the heirs of Jacob Blount, surgeon's mate in the galley service, for 690 acres of land, through Oliver Lewis, May 25th, 1784.

**BRADY, WILLIAM, SR.** Certificate of Col. E. Clark, 7th April, 1784. Entitled to a bounty. Prays for 287½ acres in Washington Co. Appoints Sanders Walker attorney to receive same.

**BEVIL.** Certificate of Col. Jas. Davis, 26th February, 1784, that he was a refugee soldier.

**BARNETT, WILLIAM.** Certificate of Col. Jas. McNiel, 3rd April, 1784. Entitled to a bounty. Prays for 250 acres in Washington Co.

**BEATY, SAMUEL.** 5th of April, 1784. Petitions for 287½ acres of land in Washington Co. as bounty for his services. Granted.

**BRYANT, BENJ.** Certificate of Col. E. Clark, 26th July, 1784. Entitled to a bounty, and prays for 287½ acres in Washington Co.

**BIRD, JOHN.** Certificate of Col. E. Clark, January, 1785, served as a soldier in the 1st Batt. of Minute Men raised for the defense of this State, although not inhabitant at the time.

**BUTLER, JOHN.** Certificate of Col. Jas. Jackson, 20th September, 1784. Entitled to a bounty. Prays for 250 acres in Washington Co.

**BEASLEY, WILLIAM.** Certificate of Col. G. Lee, and Col. E. Clark, 28th February, 1784. Entitled to a bounty. Prays for 287½ acres in Washington Co., and appoints Joshua Perry his attorney to receive his warrant for same.

**BURCH, EDWARD.** May 4th, 1784. Appoints Samuel Briggs, attorney to receive a warrant for 575 acres of land in the name of John Whitichar, deceased.

**BOWMAN, JACOB.** Certificate of Col. Jas. McNiel, 9th April, 1784. Entitled to a bounty of 250 acres.

## CERTIFICATES OF SERVICE IN AMERICAN REVOLUTION.

**BRUTON, JOHN.** Certificate of Gen. John Twiggs, 7th April, 1784. Entitled to a bounty of land as a refugee soldier, and prays for same in the county of Washington.

**BURK, THEOPHILOUS.** Certificate of Col. Jas. Jackson, 7th April, 1784. Entitled to a bounty of 250 acres.

**BRANDON, JOHN.** Petitions for 287½ acres of land as bounty for his services, in the County of Washington. Granted, 16th April, 1784.

**BUTLER, JOHN.** Certificate of Col. E. Clark, 3rd of January, 1785. Served in Batt. of Minute Men raised for defense of this State, though not at that time an inhabitant.

**BROOK, ROGER.** Certificate of Col. E. Clark, September 6th, 1784. Entitled to bounty of 250 acres of land. Prays for same in Washington Co.

**BERRYHILL, SAMUEL.** Certificate of Gen. John Twiggs, March 2, 1784. Entitled to a bounty of land as refugee, and prays for same in Washington Co.

**BECKHAM, ALLEN.** Certificate of Col. Jas. Jackson, 17th July, 1784. Entitled to a bounty, and prays for 287½ acres in Washington Co.

**BARNETT, DANIEL.** Certificate of Col. E. Clark, 2nd February, 1784, that he was a refugee soldier, and is entitled to 250 acres of bounty land.

**BARNARD, WILLIAM.** Certificate of Col. Jas. McNiel, 20th February, 1784. Refugee soldier. Entitled to bounty of 250 acres of land.

**BREWER, ERASMUS.** Certificate of Col. E. Clark, 26th March, 1784, that he was entitled to bounty of 250 acres, and prays for same in Franklin Co.

**BAKER, WILLIAM JEANS.** Certificate of Col. John Baker, 18th March, 1784. Refugee soldier. Entitled to bounty. Prays for 287½ acres in Washington Co.

**BLAYER, WILLIAM.** Certificate of Col. Francis Pew, that he was a refugee soldier, and his heirs are entitled to a bounty of 250 acres. February, 1784.

**BURNETT, JOSHUA.** Certificate of Col. E. Clark, 7th August, 1784, that he was a refugee soldier. Entitled to bounty. Prays for 287½ acres in Washington Co.

**BRUNSON, EBENEZER.** On certificate of Col. Jas. McKay, 29th January, 1784, that his heirs are entitled to his bounty of 250 acres of land, as a refugee soldier.

**BROSSARD, CELERINE.** Petitions for 920 acres of land, as bounty for his service as captain and major, in the line of this State, in 1777. Granted 20th August, 1784.

**BRADLEY, MICHAEL.** Certificate of Gen. Lachlan McIntosh, and Capt. Hillary, 19th March, 1784, that his son Abraham, is entitled to 100 acres of land as bounty for his father's services.

**BALL, WILLIAM.** Certificate of Col. E. Clark, 25th March, 1784. Refugee soldier. Entitled to 250 acres of land as bounty.

**BURGSTEINER, DANIEL.** Certificate of Col. Jenkins Davis, 9th February, 1784. Refugee soldier.

**BOLTEN, FRANCIS.** Certificate of Col. E. Clark, 29th January, 1785, that he was a Minute Man, though not an inhabitant of the State at the time of enlistment.

**BRADDOCK, JOHN.** 2nd April, 1784, was granted 600 acres of land for his services as captain, through his attorney, Nathan Brownson.

**BROWN, JOHN.** Certificate of Col. Jas. Pannill, 2nd March, 1784, that he was a soldier in the 2nd Batt. of Continental Troops, and served three years. Prays for 200 acres of land in the Continental reserve.

**BURTON, THOS.** Petitions for 287½ acres in Washington Co., as bounty for his services. March 25th, 1784.

**BRASWELL, GEORGE.** Certificate of Col. E. Clark, 25th January, 1785. Minute man, not at the time of enlistment an inhabitant of the State.

**BARNES, WILLIAM.** Certificate of Col. E. Clark, January, 1785. Minute man; was not at time of enlistment an inhabitant of this State.

**BRANTLEY, JEREMIAH.** Certificate of Col. Samuel Jacks, 7th April, 1784. Sergeant in Batt. of Minute Men on the expedition to Florida.

**BARNETT, NATHAN.** Certificate of Col. E. Clark, 25th March, 1784. Entitled to a bounty as a refugee soldier.

**BARNETT, PHILIP.** Certificate of Col. Samuel Jack, 29th April, 1784. Minute man; was not at the time inhabitant of the State. Prays for land in Franklin Co.

**BLACK, JOHN.** Certificate of Col. E. Clark, 25th March, 1784. Refugee soldier. Entitled to 250 acres of land as bounty.

**BEATY, WILLIAM.** Of Burke Co., appointed Hugh Lawson attorney to receive warrant for bounty land, 16th May, 1784.

**BOYD, JOHN.** Certificate of Col. E. Clark, 20th April, 1784, that he was a Minute man, but not an inhabitant of the State at the time of his enlistment. Prays for bounty land in Washington Co., 287½ acres.

**BUCKHALTER, JOHN.** Certificate of Col. E. Clark, 25th March, 1784. He is entitled to bounty, and prays for 287½ acres in Washington Co.

**BLOUNT, JACOB.** Certificate of Oliver Bowen, Commodore, 24th February, 1784, that he was a surgeon's mate in the galley service, and his heirs are entitled to 600 acres of land.

# CERTIFICATES OF SERVICE IN AMERICAN REVOLUTION. 41

**BANKS, REUBEN.** Certificate of Lt. Col. J. Pannill, June 7th, 1784, that he was a soldier in the 2nd regt. of Continental Troops of Ga., and served three years. Prays for 230 acres in the Continental fork of the Oconee rivers.

**BARNARD, JOEL.** Certificate of Col. Jas. McNeil, 19th February, 1784, that he was a refugee soldier from Richmond county.

**BAGGS, JOHN.** Certificate of Col. Samuel Jacks, 6th April, 1784, that he was a Minute man, though not an inhabitant of the State at the time of enlistment. Appoints Hugh Lawson, of Burke Co., attorney to receive bounty land. Prays for same in Washington Co.

**BURKS, JOHN.** Certificate of Col. E. Clark, 20th April, 1784, that he was a captain of Minute Men, though not an inhabitant of this State at the time of enlistment. Prays for 575 acres of land in Washington Co.

**BURTON, RICHARD.** Certificate of J. Houston, 29th January, 1784, that he was a soldier in the Georgia line, and is entitled to 100 acres of land.

**BUSSON, JONATHAN.** Certificate of Col. Jas. Jackson, 20th September, 1784, that he was a refugee and is entitled to 250 acres of bounty land; prays for same in Washington Co.

**BURTON, RICHARD.** Appointed Mr. Nathaniel Peavie, of Chatham Co., Savannah, to receive his bounty warrant due for three years' service, on the 16th day of January, 1784.

**BURNEY, JOHN.** Certificate of Col. E. Clark, 26th March, 1784. Entitled to a bounty, and prays for same in Washington Co.

**BROOKS, JESSEY.** Certificate of Col. G. Lee, 11th March, 1784. Entitled to a bounty of 250 acres of land; prays for same in Washington Co.

**BALDWIN, WILLIAM.** Petitioned for 345 acres in Washington Co., as a bounty for his services.

**BOYD, EDWARD.** Certificate of Col. Wm. Candler, 6th April, 1784, that he was a refugee soldier.

**BAXTER, ANDREW.** Certificate of Col. Elijah Clark, 5th October, 1784, that he was a soldier under his command, and prays for bounty land in Washington Co.

**BEARD, EDMUND.** Certificate of Col. E. Clark, 5th April, 1784. Minute man, and is entitled to bounty land. Prays for 287½ acres in Franklin Co. (Though not an inhabitant of the State.)

**BRANHAM, SAMUEL.** Certificate of Col. E. Clark, 3rd April, 1784. Minute man. Entitled to bounty lands. (Not an inhabitant of the State.)

**BURTON, JOHN.** Certificate of Col. E. Clark, 3rd January, 1785. Minute man, but not an inhabitant of the State at the time of his enlistment.

**BURNS, ANDREW.** Certificate of Col. Jas. McNeil, 15th March, 1784. Entitled to a bounty of land, and prays for 250 acres in Washington Co.

**BENFIELD, RICHARD.** Certificate of Col. E. Clark, 25th March, 1784. Entitled to a bounty of 250 acres of land.

**BURNSIDES, JOHN.** Certificate of Gen. John Twiggs, March 8th, 1784. Entitled to a bounty as a refugee soldier.

**BAKER, ARTEMUS.** Petition for 287½ acres of land in Washington Co., as bounty for services. Granted 13th April, 1784. Certificate of Col. Jno. Baker.

**BURT, MOODY.** Certificate of Gen. John Twiggs, 1st of January, 1784. Refugee soldier. Entitled to 250 acres of land, and prays for same in Washington Co. Appoints Col. Samuel Jack to take out warrant for same.

**BAKER, WHITMARSH.** Certificate of Col. John Baker, 22d February, 1784. Refugee soldier. Entitled to a bounty of land.

**BARNETT, JOHN.** Certificate of Col. E. Clark, 2nd February, 1784. Refugee soldier.

**BRADFORD, OSIAH.** Certificate of Col. E. Clark, 20th April, 1784. Entitled to a bounty of 250 acres of land. Prays for same in Franklin Co.

**BUTRY, ZACHARIAH.** Certificate of Maj. B. Porter, 26th July, 1784. A private soldier in the 2nd Ga. Continental Batt., and served three years. Petitioner prays for bounty of 230 acres in the Continental fork of the Oconee River.

**BARRON, WILLIAM.** Certificate of Col. Jas. McNeil, 15th March, 1784. Entitled to a bounty of 250 acres of land, and prays for same in Washington Co.

**BEARD, JOHN.** Certificate of Col. E. Clark, 2nd February, 1784. Minute man, though not an inhabitant of the State at the time of enlistment.

**BROWN, JAMES.** Certificate of Col. E. Clark, January, 1785. Minute man, though not an inhabitant of the State at the time of enlistment.

**BROWN, JOHN.** Certificate of Col. E. Clark, 17th August, 1781. Refugee soldier. Entitled to 250 acres of land.

**BEVIL, PAUL.** Certificate of Cols. Howell and J. Davis, 24th February, 1784. Refugee soldier. Entitled to 500 acres of land.

**BARNETT, WILLIAM.** Refugee soldier. Prays for bounty land in Washington Co., 6th April, 1784. Appoints Thos. Bush, attorney to receive 250 acres on the 5th April, 1784. On certificate of Col. Jas. McNeil.

**BARNETT, JOEL.** Petition for 287½ acres of land in Washington Co., April 7, 1784, as bounty for his services.

## CERTIFICATES OF SERVICE IN AMERICAN REVOLUTION. 43

**BARNETT, JOHN.** Certificate of Col. E. Clark, 25th March, 1784. Refugee soldier. Entitled to bounty, 250 acres of land.

**BANKSTON, DANIEL.** Petition for 287½ acres of land in Washington Co., as bounty for his services.

**BARKELOE, RICHARD.** Certificate of Gen. John Twiggs, 26th April, 1784. Entitled to a bounty as a worthy refugee.

**BOSTICK, NATHAN.** Certificate of Col. Jas. McNeil, 24th March, 1784. Refugee soldier. Entitled to a bounty, and prays for same.

**BRASWELL, JOSEPH.** Certificate of Col. E. Clark, 25th January, 1785. Minute man, though not an inhabitant of the State at time of enlistment.

**BLACK, WILLIAM.** Certificate of Col. E. Clark, 7th February, 1784. Refugee soldier. Entitled to bounty of 250 acres.

**BRANDON, JOHN.** Certificate of Col. Jas. McNeil, 15th March 1784. Entitled to a bounty of 250 acres of land.

**BAIN, REUBEN.** Certificate of Col. John Stewart, 19th April, 1784. That he was a minute man in Col. Stewart's battalion though not an inhabitant of the State at the time of enlistment, and that he went on the Florida expedition and was discharged. The dicharge was signed by Col. E. Clark, in Liberty county shows that he was in Capt. Henry Kar's company and was discharged 27th July, 1778. Prays for bounty in Franklin county.

**BURCH, CHARLES.** Certificate of Gen. John Twiggs, 6th February, 1784. That he was a refugee soldier and was entitled to two bounties equalling 500 acres.

**BURKALOW, WILLIAM.** Certificate of Gen. John Twiggs, 8th March 1784. That he was entitled to a bounty of 250 acres of land, and prays for same in Franklin county. Assigns his title to same to Robert Killcreast, 21st June 1784. Robert Killcreast assigns his right to James Hogg, on the 6th July, 1784.

**BRASWELL, WILLIAM.** Certificate of Col. E. Clark, 10th December, 1784. That he was entitled to a bounty of 250 acres.

**BUTLER, ROBERT.** Certificate of Col. John Stewart, 27th July, 1784. Minute man though not an inhabitant at the time of enlistment, entitled to a bounty of land and prays for 287½ acres in Franklin county.

**BENDER, JOHN.** Certificate of Col. G. Lee, 26th April. Entitled to 250 acres of land, and prays for same in Flanklin Co.

**BAKER, NATHANIEL.** Certificate of Col. John Baker, 28th April, 1784, refugee soldier.

**BROOM, THOMAS.** Certificate of Brig. Gen. John Twiggs, 22nd March, 1784. Entitled to a bounty of land as a refugee soldier and prays for same in Franklin Co. Assigns his right to Philip Lamar, on March 10th, 1784.

**BECKHAM, SAMUEL.** Certificate of Col. G. Lee, 5th March, 1784. Entitled to a bounty of 287½ acres.

**BRACK, BENJ.** Certificate of Gen. John Twiggs, 26th April, 1784. Entitled to a bounty of land.

**BECKHAM, SOLOMAN.** Certificate of Col. G. Lee, 2nd March, 1784. Entitled to bounty.

**BRASWELL, JAMES.** Certificate of Col. E. Clark, 25th January, 1784. Minute man, though not at the time of enlistment an inhabitant of State.

**BRANTLEY, THOS.** Certificate of Col. E. Clark, 26th March, 1784. Entitled to a bounty, 287½ acres, prays for same in Washington Co.

**BURNETT, ANDREW.** Petitions for bounty of land that he bought of Jos. Kirkham, May 1784.

**BROWN, THOS.** Certificate of Col. E. Clark, 25th March, 1784. Entitled to a bounty of land, and prays for 287½ acres in Washington Co.

**BENTLEY, JOHN.** Certifiicate of Col. E. Clarke, 25th February, 1784. Entitled to a bounty of land, prays for 287½ acres in Washington Co.

**BALDWIN, WILLIAM.** Certificate of Col. E. Clark, 25th February, 1784. As Serge. in Batt. of Minute men, though not at the time of enlistment an inhabitant of this State. Entitled to bounty and prays for 287½ acres in Washington Co.

**BOWIN, EPHRIAM.** Certificate of Col. E. Clark, 2nd February, 1784. Refugee soldier, entitled to 250 acres of land.

**BLACK, EDWARD.** Certificate of Col. E. Clark, 8th September, 1784. Entitled to a bounty and prays for 287½ acres in Washington Co.

**BANKSTON, JOHN.** Certificate of Col. E. Clark, 26th March, 1784. Entitled to a bounty and prays for 287½ acres in Washington Co.

**BEATY, WILLIAM.** Certificate of Col. Twiggs, 24th February, 1784. Entitled to a bounty and prays for 287½ acres in Washington Co.

**BISHOP, JOSHUA.** Certificate of Col. E. Clark, 26th March, 1784. Entitled to a bounty, and prays for same in Washington Co.

**BUTLER, DANIEL.** Certificate of Col. E. Clark, 25th March, 1784. Entitled to a bounty of 250 acres of land.

**BRASWELL, ALLIN.** Certificate of Col. E. Clark, 10th December, 1784. Entitled to a bounty of 250 acres of land, and prays for same in Washington Co.

**BARDEN, GILBERT.** Certificate of Col. E. Clark, 20th April, 1784. Entitled to a bounty and prays for 287½ acres in Franklin Co.

## CERTIFICATES OF SERVICE IN AMERICAN REVOLUTION. 45

**BONNER, WILLIAM.** Certificate of Col. E. Clark, 25th March, 1784. Entitled to 250 acres as a bounty and prays for same in Washington Co.

**BROWN, JOHN.** Of Wilkes Co. Certificate of E. Clark, 2nd December, 1783. Entitled to bounty land as a refugee soldier, granted.

**BROWN, ANDREW.** Certificate of Col. E. Clark, 20th May, 1784. Refugee soldier, prays for bounty in Washington Co. Petition presented by Thomas Glascock.

**BROWN, SAMUEL.** Certificate of Col. G. Lee, 26th April, 1784. Entitled to a bounty of 250 acres of land, and prays for same in Washington Co.

**BROWN, FRANCIS.** Certificate of Lt. Col. J. Pannill, 7th September, 1784. Entitled as a private soldier 2nd Ga. Continental Batt., and served three years, and prays for 230 acres of land in the Continental fork of the Oconee river.

**BROWN, ALLEN.** Certificate of Col. Twiggs, 21st April, 1784. Refugee soldier entitled to a bounty of land, and prays for same in Franklin Co.

**BERRIAN, JOHN.** Certificate of Maj. John McIntosh, 3rd April 1784. That he was a Maj. in the Continental line and is entitled to 800 acres of land.

**BURKHALTER, JOSHUA.** Certificate of Col. E. Clark, 20th May, 1784. Entitled to a bounty of 287½ acres, and prays for same in Washington Co.

**BRASWELL, JOSEPH.** Certificate of Col. E. Clark, 10th December, 1784. Entitled to a bounty of 250 acres and prays for same in Washington Co.

**BUTLER, FORD.** Certificate of Col. E. Clark, 2nd February, 1784. Refugee soldier.

**BEATY, SAMUEL.** Certificate of Col. Samuel Jack, 6th April, 1784. That he was a Minute man, and not an inhabitant of the State at the time of enlistment.

**BURKES, JOSEPH.** Certificate of Col. E. Clark, 20th April, 1784. That he was a Minute man and not an inhabitant of the State at time of enlistment.

**BOWEN, OLIVER.** Commodore, "State of Georgia, in convention, Thursday January 30th, 1777, ordered, that the House do proceed immediately to ballot for a Commodore—The House proceeded to ballot accordingly, when on closing the poll it appeared that Oliver Bowen, Esqr., was duly elected Commodore or Commander of our Naval Dept. A true extract from the Minutes of the Convention—J. Wood, Jr., Clerk, House of Assembly."

**BUTLER, EDWARD.** At a court held for Hanover Co. Va., November 6th, 1783, the court being informed of a law passed by the State of Georgia, requiring any persons emigrating from other States in the Union to the said State of Georgia, before they become citizens of the same to bring with them a certificate from the court of the county where they reside, of their being good citizens and, a friend to the rights and liberties of America."

"Edward Butler, who informs the said court of his intention of moving himself to the state of Georgia have desired a certificate of the same. Therefore, this court do certify that the said Edward Butler, hath been long an inhabitant of the said county of Hanover, and hath conducted himself in every instance as a good and worthy citizen, and uniformly given, undeniable of his attachment to the cause of America, and the independence thereof. Richard Chapman, (Jsyms, Lt. H. Co.) Thos. Travilian William Johnson, George Clough. Park Goodall."

**BOYKIN, BYUS.** Appoints Jonathan Hemp, Esq., of Burke Co., to obtain his bounty of land, due for his services, on 29th February, 1784. Prays for 575 acres.

**BRADSHAW, PETER.** Certificate of Col. E. Clark, 24th January, 1785. That he was a Minute man, though not an inhabitant of the state at the time of enlistment.

**BLACKSELL, THOMAS.** Certificate of Col. John Baker, 16th March, 1784, That he was a refugee soldier entitled to 500 acres of land, granted 575 acres in Washington Co., 13th April, 1784.

**BALDWIN, DAVID.** Capt., Sr. Certificate of Col. John Stewart, 15th May, 1784, Captain of a company of Minute men, on the Florida expedition, and is entitled to bounty of land.

**BALDWIN, MORDECAI.** Certificate of Col. E. Clark, 20th February, 1784. That he was a Lieutenant of Minute Men, though not an inhabitant of the State at time of enlistment.

**BRAKER, WILLIAM.** Certificate of Col. E. Clark, 16th November, 1784, that he was a Minute Man, though not an inhabitant of the State.

**BUTLER, WILLIAM.** Certificate of E. Clark, 14th May, 1784, that he was entitled to a bounty of 250 acres and prays for same in Washington Co.

**BALL, SAMPSON.** Certificate of Col. John Baker, 19th May, 1784, entitled to bounty, and prays for 287½ acres in Washington Co.

C.

**COATS, LESLEY.** Certificate of Col. E. Clarke, 2nd February, 1784, entitled to a bounty of 250 acres of land, and appoints Sanders Walker to receive warrant for same.

**CONE, WILLIAM, Sr.** Certificate of Col. Jas. Martin, 24th April, 1784, that he was in the 1st Batt. of Richmond Co., militia, is an invalid, and entitled to 287½ acres of land bounty.

**CONE, WILLIAM, Jr.** Certificate of Col. Jas. McNeil, 28th February, 1784, entitled to a bounty and prays for 250 acres in Washington Co.

**COX, JOHN.** Certificate of Col. E. Clark, 22nd May, 1784. Entitled to a bounty of land, and prays for 287½ acres in Franklin Co.

## CERTIFICATES OF SERVICE IN AMERICAN REVOLUTION. 47

**COX, BENJ.** Certificate of Col. E. Clark, 3rd February, 1785. That he was in the Minute men, though not an inhabitant of the State and is entitled to a bounty.

**CRIDINGTON, JOHN.** Certificate of Col. Jas. McNeil, 1st February, 1784. That he is entitled to a bounty of 250 acres of land.

**COBB, EZEKIEL.** Certificate of Col. E. Clark, 2nd February, 1784. Entitled to a bounty, and prays for 287½ acres in Washington Co.

**CULBREATH, JAMES.** Certificate of Col. James McNeil, 19th February, 1784. That he was a refugee soldier entitled to a bounty.

**CASTLEBERRY, PETER.** Certificate of Col. Wm. Few, 28th October, 1784. That he is entitled to a bounty, and prays for 287½ acres in Washington Co. Served under Capt. James Daneley.

**COLE, JOHN, Sr.** Certificate of Col. E. Clarke, 2nd February, 1784. That he is entitled to a citizen's bounty.

**CHANEY, EMANUEL.** Certificate of Col. E. Clarke, 20th May, 1784. Entitled to a bounty as a refugee soldier and prays for same in Franklin Co.

**CHAMBLISS, (CHAMBERS) JOHN.** Certificate of Col. Jas. McNeil, 21 July, 1784. Entitled to a bounty, and prays for 287½ acres in Washington Co.

**CROKER, WILLIAM.** Certificate of H. Allison, 21st April, 1784. That he served three years in the 2nd Ga. Continental Regt. Prays for 200 acres of land in the Continental Reserve.

**CRONBERGER, CHRISTOPHER.** Certificate of Col. Jenkins Davis, 16th February, 1784. That he was a refugee soldier and was killed in service, and that Barbara Cronberger is his widow, and he left no children.

**COSSINS, DAVID.** On the 18th day of May, 1784, appoints William Chiles attorney to receive his warrant for bounty land.

**CLEMMONS, ISAAC.** Certificate of Col. John Twiggs, 24th May, 1784. That he was a refugee soldier entitled to a bounty. Granted to Elizabeth Clements, executor.

**CLEMENTS, SAMUEL.** Certificate of Col. John Twiggs, 30th March, 1784. Entitled to a bounty, and prays for 287½ acres in Washington Co., and appoints John Clements of Burke Co., attorney to receive warrant.

**CHISOLM, THOS., ESQR.** On Certificate of Gen. John Twiggs, May, 1784. That he was a refugee soldier entitled to a bounty of 287½ acres and prays for same in Washington Co.

**COUSINS, WILLIAM.** Certificate of Col. Jas. McNeil, 5th April, 1784. Entitled to a bounty of 287½ acres.

**COLSON, WILLIAM.** Certificate of Col. Caleb Howell, 20th February, 1784, Effingham Co. Entitled to a bounty of 287½ acres, and prays for same in Washington Co.

**CAMPBELL, GILBERT.** Petitions for bounty of 250 acres of land in Washington Co., for his service as a private in the Minute Batt. of the State, granted 15th April, 1784.

**CRAWFORD, CHARLES.** Petitions for 287½ acres in Washington Co., as bounty, granted 16th April, 1784.

**CAMPBELL, WILLIAM.** Certificate of Col. Samuel Jack, 6th April, 1784. That he served as a private in the Batt. of Minute Men, though not at the time of enlistment an inhabitant of the State, and prays for bounty land in Washington Co.

**COTHRON, JOSIAH.** Certificate of Gen. John Twiggs, 15th March, 1784. That he was entitled to a bounty as a refugee soldier and prays for same in Washington Co.

**CURL, HENRY.** Certificate of Col. E. Clark, 1st of April, 1784. That he was a Minute man, though not an inhabitant of the State at the time of enlistment, and prays for bounty of land in Washington Co.

**CURL, JOHN.** Certificate of Col. E. Clark, 1st of April, 1784. That he was a Minute man, though not an inhabitant of the State at the time of enlistment, and prays for bounty of land in Washington Co.

**CONE, JAMES.** Certificate of Col. G. Lee, 26th February, 1784. That he is entitled to a bounty of land, 250 acres.

**CADY, JOHN.** Certificate of Col. E. Clark, 2nd February, 1784. Entitled to a bounty of 250 acres of land.

**CARTER, DAVID.** Certificate of Col. Jas. McNeil, 15th March, 1784. Entitled to bounty, and prays for 287½ acres in Washington Co.

**CARTER, PATRICK.** Certificate of Col. E. Clark, 1st April, 1784. That he was a Minute man, though not an inhabitant of the State at the time of enlistment, entitled to a bounty, and prays for 287½ acres in Washington Co.

**CORUTHERS, (CRUDDERS) WILLIAM.** Certificate of Col. Samuel Jack, 22nd April, 1784. That he was a Minute man, though not an inhabitant of the State, prays for 287½ acres in Washington Co.

**CHANDLER, MORDECAI.** Certificate of Col. Samuel Jack, 13th March, 1784. That he was a Minute man, though not at the time of enlistment, an inhabitant of the State.

**CALK, JAMES.** Certificate of Col. E. Clark, 6th April, 1784. That he was a Minute man, though not an inhabitant of the State at the time of enlistment. Prays for bounty in Washington Co.

**CARSWELL, ALEXANDER, SR.,** Power of attorney to Benjamin Blount of Southampton, Va., to take out a warrant for bounty land, 21st of April, 1784.

## CERTIFICATES OF SERVICE IN AMERICAN REVOLUTION. 49

Witnesses, Samuel Briggs, and Absolom Harris. On certificate of Gen. Jas. Twigg.

**CUNNINGHAM, JAMES.** Certificate of Col. E. Clark, 28th February, 1784. That he was entitled to a bounty of 250 acres of land as a refugee soldier.

**CAULEY, RICHARD.** Certificate of Col. E. Clark, 25th January, 1785. That he was a Minute man, though not at the time of enlistment an inhabitant of the State.

**CORBIN, WILLIAM.** Of Virginia. Certificate of Gen. Samuel Elbert, 5th March, 1784. That he was a soldier for three years in the 3rd Ga. Regt. Prays for 230 acres in the Continental Reserve. Appoints Capt. J. W. Wagnon attorney, to receive his warrant.

**COLLINS, JOHN.** On certificate of Col. Samuel Jack, 7th April, 1784. That he was a Minute man, though not an inhabitant of the State, prays for bounty land in Washington Co.

**CARTLEDGE, JAMES.** On certificate of Col. James McNeil, 5th April, 1784. That he served in the Richmond Co. Militia.

**CARTER, HENRY.** Certificate of Col. E. Clark, 1st April, 1784. That he was a Minute man, though not an inhabitant of the State, entitled to bounty, and prays for same in Washington Co.

**CARTER, THOMAS.** Certificate of Col. E. Clark, 12th April, 1784. That he was entitled to a bounty of land, and prays for 287½ acres in Flanklin Co.

**CARLYLE, JOHN.** Certificate of Col. Clark, 25th March, 1784. That he was entitled to a bounty, and prays for 250 acres of land in Washington Co.

**CONE, JAMES.** Certificate of Col. Wm. Candler, that he served in his regt. of refugees from this State. Granted a bounty of land on the 20th February 1784.

**CARSON, JOSEPH.** Certificate of Col. E. Clark, 7th April, 1784. That he was a refugee soldier entitled to a bounty of land.

**COCK, CALEB.** Petitions for 287½ acres of land in Washington Co., as bounty for his services. On certificate of Gen. Jno. Twiggs.

**CUP, MICHAEL.** Certificate of Col. E. Clark, 10th September, 1784. That he was a Minute man, though not an inhabitant of the State at time of enlistment, entitled to bounty, and prays for 287½ acres in Franklin Co.

**COATS, HENRY.** Certificate of Col. E. Clark, 9th April, 1784. Entitled to a bounty of land, and prays for 287½ acres in Washington Co.

**COBB, JOSEPH.** Certificate of Col. E. Clark, 26th March, 1784. Entitled to a bounty of 250 acres of land. Prays for same in Washington Co.

**CHILDERS, DAVID.** Certificate of Gen. Samuel Elbert, 20th March, 1784. That he was a private in the 2nd Batt. of Continental troops, and is entitled to bounty.

**CLARK, LEWIS.** Certificate of Col. E. Clark, 9th April, 1784. Entitled to two bounties of land as a refugee and citizen, and prays for same in Washington Co.

**CARTLEDGE, JAMES.** Certificate of Col. E. Clark, 1st April, 1784. That he was a Minute man, though not an inhabitant of the State at the time of enlistment, granted 287½ acres of land in Franklin Co.

**CURRY, JACOB.** Certificate of Col. E. Clark, 3rd January, 1785. Entitled to a bounty as a Minute man, though not an inhabitant of the State at the titme of enlistment.

**CROSBY, WILLIAM.** Certificate of Col. E. Clark, 1st April, 1784. That he was a Minute man, though not an inhabitant of the State at the time of enlistment. Prays for 287½ acres in Washington Co.

**CRAB, SAMUEL.** Certificate of Col. G. Lee, 11th March, 1784. That he is entitled to a bounty, and prays for 287½ acres in Washington Co.

**CLARK, JAMES, SR.** Certificate of Col. E. Clark, 6th April, 1784. That he was a Minute man, and prays for bounty land in Washington Co.

**CLEMENTS, WILLIAM.** Certificate of Brig. Gen. John Twiggs, 3rd February, 1784. Entitled to bounty, and prays for 287½ acres in Washington Co. On the 2nd April, 1784, William Clements of Burke Co., appoints Mr. John Clements of the same county, attorney to receive his warrant.

**CURREY, PETER.** Certificate of Col. E. Clarke, 25th February, 1784. That he was a Minute man, but not an inhabitant at the time of enlistment.

**CHAMBLISS, LITTLETON.** On 25th January, 1784, appoints Col. James McNeil, attorney to receive bounty land due me for service in militia.

**CHAPMAN, JOHN,** of 96th Dist. South Carolina, appoints John Stewart, attorney, 5th February, 1784, to receive his bounty as Sergt. in the Minute Service of Georgia.

**CIMBRO, WILLIAM.** On the 9th February, 1784, appoints Sanders Walker, attorney to receive his bounty of land, as per certificate of Capt. Heard, witness, John Kimbry.

**CANNON, THOMAS.** Certificate of Col. E. Clarke, 20th December, 1784. That he served in the Minute Batt. of the State, and is entitled to a bounty of 250 acres.

**CASTLEBERRY, JOHN.** Certificate of Col. G. Lee, 16th April, 1784. Entitled to a bounty, and prays for 287½ acres in Washington Co.

**CANDLER, WILLIAM, JR.** Certificate of Col. G. Lee, 20th February, 1784. Entitled to a bounty of 250 acres of land.

**CATCHING, BENJ.** Certificate of Col. E. Clarke, 2nd February, 1784. Entitled to a citizen's bounty of 287½. The House of Assembly, August 7,

## CERTIFICATES OF SERVICE IN AMERICAN REVOLUTION. 51

1783, granted his 500 acres in consideration of his being a cripple, making in all 787½ acres, and he prays for same in Washington Co.

**CANNON, ROGER,** Certificate of Col. E. Clark, 13th April, 1784. Entitled to a bounty, and prays for 287½ acres.

**CLARKE, JOHN, JR.** Certificate of Col. E. Clarke, August 19th, 1784. Entitled to a bounty as a refugee and prays for same in Washington Co. Also certificate of Col. Samuel Jack, that he was a Minute man, though not an inhabitant at the time of enlistment.

**CLARKE, JOHN, CAPT.** Certificate of Col. E. Clark, 2nd February, 1784. That he was a refugee captain, and is entitled to 500 acres of land.

**COHRON, CORNELIUS.** Certificate of Col. E. Clark, 20th April, 1784. Entitled to bounty and prays for same in Washington Co.

**CARTER, JAMES.** Certificate of Col. E. Clarke, 12th April, 1784. That he was a refugee soldier, and served as aid-de-camp at the time he was slain in battle, therefore is entitled the bounty of a captain.

**COLEMAN, HARRIS.** Certificate of Col. Elijah Clarke, 24th February, 1784. That he was a refugee soldier entitled to a bounty of 250 acres of land.

**CAMP, (KEMP), WILLIAM.** Certificate of Col. E. Clark, 8th April, 1784. That he was a refugee soldier entitled to bounty, and prays for same in Washington Co.

**CRAIN, LEWIS.** Certificate of Col. Jas. Jackson, 30th July, 1784. That he served in the Georgia State Legion, entitled to 287½ acres of land, and prays for same in Washington Co

**CRESWELL, SAMUEL.** Certificate of Col. E. Clark, 5th April, 1784. That he was a refugee soldier and served as a surgeon, and should have a surgeon's bounty, prays for 500 acres in Washington Co.

**CLOUD, JOHN.** Certificate of Col. E. Clarke, 24th February, 1784. Refugee soldier, entitled to a bounty of 500 acres, prays for same in Flanklin Co.

**CLOUD, NEOUGH.** (or Nenouh of Wilkes Co.) Certificate of Col. E. Clark, 7th April, 1784. Entitled to bounty of land. Appoints Geo. Matthews attorney, to receive same.

**CARR, PATRICK.** Certificate of Gen. John Twiggs, 13th April, 1784. Entitled to a bounty of land as refugee captain, appointment of Gen. John Morgan, and prays for same in Washington Co.

**CROFORD, JOHN.** Granted 287½ acres, bounty, in Washington Co., through Francis Tennill, Granted 17th April, 1784.

**CARSON, THOMAS.** Certificate of Col. E. Clark, 7th April, 1784. Refugee soldier entitled to bounty.

**CHISSOME, BENJ.** Certificate of Col. Benj. Few, 7th April, 1784. That he was a refugee soldier entitled to bounty, and prays for same in Flanklin Co.

**CARDIN, CORNELIUS.** Certificate of Col. Greenbury Lee, 21st February, 1784. Entitled to 250 acres of bounty land.

**CASTLEBURY, HENRY.** Certificate of Col. E. Clarke, 2nd February, 1784. Entitled to 250 acres of bounty land, granted in Washington Co.

**CROOCK, WILLIAM.** Certificate of Col. Samuel Jack, 17th May, 1784. In the Batt. of Minute men, but not at the time of enlistment, an inhabitant of the State.

**CARNEY, ONSBY.** Certflicate of Col. E. Clark, 20th April, 1784. That he was a Minute man, but not an inhabitant of the State at the time enlistment, prays for 287½ acres of land in Washington Co.

**CHESSER, JOHN.** Certificate of Col. E. Clarke, 16th November, 1784. That he was a Minute man, though not an inhabitant of the State at time of enlistment.

**CARTOR, HEPWORTH.** Grant of 1000 acres on the 21st of January, 1784, signed by John Houton, for marking the lines south of the Ogeechee river, etc. Prays for said land in Washington Co.

**CORNANT, JOHN.** On certificate of Col. E. Clark, 25th March, 1784, granted 250 acres of bounty land.

**CURETON, WILLIAM.** Certificate of Col. G. Lee, 26th April, 1784. Entitled to a bounty of 250 acres of land, and prays for same in Washington Co.

**CRUMLY, ANTHONY.** Certificate of Col. E. Clark, 2nd February, 1784. Entitled to a bounty of 250 acres, and prays for same in Washington Co.

**CATO, WILLIAM.** Certificate of Capt. Jas. McCay, 1st July, 1784. Refugee soldier and is entitled to bounty, and prays for same in Washington Co.

**COLLINS, CHARLES.** Certificate of Col. G. Lee, 11th March, 1784. Entitled to a bounty, and prays for 287½ acres in Washington Co. 17th March, 1784, Charles Collins sold said bounty to William Walker.

**CHAMBERS, JOHN.** Certificate of Col. G. Lee, 25th February, 1784. Entitled to a bounty of 250 acres of land.

**CLOUDAS, GEORGE.** Certificate of Col. E. Clark, 13th April, 1784. Entitled to a bounty, and prays for 287½ acres in Franklin Co.

**COOK, GEORGE,** Certificate of Col. E. Clark, 16th December, 1784. That he was a Minute man, though not at the time of enlistment an inhabitant of the State.

## CERTIFICATES OF SERVICE IN AMERICAN REVOLUTION. 53

**CONYERS, WILLIAM.** Certificate of Col. Francis Pugh, 1st of December, 1784, in Burke Co., that he was a refugee soldier in South Carolina, and served in defense of his country until his death. On this certificate Margaret Conyers, petitions for 250 acres of land in Washington Co.

**COATS, JOHN.** Certificate of Col. E. Clarke, 2nd February, 1784. Entitled to a bounty of land, and prays for 287½ acres in Washington Co., and appoints Sanders Walker attorney to receive same.

**CARR, HENRY, LT.** Certificate of Col. E. Clark, 7th April, 1784. That he served as a lieutenant in the Batt. of Minute men, though not at the time of appointment, an inhabitant of the State, and prays for bounty land in Franklin Co.

**CRAWFORD, JOHN.** Certificate of Col. James McNeil, 2nd February, 1784. Entitled to a bounty of land, and prays for 287½ acres in Washington Co., and appoints Col. James McNeil, attorney to receive the warrant for same.

**CRAWFORD, DAVID.** On the 10th of June, 1784, John Crawford, heir to David Crawford, of Albermarle Co., Va., appoints John Morrison attorney, to receive his warrant for 230 acres for his services in the 2nd Georgia Batt.

**CLOUD, JEREMIAH, JR.** Certificate of Col. E. Clarke, 7th December, 1784. That he was a refugee soldier entitled to a bounty, and prays for 287½ acres in Washington Co.

**COOK, GEORGE** (deceased). Certificate of Gen. John Twiggs, 7th April, 1784. That he is entitled to a bounty of 250 acres of land. Eleanor Cook, widow of George Cook, in behalf of her son, Ferguson Cook, prays for a grant of the above land to her son in Washington Co.

**CADE, DREWRY, CAPT.** Certificate of Col. E. Clarke, 7th April, 1784. That he is entitled to a bounty of 500 acres of land, and prays for same in Washington Co.

**CURETON, WILLIAM, JR.** Certificate of Col. Samuel Jack. That he was a Minute man, though not at the time of enlistment, an inhabitant of the State, entitled to a bounty of 250 acres.

**CHILDREY, THOMAS.** Certificate of Col. G. Lee, 23rd February, 1784. That he is entitled to a bounty, and prays for 287½ acres in Washington Co.

**CARSEY, STEPHEN, JR.** Certificate of Col. E. Clark, 2nd February, 1784. Refugee soldier.

**COLE, JOHN, JR.** Certificate of Col. E. Clark, 2nd February, 1784. Entitled to a bounty of 250 acres of land.

**COLE, JOHN.** Certificate of Col. J. Jackson, 10th September, 1784. That he was entitled to a bounty of 250 acres, and prays for same in Franklin Co.

**COTHORN, JOSIAH**, of Burke Co. Certificate of Gen. John Twiggs, 17th May, 1784. That he was killed in the service, and his heirs are entitled to a bounty of land.

**CHAMBLESS, CHRISTOPHER.** Certificate of Col. James McNeil, 2nd February, 1784. That he is entitled to a bounty of 250 acres.

**CLARK, BENJAMIN.** Certificate of Col. E. Clark, 10th May, 1784. Entitled to a bounty, prays for 287½ acres in Franklin Co.

**COLEMAN, JAMES.** Certificate of Col. E. Clarke, 2nd February, 1784. Refugee soldier and prays for bounty land in Washington Co.

**CHAMBLESS, LITTLETON.** Certificate of Col. Jas. McNeil, 9th February, 1784. Entitled to a bounty of 250 acres of land.

**CASTLEBERRY, JACOB.** Certificate of Col. G. Lee, 16th April, 1784. Entitled to a bounty, and prays for 287½ acres in Washington Co. Prays for it per Ninian Magruder.

**CORSIA, WILLIAM.** Certificates of Col. Jas. McNeil, 28th February, 1784. Entitled to a bounty, and prays for 287½ acres in Washington Co.

**COAN, JOHN.** Certificate of Col. G. Lee, 11th March, 1784. Entitled to a bounty of 250 acres.

**COLLINS, MOSES.** Certificate of Col. E. Clark, 2nd February, 1784. Entitled to 250 acres of land, and prays for same in Franklin Co.

**COLLINS, JOSEPH.** Certificate of Col. E. Clark, 25th March, 1784. Entitled to a bounty of 250 acres, and prays for same in Washington Co.

**CONNOR, DANIEL.** Certificate of Col. E. Clark, 5th April, 1784. Entitled to a bounty of 250 acres, and prays for same in Washington Co.

**COATES, NATHANIEL.** Certificate of Col. E. Clark, 2nd February, 1784. Entitled to bounty of 250 acres of land, and prays for same in Washington Co. and appoints Sanders Walker to receive warrant for same.

**CARLYLE, JOHN.** Certificate of Col. E. Clark, 2nd February, 1784. Entitled to a bounty of 250 acres of land.

**CARRELL, WILLIAM.** Elizabeth Carrell appoints Edward Keating, attorney to obtain bounty land due William Carrell, deceased, 10th April, 1784.

**CRAINE, SPENCER.** Certificate of Col. E. Clark, 6th April, 1784. That he is entitled to a bounty, and prays for 287½ acres in Washington Co.

**CONNER, DANIEL.** "Resolve of the House of Assembly, granting him 500 acres of land, as a gratuity on account of his pension."

**CARNEY, MATTHEW.** Certificate of Col. J. Pannill, 17th September, 1784. That he was a private soldier in the 2nd Georgia Continental Batt. and served three years, and prays for 250 acres in the Continental reserve.

**CLARK, LEWIS.** Certificate of Col. E. Clark, 2nd February, 1784. Refugee soldier.

## CERTIFICATES OF SERVICE IN AMERICAN REVOLUTION. 55

**COLLINS, SOLOMON.** Certificate of Col. E. Clark, 19th May, 1784. Entitled to a bounty of 250 acres, and prays for same in Washington Co.

**CARSON, THOS., JR.** Certificate of Col. E. Clark, 7th April, 1784. Entitled to a bounty and prays for 287½ acres in Franklin Co.

**CARR, PATRICK, MAJ.** Certificate of Gov. J. Houston, 27th April, 1784. Entitled as a refugee Major to 650 acres of land and to 250 as a citizen.

**CLARKE, E., Col.** Granted 1000 acres in Washington Co., for being a refugee Colonel, 16th April, 1784.

**CARTLIDGE, JAMES.** On certificate of Col. G. Lee, 28th February, 1784. Granted 287½ acres in Washington Co.

**CATCHING, SEYMORE.** On certificate of Col. Clark, 24th February, 1784. Granted bounty of 250 acres of land in Washington Co.

**CURRY, NICHOLAS.** Petition for bounty of 250 acres of land for his services.

**CARSON, JOSEPH,** of Wilkes Co. Petitions for 287½ acres of bounty land in Washington Co. Certificate of Col. E. Clark, 7th April, 1784.

**CHAPMAN, JOHN.** On certificate of Col. Samuel Jack, 5th April, 1784. That he enlisted as a sergeant in the Batt. of Minute men, though not at the time of enlistment an inhabitant of this State. Granted 300 acres.

**CARLTON, PATRICK.** Certificate of Col. Samuel Jack. That he was a minute man, though not at the time of enlistment an inhabitant of this State.

**CONNELL, THOMAS.** On certificate of Col. E. Clark. That he is entitled to a bounty of 250 acres of land, granted in Flanklin Co., 25th March, 1784.

**CLOWERS, PETER.** Certificate of Col. E. Clark, 10th December, 1784. Entitled to a bounty of 250 acres of land.

**CADE, DRURY.** On certificate of Col. E. Clark, 2nd February, 1784. That he was a refugee soldier and is entitled to 250 acres of bounty land, and prays for same in Franklin Co.

**COURSON, WILLIAM.** Certificate of Col. James McNeil, 21st February, 1784. That he is entitled to a bounty of 250 acres of land, appoints Thomas Buch attorney to receive same.

**CALDWELL, JAMES.** Certificate of Col. Jas. McNeil, 15th March, 1784. That he was entitled to a bounty of 250 acres of land, and prays for same in Franklin Co.

**CRAWFORD, JOHN.** Certificate of Col. Jas. McNeil, 20th February, 1784. That he was a refugee soldier and entitled to a bounty of 250 acres of land.

**COLEMAN, JAMES.** Certificate of Col. E. Clark, 14th April, 1784. That he is entitled to a bounty of 250 acres of land.

**CRAWFORD, ANDERSON.** Certificate of Col. Jas. McNeil, 17th February, 1784. That he was entitled to 250 acres of bounty land, and prays for same in Washington Co.

**CARSON, SAMUEL.** Certificate of Col. E. Clark, 2nd February, 1784. That he was a refugee soldier.

**CARSON, THOS, SR.** Certificate of Col. E. Clark, 7th April, 1784. Entitled to a refugee's bounty, and prays for same in Washington Co.

**CARSON, JOHN.** Certificate of Col. E. Clark, 3rd April, 1784. That he was a Minute man, though not at the time of enlistment an inhabitant of this State.

**CUNNINGHAM, JOHN.** On certificate of Col. E. Clark. Entitled to a bounty of 250 acres of land, granted 2nd February, 1784.

**CHISOLM, JOHN.** Certificate of Lt. Col. J. Pannill, 12th July, 1784. That he was a sergeant in the Continental troops for the State of Georgia, served three years, and prays for 230 acres of land reserved for the Continental troops in the forks of the Oconee river.

**COWIN, WILLIAM.** Certificate of Col. E. Clarke, 2nd February, 1784. Entitled to a bounty of land, and prays for 287½ acres in Washington Co.

**CONE, WILLIAM.** Certificate of Col. Jas. McNeil, 22nd March, 1784, that he served in the first Batt. of Richmond Co. Militia, and prays for 287½ acres in Washington Co.

**CHILDERS, THOS.** and Henry Childers, of Henry Co., Va., appoints Col. Jos. Pannill, of Richmond Co., Ga., "to receive all bounty lands due us in the State of Georgia for military service in the late war," 24th February, 1784.

**CRONBERGER, BARBARA,** appoints Jenkin Davis, Esqr., "to get a certificate for land as a bounty granted by the Hon. House of Assembly, to my deceased husband," 16th February. Witness, Jacob Cronberger.

**CONNELL, JOHN.** On certificate of Col. Francis Pugh, 25th February, 1784. That he is entitled to 250 acres of bounty land.

**CONNELL, JESSE.** On certificate of Col. E. Clark, 20th April, 1784. That he is entitled to a bounty of land, and prays for 287½ acres in Washington Co.

**CRISPUSS, JAMES.** On certificate of Col. E. Clark, 7th April, 1784. Entitled to a bounty, and prays for 287½ acres in Washington Co.

**CARRELL, WILLIAM.** On certificate of Col. G. Lee, 11th March, 1784. That he is entitled to a bounty of land, and prays for same in Washington Co.

**CLARKE, ELIJAH.** Granted a citizen's bounty of 250 acres in Washington Co. 16th April, 1784.

## CERTIFICATES OF SERVICE IN AMERICAN REVOLUTION.    57

**COLLIER, WILLIAM.** On certificate of Capt. Littlebury Bostick, and Col. James Martin, 23rd March, 1784. That he joined the station at Spirit Creek, immediately after the fall of Augusta, and was a good and faithful soldier in my company, and he prays for bounty in Washington Co.

**CALDWELL, GEORGE,** of Liberty Co. Certificate of Col. John Baker, 13th July, 1784. That he was a good soldier, entitled to bounty. Appoints Maj. Philip Low, attorney to receive warrant for the land.

**CARTLEDGE, JAMES.** On certificate of Col. G. Lee, 25th February, 1784, is entitled to a citizen's bounty of 250 acres of land.

**CRUTCHFIELD, JOHN.** On certificate of Col. E. Clark, 2nd February, 1784. That he is entitled to a bounty of 250 acres.

**COLESON, WILLIAM.** Certificate of Col. Jenkins Davis, 20th February, 1784. That he was a refugee soldier.

**CONNELL, DANIEL.** Certificate of Col. James Jackson, April 7, 1784. That he was entitled to a citizen's bounty, and prays for same in Washington Co.

**CONLEY, CALEB.** On certificate of Col. E. Clark, 16th November, 1784. That he was a Minute man, though not an inhabitant of the State at the time of enlistment.

**CAMPBELL, WILLIAM.** Certificate of Col. E. Clark, 2nd February, 1784. That he is entitled to bounty, and prays for 287½ acres in Washington Co. On the 3rd of February, 1784, he appoints Sanders Walker, attorney to receive his warrant for bounty land.

**CANDLER, HENRY.** On certificate of Col. G. Lee, 2nd February, 1784. Entitled to a bounty and prays for 250 acres in Washington Co.

**CHAVOS, JEREMIAH.** Certificate of Col. E. Clark, 2nd February, 1784. That he was a refugee soldier, entitled to bounty, and prays for 287 ½ acres in Washington Co.

**CLARKE, GIBSON.** Certificate of Col. E. Clark, 8th April, 1784. That he was a refugee soldier entitled to a bounty, and granted the same in Washington Co. ("Dismissed, he being on the Mississippi.")

**CRAWFORD, ANDERSON.** Certificate of Col. James McNeil, 2nd February 1784. Entitled to a bounty of 250 acres.

**CANE, JOHN.** Certificate of Col. E. Clark, 2nd February, 1784. Entitled to a bounty of 250 acres, and prays for same in Washington Co.

**COLE, JOHN, JR.** Certificate of Col. E. Clark, 25th March, 1784. Entitled to 250 acres of bounty land.

**CURREY, PETER,** Certificate of Col. E. Clark, 3rd January, 1785. That he was a Minute man, though not at the time of enlistment an inhabitant of the State.

ROSTER OF THE REVOLUTION.

**CARSON, JOHN.** Certificate of Col. E. Clark, 9th April, 1784. That he was entitled to a bounty of land, and prays for same in Franklin Co.

**CONNER, JOHN.** Certificate of Col. E. Clark, 2nd February, 1784. That he is entitled to a bounty, and prays for same in Washington Co.

**CASSELLS, JOHN.** Certificate of Col. G. Lee, 21st February, 1784. Entitled to a bounty of 250 acres of land.

**CONYERS, JOHN, CAPT.** Certificate of Col. Francis Pugh, 9th February, 1784. Refugee officer, and is entitled to a bounty.

**CURTIS, JOHN.** Certificate of Col. L. Jackson, that he is entitled to 250 acres of bounty land.

**CARSON, SAMUEL.** Certificate of Col. E. Clark, 2nd February, 1784. Entitled to a bounty, and prays for 287½ acres of land in Washington Co.

**CARSON, DAVID.** Certificate of Col. E. Clark, 3rd April, 1784. That he was a Minute man, though not at the time of enlistment an inhabitant of the State.

**COOK, JOSHUA.** (deceased.) Certificate of Gen. John Twiggs, 7th April, 1784. Entitled to a bounty of land. 287½ acres in Washington Co. granted to the heirs, and received by Dal McMurphy.

**CLARK, WILLIAM.** Certificate of Col. E. Clark, 2nd February, 1784. Entitled to a bounty, and prays for 287½ acres in Washington Co.

**CUNNINGHAM, JOHN.** Petitions for 690 acres of land in the reserve for his service as captain in the 2nd Georgia Continental Batt. Served nearly 4 years.

**CURETON, BOLING.** Certificate of E. Clark, 25th March, 1784. Entitled to a bounty, and prays for 287½ acres in Washington Co.

**CLARKE, CHARLES.** Certificate of Col. James Jackson, April 7, 1784. That he served from the fall of Augusta until the evacuation of Savannah as a good and faithful soldier. Prays for a bounty of 287½ acres in Washington Co.

**CARTLEDGE, SAMUEL.** Certificate of Col. G. Lee, 11th March, 1784. Entitled to a bounty of 250 acres, and prays for same in Washington Co.

**CARLTON, PATRICK,** of Camden District, S. C., on the 13th November, 1783, appoints David Brown, of the same Dist. to obtain his bounty land for military service in the State of Georgia. Prays for 250 acres of land in Washington Co.

**CUNNINGHAM, JOHN, MAJ.** Certificate of Col. E. Clarke, 2nd February, 1784. A refugee Major.

**CARTER, PATRICK.** Certificate of Col. Jas. Jackson, March 23rd, 1784. That he served under him from the fall of Augusta, to the evacuation of Savan-

## CERTIFICATES OF SERVICE IN AMERICAN REVOLUTION. 59

nah, and prays for 287½ acres of land in Washington Co., assigns his warrant to Henry Allison, March 23rd, 1784.

**CAMP, L.** Note to Wm. Freeman, Esqr., at Augusta, to deliver to the bearer certificates which were in his office in the name of L. Camp, and Reuben Banks, 8th August, 1784.

**CATCHINGS, MERIDETH.** Certificate Col. E. Clark, 7th April, 1784. Entitled to a bounty and prays for 287½ acres in Washington Co.

**COTHORN, WILLIAM.** Certificate of Gen. John Twiggs, 15th March, 1784. Refugee soldier entitled to bounty land.

**CHILDERS, THOMAS.** Certificate of Gen. Saml. Elbert, 23rd March, 1784. That he was one of the Georgia Continental soldiers, and entitled to 200 acres of bounty land.

**COSTELLO, EDWARD.** Certificate of Col. E. Clark, 6th April, 1784. That he was a Minute man in Georgia, though not at time an inhabitant of the State. Prays for bounty land in Washington Co.

**COSTELLO, MICHAEL.** Certificate of Col. E. Clark, 6th April, 1784. That he was a Minute man in Georgia, though not at time an inhabitant of the State. Prays for bounty land in Washington Co.

**CARDEN, CORNELIUS.** Certificate of Col. E. Clark, 3rd January, 1785. That he was a Minute man, though not at the time of enlistment, an inhabitant of the State.

**COLLINS, JOHN.** Certificate of Lt. Francis Tennill, 21st April, 1784. That he served three years in the 2nd Georgia Continental Regt. as a private, and is entitled to bounty. Prays for 200 acres of land in the reserve.

**COOK, RAINS, CAPT.** Certificate of Maj. John Habersham, 27th April, 1784. That he served in the line of this State until the end of the war. Prays for bounty land.

**CAMPBELL, DRURY.** Certificate of Col. Samuel Jack, 6th April, 1784. That he served as Lieutenant in the Batt. of Minute Men, though not an inhabitant of this State at the time of enlistment. He prays for bounty land in Washington Co.

**COLLINS, STEPHEN.** Certificate of Col. Samuel Elbert, 10th March, 1784. That he served as a soldier in the Regt. of Light Dragoons of this State, and is entitled to receive his Continental and State bounty of land accordingly. Belonged to Capt. Samuel Scott's troop.

**CURRY, CARY.** Certificate of Col. Samuel Jack, 13th April, 1784. That he was one of the Minute Men, though not at the time of enlistment an inhabitant of the State. Prays for bounty land in Washington Co.

**CHAPMAN, WILLIAM.** Certificate of Col. E. Clark, 24th December, 1784. That he is entitled to a bounty of 250 acres of land, and prays for 287½ acres of land in Flanklin Co.

ROSTER OF THE REVOLUTION.

**COOK, ISHAM.** Certificate of Col. Jos. Pannell, 25th May, 1784. That he served as a captain in the Continental line raised for the defense of this State, and died in service. His heirs pray for 500 acres in the reserve.

**CARR, HENRY.** Certificate of Col. E. Clark, 7th February, 1784. That he was a refugee soldier and is entitled to a bounty of 250 acres, and prays for same in Washington Co.

**CRIBS, THOS.** Gives power of attorney to Col. Jas. McNeil, to receive his warrant for bounty land, 9th January, 1784.

**COUP, HENRY.** Certificate of Col. E. Clark, 28th February, 1784. That he was a Minute man, though not an inhabitant of the State, entitled to a bounty and prays for same in Washington Co.

**CHANEY, GREENBURY.** Certificate of Col. E. Clark, 20th May, 1784. That he was a refugee soldier. Granted bounty.

**COLEMAN, DANIEL, ESQR.** Certificate of Col. E. Clark, 2nd February, 1784. That he was entitled to a bounty of 250 acres of land.

**CHAMBLESS, CHRISTOPHER.** Certificate of Col. Jas. McNeil. Petitions for 575 acres of bounty land, as per certificate from "the honorable John Houston, Esqr.," 5th April, 1784. Prays for same in Washington Co.

**CLEM, JOHN.** Certificate of Col. E. Clark, 3rd April, 1784. That he was a Minute man, though not an inhabitant of the State at the time of enlistment. Entitled to bounty, and prays for 287½ acres in Washington Co.

**CATCHING, JOSEPH.** Petitions for 287½ acres of land as bounty for his services, and prays for same in Washington Co. on certificate of Col. E. Clark, 24th February, 1784.

**CULPEPPER, JOSEPH, JR.** On certificate of Col. E. Clark, 29th January, 1785. Entitled to bounty as a refugee soldier, and prays for 575 acres of land in Washington Co.

**COURSEY, (CORSIA), DAVID.** On certificate of Col. James McNeil. Entitled to a bounty of 250 acres, and prays for same in Washington Co.

**COLLINS, STEPHEN.** Entitled to 287½ acres, prays for same in Washington Co., and appoints Thos. Bush, attorney, to receive the warrant, April 3, 1784.

**CLARK, BENJ.** Certificate of Col. E. Clark, 15th May, 1784. That he was a refugee soldier entitled to a bounty of 250 acres, prays for same in Franklin Co.

**CAMP, JOSEPH.** On certificate of Col. G. Lee, that he was entitled to a bounty of 250 acres of land, prays for same in Washington Co.

**CLOUD, EZEKIEL.** On certificate of Col. E. Clark, 25th March, 1784. That he was a refugee soldier entitled to 250 acres of bounty land, and prays for same in Flanklin Co.

## CERTIFICATES OF SERVICE IN AMERICAN REVOLUTION. 61

**CRAWFORD, NATHAN.** Certificate of Col. Jas. McNeil, that he was entitled to a bounty of 250 acres, and prays for same in Washington Co., 8th May, 1784.

**CLARK, JOHN, SR.** Certificate of Col. E. Clark, 25th March, 1784. Entitled to a bounty, and prays for 287½ acres in Washington Co.

**CLARK, JAMES,** Certificate of Col. E. Clark, 10th December, 1784. Entitled to a bounty of land, and prays for 250 acres in Washington Co.

**CLARK, MOSES.** Certificate of Col. John Stewart, 10th July, 1784. That he was in his Batt. of Minute Men, and prays for bounty land in Washington Co.

**CULBREATH, JOHN.** Certificate of Cols. G. Lee, and James McNeil, 11th March, 1784. That he is entitled to a bounty of land, and prays for same in Franklin Co.

**CURETON, RICHARD.** Certificate of Col. E. Clark, 2nd February, 1784. That he is entitled to a bounty of 250 acres of good land.

**CRUSE, THOMAS.** Certificate of Col. E. Clark, 8th April, 1784. Entitled to a bounty, and prays for 287½ acres in Washington Co.

**CARSON, ADAM.** Petitions for 287½ acres in Washington Co., as bounty for his services, granted 24th May, 1784.

**CUNNINGHAM, JAMES.** Certificate of Col. E. Clark, 2nd February, 1784. Refugee soldier.

**CAMPBELL, ALEXANDER.** Certificate of Col. E. Clark, 3rd January, 1785. That he was a Minute man, though not at the time of enlistment, an inhabitant of the State.

**CULLARD, HENRY.** Certificate of Col. E. Clark, 16th December, 1784. That he was a Minute man, though not at the time of enlistment, an inhabitant of the State.

**CUNNINGHAM, PATRICK.** Certificate of Col. E. Clark, 20th May, 1784. Entitled to a bounty, and prays for 250 acres of land in Franklin Co.

**COMBS, JOHN.** Certificate of Col. E. Clark, 2nd February, 1784. Entitled to a bounty of 250 acres of land.

**COBB, JAMES, SR.,** gave power of attorney to James Gilbert to draw his citizen's certificate for bounty land, 10th April, 1784.

**CHANDLER, ABEDNEGO,** of 96th Dist. South Carolina, appoints John Clark, of same District, attorney to receive his bounty land due for service in Col. Jack's Batt. of Minute Men, 29th August, 1783.

**CLEMENTS, JOHN.** Certificate of Gen. John Twiggs, 26th November, 1783. Refugee soldier in North Carolina.

**CLOUD, JEREMIAH, SR.** Certificate of Col. E. Clark, 2nd February, 1784. Entitled to a bounty, prays for 287½ acres in Washington Co.

**CRESWELL, DAVID.** Certificate of Col. G. Lee, 15th March, 1784. Entitled to a bounty, and prays for same in Washington Co. Assigns his right on March 7, 1784, to Joel Rees.

**CONNALLY, PATRICK.** Certificate of Gen. John Twiggs, 27th February, 1784. Entitled to a bounty, and prays for 287½ acres in Washington Co.

**CATTERATZ, STEPHEN.** Certificate of Col. E. Clark, 24th April, 1784. That he was a Minute man, though not at the time of enlistment an inhabitant of this State. Prays for 250 acres of land in Franklin Co.

**D.**

**DENTHAM, JOHN.** Certificate of Col. E. Clark, 16th November, 1784. That he was a Minute man, though not an inhabitant of the State at the time of enlistment.

**DANNELLY, JOHN.** Certificate of Col. G. Lee, 11th March, 1784. Entitled to bounty, and prays for 287½ acres in Washington Co.

**DAVISON, JOSEPH.** Certificate of Col. E. Clark, 7th April, 1784. Entitled to a bounty, and prays for 287½ acres in Washington Co.

**DUKE, JOHN TAYLOR, SR.** Certificate of Col. E. Clarke, 7th April, 1784. Entitled to a bounty, and prays for 287½ acres in Washington Co.

**DENNIS, JACOB.** Certificate of Col. James Jackson, 23rd July, 1784. That he is entitled to a bounty, and prays for 287½ acres in Washington Co.

**DUNN, JOSIAH.** Certificate of E. Clarke, 20th May, 1784, that he was appointed colonel of Richmond Co. Batt. at the siege of Augusta, and faithfully discharged his duties until his decease, and is entitled to a bounty. Petition of Nehemiah Dunn, executor of Josiah Dunn, for bounty land in Washington Co. Granted to the heirs of the deceased.

**DOLLY, BENJ.** Petitions for 287½ acres of bounty land in Washington Co. for his services. Granted 13th April, 1784.

**DARBY, JOHN.** Certificate of Gen. John Twiggs, 2nd February, 1784. Entitled to a bounty of 250 acres of land.

**DOOLY, WILLIAM.** Certificate of Col. E. Clarke, 2nd February, 1784. Entitled to a bounty of 250 acres.

**DUNCAN, JAMES.** Lieutenant. Certificate of Col. E. Clarke, 25th December, 1784, that he was a lieutenant in the Minute Batt. of this State, and is entitled to a bounty of 400 acres of land, and prays for same in Washington Co.

**DUHART, JOHN.** Certificate of Gen. John Twiggs, February 20, 1784. Entitled to a bounty and prays for 287½ acres in Franklin Co.

# CERTIFICATES OF SERVICE IN AMERICAN REVOLUTION. 63

**DAWSON, BRITTON.** Certificate of Col. Jas. McNeil, 25th March, 1784. Entitled to a bounty, and prays for 287½ acres in Washington Co.

**DONOWAY, WILLIAM.** Certificate of Col. E. Clarke, 2nd February, 1784. Entitled to a bounty, and prays for 250 acres in Franklin Co.

**DASHER, CHRISTIAN.** Certificate of Col. Caleb Howell, 16th February, 1784. Steadfastly did his duty until killed by the enemy, and his heirs are entitled to 250 acres bounty land.

**DANIEL, BENJ.** Certificate of Col. James McNeil, 7th April, 1784. Entitled to a bounty, and prays for 287½ acres in Washington Co.

**DYER, HENRY.** Certificate of Col. E. Clarke, 1st April, 1784; that he was a Minute man, though not at the time of enlistment an inhabitant of the State. Prays for 287½ acres in Washington Co. Granted to the heirs of Henry Dyer, 14th April, 1784.

**DEVEAUX, PETER, ESQR.** Certificate of John Armstrong, Adjt. Gen. Southern Dept., Philadelphia, 14th May, 1781, that he was appointed an aide-de-camp to Hon. Maj. Gen. Gates, on the 2nd August last, at Mask's Ferry, on the Peedee River, and continued to serve in that capacity during the general's command of the Southern Dept.

**DAY, JOSEPH.** Certificate of Maj. Gen. McIntosh, 6th April, 1784, that he was a captain, and entitled to 600 acres of bounty land.

**DENNIS, ISAAC.** Certificate of Col. G. Lee, 30th March, 1784. Entitled to bounty, and prays for 287½ acres in Washington Co.

**DAWSON, DAVID.** Certificate of Col. Jas. McNeil, 15th March, 1784. Entitled to bounty, and prays for 287½ acres in Washington Co.

**DUNCAN, JOSEPH.** Certificate of Col. E. Clarke, 1st April, 1784, that he was a captain in the Batt. of Minute Men, though not at the time of enlistment an inhabitant of the State. His brother, Matthew Duncan, prays for warrant as heir in Washington Co.

**DAVIES, MYRICK, ESQR.** Certificate of Col. Asa Emanuel, and Gen. John Twiggs, 7th April, 1784, that he served in their regiment from August to December, 1781, when he was killed by a party of Tories. Sara Davies, widow of the soldier, prays for bounty land in Washington Co. Certificate of Richard Howley, 23rd February, 1784, that Myrick Davies, Esqr., acted as member of the Executive Council during his administration, and was a refugee from this State.

**DUNSMORE, JAMES.** Certificate of E. Clarke, 11th February, 1785, that he was a Minute man, though not at the time of enlistment an inhabitant of this State.

**DENNISON, DANIEL.** Certificate of Col. E. Clarke, 24th April, 1784. Entitled to a bounty, and prays for 250 acres of land in Washington Co.

**DOWNS, GEORGE.** Certificate of Col. Jas. McNeil, 22nd March, 1784, that he was in the Richmond Co. Militia; served as a refugee, and is entitled to a bounty, and prays for same in Franklin Co.

**DENNIS, JOHN, SR.** Certificate of Col. G. Lee, 16th April, 1784, that he is entitled to a bounty of 250 acres.

**DELANY, DANIEL.** Certificate of Col. E. Clarke, 2nd February, 1784. Entitled to a bounty of 250 acres.

**DAVIS, JOHN, SR.** Certificate of Col. E. Clarke, 7th April, 1784. Entitled to a bounty, and prays for 287½ acres in Washington Co.

**DEAN, THOMAS.** Certificate of Col. E. Clarke, 21st April, 1784. Entitled to a bounty, and prays for 250 acres in Washington Co.

**DOUGLASS, GEORGE.** Certificate of Col. E. Clarke, 2nd February, 1784. Entitled to a bounty of 250 acres, and prays for same in Franklin Co.

**DAVID, WILLIAM.** Certificate of Col. Jas. McKay, and Gen. John Twiggs, 20th April, 1784. Entitled to a bounty, and prays for same in Washington Co.

**DUNCAN, WILLIAM.** Certificate of Col. E. Clarke, 3rd January, 1785, that he was a Minute man, though not an inhabitant of the State at the time of enlistment. Prays for 250 acres of land in Franklin Co.

**DICK, DAVID.** Certificate of Col. John Baker, Liberty Co. Militia, 18th March, 1784, that he was a refugee soldier, and died a short time after he left State. His heirs are entitled to 250 acres of land.

**DENHAM, CHARLES.** Certificate of Col. G. Lee, 11th March, 1784. Entitled to a bounty of 250 acres. Sold land to William Walker.

**DICKSON, HUGH.** Certificate of Col. Samuel Jack, 5th April, 1784, that he served as a sergeant in the Batt. of Minute Men, though not an inhabitant of the State.

**DELK, DAVID.** Certificate of Col. E. Clarke, 3rd January, 1785, that he was a Minute man, though not at the time of enlistment an inhabitant of the State.

**DARCEY, JAMES.** Of Burke Co. On the 17th May, 1784, appoints Mr. Hugh Lawson, Esqr., to receive his warrant for bounty land in Washington Co. Certificate of J. Twiggs.

**DUNAWAY, JOHN, SR.** Certificate of Col. E. Clarke, 19th May, 1784. Entitled to a bounty, and prays for 287½ acres in Washington Co.

**DAVIS, WILLIAM.** Certificate of E. Clarke, 7th April, 1784. Entitled to a bounty of land, and prays for same in Washington Co.

**DOWDY, RICHARD.** Certificate of Col. McNeil, 28th February, 1784. Entitled to a bounty, and prays for 287½ acres in Washington Co. Was a soldier in the late Continental Batt.

## CERTIFICATES OF SERVICE IN AMERICAN REVOLUTION.

**DENNIS, JOHN, JR.** Certificate of Col. G. Lee, 12th April, 1784. Entitled to bounty, and prays for 287½ acres in Washington Co.

**DAVIS, JENKIN.** Colonel. Certificate of L. Hall, 8th January, 1784, that Col. Jenkin Davis, of Effingham Co., is entitled to 1,050 acres of bounty land, and prays for same in Washington Co.

**DENNIS, ABRAHAM.** Certificate of Col. G. Lee, 30th March, 1784. Entitled to a bounty of 250 acres of land, and prays for same in Washington Co.

**DOWNS, JONATHAN.** Certificate of Col. E. Clarke, 6th April, 1784. Entitled to a bounty of 250 acres and prays for same in Washington Co.

**DOWNS, GEORGE.** Certificate of Col. Jas. McNeil, 23rd March, 1784. Entitled to a bounty of 250 acres of land, and prays for same in Washington Co.

**DAVIS, SAMUEL.** Certificate of Gen. John Twiggs, and Col. E. Clarke, 2nd February, 1784, that he is entitled to bounties as citizen and refugee soldier, and prays for same in Washington Co. 27th April, 1784. Appoints James Fontaine attorney to receive land.

**DABNEY, AUSTIN.** Certificate of Col. E. Clarke, 2nd February, 1784. Entitled to a bounty of 250 acres.

**DUNNISON, ELIJAH.** Certificate of Col. E. Clarke, 24th April, 1784, that he served as a sergeant in the Batt. of Minute Men, though not at the time an inhabitant of the State. Prays for 250 acres of land in Franklin Co.

**DASHER, JOHN MARTIN.** Certificate of Col. Caleb Howell, 16th February, 1784, that he was entitled to a bounty of 250 acres. John Martin Dasher, of Effingham Co., appoints Jenkin Davis, Esqr., to get the certificates for me, and the certificate of Christian Dasher.

**DAVIS, DAVID.** Certificate of Col. James Jackson, 26th July, 1784, that he served under his command in the Ga. State Legion, and is entitled to a bounty. He prays for 287½ acres in Franklin Co. "House of Assembly, July 22nd, 1782. Resolved, that a complete suit of clothes, a good horse, saddled and bridled, a likely negro, and 300 acres of land be given to David Davis, of Col. Jackson's Corps, as a testimony of the approbation of this House for his faithful services and for his discovering a conspiracy formed against the government." Extract from the Minutes.

**DANIELLY, JAMES.** Certificate of Col. Wm. Candler, that he was a refugee soldier under my command.

**DUKES, BUCKNER.** Certificate of Col. E. Clarke, 2nd February, 1784, that he is entitled to a bounty of 250 acres, and prays for same in Washington Co., and appoints William Anderson attorney to receive his certificate.

**DUKES, TAYLOR.** Certificate of Col. E. Clarke, 24th April, 1784, that he is entitled to a bounty, and prays for same in Washington Co.

**DAVIS, BENJ.** (Of Burke Co.) Certificate of Gen. John Twiggs, 2nd March, 1784, that he was a refugee soldier. Entitled to a bounty, and prays for 287½ acres in Washington Co., and appoints William Daniel attorney to receive same.

**DENNIS, RICHMOND.** Certificate of Col. G. Lee, 11th March, 1784. Entitled to a bounty, and prays for 287½ acres in Franklin Co. Also prays for 200 acres of land for the two children of Solomon Vickers, whose widow he had married.

**DAVIS, JOHN.** Certificate of Col. G. Lee, 23rd February, 1784, that he is entitled to a bounty of land.

**DAVIES, JOHN.** (Of Burke Co.) Certificate of Gen. John Twiggs, 26th November, 1783, that he was a refugee soldier in North Carolina, after the reduction of Charleston. Prays for bounty lands in Washington Co.

**DAVIS, JAMES.** (Of Wilkes Co.) Certificate of Col. E. Clarke, 22nd April, 1784, that he is entitled to a bounty of land, and prays for 287½ acres in Washington Co.

**DAVIS, CLEMENTUS.** Certificate of Col. G. Lee, 12th April, 1784. Entitled to a bounty. Prays for 287½ acres in Washington Co.

**DAVIS, LEWIS.** Certificate of Col. E. Clarke, 2nd February, 1784. Entitled to a bounty, and prays for 250 acres of land in Washington Co.

**DAVIS, ABSOLOM.** Certificate of Col. E. Clarke, 2nd February, 1784. Refugee soldier. Entitled to bounty, and prays for 287½ acres in Washington Co., April 4th, 1784. Sold same to William Swanson.

**DARCEY, WILLIAM.** Certificate of Gen. John Twiggs, 4th March, 1784. Entitled to bounty, and prays for 287½ acres in Washington Co.

**DOUGLASS, WILLIAM.** Certificate of Col. E. Clarke, 19th May, 1784. Entitled to a bounty, and prays for same in Washington Co.

**DAY, ROBERT, JR.** Certificate of Col. E. Clarke, 6th April, 1784. Entitled to bounty, and prays for 287½ acres in Washington Co.

**DANNELLY, FRANCIS.** Certificate of Col. G. Lee, 10th April, 1784. Entitled to bounty, and prays for same in Washington Co.

**DARCEY, JOEL.** Certificate of Gen. John Twiggs, 4th March, 1784. Entitled to bounty, and prays for same in Washington Co.

**DARBY, JOHN.** Certificate of Gen. J. Twiggs, February, 1784. Entitled to a bounty, and prays for 287½ acres in Washington Co.

**DEAN, JOHN.** Certificate of Col. J. McNeil, 12th August, 1784. Entitled to a bounty, and prays for same in Washington Co.

**DALLY, BENJ.** Certificate of Col. Jas. Martin, 30th January, 1784. Entitled to a bounty of land, and prays for same in Franklin Co.

## CERTIFICATES OF SERVICE IN AMERICAN REVOLUTION.

**DUKES, JOHN TAYLOR, SR.** Certificate of Col. E. Clarke, 3rd April, 1784, that he served as a soldier in the Batt. of Minute Men, though not an inhabitant of the State, and prays for 250 acres of land in Washington Co.

**DARCEY, JAMES.** Certificate of Gen. John Twiggs, 4th March, 1784, that he was a refugee soldier, entitled to bounty.

**DUNN, NEHEMIAH.** Certificate of Col. Wm. Candler, that he was a refugee soldier. Entitled to bounty. Granted 25th May, 1784.

**DOWNS, AMBROSE, JR.** Certificate of Col. Jas. McNeil, 22nd March, 1784, that he served in the first Batt. of Rich. Co. Militia, as a refugee soldier, and prays for bounty in Franklin Co.

**DUHART, JOHN.** Certificate of Gen. John Twiggs, 27th November, 1783, that he was a refugee soldier in North Carolina. John Duhart, of Burke Co., appoints his friend, Hugh Lawson, Esqr., to receive said bounty.

**DAY, STEPHEN.** Certificate of Col. Jas. McNeil, 2nd February, 1784, that he is entitled to a bounty of 250 acres, and prays for same in Washington Co.

**DAVIS, WILEY...** Certificate of Col. E. Clarke, 2nd February, 1784, that he is entitled to a bounty, and prays for same in Washington Co.

**DUKES, JAMES.** Certificate of Col. E. Clarke, 3rd April, 1784, that he served in the Batt. of Minute Men, though not an inhabitant of the State. Prays for 250 acres in Washington Co. Granted to the heirs.

**DELANY, JAMES.** Certificate of Col. Samuel Jack, 10th February, 1784, that he was a Minute man, though not an inhabitant of the State at the time of enlistment. Entitled to bounty and prays for same in Washington Co.

**DOLLAR, ANSON.** Certificate of Gen. Jas. Jackson, July 16, 1784, that he served in the Ga. State Legion, and is entitled to a bounty, and prays for 287½ acres in Washington Co.

**DAVIS, BLANDFORD.** Certificate of Col. Wm. Candler, that he was a refugee soldier in his command. Prays for bounty land in Washington Co.

**DAVIS, VATHAEL.** Certificate of Col. Wm. Candler, that he was a refugee soldier. Entitled to bounty. Granted 15th April, 1784.

**DAVIS, MERIDETH.** On certificate of Gen. Samuel Elbert, 15th April, 1784, that he is entitled to a bounty for service as a sergeant in the Continental Line of Ga.

**DAVIS, CHARLES.** On certificate of Gen. Sam. Elbert, 15th April, 1784, that he is entitled to a bounty for service as a sergeant in the Continental Line of Ga.

**DAVIS, CHESLEY.** Certificate of Col. E. Clarke, 2nd February, 1784, that he was entitled to a bounty, prayed for same in Washington Co.

**DAVIS, CHESLEY, JR.** Certificate of Col. E. Clarke, 2nd February, 1784, that he is a refugee soldier. Entitled to a bounty. Prayed for same in Washington Co.

ROSTER OF THE REVOLUTION.

**DANELLY, JAMES.** Certificate of Col. E. Clarke, 1st April, 1784, that he was a Minute man, though not an inhabitant of the State at the time of enlistment, and prays for bounty of 250 acres in Washington Co.

**DOLLARS, JOHN.** Certificate of Gen. Lachlan McIntosh, 1st October, 1783, that he was appointed 2nd Lt. in Capt. Thomas Morris' Co. of Artillery, 22nd July, 1776, and that he resigned the 26th July, 1780.

**DAVIES, JOHN, SR.** Of Burke Co. Gentleman. Certificate of Col. E. Clarke, 22nd May, 1784, that he is entitled to a bounty, and appoints Hugh Lawson, of Burke Co., attorney to receive warrant for same.

**DORTON, THOMAS.** Certificate of Col. E. Clarke, 14th April, 1784, that he is entitled to a bounty, and prays for 250 acres in Washington Co.

**DARBE, RICHARD.** Certificate of Col. G. Lee, 11th March, 1784, that he is entitled to a bounty, and prays for 287½ acres in Washington Co.

**DeCLANDENESS, MATTHEW.** Certificate of Col. Samuel Jack, 7th April, 1784, that he served as a sergeant in the Batt. of Minute Men, though not an inhabitant of the State at the time of enlistment, and prays for bounty land in Washington Co.

**DUCKWORTH, JACOB.** Certificate of Col. Jas. McNeil, 4th September, 1784. entitled to a bounty of 250 acres of land.

**DUCKWORTH, JEREMIAH.** Certificate of Col. Jas. McNeil, 2nd February, 1784. Entitled to a bounty, and prays for 287½ acres in Washington Ca.

**DAVIS, ABSOLOM.** Certificate of Col. E. Clarke, 25th March, 1784, that he is entitled to a bounty of 250 acres.

**DUKES, WILLIAM.** Certificate of Col. E. Clarke, 3rd April, 1784. Served as a lieutenant in the Batt. of Minute Men, though not an inhabitant of the State.

**DICKSON, NATHAN.** Certificate of Col. E. Clarke, 4th January, 1785, that he was a soldier in the Batt. of Minute Men, though not an inhabitant of the State at the time of enlisment.

**DOSS, JOEL.** Certificate of Col. E. Clarke, 8th April, 1784, that he was a refugee lieutenant, and is entitled to 350 acres, and prays for same in Franklin Co.

**DALTON, MATHIAS.** Certificate of Col. E. Clarke, 7th April, 1784, that he is entitled to a bounty of 250 acres. Statement from Mathias Dalton, that he had sold his bounty land to William Veazey, and requests that it be put in his name.

**DAVIS, WARE.** Certificate of Col. E. Clarke, 16th November, 1784, that he was a soldier in Batt. of Minute Men, though not an inhabitant of the State.

## CERTIFICATES OF SERVICE IN AMERICAN REVOLUTION.

**DAVIS, SOLOMON.** Certificate of Gen. John Twiggs, 2nd March, 1784, that he is entitled to a bounty of 250 acres; appoints Francis Willis to take up said land in Washington Co.

**DAVIS, HARDY.** Certificate of Col. E. Clarke, 16th December, 1784, that he was a Minute man, though not an inhabitant of the State at the time of enlistment. Entitled to bounty of land.

**DONNELLY, JAS.** Captain. Certificate of Col. G. Lee, 23rd February, 1784, that he is entitled to a bounty of 500 acres, and prays for same in Washington Co.

**DOWNS, WILLIAM, ESQR.** Certificate of Col. E. Clarke, 2nd February, 1784, that he is entitled to a bounty of 250 acres of land, and prays for same in Washington Co.

**DAVIS, JOHN WADE, JR.** Petitions by Meredith Davis, his father, John being a minor, showing that he is entitled to 287½ acres bounty for service in the Continental line. Prays for said land in Franklin Co.

**DURBAN, LUKE.** Certificate of Col. G. Lee, 25th March, 1784. Entitled to a bounty of 250 acres, and prays for same in Washington Co.

**DANIELLY, DANIEL.** Certificate of Col. Jas. McNeil, 15th March, 1784, that he is entitled to a bounty; granted 600 acres in Washington Co. for service as a lieutenant.

**DARBY, JOHN.** Of Burke Co. Planter. On the 16th May, 1784, appoints Hugh Inwin, to receive a warrant for 287½ acres of bounty land due for service.

**DUGAN, THOMAS.** Certificate of Col. E. Clarke, 2nd February, 1784, that he is entitled to a bounty as captain of a Continental Militia under my command, and prays for same in Franklin Co.

**DICKSON, HUGH.** Of 96th Dist., S. C., 27th March, 1784, appoints Capt. David Dickson attorney to apply for his bounty of land in the State of Georgia, due as a sergeant in the Minute Service of that State. Prays for 300 acres in Washington Co.

**DAY, ROBT., JR.** Certificate of Col. E. Clarke, 7th April, 1784, that he was a refugee soldier, and is entitled to 250 acres of bounty.

**DUNCAN, JAMES.** Certificate of Col. E. Clarke, 25th December, 1784, that he was a lieutenant in the Militia of Wilkes Co., and fled from the British enemy and took refuge in N. C. and served in the refugee service, and is entitled to a bounty of 400 acres. Granted 460.

**DEVEAUS, PETER, ESQR.** Certificate of John Armstrong, D. A. G. So. Dept., and letter of Maj. Gen. Gates, that he was a refugee captain, and entitled to 750 acres of land, 13th February, 1784.

ROSTER OF THE REVOLUTION.

**DOLLY, BENJAMIN.** Certificate of L. Hall, 22nd December, 1783, that he was a refugee soldier, and entitled to 250 acres of land.

**DICKS, ANDREW.** Certificate of Col. John Baker, 19th March, 1784, that he was a refugee soldier. Entitled to a bounty, and prays for 250 acres in Washington Co.

**DICKS, DAVID.** Petition of Luke Mann, for the heirs of David Dicks, deceased, that they are entitled to 250 acres of land as bounty for his services. Prays for same in Washington Co.

**DAY, HARRY.** Certificate of Col. Wm. Candler, that he was a refugee soldier under my command. Prays for bounty land in Washington Co., through Reuben Frazer.

**DICKSON, DAVID.** Certificate of Col. Samuel Jack, 13th March, 1884, that he served as a captain in the Batt. of Minute Men, though not at the time an inhabitant of the State, and that he is entitled to 500 acres of land as bounty, and prays for same in Washington Co.

**DAY, ROBERT, SR.** Certificate of Col. E. Clarke, 4th August, 1884, that he was entitled to a bounty of 250 acres of land, and prays for same in Washington Co.

**DICKSON, NATHANIEL.** Certificate of Col. Samuel Jack, 13th March, 1784, that he was entitled to bounty for service as a Minute man. John Dickson, of 96th Dist. of S. C., appoints his brother, Maj. Michael Dickson, of Camden Dist., S. C., attorney to obtain the bounty due me for my son, Samuel Dickson, for service, he being a minor, and only doing my service. 1st of April, 1784. Witnesses, David Dickson, and Reuben Jones.

**DARCEY, BENJ.** On certificate of Gen. John Twiggs, 4th March, 1784, that he is entitled to a bounty, and prays for 287½ acres in Washington Co.

**DANIEL, JOHN.** Certificate of Gen. John Twiggs, 29th March, 1784, that he is entitled to a bounty, and prays for 287½ acres in Franklin Co.

**DEAN, WILLIAM.** Certificate of Col. E. Clarke, 2nd February, 1784, that he is entitled to a bounty, and prays for 250 acres of land in Washington Co. Served as sergeant under Col. Marberry.

**DICKSON, WILLIAM.** Certificate of Col. Samuel Jack, 13th March, 1784, that he was a sergeant in the Batt. of Minute Men of this State, though not an inhabitant at the time of enlistment, on the 29th of March, 1784. Said Wm. Dickson, of 96th Dist., S. C., appoints Capt. David Dickson, attorney to receive his warrant for bounty land in Washington Co.

**DAVIS, ISAAC.** Petition of Col. G. Lee, 14th March, 1784, that he is entitled to a bounty, and prays for same in Washington Co.

**DUKES, HENRY.** Captain. Certificate of Col. E. Clarke, 8th September, 1784, that he was commissioned a captain in the Batt. of Minute Men.

## CERTIFICATES OF SERVICE IN AMERICAN REVOLUTION. 71

**DUNNISIN, DARBY.** Certificate of Col. E. Clarke, 24th April, 1784, that he is entitled to bounty, and prays for 250 acres in Washington Co.

**DAVIS, JOEL.** Certificate of Col. E. Clarke, 2nd February, 1784, that he was a refugee soldier. Entitled to 250 acres of bounty land.

**DAY, ROBT., SR.** Certificate of Col. E. Clarke, that he is entitled to a bounty of 287½ acres, and prays for same in Washington Co.

**DOOLY, GEORGE, MAJ.** Certificate of Col. E. Clarke, 8th April, 1784. Entitled to a bounty and prays for same in Washington Co. On the 5th April, 1784, George Dooly, of Wilkes Co., appoints Thomas Mitchell, attorney to receive his certificate for bounty, and also for his brother, Thomas Dooly, who was killed in the Continental Service.

**DOOLY, JOHN.** Col. February 23rd, 1784. Resolved, that Thomas and John Mitchell Dooly, sons of Col. John Dooly, who was cruelly murdered in his own house, while on parole, be allowed 500 acres each, in lieu of the land due their father, to be laid out in Washington Co.

**DARDEN, GEORGE, SR.** Certificate of Col. E. Clarke, 20th April, 1784, that he was a refugee soldier. Entitled to 287½ acres, and prays for same in Washington, Ga.

**DAVIES, EDWARD.** Captain. Certificate of Gen. John Twiggs, 1st July, 1784, that he was a refugee captain, and is entitled to 500 acres of land, and prays for same in Washington Co.

**DAVID, WILLIAM.** Certificate of Gen. John Twiggs, 20th April, 1784, that he was a refugee soldier. Entitled to bounty. Wm. David was clerk of Burke Co. at that time.

**DICKSON, MICHAEL.** Of South Carolina. Certificate of Col. Samuel Jack, 13th March, 1784, that he served as a captain in the Batt. of Minute Men, though not an inhabitant of the State.

**DELANEY, DANIEL.** Certificate of Col. E. Clarke, 25th March, 1784, that he is entitled to a bounty, and prays for 250 acres in Washington Co.

**DUNWOODY, JAMES.** Certificate of Nathan Brownson, 29th March, 1784, that he is entitled to a bounty of 250 acres as a refugee soldier.

**DARDEN, GEORGE.** Certificate of Col. E. Clarke, 20th April, 1784, that he was a refugee soldier. Entitled to bounty, and prays for 287½ acres in Washington Co.

**DAVIS, MOSES.** Certificate of Gen. John Twiggs, 4th March, 1784, that he is entitled to a bounty, and prays for 250 acres in Washington Co.

**DAVIS, JACOB.** Certificate of Col. Jas. Jackson, 23rd July, 1784, that he is entitled to a bounty, and prays for 287½ acres in Franklin Co.

**DAVIS, THOMAS.** Certificate of Col. Samuel Jack, 7th April, 1784, that he was in the Batt. of Minute Men, though not an inhabitant of the State, and prays for 287½ acres in Franklin Co.

**DAVIS, GIDEON.** Certificate of Col. E. Clarke, 2nd February, 1784, that he is entitled to a bounty of 250 acres of land.

**DUFFEY, JOHN.** Certificate of Col. Samuel Jack, 24th June, 1784, that he was a Minute man, though not an inhabitant of the State at the time of enlistment, and prays for bounty in Franklin Co.

**DINKINS, SEBREE.** Certificate of Col. E. Clarke, 16th November, 1784, that he was a Minute man, though not an inhabitant of the State at the time of enlistment.

**DAMPIER, DANIEL.** Certificate of Jos. Pannill, that he was a sergeant in the Ga. Line, and is entitled to 230 acres of land as bounty, and sold said bounty to Jos. Pannill.

**DAWSON, WILLIAM.** Certificate of Lieut. Jos. Pannill, 8th April, 1784, that he was a soldier in the Ga. Line, and died in the service. By certificate of Josiah Carter, executor, that Martin Dawson, of the State of Virginia, is the heir of said William Dawson.

**DRIVER, HENRY.** Certificate of Col. E. Clarke, 10th May, 1784, that he was a Minute man, though not an inhabitant of the State, prays for 287½ acres in Franklin Co.

**DUNCAN, MATTHEW.** Certificate of Col. E. Clarke, 1st April, 1784, that he served as a lieutenant in the Batt. of Minute Men, though not an inhabitant of the State at the time of enlistment. Prays for bounty in Washington Co.

**DAVENPORT, THOMAS.** Certificate of Maj. John Habersham, 19th April, 1784, that he was a surgeon in the 3rd Continental Batt. of this State until he died in captivity the beginning of 1780. Thomas Davenport, his son, appoints Thos. Glascock, attorney to receive a warrant for bounty due his father as a soldier. Prays for 800 acres.

**DAVIS, JAMES.** Certificate of Col. E. Clarke, 2nd February, 1784, that he is entitled to a bounty of 250 acres, and he appoints John Rutherford, Esqr., to receive the same, on the 30th December, 1785.

**DAVIS, JAMES.** Certificate of Gen. John Twiggs, 28th February, 1784, that he is entitled to a bounty, and prays for same through his friend, Francis Willis.

**DOWDY, RICHARD.** Certificate of Col. Jas. McNeil, 21st February, 1784. Entitled to a bounty of 250 acres, and appoints Thomas Bush attorney to receive same.

**DOUGLAS, ALEXANDER.** Certificate of Col. E. Clarke, 3rd April, 1784, that he was a Minute man, though not an inhabitant of the State at time of enlistment, and prays for bounty land in Washington Co.

**DUMAPLIN, ELIJAH.** Certificate of Col. E. Clarke, 16th November, 1784, that he was a Minute man, though not an inhabitant of the State at time of enlistment.

## CERTIFICATES OF SERVICE IN AMERICAN REVOLUTION. 73

**DANIEL, WILLIAM.** Certificate of Col. E. Clarke, 2nd February, 1784, that he was a refugee soldier. Entitled to a bounty of 250 acres.

**DUNCAN, THOMAS.** Certificate of Col. E. Clarke, 10th December, 1784, that he was entitled to a bounty of 250 acres of land, and prays for same in Washington Co.

**DOUGLAS, JOHN.** Certificate of Gen. John Twiggs, 19th April, 1784, that he is entitled to a bounty of 250 acres and prays for same in Washington Co.

**DeROCHE, ABRAHAM.** Certificate of Col. Jenkins Davis, 2nd March, 1784, that he was a refugee soldier.

**DAY, HENRY.** 28th April, 1784, appoints Thos. Glascock, attorney to receive his bounty as a refugee soldier.

**DAVISON, JOSEPH.** Certificate of Col. E. Clarke, 7th April, 1784, that he is entitled to a bounty and prays for 287½ acres in Washington Co.

**DOOLY, GEORGE.** Certificate of Col. E. Clarke, 2nd February, 1784, that he was a refugee captain, and is entitled to 500 acres of bounty land, and prays for same in Washington Co.

**DEMNON, CHARLES.** A petition for 287½ acres of land in Washington Co., as bounty for his services.

**DAY, JOSEPH.** Captain. Prays for 600 acres of land as bounty for his services as captain of the Line for this State.

**DOOLY, HULL.** Certificate dated 6th February, 1784, that he was a lieutenant in the navy.

**DASHER, CHRISTAIN.** Certificate of Col. Jenkins Davis, 14th February, 1784, that he was a refugee soldier and killed in service, and that John Martin Dasher is guardian for his heirs. Christian Dasher left one son.

### E.*

**EVANS, BENJAMIN.** This is to certify that Benjamin Evans has served out his time of enlistment as sergeant in the 1st Continental Regt. of Light Dragoons and is honorably discharged from service. Leo. Marbury, S. C. C., March 9, 1779.

**EVES, NATHANIEL.** Ex. order for 230 acres in the Reserve. May 17, 1784.

**EVANS, WILLIAM.** Certificate of E. Clarke, Lt. Col., January 25, 1785. Petitioner prays 287½ acres in Washington Co.

**EMANUEL, LEVI.** Certificate of John Twiggs, Brig. Gen., February 3, 1784. Petitioner prays for 575 acres in Washington Co.

**EVANS, DANIEL.** Certificate of 3 years' service in 2d Ga. Battalion, Litt. Mosby, Captain. June 10, 1785.

**EDMONDS, ABSOLEM.** Ex. order on certificate of Col. Clarke, March 26, 1784.

**EVANS, DANIEL**...Certificate of E. Clarke, Col., May 18, 1784. Petitioner prays 287½ acres in Washington Co.

**EVANS, BENJAMIN.** Certificate of Elijah Clarke, Col., April 20, 1784. Petitioner prays 287½ acres in Washington Co.

**ELLIS, ROBERT.** Certificate of 3 years' service in 4th Ga. Batalion, Jos. Pannill, Lt. Col., April 13, 1784. Petitioner prays bounty in Washington Co. Warrant 141.

**EIGLE, JOHN.** Certificate of Elijah Clarke, Col., February 2, 1724. Warrant 1117.

**EADS, ——.** Petition of Mary, relict of —— Eads, for bounty on his service as soldier. Granted April 15, 1784.

**EARNEST, WILLIAM.** Certificate of Elijah Clarke, Col., February 2, 1784.

**EMANUEL, DAVID.** Certificate of John Twiggs, Brig. Gen., March 4, 1784, 2d certificate as captain, John Twiggs, Brig. Gen., March 5, 1784. Petitioner prays two bounties, 575 acres in Washington Co.

**EVANS, WILLIAM.** Certificate of E. Clarke, Col., January 15, 1785. Warrant 1121.

**EVANS, DANIEL.** Certificate of Wm. Candler, Col. Regt. Refugees, R. C. Petitioner prays bounty in Washington Co. Warrant 1122.

**ELLIOTT, DANIEL.** Certificate of 3 years' service in 2d Batt. Ga. Cont. Line, and lost his life in said service. Elisha Miller, Capt. Comdg., November 15, 172. Granted to Elizabeth, relict of Daniel Elliott, March 19, 1784.

**EVANS, DAVID.** Certificate of Elijah Clarke, Col., August 24, 1784. Petitioner prays bounty in Franklin Co.

### E.*

Beginning with the letter "E," the remaining part of this list is the work of Mr. Wm. L. LeConte, of Atlanta, one of the most careful of investigators. It is all based upon actual certificates of service, on file in the office of Secretary of State.

Mr. LeConte was born December 28th, 1838, in Liberty County, Ga. His paternal stock was French Huguenot. Guillaume LeConte, his ancestor, came to America in 1698, after fifteen years' service in the armies of William of Orange. The family settled in St. John's Parish—now Liberty County—Georgia, in 1760. His father, William LeConte, was the elder brother of the distinguished scientists, John and Joseph LeConte.

His mother was Sarah A. Nisbet, of a Scotch-Irish family which settled in North Carolina, about 1750. His great-grandfather, John Nisbet, was a member of the first Constitutional Convention of North Carolina; his grandfather, Dr. James Nisbet, helped make the Georgia Constitution of 1798, and his uncle, Eugenius A. Nisbet, was a member of Congress, a Supreme Court justice, and a delegate to the Secession Convention. He also wrote the Ordinance of Secession, which separated Georgia from the Union.

Mr. LeConte was born in Liberty County, but on the death of his father, the family removed to Macon, where he grew up. He was educated at Franklin College (now the U. of G.), and Oglethorpe, receiving his A.B. degree from the latter in 1858.

He served through the late war, coming out as Adjutant of the 66th Georgia Regiment. He married, in 1866, Miss Virginia Trimble, of which union there were two sons, James A. and the late Dr. J. N. LeConte.

# CERTIFICATES OF SERVICE IN AMERICAN REVOLUTION.

**ELLIOTT, WILLIAM, JR.** Certificate of John Twiggs, Brig. Gen., April 2, 1784. Petitioner prays 287½ acres in Washington Co. 2d certificate, as order on Joseph Pannill, surveyor, for 287½ acres, by John Habersham, Pres. Ex. Council, May 17, 1784. Petitioner asks warrant in Franklin Co.

**ELLIOTT, HENRY.** Certificate of John Twiggs, Brig. Gen., April 2, 1784. Warrant 1125.

**ELLIOTT, JOHN.** Certificate of John Baker, Col. Warrant 1124.

**EMANUEL, ASA.** Certificate as soldier, John Twiggs, Brig. Gen., February 2, 1784. Warrant 1115.

**EMANUEL, LEVI.** Certificate as sergeant major, John Twiggs, Brig. Gen., November 27, 1785. Warrant 1112.

**EMANUEL, AMOS.** Certificate as soldier, John Twiggs, Brig. Gen., Feb. 2, 1784. Warrant 1113.

**EMANUEL, ASA.** Certificate of John Twiggs, Brig. Gen., February 2, 1784. Petitioner prays 287½ acres in Washington Co.

**ESPEY, WILLIAM.** Certificate of Benjamin Few, Col., February 20, 1784. Petitioner prays bounty in Washington Co. Warrant 1114.

**ESPEY, THOMAS.** Certificate as captain (missing) with ex. order for 500 acres, February 28, 1784. Warrant 911.

**EMBRICK, GEORGE.** Barrack master as per certificate of Brig. Gen. Samuel Elbert (missing), March 12, 1784. Petitioner prays 690 acres in reserve. Warrant 60.

**EADES, JOHN.** Certificate of Elijah Clarke, Col., February 2, 1784. Ex. order for two bounties of 250 acres each. Warrants 118 and 119.

**EADY, JOHN.** Ex. order for bounty on certificate of E. Clarke, Col., (missing), March 25, 1784. Petitioner prays warrant in Washington Co.

**ECKLES, EPHRAIM.** I certify that Ephraim Eckles, deceased, was a soldier in my company in 3d Regt. Cont. troops. He died in service and that his son, John Eckles, is entitled to his bounty. Signed, Capt. Rawleigh P. Dowman, February 2, 1784. Warrant 189.

**EVANS, STEPHEN.** Certificate as refugee and soldier, John Twiggs, Brig. Gen., December 3, 1783. Petitioner prays 250 acres Washington Co. Warrant 1120.

**EARNEST, JACOB.** Certificate of Jas. Jackson, Lt. Col., July 2, 1784. Petitioner prays land in Franklin Co.

**EUSTACE, JOHN J. KEY.** Certificate of governor that John J. Key Eustace (Major), of the American Army, is entitled to 400 acres by resolution of Congress, September 16, 1776, as per his commission by Congress. Granted bounty as a major. Warrant 38.

**EMBRY, JESSEY.** Certificate of Jas. Jackson, Lt. Col., September 18, 1784. Petitioner prays 287½ acres in Washington Co.

**ELLIOTT, DANIEL,** deceased. Ex. order for bounty to his heirs of 200 acres, March 19, 1784. Warrant 137.

**EMMETT, JAMES.** Certificate as refugee and soldier, Greenberry Lee, Col., April 7, 1784. Petitioner prays 287½ acres in Franklin Co.

**ELBERT, BRIG. GEN. SAMUEL.** Of Georgia. Certificate of Gov. Houstoun, of his service in Continental Line as per his commission, dated November 4, 1783. Petitioner prays land in the reserve. Warrant No. 12.

**EASTER, JAMES.** Certificate of Elijah Clarke, Col., April 20, 1784. Petitioner prays 287½ acres in Franklin Co.

**EASTWOOD, JOHN.** Certificate of Ob. Lee, Col., April 22, 1784. Petitioner prays bounty in Franklin Co.

**ENTICHENS, WILLIAM.** Personally appeared Mrs. Susannah Burnes, who being duly sworn saieth that she had in her hands a certificate of Wm. Entichens for bounty and that said certificate is lost. Given this 15th day of July, 1784. Zacheus Frewn, J. P. Petitioner prays 287½ acres in Washington Co.

**ELLIS, WILLIAM.** Certificate of Elijah Clarke, Col., June 16, 1784. Petitioner prays bounty in Washington Co. Warrant 1126.

**ELMONDS, ABSOLEM.** Certificate of Elijah Clarke, Col., February 2, 1784.

**ELLISON, JAMES.** Ex. order as per certificate of Col. E. Clarke (missing), March 25, 1784. Warrant 1127.

**EDWARDS JOHN.** Certificate as refugee and soldier, from this State into North Carolina as a soldier. John Twiggs, Brig. Gen., April 6, 1784. Petitioner prays bounty in Washington Co.

**EARNEST, WILLIAM.** Certificate of Elijah Clarke, Col., February 2, 1784. Petitioner prays two bounties, 575 acres in Washington Co.

**ELLIOTT, WILLIAM, SR.** Certificate of John Twiggs, Brig. Gen., February 26, 1784. Petitioner prays 287½ acres in Washington Co.

**EMBRICKEN, WILLIAM.** Certificate of Jas. Jackson, Lt. Col., March 15, 1784.

**EAVES, NATHANIEL.** Certificate as a soldier in 3d Batt. Ga. Cont. Line. Born in Brunswick Co., Va. Discharged August 26, 1779, by Nathl. Peavie, Commanding 3d Ga. Batt.

**ELLIOTT, HENRY.** Certificate of John Twiggs, Brig. Gen., February 26, 1784. Petitioner prays two grants—575 acres—in Washington Co. Warrant 24.

**EVANS, SERGEANT JOHN.** Certificate of service as a sergeant and that he died in the service. Certificate of major illegible. Petitioner prays 287½ acres in reserve. Warrant 138.

## CERTIFICATES OF SERVICE IN AMERICAN REVOLUTION. 77

**EVANS, DANIEL.** Certificate of John Twiggs, Brig. Gen., March 20, 1784. Petitioner prays 250 acres in Washington Co.

**ELLIS, STEPHEN.** Certificate of Gb. Lee, Col., March 11, 1784. Petitioner prays 287½ acres in Washington Co.

### F.

**FOSTER, FRANCIS.** Certificate as soldier and that his heirs are entitled to bounty. Elijah Clarke, Col., Aug. 4, 1784. Warrant 1141.

**FOSTER, WILLIAM.** Certificate as refugee and soldier. E. Clarke, Col. (missing). Ex. order thereon, March 25, 1784. Petitioner prays bounty in Washington Co.

**FARRELL, LT. COL. WILLIAM.** Petition upon his commission in Minute Regt., under Col. Samuel Jack. Prays two grants of 400 and 287½ acres in Franklin Co.

**FENN, ZACHARIAS.** Certificate of Gb. Lee, Col., February 3, 1784.

**FORT, OWEN.** Certificate of E. Clarke, Col., April 7, 1784. Petitioner prays warrant in Washington Co.

**FINLEY, JAMES.** Certificate of Elijah Clarke, Col., April 7, 1784. Petitioner prays 287½ acres in Washington Co.

**FARE, JACOB.** Certificate of Gb. Lee, Col., March 6, 1784. Petitioner prays 287½ acres in Washington Co.

**FORTENE, JACOB.** Certificate of Greenberry Lee, Col., May 6, 1784. Petitioner prays warrant in Washington Co.

**FORT, ARTHUR.** Certificate of Jas. McNeil, Col., March 15, 1784. Petitioner prays bounty in Washington Co.

**FORD, OWEN.** Certificate of Elijah Clarke, Col., February 2, 1784.

**FREEMAN, HOLMAN.** Certificate of Elijah Clarke, Col., February 2, 1784. Petitioner prays 287½ acres in Washington Co.

**FERKERSON, JOHN.** Certificate of Elijah Clarke, Col., January 25, 1785. Petitioner prays 250 acres in Washington Co.

**FREEMAN, HOLMAN.** ed. Certificate as adjutant, Elijah Clarke, Col., April 2, 1784. Ex. order for 350 acres. Warrant 877.

**FRANCIS, FREDERICK.** Certificate as refugee and soldier, Jas. McKay, Col., July 1, 1784. Petitioner prays 250 and 287½ acres in Washington Co.

**FUSSELL, THOMAS.** Certificate as refugee and soldier, John Twiggs, Brig. Gen., March 3, 1784. Petitioner prays warrant in Washington Co.

**FULSON, JOHN.** Certificate of Greenberry Lee, Col., April 10, 1784. Petitioner prays warrant in Washington Co.

**FREEMAN, JOHN.** Certificate of Elijah Clarke, Col., February 2, 1784. Two grants of 250 acres each. Warrants (ex. orders) 1018 and 1021.

**FREDONIA, CONRAD.** Certificate of Geo. Handley, Major, April 6, 1784. Warrant 142.

**FERGUSON, CHARLES.** Certificate of Gb. Lee, Col., February 23, 1784. 2d certificate of Gb. Lee, April 6, 1784. Petitioner prays two bounties, 287½ acres each, in Washington Co.

**FULTON, SAMUEL, SR.** Certificate of Elijah Clarke, Col., March 13, 1784. Warrant 502.

**FOWLER, NATHAN.** Certificate of Jas. McNeil, Col., February 5, 1784. Petitioner, Ruth Wilkes, prays 287½ acres in Washington Co. Granted April 15, 1784.

**FORD, WILLIAM.** Certificate as refugee and soldier, E. Clarke, Col., April 8, 1784. Petitioner prays warrant in Franklin Co. Warrant 1144.

**FELPS, DAVID.** Certificate of Gb. Lee, Col., February 20, 1784. Petitioner prays warrant in Washington Co.

**FANN, JOHN.** Certificate as refugee and soldier, John Twiggs, Brig. Gen., March 4, 1784. Warrant 1135.

**FORD, THOMAS.** Certificate of Gb. Lee, Col., February 23, 1784.

**FOSTER, WILLIAM.** Ex. order upon certificate of Col. E. Clarke (missing), March 25, 1784.

**FRIER, JOHN.** Certificate of Gb. Lee, Col., February 25, 1784. 2d certificate of Elijah Clarke, Col., April 7, 1784. Warrant No. 520. Petitioner prays two grants of 287½ acres each, in Washington Co.

**FULSOME, LAURANCE.** Certificate of Elijah Clarke, Col., November 16, 1784. Warrant 524.

**FRANCIS, FREDERICK.** Certificate as refugee and soldier (no date), John Twiggs, Brig. Gen. Warrant 1137.

**FETLER, NATHANIEL.** Certificate as refugee and soldier, Jenkins Davis, Lt. Col., March 2, 1784. Warrant 1478.

**FETLER, MATTHEW.** Certificate as refugee and soldier, Jenkin Davis, Lt. Col., March 2, 1784. Warrant 1477.

**FEW, WILLIAM, SR.** Certificate of Gb. Lee, Col., February 25, 1784. Petitioner prays warrant for 287½ acres in Washington Co. 2d certificate to Wm. Few, Gb. Lee, Col., February 25, 1784. Warrant 858. 3d certificate to Wm. Few as lieutenant colonel, Benjamin Few, Col. Commanding, Feb. 27, 1784. Petitioner prays 1207 acres on the three in Washington Co.

## CERTIFICATES OF SERVICE IN AMERICAN REVOLUTION. 79

**FEW, IGNATIUS.** Certificate of Gb. Lee, Col., March 11, 1784. Petitioner prays warrant in Washington Co. Also 900 acres in Washington Co. in head rights of himself and family.

**FEW, COLONEL BENJAMIN.** "We certify that Col. Benjamin Few commanded the Georgia Refugees and South Carolina Militia and is entitled to bounty of land according to that rank. Certified this February 20th, 1784." Lt. Col. M. Williamson and Major S. Cunningham. Petitioner prays 1150 acres in Washington Co. Warrant 855.

**FOLSOM, BENJAMIN.** Certificate of service as captain, Elijah Clarke, Col., April 20, 1784. Also certificate of Wm. Lowns that Benj. Folsom was killed by Indians while bravely fighting, and his heirs should be granted bounty land. Petitioner, Easter Folsom, prays warrant in Washington Co. Granted to heirs.

**FIELDS, WILLIAM.** Certificate of Elijah Clarke, Col., May 22, 1784. Petitioner prays warrant in Franklin Co.

**FLYNN, JAMES.** Certificate (duplicate-original lost) of Elijah Clarke, Col., November 23, 1784. Petitioner prays grant in Franklin Co.

**FRAZER, LIEUT. JOHN.** Certificate of John Habersham, Major, January 18, 1784 Warrant 77.

**FULLER, STEPHEN.** Certificate as refugee and soldier, Wm. Candler, Col. Comdg. Regt. R. C. Petitioner prays 287½ acres in Franklin Co.

**FORD, JOSHUA.** Certificate of E. Clarke, Col., April 8, 1784. Petitioner prays warrant in Washington Co.

**FRENCH, JAMES.** Certificate of E. Clarke, Col., December 10, 1784. Petitioner prays 287½ acres in Washington Co.

**FAVOURS, JOHN.** Certificate of Elijah Clarke, Col., February 2, 1784.

**FERRINGTON, JACOB.** Certificate of Elijah Clarke, Col., April 10, 1784. Petitioner prays 230 acres in Washington Co.

**FLYNN, JOHN.** Certificate as refugee and soldier, Elijah Clarke, Col., April 19, 1784. Petitioner prays 575 acres in Washington Co. Warrant 1146.

**FLYNN, JAMES.** Certificate as refugee and soldier, Elijah Clarke, Col., May 24, 1784. Petitioner prays land in Franklin Co. Warrant 1145.

**\*FULTON, CAPT. SAMUEL, JR.** Petition for 250 acres as per certificate of Col. John Baker, November 18, 1784 (missing). Warrant 894.

**FINSHWELL, JOSEPH.** Petition for 287½ acres in Washington Co., as per certificate of Col. Jas. Jackson, May 18, 1784 (missing). Granted, May 25, 1784.

---

\*The Secretary of State says that these are sufficient evidence of service, as applications would not be on file unless originally accompanied by certificates of service, signed by the proper military officer.

**FORD, JOHN, JR.** Petition for bounty of 287½ acres in Washington Co. upon annexed certificate (missing).

**FREEMAN, JOHN.** Two petitions for 500 acres in Washington Co. and 287½ acres in Franklin Co., upon certificates annexed (missing).

**FLOWERS, WILLIAM.** Certificate of Elijah Clarke, Col., April 6, 1784. Petitioner prays 250 acres in Washington Co. Warrant 519.

**FULLER, JOHN, SR.** Certificate of Jas. McNeil, Col., April 27, 1784.

**FLUKER, OWEN.** Certificate of Gb. Lee, Col., March 22, 1784. Petitioner prays 287½ acres in Washington Co.

**FUQUA, PRATER.** Certificate of Gb. Lee, Col., March 11, 1784. Petitioner prays 287½ acres in Washington Co.

**FENN, WILLIAM.** Petition for 287½ acres in Washington Co., as per certificate annexed (missing). Granted April 13, 1784. 2d certificate of John Twiggs, Brig. Gen., April 12, 1784. Petitioner prays 287½ acres in Franklin Co.

**FLEMING, MAJOR JAMES.** Certificate of Benj. Few, Col., March 14, 1784. Petitioner prays warrant in Washington Co. Warrant 870.

**FRAZER, ANDREW.** Certificate of Jas. McNeil, Col., August 6, 1784. Petitioner prays warrant in Franklin Co. Warrant 1139.

**FENN, TRAVIS.** Certificate of John Twiggs, Brig. Gen., March 4, 1784. Petitioner prays 250 acres in Washington Co.

**FULTON, JOHN.** Certificate of John Baker, Col., January 29, 1785. Warrant 1138.

**FREEMAN, JOHN.** Certificate as refugee and soldier, E. Clarke, Col., March 25, 1784. Petitioner prays 287½ acres in Washington Co. Warrant 1131.

**FLEMING, WILLIAM.** Certificate of John Twiggs, Brig. Gen., February 2, 1784. Petitioner prays 287½ acres in Washington Co.

**FRAZIER, DYER.** Certificate of ———. Petitioner prays 287½ acres in Washington Co. Granted April 16, 1784.

**FRANKLIN, WILLIAM, JR.** Certificate of Gb. Lee, Col., April 7, 1784. Petitioner prays warrant in Washington Co.

**FRAZIER, JOHN.** Petition for bounty warrant in Washington Co., January 17, 1785. Granted.

**FORD, JOHN.** Certificate of John Twiggs, Brig. Gen., April 5, 1785. Petitioner prays 575 acres in Washington Co.

**FAVOURS, JOHN.** Ex. order for bounty as per certificate of Col. E. Clarke (missing), February 25, 1784. Petitioner prays 250 acres in Washington Co.

## CERTIFICATES OF SERVICE IN AMERICAN REVOLUTION. 81

**FITZGERALD, CHARLES.** Certificate of J. W. Ellison, Capt., April 26, 1784 Petitioner prays 287½ acres in Franklin Co.

**FLEMING, SAMUEL.** Certificate of John Twiggs, Brig. Gen., March 30, 1784. Petitioner prays 287½ acres in Washington Co.

**FERREL, JAMES.** Certificate of Gb. Lee, Col., March 30, 1784. Petitioner prays 287½ acres in Washington Co.

**FERRILL, WILLIAM.** Certificate as refugee and soldier, James Martin, Col., July 22, 1784. Warrant 1142.

**FREEMAN, WILLIAM.** Certificate of Elijah Clarke, February 2, 1784. Warrant 1130.

**FREEMAN, JOHN.** Certificate of Elijah Clarke, Col., Feb. 2, 1784.

**FREEMAN, JAMES.** Certificate of Elijah Clark, Col., February 2, 1784. Petitioner prays bounty (2) of 575 acres in Washington Co.

**FLEMING, ROBERT.** Certificate of John Twiggs, Brig. Gen., March 4, 1784. Petitioner prays bounty in Washington Co.

**FOLDS, GEORGE, SR.** Certificate of Gb. Lee, Col., May 17, 1784. Petitioner prays warrant in Washington Co.

**FREEMAN, JAMES.** Ex. order for bounty as refugee and soldier as per certificate of Col. E. Clarke (see above), March 25, 1784. Warrant 1132.

**FRAZIER, ALEXANDER.** Certificate of Gb. Lee, Col., April 2, 1784. Petitioner prays 287½ acres in Washington Co.

**FREEMAN, JOHN.** Certificate as refugee and soldier, Jas. McKay, Col., April 24, 1784.

**FARMER, ASAEL.** Certificate as refugee and soldier, Elijah Clarke, Col., January 24, 1784. Warrant 1133.

**FRANCIS, ABRAM.** Certificate as refugee and soldier, Elijah Clarke, Col., May 22, 1784. Petitioner prays warrant in Franklin Co. Warrant 1136. 2d certificate of Elijah Clarke, Col., May 2, 1784. Petitioner prays 287½ acres in Franklin Co.

**FREEMAN, WILLIAM.** Certificate of (signature gone), February 2, 1784. Endorsed by governor for 250 acres March 26, 1784. Petitioner prays 575 acres in two bounties in Washington Co.

**FOSTER, WILLIAM.** Certificate of Elijah Clarke, Col., February 2, 1784. Warrant 1128.

**FREYER, HUMPHRY.** Certificate of Gb. Lee, Col., March 30, 1784. Petitioner prays 287½ acres in Franklin Co.

**FIELDS, LEWIS.** Certificate of Gb. Lee, Col., May 13, 1784. Petitioner prays warrant in Washington Co.

ROSTER OF THE REVOLUTION.

**FLENNEKIN, JAMES.** Certificate of Elijah Clarke, Col., October 5, 1784. Petitioner prays warrant in Washington Co.

**FOSTER, WILLIAM.** Certificate of Elijah Clarke, Col., February 2, 1784.

**FANNER, WILLIAM.** Certificate of John Twiggs, Brig. Gen., April 3, 1784. Petitioner prays 287½ acres in Washington Co.

**FULLER, JOSHUA.** Certificate of Jas. McNeil, Col., April 5, 1784. Petitioner prays 287½ acres in Washington Co.

**FOSTER, FRANCIS.** Petition of Penelope, widow of Francis Foster, who died on field of battle, asking warrant for 287½ acres as per annexed certificate (missing).

**FORD, JOHN, JR.** Certificate as refugee and soldier, Asa Emanuel, Colonel, April 12, 1784.

**FLOYD, PENMON.** Certificate of Elijah Clarke, Col., Dec., 1784. Warrant 523.

**FULTON, SAMUEL, JR.** Certificate of Samuel Jack. Col., March 13, 1784. Warrant 521.

**FARRELL, LIEUT. WILLIAM.** Certificate of Samuel Jack, Col. February 10, 1784. Warrant 250.

**FOULDS, GEORGE.** Certificate of Gb. Lee, Col., April 6, 1784. Petitioner prays 287½ acres in Washington Co.

**FULLER, ISAAC.** Certificate of Jas. McNeil, Col., February 2, 1784. Petitioner prays 287½ acres in Washington Co.

**FARMER, ASAEL.** Certificate of Daniel Howell, Major, January 24, 1784.

**FENN, WILLIAM.** Certificate of John Twiggs, Brig. Gen., March 4, 1784. Warrant 1134.

**FLUKEWAY, THOMAS.** Certificate of Jas. Jackson, Lt. Col., G. S. L., April 6, 1784. Petitioner prays 287½ acres in Franklin Co.

**FENN, JOHN.** Certificate of John Twiggs, Brig. Gen., April 12, 1784. Petitioner prays 2 bounties, 287½ acres each, in Washington Co.

**FLY, JEREMIAH.** Certificate of John Twiggs, Brig. Gen., February 28, 1784. Petitioner prays 287½ acres in Washington Co.

**FRIGONIER, CONRAD.** Certificate of James Martin, Col., April 23, 1784. Petitioner prays 287½ acres in Franklin Co.

**FUSSELL, EZRA.** Certificate of Benj. Lewis, Capt., endorsed by John Twiggs, Brig. Gen., April 13, 1784. Petitioner prays bounty in Washington Co.

**FORD, JOHN.** Certificate of John Twiggs, Brig. Gen., April 5, 1784. Petitioner prays 287½ acres in Washington Co. Warrant 1143.

# CERTIFICATES OF SERVICE IN AMERICAN REVOLUTION. 83

**FREDONIER, CONRAD.** Petition for 287½ acres in the Reserve between the forks of the Oconee River, as per certificate attached (missing). Granted April 15, 1784.

**FLUKER, JOHN.** Certificate of Gb. Lee, Col., March 22, 1784. Petitioner prays warrant in Washington Co.

**FULLER, ISAACK.** Certificate as Refugee and Soldier, Jas. McNeil, Col., February 19, 1784. Petitioner prays bounty in Franklin Co. Warrant 1129.

**FORD, THOMAS, JR.** Certificate of Gb. Lee, Col., March 26, 1784. Petitioner prays 287½ acres in Washington Co.

**FRANKLIN, GEORGE.** Certificate of Gb. Lee, Col., April 7, 1784. Petitioner prays warrant in Franklin Co.

**FREDERICK, THOMAS.** Certificate of John Twiggs, Brig. Gen., April 20, 1784. Petitioner prays bounty in Washington Co.

**FRASSER, MALACHIAH.** Certificate of Jas. Jackson, Lt. Col., June 3, 1784. Petitioner prays bounty in Washington Co.

**FRANKLIN, WILLIAM, SR.** Certificate of Gb. Lee., Col., April 7, 1784. Petitioner prays warrant in Washington Co.

**FUQUA, THOMAS.** Certificate of Gb. Lee , Col., March 11, 1784. Petitioner prays 287½ acres in Washington Co.

**FURLOW, WILLIAM.** Certificate of Elijah Clarke, Col., September 6, 1784. Petitioner prays 287½ acres in Washington Co. Also prays 650 acres in Washington Co. on head rights for self and family.

G.

**GRAHAM, WILLIAM.** Petition for bounty of 575 acres, endorsed by Gov. Edward Telfair, who certifies that Graham gave faithful service for three years as a soldier. Petition dated Burke Co., Ga., May 5, 1784.

**GARDINER, WILLIAM.** Certificate of Gb. Lee, Col., April 6, 1784. Petitioner prays bounty in Washington Co. He also prays 850 acres in Franklin Co. on Head Rights of self, wife, 11 children, and 1 negro.

**GRAVES, RICHARD.** Certificate of Elijah Clarke, Col., February 2, 1784.

**GRIFFIN, MICHAEL.** Certificate of Jas. Jackson, Col., April 7, 1784. Petitioner prays 287½ acres in Washington Co.

**GIFT, JONATHAN.** Certificate of Gb. Lee, Col., February 23, 1784. Petitioner prays 287½ acres in Washington Co.
2d Certificate of Gb. Lee, Col., April 29, 1784.

**GRAVAT, OBEDIAH.** Certificate of service as Private in 3d Ga. Batt., Gideon Booker, Capt., 3d Ga. Batn., March 5, 1785. Warrant 148.

ROSTER OF THE REVOLUTION.

**GWALTNERY, JEHU.** Certificate of Gb. Lee, Col., February 20, 1784.

**GARBETT, GEORGE.** Certificate of Jas. Jackson, Lt. Col., September 5, 1784. Petitioner prays 287½ acres in Washington Co.

**GREASELL, ELAM.** Certificate of Jas. Jackson, Col. Ga. State Legion, April 6, 1784. Petitioner prays warrant in Franklin Co.

**GREASELL, GEORGE.** Certificate of Jas. Jackson, Lt. Col. G. S. L., April 6, 1784. Petitioner prays warrant in Washington Co.

**GRIMSEY, RICHARD.** Certificate of E. Clarke, Col., December 10, 1784.

**GRIFFITH, SAMUEL.** Certificate of John Twiggs, Brig. Gen., February 27, 1784. Petitioner prays warrant in Washington Co.

**GRINER, PHILIP.** Certificate of John Twiggs, Brig. Gen., April 3, 1784. Petitioner prays 575 acres in Washington Co.

**GRAY, ROBERT.** Certificate of Capt. James Danely, July 20, 1784, endorsed by Benj. Few, Col. Petitioner prays 287½ acres.

**GILBERT, JAMES.** Certificate of Elijah Clarke, Col., January 25, 1785.

**GAY, ALLEN.** Certificate of Elijah Clarke, Col., December 10, 1784.

**GALASPY, JOHN.** Certificate of Elijah Clarke, Col., April 8, 1784. Petitioner prays bounty in Washington Co.

**GRIMSBY, ADAM.** Certificate of E. Clark, Col., Dec. 10, 1784. Petitioner prays bounty in Washington Co.

**GAY, JOSHUA.** Certificate of E. Clarke, Col., December 10, 1784.

**GAMBLE, JOHN.** Certificate of E. Clarke, Col., February 2, 1784. Petitioner prays 287½ acres in Washington Co.; 2d Certificate as Refugee and Soldier, John Twiggs, Brig. Gen., February 3, 1784.

**GILBERT, WILLIAM.** Certificate of E. Clarke, Col., January 25, 1785.

**GREY, ROBERT M.** Certificate of E. Clarke, Col., January 3, 1785. Warrant 675.

**GIRARDEAU, JOHN.** Certificate of John Baker, Col., February 11, 1785. Warrant 1168.

**GODBE, WILLIAM.** Certificate as Refugee and Soldier, John Twiggs, Brig. Gen., March 4, 1784. Petitioner prays 287½ acres in Washington Co.

**GIRARDEAU, WILLIAM.** Certificate of John Baker, Col., March 8, 1784.

**GRAHAM, WILLIAM.** Certificate of Geo. Walton, Col., July 15, 1784. Warrant 1150.

**GOLDWIRE, JAMES.** Certificate as Refugee and Soldier, B. Few, Col. Comdg., March 12, 1784. Petitioner, Abraham Marshall, Executor, prays 250 acres

## CERTIFICATES OF SERVICE IN AMERICAN REVOLUTION. 85

in Washington Co. for James and John Goldwire, heirs of Jas. Goldwire, deceased. Warrant 1149.

**GREGG, THOMAS.** Certificate of Elijah Clarke, Col., February 2, 1784. Warrant 1152.

**GRANT, PETER.** Certificate as Refugee and Soldier, John Twiggs, Brig. Gen., December 29, 1783. Warrant 1147.

**GLASCOCK, THOMAS.** To Capt. Geo Handley: Savannah, Dec. 21, 1783. Sir:—I beg the favor of you to endeavor to procure of His Honor, the Governor, a certificate of the lands due me as a Lieutenant in the Continental Line (This paper on file with the Secretary of State). Your humble servt., Thomas Glascock.

**GRIER, ROBERT.** Certificate of John Twiggs, Brig. Gen., April 6, 1784. Warrant 1159.

**GIDEONS, WILLIAM.** Certificate as refugee and soldier, Elijah Clarke, Col., April 19, 1784. Petitioner prays 250 acres in Franklin Co. Warrant 1158.

**GIFT, JONATHAN.** Certificate as refugee and soldier, Wm. Candler, Col. of Refugee Regt. Petitioner prays 287½ acres in Washington Co. Warrant 1157.

**GILLILAND, HUGH.** Certificate as refugee and soldier, Elijah Clarke, Col., May 15, 1784. Petitioner, Thomas McDowell, Administrator, prays warrant in Washington Co. for heirs. Warrant 1156.

**GREEN, JAMES.** Certificate of Elijah Clarke, Col., February 2, 1784. Petitioner prays warrant in Washington Co. Warrant 1171.

**GREEN, SULIVAN.** Ex. order for bounty on certificate of John Twiggs, Brig. Gen. (missing), February 6, 1784. Petitioner prays warrant in Washington Co.

**GERMANY, WILLIAM, JR.** Certificate of Jas. McNeil, Col., February 2, 1784. Petitioner prays 287½ acres in Washington Co.

**GERMANY, WILLIAM, SR.** Certificate of Jas. McNeil, Col., February 4, 1784. Petitioner prays warrant in Washington Co.

**GUALTNEY, JEHU.** Ex. order for bounty on certificate of Greenberry Lee, Col., February 20, 1784. Petitioner prays 250 acres in Washington Co.

**GRIER, WILLIAM.** Certificate of Jas. McNeil, Col., February 2, 1784. Petitioner prays 287½ acres in Washington Co.

**GAMBLE, JOHN.** Certificate as refugee and soldier, John Twiggs, Brig. Gen., December 2, 1783. Petitioner prays 2 bounties, 287½ and 575 acres in Washington Co.

**GRIFFIN, MATHEW.** Ex. order for bounty as per certificate of Col. R. Willy, December 24, 1783. Petitioner prays 287½ acres in Washington Co.

GRAVES, JOHN. Certificate of Elijah Clarke, Col., April 9, 1784. Petitioner prays bounty in Washington Co.

GENT, WILLIAM. Ex. order for bounty upon certificate of Col. Clarke, March 25, 1784.

GREEN, THOMAS. Certificate of Elijah Clarke, Col., February 2, 1784. Petitioner prays 287½ acres in Washington Co.

GREEN, SULIVA. Certificate of John Twiggs, Brig. Gen., February 4, 1784.

GREEN, FREDERICK. Certificate of Elijah Clarke, Col., April 20, 1784. Petitioner prays 287½ acres in Washington Co.

GRAY, MATTHEW. Certificate of John Twiggs, Brig. Gen., March 15, 1784. Petitioner prays bounty in Washington Co.

GREEN, BENJAMIN. Certificate of John Twiggs, Brig. Gen., February 4, 1784. Petitioner prays 287½ acres in Washington Co.

GLASCOCK, THOMAS. Ex. order for bounty as lieut. in Ga. Line as per certificate of Maj. Gen. McIntosh, 200 acres by Act of Legislature, and 200 acres by Act of Congress, February 11, 1784. Warrant 78.

GOODSON, WILLIAM. Certificate of Samuel Jack, Col., April 6, 1784. Petitioner prays 250 acres in Washington Co. Warrant 535.

GILES, WILLIAM. Certificate of Samuel Jack, Col., May 14, 1784. Petitioner prays 287½ acres in Franklin Co. Warrant 528.

GRANT, WILLIAM. Certificate of John Twiggs, Brig. Gen., February 2, 1784. Petitioner prays warrant in Washington Co.

GERMANY, JOHN. Certificate of Jas. McNeil, Col., February 2, 1784.

GENT, CHARLES. Certificate of Elijah Clarke, Col., February 2, 1784.

GUNNELS, NICHOLAS. Certificate of Elijah Clarke, Col., November 16, 1784. Petitioner prays 287½ acres in Franklin Co.

GUNNELLS, DANIEL. Certificate of Elijah Clarke, Col., February 2, 1784. Petitioner prays 250 acres in Washington Co.

GRIER, AARON. Certificate of Gb. Lee, Col., April 9, 1784. Petitioner prays 287½ acres in Washington Co. 2d certificate of Gb. Lee, Col., February 20, 1784.

GIBBS, RICHARD. Certificate of Elijah Clarke, Col., January 3, 1785. Warrant 533.

GASTON, SERGEANT DAVID. Certificate of Samuel Jack, Col., April 5, 1784. Petitioner prays 300 acres in Washington Co. Warrant 292.

GAINES, BAGLY. Certificate of Elijah Clarke, Col., January 25, 1785. Warrant 526.

# CERTIFICATES OF SERVICE IN AMERICAN REVOLUTION.

**GREEN, HENRY.** Certificate of Elijah Clarke, Col., November 21, 1784. Warrant —.

**GOLDSBERRY, JONATHAN.** Certificate of Elijah Clarke, Col., February 7, 1784. Petitioner prays 250 acres in Washington Co.

**GRANT, JOHN.** Certificate as captain and soldier, Asa Emanuel, Col., January 22, 1784.

**GROTEHOUSE, JACOB.** Certificate of Gb. Lee, Col., May 15, 1784. Petitioner prays 250 acres in Franklin Co.

**GROTEHOUSE, JACOB, JR.** Certificate of Jas. Jackson, Col., July 7, 1784. Petitioner prays bounty in Franklin Co.

**GRAY, JOHN.** Certificate of Gb. Lee, Col., April 7, 1784. Petitioner prays bounty in Washington Co.

**GRAY, THOMAS.** Certificate of Gb. Lee, Col., March 11, 1784. Petitioner prays 287½ acres in Washington Co.

**GRAVES, THOMAS.** Certificate of E. Clarke, Col., March 25, 1784. Petitioner prays 287½ acres in Washington Co.

**GIDIONS, FRANCIS.** Certificate of Elijah Clarke, Col., July 6, 1784. Petitioner prays 287½ acres in Franklin Co.

**GILES, JOHN.** Certificate of Elijah Clarke, Col., April 20, 1784. Petitioner prays 287½ acres in Franklin Co.

**GILLILAND, THOMAS.** Ex. order for bounty on certificate of Col. E. Clarke, March 25, 1784. Petitioner prays 287½ acres in Washington Co.

**GIDEON, CAPT. FRANCIS.** Certificate as refugee and soldier, Elijah Clarke, Col., April 19, 1784. Warrant 919.

**GRAVES, WILLIAM.** Certificate of Elijah Clarke, Col., April 9, 1784. Petitioner prays bounty in Washington Co.

**GRAVES, JAMES.** Certificate of Elijah Clarke, Col., April 24, 1784. Petitioner prays 250 acres in Franklin Co.

**GRIMSLY, JOHN.** Certificate of Elijah Clarke, Col., April 7, 1784. Petitioner prays 287½ acres in Washington Co.

**GODBY, WILLIAM.** Certificate of John Twiggs, Brig. Gen., March 19, 1784.

**GIDDENS, WILLIAM.** Certificate of E. Clarke, Col., August 16, 1784. Petitioner prays bounty in Franklin Co.

**GAMEST, WILLIAM.** Ex. order as per certificate of E. Clarke, Col. (missing), March 25, 1784.

**GORDEN, JESSE.** Certificate of Elijah Clarke Col., January 3, 1785. Warrant 534.

GRIMSLEY, ELIJAH. Certificate as sergeant and soldier, Elijah Clarke, Col., May 6, 1784. Petitioner prays 345 acres in Franklin Co. Warrant 291.

GARDNER, LEWIS. Ex. order on certificate of Gb. Lee, Col. (missing), February 28, 1784. Petitioner prays bounty in Washington Co.

GRANT, THOMAS. Ex. order for bounty as per certificate of Col. E. Clarke (missing), February 28, 1784. Petitioner prays bounty in Washington Co.

GLASS, JOSEPH. Certificate of E. Clarke, Col., December 20, 1784.

GRUBS, FRANCIS. Certificate of Elijah Clarke, Col., February 2, 1784. Petitioner prays bounty in Washington Co.

GEDEON, WILLIAM. Certificate of Elijah Clarke, Col., December 27, 1784. Petitioner prays 287½ acres in Washington Co.

GLOVEYER, STEPHEN. Certificate of Jas. McNeil, Col., March 15, 1784. 2d certificate of Jas. McNeil, Col., March 22, 1784. Petitioner prays 690 acres in Washington Co.

GILLILAND, WILLIAM. Certificate of Elijah Clarke, Col., February 2, 1784. 2d certificate of E. Clarke, Col., April 8, 1784. Petitioner prays 575 acres in Washington Co.

GRIMSLEY, JOSEPH. Certificate of E. Clarke, Col., December 10, 1784. Petitioner prays bounty in Washington Co.

GINKINS, ROBERT. Certificate of Elijah Clarke, Col., February 2, 1784.

GOLDEN, WILLIAM. Ex. order for bounty as per certificate of E. Clarke, Col., March 26, 1784.

GRAGZ, THOMAS. Certificate of E. Clarke, Col., April 7, 1784. Petitioner prays 575 acres in Franklin Co.

GREESON, JOHN. Certificate of Gb. Lee, Col., February 23, 1784.

GRIER, THOMAS. Certificate of Jas. McNeil, Col., March 15, 1784. Petitioner prays 287½ acres in Washington Co. 2nd certificate of Jas. McNeil, Col., February 2, 1784. Petitioner prays 575 acres in Washington Co.

GARNETT, ELI. Certificate of Jas. McNeil, Col., February 2, 1784. 2d certificate of Jas. McNeil, Col., March 22, 1784. Petitioner prays 575 acres in Washington Co.

GIBSON, JOHN. Certificate of Jas. McNeil, Col., February 2, 1784. Petitioner prays 287½ acres in Washington Co.

GORDEN, JESSE. Certificate of Elijah Clarke, Col., February 2, 1784. Petitioner prays 287½ acres in Washington Co.

GERMANY, JOHN, JR. Certificate as soldier endorsed by Gov. Houstoun, February, 1784. Petitioner prays 287½ acres in Washington Co.

## CERTIFICATES OF SERVICE IN AMERICAN REVOLUTION.

**GRAVES, RICHARD.** Certificate of Elijah Clarke, Col., April 16, 1784. Petitioner prays bounty in Washington Co.

**GLASS, JOHN.** Certificate of Elijah Clarke, Col., February 2, 1784. 2d. certificate of E. Clarke, Col., December 20, 1784. Petitioner prays 287½ acres in Washington Co.

**GODBE, CARY.** Certificate of John Twiggs, Brig. Gen., April 12, 1784. Petitioner prays 287½ acres in Washington Co.

**GILES, SAMUEL.** Certificate of Elijah Clarke, Col., February 2, 1784. Warrant 1166.

**GORHAM, JOHN.** Certificate of Benj. Few, Col., February 20, 1784. Warrant 1163.

**GRAVES, THOMAS.** Certificate of Elijah Clarke, Col., February 2, 1784.

**GRAVES, JOHN.** Certificate as refugee and soldier, John Baker, Col., November 5, 1784. Warrant 1154.

**GRAVES, ROBERT, JR.** Certificate of E. Clarke, Col., February 20, 1784. Petitioner prays 250 acres in Washington Co.

**GORHAM, JOHN.** Certificate of Elijah Clarke, Col., May 20, 1784. Petitioner prays 250 acres in Franklin Co.

**GOODALL, PLEASANT.** Certificate of John Twiggs, Brig. Gen., March 4, 1784. Petitioner prays bounty in Washington Co. Warrant 1155.

**GILES, ARTHUR.** Certificate of Samuel Jack, Col., May 17, 1784. Warrant 527.

**GILES, SAMUEL.** Certificate of Elijah Clarke, Col., February 2, 1784. Petitioner prays bounty in Franklin Co.

**GREEN, WILLIAM.** Certificate of Jas. McNeil, Col., May 22, 1784. Petitioner prays 287½ acres in Washington Co.

**GREEN, WILLIAM.** 2d certificate of Elijah Clarke, Col., April 8, 1784. Wm. Green on oath before 3 Justices of the Peace makes application for two warrants of 500 acres each in Washington Co. as Head Rights, he having 20 in family.

**GREEN, McKEEN.** Certificate of Jas. McKay, Col., January 29, 1784. Petitioner prays bounty in Washington Co. 2d certificate of Caleb Howell, Col., January 15, 1784. Petitioner prays warrant in Washington Co.

**GREEN, ISAAC.** Certificate of Gb. Lee, Col., February 20, 1784. 2d certificate of Elijah Clarke, Col., September 8, 1784. Petitioner prays 287½ acres in Washington Co.

**GREEN, THOMAS, JR.** Certificate of Samuel Jack, Col., March 13, 1784, that he enlisted in the Ga. Line from 96 Dist. S. C., and served as a soldier. Warrant 537.

**GRIZZEL, JOHN.** Certificate of Elijah Clarke, Col., October 10, 1784. Warrant 539.

**GAY, WILLIAM.** Certificate of Elijah Clarke, Col., December 10, 1784. Petitioner prays bounty in Washington Co.

**GRANT, PETER.** Certificate of John Twiggs, Brig. Gen., February 2, 1784. Petitioner prays bounty in Washington Co.

**GREY, JOHN.** Certificate of Elijah Clarke, Col., April 1, 1784. Petitioner prays bounty in Washington Co. Warrant 530.

**GREY, JAMES.** Certificate of E. Clarke, Col., April 1, 1784. Petitioner prays bounty in Washington Co. Warrant 531.

**GRAY, JACOB.** Certificate of Elijah Clarke, Col., February 2, 1784. Petitioner prays bounty in Franklin Co.

**GUNNELS, NICHOLAS.** Certificate of Elijah Clarke, Col., April 20, 1784. Petitioner prays bounty in Franklin Co. Warrant 529.

**GOLDEN, WILLIAM.** Certificate of Elijah Clarke, Col., February 2, 1784.

**GREER, LIEUT. ROBERT.** Certificate of Samuel Jack, Col., January 1, 1784. 2d certificate of Samuel Jack, Col., February 1, 1784.

**GREER, JOHN.** Certificate of Elijah Clarke, Col., February 2, 1784. 2d certificate of Elijah Clarke, Col., January 29, 1785. Petitioner prays warrant for 500 acres plus 15% in Washington Co.

**GRIFFIN, SAMUEL.** Certificate of Elijah Clarke, Lt. Col., November 16, 1784. Warrant 538.

**GRIFFIN, RANDAL.** Certificate as refugee and soldier, Elijah Clarke, Col., February 2, 1784. Warrant 1161.

**GRIFFIN, RANDOLPH.** Certificate of Elijah Clarke, Col., February 2, 1784. Petitioner prays warrant in Washington Co.

**GLASS, JOSHUA.** Certificate of Elijah Clarke, Col., February 2, 1784. Petitioner prays 287½ acres in Washington Co.

**GLASS, JOEL.** Certificate of E. Clarke, Col., February 2, 1784. Petitioner prays 287½ acres in Washington Co.

**GRINER, PHILIP.** Certificate as refugee soldier, John Twiggs, Brig. Gen., April 3, 1784. Warrant 1151.

**GENT, CHARLES.** Certificate of Elijah Clarke, Col., February 2, 1784. Petitioner prays warrant in Washington Co. Warrant 1172.

**GAINES, ABSOLEM.** Certificate of E. Clarke, Col., October 11, 1784. Warrant 525.

**GILLAND, THOMAS.** Certificate of E. Clarke, Col., February 2, 1784.

## CERTIFICATES OF SERVICE IN AMERICAN REVOLUTION. 91

**GORLEY, AYRES.** Certificate of Elijah Clarke, Col., April 14, 1784. Petitioner prays bounty in Washington Co.

**GOOLSBY, ISAIAH.** Certificate of Elijah Clarke, Col., April 20, 1784. Petitioner prays 287½ acres in Franklin Co.

**GARRETT, JOHN.** Certificate of Jas. McNeil, Col., April 5, 1784. Petitioner prays bounty in Washington Co. 2d certificate of John Twiggs, Brig. Gen., April 14, 1784. Petitioner prays bounty in Washington Co.

**GALPHIN, THOMAS.** Certificate of John Twiggs, Brig. Gen., March 29, 1784. Petitioner prays 287½ acres.

**GASTON, LIEUT. ALEXANDER.** Certificate that he enlisted in Ga. Line from S. C. and served as a soldier. Prays 400 acres bounty. Warrant 252.

**GLAMKIN, JOHN.** Certificate of Jas. Jackson, Col., May 18, 1784. Petitioner prays 287½ acres in Washington Co.

**GORE, THOMAS.** Certificate of Elijah Clarke, Lt. Col., August 4, 1784. Warrant 532.

**GRUBBS, BENJAMIN.** Certificate of Jas. McNeil, Col., February 2, 1784. Petitioner prays 287½ acres in Washington Co.

**GREEN, JAMES.** Certificate of Elijah Clarke, Col., April 8, 1784. 2d certificate of Elijah Clarke, Col., February 2, 1784. 3d certificate of Elijah Clarke, Col., on this petitioner prays 287½ acres in Washington Co.

**GREER, GILBERT.** Certificate of Jas. McNeil, Col., March 15, 1784. Petitioner prays 287½ acres in Washington Co.

**GLASCOCK, WILLIAM.** Certificate of Jas. McNeil, Col., February 22, 1784. Petitioner prays bounty in Franklin Co. Also prays Head Rights of 1000 acres in Washington on self and 16 negroes.

**GOLDING, JOHN.** Certificate of Elijah Clarke, Col., April 24, 1784. Petitioner prays 287½ acres in Washington Co.

**GREEN, JOHN.** Certificate of Col. Jas. McKay. 2d certificate of E. Clarke, Col., December 10, 1784. Petitioner prays 250 acres in Washington Co.

**GERMANY, SAMUEL.** Certificate of Jas. McNeil, Col., March 10, 1784. Petitioner prays bounty in Washington Co.

**GUNNELS, JOSEPH.** Certificate of Elijah Clarke, Col., February 2, 1784. Petitioner prays bounty in Franklin Co.

**GRAY, JAMES.** Certificate of Gb. Lee, Col., March 11, 1784. Petitioner prays 287½ acres in Washington Co. Also prays 1000 acres on head rights on self and 16 negroes. Expects to remove from North Carolina and reside in Franklin Co.

**GRAYBILL, HENRY.** Certificate of Elijah Clarke, Lt. Col., April 7, 1784. Petitioner prays 287½ acres in Washington Co.

**GARDNER, LEWIS.** Certificate of Gb. Lee, Col., February 25, 1784. Petitioner also prays head rights of 1000 acres in Washington Co., on self, wife, ten children and one negro slave.

**GREEN, JOHN.** Certificate of Jas. McKay, Col., February 21, 1784.

**GRAVES, ROBERT, SR.** Certificate of Elijah Clarke, Col., February 20, 1784. Petitioner prays 250 acres in Washington Co.

**GRAVES, ROBERT.** Certificate of Elijah Clarke, Col., April 6, 1784. Petitioner prays 287½ acres in Washington Co.

**GREEN, ANDREW M.** Certificate of Elijah Clarke, Col., January 25, 1785. Warrant 665.

**GORLEY, JAMES.** Certificate of Elijah Clarke, Col., August 20, 1784. Petitioner prays 287½ acres in Franklin Co. Warrant 629.

**GLASCOCK, LIEUT. THOMAS.** Certificate of service as lieut. in 1st Ga. Continental Regt., Lachlan McIntosh, Maj. Gen., February 3, 1784.

**GREEN, JOHN.** Certificate of John Twiggs, Brig. Gen., April 26, 1784. Petitioner prays bounty in Washington Co. Warrant 920.

**GREEN, CAPT. JOHN.** Certificate as refugee and soldier, James McKay, Col., April 6, 1784. Petitioner prays 287½ acres in Washington Co.

**GODBY, CARRY.** Certificate of John Twiggs, Brig. Gen., March 4, 1784. Petitioner prays 287½ acres in Washington Co. Warrant 1164.

**GENT, WILLIAM.** Two certificates as soldier, Elijah Clarke, Col., February 2, 1784. Petitioner prays bounty in Washington Co. Warrant 1173.

**GRIER, THOMAS.** Certificate of Jas. McNeil, Col., February 19, 1784. Warrant 1162.

**GREEN, BENJAMIN.** Certificate of John Twiggs, Brig. Gen., February 4, 1784. Warrant 1170.

**GILES, ROBERT.** Certificate of Elijah Clarke, Col., February 2, 1784. Petitioner prays bounty in Franklin Co.

**GOSSET, JACOB.** Certificate of Elijah Clarke, Col., February 2, 1784. Petitioner prays 287½ acres in Franklin Co.

**GRANT, ANDREW.** Certificate of John Twiggs, Brig. Gen., February 2, 1784. Petitioner prays bounty in Washington Co.

**GLOVER, HARDY.** Certificate of Jas. McNeil, Col., April 6, 1784. Petitioner Sarah, widow of Andrew Glover, prays 287½ acres in Washington Co.

**GREEN, WILLIAM.** Certificate as refugee to the State of N. C. and did faithful service as a soldier. John Twiggs, Brig. Gen., January 24, 1784. Petitioner prays 287½ acres in Washington Co. Warrant 1160.

CERTIFICATES OF SERVICE IN AMERICAN REVOLUTION. 93

### H.

**HARRIS, SAMUEL.** Certificate of E. Clarke, Col., May 3, 1784. Petitioner prays bounty in Washington Co. Warrant 1210.

**HARRIS, BUCKNER.** Certificate of Elijah Clarke, Col., February 2, 1784. Warrant 1212.

**HARRIS, JOHN.** Certificate as refugee and soldier, Elijah Clarke, Col., May 3, 1784. Petitioner prays bounty in Washington Co. Warrant 1209.

**HARRIS, TYREE GLEN.** Certificate of 3 years' service under Capt. Thomas Scott, Jas. McFarland, J. P. Prays 287½ acres. Warrant 145.

**HARRIS, DAVID.** Certificate of E. Clarke, Col., May 3, 1784. Petitioner prays bounty in Washington Co. 2d certificate of Elijah Clarke, Col., February 2, 1784. Warrant 1211.

**HARRIS, DAVID.** Certificate as refugee soldier, Jas. McNeil, Col., February 19, 1784. Ex. order for 500 acres to Captain David Harris as refugee soldier, February 20, 1784. 2d certificate as refugee and soldier, Caleb Howell, Col., April 25, 1784. (Certificate states that he was from Effingham Co.) Petitioner prays bounty in Washington Co.

**FRANKLIN, GEORGE.** Certificate of Gb. Lee, Col., April 7, 1784. Petitioner Washington Co. on Head Rights for self and family.

**GALASPY, JOHN.** Certificate of Elijah Clarke, Col., April 8, 1784. Petitioner Gen., March 4, 1784. Petitioner prays 287½ acres in Washington Co.

**HUBBARD, JOHN.** Ex. order for bounty upon certificates of Col. E. Clarke (missing), Mar. 25, 1784. Petitioner prays 287½ acres in Washington Co. Warrant 1241.

**HUDSON, JAMES.** Certificate as refugee and soldier, Jenkins Davis, Lt. Col., Dec. 29, 1783. Warrant 1228.

**HOUSTOUN, DR. JAMES.** Certificate as surgeon, 1st Georgia Cont. Regt.. Lachlan McIntosh, Maj. Gen., Feb. 2d, 1784. Warrant 34.

**HODGE, ROGER.** Certificate as refugee and soldier, Jenkins Davis, Lt. Col., March, 1785. Warrant 1213.

**HODGE, ROBERT.** Certificate as refugee and soldier, Col. Howell and Davis (missing), and Ex. Order, Feb. 28, 1784. Petitioner prays 287½ acres in Washington Co. Warrant 1216.

**HEARD, STEPHEN.** Certificate as refugee and soldier, Richard Hawley, Col. Warrant 1220.

**HODGE, JOHN.** Certificate as refugee and soldier, Jenkins Davis, Lt. Col., Effingham Co. Feb. 5, 1784. Warrant 1215.

**HEARD, CAPT. RICHARD.** Certificate of Elijah Clarke, Col., Mar. 3, 1784. Petitioner prays 862½ acres in 2 warrants in Washington Co. Also prays head rights of 300 acres in Washington Co. for self, wife and one child. Granted Mar. 5, 1784.

**HARVEY, BLASINGAME.** Certificate as refugee and soldier, John Twiggs, Brig. Gen., April 8, 1784. Warrant 1197.

**HALE, GEORGE.** Certificate of Lt. Col. James Jackson of Ga. Legion, Mar. 25, 1784. Petitioner prays bounty in Washington Co.

**HAMPTON, JOHN.** Certificate of Elijah Clarke, Col., Feb. 2, 1784.

**HOWSLEY, WILLIAM.** Certificate as citizen soldier, E. Clarke, Col., April 21, 1784. Petitioner prays bounty in Washington Co.

**HUBBARD, JACOB.** Certificate as refugee soldier, Elijah Clarke, Col., April 14, 1784. Petitioner prays bounty in Franklin Co. Warrant 1187.

**HODGE, ROBERT.** Certificate as refugee soldier, Jenkins Davis, Lt. Col., Feb. 25, 1784.

**HEATLY, HENRY.** Certificate of Jas. Jackson, Lt. Col., Ga. State Legion, April, 1734. Petitioner prays bounty in Washington Co.

**HATCHER, WILLIAM.** Certificate as refugee soldier, Wm. Candler, Col. Regt. Refugees. Petitioner prays bounty in Franklin Co. Warrant 1227.

**HUGES, LIEUT. NATHANIEL.** Ex. order for bounty to heirs of Lt. Nathaniel Huges, as per certificate of his service in Georgia Artillery, signed by Gen. Lachlan McIntosh. 1784. Petition of Elizabeth Watson, his heir, for 460 acres in reserve.

**HICKS, CAPT. ISAAC.** Certificate of his service as Capt. in 3d Ga. Continental Regt. from 1776 to end of the war, John McIntosh, Lt. Col., ed. Ga. Regt. Petitioner prays 930 acres (grade of Major) in reserve. Warrant 59

**HANDSHAW, THOMAS.** Certificate that he served his time in the 1st Ga. Regt. and lost his sight therein. Geo. Handley, Capt. 1st Ga. Regt., Sept. 24, 1785. Warrant 144.

**HOWARD, WILLIAM.** Certificate of Jas. Jackson, Lt. Col., Ga. Legion, April 6, 1784.

**HOLT, BEVERLY.** Certificate of Francis Tennill, Capt. 2d Ga. State Line. Jan. 9, 1786.

**HAMMOND, CHARLES.** Certificate as refugee and soldier in my command, Wm. Candler, Col. Ref. Regt. Petitioner prays 287½ acres in Washington Co. Warrant 1178.

**HOWELL, CALEB.** Certificate as refugee and soldier, Jenkins Davis, Lt. Col., Feb. 9, 1784. Warrant 1185.

**HANSON, SAMUEL.** Certificate of Jas. Jackson, Lt. Col. Ga. Legion, April 6, 1784. Petitioner prays 500 acres in Washington Co.

## CERTIFICATES OF SERVICE IN AMERICAN REVOLUTION.

**HANNAH, THOMAS.** Certificate as refugee and soldier, Elijah Clarke, Col., Aug. 10, 1784. Warrant 1196.

**HARDY, JOHN.** Certificate of John Baker, Col., April 3, 1784. Warrant 1183.

**HODGE, WILLOUGHBY.** Certificate as refugee soldier, Jenkins Davis, Lt. Col., Jan. 15, 1784. Warrant 1214.

**HADDEN, WILLIAM.** Certificate as refugee soldier, John Twiggs, Brig. Gen., Nov. 23, 1783. Warrant 1184.

**HAMEL, CAPT. DANIEL.** Certificate as refugee soldier, Jenkins Davis, Lt. Col., Jan. 30, 1784. Warrant 895.

**HUDSON, NATHANIEL.** Ex. order for bounty on certificate of Col. J. Davis and Col. Howell, Jan. 3, 1784. Warrant 1232.

**HUDSON, SAMUEL.** Certificate as refugee soldier, Jenkins Davis, Lt. Col., Emanuel Co., March, 1784.

**HICKS, JOHN.** Certificate as refugee soldier, James McKay, Col., Feb. 18, 1784. Petitioner prays bounty in Washington Co. Warrant 1242.

**HILLARY, LIEUT. CHRISTOPHER.** House of Assembly, Feb. 21, 1785. Resolved: that Christopher Hillary be allowed a warrant agreeable to his rank as lieutenant and that the Governor be empowered to grant a warrant for land agreeable to his rank in the Continental Army. Extract from minutes of Assembly, John Wilkinson, Sec. Gen. Assem.

**HART, JOHN.** Certificate of Elijah Clarke, Col., Feb. 2, 1784. Warrant 1238.

**HALWELL, LUTHER.** Certificate of John Twiggs, Brig. Gen., Feb. 16, 1784. Warrant 1174.

**HOLTZENDORF, WILLIAM.** Certificate as refugee soldier, Jenkins Davis, Lt. Col., Mar. 2, 1784. Petitioner prays 287½ acres in Washington Co. Warrant 1235.

**HAWKINS, THOMAS.** Certificate as refugee soldier, Elijah Clarke, Col., Jan. 25, 1785. Warrant 1181.

**HILL, WILLIAM.** Certificate as refugee soldier, Col. E. Clarke (missing), and Ex. Order thereon. Warrant 1203.

**HOLLIMAN, ABSOLEM.** Certificate a refugee soldier, Elijah Clarke, Col., April 20, 1784. Warrant 1191.

**HATCHER, JOHN.** Certificate as refugee soldier, Wm. Candler, Col., Refugee Regt. Warrant 1225.

**HEARD, CAPT. RICHARD.** Ex. order for 500 acres upon certificate of Col. Clarke (see above). Warrant 896.

**HAWKINS, JAMES.** Certificate as soldier in Ga. State Legion, Jas. Jackson, Lt. Col., Ga. Legion, July 27, 1784. Nicholas Hawkins, lawful heir, prays 287½ acres in Washington Co.

**HAWKINS, NICHOLAS.** Certificate of Jas. Jackson, Lt. Col., Ga. State Legion, July 27, 1784. Petitioner prays 287½ acres in Washington Co.

**HORNSBY, PHILIP.** Certificate of Elijah Clarke, Col., Feb. 2, 1784. Warrant 1233.

**HENSON, SAMUEL.** Certificate of Jas. McNeil, Col., April 7, 1784. Warrant 1189.

**HOGGATT, JOHN.** Certificate of service as sergeant in 3d Ga. Batn., Gideon Booker, Capt., Mar. 7, 1785. Warrant 147.

**HEYMAN, STEPHEN.** Certificate of John Twiggs, Brig. Gen., Mar. 4, 1784. Warrant 1186.

**HATCHET, CAPT. ARCHIBOLD.** Certificate as captain and sailor, Oliver Bowen, Commodore, Feb. 6, 1784. Warrant 3.

**HARDY, CAPT. JOHN.** Certificate as captain and sailor on Continental Galleys, Oliver Bowen, Commodore, Feb. 6, 1784. Warrant 4.

**HATCHER, JOSIAH.** Certificate of John Twiggs, Brig. Gen., Jan. 25, 1784. Warrant 1223.

**HAMILTON, THOMAS.** Certificate as refugee and soldier, Jenkins Davis, Lt. Col., Feb. 20, 1784. Prays 500 acres in Washington Co. Warrant 1237.

**HUNT, WILLIAM.** Certificate of Wm. Candler, Col., Ref. Regt., Feb. 27, 1784. Petitioner prays 575 acres in Washington Co. Warrant 1236.

**HATCHER, HENRY.** Certificate of Wm. Candler, Col., Ref. Regt. Petitioner prays 287½ acres. Warrant 1222.

**HILL, JOSHUA.** Certificate of Elijah Clarke, Col., April 8, 1784. Petitioner prays 287½ acres in Washington Co. Warrant 1205.

**HATCHER, ROBERT.** Certificate of Wm. Candler, Col., Ref. Regt. Warrant 1221.

**HERD, GEORGE.** Certificate of Elijah Clarke, Col., Mar. 2, 1784. Petitioner prays 287½ acres in Washington Co. Warrant 1219.

**HARVEY, JOEL.** Certificate of Elijah Clarke, Col., April 7, 1784. Warrant 1201.

**HARVEY, JAMES HILL.** Certificate of John Twiggs, Brig. Gen., April 8, 1784. Warrant 1200.

**HILL, JAMES.** Certificate of Elijah Clarke, Col., Feb. 2, 1784. Petitioner prays 287½ acres in Washington Co. Warrant 1204.

**HARVILL, JOSEPH.** Certificate as refugee and soldier, Wm. Candler, Col., Ref. Regt. Petitioner prays bounty in Washington Co. Warrant 1190.

## CERTIFICATES OF SERVICE IN AMERICAN REVOLUTION. 97

**HOLT, REUBEN.** Certificate of Capt. F. Tennill, countersigned by Lt. Col. Pannill, Jan. 9, 1786.

**HUNT, FITZMAURICE.** Certificate of Wm. Candler, Col., Mar. 22, 1784. Warrant 1195.

**HATCHER, JOSEPH.** Certificate of John Twiggs, Brig. Gen., Feb. 6, 1784. Warrant 1226.

**HARPER, LIEUT. ROBERT.** Certificate of Elijah Clarke, Col., Feb. 2, 1784. Warrant 933.

**HARPER, ROBERT.** Ex. order for bounty as per certificate of Col. E. Clarke (missing), Mar. 25, 1784. Petitioner prays 287½ acres in Washington Co. Warrant 1193.

**HUDSON, ROBERT.** Certificate as refugee soldier, Jenkins Davis, Lt. Col., Jan. 14, 1784. Petitioner prays 287½ acres in Washington Co. Warrant 1231.

**HUTSON, JOSEPH.** Certificate as soldier in 1st Regt. Ga. Troops, John Hereat, Auditor State of Ga., Nov. 30, 1783. Ordered bounty of 640 acres.

**HOUSE, JOHN.** Certificate as soldier in Ross' Co., 3d Ga. Regt., Nathan'l Pearre, Lt. Comdg. Company, Sep. 7, 1784. Warrant 146.

**HUBBARD, JOHN.** Certificate of Elijah Clarke, Col., Feb. 2, 1784.

**CARR, HENERY.** Certificate of Elijah Clarke, Col., April 3, 1784.

**HARPER, CAPT. SAMUEL.** Certificate as Captain, Elijah Clarke, Col., Feb. 2, 1784. Warrant 897.

**HUNTSMAN, WILLIAM.** Certificate as soldier, endorsed by Gov. Houstoun, Mar. 25, 1784. Warrant 1239.

**HILL, WILLIAM.** Certificate of Elijah Clarke, Col., Feb. 2, 1784. 2d. certificate as refugee and soldier, John Twiggs, Brig. Gen., Mar. 8, 1784. Petitioner prays 250 acres in Washington Co.

**HOLLIDAY, AMBROSE.** Certificate as refugee soldier, Wm. Candler, Col., Refugee Regt. Petitioner prays 287½ acres in Washington Co. Warrant 1208.

**HAMPTON, JOHN.** Certificate as refugee soldier, E. Clarke, Col., Mar. 25, 1784. Warrant 1234.

**HAWTHORN, STEPHEN.** Certificate of John Baker, Col., Oct. 15, 1784. Warrant 1182.

**HUGHES, NATHANIEL.** Was 1st Lieut. in 1st Company Artillery and died in the service, Lieut. Matthew Roche, Mar. 22, 1784, endorsed by Maj. Gen. Lachlan McIntosh. Warrant 80.

**HAYMAN, HENRY.** Certificate of John Twiggs, Brig. Gen., Mar. 4, 1784. Petitioner prays 287½ acres in Washington Co. Warrant 1175.

**HUDSON, SAMUEL.** Certificate as refugee soldier, Jenkins Davis, Col., Mar. 19, 1784. Warrant 1229.

**HALLIDAY, WILLIAM.** Certificate of E. Clarke, Col., April 6, 1784. Warrant 1206.

**HUDSON, JOSEPH.** Certificate of Elijah Clarke, Col., Feb. 2, 1784. Warrant 1230.

**HAYMEN, STOUTON.** Certificate as refugee soldier, John Twiggs, Brig. Gen., Mar. 2, 1784. Warrant 1176.

**HAMMOND, GEORGE.** Certificate as refugee soldier, Wm. Candler, Col., Refugee Regt. Petitioner prays bounty in Washington Co. Warrant 1179.

**HAWKINS, JAMES.** Certificate as refugee soldier, E. Clarke, Col., April 7, 1784. Petitioner, Nicholas Hawkins, his heir, prays 287½ acres in Washington Co. Warrant 1180.

**HAMMOCK, ROBERT.** Certificate of Benj. Few, Col. Commanding, Feb. 2, 1784. Petitioner prays bounty in Washington Co. Warrant 1240.

**HARVEY, JOHN.** Certificate of Jas. McNeil, Col., May 10, 1784. Petitioner prays bounty in Franklin Co. Warrant 1202.

**HERNBY, DENNIS.** Certificate as refugee soldier, Elijah Clarke, Col., Petitioner prays bounty in Franklin Co. Warrant 1192.

**HATCHER, JEREMIAH.** Certificate as refugee soldier, Wm. Candler, Col., Regt. Refugees. Warrant 1224.

**HAGAN, EDWARD.** Certificate as refugee soldier, Elijah Clarke, Col., April 7, 1784. Petitioner prays 287½ acres in Washington Co. Warrant 1188.

**HERD, JOSEPH._** Certificate of Elijah Clarke, Col., Feb. 2, 1784. Warrant 1218.

**HEARD, BERNARD.** Certificate of Elijah Clarke, Col., Feb. 25, 1784. Petitioner prays 575 acres in Washington Co. Warrant 1217.

**HARVEY, LITTLEBERRY.** Certificate of M. Williamson, Lt. Col., Ga. Refugee Regt., July 27, 1784. Petitioner prays 287½ acres in Franklin Co. Warrant 1199.

**HOLLIDAY, THOMAS.** Certificate of Elijah Clarke, Col., April 7, 1784. Warrant 1207.

**HAMMOND, ABNER.** Certificate as refugee soldier, Wm. Candler, Col., Refugee Regt. Petitioner prays bounty in Washington Co. Warrant 1177.

## CERTIFICATES OF SERVICE IN AMERICAN REVOLUTION.

### I.

**IRWIN, JOHN.** Certificate of John Twiggs, Brig. Gen., Mar. 27, 1784. Petitioner prays 287½ acres in Washington Co. and constitutes his brother, Hugh, of Burke Co., his Atty. to receive same.

**IRWIN, JOHN LAWSON.** Served in my company and Col. Asa Emanuel's Reg't., Alexander Irwin, Capt., Nov. 26, 1783.

**IRWIN, WILLIAM** (of Burke Co.). Certificate of John Twiggs, Brig. Gen., Feb. 17, 1784. Petitioner prays 287½ acres in Washington Co. and gives two powers of attorney to Jared and Hugh Irwin, both of Burke Co.

**IGLE, JOHN.** Certificate of Caleb Howell, Col., Feb. 20, 1784, 2d certificate as refugee soldier, Jenkins Davis, Lt. Col., Feb. 20, 1784. Warrant 1249.

**INMAN, CAPT. JOSHUA.** Two certificates as refugee soldier, John Twiggs, Brig. Gen., Feb. 2, 1784. Petitioner prays 750 acres in Washington Co.

**INMAN, CAPT. SHADROCK.** Certificate that he was killed in battle. His wife, of South Carolina, prays 575 acres in Washington Co.

**INLOW, SEVASTIN.** Certificate of Elijah Clarke, Col., May 20, 1784. Petitioner prays 287½ acres in Franklin Co.

**INGRAM, RICHARD.** Certificate of John Twiggs, Brig. Gen., April 9, 1784. Petitioner prays bounty in Washington Co.

**ISLAND, JOHN.** Two certificates of E. Clarke, Col., Feb. 2, 1784. Petitioner prays 287½ acres in Washington Co.

**ISLAND, ABSOLEM.** Certificate of Elijah Clarke, Col., Feb. 2, 1784.

**IRWIN, ALEXANDER.** Certificate of John Twiggs, Brig. Gen., Feb. 2, 1784. Powers of attorney to brothers, Jared and Hugh Irwin, of Burke Co. Warrant 1252.

**IRWIN, HUGH.** Certificate of John Twiggs, Brig. Gen., Feb. 2, 1784. Petitioner prays 287½ acres in Washington Co.

**IRWIN, JARED.** Certificate of John Twiggs, Brig. Gen., Feb. 2, 1784. Petitioner prays 287½ acres in Washington Co. Also proves his rights for self, wife and 3 children, and prays head rights for same.

### J.

**JARVIS, NICHOLAS.** Certificate as refugee soldier, Francis Boykin, Major, April 6, 1784. Warrant 1245.

**JORDAN, SAMUEL.** Certificate of Elijah Clarke, Col., Feb. 2, 1784.

**JORDAN, JACOB.** Two petitions for bounties of 250 acres each as per certificates annexed (missing).

**JACK, SAMUEL.** Certificate as refugee soldier, John Twiggs, Brig. Gen., Jan. 31, 1784. Also petitioner prays 1,000 acres on Oconee river in head rights for self and family. Warrant 1250.

**JEFFERS, JAMES.** Certificate of John Baker, Col., April 13, 1784. 2d certificate of John Baker, Col., April 30, 1784. Warrant 1246.

**JARRETT, ROBERT.** Certificate as refugee soldier, John Twiggs, Brig. Gen., April 26, 1784. Petitioner prays bounty in Franklin Co. Warrant 1244.

**JOHNSON, CAPT. RICHARD.** Certificate as captain in Refugee Regt., S. Hammond, Col., Jan. 18, 1784. Warrant 917.

**JACK, SAMUEL.** Petition for bounty of 287½ acres in Washington Co. as per certificate as refugee and soldier. 2d petition for bounty as colonel, 920 acres in Washington Co.

**JENKINS, BENJAMIN.** Certificate of Jas. McNeil, Col., Feb. 2, 1784.

**JORDEN, JACOB.** Certificate of Elijah Clarke, Col., Feb. 2, 1784.

**JOINER, THOMAS.** Certificate of Elijah Clarke, Col., April 24, 1784. Petition of Sarah Joiner for bounty, stating that "Joiner was killed, and has no heirs," seems to have been a sister.

**JONES, ABRAHAM.** Certificate of Jas. McNeil, Col., April 6, 1784. Petitioner, Seaborn Jones, for Abraham Jones, prays 575 acres in Washington Co.

**JACKSON, THOMAS.** Certificate of Gb. Lee, Col., Mar. 30, 1784. Petitioner prays 287½ acres in Washington Co.

**JACKSON, JOHN.** Certificate of E. Clarke, Col., Jan. 2, 1785.

**JONES, THOMAS.** Certificate of Elijah Clarke, Col., Feb. 2, 1784.

**JUSTIS, ISAAC.** Certificate of Gb. Lee, Col., Mar. 11, 1784. Petitioner prays 287½ acres in Washington Co.

**JORDAN, BAXTON.** Certificate of John Twiggs, Brig. Gen., Feb. 26, 1784. Petitioner prays bounty in Washington Co.

**JONES, ELIAS.** Certificate of Gb. Lee, Col., Mar. 20, 1784. Endorsed by Ignatius Few, Col. Petitioner prays bounty in Washington Co.

**JOURDINE, LEWIS.** Certificate of Jas. McNeil, Col., Mar. 15, 1784. Petitioner prays 287½ acres in Washington Co.

**JENKINS, BENJAMIN.** Certificate of Jas. McNeil, Col., April 17, 1784. Petitioner prays 575 acres in Washington Co.

**JACKSON, JAMES, LIEUT. COLONEL.** Certificate as refugee soldier, Wm. Candler, Feb. 17, 1784. (Col. Refugee Regt.) Certificate of Elijah Clarke, Col., Feb. 7, 1784.

CERTIFICATES OF SERVICE IN AMERICAN REVOLUTION. 101

**JENKINS, STERLING.** Certificate of E. Clarke, Col., Mar. 25, 1784. Petitioner prays bounty in Washington Co. Also prays 700 acres head rights in Washington Co. on self, wife, 4 children and 3 negroes.

**JACKSON, PETER.** Certificate of Elijah Clarke, Col., April 7, 1784. Petitioner prays 287½ acres in Washington Co.

**JOURDAN, CHARLES.** Certificate of Elijah Clarke, Col., Feb. 2, 1784.

**JONES, MARK, SR.** Certificate of Gb. Lee, Col., April 24, 1784. Petitioner prays bounty near head of Shoulder Bone Ck., Washington Co.

**JONES, JONATHAN.** Ex. order for bounty as per certificate of Col. Greenberry Lee, Feb 20, 1784. Petitioner prays 287½ acres in Washington Co.

**JACKSON, BENJAMIN.** Certificate of Jas. Jackson, Lt. Col., Mar. 30, 1784. Petitioner prays 287½ acres in Franklin Co.

**JACKSON, RANDOLPH.** Certificate of Elijah Clarke, Col., April 7, 1784. Petitioner prays 287½ acres in Washington Co.

**JOHNSON, RICHARD.** Certificate of Elijah Clarke, Col., Feb. 2, 1784.

**JORDAN, JACOB.** Certificate of Elijah Clarke, Col., Feb. 2, 1784. Warrant 1253.

**JONES, JOHN.** Certificate of Gb. Lee, Col., Feb. 23, 1784. Petitioner prays 287½ acres in Washington Co.

**JACKSON, DAVID.** Certificate of Gb. Lee, Col., April 9, 1784. Petitioner prays bounty in Washington Co.

**JACKSON, DANIEL.** Certificate of Elijah Clarke, Col., Feb. 2, 1784. Warrant 1256. 2d certificate as refugee soldier, Elijah Clarke, Col., Jan. 25, 1785. Petitioner prays 287½ acres in Washington Co.

**JERVIS, PATRICK.** Certificate of Jas. McNeil, Col., Mar. 24, 1784. Petitioner prays 290 acres in Washington Co. Also makes oath to number in family, self, wife, 4 children and 4 negroes, and prays on head rights, 650 acres in Washington Co.

**JONES, WILLIAM.** Certificate as soldier in Ga. State Legion, Jas. Jackson, Col., Ga. State Legion, July 30, 1784. Petitioner prays 287½ acres in Washington Co. 2d certificate of John Twiggs, Brig. Gen., April 3, 1784. Petitioner prays 250 acres in Washington Co.

**JONES, THOMAS** (son of William). Certificate as refugee soldier, John Twiggs, Brig. Gen., April 6, 1784. Petitioner prays 500 acres bounty.

**JONES, THOMAS.** Certificate as refugee soldier, Greenberry Lee, Col., Feb. 23, 1784. Petitioner prays 287½ acres in Washington Co. 2d certificate of Gb. Lee, Col., April 6, 1784. Petitioner prays 287½ acres in Franklin Co.

102 ROSTER OF THE REVOLUTION.

**JONES, SIMEON.** Certificate of Jas. Jackson, Lt. Col., Sep. 18, 1784. Petitioner prays bounty in Washington Co.

**JONES, SEABORN.** Certificate as refugee soldier, John Twiggs, Brig. Gen., April 7, 1784. Petitioner prays 575 acres in Washington Co.

**JONES, PHILIP.** Certificate of Elijah Clarke, Col., Feb. 2, 1784. Petitioner prays 287½ acres in Washington Co.

**JONES, PETER.** Petition for bounty upon annexed certificate (missing). Upon evidence the Board orders survey in Washington Co., May 25, 1784.

**JONES, ROBERT.** Certificate of John Twiggs, Brig. Gen., April 3, 1784. Petitioner prays 287½ acres in Washington Co. 2d certificate of Jas. Jackson, Lt. Col., Ga. State Legion, July 17, 1784. Petitioner prays 287½ acres in Washington Co.

**JONES, MATTHEW.** Certificate of Elijah Clarke, Col., Feb. 2, 1784. Petitioner prays 287½ acres in Washington Co. Warrant 1258.

**JONES, NATHAN.** Certificate of Gb. Lee, Col., Feb. 23, 1784. Petitioner prays 287½ acres in Washington Co.

**JONES, CAPT. MICHAEL.** Certificate as refugee soldier, John Twiggs, Brig. Gen., Jan. 24, 1784. Warrant 1257. 2d certificate as soldier and citizen, John Twiggs, Brig. Gen., Jan. 24, 1784. Petitioner prays 575 acres in Washington Co.

**JONES, JESSE.** Certificate of Benj. Few, Col., Feb. 20, 1784. Petitioner prays bounty in Washington Co.

**JONES, JESSE.** Certificate of Gb. Lee, Col., Mar. 20, 1784. Petitioner prays 287½ acres in Washington Co.

**JONES, JESSE.** Certificate of Jas. Jackson, Lt. Col., Ga. St. Legion, May 3, 1784. Petitioner prays bounty in Franklin Co.

**JONES, JAMES.** Certificate of Gb. Lee, Col., Mar. 30, 1784. Petitioner prays bounty in Washington Co. 2d certificate of Samuel Jack, Col., April 13, 1784. Petitioner prays 287½ acres in Washington Co.

**JONES, JAMES.** Certificate of Elijah Clarke, Col., Feb. 2, 1784. Petitioner prays 287½ acres in Washington Co.

**JONES, JAMES.** Certificate as refugee and soldier, John Twiggs, Brig. Gen., April 15, 1784. 2d certificate as citizen and soldier, John Twiggs, Brig. Gen., April 15, 1784. Petitioner prays 575 acres in Washington Co.

**JONES, ABRAHAM.** Certificate as refugee soldier, John Twiggs, Brig. Gen., April 7, 1784. Attached is the following: Georgia, Jefferson Co.—Appeared before me Abraham P. Jones, who, being duly sworn, deposed, that he served as lieutenant in 2d Ga. Regt. under Col. Elbert. Before me, Nov. 8, 1806. Wm. Wright, J. P.

## CERTIFICATES OF SERVICE IN AMERICAN REVOLUTION. 103

**JONES, BENJAMIN, JR.** Certificate of Gb. Lee, Col., Mar. 11, 1784. Petitioner prays bounty in Franklin Co.

**JONES, BENJAMIN, SR.** Certificate of Gb. Lee, Col., Mar. 11, 1784. Petitioner prays bounty in Franklin Co.

**JONES, DAVID.** Certificate of Elijah Clarke, Col., Dec. 27, 1784. Petitioner prays 287½ acres in Washington Co.

**JONES, DAVID.** Certificate as citizen and soldier, Elijah Clarke, Col., Mar. 29, 1784. Petitioner prays 250 acres in Washington Co.

**JONES, EDWARD.** Certificate of service in 1st Battalion State Troops as refugee and served as Judge Advocate, Jas. McNeil, Col., Feb. 15, 1784. Petitioner prays 2 warrants adjoining in Washington Co.

**JONES, FREDERICK.** Certificate as refugee and soldier, John Twiggs, B. G., April 5, 1784. Petitioner prays 287½ acres in Washington Co.

**JONES, CAPT. JONATHAN.** Certificate of Gb. Lee, Col., Feb. 23, 1784.

**JONES, HUGH.** Two certificates of Elijah Clarke, Col., Feb. 2, 1784.

**JONES, JOHN.** Certificate of Elijah Clarke, Col., April 20, 1784. Petitioner prays 287½ acres in Washington Co.

**JONES, LIEUT. COL. JOHN.** Certificate as refugee and soldier, John Twiggs, B. G., April 6, 1784. Petitioner prays 575 acres in Washington Co. Warrant 1262.

**JACKSON, WILLIAM.** Certificate of Elijah Clarke, Col., Feb. 25, 1784. Petitioner prays 287½ acres in Washington Co. 2d certificate of Elijah Clarke, Col., April 9, 1784. Petitioner prays 287½ acres in Franklin Co.

**JACKSON, ABSOLEM.** Certificate as refugee and soldier, James Jackson, Col., Mar. 30, 1784. Petitioner prays 287½ acres in Washington Co.

**JACKSON, DANIEL.** Certificate of Elijah Clarke, Col., Feb. 2, 1784. 2d certificate of Elijah Clarke, Col., Jan. 25, 1785.

**JACKSON, DRURY.** Certificate of Elijah Clarke, Col., Dec. 24, 1784.

**JACKSON, HENRY.** Certificate of Gb. Lee, Col., April 9, 1784. Petitioner prays bounty in Washington Co.

**JACKSON, MAJOR ISAAC.** Certificate of Benj. Few., Col., Feb. 20, 1784. Petitioner prays 650 acres in Washington Co. Warrant 871.

**JACKSON, COL. ISAAC.** Certificate of Gb. Lee, Col., April 9, 1784. Petitioner prays bounty in Washington Co.

**JACKSON, JOB.** Certificate of Gb. Lee, Col., Mar. 30, 1784. Petitioner prays 287½ acres in Washington Co.

**JACKSON, LIEUT. COL. JAMES.** Certificate as refugee and soldier, E. Clarke, Col. (missing). Ex. order for 1,050 acres, Mar. 19, 1784. Petitioner prays 1,207 acres in Washington Co. Warrant 859.

**JACKSON, REUBEN.** Certificate of Elijah Clarke, Col., Jan. 25, 1785. 2d certificate of Elijah Clarke, Col., April 20, 1784. Petitioner prays 287½ acres in Washington Co.

**JOHNSON, HENRY.** Certificate of Elijah Clarke, Col., April 20, 1784. Petitioner prays 250 acres in Franklin Co.

**JOHNSON, JOHN HUTCHINS.** Certificate of Elijah Clarke, Col., April 8, 1784. Petitioner prays 550 acres in Franklin Co.

**JOHNSTON, JACOB.** Ex. order for bounty as per certificate of Col. E. Clarke (missing), Mar. 25, 1784. Petitioner prays bounty in Washington Co.

**JOHNSON, JOHN HUTCHENS.** 2d certificate of Elijah Clarke, Col., Feb. 2, 1784. Warrant 1254.

**JOHNSON, JOHN.** Certificate of Elijah Clarke, Col., May 20, 1784. Petitioner prays 250 acres in Franklin Co.

**JOHNSON, JOHN.** Two certificates of Elijah Clarke, Col., Feb. 2, 1784.

**JOHNSON, CAPT. JOHN.** Certificate of Jas. McNeil, Col., Mar. 17, 1784. Petitioner prays bounty in Washington Co.

**JOHNSON, JAMES.** Certificate of Elijah Clarke, Col., Feb. 2, 1784. Petitioner prays bounty in Washington Co.

**JACKSON, JOSEPH.** Certificate of James Jackson, Col., April 7, 1784.

**JOHNSTON, RICHARD.** Certificate as refugee soldier, John Twiggs, B. G., Jan. 3, 1784.

**JOHNSON, CAPT. STEPHEN.** Certificate of Elijah Clarke, Col., Mar. 18, 1784. Warrant 898.

**JOHNSON, THOMAS.** Certificate of Jas. McNeil, Col., Mar. 15, 1784. Petitioner prays 287½ acres in Washington Co.

**JOHNSTONE, LIEUT. WILLIAM.** Ex. order for bounty as soldier in Ga. State Line as per certificate of Major Jas. Habersham (missing), Mar. 19, 1784. David Reese, for widow and heirs, prays bounty.

**JOINER, BENJAMIN.** Certificate of Elijah Clarke, Feb. 2, 1784. 2d certificate of Elijah Clarke, Col., Feb. 2, 1784. Petitioner prays 575 acres in Washington Co. Warrant 1251.

**JOINER, THOMAS.** Certificate of Elijah Clarke, Col., Feb. 2, 1784.

**JENKINS, ARTHUR.** Certificate of Jas. McNeil, Col., April 7, 1784. Petitioner prays 287½ acres in Washington Co.

## CERTIFICATES OF SERVICE IN AMERICAN REVOLUTION.

**JENKINS, RICHARD.** Certificate of Jas. Jackson, Lt. Col., Ga. St. Legion, April 6, 1784. Petitioner prays 287½ acres in Washington Co. 2d certificate of Gb. Lee, Col., Mar. 11, 1784. Petitioner prays 287½ acres in Washington Co.

**JENKINS, ROBERT.** Ex. order for bounty upon certificate of Col. E. Clarke (missing), Mar. 25, 1784. Petitioner prays 250 acres in Washington Co.

**JENKINS, STERLING.** Certificate of Elijah Clarke, Col., Feb. 2, 1784. Petitioner prays 400 acres in Franklin Co. as head rights for self and family.

**JENKINS, FRANCIS, JR.** Certificates as refugee and soldier, John Twiggs, B. G., April 6, 1784. Petitioner prays bounty in Washington Co. Warrant 1243.

**JUSTICE, DEMPSEY.** Certificate of Gb. Lee, Col., Mar. 11, 1784. Petitioner prays 287½ acres in Washington Co.

**JARRETT, ROBERT.** Certificate of Elijah Clarke, Col., May 22, 1784. Petitioner prays 287½ acres in Washington Co.

**JETER, JOSEPH.** Certificate of Jas. Jackson, Lt. Col., Sep. 18, 1784. Petitioner prays 287½ acres in Franklin Co.

**JORDAN, STARLING.** Certificate of John Twiggs, Bg. Gen., Feb. 19, 1784. Petitioner prays 287½ acres in Washington Co.

**JOHNSON, LIEUT. THOMAS.** Certificate of Elijffiah Clarke, Col., Feb. 2, 1784. Petitioner prays 287½ acres in Washington Co.

**JOHNSON, THOMAS.** Certificate of Jas. McNeil, Col., Mar. 22, 1784. Petitioner prays 287½ acres in Washington Co. Warrant 1247.

**JORDON, DEMPSEY.** Certificate of Elijah Clarke, Col., Feb. 2, 1784. Petitioner prays 287½ acres in Washington Co.

**JONES, SEABORN.** Certificate as refugee soldier, John Twiggs, Brig. Gen., April 25, 1784. Warrant 1260.

**JOHNSON, LT. COL. STEPHEN.** Certificate of Elijah Clarke, Col., Mar. 18, 1784. Petitioner prays 862½ acres in Washington Co.

**JOHNSON, SERGEANT JAMES.** Petition for bounty as sergeant in Minute Men as per certificates of Capt. Sam'l Thompson and Col. Samuel Jack (missing), prays 300 acres, Jan. 15, 1784.

**JOSLING, DANIEL.** Certificate as refugee and soldier, from Richmond Co., Wm. Candler, Col. Refugee Regt. Petitioner prays bounty in Washington Co. Warrant 1248.

**JOHNSON, ENSIGN WILLIAM.** Certificate as soldier, afterward 2d Lieut. and lastly Captain 1st Artillery, died in 1780 a prisoner of war, John Habersham, Major, Ga. Line, Mar. 11, 1784.

**JONES, HENRY.** Certificate of Elijah Clarke, Col., April 7, 1784. Petitioner prays 287½ acres in Washington Co.

**JACKSON, WILLIAM.** Certificate of Elijah Clarke, Col., Feb. 2, 1784. 3d certificate of Elijah Clarke, Col., Feb. 2, 1784. Petitioner prays two bounties in Washington Co.

**JOHNSTON, JACOB.** Certificate of Elijah Clarke, Col., Feb. 2, 1784.

### K.

**KENDRICK, NATHANIEL.** Certificate of Gb. Lee, Col., April 10, 1784. Petitioner prays bounty in Washington Co.

**KENDRICK, JOHN.** Certificate of Jas. McNeil, Col., April 27, 1784. Petitioner prays 287½ acres in Washington Co.

**KENDRICK, HEZEKIAH.** Certificate of Gb. Lee, Col., Feb. 20, 1784. 2d certificate as refugee soldier, Wm. Candler, Col., Refugee Regt. Petitioner prays 287½ acres in Franklin Co.

**KELLY, EDWARD.** Certificate of Elijah Clarke, Col., Feb. 2, 1784.

**KELLY, JACOB.** Certificate as refugee soldier, Elijah Clarke, Col., April 7, 1784. Petitioner prays 287½ acres in Washington Co. Warrant 1270. 2d certificate of Elijah Clarke, Col., April 1784. Petitioner prays 287½ acres in Washington Co.

**KELLEY, JOHN.** Certificate of Gb. Lee, Col., Mar. 20, 1784. Petitioner prays 287½ acres in Washington Co.

**KELLEY, JOHN.** Certificate of Benj. Few, Col., April 20, 1784. Petitioner prays 287½ acres in Washington Co. Also prays head rights of 600 acres in Washington Co. on self and 8 members of his family.

**KELLEY, THOMAS.** Certificate of Elijah Clarke, Col., Feb. 2, 1784.

**KINNEBREW, JACOB.** Certificate as refugee soldier, Elijah Clarke, Col., April 8, 1784. Petitioner prays bounty in Washington Co. Warrant 1268. 2d certificate of Elijah Clarke, Col., Feb. 2, 1784. Petitioner prays 287½ acres in Washington Co.

**KILPATRICK, THOMAS.** Certificate of John Twiggs, Brig. Gen., May 18, 1784. Petitioner prays 287½ acres in Washington Co.

**KING, JOHN.** Certificate of 3 years' service as soldier in 1st Regt. Continental Troops, Geo. Handley, Major, Dec. 22, 1784. Countersigned by Lachn. McIntosh, Maj. Gen. Warrant 168. Also prays head rights of 450 acres in Washington Co. upon nine in family.

**KASEY, STEPHEN, JR.** Certificate of Elijah Clarke, Col., Feb. 2, 1784. Warrant 1265. 2d certificate of Elijah Clarke, Col., Mar. 25, 1784. Warrant 1266.

# CERTIFICATES OF SERVICE IN AMERICAN REVOLUTION. 107

**KNEEL, PATRICK.** Petition for bounty as soldier of late Georgia Line, prays 287½ acres in reserve on certificate annexed (missing). Granted May 25, 1784.

**KILGORE, WILLIAM.** Certificate of Jas. McNeil, Col., Mar. 15, 1784. Petitioner prays 287½ acres in Washington Co.

**KILGORE, RALPH.** Certificate of Elijah Clarke, Col., Feb. 2, 1784. Petitioner prays 250 acres in Washington Co.

**KILGORE, RALPH, SR.** Certificate of Elijah Clarke, Col., April 8, 1784. Petitioner prays 250 acres in Washington Co.

**KIMBROUGH, WILLIAM, SR.** Certificate of Elijah Clarke, Col., Feb. 2, 1784. Petitioner prays 287½ acres in Washington Co.

**KIMBROUGH, WILLIAM, JR.** Petition for bounty as per certificate annexed (missing).

**KENEDY, JOHN.** Certificate of John Twiggs, Brig. Gen., April 13, 1784. Petitioner prays bounty in Washington Co. Warrant 1267.

**KILPATRICK, THOMAS.** Certificate as refugee soldier, John Twiggs, B. G., Mar. 2, 1784. Warrant 1269.

**KEMP, JOSEPH, JR.** Certificate of Greenberry Lee, Col., April 20, 1784. Petitioner prays 287½ acres in Washington Co.

**KEMP, THOMAS.** Certificate of W. Few for Gb. Lee, Col., April 20, 1784. Petitioner prays 287½ acres in Washington Co.

**KITTS, JOHN.** Certificate of John Twiggs, B. G., Mar. 2, 1784. Petitioner prays bounty in Washington Co.

**KEITH, SAMUEL, SR.** Certificate of Gb. Lee, Col., Mar. 11, 1784. Petitioner prays bounty in Washington Co.

**KILGORE, JOHN.** Certificate of Jas. McNeil, Col., Mar. 15, 1784. Petitioner prays 287½ acres in Washington Co. Warrant 5.

**KEITH, DAVID.** Certificate of Elijah Clarke, Col., April 9, 1784. Petitioner prays 250 acres in Washington Co,

**KARR, CAPT. HENRY.** Ex. order for 460 acres in Franklin Co. on certificate, by John Habersham, Pres. Ex. Council, May 17, 1784.

**KELSEY, SERGEANT HUGH; KELSEY, PRIVATE THOMAS.** Their petition for bounty of 550 acres on certificate annexed (missing).

**KELLEY, JOHN.** Certificate of Elijah Clarke, Col., Feb. 2, 1784. 2d certificate of Gb. Lee, Col., April 10, 1784.

**KELLEY, WILLIAM.** Ex. order for bounty as per certificate of Col. E. Clarke (missing), Mar. 26, 1784. Petitioner prays 287½ acres in Washington Co.

108                ROSTER OF THE REVOLUTION.

**KEILOCH, JOHN.** Certificate of Elijah Clarke, Col., April 20, 1784. Petitioner prays 287½ acres in Washington Co.

**KELLEY, WILLIAM.** Certificate of Elijah Clarke, Col., April 7, 1784. Petitioner prays 287½ acres in Washington Co.

**KIRKHAM, JOSEPH.** Certificate of Jas. Jackson, Lt. Col., Ga. State Legion, Mar. 26, 1784. Petitioner prays 287½ acres in Washington Co.

**KENNEDY, JOHN.** Certificate of Gb. Lee, Col., Feb. 25, 1784. Petitioner prays 287½ acres in Washington Co.

**KIMBROUGH, LIEUT. JOHN.** Certificate of Elijah Clarke, Col., Feb. 2, 1784. Petitioner prays 287½ acres in Washington Co.

**KING, JOEL.** Certificate of Greenberry Lee, Col., Feb. 21, 1784.

**KENDALL, JEREMIAH.** Certificate of Jas. McNeil, Col., April 5, 1784. Petitioner prays 250 acres in Washington Co. Also prays head rights of 650 acres in Washington Co., for self and nine in family.

**KERZY, STEPHEN, JR.** Certificate of Elijah Clarke, Col., April 24, 1784. Petitioner prays 287½ acres in Washington Co.

**KEITH, SAMUEL, JR.** Certificate of Gb. Lee, Col., Mar. 11, 1784. Petitioner prays bounty in Franklin Co.

**KERSEY, STEPHEN.** Certificate of Elijah Clarke, Col., Feb. 2, 1784.

**KILGORE, ROBERT, SR.** Certificate of Elijah Clarke, Col., May 14, 1784. Petitioner prays 250 acres in Franklin Co.

**KILGORE, ROBERT.** Certificate of Elijah Clarke, Col., April 24, 1784. Petitioner prays 250 acres in Franklin Co.

**KEELOCK, EBENEZER.** Certificate of Elijah Clarke, Col., April 20, 1784. Petitioner prays 287½ acres in Washington Co.

L.

**LEDBETTER, FREDERICK.** Certificate of Jas. McNeil, Col., Feb. 2, 1784. Petitioner prays 287½ acres in Washington Co.

**LAZARUS, NICHOLAS.** Ex. order for 200 acres as soldier. Petitioner prays bounty in reserve. Warrant 164.

**LETT, JAMES** (deceased). Certificate of Asa Emanuel, Col., Jan. 15, 1784, endorsed by John Twiggs, B. G. Petitioner, Hannah Lett, widow, of Burke Co., prays bounty and gives power of attorney to Francis Pugh.

**LINDSEY, DENNIS.** Certificate of Elijah Clarke, Col., Feb. 2, 1784.

**LEGIT, JOHN.** Certificate of Elijah Clarke, Col., April 13, 1784. Petitioner prays 287½ acres in Washington Co. 2d certificate of Elijah Clarke, Col., April 20, 1784. Petitioner prays bounty in Washington Co.

CERTIFICATES OF SERVICE IN AMERICAN REVOLUTION. 109

**LINN, JOHN.** Certificate as soldier in 1st Ga. Regt., Geo. Handley, Capt., Aug. 24, 1785. Warrant 151.

**LUCAS, JAMES.** Certificate of Gb. Lee, Col., April 12, 1784. Petitioner prays 287½ acres in Washington Co.

**LEONARD, ELIJAH.** Certificate of Greenberry Lee, Col., April 22, 1784. Petitioner prays bounty in Washington Co.

**LANCASTER, WILLIAM.** Certificate of Gb. Lee, Col., Mar. 11, 1784. Petitioner prays 287½ acres in Washington Co.

**LANGSTON, SAMUEL.** Certificate of Gb. Lee, Col., April 26, 1784. Petitioner prays 2 bounties of 287½ acres each in Franklin Co.

**LOW, DANIEL.** Certificate of G. B. Lee, Col., Mar. 11, 1784. 2d certificate of Samuel Jack, Col., April 6, 1784. Petitioner prays 2 bounties of 250 acres each in Washington Co.

**LANCASTER, LEVI.** Certificate of Greenberry Lee, Col., Mar. 11, 1784. Petitioner prays 287½ acres in Washington Co.

**LOWE, MAJOR PHILIP.** Ex. order for bounty for service in Ga. Line, 800 acres. Warrant 26.

**LACKEY, THOMAS.** Petition for 287½ acres in Washington Co. as per certificate annexed (missing). Granted April 13, 1784.

**LAWSON, CAPT. HUGH.** Ex. order for bounty on certificate of Gen. Twiggs (missing), Dec. 27, 1783. Petitioner prays 575 acres in Washington Co. Warrant 901.

**LANE, THOMAS.** Certificate as refugee soldier, Jenkins Davis, Lt. Col., Dec. 8, 1783. Warrant 1274.

**LANE, WILLIAM** (deceased). Certificate of service in 3d Ga. Continental Battalion, Nathaniel Pearce, Lieut. and Adj., Feb. 15, 1785. Grant made to heirs of Wm. Lane.

**LANIER, LEMUEL.** Certificate as refugee soldier, John Twiggs, B. G., Dec. 30, 1783.

**LANE, JAMES.** Certificate of service in 3d Ga. Continental Battalion, Nathaniel Pearce, Lieut. and Adj., Feb. 15, 1784. Warrant 160.

**LITTLE, ARCHIBALD.** Ex. order for bounty as per certificate of Col. Emanuel (missing), April 27, 1784. Petitioner prays 287½ acres in Washington Co.

**LEVERETT, Aaron.** Certificate of Elijah Clarke, Col., April 19, 1784. Petitioner prays 287½ acres in Washington Co. Also prays head rights of 500 acres in Franklin Co. for self, wife and five children.

**LINTON, JOHN.** Certificate of Elijah Clarke, Col., Aug. 4, 1784. Petitioner prays 287½ acres in Franklin Co.

**LYNN, THOMAS.** Certificate of James Jackson, Lt. Col., July 7, 1784. Petitioner prays 287½ acres in Washington Co.

**LOWE, ISAAC.** Ex. order for bounty on certificate of Jas. McNeil, Col. (missing), Feb. 24, 1784. Petitioner prays 287½ acres in Washington Co.

**LEWIS, REV. JOSIAH, CHAPLAIN** (deceased). Is entitled to a bounty of 750 acres as a refugee from North Carolina, and 250 acres as a citizen after his return to this state, John Twiggs, B. G., April 10, 1784. Petition of Susannah, widow of Josiah Lewis, for self, Jonathan Rees Lewis, 10 years old, Benjamin Thomas Lewis, 8 years old, Susannah Lewis, Jr., 3 years old, and Josiah Lewis, 1 year old, praying that four separate bounties in Washington Co. be granted to Benjamin Lewis, brother of Josiah Lewis, deceased, in trust for the four minors.

**LAWSON, ROGER, JR.** Certificate as refugee soldier, John Twiggs, B. G., Feb. 20, 1784 (missing), and ex. order for bounty. Warrant 1293.

**LAWSON, THOMAS.** Certificate of Elijah Clarke, Col., April 3, 1784. 2d certificate of Elijah Clarke, Col., April 8, 1784.

**LAWSON, JOHN, JR.** Certificate of John Baker, Col., Mar. 22, 1784. 2d certificate of John Baker, Col.

**LOWE, ISAAC, SR.** Certificate of Capt. Parnell, endorsed by Jas. McNeil, Col., April 7, 1784. Petitioner prays 287½ acres in Washington Co.

**LEVERETT, HENRY.** Certificate of Elijah Clarke, Col., Feb. 2, 1784. 2d certificate of Elijah Clarke, Col., April 19, 1784.

**LEVERETT, AARON.** Certificate of Elijah Clarke, Col., Feb., 2, 1784.

**LEVERETT, ROBERT.** Certificate of Elijah Clarke, Col., Feb. 2, 1784. Warrant 1301.

**LEVERETT, JOHN.** Certificate as soldier, and was killed by the enemy, E. Clarke, Col., Sep. 6, 1784. Warrant 1300.

**LEVERETT, HENRY.** Certificate as refugee soldier, Elijah Clarke, Col., April 19, 1734. Petitioner prays 287½ acres in Washington Co. Warrant 1302.

**LAWSON, ANDREW.** Certificate as refugee soldier, John Twiggs, B. G., Nov. 23, 1783. Warrant 1292. 2d certificate of Asa Emanuel, Captain, Dec. 24, 1783, endorsed by John Twiggs, B. G. 3d certificate of John Twiggs, B. G., Mar. 13, 1784. Petition of heirs for 287½ acres in Washington Co.

**LAWSON, THOMPSON.** Certificate of John Twiggs, B. G., March 30, 1784. Petitioner prays 287½ acres in Washington Co.

**LAWSON, HUGH.** His petition to have the following warrants renewed: Heirs of Andrew Lawson, 2 warrants; Roger Lawson, Roger Lawson, Jr., John Lawson, Thompson Lawson and Hugh Lawson (2 warrants), Oct. 19, 1784.

# CERTIFICATES OF SERVICE IN AMERICAN REVOLUTION. 111

**LAWSON ROGER, JR.** Certificate as refugee soldier into North Carolina, John Twiggs, B. G., Nov. 23, 1783.

**LOWE, BEVERLY.** Certificate of Jas. McNeil, Col., Mar. 15, 1784. Petitioner prays 287½ acres in Washington Co.

**LAW, GEORGE.** Certificate of John Baker, Col., Oct. 18, 1784. Warrant 1272.

**LOWE, ISAAC.** Certificate of Jas. McNeil, Col., Feb. 2, 1784.

**LOWE, OBEDIAH.** Certificate as refugee soldier, Jas. McNeil, Col., Feb. 20, 1784. 2d certificate of Jas. McNeil, Col., Feb. 19, 1784.

**LOWE, JOHN.** Certificate of Elijah Clarke, Col., Feb. 2, 1784.

**LEWIS, THOMAS, SR.** Certificate as refugee soldier, Asa Emanuel, Capt., and John Twiggs, B. G., Nov. 26, 1783. Petitioner, Thomas Lewis, Jr., prays bounty in Washington Co. 2d certificate of John Twiggs, Brig. Gen., Mar. 4, 1784. Petitioner prays bounty in Washington Co.

**LEWIS, BENJAMIN.** Certificate as refugee soldier, John Twiggs, B. G., April 10, 1784. Petitioner prays 575 acres in Washington Co.

**LEWIS, DAVID** (deceased). Certificate as refugee soldier, John Twiggs, B. G., April 12, 1784. Petitioner, Kesiah Lewis (widow), prays bounty in Washington Co.

**LEWIS, DAVID, JR.** Certificate as refugee and soldier, John Twiggs, B. G., Feb. 26, 1784. Warrant 1296.

**LEWIS, ELIEZER.** Certificate of Asa Emanuel, Col., Feb. 23, 1784. Petitioner prays 575 acres in Washington Co. Warrant 1286.

**LEWIS, JOEL** (deceased). Certificate as refugee soldier, Jacob Lewis, lawful heir, prays 287½ acres in Washington Co.

**LEWIS, DR. EVAN.** Certificate that he was regularly appointed Surgeon's Mate in Southern Hospital of Continental Army and served until time of his death, William Read, Feb. 28, 1784. Petitioners, Thomas and Jacob Lewis, brothers and lawful heirs, pray 600 acres in the reserve.

**LEWIS, JACOB.** Certificate as refugee soldier, John Twiggs, Brig. Gen., Nov. 28, 1783. Warrant 1294. 2d certificate of John Twiggs, Brig. Gen., Feb. 26, 1784. Petitioner prays bounty in Washington Co.

**LEWIS, JAMES.** Certificate of John Twiggs, Brig. Gen., Feb. 26, 1784. Petitioner prays 287½ acres in Washington Co.

**LANIER, BENJAMIN.** Certificate as refugee soldier, Jenkins Davis, Lt. Col., Feb. 9, 1784. Petitioner prays 250 acres in Washington Co. Warrant 1291.

**LANIER, CLEMENT.** Certificate as refugee soldier, Jenkins Davis, Lt. Col., Jan. 30, 1784. Warrant 1290. 2d certificate of John Twiggs, B. G., Feb. 3, 1784. Petitioner prays 575 acres in Washington Co.

**LAMAR, BENJAMIN.** Certificate of E. Clarke, Col., Dec. 10, 1784. Petitioner prays bounty in Washington Co.

**LAMAR, BASIL.** Certificate of Elijah Clarke, Col., Feb. 2, 1784. Petitioner prays 287½ acres in Washington Co. Also prays head rights of 650 acres in Franklin Co. on self, wife, 3 children and 5 negroes.

**LAMAR, JOEL.** Certificate of Elijah Clarke, Col., Dec. 10, 1784. Petitioner prays bounty in Washington Co.

**LAMAR, LUKE.** Petition for bounty as per certificate annexed (missing), 287½ acres in Washington Co.

**LAMAR, SAMUEL.** Certificate of Elijah Clarke, April 7, 1784. Petitioner prays 250 acres in Washington Co.

**LAMAR, THOMAS.** Certificate of Elijah Clarke, Col., April 7, 1784. Petitioner prays 287½ acres in Washington Co. Also prays head rights of 450 acres in Washington Co. for self, wife and 4 children.

**LAMAR, WILLIAM.** Ex. order for bounty upon certificate of Col. E. Clarke (missing). Petitioner prays 287½ acres in Washington Co.

**LAMAR, ZACHARIAH.** Certificate as refugee soldier, Elijah Clarke, Col., April 7, 1784. Warrant 1275.

**LONG, DAVID.** Certificate of E. Clarke, Col., Dec. 10, 1784.

**LUNDAY, THEOPHILUS.** Certificate of Caleb Howell, Col., Feb. 5, 1784.

**LINDSAY, DENNIS.** Ex. order for bounty upon certificate of Col. E. Clarke (missing), Mar. 1, 1784. Warrant 1304.

**LINN, CHARLES.** Certificate of Greenberry Lee, Col., Mar. 30, 1784. Petitioner prays bounty in Washington Co. Also prays head rights of 550 acres in Washington Co. for self and 7 others in family.

**LEGETT, ABNER.** Certificate as refugee soldier. Elijah Clarke, Col., April 14, 1784. Petitioner prays 287½ acres in Washington Co.

**LEATH, JOHN.** Certificate of Jas. McNeil, Col., Mar. 15, 1784. Petitioner prays bounty in Washington Co. Also prays 550 acres in Washington Co. as head rights for self, wife, five children and one negro.

**LINN, JOHN.** Certificate of 3 years' service as enlisted soldier in 3d Ga. Regt., Isaac Hicks, Captain, John McIntosh, Col., served faithfully until his death. Petitioner, Curtis Linn, brother and legal heir to deceased, asks Capt. Hicks to secure bounty on above. 2d certificate of Jas. Jackson, Col., Sep. 4, 1784. Petitioner prays bounty in Franklin Co.

**LINN, CURTIS.** Petition for bounty of 230 acres in the reserve, for his services; also as heir of his brother, John Linn, prays 280 acres in reserve.

**LITTLE, DAVID.** Certificate of Elijah Clarke, Col., July 19, 1784. Petitioner prays warrant in Washington Co.

## CERTIFICATES OF SERVICE IN AMERICAN REVOLUTION.

**LITTLE, JAMES.** Certificate as refugee soldier, E. Clarke, Col., April 8, 1784. Warrant 1277.

**LITTLE, WILLIAM.** Ex. order for bounty as per certificate of Col. Emanuel (missing), April 27, 1784. Petitioner prays 287½ acres in Washington Co.

**LANKFORD, JOSEPH.** Certificate of Elijah Clarke, Col. (no date). Petitioner prays 250 acres in Washington Co. Warrant 163.

**LANKFORD, JOHN.** Certificate of Elijah Clarke, Col., April 7, 1784. Petitioner prays 250 acres in Washington Co.

**LANKFORD, JONATHAN.** Certificate of Elijah Clarke, Col., April 10, 1784. Petitioner prays 287½ acres in Franklin Co.

**LANKFORD, MOSES.** Certificate as 3 years' service as soldier in 3d Ga. Regt. under Capt. Isaac Hicks. Warrant 162.

**LOFTIN, CORNELIUS.** Certificate of Elijah Clarke, Col., Feb. 2, 1784. Petitioner prays 287½ acres in Washington Co.

**LACKEY, THOMAS.** Ex. order for bounty upon certificate of Col. E. Clarke (missing), Mar. 25, 1784. Petitioner also prays 200 acres in Washington Co. as head rights for self.

**LACKEY, WILLIAM.** Certificate of E. Clarke, Col., Feb. 2, 1784. Petitioner prays 287½ acres in Washington Co. Warrant 1303.

**LEE, ANDREW.** Certificate of Elijah Clarke, Col., Feb. 2, 1784. Warrant 288.

**LEE, TIMOTHY.** Certificate of Jas. McNeil, Col., Feb. 19, 1784. Petitioner prays 287½ acres in Washington Co. Warrant 1287.

**LIVINGSTON, WILLIAM.** Certificate of John Twiggs, Brig. Gen., April 26, 1784. Petitioner prays bounty in Washington Co.

**LEDBETTER, JOHN.** Certificate of Jas. McNeil, Col., April 26, 1784. Petitioner prays bounty in Washington Co. Warrant 1281.

**LETT, REUBEN.** Certificate as refugee soldier, John Twiggs, B. G., Feb. 2, 1784. Petitioner prays 287½ acres in Washingtotn Co.

**LINN, CURTIS.** Certificate of 3 years' service in 3d Ga. Regt., Isaac Hicks, Capt., endorsed by John McIntosh, Col., 3d Ga. Regt., Warrant 158. Jan. 1, 1785.

**LAUDERDALE, JOHN.** Certificate as refugee soldier, John Twiggs, B. G., May 24, 1784. Petitioner prays 250 acres in Franklin Co. Warrant 1282.

**LAREMORE, JOHN.** Ex. order for bounty as per certificate of Col. E. Clarke (missing), Mar. 25, 1784. Petitioner prays 287½ acres in Washington Co.

**LONG, ROBERT.** Certificate of John Twiggs, B. G., April 3, 1784. Petitioner prays 287½ acres in Washington Co.

**LUNDY, THEOPHILUS.** Certificate as refugee soldier, Joshua Davis, Lt. Col., Jan. 30, 1784. Petitioner prays 575 acres in Washington Co. Warrant 1284 and 1371.

**LINDSAY, MAJOR JOHN.** Certificate as refugee soldier, Elijah Clarke, Col., April 6, 1784. Petitioner prays 900 acres in Washington Co.

**LINDSAY, DENNIS.** Certificate of Elijah Clarke, Col., Mar. 2, 1784. See above.

**LEGGETT, ABNER.** Ex. order for bounty as per certificate of Col. Clarke, Mar. 25, 1784. Petitioner prays 287½ acres in Washington Co.

**LEGGETT, JOHN.** Certificate as refugee soldier, Elijah Clarke, Col., April 11, 1784. Petitioner prays 287½ acres in Washington Co. Warrant 1298.

**LANE, MAJOR JOSEPH.** Of 3d Ga. Regt. His petition for 800 acres in Washington Co. as per annexed certificate (missing).

**LOCKHART, ISAAC.** Certificate as refugee soldier, John Twiggs, B. G., Dec. 29, 1783. Warrant 1275. 2d certificate of John Twiggs, B. G., Feb. 14, 1784. Petitioner prays 575 acres in Washington Co.

**LANDRUM, JOHN.** Certificate as Capt. of a Company in 1st Regt., Ga. State Troops, John Clarke, Lt. Col., Feb, 9, 1790. Warrant 501.

**LANDRUM, ZACHARIAH.** Certificate of Jas. Jackson, Col., July 13, 1784. Petitioner prays bounty in Franklin Co. Warrant No. 6.

**LAMBETH, LIEUT. WILLIAM.** Certificate as Lieut. in Galley Service, Gov. Houston, 460 acres ordered. Petition of Elizabeth Watson, Legal Heir, for bounty in reserve.

**LINDEN, SERGEANT JOSEPH.** Certificate as sergeant in Ga. Line, Jos. Pannell, Col., April 8, 1784. Petition of Mary, widow of Joseph Linden, for bounty. Warrant 167.

**LESLIE, JOSEPH.** Certificate as refugee soldier, Jas. Jackson, Lt. Col., Ga. Legion, April 7, 1784. Petitioner prays bounty in Washington Co.

**LEVINS, RICHARD.** Petition for 287½ acres in Franklin Co. as per certificate annexed (missing).

**LONG, JOHN.** Two certificates of Elijah Clarke, Feb. 2, 1784.

**LARKEY, WILLIAM.** Certificate of Elijah Clarke, Col., Feb. 2, 1784.

**LANTERN, THOMAS.** Certificate of Jas. McNeil, Col., Mar. 15, 1784. Petitioner prays 287½ acres in Washington Co.

**LUCAS, WILLIAM.** Certificate as refugee soldier, Jas. McNeil, Col., Feb. 19, 1784. Warrant 1305. 2d certificate to Lieut. William Lucas, Jas. McNeil, Col., Mar. 17, 1784.

## CERTIFICATES OF SERVICE IN AMERICAN REVOLUTION.

**LORN, THOMAS.** Certificate as refugee soldier, John Twiggs, Brig. Gen., April 12, 1784. Petitioner prays 287½ acres in Washington Co. Warrant 1279.

**LANKFORD, PARISH.** Certificate of Isaac Hicks, Capt., 3d Ga. Regt., Aug. 12, 1784.

**LINCH, JOHN.** Certificate of 3 years' faithful service in 2d Ga. Regt., Francis Tennill, Lt. 2d Regt., April 6, 1784. Petitioner prays bounty in Franklin Co. Warrant 161. 2d certificate as soldier in 2d Regt., Litleberry Moseley, Captain and Paymaster, 2d Ga. Batn., Sep. 6, 1784.

**LANKSTON, SAMUEL.** Certificate of Jas. Jackson, Col., Ga. State Legion, April 6, 1784.

**LAMBERT, WILLIAM.** Certificate of service as Lieut. on Gallies, and died in discharge of his duties, Oliver Bowen, Commodore, Aug. 26, 1784.

**LEDBETTER, JOHN.** Certificate of Jas. McNeil, Col., Feb. 5, 1784. Petitioner prays bounty in Washington Co. 2d certificate of Jas McNeil, Col., July 21, 1784. Richard Wilkes, lawful heir, prays 287½ acres in Washington Co.

**LOGAN, PHILIP.** Certificate as refugee soldier, Elijah Clarke, Col., Dec. 7, 1784. Petitioner prays bounty in Washington Co. Warrant 1283.

**LEAPHAM, LIEUT. FREDERICK.** Certificate of Samuel Jack, Col., Mar. 31, 1784. Petitioner prays 460 acres in Washington Co.

**LAMBREECH, JOHN.** Certificate as refugee soldier, Jenkins Davis, Lt. Col., Jan. 27, 1784. Warrant 1285.

**LEVEN, RICHARD.** Certificate as refugee soldier, Elijah Clarke, Col., April 12, 1784. Warrant 1273.

### M.

**MILLER, LIEUT. NICHOLAS.** Certificate of Jas. Jackson, Lt. Col., Ga. State Legion, Sep. 5, 1784. Petitioner prays 460 acres in Washington Co.

**MILLER, ALEXANDER.** Ex. order for bounty upon certificate of Col. Elijah Clarke (missing), Feb. 25, 1784. Petitioner prays 287½ acres in Washington Co.

**MILLER, SAMUEL** (of Sunbury; deceased). Petition of Mary, widow of deceased. Her husband served as Asst. Dep. Commissary of Purchases, American Army. Granted 500 acres, Mar. 26, 1784. Warrant 879.

**MILLER, NICHOLAS.** Certificate as refugee soldier, Jas. McNeil, Sep. 5, 1784. Petitioner prays 287½ acres in Washington Co. Warrant 1337.

**MILLER, ALEXANDER.** Certificate of Elijah Clarke, Col., Feb. 2, 1784.

**MILLER, CHARLES** (of Camden Dist., S. C.). Petition for bounty as soldier in Col. Samuel Jack's Batn. as per certificate of Col. Samuel Jack, Mar. 13, 1784. Warrant 628.

**MILLER, DAVID.** Certificate of Jas. McNeil, Col., Feb. 2, 1784. Petitioner prays 250 acres in Washington Co.

**MILLER, EZEKIEL.** Certificate of Gb. Lee, Col., Feb. 23, 1784. Petitioner prays 287½ acres in Washington Co.

**MILLER, GEORGE.** Certificate of Elijah Clarke, Col., Jan. 3, 1784. Warrant 627. 2d certificate of Elijah Clarke, Col., Jan. 3, 1784. Warrant 626.

**MILLER, JOSHUA.** Certificate of Greenberry Lee, Col., Feb. 25, 1784. Petitioner prays 287½ acres in Washington Co.

**MILLER, JESSE.** Certificate of Greenberry Lee, Col., Feb. 25, 1784. Petitioner prays 287½ acres in Washington Co.

**MILLER, MOSES.** Certificate as refugee soldier, Francis Pugh, Col., Dec. 2, 1784. Warrant 1339.

**MILLER, NATHANIEL.** Certificate as refugee soldier, James McCay, Col., Burke Co., April 5, 1784. Warrant 1336.

**MILLER, SAMUEL.** Certificate of Elijah Clarke, Col., April 20, 1784. Petitioner prays 287½ acres in Washington Co.

**MILLER, WILLIAM.** Certificate as refugee soldier, Jas. McCay, Col., April 7, 1784. Warrant 1335. 2d certificate as soldier, Elijah Clarke, Col., Jan. 2, 1784. Warrant 629.

**McMURRY, FREDERICK.** Certificate of Elijah Clarke, Col., Dec. 20, 1784. Petitioner prays bounty in Washington Co.

**MELLONE, MARTIN.** Certificate of Capt. James Donally and Col. Benj. Few, July 2, 1784.

**McDOWELL, JAMES.** Certificate of Francis Tennell, Col., Feb. 21, 1784. Warrant 173.

**McCLUNG, JOHN.** Certificate of Gb. Lee, Col., Mar. 12, 1784. Petitioner prays 287½ acres in Washington Co. 2d certificate of Gb. Lee, Col., Feb. 23, 1784.

**McHAMEY, TERRY.** Certificate of Gideon Booker, Capt., 3d Ga. Battalion, Mar. 7, 1785. Warrant 175.

**MILLS, WILLIAM.** Certificate of Elijah Clarke, Col., Feb. 2, 1784.

**MUSTEEN, WILLIAM.** Petition for bounty as per certificate of Capt. Gideon Booker, 3d Ga. Battalion, Jan. 6, 1785. Warrant 70.

**MOSS, LEONARD.** Certificate as soldier in Ga. State Legion, James Jackson, Lt. Col., April, 1784. Petitioner prays bounty in Washington Co.

## CERTIFICATES OF SERVICE IN AMERICAN REVOLUTION. 117

**MELVIN, CAPT. GEORGE.** Certificate as Capt. 4th Ga. Regt., Lachlan McIntosh, Maj. Gen., Feb. 20, 1784. Warrant 49.

**McLAIN, LEWIS.** Certificate as soldier in Sumter's Brigade, Francis Tennill, Major, and Thos. Sumter, Col.

**MYERS, THOMAS.** Certificate as sailor on board Gallies, Oliver Bowen, Commodore, Feb. 13, 1784. Warrant No. 9.

**McLAIN, JOHN.** Certificate of Elijah Clarke, Col., Feb. 2, 1784. Petitioner prays 287½ acres in Washington Co.

**MONCRIEF, SAMPSON.** Certificate of Jas. McNeil, Col., July 27, 1784. Petition of Mary Moncrief, widow, for 287½ acres in Washington Co.

**McMURRY, WILLIAM.** Petition for 287½ acres in Washington Co. as per certificate annexed (missing). Granted Oct. 26, 1784.

**McFARLAND, JOHN, JR.** Certificate of Jas. Jackson, Col., Richmond Co., April 8, 1784. Petitioner prays 287½ acres.

**MURPHY, EDWARD.** Certificate of Jas. McNeil, Col., Mar. 15, 1784. Petitioner prays bounty in Washington Co. Also prays head rights in Washington Co. for six whites in family.

**MURPHY, EDWARD.** Certificate of Gb. Lee, Col., Feb. 23, 1784.

**McKINNEY, WILLIAM.** Petition for 250 acres in Washington Co. as per certificate annexed (missing).

**MIMS, DRURY.** Certificate of Elijah Clarke, Col., April 6, 1784. Petitioner prays 287½ acres.

**MIMS, JOSEPH.** Certificate of Elijah Clarke, Col., Feb. 2, 1784. Petitioner prays 287½ acres in Washington Co.

**MIMS, WILLIAM.** Certificate of E. Clarke, Col., April 6, 1784. Petitioner prays 287½ acres in Washington Co.

**McGRUDER, ZADOCK.** Certificate of Benjamin Few, Col., July 20, 1784. Petitioner prays 250 acres in Washington Co.

**MAGRUDER, NINIAN OFFUTT.** Certificate of Gb. Lee, Col., Feb. 23, 1784. Petitioner prays 250 acres in Washington Co.

**MOORE, GEORGE.** Certificate of Elijah Clarke, Col., Sept. 8, 1784. Petitioner prays bounty in Franklin Co.

**MOORE, MORDECAI.** Certificate of Gb. Lee, Col., Feb. 23, 1784. Petitioner prays 287½ acres in (no county named).

**McKINNEY, MATTHEW.** Petition for 250 acres Washington Co. as per certificate annexed (missing). Petition states that he was a citizen of Camden Dist., S. C.

**MOORE, THOMAS.** Certificate of Greenberry Lee, Col., Feb. 23, 1784. Petitioner prays 287½ acres.

**MOBLEY, JOHN.** Certificate of Benj. Few, Col., July 20, 1784. Petitioner prays 287½ acres in Washington Co.

**MERCER, JAMES.** Certificate of Elijah Clarke, Col., Mar. 31, 1784. Petitioner prays bounty in Washington Co.

**MESSER, THOMAS.** Certificate of E. Clarke, Col., Feb. 2, 1784. Petitioner prays 287½ acres in Washington Co. 2d certificate of Gb. Lee, Col., Feb. 23, 1784.

**MERCER, JACOB.** Certificate of E. Clarke, Col., Feb. 25, 1784. Petitioner prays 287½ acres in Washington Co.

**MANNEN, JAMES.** Certificate of Gb. Lee, Col., April 26, 1784. Petitioner, Thomas Mannen (brother), prays bounty in Franklin Co.

**MANNEN, JOHN.** Certificate of Gb. Lee, Col., April 26, 1784. Petitioner prays bounty in Washington Co.

**MANNEN, DRURY.** Ex. order for bounty as per certificate of Col. E. Clarke (missing), Mar. 25, 1784. Petitioner prays 287½ acres in Washington Co.

**MANNEN, JOSEPH.** Certificate of Elijah Clarke, Col., Feb. 2, 1784.

**MANNEN, JOHN.** Certificate of Elijah Clarke, Col., Feb. 2, 1784.

**MORAN, WILLIAM.** Certificate of Elijah Clarke, Col., Jan. 28, 1785.

**MAISE, SERGEANT JOSEPH.** Petition for 287½ acres in the reserve as per certificate annexed (missing). Warrant 168.

**MAY, BAILEY.** Certificate of Jas. Jackson, Col., July 3, 1784. Petitioner prays bounty in Franklin Co.

**MAY, WILLIAM.** Power of attorney to Col. McNeil to draw his bounty warrant.

**MIMS, FREDERICK.** Certificate of Elijah Clarke, Col., Feb. 2, 1784.

**MOATS, DANIEL.** Certificate of Gb. Lee, Col., Mar. 29, 1784. Petitioner prays bounty in Washington Co.

**MOATS, LEVI.** Certificate of Elijah Clarke, Col., Feb. 2, 1784. Petitioner prays bounty in Washington Co.

**MOATS, SIMEON.** Certificate of Elijah Clarke, Col., Feb. 2, 1784. Petitioner prays 287½ acres in Washington Co.

**MOATES, WILLIAM.** Certificate of Elijah Clarke, Col., April 6, 1784. Petitioner prays 287½ acres in Washington Co.

**McGEHEE, THOMAS.** Certificate of Jas. Jackson, Lt. Col., Ga. State Legion, July 8, 1784. 2d certificate of Elijah Clarke, Col., Feb. 2, 1784. Petitioner prays 287½ acres in Washington Co.

# CERTIFICATES OF SERVICE IN AMERICAN REVOLUTION. 119

**MORGAN, PHILIP & JOHN.** This is to certify that John and Philip Morgan served three years under me and were properly discharged. Virginia, Dec. 23, 1782, Isaac Hicks, Capt., Lachn. McIntosh, B. Gen. Warrants 177 and 178.

**MORGAN, ROBERT.** Certificate of Jas. Jackson, Col., Sep. 2, 1784. Petition of Elizabeth, widow of Robt. Morgan, for bounty in Washington Co. for his heirs.

**MORGAN, CHRISTOPHER.** Petition for bounty as soldier in Minute Men as per certificate annexed (missing).

**MORGAN, JEREMIAH.** Certificate of Elijah Clarke, Col., April 19, 1784. Petitioner prays 575 acres in Washington Co.

**MORGAN, ASA.** Certificate of Elijah Clarke, Col., Feb. 2, 1784. Petitioner prays 287½ acres in Washington Co.

**MORGAN, LIEUT. WILLIAM.** Certificate of Greenberry Lee, Col., Mar. 10, 1784. Petitioner prays bounty in Washington Co.

**McCLENDON, JACOB.** Certificate of Elijah Clarke, Col., April 10, 1784. Petitioner prays 287½ acres in Washington Co.

**McCLENDON, SAMUEL.** Certificate of Elijah Clarke, Col., Feb. 2, 1784. Petitioner prays 287½ acres in Washington Co.

**McKEEN, WILLIAM.** Certificate of Elijah Clarke, Col., Feb. 2, 1784.

**McCAY, CAPT. JAMES.** Certificate of John Twiggs, Brig. Gen., Feb. 6, 1784. Petitioner prays 750 acres in Washington Co.

**McKOY, DANIEL.** Certificate of Greenberry Lee, Col., Mar. 13, 1784. Petitioner prays 287½ acres in Washington Co.

**McCALPIN, ALEXANDER.** Certificate of Elijah Clarke, Col., Feb. 2, 1784. 2d certificate as refugee and soldier, Elijah Clarke, Col., Mar. 25, 1784. Petitioner prays bounty of 575 acres.

**MARCUS, JOHN.** Certificate of Jas. Jackson, Lt. Col., April 16, 1784. Petitioner prays 250 acres in Washington Co.

**MARCUS, ELLIS.** Certificate of Jas. Jackson, Lt. Col., Sep., 1784. Petitioner prays bounty in Franklin Co.

**MOSLEY, BENJAMIN.** Certificate of Elijah Clarke, Col., Feb. 2, 1784. Petitioner prays 250 acres in Washington Co. 2d certificate of John Twiggs, Brig. Gen., April 12, 1784.

**MOSBY, ROBERT.** Certificate of service in Continental Line, John Habersham, Major, Line. Petitioner prays 287½ acres in the reserve. Warrant 88.

**MOSELEY, JOHN.** Certificate as soldier in Light Dragoons, Lee DeKeyser, Major, J. Marbury, Col., Feb. 13, 1784.

**MOSELEY, JESSE.** Certificate as soldier in Light Dragoons, Lee DeKeyser, Major, J. Marbury, Col., Feb. 13, 1784.

**MOSELEY, WILLIAM.** Certificate of Elijah Clarke, Col., Feb. 2, 1784. 2d certificate of Elijah Clarke, Col., April 7, 1784. Petitioner, Benjamin Moseley (father), for Wm. Moseley, prays bounty in Washington Co.

**McNEELY, DANIEL.** Certificate of Jas. Jackson, Col., Mar. 27, 1784. Petitioner prays 287½ acres in Washington Co. 2d certificate of John Twiggs, Brig. Gen., Mar. 30, 1784. Petitioner prays 287½ acres in Washington Co.

**McNEIL, JAMES & MICHAEL.** Certificate of Jas. McNeil, Col., April 8, 1784.

**MAXWELL, LIEUT. JOSIAH.** Ex. order for bounty, Jan. 24, 1784. Warrant 90.

**MAXWELL, MAJOR THOMAS.** Certificate as Major 1st Battalion Minute Men, J. Houstoun, Gov., June 25, 1784. 600 acres. Warrant 221.

**MAXWELL, THOMAS.** This is to certify that Thomas Maxwell was Captain under me on board the Gallies in the Line of this State, Oliver Bowen, Commodore, May 16, 1785. Petitioner prays 977½ acres in Washington Co.

**MOORE, JAMES.** Certificate of Gb. Lee, Col., Feb. 23, 1784. Petitioner prays 287½ acres in Franklin Co. 2d certificate of Gb. Lee, Col., Mar. 30, 1784. Petitioner prays 287½ acres in Washington Co.

**MOORE, THOMAS.** Certificate of Asa Emanuel, Col., Oct. 18, 1784. Petitioner prays 287½ acres in Washington Co.

**MOORE, THOMAS.** Certificate of Elijah Clarke, Col., Jan. 29, 1785. Petitioner prays 287½ acres in Washington Co. Also prays 1,000 acres head rights in Franklin Co. upon self, wife, 4 children and 14 negroes.

**MARSH, NATHAN.** Certificate of Elijah Clarke, Col., Sep. 8, 1784. Petitioner prays bounty in Washington Co.

**MARSH, JOHN.** Certificate of Elijah Clarke, Col., Sep. 8, 1784. Petitioner prays 287½ acres in Washington Co.

**McGILTON, VANCE.** Ex. order for bounty upon certificate of Gen. McIntosh (missing), April 21, 1784. Warrant 169. Heirs of Vance McGilton pray bounty in reserve.

**McGILTON, JAMES.** Certificate of Lachn. McIntosh, Maj. Gen., April 21, 1784. Petitioner prays bounty in the reserve. Warrant 176.
State of South Carolina, 96 District: I do certify that James McGilton was a refugee of Ga., made his escape from that State with me, and served during the war except when a prisoner. Wm. Farr, Lt. Col., Thos. Brandon, Col., Mar. 8, 1784. Warrant 319. Certificate to Jas. McGilton as refugee from Georgia, and did his duty faithfully in S. C. as a soldier. Wm. Candler, Col., Refugee Regt.

# CERTIFICATES OF SERVICE IN AMERICAN REVOLUTION.

**McINTOSH, BRIG. GEN. LACHLAN.** Petition for 977½ acres in Washington Co. Granted April 17, 1785, in two warrants. Petition of Major Gen. Lachlan McIntosh for 575 acres in Washington Co. on difference of rank. Granted April 17, 1785. Warrant No. 11. Petition of heirs of Lachlan McIntosh, by Lachlan McIntosh, Jr., for bounty of father, Maj. Gen. Lachlan McIntosh, 920 acres in Washington Co. Granted April 17, 1785.

**MARSHALL, JOHN.** Certificate of Gb. Lee, Col., Feb. 21, 1784. 2d certificate of Elijah Clarke, Col., April 6, 1784. 3d certificate of Elijah Clarke, Col., April 9, 1784. Petitioner prays bounty in Washington Co. Also prays head rights of 350 acres in Washington Co. for self and 3 negroes.

**MARSHALL, MATTHEW.** Certificate of E. Clarke, Col., April 6, 1784. Petitioner prays bounty in Washington Co.

**MARSHALL, SOLOMON.** Petition for 287½ acres in Washington Co. as per certificate annexed (missing).

**McCULLOCH, SAMUEL.** Certificate of Jas. McNeil, Col., Mar. 24, 1784. Petitioner prays 250 acres in Washington Co.

**MANN, JOHN.** Certificate of Elijah Clarke, Col., Feb. 2, 1784. Petitioner prays bounty in Washington Co.

**MANN, LUKE.** Certificate of John Baker, Col., Mar. 18, 1784. Luke Mann files power of attorney to draw bounties for: Abraham Lamb, Andrew Walthour, Laban Thompson, Joseph Plumer, Josiah Naylor, William Sapp, John Sapp, Eliger Sapp, Emanuel Sapp, Andrew Dick, Susannah Dick.

**MITCHELL, LIEUT. JOHN.** Ex. order for bounty of 400 acres, Jan. 24, 1784. Warrant 89.

**MITCHELL, WILLIAM.** Certificate of Major Carr, endorsed by John Twiggs, B. G., Feb. 20, 1784. Petitioner prays 287½ acres in Franklin Co. and 287½ acres in Washington Co.

**MITCHELL, ROBERT.** Certificate of Elijah Clarke, Col., Feb. 2, 1784. 2d certificate of Elijah Clarke, Col., May 20, 1784. Petitioner prays 575 acres in Franklin Co.

**MATTOX, JOHN.** Petition for bounty for services as Minute Man in service of the State, as per annexed certificate (missing), Mar. 20, 1784.

**MIDDLETON, BENEDICK.** Certificate of Elijah Clarke, Col., May 21, 1784. Petitioner prays bounty in Franklin Co.

**MORRISON, CAPT. JOHN.** Certificate as Capt. in Ga. State Legion, Jas. Jackson, Lt. Col., Ga. Legion, July 13, 1784. Petitioner prays 575 acres in Franklin Co. Warrant 655.

**MIDDLETON, HOLLAND, SR.** Certificate of Elijah Clarke, Col., Feb. 20, 1784. Petitioner prays bounty in Washington Co. 2d certificate of Elijah Clarke,

Col., Jan. 29, 1785. Petitioner prays 287½ acres in Washington Co. 3d
certificate of Gb. Lee, Col., April 7, 1784. Petitioner prays bounty in
Washington Co.

**MIDDLETON, HOLLAND, JR.** Certificate of Elijah Clarke, Col., Feb. 20,
1784. Petitioner prays bounty in Washington Co. 2d certificate of Jas.
McNeil, Col., April 3, 1784. Petitioner prays bounty in Washington Co.

**MATHEWS, WILLIAM.** Certificate that he was appointed Assistant to Col.
William Massey, Deputy Muster Master General for South Carolina and
Georgia, with rank of Captain, by Major Gen. Howe, N. B. Capt. Mathews
was made prisoner Dec. 29, 1778; continued a prisoner of war until peace
was declared, for want of an officer of similar rank to exchange for him.
Major Gen. John Habersham, Nov. 5, 1780. Warrant 54.

**MATHEWS, ISHAM.** Certificate of E. Clarke, Col., April 16, 1784. Petitioner
prays bounty in Franklin Co. Warrant 13.

**MATHEWS, BRI. GEN. GEORGE.** Petition on becoming a citizen of the
State of Georgia, asks 2 warrants in the reserve. Granted 850 acres.

**MILTON, NATHANIEL.** Certificate of Capt. Inman, countersigned by John
Twiggs, B. G., May 20, 1784. Petitioner prays bounty in Washington Co.

**MARBURY, LEONARD, SR.** Certificate of E. Clarke, Lt. Col., Jan. 28, 1785.

**MILLEDGE, JOHN.** Certificate of John Twiggs, B. G., Mar. 29, 1784. Petitioner prays 287½ acres in Washington Co.

**McILHENNY, JOHN.** Petition for bounty of 287½ acres in Washington Co.
as per certificate of Brig. Gen. John Twiggs (missing), July 15, 1784.

**MIDDLETON, ROBERT.** Certificate of Gb. Lee, Col., Mar. 11, 1784. Petitioner
prays 287½ acres in Washington Co. 2d certificate of Elijah Clarke, Col.,
May 21, 1784. Petitioner prays bounty in Franklin Co.

**MORPHET, JAMES.** Ex. order for bounty as per certificate of Col. E. Clarke
(missing), Mar. 25, 1784. Petitioner, through his attorney, Edward Pharr,
prays 287½ acres in Washington Co.

**MORRIS, PATRICK.** Certificate of Gb. Lee, Col., Feb. 23, 1784.

**MONEY, JOSEPH.** Certificate of Greenberry Lee, Col., Mar. 30, 1784. Petitioner prays 287½ acres in Franklin Co.

**McCLENDON, ISAAC.** Certificate of Elijah Clarke, Col., Feb. 2, 1784. 2d
certificate of Elijah Clarke, Col., Feb. 2, 1784.

**MILICAN, HUGH.** Certificate of Gb. Lee, Col., Feb. 23, 1784. Petitioner prays
bounty in Washington Co.

**MURPHY, EDWARD.** Ex. order for bounty on certificate of Col. Gb. Lee
(missing), Feb. 25, 1784. Petitioner prays bounty in Washington Co.

**MORRIS, REESE.** Ex. order for bounty upon certificate of Col. James McNeil (missing), Feb. 20, 1784. Petitioner prays 287½ acres in Franklin Co.

**McGARRY, ROBERT.** Certificate of Elijah Clarke, Col., Feb. 2, 1784.

**McNABB, ROBERT.** Certificate of Elijah Clarke, Col., Feb. 2, 1784. 2d certificate of Elijah Clarke, Col., April 20, 1784. Warrants granted in Franklin Co.

**McMULLEN, ROLEN.** Certificate of Jas. Jackson, Lt. Col., Ga. State Legion, April 6, 1784. Petitioner prays bounty in Washington Co.

**McMUNN, JOHN.** Certificate of Gb. Lee, Col., Mar. 11, 1784.

**MARSHALL, REV. ABRAHAM.** State of Georgia: This is to certify that the Rev. Mr. Abraham Marshall, early espoused the cause of the United States of America, and has rendered the Commonwealth essential services by his zeal and activity as a chaplain for Col. Stewart's regiment of Minute Men and for General Williamson's Brigade, when lying in camp opposite Augusta, by exciting the officers and soldiers to stand up in defense of their country, and is in our opinion entitled to a bounty as a chaplain, agreeable to an Act of the General Assembly of this State, in that respect made and provided, etc. Given under our hands, this 6th day of April, 1784. (Signed) Elijah Clarke, Col., Greenberry Lee, Col. 2d certificate as a refugee and chaplain, Benj. Few, Col., Mar. 12, 1784. Petitioner prays 287½ acres in Washington Co. and 747½ acres on 1st certificate. Warrant 874.

**MARSHALL, JOHN.** Ex. order for bounty as per certificate of Col. Gb. Lee (missing), Feb. 25, 1784. Petitioner prays 287½ acres in Washington Co.

**MAXWELL, EDWARD.** Certificate of Jas. McNeil, Col., April 26, 1784. Petitioner prays bounty in Washington Co.

**MAXWELL, JAMES.** Certificate as refugee soldier, John Baker, Col., April 12, 1784.

**MAXWELL, JOSIAH.** Certificate as soldier and ensign, served 5 years in 3d Regt., Ga. Continental Troops, Lachlan McIntosh, Maj. Gen., Jan. 14, 1784.

**MANNON, WILLIAM.** Certificate as soldier in 1st Batt. Minute Men, Elijah Clarke, Col., Feb. 11, 1785. Warrant 672.

**MAXWELL, THOMAS.** Certificate as refugee soldier, John Baker, Col., June 25, 1784. Warrant 1322.

**MANNEN, DRURY.** Certificate of Elijah Clarke, Col., Feb. 2, 1784.

**MANNON, JOHN, JR.** Certificate of Gb. Lee, Col., Feb. 23, 1784.

**MABRY, REPS.** Virginia, Feb. 18, 1783: This is to certify that Reps. Mabry of North Carolina enlisted as sergeant in my company and served 3 years in Continental Army, Isaac Hicks, Capt. in 3d Ga. Continental Battalion. Warrant 171.

ROSTER OF THE REVOLUTION.

**MANNING, ROBERT.** Certificate of Elijah Clarke, Col., April 8, 1784. Petitioner prays bounty in Washington Co. Warrant 1309.

**MATTOX, BENJAMIN.** Certificate of Samuel Jack, Col., April 5, 1784.

**MATTOX, JOHN.** Certificate of Samuel Jack, Col., April 5, 1784. Warrant 631.

**MADDOX, JOHN.** Certificate of Jas. McNeil, Col., Feb. 2, 1784. Petitioner prays 275 acres in Washington Co. 2d certificate to John Maddox, refugee soldier, Jas. McNeil, Col., Feb. 19, 1784.

**MADDOX, WILLIAM.** Certificate of Samuel Jack, Col., April 3, 1784. Petitioner prays 287½ acres in Franklin Co. Warrant 630.

**MADDOX, WILLIAM; PEAVY, JOHN, and McNEIL, JESSE.** Certificate that each is entitled to 287½ acres as soldiers, Jas. McNeil, Col., April 3, 1784.

**McNEIL, JESSE.** Certificate of Greenberry Lee, Col., April 7, 1784.

**MADEN, LIEUT. DAVID.** Certificate of Elijah Clarke, Col., Feb. 2, 1784. Warrant 926.

**MARBURY, THOMAS.** Certificate of Jas. McNeil, Col., May 15, 1784. Petitioner prays bounty in Washington Co. Warrant 1326.

**MARBURY, HORATIO.** Certificate of Leonard Marbury (rank not given), Petitioner prays 287½ acres in Washington Co.

**MARBURY, LEONARD, SR.** Certificate as refugee soldier, Jas. McNeil, Col., May 15, 1784. Petitioner prays bounty in Washington Co. Warrant 1325.

**MARBURY, HORATIO.** 2d certificate as refugee soldier, Elijah Clarke, Col., Warrant 1324.

**MAHAN, ARCHIBALD.** Certificate of Elijah Clarke, Col., Feb. 2, 1784. 2d certificate of Elijah Clarke, Col., April 20, 1784. Petitioner prays 287½ acres in Washington Co. Warrant 659.

**MAHAN, SAMUEL.** Certificate of E. Clarke, Col., April 9, 1784. Petitioner prays bounty in Washington Co.

**METCALF, DANZA.** Certificate of Samuel Jack, Col., Jan. 20, 1784. Warrant 650.

**MOSELEY, THOMAS, JR.** Certificate of Elijah Clarke, Col., April 20, 1784.

**MATHEWS, DANIEL, JR.** Certificate of Samuel Jack, Col., Mar. 31, 1784. Petitioner prays bounty in Franklin Co. Warrant 633.

**MATHEWS, DANIEL.** Certificate of Samuel Jack, Col., Mar. 25, 1784. Petitioner prays bounty in Franklin Co. Warrant 634.

**MATHEWS, ISHAM.** Certificate of Samuel Jack, Col., Mar. 31, 1784. Petitioner prays bounty in Franklin Co. Warrant 636. 2d certificate as refugee soldier, E. Clarke, Col., April 26, 1784. Petitioner prays bounty in Franklin Co.

**MATHEWS, JOHN.** Certificate of Gb. Lee, Col., April 10, 1784. Petitioner prays 287½ acres in Washington Co.

**MATHEWS, JAMES.** Certificate of Gb. Lee, Col., Mar. 11, 1784. Petitioner prays bounty in Washington Co.

**MATHEWS, MESHACK.** Certificate of Gb. Lee, Col., April 22, 1784. Petitioner prays bounty in Washington Co.

**MATHEWS, REUBEN.** Certificate of Samuel Jack, Col., Mar. 30, 1784. Petitioner prays bounty in Franklin Co. Warrant 635.

**MATHEWS, WILLIAM.** Certificate of John Baker, Col., Mar. 19, 1784. Petitioner prays 250 acres in Washington Co. Warrant 1351.

**MATHEWS, WILLIAM.** Certificate of Samuel Jack, Col., Mar. 31, 1784. Petitioner prays bounty in Franklin Co. Warrant 637.

**MATHEWS, WILLIAM.** Certificate of Gb. Lee, Col., May 6, 1784. Petitioner prays bounty in Washington Co.

**MARTIN, AUSTIN.** Certificate of Elijah Clarke, Col., May 17, 1784. Petitioner prays 287½ acres bounty.

**MARTIN, CORNELIUS.** Certificate of Elijah Clarke, Col., Jan. 29, 1785. Warrant 656.

**MARTIN, LIEUT. EDMOND.** Certificate of Wm. Candler, Col., Refugee Regt. Petitioner prays bounty in Washington Co.

**MARTIN, GANOWAY.** Ex. order for bounty upon certificate of Col. E. Clarke (missing), Feb. 25, 1784. Petitioner prays 287½ acres in Washington Co.

**MARTIN, JACOB.** Certificate of Elijah Clarke, Col., Jan. 17, 1784. Petitioner prays 287½ acres in Washington Co.

**MARTIN, JAMES.** Certificate as 2d Lieut., Wm. Candler, Col., Refugee Regt., Feb. 24, 1784. Petitioner prays 287½ acres in Washington Co. Warrant 1344.

**MARTIN, JAMES.** Certificate as Lieut.- Col., refugee soldier, Wm. Candler, Col., Refugee Regt. Petitioner prays 800 acres in Washington Co. Warrant 861.

**MARTIN, JAMES.** Certificate of Elijah Clarke, Col., Feb. 2, 1784. Petitioner prays bounty in Washington Co.

**MARTIN, JAMES.** Certificate of John Twiggs, Brig. Gen., Feb. 3, 1784. Petitioner prays 250 acres in Washington Co.

**MARTIN, JOHN, JR.** Certificate of John Twiggs, Brig. Gen., Dec. 2, 1783. Petitioner prays 287½ acres in Washington Co. Warrant 1349. 2d certificate of John Twiggs, B. G., Feb. 22, 1784. Petitioner prays 287½ acres in Washington Co.

**MARTIN, JOHN.** Certificate as Lieut. Col. of Chatham Co. Regt., Geo. Walton, Col., Commanding, April 23, 1784. Petitioner prays bounty in Washington Co. as Lieut. Col.

**MARTIN, JOHN.** Certificate of Elijah Clarke, Col., Feb. 11, 1785.

**MARTIN, MARSHALL.** Certificate as refugee soldier, Wm. Candler, Col., Refugee Regt. Petitioner prays bounty in Franklin Co. Warrant 1346.

**MARTIN, MATTHEW.** Certificate as refugee soldier, Wm. Candler, Col., Refugee Regt. Petitioner prays bounty in Franklin Co. Warrant 1347.

**MARTIN, SIMON.** Certificate as refugee soldier, Wm. Candler, Col., Refugee Regt. Petitioner prays bounty in Washington County. Warrant 1348.

**MARTIN, WILLIAM.** Certificate of John Twiggs, B. G., Feb. 26, 1784. Petitioner prays bounty in Washington Co.

**MARTIN, LIEUT. WILLIAM.** Certificate showing that he was killed prior to the passing of the Act, Elijah Clarke, Col., April 8, 1794. Warrant 260. 2d certificate identical with above. Upon each Betty, relict of Wm. Martin, prays bounty in Franklin Co. for Robert, William and Elizabeth, heirs of Wm. Martin, deceased.

**MAY, WILLIAM.** Certificate of James McNeil, Col., Feb. 2, 1784. Petitioner prays 287½ acres in Washington Co.

**MAY, WILLIAM.** Certificate of Elijah Clarke, Col., April 7, 1784. 2d certificate of Elijah Clarke, Col., same date. Petitioner prays 575 acres in Washington Co.

**MAY, MOSES.** Certificate of Elijah Clarke, Col., April 21, 1784. Petitioner prays bounty in Washington Co.

**MANN, JOHN.** Certificate as refugee soldier, Francis Pugh, Col., April 7, 1784. Also certificate of John Green, J. P., that he saw John Mann, a refugee in south Carolina. Warrant 1312.

**MABAN, MATTHEW.** Petition of Matthew Maban, a Minute Man, as per certificate annexed (missing). Power of attorney from Matthew Maban of Rutherford Co., N. C., to John Clarke, of 96 Dist., S. C., to draw his bounty. Warrant 642.

**MABEN, MATTHEW.** Certificate of Samuel Jack, Col., April 5, 1784 (belongs with above).

**MAYBEN, WILLIAM.** Certificate of Samuel Jack, Col., Mar. 13, 1784. Warrant 641.

**MALLARD, LAZARUS.** Certificate as refugee soldier, John Baker, Col., Mar. 22, 1784. Warrant 1306.

## CERTIFICATES OF SERVICE IN AMERICAN REVOLUTION.     127

**McMURRAY, JOHN.** Certificate of Elijah Clarke, Col., Feb. 25, 1784. Petitioner prays 287½ acres in Washington Co. Warrant 644.

**MIDDLETON, CAPT. ROBERT.** Certificate of Elijah Clarke, Col., April 1, 1784. Petitioner prays 500 acres in Washington Co. Warrant 225.

**McGILL, JOHN.** Certificate of Elijah Clarke, Col., Feb. 25, 1784. Petitioner prays 287½ acres in Washington Co. Warrant 640. 2d certificate of John McGill, Elijah Clarke, Col.

**McFIELD, WILLIAM.** Certificate of Elijah Clarke, Col., April 24, 1784. Petitioner prays 250 acres in Franklin Co.

**McNATT, SOLOMON.** Certificate of E. Clarke, Col., Jan. 3, 1785. Warrant 658.

**McDONALD, HUGH.** Certificate of Elijah Clarke, Lt. Col., Jan. 25, 1785. Warrant 639.

**McNIEL, ARCHIBALD.** Certificate that he fell in the service of his country as a refugee from the State of Georgia. John Twiggs, B. G., Feb. 3, 1784. Warrant 1327.

**McNEIL, COL. JAMES.** Certificate as refugee soldier, John Twiggs, Brig. Gen., Feb. 3, 1784. Granted bounty as a Major. Warrant 868. 2d certificate of John Twiggs, B. G., Feb. 3, 1784.

**McNEIL, COL. JAMES.** With power of attorney, acknowledges receipt of warrants in Washington Co. for: John Culbreath, Wm. Hogg, heirs of Archibald McNeil, Daniel McNair, James McNeil, Daniel McNeil, Joshua Woods, John Salis, Duncan McNeil, John Averett, Isaac Skinner, Samuel Ramsey, Christopher Chambless, John Maddox, William Hogg, William Maddox, Bartley Anderson, Peter Culbreath, Daniel McNeil, Sr., Daniel McNeil, Jr., heirs of Samuel Ramsey, Burros Hickinbottom, Elijah Anderson, Francis Holton, Stephen Gloveyer, Jas. Simpson, Jesse McNeil, Obediah Lowe, James Culbreath, Randal Bamby, William Cone, Michael McNeil, William Ramsey and David Carter, 35 in all.

**McCOY, CAPT. JAMES.** Certificate as refugee soldier, John Twiggs, B. G., Feb. 6, 1784. Certificate of Jas. McCoy on oath that he lost warrant for 575 acres in Washington Co. in a cane brake, with no probability of its ever being found, July 6, 1784.

**McLAIN, JAMES.** Certificate of Elijah Clarke, Col., Feb. 2, 1784. Petitioner prays 250 acres in Washington Co. Warrant 1334.

**McLAIN, JOHN.** Certificate of Elijah Clarke, Col., Feb. 2, 1784. Petitioner prays bounty in Washington Co. Warrant 1333.

**McDANIEL, TOKIAH.** Certificate of Elijah Clarke, Col., Jan. 25, 1785. Warrant 638.

McCOWEN, DANIEL. Certificate of Gb. Lee, Col., Feb. 23, 1784. Petitioner prays 250 acres in Franklin Co.

Mc CAIN, THOMAS. Certificate of Elijah Clarke, Col., April 24, 1784. Petitioner prays 287½ acres in Franklin Co.

McDOWELL, THOMAS. Certificate of Elijah Clarke, Col., April 7, 1784. Petitioner prays 287½ acres in Washington Co. Warrant 663. 2d certificate as refugee soldier, E. Clarke, Col., April 12, 1784. Petitioner prays bounty in Washington Co. Warrant 1318.

McDOWELL, LIEUT. THOMAS. Certificate of Elijah Clarke, Col., Feb. 2, 1784. Petitioner prays 287½ acres in Washington Co.

McCULLOUGH, SAMUEL. Certificate of service as sergeant in Minute service of the State of Georgia, being from Camden Dist., S. C. Served in Capt. Michael Dickson's company and Lieut. Col. Samuel Jack's battalion. Prays bounty in reserve. Warrant 283.

McCULLOUGH, JOHN. Certificate as refugee soldier, Francis Pugh, Col., Mar. 6, 1784. Warrant 137.

McCULLOUGH, PATRICK. Certificate of Samuel Jack, Col., April 5, 1784. Warrant 664.

McGENTY, ROBERT. Certificate of Elijah Clarke, Col., Feb. 2, 1784.

McGARY, EDWARD. Certificate of Elijah Clarke, Col., Feb. 2, 1784. Warrant 1352.

McGEARY, ROBERT. Certificate of Elijah Clarke, Col., April 5, 1784. Warrant 670.

McDOUGAL, ALEXANDER. Certificate of Elijah Clarke, Col., Feb. 2, 1784. Petitioner prays 287½ acres in Washington Co.

McCLURE, SAMPSON. Certificate of Elijah Clarke, Col., Oct. 10, 1784. Warrant 671.

McKINNEY, HENRY. Certificate of Elijah Clarke, Col., Feb. 2, 1784. Warrant 1354.

McKINNEY, JOHN. Certificate of Elijah Clarke, Col., Feb. 2, 1784.

McKINNEY, MATTHEW. Certificate of Elijah Clarke, Col., April 7, 1784. Warrant 647.

McKINNEY, NATHAN. Certificate of Elijah Clarke, Col., June 3, 1784. Warrant 645.

McKINNEY, TRAVIS. Certificate of Elijah Clarke, Col., Feb. 2, 1784.

McKINNEY, THOMAS. Certificate of Elijah Clarke, Col. Petitioner prays 287½ acres in Franklin Co. Warrant 648.

McKINNEY, WILLIAM. Certificate of Elijah Clarke, Col., Jan., 1785. Warrant 646. 2d certificate as refugee soldier, William Candler, Col., Refugee Regt.

**McCARTEY, DANIEL.** Certificate of Greenberry Lee, Col., Feb. 23, 1784.

**McCARDEL, CORNELIUS.** Certificate of Elijah Clarke, Col., April 7, 1784. Petitioner prays bounty in Franklin Co. Warrant 660.

**McCLAIN, NICHOLAS.** Certificate of Elijah Clarke, Col., Nov. 16, 1784. Warrant 666.

**McCALVEY, JOHN.** Certificate of Elijah Clarke, Col., April 2, 1784. Petitioner prays 287½ acres in Washington Co. Warrant 668.

**MANADUE, CAPT. HENRY.** Certificate that he is entitled to two bounties, one hundred acres as captain of refugees, and 250 acres as a citizen. Petitioner prays bounties in Washington Co. Warrant 904.

**MERCER, REV. SILAS.** This is to certify that the Rev. Silas Mercer, in the beginning of these times, was very active and useful in convincing the people of the justice of the cause of America, and after the British took possesion of Savannah he spent much of his time in preaching to the armies, and obtained an excellent recommendation from Colonel Hammond to General Lincoln in order that he might preach to his army, and as he was on his way to Purisburg he came to Burke Jail to preach to my regiment and was there in the time of a very warm engagement, and behaved himself exceedingly well in time of the action, and soon afterward he left the State at the expense of the chief of his property, rather than surrender to the British Government: and I have been creditably informed that he has behaved himself honorably during his absence, and has spent much of his time in preaching to armies, and has at all times supported the character of a good Whigg. Therefore, I believe he is entitled to as much land as any gentleman of his rank. Benjamin Few, Col. Richmond Co., Daniel Coleman, Zacheus Fenn. Granted 650 acres as a refugee chaplain, with rank of Major, Feb. 24, 1784. Warrant 875.

**MERCER, JACOB.** Certificate of Elijah Clarke, Col., Feb. 2, 1784.

**METCALF, LIEUT. ANTHONY.** Certificate of Samuel Jack, Col., Jan. 20, 1784.

**METCALF, WILLIAM.** Certificate of Samuel Jack, Col., Feb. 2, 1784. Warrant 649.

**MITCHELL, DAVID.** Certificate of Elijah Clarke, Col., April 8, 1784. Warrant 662.

**MITCHELL, JOHN.** Certificate of Greenberry Lee, Col., Feb. 25, 1784. Petitioner prays 287½ acres in Washington Co. Also prays 200 acres in Franklin Co. on head rights.

**MITCHELL, ROBERT.** Certificate as refugee soldier, Elijah Clarke, Col., May 20, 1784. Warrant 1353.

**MITCHELL, THOMAS.** Certificate of Elijah Clarke, Col., Feb. 2, 1784. Petitioner prays 250 acres in Washington Co.

**MITCHELL, WILLIAM.** Certificate of Elijah Clarke, Col., Feb. 2, 1784. Petitioner prays 287½ acres in Washington Co.

**MITCHELL, WILLIAM.** Certificate of Gb. Lee, Col., Feb. 23, 1784. 2d certificate as refugee soldier, John Twiggs, B. G., Mar. 8, 1784. Petitioner prays 230 acres in reserve.

**MOORE, ALEXANDER.** Certificate as refugee soldier, Elijah Clarke, Col., May 14, 1784. Petitioner prays bounty in Washington Co. Warrant 1314.

**MOORE, SERGEANT JOHN.** Certificate of Samuel Jack, Col., May 14, 1784. Petitioner prays bounty in Franklin Co.

**MOORE, MARTIN.** Certificate of John Twiggs, B. G., Feb. 23, 1784. Petitioner prays 287½ acres in Washington Co.

**MOORE, RICHARD.** Certificate of Samuel Jack, Col., May 14, 1784. Petitioner prays 287½ acres in Franklin Co. Warrant 651.

**MOORE, WILLIAM.** Certificate of John Twiggs, B. G., April 3, 1784. Petitioner prays 250 acres in Washington Co. 2d certificate as refugee soldier, E. Clarke, Col., April 16, 1784. Petitioner prays 250 acres in Franklin Co.

**MOORE, WILLIAM.** Certificate of Samuel Jack, Col., April 14, 1784. Petitioner prays bounty in Franklin Co. Upon oath, William Moore, of Virginia, asks head rights of 1,000 acres in Washington Co. upon 20 in family.

**MOSS, JAMES.** Certificate of Jas. McNeil, Col., Mar. 24, 1784.

**MORIS, JAMES.** Certificate of John Stewart, Colonel, July 27, 1784. Petitioner prays 287½ acres in Franklin Co. Warrant 654.

**MORRIS, PATRICK.** Certificate of Eliah Clarke, Col., Mar. 2, 1784. Petitioner prays 250 acres. 2d certificate of Elijah Clarke, Col., April 7, 1784. Petitioner prays 287½ acres in Washington Co.

**MORRIS, REESE.** Certificate of Jas. McNeil, Col., Feb. 2, 1784.

**MORRIS, SERGEANT WILLIAM.** Certificate of Elijah Clarke, Col., April 3, 1784. Petitioner prays bounty in Washington Co. Warrant 285.

**MOATES, SILAS.** Certificate of Elijah Clarke, Col., Feb. 2, 1784. Petitioner prays 287½ acres in Washington Co.

**MORPHET, JAMES.** Certificate of Elijah Clarke, Col., Feb. 2, 1784.

**MOFFETT, THOMAS.** Certificate of Elijah Clarke, Col., Feb. 2, 1784. Petitioner prays 287½ acres in Franklin Co. Warrant 1358.

## CERTIFICATES OF SERVICE IN AMERICAN REVOLUTION.

**MORPHET, THOMAS.** Certificate of Elijah Clarke, Col., Feb. 2, 1784. Petitioner prays 250 acres in Franklin Co.

**MOTT, JOSEPH.** Certificate of Jas. McNeil, Col., Feb. 2, 1784. Petitioner prays bounty in Washington Co.

**MOTT, ZEPHENIAH.** Certificate of Jas. McNeil, Col., Feb. 21, 1784. Petitioner prays 250 acres in Washington Co.

**MOTT, URIAH.** Certificate of Jas. McNeil, Col., Feb. 21, 1784. Petitioner prays bounty in Washington Co.

**MOTT, WILLIAM.** Power of attorney from Joseph and William Mott to Col. Jas. McNeil, to draw their bounties.

**MORTEN, JOHN.** Certificate of John Twiggs, Brig. Gen., Feb. 3, 1784.

**MILLER, DANIEL.** Certificate as refugee soldier, John Baker, Col., Mar. 19, 1784. Warrant 1338.

**MILLER, CAPT. ELISHA.** Ex. order for bounty upon certificate of Maj. Gen. McIntosh, Mar. 16, 1784. Warrant 51.

**MILLER, JOSEPH.** Certificate of Gb. Lee, Col., Feb. 25, 1784.

**MILNER, JOHN.** Certificate of Elijah Clarke, Col., April 6, 1784. Petitioner prays 287½ acres in Washington Co. Warrant 1313.

**MORGAN, CHRISTOPHER.** Certificate of Samuel Jack, Col., April 5, 1784. Warrant 674.

**MORGAN, JEREMIAH.** Certificate of Elijah Clarke, Col., April 19, 1784. Warrant 1343.

**MORGAN, JESSE.** Certificate of John Twiggs, Brig. Gen., April 6, 1784. 2d certificate as refugee soldier, Wm. Candler, Col. Refugee Regt. Petitioner prays 500 acres in Washington Co.

**MORGAN, JOHN.** Certificate of Elijah Clarke, Col., Feb. 2, 1784. Petitioner prays 287½ acres in Franklin Co. Warrant 636. 2d certificate of Elijah Clarke, Col., Feb. 2, 1784. Petitioner prays 287½ acres in Franklin Co. Petitioner upon oath prays head rights of 200 acres in Franklin Co., and gives power of attorney to draw his bounties to Richard Benton of Mecklenburg Co., Va.

**MORGAN, LUKE.** Certificate of Elijah Clarke, Col., Feb. 2, 1784. Petitioner prays bounty in Washington Co.

**MORGAN, MALACHIA.** Certificate as refugee soldier, Elijah Clarke, Col., Jan. 10, 1784. Petitioner prays bounty in Washington Co. Warrant 1241.

**MORGAN, STEPHEN.** Certificate of James Jack, Lieut. Col., Sep. 20, 1784. Petitioner prays 250 acres in Washington Co.

**MORGAN, WILLIAM.** Certificate as refugee soldier, Elijah Clarke, Col., April 8, 1784. Petitioner prays 250 acres in Washington Co. Warrant 1342.

**MURPHEY, MILLS.** Certificate as refugee soldier, John Twiggs, B. G., Dec. 29, 1783. Petitioner prays bounty in Washington Co. Warrant 1357. 2d certificate of John Twiggs, B. G., Feb. 2, 1783.

**McMURPHY, DANIEL.** Certificate as refugee soldier, John Twiggs, B. G., Jan. 27, 1784. Ex. order for bounty upon 2d certificate of John Twiggs, B. G. (missing), Jan. 29, 1784. Petitioner prays 575 acres in Washington Co.

**MEYERS, THOMAS.** Certificate of John Baker, Col., Mar. 18, 1784. Warrant 1306.

**MOCOCK, HENRY.** Certificate of Elijah Clarke, Col., April 7, 1784. Petitioner prays bounty in Washington Co. Warrant 669.

**MADKINS, WILLIAM.** Petition for 250 acres in Franklin Co. as per certificate annexed (missing).

**MOSELY, WILLIAM H.** Certificate as refugee soldier, Elijah Clarke, Col., April 8, 1784. Warrant 1311.

**MAGAR, OWEN.** Certificate of Jas. McNeil, Col., April 5, 1784. Petitioner prays bounty in Washington Co.

**MONTGOMERY, JAMES.** Certificate as refugee soldier, James McCoy, Captain, July 1, 1784. Petitioner prays 575 acres in Washington Co.

**MIDDLETON, WILLIAM.** Certificate of Elijah Clarke, Col., April 7, 1784. Petitioner prays bounty in Franklin Co.

**METCALF, DANZA.** Certificate of Samuel Jack, Col., Liberty Co., July 27, 1778.

**MOSELEY, WILLIAM.** Ex. order for bounty on certificate of Col. Elijah Clarke (missing), Mar. 25, 1784. Petitioner prays 500 acres in Washington Co.

**MAINER, JOHN.** Certificate of Elijah Clarke, Col., Feb. 2, 1784.

**MIDDLETON, CAPT. HATTON.** Certificate of Samuel Jack, Col., Mar. 26, 1784. Warrant 224.

**MORRISON, JOHN.** Petition for 460 acres in reserve as per certificate annexed (missing). Also prays head rights of 750 acres in Washington Co. for self and 11 others in family.

**MAY, JOSEPH.** Certificate of Elijah Clarke, Col., Feb. 2, 1784.

**MIMS, JOHN.** Certificate of Elijah Clarke, Col., Feb. 2, 1784.

**MOREMOUTH, JOSEPH.** Certificate of Elijah Clarke, Col., Feb. 2, 1784.

**MASH, THOMAS.** Certificate of Elijah Clarke, Col., Feb. 2, 1784. Warrant 657.

CERTIFICATES OF SERVICE IN AMERICAN REVOLUTION.  133

McBRIDE, EDWARD. Enlisted as a soldier in 2d Battalion Continental troops for the State of Georgia, to serve 3 years, and faithfully performed his duty until he was made a prisoner of war by the British troops, S. Gilbert, Brig. Gen., Oct. 29, 1784. Countersigned by Capt. John Morrison. Petitioner prays 230 acres in the reserve.

McGEE, THOMAS. Certificate of Elijah Clarke, Col., Feb. 2, 1784. Petitioner prays 287½ acres in Washington Co. Warrant 1317.

McGEE, LEWIS. Certificate as refugee soldier, John Twiggs, B. G., Mar. 22, 1784. Petitioner prays bounty in Washington Co. Warrant 1316.

McGEE, CAPT. HUGH. Ex. order for bounty as per certificate of John Twiggs, B. G. (missing), Feb. 6, 1784. Warrant 902. Certificate of Col. Jas. Martin that he is entitled to 500 acres as a soldier and 200 acres as a citizen soldier. Petitioner prays bounty in Washington Co.

McNELLY, DANIEL. Certificate of Samuel Jack, Col., April 3, 1784. Warrant 667. 2d certificate as refugee soldier, John Twiggs, B. G., Mar. 29, 1784. Warrant 1329.

McNELLY, HUGH. Certificate of John Twiggs, B. G., Mar. 30, 1784. Petitioner prays 287½ acres in Washington Co.

McCLENDON, JOSEPH. Certificate of Elijah Clarke, Col., Jan. 29, 1785. Warrant 665.

McCLENDON, TRAVIS. Certificate as refugee soldier, Elijah Clarke, Col., April 8, 1784. Petitioner prays 575 acres in Washington Co. Warrant 1310.

McCARTEY, DANIEL. Certificate of Gb. Lee, Col., Mar. 5, 1784. Petitioner prays 287½ acres in Washington Co.

McCARTHY, DANIEL. Certificate as refugee soldier, Elijah Clarke, Col., April 6, 1784. Warrant 1359.

McCARTEY, JOHN. Certificate of Gb. Lee, Col., Feb. 23, 1784. Petitioner prays 287½ acres in Washington Co.

McCARTY, ADJUTANT JOHN. Certificate as refugee soldier, Wm. Candler, Col., Refugee Regt. Warrant 1360.

McCARTHY, DRUM MAJOR JOHN. Certificate of John Stewart, Col., 1st Batt. Minute Men, April 22, 1784. Warrant 273.

McCORMICK, BENJAMIN. Certificate of Elijah Clarke, Col., Feb. 2, 1784. Warrant 1331. 2d certificate of Elijah Clarke, Col., Feb. 2, 1784. Petitioner prays 287½ acres in Washington Co.

McCORMICK, JOHN. Certificate of Elijah Clarke, Col., Feb. 2, 1784. Petitioner prays bounty in Washington Co.

ROSTER OF THE REVOLUTION.

**McCORMICK, JOSEPH.** Certificate of Elijah Clarke, Col., Feb. 2, 1784. Petitioner prays 287½ acres in Washington Co. Warrant 1332. 2d certificate of Elijah Clarke, Col., Feb. 2, 1784. Petitioner prays 287½ acres in Washington Co.

**McCORMICK, THOMAS.** Certificate of Elijah Clarke, Col., Feb. 2, 1784. Warrant 1330. 2d certificate of Elijah Clarke, Col., Feb. 2, 1784. Petitioner prays 287½ acres in Washington Co.

**McDUFFY, JOHN.** Certificate of Greenberry Lee, Col., Feb. 23, 1784. Petitioner prays 287½ acres in Washington Co.

**McCALL, THOMAS.** Certificate as refugee soldier, Elijah Clarke, Col., May 22, 1784. Warrant 1320. 2d certificate of Elijah Clarke, Col., April 7, 1784. Petitioner prays 575 acres in Franklin Co.

**McMAN, MATTHEW.** Certificate of Elijah Clarke, Col., April 3, 1784. Warrant 676.

**McMURRY, DAVID.** Certificate of Elijah Clarke, Col., Feb. 2, 1784.

**McMURRY, WILLIAM.** Certificate of Elijah Clarke, Col., Sep. 8, 1784. Warrant 643.

**MARTIN, LIEUT. BARTLETT.** Certificate of Samuel Jack, Col., April 26, 1784. Petitioner prays bounty in Franklin Co. Warrant 261.

**McCELVEY, WILLIAM.** Certificate of Elijah Clarke, Col., Oct. 10, 1784. Warrant 673.

**McKINNEY, HENRY.** Petition for 287½ acres in Washington Co. as per certificate annexed (missing).

**McMULLEN, PATRICK.** Certificate of Samuel Jack, Col., June 4, 1784. Petitioner prays bounty in Washington Co. Warrant 661.

**McBURNETT, DANIEL.** Certificate of Elijah Clarke, Col., Feb. 2, 1784.

**McGARY, EDWARD.** Certificate of Elijah Clarke, Col., July 16, 1784. Petitioner prays bounty in Franklin Co.

**McMATT, JOSEPH.** Certificate of James Jackson, Lt. Col., July 23, 1784. Petitioner prays bounty in Franklin Co.

### N.

**NIX, GEORGE.** Certificate of 3 years' service of George Nix and James McDowell, Francis Tennill, Lieut., Feb. 21, 1784. Petitioner prays 230 acres in Washington Co.

**NASH, CAPT. CLEMENT.** Petition of Mary, widow of Captain Clement Nash, of the Ga. Line, for 690 acres in the reserve, with power of attorney to Capt. Francis Tennill to draw bounty. Warrant 23.

# CERTIFICATES OF SERVICE IN AMERICAN REVOLUTION. 135

**NAIL, BENJAMIN.** Certificate as Sergeant, Elijah Clarke, Col., Sep. 10, 1784. Warrant 1364.

**NAIL, HENRY.** Certificate of Elijah Clarke, Col., Feb. 2, 1784. Warrant 1361.

**NAIL, CAPT. JOSEPH.** Certificate of Elijah Clarke, Col., Feb. 2, 1784. Petitioner prays bounty in Franklin Co. Warrant 905. 2d certificate of Elijah Clarke, Col., Feb. 2, 1784. Warrant 1363.

**NEIDLINGER, JOHN GODLEIB.** Certificate as refugee soldier, Jenkins Davis, Lt. Co., Effingham Co. Regt., Jan. 20, 1784. Warrant 1368.

**NEILLY, JOHN.** Certificate of Samuel Jack, Col., April 14, 1784. Petitioner prays bounty in Franklin Co. Warrant 685.

**NAIL, REUBEN.** Certificate of Elijah Clarke, Col., Feb. 2, 1784. Warrant 1362.

**NETTLES, ELISHA.** Certificate of Elijah Clarke, Col., April 6, 1784. Petitioner prays bounty in Washington Co. Warrant 684.

**NELSON, JAMES.** Certificate of Samuel Jack, Col., May 17, 1784. Warrant 672.

**NELSON, JOHN.** Certificate as refugee soldier, John Twiggs, B. G., Mar. 16, 1784. Petitioner prays 287½ acres Franklin Co. Warrant 1365.

**NELSON, WILLIAM.** Certificate of Elijah Clarke, Col., April 7, 1784. Petitioner prays 287½ acres in Franklin Co. Warrant 679.

**NEPHEW, JAMES.** Certificate of John Baker, Col., Liberty Co. Regt., Mar. 18, 1784. Warrant 1366.

**NESLER, ADAM.** Certificate as refugee soldier, Jenkins Davis, Lt. Col., June 23, 1784. Warrant 1367.

**NEWSOME, SOLOMON.** Certificate of Elijah Clarke, Col., Feb. 2, 1784. Petitioner prays bounty in Washington Co. Also prays head rights of 600 acres in Washington Co. for self, wife, 9 children and 7 negroes.

**NEWMAN, JOHN.** Certificate of 3 years' service in 2d Ga. Regiment, Continental Army, and lost his arm in the service. Francis Tennill, Lieut. April 27, 1784. Countersigned, June 4, 1784, Samuel Elbert, Brig. Gen. Warrant 180.

**NEVEL, THOMAS.** Certificate of Elijah Clarke, Col., Feb. 2, 1784. Warrant 683.

**NICHOLSON, BENJAMIN.** Certificate of Elijah Clarke, Col., Jan. 3, 1785. Warrant 682.

**NICKSON, ARCHIBALD.** Certificate of Elijah Clarke, Col., Jan. 25, 1785. Warrant 680.

**NORWOOD, RICHARD.** Certificate of Elijah Clarke, Col., May 6, 1784. Petitioner prays 287½ acres in Franklin Co. Warrant 677.

**NUGAN, MICHAEL.** Certificate of J. Pannill, Lt. Col., Sept. 27, 1784. Petitioner prays bounty in forks of Oconee river. Warrant 181.

**NEWMAN, WILLIAM.** Certificate of Samuel Jack, Col., April 6, 1784. Warrant 681.

**NETTLES, ELISHA.** Certificate of Elijah Clarke, Col., April 6, 1784. Petitioner prays 250 acres in Washington Co. Warrant 684.

O.

**OATES, RICHARD.** Certificate of Elijah Clarke, Col., April 20, 1784. Petitioner prays 287½ acres in Washington Co.

**OATES, JEREMIAH.** Certificate of Jas. McNeil, Col., Mar. 15, 1784. Petitioner prays 250 acres in Washington Co. Also prays he had a right of 250 acres in Washington Co. for self, wife, 2 children and 2 negroes.

**OAKMAN, WILLIAM.** Certificate of 3 years' service as Fife Major in 2d Ga. Continental Regt., Francis Tennill, Lieut. in 2d Regt., Jan. 3, 1784.

**O'BRYANT, DUNKIN.** Certificate of Elijah Clarke, Col., April 6, 1784. Petitioner prays 287½ acres in Washington Co. Warrant 687.

**O'BRYAN, JAMES.** Certificate of 3 years' service in 3d Ga. Battalion, Cont. Line, Nathaniel Pierce, Lieut., Nov. 21, 1783. Endorsed by Lachlan McIntosh, Brig. Gen.

**O'BARN, WILLIAM.** Certificate of Elijah Clarke, Col., Oct. 16, 1784. Warrant 686.

**O'DAIR, WILLIAM.** Certificate of Elijah Clarke, Col., Feb. 2, 1784.

**ODAM, URIAH.** Certificate of Elijah Clarke, Col., April 7, 1784. Petitioner prays 287½ acres in Washington Co. Warrant 688.

**ODINGFIELD, CHARLES.** Certificate that he served under me, L. Hall. Petitioner transfers his right to Maj. Richard Call.

**OFFUTT, EZEKIEL.** Certificate as refugee soldier, Wm. Candler, Col., Refugee Regt. Warrant 906. 2d certificate of Gb. Lee, Col., May 17, 1784. Petitioner prays 575 acres in Washington Co.

**OFFUTT, NATHANIEL.** Certificate as refugee soldier, Wm. Candler, Col., Refugee Regt. Warrant 1372.

**OFFUTT, JESSE.** Certificate as refugee soldier, Wm. Candler, Col. Petitioner prays 287½ acres in Washington Co. Warrant 1373.

**O'HEARN, JOSIAH.** Certificate as refugee soldier into North Carolina, John Twiggs, B. G., Nov. 27, 1783. Petitioner prays 287½ acres in Washington Co. Warrant 1374.

**OFFUTT, JOHN.** Certificate of Benj. Few, Col., July 20, 1784.

# CERTIFICATES OF SERVICE IN AMERICAN REVOLUTION.

**OLIVER, JOHN.** Certificate of Elijah Clarke, Col., April 14, 1784.

**OLIVER, JAMES.** Certificate of Benj. Few, Col. Petitioner prays bounty in Franklin Co. Also prays 1,000 acres in Washington Co. on head rights for self, wife and 4 children.

**OLIVER, PETER.** Certificate of Elijah Clarke, Col., Feb. 2, 1784. Petitioner prays 287½ acres in Washington Co.

**O'NEAL, LIEUT. AXAM.** Certificate of Elijah Clarke, Col., Feb. 2, 1784. Petitioner prays 287½ acres in Washington Co.

**O'NEAL, JOHN.** Certificate of Elijah Clarke, Col., Feb. 2, 1784.

**ORNSBY, DANIEL.** Certificate of 3 years' service as Fife Major, 2d Ga. Continental Battalion, and died in service, J. Pannill, Lt. Col., April 10, 1784. He further certifies that Daniel Ornsby left a daughter Isabel, now living with her mother, Mary Berry, and that Mary Berry—now so-called—was his wife before and at the time of his death. Warrant 184.

**OWENS, THOMAS.** Certificate of Elijah Clarke, Col., April 7, 1784. Petitioner prays 250 acres in Washington Co.

**OUTLAW, EDWARD.** Certificate as refugee soldier, John Twiggs, B. G., Feb. 16, 1784. Warrant 1370.

**OUTLAW, LEUDOVICK.** Certificate as refugee soldier, who died on retreat from Augusta to Savannah, and left one son, James Outlaw, who is entitled to his bounty. John Twiggs, B. G., Feb. 16, 1784. Warrant 1371.

**OWENS, ROBERT.** Certificate of Elijah Clarke, Col., Feb. 2, 1784. Petitioner prays 287½ acres in Washington Co. Warrant 1369.

**O'HERN, JOSIAH.** Certificate as refugee soldier, John Twiggs, B. G., Nov. 27, 1784. Petitioner prays 287½ acres in Washington Co.

**OUTLAW, EDWARD.** 2d certificate of John Twiggs, B. G., Feb. 13, 1784.

**OWENS, EPHRAIM.** Certificate of Greenberry Lee, Col., April 26, 1784. Petitioner prays bounty in Washington Co.

**OAKMAN, WILLIAM.** Ex. order for bounty as Fife Major in Ga. Line as per certificate of Gen. McIntosh (see above). Petitioner prays 250 acres in Washington Co. Warrant 683.

**OFFUTT, JOHN.** Certificate of Benj. Few, Col., July 2, 1784.

**O'NEAL, NATHANIEL.** Ex. order for bounty upon certificate of Col. Elijah Clarke (missing), Feb. 2, 1784. Petitioner prays bounty in Washington Co.

**OWENS, EPHRAIM.** Certificate of Greenberry Lee, Col., April 26, 1784. Petitioner prays bounty in Washington Co.

**OWENS, THOMAS.** Certificate of Elijah Clarke, Col., April 7, 1784. Petitioner prays 250 acres in Franklin Co.

## P.

**PALMER, GEORGE.** Certificate of John Twiggs, B. G., Feb. 19, 1784. Petitioner prays 287½ acres in Washington Co.

**PALMER, JOHN.** Certificate of Elijah Clarke, Col., April 3, 1784. Petitioner prays 575 acres in Washington Co. 2d certificate as refugee soldier, Elijah Clarke, Col., Feb. 2, 1784. Warrants 702 and 1392. 2d endorsement of Gov. upon certificate of Maj. Francis Boykin, Jan 29, 1784. Petitioner prays 250 acres in Washington Co.

**PALMER, JOHN.** Certificate of Jas. McNeil, Col., Mar. 19, 1784. Petitioner prays 287½ acres in Washington Co.

**PALMER, SOLOMON.** Certificate of Elijah Clarke, Col., Feb., 2, 1784. Petitioner prays 287½ acres in Washington Co. 2d certificate of Elijah Clarke, Col., April 6, 1784. Petitioner prays 287½ acres in Washington Co.

**PAULK, MICAJAH.** Ex. order for bounty upon certificate of Col. Jas. McNeil, Feb. 20, 1784 (missing). Petitioner prays 287½ acres in Washington Co.

**PARKER, ALLEN.** Certificate of E. Clarke, Col., Jan. 25, 1785.

**PARKER, GEORGE.** Certificate of E. Clarke, Col., Feb. 1, 1784.

**PARKER, JAMES.** Certificate of Elijah Clarke, Col., Jan. 25, 1785.

**PARKER, JOHN.** Certificate of James Jackson, Lt. Col., Ga. State Legion, April 6, 1784. Petitioner prays bounty in Washington Co.

**PARKER, JOSEPH.** Certificate of Gb. Lee, Col., Feb. 23, 1784.

**PARKER, WILLIAM.** Bringing good character from N. C., prays 550 acres in Washington Co. as head rights on self, wife and six children (not a bounty).

**PATILLO, JOHN.** Petition of his heirs for 230 acres in reserve upon certificate annexed (missing), petition signed by James, son of John Patillo, late of Brunswick Co., Va., Jan. 31, 1785. Warrant 190.

**PULLIAM, WILLIAM.** Ex. order for bounty as refugee soldier as per certificate of Col. Clarke, Feb. 25, 1784 (missing). Petitioner prays 287½ acres in Franklin Co. Warrant 1399.

**PATTON, THOMAS.** Certificate of Elijah Clarke, Col., May 18, 1784. Petitioner prays 287½ acres in Franklin Co. Warrant 606.

**PANNILL, JOSEPH.** Certificate as captain in 2d Ga. Continental Regt. on 20th Aug., 1776; major on Sep. 17, 1777, and Lt. Col., in 4th Ga., May 27, 1778. Lachlan McIntosh, Maj. Gen., Feb. 1, 1784. Warrant 18.

**PEAL, JOHN.** Certificate as refugee soldier, John Twiggs, B. G., April 12, 1784. Warrant 1395.

**PAINE, SAMUEL.** Certificate of Elijah Clarke, Col., April 1, 1784. Petitioner prays bounty in Franklin Co. 2d certificate of Samuel Jack, Col., April 6, 1784. Petitioner prays bounty in Washington Co. Warrant 689.

**PAYNE, WILLIAM.** Certificate of Gb. Lee, Col., April 20, 1784. Petitioner prays 287½ acres in Washington Co.

**PAXTON, LIEUT. WILLIAM.** Certificate of Elijah Clarke, Col., April 6, 1784. Petitioner prays 400 acres in Washington Co. Warrant 262.

**PARKER, LIEUT. JOHN.** Certificate of Elijah Clarke, Col., Feb. 2, 1784. Warrant 930.

**PARKS, CHARLES, JR.** Certificate of Elijah Clarke, Col., Feb. 2, 1784. Petitioner prays bounty in Washington Co.

**PARKS, CHARLES, SR.** Certificate of Elijah Clarke, Col., April 24, 1784. Petitioner prays 287½ acres in Washington Co.

**PARKS, LIEUT. JOHN.** Certificate of Elijah Clarke, Col., Feb. 2, 1784.

**PEARCE, JOHN.** Certificate as soldier in 1st Battalion, Elijah Clarke, Col., April 17, 1784. Warrant 699. 2d certificate of Elijah Clarke, Col., Feb. 11, 1784. Warrant 698.

**PEARCE, WILLIAM.** Certificate as soldier, 1st Battalion, Ga. Line, Elijah Clarke, Col., Feb. 11, 1784. Warrant 697. Petitioner prays head rights of 650 acres in Washington Co. on self, wife and 8 negroes.

**PEAVY, ABRAHAM.** Ex. order from Gov. Houstoun for bounty upon personal knowledge of him as a soldier, Jan. 2, 1784.

**PEAVY, DYAL.** Certificate of Jas. McNeil, Col., April 3, 1784. Petitioner prays bounty in Washington Co.

**PEAVY, JOHN.** Certificate of Jas. McNeil, Col., Feb. 2, 1784.

**PEAVY, JOSEPH.** Certificate of Jas. McNeil, Col., Mar. 18, 1784. Petitioner prays bounty in Washington Co.

**PEAVY, PETER.** Certificate of Jas. McNeil, Col., Feb. 22, 1784. Petitioner prays 287½ acres in Washington Co.

**PEAK, JOHN.** Certificate of Jas. McNeil, Col., Feb. 2, 1784. Petitioner prays bounty in Washington Co.

**PENNINGTON, STEPHEN.** Certificate of Elijah Clarke, Col., June 12, 1784.

**PENNINGTON, THOMAS.** Certificate of John Twiggs, B. G., Mar. 15, 1784. Petitioner prays 287½ acres in Washington Co.

**PERRY, ISAAC.** Certificate of Elijah Clarke, Col., Feb. 2, 1784. Petitioner prays bounty in Washington Co. Also prays head rights of 350 acres in Washington Co. for self, wife, 2 children and 10 negroes.

**PERRIT, WILLIAM.** Certificate of Gb. Lee, Col., Feb. 23, 1784.

**PERKINS, ABRAHAM.** Certificate of Greenberry Lee, Col., Feb. 23, 1784.

**PERKINS, BENJAMIN.** Certificate of Elijah Clarke, Col., Jan. 3, 1785. 2d certificate of Elijah Clarke, Col., Feb. 2, 1784.

**PERKINS, ELISHA.** Certificate of Elisha Clarke, Col., Feb. 2, 1784.

**PERKINS, JOHN.** Certificate of Gb. Lee, Col., Feb. 23, 1784. Petitioner prays 287½ acres in Washington Co. 2d certificate of Gb. Lee, Col., Mar. 11, 1784. Petitioner prays bounty in Washington Co.

**PERKINS, RICHARD.** Certificate of Gb. Lee, Col., April 10, 1784. Petitioner prays 287½ acres in Franklin Co.

**PERKINS, PETER.** Certificate of Gb. Lee, Col., Mar. 30, 1784. Petitioner prays 287½ acres in Washington Co.

**PETITE, BENJAMIN.** Certificate of John Habersham, Capt., and Jos. Habersham, Colonel, 1st Batt., Cont. Troops of Ga., May 22, 1777. This man, when taking the oath, stated that he was a tailor and from Pyerdy, France.

**PETTY, WILLIAM.** Certificate as soldier in 1st Battalion, Elijah Clarke, Col., April 6, 1784. Petitioner prays 287½ acres in Washington Co. Warrant 704.

**PUTNALL, CHRISTOPHER.** Certificate of Elijah Clarke, Col., Feb. 2, 1784. Petitioner prays 287½ acres in Washington Co.

**PENDAL, JOHN.** Certificate of Elijah Clarke, Col., May 24, 1784. Petitioner prays 287½ acres in Franklin Co.

**PETERS, JOHN.** Certificate of Elijah Clarke, Col., Feb. 2, 1784.

**PETERS, JOSIAH.** Certificate of Elijah Clarke, Col., Feb. 2, 1784.

**PHELPS, LIEUT. DAVID.** Certificate of Elijah Clarke, Col., Feb. 2, 1784. Warrant 1380. 2d certificate of Elijah Clarke, Col., Feb. 2, 1784. Petitioner prays 287½ acres in Washington Co.

**PHELPS, SERGEANT DAVID.** Certificate of Elijah Clarke, Col., April 7, 1784. Petitioner prays 345 acres in Washington Co. Warrant 693.

**PITMAN, JOHN.** Certificate of Gb. Lee, Col., Mar. 26, 1784. Petitioner prays 287½ acres in Washington Co.

**PHILLIPS, BURIEL.** Certificate of Elijah Clarke, Col., Dec. 10, 1784. Petitioner prays bounty in Washington Co.

**PHILLIPS, DEMPSEY.** Certificate of Elijah Clarke, Col., Feb. 2, 1784.

**PHILLIPS, DEMPSEY.** Certificate of Greenberry Lee, Col., Feb. 23, 1784. 2d certificate of Greenberry Lee, Col., Mar. 25, 1784. Petitioner prays two bounties of 287½ acres each, one in Washington Co. and one in Franklin Co.

**PHILLIPS, HILLERY.** Certificate of John Twiggs, B. G., Mar. 6, 1784. Petitioner prays 287½ acres in Washington Co.

**PHILLIPS, ISHAM.** Certificate of Gb. Lee, Col., April 26, 1784. Petitioner prays bounty in Washington Co.

**PHILLIPS, JOSEPH.** Certificate of Elijah Clarke, Col., Feb. 2, 1784. Warrant 1385. 2d certificate of Elijah Clarke, Col., Feb. 2, 1784. Casander, widow of Joseph Phillips, prays that a warrant issue to her son, Isham Phillips, for 575 acres in Washington Co.

**PHILLIPS, JOEL.** Certificate of Elijah Clarke, Col., Feb. 2, 1784.

**PHILLIPS, JOEL, JR.** Certificate of Elijah Clarke, Col., Feb. 2, 1784. 2d certificate as soldier in Minute Men, Elijah Clarke, Col., Nov. 16, 1784. Warrant 694.

**PHILLIPS, JOSH.** Certificate as refugee soldier (missing), with Ex. order for bounty, Mar. 25, 1784. Warrant 1379.

**PHILLIPS, JOSIAH.** Certificate of Elijah Clarke, Col. Petitioner prays 287½ acres in Washington Co.

**PHILLIPS, JOHN.** Certificate of Elijah Clarke, Col., Jan. 3, 1785. Warrant 696.

**PHILLIPS, REUBEN.** Certificate as refugee soldier, Elijah Clarke, Col., April 8, 1784. Petitioner prays 575 acres in Washington Co.

**PHILLIPS, WILLIAM, SR.** Certificate of Elijah Clarke, Col., Feb. 2, 1784. Wm. Phillips, Sr., of Amherst Co., Va., makes oath and prays head rights of 200 acres in Washington Co.

**PHILLIPS, WILLIAM.** Certificate of Elijah Clarke, Col., Feb. 2, 1784. Petitioner prays bounty in Washington Co. 2d certificate of Elijah Clarke, Col., Feb. 2, 1784. Petitioner also prays head rights of 300 acres in Franklin Co. on self, wife and one child.

**PHILLIPS, JOEL, SR.** Certificate of Elijah Clarke, Col., Feb. 2, 1784. Petitioner prays 575 acres in Washington Co.

**PHILLIPS, JOEL, JR.** Certificate of Elijah Clarke, Col., Feb. 2, 1784. Petitioner prays 575 acres in Washington Co.

**PHILLIPS, MARK.** Certificate of Elijah Clarke, Col., Feb. 2, 1784. Warrant 1378. 2d certificate of Elijah Clarke, Col., Feb. 2, 1784. Petitioner prays 575 acres in Franklin Co.

**PHILLIPS, REUBEN.** Certificate of Elijah Clarke, Col., Feb. 2, 1784. Warrant 1384. 2d certificate of Elijah Clarke, Col., April 8, 1784. Petitioner prays 575 acres in Washington Co.

PHILLIPS, SAMUEL. Certificate of John Twiggs, B. G., Feb. 2, 1784. Petitioner prays bounty in Washington Co. 2d certificate of Elijah Clarke, Col., Jan. 3, 1785. Warrant 695.

PHILLIPS, WILLIAM. Certificate of Elijah Clarke, Col., Feb. 2, 1784. Warrant 1382.

PHILLIPS, WILLIAM (son of Zachariah). 2d certificate of Elijah Clarke, Col., Feb. 2, 1784. Petitioner prays 575 acres in Washington Co. William Phillips, a citizen of Virginia, prays head rights of 800 acres in Franklin Co. for self and 12 others in family. Granted May 26, 1784. Warrant 1383.

PHILLIPS, ZACHARIAH. Certificate of Elijah Clarke, Col., Feb. 2, 1784. Warrant 907. 2d certificate to Capt. Zachariah Phillips, Elijah Clarke, Col., Feb. 2, 1784. Petitioner prays 287½ acres in Washington Co.

PHILLIPS, ZACHARIAH. Certificate of Elijah Clarke, Col., Feb. 2, 1784. Petitioner prays 575 acres in Washington Co. Warrant 1377. Capt. Zachariah Phillips prays head rights of 400 acres in Washington Co. for self, wife, five children and 2 negroes.

PAINE, SAMUEL, SR. Certificate of Greenberry Lee, Col., Mar. 11, 1784. Petitioner prays bounty in Washington Co.

PITMAN, PHILIP. Certificate of Gb. Lee, Col., Feb. 23, 1784. Petitioner prays 250 acres in Washington Co.

PITMAN, JOHN. Ex. order for bounty upon certificate of Col. Gb. Lee (missing), Feb. 25, 1784. Petitioner prays 287½ acres in Washington Co.

PLUMOR, JOSEPH. Certificate as refugee soldier, John Baker, Col., Mar. 15, 1784. Petitioner prays 250 acres in Washington Co. Warrant 1393.

PINSON, ISAAC. Certificate of Gb. Lee, Col., Feb. 20, 1784.

PAULK, MICAJAH. Certificate of Jas. McNeil, Col., Feb. 2, 1784.

POTTS, JOHN. Petition for bounty as soldier in Minute Men as per certificate annexed (missing).

PERRETT, ROBERT. Certificate of Elijah Clarke, Col., April 20, 1784. Petitioner prays 575 acres in Washington Co.

PORTER, BENJAMIN. Petition for bounty as Major 2d Ga. Continental Battalion. Prays 920 acres in reserve. Granted May 24, 1784. Warrant 22.

PORTER, BENJAMIN. Certificate of Elijah Clarke, Col., April 9, 1894. Petitioner prays 637 acres in Washington Co. Granted 575 acres as citizen and soldier. Petitioner also prays head rights of 1,000 acres in Washington Co., upon oath that he has one white and six negroes in this State, and nine other negroes in the State of Va.

CERTIFICATES OF SERVICE IN AMERICAN REVOLUTION.    143

**PORTER, JOHN.** Ex. order for bounty upon certificate of Col. E. Clarke (missing), Mar. 25, 1784.

**PORTER, JOSIAH.** Power of attorney from Josiah Porter of Camden Dist., S. C., to John Gill, to receive his bounty of 250 acres for Minute service in Michael Dickson's Co., Colonel Jack's Battalion.

**PORTER, LIEUT. THOMAS.** Petition for bounty upon certificate annexed (missing). Granted.

**POWELL, BENJAMIN.** Certificate of Elijah Clarke, Col., April 9, 1784. 2d certificate of Elijah Clarke, Col., Jan. 3, 1785. Petitioner prays bounty in Washington Co. Warrant 670.

**POWELL, CADER.** Certificate of Elijah Clarke, Col., Feb. 2, 1784. Petitioner prays 250 acres in Washington Co.

**POWELL, GEORGE.** Certificate of Elijah Clarke, Col., April 20, 1784. Petitioner prays 287½ acres in Washington Co. 2d certificate of Elijah Clarke, Col., Sep. 8, 1784. Petitioner prays 287½ acres in Franklin Co.

**POWELL, JOSHUA.** Certificate of Elijah Clarke, Col., Jan. 3, 1785. Warrant 692.

**POWELL, JOSIAH.** Ex. order for bounty upon certificate of Col. John Baker, Feb. 22, 1784 (missing). Petitioner prays 287½ acres in Washington Co. Warrant 1375.

**POWELL, JAMES.** Certificate that he was a prisoner and subsequently a refugee soldier, John Baker, Col., Aug. 19, 1784. Warrant 1376. 2d certificate of John Baker, Col., Feb. 21, 1784. Petitioner prays 575 acres in Washington Co.

**POWELL, LEWIS.** Certificate of Jas. McNeil, Col., Feb. 2, 1784. Petitioner prays 287½ acres in Washington Co.

**POWELL, LEWIS.** Certificate of Elijah Clarke, Col., Jan. 29, 1785. Petitioner prays 287½ acres in Washington Co. 2d certificate of Elijah Clarke, Col., Feb. 16, 1784. Warrant 691.

**POWELL, MOSES.** Certificate of Elijah Clarke, Col., Feb. 2, 1784. Petitioner prays bounty of 250 acres in Washington Co. 2d certificate of Elijah Clarke, Col., April 7, 1784. Petitioner prays 287½ acres in Washington Co.

**PRICE, LIEUT. JOHN.** Certificate as refugee soldier, Elijah Clarke, Col., Mar. 2, 1784. Warrant 1389. 2d certificate to Lieut. John Price, John Cunningham, Lt. Col., Aug. 4, 1784. Petitioner prays 460 acres in Franklin Co. Warrant 934.

**PRATHER, EDWARD.** Certificate of Elijah Clarke, Col., Mar. 20, 1784. Petitioner prays 250 acres in Washington Co.

**PRATHER, DANIEL.** Certificate of Jas. McNeil, Col., April 22, 1784. Petitioner prays bounty in Franklin Co.

144   ROSTER OF THE REVOLUTION.

**POUNDS, SAMUEL.** Certificate as refugee soldier, Elijah Clarke, Col., April 20, 1784. Petitioner prays 287½ acres in Washington Co. Warrant 1398.

**POUNDS, REUBEN.** Certificate as soldier in 2d Ga. Batt., J. Pannill, Lt. Col., July 12, 1784. Petitioner prays 230 acres in reserve. Warrant 186.

**PULLIAM, JAMES.** Certificate of Elijah Clarke, Col., Feb. 2, 1784. Petitioner prays 287½ acres in Franklin Co.

**PARHAM, RICHARD.** Certificate of Isaac Hicks, Capt., 3d Ga. Battalion, Virginia, Feb. 18, 1783. Also certificate of Ann Ross of Warren Co., N. C., that Wm. Ross is legitimate heir to his brother, Richard Parham. Warrant 189.

**PULLIAM, WILLIAM.** Certificate of Elijah Clarke, Col., Feb. 2, 1784. 2d certificate of Elijah Clarke, Col., Mar. 2, 1784.

**PEW, ELIJAH.** Certificate of Elijah Clarke, Col., Mar. 25, 1784. Petitioner prays bounty in Washington Co.

**PUGH, FRANCIS.** Ex. order for bounty as per certificate of John Twiggs, B. G. (missing). Petitioner prays 287½ acres in Washington Co.

**PUGH, JAMES, JR.** Ex. order for bounty as refugee soldier as per certificate of John Twiggs, B. G., Feb., 1784 (missing). Warrant 1391.

**PUGH, FRANCIS.** 2d certificate of John Twiggs, B. G., Feb. 2, 1784. Petitioner prays 287½ acres in Washington Co.

**PETERS, ELIJAH.** Certificate as refugee soldier, Elijah Clarke, Col., May 16, 1784. Petitioner prays 287½ acres in Washington Co.

**PACE, THOMAS.** Ex. order for bounty. Petitioner prays 287½ acres in Washington Co.

**PERSETT, JOHN.** Certificate as refugee soldier, Elijah Clarke, Col., April 24, 1784. Warrant 1396.

**PEAL, JOHN.** Certificate of John Twiggs, B. G., Mar. 4, 1784. Petitioner prays 287½ acres in Washington Co.

**PERSONS, JONES.** Two certificates of Elijah Clarke, Col., May 17, 1784. Petitioner prays 500 acres in Franklin Co.

**POLK, JOHN.** Ex. order for bounty as per certificate of Jas. McNeil, Col. (missing), Feb. 24, 1784. 2d cretificate of Gb. Lee, Col., Feb. 3, 1784. Petitioner prays 287½ acres in Washington Co.

**PATTISON, GIDEON.** Certificate of Elijah Clarke, Col., April 6, 1784. Petitioner prays 250 acres in Washington Co. 2d certificate as refugee soldier, Elijah Clarke, Col., April 9, 1784. Petitioner prays 250 acres in Washington Co. Warrant 1337.

**PATTISON, LIEUT. GIDEON.** Certificate of Samuel Jack, Col., April 5, 1784. Petitioner prays 460 acres in Washington Co.

## CERTIFICATES OF SERVICE IN AMERICAN REVOLUTION. 145

**PATTERSON, JOHN, JR.** Certificate of John Twiggs, B. G., Feb. 6, 1784. Warrant 1386. 2d certificate as refugee soldier, John Twiggs, B. G., Feb. 6, 1784. Petitioner prays 575 acres in Washington Co.

**PATTERSON, JOHN.** Certificate of John Twiggs, B. G., Feb. 6, 1784. Petitioner prays 287½ acres in Washington Co.

**PATTERSON, ROBERT.** Certificate as refugee soldier, John Twiggs, B. G., Jan. 20, 1784. 2d certificate of John Twiggs, B. G., Feb. 3, 1784. Petitioner prays 287½ acres in Washington Co.

**PATTERSON, ROBERT.** Two certificates of John Twiggs, B. G., Mar. 4, 1784. Petitioner prays 287½ acres in Washington Co. Warrant 1388.

**PATTERSON, JOHN.** Certificate as refugee soldier, Elijah Clarke, Col., Aug. 20, 1784. Petitioner prays 575 acres in Washington Co.

**PATTERSON, WILLIAM.** Certificate of John Twiggs, B. G., Feb. 27, 1784. Petitioner prays 287½ acres in Washington Co.

**PACE, THOMAS.** Certificate of Jas. McNeil, Col., Feb. 21, 1784. 2d certificate—taken prisoner by the British, but finally escaped and renewed service under Col. Jas. Martin, July 26, 1784. Prays two bounties of 287½ acres each in Washington Co.

**PAINE, SAMUEL, SR.** Power of attorney to John Cobb to draw bounty allowed him as a soldier.

**PAYNE, SAMUEL, JR.** Certificate of Gb. Lee, Col., April 20, 1784. Petitioner prays 287½ acres in Washington Co.

**PULLIUM, JOSEPH.** Ex. order for bounty upon certificate of Elijah Clarke, Col., Feb. 15, 1784 (missing). Petitioner prays 287½ acres in Franklin Co.

**PARIS, PETER.** Certificate of Jas. McNeil, Col., Mar. 23, 1784. Petitioner prays bounty in Washington Co. Also prays head rights of 1,000 acres in Washington Co. for self, wife, three children and 12 negroes.

**PITTMAN, TIMOTHY.** Certificate of Gb. Lee, Col., Mar. 26, 1784. Petitioner prays 287½ acres in Washington Co.

**PHINEY, LACHLAN.** Certificate of Elijah Clarke, Col., May 20, 1784. Warrant 1397.

**PUSLEY, DAVID.** This is to certify that David Pusley, Edmond Camp, Machael Jackson, Smith Miller and John Bardd were soldiers in my command, Continental Regt., Light Horse, State of Georgia, Leonard Marbury, Capt., Dec. 24, 1784.

**PORTERRE, SIMON.** Certificate of Elijah Clarke, Col., Jan. 25, 1785. Warrant 700.

**PETERE, BERIEMAN.** Certificate of Elijah Clarke, Col., July 27, 1776.

**POLLARD, ROBERT.** Certificate of Jas. Jackson, Lt. Col., June 23, 1784. Petitioner prays bounty in Washington Co.

**PACE, BARNARD.** Certificate of Elijah Clarke, Col., Feb. 2, 1784. Petitioner prays 287½ acres in Franklin Co.

**PARISH, ROBERT.** Certificate of service as Lieut. in Light Dragoons, Leonard Marbury, Col., Feb. 14, 1785. Warrant 76.

**PITMAN, JOHN.** Certificate of Gb. Lee, Col., Feb. 23, 1784.

**PARTIN, JOHN.** Certificate of Elijah Clarke, Col., Feb. 2, 1784. Petitioner prays bounty in Franklin Co. Warrant 1390. 2d certificate as refugee soldier, Elijah Clarke, Col., Feb. 2, 1784.

**PHINNEY, LACHLAN.** Certificate of Francis Tennill, Lieut., 2d Regt., April 7, 1784. Warrant 188.

**PINSON, WILLIAM.** Certificate of Jas. Jackson, Lt. Col., July 17, 1784. Petitioner prays bounty in Franklin Co.

**PLATTEN, BENJAMIN.** Certificate of Elijah Clarke, Col., Nov. 16, 1784. Warrant 701.

**PERRETT, ROBERT.** Certificate of Gb. Lee, Col., Mar. 30, 1784. Petitioner prays bounty in Washington Co.

**PRICE, JOB.** Certificate as refugee soldier, John Twiggs, B. G., May 25, 1784. Petitioner prays bounty in Franklin Co.

## Q.

**QUEENS, JOHN.** Certificate of Elijah Clarke, Col., Feb. 2, 1784. Petitioner prays 287½ acres in Washington Co.

**QUEEN, WILLIAM.** Certificate of Elijah Clarke, Col. Petitioner prays bounty in Franklin Co.

**QUARLES, PETER.** Certificate of Gb. Lee, Col., May 3, 1784. Petitioner prays bounty in Franklin Co.

**QUARLES, ROGER.** Certificate of Gb. Lee, Col., Feb. 23, 1784. Petitioner prays 287½ acres in Washington Co.

## R.

**RANN, FRANCIS.** Certificate of Elijah Clarke, Col., April 9, 1784. Petitioner prays 250 acres in Washington Co.

**RAGGAN, JOHN.** Ex. order for bounty upon certificate of Elijah Clarke, Col., Feb. 25, 1784 (missing). Petitioner prays 287½ acres in Washington Co. 2d certificate of Elijah Clarke, Col., Feb. 2, 1784.

**RAGGAN, JONATHAN.** Certificate of Elijah Clarke, Col., Feb. 2, 1784. Petitioner prays 287½ acres in Washington Co.

## CERTIFICATES OF SERVICE IN AMERICAN REVOLUTION. 147

**RAGAN, FELIX.** Ex. order to surveyor to lay out plat of 275 acres (two bounties) as per certificate rendered (missing).

**RAGLAND, BENJAMIN.** Certificate of Elijah Clarke, Col., Feb. 2, 1784. Petitioner pray 575 acres in Washington Co.

**RAGLAND, LIEUT. EVAN.** Certificate of Elijah Clarke, Col., Feb. 2, 1784. Warrant 935. 2d certificate as refugee soldier, Elijah Clarke, Col., Feb. 2, 1784. Petitioner prays 575 acres in Washington Co. Also prays 200 acres in head rights for four in family.

**RAMSEY, ISAAC, SR.** Certificate of Gb. Lee, Col., Feb. 23, 1784. Petitioner prays 287½ acres in Washington Co. 2d certificate of Elijah Clarke, Col., Mar. 2, 1784.

**RAMSEY, ISAAC, JR.** Certificate of Elijah Clarke, Col., Mar. 2, 1784. 2d certificate to Isaac Ramsey, Gb. Lee, Col., April 12, 1784. Petitioners, father and son, pray 862 acres in one tract in Washington Co.

**RAMSEY, JOHN, SR.** Certificate of Jas. McNeil, Col., April 27, 1784. Petitioner prays 287½ acres in Washington Co. 2d certificate of Elijah Clarke, Col., June 21, 1784. Petitioner prays 287½ acres in Franklin Co. Warrant 727.

**RAMSEY, JOHN, JR.** Certificate of Jas. Jackson, Col., Ga. State Legion, Mar. 24, 1784. Your petitioner is heir and surviving brother to Samuel Ramsey, who fell fighting for the independence of the country. Prays two bounties of 287½ acres each in Franklin Co.

**RAMSEY, RANDAL, JR.** Certificate of Jas. McNeil, Col., Feb. 2, 1784. Petitioner prays 287½ acres in Washington Co. 2d certificate of Jas. McNeil, Col., Mar. 1, 1784. Petitioner prays 287½ acres in Washington Co.

**RAMSEY, SAMUEL, JR.** I hereby certify that Samuel Ramsey, Jr., served under me as a good and faithful soldier and citizen, and was killed in the service of this State under my command, doing his duty. Jas. Jackson, Col., Mar. 24, 1784.

**RAMSEY, THOMAS.** Certificate of Elijah Clarke, Col., Mar. 2, 1784. 2d certificate of Elijah Clarke, Col., April 7, 1784. Petitioner prays 287½ acres in Washington Co.

**RAMSEY, THOMAS, JR.** Certificate of Gb. Lee, Col., April 22, 1784. Petitioner prays bounty in Washington Co.

**RAMSEY, WILLIAM.** Certificate of Jas. McNeil, Col., Feb. 2, 1784. Petitioner prays 287½ acres in Washington Co.

**RAY, BENJAMIN.** Certificate of Greenberry Lee, Col., April 20, 1784. Petitioner prays 250 acres in Washington Co.

**RAY, GEORGE.** Certificate of Gb. Lee, Col., Feb. 23, 1784. Petitioner prays 250 acres in Washington Co. 2d certificate of Gb. Lee, Col., April 21, 1784.

148   ROSTER OF THE REVOLUTION.

**RAE, JAMES.** Certificate of Jas. McNeil, Col., Mar. 15, 1784. Petitioner prays 287½ acres.

**RAY, JOHN.** Certificate of Benjamin Few, Col., July 20, 1784, on certificate of Capt. James Darnley. Petitioner prays 287½ acres in Washington Co.

**RAY, WILLIAM.** Certificate of Jas. Jackson, Lt. Col., Ga. State Legion, July 30, 1784. Petitioner prays 287½ acres in Washington Co.

**RAY, ZACHARIAH.** Certificate of Gb. Lee, Col., Mar. 11, 1784. Petitioner prays bounty in Washington Co.

**RAY, AMBROSE.** Certificate of Elijah Clarke, Col., Feb. 2, 1784. Warrant 1423.

**ROAN, JAMES.** Certificate of Elijah Clarke, Col., April 9, 1784. Petitioner prays 287½ acres in Washington Co.

**RIGGANS, DARBY.** Certificate of Gb. Lee, Col., Mar. 20, 1784. Petitioner prays bounty in Franklin Co.

**REDDING, GEORGE.** Petition for 287½ acres in Washington Co. as per certificate annexed (missing).

**RIDDLE, WILLIAM.** Certificate of Samuel Jack, Col., Mar. 13, 1784. Petitioner prays 250 acres in Washington Co. Warrant 739.

**RICHARDSON, JOSEPH.** Certificate of Jas. McNeil, Col., Feb. 2, 1784.

**RICHARDSON, MARMADUKE.** Certificate of Jas. McNeil, Col., April 19, 1784. Petitioner prays 287½ acres in Washington Co.

**REEVES, CORPORAL DAVID.** Certificate of Samuel Jack, Col., April 6, 1784. Petitioner prays 250 acres in Franklin Co.

**RICHARDSON, ENOS.** Certificate of Jas. McNeil, Col., Mar. 15, 1784. Petitioner prays 287½ acres in Franklin Co.

**RICHARDSON, TIMOTHY.** Certificate of Jas. McKay, Col., April 7, 1784. Petitioner prays bounty in Washington Co.

**REED, JAMES.** Certificate of John Twiggs, B. G., April 19, 1784. Petitioner prays bounty in Washington Co.

**READ, JOHN.** Certificate of Jas. McNeil, Col., Mar. 15, 1784. Petitioner prays 287½ acres in Washington Co.

**POTTS, JOHN.** Certificate of Samuel Jack, Col., Mar. 13, 1784. Warrant 703.

**PERRETT, ROBERT.** Certificate of Elijah Clarke, Col., Mar. 29, 1784. Warrant 794.

**ROAN, TUDSTALL.** Certificate of Elijah Clarke, Col., Feb. 2, 1784. Petitioner prays 287½ acres in Washington Co.

# CERTIFICATES OF SERVICE IN AMERICAN REVOLUTION.

**REEVES, JAMES.** Certificate of E. Clarke, Col., Nov. 4, 1784. Warrant 731.

**REEVES, SPENCER.** Certificate of Benj. Few, Col., July 17, 1784. Petitioner prays 287½ acres.

**REEVES, THOMAS.** Certificate of Benj. Few, Col., July 20, 1784. Petitioner prays 287½ acres.

**RHODES, JOHN.** Certificate of Jas. McNeil, Col., Mar. 15, 1784. Petitioner prays 287½ acres in Washington Co.

**RICHIE, LIEUT. JOHN.** Certificate of Samuel Jack, Col., Jan. 31, 1784. Warrant 264.

**REED, SAMUEL.** Certificate of John Twiggs, B. G., April 20, 1784. Petitioner prays 287½ acres in Washington Co. Also prays head rights of 900 acres in Washington Co. for self, wife, 7 children and 6 negroes.

**READ, WILLIAM.** This is to certify that Wm. Read was appointed second surgeon of the General Hospital in the Middle District, 9th July, 1778, was promoted to be Hospital Physician, 15th May, 1781, and continued to serve in that capacity to the end of the war. Lachlan McIntosh, Maj. Gen., Feb. 26, 1784. Petitioner prays bounty in forks of the Oconee river. Warrant 38.

**ROGERS, BRITTAIN.** Certificate of Elijah Clarke, Col., Feb. 2, 1784. Petitioner prays 250 acres in Washington Co. Warrant 1410. 2d certificate as refugee soldier, Elijah Clarke, Col., Feb. 2, 1784. Petitioner prays 250 acres in Washington Co.

**ROGERS, DRURY.** Certificate of Elijah Clarke, Col., Feb. 2, 1784. Petitioner prays 250 acres in Washington Co.

**ROGERS, DRURY, JR.** Certificate of Elijah Clarke, Col., Nov. 6, 1784. Petitioner prays 287½ acres in Washington Co.

**ROGERS, DREAD.** Certificate of Elijah Clarke, Col., Feb. 2, 1784. Warrant 1412. 2d certificate of Elijah Clarke, Col., Mar. 25, 1784. Petitioner prays 250 acres in Washington Co.

**ROGERS, EDWARD.** Certificate of Samuel Jack, Col., April 7, 1784. Petitioner prays 287½ acres in Washington Co.

**ROGERS, JEREMIAH.** Certificate of John Twiggs, B. G., Mar. 22, 1784. Petitioner prays bounty in Washington Co.

**ROGERS, JOHN.** Certificate of Elijah Clarke, Col., Feb. 2, 1784. Warrant 1417. 2d certificate of Elijah Clarke, Col., Feb. 2, 1784. Petitioner prays 287½ acres in Washington Co. Also prays 450 acres in Franklin Co. in head rights for self and 5 in family.

**ROGERS, PELEG.** Certificate of Jas. McNeil, Col., Mar. 15, 1784. Petitioner prays 287½ acres in Washington Co. Also prays 650 acres in Washington Co. on head rights for self, wife, 2 children and 6 negroes.

**ROGERS, REUBEN.** Certificate of Elijah Clarke, Col., Feb. 2, 1784. Petitioner prays bounty in Washington Co.

**ROGERS, JOHN** (deceased). Certificate of John Twiggs, B. G., Mar. 24, 1784. Petition of Mary, relict of John Rogers, for 287½ acres in Washington Co.

**ROGERS, SERGEANT WILLIAM.** Certificate of Elijah Clarke, Col., April 20, 1784. Warrant 712.

**ROGERS, WILLIAM.** Certificate of Elijah Clarke, Col., Feb. 2, 1784. Petitioner prays 287½ acres in Washington Co. Warrant 1409.

**ROGAN, FELIX.** Certificate of Elijah Clarke, Col., Feb. 2, 1784. Petitioner prays bounty in Franklin Co. Warrant 1424.

**ROBERSON, ALEXANDER.** Certificate of Nat. Pierre, 2d Lieut., 3d Ga. Cont. Regt., Jan. 13, 1784. Countersigned by Lachlan McIntosh, Maj. Gen. Warrant 192.

**ROBERSON, DAVID, JR.** Certificate of Gb. Lee, Col., April 20, 1784. Petitioner prays bounty in Washington Co.

**ROBINSON, DAVID.** Certificate of E. Clarke, Lt. Col., Jan. 3, 1785. Warrant 717.

**ROBERSON, GEORGE.** Certificate of E. Clarke, Col., Dec. 20, 1784.

**ROBERTSON, JOSEPH.** Certificate of Samuel Jack, Col., Mar. 13, 1784. Warrant 718.

**ROBERTSON, JOHN.** Certificate of Elijah Clarke, Col., April 20, 1784. Petitioner prays 287½ acres in Washington Co.

**ROBERTSON, ARCHIBALD.** Certificate of E. Clarke, Col., Aug. 20, 1784. Petitioner prays bounty in Washington Co.

**ROBERTSON, JOHN** (see above). From South Carolina; prays head rights of 300 acres in Washington Co. for self, wife and one child.

**ROBERSON, SAMUEL.** Certificate of Gb. Lee, Col., Mar. 3, 1784. Petitioner prays bounty in Washington Co.

**ROBESON, SILVANUS.** Certificate of Gb. Lee, Col., Mar. 30, 1784. Petitioner prays bounty in Washington Co.

**ROBERTSON, WILLIAM.** Certificate of John Twiggs, B. G., Mar. 23, 1784. Petitioner prays 287½ acres in Washington Co. 2d certificate of Elijah Clarke, Col., April 20, 1784. Petitioner prays 287½ acres in Washington Co.

**ROBERTSON, ZADOCK.** Of 96 Dist., S. C., certificate as soldier in battalion of Minute Men, Samuel Jack, Col., Mar. 13, 1784. Petitioner prays 250 acres in Washington Co. Warrant 719.

# CERTIFICATES OF SERVICE IN AMERICAN REVOLUTION. 151

**ROSEBOROUGH, GEORGE** (deceased). Certificate of service in 1st Battalion of Minute Men, and fell in defense of this State. Jas. McNeil, Col., Feb. 27, 1784. Warrant 1402.

**ROSEBOROUGH, WILLIAM.** Certificate of Jas. McNeil, Col., April 5, 1784. Petitioner prays 287½ acres in Washington Co.

**REYNOLDS, ABSOLEM.** Certificate as Fifer in 2d Ga. Cont. Regt., Lachlan McIntosh, Bg. Gen., Sep. 3, 1784. Petitioner prays 230 acres in the reserve. Warrant 191.

**REYNOLDS, COLEMAN.** Certificate of Elijah Clarke, Col., Feb. 2, 1784. Warrant 1404. 2d Ex. order for bounty as refugee soldier, Mar. 25, 1784. Petitioner prays 2 warrants, 575 acres, in Washington Co.

**REYNOLDS, GEORGE.** Certificate as refugee soldier, Elijah Clarke, Col., July 29, 1784. Petitioner prays 287½ acres in Washington Co.

**RUNNALS, FREDERICK.** Certificate of Elijah Clarke, Col., Feb. 2, 1784. Petitioner prays 287½ acres in Washington Co.

**RUNNALS, HAMILTON.** Certificate of Elijah Clarke, Col., July 9, 1784. Petitioner prays 287½ acres in Washington Co.

**ROLLING, DAVID.** Certificate of E. Clarke, Lt. Col., Feb. 2, 1784. Warrant 722.

**ROLLING, JOHN, JR.** Certificate of Elijah Clarke, Col., Oct. 10, 1784. Warrant 721.

**ROLLING, JOHN.** Certificate of Elijah Clarke, Col., Feb. 2, 1785. Warrant 720.

**ROQUEMORE, PETER.** Certificate of Elijah Clarke, Col., Feb. 2, 1784. Warrant 737. 2d certificate of Elijah Clarke, Col., April 3, 1784. Petitioner prays 575 acres in Washington Co.

**ROQUEMORE, LIEUT. PETER.** Certificate of Elijah Clarke, Col., Feb. 2, 1784. Warrant 927.

**ROQUEMORE, JAMES.** Certificate of Elijah Clarke, Col., Feb. 2, 1784. Petitioner prays 287½ acres in Washington Co.

**ROCK, JAMES.** Certificate of Elijah Clarke, Col., Feb. 2, 1784. Warrant 729.

**ROSS, JOHN.** Certificate of Elijah Clarke, Col., Feb. 2, 1784.

**ROSE, HENRY.** Certificate of Elijah Clarke, Col., Feb. 2, 1784. Petitioner prays bounty in Franklin Co.

**ROSS, THOMAS, SR.** Certificate of Elijah Clarke, Col., May 20, 1784. Petitioner prays 287½ acres in Franklin Co.

**ROSS, THOMAS.** Certificate of Elijah Clarke, Col., Feb. 2, 1784. Petitioner prays bounty in Franklin Co.

**ROSE, JOHN.** Certificate of Elijah Clarke, Col., Feb. 2, 1784. Petitioner prays bounty in Franklin Co. Warrant 1422. 2d certificate as refugee soldier, Elijah Clarke, Col., April 20, 1784. Petitioner prays 287½ acres in Franklin Co.

**ROSE, WILLIAM.** Certificate of Elijah Clarke, Col., Feb. 2, 1784. Warrant 732.

**RIDING, GEORGE.** Certificate as refugee soldier, John Twiggs, B. G., Feb. 19, 1784. Warrant 1403.

**ROBERTS, FRANCIS.** Certificate of E. Clarke, Col., April 6, 1784. Petitioner prays bounty in Franklin Co. Warrant 716.

**ROBERTS, JAMES.** Certificate as refugee soldier, James McCoy, Col., April 5, 1784. Petitioner prays 250 acres in Washington Co. Warrant 1413.

**ROBERTS, JOHN.** Certificate of Elijah Clarke, Col., Feb. 2, 1784. Petitioner prays 287½ acres in Washington Co. 2d certificate of Elijah Clarke, Col., April 9, 1784. Petitioner prays 287½ acres in Washington Co. Warrant 715.

**ROBERTS, JOHN.** Certificate as refugee soldier, James McCoy, Col., April 5, 1784. Warrant 1414. 2d certificate of James McCoy, Col., April 7, 1784. Petitioner prays 250 acres in Washington Co.

**ROBERTS, JOHN.** Certificate of Gb. Lee, Col., Mar. 11, 1784. Petitioner prays 287½ acres in Washington Co.

**ROBERTS, JONAS.** Certificate of John Twiggs, B. G., April 27, 1784. Petitioner prays bounty in Washington Co.

**ROBERTS, THOMAS.** Certificate of Gb. Lee, Col., Mar. 30, 1784. Petitioner prays 287½ acres in Washington Co.

**ROBERTS, THOMAS.** Certificate of Elijah Clarke, Col., April 6, 1784. Petitioner prays 287½ acres in Washington Co. Thomas Roberts from Lincoln Co., N. C., prays head rights of 400 acres in Washington Co. for self, wife and 3 children.

**ROE, JAMES.** Certificate as refugee soldier, Wm. Candler, Col., Refugee Regt. Petitioner prays 287½ acres in Franklin Co. Warrant 1405.

**RAE, JAMES.** His petition for bounty as deputy commissary general from 1776 to Feb., 1780. Granted.

**ROE, WALTER.** Certificate of Elijah Clarke, Col., April 24, 1784. Warrant 707.

**RICE, JOHN.** Certificate of Elijah Clarke, Col., April 6, 1784. Petitioner prays bounty in Washington Co. Warrant 708.

**RICE, NATHAN.** Certificate of Elijah Clarke, Lt. Col., Jan. 29, 1785. Warrant 709.

# CERTIFICATES OF SERVICE IN AMERICAN REVOLUTION.

**RICE, DAVID.** Certificate of E. Clarke, Lt. Col., Jan. 29, 1785. Warrant 710.

**RYLEY, BARNARD.** Certificate of Elijah Clarke, Lt. Col., Feb. 2, 1784.

**RILEY, JOSEPH.** Certificate of Elijah Clarke, Col., Feb. 2, 1784.

**RILEY, WILLIAM.** Certificate of Elijah Clarke, Col., Feb. 2, 1784. Petitioner prays 287½ acres in Franklin Co.

**RASER, ISAAC.** Certificate as refugee soldier, Jenkins Davis, Lt. Col., Mar. 2, 1784. Petitioner prays 287½ acres in Washington Co. Warrant 1420.

**ROZER, AMOS.** Certificate of Elijah Clarke, Lt. Col., Jan. 25, 1784. Warrant 735.

**ROZER, CALEB.** Certificate as refugee soldier, Elijah Clarke, Col., Jan. 25, 1785. Warrant 1408. 2d certificate of Elijah Clarke, Col., Jan. 25, 1785.

**ROZER, EDWARD.** Certificate of Elijah Clarke, Lt. Col., Jan. 25, 1785.

**ROZER, JOHN.** Certificate of E. Clarke, Col., Jan. 25, 1785.

**ROZER, SHADRACK** (not a bounty). From Halifax Co., N. C., prays head rights of 600 acres in Washington Co. for 9 in family.

**RIDER, BENJAMIN.** Certificate of Jas. Jackson, Col., April 2, 1784. Petitioner prays 287½ acres in Franklin Co.

**RIDER, JOSEPH S.** Certificate as refugee soldier, E. Clarke, Col., April 19, 1784.

**ROWLAND, JOHN.** Certificate of Elijah Clarke, Col., Nov. 16, 1784.

**ROWLAND, SAMUEL.** Certificate of Samuel Jack, Col., April 5, 1784. Warrant 723.

**ROUNTREE, ABNER.** Certificate as refugee soldier, Wm. Candler, Col. Refugee Regt. Petitioner prays 287½ acres in Washington Co. Warrant 1417.

**ROUNTREE, JOB.** Certificate as refugee soldier, Wm. Candler, Col., R. Regt. Petition of Jesse Rountree for heirs of Job Rountree for 287½ acres in Washington Co.

**ROUNTREE, JESSE.** Certificate as refugee soldier, Wm. Candler, Col., Refugee Regt. Petitioner prays 287½ acres in Washington Co. Warrant 1416.

**ROWELL, EDWARD.** Certificate of Jas. McNeil, Col., Mar. 15, 1784. Petitioner prays bounty in Washington Co. Also prays head rights of 1,000 acres in Washington for self and 20 negroes.

**ROWELL, HOWELL.** Certificate of John Twiggs, B. G., April 3, 1784. Petitioner prays bounty in Washington Co.

**RUSHING, MALACHI.** Certificate of Caleb Howell, Col., Dublin, Mar. 14, 1784.

**RUSHING, MATTHEW.** Certificate of Caleb Howell, Col., Mar. 1, 1784. 2d certificate of Jenkins Davis, Col., Mar. 5, 1784. Petitioner prays 575 acres in Washington Co.

**RUTHERFORD, SAMUEL, JR.** Certificate as refugee soldier, Elijah Clarke, Col., Aug. 9, 1784. Petitioner prays bounty in Franklin Co. 2d certificate of Elijah Clarke, Col., Feb. 2, 1784.

**RYAN, JAMES.** Certificate of Elijah Clarke, Col., Feb. 25, 1784. Petitioner prays 287½ acres in Washington Co. Warrant 713.

**RYAN, JOHN.** Certificate of Gb. Lee, Col., April 2, 1784. Petitioner prays bounty in Franklin Co.

**RYAN, RICHARD.** Certificate of Elijah Clarke, Col., Feb. 2, 1784. Petitioner prays 575 acres in 2 certificates, in Washington Co.

**REDIX, ABSOLEM.** Certificate of E Clarke, Col., April 9, 1784. Petitioner prays bounty in Washington Co.

**ROBARDS, THOMAS.** Certificate of Elijah Clarke, Col., April 7, 1784. Petitioner prays 287½ acres in Washington Co.

**REYFIELD, ISAAC.** I do certify that Rowling Lancaster, Isaac Reyfield, David Crawford and Bazil Maxwell, four soldiers, enlisted for 3 years in 2d Battalion, Continental Troops, in defense of the State of Georgia, and all died in the service, and that the heirs of said soldiers are entitled to the benefit of Continental and State bounties of land. S. Elbert, Brig. Gen., Cont. Army, July 15, 1784.

**ROWLEY, JOHN.** Certificate of Elijah Clarke, Col., Jan. 25, 1785. Warrant 474.

**RUSSELL, WILLIAM.** Certificate of Elijah Clarke, Col., Jan. 25, 1785. Warrant 734.

**RICHARDS, JACOB.** Certificate of Elijah Clarke, Col., Nov. 16, 1784. Warrant 733.

**RAVOT, ABRAHAM.** Certificate of Caleb Howell, Col., Feb. 5, 1784. Petitioner prays 287½ acres in Washington Co.

**RANEY, WILLIAM.** Certificate of John Twiggs, B. G., Mar. 22, 1784. Petitioner prays 250 acres in Washington Co.

**RESSETO, WILLIAM.** Certificate of Elijah Clarke, Col., April 20, 1784. Petitioner prays bounty in Washington Co.

**RAFFERTY, MICHAEL.** Certificate as refugee soldier, Elijah Clarke, Col., April 8, 1784. Petitioner prays 2 warrants of 287½ acres each in Washington Co. Warrant 1406.

**RENCH, JOHN.** Certificate of Elijah Clarke, Col., April 8, 1784. Warrant 728.

# CERTIFICATES OF SERVICE IN AMERICAN REVOLUTION. 155

**RATLETT, JAMES.** Certificate of Elijah Clarke, Col., Jan. 28, 1785.

**RUROY, JAMES.** Certificate of Elijah Clarke, Col., Nov. 19, 1784. Warrant 706.

S.

**SANDERS, SIMON.** Certificate of Elijah Clarke, Col., Jan. 3, 1785. Warrant 770.

**SANDERS, CAPT. ABRAHAM.** Certificate of Elijah Clarke, Col., May 20, 1784. Petitioner prays 262½ acres ―――――. Warrant 900.

**SAPP, ELIJAH.** Certificate of Asa Emanuel, Capt., and John Twiggs, B. G., April 6, 1784. Petitioner prays 250 acres in Washington Co.

**SAPP, EMANUEL.** Certificate of Asa Emanuel, Capt., and John Twiggs, B. G., April 6, 1784. Petitioner prays 250 acres in Washington Co.

**SAPP, WILLIAM.** Certificate of Asa Emanuel, Capt., and John Twiggs, B. G., April 6, 1784. Petitioner prays 250 acres in Washington Co.

**SANDERS, JACOB.** Certificate of Elijah Clarke, Col., Feb. 2, 1784. Petitioner prays bounty in Washington Co. Warrant 1299.

**SANDERS, JOSHUA.** Ex. order for bounty upon certificate of Col. E. Clarke (missing), Feb. 24, 1784. Petitioner prays 287½ acres in Washington Co.

**SANDERS, MARK.** Certificate of Elijah Clarke, Col., April 1, 1784. Petitioner prays 287½ acres in Washington Co.

**SALTER, SIMON.** Certificate as refugee soldier, Elijah Clarke, Col., Feb. 2, 1784. 2d Ex. order for bounty upon certificate of Col. E. Clarke (missing), Mar. 26, 1784. Petitioner prays head rights of 1,000 acres in Washington for self and 16 in family.

**SHANNON, THOMAS.** Ex. order for bounty upon certificate of Col. E. Clarke (missing), Feb. 25, 1784. Petitioner prays 250 acres in Washington Co.

**SAPP, DILL.** Certificate of John Twiggs, B. G., Mar. 23, 1784. Petitioner prays 2 warrants of 287½ acres each in Washington Co.

**SAPP, WILLIAM, JR.** Certificate of John Twiggs, B. G., Mar. 23, 1784. Petitioner prays 287½ acres in Washington Co.

**SALTER, SIMON.** Certificate of Gb. Lee, Col., April 7, 1784. Petitioner prays bounty in Washington Co.

**SAVAGE, REV. LOVELESS.** Certificate as chaplain, Wm. Candler, Col., Refugee Regt. Petitioner prays 747½ acres in Washington Co. Warrant 873. 2d certificate of Jas. McNeil, Col., Mar. 15, 1784. Petitioner prays 287½ acres in Washington Co.

**SATTERWHITE, WILLIAM.** Certificate of Gb. Lee, Col., Mar. 20, 1784. Petitioner prays bounty in Washington Co.

**SUMMERFORD, JACOB.** Power of attorney of Jacob Summerford of Camden Dist., S. C., to Joseph Ratchford of Ga., to apply for 250 acres bounty for his services in Col. Clarke's battalion of Minute Men of Ga., April 8, 1784.

**STRADFORD, SAMUEL.** Petition for 287½ acres in Washington Co. as per certificate annexed (missing). Granted April 13, 1784.

**SAFFOLD, DANIEL.** Petition for 287½ acres in Franklin Co. as per certificate of Col. E. Clarke, Sep. 8, 1784 (missing).

**SAWYER, JOHN.** Ex. order for bounty as per certificate of Col. E. Clarke, (missing), Mar. 25, 1784. Petitioner prays 250 acres in Washington Co.

**SCOTT, ABRAHAM.** Certificate of John Twiggs, B. G., Mar. 20, 1784. Petitioner prays 287½ acres in Washington Co.

**SCOTT, REV. ALEXANDER.** Certificate as chaplain, Caleb Howell, Col., May 10, 1784. Petitioner prays 750 acres in Washington Co.

**SCOTT, BENJAMIN.** Ex. order for bounty as per certificate of Col. E. Clarke (missing), Mar. 25, 1784. Petitioner prays 287½ acres in Washington Co.

**SCOTT, CORNELIUS.** Certificate of Elijah Clarke, Col., April 3, 1784. Petitioner prays 287½ acres in Washington Co. Warrant 751.

**SCOTT, JOSEPH.** Certificate as refugee soldier, Elijah Clarke, Col., April 8, 1784. Petitioner prays bounty in Washington Co. Also prays head rights of 1,000 acres in Washington Co. on self and 17 in family.

**SCOTT, JOHN, SR.** Certificate of Elijah Clarke, Col., April 7, 1784. Petitioner prays bounty in Washington Co. Warrant 749.

**SCOTT, JOHN, JR.** Certificate of Elijah Clarke, Col., April 7, 1784. Petitioner prays bounty in Washington Co. Warrant 750.

**SCOTT, SERGEANT PETER.** Petition for 287½ acres in Washington Co. as per certificate annexed. Warrant 752.

**SCOTT, PHILIP.** Certificate as refugee soldier, Patrick Carr, Comdg. Independent Corps.

**SCOTT, WILLIAM.** Certificate of Elijah Clarke, Col., Jan., 1785.

**SCOTT, CAPT. WILLIAM.** Of the Ga. Line. Certificate of John Habersham, Maj. Gen., Ga. Line, Mar. 1, 1785. Warrant 44.

**SCOTT, WILLIAM, JR.** Certificate of Elijah Clarke, Col., April 7, 1784. Petitioner prays bounty in Washington Co. Warrant 753.

**SESSOMS, WILLIAM, JR.** Certificate that he enlisted for 3 years under Capt. Dooly of 3d Batt. of Foot, Col. James Screven; Thos. Mitchell, 1st Lieut., and Geo. Dooly, 2d Lieut., May 21, 1784. Warrant 194.

**SESSOMS, WILLIAM.** Certificate of Elijah Clarke, Col., Feb. 2, 1784. Petitioner prays 287½ acres in Washington Co.

# CERTIFICATES OF SERVICE IN AMERICAN REVOLUTION.

**SHECK, FREDERICK.** Petition for 460 acres in reserve, as a lieutenant, as per certificate annexed (missing). Granted.

**SHEFFEL, MARK.** Certificate as refugee soldier, John Twiggs, B. G., Mar. 27, 1784. Warrant 1459.

**SHARPE, JAMES BOYD.** Certificate as surgeon from 6 Dec., 1782, to close of the war, John Habersham, Major, Comdg. Ga. Batt., Mar. 18, 1784. Petitioner prays 600 acres in the reserve.

**SHAW, DAVID.** Certificate of Gb. Lee, Col., April 21, 1784. Petitioner prays 287½ acres in Washington Co.

**SHAW, THOMAS, SR.** David Shaw further prays bounty of 345 acres due Thomas Shaw, deceased.

**SETTLER, CAPT. DANIEL.** Certificate of Jenkins Davis, Lt. Col., and that Godleib Neidlinger is trustee for his heirs. Warrant 882.

**SHIELDS, WILLIAM.** Certificate of Gb. Lee, Col., April 20, 1784. Petitioner prays bounty in Franklin Co.

**SHIELDS, WILLIAM, JR.** Certificate of Gb. Lee, Col., April 10, 1784. Petitioner prays 287½ acres in Washington Co.

**SHIELDS, ANDREW.** Certificate of Jas. McNeil, Col., Mar. 24, 1784. Petitioner prays 287½ acres in Washington Co. Warrant 1456. 2d certificate of Jas. Jackson, Col., Ga. State Legion, April 7, 1784. Petitioner prays 250 acres in Washington Co. 3d certificate as private in 1st Ga. Cont. Batt., Geo. Handley, Capt., Mar. 4, 1784. Petitioner, through Col. Pannill, prays 230 acres in the reserve.

**SHIELDS, MAJOR JOHN.** Certificate that he lost his life gloriously fighting for the State, Wm. Candler, Col., R. R. Petitioner, Margaret Shields, prays bounty in Washington Co. Warrant 863.

**SHIELDS, WILLIAM.** Certificate as refugee soldier, Gb. Lee, Col., Feb. 20, 1784. 2d certificate of Gb. Lee, Col., Mar. 11, 1784. Petitioner prays 575 acres in Washington Co.

**SHIELDS, WILLIAM.** Certificate as refugee soldier, Benj. Few, Col., Aug. 19, 1784. Warrant 1457.

**SHACKLEFORD, JOHN.** Certificate of Jas. McNeil, Col., Feb. 22, 1784. Petitioner prays 575 acres in Washington Co.

**SHADDOCK, THOMAS.** Certificate as refugee soldier, James McCay, Col., April 5, 1784. 2d certificate of James McCay, Col., April 6, 1784. Petitioner prays 575 acres in Washington Co.

**SHARPE, JOHN, SR.** Certificate of John Twiggs, B. G., Feb. 26, 1784.

**SHARPE, MICHAEL.** Certificate of John Twiggs, B. G., Feb. 26, 1784. John Sharpe, for petitioner, prays 287½ acres in Washington Co.

**SHAFFER, DAVID.** Certificate of Elijah Clarke, Col., Feb. 2, 1784. Petitioner prays 287½ acres in Washington Co.

**SHAW, ADAM.** Certificate of James Jackson, Col., April 7, 1784. Petitioner prays 287½ acres in Washington Co.

**SHAW, THOMAS.** Certificate as Minute Man, Gb. Lee, Col., April 4, 1784. Petitioner prays 287½ acres in Washington Co.

**SHAW, SERGEANT THOMAS.** Certificate of Elijah Clarke, Col., April 6, 1784. Warrant 282.

**SHAW, THOMAS, JR.** Certificate of Elijah Clarke, Col., April 6, 1784. Warrant 769.

**SHEPHERD, STEPHEN.** Certificate of Elijah Clarke, Col., April 1, 1784. Petitioner prays 287½ acres in Washington Co.

**SHANNON, THOMAS, SR.** Certificate of Elijah Clarke, Col., July 22, 1784. Petitioner prays 287½ acres in Washington Co.

**SHANNON, THOMAS.** Certificate of Elijah Clarke, Col., Feb. 2, 1784.

**SHERRELL, DAVID.** Certificate of Elijah Clarke, Col., May 18, 1784. Petitioner prays 2 bounties in Franklin Co. Warrant 1434.

**SHELTON, HENRY.** Certificate of Elijah Clarke, Col., Feb. 2, 1784. Petitioner prays 287½ acres in Washington Co.

**SHEFFEL, WILLIAM.** Certificate as refugee soldier, John Twiggs, B. G., Mar. 27, 1784. Warrant 1458.

**SHEFFEL, JOHN.** Certificate of John Twiggs, B. G., Mar. 27, 1784. Petitioner prays 287½ acres in Washington Co.

**SHEFTALL, MORDECAI.** Petition for bounty in reserve, as per certificate annexed (missing).

**SHEFFEL, WILLIAM.** 2d certificate of John Twiggs, B. G., Mar. 27, 1784. Petitioner prays 575 acres in Washington Co.

**SIMMONS, CHARLES.** Certificate as refugee soldier, John Twiggs, B. G., Jan. 1, 1783. Warrant 1460. 2d certificate of James McNeil, Col., April 5, 1784. Petitioner prays 575 acres in Washington Co.

**SIMMONS, JAMES.** Certificate as refugee soldier, Elijah Clarke, Col., Nov. 16, 1784. Warrant 1425. 2d certificate of Elijah Clarke, Col., Jan. 25, 1784.

**SIMMONS, JAMES.** Certificate as refugee soldier, Elijah Clarke, Col., April 8, 1784.

**SIMMONS, JAMES.** Certificate of Elijah Clarke, Col., Dec. 10, 1784. Petitioner prays bounty in Washington Co.

CERTIFICATES OF SERVICE IN AMERICAN REVOLUTION. 159

SIMMONS, JAMES. Certificate of Elijah Clarke, Col., Jan. 3, 1785. Petitioner prays 287½ acres in Washington Co. Warrant 746.

SIMMONS, MALBOURN. Certificate of Elijah Clarke, Col., Feb. 2, 1784.

SIMMONS, STERNS. Certificate of Elijah Clarke, Col., Feb. 2, 1784. Petitioner prays bounty in Washington Co.

SIMMONS, THOMAS. Certificate of Elijah Clarke, Col., April 7, 1784. Petitioner prays 250 acres in Washington Co.

SIMMONS, RICHARD. Certificate of E. Clarke, Col., Jan. 3, 1785. Warrant 745.

SIMMONS, WILLIAM, SR. Certificate of Elijah Clarke, Col., Feb. 3, 1784. Petitioner prays 250 acres in Franklin Co.

SIMMONS, WILLIAM, JR. Certificate of Elijah Clarke, Col., Dec. 10, 1784.

SHARPE, J. Z. Surgeon's Mate. Ex. order for bounty, Mar. 19, 1784. Warrant 33.

SNELSON, SERGEANT THOMAS. Certificate of Elijah Clarke, Col., April 1, 1784. Petitioner prays bounty in Washington Co. Warrant 295.

SNELSON, JAMES. Certificate of Elijah Clarke, Col., April 1, 1784. Petitioner prays 287½ acres in Washington Co. Warrant 777.

SIMPSON, SAMUEL. Petition for 230 acres on certificate annexed (missing). Granted Nov. 23, 1784.

SELLS, JOHN. Certificate of Gb. Lee, Col., Mar. 11, 1784. Petitioner prays bounty in Franklin Co.

SNEED, DUDLEY. Certificate as refugee soldier, Elijah Clarke, Col., April 19, 1784. Petitioner prays 287½ acres in Washington Co. Warrant 1431.

SIMMS, ROBERT. This is to certify that Robert Simms was a soldier in 2d Ga. Battalion and served faithfully his enlistment, 3 years. Lieut. G. Moseley, Capt. and Paymaster, J. Pannill, Lt. Col., 2d Ga.

SIMMS, MANN. Certificate as refugee soldier, James Martin, Col., April 27, 1784. Petitioner prays bounty in Washington Co.

SIMMS, WILLIAM. Certificate of Jas. McNeil, Col., April 7, 1784. Petitioner prays bounty in Washington Co.

SIZEMORE, WILLIAM. Certificate of Elijah Clarke, Col., April 20, 1784. Petitioner prays 287½ acres in Washington Co. Warrant 784.

SIMPSON, JAMES. Certificate of Jas. McNeil, Col., Feb. 2, 1784. Petitioner prays 287½ acres in Washington Co.

SIMPSON, JAMES. Certificate of Elijah Clarke, Col., Feb. 2, 1784.

**SINQUEFIELD, SAMUEL.** Certificate of Elijah Clarke, Col., April 7, 1784. Petitioner prays 287½ acres in Washington Co.

**SINQUEFIELD, JAMES.** Certificate as refugee soldier, Elijah Clarke, Col., Nov. 16, 1784. Warrant 1430.

**SINQUEFIELD, SAMUEL, JR.** Certificate of Elijah Clarke, Col., April 6, 1784. Petitioner prays 287½ acres in Washington Co.

**SHICK, LIEUT. FREDERICK.** Certificate of John Habersham, Major Ga. Line, Sept. 29, 1784. Warrant 94.

**SITTON, JOHN.** Certificate of E. Clarke, Col., April 6, 1784. Petitioner, Sarah Sitton, prays bounty in Washington Co.

**STONE, CHARLES.** Certificate of Elijah Clarke, Col., Feb. 2, 1784.

**SNELL, DAVID.** Ex. order for 287½ acres in Washington Co. as per certificate annexed (missing), May 17, 1784.

**SIGMAN, JOHN.** Certificate of Elijah Clarke, Col., Feb. 2, 1784. Warrant 1462.

**SIDMAN, JOHN SR.** Certificate of Elijah Clarke, Col., June 21, 1784. Petitioner prays 287½ acres in Franklin Co. Warrant 778.

**SHEFFEL, MARK.** Certificate of John Twiggs, B. G., Mar. 27, 1784. Petitioner prays 575 acres in Washington Co.

**SKINNER, CAPT. ISAAC.** Certificate as refugee soldier, Jas. McNeil, Col., Feb. 9, 1784. Warrant 1492.
2d certificate of Elijah Clarke, Col., Feb. 20, 1784. Warrant 909.

**SLEEKER, GEORGE.** Certificate to GEO. SLEEKER, soldier of Camden Dist., S. C., May 10, 1784, Elijah Clarke, Col., Warrant 782. Petitioner prays 287½ acres in Franklin Co.

**SMART, ROBERT.** Certificate of Samuel Jack, Col., Mar. 13, 1784. Warrant 780.

**SHIRLEY, JOHN.** Certificate of Samuel Jack, Col., April 10, 1784. Petitioner prays 287½ acres in Washington Co. Warrant 768.

**SMITH, ARTHUR.** Certificate as refugee soldier, Elijah Clarke, Col., May 12, 1784. Petitioner prays 250 acres in Franklin Co. Warrant 1444.

**SMITH, ANDREW.** Order of Ex. Council for 2 bounties of 287½ acres each in Washington Co. as per certificate annexed. May 17, 1784.

**SMITH, CORNELIUS.** Certificate as refugee soldier, Elijah Clarke, Col., April 14, 1784. Warrant 1439.

**SMITH, DAVID.** Certificate of Elijah Clarke, Col., Feb. 2, 1784.

**SMITH, EBENEZER.** Certificate as refugee soldier, Elijah Clarke, Col., April 8, 1784. Petitioner prays bounty in Franklin Co. Warrant 1441.

# CERTIFICATES OF SERVICE IN AMERICAN REVOLUTION. 161

**SMITH, FRANCIS.** Certificate of Elijah Clarke, Co., April 22, 1784. Petitioner prays 250 acres in Washington Co.

**SMITH, GEORGE.** Certificate of Jas. McNeil, Col., Mar. 9, 1784. Petitioner prays 287½ acres in Washington Co.

**SMITH, ISRAEL.** Certificate of Elijah Clarke, Col., Feb. 2, 1784. Petitioner prays 287½ acres in Washington Co.

**SMITH, JACOB.** Certificate of Elijah Clarke, Col., Feb. 2, 1784. Petitioner prays 287½ acres in Washington Co.
2d certificate of Elijah Clarke, Col., Dec. 2, 1784—also signed by Capt. John Autrey. Petitioner prays 287½ acres in Washington Co.

**SMITH, JAMES.** Certificate as refugee soldier, Elijah Clarke, Col., April 8, 1784.
2d certificate of Elijah Clarke, Col., April 21, 1784. Petitioner prays two bounties in Washington Co.

**SMITH, JAMES.** Certificate as refugee soldier, John Twiggs, B. G., April 6, 1784. Petitioner prays bounty in Franklin Co. Warrant 1447.

**SMITH, JOHN SR.** Certificate of Gb. Lee, Col., Feb. 23, 1784. Petitioner prays 287½ acres in Washington Co.

**SMITH, JOHN.** Ex. order for bounty upon certificate of Col. Gb. Lee, Ex. No. 420.

**SMITH, JOHN.** Certificate of Elijah Clarke, Col., Feb. 10, 1784. Petitioner prays bounty in Washington Co.

**SMITH, JOHN.** Certificate of Jas. McNeil, Col., April 7, 1784. Petitioner prays bounty in Franklin Co.

**SMITH, JOHN.** Certificate of John Twiggs, B. G., Mar. 3, 1784. Petitioner prays 287½ acres in Washington Co.

**SMITH, JOHN.** Certificate of Elijah Clarke, Lt. Col., April 1, 1784. Petitioner prays 287½ acres in Franklin Co. Warrant 757.
2d certificate of Elijah Clarke, Col., April 6, 1784. Petitioner prays bounty in Franklin Co.

**SMITH, MOSES.** Certificate of Elijah Clarke, Lt. Col., Nov. 4, 1784. Warrant 756.

**SMITH, MAJOR BURRELL.** Petition for bounty in Washington Co. Warrant 864.

**SMITH, NATHAN.** Certificate of Elijah Clarke, Col., Feb. 2, 1784. Warrant 1442.
2d Certificate of Elijah Clarke, Col., Feb. 2, 1784.

**SMITH, NATHANIEL.** Certificate of Elijah Clarke, Col., Feb. 2, 1784. Warrant 1443.

**SMITH, REDICK.** Certificate of Elijah Clarke, Col., Dec. 24, 1784.

**SMITH, LIEUT. RANDOLPH** of Capt. Thos. Dooly's Co., Capt. John Dooly, July 31, 1784. Warrant 95. Also a certificate to John Tomberlin on same sheet.

**SMART, ROBERT,** of 96 Dist. S. C., Petitions for bounty upon certificate annexed (missing).

**SMITH, SAMUEL.** Certificate of E. Clarke, Col., Feb. 2, 1784. Petitioner prays 287½ acres in Washington Co. 2d Certificate as refugee soldier Elijah Clarke, Col., April 8, 1784. Petitioner prays bounty in Franklin Co.

**SMITH, SIMON.** Certificate of Gb. Lee, Col., Mar. 11, 1784. Petitioner prays 287½ acres in Washington Co. 2d certificate to Sergeant Simon Smith, Elijah Clarke, Col., April 20, 1784. Petitioner prays 345 acres in Washington Co. Warrant 281.

**SMITH, SAMUEL.** Certificate as refugee soldier, Elijah Clarke, Col., Sep. 8, 1784. Petitioner prays 287½ acres in Washington Co. Warrant 1445.

**SMITH, THOMAS.** Certificate of Elijah Clarke, Col., Feb. 2, 1784.

**SMITH, THOMAS.** Certificate of Elijah Clarke, Col., Mar. 2, 1784. Said Thomas Smith of Virginia, having served in Ga. Troops and being desirous to settle in Georgia prays Head Rights of 600 acres in Washington Co., for self, wife, two children and five negroes.

**SMITH, THOMAS, JR.** Certificate of Elijah Clarke, Col., Feb. 2, 1784.

**SMITH, THOMAS.** Certificate of Elijah Clarke, Col., Feb. 25, 1784.

**SMITH, THOMAS, JR.** Ex. order for bounty as refugee soldier as per certificate of Col. Clarke, (see above) March 25, 1784. Petitioner prays 287½ acres in Washington Co. Warrant 755.

**SMITH, THOMAS.** Certificate of Elijah Clarke, Col., Feb. 2, 1784. Petitioner prays 287½ acres in Washington Co. Warrant 1446.

**SMITH, THOMAS.** Certificate as soldier in Minute Men, Elijah Clarke, Col., April 7, 1784. Petitioner prays 287½ acres in Franklin Co. Warrant 754.

**SPRADLING, JAMES.** Power of attorney to Thos. Bush to draw his bounty upon certificate attached (missing)

**SPURLOCK, ROBERT.** Certificate Wm. Candler, Col., refugee Regt., Feb. 24, 1784. Petitioner prays 287½ acres in Washington Co. Warrant 1461.

**SPURLOCK, ROBERT.** Certificate of Gb. Lee, Col., Feb. 23, 1784. Petition of Mary, widow of Robert Spurlock for 250 acres in Franklin Co. Certificate calls him "Major Robert Spurlock."

**SPENCER, WILLIAM.** Certificate of John Baker, Col., April 21, 1784. Petitioner prays bounty in Franklin Co. Warrant 1427.

CERTIFICATES OF SERVICE IN AMERICAN REVOLUTION. 163

**SPIKES, ELIAS.** Certificate of Elijah Clarke, Col., Dec. 10, 1784. Petitioner prays bounty in Washington Co.

**SPIKES, JOSIAH.** Certificate of Elijah Clarke, Col., Dec. 10, 1784. Petitioner prays bounty in Washington Co.

**STATTEN, JOSEPH.** Certificate of Jas. McNeil, Col., Feb. 4, 1784. Petitioner prays 287½ acres in Washington Co.

**STANFORD, WILLIAM.** Certificate of Benjamin Few, Col., Sep. 20, 1784. Petitioner prays 287½ acres in Washington Co.

**STAFFORD, SAMUEL.** Order from Ex. Council for survey of 287½ acres in Washington Co. May 17, 1784. Petitioner prays exchange into Franklin Co.

**STALLINGS, JOHN.** Certificate as refugee soldier, John Twiggs, B. G., Feb. 26, 1784. Warrant 1454.

**STALLINGS, JESSE.** Certificate of Elijah Clarke, Col., Feb. 2, 1784.

**STALLINGS, EZEKIEL.** Ex. order for bounty upon certificate of Col. Wm. Candler, Feb. 24, 1784 (missing). Warrant 1455.

**STALLINGS, CAPT. FREDERICK.** Petition of Hannah, widow of Capt Frederick Stallings for 575 acres in Washington Co. for self and only child Mary, upon certificate annexed (missing).

**STAPLER, JOHN.** Certificate of Gb. Lee, Col., Feb. 20, 1784.

**STEDMAN, JOHN.** Certificate of Elijah Clarke, Lt. Col., June 21, 1784. Petitioner prays 287½ acres in Franklin Co. Warrant 781.

**STEPHENS, BENJAMIN.** Certificate of E. Clarke, Col., Jan., 1785. Warrant 740.

**STEVENS, JOHN.** Certificate as refugee soldier, John Twiggs, B. G., Mar. 27, 1784. Warrant 1433.

**STEPHENS, THOMAS.** Certificate of E. Clarke, Lt. Col., Jan. 3, 1785. Warrant 741.

**STEPHENS, JOHN.** Certificate of Elijah Clarke, Col., Feb. 2, 1784. 2d certificate of Elijah Clarke, Col., Jan. 11, 1785. Petitioner prays 250 acres in Washington Co.

**STEWART, JAMES.** Certificate of E. Clarke, Col., Feb. 2, 1784. Warrant 1453.

**STEWART, JAMES.** Certificate of Elijah Clarke, Col., March 26, 1784. Petitioner prays bounty in Franklin Co.

**STEWART, JAMES.** Certificate of Elijah Clarke, Col., April 25, 1784. Petitioner prays bounty in Washington Co.

**STEWART, ADJUTANT JAMES.** His petition for 500 acres in Washington Co., as per certificate annexed (missing).

**STEWART, JAMES SR.** Certificate as refugee soldier, John Baker, Col., Liberty Co. Militia, Mar. 3, 1784. Warrant 1452. 2d certificate of John Baker, Col., Jan. 20, 1785.

**STEWART, JOHN.** Certificate as refugee soldier, John Baker, Col., Jan. 20, 1785.

**STUART, WILLIAM.** Certificate of Elijah Clarke, Col., Dec. 24, 1784. Petitioner prays through Holland Middleton, 287½ acres in Washington Co. Warrant 607.

**STRAM, JAMES.** Certificate of Elijah Clarke, Col., Feb. 2, 1784. Warrant 773.

**STIFF, WILLIAM.** His petition (through Col. Francis Tennill) for 230 acres in the Reserve, as a soldier of the Ga. Continental Line. Warrant 6.

**STUDSTILL, JOHN.** Certificate of Elijah Clarke, Col., Jan. 29, 1785. Warrant 772.

**STRINGER, JOHN.** Certificate of Elijah Clarke, Col., April 1, 1784. Warrant 785.

**STROHACKER, RANDOLPH.** Certificate as refugee soldier, Jenkins Davis, Lt. Col., Mar. 2, 1784. Petitioner prays 287½ acres in Washington Co. Warrant 1467.

**STRONG, JOHN.** Certificate as refugee soldier, Jenkins Davis, Lt. Col., Emanuel Co. Militia, Mar, 9, 1784. Warrant 1428.

**STOAT, DAVID.** Certificate of Elijah Clarke, Col., Oct. 10, 1784. Warrant 771.

**STRIPLING, FRANCIS.** Certificate of Elijah Clarke, Col., Feb, 2, 1784. Petitioner prays 250 acres in Washington Co.

**STANFORD, JOHN.** Certificate of Gb. Lee, Col., April 7, 1784. Petitioner prays 287½ acres in Franklin Co.

**STANLEY, DEMPSEY.** Certificate of Elijah Clarke, Col., April 20, 1784.

**STEWART, ISAAC.** Certificate of Elijah Clarke, Col., Feb. 2, 1784. Petitioner prays bounty in Washington Co.

**STALLINGS, LIEUT. JAMES.** Certificate of Wm. Candler, Col., Refugee Regt. Warrant 928.

**STALLINGS, CAPT. FREDERICK.** (deceased). Certificate of Wm. Candler, Col. R. R. Warrant 908.

**STROZIER, PETER.** Ex. order for bounty on certificate of Col. E. Clarke, Mar. 25, 1784. Warrant 1435.

## CERTIFICATES OF SERVICE IN AMERICAN REVOLUTION.

**STEED, PHILIP.** Certificate of Elijah Clarke, Lt. Col., April 6, 1784. Petitioner prays bounty in Washington Co. Warrant 762.

**STEED, EDWARD.** Certificate of E. Clarke, Lt. Col., Jan. 3, 1785. Warrant 761.

**STONE, JOSHUA.** Certificate of Elijah Clarke, Lt. Col., Jan. 3, 1785. Warrant 766.

**STALL, JOHN.** Certificate of E. Clarke, Lt. Col., Jan. 3, 1785. Warrant 747.

**STALL, PETER.** Certificate of E. Clarke, Lt. Col., Jan. 3, 1785. Warrant 748.

**STALLINGS, FREDERICK.** (Killed by the enemy) Certificate of Jas. McNeil, Col., Feb. 17, 1784.

**SIMMONS, BENJAMIN.** Certificate of E. Clarke, Col., Dec. 10, 1784. Also prays head rights of 850 acres in Washington Co. for self, wife, 5 children and seven negro slaves.

**STALLINGS, EZEKIEL.** Certificate as refugee soldier, Wm. Candler, Col., Ref. Regt. (no date).

**STANLEY, SHADRACK.** Certificate of Elijah Clarke, Col., Feb. 2, 1784. Petitioner prays bounty in Washington Co. Desiring to remove from South Carolina to Georgia, he also prays head rights for self and six in family in Washington Co.

**STEVENS, JOHN.** Certificate of John Twiggs, B. G., Mar. 27, 1784. Petitioner prays 575 acres in Washington Co.

**STRENGTH, JOHN.** Ex. order for bounty upon certificate of Col. Gb. Lee, Feb. 26, 1784. Petitioner prays 287½ acres in Washington Co. through Ignatius Few.

**STOCKS, BENTLEY.** Certificate of Elijah Clarke, Col., April 1, 1784.

**SUMMERFORD, JACOB JR.** Certificate of Elijah Clarke, Lt. Col., May 10, 1784. Petitioner prays 287½ acres in Franklin Co. Warrant 765.

**SIOCUMB, SETH.** Certificate as refugee soldier, John Twiggs, B. G., Feb. 4, 1784. Petitioner prays 287½ acres in Washington Co. Warrant 1470.

**SALSBERY, THOMAS.** Petition as a soldier in 2d Ga. Battalion, for 230 acres in the reserve, as per certificate of Jas. Pannill, Lt. Col. (missing), April 8, 1784. Warrant 196. For a consideration he sells grant to Geo. Mathews.

**STALLINGS, EZEKIEL.** Ex. order for bounty as per certificate of Col. James Jackson (missing), Dec. 24, 1783. Petitioner prays 575 acres in Washington Co.

**STALLINGS, FREDERICK.** Petition of Hannah, widow, and Mary, only child of Frederick Stallings, for 287½ acres in Washington Co. See certificate above.

**STALLINGS, LIEUT. JAMES.** .Ex. order for bounty upon certificate of Col. Jas. Jackson, Dec. 1783 (missing). Upon Col. Jackson's recommendation, granted 690 acres in Washington Co.

**STALLINGS, JAMES.** Certificate of Elijah Clarke, Col., certificate annexed (missing), May 20, 1784.

**STALLINGS, JOHN.** Certificate as refugee soldier, John Twiggs, B. G., Feb. 26, 1784. Warrant 1454.

**STEADMAN, LIEUT. JAMES** (deceased). Ex. order for bounty. Petition of David Reese for widow.

**STIRK, SAMUEL.** Petitioner for 575 acres in Washington Co. as per certificate annexed (missing).

**STOCKHAM, SETH.** Certificate of Elijah Clarke, Col., Dec. 16, 1784. Warrant 776.

**STONE, THOMAS.** Order to surveyor to lay out 575 acres as bounty in Washington Co. As per certificate. May 25, 1784.

**STRIPPLING, FRANCIS.** Order to surveyor of Washington Co. to lay out 287½ acres bounty as per certificate.

**STRONG, JOHN.** Certificate of John Martin, Col., March 1, 1784.

**STROZIER, PETER.** Certificate of Elijah Clarke, Col., Feb. 2, 1784.

**SPIKES, NATHAN.** Certificate of Elijah Clarke, Col., Dec. 10, 1784. Petitioner prays bounty in Washington Co.

**STUART, CLEMENT.** Certificate of E. Clarke, Lt. Col., April 5, 1784. Petitioner prays bounty in Franklin Co. Warrant 758.

**STEWART, CHARLES.** Certificate of Elijah Clarke, Col., Feb. 2, 1784. Petitioner prays bounty in Franklin Co.

**STEWART, CHARLES.** Certificate of Elijah Clarke, Col., April 20, 1784. Petitioner prays 287½ acres in Washington Co.

**STEWART, CHARLES.** Certificate of services as Lieut. of Capt. Walker's Company of Minute Men, E. Clarke, Col., April 7, 1784. Petitioner prays bounty in Washington Co.

**STEWART, ADJUTANT JAMES.** Certificate of Elijah Clarke, Col., March 29, 1784. Petitioner prays 400 acres bounty. Warrant 271.

**STEWART, JOHN.** (deceased). Certificate as refugee soldier, Elijah Clarke, Col., April 7, 1784. James Stewart, executor prays bounty in Franklin Co.

**STEWART, COL. JOHN.** Certificate of Gb. Lee, Col. Petitioner prays bounty (800 acres) in Washington Co.

# CERTIFICATES OF SERVICE IN AMERICAN REVOLUTION. 167

**STEWART, JOHN.** Certificate of Elijah Clarke, Col., April 21, 1784. Petitioner prays bounty in Washington Co.

**STEWART, ROBERT.** Certificate of Elijah Clarke, Col., Feb. 2, 1784.

**STUART, SAMUEL.** Certificate of Elijah Clarke, Col., Feb. 2, 1784. Warrant 759.

**STEDMAN, LIEUT. JAMES.** Certificate of service in 4th Battalion Ga. Line; killed by the enemy near 96, South Carolina in 1780. John Habersham, Major, April 4, 1784.

**SHEFFIELD, JOHN.** Certificate of Jas. Jackson, Lt. Col., Ga. Legion, April 3, 1784. Petitioner prays 287½ acres in Franklin Co.

**SULLAVAN, OWEN, SR.** Certificate of Greenberry Lee, Col., Mar. 11, 1784. Petitioner prays 287½ acres in Washington Co.

**SULLIVAN, WILLIAM.** Certificate of Elijah Clarke, Col., Feb. 2, 1784. Petitioner prays 575 acres in Washington Co. Warrant 1466. 2d certificate of Elijah Clarke, Col., Feb. 2, 1784.

**SULLIVAN, WILLIAM.** Certificate as refugee soldier, Elijah Clarke, Col., Feb. 28, 1784. Warrant 1465.

**SUMMERS, DEMPSEY.** Certificate of Elijah Clarke, Col., Jan. 24, 1785. Warrant 744.

**SUMMERS, JOHN.** Certificate of Elijah Clarke, Col., Jan. 24, 1785. Warrant 742.

**SUMMERS, SAMUEL.** Certificate of Elijah Clarke, Col., Jan. 3, 1785. Warrant 743.

**SUMMERFORD, JACOB.** Certificate of Elijah Clarke, Lt. Col., May 10, 1784. Petitioner prays 287½ acres in Franklin Co. Warrant 764.

**SUMMERFORD, RICHARD.** Certificate of Elijah Clarke, Lt. Col., May 10, 1784. Petitioner prays 287½ acres in Franklin Co. Warrant 763.

**SUMMERLIN, JAMES.** Certificate as refugee soldier, Elijah Clarke, Col., Jan. 24, 1785. Warrant 1436.

**SUMMERLIN, WILLIAM.** Certificate of Benj. Few, Col., July 20, 1784. Petitioner prays 287½ acres bounty.

**SALLET, ROBERT.** Certificate as refugee soldier (missing), with ex. order for bounty. Petitioner prays 575 acres in Franklin Co. Warrant 1432.

—T—

**TANYHILL, JOHN.** Certificate of Samuel Jack, Col., March 25, 1784. Warrant 793.

**TUNUS, NEHEMIAH.** Certificate of Elijah Clarke, Col., Feb. 20, 1784. Petitioner prays 287½ acres in Franklin Co.

**TATE, RICHARD.** Certificate of Elijah Clarke, Col., Dec. 10, 1784. Petitioner prays bounty in Washington Co.

**TARVIN, GEORGE.** Certificate of Gb. Lee, Col., Feb. 23, 1784. Petitioner prays 287½ acres in Washington Co.

**TAYLOR, EDMUND.** Certificate of Littleberry Moseley, Capt and Paymaster, May 5, 1785.

**TAYLOR, HENRY.** Certificate of Gb. Lee, Col., Feb. 23, 1784. Petitioner prays 287½ acres in Washington Co.

**TAYLOR, CAPT. JAMES.** Certificate of Samuel Jack, Col., April 22, 1784. Warrant No. 227 for 575 acres in Washington Co.

**TAYLOR, JOHN.** Certificate of John Twiggs, B. G., March 29, 1784. Petitioner prays 287½ acres in Washington Co.

**TAYLOR, JOSIAH.** Certificate of John Twiggs, B. G., March 23, 1784. Petitioner prays bounty in Washington Co.

**TAYLOR, RANDOLPH.** Certificate of Elijah Clarke, Col., May 27, 1784. Robert Taylor (brother) prays bounty on above certificate. Warrant 1497.

**TAYLOR, ROBERT JR.** Certificate of Elijah Clarke, Col., July 26, 1784. Petitioner prays 287½ acres in Franklin Co.

**TAYLOR, ROBERT.** Certificate of Elijah Clarke, Col., April 22, 1784. Petitioner prays 250 acres in Franklin Co.

**TAYLOR, THOMAS.** Certificate of Jas. Jackson, Col., Ga. State Legion, April 7, 1784. Petitioner prays 287½ acres in Washington Co.

**TERONDEL, DANIEL.** Order to surveyor of Franklin Co., to lay out 575 acres as bounty, June 6, 1785.

**TANKERFIELD, JOHN.** Certificate of Elijah Clarke, Col., Sept. 8, 1784. Petitioner prays bounty in Washington Co.

**TANNER, JOEL.** Certificate of Elijah Clarke, Col., Sept. 8, 1784. Petitioner ,prays bounty in Washington Co.

**THORP, JOHN.** Certificate as refugee soldier, John Baker, Col., August 2, 1784. Warrant 1484.

**THEGOTT, JOHN.** Certificate of Elijah Clarke, Col., Jan. 25, 1785. Warrant 796.

**THORN, WILLIAM.** Certificate of Caleb Howell, Col., Feb. 29, 1784. Petitioner prays 575 acres in Washington Co.

**THORNTON. WILLIAM.** Certificate of Elijah Clarke, Col., Feb. 2, 1784. 2d certificate of Elijah Clarke, Col., May 17, 1784. Petitioner prays bounties in Franklin Co.

# CERTIFICATES OF SERVICE IN AMERICAN REVOLUTION. 169

**THORNTON, SAMUEL.** Certificate of Elijah Clarke, Col., April 20, 1784. Petitioner prays 250 acres in Washington Co.

**THORNTON, SOLOMON.** Certificate of Elijah Clarke, Col., Feb. 2, 1784. Petitioner prays 287½ acres in Washington Co.

**THOMAS, SERGEANT BENJAMIN.** Certificate as soldier in Dragoons, signed by George Marbury.

**THOMAS, ALLEN.** Augusta, Oct. 31, 1789. These are to certify that I have audited the claims and demands of Allen Thomas against the State of Georgia for services amounting to 2 pounds, 17 shillings; John Wereat, auditor.

**THOMAS, SERGEANT BENJAMIN.** Petition for bounty as Sergeant in the Continental Line on certificate (missing). See above.

**THOMAS, GIDEON.** Certificate of John Twiggs, B. G., April 6, 1784. Petitioner prays 287½ acres in Washington Co.

**THOMAS, SAMUEL.** Certificate as refugee soldier, John Twiggs, B. G., March 17, 1784. Petitioner prays 287½ acres in Washington Co. 2d certificate of John Twiggs, B. G., March 23, 1784. Petitioner prays 287½ acres in Washington Co.

**THOMPSON, BENJAMIN.** Certificate of Elijah Clarke, Col., Feb. 2, 1784. 2d certificate of Elijah Clarke, Col., Feb. 2, 1784. Petitioner prays on 2 above certificates 575 acres in Washington Co. Warrant 1487.

**THOMPSON, ISHAM.** Certificate of Elijah Clarke, Col., Feb. 2, 1784.

**THOMPSON, JOHN.** Certificate of Elijah Clarke, Col., Feb. 2, 1784.

**THOMPSON, JESSE.** Certificate of Gb. Lee, Col., April 6, 1784. Petitioner prays 287½ acres in Washington Co.

**THOMPSON, LABAN.** Certificate of John Twiggs, B. G., March 23, 1784. Petitioner prays 250 acres in Washington Co. Savannah, Nov. 10, 1784. I have audited the claims of Laban Thompson against the State of Georgia, amounting to 2 pounds, 17 shillings for services. (signed) John Wereat, auditor.

**THOMPSON, PETER.** Certificate of Elijah Clarke, Col., Feb. 2, 1784. Petitioner prays bounty in Franklin Co.

**THOMPSON, BENJAMIN.** Certificate of Elijah Clarke, Col., Feb. 2, 1784. 2d certificate of Elijah Clarke, Col., Feb. 2, 1784. Petitioner prays 575 acres in Washington Co.

**THOMPSON, DRURY.** Certificate of Elijah Clarke, Col., Feb. 2, 1784. Petitioner prays bounty in Franklin Co. Warrant 1489.

**THOMPSON, ISHAM.** Certificate of Elijah Clarke, Col., Feb. 2, 1784. Petitioner prays bounty in Franklin Co. Warrant 1491.

170  ROSTER OF THE REVOLUTION.

THOMPSON, JAMES. Certificate of Greenberry Lee, Col., Feb., 2, 1784. Petitioner prays 287½ acres in Franklin Co.

THOMPSON, JAMES. Certificate of Elijah Clarke, Col., April 7, 1784. Petititioner prays 287½ acres in Washington Co.
2d certificate of Elijah Clarke, Col., Jan. 25, 1785.

THOMPSON, CAPT. JOHN. Certificate of Elijah Clarke, Col., April 24, 1784. Warrant 910. 2d certificate of Elijah Clarke, Col., April 24, 1784. Petitioner prays 500 acres in Franklin Co.

THOMPSON, JOHN. Certificate as refugee soldier, Elijah Clarke, Col., April 7, 1784. Petitioner prays 287½ acres in Washington Co.

THOMPSON, PETER. Certificate of Elijah Clarke, Col., Feb. 2, 1784. Warrant 1490.

THOMPSON, ROBERT. Certificate of Elijah Clarke, Col., Feb. 2, 1784. Petitioner prays bounty in Franklin Co. Warrant 1492. 2d certificate of Elijah Clarke, Col., Feb. 2, 1784. Petitioner prays bounty in Franklin Co.

THOMPSON, REUBEN. Certificate of Elijah Clarke, Col., Feb. 2, 1784.

THOMPSON, WILLIAM. Certificate of Jas. McNeil, Col., Feb. 2, 1784. 2d certificate as refugee soldier, Jas. Jackson, Col., Ga. State Legion, April 6, 1784. Petitioner prays 575 acres in Washington Co.

THOMPSON, WILLIAM. Certificate of Elijah Clarke, Col., Feb. 2, 1784. 2d certificate of Elijah Clarke, Col., Feb. 2, 1784.

THOMPSON, WILLIAM. Certificate of Elijah Clarke, Col., Feb. 2, 1784. 2d certificate of Elijah Clarke, Col., Feb. 2, 1784. Petitioner prays on two above certificates 575 acres in Franklin Co.

THOMPSON, ZACHARIAH. Certificate of Elijah Clarke, Col., April 30, 1784. Petitioner prays 287½ acres in Washington Co.

THOMAS, BENJAMIN. Certificate of Elijah Clarke, Col., April 7, 1784. Petitioner prays 287½ acres in Washington Co. Warrant 790.

THOMAS, GILSHOT. Certificate of Jas. McKay, Col., and John Twiggs, B. G., April 30, 1784. Petitioner prays 500 acres in Washington Co.

THOMAS, JAMES. Certificate of E. Clarke, Lt. Col., Jan. 3, 1785. Warrant 791.

THOMAS, PETER. Certificate of Jenkins Davis, Col., Mar. 24, 1784. Petitioner prays 500 acres in Washington Co. 2 Warrants.

THORNTON, WILLIAM. Ex. order for bounty upon certificates of Col. E. Clarke, March 25, 1784. Petitioner prays 287½ acres in Washington Co.

THORN, DAVID. Certificate of Lyman Hall, Gov., Dec. 31, 1783.

**THORN, DAVID.** Certificate of Caleb Howell, Col., Jan. 16, 1784. Petitioner prays 575 acres in Washington Co.

**THORN, WILLIAM.** Certificate as refugee soldier, Jenkins Davis, Lt. Col., Dec. 8, 1783. Warrant 1493.

**THREADGILL, GEORGE.** Petition for 230 acres in the Reserve, as per certificate annexed (missing). Granted Jan. 31, 1785.

**THREADGILL, CAPT. THOMAS.** Petition for bounty of 690 acres in the Reserve. Granted Jan. 31, 1785.

**THURMON, ABSOLEM.** Certificate of Elijah Clarke, Col., Feb. 2, 1784. Petitioner prays 250 acres in Washington Co.

**THURMON, JOHN.** Certificate of Elijah Clarke, Col., Feb. 2, 1784. Warrant 1483. 2d certificate of Elijah Clarke, Col., Feb. 2, 1784. Petitioner prays both bounties in Washington Co. John Thurmon of Virginia prays 500 acres in Franklin Co. and 500 acres in Washington Co. for self, wife, 4 children and 19 slaves.

**TEMPLE, CAPT. ANDREW.** Petition of Edward Cowan, administrator of estate of the late Capt. Andrew Temple of the Ga. Line, for 920 acres for his heirs.

**THOMPSON, JESSE.** Certificate of Elijah Clarke, Col., Dec. 17, 1784. Warrant 795.

**THOMPSON, JAMES.** Certificate as refugee soldier, Elijah Clarke, Col., Jan. 25, 1785. Warrant 1486.

**THOMPSON, JOSHUA.** Certificate of Gb. Lee, Col., March 26, 1784. Petitioner prays 287½ acres in Washington Co.

**THOMPSON, WILLIAM.** Certificate of Jas. McNeil, Col., Feb. 20, 1784. Petitioner prays bounty in Washington Co. Warrant 1473. 2d certificate of Jas. McNeil, Col., Feb. 20, 1784 (missing), with ex. order for bounty. Petitioner prays 250 acres in Washington Co. Warrant No. 3.

**TINE, HENRY.** Petition stating he deserted the British and enlisted in the Continental Army, as per certificate annexed (missing). Prays 230 acres in Washington Co.

**TINDALL, JOHN.** Certificate of Jas. Jackson, Lt. Col., Ga. Legion, Mar. 23, 1784. Petitioner (of Richmond Co.) prays 200 acres in Franklin Co.

**TINDALL, WILLIAM.** Certificate of Jas. McNeil, Col., Feb. 2, 1784. Petitioner prays 287½ acres in Franklin Co.

**TODD, WILLIAM.** Certificate of Jas. Jackson, Lt. Col., Ga. Legion, Sep. 18, 1784.

**TOLAR, DEMPSEY.** Certificate of Greenberry Lee, Col., April 26, 1784. Petitioner prays bounty in Franklin Co.

**TOMLINSON, LIEUT. DAVID.** Certificate of Wm. Ames, Capt., countersigned by Elijah Clarke, Col., April 20, 1784. Petitioner prays 287½ acres in Washington Co. Warrant 267.

**TOMME, JOSEPH.** Certificate of Jas. McNeil, Col., April 5, 1784. Petitioner prays 287½ acres in Washington Co.

**TOMKINS, WILLIAM.** Petition for bounty as per certificate of Col. Jas. McNeil, Jan. 12, 1784. (missing).

**THOMAS, JAMES.** Certificate of Jas. McNeil, Col. Feb. 2, 1784. Petitioner prays 287½ acres in Washington Co.

**TORRENCE, JOHN.** Certificate as refugee soldier, Wm. Candler, Col., Ref. Regt. Petitioner prays 287½ acres in Franklin Co. Warrant 1469.

**TOWNS, JOHN.** Ex. order for bounty upon certificate of Samuel Jack, Col., March 13, 1784 (missing). Petitioner prays 250 acres in Washington Co. Also prays head rights of 900 acres in Washington Co., having brought from South Carolina himself, wife, 10 children and 3 negroes. Warrant 799.

**TOWNSEND, HENRY.** Certificate as refugee soldier, Elijah Clarke, Col., Sep. 2, 1784. Petitioner prays bounty in Washington Co. Also prays head rights of 550 acres in Washington Co. for self, wife, 5 children and one negro, coming from Camden Dist., S. C.

**TOWNSEND, THOMAS.** Certificate of Jas. McNeil, Col., Mar. 15, 1784. Petitioner prays 250 acres in Washington Co.

**TRAPP, JOHN.** Certificate of Elijah Clarke, Col., Feb. 2, 1784. Petitioner prays 287½ acres in Washington Co.

**TRAPP, JOSEPH.** Certificate of Elijah Clarke, Col., April 24, 1784. Petitioner prays bounty in Franklin Co. and 2d bounty of 287½ acres in Washington Co.

**TWEEDLE, JOHN.** Certificate of Elijah Clarke, Col., May 20, 1784. Petitioner prays 250 acres in Franklin Co.

**TRIMBLE, MOSES.** Certificate of Elijah Clarke, Col., May 20, 1784. Petitioner prays bounty in Franklin Co.

**TRAMMEL, DENNIS.** Certificate as refugee soldier, Benjamin Few, Col., May 15, 1784. Petitioner prays 287½ acres in Washington Co.

**TRUEMAN, GARRETT.** Certificate of Elijah Clarke, Col., April 14, 1784. Petitioner prays 287½ acres in Franklin Co.

**TRUEMAN, JAMES.** Certificate of Elijah Clarke, Col., Feb. 2, 1784.

**TUREMAN, JOHN.** Certificate of Elijah Clarke, Col., Feb. 2, 1784.

**TRAYWICK, FRANCIS.** House of Representatives, Feb. 21, 1785. The committee to whom petition No. 40 was referred wherein Francis Traywick

CERTIFICATES OF SERVICE IN AMERICAN REVOLUTION. 173

set forth that he was wounded in service and rendered incapable of supporting himself and family—The Committee are of opinion the prayer of petitioner should be granted; and the Governor be empowered to grant a warrant for same. Agreed to by Assembly. Extract from the Minutes. John Wilkinson, Sec. Gen. Assembly. Granted 500 acres.

**TROY, JOHN.** Certificate of Elijah Clarke, Col., Feb. 2, 1784. Warrant 1496. 2d certificate of Elijah Clarke, Col., Feb. 2, 1784. Petitioner prays 287½ acres in Washington Co.

**TROY, JOHN.** Certificate of Elijah Clarke, Col., April 1, 1784. Warrant 798. 2d certificate of Elijah Clarke, Col., April 24, 1784. Petitioner prays 250 acres in Franklin Co. Warrant 800.

**TURNER, CHARLES.** Certificate to Charles Turner from Brunswick Co., Va. as refugee soldier and died in the service, Isaac Hicks, Capt. 3rd Ga. Cont. Battalion, Jan. 27, 1784. Granted 200 acres in the Reserve.

**TURNER, CAPT. DAVID.** Certificate as Capt-Lieut. of Capt. Morris' Co. Artillery and died in service Dec. 1778. John Habersham, Major Ga. Line, March 19, 1784. David Rees, executor of David Turner, late Capt-Lieut. in Ga. Continental Line of Artillery, prays 690 acres bounty. Warrant 97.

**FARRELL, JOHN.**
**TURNER, THOMAS, SR.**
**TURNER, THOMAS, JR.**
**TURNER, PETER.**
**TURNER, DENNIS.**
This is to certify that John Farrell, Thomas Turner, Sr., Thomas Turner, Jr. Peter Turner and Dennis Turner were soldiers under me in Continental Regt. Light Horse. Leonard Marbury, Lt. Col., Jan. 24, 1785.

**TURNER, GEORGE.** Certificate of 3 years' service in 3d Ga. Cont. Line, Francis Tennill, Col., Ga. Line, April 7, 1784. Warrant 203.

**TURNER, HENRY.** Certificate of Elijah Clarke, Col., Jan., 1785. Warrant 786.

**TURNER, JOHN.** Certificate of Elijah Clarke, Lt. Col., Jan. 25, 1785. Warrant 787. 2d certificate as refugee soldier, Elijah Clarke, Col., Jan. 25, 1785. Warrant 1476.

**TURNER, NEHEMIAH.** Certificate of Elijah Clarke, Lt. Col., March 29, 1784. Warrant 806.

**TURNER, SAMPSON.** Certificate of Elijah Clarke, Col., Jan. 25, 1785.

**TYNER, RICHARD.** Certificate of Elijah Clarke, Col., Feb. 2, 1784.

**TURNER, GEORGE.** Petition for 200 acres in Reserve as soldier in 3d Bat. Cont. Troops, State of Ga. As per certificate annexed (missing).

**TUCKER, GEORGE.** Certificate of Elijah Clarke, Col., Feb. 2, 1784. Warrant 1494. 2d certificate of Elijah Clarke, Col., Feb. 2, 1784. Petitioner prays 2 warrants of 287½ acres each in Washington Co.

**TUCKER, PASCHAL.** Certificate as soldier in 3d Ga. Battalion, John McIntosh, Lt. Col., 3rd Batt. April 30, 1785. Warrant 201.

**TUCKER, ROBERT.** Certificate of Elijah Clarke, Col., April 12, 1784. Petitioner prays 287½ acres in Washington Co.

**TRAPP, JOSEPH.** Certificate of Elijah Clarke, Lt. Col., Feb. 25, 1784.

**TUCKER, THOMAS, SR.** Certificate of Elijah Clarke, Col. May. 10, 1784. Warrant 797. 2d certificate of Elijah Clarke, Col., Feb. 2, 1784. Petitioner prays 287½ acres Washington Co.

**THOMAS TUCKER, JR.** Certificate of Elijah Clarke, Col., Feb. 2, 1784. Petitioner prays 287½ acres in Washington Co. 2d certificate as refugee soldier, Elijah Clarke, Col., April 12, 1784. Petitioner prays 287½ acres in Washington Co.

**TULLY, WILLIAM.** Certificate as refugee, Francis Pugh, Col., March 22, 1784. Petitioner prays 250 acres in Washington Co. Warrant 1495.

**TURKINETT, GEORGE.** Certificate as refugee soldier, Jas. McNeil, Col., March 15, 1784. Petitioner prays 287½ acres in Washington Co.

**TURKINETT, HENRY.** Certificate as refugee soldier, Jas. McNeil, Col., March 23, 1784. Petitioner prays 250 acres in Washington Co.

**TRUEMAN, GEORGE.** Certificate as refugee soldier, Elijah Clarke, Col., April 20, 1784. Petitioner prays 287½ acres in Franklin Co.

**TWEDLE, JOHN.** Certificate as Sergeant in 1st Ga. Battn., George Handley, Capt. Ga. Regt., Feb. 25, 1784. Warrant 205.

**TWIGGS, BRIG. GEN. JOHN.** Certificate of Gov. Houstoun, Feb. 6, 1784. Petitioner prays 3 grants of 500 acres, 500 acres and 437½ acres in Washington Co. Warrant 853.

—U—

**UPTON, EDWARD.** Certificate as refugee soldier, Jas. Jackson, Lt. Col., Ga. State Legion, April 6, 1784. Petitioner prays 287½ acres in Franklin Co.

**UPTON, PHILIP.** Certificate of Gb Lee, Col., March 11, 1784. Petitioner prays 287½ acres in Washington Co.

**UNDERWOOD, SAMUEL.** Certificate of Jas. McNeil, Col., March 15, 1784. Petitioner prays 287½ acres in Washington Co.

—V—

**VANCE, PATRICK.** Certificate as refugee soldier, Elijah Clarke, Col., April 21, 1784. Petitioner prays bounty in Washington Co.

**VANN, CADER.** Certificate of Elijah Clarke, Col., Dec. 16, 1784. Warrant 802.

# CERTIFICATES OF SERVICE IN AMERICAN REVOLUTION.

**VAN ZANT, ISAAC.** Certificate as refugee soldier, John Twiggs, B. G., Jan. 8, 1784. Petitioner prays 250 acres in Franklin Co. Warrant 1505.

**VANN, JAMES.** Certificate as refugee soldier, Elijah Clarke, Col., Feb. 2, 1784. Petitioner prays bounty in Washington Co.

**VEAZEY, JAMES.** Certificate of E. Clarke, Col., April 6, 1784. Petitioner prays 287½ acres in Washington Co.

**VEAZEY, JACOB.** Power of Atty. to Jere. Oates to draw his Bounty Warrant.

**VICKERS, SOLOMON.** Certificate as soldier in 1st Battn. Ga. Cont. Troops and died in service of this State, Ignatius Few, Capt. Cont. Line. Warrant 206.

**VICKERS, THOMAS.** Certificate of Greenberry Lee, Col., March 11, 1784. Petetioner prays bounty in Washington Co.

—W—

**WELLS, ANDREW.** Certificate as refugee soldier, Elijah Clarke, Col., Aug. 21, 1784. Warrant 1531.

**WELLS, BENJAMIN.** Certificate of Gb. Lee, Col., March 11, 1784. Petitioner prays bounty in Washington Co. 2d certificate of Gb. Lee, Col., Feb. 27, 1784.

**WELLS, JOURDAN.** Petitions of Benjamin and Jourdan Wells upon annexed certificates (missing) for 287½ acres each in Washington Co.

**WELLS, SURGEON HUMPHREY.** Certificate of Elijah Clarke, Col., Jan. 2, 1784. Endorsed by Jas. Jackson, Col., Ga. State Legion. 2d certificate of Jas. McNeil, Col., April 13, 1784. Petitioner, Mrs. Abigail Wells, prays bounty in Washington Co.

**WELLS, JACOB.** Certificate of Elijah Clarke, Lt. Col., Dec. 16, 1784. Warrant 829.

**WELLS, JOHN.** Certificate of Asa Emanuel, Col., April 7, 1784. Petitioner prays 287½ acres in Washington Co.

**WELLS, JOSEPH.** Certificate of Elijah Clarke, Col., April 3, 1784. Petitioner prays 287½ acres in Washington Co. Warrant 828. 2d certificate of Elijah Clarke, Col., June 28, 1784. Petitioner prays 287½ acres in Franklin Co.

**WELLS, MESHECK.** Certificate of Joseph Pannill, Col., Feb. 3, 1784. Warrant 213.

**WELLS, ROBERT.** Certificate as refugee soldier, Elijah Clarke, Col., August 24, 1784. On Sept. 7, 1784, petitioner transfers his rights to Robt. Correy. Warrant 1530.

**WADE, HEZEKIAH.** Petition for 575 acres in Washington Co. upon certificate of Samuel Jack, Col., Feb. 1, 1784. (missing).

**WADE, JOHN.** Certificate as refugee Soldier, Wm. Candler, Col., Ref. Regt. Feb. 21, 1784. Petitioner prays 287½ acres in Washington Co. Warrant 1539.

**WADE, NATHANIEL.** Certificate as refugee soldier, Wm. Candler, Col., Ref. Regt. Feb. 21, 1784. Petitioner prays 287½ acres in Washington Co. Warrant 1541.

**WADE, NEHEMIAH.** Certificate as refugee soldier, Wm. Candler, Col., Ref. Regt., Feb. 21, 1784.

**WELBORN, DAVID.** Certificate as refugee soldier, Elijah Clarke, Col., Feb. 2, 1784. Petitioner prays 250 acres in Washington Co.

**WELBORN, EDWARD.** Certificate as refugee soldier, Elijah Clarke, Col., Feb. 2, 1784. Petitioner prays 250 acres in Washington Co.

**WELBORN, THOMAS.** Certificate of Elijah Clarke, Col., Feb. 2, 1784. Petitioner prays 287½ acres in Washington Co.

**WEBSTER, ABNER.** Certificate of Samuel Jack, Col., April 6, 1784. Petitioner prays 287½ acres in Washington Co.

**WEBSTER, BENJAMIN.** Certificate of 3 years service in 2d Ga. Cont. Battn. J. Stirk, Lt. Col., 2d Ga. Battn. Petitioner prays 200 acres in the Reserve. Warrant 210. 2d certificate of Jas. McNeil, Col., March 15, 1784.

**WEBSTER, JOHN.** Certificate of Elijah Clarke, Col., Sept. 8, 1784. Petitioner prays bounty in Franklin Co.

**WEBSTER, JONATHAN.** Certificate of Elijah Clarke, Col., Sept. 8, 1784. Petitioner prays bounty in Washington Co.

**WEBSTER, SAMUEL.** Certificate of Samuel Jack, Col., April 6, 1784. Petitioner prays 250 acres in Washington Co. Warrant 849.

**WEBSTER, THOMAS.** Certificate as drummer in Ga. Line, John Habersham, Major Ga. Line, Nov. 23, 1784. Petitioner, Peter Webster, prays 230 acres in the reserve. Warrant 217.

**WEBSTER, WILLIAM.** Ex. order for bounty on certificate of Col. E. Clarke, March 25, 1784. (missing). Petitioner prays 250 acres in Washington Co.

**WEATHERS, EDWARD.** Certificate of John Twiggs, B. G., April 9, 1784. Petitioner prays bounty in Washington Co.

**WEBB, JESSE.** Certificate of Elijah Clarke, Col., Feb. 2, 1784. Warrant 1548.

**WEBB, JOHN.** Certificate of service in 2d Co. Cont. Artillery of Ga. John Dollar, Capt. Talbot, Brig. Gen., March 3, 1784. Petitioner prays 230

## CERTIFICATES OF SERVICE IN AMERICAN REVOLUTION.

acres in the reserve. 2d certificate of Elijah Clarke, Col., April 8, 1784. Petitioner prays 575 acres in Franklin Co. Warrant 1550.

**WEBB, WILLIAM.** Certificate of Elijah Clarke, Col., Feb. 2, 1784. Warrant 1549. 2d certificate of Elijah Clarke, Col., April 3, 1784. Petitioner prays 575 acres in Franklin Co.

**WAGONON, GEORGE.** Certificate of Elijah Clarke, Col., April 20, 1784. Petitioner prays bounty in Washington Co.

**WAGNON, JOHN MICHAEL.** Certificate of Elijah Clarke, Col., May 22, 1784. Petitioner prays 287½ acres in Washington Co. Warrant 1515.

**WAGNON, THOMAS.** Ex. order for bounty upon certificate of Col. Samuel Elbert, Feb. 13, 1784. (missing). Petitioner prays 230 acres in the reserve. Warrant 208.

**WAGNON, WILLIAM.** Certificate of Elijah Clarke, Col., Feb. 2, 1784. Petitioner prays bounty in Washington Co.

**WESTBROOK, LIEUT. STEPHEN.** Certificate of Elijah Clarke, Col., Feb. 2, 1784. 2d certificate of Elijah Clarke, Col., Feb. 2, 1784. Petitioner prays 690 acres in 2 certificates in Washington Co. Warrant 1508.

**WEST, CAPT. SAMUEL.** Certificate of Jas. Jackson, Col., July 16, 1784. Petitioner prays bounty in Franklin Co. Warrant 914.

**WEST, MAJOR SAMUEL.** Certificate of Jas. Jackson, Col., 1st Regt. Cont. Line Ga.

**WEST, JAMES.** Certificate of Gb. Lee, Col., Feb. 2, 1784. Petitioner prays 287½ acres in Washington Co.

**WEST, JOHN.** Certificate of James Jackson, Col., April 2, 1784. Petitioner prays 287½ acres in Washington Co.

**WELBORN, CURTIS, JR.** Certificate of Elijah Clarke, Col., Jan. 29, 1785. Warrant 846.

**WELDEN, ANDREW.** Certificate of E. Clarke, Col., April 9, 1784. Petitioner prays 250 acres in Washington Co.

**WALLACE, WILLIAM.** Certificate of Jas. Jackson, Lt. Col. Ga. St. Legion, March 26, 1784. Petitioner prays 287½ acres in Washington Co. 2d certificate of Elijah Clarke, Col., Feb. 2, 1784.

**WALLIS, ABSOLEM.** Petition as refugee soldier as per certificate annexed (missing). Prays 2 warrants of 287½ acres each in Washington Co.

**WELCH, CALEB.** Certificate of Gb. Lee, Col., March 1, 1784. Petitioner prays bounty in Washington Co.

**WELCH, NICHOLAS.** Certificate of Gb. Lee, Col., March 11, 1784. Petitioner prays bounty in Washington Co.

**WELCH, SERGEANT JOSHUA.** Certificate of John Stewart, Col., April 20, 1784. Petition of Mrs. Mary Welch, widow, in the name of Nicholas Welch father of Joshua Welch, deceased. Warrant 280.

**WELCH, JOSHUA.** Certificate of Elijah Clarke, Col., Feb. 2, 1784. Petitioner prays 287½ acres in Washington Co.

**WELCHER, JOHN.** Certificate of Col. Gb. Lee and Col. Benj. Few, April 6, 1784. Bounty granted in Washington Co. 2d certificate of Jas. Jackson, Col., Sept. 18, 1784. Petitioner prays bounty in Franklin Co.

**WELCHER, JORDAN.** Certificate as refugee soldier, Gb. Lee, Col., April 6, 1784. Petitioner prays 287½ acres in Washington Co.

**WAGNON, THOMAS.** Certificate as soldier in 3d Ga. Cont. Line, J. P. Wagnon, Lt. 3d Ga. Regt. Endorsed by Samuel Elbert, Col. Comdg. Regt.

**WALKER, BENJAMIN.** Certificate of Elijah Clarke, Col., Feb. 2, 1784. Warrant 1506. 2d certificate of Elijah Clarke, Col., Feb. 2, 1784. Warrant 1533.

**WALKER, EDWARD,**
**WALKER, WILLIAM.** Certificate that Edward Walker and William, his son, served faithfully as refugee soldiers. Gb. Lee, Col., May 25, 1784. Each granted bounty in Washington Co.

**WALKER, DAVID.** Power of Atty. to Jas. McNeil to receive his bounty.

**WALKER, ELISHA.** Certificate of Jas. McNeil, Col., Feb. 2, 1784. Petitioner prays bounty in Washington Co.

**WALKER, ISAAC.** Certificate as refugee soldier, Asa Emanuel, Col., April 7, 1784. Petitioner prays 287½ acres in Washington Co.

**WALKER, JOHN.** Certificate as refugee soldier, John Baker, Col., May 10, 1784. Petitioner prays 287½ acres in Franklin Co. Warrant 1532.

**WALKER, JOSEPH.** Certificate of Elijah Clarke, Col., Feb. 2, 1784. Petitioner prays 287½ acres in Washington Co.

**WALKER, SILVANUS.** Certificate of Elijah Clarke, Col., Feb. 2, 1784. Petitioner prays 287½ acres in Washington Co. Also prays head rights of 300 acres in Washington Co. on self, 3 children and 3 negroes.

**WALKER, CHAPLAIN SANDERS.** Certificate of Col. E. Clarke, that he was enlisted as Chaplain by Col. Dooley, that he lost considerable property by the Tories—had twice left the State—that at Col. Clarke's earnest solicitation he returned to use his influence with Maddox Williams and Waters on behalf of the prisoners and distressed inhabitants—that he not only undertook the hazzardous enterprise, but was of signal service to his country in prosecuting the instructions given him. Certificate signed by Col. Clarke, Daniel Coleman and Geo. Walton. Petitioner prays 747½ acres in Washington Co.

**WALKER, THOMAS.** Certificate of Elijah Clarke, Col., Nov. 2, 1784. Petitioner prays bounty in Washington Co.

# CERTIFICATES OF SERVICE IN AMERICAN REVOLUTION. 179

**WALKER, WILLIAM SR.** Certificate of Elijah Clarke, Col., April 12, 1784. Petitioner prays 287½ acres in Washington Co.

**WALKER, WILLIAM.** Certificate of Samuel Jack, Col., April 26, 1784. Petitioner prays 287½ acres in Franklin Co.

**WALKER, CAPT. WILLIAM.** Certificate of Elijah Clarke, Col., Feb. 2, 1784. 2d certificate as refugee soldier, Benj. Few. Col., Aug. 19, 1784. Petitioner prays 575 acres in Washington Co. Warrant 881.

**WALDEN, ROBERT.** Certificate of Gb. Lee, Col., March 30, 1784. Petitioner prays 250 acres in Franklin Co.

**WOLICON, DANIEL, SR.** Certificate of Jas. Martin, Col., April 13, 1784.

**WALLER, WILLIAM.** Certificate of ——————. Petitioner prays bounty in Washington Co.

**WALSH, EDWARD.** Petition for 690 acres in the reserve, as per certificate annexed. (missing).

**WOLICON, DANIEL.** Certificate as refugee soldier, John Twiggs, B. G., April 13, 1784. Petitioner prays bounty in Washington Co.

**WALL, ARTHUR.** Certificate of Elijah Clarke, Col., Sept. 6, 1784. Petitioner prays 287½ acres in Washington Co. Warrant 1514.

**WALL, DAVID.** Certificate of Samuel Jack, Col., April 7, 1784. Petitioner prays 287½ acres in Washington Co. Warrant 817.

**WALL, JOHN.** Certificate of Samuel Jack, Col., April 20, 1784. Petitioner prays 250 acres in Washington Co. Warrant 819.

**WATERS, CHARLES.** Certificate of Elijah Clarke, Col., Feb. 2, 1784.

**WELLS, JORDAN.** Certificate of Gb. Lee, Col., Feb. 25, 1784.

**WICKMAN, JOHN.** Certificate of E. Clarke, Col., Nov. 16, 1784. Warrant 852.

**WILCHER, JEREMIAH.** Certificate of Gb. Lee, Col., April 6, 1784. Petitioner prays 287½ acres in Washington Co.

**WIDEMAN, ADAM.** Certificate of Elijah Clarke, Col., Feb. 2, 1784. Petitioner prays 287½ acres in Washington Co. Warrant 1554.

**WILLIS, BRITTAIN.** Certificate of Elijah Clarke, Col., Feb. 2, 1784. Petitioner prays bounty in Washington Co. 2d certificate of Elijah Clarke, Col., April 12, 1784. Petitioner prays 287½ acres in Washington Co. Warrant 844.

**WILLIS, JOSEPH.** Certificate of Elijah Clarke, Col., Jan. 3, 1785. Warrant 845.

**WILLIS, ISAIAH.** Certificate of Elijah Clarke, Col., April 10, 1784. Petitioner prays 250 acres in Washington Co.

**WILLIE, ROBERT.** Certificate of Elijah Clarke, Col., May 24, 1784. Petitioner prays 250 acres in Washington Co.

**WILFORD, PHILIP.** Certificate as Minute Man, E. Clarke, Col., Nov. 1784. Warrant 874.

**WILLIE, RICHARD.** Certificate as refugee soldier, John Twiggs, B. G., April 17, 1784. Petition of Joshua Inman, guardian, for Sarah, widow and James and Patty, orphans of Richard Willis, dec'd, for land in Washington Co. Warrant 1552.

**WILLIE, WILLIAM.** Certificate as refugee soldier, John Twiggs, B. G., April 17, 1784. Petition of Joshua Inman for James Willie, nephew, and heir of Wm. Willie dec'd for land in Washington Co. Warrant 1551.

**WILLIAMS, BURTON.** Certificate of Elijah Clarke, Col., Feb. 2, 1784.

**WILLIAMS, BUTLER.** Certificate as Minute Man, Elijah Clarke, Col., Jan. 3, 1785. Warrant 815.

**WILLIAMS, CARROL.** Ex. order for bounty as per certificate of Brig. Gen. Elbert, May 25, 1784. (missing). Petitioner prays 230 acres in the reserve.

**WILLIAMS, CHARLES.** Certificate of Elijah Clarke, Col., April 8, 1784. Petitioner prays 250 acres in Washington Co.

**WILLIAMS, EDWARD.** Certificate of Elijah Clarke, Col., Jan. 3, 1784. Petitioner prays 230 acres in Washington Co. Warrant 813.

**WILLIAMS, FREDERICK.** Certificate of Elijah Clarke, Col., April 7, 1784. Petitioner prays 287½ acres in Washington Co.

**WILLIAMS, GEORGE.** Certificate of Elijah Clarke, Col., Feb. 28, 1784. Warrant 816. 2d certificate of Elijah Clarke, Col., April 1, 1784. 3d certificate as soldier in 1st Battn. Minute Men, Elijah Clarke, Col., April 9, 1784. Warrant 837. Petitioner prays 3 warrants, 787 acres in Washington Co.

**WILLIAMS, JAMES.** Certificate of Jas. McNeil, Col., April 2, 1784. Petitioner prays bounty in Washington Co. 2d certificate of Elijah Clarke, Col. April 12, 1784. Petitioner prays 287½ acres in Washington Co.

**WILLIAMS, JOSEPH.** Certificate of Samuel Jack, Col. April 5, 1784. Warrant 811.

**WILLIAMS, JOHN.** Certificate of Jas. McNeil, Col., Feb. 2, 1784. Petitioner prays 287½ acres in Washington Co.

**WILLIAMS, JOHN.** Certificate of Jas. McNeil, Col., March 9, 1784. Petitioner prays 287 ½ acres in Washington Co.

**WILLIAMS, JOHN.** Certificate as soldier in 1st Battn. Minute Men, Elijah Clarke, Col., March 5, 1784.

CERTIFICATES OF SERVICE IN AMERICAN REVOLUTION. 181

**WILLIAMS, JOHN.** 2d certificate of Elijah Clarke, Col., Sept. 21, 1784. Petitioner prays 287½ acres in Washington Co.

**WILLIAMS, JOHN.** Certificate of Elijah Clarke, Col., Jan. 29, 1785. Warrant 812.

**WILLIAMS, JOSHUA.** Certificate of Gb. Lee, Col., April 20, 1784. Petitioner prays bounty in Franklin Co.

**WILLIAMS, LITTLETON.** Littleton Williams of Virginia, through his friend, Capt. John Peter Wagnon of Chatham Co. prays bounty for services as soldier in the Ga. Line.

**WILLIAMS, NATHANIEL.** Certificate of E. Clarke, Col., June 21, 1784. Petitioner prays 287½ acres in Franklin Co. Warrant 814.

**WILLIAMS, SAMUEL.** Certificate as refugee soldier. Capt. Green, endorsed by John Twiggs, B. G., April 26, 1784. Petitioner prays bounty in Washington Co.

**WILLIAMS, SAMUEL.** Certificate of Elijah Clarke, Col., Oct. 10, 1784. Warrant 838.

**WILLIAMS, THOMAS.** Certificate of Elijah Clarke, Col., Nov. 16, 1784. Petitioner prays 287½ acres in Washington Co.

**WILLIAMS, THOMAS, JR.** Certificate of Elijah Clarke, Lt. Col., Feb. 25, 1784. Warrant 810.

**WILLIAMS, ROBERT.** Certificate as refugee soldier, John Twiggs, B. G., April 5, 1784. 2d certificate of Col. McKay, endorsed by John Twiggs, B. G., April 7, 1784. Petitioner prays 2 warrants of 287½ acres each in Washington Co.

**WILDER, WILLIAM.** Certificate of Elijah Clarke, Col., Feb. 2, 1784. Petitioner prays 287½ acres in Washington Co.

**WILDER, DREAD.** Certificate of Elijah Clarke, Col., Feb. 2, 1784. Petitioner prays bounty in Washington Co.

**WILDER, MALACHI.** Certificate of Elijah Clarke, Col., Feb. 2, 1784.

**WILDER, SAMPSON.** Certificate of Elijah Clarke, Col., Feb. 2, 1784.

**WILLEBY, WILLIAM.** Certificate of Francis Tennill, Lieut. in 2d Regt., April 7, 1784. Warrant 214.

**WILLSON, ANDREW.** Certificate of E. Clarke, Col., April 7, 1784. Petitioner prays bounty in Washington Co. 2d certificate of Elijah Clarke, Col., April 6, 1784. Petitioner prays bounty in Washington Co.

**WILLSON, DAVID.** Certificate of Elijah Clarke, Col., April 20, 1784. Petitioner prays 287½ acres in Washington Co. Warrant 824.

**WILSON, HUGH.** Certificate of Elijah Clarke, Col., April 7, 1784. Petitioner prays 250 acres in Franklin Co. Warrant 827.

**WILSON, JAMES.** Certificate of Elijah Clarke, Col., April 20, 1784. Petitioner prays 287½ acres in Washington Co. 2d certificate as refugee soldier, Wm. Candler, Col., July 23, 1784. Warrant 1513.

**WILSON, CAPT. JOHN.** Certificate of Gb. Lee, Col., Feb. 25, 1784. Petitioner prays bounty in Washington Co.

**WILSON, LIEUT. JOHN.** Certificate as refugee soldier, Wm. Candler, Col., Ref. Regt. Petitioner prays bounty in Washington Co. Warrant 923.

**WILSON, ROBERT.** Certificate of Elijah Clarke, Col., Feb. 2, 1784. Petitioner prays 250 acres in Washington Co.

**WILSON, ROBERT.** Certificate of Elijah Clarke, Col., May 20, 1784. Warrant 823.

**WILSON, ROBERT.** Certificate as sergeant. Elijah Clark, Lt. Col., April 1, 1784, Warrant 270.

**WILSON, ROBERT.** Certificate as sergeant. Elijah Clark, Lt. Col., April 1, prays bounty in Washington Co.

**WILSON, SAMUEL.** Certificate of Gb. Lee, Col., Feb. 24, 1784. Petitioner prays bounty in Washington Co.

**WILSON, SAMUEL.** Certificate of Elijah Clarke, Col., Dec. 4, 1783.

**WILSON, SAMUEL.** Certificate of Elijah Clarke, Lt. Col., Jan. 25, 1785. 2d certificate of Elijah Clarke, Lt. Col., Jan. 25, 1785.

**WILKINS, DAVID.** Certificate of Elijah Clarke, Col., Feb. 25, 1784.

**WILKINS, JOHN.** Certificate of E. Clarke, Lt. Col., Jan. 3, 1785. Warrant 821.

**WILKINS, GABRIEL.** Certificate of Elijah Clarke, Lt. Col., June 21, 1784. Petioner prays 287½ acres in Franklin Co. Warrant 822.

**WILKINS, WILLIAM.** Certificate of Gb. Lee, Col., April 5, 1784. Petitioner prays 250 acres in Washington Co.

**WILKINS, GABRIEL.** Certificate of Jas. Jackson, Col., April 7, 1784. Petitioner prays 287½ acres in Washington Co.

**WILCASON, JOHN.** Certificate of Gb. Lee, Feb. 23, 1784.

**WINNINGHAM, ABNER.** Certificate of Gb. Lee, Col., Feb. 23, 1784. Petitioner prays 287½ acres in Washington Co.

**WINNINGHAM, JOHN.** Certificate of Gb. Lee, Col., Feb. 23, 1784. Petitioner prays 287½ acres bounty.

**WISENOR, JOHN.** Certificate of E. Clarke, Lt. Col., April 6, 1784. Petitioner prays 250 acres in Washington Co. Warrant 851.

**WILLIAMSON, LIEUT. COL. MICAJAH.** Certificate of Elijah Clarke, Col., Feb. 2, 1784. Warrant 860.

# CERTIFICATES OF SERVICE IN AMERICAN REVOLUTION. 183

**WILLIAMSON, MICAJAH, JR.** Certificate of Elijah Clarke, Col., April 8, 1784. Petitioner prays 287½ acres in Washington Co.

**WILLIAMSON, CHARLES.** Certificate of Elijah Clarke, Col., Feb. 2, 1784.

**WILLIAMSON, CHARLES.** Certificate of Elijah Clarke, Col. Feb. 2, 1784. Petitioner prays 575 acres on 2 certificates in Washington Co. Warrant 1538.

**WILLIAMSON, LIEUT. CHARLES.** Certificate of Elijah Clarke, Col., May 22, 1784. Petition of Susannah, widow of Charles Williamson, for 400 acres in Washington Co. Warrant 209.

**WILLIAMSON, GEORGE.** Certificate as refugee soldier, John Twiggs, B. G., April 5, 1784. Petitioner prays bounty in Washington Co. Warrant 1537.

**WILLIAMSON, LITTLETON.** Certificate of Francis Tennill, Lieut, 2d Regt., countersigned by S. Elbert, Brig. Gen., Feb. 22, 1784. 2d certificate of Lt. Col. John McIntosh, March 5, 1784. Petitioner prays 230 acres in the reserve. Warrant 216.

**WAINWRIGHT, GEORGE.** Certificate of Gb. Lee, Col., Feb. 21, 1784. 2d certificate, same signature and date. Petitioner prays bounty in Washington Co.

**WHIGGAM, JOHN.** Certificate of Jas. McNeil, Col., April 5, 1784. Petitioner prays 287½ acres in Washington Co.

**WIGGANE, WILLIAM, SR.** Certificate of Elijah Clarke, Col., April 7, 1784. Petitioner prays 287½ acres in Washington Co.

**WIGGINS, WILLIAM, JR.** Certificate of Elijah Clarke, Col., April 7, 1784.

**WIGGINS, WILLIAM.** Certificate of Elijah Clarke, Col., Feb. 2, 1784. Petitioner prays 287½ acres in Washington Co.

**WIGGINS, WILLIAM.** Certificate of Gb. Lee, Col., Feb. 23, 1784. Petitioner prays 287½ acres in Washington Co.

**WINN, BENJAMIN.** Certificate of Elijah Clarke, Col., Dec. 10, 1784.

**WINN, JOHN.** Certificate of Elijah, Clarke, Col., Dec. 10, 1784.

**WINN, JOSEPH.** Certificate as refugee soldier, John Baker, Col., June 5, 1784. Warrant 1521.

**WINN, PETER.** Certificate of John Baker, Col., Nov. 5, 1784. Warrant 1522.

**WINN, ROBERT.** Certificate of Gb. Lee, Col., Feb. 23, 1784. Petitioner prays 287½ acres in Franklin Co.

**WISE, JAMES.** Certificate of Elijah Clarke, Col., Dec. 10, 1784. Petitioner prays bounty in Washington Co.

**WISE, JOSEPH.** Certificate of Elijah Clarke, Col., July 5, 1784. Petitioner prays 287½ acres in Franklin Co.

**WINN, JOSHUA.** Ex. order for bounty upon certificate of Col. Wm. Candler, March 20, 1784. Warrant 1520.

**WISE, WILLIAM.** Certificate as refugee soldier, Elijah Clarke, Col., Jan. 25, 1785. Warrant 1511. 2d certificate of Elijah Clarke, Col., Jan. 25, 1785.

**WILKERSON, JOHN.** Certificate of Jas. Jackson, Lt. Col., Sept. 17, 1784. Petitioner prays bounty in Washington Co.

**WILCASON, JOHN.** Ex. order for bounty upon certificate of Col. Greenberry Lee, Aug. 20, 1781. (missing).

**WILKINSON, WILLIAM.** Power of attorney from Wm. Wilkinson of Mecklenburg Co. Va., to Samuel Burnley of Liberty Co., Ga.; to secure his bounty for services as a soldier in 3d Continental Regt. Ga. State Troops, Jan. 1, 1785. Certificate endorsed by Isaac Hicks, Capt. 3d Ga. Continental Battalion.

**WOLECON, DANIEL, JR.** This is to certify that I have issued to Danl. Wolecon, Jr., 2 certificates, 1st as a refugee soldier, 2d as a citizen. Jas. McNeil, Col., April 10, 1784. Granted 575 acres.

**WOMACK, JESSE.** Certificate of John Twiggs, B. G., Oct. 19, 1784. Petitioner prays 287½ acres in Washington Co.

**WOOD, ABRAHAM.** Certificate of Elijah Clarke, Col., Sept. 8, 1784. Petitioner prays 287½ acres in Washington Co.

**WOOD, CHRISTOPHER.** Certificate of Elijah Clarke, Col., Jan. 11, 1784. Petitioner prays 287½ acres in Washington Co.

**WOOD, HENRY.** Certificate as refugee soldier, John Baxter, Col., Feb. 21, 1784. Petitioner prays 287½ acres in Washington Co. Warrant 1527.

**WOOD, CORPORAL JAMES.** Certificate of service in 3d Ga. Regt., Nat. Peavie, Lieut., endorsed by Lachlan McIntosh, Brig. Gen., Jan. 29, 1784. Warrant 207.

**WOOD, JAMES.** Certificate as Lieut. in Minute Men, Elijah Clarke, Col., March 16, 1784.

**WOOD, JAMES.** Certificate of Elijah Clarke, Col., Sept. 6, 1784. Petitioner prays 287½ acres in Washington Co.

**WOOD, JOSHUA.** Certificate of Jas. McNeil, Col., March 22, 1784. Warrant 1528.

**WOODS, JOSHUA, JR.** Certificate of John Stewart, Col., June 21, 1784. Petitioner prays 287½ acres in Franklin Co. Warrant 835.

**WOODS, JOSHUA, SR.** Certificate of John Stewart, Col., July 27, 1784. Petitioner prays 287½ acres in Franklin Co. Warrant 836.

# CERTIFICATES OF SERVICE IN AMERICAN REVOLUTION. 185

**WOODS, JOSEPH.** Certificate as paymaster 1st Ga. Regt., Lachlan McIntosh, Brig. Gen., July 1, 1784. Endorsed by Maj. Handley and Col. John Melton. Warrant 84.

**WOODS, RICHARD.** Certificate as refugee soldier, E. Clarke, Col., March 25, 1784. Warrant 1526.

**WOOD, WILLIAM.** Certificate of Elijah Clarke, Col., Feb. 2, 1784. 2d certificate of Elijah Clarke, Col., April 16, 1784. Petitioner prays bounty in Franklin Co.

**WOODRUFF, JOSEPH.** Certificate as Major of Artillery, John Martin, Col., Feb. 22, 1784. Petitioner prays 650 acres in Washington Co. Warrant 869.

**WALLER, SAMUEL.** Certificate of Elijah Clarke, Col., April 18, 1784. Petitioner prays bounty in Washington Co.

**WOOTEN, ROBERT.** Certificate as refugee soldier, John Twiggs, B. G., Feb. 6, 1784.

**WOOTEN, THOMAS.** Certificate of Elijah Clarke, Col., Feb. 2, 1784.

**WOOTEN, LIEUT. THOMAS.** Certificate of Elijah Clarke, Col., Feb. 2, 1784. Petitioner prays 250 acres in Washington Co.

**WARDMAN, JACOB.** Certificate of E. Clarke, Lt. Col., Jan. 3, 1785. Warrant 848.

**WRIGHT, ABENDAGO.** Certificate as refugee soldier, Elijah Clarke, Col. 2d certificate of Gb. Lee, Col., Feb. 23, 1784. Petitioner prays 2 grants of 575 acres in all, in Washington Co.

**WOODSWORTH, THOMAS.** Certificate of Elijah Clarke, Col., May 17, 1784. Petitioner prays bounty in Franklin Co.

**WRIGHT, HABAUK.** Certificate as refugee soldier, Wm. Candler, Col. Regt. Petitioner prays 2 bounties in Washington Co. Warrant 1525.

**WRIGHT, JAMES.** Certificate of Gb. Lee, Col., Feb. 23, 1784. Petitioner prays 287½ acres in Washington Co.

**WRIGHT, JOHN.** Certificate of Gb. Lee, Col., Feb. 23, 1784. Petitioner prays 287½ acres in Washington Co.

**WRIGHT, ISAIAH.** Certificate of Gb. Lee, Col., April 5, 1784. Petitioner prays 250 acres in Washington Co.

**WRIGHT, MESHACK.** Certificate as refugee soldier, Wm. Candler, Col. Ref. Regt. Petitioner prays bounty in Washington Co. Warrant 1524.

**WRIGHT, SHADRACK.** Certificate that he enlisted as Captain in 1st Ga. Continental Line and died in service. Lachlan McIntosh, Maj. Gen., Feb. 3, 1784. 300 acres granted heirs of Shadrack Wright, Warrant 39.

**WYCHE, GEORGE.** Certificate of John Twiggs, B. G., March 11, 1784. Petitioner prays 250 acres in Washington Co.

**WYCHE, SAMUEL.** Petition for 250 acres in Washington Co., as per certificate annexed (missing). Power of attorney from Batt Wyche, heir of Saml. Wyche, deceased, to Capt. Hugh Magee, to draw bounty.

**WARD, JOHN.** Certificate as refugee soldier, John Twiggs, B. G., April 6, 1784. Petitioner prays bounty in Washington Co.

**WARD, SAMUEL.** Certificate of Elijah Clarke, Col., Feb. 2, 1784.

**WARNOCK, JESSE.** Certificate of John Twiggs, B. G., April 6, 1784. Petitioner prays 287½ acres in Washington Co.

**WARREN, JEREMIAH.** Certificate of Elijah Clarke, Col., April 21, 1784. Warrant 1535.

**WEREAT, JOHN.** Certificate of Jas. McNeil, Col., May, 17, 1784. Petitioner prays 575 acres as a soldier and a citizen, in Washington Co.

**WASONE, JOHN PALMER.** Certificate of —— Boykin, Major, Dec. 10, 1783.

**WATERS, RAWLEY.** Certificate of Elijah Clarke, Col., Feb. 2, 1784. Warrant 830.

**WADE, NEHEMIAH.** Certificate of Wm. Candler, Col., Feb. 20, 1784. Warrant 1540.

**WALLS, FRANCIS.** Certificate of Samuel Jack, Col., April 20, 1784. Petitioner prays 250 acres in Washington Co. Warrant 818.

**WALTON, CAPT. GEORGE.** Certificate of Elijah Clarke, Col., Feb. 2, 1784. Warrant 913. 2d certificate as refugee Captain, Elijah Clarke, Col., Feb. 2, 1784. Petitioner prays on 2 above certificates 862½ in two surveys in Washington Co.

**WALTON, LIEUT. GEORGE, JR.** Certificate of Elijah Clarke, Col., Feb. 2, 1784. Warrant 98. 2d certificate to Lieut. Geo. Walton Jr., Lachlan McIntosh, Maj. Gen., March 18, 1784. Petitioner prays 575 acres in Washington Co.

**WALTON, NEWELL.** Certificate of Elijah Clarke, Col., Feb. 2, 1784. Warrant 1536. 2d certificate of Elijah Clarke, Col. Petitioner prays 575 acres in Washington Co.

**WALTON, ROBERT.** Petition for 287½ acres in Franklin Co. as per certificate annexed (missing). Granted May 17, 1784.

**WALTHOUR, ANDREW.** Certificate as refugee soldier, John Baker, Col., March 15, 1784. Warrant 1560. 2d certificate of John Baker, Col., May 19, 1784. Petitioner prays bounty in Washington Co.

**WALLIS, ABSOLEM.** Certificate as refugee soldier, John Twiggs, B. G., Feb. 16, 1784. Warrant 1559. 2d certificate of John Twiggs, B. G., Feb. 16, 1784.

## CERTIFICATES OF SERVICE IN AMERICAN REVOLUTION. 187

**WALLER, BENJAMIN.** Certificate of Elijah Clarke, Col., Feb. 2, 1784.

**WALLIS, CHARLES.** Certificate of Elijah Clarke, Col., Jan. 25, 1785.

**WALLIS, JAMES.** Certificate of Elijah Clarke, Col., June 22, 1784. Petitioner prays 287½ acres in Washington Co.

**WALLACE, WILLIAM.** Ex. order for bounty upon certificate of Col. E. Clarke, Feb. 20, 1784. (missing). Petitioner prays 250 acres in Washington Co.

**WALLER, JEREMIAH.** Certificate of Elijah Clarke, Col., Dec. 10, 1784. Petitioner prays bounty in Washington Co.

**WALSH, MAJOR EDWARD.** Certificate of Col. Seth Cuthbert and Brig. Gen. S. Elbert, March 15, 1784. Warrant 20.

**WALSH, MAJOR PATRICK.** This is to certify that Major Patrick Walsh, Ga. Regt. Light Dragoons is entitled to a bounty of 600 acres of land. J. Houstoun, Gov., June 4, 1784. Warrant 21.

**WALTER, JOSEPH.** Order of John Habersham, Pres. Ex. Council, to Suveyor of Washington Co. to lay out a bounty of 230 acres for Joseph Walter, soldier—a deserter from the British. May 17, 1784.

**WATERS, JAMES.** Certificate as refugee soldier, Benj. Few. Col., July 2, 1784. Petitioner prays 250 acres in Washington Co.

**WATTS, GEORGE.** Certificate of Elijah Clarke, Col., Jan. 3, 1785. Warrant 842.

**WATTS, JACOB.** Certificate of Elijah Clarke, Col., Petitioner prays bounty in Franklin Co. Warrant 841.

**WARD, BENJAMIN.** Petition for bounty in Washington Co. upon certificate of John Twiggs, B. G., April 6, 1784. (missing).

**WARD, CHARLES.** Certificate as refugee soldier, John Twiggs, B. G., April 14, 1784. Petitioner prays 250 acres in Washington Co.

**WARD, HUGH.** Certificate of Elijah Clarke, Col., Jan. 3, 1785. Warrant 834.

**WARD, JOHN.** Certificate of E. Clarke, Col., Jan. 3, 1785. Warrant 833.

**WARDEN, JOHN.** Certificate as surgeon of the Ga. Line (signature and date gone). Petitioner prays 800 acres in the reserve. Warrant 36.

**WARE, ROBERT.** Ex. order for bounty upon certificate of Col. E. Clarke, March 25, 1784. Petitioner, an emigrant from Caroline Co. Va., also prays head rights of 1,000 acres in Washington Co. on self and 24 in family.

**WATSON, BENJAMIN.** Certificate of Elijah Clarke, Col., Dec. 10, 1784. Petitioner prays bounty in Washington Co.

**WATSON, GEORGE.** Certificate of Gb. Lee, Col., Feb. 21, 1784. Petitioner prays bounty in Washington Co.

ROSTER OF THE REVOLUTION.

**WATSON, JACOB.** Certificate of E. Clarke, Col., June 25, 1784. Petitioner prays 287½ acres in Franklin Co. Warrant 839.

**WATSON, JOHN.** Certificate of Elijah Clarke, Col., June 21, 1784. Petitioner prays bounty in Franklin Co. Warrant 840. 2d certificate of E. Clarke, Col., Dec. 10, 1784. Petitioner prays bounty in Washington Co.

**WATSON, THOMAS.** Certificate of Gb. Lee, Col., April 20, 1784. Petitioner prays bounty in Washington Co.

**WATSON, ELEVIN.** Certificate of Elijah Clarke, Col., Feb. 2, 1784. Petitioner prays 287½ acres in Washington Co. Warrant 1553.

**WAY, EDWARD.** Certificate as refugee soldier, John Baker, Col., March 22, 1784. Petitioner prays 287½ acres in Washington Co. Warrant 1546.

**WAY, JOSEPH.** Certificate as refugee soldier, John Baker, Col., March 22, 1784. Warrant 1545.

**WAY, JOSEPH.** This is to certify that Joseph Way, son of Thomas, was a good soldier under me, John Baker, Col., April 14, 1785. Warrant 1544.

**WAY, JOHN, SR.** Ex. order for two bounties on certificate of Col. John Baker, June 1, 1784. (missing). Petitioner prays two warrants in Franklin Co. Warrant 1542.

**WAY, JOHN, JR.** Ex. order for bounty upon certificate of Col. John Baker, April 21, 1784 (missing). As refugee soldier. Petitioner prays bounty in Franklin Co. Warrant 1543.

**WAY, WILLIAM.** Certificate as refugee soldier, John Baker, Col., June 5, 1784. Warrant 1547.

**WHATLEY, MICHAEL.** Certificate of Elijah Clarke, Col., April 7, 1784. Petitioner prays 287½ acres in Washington Co. Petitioner further prays (as former citizen of North Carolina) on 9 head rights, 200 acres in Franklin Co. and 250 acres in Washington Co.

**WHATLEY, SAMUEL.** Certificate of Elijah Clarke, Col., Feb. 2, 1784. Warrant 1558. 2d certificate of Elijah Clarke, Col., Feb. 2, 1784. Petitioner prays warrants for 575 acres in Washington Co.

**WHATLEY, RICHARD.** Certificate of Elijah Clarke, Col., Feb. 2, 1784. Petitioner prays 250 acres in Washington Co. 2d certificate of Elijah Clarke, Col., April 7, 1784. Petitioner prays 287½ acres in Washington Co.

**WHATLEY, RICHARD, SR.** Certificate of John Cunningham, Lt. Col., Aug. 4, 1784. Petitioner prays 287½ acres in Washington Co. Warrant 1557.

**WHATLEY, WALTON.** Certificate as refugee soldier, E. Clarke, Col., August 19, 1784. Petitioner prays 287½ acres in Washington Co. Warrant 1556.

**WHEAT, HEZEKIAH.** Certificate as refugee soldier, E. Clarke, Col. Petitioner prays 250 acres in Franklin Co. Warrant 1507.

## CERTIFICATES OF SERVICE IN AMERICAN REVOLUTION.

**WHEAT, JOHN.** Certificate of Elijah Clarke, Col., Feb. 2, 1784.

**WHEELER, ZACHARIAH.** Certificate of E. Clarke, Col., April 20, 1784. Petitioner prays bounty in Washington Co.

**WHERE, WILLIAM.** Certificate as refugee soldier, Wm. Candler, Col., R. R. C. Petitioner prays 250 acres in Washington Co. Warrant 1510.

**WARE, HENRY, SR.** Cetificate of Elijah Clarke, Col., April 12, 1784. Petitioner prays 250 acres in Washington Co.

**WARE, HENRY, JR.** Ex order for bounty upon certificate of Col. E. Clarke, March 25, 1784. (missing)). Petitioner prays 250 acres in Washington Co.

**WARE, JAMES.** Certificate of Elijah Clarke, Col., April 2, 1784. Petitioner prays 250 acres in Washington Co.

**WARE, JOHN.** Certificate as refugee soldier, Elijah Clarke, Col., April 20, 1784. Petitioner prays 287½ acres in Franklin Co. Warrant 1519.

**WARE, NICHOLAS.** Certificate of Elijah Clarke, Col., Feb. 2, 1784. Petitioner prays 250 acres in Washington Co.

**WARE, WILLIAM.** Certificate of Gb. Lee, Col., Feb. 23, 1784. Petitioner prays 287½ acres in Washington Co.

**WHITT, RICHARD.** Certificate of E. Clarke, Col. Petitioner prays 250 acres in Franklin Co. Warrant 850.

**WHITBY, THOMAS.** Certificate of Elijah Clarke, Col., Feb. 2, 1784. 2d certerficate of Gb. Lee, Col., March 15, 1784. Petitioner prays bounty in Washington Co.

**WHITMORE, JONATHAN.** Petition of John Frazier, Atty. for Humphrey Whitmore, administrator of estate of Jonathan Whitmore, dec'd who served in 3d Battalion Ga. Infantry, for bounty for heirs of 230 acres in Washington Co.

**WHITE, DEMPSEY.** Petition for 287½ acres in Washington Co. as per certificate annexed (missing). Warrant 2774. Certificate of James Jackson, Col., Ga. State Legion, March 26, 1784.

**WHITE, JOHN.** Certificate of Elijah Clarke, Col., Feb. 2, 1784. Warrant 1555. 2d certificate of Elijah Clarke, Col., Feb. 2, 1784.

**WHITE, JOSEPH.** Certificate of Elijah Clarke, Col., Aug. 9, 1784. Petitioner prays bounty in Washington Co.

**WHITE, CAPT. JAMES.** Certificate of Elijah Clarke, Col., Aug. 4, 1784. Petitioner prays bounty in Washington Co. Warrant 880.

**WHITE, NICHOLAS.** Certificate of Jas. Jackson, Lt. Col., July 23, 1784. Petitioner prays bounty in Franklin Co.

**WHITE, THOMAS.** Certificate of Wm. Few. for Gb. Lee, Col., July 23, 1784. Petitioner prays bounty in Franklin Co.

**WAGONER, HENRY.** Certificate of Elijah Clarke, Col., April 20, 1784. Petitioner prays bounty in Washington Co.

**WHITESIDES, JOHN.** Ex. order for bounty upon certificate of Col. Clarke, (missing). March 25, 1784. Petitioner prays 287½ acres in Washington Co.

**WHITICEL, DR. JOHN.** This is to certify that Dr. John Whiticel of South Carolina was a refugee, and did many singular services in my camp for my regiment, and I recommend a bounty for him. Elijah Clarke, Col., May 20, 1784. Referred by Land Court to Legislature for action.

**WHITSET, JOHN.** Certificate as refugee soldier, Elijah Clarke, Col., Nov. 24, 1784. Petitioner prays bounty in Franklin Co. Warrant 1516.

**WHITTON, ROBERT.** Certificate of Jas. McNeil, Col., April 2, 1784. Petitioner prays 287½ acres in Washington Co.

**WHITTON, AUSTIN.** Certificate of Elijah Clarke, Col., and Capt. Martin, May 25, 1784. Petitioner prays 250 acres in Franklin Co. 2d certificate of Elijah Clarke, Col., April 23, 1784. Petitioner prays 287½ acres in Washington Co. Warrant 832.

**WHITTON PHILIP.** Certificate of E. Clarke, Col., Nov. 16, 1784. Warrant 831.

**WHITTINGTON, CORNELIUS.** Certificate of Jas. Mc.Neil, Col., March 15, 1784. Petitioner prays 287½ acres in Washington Co.

**WHATLEY, EDWARD.** Certificate of Jas. Jackson, Col., July 19, 1784. Petitioner prays bounty in Franklin Co.

**WHITAKER, CAPT. JOHN.** Certificate of John Twiggs, B. G., April 6, 1784. Petitioner prays bounties of 575 acres in Franklin Co. Warrant 912.

**WHITAKER, SAMUEL.** Certificate of Gb. Lee, Col., Sept. 6, 1784. Petitioner prays 287½ acres in Washington Co.

**WILDS, CHARLES.** Certificate as refugee soldier, Gb. Lee, Col., April 17, 1784. Petitioner prays bounty in Washington Co.

—Y—

**YARBOROUGH, JAMES.** Certificate of Elijah Clarke, Col., Feb. 2, 1784. Petitioner prays 287½ acres in Washington Co. 2d certificate of Elijah Clarke, Col., June 24, 1784. Petitioner prays 287½ acres in Franklin Co.

**YARBOROUGH, JAMES.** Certificate of Samuel Jack, Col., April 24, 1784. Warrant 808. 2d certificate of Elijah Clarke, Col., Sept. 8, 1784. Petitioner prays 287½ acres in Washington Co.

## CERTIFICATES OF SERVICE IN AMERICAN REVOLUTION.

**YARBOROUGH, LITTLETON.** Certificate as refugee Soldier, James Jackson, Lt. Col., March 22, 1784. Petitioner prays Bounty in Washington Co.

**YARBOROUGH, THOMAS.** Certificate as refugee soldier, Asa Emanuel, Col., April 7, 1784. Petitioner prays bounty in Washington Co.

**YARBOROUGH, WILLIAM.** Certificate of E. Clarke, Col., June 24, 1784. Petitioner prays bounty in Franklin Co. 2d certificate as refugee soldier, Elijah Clarke, Col., Nov. 16, 1784. Warrant 1500.

**YARBOROUGH, WILLIAM.** Certificate of Elijah Clarke, Col. Sept. 8, 1784. Petitioner prays bounty in Franklin Co.

**YARBOROUGH, WILLIAM.** Certificate of Elijah Clarke, Col., Jan. 1785.

**YORK, JAMES.** Certificate of Elijah Clarke, Col., Feb. 2, 1784. Warrant 1499. 2d certificate of Elijah Clarke, Col., Feb. 2, 1784. Petitioner prays 287½ acres bounty.

**YORKE, JAMES.** Certificate of Elijah Clarke, Lt. Col., April 24, 1784. Warrant 809. 2d certificate of Elijah Clarke, Col., May 24, 1784. Petitioner prays 287½ acres in Washington Co.

**YORK, JOHN.** Certificate of Elijah Clarke, Col., Feb. 2, 1784. Warrant 1498. 2d certificate of Elijah Clarke, Col., Feb. 2, 1784. Petitioner prays 2 warrants—500 acres—in Franklin Co.

**YOUNG, EDWARD.** Certificate as refugee soldier, Elijah Clarke, Col., April 7, 1784. Petitioner prays 287½ acres in Washington Co. Warrant 1502. 2d certificate of Elijah Clarke, Col., April 7, 1784. Petitioner prays bounty in Washington Co.

**YOUNG, EDWARD.** Certificate of Elijah Clarke, Col., Sept. 8, 1784. 2d certificate of Elijah Clarke, Col., Sept, 8, 1784. Petitioner prays 575 acres in Washington Co.

**YOUNG, EDWARD.** Certificate as soldier in Minute Men, Samuel Jack, Col., April 26, 1784. Petitioner prays 287½ acres in Washington Co. Warrant 803.

**YOUNG, WILLIAM.** Certificate as soldier in Minute Men, Samuel Jack, Col., April 6, 1784. Warrant 804. 2d certificate of John Twiggs, B. G., March 4, 1784. Petitioner prays 287½ acres in Washington Co.

**YOUNG, WILLIAM.** Certificate as refugee soldier. Elijah Clarke, Col., April 19, 1784. 2d certificate of Elijah Clarke, Col., Jan. 11, 1785. Petitioner prays 575 acres in Washington Co.

**YOUNG, DANIEL.** Certificate as Lieutenant, Elijah Clarke, Col., Feb., 20, 1784. Petitioner prays 287½ acres in Washington Co. 2d certificate to Lieut. Daniel Young, Elijah Clarke, Col., April 7 ,1784. Petitioner prays bounty in Washington Co. Warrant 270.

**YOUNG, ISHAM.** Certificate as soldier in Minute Men, E. Clarke, Lt. Col., April 7, 1784. Warrant 805. 2d certificate as refugee soldier, Elijah Clarke, Col., April 7, 1784. Petitioner prays bounty in Washington Co. Warrant 1503.

**YOUNG, ISHAM.** Certificate of Elijah Clarke, Col., April 7, 1784. Petitioner prays bounty in Washington Co.

**YOUNG, JAMES.** Certificate of John Twiggs, B. G., March 4, 1784. Petitioner prays 287½ acres in Washington Co.

**YOUNG, JAMES.** Certificate of Elijah Clarke, Col., April 24, 1784. Petitioner prays 287½ acres in Franklin Co.

**YOUNG, JOHN, JR.** Certificate of Samuel Jack, Col., April 6, 1784. Petitioner prays 287½ acres in Washington Co. Warrant 807. 2d certificate of Elijah Clarke, Col., Dec. 10, 1784. Petitioner prays bounty in Washington Co.

**YOUNG, JOHN, SR.** Certificate of Samuel Jack, Col., April 6, 1784. Petitioner prays 250 acres in Washington Co. Warrant 806. 2d certificate of Elijah Clarke, Col., Jan. 27, 1785. Petitioner prays 287½ acres in Washington Co.

**YOUNGBLOOD, ABRAHAM.** Certificate of Jas. McNeil, Col., April 3, 1784. Petitioner prays bounty in Washington Co.

**YOUNGBLOOD, ISAAC.** Certificate of Jas. McNeil, Col., April 3, 1784. Petitioner prays 287½ acres in Washington Co.

**YOUNGBLOOD, JAMES.** Certificate of Jas. McNeil, Col., Feb. 2, 1784.

**YOUNGBLOOD, JOHN.** Certificate of Jas. McNeil, Col., May 28, 1784. Petitioner prays 287½ acres in Washington Co.

**YOUNGBLOOD, JOHN.** Certificate of Jas. McNeil, Col., Sep. 16, 1784.

**YOUNGBLOOD, JONATHAN.** Certificate of Gb. Lee, Col., Feb. 23, 1784. Petitioner prays 287½ acres in Washington Co.

**YOUNGBLOOD, PETER.** Certificate as soldier in 1st Battn. Ga. Troops, Jas. McNeil, Col., March 21, 1784. Warrant 1501. 2d Certificate of Jas. McNeil, Col., Mar. 15, 1784. Petitioner prays 575 acres in Washington Co.

—Z—

**ZACHARY, JAMES.** Certificate as refugee soldier, Wm. Barnett, Capt. and Jas. McNeil, Col., April 6, 1784. Petitioner prays 287½ acres in Washington Co.

**ZETTLER, NATHANIEL.** Power of attorney to Capt. Jenkins to secure certificate "For me and my brother" for land granted us by the General Assembly for services.

**ZINN, JACOB.** Certificate as refugee soldier, Wm. Candler, Col., Ref. Regt. Petitioner prays 287½ acres in Washington Co. Warrant 1562.

## EXPLANATORY.

### HEAD-RIGHTS AND LOTTERY LAND GRANTS OF GEORGIA.

There are two characters of land in this State; one known as Head-Rights, the other as Lottery Lands.

All of that territory of the State lying west of the Savannah River, and extending to the Apalachie and Oconee rivers, and also all lands east of original Wayne County, extending to the Atlantic Ocean, are known as Head-Right Lands. Grants to the same were first issued by the Trustees of the Colony of Georgia, under and by authority of King George the Third, of England; also by John Reynolds, Henry Ellis and James Wright, Governors of the Colony, under and by same authority.

During Henry Ellis' administration as Governor of the Colony, there was a good deal of dispute about the titles made by the Lord proprietors of Carolina, who claimed a considerable territory of the Colony of Georgia. He caused the following Act to be passed:

"An Act for establishing and confirming the titles of the several inhabitants of this Province to their respective lands and tenements.

"Forasmuch as many suits and contests may arise by means of pretended ancient titles to lands and tenements derived from and under the late Lord proprietors of Carolina, the conditions of which titles have not been complied with, and the lands have since been re-granted, for remedy and prevention thereof,

"Be it enacted, That all and every person or persons, that are now possessed of, or do hold any lands or tenements whatsoever within the said Province of Georgia, by and under grants from the late Honorable Trustees for establishing the Colony of Georgia, or by and under grants from his Majesty, obtained since the surrender of his charter of the said Trustees, are hereby established and confirmed in the possession of their several and respective lands and tenements; and such grants thereof are hereby accordingly ratified and confirmed, and declared to be good and valid to all intents and purposes whatsoever, against all, and all manner of persons claiming any estate or interest therein, by and under the said Lords proprietors of Carolina, or by or under any former grants obtained before the date of his Majesty's charter to said Trustees for establishing the Colony of Georgia, any Act, law or statute to the contrary notwithstanding.

"By order of the Upper House:
"PATRICK HOUSTON.
"By order of the Common House:
"DAVID MONTAIGUT, Speaker.
"Council Chamber, 24th September, 1759.
"Assented to, HENRY ELLIS."

This Head-Right territory, extending from Camden County to the south line of Wilkes County, was divided up during the Colonial period of Georgia, into parishes, viz.: Christ Church, St. Andrew, St. David, St. George, St. James,

St. John, St. Mary, St. Mathew, St. Patrick, St. Paul, St. Philip, and St. Thomas. After our independence the parishes were abolished and the territory divided up into counties.

There was passed at Savannah on the 7th day of June, 1777, "An Act for opening a land office, and for the better settling and strengthening this State." Under this Act every free white person, or head of a family, was entitled to two hundred acres of land, and for every other white person of same family, fifty acres of land, and fifty acres for every negro owned by said family, not to exceed ten.

This Act has been amended several times by the General Assembly, so any person, resident of the State, could head-right and have granted him, not exceeding one thousand acres of land (unless by special act of the Legislature).

The bounties of the Revolutionary soldiers were paid for their services in this Head-Right territory; most of them in the counties of Washington and Franklin.

An Act passed August 20th, 1781, entitled, "An Act to amend the several Acts for the better regulation of the militia of this State." Section 8 reads as follows: "And, Whereas, numbers of persons are daily absenting themselves and leaving their fellow citizens to encounter the difficulties of the present crisis, Be it enacted, etc., That any person or persons who shall produce a certificate from the commanding officer of the district to which he belongs, to the Legislature (on the total expulsion of the enemy from it), of his having steadfastly done his duty from the time of passing this Act, shall be entitled to two hundred and fifty acres of good land (which shall be exempt from taxes for the space of ten years thereafter); Provided, such person or persons can not be convicted of plundering or distressing the country."

Also, "An Act for opening the land office, and for other purposes therein mentioned," passed 17th February, 1783. Section 2, "Be it therefore enacted, That in case any officer or soldier or other person, claiming under such engagements as aforesaid, shall produce a certificate from his Honor the Governor, for the time being, that a tract of land is, or are due to him, that then such officer, soldier or other person, shall be entitled to a warrant and grant for any unlocated lands (agreeable to the quantity contained in his certificate) within this State."

Section 14 (same Act), "All the officers and soldiers, all the officers and marines of the navy, officers of the medical department, refugees and citizens, who are entitled to land in this State, as bounties for their service, in manner as above mentioned, shall be entitled to have included in their grants an additional quantity of fifteen acres to each hundred acres in full for and in lieu of any exemption of taxes. And every Act, and clause of an Act, allowing such exemption from taxation, shall be, and the same is hereby repealed, and declared null and void, anything to the contrary notwithstanding."

All soldiers were entitled to 250 acres of good land, free of taxes, for ten years. Under the above section he could have granted him 15 per cent more land, making 287½ acres, and commence to pay taxes on same.

Section 2 of the Act of February 17th, 1783, was amended so all officers, soldiers, seamen, etc., could present their certificates of service from their commanding officer to the land court, at Augusta, Georgia, instead of to the Governor. Section 9 of an Act passed February 22, 1785, reads as follows: "Be it therefore enacted by authority aforesaid, That in future, all and every person or persons whatsoever, who conceive himself and themselves entitled to a bounty, shall lay his or their vouchers or credentials before the said Land Court, where they apply for the same; on a full consideration of all circumstances respecting the petitioner, either grant or reject the application, as coming or not coming within the scope and intention of the several laws of this State for granting bounties, and as no surveys of land due as bounties from this State shall be allowed, unless brought in and claimed within one year from and after the passing of this Act."

The above Act in regard to bounties was amended by subsequent legislation, relieving bounty warrants of being returned within the period of one year, but declaring bounty warrants never out of date.

But an Act passed December 10th, 1818, entitled, "An Act to limit the time for persons to take out their grants in this State so far as relates to land surveyed on Head-Rights and bounty warrants." Section 2 (of said Act) reads as follows: "The time hereafter to be allowed to persons who may hereafter have any land surveyed in this State, on Head-Right or bounty, shall be three years from the time of making such survey; and in case of failure of neglect to take out the grant, it shall revert and become the property of the State, and be subject to be surveyed and granted to any person or persons, who are hereby authorized to survey the same; Provided, nevertheless, that nothing herein contained shall be so construed as to operate against or prejudice the claim of any orphan or orphans."

This Head-Right territory of the State consists now of thirty-five (35) counties, viz.: Bryan, Bulloch, Burke, Camden, Chatham, Clarke, Columbia, Effingham, Elbert, Emanuel, Franklin, Glascock, Glynn, Greene, Hancock, Hart, Jackson, Jefferson, Johnson, half of Laurens, Liberty, Lincoln, Madison, McDuffie, McIntosh, half of Montgomery, Oconee, Oglethorpe, Richmond, Screven, Taliaferro, Tattnall, Warren, Washington and Wilkes.

## LOTTERY LANDS.

There were five different lotteries of land authorized by the General Assembly of the State, viz.: 1805, 1820, 1821, 1827 and 1831.

All that territory of the State situated between the Oconee and Ocmulgee rivers was first purchased from the Indians and disposed of by lottery in 1805. In this lottery every white man, widow and orphan, resident of this State, was entitled to one draw, and every Revolutionary soldier was entitled to two draws. This territory at the time of survey, was covered by only two original counties—Baldwin and Wilkinson.

It was divided into districts, and each district numbered, each district was sub-divided into land lots, and each land lot numbered and contained 202½ acres each, except fractional parts of lots occurring on the rivers.

This territory is now divided up into thirteen (13) different counties, viz.: Baldwin, part of Bibb, Dodge, Jasper, Jones, Laurens, half of Montgomery, Morgan, three-fourths of Pulaski, Putnam, Telfair, Twiggs and Wilkinson.

All that territory of the State lying south of the Altamaha River to the Florida line and west of said river to the Chattahoochee river, after purchase from the Indians, was also divided into districts, and each district sub-divided into land lots. The land lots of original Appling and Irwin contain 490 acres each, and land lots of original Early contain 250 acres each. These lands were disposed of by lottery in 1820. This territory was covered by only three original counties at the time of survey and lottery, viz.: original Appling, Early and Irwin—divided since into twenty-four counties, viz.: Appling, one-fourth of Charlton, Clinch, Coffee, Echols, Pierce, Ware, three-fourths Wayne, Berrien, Brooks, Colquitt, Irwin, Lowndes, one-half of Thomas, three-fourths of Wilcox, three-fourths of Worth, Baker, Calhoun, part of Clay, Decatur, Dougherty, Early, Miller, and Mitchell.

The land lots of original Gwinnett, Hall, Rabun and Walton, of 202½ acres each, were also disposed of by lottery in 1820.

All the territory of the State lying north of original Irwin extending from Ocmulgee River west to the Flint River, after purchase from the Indians, was laid out into districts, and each district sub-divided into land lots of 202½ acres and disposed of by lottery in 1821.

At the time of lottery this territory was covered by only five counties; original Dooly, Houston, Monroe, Henry, and Fayette. Since that date it has been divided up into twenty-one different counties, viz.: Dooly, one-fourth of Pulaski, one-fourth Wilcox, one-half Worth, one-half Bibb, Crawford, Houston, one-fourth Macon, one-fourth Butts, Monroe, Pike, one-half Spalding, Upson, Clayton, DeKalb, Fayette, part of Fulton, Henry, Newton, Rockdale and Campbell counties.

All that territory of the State north of original Early county and lying between the Flint and Chattahoochee Rivers, composing the five original counties of Lee, Muscogee, Troup, Coweta, and Carroll, after purchase from the Indians, was also divided into districts and each district sub-divided into land lots of 202½ acres and disposed of by lottery in 1827. This territory, since the lottery, has been divided up into twenty-two different counties, viz.: part Clay, Lee, part Macon, Quitman, Randolph, part Schley, Stewart, Sumter, Terrell, Webster, three-fourths Chattahoochee, part Harris, Marion, Muscogee, Talbot, Taylor, part Heard, Meriwether, Troup, Coweta, Carroll, part Douglas, and three-fourths Haralson counties.

The remaining territory of the State lying north of the Chattahoochee river, bounded on the west by the State of Alabama and north by the States of Tennessee and North Carolina, is known as the "Cherokee Purchase." After purchase from the Cherokee Tribe of Indians it was laid out into sections, numbers 1, 2, 3, 4. These sections were sub-divided into districts, nine miles square, and each district sub-divided into square land lots of forty, and one hundred and sixty acres each. At the time of survey the forty-acre lots were supposed to contain gold and are known as "gold lots." The one hundred and sixty acre-lots are known as "land lots."

## EXPLANATORY.

The "Cherokee Purchase" is now covered by twenty-three different counties, viz.: Bartow, Catoosa, Chattooga, Cherokee, Cobb, Dade, Dawson, part Douglas, Floyd, Forsyth, Gilmer, Gordan, part Haralson, Lumpkin, Milton, Murray, Pauling, Pickens, Polk, Towns, Union, Walker, and Whitfield counties.

Grants to a great many lots in the different lotteries were not taken out by the fortunate drawers, although the State extended the time by appropriate legislation several times, and the land lots finally reverted to the State by Acts of the General Assembly of Georgia.

These lots were then sold to different parties and regranted.

PHILIP COOK.

---

Copied from "Historical Collections of the Joseph Habersham Chapter, D. A. R.," Vol. I, pages 303-309.

## THE LE CONTE LIST.

**BOUNTY SURVEYS RECORDED BY THE SURVEYOR GENERAL AND PRESERVED IN THE OFFICE OF SECRETARY OF STATE, ATLANTA, GA.**

Copied 1911, by Wm. L. Le Conte and Presented to the State.

### SURVEYOR GENERAL'S BOOK A.

**GREEN, WILLIAM.** 287½ acres, Washington Co., bounded N., E. & S. unknown, W. by academy land. No. 330, July 3rd, 1784. Warrant No. 2658. p. 112.

**DAVIS, BENJAMIN.** 287½ acres, Washington Co., bounded N. vacant, E. by Johnson, S. by academy land, W. vacant lot 291. Warrant No. 2034, June 26th, 1784. p. 114.

**PITTMAN, TIMOTHY.** 287½ acres, Washington Co., bounded N. & E. vacant, S. by Peter Watson, W. by Oconee river, lot —. Warrant No. 1873, June 2, 1784. p. —.

**SHIELDS, ANDREW.** 287½ acres, Washington Co., bounded N. & E. vacant, S. by Bacon's land, W. by Oconee river, lot 314. Warrant —, May 17, 1784. p. 122.

**MARGANTON, ASA.** 287½ acres, Washington Co., bounded N. & E. vacant, S. by Pannill, W. by Oconee river, lot 360, July 6, 1784. p. 122.

**BACON, JOHN.** 287½ acres, Washington Co., bounded N. & E. vacant, S. by Morganson, W. by Oconee river, lot 318, May 17, 1784. p. 123.

**CHILDERS, DAVID.** 230 acres, Washington Co., bounded N. & E. vacant, S. surveyed, W. Oconee river, lot 321. May 17, 1784. p. 124.

**SHIELDS, ANDREW.** 287½ acres, (2d bounty) Washington Co., bounded N., E. & S. vacant, W. Oconee river, lot 323. June, 21st, 1784. p —.

**EVANS, DANIEL.** 287½ acres, Washington Co., bounded N. & E. vacant, S. Hezekiah, Beal, W. vancant, lot 253. May 17, 1784. p. —.

**ROWELL, EDWARD.** 287½ acres, Washington Co., bounded N. Howell Rowell, E. vacant, S. Jacob Bugg, W. Oconee river, lot 390. June 9th, 1784, p. 132.

**FORT, OWEN.** 287½ acres, Washington Co., bounded N. & E. vacant, S. Wm. Jones, W. vacant, lot 259. May 17, 1784. p. 133.

**KELLY, JAMES.** 287½ acres, Washington Co., bounded N. Simmons, E. vacant, S. Walker, W. Oconee river, lot 269. June 5, 1784. p. 137.

**WILDS, CHARLES.** 287½ acres, Washington Co., bounded N. vacant, E. Samuel Wilson, S. & W. Oconee river, lot 272. May 17, 1784, p. 138.

# BOUNTY SURVEYS.

**BEAL, HEZIKIAH.** 287½ acres, Washington Co., bounded N. Daniel Evans, E., S. & W. vacant, lot 274. June 8th, 1784. p. 139.

**BESONS, PETER.** 287½ acres, Washington Co., bounded N., E. & W. vacant, S. James Harrison, lot 275. July 2, 1784. p. 139.

**HARRIS, JAMES.** 287½ acres, Washington Co., bounded N. Peter Beson, E. & S. vacant, W. Limestone creek, lot 276. May 17, 1784. p. 139.

**LEVERETT, HENRY.** 287½ acres, Washington Co., bounded N. Benj. Catchings, E. & S. vacant, W. Oconee river, lot 374. May 17, 1784. p. 141.

**FINDLEY, JAMES.** 287½ acres, Washington Co., bounded all sides, by vacant lands, lot 377. June 17, 1784. p. 142.

**PHILLIPS, ZACHARIAH.** 287½ acres, Washington Co., bounded N. vacant, E. Leggett and Phillips, S. Oconee river, W. Jacob Landers, lot 381. Surveyed May 17, 1784. p. 144.

**DAVIS, LEWIS.** 287½ acres, Washington Co., bounded N. vacant, E. Arthur Fort, S. Ogeechee river, W. James Bowers, lot 382. May 17, 1784, p. 143.

**NIELS, GEORGE.** 287½ acres, Washington Co., bounded S. by Thos. Snelson, other sides, vacant, lot 383. May 17, 1784. p. 145.

**JONES, JOHN.** 287½ acres, Washington Co., bounded N. Jones swamp, E. by Richard Bowie, S. & W. vacant, lot 384. May 17, 1784. p. 145.

**BUGG, NICHOLAS.** 287½ acres, Washington Co., bounded N. Williamson's swamp, E. Jesse Morgan, S. & W. vacant, lot 430. May 17, 1784, p. 145.

**GALASPY, JOHN.** 287½ acres, Washington Co., bounded N. Ogeechee river— other sides vacant, lot 386. May 17, 1784, p. 145.

**BOWIE, JAMES.** 287½ acres, Washington Co., bounded N. vacant, E. Lewis Davis, S. Ogeechee river, W. vacant, lot 389. May 17, 1784. p. 146.

**SHADDOCKS, THOMAS.** 575 acres, Washington Co., bounded on all sides by vacant lands, lot 388. Warrant 567. May 17, 1784. p. 146.

**MORGAN, JESSE.** 575 acres, Washington Co., bounded N. Williamson's swamp, E. surveyed, S. vacant, W. Nich. Bugg, lot 390. Warrant 1911. May 17, 1784. p. 147.

**BOWIE, REASON.** 287½ acres, Washington Co., bounded N. Williamson's swamp, E. vacant, S. Wiliam Jones, W. John Jones, lot 391. Warrant 2167. May 17, 1784. p. 147.

**PHILLIPS, WILLIAM.** 575 acres, Washington Co., bounded N. & S. vacant, E. & W. surveyed, crossed by Williamson's swamp, lot —. Warrant 888. May 17, 1784. p. 147.

**WHERE, WILLIAM.** 287½ acres, Washington Co., bounded N. swamp, E. John Roberts, S. vacant, W. Harris, lot 393. Warrant 1833. May 17, 1784. p. 148.

ROSTER OF THE REVOLUTION.

**KENDALL, JEREMIAH.** 287½ acres, Washington Co., bounded N., E. & S. vacant, W. William Glascock, lot 394. Warrant 1460. May 17, 1784. p. 148.

**McMULLEN, ROBERT.** 287½ acres, Washington Co., bounded N E. & S E. vacant, N W, Oconee river, S W. Simmons, lot 440. Warrant 70. May 17, 1784. p. 148.

**JACKSON, WILLIAM.** 287½ acres, Washington Co., bounded N. Wilkes Co. line, other sides vacant, lot 401. Warrant 1907. May 17, 1784. p. 148.

**JACKSON, REUBEN.** 287½ acres, Washington Co., bounded S. by Oconee river, other sides vacant, lot 403. Warrant 2097. May 17, 1784. p. 152.

**ANDERSON, ALEXANDER.** 287½ acres, Washington Co., bounded all sides by vacant lands, lot 406. Warrant 430. May 17, 1784. p. 153.

**YOUNG, DANIEL.** 287½ acres, Washington Co., bounded W. John Oliver, other sides vacant, lot 407. Warrant 104. May 17, 1784. p. 153.

**STOCKS (OR STOKES), BENTLEY.** 287½ acres, Washington Co., bounded N. Anthony Metcalf, E. & S. vacant, W. David Shaffer, lot 409. Warrant 1160. May 17, 1784. p. 154.

**HAMMET, JAMES.** 287½ acres, Washington Co., bounded N. & S. M. Williamson, E. vacant, W. Dukes, lot 410. Warrant 716. May 17, 1784. p. 154.

**PATTERSON, GIDEON.** 287½ acres, Washington Co., bounded N. Shaffer, W. by College lands, other sides vacant, lot 411. Warrant 2306. May 17, 1784. p. 155.

**DUKE, JOHN TAYLOR.** 287½ acres, Washington Co., bounded N. vacant, E. Elijah Clarke, S. Jno. Heard, W. M. Williamson, lot 412. Warrant 599. June 8, 1784. p. 155.

**DUKE, JOHN TAYLOR, SR.** 287½ acres, Washington Co., bounded N. Wm. Hammock, E. M. Williamson, lot 413. Warrant 2208. May 17, 1784, p. 155.

**DUKE, JOHN TAYLOR.** 287½ acres, (2d bounty) Washington Co., bounded N. College lands, E. vacant, S. Wiliamson, W. Hammock, lot 414. Warrant 1631. May 17, 1784, p. 156.

**SULLIVAN, WILLIAM.** 575 acres, Washington Co., bounded all sides by vacant lands, bisected by Shoulderbone Ck., lot 460. Warrant 1551. June 6, 1784. p. 156.

**SHAFFER, DAVID.** 287½ acres, Washington Co., bounded N. by Wiliam Brown, E. Bentley Stokes, S. Geo. Patterson, W. College lands, lot 416. Warrant 2360. May 17, 1784. p. 156.

**BROWN, WILLIAM.** 287½ acres, Washington Co., bounded N. David, Shaffer, E. Shoulderbone Ck., W. Anthony Metcalf, lot 417. Warrant 1749. June 7, 1784. p. 157.

BRAIDY, WILLIAM. 287½ acres, Washington Co., bounded N. Danza Metcalf, E. Richard Call, S. James Alexander, W. vacant, lot 418. Warrant 2646. June 9, 1784. p. 157.

PHELPS, DAVID. 287½ acres, Washington Co. bounded all sides by vacant lands, lot 473. Warrant 1309. July 25, 1784. p. 172.

WATSON, PETER. 287½ acres, Washington Co., bounded W. by Oconee river, other sides vacant, lot 474. Warrant 767. May 17, 1784, p. 172.

LEGET, ABNER. 287½ acres, Washington Co., bounded N. vacant, E. Morgan, S. Academy lands, W. vacant, lot —. Warrant 1072. June 27th, 1784. p. 172.

AUTREY, JACOB. 287½ acres, Washington Co., bounded N. John Holmes, E. vacant, S. John Wiggins, W. Henry Allison, lot 476. Warrant 965. June 17, 1784. p. 173.

MARSHALL, SOLOMON. 287½ acres, Washington Co., bounded N. vacant, E. John Cowles, & Youngblood, S. Jesse Harris, W. Autrey, lot —. Warrant 1046. June 25, 1784. p. 173.

BUCKNER, HARRIS. 575 acres, Washington Co. bounded N. Henry Anglin, E. Solomon, S. vacant, W. John & Alexander Autrey, lot 479. Warrant 1177. June 22, 1784. p. 174.

HOLMES, JOHN. 287½ acres, Washington Co., bounded all sides by vacant lands, lot 479. Warrant 2458. June 5, 1784. p. 174.

HARRIS, WALTER. 287½ acres, Washington Co., bounded W. Oconee river, other sides vacant, lot 481. Warrant 787. June 3rd, 1784. p. 174.

ALISON, HENRY. 287½ acres, Washington Co., bounded N. Jacob Autrey, E. Kendrick, S. & W. vacant, lot 483. Warrant 2653. June 2, 1784. p. 175.

WHIGGAMS, JOHN. 287½ acres, Washington Co., bounded N. vacant, E. Alexander Autrey, S. Kendrick, W. Jacob Autrey, lot 484. Warrant 1181. June 16, 1784. p. 175.

BUGG, JERE, 287½ acres, Washington Co., bounded N. & W. vacant, E. Jno. Beckham, S. Altamaha river, lot 337. Warrant 282. June 3, 1784. p. 189.

HATCHER, ARCHIBALD. 287½ acres, Washington Co., bounded N. Oconee river, E. & S. vacant, W. Bugg, lot 339. Warrant 1085. June 5th, 1784. p. 190.

TAYLOR, JOHN. 287½ acres, Washington Co., bounded N. Oconee river, other sides vacant, lot 580. Warrant 55. June 5th, 1784. p. 190.

BURCH, EDWARD. 575 acres, Washington Co., bounded N. Oconee river, E. Charles Burch, S. & W. vacant, lot 341. Warrant 2150. June 5th, 1784. p. 191.

BURCH, CHARLES. 575 acres, Washington Co., bounded N. Oconee river, other sides vacant, lot 343. Warrant 2444. June 5, 1784, p. 191.

**BOYD, EDWARD.** 287½ acres, Washington Co., bounded N. & E. vacant, S. Will Thompson, W. Oconee river, lot 343. Warrant 868. June 23, 1784 p. 191.

**WILLIAMS, CHARLES.** 287½ acres, Washington Co., bounded W. Oconee river, other sides vacant, lot 346. Warrant 1914. June 5th, 1784. p. 192.

**RAZOR, ISAAC.** 287½ acres, Washington Co., bounded N. & E. vacant, S. Edward Boyd, W. Altamaha river, lot 347. Warrant 186. June 23rd, 1784. p. 193.

**RICE, JOHN.** 287½ acres, Washington Co., bounded N. & E. vacant, S. Jeremiah Bugg, W. Altamaha river, lot 348. Warrant 1410. June 23, 1784. p. 193.

**CHAMBLESS, CHRISTOPHER.** 575 acres, Washington Co., bounded E. Ambrose Jones, other sides vacant, lot 349. Warrant 2439. June 5, 1784. p. 193.

**WOODS, JOSHUA.** 575 acres, Washington Co., bounded S. James Culbreath and Thos. Brannon, other sides vacant, lot 590. Warrant 1393. June 3, 1784. p. 193.

**CULBREATH, JOHN.** 287½ acres, washington Co., bounded N. David McNeil, E. unknown, S. Christopher Chambless, W. States land, lot 351. Warrant 377. July 1st, 1784. p. 194.

**JOHNSON, THOMAS.** 287½ acres, Washington Co., bounded all sides by vacant lands, lot 352. Warrant 1563. June 2, 1784. p. 194.

**PARKER, JOHN.** 287½ acres, Washington Co., bounded N. & E. vacant, S. Carter, W. Oconee river, lot —. Warrant 607. June 4th, 1784. p. 194.

**McNEIL, JESSE.** 287½ acres, Washington Co., bounded N. Academy lands, E. Bever Dam ck., S. Isaac Skinner, W. Samuel Alexander, lot 554. Warrant 449. June 3, 1784. p. 195.

**AVERAT, JOHN.** 287½ acres, Washington Co., bounded E. Christopher Chambless, other sides vacant, lot —. Warrant 1297. June 6, 1784, p. 195.

**SHOAWE, THOMAS, JR.** 287½ acres, Washington Co., bounded W. Beaver Dam ck., other sides vacant, lot 556. Warrant 2236. July 4, 1784. p. 195.

**McNAIR, DANIEL.** 287½ acres, Washington Co., bounded E. Isaac Skinner, other sides vacant, lot 558. Warrant 856. June 3, 1784. p. 196.

**RAMSEY, SAMUEL.** 287½ acres, Washington Co., bounded N. Wm. Ramsey, E. vacant, lot 559. Warrant 1855. June 1, 1784. p. 196.

**MANN, JOHN.** 287½ acres, Washington Co., bounded N. John Mills, E. vacant, S. Will White, W. Altamaha river, lot 600. Warrant 1051. July 26, 1784. p. 196.

## BOUNTY SURVEYS.

**FORD, JOSHUA.** 287½ acres, Washington Co., bounded S. John Hill & John Martin, other sides vacant, lot 561. Warrant 1681. June 26, 1784. p. 196.

**PAIN, SAMUEL.** 287½ acres, Washington Co., bounded S. Joshua Ford, other sides vacant, lot 562. Warrant 747. June 26, 1784. p. 197.

**NEWBERRY, WILLIAM.** 287½ acres, Washington Co., bounded N. Charles Odingsell, E. & S. vacant, W. Ohoopee ck, lot 563. Warrant 2133. June 22, 1784. p. 197.

**BOSTIC, LITTLEBERRY.** 575 acres, Washington Co., bounded N. Ohoopee ck., E. vacant, S. James Donally, W. Altamaha river, lot 564. Warrant 995. June 25, 1784. p. 197.

**WALTON, GEORGE.** 575 acres, Washington Co., bounded N. & E. vacant, S. Charles Odinsell, W. Ohoopee ck, lot —. Warrant 2397. June 17, 1784. p. 197.

**BROWN, EPHRAIM.** 575 acres, Washington Co., bounded N. & E. vacant, S. Geo. Walton, W. Ohoopee ck., lot 566. Warrant 2392. June 24, 1784. p. 197.

**STEPHENS, JOHN.** 575 acres, Washington Co., bounded W. James Roberts, other sides vacant, lot 567. Warrant 1910. June 26, 1784. p. 198.

**SATTERWHITE, WILLIAM.** 287½ acres, Washington Co., bounded S. Robert Hudson, other sides vacant, lot 568. Warrant 2060. June 18, 1784. p. 198.

**HOLLINGER, WILLIAM.** 287½ acres, Washington Co., bounded N. & E. vacant, S. Sam'l McCulloch, W. Anthony Elumbley, lot 610. Warrant 2424. June 21, 1784. p. 198.

**TAYLOR, THOMAS.** 287½ acres, Washington Co., bounded N. Wm. Willis, E. vacant, S. James Martin, W. Altamaha river, lot 571. Warrant 2064. June 18, 1784. p. 199.

**MARTIN, JAMES.** 287½ acres, Washington Co., bounded N. Thos. Taylor, E. & S. vacant, W. Altamaha river, lot 572. Warrant 460. June 18, 1784. p. 199.

**HOLLIMAN, RICHARD.** 287½ acres, Washington Co., bounded N. Sam'l McCulloch, E. vacant, S. Ebeneezer Brunson, W. Altamaha river, lot 574. Warrant 574. June 20, 1784. p. 199.

**PUGH, ELIJAH.** 287½ acres, Washington Co., bounded N. Joseph Williams, E. & S. vacant, W. Cobb's ck., lot 575. Warrant 2128. June 25, 1784. p. 200.

**WILLIAMS, JOSEPH.** 287½ acres, Washington Co. bounded N. & E. vacant, S. Jo. Robertson, W. Mark Holliman, lot 567. Warrant 1603, June 20, 1784. p. 200.

**ROBERTSON, JOSEPH.** 287½ acres, Washington Co., bounded N. Tyre Glenn Harris, E. & S. vacant, W. Altamaha river, lot 577. Warrant 710. June 20, 1784. p. 200.

## ROSTER OF THE REVOLUTION.

**HOLLIMAN, DAVID,** 287½ acres, Washington Co., bounded N. John Chandler, E. & S. vacant, W. Ohoopee ck., lot 578. Warrant 131. June 11, 1784. p. 200.

**CHUMBLY, ANTHONY.** 287½ acres, Washington Co., bounded N. & E. vacant, S. Jas. Johnson, W. Joe Williams, lot 579. Warrant 2394. June 17, 1784. p 201.

**ODINGSELLS, CHARLES.** 575 acres, Washington Co., bounded all sides vacant, lot 260. Warrant 2649. June 15, 1784. p. 201.

**HUDSON, ROBERT.** 287½ acres, Washington Co., bounded S. James Martin, other sides vacant, lot 581. Warrant 2102. June 18, 1784. p. 201.

**HOLLIMAN, MARK.** 287½ acres, Washington Co., bounded S. Tyre Glenn Harris, other sides vacant, lot 582. Warrant 362. May 17, 1784. p. 201.

**CHANDLER, JOHN.** 287½ acres, Washington Co., bounded N. vacant, E. Ohoopee river, S. Michael Castell, W. Dead river and vacant. Lot No. 583 Warrant 34. May 17, 1784, p. 202.

**KELL, JOHN.** 287½ acres, Washington Co., bounded S. by Castell, other sides by Altamaha river, lot 584. War. —. May 17, 1784, p. 202.

**RUSHING, MATTHEW.** 575 acres, Washington Co., bounded E. by Oconee river, other sides vacant, lot 585. Warrant 2703. June 19, 1784. p. 202.

**HOLLINGER, TITUS.** 287½ acres, Washington Co., bounded N. & E. vacant, S. by Will Green, W. by Altamaha river, lot 586. Warrant 1418, May 17, 1784. p. 202.

**DAVIS, HEIRS of,** 287½ acres, Washington Co., bounded N. Seaborn, Jones, E. vacant, S. Isaac Razor, W. Altamaha river. Lot 587. War. 2638. June 24, 1784, p. 203.

**BRANDON, JOHN.** 287½ acres, Washington Co., bounded N. & E. vacant, S. Abraham Lamb, W. Altamaha, river, lot 588. Warrant 238, June 23, 1784. page 203.

**O'NEIL, JOHN.** 287½ acres, Washington Co., bounded all sides vacant, bisected by Ohoopee river, lot 630. Warrant 2358. June 1784. p. 203.

**MATTHEWS, WILLIAM.** 287½ acres, Washington Co., bounded W. Altamaha river, other sides vacant, lot 591. Warrant 2623. June 6, 1784, p. 204.

**MATTHEWS, WILLIAM.** 287½ acres, (2d bounty) Washington Co., bounded W. by Altamaha river, other sides vacant, lot 592. Warrant 2622. June 5, 1784. p. 204.

**PAIN, SAMUEL.** 287½ acres, Washington Co., bounded E. William Satterwhite, S. Wiliam Wallace, other sides vacant, lot 593. Warrant 687. June 19, 1784. p. 204.

**WALLACE, WILLIAM.** 287½ acres, Washington Co., bounded E. Robert Hudson, other sides vacant, lot 594. Warrant 935. June 19, 1784, p. 204.

## BOUNTY SURVEYS.

**GERMANY, JOHN.** 287½ acres, Washington Co., bounded N. vacant, E. Wm. Wallace, S. John Crawford, W. Altamaha river, lot 505. Warrant 1182. June 19, 1784. p. 205.

**HUDSON, NATHANIEL.** 287½ acres, Washington Co., bounded N. Rushing, E. & S. vacant, W. Oconee river, lot 596. Warrant 2701. June 15, 1784. p. 205.

**BARTEMORE, BENJ.** 575 acres, Washington Co., bounded N. & E. vacant, S. Titus Hollinger, W. Altamaha river, lot 597. Warrant 28. May 17, 1784. p. 205.

**McKEEN, GREEN.** 287½ acres, Washington Co., bounded N. & E. vacant, S. Richard Call, W. Altamaha river, lot 598. Warrant 270. June 9, 1784. p. 206.

**WILLIE, HEIRS OF WILLIAM.** 287½ acres, Washington Co., bounded W. Altamaha river, other sides vacant, lot 640. Warrant 1872. May 17, 1784. p. 206.

**GREEN, JOHN.** 287½ acres, Washington Co., bounded N. & E. vacant, S. John Hicks, W. Altamaha river, lot 604. Warrant 2356. May 17, 1784. p. 207.

**BRUNSTON, WILLIAM.** 287½ acres, Washington Co., bounded N. & E. vacant, S. John Brunson, W. McKeen, lot 601. Warrant 953. June 9, 1784, p. 206.

**BRUNSON, JOHN.** 287½ acres, Washington Co., bounded N. Richard Call, E. Green McKeen, S. & W. vacant, lot 602. Warrant 2095. May 8, 1784 p. 207.

**JOHNSTON, WILLIAM.** 287½ acres, Washington Co., bounded N. Sam Underwood, E. & S. vacant, W. Ohoopee river, lot 603. Warrant 2403. June 5, 1784. p. 207.

**THOMPSON, WILLIAM.** 287½ acres, Washington Co., bounded N. & E. vacant, S. William Thompson, W. Altamaha river, lot 605. Warrant 545. May 17, 1784. p. 207.

**THOMPSON, WILLIAM.** 287½ acres, (2d bounty) Washington Co., bounded N. & E. vacant, S. John Rice, W. Altamaha river, lot 606. Warrant 185. May 17, 1784. p. 208.

**PERRIT, ROBERT.** 287½ acres, Washington Co., bounded N. Will Green, E. vacant, S. Wm. David, W. Altamaha river, lot 607. Warrant 1044. June 28, 1784. p. 208.

**UNDERWOOD, SAMUEL.** 287½ acres, Washington Co., bounded W. Ohoopee river, other sides vacant, lot 608. Warrant 677. June 5, 1784, p. 208.

**WILLIE, HEIRS OF RICHARD.** 287½ acres, Washington Co., bounded N. & E. vacant, S. Wm. Wilie, W. Altamaha river, lot 609. Warrant 1133. May 17, 1784. p. 208.

**BRANHAM, SAMUEL.** 287½ acres, Washington Co., bounded W. Ohoopee river, other sides vacant, lot 650. Warrant 2074. May 17, 1784. p. 209.

**BRUNSON, HEIRS OF EBENEZER.** 575 acres, Washington Co., bounded N. & E. vacant, S. Joshua Freeman, W. Altamaha river, lot 611. Warrant 1331. May 17, 1784. p. 209.

**KILGORE, JOHN,** 287½ acres, Washington Co., bounded N. Sam'l Brunson, E. & S. vacant, W. Ohoopee river, lot 612. Warrant 1035. June 26, 1784. p. 209.

**HIX, JOHN.** 287½ acres, Washington Co., bounded N. & W. vacant, E. Mark Holliman, S. John Hix, lot 613. Warrant 1598. June 23, 1784. p. 209.

**JONES, SEABORN.** 575 acres, Washington Co., bounded N. Nath'l Hudson, E. vacant, W. heirs of John Davis, W. Altamaha river, lot 614. Warrant 117. June 24, 1784. p. 210.

**BRANDON, DAVID.** 287½ acres, Washington Co., bounded N. & E. vacant, S. John Hix, W. John Givins, lot 615. Warrant 2255. June 23, 1784. p. 210.

**GREEN, WILLIAM.** 287½ acres, Washington Co., bounded W. Altamaha river, other sides vacant, lot 617. Warrant 808. May 17, 1784. p. 210.

**ADAMS, HEIRS OF ROBERT.** 575 acres, Washington Co., bounded N. & E. vacant, S. Philips Oriner, W. Altamaha river, lot 618. Warrant 211 May 17, 1784. p. 211.

**GRINER, PHILIP.** 575 acres, Washington Co., bounded W. Altamaha river, other sides vacant, lot 619. Warrant 250. May 17, 1784, p. 211.

**ROBERTS, JOHN.** 287½ acres, Washington Co., bounded N. & E. vacant, S. Wm. Where, W. Williamson's swamp, lot 621. Warrant 1892. June 28, 1784. p. 212.

**JACK, SAMUEL.** 287½ acres, Washington Co., bounded N. & E. vacant, S. Lawson, W. Oconee river, lot 622. Warrant 1617. May 17, 1784. p. 212.

**CASTLEBERRY, HENRY.** 287½ acres, Washington Co., bounded all sides vacant, lot 623. Warrant 2391. June 17, 1784. p. 212.

**WOOTEN, NATHANIEL.** 287½ acres, Washington Co., bounded N. Oliver, E. Lanear, S. Lamar, W. Ohoochee river, lot 624. Warrant 5. June 10, 1784.

**MOATES, WILLIAM.** 287½ acres, Washington Co., bounded, N. Few, E. Glenn, S. Castleberry, W. Simon Moates, lot 625. Warrant 60. June 30, 1784. p. 213.

**FULLER, JOHN.** 287½ acres, Washington Co., bounded all sides vacant, bisected by Camp's branch, lot 627. Warrant 2259. May 17, 1784, p. 213.

## BOUNTY SURVEYS.

**DEAN, JOHN.** 287½ acres, Washington Co., bounded W. Ohoopee river, other sides vacant, lot 628. Warrant 1951. June 7, 1784. p. 214.

**MOATES, SILAS.** 287½ acres, Washington Co., bounded N. Castleberry, other sides vacant, lot 629. Warrant 1425. June 30, 1784. p. 214.

**ISLAND, ABSOLEM.** 287½ acres, Washington Co., bounded all sides vacant, lot 630. Warrant 573. May 17, 1784. p. 214.

**ALLEN, THOMAS,** 287½ acres, Washington Co., bounded N. & E. vacant, S. & W. Elijah Gillett, lot 631. Warrant 1997. May 17, 1784. p. 214.

**GUSTAVOUS, MICAJAH.** 287½ acres, Washington Co., bounded N. Snelson, E. & W. vacant, S. Glenn, lot 632. Warrant 268. May, 17, 1784. p. 214.

**CARROLL, WILLIAM.** 287½ acres, Washington Co., bounded W. Long and vacant, other sides vacant, lot 633. Warrant 1970. May 17, 1784. p. 215.

**SNELSON, THOMAS.** 287½ acres, Washington Co., bounded S. Micajah Gustavous, other sides vacant, lot 634. Warrant 2467. June 29, 1784. p. 215.

**MOATES, SIMON.** 287½ acres, Washington Co., bounded N. Wm. Moates, E. Silas Moates, S. Absolem Island, W. vacant, lot 635. Warrant 1078. July 1, 1784. p. 215.

**MADDOX, WILLIAM.** 287½ acres, Washington Co., bounded N. Culbresth, other sides vacant, bisected by Richard ck., lot 636. Warrant 549. May 17, 1784, p. 216.

**RAMSEY, RANDAL.** 287½ acres, Washington Co., bounded N. David Carter, E. Isaac Manners, S. vacant, W. Wm. Cone, bisected N. & S. by Beaverdam ck, lot 637. Warrant 1148. June 5, 1784. p. 216.

**BUSH, JOHN.** 287½ acres, Washington Co., bounded N. James McKey, E. Ohoopee river, S. & W, vacant, lot 638. Warrant (old warrant number) Oct. 12, 1785. p. 216.

**CARTER, DAVID.** 287½ acres, Washington Co., bounded N. Jesse McKee, E. & S. vacant, W. Skinner, bisected, E. & W. by Richland ck., and dotted line marked "Indian War Trail," lot 639. Warrant 2585. May 24, 1784. p. 216.

**RICHARDSON, JOSEPH.** 287½ acres, Washington Co., bounded E. Sam Hicks, other sides vacant, lot 640. Warrant 180. May 17, 1784. p. 217.

**POWELL, LEWIS.** 287½ acres, Washington Co., bounded all sides vacant, cut on E. by branch of Town creek and on W. by branch of Richland creek, lot 641. Warrant 1010. June 1, 1784. p. 217.

**McCALL, THOMAS.** 287½ acres, Washington Co., bounded all sides vacant, quartered by Long Branch Town creek, lot 642. Warrant 587. June 12, 1784. p. 217.

**CARLISLE, JOHN.** 287½ acres, Washington Co., bounded N. Thos. Frederick, E. Oconee river, S. Jacob Linn, W. vacant, lot 643. Warrant 2336. June 9, 1784. p. 217.

## ROSTER OF THE REVOLUTION.

**COWINS, WILLIAM.** 287½ acres, Washington Co., bounded W. unknown, other sides vacant, lot 644. Warrant 300. June 5, 1784. p. 218.

**FREDERICK, THOMAS.** 287½ acres, Washington Co., bounded N. & W. vacant, E. Oconee river, S. John Carlisle, lot 645. Warrant 1924. June 27, 1784. p. 218.

**COOK, JOHN.** 287½ acres, Washington Co., bounded all sides vacant, traversed by Rocky creek, lot 646. Warrant 691. May 17, 1784. p. 218.

**McKINNEY, HENRY.** 287½ acres, Washington Co., bounded N. vacant, E. Alex Douglas, S. Sam'l Carson, W. Wm. Anderson, lot 647. Warrant 1733. June 8, 1784. p. 218.

**CARSON, SAM'L.** 287½ acres, Washington Co., bounded N. McKinney & McDouglas, E. vacant, S. Wade W. Oconee river, lot 648. Warrant 1641. June 8, 1784. p. 219.

**McDOUGLAS, ALEXANDER.** 287½ acres, Washington Co., bounded S. Henry McKinney, other sides vacant, lot 689. Warrant 1785. May 17, 1784. p. 219.

**SHIFFEL, MARK.** 575 acres, Washington Co., bounded N. Silas Moates, E. & S. vacant, W. Simon Moates, lot 650. Warrant 897. May 17, 1784. p. 219.

**WADE, NEHEMIAH,** 287½ acres, Washington Co., bounded N. Samuel Carson, E. vacant, S. Richard Call, W. Oconee river, lot 651. Warrant 1685. June 8, 1784. p. 219.

**WILSON, LEVIN.** 287½ acres, Washington Co., bounded E. Williamson's creek, other sides vacant, lot 652. Warrant 14. May 17, 1784. p 220.

**CONNELLY, WILLIAM.** 230 acres, Washington Co., bounded N. & E. vacant, S. Gen. McIntosh, W. Oconee river, lot 654. Warrant —. May 17, 1784. p. 220.

**HOUSE, LAWRENCE.** 230 acres, Washington Co., bounded W. Oconee river, other sides vacant, lot 655. Warrant —. May 17, 1784. p. 220.

**McKINNEY, MATTHEW.** 287½ acres, Washington Co., bounded N. Moses Collins, E. & S. vacant, W. Robert Holmes, lot 656. Warrant 1800. May 17, 1784. p. 221.

**CARTLAGE, JAMES.** 287½ acres, Washington Co., bounded N. Franklin Co. line, E. & S. vacant, W. Peter Werber, lot 657. Warrant 1394. May 17, 1784. p. 221.

**GERMANY, SAMUEL.** 287½ acres, Washington Co., bounded N. unknown, E. Fitzpatrick, S. Garnet & Johnson, W. Dannelly, lot 658. Warrant 1207. June 19, 1784. p. 221

**CARTLEDGE, JAMES.** 287½ acres (2d bounty), Washington Co., bounded W. Frederick, other sides vacant, lot 659. Warrant 2109. June 1, 1784. p. 221.

BOUNTY SURVEYS. 209

BURTON, RICHARD. 230 acres, Washington Co., bounded W. Oconee river, other sides vacant, lot 661. Warrant —. May 17, 1784. p. 222.

STEWART, CLEMENT. 287½ acres, Washington Co., bounded E. Thos. McCall, other sides vacant, lot 663. Warrant 619. May 17, 1784, p. 222.

BARNETT, JOEL. 287½ acres, Washington Co., bounded all sides vacant, crossed by N. fork Shoulderbone creek, lot 664. Warrant 949. May 17, 1784. p. 223.

McNEIL, HEIRS OF ARCHIBALD. 287½ acres, Washington Co., bounded N. Archibald McNeil, other sides vacant, lot 671. Warrant 672. May 17, 1784. p. 222.

McNEIL, MICHAEL. 287½ acres, Washington Co., bounded all sides vacant, lot 666, Warrant 1952. June 25, 1784. p. 223.

RAMSEY, WILLIAM, 287½ acres, Washington Co., bounded N. & W. vacant, E. William Collins, S. Richland creek, lot 667. Warrant 1010. June 1, 1784. p. 223.

STUART, CHARLES. 287½ acres, Washington Co., bounded N. & S. vacant, E. Hickinbottom, W. unknown, lot 669. Warrant 1975. May 17, 1784, p. 224.

McNEIL, DANIEL. 287½ acres, Washington Co., bounded N. Gillet, E. & S. vacant, W. Oconee river, lot 670. Warrant 35. May 17, 1784, p. 224.

ANDERSON, ELIJAH, 287½ acres, Washington Co., bounded N. Arch. McNeil, other sides vacant, lot 671. Warrant 672. May 17, 1784, p. 224.

FUQUA, THOMAS. 287½ acres, Washington Co., bounded all sides vacant, lot 672. Warrant 1213. May 17, 1784. p. 225.

CRIBBS, THOMAS. 287½ acres, Washington Co., bounded E. Thos. Johnson, other sides vacant, lot 673. Warrant 947. May 17, 1784, p. 255.

BARNETT, WILLIAM, 287½ acres, Washington Co., bounded N. Nathan Hicks, E. & W. vacant, S. Peter Culbreath, lot 675. Warrant 2275. May 17, 1874, p. 226.

JUSTICE, DEMPSEY, 287½ acres, Washington Co., bounded all sides vacant, lot 676, Warrant 1920. May 17, 1784. p. 226.

SIMPSON, JAMES. 287½ acres, Washington Co., bounded all sides vacant bisected by fork of Oconee river, lot 678. Warrant 476. June 25, 1784, p. 226.

CONE, WILLIA. 287½ acres, Washington Co., bounded W. Thos. Johnston, other sides vacant, lot 720. Warrant —. May 17, 1784. p. 227.

HIGGINBOTHAM, BURROUGHS. 287½ acres, Washington Co., bounded all sides vacant, lot 680. Warrant 276. May 17, 1784. p. 227.

ROSTER OF THE REVOLUTION.

SMITH, NATHANIEL. 287½ acres, Washington Co., bounded W. Thos. Farqua, other sides vacant, lot 681. Warrant 1015. June 17, 1784. p. 227.

HOLTON, FRANCIS, 287½ acres, Washington Co., bounded all sides vacant, lot 682. Warrant 179. May 17, 1784. p. 227.

COLLIER, WILLIAM. 287½ acres, Washington Co., bounded S. Lewis Powell, other sides vacant, lot 684. Warrant 2520. June 1, 1784. p. 227.

CULBREATH, PETER. 287½ acres, Washington Co., bounded S. James Culbreath, other sides vacant, bisected by Richland creek, lot 685. Warrant 2012. June 7, 1784. p. 228.

BRANNON, THOMAS. 287½ acres, Washington Co., bounded E. Thos. Hill, W. Wm. Maddox, other sides vacant, touched by Richland creek, lot 686. Warrant 1909. May 17, 1784. p. 228.

BARNETT, WILLIAM. 287½ acres, Washington Co., bounded all sides vacant, lot 687. Warrant 2529. May 17, 1784. p. 229.

McNEIL, DANIEL. 287½ acres, Washington Co., bounded E. John Hill, other sides vacant, lot 688. Warrant 984. May 24, 1784. p. 229.

CULBREATH, JAMES. 575 acres, Washington Co., bounded all sides vacant cut by Richland creek, lot 730. Warrant 1606. May 17, 1784. p. 230.

PENNINGTON, THOMAS. 287½ acres, Washington Co., bounded N. Jacob Zinn, E. Oconee river, S. Travis Fenn, W. vacant, lot 697. Warrant 2022. May 17, 1784. p. 232.

FENN, TRAVIS. 287½ acres, Washington Co., bounded N. Thos. Pennington, E. Oconee river, S. Sam'l Berry, W. vacant, lot 698. Warrant 2503. May 17, 1784. p. 232.

ZINN, JACOB. 287½ acres, Washington Co., bounded N. John Carlyle, E. Oconee river, S. Thos. Pennington, W. vacant, lot 740. Warrant 2390. June 8, 1784. p. 232.

BISHOP, JAMES. 287½ acres, Washington Co., bounded N. Stephen Bishop, E. unknown, S. Leonard Switzer, W. vacant, lot 700. War. 987. June 10, 1784, p. 233.

TUCKER, THOMAS. 287½ acres, Washington Co., bounded W. Oconee river, other sides vacant, lot 701. Warrant 263. June 2, 1784. p. 233.

BERRYHILL, SAMUEL. 287½ acres, Washington Co., bounded N. Oconee river, E. & S. vacant, W. Travis Fenn, lot 702. Warrant 1146. May 17, 1784. p. 233.

CURETON, RICHARD. 287½ acres, Washington Co., bounded all sides vacant, lot, 703. Warrant 491. May 17, 1784. p. 233.

AVENT, JOSEPH. 287½ acres, Washington Co., bounded all sides vacant, lot 704. Warrant 2244. June 26, 1784. p. 234.

## BOUNTY SURVEYS. 211

**CHILDRY, THOMAS.** 287½ acres, Washington Co., bounded N. Sam Holliman, E. Few, S. & W. Oconee river, lot 705. Warrant 818. May 17, 1784. p. 234.

**EVANS, JOHN,** 287½ acres, Washington Co., bounded S. Few and Rutherford, other sides vacant, lot 706. Warrant 676. May 17, 1784. p. 234.

**HOLLIMAN, SAMUEL.** 287½ acres, Washington Co., bounded N. Ayres and Irvin, E. Few, S. Thos Childry, W. Oconee river, lot 707. Warrant 1229. May 17, 1784. p. 234.

**SINQUEFIELD, AARON.** 287½ acres, Washington Co., bounded N. Wm. Buckhalter, E. & S. vacant, W. Williamson's swamp, lot 750. Warrant 2404. July 2, 1784. p. 236.

**ROBERTS, JOHN.** 575 acres, Washington Co., bounded N. Few, other sides vacant, lot 710. Warrant 2625. May 5, 1784. p. 236.

**SALTER, SIMON.** 287½ acres, Washington Co., bounded all sides vacant, containing two ponds, lot 711. Warrant 1314. July 1, 1784. p. 236.

**FREEMAN, WILLIAM.** 575 acres, Washington Co., bounded W. Burrell Pope, other sides vacant, Bigg creek on W., lot 717. Warrant 114. May 17, 1784. p. 238.

**BURNETT, JOHN.** 575 acres, Washington Co., bounded N. Smith, E. vacant, S. Freeman, W. Oconee river, lot 760. Warrant 1480. June 3, 1784. p. 239.

**FREEMAN, JOHN.** 575 acres, Washington Co., bounded N. Burnett, E. & S. vacant, W. Oconee river, lot 720. Warrant 2129. June 3, 1784. p. 239.

**HENDERSON, ZACHARIAH.** 260 acres, (bounty) Washington Co., bounded N. & E. vacant, S. Oconee river, W. vacant, lot 723. Warrant —. Aug. 1, 1784. p. 240.

**SIMMS, MANN.** 287½ acres, Washington Co., bounded S. John Jones, other sides vacant, lot 725. Warrant 2348. June 12, 1784. p. 240.

**HUGHES, NICHOLAS.** 287½ acres, Washington Co., bounded S. Wm. Mitchell, other sides vacant, cut by Buffalo creek, lot 737. Warrant 1017. June 8, 1784. p. 246.

**PUGH, JESSE.** 287½ acres, Washington Co., bounded S. D. Robertson, other sides vacant, cut by fork of Buffalo creek, lot 738. Warrant 2468. July 16, 1784. p. 276.

**CLOWER, JOHN.** 287½ acres, Washington Co., bounded all sides vacant. Bisected N. & S. by Buffalo creek, lot 739. Warrant 262. June 17, 1784. p. 246.

**McFARLAND, JOHN.** 287½ acres, Washington Co., bounded N. Jas. McFarland, E. & W. vacant, S. Ben Scott, lot 780. Warrant 1055. June 28, 1784. p. 246.

ROSTER OF THE REVOLUTION.

**McFARLAND, JAMES.** 287½ acres, Washington Co., bounded N. Sam'l Wilson, E. vacant, S. Gilbert Dinkins, W. Oconee river, lot 741. Warrant 2027. May 17, 1784. p. 247.

**BERRY, JOHN.** 287½ acres, Washington Co., bounded W. John Bryant, other sides vacant, cut by Big creek, lot 743. Warrant 1628. June 9, 1784. p. 247.

**NAIL, JOSEPH.** 575 acres, Washington Co., bounded W. Stephen Westbrook, other sides vacant, lot 755. Warrant 248. June 14, 1784. p. 250.

**McFARLAND, JOHN.** 287½ acres, Washington Co., bounded W. Jonas, other sides vacant, bisected by Little Beaverdam creek, lot 758. Warrant —. June 24, 1784. p. 251.

**CATCHINGS, JOSEPH.** 287½ acres, Washington Co., bounded N. & E. vacant, S. Parks, W. Oconee river, lot 782. Warrant 285. June 5, 1784. p. 258.

**COBB, JOSEPH.** 287½ acres, Washington Co., bounded N. & E. vacant, S. Wm. Brunston, W. Moses Lepham, lot 788. Warrant 1415. June 25, 1784. p. 260.

**LEAPHAM, MOSES.** 287½ acres, Washington Co., bounded N. & E. vacant, S. McKeen Green, W. Altamaha river, lot 789. Warrant 2261. June 25, 1784. p. 261.

**TUREMAN, GARRETT.** 287½ acres, Franklin Co., bounded all sides vacant, cut by Broad river, lot 830. Warrant 146. June 3, 1784. p. 261.

**TRIMBLE, MOSES.** 287½ acres, Franklin Co., bounded N. Tugalo river, E. Spurlock, other sides vacant, lot 793. Warrant —. July 22, 1784. p. 262.

**TAYLOR, ROBERT.** 287½ acres, Franklin Co., bounded W. College lands, other sides vacant, lot 794. Warrant 102. June 25, 1784, p. 262.

**TUREMAN, JOHN.** 287½ acres, Franklin Co., bounded E. Westbrook, other sides vacant, lot 795. Warrant 321.. May 17, 1784. p. 262.

**YARBOROUGH, JAMES.** 287½ acres, Washington Co., bounded N. & W. vacant, E. Shiffell, S. Rutherford, lot 801. Warrant 1238. June 16, 1784. p. 263.

**YARBROUGH, JAMES.** 287½ acres, Franklin Co., bounded E. Henry Nails, other sides vacant, cut by Broad river and Paynes creek, lot 802. Warrant 797. Sept. 17, 1784. p. 264.

**LANDERS, JACOB.** 575 acres, Washington Co., bounded N. Thos. Napier, E. & S. vacant, W. Oconee river, lot 808. Warrant 1652. June 17, 1784. p. 265.

**IRVIN, WILLIAM,** 287½ acres, Washington Co., bounded N. vacant, lies in fork of Big creek, pointing N., lot 811. Warrant 261. May 17, 1784. p. 266.

**IRVIN, JARED.** 287½ acres, Washington Co., bounded N. & E. Bigg creek, S. vacant, W. Hadden, lot 812. Warrant 1305. July 3, 1784. p. 267.

# BOUNTY SURVEYS. 213

**KELLY, EDWARD.** 575 acres, Washington Co., bounded N. Shoulderbone creek, E. Oconee river, S. vacant, W. Daley, lot 814. Warrant 697. July 20, 1784. p. 267.

**JARVIS, NICHOLAS.** 575 acres, Franklin Co., bounded all sides vacant, cut N. & S. by Town creek, lot, 816. Warrant 440. June 19, 1784. p. 268.

**JOINER, BENJAMIN.** 575 acres, Washington Co., bounded N. Jno. Bryant, E., S. & W. vacant, cut by Bigg creek, lot 817. Warrant 798. June 9, 1784, p. 268.

**FERRIN, GEORGE.** 287½ acres, Washington Co., bounded N. vacant, E. Jno. McFarland, S. McFarland, W. Adam Shone, lot 818. Warrant 842. June 24, 1784. p. 269.

**JARVIS, PAT.** 287½ acres, Washington Co., bounded E. John Wilson, other sides vacant, lot 819. Warrant 1458. June 27, 1784. p. 269.

**IRVIN, JOHN LAWSON.** 287½ acres, Washington Co., bounded all sides vacant, lot 860. Warrant 360. July 1, 1784. p. 269.

**IRVIN, HUGH.** 287½ acres, Washington Co., bounded N. & E. vacant, W. fork of Williamson's creek, W. Joel Harris, lot 821. Warrant 225. June 28, 1784, p. 270.

**LYNCH, JOHN.** 230 acres, Franklin Co., bounded N. Oconee river, other sides vacant, lot 833. Warrant —. July 21, 1784. p. 273.

**POWELL, MOSES.** 287½ acres, Washington Co., bounded all sides vacant, cut E. & W. by Williamson's swamp, lot 836. Warrant 418. July 6, 1784. p. 273.

**MARSHALL, REV. ABRAHAM.** 287½ acres, Washington Co., bounded N. Oconee river, E. Carter, S. vacant and Campbell, lot 836. Warrant 312. June 4, 1784. p. 273.

**SHAW, DAVID.** 287½ acres, Washington Co., bounded N. vacant, E. David Kelly. S. Moses Lepham, W. Altamaha river, lot 845. Warrant 403. June 2, 1784. p. 275.

**KELLY, WILLIAM,** 287½ acres, Washington Co., bounded N. & E. vacant, S. Joseph Cobb, W. David Shaw, lot 842. Warrant 961. June 2, 1784. p. 275.

**KNEAL, PATRICK.** 230 acres, Franklin Co., bounded N. vacant, E. William Corbin, S. Oconee river, W. John Lynch, lot 844. Warrant —. July 8, 1784. p. 275.

**CORBIN, WILLIAM.** 230 acres, Franklin Co., bounded N. & E. vacant, S. Oconee river, W. Patrick Kneal, lot 845. Warrant —. July 8, 1784. p. 275.

**KNEAL, HENRY,** 287½ acres, Franklin Co., bounded N. Yarborough, other sides vacant, lot 847. Warrant 795. Sept. 17, 1784. p. 276.

**NAIL, REUBEN.** 287½ acres, Franklin Co., bounded N. & S. vacant E. John Burke, W. Robert Graves, bisected by Broad river, lot 848. Warrant 745. July 30, 1784. p. 276.

**O'NEAL, AXUM.** 287½ acres, Washington Co., bounded all sides vacant, source of Shoulderbone creek, lot 852. Warrant 631. June 7, 1784. p. 227.

**QUERNS, JOHN.** 287½ acres, Washington Co., bounded N. by College lands, on Falling creek, E. vacant, S. Hopkins, W. Querns, lot 643. June 20, 1784. p. 278.

**RAFFERTY, MICHAEL.** 287½ acres, Washington Co., bounded E. John Laramore, other sides vacant, lot 900. Warrant 1518. July 22, 1784. p. 279.

**KIMBROUGH, JOHN.** 287½ acres, Washington Co., bounded all sides vacant, lot, 865. Warrant 238. Nov. 17, 1784. p. 281.

**KIMBROUGH, WILLIAM.** 287½ acres, Washington Co., bounded N. & S. vacant, E. Robt. Holliman, W. grantee, lot 866. Warrant 207. Nov. 15, 1784, p. 281.

**KIMBROUGH, WILLIAM,** 287½ acres, (2d bounty) Washington Co., bounded E. Kimbrough, other sides vacant, lot 867. Warrant 1176. November 15, 1784. p. 281.

**DUHART, JOHN.** 287½ acres, Washington Co., bounded N. vacant, E. Robt. Pattison, S. Oconee river, W. Stringer, lot 876. Warrant 2148. June 7, 1784. p. 284.

**GALPHIN, THOMAS.** 287½ acres, Washington Co., bounded E. Ogeechee river, other sides vacant, lot 877. Warrant 429. July 17, 1784. p. 285.

**EMAMUEL, DAVID.** 575 acres, Washington Co., bounded N. & W. vacant, E. heirs of Joel Lewis, S. Wm. Wash, lot 578. Warrant —. June 3, 1784. p. 285.

**ALEXANDER, ASA.** 287½ acres, Washington Co., bounded E. Stephen Bishop (on Shoulderbone creek), other sides vacant, lot 897. Warrant 1944. June 25, 1784. p. 286.

**ROSEBOROUGH, GEORGE.** 287½ acres, Washington Co., bounded N. Sanders and Wright, E. Ben McCormick, other sides vacant, lot 920. Warrant —. Nov. 1, 1894. p. 286.

**ALLEN, ROBERT,** 287½ acres, Washington Co., bounded N.-E. vacant, S.-E. Asa Emanuel, S.-W. Oconee river, N.-W. Howell, lot 881. Warrant 1419. June 7, 1784. p. 287.

**RICKETSON, TIMOTHY.** 287½ acres, Washington Co., bounded N. Isaac Wells, E. & S. vacant, W. Wm. Smith, on Shoulderbone creek waters, lot 904. Warrant 1574. Nov. 20, 1784, p. 298.

## BOUNTY SURVEYS.

**McGREGOR, ALEXANDER.** 287½ acres, Washington Co., bounded E. & S. unknown, N. & W. vacant, lot 905. Warrant 1752. Nov. 21, 1784. p. 299.

**MOTT, ZEPHANIA.** 287½ acres, Washington Co., bounded W. Wm. Smith, on Shoulderbone creek waters, lot 906. Warrant 525. Nov. 21, 1784. p. 299.

**FRAZIER, MALAKIAH.** 287½ acres, Washington Co., bounded N. & E. vacant, S. Abraham Marshall, W. Carter, lot 908. Warrant 196. Oct. 30, 1784. p. 300.

**PUGH, FRANCIS.** 287½ acres, Washington Co., bounded S. Ogeechee river, other sides vacant, cut by Baker Springs creek, lot 917. Warrant 2660. July 3, 1784. p. 305.

**CUTHBERT, MAJOR A. DANIEL.** 920 acres, Washington Co., bounded S. Jas. Houston, other sides vacant, cut by Sugar creek, lot 960. Warrant —. Dec. 8, 1784. p. 306.

**DENHAM, CHARLES.** 827½ acres, Washington Co., bounded S. Richland creek, other sides vacant, lot 924. Warrant 2276. June 17, 1784. p. 308.

**BALDWIN, WILLIAM.** 287½ acres, Washington Co., bounded W. Zach Wheeler, other sides unknown, lot 925. Warrant 1683. June 22, 1784. p. 309.

**PACE, THOMAS.** 287½ acres, Washington Co., bounded W. Thos. Moseley, other sides vacant, lot 928. Warrant 120. July 14, 1784. p. 310.

**McINTOSH, COL. JOHN.** 1150 acres, Washington Co., bounded W. Thos. Glascock and Gen. McIntosh, other sides vacant, cut by Oconee river, lot 928. Warrant —. Nov. 16, 1784. p. 315.

**LINN, JOHN.** 287½ acres, Franklin Co., bounded N. vacant, E. John Ware, S. Jo. Jeter, W. Wm. Mose, lot 939. Warrant 827, Dec. 10, 1784. p. 316.

**BARLOW, WILLIAM.** 287½ acres, Franklin Co., bounded N. & E. vacant, S. Welcher, W. Amb. Bradley, lot 980. Warrant 818. Dec. 3, 1784. p. 316.

**BRADLEY, JOSHUA.** 287½ acres, Franklin Co., bounded N. Abr. Bradley, E. John Welcher, S. E. Bugg Hicks, W. vacant, cut by fork of Bear creek, lot 941. Warrant 817. Dec. 3, 1784. p. 317.

**BRADLEY, ABRAHAM.** 287½ acres, Franklin Co., bounded N. & W. vacant, E. Wm. Barlow, S. Joshua Bradley, lot 942. Warrant 819. Dec. 3, 1784. p. 317.

**WELCHER, JOHN.** 287½ acres, Franklin Co., bounded E. Wm. Barlow, S. Joshua Bradley, N. & W. vacant, cut by fork of Bear creek, lot 943. Warrant 826. Dec. 3, 1784. p. 318.

**DOUGLAS, GEORGE.** 287½ acres, Franklin Co., bounded N. John Ware, E. & S. vacant, W. Jo. Jeter, cut N-W. & S-E. by Clarkes creek, lot 944. Warrant 830. Dec. 10, 1784. p. 318.

**JETER, JOSEPH.** 287½ acres, Franklin Co., bounded N. & E. vacant, S. Geo. Douglas, W. John Lynn, cut by Clarkes creek, lot 945. Warrant 828. Dec. 10, 1784. p. 319.

**KING, JOHN.** 287½ acres, Washington Co., bounded N. & W. vacant, E. Champain, S. Johnston, Rose creek, fork of Oconee river, lot 990. Warrant —. Jan. 3, 1785. p. 321.

**ELBERT, GEN. SAMUEL.** 575 acres, Washington Co., bounded S. by grantee, other sides vacant, lot 954. Warrant —. Nov. 30, 1784. p. 323.

**ELBERT, SAMUEL.** 977½ acres, Washington Co., bounded N. grantee, E. Geo. & Jos. Maxwell, S-W. Oconee river, and grantee, lot 955. Warrant —. Nov. 30, 1784. p. 323.

**ELBERT, GEN. SAMUEL.** 402½ acres, Washington Co., bounded N-E. grantee, S. Oconee river, S-W. Gen. McIntosh, lot 956. Warrant —. Nov. 30, 1784. p. 323.

**HOWE, HEIRS OF LIEUT. ROBERT.** 460 acres, Washington Co., bounded all sides vacant, Rocky creek, lot 957. Warrant —. Nov. 28, 1784. p. 324.

**THORN, DAVID.** 287½ acres, Effingham Co., bounded all sides vacant, lot 966. Warrant —. Feb. 14, 1785. p. 329.

**McGETTON, VANCE.** 230 acres, Franklin Co., bounded S. Oconee river, other sides vacant, lot 972. Warrant —. July 17, 1784. p. 329.

**PEARCE, NATHANIEL.** 500 acres, Franklin Co., bounded N. Richd. Call, E. & W. vacant, S. Glascock and Walton, lot 977. Warrant —. Dec. 3, 1784. p. 330.

**CORSEY, STEPHEN.** 575 acres, Franklin Co., bounded all sides vacant, cut by Broad river, lot 978. Warrant —. June 10, 1784. p. 331.

**HUDSON, JAMES.** 287½ acres, Washington Co., bounded N. Jas. Pugh, E. & S. vacant, W. Ogeechee river, lot 979. Warrant —. July 4, 1784. p. 331.

**FLING, JOHN.** 575 acres, Washington Co., bounded E. Evan Harvey, other sides vacant, cut by ford of Oconee river, lot 1020. Warrant —. Sept. 17, 1784. p. 31.

**BROWN, JOHN.** 575 acres, Washington Co., bounded N. vacant, no other boundaries given, lot 981. Warrant —. May 30, 1784, p. 332.

**WHITBY, THOMAS.** 287½ acres, Franklin Co., bounded S. Sam'l Stafford, other sides vacant, lot 1030. Warrant 701. Aug. 27, 1784. p. 335.

**LAMB, BETHIEL,** 287½ acres, Franklin Co., bounded N. vacant, lies in forks of Mulberry and Bigg Pond (forks of Oconee river,) lot 991. Warrant 448. July 30, 1784. p. 335.

**WILLIAMSON, MICAJAH.** 287½ acres, Franklin Co., bounded E. G. Walton, other sides vacant, on waters of South Broad river, lot 992. Warrant 691. Aug. 20, 1784. p. 335.

**RICKETSON, MARMADUKE.** 287½ acres, Franklin Co., bounded N. & E. vacant, S. Thos. McDowell, W. Fork of Broad river, lot 993. Warrant 696. Aug. 27. 1784. p. 336.

**McDOWELL, THOS.** 287½ acres, Franklin Co., bounded N. Richetson, E. & S. vacant, W. Wm. Fanner, lot 994. Warrant 694. Aug. 26, 1784. p. 336.

**ADKIN, WILLIAM.** 287½ acres, Franklin Co., bounded S. Simon Beck, other sides vacant, cut N. & S. by fork of Board river, lot 966. Warrant 342. June 30, 1784. p. 336.

**LONG, HENRY.** 460 acres, Franklin Co., bounded S. Thos. Greer, other sides vacant, lot 977. Warrant 695. Aug. 19, 1784. p. 337.

**BECK, SIMON.** 287½ acres, Franklin Co., bounded S. Adkin, other sides vacant, cut by north fork of Broad river, lot 995. Warrant 342. July 4, 1784. p. 336.

**WAY, JOHN, SR.** 575 acres, Franklin Co., bounded all sides vacant, bisected N. & S. by middle fork of Board river, lot 999. Warrant 687. Oct. 5, 1784. p. 337.

**EDWARDS, JOSEPH.** 287½ acres, Washington Co., bounded N. & E. vacant, S. branch of Town creek and Jno. Brown, W. surveyed, lot 1040. Warrant 3109. Oct. 19, 1784. p. 338.

**WILLIAMS, JAMES.** 287½ acres, Washington Co., bounded N. & W. vacant, E. surveyed, S. Furlow and Phillips, lot 1001. Warrant 528. Oct. 20, 1784, p. 338.

**SHARP, MICHAEL.** 287½ acres, Washington Co., bounded N. & W. vacant, E. Jno. Sharp, S. Ogeechee river, lot 1002. Warrant 304. July 24, 1784. p. 339.

**MITCHELL, THOMAS.** 287½ acres, Washington Co., bounded E. Geo. Dooley, other sides vacant, lot 838. Warrant 692. June 10, 1784. p. 274.

**LEAPHAM, MOSES.** 287½ acres, Washington Co., bounded all sides vacant, on Williamson's Swamp. Lot 1003. Warrant 1003. July 23, 1784. p. 339.

**HODGE, ROBERT.** 575 acres, Washington Co., bounded E. Williamson's swamp creek, other sides vacant, lot 1004. Warrant 1274. July 5, 1784. p. 339.

**FURLOW, WILLIAM.** 287½ acres, Washington Co., bounded N. & W. vacant, E. College lands, S. Harper, lot 1005. Warrant 3024. Oct. 20, 1784. p. 339.

**HOPKINS, LAMBETH.** 287½ acres, Washington Co., bounded N. vacant, E. Pittman, S. Oconee river, W. Harris, lot 1006. Warrant 2910. July 23, 1784. p. 340.

**WILLIAMS, JOHN.** 287½ acres, Washington Co., bounded N. & W. vacant, E. Joe Mooney, S. Phillips, on waters of Town creek, lot 1007. Warrant 452. Oct. 20, 1784. p. 340.

**HUNTER, MILES.** 287½ acres, Washington Co., bounded N. & E. vacant, S. Oconee river, W. Sam'l Whatley, lot 1008. Warrant 2605. June 1, 1784. p. 340.

**GREENE, JAMES.** 287½ acres, Washington Co., bounded S. Adam Mannin, other sides vacant, cut by fork of Town creek, lot 1009. Warrant 555. Jan. 3, 1785. p. 341.

**DANIELLY, JAMES.** 287½ acres, Washington Co., bounded N. Grantee, E. & S. vacant, W. surveyed, lot 1050. Warrant 971. Jan, 3, 1785. p. 341.

**CUP, MICHAEL.** 287½ acres, Washington Co., bounded S. Jas. Dannielly, other sides vacant, lot 1011. Warrant 2995. Jan. 2, 1785. p. 341.

**WALLACE, WILLIAM.** 287½ acres, Washington Co., bounded N. Greene and Manning, other sides surveyed, lot 1012. Warrant 2148. Jan. 3, 1785, p. 342.

**DANIELLY, JAMES.** 287½ acres, Washington Co., bounded N. Michael Cup, E. & W. surveyed, S. vacant, bisected by north fork of Town creek, lot 1013. Warrant 1955. Jan. 2, 1785. p. 342.

**EADES, JOHN.** 287½ acres Washington Co., bounded N. Jesse Morgan, E. Thos, Shaddock, S. Youngblood, W. vacant, lot 1014. Warrant 1235. June 29, 1785. p. 342.

**YOUNG, WILLIAM.** 287½ acres, Washington Co., bounded N. & E. vacant, S. Stugis, W. Cunningham, cut E. & W. by Shoulderbone creek, lot 1015. Warrant 1276. Nov. 20, 1784. p. 343.

**KELLY, THOS.** 287½ acres, Washington Co., bounded N. vacant, E. B. Heard, S. William Thompson, W. J. M. Simmons, lot 1016. Warrant 221. Nov. 15, 1784. p. 343.

**BURKE, ISHAM.** 287½ acres, Washington Co., bounded N. Jas. Hogg, E. Ben Nicholas, S. Holliman, W. vacant, lot 1017. Warrant 155. Nov. 15, 1784. p. 343.

**SESSUNS, WILLIAM, SR.** 230 acres, Franklin Co., bounded S. Wm. Dean, other sides vacant, lot 1018. Warrant —. Dec. 11, 1784. p. 344.

**COLLINS, STEPHEN.** 230 acres, Franklin Co., bounded E. Wm. Sessuns, Sr., other sides vacant, lot 1019. Warrant (reserve). Dec. 7, 1784. p. 344.

**PHILLIPS, MARK.** 575 acres, Franklin Co., bounded N. & E. vacant, S. College lands, W. Oconee river, lot 1060. Warrant 717. Aug. 1784. p. 344.

**MIDDLETON, ROBERT.** 287½ acres, Franklin Co., bounded all sides vacant, cut E. & W. by Broad river, lot 1021. Warrant 670. Aug. 17, 1784. p. 345.

## BOUNTY SURVEYS.

**HARVEY, BLASINGAME.** 287½ acres, Washington Co., bounded N. & E. vacant, S. Clarke, W. Oconee river, lot 1023. Warrant 1024 and 1865. June 10, 1784. Covers 2 warrants as above. p. 345.

**HARVEY, JAMES HILL.** 287½ acres, Washington Co., bounded N. & E. vacant, S. B. Harvey, W. Oconee river, lot 1024. Warrant 915. June 10, 1784. p. 345.

**BAGBY, GEORGE.** 287½ acres, Washington Co., bounded N. Buffalo creek, E. & S. vacant, W. Greene, lot 1025. Warrant 395. Nov. 6, 1784. p. 346.

**JOHNSTON, WILLIAM.** 287½ acres, Franklin Co., bounded W. Robt. Middleton, other sides vacant, lot 1026. Warrant 594. Aug. 20, 1784. p. 346.

**JONES, DAVID.** 287½ acres, Franklin Co., bounded N. Wm. Field, other sides vacant. On Broad river, lot 1027. Warrant 688. Aug. 17, 1784, p. 346.

**YOUNGE, JOHN.** 287½ acres, Washington Co., bounded N. & W. vacant, E. H. Middleton, S. Crutchfield, lot 1028. Warrant 964. Nov. 15, 1784. p. 347.

**HILL, RICHARD.** 287½ acres, Franklin Co., bounded all sides vacant. On Broad river, lot 1029. Warrant 685. Aug. 24, 1785. p. 347.

**BACON, JOHN.** 287½ acres, Liberty Co., bounded N. Elijah Lewis, E. vacant, S. Thos. Bacon, W. vacant, lot 1031. Warrant —. Dec. 10, 1784. p. 348.

**RUSSEL, JACOB.** 230 acres, Franklin Co., bounded N. unknown, E. Oconee river, S. Tierce, W. vacant, cut N. & S. by Beaverdam creek, lot 1062. Warrant (reserve) Feb. 28, 1785. p. 360.

**TIERCE, BRANDETH.** 230 acres, Franklin Co., bounded N. Joel Russel, E. Oconee river, S. Wallace, W. vacant, cut by Beaverdam crek, N. & S., lot 1063. Warrant (reserve). Feb. 28, 1785. p. 360.

**JAMESON, WILLIAM.** 287½ acres, Camden Co., bounded N. Isaac Bugg, E. & W. vacant, S. Samuel Murs, lot 1064. Warrant —. Oct. 10, 1785. p. 360.

**BUGG, ISAAC.** 287½ acres, Camden Co., bounded N. Benj. Andrews, E. vacant, S. Wm. C. Jameson, lot 1065. Warrant —. Oct. 10, 1785, p. 360.

**JEFFERS, JAMES.** 287½ acres, Camden Co., bounded N. Crooked river, other sides vacant, lot 1110. Warrant —. June 17, 1785. p. 360.

**MEERS, SAMUEL.** 575 acres, Camden Co., bounded N. Alex Bessett, E. & W. vacant, S. Wm. Jameson, lot 1075. Warrant —. Oct. 10, 1785. p. 364.

**PENDLETON, SOLOMON.** 1150 acres, Camden Co., bounded N. & E. vacant, S. St. Marys river, W. Thos. Wetherclift, lot 1076. Warrant —. Oct. 14, 1785. p. 365.

**McMATH, JOSEPH.** 287½ acres, Washington Co., bounded N. vacant, E. Robt. Pollard, S. Ogeechee river, W. vacant, lot 1079. Warrant —. March 11, 1785, p. 336.

POLLARD, ROBERT. 287½ acres, Washington Co., bounded N. vacant, E. Wm. Davis, S. Ogeechee river, W. Joe McMath, lot 1080. Warrant —. Mar. 11, 1785, p. 366.

DAVIS, WILLIAM. 287½ acres, Washington Co., bounded N. vacant, E. Thos. Galphin, S. Ogeechee river, W. Pollard, lot 1081. Warrant —. Mar. 11, 1785, p. 366.

THORN, DAVID. 575 acres, Washington Co., bounded N. vacant, E. Ogeechee river, S. Wm. Scott, W. vacant, lot 1082. Warrant —. Mar. 11, 1785, p. 366.

EARNEST, JACOB. 287½ acres, Washington Co., bounded N. & E. vacant, S. Joe McMath, W. Ogeechee river, lot 1083. Warrant —. Mar. 12, 1785, p. 367.

JONES, BENJAMIN. 287½ acres, Washington Co., bounded N. & W. vacant, E. Jacob Earnest, S. Ogeechee river, lot 1084. Warrant —. April 2, 1785, p. 367.

WILLIAMS, JOHN. 287½ acres, Washington Co., bounded all sides vacant, lot 1085. Warrant —. April 2, 1785, p. 367.

COATS, JOHN. 287½ acres, Washington Co., bounded all sides vacant, bisected N. & S. by Williamson's creek, lot 1086. Warrant —. April 13, 1785, p. 368.

SIMMONSON, ISAAC. 287½ acres, Washington Co., bounded all sides vacant. Large amount of cypress swamp. Lot 1087. Warrant —. Mar. 12, 1785, p. 368.

MILLER, NICHOLAS. 287½ acres, Washington Co., bounded N. unknown, E. Williamson's creek, S. grantee, W. vacant, lot 1088. Warrant —. Mar. 23, 1785, p. 368.

CHELDNEY, WILLIAM. 287½ acres, Washington Co., bounded N. Miller, E. Williamson's creek, W. Beaverdam creek, lot 1090. Warrant —. Mar. 23, 1785, p. 268.

HUGELLY, ALEXANDER. 287½ acres, Washington Co., bounded N. vacant, E. Simon Jones, S. Ogeechee river, W. Williamson's creek, lot 1091. Warrant —. March 14, 1785, p. 369.

JONES, SIMEON. 287½ acres, Washington Co., bounded N. vacant, E. Sam Howell, S. Ogeechee river, W. Angelly, lot 1092. Warrant —. March 14, 1785, p. 369.

HOWELL, SAMUEL. 287½ acres, Washington Co., bounded N. vacant, E. Benj. Jones, S. Ogeechee river, W. Simeon Jones, lot 1093. Warrant —. March 14, 1785, p. 369.

SCOTT, WILLIAM. 287½ acres, Washington Co., bounded N. & W. vacant, E. Ogeechee river, S. Galphin, lot 1094. Warrant —. March 10, 1785, p. 369.

## BOUNTY SURVEYS.

**EARLY, JEFFERY.** 575 acres, Franklin Co., bounded N. Wm. Thompson, other sides vacant. Cut by Eastanola creek, lot 1103. Warrant —. June 9, 1785, p. 372.

**FRAZER, BARBANY.** 230 acres, Franklin Co., bounded N. Marbury, E. & S. vacant, W. Frazer. Cut by fork of Oconee river, lot 1104. Warrant (reserve), Oct. 9, 1785, p. 373.

**FRAZER, MARY.** 230 acres, Franklin Co., bounded N. Marbury, E. Griggs, S. vacant, W. Barbary Frazer (reserve), lot 1105, Oct. 11, 1785, p. 373.

**FRAZER, PENELOPE.** 230 acres, Franklin Co., bounded N. Marbury, E. Barbary Frazer, S. vacant, W. Oconee river, lot 1107 (reserve), Oct. 11, 1785, p. 374.

**GRAY, JACOB.** 287½ acres, Franklin Co., bounded N. & E. vacant, S. John Wingfield, W. Fork of Oconee river, lot 1108, Warrant —. March 1, 1785, p. 374.

**GORHAM, JOHN.** 287½ acres, Franklin Co., bounded S. Oconee river, other sides vacant, lot 1109. Warrant —. June 2, 1784, p. 374.

**HUDSON, CUTHBERT.** 287½ acres, Franklin Co., bounded all sides vacant. Cut S-E. & N-W. by Eastanola creek, lot 1114. Warrant —. May 6, 1785, p. 376.

**HARRISON, THOMAS.** 575 acres, Franklin Co., bounded N. & S. vacant, E. Ben Harrison, W. Walker Richardson. Cut by Beaverdam creek, lot 1115. Warrant —. June 10, 1785, p. 376

**HOLLAND, JACOB.** 287½ acres, Franklin Co., bounded all sides vacant. Cut by Beaverdam creek, lot 1116. June 8, 1785, p. 377.

**HUBBARD, JOHN.** 287½ acres, Franklin Co., bounded all sides vacant. Cut by fork of Oconee river, lot 1117, Aug. 30, 1784, p. 377.

**HORN, JOHN.** 287½ acres, Franklin Co., bounded all sides vacant. On waters of Oconee river, lot 1118. Warrant —. May 17, 1784, p. 377.

**HARRISON, BENJAMIN.** 287½ acres, Franklin Co., bounded E. Holland, other sides vacant. Cut N. & S. by Beaverdam creek, lot 1119. June 10, 1785, p. 378.

**JONES, SEABORN.** 1150 acres, Franklin Co., bounded S. Col. Leonard Marbury, other sides vacant. Cut N. & S. by Middle creek, lot 1160. Oct. 7, 1785, p. 378.

**JONES, ALETHEA ANDERSON.** 1,150 acres, Franklin Co., bounded N. E. & W., H. Marbury, S. Jas. Jones, on Dove creek, lot 1121. Oct. 10, 1785, p. 378.

**JONES, JAMES.** 1,150 acres, Franklin Co., bounded N. Dr. Baker, E. & W. Marbury, S. A. Jones, lot 1122, Oct. 10, 1785, p. 379.

**JONATHAN, JOHN.** 287½ acres, Franklin Co., bounded S. Lucas, other sides vacant. Cut by N. fork of Oconee river, lot 1123. Aug. 18, 1784, p. 379.

**JARRET, ROBERT.** 287½ acres, Franklin Co., bounded W. Austin Webb, other sides vacant, lot 1124. June 10, 1784, p. 379.

**LAMAR, BASIL.** 287½ acres, Franklin Co., bounded N. Broad river, other sides vacant, lot 1126. May 6, 1785, p. 380.

**LANCASTER, ROWLAND.** 230 acres, Franklin Co., bounded N. & W. vacant, E. Michael Nugan, S. Mulberry Fork and vacant, lot 1127. March 10, 1785, p. 381.

**LEITCH, DAVID.** 287½ acres, Franklin Co., bounded all sides vacant. Cut N. & S. by Beaverdam creek, lot 1128. June 10, 1785, p. 381.

**MARBURY, LEONARD.** 1,380 acres, Franklin Co., bounded N. H. Marbury, other sides vacant. Cut by Big creek, lot 1131. Sept. 8, 1781, p. 382.

**MARBURY, HORATIO.** 1,150 acres, Franklin Co., bounded N. Horatio, Garrett, E. McCracken, S. & W. Collier. Cut by Lamar's creek, lot 1132. Aug. 8, 1785, p. 383.

**MOSS, WILLIAM.** 1,150 acres, Franklin Co., bounded W. James Shepherd, other sides vacant. Cut by Beaverdam creek, lot 1142. Sept. 15, 1785, p. 386.

**MARBURY, THOMAS.** 460 acres, Franklin Co., bounded N. & W. vacant, E. Jesse Johnston, S. H. Marbury, on Oconee river, lot 1143. Oct. 10, 1785, p. 387.

**NUGAN, MICHAEL.** 230 acres, Franklin Co., bounded S. Oconee river, other sides vacant, lot 1144 (reserve). Mar. 10, 1785, p. 387.

**POTTS, STEPHEN.** 690 acres, Franklin Co., bounded N. L. Marbury, E. vacant, S. Handley, W. Dr. Baker, lot 1146. Sept. 15, 1785, p. 388.

**PAYNE, THOMAS,** 287½ acres, Franklin Co., bounded all sides vacant. Cut N. & S. by Tocca creek, lot 1155. Aug. 10, 1785, p. 391.

**PAYNE, THOMAS.** 287½ acres, Franklin Co., bounded E. Wm. Payne, other sides vacant. Cut E. & W. by Doss' creek, p. 391.

**RICHARDSON, WALKER.** 287½ acres, Franklin Co., bounded E. Tugalo river, other sides vacant, lot 1166. May 10, 1785, p. 395.

**STEWART, JOHN.** 287½ acres, Franklin Co., bounded all sides vacant. Cut by Eastanola creek, lot 1171. Dec. 13, 1784, p. 395.

**STEWART, CHARLES.** 460 acres, Franklin Co., bounded N. Count D'Estaing, other sides vacant. Cut N. & S. by Trall creek, lot 1176. June 4, 1784, p. 398.

**STURGIS, ANDREW.** 287½ acres, Franklin Co., bounded N. Middle Fork Oconee river, E. Ignatius Few, S. Peter Roseseau, W. vacant, lot 1175. Aug. 8, 1785, p. 398.

**THOMPSON, WILLIAM.** 230 acres, Franklin Co., bounded N. Alex Scott, E. John Clarke, S. & W. vacant, lot 1178. May 12, 1785, p. 399.

**THOMPSON, JAMES.** 287½ acres, Franklin Co., bounded S. Mulberry Fork of Oconee river, other sides vacant, lot 1179. Aug. 1, 1784, p. 399.

**TINDALL, JOHN.** 287½ acres, Franklin Co., bounded all sides vacant. Cut by Walnut creek, lot 1220. June 13, 1784, p. 400.

**TROY, JOHN.** 575 acres, Franklin Co., bounded W. Wm. Pulliam, other sides vacant. Cut by N. Fork of Broad river, lot 1182. July 8, 1784, p. 400.

**THOMPSON, ISHAM.** 575 acres, Franklin Co., bounded all sides vacant. Cut by fork of Cane creek, lot 1184. June 21, 1784, p. 401.

**TWEEDIE, JOHN.** 287½ acres, Franklin Co., bounded N. & W. vacant, E. Pulliam, S. Richard Call. Cut by fork of Clarke's creek, lot 1185. Dec. 6, 1784, p. 401.

**TANNER, WILLIAM.** 287½ acres, Franklin Co., bounded N. Samuel Stafford, other sides vacant. Cut by fork of Broad river, lot 1186. Aug. 25, 1784, p. 402.

**TOWNS, JOHN.** 287½ acres, Franklin Co., bounded all sides by surveyed lands. Cut by fork of Sandy river, lot 1187. July 21, 1785, p. 402.

**TELFAIR, EDWARD.** 575 acres, Franklin Co., bounded W. grantee, other sides vacant. On head-waters of Oconee river, lot 1188. May 28, 1785, p. 402.

**THOMPSON, WILLIAM.** 287½ acres, Franklin Co., bounded W. John Mays, other sides vacant. On Oconee river, lot 1193. June 10, 1785, p. 404.

**TORRENCE, JOHN.** 287½ acres, Franklin Co., bounded N. fork of Oconee river, E. Andrew Sturgis, S. & W. vacant, lot 1194. Jan. 25, 1785, p. 404.

**TRAPP, JOSEPH.** 287½ acres, Franklin Co., bounded N. & E. surveyed, S. & W. vacant. Cut by Sandy creek, lot 1196. Aug. 14, 1784, p. 405.

**TERONDET, DANIEL.** 575 acres, Franklin Co., bounded S. McCracken, other sides vacant. Cut by fork of Broad river, lot 1197. June 6, 1785, p. 405.

**UPTON, EDWARD.** 287½ acres, Franklin Co., bounded al sides vacant, lot 1198. Jan. 7, 1785, p. 406.

**WISENER, JOHN.** 287½ acres, Franklin Co., bounded N. Jno. Shaw, E. McCoy, S. vacant, W. Wm. Pulliam, lot 1240, June 6, 1784, p. 406.

**WALTON, ROBERT.** 287½ acres, Franklin Co., bounded S. Ezekiel Offutt, other sides vacant. Cut by Cobb creek of Tugalo river, lot 1201. July 20, 1784, p. 407.

**WISE, JOSEPH.** 287½ acres, Franklin Co., bounded S. Gregg, other sides vacant. On S. fork of Broad river, lot 1202. Aug. 18, 1784, p. 407.

**WEBB, JOHN.** 575 acres, Franklin Co., bounded S. Wm. Black, other sides vacant. Cut by Webb's creek and Williams' Fork of Oconee river, lot 1203. July 14, 1784, p. 407.

**WEBB, AUSTIN.** 575 acres, Franklin Co., bounded all sides vacant. Cut by Nails creek, lot 1204. July 8, 1784, p. 408.

**WEBB, WILLIAM.** 575 acres, Franklin Co., bounded all sides vacant. Cut by Little creek, lot 1205. July 7, 1784, p. 408.

**WAY, JOHN, JR.** 287½ acres, Franklin Co., bounded all sides vacant, lot 1206. May 24, 1784, p. 408.

**WESTBROOK, JOHN.** 287½ acres, Franklin Co., bounded E. John Stanford, other sides vacant. Evenly divided, S-W. to N-E. by N. fork Oconee river, lot 1207. Feb. 10, 1785, p. 409.

**WASH, WILLIAM.** 230 acres, Franklin Co., bounded W. Rowland Lancaster, other sides vacant. Cut N. & S. by Cedar creek, lot 1208. April 10, 1785, p. 409.

**WALKER, WILLIAM.** 287½ acres, Franklin Co., bounded W. Glascock, other sides vacant, lot 1250. Oct. 30, 1784, p. 410.

**WALTON, GEORGE.** 400 acres Franklin Co., bounded E. Henry Long, other sides vacant, lot 1211. Aug. 20, 1784, p. 410.

**WATSON, WILLIS.** 287½ acres, Franklin Co., bounded all sides vacant, on Broad river, lot 1216. March 16, 1785, p. 412.

**WALTON, WILLIAM.** 287½ acres, Franklin Co., bounded W. Jesse Walton, other sides vacant, lot 1217. June 23, 1785, p. 412.

**WARD, BRYAN.** 920 acres, Franklin Co., bounded all sides vacant. Cut by Beaverdam and Ward creeks, forks of Oconee river, lot 1218. June 15, 1785, p. 412.

**WALTON, WILLIAM.** 287½ acres, Franklin Co., bounded S. Edward Telfair, other sides vacant, lot 1221. May 21, 1785, p. 413.

## SURVEYOR GENERAL'S BOOK "B."

**ABBOTT, JOHN.** 575 acres, Washington Co., bounded N. Clarke, E. vacant, S. Good, W. Oconee river, survey 1. June 7, 1784. Warrant 2185, p. 1.

**MAY, WILLIAM.** 287½ acres, Washington Co., bounded W. Anderson, other sides vacant, survey 2. May 17, 1784. Warrant 2455, p. 1.

## BOUNTY SURVEYS.

**CARSON, DAVID.** 287½ acres, Washington Co., bounded all sides vacant. Cut by Buffalo creek, survey 3. May 27, 1784. Warrant 2720, p. 2.

**WILLIAMS, CHARLES.** 287½ acres, Washington Co., bounded S. Wm. Hunt, other sides vacant, survey 4. May 25, 1784. Warrant 2688, p. 2.

**HUNT, WILLIAM.** 575 acres, Washington Co., bounded N. Chas. Williams, other sides vacant, survey 5. June 10, 1784. Warrant 2310, p. 2.

**CARSON, DAVID.** 287½ acres, Washington Co., bounded E. Wm. Dennis, other sides vacant. Cut by Buffalo creek, survey 6. June 7, 1784. Warrant 2718, p. 3.

**ABBOTT, JOHN.** 287½ acres, Washington Co., bounded N. Oconee river, E. vacant, S. Fredk. Braswell, W. McCall, survey 7. June 9, 1784. Warrant 2264, p. 3.

**SIKES, WILLIAM.** 287½ acres, Washington Co., bounded N. vacant, E. Lockhart, S. Oconee river, W. Paulett, survey 8. May 17, 1784. Warrant 2464, p. 3.

**GRAVES, WILLIAM.** 287½ acres, Washington Co., bounded S. Ralph Kilgore, other sides vacant. Cut by Clarke's creek, survey 9. June 11, 1784. Warrant 1192, p. 4.

**KILGORE, RALPH.** 287½ acres, Washington Co., bounded N. Wm. Graves, E. John Marshall, S. Jno. Braswell, W. vacant, survey 10. June 11, 1784. Warrant 721, p. 4.

**BRASWELL, JOHN.** 287½ acres, Washington Co., bounded N. Ralph Kilgore, E. Gray, S. Fred Braswell, W. vacant, survey 11, June 11, 1784. Warrant 2635, p. 4.

**BRASWELL, FREDERICK.** 287½ acres, Washington Co., bounded N. Jno. Braswell, E. Elijah Anderson, S. & W. vacant. Cut by Clarke's creek, survey 12. June 11, 1784. Warrant 2307, p. 4.

**BRASWELL, FERDINAND.** 287½ acres, Washington Co., bounded N. & W. vacant, E. Jno. Lewis, S. Jno. Abbott, survey 13. June 9, 1784. Warrant 2633, p. 5.

**HARVEY, HEIRS OF RICHARD.** 287½ acres, Washington Co., bounded S. H. Irvin, other sides vacant. Cut by Walnut creek, survey 14. May 17, 1784. Warrant 370, p. 5.

**STONE, CHARLES.** 575 acres, Washington Co., bounded W. surveyed, other sides vacant. Cut by fork of Oconee river, survey 15. July 24, 1784. Warrant 1695, p. 5.

**MANADUE, HENRY.** 575 acres, Washington Co., bounded S. Oconee river, other sides vacant, survey 16. June 10, 1784. Warrant 2147, p. 6.

**PERKINS, WILLIAM.** 287½ acres, Washington Co., bounded N. Massey, E. Clarke, S. Jno. Clarke, W. Harvey, survey 17. June 9, 1784. Warrant 1669, p. 6.

**CLARKE, JOHN.** 287½ acres, Washington Co., bounded N. Perkins, E. Clarke, S. Ohoopee river, W. Harvey, survey 18. June 9, 1784. Warrant 2135, p. 6.

**GRAY, JOHN.** 287½ acres, Washington Co., bounded N. & E. vacant, S. Elijah Anderson, W. Braswell, survey 19. June 11, 1784. Warrant 1630, p. 7.

**ANDERSON, ELIJAH.** 287½ acres, Washington Co., bounded N. Gray, E. & S. vacant, W. Clarke's creek and Fred Braswell, survey 20. June 11, 1784. Warrant 672, p. 7.

**LOWE, JOHN.** 287½ acres, Washington Co., bounded N. vacant, E. McCall, S. Joshua Lee, W. Elijah Clarke, survey 21. June 9, 1784. Warrant 1558, p. 7.

**LEE, JOSHUA.** 287½ acres, Washington Co., bounded N. Jno. Lowe, E. McCall, S. Oconee river, W. vacant, survey 22. June 9, 1784. Warrant 1013, p. 7.

**MARSHALL, JOHN.** 287½ acres, Washington Co., bounded W. Wm. Graves, other sides vacant, survey 23. June 11, 1784. Warrant 1438, p. 8.

**SIZEMORE, WILLIAM.** 287½ acres, Washington Co., bounded N. Wade, E. vacant, S. & W. Oconee river, survey 24. June 10, 1784. Warrant 1931, p. 8.

**LOCKHART, ISAAC.** 287½ acres, Washington Co., bounded N. vacant, E. Chas. Harvey, S. Oconee river, W. Paulette, survey 25. June 9, 1784. Warrant 1503, p. 8.

**MANNING, ROBERT.** 287½ acres, Washington Co., bounded S. Lawson, other sides vacant, survey 26. June 25, 1784. Warrant 594, p. 9.

**WELCHER, JEREMIAH.** 287½ acres, Washington Co., bounded all sides vacant, survey 27. June 27, 1784. Warrant 1037, p. 9.

**PRATHER, EDWARD.** 200 acres, Washington Co., bounded—on an island formed by Ohoopee river. Warrant calls for 287½ acres, but not enough land to make it, survey 28. June 9, 1784. Warrant 741.

**CLARKE, ELIJAH.** 805 acres, Washington Co., N. vacant, E. vacant and Irvin, S. Irvin, W. Lamar, survey 29. June 25, 1784. Warrant 68, p. 10.

**IRVIN, ALEXANDER.** 575 acres, Washington Co., bounded N. vacant, E. Rutherford, S. Rutherford and Ayres, W. Ayres and Clarke, survey 30. June 25, 1784. Warrant 21, p. 10.

**NIMMS, DRURY.** 287½ acres, Washington Co., bounded N. district line, E. vacant. Cut N. & S. by Town creek, survey 31. June 7, 1784. Warrant 1809, p. 11.

## BOUNTY SURVEYS.

**HARVEY, CHARLES.** 287½ acres, Washington Co., bounded N. Hadden and vacant, other sides vacant, survey 32. June 27, 1784. Warrant 976, p. 11.

**AYRES, DANIEL.** 460 acres, Washington Co., bounded N. Lamar, E. Irvin, S. Holliman, W. Oconee river and Qualls, survey 33. June 25, 1784. Warrant 149, p. 11.

**CLARKE, ELIJAH.** 1,150 acres, Washington Co., bounded S. Oconee river, other sides vacant, survey 34. June 25, 1784. Warrant 149.

**WELLS, BENJAMIN.** 575 acres, Washington Co., bounded all sides vacant. Cut by Great and Little Buffalo rivers, survey 36. June 6, 1784. Warrant 553, p. 13.

**SITTON, HEIRS OF JOHN.** 287½ acres, Washington Co., bounded N. Mathew Marshall, E. vacant. Cut N. & S. by Buffalo creek, survey 37. June 3, 1784. Warrant 502, p. 13.

**MARSHALL, MATTHEW.** 287½ acres, Washington Co., bounded S. Wm. Few, other sides vacant. Cut by Buffalo creek, survey 38. June 29, 1784. Warrant 1971, p. 13.

**CHAMBERS, JOHN.** 287½ acres, Washington Co., bounded N. Jos. Anderson, E. Jesse Jones, S. & W. vacant, survey 30. June 9, 1784. Warrant 1835, p. 14.

**MILLER, JOSHUA.** 287½ acres, Washington Co., bounded all sides vacant. Cut by Big Buffalo creek, survey 40. June 7, 1784. Warrant 677, p. 14.

**WELSH, JOSHUA.** 287½ acres, Washington Co., bounded E. Kelly, other sides vacant. Cut N-W. to S-E. by Big Buffalo creek, survey 41. June 12, 1784. Warrant 572, p. 14.

**WATSON, THOMAS.** 287½ acres, Washington Co., bounded N. Jesse Brooks, other sides vacant. Divided E. to W. Buffalo creek, survey 42. June 23, 1784. Warrant 2065, p. 15.

**RAMSEY, ISAAC.** 287½ acres, Washington Co., bounded all sides vacant. Cut N. to S. by Buffalo creek, survey 43. June 22, 1784. Warrant 1183, p. 15.

**SMITH, THOMAS.** 287½ acres, Washington Co., bounded E. by Perry, other side vacant. Divided W. to E. by Buffalo creek, survey 44. June 7, 1784. Warrant 1484, p. 15.

**BROOKS, JESSE.** 287½ acres, Washington Co., bounded all sides vacant, survey 45. June 25, 1784. Warrant 2003, p. 16.

**SMITH, THOMAS.** 287½ acres, Washington Co., bounded all sides vacant. On Buffalo creek, survey 46. June 8, 1784. Warrant 2124, p. 16.

**WAINWRIGHT, GEORGE.** 287½ acres, Washington Co., bounded N. & E. vacant, S. Oconee river, W. Benj. Few, survey 47. June 6, 1784. Warrant 2160, p. 16.

**FREIL, JOHN.** 287½ acres, Washington Co., bounded S. Oconee river, other sides vacant. Cut E. to W. by Buffalo creek, survey 48. June 10, 1784. Warrant 1622, p. 17.

**HUKENBOTTOM, JOSEPH.** 287½ acres, Washington Co., bounded N. and E. vacant, S. Wilcher, W. Thos. Johnston. Cut E. to W. by branch of Oconee river, survey 51. June 27, 1784. Warrant 2474, p. 18.

**HAMMOCK, BENEDICT.** 287½ acres, Washington Co., bounded S. Lick creek, other sides vacant, survey 53. July 1, 1784. Warrant 191, p. 19.

**ANDERSON, WILLIAM.** 287½ acres, Washington Co., bounded N. Jas. Dunbar, E. & W. vacant, S. Oconee river, survey 54. Jan. 23, 1784. Warrant 2516, p. 19.

**JOHNSTON, THOMAS.** 287½ acres, Washington Co., bounded S. David Jones, other sides vacant, survey 55. June 27, 1784. Warrant 1349, p. 19.

**BLACK, HENRY.** 575 acres, Franklin Co., bounded all sides vacant. Cut E. to W. by Black creek, survey 62. June 7, 1784. Warrant 114, p. 22.

**FENN ZACHARIAH.** 287½ acres, Richmond Co., bounded N. & W. vacant, E. Sol. Willey, S. Ogeechee river, survey 66, 1784. Warrant —, p. 23.

**ANDERSON, HENRY.** 287½ acres, Franklin Co., bounded N. & E. vacant, S. Ezekiel Offutt, W. Jno. Shannon, survey 80, Aug. 16, 1784. Warrant 480, p. 28.

**ALLISON, JAMES.** 575 acres, Washington Co., bounded all sides vacant. Cut by Shoulderbone creek, survey 83. June 27, 1784. Warrant 664, p. 29.

**BRANTLEY, THOMAS,** 287½ acres, Washington Co., bounded all sides vacant. Cut E. & W. by Shoulderbone creek, survey 86. June 7, 1784. Warrant 1796, p. 30.

**BEASLEY, BURWELL.** 287½ acres, Washington Co., bounded N. Jno. Clarke, E. Peter Youngblood, S. & W. vacant, survey 87. June 10, 1784. Warrant 2288, p. 30.

**BONNER, ROBT.** 287½ acres, Franklin Co., bounded N. Saml. Wilson, other sides vacant. Cut N. & S. by Sandy creek, survey 96. August 14, 1784. Warrant 731, p. 33.

**BARNARD, JESSE.** 287½ acres, Franklin Co., bounded N. & W. vacant, E. unknown, S. Oconee river, survey 97. June 3, 1784. Warrant 314, p. 34.

**BURKE, JOHN.** 287½ acres, Franklin Co., bounded E. Reuben Nails, other sides unknown. Cut E. to W. by Broad river, survey 98. July 29, 1784. Warrant 755, p. 34.

**BISHOP, STEPHEN.** 287½ acres, Washington Co., bounded N. & S. vacant, E. Beaverdam creek, W. James Bishop, survey 99. June 6, 1784. Warrant 1364, p. 34.

## BOUNTY SURVEYS.

**BISHOP, JAMES.** 287½ acres, Washington Co., bounded W. Stephen Bishop, other sides vacant. On Beaverdam creek, survey 100. June 6, 1784. Warrant 1278, p. 35.

**BAGGS, JOHN.** 287½ acres, Washington Co., bounded all sides vacant. On Buffalo creek, survey 101. Warrant 1932. June 3, 1784, p. 35.

**BLOODWORTH, SAMUEL.** 287½ acres, Washington Co., bounded N. Island, E. Oconee river, S. & W. vacant, survey 102. Warrant 1545. June 4, 1784, p. 35.

**McMUNN, JOHN.** 287½ acres, Washington Co., bounded N. Jas. Moore, other sides vacant. Cut N. & S. by Buffalo creek, survey 107. Warrant 2685, June 4, 1784, p. 37.

**DARLEY, JOHN.** 287½ acres, Washington Co., bounded N. & W. vacant, E. survey, S. Oconee river, survey 120. June 29, 1784. Warrant 2498, p. 42.

**DOSE, JOEL.** 575 acres, Franklin Co., bounded N. Wilkins, E. & W. vacant, S. Hubbard. Cut by Gorham & Doss creeks, survey 122. June 10, 1784. Warrant 335, p. 42.

**DOOLEY, GEORGE.** 575 acres, Washington Co., bounded S. Shoulderbone creek, other sides vacant, survey 123. June 3, 1784. Warrant 2016, p. 43.

**DAY, ROBERT.** 287½ acres, Washington Co., bounded S. Edward Hagin, other sides vacant, survey 126. July 8, 1784. Warrant 755, p. 44.

**LAMAR, JOHN.** 287½ acres, Washington Co., bounded N. grantee, E. Thos. Glascock, S. & W. vacant, survey 129. Aug. 15, 1784. Warrant 1753, p. 45.

**MURPHY, EDMOND.** 287½ acres, Washington Co., bounded S. Oconee river, other sides vacant, survey 130. Aug. 16, 1784. Warrant 404, p. 45.

**BARRON, WILLIAM.** 287½ acres, Washington Co., bounded E. Oconee river, other sides vacant, survey 131. Aug. 16, 1784. Warrant 656, p. 45.

**FRANKLIN, WILLIAM.** 287½ acres, Washington Co., bounded N. & E. vacant, S. Oconee river, W. Blueford Davis, survey 132. Aug. 16, 1784. Warrant 1504, p. 46.

**PALMER, JOHN.** 287½ acres, Washington Co., bounded all sides vacant. Cut by fork of Oconee river, W. Blueford Davis, survey 132. Aug. 16, 1784. Warrant 1504, p. 46.

**DAVIS, BLUEFORD.** 287½ acres, Washington Co., bounded N. & E. vacant, S. Oconee river, W. Edmond Murphy, survey 134. Aug. 16, 1784. Warrant 569, p. 46.

**DIOLENDEMUS, MATTHEW.** 287½ acres, Washington Co., bounded S. Little Ogeechee river, other sides vacant, survey 135. Sept. 27, 1784. Warrant 698, p. 46.

DANNELLY, JAMES. 287½ acres, Washington Co., bounded N. vacant, E. Benj. Lockhart, S. Oconee river, W. Wm. Franklin, survey 136. Aug. 16, 1784. Warrant 137, p. 47.

LOCKHART, BENJ. 287½ acres, Washington Co., bounded S. vacant and Oconee river, other sides vacant, survey 137. Aug. 16, 1784. Warrant 1653, p. 47.

PARKS, JOHN. 640 acres, Washington Co., bounded S. Seymour Catchings, other sides vacant, survey 146. June 25, 1784. Warrant 2425, p. 52.

MOSELEY, WILLIAM. 287½ acres, Washington Co., bounded N. Jno. Parks, E. vacant, S. Phillips and Greer, W. Catchings, survey 147. June 25, 1784. Warrant 2491, p. 51.

McGEHEE, THOMAS. 575 acres, Washington Co., bounded all sides vacant. Cut by Mill Shoal creek, survey 149. June 5, 1784. Warrant 2106, p. 52.

DENNIS, JACOB. 287½ acres, Washington Co., bounded S. Wm. Baldwin, other sides vacant, survey 163. July 23, 1784. Warrant 1601, p. 56.

FRIEL, LEWIS. 287½ acres, Washington Co., bounded N. Joel Statin, other sides vacant, survey 167, June 25, 1784. Warrant 2729, p. 58.

LONG, ROBERT. 287½ acres, Washington Co., bounded all sides vacant, on Limestone creek, survey 176. July 2, 1784. Warrant 1252, p. 62.

JONES, ROBERT. 287½ acres, Washington Co., bounded W. Robt. Long, other sides vacant, survey 177. July 2, 1784. Warrant 1576, p. 62.

FEW, IGNATIUS. 287½ acres, Washington Co., bounded N. & W. vacant, E. Gardner, S. Oconee river. Cut by Buffalo creek, survey 200. June 10, 1784. Warrant 931, p. 70.

PEAL, JOHN. 287½ acres, Washington Co., bounded all sides vacant, survey 208. July 1, 1784. Warrant 948, p. 74.

LESLIE, JOSEPH. 287½ acres, Washington Co., bounded E. Ohoopee river, other sides vacant. Cut by Deep creek, survey 220. June 29, 1784. Warrant 92, p. 75.

McNEELY, DANIEL. 287½ acres, Washington Co., bounded Oconee river, other sides vacant. Cut by Deep creek, survey 220. June 29, 1784. Warrant 2043, p. 78.

MARTIN, JOHN. 287½ acres, Washington Co., bounded S. Buckeye creek, other sides vacant, survey 277. June 28, 1784. Warrant —, p. 82.

CRANE, LEWIS. 287½ acres, Washington Co., bounded N. Johnston, E. Simon Smith and Academy lands, S. vacant, W. Benj. Harris, survey 233. June 4, 1784. Warrant, —, p. 84.

JENKINS, RICHARD. 287½ acres, Washington Co., bounded N. Jesse Thompson, other sides vacant, survey 234. June 4, 1784, p. 84.

## BOUNTY SURVEYS.

**SMITH, SIMON.** 287½ acres, Washington Co., bounded N. & W. vacant, E. Johnston, S. Academy lands, survey 235. June 25, 1784, p. 85.

**FLUKER, WILLIAM.** 287½ acres, Washington Co., bounded W. George Wagner, other sides vacant. Cut E. to W. by Fishing creek, survey 236. June 23, 1784, p. 85.

**THOMPSON, JESSE.** 287½ acres, Washington Co., bounded S. Richard Jenkins, other sides vacant, survey 237. May 17, 1784, p. 85.

**CLOUD, EZEKIEL.** 575 acres, Franklin Co., bounded all sides vacant. Cut by Indian creek, branch of Mulberry creek, survey 244. May 17, 1784, p. 86.

**KILGORE, ROBERT.** 287½ acres, Franklin Co., bounded all sides vacant. Cut by Big Pond creek, fork of Oconee River, survey 240. May 17, 1784, p. 86.

**McNEILLY, HUGH.** 287½ acres, Washington Co., bounded S. Jno. Martin, other sides vacant, survey 246. May 17, 1784, p. 88.

**CLARKE, WILLIAM.** 287½ acres, Washington Co., bounded S. College lands, other sides vacant. Cut by fork of Shoulderbone creek, survey 248. June 11, 1784, p. 89.

**HILL, WILLIAM.** 287½ acres, Washington Co., bounded N. Hayman, E. Oconee river, S. Joseph Bugg, W. vacant, survey 260. May 17, 1784, p. 92.

**HAYMAN, STEPHEN.** 287½ acres, Washington Co., bounded N. Jas. Douglas, E. Oconee river, S. Stanton Hayman, W. vacant, survey 261. May 17, 1784, p. 93.

**HAYMAN, STOUTON.** 287½ acres, Washington Co., bounded N. Stephen Hayman, E. Oconee river, S. Wm. Hill, W. vacant, survey 262. May 17, 1784, p. 93.

**GAMBOL, JOHN.** 575 acres, Washington Co., bounded S. Jno. Peal, other sides vacant. Cut E. to W. by Buck creek, survey 268. June 30, 1784, p. 95.

**HADDON, WILLIAM.** 287½ acres, Washington Co., bounded all sides vacant, survey 269. May 17, 1784, p. 95.

**HINTON, JOB.** 287½ acres, Washington Co., bounded all sides vacant, survey 270. June 28, 1784, p. 96.

**GRAVES, ROBERT.** 287½ acres, Franklin Co., bounded E. Reuben Nails, other sides vacant, survey 272. Sept. 17, 1784, p. 96.

**HAGAN, EDWARD.** 287½ acres, Washington Co., bounded all sides vacant, survey 273. June 17, 1784, p. 97.

**GREZEL, GEORGE.** 287½ acres, Washington Co., all sides vacant, survey 276. June 6, 1784, p. 98.

**HATCHER, ROBERT.** 287½ acres, Franklin Co., bounded all sides vacant. Cut by Sandy creek, survey 281. Aug. 12, 1784, p. 99.

## ROSTER OF THE REVOLUTION.

**HAGAN, JAMES.** 287½ acres, Washington Co., bounded (triangle) N-E. Hagan, S. Shoulderbone creek, N-W. unknown, survey 282. June 21, 1784, p. 100.

**HAGAN, EDWARD.** 287½ acres, Washington Co., bounded N. Robert Day, other sides vacant, survey 285, June 2, 1784, p. 100.

**HARVEY, CHARLES.** 287½ acres, Franklin Co., bounded N. & E. vacant, S. & W. Samuel Wilson. Cut N. & S. by Sandy creek, survey 290. Aug. 14, 1784, p. 102.

**HARVEY, JOHN.** 287½ acres, Franklin Co., bounded S. Sam'l Wilson, other sides vacant. Cut S. E. to N. W. by Sandy creek, survey 291. Aug. 14, 1784, p. 102.

**HOWARD, BENJ.** 287½ acres, Washington Co., bounded E. Long, other sides vacant, survey 292. July 3, 1784, p. 102.

**GARDNER, WILLIAM.** 287½ acres, Washington Co., bounded E. Oconee river, S. Ignatius Few, other sides vacant, survey 295. June 8, 1784, p. 103.

**MITCHELL, WILLIAM.** 287½ acres, Washington Co., bounded N. Nich Hugh, other sides vacant, survey 297. June 7, 1784, p. 104.

**CASTLEBERRY, RICHARD.** 287½ acres, Richmond Co., bounded S. Claiborn, other sides vacant, survey 331. Aug. 15, 1784, p. 114.

**YOUNG, JOHN, JR.** 287½ acres, Washington Co., bounded N. Ed Young, E. Geo. Hart, S. & W. vacant, survey 332. June 7, 1784, p. 114.

**DAVID, WILLIAM.** 575 acres, Washington Co., bounded W. Altamaha river, other sides vacant, survey 334. June 23, 1784, p. 115.

**KELLY, THOMAS.** 287½ acres, Washington Co., bounded N. Wm. McGehee, E. Oconee river, S. Jno. Potts, W. vacant, survey 346. June 19, 1784, p. 118.

**McGEHEE, LEWIS.** 287½ acres, Washington Co., bounded N. Reuben Lett, E. & S. vacant, W. Ogeechee river, survey 352. July 15, 1784, p. 119.

**PAIN, SAMUEL.** 287½ acres, Washington Co., bounded N. & W. vacant, E. Wm. Sattewhite, S. Wm. Wallace, survey 353, June 19, 1784, p. 119.

**MATTHEWS, MESHECK.** 287½ acres, Washington Co., bounded N. Jno. Young, E. Ed. Hall, S. Wm. Matthews, W. vacant, survey 356. June 7, 1784, p. 120.

**HALL, EDWARD.** 287½ acres, Washington Co., bounded N. Geo. Hart, E. Altamaha river, S. Wm. Matthews, W. vacant, survey 355. June 7, 1784, p. 120.

**WALLACE, WILLIAM.** 287½ acres, Washington Co., bounded N. & W. vacant, E. Robt. Hudson, S. Jno. Getmany, survey 359. June 19, 1784, p. 121.

## BOUNTY SURVEYS. 233

**GERMANY, JOHN.** 287½ acres, Washington Co., bounded N. Wm. Wallace, E. Jno. Crawford, S. Altamaha river, W. vacant, survey 360. June 19, 1784, p. 121.

**HORNBY, PHILIP.** 575 acres, Washington Co., bounded S. Andrew Dick, other sides vacant, survey 361. Oct. 29, 1784, p. 122.

**MARBURY, THOMAS.** 575 acres, Washington Co., bounded E. Altamaha river, other sides vacant, survey 362. June 7, 1784, p. 122.

**FOLD, GEORGE.** 287½ acres, Washington Co., bounded N. Jno. Germany, E. Altamaha river, S. Thos. Marbury, W. vacant, survey 363. June 7, 1784, p. 122.

**BEAL, ARCHIBALD.** 862½ acres, Washington Co., bounded N. & W. vacant, E. Ogeechee river, S. Chas. Simmons, survey 364. July 6, 1784, p. 123.

**YOUNG, EDWARD.** 287½ acres, Washington Co., bounded E. Thos. Marbury, other sides vacant, survey 365. June 7, 1784. Warrant 2005, p. 123.

**CARNERY, ORNSBY.** 286½ acres, Washington Co., bounded all sides vacant. Cut by Rich creek, survey 366. Nov. 22, 1784. Warrant 1371, p. 123.

**HART, GEORGE.** 287½ acres, Washington Co., bounded N. Thos. Marbury, E. Altamaha river, S. & W. vacant, survey 367, June 7, 1784. Warrant 1642, p. 124.

**MATTHEWS, WILLIAM.** 287½ acres, Washington Co., bounded S. Wm. Matthews, other sides vacant, survey 369. June 6, 1784. Warrant 2622, p. 124.

**TALYOR, JOSIAH.** 287½ acres, Washington Co., bounded N. Gen. Twiggs, E. Titus Hollinger, S. & W. vacant, survey 371. May 17, 1784. Warrant 579, p. 125.

**GERMANY, WILLIAM.** 287½ acres, Washington Co., bounded N. & W. vacant, E. Altamaha river, S. Phil. Green, survey 375. Oct. 18, 1784. Warrant 1233, p. 126.

**PENDLETON, SOLOMAN.** 1149 acres, Effingham Co., bounded N. Jno. Galphin, E. Savannah river, S. Jos. Wiseman, W. vacant, survey 380. April 12, 1784, p. 128.

**BARNETT, NATHAN.** 575 acres, Franklin Co., bounded all sides vacant. Cut by Big Shoal creek, survey 381. June 21, 1784, p. 128.

**BARNETT, DANIEL.** 287½ acres, Franklin Co., bounded N. unknown, E. Jas. Simms, S. Richardson, W. Nathan Barnett, survey 382. June 23, 1784. Warrant 249, p. 128.

**BARNETT, JOHN.** 575 acres, Franklin Co., bounded all sides vacant. Cut E. to W. by Marshall's creek, fork of Oconee river, survey 383. Aug. 2, 1784. Warrant 285.

## ROSTER OF THE REVOLUTION.

**WEBB, JESSE.** 287½ acres, Franklin Co., bounded S. Moses Miller, other sides vacant, survey 398. June 1, 1784. Warrant 1, p. 133.

**SANDERS, JOSHUA.** 287½ acres, Washington Co., bounded all sides vacant, survey 399. June 10, 1784. Warrant 2278, p. 133.

**HODGE, JACOB.** 460 acres, Wilkes Co., bounded N. Johnston, E. Douglass & Whatley, S. survey, W. Jno. Lowe, survey 402. Nov. 10, 1784, p. 134.

**SAPP, JOHN.** 287½ acres, Washington Co., bounded N. Jno. Ragan, E. & W. vacant, S. Jno. Perkins, survey 403. Nov. 9, 1784. Warrant 105, p. 134.

**FEW, BENJAMIN.** 1,150 acres, Washington Co., bounded S. Oconee river, other sides vacant, survey 412. June 9, 1784. Warrant 2435, p. 137.

**AYRES, THOMAS.** 287½ acres, Washington Co., bounded N. & E. vacant, S. Altamaha river, W. Wm. Germany, survey 413. Oct. 18, 1784. Warrant 1066, p. 138.

**WILLIAMSON, ROBERT.** 575 acres, Washington Co., bounded W. Magehee and Reuben Lett, other sides vacant, survey 414. July 5, 1784. Warrant 830, p. 138.

**PEARRY, JOHN.** 287½ acres, Washington Co., bounded S. Ogeechee river, other sides vacant, survey 415. July 7, 1784. Warrant 1333, p. 138.

**SAPP, EMANUEL.** 287½ acres, Washington Co., bounded N. Col. Jas. Jackson, E. Thompson & Evans, S. Betsell, W. vacant, survey 416. Oct. 29, 1784. Warrant 1116, p. 139.

**SAPP, JOHN.** 287½ acres, Washington Co., bounded N. Andrew Dick, E. & W. vacant, S. James Jackson, survey 417. Oct. 29, 1784. Warrant 1568, p. 139.

**LANGSTON, SAMUEL.** 287½ acres, Washington Co., bounded N. Wm. Matthews, E. Altamaha river, S. Joshua Inman, W. vacant, survey 418. June 6, 1784. Warrant 251, p. 139.

**KAIR, HENRY.** 575 acres, Washington Co., bounded N. Washington Co. line, E. Watson, S. & W. vacant, survey 419. June 2, 1784. Warrant 787, p. 140.

**CHENEY, GREENBERRY.** 287½ acres, Franklin Co., bounded N. vacant, E. Knox, S. Wilkes Co. line, W. Fair, survey 240. June 13, 1784. Warrant 479, p. 141.

**SIMMONS, CHARLES.** 287½ acres, Washington Co., bounded N. & W. vacant, E. Ogeechee river, S. Robt. Williamson, survey 421. July 5, 1784. Warrant 232, p. 141.

**BERRY, JOHN.** 230 acres, Franklin Co., bounded N. S. fork of Oconee river, other sides vacant, survey 422. July 8, 1784. Reserve, p. 141.

**GRIFFIN, MATTHEW.** 287½ acres, Washington Co., bounded N. Jas. McGilton, E. Ogeechee river, S. Jas. Allen, W. vacant, survey 425. July 7, 1784. Warrant 243, p. 142.

## BOUNTY SURVEYS.

**DICKS, ANDREW.** 287½ acres, Washington Co., bounded N. Philip Hornby, other sides vacant, survey 426. Oct. 29, 1784. Warrant 1499, p. 142.

**WILLIAMSON, CHARLES.** 575 acres, Washington Co., bounded N. vacant, E. Sam'l Whatley, S. Oconee river, W. Jno. Burney, survey 428. June 5, 1784. Warrant 2111, p. 143.

**STAMPS, POWELL.** 287½ acres, Washington Co., bounded S. M. Ragan, other sides vacant. Cut N. & S. by Island creek, survey 429. Nov. 12, 1784. Warrant 1102, p. 142.

**WOODRUFF, JOS.** 690 acres, Washington Co., bounded N. & W. vacant, E. Williamson's Swamp, S. John & George Galphin, survey 430. July 22, 1784. Warrant 1839, p. 144.

**WHATLEY, WALTON.** 287½ acres, Washington Co., bounded N. Jno. Golson, E. vacant, S. Wm. Mayo, W. Tucker. Cut by Rocky creek, survey 431. July 14, 1784. Warrant 2510, p. 144.

**MILNER, JOHN.** 287½ acres, Washington Co., bounded W. Sanders Walker, other sides vacant, survey 432. Nov. 14, 1784. Warrant 1508, p. 144.

**WEBSTER, WILLIAM.** 287½ acres, Washington Co., bounded N. Francis Moore, E. & S. vacant, W. Wm. Walker. Cut by Island creek, survey 433. July 13, 1784. Warrant 1073, p. 145.

**McCORMICK, BENJ.** 287½ acres, Washington Co., bounded N. & E. vacant, S. Sanders, W. Beckham. Cut E. & W. by Fork creek, survey 434. July 5, 1784. Warrant 1954, p. 145.

**LARAMORE, JOHN.** 287½ acres, Washington Co., bounded all sides vacant, survey 435. July 23, 1784. Warrant 1844, p. 145.

**RAGAN, JOHN.** 287½ acres, Washington Co., bounded N. & E. vacant, S. Jno. Island, W. Powell Stamps, survey 436. Nov. 8, 1784. Warrant 144, p. 145.

**SANDERS, MARK.** 287½ acres, Washington Co., bounded N. & S. vacant, E. Christmas & Owens, W. Joshua Sanders, survey 437. June 29, 1784. Warrant 2168, p. 146.

**WELCH, BENJAMIN.** 287½ acres, Washington Co., bounded N. Wright, E. & W. vacant, S. Stern Simmons, survey 440. July 10, 1784. Warrant 1479, p. 147.

**PERRITT, WILLIAM.** 287½ acres, Washington Co., bounded N. & S. vacant, E. College lands, W. Wm. Baldwin, survey 445. July 19, 1784. Warrant 1384, p. 148.

**BALDWIN, WILLIAM.** 345 acres, Washington Co., bounded S. Wm. Kimbrough, other sides vacant. Cut by Beaverdam creek, survey 446. Nov. 16, 1784. Warrant 1965, p. 149.

**FREIL, JOHN.** 287½ acres, Washington Co., bounded N. & W. vacant, S. Jesse Brooks, S. E. by Buffalo creek, survey 447. July 14, 1784. Warrant 840, p. 149.

**FEW, WILLIAM.** 1207½ acres, Washington Co., bounded all sides vacant. Cut by branch of Buffalo creek, survey 453. June 23, 1784. Warrant 139, p. 151.

**SMITH, DAVID.** 287½ acres, Washington Co., bounded all sides vacant, survey 455. Nov. 17, 1784. Warrant 571, p. 152.

**GREENE, WILLIAM.** 287½ acres, Washington Co., bounded N. & W. vacant, E. grantee, S. Altamaha river. Cut by Deep creek, survey 465. June 15, 1784. Warrant 1198, p. 156.

**HOUSTON, DR. JAMES.** 920 acres, Washington Co., bounded N. Daniel Cuthbert, E. Montfort, S. Henry Allison, W. Jacob Blount. On waters of Oconee river, survey 486. Dec. 8, 1784. Reserve, p. 163.

**HOUSTON, WILLIAM.** 287½ acres, Washington Co., bounded N. vacant, E. John Houston, S. Oconee river, W. Sharp & Douglass, survey 493. June 10, 1784. Warrant 1851, p. 165.

**MADDEN, DAVID.** 287½ acres, Washington Co., bounded E. Benj. Thompson, other sides vacant. On waters of Buffalo creek, survey 498. Oct. 18, 1784. Warrant 614, p. 166.

**FRYAR, FIELDING.** 287½ acres, Burke Co., bounded N. Dean & Moore, E. & S. vacant, W. Luke Dean, survey 506. Nov. 23, 1784. Warrant —, p. 169.

**HUGHS, NICHOLAS.** 287½ acres, Washington Co., bounded W. John Jones, other sides vacant. Cut N. to E. by Buffalo creek, survey 511. June 5, 1784. Warrant 1205, p. 171.

**JONES, NATHAN.** 287½ acres, Washington Co., bounded S. Jonathan Jones, other sides vacant. Cut S. to N. by Buffalo creek, survey 512. June 5, 1784. Warrant 291, p. 171.

**PUGH, JEHU.** 287½ acres, Washington Co., bounded E. Burwick Rogers, other sides vacant. Cut E. to W. by Sandy creek, survey 513. June 29, 1784. Warrant 2110, p. 171.

**DENNIS, ABRAHAM.** 287½ acres, Washington Co., bounded S. James McFarland, other sides vacant. Cut by Buffalo creek, survey 515. June 7, 1784. Warrant 597, p. 172.

**JONES, JAMES.** 287½ acres, Washington Co., bounded S. Joseph Reed, other sides vacant, survey 516. June 14, 1784. Warrant 927, p. 172.

**BARNHART, JOHN.** 287½ acres, Washington Co., bounded all sides vacant. Cut E. to W. by fork of Shoulderbone creek, survey 516. June 25, 1784. Warrant 1806, p. 173.

## BOUNTY SURVEYS. 237

**WIGGINS, WILLIAM.** 287½ acres, Washington Co., bounded S. Abraham Dennis, other sides vacant, survey 518. June 7, 1784. Warrant 1399, p. 173.

**ROGERS, BRITTAIN.** 287½ acres, Washington Co., bounded N. & S. vacant, E. grantee, W. vacant and Simms. Cut by Fork creek, survey 519. June 7, 1784. Warrant 1950, p. 173.

**ROGERS, BURWICK.** 287½ acres, Washington Co., bounded E. Thos. Wooten, other sides vacant, survey 521. June 12, 1784. Warrant 1107, p. 174.

**EVANS, DANIEL.** 287½ acres, Washington Co., bounded N. & W. vacant, E. Williamson's Swamp, S. Jno. Ledbetter, survey 529. June 15, 1784. Warrant 1494, p. 177.

**LAMAR, SAMUEL.** 287½ acres, Washington Co., bounded all sides vacant, survey 530. June 9, 1784. Warrant 183, p. 177.

**LEGETT, ABNER.** 287½ acres, Washington Co., bounded all sides vacant. Cut S. to N. by Lick creek, survey 531, July 22, 1784. Warrant 2291, p. 178.

**HARKINS, THOMAS.** 287½ acres, Washington Co., bounded N. & E. vacant, S. & W. survey. Cut S. to N. by Lick creek, survey 532. July 24, 1784. Warrant 828, p. 178.

**LEGETT, JOHN.** 287½ acres, Washington Co., bounded all sides surveyed. Cut E. to W. by Lick creek, survey 533. May 17, 1784. Warrant 364, p. 178.

**EDWARDS, PETER.** 287½ acres, Washington Co., bounded N. Beaverdam creek, E. & S. vacant, W. Jas. Allison, survey 534. Oct. 21, 1784. Warrant 2417, p. 179.

**HERTSHORN, WILLIAM.** 287½ acres, Washington Co., bounded N. & E. vacant, S. Beaverdam creek, W. Wilkes Co. line, survey 535. Oct. 21, 1784. Warrant 2994, p. 179.

**ALEXANDER, EZEKIEL.** 287½ acres, Washington Co., bounded E. John Lytton, Alexander, other sides vacant. Cut E. to W. by Little Beaverdam creek, survey 536. June 26, 1784. Warrant 412, p. 179.

**GRAVES, RICHARD.** 287½ acres, Washington Co., bounded W. Whatley, other sides vacant. Cut N. & S. by Deresow's creek, survey 541. Nov. 14, 1784. Warrant 1695, p. 181.

**MOORE, RICHARD.** 287½ acres, Franklin Co., bounded N. Oconee river, other sides vacant, survey 555. June 26, 1784. Warrant 472, p. 186.

**THOMPSON, BENJ.** 575 acres, Washington Co., bounded all sides vacant. Cut by Beaverdam creek, survey 556. Oct. 18, 1784. Warrant 2,000, p. 187.

**LAMAR, WILLIAM.** 287½ acres, Washington Co., bounded all sides vacant, survey 558. June 9, 1784. Warrant 936, p. 188.

## ROSTER OF THE REVOLUTION.

**FORT, ARTHUR.** 287½ acres, Washington Co., bounded N. Little Ogeechee river and Cowpen creek, E. Ogeechee river, S. Lewis Davis, W. vacant, survey 559. June 24, 1784. Warrant 1456, p. 188.

**O'HEARN, JOSIAH.** 287½ acres, Washington Co., bounded N. vacant, E. Jno. DuHart, S. & W. Oconee river, survey 562. June 8, 1784. Warrant 1937, p. 189.

**KUPERT, JOHN.** 287½ acres, Effingham Co., bounded all sides vacant. Cut N. & S. by Bird's creek, survey 563. Oct. 12, 1784. Warrant —, p. 189.

**WOOTEN, JAMES.** 287½ acres, Washington Co., bounded all sides vacant. Cut W. to E. by Beaverdam creek, survey 750. June 11, 1784. Warrant 2521, p. 193.

**WOOTEN, THOMAS.** 287½ acres, Washington Co., bounded W. Burwell Rogers, other sides vacant, survey 571. June 12, 1784. Warrant 1657, p. 193.

**CHAPLAIN, JOSEPH.** 200 acres, Washington Co., bounded N. Night, E. Williamson's Swamp, S. & W. vacant. Cut E. & W. by Walnut creek, survey 572. June 12, 1784. Warrant —, p. 193.

**FULTON, SAMUEL.** 287½ acres, Washington Co., bounded N. vacant, E. Patterson, S. Limestone creek, W. Wiliamson's Swamp, survey 573. June 3, 1784. Warrant 1450, p. 194.

**THOMPSON, JOSHUA.** 287½ acres, Washington Co., bounded all sides vacant. Cut W. to E. by Fishing creek, survey 574. June 8, 1784. Warrant 2090, p. 194.

**RED, SAMUEL.** 287½ acres, Washington Co., bounded all sides vacant, survey 582. June 12, 1784. Warrant 1025, p. 197.

**THOMPSON, ROBERT.** 287½ acres, Franklin Co., bounded all sides vacant, survey 587. June 16, 1784. Warrant 32, p. 198.

**THOMPSON, LABAN.** 287½ acres, Washington Co., bounded N. Jno. Mann, E. vacant, S. Benj. Bartmore, W. Titus Hollinger, survey 592. May 24, 1784. Warrant 615, p. 200.

**WINTERS, FRED.** 287½ acres, Franklin Co., bounded N. Jno. Matthews, E. & S. vacant, W. Cornelius Scott, survey 598. Dec. 14, 1784. Warrant 2292, p. 202.

**SCOTT, CORNELIUS.** 287½ acres, Franklin Co., bounded N. Jno. Allen, E. Fred Winters, S. Sam'l Creswell, W. vacant. Cut by branch of Eastanola creek, survey 599. Oct. 16, 1784. Warrant 1694, p. 202.

**MATTHEWS, JOHN.** 287½ acres, Franklin Co., bounded N. & E. vacant. S. Fred Winters, W. Jno. Allen. Crossed by Indian Trading Path. Cut by Eastanaula creek, survey 600. Dec. 16, 1784. Warrant 845, p. 203.

## BOUNTY SURVEYS.

**ALLEN, JOHN.** 287½ acres, Franklin Co., bounded N. & W. vacant, E. John Matthews, S. Cornelius Scott, survey 601. Dec. 16, 1784. Warrant 829, p. 203.

**TAYLOR, HENRY.** 287½ acres, Washington Co., bounded all sides vacant, S. John Buckhalter, survey 603. June 5, 1784. Warrant 1883, p. 204.

**BUCKHALTER, JOHN.** 287½ acres, Washington Co., bounded all sides vacant. Cut W. to E. by Shoulderbone creek, survey 604. June 5, 1784. Warrant 1703, p. 204.

**BUCKHAM, SIMON.** 287½ acres, Washington Co., bounded all sides vacant. Cut by branch of Buffalo creek and Shoulderbone creek, survey 605, June 6, 1784. Warrant 2118, p. 204.

**CAMPBELL, WILLIAM.** 287½ acres, Washington Co., bounded N. & S. vacant, E. vacant, W. John Holmes, survey 606. June 17, 1784. Warrant 2141, p. 205.

**EMANUEL, ASA.** 287½ acres, Washington Co., bounded N. Wm. Blanchard, E. Oconee river, S. Robert Allen, W. vacant, survey 617. June 9, 1784. Warrant 1904, p. 210.

**STROHECKER, RUDOLPH.** 287½ acres, Washington Co., bounded N. Oconee river, E. Fred Jones, S. vacant, W. Asa Emanuel, survey 618. June 8, 1784. Warrant 906, p. 211.

**THORNTON, SOLOMAN.** 287½ acres, Washington Co., bounded N. J. Simmons, E. Shoulderbone creek, S. Rogers, W. vacant, survey 623. June 8, 1784. Warrant 906, p. 211.

**WOOD, JAMES.** 230 acres, Washington Co., bounded E. Oconee river, other sides vacant, survey 629. June, 1784. Reserve, p. 215.

**BACON, THOMAS.** 287½ acres, Liberty Co., bounded S. John Bacon, other sides vacant, survey 630. Dec. 10, 1784. Warrant —, p. 216.

**MORCE, ALEXANDER.** 287½ acres, Washington Co., bounded N. unknown, E. vacant, S. Oconee river, W. Porter, survey 642. June 10, 1784. Warrant 2713, p. 220.

**COWEN, CAPT. EDWARD.** 690 acres, Washington Co., bounded all sides vacant. Cut by Rooty creek, survey 643. Nov. 15, 1784. Reserve, p. 221.

**YOUNGBLOOD, JOHN.** 287½ acres, Washington Co., bounded N. Glascock, other sides vacant, survey 644. Jan. 4, 1785. Warrant 1830, p. 221.

**KEMP, THOMAS.** 287½ acres, Washington Co., bounded N. Matthews, E. vacant, S. John Cook, Sr., W. Reddick. Cut W. to E. by Dososow creek, survey 645. Nov. 11, 1784. Warrant 1227, p. 221.

**LOWE, CAPT. JOHN TOLSON.** 575 acres, Franklin Co., bounded E. Capt. Marbury, others vacant, survey 713. May 23, 1785, p. 250.

**MATTHEWS, WILLIAM.** 287½ acres, Franklin Co., bounded E. Hudson, others vacant, survey 717. June 7, 1785, p. 251.

**LAUDERDEAL, JOHN.** 287½ acres, Franklin Co., bounded all sides vacant. Cut by Bear creek and its forks, survey 719. Feb. 3, 1786, p. 252.

**SMALLWOOD, MIDDLETON.** 287½ acres, Franklin Co., bounded S. Robt. Middleton, other sides vacant, survey 722. Aug. 4, 1784, p. 254.

**HAWKINS, HEIRS OF JAMES.** 287½ acres, Franklin Co., bounded S. N. fork of Oconee river, other sides vacant, survey 723. June 7, 1784, p. 254.

**KELL, ARCHIBALD.** 287½ acres, Franklin Co., bounded S. Tugalo river, other sides vacant, survey 724. Dec. 14, 1784, p. 254.

**McCAIN, THOMAS.** 287½ acres, Franklin Co., bounded all sides vacant. Cut N. & S. by Allen's creek of the Oconee river, survey 724. Dec. 14, 1784, p. 254.

**MURPHY, MILLS.** 575 acres, Franklin Co., bounded S. Oconee river, other sides vacant. Cut E. to W. by Indian Cut creek, survey 728. June 28, 1784, p. 256.

**MATTHEWS, ISHAM.** 287½ acres, Franklin Co., bounded N. Jno. Bender, E. Livingston, S. Wm. Matthews, W. vacant, survey 729, p. 256.

**MOORE, WILLIAM.** 287½ acres, Franklin Co., bounded all sides vacant. Cut by N. fork of Oconee river, survey 730. Oct. 30, 1784, p. 256.

**McCORDELL, CORNELIUS.** 287½ acres, Franklin Co., bounded N. Jas. Cartledge, E. John Clarke, S. John Gorham, W. Thos. Cannon, survey 731. Dec. 21, 1784, p. 257.

**CARTLEDGE, EDMOND.** 287½ acres, Richmond Co., bounded N. & E. vacant, S. Edmond Cartledge, Sr., W. Edmond Cartledge & Galpin, survey 835. Aug. 7, 1784, p. 293.

**BAKER, WILLIAM.** 1,150 acres, Franklin Co., bounded N. & S. vacant, E. H. Marbury, W. H. Marbury, on Big creek, survey 915. Sept. 8, 1784. On Reserve, p. 323.

**BOSWOETH, OBEDIAH.** 575 acres, Franklin Co., bounded S. John Gorham, other sides vacant. Cut by Oconee river, survey 917. June 7, 1784, p. 324.

**THOMAS, CONNELL.** 287½ acres, Franklin Co., bounded E. Connell & Wash, other sides vacant, survey 931. June 2, 1785, p. 239.

**CULPEPPER, MALACHIA.** 287½ acres, Franklin Co., bounded all sides vacant. Cut by N. fork of Oconee river, survey 935. Oct. 30, 1784, p. 330.

**CLARKE, ELIJAH.** 4,600 acres, Franklin Co., bounded N. Jno. Clarke, E. Jno. Freeman, S. Oconee river, W. Freeman & Cleves, survey 936. Aug. 10, 1785, p. 331.

BOUNTY SURVEYS. 241

**CLARKE, MOSES.** 230 acres, Franklin Co., bounded N. Jno. Clarke, other sides vacant, survey 950. Sept. 8, 1785. On Reserve, p. 338.

**CLARKE, JOHN.** 230 acres, Franklin Co., bounded N. Leonard Marbury, other sides vacant, survey 952. Sept. 8, 1785. On Reserve, p. 338.

**CARNES, THOMAS.** 450 acres, Franklin Co., bounded (triangle) N. Major Cobb, E. Wiliam & Jesse Walker, W. Oconee river, survey 951. June 23, 1785. On Reserve, p. 338.

## SURVEYOR GENERAL'S BOOK "D."

**BUGG, H.** 287½ acres, Camden Co., bounded N. Dr. Wicker, other sides vacant. Cut by Pagin creek. Survey 7, July 10, 1784, p. 5.

**LAW, GEORGE.** 287½ acres, Camden Co., bounded all sides vacant, survey 63, July 9, 1785, p. 19.

**PALMER, JOHN.** 287½ acres, Camden Co., bounded all sides vacant, survey 91, Aug. 15, 1787, p. 29.

**RICKEY, JOHN.** 287½ acres, Camden Co., bounded E. Wm. Denny, other sides vacant, survey 96, June 18, 1786, p. 31.

**WINN, JOSEPH.** 287½ acres, Camden Co., bounded all sides vacant. Cut by Town creek swamp, survey 166. Aug. 5, 1785, p. 60.

**WRIGHT, JOHN.** 287½ acres, Camden Co., bounded all sides vacant, survey 172. Nov. 24, 1786, p. 62.

**WHITE, THOMAS.** 287½ acres, Camden Co., bounded N. Capt. Randolph, other sides vacant, survey 173. Sept. 18, 1786, p. 62.

**LAWSON, JOHN.** 287½ acres, Liberty Co., bounded N. & E. Altamaha river, S. Dunwoody, W. vacant, survey 258, May 25, 1790, p. 82.

**OSGOOD, JOSIAH.** 287½ acres, Liberty Co., bounded N. & W. vacant, E. Altamaha river, S. Jos. Clay, survey 281. May 25, 1790, p. 88.

**BRAY, THOMAS.** 287½ acres, Effingham Co., bounded N. vacant and Col. Howell, other sides vacant, survey 358. Mar. 30, 1790, p. 114.

**BROWNSON, NATHAN.** 287½ acres, Effingham Co., bounded N. Robt. Dunwoody, other sides vacant, survey 372. Dec. 22, 1788, p. 117.

**HOWELL, CALEB.** 387½ acres, Effingham Co., bounded N. Wade O'Brien, E. Howell, S. Joshua Pearce, Jr., W. Vacant, survey 430. Aug. 21, 1788, p. 134.

## SURVEYOR GENERAL'S BOOK "E."

**BRAZILL, SAMPSON.** 287½ acres, Washington Co., bounded N. Edward Hill, E. John McLain, S. unknown, W. Wm. Baldwin. Cut E. to W. by Shoulderbone creek, survey, Nov. 20, 1784. Warrant 2992, p. 1.

**BALDWIN, MORDECAI.** 460 acres, Washington Co., bounded N. Heard, E. vacant, S. Thos. Maxwell, W. Wm. Farrell, June 10, 1784. Warrant 2650, p. 3.

**BROWN, FREDERICK.** 287½ acres, Washington Co., bounded S. Lewis Bobough, other sides unknown. Dec. 17, 1784. Warrant 3973, p. 2.

**BOBOUGH, LEWIS.** 287½ acres, Washington Co., bounded N. Fred Brown, S. Richard Call, other sides unknown. Dec. 17, 1784. Warrant 2975, p. 4.

**BURNEY, JOHN, JR.** 287½ acres, Washington Co., bounded all sides vacant. June 14, 1784. Warrant 1687, p. 5.

**BURNEY, JOHN, SR.** 287½ acres, Washington Co., bounded N. & E. vacant, S. & W. unknown. June 30, 1784. Warrant —, p. 6.

**BRASWELL, FREDERICK.** 287½ acres, Washington Co., bounded N. unknown, E. vacant, S. Ed. Hall, W. Wm. Baldwin, survey. Nov. 15, 1784. Warrant 2307, p. 7.

**ALLISON, HENRY.** 460 acres, Washington Co., bounded N. Bartlett Martin, E. vacant, S. Robt. Moseley, W. Jas. Houston, surveyed. Dec. 7, 1784. Warrant —. On Reserve, p. 8.

**MOSELEY, CAPT. LITTLEBERRY.** 690 acres, Washington Co., bounded N. Chisholm, E. & S. vacant, W. south fork Oconee river. Oct. 15, 1784. Reserve, p. 9.

**PAYNE, CAPT. THOMAS.** 460 acres, Washington Co., bounded S. Montfort and Evans, other sides vacant, survey 10. Oct. 15, 1784. Reserve, p. 10.

**CRAIN, LEWIS.** 287 acres, Washington Co., bounded N. Thos. McGree, E. & S. vacant, W. Geo. Wycho. Nov. 6, 1784. Warrant 2971, p. 11.

**LEWIS, JOSEPH.** 287½ acres, Liberty Co., bounded N. Lewis Ledbetter, E. Altamaha river, S. Drury Ledbetter, W. vacant, survey 13. Dec. 14, 1784. Warrant —, p. 13.

**LEWIS, JOSEPH.** 287½ acres (2d bounty), Liberty Co., bounded N. & E. vacant, S. grantee, W. Drury Ledbetter, survey 15. Feb. 24, 1785, p. 15.

**LEWIS, JOSEPH.** 287½ acres (3d bounty), Liberty Co., bounded E. Wm. Jones, other sides vacant, survey 18. Mar. 9, 1785, p. 18.

**LEWIS, ELIJAH.** 287½ acres, Liberty Co., bounded N. Thos. Bacon, S. John Bacon, others vacant, survey 19, Dec. 9, 1784, p. 19.

**CONYERS, MRS. MARGARET.** 287½ acres (old bounty), Effingham Co., survey 35. March 19, 1785, p. 35.

**SUNDAY, THEOPHILUS.** 575 acres, Effingham Co., bounded N. Marlow, E. Beaverdam creek, S. Jno. McQueen, W. vacant, survey 36. May 12, 1785, p. 38.

## BOUNTY SURVEYS.

**BONNELL, DAVID.** 500 acres, Effingham Co., bounded N. Great Ogeechee river, other sides vacant, survey 42. July 11, 1784, p. 42.

**HOWELL, DANIEL.** 287½ acres, Effingham Co., bounded all sides vacant, survey 46, Jan. 25, 1785, p. 46.

**HOWELL, DANIEL.** 287½ acres (2d bounty), Effingham Co., bounded all sides vacant. Cut N. & S. by Little Ogeechee river, survey 49. Jan. 25, 1785, p. 49.

**REDDING, GEORGE.** 287½ acres, Burke Co., bounded N. Wm. Gibson, E. Abm. Sunday, S. Berry Green, W. vacant, survey 76. March 27, 1785, p. 76.

**JONES, PHILIP.** 287½ acres, Burke Co., bounded N. Handley, S. E. Newman, W. vacant, survey 77, Dec. 24, 1784, p. 77.

**GOODALL, PLEASANT.** 287½ acres, Burke Co., bounded N. & E. vacant, S. James Gray, W. James Gray, survey 153. Feb. 14, 1785, p. 153.

**WARD, HEIRS OF BENJAMIN.** 287½ acres, Burke Co., bounded N. Alex. Carswell, E. David Holmes, S. Joseph Ward, W. vacant (granted to Charles Ward in trust for Heirs of Benjamin), survey 196. Nov. 29, 1784, p. 196.

**LOWE, ISAAC.** 287½ acres, Richmond Co., bounded N. & E. vacant, S. Jackson Higgins, W. Higginbotham, survey 272. Sept. 9, 1784, p. 272.

**BUTLER, DANIEL.** 575 acres, Richmond Co., bounded N. vacant, E. Frank, S. Martin, W. Lamar, survey 323. Oct. 6, 1784, p. 323.

**APPLING, JOHN.** 1,150 acres, Franklin Co., bounded all sides vacant, survey 324. May 6, 1785, p. 324.

**APLING, JOHN.** 862½ acres, Franklin Co., bounded N. & S. survey, E. Jas. Stubble, W. unknown, survey 325. Aug. 9, 1785, p. 325.

**CALL, RICHARD.** 1035 acres, Franklin Co., bounded all sides vacant, survey 330. June 11, 1785, p. 330.

**CARNES, PETER.** 1,150 acres, Franklin Co., bounded N. Bryan Ward, others vacant, survey 338. May 12, 1785, p. 338.

**CLARKE, JOHNSTON.** 287½ acres, Franklin Co., bounded N. & E. vacant, S. Big Pond fork of Oconee river, W. Wm. Fenn, survey 342. July 30, 1784, p. 342.

**CLOUD, JOHN.** 575 acres, Franklin Co., bounded Manoah Cloud, other sides vacant, survey 346. July 18, 1785, p. 346.

**CLOUD, MANOAH.** 575 acres, Franklin Co., bounded W. Jno. Cloud, other sides vacant, survey 347. Oct. 9, 1784, p. 347.

**CURREY, PETER.** 287½ acres, Franklin Co., bounded S. Stephen Coan, other sides vacant, survey 349, May 6, 1785, p. 349.

**COURSEY, DAVID.** 287½ acres, Franklin Co., bounded all sides vacant, survey 350. May 18, 1785, p. 350.

**CULBREATH, JOHN.** 287½ acres, Franklin Co., bounded N. fork of Oconee river, W. Ignatius Few, other sides vacant, survey 352. Jan. 29, 1785, p. 352.

**BREWER, GEORGE.** 287½ acres, Franklin Co., bounded S. county line, other sides vacant, survey 353. June 1, 1784, p. 353.

**BERRY, RICHARD.** 287½ acres, Franklin Co., bounded N. unknown, E. Jos. G. Taylor, S. N. fork of Oconee river, W. vacant, survey 354, April 12, 1785, p. 354.

**BLOUNT, STEPHEN.** 575 acres, Franklin Co., bounded N. unknown, E. & W. vacant, S. Jeremiah Brantley and Peyton Wyatt, survey 355, Mar. 11, 1785, p. 355.

**CARNES, PETER.** 1,150 acres, Franklin Co., bounded all sides vacant, survey 339. May 15, 1785, p. 339.

**CASTLEBERRY, JOHN.** 287½ acres, Franklin Co., bounded E. Ch. Few, other sides vacant, survey 358. June 8, 1784, p. 358.

**BUTLER, DANIEL.** 575 acres, Franklin Co., bounded all sides vacant. Cut N. & S. by Big Shoal creek, survey 359. Sept. 25, 1784, p. 359.

**FEW, IGNATIUS.** 1,150 acres, Franklin Co., bounded N. & S. vacant, E. unknown, W. Oconee river, survey 403. Aug. 4, 1785, p. 403.

**FEW, COL. IGNATIUS.** 1,150 acres, Franklin Co., bounded N. & E. vacant, S. & W. Oconee river, survey 404. Aug. 10, 1785, p. 404.

**JONES, ALITHEA ANDERSON.** 287½ acres, Franklin Co., bounded N. grantee, E. Col. Marbury, S. Edward Telfair, W. vacant, survey 406. May 21, 1785, p. 406.

**ADKINSON, THOMAS.** 287½ acres, Franklin Co., bounded S. Jno. Bernett, other sides vacant, survey 356, Oct. 3, 1785, p. 356.

**BARBER, GEORGE.** 690 acres, Franklin Co., bounded all sides vacant, survey 357. June 10, 1784, p. 357.

**BELLAMY, RICHARD.** 287½ acres, Franklin Co., bounded W. Jas. Hodges, other sides vacant, survey 360. July 10, 1784, p. 360.

**BLACK, JOHN.** 575 acres, Franklin Co., bounded S. Wm. Black, other sides vacant, survey 361. Aug. 6, 1784, p. 361.

**BLACK, WILLIAM.** 575 acres, Franklin Co., bounded N. Jno. Webb, E. J. Black, S. Jno. Black, W. vacant, survey 362. July 16, 1784, p. 362.

**CORSEY, STEPHEN.** 575 acres, Franklin Co., bounded all sides vacant. On N. fork of Broad river, survey 363. June 30, 1784, p. 363.

## BOUNTY SURVEYS. 245

**ADCOCK, THOMAS.** 287½ acres, Franklin Co., bounded N. Wm. Ford, other sides vacant, survey 364. Oct. 28, 1784, p. 364.

**COBB, JAMES, SR.** 287½ acres, Franklin Co., bounded W. Offutt, other side vacant, survey 365. Oct. 28, 1784, p. 365.

**BARNETT, WILLIAM.** 287½ acres, Franklin Co., bounded E. John Smith, other sides vacant. On Indian creek, survey 366, Oct. 22, 1784, p. 366.

**CARTLEDGE, EDMUND.** 287½ acres, Franklin Co., bounded N. Glascock, S. Glascock, others vacant, survey 367. Oct. 30, 1784, p. 367.

**BAILEY, WILLIAM.** 287½ acres, Franklin Co., bounded N. Jesse Webb, other sides vacant, survey 368. June 8, 1784, p. 368.

**BARDIN, GILBERT.** 287½ acres, Franklin Co., bounded all sides vacant, survey 369. July 30, 1784, p. 369.

**CARTLEDGE, JAMES.** 287½ acres, Franklin Co., bounded N. Wm. Pulliam, E. Jno. Clarke, S. Cornelius McCardell, W. R. Dennis, survey 370. Dec. 21, 1784, p. 370.

**CANNON, THOMAS.** 287½ acres, Franklin Co., bounded N. R. Dennis, E. McCardell, S. John Corham, W. vacant, survey 371. Feb., 1785, p. 371.

**BRANTLEY, JEREMIAH.** 345 acres, Franklin Co., bounded W. Wyatt, others vacant, survey 372. Mar. 10, 1785, p. 372.

**BROOM, THOMAS.** 287½ acres, Franklin Co., bounded N. W. Nichols, others vacant, survey 373. June 21, 1784, p. 373.

**BRITT, CHARLES.** 287½ acres, Franklin Co., bounded all sides vacant. Cut N. & S. by Eastanaula river, survey 374. Dec. 16, 1784, p. 374.

**FEW, WILLIAM.** 575 acres, Franklin Co., bounded N. & W. unknown, E. & S. vacant, survey 375. Aug. 10, 1785, p. 375.

**FEW, WILLIAM.** 1,150 acres, Franklin Co., bounded N. & W. Scott, E. vacant, S. Jno. Apling, survey 378. Aug. 5, 1785, p. 378.

**FEW, WILLIAM.** 1,024 acres, Franklin Co., bounded S. Franklin fork Oconee river, others unknown and vacant, survey 379. Aug. 11, 1785, p. 379.

**FEW, WILLIAM.** 1,250 acres, Franklin Co., bounded S. Fork of Oconee river, others vacant, survey 380. Aug. 9, 1785, p. 380.

**FEW, WILLIAM.** 1,120 acres, Franklin Co., bounded N. unknown, E. & W. vacant, S. north fork of Oconee river, survey 381. Aug. 6, 1785, p. 381.

**FEW, WILLIAM.** 1,725 acres, Franklin Co., bounded all sides unknown, survey 376. Aug. 10, 1785, p. 376.

**FEW, WILLIAM.** 887 acres, Franklin Co., bounded all sides unknown. On branch of Oconee river, survey 377. Aug. 12, 1785, p. 377.

246     ROSTER OF THE REVOLUTION.

**EVANS, STEPHEN.** 287½ acres, Franklin Co., bounded all sides vacant, survey 382. May 6, 1785, p. 382.

**FREEMAN, JOHN.** 1,200 acres, Franklin Co., bounded N. & S. vacant, E. Christopher Orr, W. Pope, survey 384. Aug. 4, 1784, p. 384.

**FREEMAN, HOLMAN.** 920 acres, Franklin Co., bounded all sides vacant, survey 385. Aug. 4, 1785, p. 385.

**FUQUA, THOMAS.** 287½ acres, Franklin Co., bounded N. & W. vacant, E. Jas. Thompson, S. fork of Oconee river, survey 386. Aug. 1, 1784, p. 386.

**DYAR, HEIRS OF HENRY.** 287½ acres, Franklin Co., bounded N. & W. vacant, E. Richard Berry, S. Oconee river, survey 387. April 12, 1785, p. 387.

**DEAN, WILLIAM.** 230 acres, Franklin Co., bounded all sides vacant, survey 388. Dec. 13, 1784, p. 388.

**FENN, WILLIAM.** 287½ acres, Franklin Co., bounded S. Oconee river, other sides vacant, survey 389. July 30, 1784, p. 389.

**EASTER, JAMES.** 287½ acres, Franklin Co., bounded W. Wm. Hooper, others vacant. Cut by Town's creek, survey 390. Sept. 10, 1784, p. 390.

**FORD, WILLIAM.** 287½ acres, Franklin Co., bounded W. Thos. Scott, others vacant, survey 391. Oct. 28, 1784, p. 391.

**DRIVER, HENRY.** 287½ acres, Franklin Co., bounded N. & E. vacant, S. Oconee river, W. Jacob Summerford, survey 392. June 9, 1784, p. 392.

**FRANKLIN, G.** 287½ acres, Franklin Co., bounded N. & E. vacant, S. Jas. Cobb, W. Scott, survey 393. Oct. 28, 1784, p. 393.

**DAVIS, MEREDITH.** 287½ acres, Franklin Co., bounded W. Offutt, other sides vacant, survey 394. Oct. 27, 1784, p. 394.

**DOUGLAS, GEORGE.** 287½ acres, Franklin Co., bounded N. Jno. Ware, E. & S. vacant, W. Jos. Jeter. Cut by fork of Clarke's creek, survey 395. Dec. 10. 1784, p. 395.

**FULLER, JOHN.** 287½ acres, Franklin Co., bounded N. & S. vacant, E. Glascock, W. Jos. McCutchins, survey 396. Oct. 30, 1784, p. 396.

**FULLER, STEPHEN.** 287½ acres, Franklin Co., bounded N. & W. middle fork of Oconee river, other sides vacant, survey 397. Dec. 1, 1784, p. 397.

**DENNIS, RICHMOND.** 287½ acres, Franklin Co., bounded N. & W. vacant, E. Jas. Cartledge, S. Thos. Cannon, survey 398. Dec. 1, 1784, p. 397.

**DYAS, JOHN.** 287½ acres, Franklin Co., bounded W. College lands, other sides vacant, survey 399. July 20, 1784.

**DUKE, TAYLOR.** 460 acres, Franklin Co., bounded E. Wamberscies, others vacant. Cut by fork of Broad river, survey 401. July 9, 1784, p. 401.

## BOUNTY SURVEYS. 247

**FEW, COL. IGNATIUS.** 1,187½ acres, Franklin Co., bounded E. Jno Hollingsworth, other sides vacant, survey 402. Aug. 8, 1784, p. 402.

**JONES, ALITHEA ANDERSON.** 575 acres, Franklin Co., bounded N. Marbury, other sides vacant, survey 405. May 21, 1785, p. 405.

**JONES, JAMES.** 575 acres, Franklin Co., bounded S. Col. Marbury, other sides vacant, survey 407. May 20, 1785, p. 407.

**GIBBONS, WILLIAM, JR.** 1,150 acres, Franklin Co., bounded N. Edward Telfair, other sides vacant, survey 410. June 10, 1785, p. 410.

**GORHAM, JOHN.** 575 acres, Franklin Co., bounded N. & W. vacant, E. by grantee, S. Strother and Richardson, survey 411. May 11, 1785, p. 411.

**JONES, JAMES.** 575 acres, Franklin Co., bounded N. vacant, E. fork of Oconee river, S. Ignatius Few, W. John Gorham, survey 403. June 20, 1785, p. 408.

**GORHAM, JOHN.** 575 acres, Franklin Co., bounded N. grantee, W. W. Richardson, others vacant, survey 413. May 10, 1785, p. 413.

**GORHAM, JOHN.** 287½ acres, Franklin Co., bounded S. south fork of Broad river, other sides vacant, survey 414. May 30, 1784, p. 414.

**GORHAM, JOHN.** 575 acres, Franklin Co., bounded N. & S. grantee, E. & W. vacant, survey 415. May 13, 1785, p. 415.

**GARRETT, JOHN.** 575 acres, Franklin Co., bounded N. Morris, other sides vacant, survey 417. Aug. 10, 1785, p. 417.

**GARRETT, JOHN.** 287½ acres, Franklin Co., bounded all sides vacant, survey 418. Sept. 6, 1785, p. 416.

**GARRETT, JOHN.** 2,875 acres, Franklin Co., bounded all sides vacant, or unknown, survey 419. Sept. 6, 1785, p. 419.

**GARRETT, JOHN.** 287½ acres, Franklin Co., bounded all sides vacant, survey 420. Sept. 6, 1785, p. 420.

**GARRETT, JOHN.** 200 acres, Franklin Co., bounded S. Oconee river, other sides unknown, survey 421. Aug. 10, 1785, p. 421.

**GARRETT, JOHN.** 287½ acres, Franklin Co., bounded all sides vacant, survey 423. Sept. 6, 1785, p. 422.

**GARRETT, JOHN.** 287½ acres, Franklin Co., bounded N. Thos. Marshall, E. & S. vacant, W. middle fork of Oconee river, survey 423. Aug. 9, 1785, p. 423.

**GORHAM, JOHN.** 575 acres, Franklin Co., bounded N. Richardson, E. Gorham, other sides vacant, survey 412. May 10, 1785, p. 412.

**GARRETT, JOHN.** 575 acres, Franklin Co., bounded N. Collier, E. Nelson, S. & W. vacant, survey 416. Aug. 10, 1785, p. 416.

**JOHNSTON, JOHN H.** 277 acres (triangle), Franklin Co., bounded N. unknown. E. Ford Butler, S. W. Walter Richardson, survey 425. June 23, 1784, p. 425.

**HORN, JESSE.** 287½ acres, Franklin Co., bounded S. Jno. Pittman, other side vacant, survey 426. Oct. 5, 1784, p. 426.

**HARVEY, LITTLEBERRY.** 287½ acres, Franklin Co., bounded W. survey, other sides vacant, survey 427. Oct. 29, 1784, p. 427.

**HOLTON, FRANCIS.** 287½ acres, Franklin Co., bounded all sides vacant on Oconee river, survey 428. Oct. 30, 1784, p. 428.

## SURVEYOR GENERAL'S BOOK "F."

**JOHNSTON, WILLIAM.** 287½ acres, Franklin Co., bounded S. Oconee river, other sides vacant, survey 5. July 15, 1784, p. 5.

**HUDSON, SAMUEL.** 287½ acres, Franklin Co., bounded all sides vacant, survey 6. April 9, 1785, p. 5.

**HORN, JACOB.** 287½ acres, Franklin Co., bounded N. Welcher, E. Stephen Evans, S. & W. vacant, survey 7. May 6, 1785, p. 6.

**JARRETT, DEVEREAUX.** 575 acres, Franklin Co., bounded S. Big Shoal creek, other sides unknown, survey 6. Aug. 27, 1785, p. 6.

**HUDSON, JOSEPH.** 575 acres, Franklin Co., bounded all sides vacant. Cut by Hudson's fork of Oconee river, survey 9. June 8, 1784, p. 7.

**JONES, THOMAS.** 287½ acres, Franklin Co., bounded E. Geo. Barber, other sides vacant. Cut E. to W. by Connerol's creek, survey 10. Aug. 14, 1784, p. 7.

**CREGG, THOMAS.** 575 acres, Franklin Co., bounded N. & W. vacant, E. Rd. Thompson, S. Benjamin Hubbard. Cut by Hudson's fork, survey 11. June 8, 1784, p. 8.

**GLASCOCK, WILLIAM.** 287½ acres, Franklin Co., bounded all sides vacant. Cut E. to W. by Bear creek, survey 12. July 15, 1784, p. 8.

**HUBBARD, JOHN.** 287½ acres, Franklin Co., bounded N. & S. vacant, E. Wm. Thomas, W. Joel Doss. Cut W. to E. Gorham's fork Broad river, survey 13. June 8, 1784, p. 8.

**HALL, GEORGE.** 230 acres, Franklin Co., bounded S. Johnson Clarke, other sides vacant. Cut by Big Pond fork of Oconee river, survey 14. July 30, 1784, p. 9.

**HUBBARD, JACOB.** 575 acres, Franklin Co., bounded N. Jas. Little, other sides vacant. Cut by Nails creek, survey 15. June 4, 1784, p. 10.

**GREASEL, ELAM.** 287½ acres, Franklin Co., bounded S. Oconee river, other sides vacant, survey 16. June 25, 1784, p. 10.

BOUNTY SURVEYS. 249

**HEATLEY, ROBERT.** 287½ acres, Franklin Co., bounded S. Oconee river, other sides vacant, survey 17. June 11, 1784, p. 11.

**GILES, WILLIAM.** 287½ acres, Franklin Co., bounded E. Jno. Castleberry, other sides vacant. Cut by Curry's creek, survey 18. June 25, 1784, p. 11.

**JACKSON, WILLIAM.** 287½ acres, Franklin Co., bounded S. Mulberry fork of Oconee river, other sides vacant, survey 19. Aug. 1, 1784, p. 12.

**JONES, BENJAMIN.** 287½ acres, Franklin Co., bounded N. H. Hendricks, other sides vacant. Cut E. to W. by N. fork of Oconee river, survey 20. June 29, 1784, p. 12.

**McCARRY, EDWARD.** 575 acres, Franklin Co., bounded all sides vacant. Cut E. to W. by middle fork of Broad river, survey 21. Aug., 1784, p. 13.

**HILL, JOHN.** 287½ acres, Franklin Co., bounded E. J. Fountain, other sides vacant. Cut by Broad river, survey 22. Dec. 17, 1784, p. 13.

**HOWARD, JULIUS.** 287½ acres, Franklin Co., bounded all sides vacant. Cut by Bear creek and tributaries, survey 33. July 15, 1784, p. 14.

**ALEXANDER, SAMUEL.** 287½ acres, Washington Co., bounded N. College lands, other sides vacant. On Richland creek, survey 26. May 31, 1784, p. 15.

**ALEXANDER, SAMUEL.** 575 acres, Washington Co., bounded N. College lands, other sides vacant. On Richland creek, survey 26. May 31, 1784, p. 15.

**ASHMORE, JOHN.** 287½ acres, Washington Co., bounded S. Oconee river, other sides vacant, survey 27. June 1, 1784, p. 16.

**BUSSEY, HEZEKIAH.** 287½ acres, Washington Co., bounded N. Jno. Golden, E. Oconee river, S. & W. vacant. On Richland creek, survey 28. June 3, 1784, p. 16.

**BRADLEY, WILLIAM.** 287½ acres, Washington Co., bounded E. Richland creek, other sides vacant, survey 30. June 4, 1784, p. 17.

**ANDREWS, JOSHUA.** 287½ acres, Washington Co., bounded all sides vacant. Cut W. to E. by Fakling creek, survey 31. June 6, 1784, p. 16.

**ANGLIN, DAVID.** 287½ acres, Washington Co., bounded all sides vacant. Cut E. to W. by Fishing creek, survey 32. June 7, 1784, p. 18.

**BLANCHARD, WILLIAM.** 287½ acres, Washington Co., bounded N. Oconee river, E. Asa Emanuel, S. vacant, W. R. Fleming, survey 33. June 9, 1784, p. 19.

**BOYKIN, JESSE.** 287½ acres, Washington Co., bounded N. & W. vacant, E. Oconee river, S. Fred Francis, survey 34. June 10. 1784, p. 19.

**BURKE, CHARLEY.** 287½ acres, Washington Co., bounded E. Shoulderbone creek, other sides vacant. Cut E. to W. by 12 miles of Beaverdam creek, survey 35. June 10, 1784, p. 20.

**BERRY, WILLIAM.** 287½ acres, Washington Co., bounded W. Jno. Anderson, other sides vacant, on Buffalo creek, survey 36. June 10, 1784, p. 20.

**BENTLEY, JOHN.** 287½ acres, Washington Co., bounded all sides vacant. Cut S. to N. by 12 miles of Beaverdam Creek Trading Path, laid out SE. to NW., survey 37. June 10, 1784, p. 21.

**BUCKHALTER, JACOB.** 287½ acres, Washington Co., bounded N. Jas. Camp, E. & S. vacant, W. Williamson's swamp, survey 38. June 12, 1784, p. 21.

**BURNETT, JOHN.** 287½ acres, Washington Co., bounded N. Wm. Marler, E. & W. vacant, S. Jno. Roberts, on Rocky creek, survey 39. July 13, 1784, p. 22.

**BUCKHALTER, MICHAEL.** 287½ acres, Washington Co., bounded N. & E. vacant, S. Ogeechee river, W. R. Middleton, survey 40. June 15, 1784, p. 22.

**BROWN, THOMAS.** 287½ acres, Washington Co., bounded S. Allen, other sides vacant. Cut by branch of Fishing creek, survey 41. June 15, 1784, p. 23.

**BURT, MOODY.** 287½ acres, Washington Co., bounded N. Little Beaverdam of Richland creek, E. Adams, S. John White, W. vacant, survey 42. June 16, 1784, p. 23.

**BRANNAN, THOMAS.** 287½ acres, Washington Co., bounded N. Bentley, E. vacant, S. Trippe, W. Smalley, survey 43. June 30, 1784, p. 24.

**BOWEN, JOEL.** 287½ acres, Washington Co., bounded N. & W. vacant, E. Hammock, S. Lick creek, survey 44. July 1, 1784, p. 24.

**BURNETT, JOHN.** 575 acres, Washington Co., bounded N. Little creek, others vacant, survey 45. July 1, 1784, p. 25.

**BRYANT, JOHN.** 460 acres, Washington Co., bounded N. & S. vacant, E. vacant & Davenport, Jackson, Stake, on Rocky fork of Shoulderbone creek, survey 46. July 2, 1784, p. 25.

**BUCKHALTER, WILLIAM.** 287½ acres, Washington Co., bounded W. Howard, other sides vacant, on Williamson's swamp, survey 47. July 3, 1784, p. 26.

**ALLEN, JAMES.** 287½ acres, Washington Co., bounded N. & W. vacant, E. Ogeechee river, S. John Pearry, survey 48. July 7, 1784, p. 26.

**AYRES, JAMES.** 287½ acres, Washington Co., bounded N. &. E. vacant, S. Williamson's swamp, W. Weldon Houseley, survey 49. July 8, 1784, p. 27.

**ADCOCK, JAMES.** 287½ acres, Washington Co., bounded N. Sapp, E. Burke, S. Taylor, W. vacant, survey 50. July 9, 1784, p. 27.

BOUNTY SURVEYS. 251

**ALEXANDER, JAMES.** 287½ acres, Washington Co., bounded S. Wm. Bradley, other sides vacant. Cut by Rocky creek, survey 51. June 8, 1784, p. 28.

**AUTREY, ALEXANDER.** 575 acres, Washington Co., bounded all sides vacant. Cut S. to N. by Buffalo creek, survey 52. July 22, 1784, p. 28.

**ASBURY, JONATHAN.** 287½ acres, Washington Co., bounded N. Houston, other sides vacant, on branch of Fishing creek, survey 53. June 9, 1784, p. 29.

**ALEXANDER, JAMES.** 287½ acres, Washington Co., bounded all sides vacant, survey 54. July 24, 1784, p. 29.

**BRASWELL, JOHN.** 287½ acres, Washington Co., bounded N. & W. vacant, E. Williamson's Swamp creek, S. Woodruff, survey 55. July 22, 1784, p. 30.

**BOYKIN, FRANCIS.** 387½ acres, Washington Co., bounded N. & W. vacant, E. Geo. Powell, S. Ogeechee river, survey 56. April 29, 1784, p. 30.

**BROWNER, CHARLES.** 287½ acres, Washington Co., bounded W. Geo. Bassett, other sides vacant, on Shoulderbone creek, survey 57. Feb. 26, 1785, p. 31.

**BASSETT, GEORGE.** 287½ acres, Washington Co., bounded N.-W. Rae, E. Evans, S. & W. vacant, on Shoulderbone creek, survey 57. Feb. 24, 1785, p. 31.

**BROOME, THOMAS.** 287½ acres, Washington Co., bounded N. Henry Wood, E. Ogeechee river, S. & W. vacant, survey 59. July 24, 1784, p. 32.

**BROWN, ANDREW.** 287½ acres, Washington Co., bounded N. J. Thomas, E. vacant, S. Jas. Thomas, W. Jas. Catchings, survey 66. Jan. 3, 1785, p. 35.

**BURNSIDES, JOHN.** 287½ acres, Washington Co., bounded N. Breed & Nimms, E., S. & W. by Glascock, survey 67. Jan. 4, 1785, p. 36.

**BALDWIN, DAVID.** 287½ acres, Washington Co., bounded N. & W. vacant, E. Grantee, S. Cornelius, Smith, on Shoulderbone creek, survey 68. Feb. 24, 1785, p. 36.

**BARROW, REUBEN.** 287½ acres, Washington Co., bounded W. Robert Alexander, other sides vacant. Cut E. & W. by Big creek, survey 69. April 7, 1785, p. 37.

**ALEXANDER, ROBERT.** 287½ acres, Washington Co., bounded all sides vacant. Cut E. to W. by Big creek, survey 70. April 7, 1785, p. 37.

**BALDWIN, DAVID.** 287½ acres, Washington Co., bounded N. vacant, E. College lands, S. Perritt, W. grantee, survey 71. Feb. 24, 1785, p. 38.

**BARRETT, THOMAS.** 287½ acres, Washington Co., bounded all sides vacant. Cut by Richland creek, survey 74. April 16, 1785, p. 39.

**BROOKS, JACOB.** 287½ acres, Washington Co., bounded N. & W. vacant, E. Williamson's swamp, S. Grimsley, survey 75. Nov. 22, 1784, p. 40.

**BISHOP, JOSHUA.** 287½ acres, Washington Co., bounded all sides vacant. Cut S. to N. by Town creek and tributaries, survey 76. Dec. 30, 1784, p. 40.

**BUGG, JOHN, JR.** 287½ acres, Washington Co., bounded all sides vacant. Cut S. to N. by Ohoopee river, survey 77. June 10, 1784, p. 41.

**BRUTON, JOHN.** 287½ acres, Washington Co., bounded N. & W. vacant, E. Jno. Coleman, S. Soloman, Palmer, on Town's creek, survey 78. Nov. 14, 1784, p. 41.

**AYRES, ABRAM.** 287½ acres, Washington Co., bounded S. Henry Candler, other sides vacant, survey 79. Nov. 1, 1784, p. 42.

**BANKS, REUBEN.** 230 acres, Washington Co., bounded E. Jas. Gilton, other sides vacant. Cut N. & S. by Rae's creek, survey 80. Dec. 16, 1784, p. 42.

**BELL, JOHN.** 287½ acres, Washington Co., bounded N. Wm. Brown, E. College lands, S. Wm. Bryant, W. Bryant and vacant, survey 81. Oct. 11, 1784, p. 43.

**BROWN, WILLIAM.** 750 acres, Washington Co., bounded E. Wilkes Co. line, S. College lands, other sides vacant, on Falling creek survey 82. Oct. 10, 1784, p. 43.

**BUSSEY, THOMAS.** 287½ acres, Washington Co., bounded N. & E. vacant, S. John Rogers, W. Jno. Island. Cut by branch of Eland creek, survey 83. Nov. 8, 1784, p. 44.

**BEARD, EDMOND.** 287½ acres, Washington Co., bounded N. Benj. Jenkins, E. Thos. Hartshorn, S. Henry Townsend, W. Fitzpatrick, on Richland creek survey 84. Oct. 18, 1784, p. 44.

**BOSTICK, NATHAN.** 287½ acres, Washington Co., bounded N. & E. vacant, S. Andrew Gordon, W. Richard Call, survey 85. June 10, 1784, p. 45.

**BROWNSON, NATHAN.** 1,150 acres, Washington Co., bounded all sides vacant. Cut by Rooty creek bottom, survey 86. Nov. 16, 1784, p. 45.

**BOWIE, REASON.** 287½ acres, Washington Co., bounded N. Thornton, E. Fitzgerald, S. Wheeler, W. Ramsey, on Richland creek, survey 87. Oct. 19, 1784, p. 46.

**ALLEN, JAMES.** 287½ acres, Washington Co., bounded N. & W. vacant, E. Surveyed, S. 12 miles Beaverdam creek, survey 88. Oct. 21, 1784, p. 46.

**BENTLEY, JOHN.** 287½ acres, Washington Co., bounded all sides vacant. Cut S. to N. by Town creek, survey 89. Nov. 15, 1784, p. 47.

**BURKE, JOHN.** 287½ acres, Washington Co., bounded W. Reddick, other sides vacant. Cut E. to W. by forks of Buffalo creek, survey 90. Nov. 1, 1784, p. 47.

## BOUNTY SURVEYS. 253

**AYRES, WILLIAM.** 287½ acres, Washington Co., bounded N. Jno. Williams, other sides vacant. Cut S. to N. by N. fork of Buffalo creek, survey 91. Nov. 6, 1784, p. 48.

**BISHOP, WILLIAM.** 287½ acres, Washington Co., bounded S. Rocky creek, other sides vacant, survey 92. Nov. 3, 1784, p. 48.

**BARNETT, JOSHUA.** 287½ acres, Washington Co., bounded N. Williams & Perkins, E. Jno. Pitman, S. Green & Christmas, W. vacant, survey 93. Nov. 7, 1784, p. 49.

**BRADLEY, ABRAHAM.** 230 acres, Washington Co., bounded S. Tennill, other sides vacant, on Reserve, survey 94. Nov. 27, 1784, p. 49.

**BARFIELD, RICHARD.** 287½ acres, Washington Co., bounded N. Ed. Young, E. Pitman, S. & W. Rocky creek, survey 95. Nov. 7, 1784, p. 50.

**AYCOCK, RICHARD.** 575 acres, Washington Co., bounded N. Oconee river, E. & S. vacant, W. Big creek & Smith, survey 96. June 4, 1784, p. 50.

**ACORD, JOHN.** 287½ acres, Washington Co., bounded all sides vacant, survey 97. Oct. 28, 1784, p. 51.

**ALEXANDER, JOHN LISTON.** 287½ acres, Washington Co., bounded all sides vacant, survey 98. June 11, 1784, p. 51.

**BARNETT, CLABURN.** 287½ acres, Washington Co., bounded N. Shoulderbone creek, other sides vacant, survey 99. June 9, 1784, p. 52.

**RAYFIELD, SPENCER.** 230 acres, Washington Co., bounded E. Tennill, other sides vacant, on Oconee river, on Reserve, survey 100. Nov. 27, 1784, p. 52.

**BLOUNT, JACOB (HEIRS OF).** 690 acres, Washington Co., bounded N. & W. vacant, S. Robt. Mosby, E. Jas. Houston. Cut by South fork of Oconee river, survey 101. Dec. 9, 1875, p. 53.

**BATES, JOHN.** 287½ acres, Washington Co., bounded all sides vacant, on Shoulderbone creek, survey 102. June 10, 1784, p. 53.

**BROWN, ALLEN.** 287½ acres, Washington Co., bounded N. fork of Buffalo creek, E. & S. vacant, W. Wm. Welch, survey 103. Nov. 1, 1784, p. 54.

**ALEXANDER, ASA.** 287½ acres, Washington Co., bounded all sides surveyed, on Rocky creek ford of Shoulderbone creek, survey 104. Sept. 18, 1784, p. 54.

**BOOKER, CAPT. GIDEON.** 690 acres, Washington Co., bounded N. Littleberry Mosely, E. & S. vacant, W. Oconee river, survey 105. Oct. 15, 1784, p. 55.

**BELL, HUGH.** 230 acres, Washington Co. (on Reserve), bounded N. Wm. Gibson, other sides vacant, on Sugar creek, survey 106. Dec. 6, 1784, p. 55.

254          ROSTER OF THE REVOLUTION.

BUCKHALTER, JOSHUA. 690 acres, Washington Co., bounded E. Ogeechee river, other sides vacant, survey 108. Oct. 12, 1784, p. 56.

BURNEY, RANDALL. 287½ acres, Washington Co., bounded S. North fork of Ohoopee river, other sides vacant, survey 109. Mar. 25, 1785, p. 57.

BURFORD, WILLIAM. 287½ acres, Washington Co., bounded N. Buford, E. & W. unknown, S. Benj. Jenkins, on Richland creek, survey 113. Oct. 26, 1784, p. 59.

BEOHOM, WILLIAM. 287½ acres, Washington Co., bounded S. survey, E. Berkley, & Christmas, S. survey & vacant, survey 114. April 14, 1785, p. 59.

BRACK, ELEAZER. 287½ acres, Washington Co., bounded N. Williamson's Swamp creek, other sides vacant, survey 116. March 25, 1785, p. 60.

BARTLEY, JOHN. 287½ acres, Washington Co., bounded S. grantee, W. Zachariah Lamar, other sides vacant, survey 117. May 5, 1785, p. 61.

COBB, EZEKIEL. 287½ acres, Washington Co., bounded N. Geo. Powell, E. vacant, S. & W. Ogeechee river, survey 119. May 1, 1785, p. 62.

COLLINS, JOHN. 287½ acres, Washington Co., bounded all sides vacant, on Buffalo creek, survey 120. Nov. 12, 1785, p. 62.

CHISHOLM. 230 acres (on Reserve), Washington Co., bounded all sides vacant. Cut N. to S. by Ohoopee creek, survey 121. Nov. 27, 1784, p. 63.

CAMPBELL, JOHN. 230 acres (on Reserve), Washington Co., bounded N. Chisholm, E. Bradley Stennie, W. Spencer Rayfield, survey 122. Nov. 28, 1784, p. 63. All sides vacant, on Buffalo creek, survey 124. June 7, 1784, p. 64.

COATES, NATHANIEL. 287½ acres, Washington Co., bounded all sides vacant, on Buffalo creek, survey 124. June 7, 1784, p. 64.

CRESWELL, DAVID. 184 acres, Washington Co., bounded N. Wallace & Manning, E. Col. Napier, S. & W. survey, survey 126. May 9, 1785, p. 65.

CRESWELL, DAVID. 100 acres (part of bounty), Washington Co., bounded W. Pannill, E. Oconee river, S. & W. Shields, survey 129. June 8, 1785, p. 67.

COLLINS, JOHN. 230 acres (Bounty Reserve), Washington Co., bounded E. Clement Narsh, other sides vacant. Cut by Rock creek, survey 131. July 3, 1784, p. 68.

CATCHINGS, MEREDITH. 287½ acres, Washington Co., bounded S. Daniel Danielly, other sides vacant, on Fishing creek, survey 132. June 3, 1784, p. 69.

CARSON, THOMAS. 287½ acres, Washington Co., bounded N. & E. vacant, S. Wilson, W. Wooten, survey 133. July 10, 1784, p. 69.

## BOUNTY SURVEYS.

**CLARKE, JOHN SEBR.** 287½ acres, Washington Co., bounded N. & W. vacant, E. Ogeechee river, S. Pleasant Goodall. Cut by Dead river, survey 134, July 6, 1784, p. 70.

**CUNNINGHAM, COL. JOHN.** 500 acres, Washington Co., bounded N. Newill, Walton, E. & S. vacant, S. Wm. Sturgeon, on Rocky creek fork of Shoulderbone creek, survey 135. Nov. 20, 1784, p. 70.

**CAMPBELL, WILLIAM.** 287½ acres, Washington Co., bounded N. Marshall, E. vacant, S. Jno. Harrington, W. Oconee river, survey 136. June 4, 1784, p. 71.

**CAWTHORN, JOSIAH.** 287½ acres, Washington Co., bounded N. Williamson's swamp, other sides vacant, survey 138. March 25, 1785, p. 72.

**CRUTCHFIELD, JOHN.** 287½ acres, Washington Co., bounded N. Young, E. Whitaker, S. Hogg, W. vacant, on Shoulderbone creek, survey 139. Nov. 14, 1784, p. 72.

**CAWTHORN, JOSHIA.** 287½ acres, Washington Co., bounded all sides vacant, on Williamson's Swamp creek, survey 140. Mar. 26, 1785, p. 73.

**CARNEY, MATTHEW.** 230 acres (Bounty Reserve), Washington Co., bounded N. Adamson, E. & S. vacant, W. Oconee river, survey 141. Oct. 10, 1784, p. 73.

**COLEMAN, JOHN.** 287½ acres, Washington Co., bounded W. Rogers, other sides vacant, on Big creek, survey 142. June 7, 1784, p. 74.

**CASTLEBERRY, JACOB.** 287½ acres, Washington Co., on island of Oconee river, bounded N. Thrice, & Catchings, survey 143. June 2, 1784, p. 74.

**CANDLER, WILLIAM.** 287½ acres, Washington Co., bounded S. Williamson's Swamp creek, other sides vacant, survey 144. July 1, 1784, p. 75.

**COLEMAN, JOHN.** 287½ acres, Washington Co., bounded N. Palmer, other sides vacant. Cut SE. to NW. by Town creek, survey 145. Nov. 14, 1784, p. 75.

**CARTLEDGE, SAMUEL.** 287½ acres, Washington Co., bounded N. Dixon, E. & W. vacant, S. Michael Smalley, survey 146. June 29, 1784, p. 76.

**CATCHINGS, SEYMOUR.** 575 acres, Washington Co., bounded all sides vacant. Cut E. to W. by Sandy creek, survey 147. June 16, 1784, p. 76.

**CLOUD, JEREMIAH.** 287½ acres, Washington Co., bounded N. & W. vacant, E. Rocky creek, S. vacant, W. Bishop, survey 148. Nov. 4, 1784, p. 77.

**CLARKE, GIBSON.** 287½ acres, Washington Co., bounded E. Jeremiah Cloud, other sides vacant, on Oconee river, survey 149. June 27, 1784, p. 77.

Henry Hartley, S. Ogeechee river, survey 150. July 3, 1784, p. 78.

**CONE, WILLIAM**—287½ acres, Washington Co., bounded N. & W. vacant, E.

**CRAWFORD, JOHN.** 287½ acres, Washington Co., bounded N. Jas. Lesley, E. Wm. Wallace, S. Thos. Taylor, W. Altamaha river, survey 151. June 19, 1784, p. 78.

**CALK, JAMES, JR.** 287½ acres, Washington Co., bounded all sides vacant, on Griffin fork of Williamson's swamp, survey 152. July 14, 1784, p. 79.

**CANDLER, HENRY.** 287½ acres, Washington Co., bounded S. Sanders Walker, other sides vacant. Cut by Buck creek, survey 153. Nov. 10, 1784, p. 79.

**CURLE, JOHN.** 287½ acres, Washington Co., bounded N. Youngblood, E. Beasley, S. Jesse Sanders, W. vacant, survey 154. June 10, 1784, p. 80.

**CLARKE, MOSES.** 287½ acres, Washington Co., bounded all sides vacant, on Buffalo creek, survey 155. Oct. 23, 1784, p. 80.

**COLEMAN, JAMES.** 287½ acres, Washington Co., bounded N. Buffalo creek, other sides vacant, survey 156. Dec. 29, 1784, p. 81.

**CUNNINGHAM, WILLIAM.** 287½ acres, Washington Co., bounded N. Geo. Rowland, E. Oliver & Oconee river, S. Benj. Greene, W. vacant, survey 157. June 8, 1784, p. 81.

**COLEMAN, JAMES.** 287½ acres, Washington Co., bounded all sides vacant, on Swift creek branch of Buffalo creek, survey 158. April 11, 1785, p. 82.

**CAMP, JOSEPH.** 287½ acres, Washington Co., bounded N. vacant, E. Hickory creek, S. Williamson's swamp, W. Richard Night, survey 159. June 12, 1784, p. 82.

**CASTELLO, MICHAEL.** 287½ acres, Washington Co., bounded N. Jno. Kieth, E. Dead river, S. Ohoopee river & Jno. Chandler, W. Oconee river, survey 161. June 1, 1784, p. 84.

**CHAVES, JEREMIAH.** 287½ acres, Washington Co., bounded N. Wilson, Rogers, E., S. & W. vacant, on branch of Big creek, survey 162. June 23, 1784, p. 84.

**CURRY, NICHOLAS.** 287½ acres, Washington Co., bounded N. & E. vacant, S. J. H. Harvey, W. Oconee river, survey 163. June 10, 1784, p. 84.

**CALK, JAMES.** 287½ acres, Washington Co., bounded N. Candler, other sides vacant, survey 164. Nov. 1, 1784, p. 85.

**CHILDRE, THOMAS.** 287½ acres, Washington Co., bounded W. Buffalo creek, other sides vacant, survey 167. May 3, 1785, p. 86.

**COOKE, GEORGE.** 287½ acres, Washington Co., bounded N. vacant, & Oconee river, E. & S. Daniel Murphy, W. vacant, survey 169. June 11, 1784, p. 87.

**CRISPUS, JAMES.** 287½ acres, Washington Co., bounded N. Newsom, E. Long, S. & W. vacant, survey 171. Aug. 13, 1784, p. 88.

## BOUNTY SURVEYS.

**CAINE, JOHN.** 287½ acres, Washington Co., bounded S. John Eaddy, other sides vacant, on Buffalo creek, survey 172. July 6, 1784, p. 89.

**DEAN, THOMAS.** 287½ acres, Washington Co., bounded N. Daniel Young, E. Shoulderbone creek, other sides vacant, survey 173. June 6, 1784, p. 89.

**DAVIS, ABSOLEM.** 575 acres, Washington Co., bounded N. & E. vacant, S. Abm. Landers, W. Oconee river, survey 174. June 18, 1784, p. 90.

**DAY, HENRY.** 287½ acres, Washington Co., bounded E. Moses Hill, other sides vacant. Cut by branch of Buffalo creek, survey 175. June 24, 1784, p. 90.

**DARDEN, GEORGE.** 287½ acres, Washington Co., bounded all sides vacant. Cut N. & S. by fork of Buffalo creek, survey 176. April 15, 1785, p. 91.

**DARDIN, JOHN.** 287½ acres, Washington Co., bounded W. Jesse Thompson, others vacant, on Town creek, survey 177. June 4, 1784, p. 91.

**DAVIS, CLEMTIUS.** 287½ acres, Washington Co., bounded N. & W., vacant, E. Buffalo creek, S. Saml. Braswell, survey 178. Mar. 10, 1785, p. 92.

**DAVIS, MOSES.** 287½ acres, Washington Co., bounded all sides vacant, on Williamson's Swamp creek and Buffalo creek, survey 179. May 4, 1785, p. 92.

**DARDIN, GEORGE.** 287½ acres, Washington Co., bounded all sides vacant. Cut by Sandy creek and tributaries, survey 180. June 5, 1784, p. 93.

**DUKE, WILLIAM.** 287½ acres, Washington Co., bounded N. & W. vacant, E. William Pope, S. William Hammiten, on Shoulderbone creek, survey 181. June 10, 1784, p. 93.

**DOUGLAS, JOHN.** 287½ acres, Washington Co., bounded N. Jos. Tharpe, E. Oconee river, S. Stephen Hayman, W. vacant, survey 182. June 10, 1784, p. 94.

**DARSEY, JAMES.** 287½ acres, Washington Co., bounded N. vacant, E. & S. Oconee river, W. grantee, survey 183. June 3, 1784, p. 94.

**DAVIS, WILLIS.** 575 acres, Washington Co., bounded N. & E. vacant, S. 12 miles Beaverdam creek of Shoulderbone creek, survey 184. Oct. 23, 1784, p. 95.

**DENNIS, JOHN.** 287½ acres, Washington Co., bounded N. David Robertson, E. & W. vacant, S. Isaac Dennis. Cut by N. fork of Buffalo creek, survey 185, Dec. 10, 1784, p. 95.

**DUKE, BUCKNER.** 287½ acres, Washington Co., bounded S. Clarke & vacant, other sides vacant. Cut by Log Dam creek, survey 186. Jan. 6, 1785, p. 96.

**DUNCAN, MATTHEW.** 460 acres, Washington Co., bounded N. Abm. Landers, E. Gilbert Campbell, S. Wm. Anderson, W. Oconee river, survey 187. June 2, 1784, p. 96.

De La PLAIGNE, MAJOR PETER EMANUEL. 290 acres (on Reserve), Washington Co., bounded N. Major Handley, E. & W. vacant, S. Paxton & John Chisholm, on Crooked creek, survey 188. Nov. 23, 1784, p. 97.

DAY, ROBERT, JR. 287½ acres, Washington Co., bounded all sides surveyed, or vacant, survey 189. Dec. 14, 1784, p. 97.

DENNISON, DANIEL. 287½ acres, Washington Co., bounded N. Daniel Whitaker, E. Benj. Wells, S. Benj. Nichols, W. Jas. Hogg, on Rocky fork of Shoulderbone creek, survey 190. Nov. 15, 1784, p. 98.

DARBE, RICHARD. 287½ acres, Washington Co., bounded N. & W. vacant, E. Thos. Gray, S. Wm. Courton, on Fork of Buffalo creek, survey 191. Nov. 1, 1784, p. 98.

DARCEY, BENJ. 287½ acres, Washington Co., bounded N. Wm. Fleming, other sides vacant, on Ct. Ohoopee river, survey 192. April 26, 1785, p. 99.

DARCEY, JAMES. 287½ acres, Washington Co., bounded N. grantee, E. Oconee river, S. vacant, W. Wm. Wash, survey 193. June 4, 1784, p. 99.

DAVIS, BENJ.—287½ acres, Washington Co., bounded N. & W. vacant, E. Wm. Cone, S. Ogeechee river, survey 194. July 4, 1784, p. 100.

DAVIS, SAMUEL. 287½ acres, Washington Co., bounded N. vacant, E. Williamson's Swamp creek, S. Robert Owens, W. Absolom Jackson, survey 195. June 23, 1784, p. 100.

DOUGLAS, WILLIAM. 287½ acres, Washington Co., bounded S. Ogeechee river, other sides vacant, survey 196. April 12, 1784, p. 101.

DAVIS, WILLIAM. 287½ acres, Washington Co., bounded N. Island creek, other sides vacant, survey 197. Oct. 28, 1784, p. 101.

DIXON, EDWARD, SR. 287½ acres, Washington Co., bounded S. Sanders Walker, other sides vacant, on branches of Town creek, survey 198. Nov. 17, 1784, p. 102.

DUKE, HEIRS OF JAMES. 287½ acres, Washington Co., bounded W. Samuel Alexander, other sides vacant, survey 199. May 31, 1784. On branch of Richmond creek, p. 102.

DIXON, DAVID. 575 acres, Washington Co., bounded E. Moss & Greaswell, other sides vacant, on Shoulderbone creek, survey 100. June 9, 1784, p. 103.

DANIEL, BENJ. 287½ acres, Washington Co., bounded N. Fort, other sides vacant. Cut by Buckeye creek, survey 201. Aug. 13, 1784, p. 103.

DAVENPORT, DR. THOMAS. 460 acres (on Reserve), Washington Co., bounded N. & E. vacant, S. Montfort, W. Chisholm, on Oconee river, survey 207. Oct. 15, 1784, p. 106.

BOUNTY SURVEYS. 259

**DAVENPORT, DR. THOMAS.** 920 acres (triangle), Washington Co., bounded NE. grantee & Chisholm, S. Franklin Coline, NW. vacant, survey 208. Nov. 15, 1784, p. 107.

**DOUGLAS, ALEXANDER.** 287½ acres, Washington Co., bounded all sides surveyed, or vacant, survey 209. Aug. 5, 1784, p. 107.

**DUNCAN, LIEUT. DAVID.** 460 acres (on Reserve), Washington Co., bounded all sides vacant or surveyed, on branch of Oconee river, survey 210. Feb. 21, 1785, p. 108.

**DUNCAN, LIEUT. JAMES.** 460 acres (on Reserve), Washington Co., bounded all sides vacant, or surveyed, survey 211. Feb. 20, 1785, p. 108.

**ELLIS, ROBERT.** 230 acres (on Reserve), Washington Co., bounded W. South fork of Oconee river, other sides vacant, survey 212. July 7, 1784, p. 109.

**ELLIS, STEPHEN.** 287½ acres, Washington Co., bounded N. Benj. Porter, E. Richland creek, S. Col. Napier, W. Benj. Porter, survey 213. Jan. 3, 1785, p. 109.

**EADDY, JOHN.** 287½ acres, Washington Co., bounded N. Nathl. Coates, E. & W. vacant, S. John Carnes, survey 214. July 6, 1784, p. 110.

**EAVES, NATHANIEL.** 230 acres (on Reserve), Washington Co., bounded E. Oconee river, other sides vacant, survey 215. Nov. 20, 1784, p. 110.

**EILAND, JOHN.** 287½ acres, Washington Co., bounded N. Burford & Walker, other sides vacant. Cut by Island creek, survey 216. Nov. 8, 1784, p. 111.

**FULLER, JOSHUA.** 287½ acres, Washington Co., bounded NW. Thomas, NE. Glascock, & Fuller, survey 217. Jan. 4, 1784, p. 111.

**EILAND, ABSOLEM.** 287½ acres, Washington Co., bounded E. Wright, other sides vacant, survey 218. June 28, 1785, p. 112.

**EVANS, STEPHEN.** 230 acres (on Reserve), Washington Co., bounded S. Capt. Moseley, other sides vacant, survey 219. Oct. 15, 1784, p. 112.

**FLUKER, JOHN.** 287½ acres, Washington Co., bounded N. Bishop & Burke, E. vacant, S. Tripp, W. Carter, survey 221. July 5, 1784, p. 113.

**FLUKER, OWEN.** 287½ acres, Washington Co., bounded S. Wm. Ayres, other sides vacant. Cut by Buffalo creek, survey 222. Nov. 1, 1784, p. 114.

**FLEMING, WILLIAM.** 287½ acres, Washington Co., bounded N. Jared Irvin, other sides vacant, survey 223. June 10, 1784, p. 114.

**GIBBS, WILLIAM.** 230 acres (on Reserve), Washington Co., bounded N. Thos. Lester, E. & W. vacant, S. Hugh Bell, survey 224. Dec. 6, 1784, p. 115.

**FULLER, JOHN.** 287½ acres, Washington Co., bounded N. & W. vacant, E. & S. Henry, Candler, survey 225. Nov. 1, 1784, p. 115.

**PANNILL, COL. JOSEPH.** 300 acres (on Reserve), Washington Co., bounded N. grantee, E. Oconee river, S. vacant, W. Greenbrier creek, survey 226. July 2, 1784, p. 116.

**FENN, JOHN.** 287½ acres, Washington Co., bounded N. & E. vacant, S. Spencer Reeves, W. Offutt, survey 227. Nov. 16, 1784, p. 116.

**FOSTER, WILLIAM.** 575 acres, Washington Co., bounded N. & W. unknown, E. Alex Moore, S. Oconee river, survey 230. June 10, 1784, p. 118.

**FINCHWELL, JOSEPH.** 287½ acres, Washington Co., bounded N. & E. vacant, S. Jas. Wright, W. Oconee river, survey 231. June 3, 1784, p. 118.

**FLEMING, ROBERT.** 287½ acres, Washington Co., bounded N. Wm. Blanchard, E. Jas. Pugh, S. Chas. William, W. Oconee river, survey 232. June 9, 1784, p. 119.

**FUSELL, EZRA.** 287½ acres, Washington Co., bounded N. Jno. Braswell, E. & S. vacant, W. Williamson's Swamp creek, survey 233. July 22, 1784, p. 119.

**GILLILAND, WILLIAM.** 575 acres, Washington Co., bounded N. Thos. Gilliland, E. Wright & Rogers, S. & W. vacant, survey 234. Oct. 12, 1784, p. 120.

**GRAVES, RICHARD.** 287½ acres, Washington Co., bounded N. Wm. Anderson, E. vacant, S. Jno. Whitesides, W. Oconee river, survey 135. June 23, 1784, p. 120.

**GREER, THOMAS.** 575 acres, Washington Co., bounded S. Harris creek, other sides vacant, survey 236. June 17, 1784, p. 121.

**GILLILAND, THOMAS.** 287½ acres, Washington Co., bounded N. & W. vacant, E. Wm. Gilliland, S. Wm. Gilliland, survey 237. July 12, 1784, p. 121.

**FEW, IGNATIUS.** 287½ acres, Washington Co., bounded all sides vacant. Cut by Buffalo creek, survey 243, May 6, 1784, p. 124.

**FEW, BENJAMIN.** 287½ acres, Washington Co., bounded N. Williamson's Swamp creek, other sides vacant, survey 245. Sept. 5, 1785, p. 125.

**FEW, BENJAMIN.** 287½ acres, Washington Co., bounded N. Ogeechee river, E. & W. grantee, S. vacant, survey 247. May 9, 1785, p. 126.

**GARDNER, LEWIS.** 287½ acres, Washington Co., bounded N. Wm. Gardner, E. vacant, S. Haney, W. Oconee river, survey 251. June 8, 1784, p. 128.

**GRIMSLEY, JOHN.** 287½ acres, Washington Co., bounded S. Williamson's Swamp creek, other sides vacant, survey 252. July 2, 1784, p. 129.

**GRIER, ROBERT.** 287½ acres, Washington Co., bounded N. &. E. vacant, S. Thos. Vickers, W. Buffalo creek, survey 253. Oct. 6, 1784, p. 129.

**GRIER, AARON.** 287½ acres, Washington Co., bounded N. Bishop, E. Davis, S. & W. vacant, survey 255. July 1, 1784, p. 130.

## BOUNTY SURVEYS.

**GARRETT, JOHN.** 287½ acres, Washington Co., bounded N. & W. vacant, E. Benj. Davis, S. Ogeechee river, survey 156. July 4, 1784, p. 131.

**GOULSBY, JONATHAN.** 287½ acres, Washington Co., bounded N. Wm. Morgan, E. & S. vacant, W. Jno. Ragan. Cut by Eiland creek, survey 257. Nov. 8, 1784, p. 131.

**GLAMKIN, JOHN.** 287½ acres, Washington Co., bounded E. John Jones, other sides vacant, Indian trading path on West, survey 259. June 5, 1784, p. 132.

**GRIFFIN, SAMUEL.** 287½ acres, Washington Co., bounded N. Oconee river, other sides vacant, survey 260. June 5, 1784, p. 133.

**GREY, THOMAS.** 287½ acres, Washington Co., bounded E. Courton, other sides vacant. Cut by Buffalo creek, survey 261. Nov. 1, 1784, p. 133.

**GREEN, THOMAS.** 287½ acres, Washington Co., bounded S. Long & Fort, other sides vacant. Cut by Fox, survey 262. Aug. 11, 1784, p. 134.

**GAMBLE, JOHN.** 287½ acres, Washington Co., bounded N. & E. vacant, S. Beaverdam of Richland creek, W. Jno. White, survey 263. June 19, 1784, p. 134.

**GREENE, BENJAMIN.** 287½ acres, Washington Co., bounded N. Lawson, E. vacant, S. Cunningham, W. Oconee river, survey 264. June 8, 1784, p. 135.

**GLASS, JOEL.** 287½ acres, Washington Co., bounded N. Jno. Glass, E. vacant, S. Wilkes Co. Line, W. branch of Big creek, survey 265. June 10, 1784, p. 135.

**GRANT, PETER.** 575 acres Washington Co., bounded N. Oconee river, other sides vacant or surveyed, survey 266. June 10, 1784, p. 136.

**GLASS, JOHN.** 287½ acres, Washington Co., bounded N. fork of Big creek, E. & S. vacant, W. Thos. Wellborn, survey 267. June 10, 1784, p. 136.

**GASTON, ALEXANDER.** 460 acres, Washington Co., bounded N. & W. vacant, E. Matthews, S. surveyed. Cut by branch of Oconee river, survey 268. Dec. 16, 1784, p. 137.

**GREEN, THOMAS.** 287½ acres, Washington Co., bounded all sides vacant, survey 269. April 27, 1784, p. 137.

**GERMANY, WILLIAM.** 287½ acres, Washington Co., bounded N. & W. vacant, E. Altamaha river, S. Philip Griner, survey 270. Oct. 18, 1784, p. 138.

**HARVEY, JOEL.** 287½ acres, Washington Co., bounded N. branch of Williamson's creek, other sides vacant, survey 271. June 28, 1784, p. 138.

**HOGG, JAMES.** 287½ acres, Washington Co., bounded W. Wilkes Co. Line, other sides vacant, on branch of Little river, survey 272. Oct. 18, 1784, p. 139.

HOGG, WILLIAM. 287½ acres, Washington Co., bounded E. Thos. Shaw, other sides vacant. Cut by Beaverdam fork of Richland creek, survey 273. July 4, 1784, p. 139.

HARBRICK, MICHAEL. 287½ acres, Washington Co., bounded all sides vacant. Cut by branch of Williamson's Swamp creek, survey 274. June 19, 1784, p. 140.

HOUSLEY, WELDON. 345 acres, Washington Co., bounded S. Williamson's Swamp creek, other sides vacant, survey 276. July 8, 1784, p. 141.

HILL, MOSES. 287½ acres, Washington Co., bounded N. Thos. Ramsey, other sides vacant, on Buffalo creek, survey 277. June 27, 1784, p. 141.

HATCHER, JOHN. 287½ acres, Washington Co., bounded all sides vacant, on Williamson's Swamp creek, survey 278. Nov. 24, 1784, p. 142.

HADDEN, WILLIAM. 287½ acres, Washington Co., bounded N. Pig creek, E. & W. vacant, S. Long & vacant, survey 279. July 4, 1784, p. 142.

HOUSTON, JOHN. 287½ acres, Washington Co., bounded N. Frederick Francis, E. Oconee river, S. Wm. Houstoun, W. vacant, survey 281. June 10, 1784, p. 143.

HOGG, JAMES. 575 acres, Washington Co., bounded all sides vacant, on Buffalo creek, survey 282. June 30, 1784, p. 144.

HOGG, WILLIAM. 287½ acres, Washington Co., bounded all sides vacant, on N. fork Shoulderbone creek, survey 283. June 10, 1784, p. 144.

HOWELL, NATHANIEL. 287½ acres, Washington Co., bounded all sides vacant. Cut by Richland creek and tributaries, survey 285. June 3, 1784, p. 145.

HEARD, STEPHEN. 287½ acres, Washington Co., bounded N. Rocky creek & Walker, E. Jno. Eiland, S. Perkins & Sapp, W. Rocky creek, survey 287. Nov. 10, 1784, p. 146.

HARPER, JOSEPH. 345 acres, Washington Co., bounded N. Sullivan & Scott, E. vacant, S. Fluker, & Whatley, W. Oconee river, survey 288. July 13, 1784, p. 147.

HARRINGTON, THOMAS. 287½ acres, Washington Co., bounded N. & W. vacant, E. Patrk. Vance, S. Gibson Clarke, on Oconee river, survey 289. June 29, 1784, p. 147.

HAMILTON, THOMAS. 575 acres, Washington Co., bounded N. Hez. Bussey, & Wm. Wilkins, E. Jno. Tankersley, S. Abednego Wright, W. vacant & Benj. Scott, survey 290. July 13, 1784, p. 148.

HARVEY, JOHN. 287½ acres, Washington Co., bounded N. Randal Jackson, E. & W. vacant, S. James Ryan, survey 291. July 14, 1784, p. 148.

## BOUNTY SURVEYS.

**HANNAH, THOMAS.** 575 acres, Washington Co., bounded all sides vacant, or surveyed, on Island creek, survey 292. Dec. 14, 1784, p. 149.

**HOWELL, DAVID.** 287½ acres, Washington Co., bounded N. vacant, E. Robt. Allen, S. Oconee river, W. Robt. Patterson, survey 293. June 7, 1784, p. 149.

**HARVEY, MICHAEL.** 287½ acres, Washington Co. (diamond), bounded N. Peter Jackson & vacant, S. vacant & Randal Jackson, survey 295. June 7, 1784, p. 150.

**HEWITT, WILLIAM.** 287½ acres, Washington Co., bounded N. & E. vacant, S. Jas. McMinn, W. Abm. Dennis, on Buffalo creek, survey 295. June 7, 1784, p. 150.

**HARTLE, HENRY.** 287½ acres, Washington Co., bounded N. Ogeechee river, other sides vacant, survey 296. July 3, 1784, p. 151.

**HEARD, JOHN, SR.** 287½ acres, Washington Co., bounded N. Stewart, E. vacant, S. vacant, W. Heirs of Jno. Thornton, survey 297. Nov. 2, 1784, p. 151.

**HARVEY, THOMAS.** 287½ acres, Washington Co., bounded all sides vacant, on Rake creek, survey 289. Nov. 17, 1784, p. 152.

**HARRIS, TYRE GLENN.** 287½ acres, Washington Co., bounded S. Altamaha river, other sides vacant, survey 299. June 30, 1784, p. 152.

**HANDLEY, GEORGE.** 460 acres (on Reserve), Washington Co., bounded N. Paxton, & Tennill, E. & S. Oconee river, W. Croked creek & Eve, survey 301. Nov. 28, 1784, p. 153.

**HOWARD, RHESA.** 287½ acres, Washington Co., bounded N. Williamson's Swamp creek, E. Isaac Pinson, S. & W. vacant, survey 303. Aug. 30, 1784, p. 154.

**HOLLIDAY, AYRES.** 287½ acres, Washington Co., bounded N. vacant, E. Reddick, S. Thos. Shaw, W. Matthews, survey 304. Nov. 10, 1784, p. 155.

**HOOF, SAMUEL.** 287½ acres, Washington Co., bounded (triangle) NE. Richland creek, S. vacant, NW. Little Beaverdam creek, survey 305, June 9, 1784, p. 155.

**HILL, JOSHUA.** 287½ acres, Washington Co., bounded N. Jos. Langford, E. vacant, S. Wm. Shaw, W. Altamaha river, survey 306. Oct. 8, 1784, p. 156.

**HARBRICK, NICHOLAS.** 287½ acres, Washington Co., bounded E. Benj. Few, others vacant, survey 308. June 17, 1784, p. 157.

**HATCHER, HENRY.** 287½ acres, Washington Co., bounded N. Jos. Langford, E. Altamaha river, S. Thos. Ayres, W. vacant, survey 309. Oct. 18, 1784, p. 158.

**HANCOCK, GEORGE.** 690 acres (on Reserve), Washington Co., bounded all sides vacant. Cut E. to W. by Rae's creek, survey 310. Dec. 1, 1784, p. 158.

## ROSTER OF THE REVOLUTION.

**HARTSHORN, THOMAS.** 287½ acres, Washington Co., bounded N. Wilkes Co. Line, E. Jas. Hogg, S. & W. vacant. Cut by branch of Little river, survey 311. Oct. 11, 1784, p. 158.

**HARRIS, DAVID.** 862½ acres, Washington Co., bounded all sides vacant. Cut E. to W. by Big creek, survey 312. June 5, 1784, p. 159.

**HEWETT, WILLIAM.** 287½ acres, Washington Co., bounded S. Catahings, other sides vacant, on branch of Shady creek, survey 313. June 21, 1784, p. 159.

**HILL, JOHN.** 287½ acres, Washington Co., bounded N. Dysart, E. vacant, S. Jas. Hill, W. Altamaha river, survey 314. June 26, 1784, p. 160.

**HORN, JESSE,** 287½ acres, Washington Co., bounded E. Nathl. Howell, other sides vacant. Touched SE. corner by Richland creek, survey 315. June 5, 1784, p. 160.

**HILL, JAMES.** 287½ acres, Washington Co., bounded N. & E. vacant, S. Jno. Coleman, W. Wm. Rogers. Cut E. to W. by S. fork of Big creek, survey 316. June 4, 1784, p. 161.

**HILLIARD, JAMES.** 287½ acres, Washington Co., bounded N. & E. vacant, S. Candler, W. Candler, on branch of Town creek, survey 317. Nov. 1, 1784, p. 161.

**HALL, GEORGE.** 287½ acres, Washington Co., bounded S. I. Stewart, & Geo. Foulder, other sides vacant. Cut by branch of Shoulderbone creek, survey 318. Nov. 10, 1784, p. 162.

**HARPER, WILLIAM.** 287½ acres, Washington Co., bounded all sides vacant, survey 319. July 17, 1784, p. 162.

**HARPER, ROBERT.** 287½ acres, Washington Co., bounded all sides vacant. Cut by Rocky creek, a fork of Shoulderbone creek, survey 321. June 12, 1784, p. 163.

**HARPER, GEORGE.** 287½ acres, Washington Co., bounded N. Robt. Harper, other sides vacant. Cut by fork of Shoulderbone creek, survey 322. June 7, 1784, p. 164.

**HILL, JOSHUA.** 287½ acres, Washington Co., bounded N. vacant, E. Wm. Kelly, S. grantee, Jos. Langford, Henry Hatcher, W. Wm. Payne, survey 323. Oct. 18, 1784, p. 164.

**HAMMETT, SITHA.** 287½ acres, Washington Co., bounded N. survey, E. McAlpin, S. & W. vacant, survey 324. June 10, 1784, p. 165.

**HARRIS, NATHAN.** 287½ acres, Washington Co., bounded all sides vacant. Cut N. to S. by Buffalo creek, survey 325. Nov. 17, 1784, p. 165.

**HARVEY, JOHN.** 287½ acres, Washington Co., bounded N. & E. vacant, S. Little Ogeechee river, W. Jas. Averett, survey 326. June 21, 1784, p. 166.

# BOUNTY SURVEYS. 265

**HAYES, ANDREW.** 287½ acres, Washington Co., bounded all sides vacant, or survey, survey 327. May 20, 1784, p. 166.

**JARRETT, ROBERT.** 287½ acres, Washington Co., bounded W. Micajah Williamson, other sides vacant, on Shoulderbone creek, survey 330. July 1, 1784, p. 168.

**JOHNSTON, CALEB.** 287½ acres, Washington Co., bounded all sides vacant. Cut E. to W. by Town creek, survey 331. Mar. 23, 1785, p. 168.

**JACKSON, ISAAC.** 757 acres, Washington Co., bounded all sides vacant, on Shoulderbone creek, survey 332. June 10, 1784, p. 169.

**JOHNSTON, WILLIAM.** 460 acres, Washington Co., bounded (on Reserve), N. & E. vacant, S. Bartlett Martin, W. Sustale, survey 334. Dec. 14, 1784, p. 170.

**JONES, PHILLIP.** 287½ acres, Washington Co., bounded N. & E. vacant, S. Jno. Braswell, W. Jas. Woodruff, survey 337. July 22, 1784, p. 171.

**INMAN, SHADRACK.** 575 acres, Washington Co., bounded all sides vacant, on Shoulderbone creek, survey 338. July 19, 1784, p. 172.

**JACKSON, JOHN.** 287½ acres, Washington Co., bounded N. Wm. Wallace, E. Geo. Fould, S. Ed. Younge, W. vacant, survey 338. June 7, 1784, p. 172.

**JACKSON, JOB.** 287½ acres, Washington Co., bounded N. & W. vacant, E. Henry Taylor, S. McCormack, survey 340. July 5, 1784, p. 173.

**JONES, JOHN.** 287½ acres, Washington Co., bounded W. Jas. McHarland, other sides vacant, on Buffalo creek, survey 341. June 5, 1784, p. 173.

**JACKSON, RANDOLPH.** 287½ acres, Washington Co., bounded N. Jno. Harvey, E. & W. vacant, S. Michael Harvey, survey 342. July 13, 1784, p. 174.

**JOHNSTON, JOHN.** 287½ acres, Washington Co., bounded N. & E. vacant, S. Wm. Kemp, W. Oconee river, survey 343. Aug. 10, 1784, p. 174.

**JACKSON, PETER.** 287½ acres, Washington Co., bounded NW. Michael Harvey, other sides vacant, near Oconee river, survey 344. July 14, 1784, p. 175.

**JONES, FREDERICK.** 287½ acres, Washington Co., bounded N. Randolph Strohakers, E. Oconee river, S. & W. vacant, survey 345. June 8, 1784, p. 175.

**JONES, JESSE.** 287½ acres, Washington Co., bounded S. Asa Merder, other sides vacant, on Buffalo creek, survey 346. June 26, 1784, p. 176.

**JONES, JONATHAN.** 287½ acres, Washington Co., bounded N. Nathan Jones, other sides vacant. Cut N. & S. by Buffalo creek, survey 347. June 5, 1784, p. 176.

**JUSTICE, ISAAC.** 287½ acres, Washington Co., bounded S. Shoulderbone creek, other sides vacant, survey 348. July 21, 1784, p. 177.

**JONES, ELIAS.** 287½ acres, Washington Co., bounded S. Wm. Berchell, other sides vacant, on Buffalo creek, survey 349. June 12, 1784, p. 177.

**JOHNSTON, DANIEL.** 287½ acres, Washington Co., bounded N. Jas. Sanson, E. Napier, S. Jas. Grirsby, W. Barton, on Town creek, survey 350. June 28, 1784, p. 178.

**JENKINS, ARTHUR.** 287½ acres, Washington Co., bounded N. Jno. Sheffield, other sides vacant, on Buffalo creek, survey 351. June 10, 1784, p. 178.

**JACK, SAMUEL.** 520 acres, Washington Co., bounded N. & W. vacant, E. Newell Walton, S. Reeves & Stirk, on Richland creek, survey 352. Nov. 17, 1784, p. 179.

**JONES, WILLIAM.** 287½ acres, Washington Co., bounded all sides vacant, on sides vacant, on Williamson's Swamp creek, survey 353. Aug. 12, 1784, p. 179.

**JONES WILLIAM.** 287½ acres, Washington Co., bounded all sides vacant, on Shoulderbone creek, survey 355. Nov. 22, 1784, p. 180.

**KILGORE, WILLIAM.** 287½ acres, Washington Co., bounded N. Wilkes Co. Line, E. vacant, S. Joiner, W. Gray. Cut by Falling creek, survey 356. Nov. 11, 1784, p. 181.

**CARR, HENRY.** 575 acres, Washington Co., bounded N. & E. vacant, S. Richland creek, W. Wm. Bradley, survey 357. June 4, 1784, p. 181.

**KELLY, WILLIAM, SR.** 287½ acres, Washington Co., bounded N. & W. vacant, E. Ogeechee river, S. Thos. McDowell, survey 358, July 6, 1784, p. 182.

**KILGORE, JOHN.** 179 acres, Washington Co., bounded N. Saml. Hicks, E. Jos. Richardson, S. Chambless, W. unknown, survey 359. July 2, 1786, p. 182.

**KELLY, WILLIAM.** 287½ acres, Washington Co., bounded N. & W. vacant, E. Ogeechee river, S. Jas. McGilton, survey 360. July 8, 1784, p. 183.

**KEMP, WILLIAM.** 575 acres, Washington Co., bounded all sides vacant, on Oconee river, survey 361. Oct. 12, 1784, p. 183.

**KENDRICK, NATHANIEL.** 287½ acres, Washington Co., bounded S. Rocky creek, other sides vacant, survey 362. June 14, 1784, p. 184.

**KELLY, WILLIAM, SR.** 287½ acres, Washington Co., bounded N. Edw. Rogers, other sides vacant, on Foster's branch, survey 363. Aug. 16, 1784, p. 184.

**LANDERS, CAPT. ABRAHAM.** 862½ acres, Washington Co., bounded N. Oconee river, E. & S. vacant, W. John Dean, survey 364. June 17, 1784, p. 185.

**LINN, HEIRS OF JOHN.** 230 acres, Washington Co., bounded (on Reserve) N. Curtiss Linn, E. & W. vacant, S. Heirs of Jno. Patillo, on Oconee river, survey 365. Feb. 10, 1785, p. 185.

BOUNTY SURVEYS. 267

**LAWSON, ROGER.** 287½ acres, Washington Co., bounded N. Eiland, E. vacant, S. & W. Oconee river, survey 366. July 6, 1785, p. 185.

**LINN, CURTISS.** 230 acres, Washington Co. (on Reserve), bounded N. Jas. Houston, E. & W. vacant, S. Heirs of Jno. Linn, on Oconee river, survey 367. Feb. 10, 1784, p. 186.

**LAMB, ABRAHAM.** 287½ acres, Washington Co., bounded N. surveyed, E. vacant, S. Jno. Mann, W. Altamaha river, survey 368. June 22, 1784, p. 187.

**LITHGOE, ROBERT.** 287½ acres, Washington Co., bounded S. grantee, others vacant, survey 369. Oct. 19, 1784, p. 187.

**LETT, REUBEN.** 287½ acres, Washington Co., bounded N. & E. vacant, S. Ogeechee river, W. Francis Pugh, survey 370. July 15, 1784, p. 188.

**LAWSON, HEIRS OF ANDREW.** 287½ acres, Washington Co., bounded E. vacant & grantee, others vacant, on Big creek, survey 372. April 9, 1785, p. 189.

**LESTER, THOMAS.** 230 acres (on Reserve), Washington Co., bounded S. Wm. Gibbs, other sides vacant, on Oconee river, survey 374. Dec. 6, 1784, p. 190.

**LINDSAY, DENNIS.** 575 acres, Washington Co., bounded N. Sheffield, E. & S. vacant, W. Bear creek (improperly called Williamson's swamp), survey 375. July 9, 1784, p. 190.

**LAND, JOHN.** 287½ acres, Washington Co., bounded N. & W. vacant, E. Howell, S. Richland creek, survey 376. June 4, 1784, p. 190.

**LEVERETT, JOHN.** 287½ acres, Washington Co., bounded N. Jno. White, E. & S. vacant, W. Morris Findley, survey 377. April 8, 1785, p. 192.

**LEDBETTER, JOHN.** 287½ acres, Washington Co., bounded N. Bear creek, E. & S. vacant, W. Daniel Evans, survey 378. June 14, 1784, p. 102.

**LANGFORD, MOSES.** 230 acres (on Reserve), Washington Co., bounded all sides vacant, on Oconee river, survey 379. Nov. 13, 1784, p. 192.

**LANGFORD, JOSIAH.** 230 acres, Washington Co., bounded (on Reserve) E. Moses Langford, other sides vacant, on Oconee river, survey 380. Nov. 13, 1784, p. 193.

**LEONARD, ELIJAH.** 287½ acres, Washington Co., bounded N. vacant, E. Wm. Hill, S. & W. unknown, on Fort creek, survey 381. April 8, 1785, p. 193.

**LANGFORD, JOSEPH.** 287½ acres, Washington Co., bounded N. Joshua Hill, E. Altamaha river, S. Hatcher, W. vacant, survey 382. Oct. 18, 1784, p. 194

**LAWSON, THOMAS.** 287½ acres, Washington Co., bounded N. Wm. Wilder, E. vacant, S. unknown, W. Wm. Walker, survey 383. Nov. 5, 1784, p. 194.

**LEGETT, JOHN.** 287½ acres, Washington Co., bounded N. Phillips, E. Zachariah Phillips, S. vacant, W. Phillips. Cut by branch of Oconee river, survey 385. June 12, 1784, p. 195.

## ROSTER OF THE REVOLUTION.

**LEAPHAM, ABRAHAM.** 287½ acres, Washington Co., bounded N. & E. vacant, S. Adam Shaw, W. Jas. McHarland. Cut by Island creek survey 386. June 27, 1784, p. 196.

**LOWE, DANIEL.** 575 acres, Washington Co., bounded all sides vacant. Cut N. & S. by Buffalo creek, survey 387. July 12, 1784, p. 196.

**LAMAR, THOMAS.** 287½ acres, Washington Co., bounded all sides vacant, on Oconee river. June 25, 1784, p. 197.

**LITHGOE, ANDREW.** 287½ acres, Washington Co., bounded N. Dunn, E. & W. unknown, S. vacant, on Richland creek, survey 389. Nov. 20, 1784, p. 197.

**MANNING, ADAM.** 287½ acres, Washington Co., bounded all sides vacant. Cut E. to W. by S. fork of Town creek, survey 390. Jan. 2, 1785, p. 198.

**McINTOSH, HEIRS OF MAJOR LACHLAN.** 720 acres (on Reserve), Washington Co., bounded all sides vacant. Cut E. to W. by branch of Rocky creek, survey 391. Feb. 23, 1785, p. 198.

**MILTON, MAJOR JOHN.** 920 acres, Washington Co. (on Reserve), bounded all sides vacant. Cut N. to S. by Rae's creek, survey 392. Dec. 4, 1784, p. 199.

**MOORE, FRANCIS.** 287½ acres, Washington Co., bounded all sides vacant, on Island creek, survey 393. July 12, 1784, p. 199.

**McINTOSH, GENERAL LACHLAN.** 1,552 acres (on Reserve), Washington Co., bounded N. Maj. Elbert, E. Oconee river, S. grantee, W. Glascock. Cut by Rake creek & Rooty creek, survey 394. Nov. 15, 1784, p. 200.

**McINTOSH, MAJOR WILLIAM.** 920 acres (on Reserve), Washington Co., bounded S. vacant, & Little Oconee river, other sides vacant, survey 395 Nov. 17, 1784, p. 201.

**MIMMS, WILLIAM.** 287½ acres, Washington Co., bounded E. Francis Moore, other sides vacant, survey 396. July 12, 1784, p. 201.

**MOTTE, WILLIAM.** 287½ acres, Washington Co., bounded N. & W. vacant, E. vacant, & Ogeechee river, S. Ogeechee river, survey 397. June 1, 1784, p. 202.

**MOON, SAMUEL.** 287½ acres, Washington Co., bounded N. vacant, E. Oconee river, S. Jas. Red, W. Saml. Rae, survey 398. June 12, 1784, p. 202.

**MANNEN, JOHN.** 287½ acres, Washington Co., bounded all sides vacant. Cut by Buffalo creek, survey 399. June 16, 1784, p. 203.

**MOSELEY, THOMAS.** 287½ acres, Washington Co., bounded N. vacant, & Joshua Bishop, other sides vacant. Cut NW. to SE. by Town creek, survey 400. Sept. 30, 1784, p. 203.

McGILTON, JAMES. 230 acres, Washington Co. (on Reserve), bounded N. Porter, E. N. Perry, other sides vacant, on Oconee river, survey 401. Dec. 16, 1784, p. 204.

MOORE, JOHN. 287½ acres, Washington Co., bounded N. Jno. Dennis, other sides vacant, on Buffalo creek, survey 402. Mar. 1, 1784, p. 204.

McNIEL, DANIEL, JR. 287½ acres, Washington Co., bounded N. vacant, E. Nathl. Hicks, S. Daniel McNair, & Samuel Alexander, W. Ramsey, on branch of Richland creek, survey 403. June 4, 1784, p. 205.

MITCHELL, CHARLES. 850 acres, Washington Co., bounded N. Richard Farrill, other sides vacant. Cut E. to W. by branch of Shoulderbone creek, survey 404. Nov. 20, 1784, p. 205.

McCORMICK, THOMAS. 287½ acres, Washington Co., bounded N. Comer Peak, other sides vacant. Cut by Buffalo creek on N. line, survey 405. Oct. 30, 1784, p. 206.

MAXWELL, LIEUT. JOSIAH. 460 acres (on Reserve), Washington Co., bounded N. Michell, E. Oconee river, S. Pannell, W. vacant, survey 406. July 2, 1784, p. 206.

MOSELEY, BENJ. 287½ acres, Washington Co., bounded S. McClendon, other sides vacant, on branch of Fishing creek, survey 407. June 25, 1784, p. 207.

McALPHIN, ALEXANDER. 575 acres, Washington Co., bounded S. College lands, other sides vacant. Cut N. & S. by Richland creek, survey 408. June 1, 1784, p. 207.

McGILTON, JAMES. 287½ acres, Washington Co., bounded E. Ogeechee river, other sides vacant, survey 410. July 17, 1784, p. 208.

MOSEBY, ROBERT. 460 acres, Washington Co., bounded (on Reserve) N. Allison, E. & S. vacant, W. Blount & Houston. Cut by Oconee river, survey 411. Dec. 7, 1784, p. 209.

MORGAN, MALACIAH. 287½ acres, Washington Co., bounded S. College lands, other sides vacant, on Sandy creek, survey 412. June 24, 1784, p. 209.

MERCER, ASA. 287½ acres, Washington Co., bounded all sides vacant, on Buffalo creek, survey 413. June 26, 1784, p. 210.

McGARRY, ROBERT. 575 acres (triangle), Washington Co., bounded N. Franklin Co. Line, E. Wilkes Co. Line, W. vacant. Cut by Big creek, survey 414. June 11, 1784, p. 210.

MAY, WILLIAM. 287½ acres, Washington Co., bounded N. & W. vacant, E. Jno. Frie, S. Oconee river, survey 415. June 1, 1784, p. 211.

McCLENDON, ISAAC. 287½ acres, Washington Co., bounded N. Coleman & Hill, E. Freeman, S. & W. vacant. Cut by Big creek, survey 416. June 21, 1784, p. 211.

**MITCHELL, JOHN.** 460 acres, Washington Co., bounded N. & W. vacant, E. Oconee river, S. Maxwell, survey 417. July 2, 1784, p. 212.

**MOSELEY, THOMAS.** 287½ acres, Washington Co., bounded all sides vacant. Cut by Boggy Cut creek, survey 418. July 14, 1784, p. 212.

**MAY, JOHN.** 287½ acres, Washington Co., bounded N. & E. vacant, W. Dan'l McNeil (triangle), on Richland creek, survey 419. July 2, 1784, p. 213.

**McGEEHEE, THOMAS.** 287½ acres, Washington Co., bounded N. Baldwin, E. vacant, S. Lewis Crane, W. Kimbrough, survey 420. Nov. 11, 1784, p. 213.

**MARSHALL, ZACHEUS.** 287½ acres, Washington Co., bounded all sides vacant. Cut by Buffalo creek, survey 421. Oct. 26, 1784, p. 214.

**McLEAN, JOHN.** 287½ acres, Washington Co., bounded S. Dill Sapp, other sides vacant, on Rocky creek, survey 422. Nov. 17, 1784, p. 214.

**MATTHEWS, MOSES.** 287½ acres, Washington Co., bounded N. & W. vacant, E. Rocky creek, S. Jas. Matthews, survey 423. Nov. 5, 1784, p. 215.

**McCULLOCH, PATRICK.** 287½ acres, Washington Co., bounded N. Misery branch, other sides vacant, survey 424. June 28, 1784, p. 215.

**MOSS, LEONARD.** 287½ acres, Washington Co., bounded N. & E. vacant, S. Geo. Greasell, W. Thos. Brantley, on Shoulderbone creek, survey 425. June 8, 1784, p. 216.

**MITCHELL, WILLIAM.** 287½ acres, Washington Co., bounded S. Wm. Cone, other sides vacant, on Ogecchee river, survey 426. July 3, 1784, p. 216.

**MOORE, WILLIAM.** 287½ acres, Washington Co., bounded N. & E. vacant, S. Henry Hartle, W. Wm. Mitchell, on Ogeechee river, survey 427. July 3, 1784, p. 217.

**MATTHEWS, JAMES.** 287½ acres, Washington Co., bounded E. Rocky creek, other sides vacant, survey 428. Nov. 5, 1784, p. 217.

**MIMMS, SHADRACK.** 287½ acres, Washington Co., bounded all sides vacant. Cut N. to S. by Shoulderbone creek, survey 429. June 13, 1784, p. 218.

**MORGAN, WILLIAM.** 287½ acres, Washington Co., bounded N. & E. vacant, S. Jonathan, Goulsby, W. Jno. Ragan. Cut N. & S. by Island creek, survey 430. Nov. 8, 1784, p. 218.

**McGARR, CUEN.** 287½ acres, Washington Co., bounded W. Jas. Ragan, other sides vacant. Cut on N. end by Beaverdam creek, survey 431. July 16, 1784, p. 219.

**McCORMICK, BENJAMIN.** 287½ acres, Washington Co., bounded N. & W. vacant, E. Benj. Catchings, S. Jno. Frice, survey 432. July 14, 1784, p. 219.

**MARSHALL, DANIEL.** 287½ acres, Washington Co., bounded N. Dixon, other sides vacant. Cut N. & S. by Fort creek, survey 433. June 29, p. 220.

# BOUNTY SURVEYS.

**MARSHALL, JOSEPH.** 287½ acres, Washington Co., bounded S. Jas Youngblood, other sides vacant, on Deroso's creek, survey 434. Nov. 15, 1784, p. 220.

**MIDDLETON, ROBERT.** 575 acres, Washington Co., bounded N. & W. survey, E. Davis, S. 12 Mile Beaverdam creek, survey 435. Oct. 23, 1784, p. 221.

**MARSHALL, ABRAHAM.** 747½ acres, Washington Co., bounded E. Walker & Seals, other sides vacant. Cut SE. to NW. by Town creek, survey 436. Oct. 30, 1784, p. 221.

**MORGAN, JOHN.** 230 acres, Washington Co., bounded (on Reserve) N. & E. vacant, S. Greenbrier creek, W. Morgan, survey 437. July 9, 1784, p. 222.

**MORGAN, PHILIP.** 230 acres, Washington Co., bounded (on Reserve) E. Jno. Morgan, other sides vacant, on Oconee river, survey 438. July 9, 1784, p. 222.

**MOORE, JONAS.** 287½ acres, Washington Co., bounded N. Jno. Alexander, E. McFarland, S. & W. vacant. Cut by Beaverdam creek, survey 439. June 24, 1784, p. 223.

**MARLER, WILLIAM.** 287½ acres, Washington Co., bounded all sides vacant, on Rocky creek, survey 441. July 13, 1784, p. 224.

**MARTIN, JOHN, JR.** 287½ acres, Washington Co., bounded N. branch of Bear creek, other sides vacant, survey 422. March 31, 1785, p. 224.

**McGRUDER, ZADOCK.** 287½ acres, Washington Co., bounded all sides vacant, on Bear creek, survey 443. Mar. 14, 1785, p. 225.

**McKAY, JAMES.** 575 acres, Washington Co., bounded N. Jno. Bush, E. vacant, S. Jas. Reed, W. Oconee river, survey 444. July 26, 1784, p. 225.

**MIMMS, JOHN.** 287½ acres, Washington Co., bounded all sides vacant, or unknown, on Town creek, survey 445. April 21, 1785, p. 226.

**MOATES, LEVI.** 287½ acres, Washington Co., bounded N. Thomas & Glascock, E. Glascock, S. unknown, W. Wright, on Island creek, survey 446. Jan. 4, 1785, p. 226.

**MARTIN, JAMES.** 287½ acres, Washington Co., bounded E. Jno. Martin, Jr., other sides vacant, survey 447. Mar. 19, 1785, p. 227.

**MARTIN, MELOAN.** 287½ acres, Washington Co., bounded all sides unknown or vacant, on Buffalo creek, survey 449. May 3, 1785, p. 228.

**McMURPHY, DANIEL.** 575 acres, Washington Co., bounded N. Heirs of Geo. Cook, other sides vacant. Cut by Deep creek, survey 450. June 11, 1784, p. 228.

**MATTHEWS, WILLIAM.** 690 acres, Washington Co., bounded N. & W. vacant, E. Oconee river, S. Benj. Porter survey 451. Oct. 10, 1784, p. 229.

**NOLAND, PHILIP.** 287½ acres, Washington Co., bounded N. Anderson, E. vacant, S. Irvin & vacant, W. Big creek, survey 454. July 3, 1784, p. 230.

**NEIL, THOMAS.** 250 acres, Washington Co., bounded N. Awtrey, E. Oconee river, S. Wagner, W. Awtrey, survey 457. June 2, 1784, p. 233.

**OLDHAM, URIAH.** 287½ acres, Washington Co., bounded S. branch of Bear creek, other sides vacant, survey 460, April 12, 1785, p. 233.

**O'BRYAN, JAMES.** 230 acres, Washington Co. (on Reserve), bounded all sides vacant. Cut SE. to NW. by Pearres creek, survey 463. July 5, 1784, p. 235.

**OWENS, ROBERT.** 287½ acres, Washington Co., bounded N. & S. vacant, E. Bear creek, W. Moses Leapham, survey 464. July 23, 1784, p. 235.

**PEWELL, JOSIAH.** 287½ acres, Washington Co., bounded N. Michael Sharp, E. Ogeechee river, S. & W. vacant, survey 465. July 24, 1784, p. 235.

**PHILLIPS, JOEL.** 575 acres, Washington Co., bounded N. branch of Oconee river, other sides vacant, survey 466. June 19, 1784, p. 236.

**PHILLIPS, JOHN.** 287½ acres, Washington Co., bounded all sides vacant. Cut by branch of Buffalo creek, survey 467. May 8, 1785, p. 237.

**PERRETT, ROBERT.** 287½ acres, Washington Co., bounded all sides unknown or vacant, on Buckeye creek, survey 468. Aug. 13, 1784, p. 237.

**PERRETT, JOHN.** 575 acres, Washington Co., bounded N. Wash, E. Oconee river, S. & W. vacant, survey 469. June 27, 1784, p. 238.

**PERRETT, ROBERT.** 287½ acres, Washington Co., bounded N. Buckeye creek, E. & S. vacant, W. Kemp, survey 470. Aug. 4, 1784, p. 238.

**PHILLIPS, JOSEPH.** 575 acres, Washington Co., bounded N. Clayton, E. Jno. Brown, S. College lands, W. vacant. Cut by Richland creek, survey 471. Oct. 19, 1784, p. 239.

**PUGH, JAMES, JR.** 287½ acres, Washington Co., bounded N. branch of Ohoopee river, other sides vacant, survey 472. Mar. 18, 1785, p. 239.

**PATULLO, HEIRS OF JOHN.** 230 acres, Washington Co. (on Reserve), bounded N. Jno. Linn, other sides vacant, survey 473. Feb. 10, 1785, p. 240.

**PEARCE, LIEUT. NATHANIEL.** 460 acres, Washington Co. (on Reserve), bounded N. & W. vacant, E. Oconee river, S. Morrison, survey 474. Nov. 23, 1784, p. 240.

**PERRITT, JOHN.** 287½ acres, Washington Co., bounded N. vacant, other sides surveyed. Cut by Bear creek, survey 475. April 13, 1785, p. 241.

**POWELL, LEWIS.** 287½ acres, Washington Co., bounded N. Jeremiah Bugg, E. Oconee river, S. Arch Hatcher, W. vacant, survey 476. June 9, 1785, p. 241.

# BOUNTY SURVEYS.

**PERKINS, JOHN.** 287½ acres, Washington Co., bounded N. Moose Hill, other sides vacant, survey 478. June 25, 1785, p. 242.

**PERKINS, ABRAHAM.** 287½ acres, Washington Co., bounded N. Sanders Walker, S. vacant, W. vacant, on Buck creek, survey 479. Nov. 14, 1784, p. 243.

**POWELL, GEORGE.** 287½ acres, Washington Co., bounded N. vacant, E. Ezekiel Cobb, S. Ogeechee river, W. Francis Boykin, survey 480. May 1, 1785, p. 243.

**PAXTON WILLIAM.** 230 acres, Washington Co. (on Reserve), bounded N. Chisholm, E. Rayfield, S. vacant, W. De La Plainge. Cut N. & S. by Crooked creek, survey 481. Nov. 27, 1784, p. 244.

**PHILLIPS, ISHAM.** 287½ acres, Washington Co., bounded N. Glascock, E. vacant, S. Abm. Island, W. Glascock, survey 482. Jan. 5, 1785, p. 244.

**PHILLIPS, JOSIAH.** 287½ acres, Washington Co., bounded S. Reynolds, other sides vacant, on Richland creek, survey 483. June 5, 1784, p. 245.

**PINSON, ISAAC.** 287½ acres, Washington Co., bounded N. Williamson's or Bear creek, E. & S. vacant, W. R. Howard, survey 484. Aug. 31, 1784, p. 245.

**POWELL, CADER.** 287½ acres, Washington Co., bounded all sides vacant. Cut E. to W. by branch of Buffalo creek, survey 485. June 17, 1784, p. 246.

**PERRY, ISAAC.** 287½ acres, Washington Co., bounded N. & E. vacant, S. Oconee river, W. Reuben Jackson, survey 486. June 7, 1784, p. 246.

**POUND, REUBEN.** 230 acres (on Reserve), Washington Co., bounded S. Oconee river, other sides vacant, survey 487. Oct. 10, 1784, p. 246.

**PEAK, JOHN.** 287½ acres, Washington Co., bounded all sides vacant. Cut N. to S. by fork of Big creek, survey 488. June 21, 1784, p. 247.

**PERKINS, JOHN.** 287½ acres, Washington Co., bounded N. H. Horton, E. Jno. McFarland, S. vacant, W. Abhm. Leapham. Cut E. & W. by Island creek, survey 489. June 28, 1784, p. 247.

**PAYNE, WILLIAM.** 287½ acres, Washington Co., bounded S. Germany & Ayres, other sides vacant, near Atlamaha river, survey 490. Oct. 18, 1784, P. 247.

**PERKINS, PETER.** 287½ acres, Washington Co., bounded N. Rocky creek, E. Wm. Wilder, S. vacant, W. Wm. Johnston, survey 492. Nov. 7, 1784, p. 248.

**PITMAN, PHILIP.** 287½ acres, Washington Co., bounded N. Wm. Kemp, other sides vacant, survey 493. Aug. 13, 1784, p. 349.

**POPE, WILLIS.** 300 acres, Washington Co., bounded N. & W. vacant, E. John Kimbo, S. Wm. Duke. Cut by branch of Shoulderbone creek, survey 494. July 20, 1784, p. 249.

**PETRIE, DYALL.** 287½ acres, Washington Co., bounded N. & W. vacant, E. Peter Terrill, S. Jno. Oggletree, on Richland creek, survey 495. Dec. 14, 1784, p. 250.

**PHINNEY, LARKIN.** 230 acres, Washington Co., bounded E. Oconee river, other sides vacant, survey 496. June 5, 1784, p. 250.

**PEVEY, PETER.** 287½ acres, Washington Co., bounded N. Ed. Young, E. Matthews, S. vacant, W. Pitman. Cut by branch of Oconee river, survey 497. Nov. 9, 1784, p. 251.

**PATTERSON, ROBERT.** 287½ acres, Washington Co., bounded N. David Howell, E. Oconee river, S. Jno. Duhart, W. vacant, survey 489. June 17, 1784, p. 251.

**POTTS, JOHN.** 287½ acres, Washington Co., bounded N. & E. vacant, S. Wm. McGeehee, W. Oconee river, survey 499. June 11, 1784, p. 252.

**PATTERSON, GIDEON.** 287½ acres, Washington Co., bounded S. Wm. Martin, other sides vacant, survey 500. July 7, 1784, p. 252.

**PAYNE, LIEUT. THOMAS.** 460 acres, Washington Co., bounded (on Reserve) N. Evans, & Montfort, other sides vacant, survey 501. Oct. 15, 1784, p. 253.

**PUGH, JAMES, JR.** 287½ acres, Washington Co., bounded E. Robt. Flemming, other sides vacant, on Pughs Mill creek, survey 502. June 9, 1784, p. 253.

**PANNELL, JOSEPH.** 300 acres, Washington Co., bounded (on Reserve) N. Maxwell, E. Oconee river, S. Pannell, W. vacant, survey 504. July 2, 1784, p. 254.

**PALMER, SOLOMAN.** 287½ acres, Washington Co., bounded N. Jno. Bentley, other sides vacant. Cut by Town creek, survey 505. Nov. 14, 1784, p. 255.

**PALMER, JOHN.** 287½ acres, Washington Co., bounded E. Ogeechee river, other sides vacant, survey 506. July 5, 1784, p. 255.

**ROBERTS, THOMAS.** 287½ acres, Washington Co., bounded N. & W. Williamson's Swamp creek, E. vacant, S. Watson, survey 507. July 2, 1784, p. 256.

**ROWELL, HOWELL.** 287½ acres, Washington Co., bounded N. Ed. Rowell, E. Oconee river, S. Thos. Frederick, W. vacant, survey 508. June 9, 1784, p. 256.

**RED, JAMES.** 287½ acres, Washington Co., bounded N. Samuel Moon, E. Oconee river, S. Wm. Green, W. Deep creek, survey 509. June 12, 1784, p. 257.

**ROBERTS, JONAS.** 287½ acres, Washington Co., bounded N. Surveyed, E. vacant, S. Wm. Green, W. Deep creek, survey 510. June 15, 1784, p. 257.

**RYAN, RICHARD.** 575 acres, Washington Co., bounded N. Oconee river, E. Kelly, S. vacant, W. Jno. Hobbs, survey 511. June 8, 1784, p. 258.

**JACKSON, TIMOTHY.** 287½ acres, Washington Co., bounded N. & W. vacant, E. Ogeechee river, S. Wm. Kelly, Sr., survey 512. July 7, 1784, p. 258.

**ROQUEMORE, PETER.** 402½ acres, Washington Co., bounded N. Dennis Lindsay, E. & S. vacant, W. Bear creek, survey 513. July 9, 1784, p. 259.

**RAMSAY, RANDOLPH.** 287½ acres, Washington Co., bounded N. Jno. Ramsay, other sides vacant. Cut E. & W. by branch of Buffalo creek, survey 514. June 23, 1784, p. 259.

**WRIGHT, ABEDNEGO.** 575 acres, Washington Co., bounded S. Benj. Scott, other sides vacant, survey 515. Dec. 9, 1784, p. 260.

**RYAN, JAMES.** 287½ acres, Washington Co., bounded N. & S. vacant, E. Owen, McGarr, W. Jno. Harvey. Cut E. & W. by Beaverdam creek, survey 516. July 16, 1784, p. 260.

**RAMSEY, THOMAS.** 287½ acres, Washington Co., bounded N. Jesse Jones, other sides vacant. Cut E. & W. by branch of Buffalo creek, survey 517. June 26, 1784, p. 261.

**ROE, ANDREW.** 287½ acres, Washington Co., bounded W. Cobb & Powell, other sides vacant, on Ogeechee river, survey 518. May 1, 1784, p. 261.

**RAMSEY, JOHN.** 287½ acres, Washington Co., bounded N. Randolph Ramsey, other sides vacant, survey 519. June 23, 1784, p. 262.

**RUNNELLS, FREDERICK.** 287½ acres, Washington Co., bounded W. Jesse Horne, other sides vacant. Cut N. & S. by Richland creek, survey 520. June 5, 1784, p. 262.

**ROBERTS, JOHN.** 287½ acres, Washington Co., bounded N. Island, or Rock creek, E. & W. vacant, S. Williams, survey 521. July 3, 1784, p. 263.

**ROGERS, DRURY.** 287½ acres, Washington Co., bounded N. Shoulderbone creek, E. Amason, S. vacant, W. Soloman Thornton. Cut by Fort creek, survey 522. June 8, 1784, p. 263.

**RYLEY, JOSEPH.** 287½ acres, Washington Co., bounded W. Wm. Mimms, other sides vacant. Cut E. & W. by Island creek, survey 523. Jan. 4, 1785, p. 264.

**ROQUEMIRE, JAMES.** 287½ acres, Washington Co., bounded N. & W. vacant, E. Jas. Yorke, S. Jno. Garrett, survey 524. July 4, 1784, p. 264.

**READ, JOHN.** 245 acres, Washington Co., bounded N. Cribbs, other sides vacant, or surveyed. On Beaverdam of Richland creek, survey 527. Jan. 26, 1785, p. 266.

**ROBERTSON, JONATHAN.** 287½ acres, Washington Co., bounded E. Phillips, other sides vacant. On Buffalo creek, survey 530. Jan 12, 1785, p. 267.

**REDDIX, ABSOLEM.** 287½ acres, Washington Co., bounded N. Maddin, other sides vacant, on Buffalo creek, survey 530. Jan. 12, 1785, p. 267.

STEWART, ISAAC. 287½ acres, Washington Co., bounded N. & W. vacant, E. Geo. Hall, S. Geo. Fould, on Shoulderbone creek, survey 531. Feb. 12, 1785, p. 268.

SMITH, THOMAS, JR. 575 acres, Washington Co., bounded (triangle) NW. south fork of Sugar creek, E. vacant, survey 532. July 2, 1784, p. 268.

STEED, PHILIPS. 287½ acres, Washington Co., bounded N. unknown, E. Walton, S. Geo. Fould, W. vacant, on Shoulderbone creek, survey 533. Feb. 12, 1785, p. 269.

SMART, ROBERT. 287½ acres, Washington Co., bounded S. Wm. Morgan, other sides vacant, on Rocky creek, survey 535. April 7, 1785, p. 270.

SMITH, CORNELIUS. 287½ acres, Washington Co., bounded N. Willis Pope, E. vacant, S. Wm. Perritt, W. Williamson's, on Shoulderbone creek survey 536. June 5, 1784, p. 270.

SHARPE, JOHN. 287½ acres, Washington Co., bounded N. & W. vacant, E. Galpin, S. Ogeechee river, survey 541. July 24, 1784, p. 273.

STUART, CHARLES. 287½ acres, Washington Co., bounded N. Theo. Turk, other sides vacant, survey 542. Mar. 13, 1785, p. 273.

SPURLOCK, ROBERT. 287½ acres, Washington Co., bounded N. Pat Jarvis, E. vacant, S. Sanders Walker, W. Wm. Candler, on Little Beaverdam creek, survey 543. June 27, 1784, p. 274.

STUART, JAMES. 287½ acres, Washington Co., bounded all sides vacant. Cut N. & S. by Glen creek, survey 550. Oct. 23, 1784, p. 277.

STUART, JOHN (3RD). 287½ acres, Washington Co., bounded all sides vacant. Cut N. & S. by Glen's creek, survey 551. Oct. 3, 1784, p. 278.

SHELTON, HENRY. 287½ acres, Washington Co., bounded all sides vacant, on fork of Bear creek, survey 552. Nov. 25, 1784, p. 278.

STORY, EDWARD. 287½ acres, Washington Co., bounded N. Fitzpatrick, other sides vacant, survey 553. April 21, 1785, p. 279.

STRENGTH, JOHN. 287½ acres, Washington Co., bounded N. Benj. Few, other sides vacant, on Williamson's Swamp (or Bear) creek, survey 554. June 22, 1784, p. 279.

SMITH, JOSEPH. 287½ acres, Washington Co., bounded N. Jno. McCartie, E. Carter, S. & W. vacant, survey 557. Jan. 3, 1785, p. 281.

SHEFFIELD, JOHN. 287½ acres, Washington Co., bounded all sides vacant, on Buffalo creek, survey 558. June 10, 1784, p. 281.

SCOTT, PETER. 287½ acres, Washington Co., bounded N. & W. vacant, S. surveyed, E. Thos. Bussey, on Island creek, survey 560. Nov. 10, 1784, p. 282.

## BOUNTY SURVEYS.

**SHAW, ADAM.** 287½ acres, Washington Co., bounded N. Abm. Lepham, E. & S. vacant, W. Hugh Horton, on branch of Island creek, survey 561. June 29, 1784, p. 283.

**SUTTON, PHILIP.** 287½ acres, Washington Co., bounded S. main Buffalo creek, other sides vacant, survey 562. Oct. 25, 1784, p. 283.

**STEPHENS, JOHN.** 287½ acres, Washington Co., N. & W. vacant, E. Jno. Lang, S. Little Beaverdam creek of Richland creek, survey 563. June 19, 1784, p. 284.

**STALLINGS, JESSE.** 287½ acres, Washington Co., bounded N. & E. vacant, S. Jno. Williams, W. Ayres, on Buffalo creek, survey 564. Nov. 6, 1784, p. 284.

**STATENS, JOSEPH.** 287½ acres, Washington Co., bounded N. Thos. Lamar, other sides vacant, on Oconee river, survey 565. June 25, 1784, p. 285.

**SMALLEY, MICHAEL.** 287½ acres, Washington Co., bounded N. Christmas, & Bentley, E. vacant, S. Cartledge, W. Burke, survey 566. June 30, 1784, p. 285.

**SAPP, WILLIAM.** 287½ acres, Washington Co., bounded all sides vacant, on branch of Fort creek, survey 567. July 9, 1784, p. 286.

**STIFF, WILLIAM.** 230 acres, Washington Co. (on Reserve), bounded N. & E. vacant, S. Oconee river, W. Mitchell, survey 568. July 3, 1784, p. 286.

**SHAW, THOMAS.** 287½ acres, Washington Co., bounded N. Peter Perry, E. Matthews, S. vacant, W. Reddick, on Deroso creek, survey 569. Nov. 10, 1784, p. 287.

**SIMPSON, SAMUEL.** 230 acres, Washington Co., bounded (on Reserve) all sides vacant. Cut by branch of Beaverdam creek, survey 570. Nov. 29, 1784, p. 287.

**SHARPE, JOSHUA.** 287½ acres, Washington Co., bounded N. Douglas, E. & S. vacant, W. Oconee river, survey 571. June 10, 1784, p. 288.

**SULLIVAN, WILLIAM.** 287½ acres, Washington Co., bounded N. Harper, E. Oconee river, S. Bussey, W. vacant. Cut by fork of Oconee river, survey 572. June 2, 1784, p. 288.

**RIDEN, JOSEPH SCOTT.** 287½ acres, Washington Co., bounded W. Oconee river, other sides vacant. Cut N. & S. by Richland creek, survey 573. June 5, 1784, p. 289.

**SMITH, CORNELIUS.** 287½ acres, Washington Co., bounded N. Thos. Cribbs, other sides vacant. On Stewart's creek, survey 577. April 13, 1785, p. 289.

**SIMMONS, JOHN.** 287½ acres, Washington Co., bounded N. Col. Candler, E. Shoulderbone creek, S. Thornton, W. vacant, survey 578. June 8, 1784, p. 291.

**SAPP, JOHN.** 287½ acres, Washington Co., bounded N. & E. vacant, S. Wm. Sapp, W. unknown. Cut by branch of Fort creek, survey 579. July 9, 1784, p. 292.

**SAPP, DILL.** 287½ acres, Washington Co., bounded N. Jno. Sapp, E. Sanders, S. & W. vacant. On branch of Fort creek, survey 580. July 9, 1784, p. 292.

**SHEFTALL, MORDECAI.** 1,150 (on reserve), Washington Co., bounded all sides vacant. Cut N. W. to S. E. by Rocky creek, survey 581. Nov. 15, 1784, p. 293.

**SAPP, DILL.** 287½ acres, Washington Co. (2), bounded N. & E. vacant, S. Rocky creek and Jeremiah Cloud, W. Joseph Walker, survey 582. Nov. 7, 1784, p. 293.

**SNEED, DUDLEY.** 287½ acres, Washington Co., bounded W. Oconee river, other sides vacant, survey 583. June 6, 1784, p. 294.

**TUNIS, NEHEMIAH.** 345 acres, Washington Co., bounded N. Jno. Sheffield, E. & S. vacant, W. Buffalo creek, survey 584. June 10, 1784, p. 294.

**TUCKER, THOMAS.** 287½ acres, Washington Co., bounded S. Bishop, other sides vacant, survey 585. July 2, 1784, p. 295.

**TUCKER, ROBERT.** 287½ acres, Washington Co., bounded N. Sheppard and vacant, E. & S. vacant, W. Bishop, survey 586. July 2, 1784, p. 295.

**TOWNSEND, HENRY.** 287½ acres, Washington Co., bounded N. Jas. Hogg, other sides vacant. On Richland creek, survey 588. Oct. 18, 1784, p. 296.

**TRAPP, JOHN.** 287½ acres, Washington Co., bounded N. & E. vacant, S. Jno. Sapp, W. Joshua Sanders. On Fort creek, survey 590. July 9, 1784, p. 297.

**TELFAIR, HON. EDWARD.** 575 acres, Washington Co., bounded N. Ignatius Few, other sides vacant. Cut N. & S. by Buffalo creek, survey 591. June 25, 1784, p. 298.

**THORNTON, SAMUEL.** 287½ acres, Washington Co., bounded N. Benj. Jenkins, other sides unknown or vacant. On Richland creek, survey 592. June 13, 1784, p. 298.

**THOMAS, JAMES.** 287½ acres, Washingtton Co., bounded N. & E. vacant, S. Jo. Smith, W. Jno. Parker, survey 593. Jan. 3, 1785, p. 299.

**TROY, JOHN.** 287½ acres, Washington Co., bounded N. Saml. Alexander, other sides vacant. On Richland creek, survey 595. May 31, 1784, p. 300.

**TRAWICK, FRANCIS.** 287½ acres, Washington Co., bounded all sides vacant, survey 596. Oct. 20, 1784.

**THOMPSON, BENJAMIN.** 575 acres, Washington Co., bounded all sides vacant. Cut by Doctor's Branch, survey 598. Aug. 9, 1784, p. 301.

BOUNTY SURVEYS. 279

**TOWNSEND, THOMAS.** 287½ acres, Washington Co., bounded all sides vacant. On Shoulderbone creek, survey 600. Nov. 22, 1784, p. 302.

**TURKNETT, HENRY.** 287½ acres, Washington Co., bounded N. Jno. Cain, other sides vacant, survey 601. Dec. 8, 1784, p. 303.

**TENNILL, CAPT. FRANCIS.** 690 acres, Washington Co., bounded (on reserve) N. Oconee river and vacant, E. Geo. Handley, S. Campbell and Rayford, W. vacant, survey 602. Nov. 26, 1784, p. 303.

**THURMAN, ABSOLOM.** 287½ acres, Washington Co., bounded N. & E. vacant, S. Maj. Sheppard, W. Aaron Greer. Cut by Beaverdam creek, survey 603. July 1, 1784, p. 304.

**THOMPSON, WILLIAM.** 287½ acres, Washington Co., bounded N. Benj. Wells, Jr., E. Thos. Kelley, S. estate of Offutt, W. Benj. Knuckles. On Rocky creek, survey 604, Nov. 13, 1784, p. 304.

**WRIGHT, ISAIAH.** 287½ acres, Washingtotn Co., bounded N. vacant, E. Gilleland, S. Gilleland, W. Carson, survey 605. Dec. 10, 1784, p. 305.

**WILKINS, WILLIAM.** 287½ acres, Washington Co., bounded N. Oconee river, E. & S. vacant, W. Hwz. Bussey, survey 606. Dec. 3, 1784, p. 305.

**WILLIAMS, GEORGE.** 575 acres, Washington Co., bounded all sides vacant. Cut by Beaverdam fork of Richland creek, survey 607. Sept. 12, 1784, p. 306.

**WOODS, NATHANIEL.** 287½ acres, Washington Co., bounded W. Chaplain, other sides vacant, survey 608. June 14, 1784, p. 306.

**WHATLEY, JOHN.** 287½ acres, Washington Co., bounded N. Little Ogeechee river, E. Sinquefield, S. vacant, W. Michael Whatley, survey 609. Sept. 2, 1784, p. 307.

**WHATLEY, WHARTON.** 287½ acres, Washington Co., bounded N. vacant and Harvey, E. vacant, S. Burnice, W. Messaries. On Oconee river, survey 610. Sept. 22, 1784, p. 307.

**WYCHE, GEORGE.** 287½ acres, Washington Co., bounded N. Wm. Ray, E. & S. vacant, W. Lewis Crane. On Rocky fork of Shoulderbone creek, survey 611. Nov. 15, 1784, p. 308.

**WILSON, SAMUEL.** 287½ acres, Washington Co., bounded N. Oconee river, E. & S. vacant, W. Jas. McFarland, survey 612. June 5, 1784, p. 308.

**VICKERS, THOMAS.** 287½ acres, Washington Co., bounded all sides vacant. On branch of Buffalo creek, survey 614. July 9, 1784, p. 309.

**WHEELER, ZACHARIAH.** 287½ acres, Washington Co., bounded all sides vacant. Cut by Bushey creek and Richland creek, survey 617. June 26, 1784, p. 311.

**WILLIS, ISAIAH.** 287½ acres, Washington Co., bounded W. Dread Rogers, others vacant. On Shoulderbone creek, survey 618. Nov. 20, 1784, p. 311.

ROSTER OF THE REVOLUTION.

**WRIGHT, JOHN.** 287½ acres, Washington Co., bounded N. Oconee river, E. Jas. McFarland, other sides vacant, survey 619. June 2, 1784, p. 312.

**WEBSTER, THOMAS.** 230 acres, Washington Co. (on reserve), bounded W. Thos. Payne, other sides vacant. Cut by Greenbrier creek, survey 620. Nov. 29, 1784, p. 312.

**WALKER, SANDERS.** 747 acres, Washington Co., bounded S. Jno. Milner, other sides vacant. Cut N. & S. by Buck creek, survey 622. Nov. 12, 1784, p. 313.

**WATERS, CHARLES.** 287½ acres, Washington Co., bounded N. Jno. Harriman, E. William Campbell, S. vacant and Marshall, W. Tenkerson. On Tenkerson's creek, survey 613. Nov. 12, 1784, p. 314.

**WALTON, NEWILL.** 575 acres, Washington Co., bounded N. Jno. Cunningham, E. Samuel Jack, S. vacant, W. vacant. On Rocky fork of Shoulderbone creek, survey 634. Nov. 18, 1784, p. 314.

**WILSON, JOHN.** 460 acres, Washington Co., bounded E. Jas. Wootten, other sides vacant. Cut E. & W. by Beaverdam creek, survey 625. June 11, 1784, p. 315.

**WHITTEN, AUSTIN.** 287½ acres, Washington Co., bounded N. & W. vacant, E. Little Beaverdam of Richmond creek, S. Saml. Hoof, survey 626. June 18, 1784, p. 315.

**WILLIAMS, JOHN.** 287½ acres, Washington Co., bounded all sides vacant. On a fork of Buffalo creek, survey 627, Nov. 10, 1784, p. 316.

**WINFREY, HEIRS OF CAPT. JACOB.** 690 acres, Washington Co., bounded all sides vacant. On Beaverdam creek, survey 628. Jan. 12, 1785, p. 316.

**WILLIS, BRITTAIN.** 575 acres, Washington Co., bounded N. Freeman and Burrill, E. Joiner and vacant, S. Jno. Berry, W. vacant. Cut N. & S. by east fork of Big creek, survey 630. June 14, 1784, p. 317.

**WELCH, JOSHUA.** 287½ acres, Washington Co., bounded W. Jesse Jones, other sides vacant. On Buffalo creek, survey 631. June 19, 1784, p. 318.

**WHATLEY, MICHAEL.** 287½ acres, Washington Co., bounded N. Little Ogeechee river, E. Jno. Whatley, other sides vacant, survey 632. Sept. 2, 1784, p. 318.

**WHITE, JOHN.** 287½ acres, Washington Co., bounded N. & W. vacant, E. Beaverdam creek, S. Henry Carr. Cut by Richland creek, survey 633. June 19, 1784, p. 319.

**WHITAKER, SAMUEL.** 287½ acres, Washington Co., bounded N. Middleton, E. Jere Hatcher, S. Daniel Dennison, W. Crutchfield. Cut by Shoulderbone creek, survey 634. Nov. 15, 1784, p. 319.

## BOUNTY SURVEYS. 281

**WELLS, BENJAMIN, JR.** 287½ acres, Washington Co., bounded N. Hatcher, E. Jas. Simmons, S. Wm. Thompson, W. D. Dennison. On Shoulderbone creek, survey 635. Nov. 13, 1784, p. 320.

**WILSON, SAMUEL.** 287½ acres, Washington Co., bounded N. Oconee river, E. Chas. Wild, S. vacant, W. McFarland, survey 636. June 2, 1784, p. 320.

**WILLIAMS, CHARLES.** 287½ acres, Washington Co., bounded all sides vacant. On Shoulderbone creek, survey 638. June 4, 1784, p. 321.

**WOOD, JONATHAN.** 287½ acres, Washington Co., bounded N. vacant, & McClendon, E. vacant, S. Harper, W. Harris's creek, survey 637. June 26, 1784, p. 321.

**WRIGHT, HABAKUK.** 575 acres, Washington Co., bounded E. Joshua Sanders, other sides vacant. Cut diagonally by Fort creek, survey 639. Dec. 7, 1784, p. 321.

**WILLIAMS, EDWARD.** 287½ acres, Washington Co., bounded N. & S. vacant, E. Wm. Few, W. Edward Telfair. Cut by Buffalo creek, survey 640. June 22, 1784, p 322.

**WALKER, DAVID.** 287½ acres, Washington Co., bounded all sides vacant, on Williamson's Swamp creek, survey 641. July 16, 1784, p. 322.

**WALKER, JOSEPH.** 287½ acres, Washington Co., bounded N. & W. vacant, E. Jeremiah Cloud, S. Wm. Bishop, survey 642. Nov. 4, 1784, p. 322.

**WAGONER, HENRY.** 287½ acres, Washington Co., bounded N. Wm. Terrell, E. Oconee river, S. & W. vacant, survey 643. June 2, 1784, p. 323.

**WILDER, WILLIAM.** 287½ acres, Washington Co., bounded N. & W. vacant, E. Lawson, S. York. Cut N. & S. by Rocky creek, survey 644. Nov. 8, 1784, p. 323.

**WRIGHT, WILLIAM.** 287½ acres, Washington Co., bounded N. Candler, E. Henry Candler, S. & W. vacant, on Town creek, survey 645. April 14, 1785, p. 323.

**WOOTEN, THOMAS.** 287½ acres, Washington Co., bounded N. Rocky creek, E. Daniel Young, S. Peter Perkins, W. Wilder & Yorke, survey 646. May 12, 1785, p. 324.

**WELCHER, WILLIAM.** 287½ acres, Washington Co., bounded N. Watery fork of Buffalo creek, E. & S. vacant, W. Philip Sutton, survey 647. Nov. 1, 1784, p. 324.

**WEBSTER, ABNER.** 287½ acres, Washington Co., bounded E. Carson & Mimms, other sides vacant, on Sandy Run creek, survey 648. Jan. 5, 1785, p. 324.

**WELLS, JOSEPH.** 287½ acres, Washington Co., bounded NE. & W. by Glascock, S. vacant, on Deroso's creek, survey 649. Nov. 12, 1784, p. 325.

**WAGONER, GEORGE.** 287½ acres, Washington Co., bounded N. Porter, E. Jas. Wagoner, S. vacant, W. unknown, on Fishing creek, survey 653. June 23, 1784, p. 326.

**WARE, NICHOLAS.** 287½ acres, Washington Co., bounded N. Sanders Walker, E. Vinings, S. Marshall, W. vacant, on Beaverdam creek, survey 654. May 5, 1785, p. 326.

**WALLACE, WILLIAM.** 287½ acres, Washington Co., bounded N. grantee, E. Glascock, S. Jas. Thomas, W. Glascock, survey 650. Jan. 11, 1785, p. 326.

**WHITESIDES, JOHN.** 287½ acres, Washington Co., bounded N. Hamm, E. Oconee river, S. vacant, W. Ed. Hagan, survey 651. June 26, 1784, p. 326.

**WILDER, SAMPSON.** 287½ acres, Washington Co., bounded all sides vacant, on Buffalo creek, survey 655. June 28, 1784, p. 326.

**WILLIAMSON, MICAJAH.** 287½ acres, Washington Co., bounded N. & E. vacant, S. Robt. Jarrett, W. Martin, on Shoulderbone creek, survey 656. July 1, 1784, p. 327.

**WILKINS, GABRIEL.** 287½ acres, Washington Co., bounded all sides vacant, survey 657. Aug. 5, 1784, p. 327.

**YOUNG, WILLIAM.** 287½ acres, Washington Co., bounded N. & S. vacant, E. McCall, W. unknown, between Williamson's Swamp creek and Ogeechee river, survey 658. Nov. 25, 1784, p. 328.

**YANKERFIELD, JOHN.** 287½ acres, Washington Co., bounded all sides vacant, on Buffalo creek, survey 659. Nov. 13, 1784, p. 328.

**WEATHERS, EDWARD.** 287½ acres, Washington Co., bounded S. Academy lands, other sides vacant, on Shoulderbone creek, survey 660. July 19, 1784, p. 328.

**WOOTEN, JAMES.** 287½ acres, Washington Co., bounded all sides vacant, on Rocky fork of Shoulderbone creek, survey 661. July 19, 1784, p. 329.

**WALL, JOHN.** 287½ acres, Washington Co., bounded W. Tripp, other sides vacant, survey 662. July 16, 1784, p. 329.

**WOOTEN, THOMAS.** 287½ acres, Washington Co., bounded N., E. & W. by Oconee river, S. vacant, survey 663. July 20, 1784, p. 329.

**WOOD, HENRY.** 287½ acres, Washington Co., bounded N. & E. vacant, S. Joshia Powell, W. Ogeechee river, survey 664. July 24, 1784, p. 330.

**WINSKETT, SAMUEL.** 287½ acres, Washington Co., bounded N. Col. Williamson, other sides vacant. Cut N. & S. by fork of Shoulderbone creek, survey 666. June 4, 1784, p. 330.

**WILLIAMS, GEORGE.** 575 acres, Washington Co., bounded E. unknown, other sides vacant, on Oconee river, survey 668. Feb. 2, 1785, p. 331.

**WHEELIS, JOHN.** 287½ acres, Washington Co., bounded all sides vacant, on Shoulderbone creek, survey 669. June 4, 1784, p. 331.

**YOUNG, EDWARD.** 287½ acres, Washington Co, bounded N. & W. vacant, E. Rocky creek, S. Matthews, survey 670. Nov. 4, 1784, p. 332.

**YOUNGBLOOD, PETER.** 575 acres, Washington Co., bounded all sides vacant. Cut N. & S. by Harris creek, survey 671. June 10, 1784, p. 332.

**YORK, JAMES.** 287½ acres, Washington Co., bounded N. Ramsey, other sides vacant, survey 672. July 3, 1784, p. 332.

**YOUNG, DANIEL.** 287½ acres, Washington Co., bounded N. William Johnston, E. & S. vacant, W. Walker, on Rocky creek, survey 673. Nov. 4, 1784, p. 333.

**YOUNGBLOOD, JAMES.** 287½ acres, Washington Co., bounded N. Graves, E. Jos. Marshall, S. vacant, W. Deroso's creek, survey 674. Nov. 14, 1784, p. 333.

**YORK, JAMES.** 287½ acres, Washington Co., bounded N. & W. Rocky creek, E. vacant, S. Wm. Wilder, survey 675. Nov. 5, 1784, p. 333.

**YOUNG, WILLIAM.** 287½ acres, Washington Co., bounded N. Harvey, other sides vacant, on East branch creek of Ohoopee river, survey 677. Mar. 24, 1785, p. 334.

**AUTRY, JOHN.** 287½ acres, Washington Co., bounded N. Oconee river, E. Walton Harris, S. vacant, W. Sanders, survey 678. June 2, 1784, p. 334.

**AUTREY, JOHN.** 575 acres, Washington Co., bounded all sides vacant, on Town creek, survey 679. July 7, 1784, p. 335.

**ALFORD, JAMES.** 287½ acres, Washington Co., bounded N. & S. vacant, E. Wilkes county line, W. vacant, & McFarland, on Shoulderbone creek, survey 680. April 25, 1785, p. 335.

**ACORD, JOHN.** 287½ acres, Washington Co., bounded all sides vacant, on Buffalo creek, survey 683. Dec. 28, 1784, p. 336.

**AVERETT, JOHN.** 287½ acres, Washington Co., bounded S. Little Ogeechee river, other sides vacant, survey 685. Oct. 17, 1784, p. 337.

**BATTERY, ZACHARIAH.** 230 acres (on Reserve), Washington Co., bounded N. & E. vacant, S. unknown, W. fork of Oconee river, survey 690. Oct. 10, 1784, p. 338.

**BRYAN, DUNCAN.** 287½ acres, Washington Co., bounded N. Jno. Coleman, E. & S. vacant, W. Ragland, on branch of Big creek, survey 691. June 8, 1784, p. 339.

**BARTON, WILLOUGHBY.** 287½ acres, Washington Co., bounded N. Holmes & vacant, E. vacant, S. Griggsby, W. vacant. Cut N. & S. by Town creek, survey 692. June 15, 1784, p. 339.

**BRYANT, LIEUT. JOHN.** 460 acres, Washington Co., bounded N. Wilson & Ragland, other sides vacant, on Middle fork of Big creek, survey 695. June 8, 1784, p. 340.

**BUGG, JACOB.** 287½ acres, Washington Co., bounded N. vacant, E. Wm. Hill, S. Oconee river, W. Edw. Rowell, survey 696. June 9, 1784, p. 340.

**BURKE, DAVID.** 287½ acres, Washington Co., bounded N. Isaac Lowe, E. Mullins & Bulloch, S. Walker, W. vacant, survey 698. July 10, 1784, p. 341.

**BERRY, WILLIAM.** 230 acres, Washington Co., bounded (on Reserve), all sides vacant. Cut by Green Brier creek, survey 699. July 3, 1784, p. 341.

**BEASLEY, RICHARD.** 287½ acres, Washington Co., bounded W. vacant, & Walker, other sides vacant, on Stephen's creek, survey 702. April 6, 1785, p. 342.

**BOWEN, OLIVER—COMMODORE OF GEORGIA NAVY.** 1,150 acres (on Reserve), Washington Co., bounded E. Oconee river, other sides vacant, survey 703. Nov. 17, 1784, p. 343.

**CAMPBELL, WILLIAM.** 287½ acres, Washington Co., bounded N. vacant, E. Bush, S. Oconee river, W. Jno. Taylor, survey 706. June 10, 1785, p. 344.

**CRAWFORD, STROTHER.** 230 acres, Washington Co., bounded (on Reserve) N. & E. vacant, S. W. Jones, W. Wm. Croker, survey 707. July 4, 1784, p. 344.

**CONNELLY, PATRICK.** 287½ acres, Washington Co., bounded W. Beecham, other sides vacant, on Buffalo creek, survey 709. Nov. 1, 1784, p. 345.

**CHRISTMAS, NATHANIEL.** 287½ acres, Washington Co., bounded all sides vacant. Cut E. & W. by lower Town creek, survey 711. Oct. 7, 1785, p. 346.

**CROKER, WILLIAM.** 230 acres, Washington Co., bounded (on Reserve) N. & W. vacant, E. Crawford, S. C. B. Davis, survey 713. July 4, 1784, p. 346.

**CASTLEBERRY, JOHN.** 287½ acres, Washington Co., bounded N. & E. vacant, S. McFarland, W. Jos. Davidson, survey 715. June 30, 1784, p. 347.

**CASTLEBERRY, PETER.** 287½ acres, Washington Co., bounded W. Fuller, other sides vacant, on Ogeechee river, survey 722. Feb. 1, 1785, p. 349.

**CLARKE, JOHN.** 287½ acres, Washington Co., bounded all sides vacant. Cut N. & S. by Old Town creek, survey 728. June 4, 1784, p. 351.

**COLLINS, MOSES.** 287½ acres, Washington Co., bounded E. Holmes, other sides vacant. Cut N. & S. by Big creek, survey 732. June 11, 1784, p. 353.

**COLEMAN, JAMES.** 287½ acres, Washington Co., bounded all sides vacant. Cut N. & S. by Buffalo creek, survey 733. April 4, 1785, p. 353.

## BOUNTY SURVEYS.   285

**DAVIDSON, JOSEPH.** 287½ acres, Washington Co., bounded N. vacant, E. Jno. Castleberry, S. Jas. McFarland, W. Luke Durham, survey 734. June 30, 1784, p. 353.

**DURBAN, LUKE.** 287½ acres, Washington Co., bounded N. & W. vacant, E. Jos. Davidson, S. McFarland, on Buffalo creek, survey 735. June 30, 1784, p. 354.

**DANNELLY, JAMES.** 575 acres, Washington Co., bounded W. Chestley Davis, N. Altamaha river, other sides vacant, survey 737. June 25, 1784, p. 354.

**DAVIS, JAMES.** 287½ acres, Washington Co., bounded N. Greer, E. Bishop, S. Beaverdam creek, W. vacant, survey 738. July 1, 1784, p. 355.

**DUCKWORTH, JACOB.** 287½ acres, Washington Co., bounded W. branch of Williamson's swamp, other sides vacant, survey 740. Dec. 23, 1784, p. 355.

**DAVIS, SOLOMAN.** 287½ acres, Washington Co., bounded S. Wm. Goober, other sides vacant, survey 742. Nov. 1, 1784, p. 356.

**FENN, ZACHARIAH.** 287½ acres, Washington Co., bounded E. vacant, & Darby, other sides vacant. Cut by branch of Sandhill creek, survey 747. Oct. 8, 1785, p. 358.

**FLOURNOY, ROBERT.** 287½ acres, Washington Co., bounded all sides vacant. Cut E. & W. by Crooked creek, survey 748. Dec. 8, 1785, p. 358.

**FORTUNE, JACOB.** 287½ acres, Washington Co., bounded N. Carson, E. & S. vacant, W. surveyed & Mitchell, survey 749. July 3, 1784, p. 359.

**FOWLER, NATHAN.** 287½ acres, Washington Co., bounded N. & E. unknown, S. Marshall, W. Jas. Tannyhill, on Fort creek, survey 751. July 7, 1784, p. 359.

**FENN, ZACHARIAS.** 575 acres, Washington Co., bounded N. & E. vacant, S. Wamack, & Heard, W. Deep creek, survey 742. Dec. 6, 1785, p. 359.

**FENN, JOHN.** 287½ acres, Washington Co., bounded E. Jno. Gambol, other sides vacant, on Buckeye creek, survey 754. Oct. 7, 1785, p. 360.

**FOULDS, GEORGE.** 287½ acres, Washington Co., bounded N. & E. vacant, S. Jas. Bishop, W. Adcock, survey 755. July 9, 1784, p. 360.

**FAIR, JACOB.** 287½ acres, Washington Co., bounded all sides vacant, on fork of Buffalo creek, survey 756. Dec. 25, 1784, p. 361.

**FENN, JOHN.** 287½ acres, Washington Co., bounded N. Jno. & Geo. Galphin, E. & W. vacant, S. Jno. Sharp, on Ogeechee river, survey 759. July 24, 1784, p. 362.

**GODBY, WILLIAM.** 287½ acres, Washington Co., bounded all sides vacant, on branch of Town creek, survey 760. Nov. 1, 1784, p. 362.

**GRAY, JAMES.** 287½ acres, Washington Co., bounded N. Wilslet, other sides vacant, survey 761. Nov. 2, 1784, p. 362.

**GREER, WILLIAM.** 287½ acres, Washington Co., bounded N. Phillips, T. & S. vacant, W. Baker & Hughton, on Ogeechee river, survey 762. June 9, 1785, p. 363.

**GODBY, CARY.** 287½ acres, Washington Co., bounded N. Jo. Marbury, other sides vacant, survey 763. July 10, 1784, p. 363.

**GLASCOCK, CAPT. THOMAS.** 690 acres (on Reserve), Washington Co., bounded N. Gen. McIntosh, E. & S. vacant, W. Gen. McIntosh, on Oconee river, survey 764. Nov. 15, 1784, p. 363.

**GREENE, ISAAC.** 287½ acres, Washington Co., bounded all sides vacant. Cut E. & W. by Town creek, survey 766. April 25, 1785, p. 364.

**HOPKINS, LAMBERT.** 230 acres (on Reserve), Washington Co., bounded N. Phillips, E. & S. Tennill, W. Green Brier creek, survey 772. March 7, 1786, p. 366.

**HUDSPETH, CHARLES.** 287½ acres, Washington Co., bounded N. Williamson's Swamp creek, E. & S. vacant, W. Galphin's old line, survey 755. June 29, 1784, p. 367.

**HARRINGTON, JOHN.** 287½ acres, Washington Co., bounded N. Oconee river, E. Campbell, S. vacant, W. Jno. Tankersley, & Oconee river, survey 776. June 3, 1784, p. 367.

**HUDSON, JAMES.** 287½ acres, Washington Co., bounded N. vacant, E. Jno. Garrett, S. Ogeechee river, W. Jas. Hudson, survey 779. July 4, 1784, p. 368.

**HILL, EDWARD.** 287½ acres, Washington Co., bounded E. Wm. Kimbrough, W. Brazele, other sides vacant, or unknown, on Shoulderbone creek, survey 780. Nov. 15, 1784, p. 369.

**HAMMOCK, JOHN.** 287½ acres, Washington Co., bounded N. Brantley, E. Tripp, S. vacant, W. unknown, survey 782. July 7, 1784, p. 369.

**HYNES, ROBERT.** 287½ acres, Washington Co., bounded N. Wilkes Co. line, E. Ledbetter, S. Wood, W. Houston. Cut by Little Ogeechee river, survey 784. Oct. 26, 1784, p. 370.

**HOGG, JAMES.** 287½ acres, bounded N. vacant, E. Jno. Crutchfield, S. Daniel Dennison, W. Isham Burke, on Shoulderbone creek, survey 785. May 17, 1784, p. 370.

**HAYES, ANDREW.** 287½ acres, Washington Co., bounded S. Oconee river, other sides surveyed. Cut N. & S. by Sandy creek, survey 787. April 9, 1785, p. 371.

**HEARD, BERNARD.** 575 acres, Washington Co., bounded N. Ezekiel Offutt, E. Kelly, S. Rocky branch of Shoulderbone creek, survey 791. Nov. 16, 1784, p. 372.

BOUNTY SURVEYS. 287

**HAMILTON, WILLIAM.** 287½ acres, Washington Co., bounded all sides vacant, or surveyed, on Fort creek, survey 795. April 8, 1785, p. 347.

**HILL, WILLIAM.** 287½ acres, Washington Co., bounded N. & E. vacant, S. Brantley, W. Wm. Hamilton, survey 796. April 8, 1785, p. 374.

**HOPKINS, LAMBETH.** 287½ acres, Washington Co., bounded N. Harris, E. vacant, S. Timothy Pittman, W. Oconee river, survey 797. July 23, 1784, p. 374.

**HEARD, JOHN.** 287½ acres, Washington Co., bounded all sides vacant. Cut by Rocky creek, survey 798. June 27, 1784, p. 375.

**JONES, WILLIAM.** 230 acres (on Reserve), Washington Co., bounded N. Strother Crawford, E. vacant, S. Oconee river, W. Chas. B. Davis, survey 799. July 4, 1784, p. 375.

**JACK, SAMUEL.** 400 acres, Washington Co., bounded N. Newell Walton, E. Sturgis, S. vacant, W. Saml. Sterk, on Shoulderbone creek, survey 801. Nov. 18, 1784, p. 376.

**JORDAN, LEWIS.** 287½ acres, Washington Co., bounded all sides vacant. Cut in NW. corner by Buffalo creek, survey 803. Oct. 27, 1784, p. 376.

**JACKSON, THOMAS.** 287½ acres, Washington Co., bounded S. Jos. Kirkland, other sides vacant, on Shoulderbone creek, survey 804. July 15, 1784, p. 377.

**JOHNSTON, WILLIAM.** 287½ acres, Washington Co., bounded N. Rocky creek, W. Wm. Bishop, other sides vacant, survey 805. Nov. 4, 1784, p. 377.

**JONES, THOMAS.** 287½ acres, Washington Co., bounded N. near College lands, W. Long, other sides vacant, on Beaverdam creek, survey 806. Nov. 2, 1785, p. 377.

**KILPATRICK, THOMAS.** 287½ acres, Washington Co., bounded N. Glascock, other sides vacant, survey 807. Nov. 1, 1784, p. 378.

**KEMP, JOSEPH.** 287½ acres, Washington Co., bounded S. Jno. Rogers, other sides vacant, on Big creek, survey 809. April 1, 1786, p. 378.

**KENNEDY, JOHN.** 287½ acres, Washington Co., bounded N. & S. vacant, E. Jno. Felps, W. Edw. Williams. Cut by Buffalo creek, survey 810. June 26, 1784, p. 379.

**KEMP, WILLIAM.** 287½ acres, Washington Co., bounded W. Buckeye creek, other sides vacant, survey 812. Sept. 22, 1784, p. 379.

**KIRKHAM, JOSEPH.** 287½ acres, Washington Co., bounded W. Thos. Jackson, other sides vacant, on Shoulderbone creek, survey 813. July 15, 1784, p. 380.

**LEDBETTER, JOHN.** 287½ acres, Washington Co., bounded N. & S. unknown, E. Robt. Hynes, W. Allen Scott, on fork of Little Oconee river, survey 819. Oct. 26, 1784, p. 382.

**LOWE, ISAAC.** 287½ acres, Washington Co., bounded N. Isaiah Wright, E. Benj. Welch, S. McMullin, & Simmons, W. Burke, on branch of Oconee river, survey 821. July 10, 1784, p. 382.

**LEDBETTER, FREDERICK.** 287½ acres, Washington Co., bounded all sides vacant. Cut N. & S. by Town creek, survey 822. June 3, 1784, p. 383.

**LOGAN, PHILIP.** 287½ acres, Washington Co., bounded all sides vacant, on Buffalo creek, survey 823. April 7, 1785, p. 383.

**MORRIS, JOHN.** 287½ acres, Washington Co., bounded N. unknown, E. unknown, S. vacant, W. surveyed, survey 826. Dec. 23, 1784, p. 384.

**METCALF, WILLIAM.** 460 acres, Washington Co., bounded all sides vacant. Cut SW. to NE. by Clear creek, survey 827. June 12, 1784, p. 384.

**McGRUDER, NINIAN OFFITT.** 287½ acres, Washington Co., bounded all sides vacant, on Williamson's Swamp creek, survey 828. July 23, 1784, p. 385.

**MOTTE, JOSEPH.** 287½ acres, Washington Co., bounded N. Hall, E. vacant, S. Miller, W. Little Ogeechee river, survey 289. Mar. 6, 1786.

**McKINNEY, WILLIAM M.** 287½ acres, Washington Co., bounded N. Carr & Thompson, E. vacant, W. Jackson & vacant, on Shoulderbone creek, survey 833. Sept. 17, 1785, p. 386.

**MARCUS, JOHN.** 287½ acres, Washington Co., bounded N. fork of Ohoopee river, other sides vacant. Cut by Beaverdam creek, survey 835. June 8, 1785, p. 837.

**MILLER, EZEKIEL.** 287½ acres, Washington Co., bounded N. & W. surveyed, E. & S. vacant, on Ogeechee river, survey 837. Nov. 17, 1784, p. 388.

**McLENDON, JACOB.** 287½ acres, Washington Co., bounded all sides vacant, on Harris creek, survey 838. June 17, 1784, p. 388.

**MORRIS, WILLIAM.** 287½ acres, Washington Co., bounded E. Matthews, other sides vacant, survey 843. July 3, 1784, p. 390.

**McDOWELL, THOMAS.** 287½ acres, Washington Co., bounded N. & E. vacant, S. Ogeechee river, W. Jas. Clarke, Sr., survey 844. July 7, 1784, p. 390.

**MIDDLETON, HOLLAND.** 287½ acres, Washington Co., bounded N. Thos. Lamar, E. Samuel Whittaker, S. Jas. Young, W. vacant, on Rocky fork of Shoulderbone creek, survey 845. Nov. 15, 1784, p. 390.

**METCALF, LIEUT. DANZA.** 460 acres, Washington Co., bounded N. Robt. Harper, E. & W. vacant, S. Henry's fork & Wm. Brady, on Rocky creek, survey 846. July 17, 1784, p. 391.

**MARSHALL, LEVI.** 287½ acres, Washington Co., bounded W. Nicholas Long, other sides vacant, on Oconee river, survey 853. Nov. 14, 1785, p. 393.

**MIMMS, DRURY.** 287½ acres, Washington Co., bounded E. Wm. Jones, other sides vacant, on Boggy branch, survey 854. July 7, 1785, p. 393.

**MOORE, ALEXANDER.** 287½ acres, Washington Co., bounded N. vacant, & Lithgoe, E. & S. vacant, W. Jno. Wall, survey 855. July 6, 1784, p. 394.

**MARBURY, THOMAS.** 287½ acres, Washington Co., bounded N. vacant, E. Godby, S. Carson, W. Thos. Johnston, survey 856. July 10, 1784, p. 394.

**MEANLEY, LIEUT. JOHN.** 460 acres, Washington Co., bounded N. Banks & King, other sides vacant. Cut N. & S. by Roe's creek. survey ——. Mar. 10, 1785, p. —.

**McCARTHY, JOHN.** 287½ acres, Washington Co., bounded W. David Creswell, other sides vacant, on Island & Town creeks, survey 862. Oct. 26, 1785, p. 396.

**MATTHEWS, WILLIAM.** 287½ acres, Washington Co., bounded N. Tucker, other sides vacant, survey 864. July 3, 1784, p. 397.

**McCARTHY, DRUM MAJ. JOHN.** 460 acres, Washington Co., bounded N. & W. vacant, E. Jas. Catter, S. Jos. Smith, on Rocky creek, survey 865. Jan. 3, 1785, p. 397.

**MATTHEWS, MESHACK.** 287½ acres, Washington Co., bounded N. vacant, E. Tucker, S. Sheppard, W. Morris, survey 866. July 3, 1784, p. 397.

**NASH, HEIRS OF CAPT. CLEMENT.** 690 acres (on Reserve), Washington Co., bounded all sides vacant, survey 870. July 3, 1784( p. 399.

**NEWGATE, HEIRS OF CAPT. JOHN.** 690 acres (on Reserve), Washington Co., bounded S. Reuben Banks, other sides vacant, survey 871. Mar. 16, 1785, p. 400.

**NICHOLS, BENJAMIN.** 287½ acres, Washington Co., bounded N. Thompson, E. Randolph & Offutt, S. Burke, W. Dennis, on Shoulderbone creek, survey 874. Nov. 15, 1784, p. 401.

**NORTH, JOHN.** 287½ acres, Washington Co., bounded N. & S. vacant, E. south branch of Williamson's Swamp creek, W. Nicholas Scurry, survey 875. Mar. 31, 1785, p. 401.

**NEWMAN, JOHN.** 230 acres (on Reserve), Washington Co., bounded W. Meredith Davis, other sides vacant, on Beaverdam creek, survey 876. July 14, 1784, p. 402.

**ODINGSELL, CHARLES.** 575 acres, Washington Co., bounded all sides vacant. Cut N. & S. by Ohoopee river, survey 877. June 15, 1784, p. 402.

**ORRICK, JAMES.** 287½ acres, Washington Co., bounded N. Braswell, E. Buffalo creek, S. Jno. Anderson, W. Isham Phillips, survey 878. Sept. 22, 1785, p. 402.

**OFFUTT, EZEKIEL.** 575 acres, Washington Co., bounded N. Wm. Thompson, E. Bernard Heard, S. vacant, W. Jno. Kendall, on Rocky creek, survey 879. Nov. 15, 1784, p. 403.

**PALMER, JONATHAN.** 287½ acres, Washington Co., bounded all sides vacant or surveyed, on Shoulderbone creek, survey 880. Feb. 10, 1785, p. 403.

**POWELL, STEPHEN.** 287½ acres, Washington Co., bounded S. branch of Ohoopee river, other sides vacant, survey 882. April 18, 1785, p. 404.

**PHILLIPS, WILLIAM.** 230 acres, Washington Co., bounded (on Reserve) N. Oconee river, E. surveyed, S. Tennill, W. Burton, survey 884. Dec. 5, 1785, p. 404.

**PHILLIPS, ISAAC.** 230 acres (on Reserve), Washington Co., bounded N. vacant, E. Tennill, S. Hopkins, W. Greenbrier creek, survey 889. Mar. 7, 1786, p. 406.

**PEAVY, DIAL.** 287½ acres, Washington Co., bounded N. College lands, E. Nathl. Rumbley, S. vacant, W. unknown, survey 892. July 10, 1785, p. 406.

**RUNNELLS, GEORGE.** 287½ acres, Washington Co., bounded NE, Thos. Brown, SE. surveyed, W. Stephens & Autrey, on Fishing creek, survey 893. Mar. 22, 1785, p. 407.

**RAY, WILLIAM.** 287½ acres, Washington Co., bounded W. Geo. Wyche, other sides vacant, on Rocky creek, survey 901. Nov. 11, 1784, p. 409.

**REEVES, SPENCER.** 287½ acres, Washington Co., bounded N. Nathl. Wade, E. Fenn, S. & W. vacant, on Richland creek, survey 902. Nov. 16, 1784, p. 409.

**SHARPE, JOHN.** 287½ acres, Washington Co., bounded N. & W. vacant, E. Jno. Fenn, S. Michael Sharpe, near Ogeechee river, survey 909, July 24, 1784, p. 412.

**SIMMONS, STERN.** 575 acres, Washington Co., bounded NE. vacant, SE. Stewart, W. Oconee river, survey 911. June 7, 1784, p. 412.

**SCOTT, JOSEPH.** 287½ acres, Washington Co., bounded N. McFarland, E., S. & W. vacant. Cut N. & S. by Island creek, survey 912. June 20, 1784, p. 413.

**SCOTT, ABRAHAM.** 287½ acres, Washington Co., bounded E. Jno. Ledbetter, other sides unknown. Cut by branch of Little Ogeechee river, survey 913. Oct. 26, 1784, p. 413.

## BOUNTY SURVEYS.

**STALLINGS, EZEKIEL.** 575 acres, Washington Co., bounded W. Jas. Stallings, other sides vacant, on Oconee river, survey 914. June 8, 1785, p. 413.

**STEWART, JACOB.** 287½ acres, Washington Co., bounded N. south fork of Ohoopee river, E. & S. vacant, W. Jno. Marcus, survey 917. June 6, 1785, p. 414.

**STIRK, SAMUEL.** 575 acres, Washington Co., bounded N. Samuel Jack, S. vacant, W. Edw. Hail, & Reeves, on Shoulderbone creek, survey 918. Nov. 16, 1784, p. 415.

**SMITH, WILLIAM.** 287½ acres, Washington Co., bounded all sides vacant, on Oconee river, survey 919. April 10, 1785, p. 415.

**SHEFFLE, WILLIAM.** 575 acres, Washington Co., bounded S. Williamson's Swamp creek, other sides vacant, survey 921. May 6, 1784, p. 416.

**SHARPE, JOHN, SR.** 287½ acres, Washington Co., bounded N. & W. Oconee river, E. vacant, S. Jas. Stallings, survey 923. June 8, 1785, p. 416.

**TANNER, JOEL.** 287½ acres, Washington Co., bounded all sides vacant, on Buffalo creek, survey 926. May 12, 1785, p. 417.

**THOMPSON, BENJAMIN.** 287½ acres, Washington Co., bounded all sides vacant. Cut N. & S. by Deep creek, survey 933. Sept. 12, 1785, p. 419.

**VANN, EDWARD.** 287½ acres, Washington Co., bounded all sides by Oconee river (island), survey 934. Oct. 10, 1785, p. 419.

**WOMACK, JESSE.** 287½ acres, Washington Co., bounded E. Lamar, other sides vacant, on Deep creek, survey 941. Mar. 25, 1785, p. 421.

**WEST, JAMES.** 287½ acres, Washington Co., bounded all sides vacant, on Richland creek, survey 942. June 7, 1784, p. 422.

**WILLIS, GEORGE.** 690 acres (on Reserve), Washington Co., bounded N. Freeman, E. Freeman & Phillips, S. vacant, W. Joshia Cole, survey 943. June 7, 1785, p. 422.

**WALTON, ROBERT.** 287½ acres, Washington Co., bounded S. Willis, other sides vacant. Cut E. & W. by Buffalo creek, survey 944. Dec. 28, 1784, p. 422.

**WAGNER, JAMES.** 287½ acres, Washington Co., bounded W. Geo. Wagner, other sides vacant, on Fishing creek, survey 946. June 23, 1784, p. 423.

**WAGNER, GEORGE.** 287½ acres, Washington Co., bounded N. Porter, E. Jas. Wagner, S. & W. vacant, on Falling creek, survey 947. June 23, 1785, p. 423.

**WEST, WILLIAM.** 287½ acres, Washington Co., bounded N. Williamson's Swamp creek, other sides vacant or surveyed, survey 948. April 12, 1785, p. 424.

**WILLIAMSON, LITTLETON.** 230 acres, Washington Co., bounded (on Reserve) N. & E. vacant, S. Wagner, W. Chisholm, survey 949. Oct. 10, 1785, p. 424.

**WOOD, HEIRS OF CAPT. EDWARD.** 690 acres (on Reserve), Washington Co., bounded all sides vacant, on Rooty creek, survey 950. Nov. 18, 1784, p. 424.

**WAGNON, THOMAS.** 230 acres, Washington Co., bounded N. & E. vacant, S. Glascock, W. Chisholm, survey 951. Oct. 10, 1784, p. 425.

**WOOD, LIEUT. JAMES.** 460 acres, Washington Co., bounded (on Reserve) N. Houstoun & Hines, E. unknown, W. Call, survey 952. Oct. 25, 1784, p. 425.

**WILSON, SAMUEL.** 287½ acres, Washington Co., bounded N. vacant, E. Wilson, S. Carson, W. Carry, Godby, survey 953. July 10, 1784, p. 425.

**WEBSTER, SAMUEL.** 287½ acres, Washington Co., bounded N unknown, E. Jno. Burke, S. vacant, W. Rocky fork of Shoulderbone creek, survey 957. July 12, 1784, p. 427.

**YOUNG, WILLIAM.** 287½ acres, Washington Co., bounded N. Island creek, E. Breed, S. Capt. Glascock, W. vacant, survey 958. April 12, 1785, p. 427.

**YOUNG, LIEUT. DANIEL.** 460 acres, Washington Co., bounded N. Mount fork of Shoulderbone creek, E. & S. vacant, W. Anthony Metcalfe, survey 959. June 6, 1784, p. 427.

**YARBROUGH, THOMAS.** 287½ acres, Washington Co., bounded N. & W. vacant, E. Wm. Few, S. Buffalo creek, survey 960. June 25, 1784, p. 428.

**BACON, REUBEN.** 287½ acres, Washington Co., bounded N. & E. vacant, S. Ogeechee river, W. Archibald Beal, survey 961. Mar. 10, 1785, p. 428.

### SURVEYOR GENERAL'S BOOK " G."

**RAVOTT, ABRAHAM.** 287½ acres, Franklin Co., bounded N. & W. vacant, E. Robertson, S. Stafford, on upper south fork of Broad river, surveyor's No. 1. Aug. 26, 1784, p. 1.

**STUART, JAMES.** 287½ acres, Franklin Co., bounded all sides vacant, on N. fork of Oconee river, survey 2. Oct. 30, 1784, p. 1.

**PULLIAM, WILLIAM.** 287½ acres, Franklin Co., bounded N. S. Pulliam, E. & W. vacant, S. Jno. Clarke. Cut by N. fork of Broad river, survey 3. July 8, 1784, p. 2.

**PULLIAM, JOSEPH.** 287½ acres, Franklin Co., bounded N. & W. vacant, E. Robt. Pulliam, S. vacant. Cut E. & W. by Eastanaula creek, survey 4. May 24, 1784, p. 2.

## BOUNTY SURVEYS.

**PIERCE, ABRAHAM.** 287½ acres, Franklin Co., bounded N. & S. vacant, E. & W. Glascock, on north fork of Oconee river, survey 6. Oct. 30, 1784, p. 3.

**SNELSON, JAMES.** 287½ acres, Franklin Co., bounded S-W. Count DeEstang, other sides vacant, on north fork of Oconee river, survey 5. Nov. 1, 1784, p. 3.

**STUART, CLEMENT.** 287½ acres, Franklin Co., bounded all sides vacant, on north fork of Oconee river, survey 7. Oct. 30, 1784, p. 4.

**PULLIAM, WILLIAM.** 287½ acres, Franklin Co., bounded N. Jno. Troy, E. & W. vacant, S. S. Pulliam, on branch of Broad river, survey 8. July 8, 1784, p. 4.

**SCOTT, THOMAS.** 1,150 acres, Franklin Co., bounded S. north fork of Oconee river, other sides vacant. Cut by N. & S. forks of Curry's creek, survey 9. June 6, 1785, p. 5.

**STUBBS, JAMES.** 287½ acres, Franklin Co., bounded E. Simmons, other sides vacant, on Black creek of Broad river, survey 10, June 9, 1785, p. 6.

**STICKER, GEORGE.** 287½ acres, Franklin Co., bounded all sides vacant. Cut E. & W. by Curry's creek, survey 11. June 8, 1784, p. 6.

**SALLETT, ROBERT.** 575 acres, Franklin Co., bounded all sides vacant. Cut by Walnut creek of Oconee river, survey 13. June 27, 1784, p. 7.

**SWAIN, JAMES.** 287½ acres, Franklin Co., bounded N. Edw. Upton, other sides vacant, on Barber's creek, survey 15. Jan. 5, 1785, p. 8.

**O'NEIL, JOHN.** 287½ acres, Franklin Co., bounded all sides vacant, on Big Shoal creek, survey 17. June 3, 1784, p. 9.

**NICHOLS, WILLIAM.** 287½ acres, Franklin Co., bounded S. Thos. Broom, other sides vacant. Cut by north fork of Connoochee creek, survey 18. June 21, 1784, p. 10.

**OFFUTT, EZEKIEL..** 287½ acres, Franklin Co., bounded N. Robt. Walton, E. & W. vacant, S. William Pulliam. Cut N. & S. by south fork of Cobb's creek, survey 19. May 25, 1784, p. 10.

**OFFUTT, JOHN.** 287½ acres, Washington Co., bounded N. Nathl. Wade, E. Edw. Hall, S. vacant, W. John Fenn, on Rocky fork of Shoulderbone creek, survey 20. Nov. 16, 1784, p. 11.

**PALMER, JOHN.** 575 acres, Franklin Co., bounded all sides vacant. Cut by Oconee river, survey 21. July 25, 1784, p. 11.

**PITTMAN, JOHN.** 287½ acres, Franklin Co., bounded S. Middletown, other sides vacant, on Flatt creek, survey 22. Oct. 5, 1784, p. 12.

**PATTON, THOMAS.** 287½ acres, Franklin Co., bounded SW. Hardy Hinton, other sides vacant, on Gorman's fork of Broad river, survey 23. July 27, 1784, p. 12.

**QUEEN, WILLIAM.** 287½ acres, Franklin Co., bounded SE. Fuller, SW. north fork of Oconee river, other sides vacant, survey 24. June 8, 1784, p. 13.

**PAYNE, SAMUEL.** 287½ acres, Franklin Co., bounded N. Geo. Franklin, E. Thos. Adcock, other sides vacant, on Big Pond branch, survey 25. Oct. 28, 1784, p. 13.

**ROSE, JOHN.** 575 acres, Franklin Co., bounded S. Jas. Little, other sides vacant, on Broad river, survey 26. Aug. 20, 1784, p. 14.

**SIMMONS, WILLIAM.** 287½ acres, Franklin Co., bounded all sides vacant, on north fork of Broad river, survey 27. June 7, 1784, p. 14.

**STAFFORD, SAMUEL.** 287½ acres, Franklin Co., bounded all sides vacant, on south fork of Broad river, survey 28. Aug. 25, 1784, p. 15.

**SURES, JOHN.** 287½ acres, Franklin Co., bounded S. Thos. Snelson, other sides vacant, on north fork of Oconee river, survey 29. Oct. 10, p. 15.

**STANFORD, JOHN.** 287½ acres, Franklin Co., bounded N. & W. vacant, E. Thos. Snelson, S. Wm. Motte, on Oconee river, survey 30, Oct. 10, 1784, p. 16.

**ROSEBOROUGH, WILLIAM.** 287½ acres, Washington Co., bounded N. & E. vacant, S. Dan'l McCoy, W. Jno. Shaw, on Broad river, survey 31, Dec. 6, 1784, p. 16.

**SHOW, JOHN.** 287½ acres, Franklin Co., bounded N. & W. vacant, E. Roseborough, S. Jno. Wisener. Cut by Clarkes creek, survey 32. Dec. 6, 1784, p. 17.

**SNELSON, THOMAS.** 287½ acres, Franklin Co., bounded W. Wm. Motte, other sides vacant, on north fork of Oconee river, survey 33. Oct. 10, 1784, p. 17.

**SHANNON, OWEN.** 287½ acres, Franklin Co., bounded N. & E. vacant, S. Meredith Davis, W. Offutt, on Diamond fork of Oconee river, survey 34, Oct. 27, 1784, p. 18.

**SUMMERFORD, JACOB.** 287½ acres, Franklin Co., bounded N. & E. vacant, S. Oconee river, W. College lands, on middle fork of Oconee river, survey 35. June 9, 1784, p. 18.

**NELLY, JOHN.** 287½ acres, Franklin Co., bounded S. Jno. Barnett, other sides vacant, on Walnut & Pretty Run creeks, survey 36. June 25, 1784, p. 18.

**SHANNON, JOHN.** 287½ acres, Franklin Co., bounded N. & E. vacant, S. Anderson, W. Col. Clarke. Cut by Sandy creek survey 37. Aug. 16, 1784, p. 19.

## BOUNTY SURVEYS.

**PACE, BERNARD.** 287½ acres, bounded SE. Sears, SW. Walton, other sides vacant, on Oconee river, survey 38. June 2, 1784, p. 19.

**SCOTT, ALEXANDER.** 230 acres (on Reserve), Franklin Co., bounded N. & E. vacant, S. Col. Marbury, W. Wm. Thompson, survey 39. June 19, 1785, p. 19.

**RENCH, JOHN.** 287½ acres, Franklin Co., bounded W. Pope, other sides vacant, on north fork of Broad river, survey 40. July 10, 1784, p. 20.

**ROGERS, PETER.** 287½ acres, Franklin Co., bounded E. Jos. McCutchins, other sides vacant, on north fork Oconee river, survey 41. June 10, 1785, p. 20.

**SEAMAN, JOHN.** 287½ acres, Franklin Co., bounded N. & E. vacant, S. & W. Benj. Taliaferro, on Taliaferro creek, survey 42. Mar. 16, 1785, p. 21.

**RUNNELS, RICHARD.** 575 acres, Franklin Co., bounded S. Joshua Winn, other sides vacant, on middle fork of Broad river, survey 43. June 10, 1785, p. 21.

**SAFFORD, DANIEL.** 287½ acres, Franklin Co., bounded S. Jesse Webb, other sides vacant. Cut N. & S. by Shoal creek, survey 46. Sept. 30, 1784, p. 22.

**SUMMERLIN, WILLIAM.** 287½ acres, Franklin Co., bounded T. Willis Watson, other sides vacant, on Broad river, survey —. Mar. 16, 1785, p. 22.

**MILLER, MOSES.** 287½ acres, Franklin Co., bounded all sides vacant. Cut by Big Shoal creek, survey 54. June 1, 1784, p. 25.

**MARBURY, WILLIAM.** 287½ acres, Franklin Co., bounded N. & W. vacant, E. & S. north fork of Oconee river, survey 64. May 14, 1785, p. 29.

**ANDERSON, HENRY.** 287½ acres, Franklin Co., bounded all sides vacant. Cut by Chowestowe creek, survey 65. Dec. 12, 1784, p. 29.

**BEARD, EDMOND.** 287½ acres, Franklin Co., bounded all sides vacant, on Oconee river, survey 66. July 2, 1784, p. 29.

**McCOWEN, DANIEL.** 287½ acres, Franklin Co., bounded all sides vacant, Cut by Bear creek tributary of Oconee river, survey 67. Jan. 24, 1785, p. 30

**MAY, JOHN.** 287½ acres, Franklin Co., bounded all sides vacant, survey 68. June 10, 1785, p. 30.

**LINN, THOMAS.** 287½ acres, Franklin Co., bounded W. Jno. King, other sides vacant, on north fork of Oconee river, survey 69. June 10, 1785, p. 30.

**McCULLOCH, SAMUEL.** 287½ acres, Franklin Co., bounded W. Stephen Evans, other sides vacant. Cut by Gravelly creek, survey 70. **May 6, 1785, p. 31.**

**KINNEBREW, JACOB.** 287½ acres, Franklin Co., bounded N. & W. vacant, E. Saml. McCulloch, S. Peter Curry, on Gravelly Run creek, survey 71. May 6, 1785, p. 31.

ROSTER OF THE REVOLUTION.

**KENDRICK, HEZEKIAH.** 287½ acres, Franklin Co., bounded N. & W. vacant, E. unknown, S. north fork of Oconee river, survey 72. June 18, 1784, p. 31.

**MIDDLETON, WILLIAM.** 287½ acres, Franklin Co., bounded N. Saml. Payne, E. & S. vacant, W. Jas. Cobb. Cut E. & W. by Big Pond fork Oconee river, survey 73. Oct. 28, 1784, p. 32.

**MOTTE, WILLIAM.** 287½ acres, Franklin Co., bounded S. Ezekiel Offutt, other sides vacant, on Curry creek, survey 74. Oct. 10, 1784, p. 32.

**LITTLE, JAMES.** 575 acres, Franklin Co., bounded S. Jacob Hubbard, other sides vacant, on Broad river, survey 77. June 6, 1784, p. 33.

**McKOY, DANIEL.** 287½ acres, Washington Co., bounded N. Roseborough, E. & S. vacant, W. Wesener, on Clarke's creek and Broad river, survey 75. Dec. 6, 1784, p. 32.

**McLEAN, LEWIS.** 287½ acres, Franklin Co., bounded all sides vacant, on Broad river, survey 76. June 10, 1784, p. 33.

**MATTHEWS, ISHAM.** 287½ acres, Franklin Co., bounded all sides vacant. Cut E. & W. by Curry's creek, survey 78. June 11, 1784, p. 33.

**MATTHEWS, WILLIAM.** 287½ acres, Franklin Co., bounded E. Isham Matthews, other sides vacant, on Sandy creek, survey 80. June 11, 1784, p. 34.

**McCAIN, THOMAS.** 287½ acres, Franklin Co., bounded S. Tugalo river, other sides vacant, survey 81. Dec. 13, 1784, p. 34.

**MORRISON, JOHN.** 575 acres, Franklin Co., bounded N. Glascock, E. & S. vacant, W. Dr. Creswell, on Tugalo river, survey 82. Dec. 1, 1784, p. 35.

**MATTHEWS, DANIEL.** 287½ acres, Franklin Co., bounded S. Francis Gideon, other sides vacant. Cut by Sandy creek, survey 83. June 24, 1784, p. 35.

**MORGAN, JOHN.** 287½ acres, Franklin Co., bounded W. Wm. Moss, other sides vacant. Cut E. & W. by Tom creek, survey 84. July 8, 1784, p. 35.

**McLENDON, DENNIS.** 287½ acres, Franklin Co., bounded all sides vacant, on Broad river, survey 85. Dec. 11, 1784, p. 36.

**MITCHELL, WILLIAM.** 287½ acres, Franklin Co., bounded S. Oconee river, other sides vacant. Cut by Beaverdam creek, survey 87. May 17, 1784, p. 36.

**ANDERSON, WILLIAM.** 200 acres, Wilkes Co., bounded N. Joshua Miller, W. Jones, other sides vacant, on Middle creek, survey 88. Aug. 13, 1784, p. 37.

**ATKINS, ARNOLD.** 200 acres, Wilkes Co., bounded N. Creswell, other sides vacant, on Little river, survey 89. Oct. 3, 1784, p. 37.

**ARMOUR, ANDREW.** 200 acres, Wilkes Co., bounded S. grantee, other sides vacant. Cut N. & S. by Indian creek, survey 91. Sept. 10, 1784, p. 38.

## BOUNTY SURVEYS.

**ANSLEY, THOMAS.** 287½ acres, Wilkes Co., bounded all sides vacant. Touched by Curl's Folly creek, survey 113. Sept. 18, 1784, p. 46.

**BANKSTON, ELIJAH.** 287½ acres, Wilkes Co., bounded all sides vacant, survey 151. Nov. 16, 1784, p. 59.

**BENDER, JOHN.** 287½ acres, Franklin Co., bounded E. Oconee river, other sides vacant, survey 156. Jan. 25, 1785, p. 61.

**BANKSTON, DANIEL.** 287½ acres, Wilkes Co., bounded N. vacant, E. & S. Peter Smith, W. Geo. Lumpkin, marked "Lampkin's Path to Washington," survey 190. Nov. 20, 1785, p. 101.

**CANDLER, HENRY.** 575 acres, Washington Co., bounded N. Seals & Marshall, other sides vacant, survey 274. Nov. 10, 1784, p. 101.

**CLARKE, ELIJAH.** 575 acres, Wilkes Co., bounded N. William Johnston, E. & S. vacant, W. Jno. Lacy, on Long creek, survey 289. Sept. 15, 1784, p. 106.

**COLLINS, BRICE.** 287½ acres, Wilkes Co., bounded N. Shellman & Climas, other sides vacant, survey 310. Sept. 14, 1784, p. 114.

**JONES, PHILIP.** 287½ acres, Wilkes Co., bounded N. Savannah river, E. Langford, S. Robt. Walton, W. unknown. Cut N. & S. by Well's creek, survey 565. Sept. 16, 1784, p. 202.

**LUCAS, WILLIAM.** 287½ acres, Wilkes Co., bounded all sides vacant, survey 595. Aug. 18, 1784, p. 213.

### SURVEYOR GENERAL'S BOOK "H."

**BROWNFIELD, JOHN.** 287½ acres, Wilkes Co., bounded N. grantee, E. McLean, S. Brownfield, W. Geo. Calhoun, survey 459. Aug. 10, 1784, p. 237.

**THOMAS, JAMES.** 287½ acres, Wilkes Co., bounded (old Bounty Warrant) E. Long creek, S. Hutchinson, W. Williams, survey 619. Sept. 12, 1784, p. 320.

**RYAN, JOSEPH.** 287½ acres, Wilkes Co., bounded N. Hitt, E. Benj. Allen, S. surveyed, W. Banks & Vassar. Cut by Indian creek, survey 678. July 5, 1785, p. 349.

### SURVEYOR GENERAL'S BOOK "I."

**FORD, JOHN, JR.** 287½ acres, Burke Co., bounded N. Hollingsworth, E. Taylor, S. Sapp, W. Chas. Kimble, survey 23. May 12, 1786, p. 9.

**GRANT, ANDREW.** 287½ acres, Burke Co., bounded N. & W. vacant, E. Hughes, S. Stratton, on north side Buckhead creek, survey 26, Nov. 23, 1785, p. 10.

**JONES, BATT.** 287½ acres, Burke Co., bounded E. James Jones, other sides vacant, on McIntosh creek, survey 38. Feb. 5, 1785, p. 14.

**LEWIS, BENJAMIN.** 287½ acres, Burke Co., bounded N. Allday, E. & S. vacant, W. Thomas, survey 43. Mar. 13, 1785, p. 16.

**LEWIS, DAVID.** 287½ acres, Burke Co., bounded E. Henry Turner, other sides vacant, on Cheaver's creek, survey 44. Aug. 21, 1786, p. 17.

**KELLY, WILLIAM.** 287½ acres, Washington Co., bounded S. Chas. Collins, other sides vacant, near Oconee river, survey —. May 17, 1784, p. —.

**BURKE, JOSEPH.** 287½ acres, Franklin Co., bounded S. M. Gunnold, other sides vacant, on North fork of Oconee river, survey 164. Aug. 5, 1785, p. 76.

**COLLINS, JOHN.** 287½ acres, Franklin Co., bounded S. Harding, other sides unknown, on fork of Candy creek, survey 165. Sept. 5, 1784, p. 76.

**BUSSON, JONATHAN.** 287½ acres, Franklin Co., bounded S. Jas. Manon, other sides vacant, on Oconee river, survey —. Feb. 9, 1785, p. —.

**BERRY, GIDEON.** 287½ acres, Franklin Co., bounded all sides unknown or vacant, survey 169. April 26, 1785, p. 78.

**BOND, GEORGE.** 287½ acres, Franklin Co., bounded S. Elijah Dennison, other side vacant, on north fork of Broad river, survey 171. June 7, 1784, p. 79.

**AYRES, ABRAHAM.** 287½ acres, Franklin Co., bounded N. Montfort, other sides vacant. Cut by Little creek, survey 175. April 11, 1785, p. 81.

**SEGAR, GEORGE.** 287½ acres, Burke Co., bounded N. Lewis & Evans, E. vacant, W. Geo. Segars, & Wm. Barron, survey 185. May 8, 1786, p. 86.

**BECKHAM, ABNER.** 287½ acres, Burke Co., bounded N. David Lewis, other sides vacant, survey 203. July 24, 1786, p. 95.

**PERSONS, JONES.** 287½ acres, Franklin Co., bounded all sides vacant, or surveyed. Cut N. & S. by north fork of Oconee river, survey 227. Aug. 18, 1784, p. 107.

**JOHNSON, GEORGE.** 287½ acres, Glynn Co., bounded all sides vacant, survey 252. Sept. 10, 1786, p. 120.

**MORRISON, JOHN.** 287½ acres, Camden Co., bounded N. & E. vacant, S. Gt. Satilla river, W. Jno. Strong, survey 254. Dec. 28, 1785, p. 121.

**MERCER, THOMAS.** 287½ acres, Washington Co., bounded W. Benj. Few, other sides vacant, on Williamson's Swamp creek, survey 297. May 4, 1785, p. 144.

**BOSWELL, DAVID.** 287½ acres, Greene Co., bounded N. Wm. Brown, E. Benj. James, S. unknown, W. Wilkes Co., line on Big creek, survey 315. Mar. 29, 1786, p. 150.

**PULLIAM, WILLIAM.** 287½ acres, Franklin Co., bounded S. Jno. Cobb, other sides vacant. Cut N. & S. by Shoal creek, survey 325. June 10, 1785, p. 155.

# BOUNTY SURVEYS.

**NORWOOD, RICHARD.** 287½ acres, Franklin Co., bounded all sides vacant. Cut E. & W. by south fork of Broad river, survey 337. Oct. 20, 1785, p. 161.

**GREER, DAVID.** 287½ acres, Franklin Co., bounded all sides vacant. Cut E. & W. by middle fork of Broad river, survey 354. July 20, 1785, p. 170.

**FEW, BENJAMIN.** 287½ acres, Washington Co., bounded S. grantee, other sides vacant, on Buffalo creek, survey 414. Sept. 5, 1785, p. 200.

**AYRES, WILLIAM.** 287½ acres, Wilkes Co., bounded N. Maj. McCall, E. & S. Stewart, W. vacant, on branch Little River, survey 430. May 8, 1787, p. 203.

**YOUNGBLOOD, JOHN.** 287½ acres, Richmond Co., bounded all sides vacant. Cut S.-W. to N.-E. by Boggy Cutt creek, survey 439. July 13, 1785, p. 213.

**BECKHAM, SOLOMAN.** 287½ acres, Washington Co., bounded N. Thos. Moxley, E. Eiland, S. Saml. Beckham, W. vacant, on Town creek, survey 478. Dec. 31, 1784, p. 239.

**BECKHAM, SAMUEL.** 287½ acres, Washington Co., bounded N. Eiland, E. & S. vacant, W. Soloman Beckham. Cut by Town creek, survey 479. Dec. 31, 1784, p. 339.

**THORNTON, WILLIAM.** 287½ acres, Washington Co., bounded all sides vacant, survey 549. Dec. 29, 1784, p. 275.

**ADAMSON, CHARLES.** 230 acres (on Reserve), Washington Co., bounded N. & W. vacant, E. Matthew Carney, S. Oconee river, survey 568. Oct. 10, 1784, p. 286.

**BURNES, ANDREW.** 287½ acres, Franklin Co., bounded N. Jno. Kelly, E. Isham Young, other sides vacant. Cut by Eastaunola creek, survey 570. April 4, 1784, p. 287.

**HUNT, FITZMAURICE.** 287½ acres, Richmond Co., bounded N. & W. vacant, E. Ab. Davis, S. Hunt & Perkins, survey 572. May 8, 1787, p. 288.

**BEAZLEY, JOSEPH.** 287½ acres, Washington Co., bounded N.-W. Peak, S. Walker, other sides vacant, survey —. Oct. 26, 1784, p. 290.

**FUQUA, PRATER.** 287½ acres, Washington Co., bounded W. Benj. Catchings, other sides vacant, on fork of DeRozeaux creek, survey 577. July 9, 1784, p. 290.

**DAVIS, MYRICK.** 287½ acres, Richmond Co., bounded N. McBean's creek, S. Fould, other sides vacant, survey 578. Nov. 23, 1787, p. 291.

**WARD, CHARLES.** 287½ acres, Burke Co., bounded N. Simon Jackett, E. Tanner, S. Taylor, W. vacant, survey 639. Mar. 8, 1786, p. 309.

**BECKHAM, ALLEN.** 287½ acres, Washington Co., bounded N. Floyd, E. Walker, S. Shuffels, W. unknown, on south fork of Town creek, survey 650. Jan. 15, 1787, p. 309.

**HICKS, NATHANIEL.** 287½ acres, Washington Co., bounded all sides vacant. Cut by Ohoopee river, survey 628. April 23, 1787, p. 323.

**ANDREWS, BENJAMIN.** 287½ acres, Liberty Co., bounded N. Young, E. Edw. Ball, S. Wm. Bacon, W. vacant, survey 698. Dec. 26, 1785, p. 336.

**CLARKE, WILLIAM.** 287½ acres, Liberty Co., bounded N. & W. Altamaha river, E. vacant, S. grantee, p. 336.

**BACON, JOHN.** 287½ acres, Liberty Co., bounded N. & S. grantee, E. vacant, W. Francis Arthur, survey 706. Nov. 16, 1785, p. 339.

**WARREN, ELIAS.** 287½ acres, Liberty Co., bounded E. David Duke, other sides vacant, survey 717. July 22, 1785, p. 345.

**WARREN, JOHN.** 287½ acres, Liberty Co., bounded W. Ducker, other sides vacant, survey 718. July 10, 1785, p. 345.

**GRAVES, JOHN.** 287½ acres, Camden Co., bounded N. grantee, E. vacant, S. Gilbert Harrison, W. Peter Tarling, survey 725. Sept. 10, 1785, p. 349.

**McINTOSH, CAPT. LACHLIN.** 690 acres (on Reserve), Franklin Co., bounded N. north fork of Oconee river, E. Dr. Wm. Reid, other sides vacant, survey 730. March 23, 1785, p. 352.

**BROOKS, ROGER.** 240 acres, Washington Co., bounded N. unknown, E. Booker, S. Carr, W. Academy lands, on Shoulderbone creek, survey 736. July —, 1785, p. 355.

**MORRISON, CAPT. JOHN.** 690 acres (on Reserve), Washington Co., bounded N. vacant, E. Eve, S. Oconee river, W. Crawford & Lancaster, survey 742. Nov. 25, 1784, p. 358.

**DAVENPORT, STEPHEN.** 230 acres (on Reserve), Washington Co., bounded N. surveyed, other sides vacant, survey 743. Nov. 15, 1784, p. 359.

**MAXWELL, GEORGE.** 230 acres (on Reserve), Washington Co., bounded N. Morrison, E. Oconee river, S. vacant, W. Jas. Maxwell, survey 744. Nov. 28, 1784, p. 359.

**LANCASTER, WILLIAM.** 230 acres (on Reserve), Washington Co., bounded N. Morrison, E. Maxwell, S. & W. vacant. Cut by Oconee river, survey 745. Nov. 28, 1784, p. 360.

**ANDREWS, SAMUEL.** 287½ acres, Washington Co., bounded W. Buffalo creek, other sides vacant, survey 749. April 10, 1786, p. 362.

**BRIGGS, SAMUEL.** 287½ acres, Burke Co., bounded N. & E. vacant, S. Catlett, W. Pleasant Goodall. Cut in N.-W. corner by Beaverdam creek, survey 874. Feb. 14, 1785, p. 427.

**BRACK, BENJAMIN.** 287½ acres, Burke Co., bounded N. Tennison & Meadows, other sides vacant, on fork of Sandy Run creek, survey 956. April 10, 1787, p. 467.

## BOUNTY SURVEYS.

**EMANUEL, DAVID.** 287½ acres, Burke Co., bounded all sides vacant, on Major's Branch creek, survey 960. Jan. 2, 1786, p. 469.

**GOODWYN, THEODORE.** 287½ acres, Burke Co., bounded all sides vacant, on branch of McBean's creek, survey 976. May 6, 1785, p. 477.

**GRAY, MATTHIAS.** 287½ acres, Burke Co., bounded all sides vacant. Cut E. & W. by Gray's branch, survey 980. Aug. 3, 1785, p. 479.

**GREEN, JOHN.** 287½ acres, Burke Co., bounded N. & W. vacant, E. Green & Burneman, S. Jno. Green. Cut N.-W. to S.-E. by Rocky creek, survey 1,007. Aug. 9, 1785, p. 493.

**FORD, THOMAS.** 287½ acres, Burke Co., bounded all sides vacant. Cut by Brier creek, survey 1,023. Aug. 25, 1785, p. 501.

**LAWSON, ROGER.** 287½ acres, Burke Co., bounded N. Widow Rae, E. vacant, S. Rocky creek, W. Richard Johnson, survey 1,089. May 15, 1786, p. 536.

**LEWIS, JACOB.** 287½ acres, Burke Co., bounded N. grantee, other sides vacant, on Big Pond, head of Jordan's branch, survey 1,102. Jan. 13, 1785, p. 542.

**LINN, JOHN.** 287½ acres, Burke Co., bounded N. & E. vacant, S. Mulky, W. Gray & Nelson, survey 1,108. May 13, 1786, p. 545.

**MOORE, WILLIAM.** 287½ acres, Burke Co., bounded S. Richard Burkeloe, other sides vacant. Cut N. & S. by Newberry creek, survey 1,150. Feb. 1, 1785, p. 566.

**SEABERT, JOHN.** 287½ acres, Burke Co., bounded N. Jared Irwin, E. vacant, S. Samuel Elbert, W. Jas. Rae & Co., survey 1,257. Mar. 9, 1785, p. 625.

**SEGAR, SAMUEL.** 287½ acres, Burke Co., bounded N. Elizabeth Tanner, E. Duke & vacant, S. vacant, W. Ward & Kennedy, survey 1,260. June 9, 1786, p. 626.

**SAPP, PHILIP.** 287½ acres, Burke Co., bounded N. Jas. Lambeth, E. Taylor & Liverman, S. Clarg, W. D. Sapp. Cut by Peters branch, survey 1,266. April 30, 1787, p. 629.

### SURVEYOR GENERAL'S BOOK "K."

**ASHWORTH, BENJAMIN.** 575 acres, Franklin Co., bounded N. Washington Co. line, E. Benj. Brewer, S. Wooten & Walton, W. surveyed, survey 3. Jan. 27, 1786, p. 2.

**ANDERSON, JOHN.** 287½ acres, Washington Co., bounded S. Dixon, other sides vacant, on head of Buffalo creek, survey 20. June 11, 1784, p. 11.

**AYRES, WILLIAM.** 287½ acres, Washington Co., bounded N. & E. vacant, S. Jacob Davis, W. Canoocha river. Cut by Dogwood creek, survey 38. Dec. 5, 1785, p. 24.

**AVERETT, JOHN.** 287½ acres, Washington Co., bounded N. Little Ogeechee river, other sides vacant, survey 39. Mar. 4, 1785, p. 24.

**ALLISON, LIEUT. HENRY.** 460 acres (on Reserve), Washington Co., bounded N. & E. surveyed, S. vacant, W. fork of Oconee river, survey 40. Sept. 10, 1785, p. 25.

**ARMOUR, ANDREW.** 287½ acres, Greene Co., bounded N. Jas. Wilson, E. unknown, S. grantee, W. Miles Duncan. Cut by Beaverdam creek, survey 42. July 5, 1785, p. 26.

**ABERCROMBIE, CHARLES.** 230 acres (on Reserve), Greene Co., bounded N. Smith, other sides vacant, survey 50. Mar. 10, 1786, p. 31.

**ABERCROMBIE, CHARLES.** 287½ acres, Greene Co., bounded N. & E. vacant, S. grantee, W. grantee, on Buffalo creek, survey 51, May 4, 1786, p. 31.

**BUTLER, FORD.** 287½ acres, Franklin Co., bounded W. Jno. Partin, other sides vacant. Cut E. & W. by Big Shoal creek, survey 53. June 2, 1785, p. 32.

**BAILEY, WILLIAM.** 287½ acres, Franklin Co., bounded S. Jas. Easter, other sides vacant. Cut N. & S. by Tom's creek, survey 58. May 6, 1785, p. 36.

**BERRIEN, JOHN.** 920 acres (on Reserve), Franklin Co., bounded all sides vacant. Touched by middle fork of Oconee river, survey 59. Dec. 20, 1785, p. 36.

**BROWN, ALLEN.** 287½ acres, Franklin Co., bounded N. Jno. Talbot, E. & S. vacant, W. Jno. Kelly, on Eastanola creek, survey 62. Dec. 21, 1784, p. 38.

**BEDINGFIELD, CHARLES.** 287½ acres, Franklin Co., bounded W. Henry Black, other sides vacant. Cut by Gorham's fork, survey 65. June 7, 1784, p. 38.

**BURNETT, JOHN.** 287½ acres, Franklin Co., bounded all sides vacant, on N. fork of Oconee river, survey 72. Oct. 30, 1784, p. 43.

**BENDER, JOHN.** 287½ acres, Franklin Co., bounded N. fork of Oconee river, E. Jno. Hollingshead, other sides vacant, survey 76. April 10, 1786, p. 45.

**CRESWELL, SAMUEL.** 287½ acres, Franklin Co., bounded all sides vacant. Cut by Chawga creek, of Tugalo river, survey 114. May 8, 1785, p. 65.

**CONNELL, THOMAS.** 287½ acres, Franklin Co., bounded E. Geo. White, other sides vacant, on Oconee river, survey 135. April 1, 1786, p. 79.

**COLTER, JOHN.** 287½ acres, Franklin Co., bounded all sides vacant. Cut by Beaverdam creek, survey 148. Mar. 10, 1786, p. 86.

**CHAPMAN, WILLIAM.** 287½ acres, Franklin Co., bounded all sides vacant. Cut N. & S. by Indian creek, survey 155. Aug. 2, 1784, p. 90.

## BOUNTY SURVEYS. 303

**CURLE, HENRY.** 287½ acres, Franklin Co., bounded E. Edw. Upton, other sides vacant, on Barber's creek, survey 173. Jan. 23, 1785, p. 103.

**CROCKET, SAMUEL.** 287½ acres, Franklin Co., bounded all sides vacant. Cut E. & W. by Crocket's creek, survey 185. Sept. 5, 1784, p. 109.

**DUKES, TAYLOR.** 287½ acres, Franklin Co., bounded all sides vacant, on north fork of Oconee river, survey 201. Oct. 4, 1784, p. 118.

**DALTON, MATTHIAS.** 287½ acres, Franklin Co., bounded N. & E. vacant, S. north fork of Oconee river, W. Frank, survey 202. June 8, 1785, p. 118.

**DORTON, THOMAS.** 287½ acres, Franklin Co., bounded all sides vacant. Cut S.-E. to N.-W. by Bear creek, survey 203. July 15, 1784, p. 119.

**DENNISON, ELIJAH.** 287½ acres, Franklin Co., bounded N. Geo. Bond, other sides vacant, on fork of Broad river, survey 211. June 7, 1784, p. 123.

**DALTON, THOMAS.** 287½ acres, Franklin Co., bounded all sides vacant. Cut diagonally by Bear creek, survey 212. July 15, 1784, p. 123.

**DOOLEN, JOHN.** 287½ acres, Wilkes Co., bounded N. Wm. Dudley, E. Moon, S. Geo. Darden, W. unknown, on Hooley creek survey 215. Nov. 24, 1786, p. 125.

**EVANS, BENJAMIN.** 287½ acres, Washington Co., bounded N. Little Ogeechee river, E. & S. vacant, W. Samuel Sinquefield, survey 234. Sept. 2, 1784, p. 142.

**FARRISH, ROBERT.** 460 acres (on Reserve) Franklin Co., bounded N. & E. surveyed, S. Michael Long, W. Chandlers. Cut by Oconee river, survey 235. Mar. 5, 1785, p. 135.

**FREEMAN, JAMES.** 287½ acres, Franklin Co., bounded N. Savannah river, other sides vacant. Cut by Lightwood Log creek, survey 243. Oct. 10, 1785, p. 139.

**FIELDS, WILLIAM.** 287½ acres, Franklin Co., bounded all sides vacant, on south cut of Broad river, survey 247. Aug. 24, 1784, p. 142.

**FREEMAN, JAMES.** 230 acres (on Reserve), Franklin Co., bounded E. H. Freeman, other sides vacant, on Horse creek, survey 248. June 10, 1785, p. 142.

**FEW, BENJAMIN.** 287½ acres, Washington Co., bounded N. vacant, E. grantee, S. Ogeechee river, W. grantee, survey 277. May 8, 1785, p. 160.

**FEW, IGNATIUS.** 287½ acres, Washington Co., bounded N. Jesse Miller, other sides vacant. Cut by Williamson's Swamp creek, survey 282. April 9, 1785, p. 162.

**FREEMAN, JOHN.** 287½ acres, Washington Co., bounded E. Jno. Rogers, other sides vacant (W. Elisha Anderson). Cut E. & W. by Big creek, survey 295. Mar. 17, 1785, p. 160.

## ROSTER OF THE REVOLUTION.

**FITZPATRICK, RENE.** 230 acres (on Reserve), Greene Co., bounded N. Arch. Grisson, E. Curtis Welborn, S. Buchannon, W. Simonton, on Greenbrier creek, survey 323. Mar. 23, 1786, p. 187.

**FITZPATRICK, WILLIAM.** 460 acres (on Reserve), Greene Co., bounded N. Burton, E. vacant, S. Allison, W. Forsyth. Cut by Greenbrier creek, survey 323. Mar. 11, 1785, p. 188.

**GAY, WILLIAM.** 287½ acres, Franklin Co., bounded N. & S. vacant, E. McCall, W. Huntsman. Cut by Little creek, survey 352. Nov. 25, 1785, p. 204.

**GREER, DAVID.** 287½ acres, Franklin Co., bounded S. Jno. Johnston, other sides vacant. Cut E. & W. by Hudson river, survey 358. July 7, 1785, p. 208.

**GREER, DAVID.** 287½ acres, Franklin Co., bounded all sides vacant. Cut E. & W. by middle fork of Broad river, survey 368. July 10, 1785, p. 215.

**HAY, WILLIAM.** 287½ acres, Franklin Co., bounded all sides vacant. Cut by Beaverdam creek, of Broad river, survey —. Mar. 8, 1786, p. 220.

**HARGIS, JAMES.** 287½ acres, Franklin Co., bounded S. Richard Bellamy, other sides vacant. Cut N. & S. by Nails creek, survey 391. May 24, 1784, p. 229.

**HATCHER, VALENTINE.** 287½ acres, Franklin Co., bounded all sides vacant. Cut by fork of Broad river, survey 393. May 17, 1784, p. 330.

**HARRIS, THOMAS.** 230 acres (on Reserve), Franklin Co., bounded N. Jno. Smith, E. vacant, S. Woodward, W. Jno. Corham, survey 396. May 4, 1785, p. 232.

**HUNT, WILLIAM, JR.** 287½ acres, Franklin Co., bounded E. Hawkins, other sides vacant. Cut E. & W. by Shoulderbone creek, survey 403, June 30, 1784, p. 236.

**HAWKINS, ABIMELECK.** 287½ acres, Franklin Co., bounded E. College lands, other sides vacant, on Oconee river, survey 404. July 6, 1787, p. 236.

**HOLLIDAY, AMBROSE.** 287½ acres, Richmond Co., bounded E. Carmichael, other sides vacant, survey 429. Aug. 22, 1786, p. 249.

**JACK, JOHN.** 287½ acres, Franklin Co., bounded N. & E. vacant, S. surveyed, W. Oconee river, survey 448. July 2, 1787, p. 261.

**INLOW, SEVASTIN.** 287½ acres, Franklin Co., bounded S. Geo. Walton, other sides vacant, on Fork of Bear creek, survey 453. Dec. 2, 1784, p. 263.

**JENKINS, ROBERT.** 230 acres (on Reserve), Washington Co., bounded N. vacant, E. & W. surveyed, S. Continental fork of Oconee river, survey 477. Oct. 3, 1785, p. 276.

## BOUNTY SURVEYS

**JORDAN, DEMPSEY.** 287½ acres, Washington Co., bounded all sides surveyed, survey 478. July 23, 1784, p. 277.

**JOHNSTON, RICHARD.** 575 acres, Washington Co., bounded N. Gordon, E. unknown, S. Carson, & Howell, W. Phillips. Cut by Richland creek, survey 481. Sept. 13, 1785, p. 278.

**JONES, WILLIAM.** 287½ acres, Burke Co., bounded S. Jno. McQueen, other sides vacant, survey 485. April 13, 1786, p. 282.

**KELLY, JOHN.** 287½ acres, Franklin Co., bounded N. Jno. Toller, E. Allen Brown, S. H. Wilson, W. vacant. Cut by Eastanola creek, survey 499. Dec. 21, 1784, p. 288.

**KING, JOHN.** 690 acres (on Reserve), Washington Co., bounded all sides vacant, on Oconee river, survey 517. Sept. 6, 1785, p. 299.

**KELLY, JACOB.** (2nd bounty) 287½ acres, Washington Co., bounded S. Erwin, other sides vacant, survey 523. Mar. 22, 1785, p. 302.

**KENDRICK, HEZEKIAH.** 287½ acres, Washington Co., bounded N. Wiggins, E. & S. vacant, W. Henry Williams. Cut by Town creek, survey 527. June 16, 1784, p. 304.

**KENNEDY, JOHN.** 287½ acres, Washington Co., bounded N. Edw. Williams, E. & W. vacant, S. Friel. Cut by Buffalo creek, survey 529. June 26, 1784, p. 305.

**LEGETT, JOHN.** 287½ acres, Franklin Co., bounded all sides vacant. Cut N. & S. by Oconee river, survey 532. June 5, 1784, p. 308.

**LOCKHART, RICHARD.** 287½ acres, Franklin Co., bounded all sides vacant. Cut E. & W. by south fork of Broad river, survey 534. Mar. 12, 1786, p. 309.

**LAZARUS, NICHOLAS.** 230 acres (on Reserve), Franklin Co., bounded all sides vacant, survey 536. July 5, 1784, p. 310.

**LINDSAY, JAMES.** 287½ acres, Franklin Co., bounded E. Wm. Thompson, other sides vacant, on Eastanola creek, survey 537. June 12, 1785, p. 310.

**LEVINS, RICHARD.** 287½ acres, Franklin Co., bounded S. Curle, other sides vacant. Cut S.-W. to N.-E. by Barber's creek, survey 549. Mar. 11, 1785, p. 318.

**LAMAR, THOMAS.** 287½ acres, Washington Co., bounded N. & E. vacant, S. Jeremiah Hatcher, W. Middleton, on Rocky fork of Shoulderbone creek, survey 587. Nov. 13, 1784, p. 328.

**LEWIS, THOMAS.** 287½ acres, Washington Co., bounded N. Heirs of Joel Lewis, E. & S. vacant, W. Wm. Wash, survey 569. June 4, 1784, p. 329.

**LINN, CHARLES.** 287½ acres, Washington Co., bounded N. & W. vacant, E. Walker, S. Wright & Island, on Fork creek, survey 571. Dec. 14, 1785, p. 330.

ROSTER OF THE REVOLUTION.

**LOWE, JOHN.** 287½ acres, Washington Co., bounded N. Shoulderbone creek, other sides vacant, survey 572. June 5, 1784, p. 330.

**LONGSTREET, DANIEL.** 287½ acres, Washington Co., bounded N. Wagon, other sides vacant. Cut N. & S. Ogeechee river, survey 573. Jan. 1, 1787, p. 331.

**LETT, REUBEN.** 287½ acres, Washington Co., bounded S. Deep creek, other sides vacant, survey 574. Mar. 21, 1785, p. 331.

**LITHGOWE, ANDREW.** 287½ acres, Washington Co., bounded N. O'Neal, E. Melton, S. & W. vacant, survey 576. July 3, 1784, p. 332.

**LEWIS, JOEL.** 287½ acres, Washington Co., bounded N. & E. vacant, S. Thos. Lewis, W. David Emanuel. Cut by Mill creek, survey 577. June 4, 1784, p. 333.

**LEWIS, HEIRS OF DR. EVAN.** 690 acres (on Reserve), Washington Co. bounded N. Pearre, E. Oconee river, S. Jno. Maise, W. vacant, survey 579. Nov. 14, 1784, p. 334.

**LEWIS, WILLIAM, JR.** 287½ acres, Burke Co., bounded N. & S. vacant, E. Wm. Lord, W. David Ward, on Rocky creek, survey 591. Jan. 17, 1787, p. 334.

**LEWIS, WILLIAM, SR.** 287½ acres, Burke Co., bounded by Widow Bull, Brier creek, Benj. Warren, Susan Thomas, Tilly & Wolfington (odd shape), survey 593. June 21, 1786, p. 341.

### SURVEYOR GENERAL'S BOOK "L."

**CLARKE, WILLIAM.** 287½ acres, Liberty Co., bounded N. grantee, E. vacant, S. Elijah Lewis, W. Altamaha river, survey 3, March 19, 1785, p. 2.

**HOWELL, DANIEL.** 287½ acres, Effingham Co., bounded N. Thos. Howell, E. William Howell & Barton, S. Philip Dell, W. vacant, survey 55. Mar. 7, 1785, p. 29.

**HOWELL, CALEB.** 287½ acres, Effingham Co., bounded N. & E. vacant, S. Chaplin Williams, W. Philip Dell, survey 58. May 27, 1785, p. 31.

**LANIER, CLEMENT.** 287½ acres, Effingham Co., bounded N. Great Ogeechee river, E. & S. vacant, W. Chas. Mizell, survey 91. Mar. 14, 1786, p. 48.

**THOMPSON, JAMES.** 287½ acres, Effingham Co., bounded N. Thompson, other sides vacant. Cut N. & S. by Black creek, survey —. Sept. 5, 1785, p. —.

**EMBRY, JESSE.** 287½ acres, Burke Co., bounded N. vacant, E. Jacob Martin, S. Beaverdam creek, W. Tatnell & Freeman, survey 210. Mar. 30, 1786, p. 109.

**EDWARDS, JOHN.** 287½ acres, Burke Co., bounded N. Zach Fryar, E. Sheftall, S. Gray, W. vacant, survey 211. Jan. 21, 1786, p. 110.

# BOUNTY SURVEYS

**MARTIN, JACOB.** 287½ acres, Burke Co., bounded N. vacant, E. Jno. McQueen, S. Beaverdam creek, W. Jesse Embry, survey 263. Mar. 30, 1786, p. 136.

**NELSON, THOMAS.** 287½ acres, Burke Co., bounded N. Harroldson, & Bell, E. vacant, S. Jno. Walker, W. Fussell, survey 265. Oct. 15, 1785, p. 137.

**STOUT, DAVID.** 287½ acres, Burke Co., bounded W. John Sapp, other sides vacant, survey 297. April 26, 1787, p. 153.

**THOMAS, SAMUEL.** 287½ acres, Burke Co., bounded N. & W. vacant, E. Thos. Bell, S. Daniel Bullard, survey 316. Jan. 19, 1787, p. 163

**WARD, JOHN, BY ELIZABETH WARD FOR HIS HEIRS.** 287½ acres, Burke Co., bounded S. Rocky Comfort creek, other sides vacant, survey 331. Jan. 27, 1786, p. 170.

**BUGG, WILLIAM.** 287½ acres, Richmond Co., bounded N. Anderson, & Grierson, E. Wm. Simms, S. Lamar, Reynolds & Muer. Cut by Cowen's creek, survey 183. July 4, 1786, p. 183.

**BARTON, WILLOUGHBY.** 287½ acres, Richmond Co., bounded N. Wm. Lee, E. Jno. Lamar, S. vacant, W. Widow Tanner, on Spirit Tanner, on Spirit creek, survey 358. April 3, 1788, p. 184.

**BUSH, LEVI.** 287½ acres, Richmond Co., bounded N. Rocky Comfort creek, other sides vacant, survey 366. Dec. 7, 1787, p. 188.

**CARR, THOMAS.** 287½ acres, Richmond Co., bounded N. & E. vacant, S. Ambrose Holliday, W. John Lee, survey 393. July 18, 1787, p. 202.

**COX, CALEB.** 287½ acres, Richmond Co., bounded E. Benj. Jenkins, other sides vacant. Cut N. & S. by Spirit creek, survey 319. Dec. 9, 1786, p. 205.

**DAVIS, JOHN.** 287½ acres, Richmond Co., bounded S. Burche, other sides vacant, survey 410. Sept. 6, 1785, p. 211.

**MOORE, MORDECAI.** 287½ acres, Richmond Co., bounded N. Oliver Matthews, E. vacant, S. Barnett & Echols, W. Moore. Cut by Upton's creek, survey 463, p. 239.

**SMITH, JOHN.** 287½ acres, Richmond Co., bounded all sides vacant. Cut E. & W. by south fork of Spirit creek, survey 539. July 26, 1786, p. 278.

**TAPLEY, MARK.** 287½ acres, Richmond Co., bounded N. Bolling, E. & W. vacant, S. Joel Tapley. Cut N. & S. by Rocky Comfort creek, survey 543. Jan. 13, 1786, p. 280.

**GREAVES, WILLIAM.** 287½ acres, Glynn Co., bounded all sides by grantee, survey 604. Oct. 18, 1785, p. 310.

**OSGOOD, JOSHIA.** 287½ acres, Glynn Co., bounded W. grantee, other sides vacant. Cut by Cedar swamp, survey 627. April 5, 1787, p. 322.

## SURVEYOR GENERAL'S BOOK "N."

**COX, ZACHARIAH.** 287½ acres, Franklin Co., bounded S. north fork of Oconee river, other sides vacant, survey 11. Aug. 6, 1784, p. 6.

**DANIEL, WILLIAM.** 287½ acres, Franklin Co., bounded S. Samuel Creswell, other sides vacant. Cut by Eastanola creek, survey 14, June 4, 1788, p. 7.

**DAVIS, GIDEON.** 287½ acres, Franklin Co., bounded N. Wm. Thompson, other sides vacant. Cut on S. side by Eastanola creek, survey 16. June 9, 1785, p. 8.

**DARCY, JOEL.** 575 acres, Franklin Co., bounded N. Coleman, other sides vacant, on Indian creek, survey 15. Aug. 3, 1785, p. 8.

**JONES, JESSE.** 287½ acres, Franklin Co., bounded N. Burnett, E. & W. vacant, S. Joel Darcy, & Ezekiel Cloud. Cut by Indian creek, survey 23. Aug. 4, 1784, p. 12.

**McCALL, THOMAS.** 575 acres, Franklin Co., bounded N. & E. vacant, S. Mitchell, W. Stone, on Oconee river, survey 24. Mar. 10, 1786, p. 13.

**MORGAN, ISHAM.** 287½ acres, Franklin Co., bounded N. & E. vacant, S. Thurman, W. Zachariah Lamar. Cut N. & S. by Sugar creek, survey 48. June 25, 1785, p. 28.

**MITCHELL, FRANCIS.** 287½ acres, Franklin Co., bounded N. & E. vacant, S. Post, W. Lamar. Cut by branch of Oconee river, survey 52. Aug. 5, 1785, p. 30.

**MERCER, SILAS.** 287½ acres, Franklin Co., bounded N. grantee, E. Alex McNutt, other sides vacant. Cut N. & S. by Hard Labor creek, surveys 53 & 54. Mar. 12, 1786, p. 30.

**MARCUS, ELIAS.** 287½ acres, Franklin Co., bounded N. & E. vacant, S. Wm. Shields, W. Jas. Mannon. Cut N. & S. by Price's creek, survey 60. Feb. 9, 1785, p. 35.

**McDONALD, JOHN.** 287½ acres, Franklin Co., bounded W. Jones, other sides vacant, or unknown, survey 61. July 12, 1785, p. 35.

**MIDDLETOWN, BENEDICT.** 287½ acres, Franklin Co., bounded S. Richard Hill, other sides vacant, on Broad river, survey 67. Aug. 20, 1784, p. 39.

**MORPHETT, THOMAS.** 287½ acres, Franklin Co., bounded N.-E. by Keowee river, other sides vacant (in bend of river), survey 71. June 11, 1784, p. 41.

**McBURNETT, DANIEL.** 287½ acres, Franklin Co., bounded E. Jno. Carnes, other sides vacant, on north fork of Oconee river, survey 74. June 2, 1784, p. 42.

**NAIL, JULIAN.** 287½ acres, Franklin Co., bounded all sides vacant, on Mill creek branch of Broad river, survey 84. June 16, 1784, p. 48.

## BOUNTY SURVEYS

**OFFUTT, EZEKIEL.** 287½ acres, Franklin Co., bounded S. Robert Walton, other sides vacant. Cut N. & S. by Cobb's branch of Tugalo river, survey 108. Oct. 4, 1784, p. 60.

**PINSON, WILLIAM.** 287½ acres, Franklin Co., bounded S. Oconee river, other sides vacant, survey 110. Feb. 15, 1785, p. 61.

**PARTON, JOHN.** 575 acres, Franklin Co., bounded S. Big Shoal creek, other sides vacant, survey 111. June 2, 1784, p. 61.

**PARKS, HENRY.** 287½ acres, Franklin Co., bounded all sides vacant. Cut N.-E. to S.-W. by Hudson river, survey 128. Nov. 10, 1785, p. 71.

**PHILLPOT, WARREN.** 287½ acres, Franklin Co., bounded all sides vacant, on Gum Log creek, survey 131. July 11, 1785, p. 72.

**PAYNE, THOMAS.** 287½ acres, Franklin Co., bounded all sides vacant. Cut E. & W. by north fork of Broad river, survey 77. May 7, 1785, p. 77.

**SMITH, JOHN.** 287½ acres, Franklin Co., bounded W. Benj. Pulliam, other sides vacant. Cut N.-W. corner by Gum Log creek, survey 163. Aug. 16, 1785, p. 89.

**SMITH, ARTHER.** 287½ acres, Franklin Co., bounded N. vacant, E. Berry, Travis, S. Tugalo river, W. Edw. Rice, survey 165. June 2, 1784, p. 90.

**SESSUMS, WILLIAM.** 230 acres (on Reserve), Franklin Co., bounded S. Richard Call, other sides vacant, survey 170. Dec. 15, 1784, p. 92.

**SAPP, WILLIAM.** 287½ acres, Franklin Co., bounded E. Nail, other sides vacant. Cut E. & W. by Hudson's fork, survey 180. May 7, 1785, p. 98.

**STRINGER, JOHN.** 287½ acres, Franklin Co., bounded all sides vacant. Cut SW. to NE. by Camp creek, survey 181. June 3, 1784, p. 99.

**SUTTON, HEIRS OF RALPH.** 230 acres (on Reserve), Franklin Co., bounded N. unknown, other sides vacant, survey 182. Jan. 4, 1786, p. 99.

**STROZIER, PETER.** 287½ acres, Franklin Co., bounded N. grantee, E. Oconee river, other sides unknown. Cut N. & S. by Cedar creek, survey 186. July 3, 1787, p. 102.

**TALBOT, JOHN.** 287½ acres, Franklin Co., bounded N. Jas. Fountain, S. Chas. Britt, other sides vacant. Cut N. & S. by Eastanola creek, survey 189. June 12, 1785, p. 103.

**THOMPSON, ROBERT.** 287½ acres, Franklin Co., bounded all sides vacant. Cut E. & W. by Eastanola creek, survey 198. Dec. 11, 1784, p. 108.

**THURMAN, JOHN.** 575 acres, Franklin Co., bounded N. vacant, E. Lasley, S. Z. Lamar, W. grantee. Cut by Sugar creek, survey 211. Sept. 12, 1785, p. 114.

**TRIMBLE, MOSES.** 287½ acres, Franklin Co., bounded N. Savannah river, E. Spurlock, other sides vacant, survey 214. Sept. 30, 1784, p. 116.

**THORNTON, WILLIAM.** 287½ acres, Franklin Co., bounded all sides vacant. Cut by Big Pond creek, survey 217. Aug. 5, 1784, p. 117.

**TUREMAN, GEORGE.** 287½ acres, Franklin Co., bounded all sides vacant. Cut E. & W. by Eastanola creek, survey 220. April 12, 1785, p. 119.

**WALTON, WILLIAM.** 287½ acres, Franklin Co., bounded all sides vacant, on north branch of middle fork of Broad river, survey 245. Aug. 17, 1785, p. 133.

**WALTON, GEORGE.** 462½ acres, Franklin Co., bounded all sides vacant, on Barber's creek, survey 249. Jan. 25, 1785, p. 136.

**WARD, BRYANT.** 287½ acres, Franklin Co., bounded all sides vacant. Cut by north fork of Broad river, survey 255. June 5, 1785, p. 139.

**WARD, SAMUEL.** 287½ acres, Franklin Co., bounded all sides vacant. Cut W. to E. by south fork of Walton's creek, survey 260. June 8, 1785, p. 142.

**WOOD, RICHARD.** 575 acres, Franklin Co., bounded S. Wm. Hay, other sides vacant, survey 269. Jan. 5, 1786, p. 147.

**WOOD, JOHN.** 690 acres, Franklin Co., bounded E. Ignatius Few, other sides vacant. Cut E. & W. by Buck creek, survey 274. Aug. 8, 1784, p. 150.

**WALLER, JOSEPH.** 230 acres (on reserve), Franklin Co., bounded N. Appalachee river, other sides vacant, survey 277. Nov. 20, 1784, p. 151.

**WILDER, MALACHI.** 287½ acres, Franklin Co., bounded E. Jno. Wingfield, other sides vacant. Cut E. & W. by Barber's creek, survey 282. March 17, 1785, p. 155.

**WESTBROOK, STEPHEN.** 690 acres, Franklin Co., bounded N. & S. vacant, E. Jos. Nail, W. Jno. Tureman, survey 286. June 3, 1784, p. 158.

**WEST, CAPT. SAMUEL.** 862½ acres, Franklin Co., bounded S. Way, other sides vacant. Cut N. & S. by Middle Fork of Broad River, survey —. Oct. 10, 1784, p. —.

**WELCHER, JORDAN.** 287½ acres, Franklin Co., bounded E. Peter Curry, other sides vacant. On Craybill creek, survey 289. May 6, 1785, p. 159.

**WALLACE, JAMES.** 287½ acres, Franklin Co., bounded N. vacant, E. unknown, S. Oconee river, W. Wm. Pinson, survey 190. Feb. 15, 1785, p. 160.

**WALKER, WILLIAM.** 287½ acres, Franklin Co., bounded all sides vacant, survey 291. June 14, 1785, p. 160.

**YOUNG, WILLIAM.** 287½ acres, Franklin Co., bounded E. Jno. Harris, other sides vacant, survey 292. Dec. 17, 1784, p. 161.

## BOUNTY SURVEYS 311

**YOUNG, ISHAM.** 287½ acres, Franklin Co., bounded N. Allen Brown, E. & S. vacant, W. Hugh Wilson. On Eastanola creek, survey 295. Dec. 20, 1784, p. 162.

**BAXTER, ANDREW.** 230 acres (on reserve), Greene Co., bounded N. Glascock, E. & S. vacant, W. Thos. Welborne. On fork of Oconee river, survey 308. March 10, 1786, p. 169.

**BAXTER, JAMES.** 230 acres (on reserve), Greene Co., bounded all sides vacant. On north fork of Oconee river, survey —. March 10, 1786, p. —.

**CURRY, WM.** 230 acres (on reserve), Greene Co., bounded N. Daniel, E. & S. vacant, W. Franklin county line, survey 321. March 23, 1786, p. 176.

**COOK, NATHANIEL.** 460 acres (on reserve), Greene Co., bounded N. surveyed, E. Sanford, S. Heard and Thurman, W. Grier, survey —. Dec. 12, 1786, p. —.

**DANIEL, WILLIAM.** 230 acres (on reserve), Greene Co., bounded N. Franklin county line, E. Jno. Buchannon, other sides vacant, survey 326. March 24, 1786, p. 179.

**DANIEL, THOMAS.** 460 acres (on Reserve), Greene Co., bounded W. Whatley, other sides surveyed, survey 327. March 10, 1786, p. —.

**DANIEL, WILLIAM.** 1,100 acres, Greene Co., bounded N. Hawton and unknown, E. Daniel, S. unknown, W. Joshua Haughton. Cut by Beaverdam fork of Richland creek, survey 335. July 4, 1786, p. 184.

**SANFORD, JESSE.** 287½ acres, Greene Co., bounded N. north fork of Island creek, E. Riggins, S. & W. surveyed, survey 392. March 23, 1786, p. 218.

**TAYLOR, JOSEPH GROVE.** 287½ acres, Greene Co., bounded S. Taylor, other sides vacant. N.-W. corner cut by Town creek, survey 393. June 15, 1787, p. 218.

**ANDERSON, ELISHA.** 575 acres, Washington Co., bounded E. Jas. Freeman, other sides vacant. Cut E. & W. by Big creek, survey 427. March 16, 1785, p. 239.

**BARKSHAN, RICHARD.** 287½ acres, Washington Co., bounded N. M. Williamson, other sides vacant. Cut by branch of Shoulderbone creek, survey 432. Jan. 27, 1785, p. 241.

**BRAY, THOMAS.** 287½ acres, Washington Co., bounded W. Wm. Houghton, other sides vacant. On Little Ogeechee river, survey 433. Feb. 27, 1787, p. 242.

**BOWIE, JAMES.** 287½ acres, Washington Co., bounded N. vacant, E. Bowie, S. Ogeechee river, W. Benj. Few, survey 442. Aug. 28, 1784, p. 246.

**BURNS, ANDREW.** 287½ acres, Washington Co., bounded all sides vacant. On Shoulderbone creek, survey 447. May 24, 1786, p. 248.

**BENNETT, HEIRS OF JOHN.** 230 acres (on reserve), Washington Co., bounded N. Clem Nash, S. Jos. Lindon, other sides vacant, survey 460 July 5, 1784. p. 253.

Copied March 11, 1912.—J. A. Le Conte

## LAND LOTTERY GRANTS.

### IRWIN COUNTY LOTTERY LIST.

Revolutionary soldiers, and widows of Revolutionary soldiers. Names compiled by Miss Helen M. Prescott, from the original list of the drawing. Said original list copied and certified to officially by E. B. DeGraffenreid, Federal Union Power Press, Milledgeville, Ga., 1837, pamphlet in the Georgia State Library:

#### DISTRICT NO. 1.

| | | | |
|---|---|---|---|
| 55. | Ed. R. Tinney, | Chatham, | Dec. 9, 1825 |
| 117. | Isaac Bryant, | Putnam, | Sept. 23, 1822 |
| 1. | John Hill, | Hancock, | Sept. 17, 1840 |

#### DISTRICT NO. 3.

| | | | |
|---|---|---|---|
| 31. | John Willeby, | Twiggs, | Dec. 19, 1829 |
| 135. | Joseph Grant, | Hancock, | Nov. 3, 1828 |
| 218. | John Smith, Sr., | Morgan, | Aug. 23, 1841 |

#### DISTRICT NO. 4.

| | | | |
|---|---|---|---|
| 80. | James Myhand, Sr., | Morgan, | Nov. 3, 1823 |
| 87. | James Collins, | Richmond, | Dec. 22, 1821 |

#### DISTRICT NO. 5.

| | | | |
|---|---|---|---|
| 207. | John Buford, Sr., | Scriven, | Nov. 2, 1829 |

#### DISTRICT NO. 6.

| | | | |
|---|---|---|---|
| 15. | Forrest Greene, | Jackson, | Nov. 26, 1821 |
| 142. | John B. Johnston, | Clarke, | Aug. 27, 1841 |
| 235. | Daniel Connon, Sr., | Clarke, | Mar. 1, 1830 |
| 294. | Wm. Presnell, | Jackson, | Dec. 21, 1839 |

#### DISTRICT NO. 7.

| | | | |
|---|---|---|---|
| 113. | James Tison, | Effingham, | Feb. 14, 1833 |
| 117. | John Brumfield, | Elbert, | Dec. 13, 1830 |
| 230. | John Kent, | Warren, | Dec. 6, 1820 |
| 310. | Joel Rivers, | Hancock, | Nov. 23, 1835 |

#### DISTRICT NO. 8.

| | | | |
|---|---|---|---|
| 44. | Jacob Johnson, | Twiggs, | Oct. 5, 1837 |
| 169. | Claiborne Webb, | Jackson, | Dec. 19, 1826 |
| 348. | John Ballinger, Sr., | Elbert, | Dec. 3, 1839 |
| 403. | Drury Binum, | Warren, | Oct. 13, 1824 |
| 444. | Mark Snow, | Gwinnett, | Nov. 1, 1830 |

## DISTRICT NO. 9.

| | | | |
|---|---|---|---|
| 4. | Wm. Gilbert, | Morgan, | Dec. 17, 1829 |
| 352. | Wm. Thompson, | Jackson, | June 23, 1831 |
| 357. | Hardeman Rooks, | Jackson, | Nov. 5, 1827 |
| 403. | Robert Greer, | Morgan, | Nov. 4, 1829 |
| 413. | Elisha Cook, | Hancock, | Nov. 13, 1832 |
| 428. | John Wright, | Walton, | Oct. 4, 1825 |

## DISTRICT NO. 10.

| | | | |
|---|---|---|---|
| 419. | Thos. Gilbert, | Franklin, | Aug. 31, 1841 |

## DISTRICT NO. 11.

| | | | |
|---|---|---|---|
| 269. | Wm. Morris, Sr., | Jackson, | Mar. 31, 1824 |

## DISTRICT NO. 12.

| | | | |
|---|---|---|---|
| 15. | John McGamery, | Warren, | Sept. 30, 1824 |
| 75. | John Harvey, | Clark, | July 13, 1821 |
| 209. | Dan'l Casey, | Elbert, | Nov. 16, 1824 |
| 218. | Thos. Goore, Sr., | Hancock, | Dec. 23, 1828 |

## DISTRICT NO. 13.

| | | | |
|---|---|---|---|
| 263. | Isaac Hollinsworth, | Twiggs, | Oct. 30, 1827 |
| 361. | William Smith, | Walton, | Jan. 29, 1821 |
| 363. | Jas. P. Buchannan, Sr., | Jasper, | Sept. 17, 1822 |
| 408. | David Sanders, | Putnam, | Dec. 14, 1836 |
| 453. | Amos Brantley, | Hancock, | Dec. 26, 1828 |
| 469. | John Capeheart, | Jones, | Jan. 8, 1824 |
| 470. | John Inger, | Jackson, | Dec. 17, 1823 |
| 504. | Jeremiah Nelson, | Hancock, | Jan. 12, 1826 |
| 517. | Jacob Mercer, | Jasper, | Jan. 31, 1828 |

## DISTRICT NO. 14.

| | | | |
|---|---|---|---|
| 87. | Joel Rives, | Hancock, | Dec. 29, 1825 |
| 122. | John Bellinger, | Elbert, | Mar. 19, 1825 |

## DISTRICT NO. 15.

| | | | |
|---|---|---|---|
| 130. | Joseph Collins, | Morgan, | Sept. 4, 1837 |
| 138. | Rich'd Jarvell, | Baldwin, | July 20, 1824 |

## DISTRICT NO. 16.

| | | | |
|---|---|---|---|
| 58. | John Allgood, | Elbert, | Feb. 28, 1831 |

**JEFFERSON COUNTY LIST.**

Revolutionary soldiers, widows and daughters of Revolutionary soldiers, included among those entitled to draws in the Lottery of 1821. Names found

## LAND LOTTERY GRANTS. 315

in small book, in the Ordinary's office at Louisville, Ga., copied by Miss Helen M. Prescott:

| | | |
|---|---|---|
| John Boutin, R. S. | Mary Patterson, W. R. S. | Wm. Lions, R. S. |
| Jane Bostwick, W. R. S. | Esther Butt, W. & D. | Morris Murphey, R. S. |
| Ann D. Powell, W. R. S. | Polly Blunt. | Martha D. Moss, Wid. |
| Cloey Pate, W. R. S. | Michael Cowart, W. & D. | Moses Newton, R. S. |
| Mary Scott, W. R. S. | Eliz. Durouzeaux, W. & D. | Nancy Sammons, Wid. |
| John Arrington, R. S. | Stephen Durouzeaux, R. S. | Caleb Welch, R. S. |
| Hugh Alexander, R. S. | George Fowler, Sr., R. S. | Jere Welcher, R. S. |
| Rhoda Barber, W. & D. | Sarah Fountain, Wid. | Cath. Warner, W. & D. |
| Ezekiel Causey, R. S. | Cath. Girtman, Wid. | James Cook, R. S. |
| James Cotter, R. S. | Dempsey Hall, Sr., R. S. | Eliz. Fort, W. & D. |
| Wm. Clements, Sr., R. S. | John S. Holder, R. S. | Norman McCloud, R. S. |
| Eliz. Causey, Wid. | Mrs. Ann Hall, Wid. | Seth Pierce, R. S. |
| Ben Green, R. S. | Mary Spivey, Wid. | James Johnston, R. S. |
| Rebecca Garvin, W. & D. | John Thompson, R. S. | Hudson Hall, Sr., R. S. |
| Mary Haddin, W. R. S. | Sarah Thompson, Wid. | John Darby, Sr., R. S. |
| Am Montgomery, W. R. S. | Joshua Watson, R. S. | Wm. Thompson, R. S. |
| Elinor McNeely, W. R. S. | Lucretia Alford, Wid. | |

### ELBERT COUNTY LOTTERY LIST.

Revolutionary soldiers, and widows of Revolutionary soldiers. Names compiled by Miss Helen M. Prescott, from book containing list of persons entitled to draws in the Land Lottery, 1825, Ordinary's office, Elbert County:

### MAJOR DAVID DOBBS' BATTALION.

#### CAPT. HORTON'S DIST.

| | | |
|---|---|---|
| Moses Mills. | Thos. Hilley, Sr. | Katherine McConery, Wid. |
| Thomas Maxwell, Sr. | Sarah Teasley, Wid. | Nancy Murry, Wid. |
| Jacob Higginbotham. | Transilvania Gwinn, Wid. | Ann Underwood, Wid. |
| John Maxwell. | Hannah Burden, Wid. | Thomas Adams. |
| James Hunt. | Claiborne Sandridge. | James Adams, Sr. |
| Nathan Bond. | Robert Pullum. | Henry Cabenniss. |

#### CAPT. CARPENTER'S DIST.

| | | |
|---|---|---|
| Richard Rumsey. | Amos Richardson. | John Enlo. |
| Joseph Valsey, Sr. | Silas Teasley. | Isaac Alexander. |
| Lewis Stowers, Sr. | Angus McCourney, Sr. | Wm. White, Sr. |
| Wm. Rucker. | Wm. Kelly. | |

#### CAPT. DENNIS' DIST.

| | | |
|---|---|---|
| Mary Park, Wid. | Mary Alexander, Wid. | Levisa Terrell, Wid. |
| James Lockhart. | Mary Johnston, Wid. | Katherine Yoes, Wid. |
| Wm. Hailey. | John Davis. | Anderson McGuire. |

Fountain Jourdan.
Frances Ganes.
Peter Huiton.
Tabitha Shaggs, Wid.
Lucy Crawford, Wid.

Thos. King.
Moses Hunt.
John Cash.
Gabriel Smethers.
James Riley.

James Grissap.
Wayneford Underwood,Wid.
John Daniel, Sr.
Wm. Wood, Sr.
John Harris, Sr.

CAPT. BLACKWELL'S DIST.

John Rucker.
Wm. Gaines.
John Womley.
Mary Ford, Wid.
Eli Carvenson.
Elizabeth Royal, Wid.

Rebecca Harris, Wid.
Ben Brown.
Thos. Whealer, Sr.
Dozier Thornton.
Molly Hudson, Wid.
John M. White.

Eliz. Carter, Wid.
Janet Hausard, Wid.
Sally Chandler Blackwell, Wid.
Judith Mann, Wid.
Nancy Newberry, Wid.

(Above names certified to by Thos. White and John A. Verdel, receivers of names for draws, Oct. 31, 1825.)

## MAJOR ALLEN'S BATTALION.

List by Wm. Jones and Barrister R. Bray, Oct. 1, 1825:

CAPT. ALSTON'S DIST.

Susannah Gray, Wid.

Gilly Alston, Wid.
Eliz. Heard.

Sary Beck, Wid.

CAPT. TUCKER'S DIST.

Enos Tate, Sr., R. S.
Godfrey Tucker, R. S.
Jesse Tatum, R. S.
Barsheba Owens, Wid.

Eliz. Hudson, Wid.
John Childs, Citizen.
James F. Nunnalee.
Joseph Terrill.

Fanny Jones.
Nancy Davis.
Elizabeth Seals.

CAPT. BUTLER'S DIST.

Spencer Allgood.
James Dillard, Citizen.

Eliz. Kerlin.
John Dennard, Citizen.
James M. Brown.

John Wilkins.
Patrick Butler.

CAPT. BELL'S DIST.

Mary Dye, Wid.
Eliz. Bell, Wid.
Wm. B. Key.
John Allgood.

Ann Bullard.
John Cook.
Mary Cook, Wid.
Margaret Jack, Wid.
Rebecca Snelling, Wid.

Jesse Maupin.
Rebecca Clark, Wid.
Eliz. Carter, Wid.
Francis Naish, Wid.

CAPT. TATE'S DIST.

Margaret Fleming, Wid.
Susannah Colbert, Wid.

Thos. Barton.
Eliz. Evant, Wid.

Eliz. M. Saxon, Wid.
Eliz. Tate, Wid.

# LAND LOTTERY GRANTS. 317

## JACKSON COUNTY LOTTERY LIST.

Revolutionary soldiers, and widows of Revolutionary soldiers, entitled to draw in the Land Lottery of 1825, in Jackson County:

### MAJOR BOWEN'S BATTALION.
#### CAPT. RIDEN'S DIST., NO. 253.

| | |
|---|---|
| Ruth Stapler, Widow of Revolutionary Soldier, | 1 |
| Anthony M. Elton, Revolutionary Soldier, | 2 |
| Jane Stoneham, Widow of Revolutionary Soldier, | 1 |
| William Lord, Revolutionary Soldier, | 2 |
| Joseph Harris, Revolutionary Soldier, | 2 |
| William Matthews, Revolutionary Soldier, | 2 |
| Abrilla Sharp, Widow of Revolutionary Soldier, | 1 |
| Sarah Moore, Widow of Revolutionary Soldier, | 1 |
| Archibald Underwood, Revolutionary Soldier, | 2 |
| John McDonald, Revolutionary Soldier, | 2 |
| Obedience Ryan, Widow of Revolutionary Soldier, | 1 |
| Elizabeth Royal, Widow of Revolutionary Soldier, | 1 |
| Sally Baugh, Widow of Revolutionary Soldier, | 1 |

#### CAPT. McGINNIS' DIST., No. 255.

| | |
|---|---|
| Nathan Bowles, Revolutionary Soldier, | 2 |
| Thomas Barron, Revolutionary Soldier, | 2 |
| George Hanry, Revolutionary Soldier, | 2 |
| Rachel Bennett, Widow of Revolutionary Soldier, | 1 |
| Mary Anthony, Widow of Revolutionary Soldier, | 1 |
| William Gober, Sr., Revolutionary Soldier, | 2 |
| James Barr, Revolutionary Soldier, | 2 |
| Sharod Gean, Revolutionary Soldier, | 2 |
| Lucy Williams, Widow of Revolutionary Soldier, | 1 |
| Nancy York, Widow of Revolutionary Soldier, | 1 |
| Mary Ann Patterson, Widow of Revolutionary Soldier, | 1 |
| Polly Flanigan, Widow of Revolutionary Soldier, | 1 |

#### CAPT. ORR'S DIST., NO. 257.

| | |
|---|---|
| Edward Pharr, Revolutionary Soldier, | 2 |
| Alexander Morrison, Revolutionary Soldier, | 2 |
| Sherrod Thompson, Revolutionary Soldier, | 2 |
| William Potts, Revolutionary Soldier, | 2 |
| Isaac Lynch, Revolutionary Soldier, | 2 |
| Sarah Cash, Widow of Revolutionary Soldier, | 1 |
| Margarett Barnett, Widow of Revolutionary Soldier, | 1 |
| Sarah Robinson, Widow of Revolutionary Soldier, | 1 |
| Ancil Cunningham, Revolutionary Soldier, | 2 |

#### CAPT. MILLER'S DIST., NO. 455.

| | |
|---|---|
| Nancy Orr, Widow of Revolutionary Soldier, | 1 |
| Robert Henderson, Revolutionary Soldier, | 2 |

## CAPT. BAUGH'S DIST., NO. 465.

Margaret Burns, Widow of Revolutionary Soldier, . . . . . . . . . . 1
William Wilson, Revolutionary Soldier, . . . . . . . . . . . . . 2
Rachel Webb, Widow of Revolutionary Soldier, . . . . . . . . . 1
Jemima Dale, Widow of Revolutionary Soldier, . . . . . . . . . . 1
John G. Henderson, Revolutionary Soldier, . . . . . . . . . . . 2
Prudence Cowan, Widow of Revolutionary Soldier, . . . . . . . . 1

## CAPT. LIDDELL'S DIST., NO. 423.

Esther Hemphill, Widow of Revolutionary Soldier, . . . . . . . . . . 1
Elizabeth Pettyjohn, Widow of Revolutionary Soldier, . . . . . . . . . 1
Christian Boradwell, Widow of Revolutionary Soldier, . . . . . . . . . 1
John Sesson, Revolutionary Soldier, . . . . . . . . . . . . . . 2
Jane Wallis, Widow of Revolutionary Soldier, . . . . . . . . . . 1
Elizabeth Glenn, Widow of Revolutionary Soldier, . . . . . . . . . 1
Middleton Brooks, Revolutionary Soldier, . . . . . . . . . . . . 2
John King, Revolutionary Soldier, . . . . . . . . . . . . . . . 2
Hannah Boyle, Widow of Revolutionary Soldier, . . . . . . . . . 1
Medience Martin, Widow of Revolutionary Soldier, . . . . . . . . . 1
Rebecca Wright, Widow of Revolutionary Soldier, . . . . . . . . . 1
Frances Wright, Widow of Revolutionary Soldier, . . . . . . . . . 1

## MAJOR MITCHELL'S BATTALION.
## CAPT. HOLIDAY'S DIST., NO. 242.

John Muckelhannon, Revolutionary Soldier, . . . . . . . . . . . . 2
Mary Dameron, Widow of Revolutionary Soldier, . . . . . . . . . 1
Judith Brooks, Widow of Revolutionary Soldier, . . . . . . . . . 1
Eve Boggs, Widow of Revolutionary Soldier, . . . . . . . . . . 1
Elizabeth Heard, Widow of Revolutionary Soldier, . . . . . . . . . 1
Ann Reynolds, Widow of Revolutionary Soldier, . . . . . . . . . 1
Mary Thurmond, Widow of Revolutionary Soldier, . . . . . . . . . 1
Margarett Pendergrass, Widow of Revolutionary Soldier, . . . . . . . 1
Judith Shackelford, Widow of Revolutionary Soldier, . . . . . . . . 1

## CAPT. LAY'S DIST. NO. 246.

William Pentecost, Revolutionary Soldier, . . . . . . . . . . . 2
Nancy Hines, Widow of Revolutionary Soldier, . . . . . . . . . . 1
Nancy Fuller, Widow of Revolutionary Soldier, . . . . . . . . . . 1
Jesse Johnson, Revolutionary Soldier, . . . . . . . . . . . . . 2
Phoebe Boring, Widow of Revolutionary Soldier, . . . . . . . . . 1
Josiah Bondurant, Revolutionary Soldier, . . . . . . . . . . . . 2
Hannah Brooks, Widow of Revolutionary Soldier, . . . . . . . . . 1
Sarah Burson, Widow of Revolutionary Soldier, . . . . . . . . . . 1
George Slaton, Revolutionary Soldier, . . . . . . . . . . . . . 2
Daniel McDaniel, Revolutionary Soldier, . . . . . . . . . . . . 2
Sarah Lambert, Widow of Revolutionary Soldier, . . . . . . . . . 1

LAND LOTTERY GRANTS. 319

## CAPT. WITHERSPOON'S DIST., NO. 243.

Patience Bryant, Widow of Revolutionary Soldier, . . . . . . . . . 1
Elizabeth Maynard, Widow of Revolutionary Soldier, . . . . . . . . 1
Martha Cowan, Widow of Revolutionary Soldier, . . . . . . . . . 1
Martha Adams, Widow of Revolutionary Soldier, . . . . . . . . . 1

## CAPT. DEATON'S DIST., NO. 248.

Sarah K. Horton, Widow of Revolutionary Soldier, . . . . . . . . . 1
Francis Bell, Revolutionary Soldier, . . . . . . . . . . . . . 2
Solomon Saxon, Revolutionary Soldier, . . . . . . . . . . . . 2
James Cochran, Revolutionary Soldier, . . . . . . . . . . . . 2
James W. Cook, Revolutionary Soldier, . . . . . . . . . . . . 2
Jacob Brazelton, Sr., Revolutionary Soldier, . . . . . . . . . . 2
Alexander Reid, Revolutionary Soldier, . . . . . . . . . . . . 1
Mary McNeely, Widow of Revolutionary Soldier, . . . . . . . . . 1

## CAPT. MITCHELL'S DIST., NO. 245.

Tabitha Chandler, Widow of Revolutionary Soldier, . . . . . . . . 1
Elizabeth Dorris, Widow of Revolutionary Soldier, . . . . . . . . 1
Mary Thompson, Widow of Revolutionary Soldier, . . . . . . . . . 1
Sally Rawls, Widow of Revolutionary Soldier, . . . . . . . . . . 1
Martha Garner, Widow of Revolutionary Soldier, . . . . . . . . . 1

## FRANKLIN COUNTY, GA., R. S.

Copy of paper from Mrs. Jane E. Martin, which she copied from two books sent her by A. J. Neal and returned to him:
"List of names of the men who drew land in Capt. Walters' Dist., in the lottery of 1825 by act of the legislature of June 9, 1825, in Col. John A. Patrick's Regt., composed of Maj. Shackleford and Chandler's Battalion." "Taken by Jas. Chandler, Jan. 31, 1825. M. H. Payne."

We give only the Revolutionary soldiers, and widows of Revolutionary soldiers, in this list:

### CAPT. WALTERS' DIST.

Benjamin Harrison.
John Cleveland.
Ben Pulliam.
Aaron Roberts.
Elijah Walters.
James Cash.
Mary Gadden.
Isaac Gray.
Wm. Mitchell.
Henry Smith.

Jesse Thomas.
Wm. Hobgood.
Elias Burgess.
Shepperd Liddell.
Elisha Wilkison.
Jos. Edwards.
John Algood.
Thomas Covington.
Victoria Crawford, W.R.S.
Richard Harper.

Gabriel Smith.
Jesse Smith.
Jacob Setger.
Wm. Smith.
Jesse Rowell.
John Bryan.
Edward Camp.
Joyce Harper, W. R. S.
Absalom Cleveland.
Wm. Flannigan.

# ROSTER OF THE REVOLUTION.

| | CAPT. TABOR'S DIST. | |
|---|---|---|
| Levi Williams. | John Stonecypher. | Eliz. Laseby, W. R. S. |
| Samule Newby. | Mary White, W. R. S. | Mary White, W. R. S. |
| Sampson Walls. | Chas. Angle. | Moses Guest. |
| Gillam Willbank. | Joel Mabrey, Sr. | Wm. York. |
| John Tabor. | John Tate, Sr. | John McMullan. |
| Wm. Dodd. | Jas. Armstrong. | Mary Crump, W. R. S. |
| M. Lee. | Wm. Willmott. | |

| | CAPT. BENNETT'S DIST. | |
|---|---|---|
| Richard Wheeler. | Andrew Glenn. | Israel Prickett. |
| Mary Wheeler, W. R. S. | Thomas Clark. | Geo. Garner. |
| Elizabeth Henry | Thomas Akins. | Benj. Cleveland. |
| George Cockburn. | Anne Jane Sims. | |

| | CAPT. BLANKENSHIP'S DIST. | |
|---|---|---|
| Wm. Pulliam. | John Albritton. | Wm. Glover. |
| Eliz. Tate, W. R. S. | Joshua Sewell. | Henry Burroughs. |
| Nancy Chandler. | George Stovall. | Robert McFarland. |
| | Abner Jordan. | |

| | MAJ. BRUCE'S BATTALION. | |
|---|---|---|
| Barbary Crider, W. R. S. | Elijah Walley, R. S. | Mary Crump, W. R. S. |
| Malinda Durkee, W. R. S. | Mary Gaddis, W. R. S. | Mary Wheeler, W. R. S. |
| Temple Manley, W. R. S. | James Hutcherson, R. S. | Elizabeth Harvy, W. R. S. |
| James Wilson, R. S. | Mary Graddy, W. R. S. | Ann Jane Sims, W. R. S. |
| Comfort Baker, R. S. | Wm. Mitchell, R. S. | Jane Pulliam, W. R. S. |
| John Crider, R. S. | Susanna Longbridge, W.R.S. | Eliz. Tate, W. R. S. |
| John Sandiges, R. S. | Victor Crawford, R. S. | Mary Chandler, W. R. S. |
| Benjamin Harrison, R. S. | Elizabeth Lasbee, W. R. S. | Geo. Stovall, Sr., R. S. |

In Capt. Blankenship's Co.

These men were soldiers in Col. John A. Patrick's regiment, composed of Major Shackelford's and Chandler's Battalion:

| | | |
|---|---|---|
| Rhoda Young, W. R. S. | Eliz. Tate, W. R. S. | Wm. Bryan, R. S. |
| Mary Gaddens, W. R. S. | Nancy Chandler, W. R. S. | Lucy Reaves (?), W. R. S. |
| George Cockburn, R. S. | John Allbritton, R. S. | Peter Walton, R. S. |
| Thomas Clarke, R. S. | Joshua Sewell, R. S. | Mary Scott, W. R. S. |
| Ann Jane Sims, W. R. S. | Geo. Stovall, R. S. | Sarah Mitchell, W. R. S. |
| George Garner, R. S. | Wm. Glover, R. S. | Victoria Crawford, W. R. S. |
| Wm. Pulliam, R. S. | Thos. Whitlow, R. S. | Mary White, W. R. S. |
| Israel Prickett, R. S. | Mattburn Jordan, R. S. | Catherine Dodd, W. R. S. |
| George Garner, R. S. | Henry Burroughs, R. S. | Mary Wheeler, W. R. S. |
| Ben Cleveland, R. S. | Robt. M. Farley, R. S. | Matilda Carter, W. R. S. |
| Wm. Pulliam, R. S. | Abner Jordan, R. S. | Eliz. Harvey, W. R. S. |
| Jane Pulliam, W. R. S. | Wm. A. Stovall, R. S. | Mary Wheeler, W. R. S. |
| | Freeman Wheeler, R. S. | |

## BK. 2ND.

List of Revolutionary soldiers, who were pensioned by United States Government for rendering service, living in Franklin County, 1825, as taken from the Secty's (?) book in the Ordinary's office (date, 1835) of Thomas King, containing the receipt for the money paid to pensioners:

1. Jesse Holbrook.
2. Jesse Marshall.
3. Abner Shurden.
4. Samuel Mackie.
5. Robert Brown.
6. Richard B. Hooper.
7. J. Hodges.
8. Wm. Speares.
9. Elisha Dyer.
10. Wm. Allen.
11. Wm. Murdock.
12. John McMillan.
13. Thos. Clark.
14. David Carter.
15. Wm. Mitchell.
16. John Albritton.
17. Wm. Aaron.
18. Henry Smith.
19. Wm. Thomas.
20. John Tate.
21. Peter Groover.
22. Jesse Smith.
23. Wm. Glover.
24. James Cash, d. 1837.
25. Wm. Allen.
26. Thos. Clark.
27. David Carter.
28. John Stonecypher.
29. Moses Guest.
30. Leak's wife, Judith.
31. Thomas Hodges, 1836.
32. C. Addison.
33. Thos. Holmes.
34. Henry Smith.
35. John Allerton.
36. Thompson Epperson.
37. Wm. Carter.
38. John Stonecypher.
39. Henry Parks.
40. Abner Sheridan.
41. Robert K. Turner.
42. Wm. Spears.
43. Richard B. Hooper.
44. Jacob Groover.
45. Hezikiah Smith.

46. Wm. Thomas' widow, Nancy.
47. John Epperson, d. 1836; W., Mary.
48. Robert Fleming.
49. Samuel Southerland, 49.—1837.
50. Russel Dranst (?).
51. Daniel Southerland.
52. Richard B. Hooper, by Macajah Martin.
53. Stephen Fuller, by sons, Cooper B. and Geo. W. Fuller.
54. Robt. Brown, by son, Hugh Brown, 1838.
55. Richard Bond, d. Jan., 1837; son, Lindsey Bond.
56. Wm. Murdock, by son, Thos. H. Murdock, 1839.
57. Daniel Southerland, d. Feb. 20, 1838; son, Russel Davis.
58. James Blair.
59. Henry Parks.
60. Simon Terrell, by Mary Davis.
61. Henry Truitt.
62. Henry Smith, d. 1839; son, Isam Smith.
63. Robert Fleming, d. March 4, 1839; son, G. M. Fleming, 1838.
64. David Carter, d. Sept., 1839; 4th son, Lewis Carter.
65. Elisha Dyer, d. Sept. 4, 1839; W., Larinia (?).
66. Stephen Fuller, d. Sept., 1846; his sons, Geo. W. Fuller and Cooper Fuller.
67. Robert Brown, d. Jan., 1840; wife, Jane, and son, Hugh.
   (1) Mary White, recd. $300, April 9, 1841, for her husband's services.
68. Jackson Oliver, d. March, 1837.
69. Henry Park, Sept., 1840.

70. (2) Charity Holbrook, the wife, recd. pension of $300, by Berrian Holbrook, March 4, 1841.
   (3) Annie Smith, W. of Jesse Smith, who d. April, 1842.
   (4) William Mitchell, d. March, 1842; W., Eleanor, and son, Wm., Jr.
71. R. A. Ward.
72. Wm. Cheek.
73. Chas. W. Cheek.
   (5) Wid. Martha Fleming, by Joel Thomas, 1845.
74. Richard Branham, d. 1846.
   (6) Agnes Thomas, wife of Joel T.
   (7) Ann Wade, Wid., and sons, John and Thos. Wade.
   (8) Jane Ash, Wid.; son, A. F. Ash.
   (9) Martha Fleming, 1845.
75. Thos. Bush, son of Daniel Thos. Bush.
76. John Stonecypher, 1845; by son, Ben Stonecypher.
77. Allen T. Garrison, 1846.
78. T. W. E. Rucker, 1846.
79. (9) Jane Ash, Wid., and son, R. R. Ash.
   Martha Fleming; s., L. M. Fleming.
   Hugh Holland, d. May 19, 1832.
80. Thomas King, 1835.
   Secty. of Co. Court of Franklin Co.
   Dianthe Fuller, 1830, recd. pension for Hugh Fuller, March, 1838.
   In Sept., 1845, R. A. R. Neal was ap. Ordinary and gave the receipts.

## LIST OF REVOLUTIONARY SOLDIERS FROM WILKES COUNTY, GEORGIA, AS TAKEN FROM LAND LOTTERY RECORDS.

On the Land Lottery Records of Wilkes County, Georgia, Court of Ordinary, the names in this list are designated as those of "Revolutionary Soldiers." In some instances, the names of the widows of Revolutionary soldiers having been given, these were traced through the Deed Records, in office of Clerk of Superior Court, in this way, the names of the husbands of such widows having been reliably established.

While the list is not complete, it is correct thus far.

Work done by Annie M. Lane, Record Committee of " D. A. R.," 1916.

(A)
Aldrage, William.
Appling, Joel.
Anderson, William, Sr.
Anderson, John.
Arnold, John.
Arnold, James.
Appling, Ivell.

(B)
Bailey, John
Banks, William.

Bankston, Lawrence.
Barnett, William, Sr.
Barnett, Lewis.
Barnett, William.
Barrett, Lewis.
Bennett, Reuben.

## LAND LOTTERY GRANTS. 323

Bell, Arthur.
Bensen, William, Sr.
Blakey, Churchel.
Blackburn, Nathan.
Bledsoe, William.
Booker, William.
Booker, John, Sr.
Bowen, Samuel, Sr.
Bryan, Nathan.
Burks, Joseph.
Burdette, Humphrey.

(C)

Callaway, Jacob.
Carrell, Jessey.
Clemmons, Henry, Sr.
Carrol, Charles.
Carter, John.
Carter, William.
Chaffin, Isham.
Combs, John.
Combs, Philip, Sr.
Cooper, John, Sr.
Crosby, Urial.
Curry, Peter.
Coleman, Thompson.

(D)

Davis, William.
Davis, William.
Doster, Jonathan.
Downs, Ambrose.
Dyson, John.

(E)

Eason, Isaac.
Eidson, Thomas.
Eckles, Edward, Sr.
Estar, George.
Evans, Thomas.

(G)

Garrard, Anthony.
Gibson, Henry B.
Gibson, John.
Graves, John.

(H)

Hamilton, Andrew.
Hamilton, George.
Hammons, John.
Hancock, William.
Harper, John.
Harris, Ezekiel.
Harrison, Joseph.
Helmes, John.
Hood, John.
Hopkins, Isaac.
Hudgens, William.
Hughes, William.
Huling, James.
Huff, Mathew.
Huckaby, Philip.
Hurley, Joseph.

(J)

Jenkins, Sterling.
Johns, John.
Johnson, Bartholomew.
Johnson, Abraham.
Johnson, Joseph B.
Johnson, Joseph P.

(K)

Kelley, John.
Kellum, George.
Kent, Peter.
King, Richard, Sr.

(L)

Landrum, John.
Lasley, Thomas.
Lawson, John, Sr.
Lindsey, Jacob, Sr.
Lindsey, John.

(M)

Maddox, Walter.
Maddox, William.
Martin, Ganaway.
Mattox, Charles.
Mattox, Charles.
Mathews, James, Sr.
McCormick, Thomas.
McLaughlin, Peter.

Meloy, Andrew.
Miller, Lewis.
Moncreef, Mathew.
Montgomery, David.
Moore, John.
Moreman, Thomas.
Murphey, Francis.
Murphy, John.

(N)

Nelson, John.
Norman, John, Sr.
Norris, Alexander.

(O)

Orr, Christopher.
Owens, John, Sr.

(P)

Parkerson, Levin.
Perkins, John.
Peteet, Richard.
Pool, William.
Pool, Dudley.
Pollard, Thomas.
Pope, John.
Porter, Thomas.
Poss, Christopher.
Proctor, William.
Pullen, Joseph, Sr.

(R)

Ray, John.
Ridley, John, Sr.

(S)

Sappington, John.
Sandeford, Elemerick.
Shank, John.
Sherrer, James.
Simons, Abraham.
Smith, John.
Snider, Cristian.
Sowel, Zadok.
Springer, John.
Snelson, William, Sr.
Stewart, Amos.
Strozier, Peter.

## ROSTER OF THE REVOLUTION.

(T)
Taliafero, Benjamin.
Trammell, Peter.
Triplett, William.
Truitt, Pernal.

(W)
Waggoner, William.
Walton, Josiah.
Whatley, Samuel.
Williams, John.
Williams, William.
Willis, George, Sr.

Webster, Abner.
Wolfe, Andrew, Sr.
Wood, John.
Woodroof, Richard.
Wright, John.
Woolbright, Jacob.

State of Georgia, Wilkes County:
In the Court of Ordinary:
I, S. D. Fanning, Ordinary of said County, and Ex-Officio Clerk of the Court of Ordinary, certify that the attached and foregoing pages of printing contain a full, true and complete copy of the names of Revolutionary Soldiers from Wilkes County, Georgia, as the same appear on record in this office, Land Lottery Records.

Witness my hand and the Seal of said Court at Washington, Georgia, this 18th day of October, 1916.

S. D. FANNING, Ordinary,
and Ex-Officio Clerk of the Court of Ordinary
of Wilkes County, Georgia.

State of Georgia, Wilkes County:
Not having been able to establish, in any way, the names of the husbands of all the widows of Revolutionary soldiers occurring on the Land Lottery Records, we herewith respectively submit those remaining, that at least the surnames of the soldiers may be known:

**WIDOWS OF REVOLUTIONARY SOLDIERS.**

| | |
|---|---|
| Allison, | Agnes. |
| Arnold, | Elizabeth. |
| Bell, | Elizabeth. |
| Brinton, | Mary. |
| Brown, | Elizabeth. |
| Bruce, | Elizabeth. |
| Carlton, | Mildred. |
| Cofer, | Elizabeth. |
| Dukes, | Kesiah. |
| Edmonds, | Winney. |
| Edwards, | Precious E. |
| Flynt, | Sarah. |
| Freeman, | Sarah. |
| Gideons, | Elizabeth. |
| Heard, | Elizabeth A. |
| Huskey, | Rebeccah. |
| Lee, | Margaret. |
| Lockhart, | Polly. |

**REVOLUTIONARY SOLDIERS.**

...... Allison.
...... Arnold.
...... Bell.
...... Brinton.
...... Brown.
...... Bruce.
...... Carlton.
...... Cofer.
...... Dukes.
...... Edmonds.
...... Edwards.
...... Flynt.
...... Freeman.
...... Gideons.
...... Heard.
...... ......
...... Lee.
...... Lockhart.

| | | | |
|---|---|---|---|
| Macklin, | Jane. | ...... | Macklin. |
| Mallory, | Mary. | ...... | Mallory. |
| Mathews, | Rebecca. | ...... | Mathews. |
| Murphy, | Martha. | ...... | Murphy. |
| Matthews, | Winnefred. | ...... | Matthews. |
| Nelms, | Nancy. | ...... | Nelms. |
| Nunnelly, | Margaret. | ...... | Nunnelly. |
| Paschall, | Mary. | ...... | Paschall. |
| Piggot, | Susanna. | ...... | Piggot. |
| Pool, | Elizabeth. | ...... | Pool. |
| Randolph, | Dorothy. | ...... | Randolph. |
| Ruddell, | Lee Ann. | ...... | Ruddell. |
| Runnels, | Sarah T. | ...... | Runnels. |
| Runnels, | Sallie. | ...... | Runnels. |
| Shoemaker, | Catherine. | ...... | Shoemaker. |
| Simpson, | Hester. | ...... | Simpson. |
| Simpson, | Lucy. | ...... | Simpson. |
| Speller, | Martha. | ...... | Speller. |
| Whitlock, | Mary. | ...... | Whitlock. |
| ........ | ..... | Moses | Wade. |

Failed to state that WILLIAM BARNETT, SR., whose name occurred on List of Revolutionary Soldiers previously submitted, was an officer in the Revolution.

State of Georgia, County of Wilkes:

I, S. D. Fanning, Ordinary, certify that the foregoing pages are true and correct, as taken from the Land Lottery Records of said County.

Given under my official hand and the Seal of said Court, this, the 26th day of October, 1916.

S. D. FANNING, Ordinary.
Wilkes County, Georgia.

## REVOLUTIONARY SOLDIERS AND THE WIDOWS OF REVOLUTIONARY SOLDIERS

Listed in "The Cherokee Land Lottery," James F. Smith, Harper Bros., 1838.

| Dis. | Sec. | Lot. | Name. | District. | County. |
|---|---|---|---|---|---|
| 6 | 1 | 27 | James, Blair, | Whitehead's, | Habersham. |
| 6 | 1 | 63 | John Turner, | 374th, | Putnam. |
| 6 | 1 | 92 | Eleanor Blalock, | 588th, | Upson. |
| 6 | 1 | 127 | Jas. Key Kendall, | Stephens', | Habersham. |
| 6 | 1 | 156 | William Matthews, | Riden's, | Jackson. |
| 6 | 1 | 180 | Richard Gregory, | Hargrove's, | Oglethorpe. |
| 6 | 1 | 205 | Samuel Warden, | Morgan's, | Madison. |
| 6 | 1 | 238 | Samuel Wilson, | 34th, | Screven. |

ROSTER OF THE REVOLUTION.

| Dis. | Sec. | Lot. | Name. | District. | County. |
|---|---|---|---|---|---|
| 6 | 1 | 246 | Claborn Sandridge, | Seal's, | Elbert. |
| 6 | 1 | 263 | Lucy Windham, | Downs, | Warren. |
| 6 | 1 | 265 | Mary Rutherford, | Barker's, | Gwinnett. |
| 6 | 1 | 271 | Isabella Estes, | McClendon's, | Putnam. |
| 6 | 1 | 289 | Moses Beard, | Athens', | Clarke. |
| 6 | 1 | 290 | Richard Simmons, | 404th, | Gwinnett. |
| 6 | 1 | 304 | Stephen Clayton, Sr., | Burgess', | Carroll. |
| 7 | 1 | 28 | Sarah Harvey, | 47th, | Upson. |
| 7 | 1 | 86 | Mary Wheeler, | White's, | Franklin. |
| 7 | 1 | 123 | Frances Barron, | 589th, | Upson. |
| 7 | 1 | 125 | Martha Murphy, | 177th (Wilkes'), | Wilkes. |
| 7 | 1 | 181 | James Rylee, Sr., | Blackstock's | Hall. |
| 7 | 1 | 196 | John Westbrook, | Mangum's, | Franklin. |
| 7 | 1 | 239 | James Scott, | Baker's, | Liberty. |
| 7 | 1 | 245 | Jemina Lovejoy, | Madden's, | Pike. |
| 7 | 1 | 249 | William Downs, | 10th, | Effingham. |
| 7 | 1 | 261 | Jane McMinn, | Stephens', | Habersham. |
| 7 | 1 | 276 | James Comer, | Comer's, | Jones. |
| 7 | 1 | 300 | John Dunn, | Lamberth's, | Fayette. |
| 8 | 1 | 31 | John Thomas, | Stewart's, | Troup. |
| 8 | 1 | 64 | Sarah Simmons, | 555th, | Upson. |
| 8 | 1 | 126 | Edmond Collins, | Ross', before 1838, | Monroe. |
| 8 | 1 | 149 | Sarah Commins, | 143d, " " | Greene. |
| 8 | 1 | 152 | Lewis Wilhite, | Wilhites, " " | Elbert. |
| 8 | 1 | 190 | Nancy Lewis, | Hines', " " | Coweta. |
| 8 | 1 | 239 | Sugars Bynum, | Chambers', " | Houston. |
| 8 | 1 | 232 | Sarah Cheshire, | Brewer's, " " | Monroe. |
| 8 | 1 | 255 | Isaac Horton, | Barker's, " " | Gwinnett. |
| 8 | 1 | 318 | Zacharia White, | 10th, " " | Effingham. |
| 9 | 1 | 6 | Henry Varnadore, | 535th, " " | Dooly. |
| 9 | 1 | 27 | Mary Buchannan, | Wilson's, | Jasper. |
| 9 | 1 | 103 | George Cotton, Sr., | Lynn's, | Warren. |
| 9 | 1 | 107 | Wm. McGruder, | 119th, | Richmond. |
| 9 | 1 | 133 | David Smith, | Bush's, | Burke. |
| 9 | 1 | 145 | James Denmer, | Welche's, | Habersham. |
| 9 | 1 | 176 | Joshua Smith, Sr., | Dobb's, | Hall. |
| 9 | 1 | 181 | Elizabeth Matthews, | Gunn's, | Jefferson. |
| 9 | 1 | 205 | Elizabeth Keen, | Blackshear's, | Laurens. |
| 9 | 1 | 211 | Celia Morris, | Sims', | Troup. |
| 9 | 1 | 290 | Elizabeth Tabor, | Whites', | Franklin. |
| 9 | 1 | 313 | Joshia Burgess, | 373d, | Jasper. |
| 10 | 1 | 14 | Edmond Raines, | Jones', | Morgan. |
| 10 | 1 | 43 | Thomas Bryan, Sr., | Sewell's, | Franklin. |
| 10 | 1 | 91 | Ursula Harvey, | Kendricks', | Putnam. |
| 10 | 1 | 136 | Stephen Tredwell, | 702d, | Heard. |

## LAND LOTTERY GRANTS.

| Dis. | Sec. | Lot. | Name. | District. | County. |
|---|---|---|---|---|---|
| 10 | 1 | 151 | Jonathan Stockley, | Ross', | Monroe. |
| 10 | 1 | 183 | Christian Broadwell, w.r.s. | Liddell's, | Jackson. |
| 10 | 1 | 184 | Hannah Terry, | Newsom's, | Warren. |
| 10 | 1 | 193 | William Fason, | 117th, | Hancock. |
| 10 | 1 | 194 | William Arnold, Sr., | Scroggins', | Oglethorpe. |
| 10 | 1 | 198 | David Patrick, | Hall's, | Oglethorpe. |
| 10 | 1 | 299 | John Sappington, | House's, | Henry. |
| 10 | 1 | 250 | Jane Clarke, | Burnett's, | Lowndes. |
| 16 | 1 | 7 | Mary Goolsby, | Green's, | Oglethorpe. |
| 16 | 1 | 38 | Barbara Merritt, | 364th (Jasper), | Jasper. |
| 16 | 1 | 39 | Anna Moody, | Hatchett's, | Oglethorpe. |
| 16 | 1 | 40 | John Wright, | McLin's, | Butts. p. 44. |
| 16 | 1 | 89 | Conrad Augley, | Hicks', | Decatur. |
| 16 | 1 | 111 | Alice Deadwiler, | Wilhites, | Elbert. |
| 16 | 1 | 118 | John Barton, | Martin's, | Hall. |
| 16 | 1 | 126 | Nancy Williamson, | Newman's, | Thomas. |
| 16 | 1 | 137 | Thomas Garner, | Dobb's, | Hall. |
| 16 | 1 | 157 | Mary Bolton, | Parham's, | Warren. |
| 16 | 1 | 191 | Samuel Roach, | 510th, | Early. |
| 16 | 1 | 224 | Jesse Brown, | 430th, | Early. |
| 17 | 1 | 26 | Mary Fitts, | Nellums', | Elbert. |
| 17 | 1 | 32 | John Guise, | McDowell's, | Lincoln. |
| 17 | 1 | 58 | J. Cartledge, Sr., | Hutchinson's, | Columbia. |
| 17 | 1 | 60 | Jane Evans, | Evans', | Fayette. |
| 17 | 1 | 77 | Stephen H. Renfroe, | Comer's, | Jones. |
| 17 | 1 | 97 | Jane Baker, | Valleau's, | Chatham. |
| 17 | 1 | 125 | Eben. Jackson, Sr., | Valleau's, | Chatham. |
| 17 | 1 | 127 | Thomas Epperson, | Mangum's, | Franklin. |
| 17 | 1 | 140 | Richard Dean, | Chambers,' | Houston. |
| 17 | 1 | 150 | Dial Peavy, | Lamberth's, | Fayette. |
| 17 | 1 | 178 | Agnes Lawless, | Sea's, | Madison. |
| 17 | 1 | 185 | Nathaniel Handy, | Stephen's, | Habersham. |
| 17 | 1 | 192 | Elizabeth Talbot, | Morgan's, | Clarke. |
| 17 | 1 | 204 | James, Gray, | Madden's, | Pike. |
| 17 | 1 | 217 | John Connell, | Peterson's, | Montgomery. |
| 17 | 1 | 221 | George Slatin, | Lay's, | Jackson. |
| 17 | 1 | 231 | Peril Sinar, | 121st, | Richmond. |
| 18 | 1 | 23 | Nancy Duke, | Night's, | Morgan. |
| 18 | 1 | 42 | Jacob C. Dyer, | Tompkin's, | Putnam. |
| 18 | 1 | 48 | Elizabeth Roberts, | 417th, | Warren. |
| 18 | 1 | 91 | John Ray, Sr., | Hill's, | Harris. |
| 18 | 1 | 118 | Jesse Coleman, | 73d, | Burke. |
| 18 | 1 | 124 | Mary Grady, | Willis', | Franklin. |
| 18 | 1 | 166 | Susanna Wheeler, | 249th, | Walton. |
| 18 | 1 | 235 | Elizabeth Freeman, | Wilson's, | Jasper. |

| Dis. | Sec. | Lot. | Name. | District. | County. |
|---|---|---|---|---|---|
| 18 | 1 | 247 | Samuel Smith, | Sanderlin's, | Chatham. |
| 18 | 1 | 259 | William King, | Sweat's, | Ware. |
| 18 | 1 | 285 | Elizabeth Arrant, | 561st, | Upson. Avant? |
| 18 | 1 | 313 | Sarah Lambert, | Lay's, | Jackson. |
| 19 | 1 | 18 | Sarah Alexander, | Chambers', | Gwinnett. |
| 19 | 1 | 120 | Philips Crawford, | Nesbit's, | Newton. |
| 4 | 2 | 39 | James Mikell, | Slater's, | Bulloch. |
| 4 | 2 | 146 | Thomas Millican, | Johnson's, | DeKalb. |
| 4 | 2 | 274 | Martha Hinds, | 3d, | Chatham. |
| 4 | 2 | 316 | Frances B. Golden, | Anderson's, | Wilkes. |
| 5 | 2 | 47 | Henry Dobson, | Price's, | Hall. |
| 5 | 2 | 78 | John Prince, | Dyers', | Habersham. |
| 5 | 2 | 95 | Henry Cabaness, | Wilhite's, | Elbert. |
| 5 | 2 | 108 | William Ragland, | Peurifoy's, | Henry. |
| 5 | 2 | 116 | Martha Copeland, | Rutland's, | Bibb. |
| 5 | 2 | 127 | Catherine Lewis, | Russell's, | Henry. |
| 5 | 2 | 192 | Absalum Joiner, | Rutland's, | Bibb. |
| 5 | 2 | 225 | Moses Pinson, | Welchel's, | Hall. |
| 5 | 2 | 284 | Jesse Johnson, | Say's, | Jackson. |
| 5 | 2 | 307 | Celia Culbertson, | Talley's, | Troup. |
| 6 | 2 | 16 | Martha Chambers, | Griffin's, | Fayette. |
| 6 | 2 | 33 | Elizabeth Farechild, | Whipple's, | Wilkinson. |
| 6 | 2 | 74 | Susan Smith, | Morrison's, | Montgomery. |
| 6 | 2 | 129 | Mary Cannon, | Jones', | Bulloch. |
| 6 | 2 | 130 | Isaac Durham, | Latimer's, | DeKalb. |
| 6 | 2 | 161 | Lewis Goodman, | Bostick's, | Twiggs. |
| 6 | 2 | 194 | Moses Holcomb, | 3d Sec., | Cherokee. |
| 6 | 2 | 238 | Mary Bostwick, | Jones', | Morgan. |
| 6 | 2 | 273 | Levi Jester, | Tnaxton's, | Butts. |
| 6 | 2 | 276 | Sarah Dubose, | 69th, | Burke. |
| 6 | 2 | 287 | Joseph Griffin, | Haralson's, | Troup. |
| 6 | 2 | 317 | Elizabeth Rye, | Hucy's, | Harris. |
| 7 | 2 | 6 | William Pentecost, | Lay's, | Jackson. |
| 7 | 2 | 91 | Isam Hancock, | Welche's, | Habersham,p.89 |
| 7 | 2 | 160 | John Landrum, | Hinton's, | Wilkes. |
| 7 | 2 | 265 | Elizabeth Cannon, | 373d, | Jasper. |
| 8 | 2 | 34 | Charles Gates, Sr., | 406th, | Gwinnett. |
| 8 | 2 | 59 | Isaac Moore, | Collins', | Henry. |
| 8 | 2 | 73 | Sarah Head, | Lunceford's, | Elbert. |
| 8 | 2 | 145 | Gabriel Jones, | Groce's, | Bibb. |
| 8 | 2 | 184 | John Hendrick, | Bustin's, | Pike. |
| 8 | 2 | 197 | Mary Warren, | Herndon's, | Hall. |
| 8 | 2 | 297 | John Maginty, | Bustin's, | Pike. |
| 8 | 2 | 304 | Arthur Harrup, | Barefield's, | Jones. |
| 9 | 2 | 4 | Sarah Smith, | 277th, | Morgan. |

## LAND LOTTERY GRANTS.

| Dis. | Sec. | Lot. | Name. | District. | County. |
|---|---|---|---|---|---|
| 9 | 2 | 22 | William Mitchell, | Willis', | Franklin. |
| 9 | 2 | 35 | Henry Dickerson, | Everett's, | Washington. |
| 9 | 2 | 40 | Jane Wiley, | Crow's, | Pike. |
| 9 | 2 | 75 | Benjamin Phillips, | Brown's, | Camden. |
| 9 | 2 | 93 | Jane Willingham, | Colley's, | Oglethorpe. |
| 9 | 2 | 96 | John McVicker, | Smith's, | Henry. |
| 9 | 2 | 118 | Susannah Hicks, | 589th, | Upson. |
| 9 | 2 | 135 | Robert Carithers, | Sea's, | Madison. |
| 9 | 2 | 163 | Margaret McCollum, | Crawford's, | Franklin. |
| 9 | 2 | 189 | George Grumbles, | Bush's, | Burke. |
| 9 | 2 | 202 | Elizabeth Wilcher, | Cnestnut's, | Newton. |
| 9 | 2 | 225 | Hardy Johnson, | 55th, | Emanuel. |
| 9 | 2 | 246 | John Callahan (sic), | Jenkins', | Oglethorpe. |
| 9 | 2 | 259 | Stephen Hayman, | Bryant's, | Burke. |
| 9 | 2 | 298 | Ralph Bozeman, | Swain's, | Thomas. |
| 9 | 2 | 305 | Rosanna Jenkins, | Bragaw's, | Oglethorpe. |
| 9 | 2 | 314 | Patsey Vernon, | Collins', | Oglethorpe. |
| 10 | 2 | 35 | Lydia Cook, | 12th, | Effingham. |
| 10 | 2 | 88 | Leonard Wills, | Chambers', | Gwinnett. |
| 10 | 2 | 99 | Lavina Harris, | Guice's, | Oglethorpe. |
| 10 | 2 | 155 | John Sappington, | House's, | Henry. |
| 10 | 2 | 160 | Sarah Brack, | Cannon's, | Wilkinson. |
| 10 | 2 | 203 | Elizabeth Matthews, | Silman's, | Pike. |
| 10 | 2 | 241 | Elizabeth Gideons, | Phillips', | Talbot. |
| 10 | 2 | 243 | Thomas Pledger, | Luncefords', | Elbert. |
| 10 | 2 | 259 | Sarah Thrower, | ............ | ............ |
| 10 | 2 | 297 | Susannah Hewell, | Fenn's, | Clarke. |
| 11 | 2 | 4 | Mary C. Butler, | Bridges', | Gwinnett. |
| 11 | 2 | 35 | William Little, Sr., | 307th, | Putnam. |
| 11 | 2 | 57 | Samuel Moseley, | White's, | Franklin. |
| 11 | 2 | 83 | Adam Carson, | Alsabrook's, | Jones. |
| 11 | 2 | 85 | Mary Bennett, | Morgan's, | Appling. |
| 11 | 2 | 94 | Moses Hunter, | Whitehead's, | Habersham. |
| 11 | 2 | 118 | Mary Nash, | Sander's, | Jones. |
| 11 | 2 | 128 | Rebecker Nix, | Mizell's, | Talbot. |
| 11 | 2 | 218 | Wm. Mitchell, Sr., | Willis', | Franklin. |
| 11 | 2 | 230 | Sarah Lacy, | Hargrove's, | Newton. |
| 11 | 2 | 243 | Tully Choice, | 101st, | Hancock, p. 120 |
| 11 | 2 | 247 | Hugh M. Comer, | Stewart's, | Jones. |
| 12 | 1 | 6 | Rachel Magbee, | Hall's, | Butts. |
| 12 | 2 | 19 | Elizabeth Darrys, | 245th, | Jackson. |
| 12 | 2 | 54 | Willis Cason, Sr., | Lester's, | Pulaski. |
| 12 | 2 | 66 | William Buford, | Berry's, | Butts. |
| 12 | 2 | 106 | Lucretia Miller, | 458th, | Early. |
| 12 | 2 | 133 | William Allen, | Smith's, | Franklin. |
| 12 | 2 | 143 | Isam Watson, | Folsom's, | Lowdnes. |

ROSTER OF THE REVOLUTION.

| Dis. | Sec. | Lot. | Name. | District. | County. |
|---|---|---|---|---|---|
| 12 | 2 | 149 | Rebecca Brown, | Bishop's, | Henry. |
| 12 | 2 | 223 | Absolom Auldridge, | Walker's, | Houston. |
| 12 | 2 | 246 | Jane Oliver, | Lunceford's, | Elbert. |
| 12 | 2 | 248 | Zipporah Tammons, | 2d. Sec., | Cherokee. |
| 12 | 2 | 256 | William Vickers, | Griffin's, | Merriwether. |
| 12 | 2 | 261 | James Arkins, | Lamberth's, | Fayette. |
| 12 | 2 | 270 | Joseph Denson, Sr., | Underwood's, | Putnam. |
| 12 | 2 | 298 | Willis Caison, Sr., | Green's, | Ware. |
| 12 | 2 | 319 | James St. John, Sr., | McCuller's, | Newton. |
| 13 | 2 | 8 | John Turner, | Colley's, | Oglethorpe. |
| 13 | 2 | 56 | Jane McCutchen, | Griffin's, | Hall. |
| 13 | 2 | 67 | Jane Gammill, | Calhoun's, | Harris. |
| 13 | 2 | 145 | Robert Henderson, | Miller's, | Jackson. |
| 13 | 2 | 219 | Frederick Metts, | Martin's, | Washington. |
| 13 | 2 | 295 | Ephraim Liles, | Bostick's, | Twiggs. |
| 13 | 2 | 319 | Rebecca Creemmy, | Hand's, | Appling. |
| 14 | 2 | 5 | John Carroll, | 393d, | Jasper. |
| 14 | 2 | 12 | Henry Stone, | Sweat's, | Ware. |
| 14 | 2 | 31 | Thos. Merriwether, | McKorkles, | Jasper, p. 137. |
| 14 | 2 | 45 | William Thompson, | Smith's, | Habersham. |
| 14 | 2 | 69 | Jane Tool, | Baismore's, | Jones. |
| 14 | 2 | 99 | Fredrick Daniel, | Wilson's, | Pike. |
| 14 | 2 | 160 | Mary Brown, | Woodruff's, | Campbell. |
| 14 | 2 | 191 | Neddy Pennington, | Sullivan's, | Jones. |
| 14 | 2 | 193 | John Roberts, | Tower's, | Gwinnett. |
| 14 | 2 | 207 | Mary Crawford, | Mullen's, | Carroll. |
| 14 | 2 | 273 | Samuel Elrod, Sr., | Jones' | Habersham. |
| 14 | 2 | 288 | Michael Brannon, | Chamber's, | Gwinnett. |
| 14 | 2 | 308 | Sarah Harvey, | Bostick's, | Twiggs. |
| 14 | 2 | 314 | Ivey Smith, | George's, | Appling. |
| 20 | 2 | 1 | Unity Willoughby, w., | Rutland's, | Bibb. |
| 20 | 2 | 57 | Margaret Browning, | Morgan's, | Clarke. |
| 20 | 2 | 65 | Nancy Cunningham, | 192d, | Elbert. |
| 20 | 2 | 73 | Peny Pruitt, w.r.s., | Martin's, | Newton. |
| 20 | 2 | 81 | Thomas Cannup, | Hughes', | Habersham. |
| 20 | 2 | 97 | James Blair, | Whitehead's, | Habersham. |
| 20 | 2 | 101 | Benjamin Dorton, | Martin's, | Pike. |
| 20 | 2 | 121 | Elizabeth Brown, | 73d, | Burke. |
| 20 | 2 | 128 | Elijah Bowen, | Clifton's, | Tattnall. |
| 20 | 2 | 157 | Mary Levar, | Will's, | Twiggs. |
| 20 | 2 | 209 | Sarah Bayles, | Down's, | Warren. |
| 20 | 2 | 231 | Lydia Bohannon, | Morgan's, | Appling. |
| 20 | 2 | 249 | Humphrey Bearden, | Barnett's, | Clarke. |
| 20 | 2 | 282 | Baker Ayres, | Whitehead's, | Habersham. |
| 20 | 2 | 300 | Cealey Leverett, | Griffin's, | DeKalb, p. 149. |
| 20 | 2 | 302 | James Keak, Sr., | Belcher's, | Jasper. |

LAND LOTTERY GRANTS. 331

| Dis. | Sec. | Lot. | Name. | District. | County. |
|---|---|---|---|---|---|
| 20 | 2 | 321 | Amis Wright, w.r.s., | Hearn's, | Butts. |
| 20 | 2 | 333 | Thomas Glenn, | Baismore's, | Jones. |
| 22 | 2 | 78 | Jacob Setzer, | Edward's, | Franklin. |
| 22 | 2 | 97 | John Potts, | Jones', | Habersham. |
| 22 | 2 | 99 | John Arnett, | Groover's, | Thomas. |
| 22 | 2 | 107 | Robert Mitchell, | Rutland's, | Bibb. |
| 22 | 2 | 165 | Jane Stewart, | Bryan's, | Monroe. |
| 22 | 2 | 169 | Benjamin Phillips, | Brown's, | Camden. |
| 22 | 2 | 184 | Needham Chestnut, | Pearce's, | Houston. |
| 22 | 2 | 198 | James Rylee, Sr., | Blackstock's, | Hall. |
| 22 | 2 | 214 | Richard W. Oates, | 672d, | Harris. |
| 22 | 2 | 227 | Ann Sager, | 163d, | Greene. |
| 22 | 2 | 266 | Elias Hendricks, | Wilson's, | Madison. |
| 22 | 2 | 282 | Lydia Bohannon, | Morgan's, | Appling. |
| 23 | 2 | 36 | William Spears, | Edward's, | Franklin. |
| 23 | 2 | 66 | Baker Ayres, | Whitehead's, | Habersham. |
| 23 | 2 | 69 | Robert Brooks, | Taylor's, | Houston. |
| 23 | 2 | 102 | Biddy Procter, | 406th, | Gwinnett. |
| 23 | 2 | 158 | John Moore, | 116th, | Hancock. |
| 23 | 2 | 168 | Rebecca Wilson, | 138th, | Greene. |
| 23 | 2 | 171 | Samuel Holliman, | Dozier's, | Columbia. |
| 23 | 2 | 181 | Mordecai Brown, | Bishop's, | Henry. |
| 23 | 2 | 212 | James Wadsworth, | Davis', | Jones. |
| 23 | 2 | 217 | Mary Daniel, | Mason's, | Washington. |
| 23 | 2 | 243 | Edward Burch, | Delmon's, | Pulaski. |
| 23 | 2 | 295 | Tabithy Stewart, | 34th, | Screven. |
| 23 | 2 | 306 | Samuel Brady, | Watson's, | Marion. |
| 24 | 2 | 8 | Calra Harris, | Talley's, | Troup. |
| 24 | 2 | 17 | Susannah Gray, | Clark's, | Elbert. |
| 24 | 2 | 26 | Ethelred Harrell, Sr., | McDaniels,' | Pulaski. |
| 24 | 2 | 40 | Mary Carroll, | 167th. | Wilkes. |
| 24 | 2 | 67 | Rebecca Derracott, | Canning's, | Elbert. |
| 24 | 2 | 126 | Jacob Stillwell, | 735th, | Troup. |
| 24 | 2 | 137 | John Sanders, | Griffin's, | DeKalb. |
| 24 | 2 | 184 | Elizabeth Jourdan, | Camps', | Warren. |
| 24 | 2 | 190 | Shadrack Ellis, | Coxe's, | Talbot. |
| 24 | 2 | 227 | James Bowden, | Hill's, | Monroe. |
| 24 | 2 | 273 | Isham Hancock, | Welches', | Habersham. |
| 24 | 2 | 309 | John M. LeGrand, | Nellum's, | Elbert. |
| 24 | 2 | 312 | Luraney Luker, w.r.s., | Arrington's, | Merriwether. |
| 24 | 2 | 313 | Martha Lawson, | Whipple's, | Wilkinson. |
| 25 | 2 | 4 | Loami Brown, r.s., | 535th, | Dooly. |
| 25 | 2 | 20 | Margaret England, | Brook's, | Habersham. |
| 25 | 2 | 23 | Jesse Richardson, | Barnett's, | Habersham. |
| 25 | 2 | 30 | Robert Colquitt, | . . . . . . . . . . . | Oglethorpe. |
| 25 | 2 | 71 | John Barton, | Martin's, | Hall. |

ROSTER OF THE REVOLUTION.

| Dis. | Sec. | Lot. | Name. | District. | County. |
|---|---|---|---|---|---|
| 25 | 2 | 95 | Nancy Culver, | 111th | Hancock. |
| 25 | 3 | 106 | Mary Mappin, | Dozier's, | Columbia. |
| 25 | 2 | 128 | Miner Mead, | Wisenhunt's, | Carroll. |
| 25 | 2 | 140 | Susannah Monk, | Kendrick's, | Putnam. |
| 25 | 2 | 171 | Charlotte Lockhart, | Brewer's, | Monroe. |
| 25 | 2 | 173 | Philemon Hodges, | Few's, | Muscogee. |
| 25 | 2 | 183 | James Fould, | Smith's, | Wilkinson. |
| 25 | 2 | 199 | Colesby Smith, | Peacock's, | Washington. |
| 25 | 2 | 204 | Jane Ray, | Durham's, | Talbot. |
| 25 | 2 | 209 | Mary Mophett, | Tuggle's, | Merriwether. |
| 25 | 2 | 228 | J. Cartledge, Sr., | Hutchinson's, | Columbia. |
| 25 | 2 | 234 | Daniel Parker, Sr., | 555th, | Upson. |
| 25 | 2 | 275 | John West, | Kellum's, | Talbot. |
| 25 | 2 | 282 | Lucy Duffil, | Colley's, | Oglethorpe. |
| 25 | 2 | 306 | Mary Williams, | Slater's, | Bulloch. |
| 25 | 2 | 314 | John Nix, Sr., | Herndon's, | Hall. |
| 25 | 2 | 324 | James Swords, | Parks', | Walton. |
| 26 | 2 | 75 | John Williams, | Welche's, | Habersham. |
| 26 | 2 | 96 | William Holliday, | Prescott's, | Twiggs. |
| 26 | 2 | 98 | Rachael Cronick, | 417th, | Walton. |
| 26 | 2 | 101 | Mary Brown, | Mobley's, | DeKalb. |
| 26 | 2 | 142 | W. Jordan, w.r.s., | Sinquefield's, | Washington. |
| 26 | 2 | 150 | James Branch, | Ricks', | Laurens. |
| 26 | 2 | 163 | Daniel McCollum, | Jones', | Habersham. |
| 26 | 2 | 165 | Benjamin Jordan, | Tughles', | Merriwether. |
| 26 | 2 | 232 | Mary Weaver, | Moore's, | Randolph. |
| 26 | 2 | 274 | Thomas Higgs, Sr., | Daniel's, | Hall. |
| 26 | 2 | 276 | Margaret McWhorter, | Beasley's, | Oglethorpe. |
| 26 | 2 | 278 | John Tillary, Sr., | Hearn's, | Butts. |
| 26 | 2 | 317 | Elizabeth Coleman, | Ellsworth's, | Bibb. |
| 27 | 2 | 9 | Joseph Dawson, | Baley's, | Butts. |
| 27 | 2 | 16 | Mary Wingate, | 600th, | Richmond. |
| 27 | 2 | 22 | Ann Games, | Jones', | Thomas. |
| 27 | 2 | 73 | Elisabeth Doles, | 318th, | Baldwin. |
| 27 | 2 | 99 | Larkin Smith, Sr., | Jankin's. | Oglethorpe. |
| 27 | 2 | 117 | Thomas, Slay, | Johnson's, | DeKalb. |
| 27 | 2 | 175 | Henry Zinn, | 122d, | Richmond. |
| 27 | 2 | ... | Silva Reese, w.r.s., | Seay's, | Hall. |
| 27 | 2 | ... | John Tubett, | Silman's, | Pike. |
| 27 | 2 | ... | George Habersham, | Thames', | Crawford. |
| 27 | 2 | ... | Richard Hooper, | Chandler's, | Franklin. |
| 27 | 2 | ... | Amos Richardson, | Stewart's, | Elbert. |
| 27 | 2 | ... | James Starrell, | Dyer's, | Habersham. |
| 27 | 2 | ... | William Terrill, | Footes', | DeKalb. |
| 27 | 2 | ... | John Conden, | Howard's, | Oglethorpe. |
| 27 | 2 | ... | Mary Smith, | Strickland's, | Merriwether. |

## LAND LOTTERY GRANTS.

| Dis. | Sec. | Lot. | Name. | District. | County. |
|---|---|---|---|---|---|
| 27 | 2 | ... | Elizabeth Magee, | Rook's, | Putnam. |
| 5 | 3 | ... | Mary McClain, | Towers', | Gwinnett. |
| 5 | 3 | ... | C. Hamilton, w.r.s., | Peterson's, | Montgomery. |
| 5 | 3 | ... | Nancy Bachelder, | Young's, | Wilkinson. |
| 5 | 3 | ... | Rachael Yarbrough, | Moffett's, | Muscogee. |
| 5 | 3 | ... | Josiah Burgess, | 373d, | Jasper. |
| 5 | 3 | ... | Lazarus Hinson, | Smith's, | Franklin. |
| 5 | 3 | ... | Sarah Dobbs, | Dobbs', | Hall. |
| 6 | 3 | ... | William Thompson, | Smith's, | Habersham. |
| 6 | 3 | ... | Martha W. Johnson, | Compton's, | Fayette. |
| 6 | 3 | ... | John Maginty, | Bustin's, | Pike. |
| 6 | 3 | ... | Nathaniel Miller, | Perry's, | Baldwin. |
| 6 | 3 | ... | Joshia Walton. | Hinton's, | Wilkes. |
| 6 | 3 | ... | Howell Mangum, | ............ | ............ |
| 6 | 3 | ... | Lewis Jenkins, | ............ | ............ |
| 6 | 3 | ... | Soloman Sellers, | Hand's, | Appling. |
| 6 | 3 | ... | Elizabeth Hubbard, | Guice's, | Oglethorpe. |
| 6 | 3 | ... | Nathan Bowles, | McGinnis', | Jackson. |
| 6 | 3 | ... | Sarah Battle, | 602d, | Taliaferro. |
| 6 | 3 | ... | Mary Worsham, | Parks', | Walton. |
| 6 | 3 | ... | John Potts, | Jones', | Habersham. |
| 6 | 3 | ... | Mary Ross, | Robinson's, | Harris. |
| 6 | 3 | ... | Jean Higginbotham,w.r.s., | Canning's, | Elbert. |
| 6 | 3 | ... | Michael Barnwell, | Chambers', | Houston. |
| 6 | 3 | ... | Elizabeth Tyler, | Prophett's, | Newton. |
| 6 | 3 | ... | Robert Tucker, | Stower's, | Elbert. |
| 7 | 3 | ... | Richard Woodruff, | Norman's, | Houston. |
| 7 | 3 | ... | Ebenezer Fain, Sr., | Burnett's, | Newton. |
| 7 | 3 | ... | William Patrick, | 49th, | Elbert. |
| 7 | 3 | ... | Elizabeth Ward, | Lawrence's, | Wilkes. |
| 7 | 3 | ... | Elvilah Slatter, w.r.s., | Will's, | Habersham. |
| 7 | 3 | ... | Thomas Usery, | Turner's, | Crawford. |
| 7 | 3 | ... | John Cross, Sr., | Brooks, | Muscogee,p.212 |
| 7 | 3 | ... | Anthony M. Elton, | Riden's, | Jackson. |
| 7 | 3 | ... | Seth Thompson, | Curry's, | Merriwether. |
| 7 | 3 | ... | William Wetter, | Athens, | Clarke. |
| 7 | 3 | ... | William G. Hall, | Kendrick's, | Putnam. |
| 7 | 3 | ... | Milly Middlebrook, | Stanton's, | Newton. |
| 8 | 3 | ... | Frances Bruson, | Sinclair's, | Houston. |
| 8 | 3 | ... | Nancy Newson, | Crawford's, | Morgan. |
| 8 | 3 | ... | Specey Rusheon, | Sweat's, | Ware. |
| 8 | 3 | ... | Lewis Goodman, | Bostick's, | Twiggs. |
| 8 | 3 | ... | William Ham, | Whitaker's, | Crawford. |
| 8 | 3 | 129 | John Doby, | McKorkle's, | Jasper, |
| 8 | 3 | 155 | Elizabeth Visage, | Elli's, | Rabun, |
| 8 | 3 | 175 | William Thompson, | Thomas', | Ware, |

| Dis. | Sec. | Lot. | Name. | District. | County. |
|---|---|---|---|---|---|
| 8 | 3 | 201 | Molly Burnett, | Burnett's, | Lowdnes, |
| 8 | 3 | 215 | Joel Barnett, | Hargrove's, | Oglethorpe, |
| 8 | 3 | 221 | Robert Smith, Sr., | Hearn's, | Butts, |
| 8 | 3 | 264 | Elizabeth Barr, | Sinclair's, | Houston, |
| 8 | 3 | 274 | Easter Chester, Sr., | Jenning's, | Clarke. |
| 9 | 3 | 42 | John Hammett, | Newsom's, | Warren. |
| 9 | 3 | 160 | Benjamin Adams, | Fate's, | Warren. |
| 9 | 3 | 165 | Mary Brantley, | Gorley's, | Putnam. |
| 9 | 3 | 194 | James Lockhart, | Taylor's, | Elbert. |
| 9 | 3 | 195 | Dorothy Randolph, | Moseley's, | Wilkes. |
| 9 | 3 | 218 | Sarah Sutton, | Vining's, | Putnam. |
| 9 | 3 | 240 | Susannah Grizzard, | Camp's, | Warren. |
| 9 | 3 | 256 | Catherine Garr, | Wood's, | Morgan. |
| 9 | 3 | 272 | Isam Watson, | Folsom's, | Lowdnes. |
| 9 | 3 | 285 | John McClain, | Thomas', | Ware. |
| 9 | 3 | 314 | Margaret Turke, | Fleming's, | Franklin. |
| 10 | 3 | 62 | Edy Halbrooks, r.s., | Crawford's, | Franklin. |
| 10 | 3 | 99 | James Mikell, | Slater's, | Bulloch. |
| 10 | 3 | 120 | Samuel Waits, | McGeehee's, | Troup. |
| 10 | 3 | 129 | Michael Barnwell, | Chamber's, | Houston. |
| 10 | 3 | 142 | Isaad Hall, | Payne's, | Merriwether. |
| 10 | 3 | 215 | William Scott, | Atkinson's, | Coweta. |
| 10 | 3 | 264 | David McMurran, | ............ | ............ |
| 10 | 3 | 269 | John Cooksey, | McCuller's, | Newton. |
| 10 | 3 | 293 | John Davis, | McCraney's, | Lowdnes. |
| 10 | 3 | 320 | Thomas Holmes, | David's, | Franklin. |
| 11 | 3 | 2 | Kesse Smith, Sr., | Edward's, | Franklin. |
| 11 | 3 | 39 | William Jones, Sr., | Wilson's, | Jasper. |
| 11 | 3 | 51 | Eve Boggs, | 242d, | Jackson. |
| 11 | 3 | 63 | Charles Atkins, Sr., | 558th, | Upson. |
| 11 | 3 | 72 | Sally Linn, | Williams', | Jasper. |
| 11 | 3 | 75 | George Varner, | Smith's, | Franklin. |
| 11 | 3 | 80 | John R. McMullions, | Smith's, | Franklin. |
| 11 | 3 | 111 | Mary Jackson, | Martin's, | Washington. |
| 11 | 3 | 115 | Dicey Pool, | Crow's, | Pike. |
| 11 | 3 | 146 | Anne Springer, | Moseley's, | Wilkes. |
| 11 | 3 | 157 | Zacharia Cowart, Sr., | 510th, | Early. |
| 11 | 3 | 169 | Richard Speak, Sr., | McLinn's, | Butts. |
| 11 | 3 | 182 | Charles Jordan, Sr., | Crow's, | Merriwether. |
| 11 | 3 | 259 | Martha Long, | 114th, | Hancock. |
| 11 | 3 | 277 | James Walker, Sr., | 470th, | Upson. |
| 11 | 3 | 286 | Robert Jennings, | Hatchertt's, | Oglethorpe. |
| 11 | 3 | 292 | James Gilmore, | Spark's, | Washington. |
| 12 | 3 | 1 | William Selman, | 555th, | Upson. |
| 12 | 3 | 29 | Patsey Vernon, | Colley's, | Oglethorpe. |
| 12 | 3 | 63 | Nancy Gordon, | Gunn's, | Jones. |

## LAND LOTTERY GRANTS. 335

| | | | | | |
|---|---|---|---|---|---|
| 12 | 3 | 75 | Jane Paris, | Whitehead's, | Habersham. |
| 12 | 3 | 160 | William Tedder, | Morrison's, | Montgomery. |
| 12 | 3 | 310 | Elizabeth Fuller, | 148th, | Greene. |
| 12 | 3 | 311 | Caroline Barnett, | Davis', | Clarke. |
| 12 | 3 | 312 | Allen Tucker, | 148th. | Greene. |
| 12 | 3 | 347 | Priscilla Strad, | Bryan's, | Monroe. |
| 12 | 3 | 349 | William M. Harper, | Chastain's, | Habersham. |
| 12 | 3 | 355 | Elizabeth Childs, | Sander's, | Jones. |
| 13 | 3 | 8 | Elizabeth Lansford, | Dawson's, | Jasper. |
| 13 | 3 | 42 | Susannah Eubanks, | Herndon's, | Hall. |
| 13 | 3 | 52 | David Mitzher, | 11th, | Effingham. |
| 13 | 3 | 147 | Thomas Howell, | Brown's, | Camden. |
| 13 | 3 | 156 | John R. McMillan, | Smith's, | Franklin. |
| 13 | 3 | 159 | Charles Gates, Sr., | 406th, | Gwinnett. |
| 13 | 3 | 189 | Mary Nichols, | Bostick's, | Twiggs. |
| 13 | 3 | 215 | Reuben Nail, | Carpenter's, | Tattnall. |
| 13 | 3 | 220 | Nathaniel Affut, | William's, | Washington. |
| 13 | 3 | 239 | William Jordan, | McClain's, | Newton. |
| 13 | 3 | 293 | Frances Scott, w.r.s., | 143d, | Greene. |
| 13 | 3 | 312 | David Monroe, Sr., | 73d, | Burke. |
| 14 | 3 | 15 | Henry Tulley, Sr., | McCuller's, | Newton. |
| 14 | 3 | 30 | William Davis, | Nichols,' | Fayette. |
| 14 | 3 | 35 | Elizabeth Trainum, | 278th, | Morgan. |
| 14 | 3 | 40 | John Mattox, | 464th, | Gwinnett. |
| 14 | 3 | 56 | George Wilson, | 454th, | Walton. |
| 14 | 3 | 64 | Thomas Murray, | Murphy's, | Columbia. |
| 14 | 3 | 134 | Ann McGoy, | 603d, | Taliaferro. |
| 14 | 3 | 170 | Tabitha Bateman, | Smith's, | Houston. |
| 14 | 3 | 182 | Sarah Cash, | Orr's, | Jackson. |
| 14 | 3 | 236 | Thomas Tanner, | Griffin's, | DeKalb. |
| 14 | 3 | 279 | Robert Henderson, Sr., | Jones', | Hall. |
| 14 | 3 | 294 | William Suttles, | Mobley's, | DeKalb. |
| 14 | 3 | 314 | John Dowd, | Newsom's, | Warren. |
| 15 | 3 | 22 | John Hames, Sr. (Haines?), | Daniel's, | Hall. |
| 15 | 3 | 24 | James Adams, | Seals', | Elbert. |
| 15 | 3 | 32 | Mary Lloyd, | 404th, | Gwinnett. |
| 15 | 3 | 38 | Lazarus Telly, | Keener's, | Rabun. |
| 15 | 3 | 64 | Jane Ward, | 190th, | Elbert. |
| 15 | 3 | 71 | John Hayes, | Latimers', | DeKalb. |
| 15 | 3 | 164 | William Tomalson, | Everett's, | Washington. |
| 15 | 3 | 171 | George Young, Sr., | Howard's, | Oglethorpe. |
| 15 | 3 | 183 | Patrick Butler, Sr., | Smith's, | Elbert. |
| 15 | 3 | 205 | John Hines, | 73d, | Burke. |
| 15 | 3 fr. | 6 | Mary Napp, | 160th, | Greene. |
| 15 | 3 | 28 | Elizabeth Watson, | Murphy's, | Columbia. |
| 16 | 3 | 48 | Thomas McCall, | Hobb's, | Laurens. |

| Dis. | Sec. | Lot. | Name. | District. | County. |
|---|---|---|---|---|---|
| 16 | 3 | 63 | John Bowen, | Barker's, | Gwinnett. |
| 16 | 3 | 76 | James W. Cook, | 248th, | Jackson. |
| 16 | 3 | 78 | Jonathan Rhan, | 11th, | Effingham. |
| 16 | 3 | 85 | Ann Bryan, | 73d, | Burke. |
| 16 | 3 | 104 | Rebecca Williams, | Welchel's, | Hall. |
| 16 | 3 | 116 | John Gilbert, | 243d, | Jackson. |
| 16 | 3 | 120 | Robert Barnwell, | Griffin's, | Hall. |
| 16 | 3 | 126 | Ann Wilson, | 12th, | Effingham. |
| 16 | 3 | 224 | Clement Waters, | Welches', | Habersham. |
| 16 | 3 | 233 | Samuel Brady, | Watson's, | Marion. |
| 16 | 3 | 244 | Isaac Hopkins, | Norman's, | Wilkes. |
| 22 | 3 | 19 | Pester Hinton, | Taylor's, | Elbert. |
| 22 | 3 | 29 | Robert Carter, | McClain's, | Newton. |
| 22 | 3 | 52 | Henry Dobson, | Price's, | Hall. |
| 22 | 3 | 58 | Mary Kirklin, | Stewart's, | Troup. |
| 22 | 3 | 91 | M. W. Tomlinson, | Chustus', | Jefferson. |
| 22 | 3 | 112 | Susannah Sett, | Johnson's, | DeKalb. |
| 22 | 3 | 129 | M. Watkins, Sr., | Garner's, | Jefferson. |
| 22 | 3 | 154 | Samuel Shephard, | Seal's, | Elbert. |
| 22 | 3 | 182 | Sarah Rushing, | Haygood's, | Washington. |
| 22 | 3 | 194 | Elizabeth Richardson, | 396th, | Emanuel. |
| 22 | 3 | 255 | Ica Atkins, Sr., | Mitchell's, | Pulaski. |
| 22 | 3 | 335 | Elizabeth Porter, | Dozier's, | Columbia. |
| 22 | 3 | 338 | Margarette McCibben, | Hood's, | Henry. |
| 23 | 3 | 47 | Betahny Knight, w.r.s., | 57th, | Emanuel. |
| 23 | 3 | 53 | Josiah Hatcher, | Allison's, | Pike. |
| 23 | 3 | 103 | George Harper, | Gunn's, | Jones. |
| 23 | 3 | 113 | Cornelius Gibbs, | Henson's, | Rabun. |
| 23 | 3 | 128 | Elizabeth Glenn, | McGeehee's, | Troup. |
| 23 | 3 | 188 | Diana Hester, | Bivins, | Jones. |
| 23 | 3 | 192 | Diana Gray, | Willis', | Franklin. |
| 23 | 3 | 210 | Frances Herndon, w.r.s., | 778th, | Heard. |
| 23 | 3 | 213 | Nathaniel Lewis, | Cleland's, | Chatham. |
| 23 | 3 | 215 | George Grumbles, | Bush's, | Burke. |
| 23 | 3 | 292 | Easther Dyson, | 734th, | Lee. |
| 23 | 3 | 305 | Mary Jones, | Jones', | Hall. |
| 23 | 3 | 343 | Ann Glenn, | Phillip's, | Jasper, p. 290. |
| 23 | 3 | 346 | Benjamin Smith, | Craven's, | Coweta. |
| 24 | 3 | 6 | Henry Huey, | Latimer's, | DeKalb. |
| 24 | 3 | 23 | William Stone, | Phillips', | Jasper. |
| 24 | 3 | 34 | William Lard, | Riden's, | Jackson. |
| 24 | 3 | 45 | Charles Arnold, | Carpenter's, | Tattnall. |
| 24 | 3 | 57 | Sarah Johnson, | 693d, | Heard. |
| 24 | 3 | 73 | Samuel Ewing, | 102d, | Hancock. |
| 24 | 3 | 103 | David Anthony, | David's, | Franklin. |
| 24 | 3 | 150 | Elizabeth Glenn, | Liddell's, | Jackson. |

## LAND LOTTERY GRANTS.

| Dis. | Sec. | Lot. | Name. | District. | County. |
|---|---|---|---|---|---|
| 24 | 3 | 188 | James Wood, | Collier's, | Monroe. |
| 24 | 3 | 222 | Thomas Glenn, | Baismore's, | Jones. |
| 24 | 3 | 294 | Margery Hobbs, | Hughes', | Habersham. |
| 24 | 3 | 250 | Wiloughy Gaison, | Green's, | Ware. |
| 24 | 3 | 255 | Susan Wright, | 104th, | Hancock. |
| 24 | 3 | 286 | Uriah Skinner, | Roe's, | Burke. |
| 25 | 3 | 15 | Thomas Simmons, | Williams', | Ware. |
| 25 | 3 | 19 | John King, | Liddell's, | Jackson. |
| 25 | 3 | 54 | John Dalton, | Ellsworth, | Bibb. |
| 25 | 3 | 95 | Mary Stamper, | Parham's, | Warren. |
| 25 | 3 | 109 | Peter Guise, | Stoke's, | Lincoln. |
| 25 | 3 | 119 | Nathaniel Bond, | Seal's, | Elbert. |
| 25 | 3 | 126 | M. A. Douglas, w.r.s., | Arrington's, | Merriwether. |
| 25 | 3 | 132 | Job Jordan, | Watson's, | Marion. |
| 25 | 3 | 146 | Mary Lucas, | 102d, | Hancock. |
| 25 | 3 | 150 | William Ham, | Whitaker's, | Crawford. |
| 25 | 3 | 155 | John Harris, | Hargroves', | Newton. |
| 25 | 3 | 161 | William Lesley, | Bragaw's, | Oglethorpe. |
| 25 | 3 | 228 | Kesiah Bailey, | Martin's, | Washington. |
| 26 | 3 | 11 | Susannah Hubbard, | Guice's, | Oglethorpe. |
| 26 | 3 | 29 | Edmond Shackleford, | Taylor's, | Elbert. |
| 26 | 3 | 36 | Richard Speak, Sr., | McLinn's, | Butts. |
| 26 | 3 | 42 | Winiford Dyess, | Miller's, | Ware. |
| 26 | 3 | 48 | Nancy Keslerson, | Rutland's, | Bibb. |
| 26 | 3 | 54 | William Wilson, | Baugh's, | Jackson. |
| 26 | 3 | 55 | John Wilson, Sr., | 148th, | Greene. |
| 26 | 3 | 64 | John Lawrence, | Taylor's, | Putnam. |
| 26 | 3 | 67 | Sarah Daniel, | 121st, | Richmond. |
| 26 | 3 | 87 | Levicey Holloman, w.r.s., | 6th, Mitchell's, | Pulaski. |
| 26 | 3 | 124 | Archibald Perkins, | 141st, | Greene. |
| 26 | 3 | 143 | John Higgs, | Edward's, | Montgomery. |
| 26 | 3 | 168 | Mary Ann Davis, | Rhode's, | DeKalb. |
| 26 | 3 | 170 | Martha Allison, | 143d, | Greene. |
| 26 | 3 | 186 | Elizabeth Parish, | Lynn's, | Warren. |
| 26 | 3 | 194 | Josiah Walton, | Hinton's, | Wilkes. |
| 26 | 3 | 225 | Rosannah Carnes, | Keener's, | Rabun. |
| 26 | 3 | 255 | Polly Robinson, | Burgess', | Carroll. |
| 26 | 3 | 267 | Mary Rooks, | 353d, | Wayne. |
| 26 | 3 | 278 | Mary Harper, | 101st, | Hancock. |
| 26 | 3 | 280 | Elizabeth Conaway, | Herndon's, | Hall. |
| 26 | 3 | 281 | Amy Peacock, | 454th, | Walton. |
| 26 | 3 | 282 | John Morris, | Bush's, | Pulaski. |
| 26 | 3 | 293 | Jesse Coleman, | 73d, | Burke. |
| 26 | 3 | 320 | Mary Davis, | Peterson's, | Montgomery. |
| 26 | 3 | 323 | Isaac Coker, | Hood's, | Henry. |
| 27 | 3 | 4 | John Moore, | Merck's, | Hall. |

| Dis. | Sec. | Lot. | Name. | District. | County. |
|---|---|---|---|---|---|
| 27 | 3 | 7 | S. Golightly, | William's, | Washington. |
| 27 | 3 | 40 | Sally Twitty, | Lamberth's, | Fayette. |
| 27 | 3 | 83 | Mary Clarke, | Hannah's, | Jefferson. |
| 27 | 3 | 145 | Hugh M. Comer, | Stewart's, | Jones. |
| 27 | 3 | 152 | William Lesley, | Bragaw's, | Oglethorpe. |
| 27 | 3 | 153 | Walter Been, | Belcher's, | Jasper. |
| 27 | 3 | 174 | Susannah Yates, | Lamberth's, | Fayette. |
| 27 | 3 | 182 | Robert Smith, Sr., | Hearn's, | Butts. |
| 27 | 3 | 183 | Benjamin Dorton, | Martin's, | Pike. |
| 27 | 3 | 190 | Sarah Highsmith, | 335th, | Wayne. |
| 27 | 3 | 195 | Elender Golden, | 417th, | Walton. |
| 27 | 3 | 243 | Elizabeth Rudolph, | Hobkerks', | Camden. |
| 27 | 3 | 270 | W. Edmonds, | Lunceford's, | Wilkes. |
| 27 | 3 | 293 | Nathaniel Beall, | 124th, | Richmond. |
| 27 | 3 | 300 | Joshua Elder, | Robinson's, | Fayette. |
| 27 | 3 | 332 | Elizabeth Doherty, | Say's, | DeKalb. |
| 27 | 3 | 341 | Ann Bradford, | Robinson's, | Putnam. |
| 28 | 3 | 18 | Mary McRee, | Barnett's, | Clarke. |
| 28 | 3 | 22 | Elizabeth Hughton, | Athen's, | Clarke. |
| 28 | 3 | 46 | Mary Chicoming, | Lester's, | Monroe. |
| 28 | 3 | 54 | James Epsy, | Buckbranch, | Clarke. |
| 28 | 3 | 83 | Zachariah Cowart, Sr., | 510th, | Early. |
| 28 | 3 | 99 | William Palmer, | Rhode's, | DeKalb. |
| 28 | 3 | 158 | Alston S. Massey, | Robinson's, | Harris. |
| 28 | 3 | 167 | David Patrick, | Hall's, | Oglethorpe. |
| 28 | 3 | 175 | John Litton, | Hughes', | Habersham. |
| 28 | 3 | 199 | Winefred Paine, | Morris', | Crawford. |
| 28 | 3 | 202 | Jesse Miller, | Jordan's, | Harris. |
| 28 | 3 | 214 | Samuel Carruthers, | Towers', | Gwinnett. |
| 28 | 3 | 220 | Margaret Buice, | Hutson's, | Newton. |
| 28 | 3 | 245 | John Rutherford, | Perry's, | Baldwin. |
| 28 | 3 | 293 | Thomas Leansley, | Ware's, | Coweta. |
| 4 | 4 | 24 | Elizabeth Haney, | Winn's, | Gwinnett. |
| 4 | 4 | 29 | Deborah Cook, | Lightfoot's, | Washington. |
| 4 | 4 | 37 | Emily Denton, | Hart's, | Jones. |
| 4 | 4 | 42 | Lewis S. Nobles, | Peterson's, | Montgomery. |
| 4 | 4 | 43 | Sarah Glazier, | Hampton's, | Newton. |
| 4 | 4 | 56 | Burdett Leach, | Hammond's, | Franklin. |
| 4 | 4 | 84 | Sally Grissam, | Trout's, | Hall. |
| 4 | 4 | 93 | Mary Dickson, | 80th, | Screven. |
| 4 | 4 | 107 | John McDonald, | Riden's, | Jackson. |
| 4 | 4 | 122 | Frederick Thompson, | 249th, | Walton. |
| 4 | 4 | 123 | Sherwood Stroud, | 249th, | Walton. |
| 4 | 4 | 134 | Lee Ann Ruddell, w.r.s., | Moseley's, | Wilkes. |
| 4 | 4 | 171 | Mary King, | Phillip's, | Talbot. |
| 4 | 4 | 172 | Eliza A. Taliferro, | Hinton's, | Wilkes. |

LAND LOTTERY GRANTS. 339

| Dis. | Sec. | Lot. | Name. | District. | County. |
|---|---|---|---|---|---|
| 4 | 4 | 255 | Mary Spence, | 74th, | Burke. |
| 4 | 4 | 306 | James Smith, | Guices, | Oglethorpe. |
| 4 | 4 | 311 | Thomas Newman, | 121st, | Richmond. |
| 5 | 4 | 6 | George Kellum, | Kellum's, | Talbot. |
| 5 | 4 | 44 | William Flanagan, | Martin's, | Hall. |
| 5 | 4 | 58 | Henry Hayman, | Blair's, | Lowdnes. |
| 5 | 4 | 68 | Benjamin Joiner, | Covington's, | Pike. |
| 5 | 4 | 84 | Celia Stringer, | Peterson's, | Burke. |
| 5 | 4 | 85 | Rosannah Johnson, | Harris', | DeKalb. |
| 5 | 4 | 103 | Jane Flood, | Allen's, | Henry. |
| 5 | 4 | 121 | Thomas Cobbett, | Clark's, | Elbert. |
| 5 | 4 | 128 | Phebe Park, | 161st, | Greene. |
| 5 | 4 | 150 | John Norman, Sr., | Hinton's, | Wilkes. |
| 5 | 4 | 185 | Mary Jernigan, | 106th, | Hancock. |
| 5 | 4 | 189 | Abel Gower, | Reed's, | Gwinnett. |
| 5 | 4 | 220 | Benjamin Thompson, | 113th, | Hancock. |
| 5 | 4 | 231 | Elizabeth McDaniel, | Gunn's, | Jones. |
| 5 | 4 | 243 | Urill Crosby, | Lunceford's, | Wilkes. |
| 5 | 4 | 247 | William Aldrige, | Norman's, | Wilkes. |
| 5 | 4 | 263 | Celia Lewis, | 406th, | Gwinnett. |
| 5 | 4 | 283 | Winny Verdib, w.r.s., | Goodwin's, | Houston. |
| 5 | 4 | 284 | John Kent, | Bostick's, | Twiggs. |
| 5 | 4 | 295 | John Hickman, | Kendrick's, | Monroe. |
| 5 | 4 | 304 | Anthony Seal, | Huey's, | Harris. |
| 5 | 4 | 322 | Daniel Greene, | Greene's, | Ware. |
| 6 | 4 | 49 | John McDade, | Reid's, | Gwinnett. |
| 6 | 4 | 93 | George Eubanks, | Dearing's, | Butts. |
| 6 | 4 | 117 | Mary Phillips, | Sam Sweetman's, | Twiggs. |
| 6 | 4 | 139 | Soloman Williams, | Rick's, | Laurens. |
| 6 | 4 | 170 | Judith McFail, | Gouodings, | Lowdnes. |
| 6 | 4 | 234 | Littleberry Daniel, | 693d, | Heard. |
| 6 | 4 | 265 | Sarah Wesson, | Lightfoot's, | Washington. |
| 7 | 4 | 60 | Lewis Jenkins, | Peacock's, | Washington. |
| 7 | 4 | 71 | John Davis, Sr., | Welche's, | Habersham. |
| 7 | 4 | 74 | Hannah Holbrook, | Towers', | Gwinnett. |
| 7 | 4 | 181 | George Haynie, | McGinnis', | Jackson. |
| 7 | 4 | 207 | John Conyers, | 37th, | Screven. |
| 7 | 4 | 245 | Jesse Pollock, | Buck's, | Houston. |
| 7 | 4 | 301 | Mary Dunaway, | Perryman's, | Warren. |
| 8 | 4 | 49 | Ann Morrow, | Hampton's, | Newton. |
| 8 | 4 | 64 | William Dugger, Sr., | Groover's, | Thomas, p. 355. |
| 8 | 4 | 94 | Uriah Burkett, | 535th, | Dooly. |
| 8 | 4 | 97 | John Hudson, | Colquohoun's, | Henry. |
| 8 | 4 | 107 | John Peter Arnand, | 3d, | Chatham. |
| 8 | 4 | 183 | Elizabeth P. Kendall, | Brook's, | Muscogee. |
| 8 | 4 | 246 | Martha Fowler, | Griders', | Morgan. |

## ROSTER OF THE REVOLUTION.

| Dis. | Sec. | Lot. | Name. | District. | County. |
|---|---|---|---|---|---|
| 8 | 4 | 281 | Isaac Baldasee, | Wright's, | Tattnall. |
| 9 | 4 | 1 | Celia Giles, | Everett's, | Washington. |
| 9 | 4 | 54 | Ann Cannon, | 417th, | Walton. |
| 9 | 4 | 65 | Charity Gamade, | Pearces', | Houston. |
| 9 | 4 | 70 | Ann Hendry, | Laker's, | Liberty. |
| 9 | 4 | 108 | Kesiah Fuller, | Adams', | Columbia. |
| 9 | 4 | 132 | Hannah Butler, | 687th. | Lee. |
| 9 | 4 | 152 | Dorcas Horn, | Crow's, | Pike. |
| 9 | 4 | 157 | John Harper, | M. Brown's, | Habersham. |
| 9 | 4 | 161 | Susannah Alexander, | Seally's, | Talbot. |
| 9 | 4 | 173 | J. Alsobrook, Sr., | Alsobrook's, | Jones. |
| 9 | 4 | 182 | Willmouth Fox, | 362d, | Jasper. |
| 9 | 4 | 213 | Josiah Dennis, | Night's, | Morgan. |
| 9 | 4 | 219 | Jemina Fincher, | Smith's, | Henry. |
| 9 | 4 | 248 | Matthew Alexander, | Brown's, | Habersham. |
| 9 | 4 | 304 | John Barnwell, | Dearing's, | Henry. |
| 10 | 4 | 44 | John Cask, | Peurifoy's, | Henry. |
| 10 | 4 | 46 | Mary Wence, | 1st, | Chatham. |
| 10 | 4 | 96 | John Grace, | Carpenter's, | Tattnall. |
| 10 | 4 | 142 | Jesse McNeill, | Johnson's, | Bibb. |
| 10 | 4 | 146 | John Austin, Sr., | 250th, | Walton. |
| 10 | 4 | 173 | Nancy Hiner, | Lay's, | Jackson. |
| 10 | 4 | 174 | William Glasgow, | Wilson's, | Madison. |
| 10 | 4 | 187 | Alexander Martin, | Mantooth's, | Oglethorpe. |
| 10 | 4 | 260 | James Barber, | 406th, | Gwinnett. |
| 10 | 4 | 304 | Wiatt Hewell, | Hargroves', | Newton. |
| 10 | 4 | 4 | Matthew Varner, Sr., | Hall's, | Oglethorpe. |
| 11 | 4 | 36 | Nancy Jones, | Griffin's, | Fayette. |
| 11 | 4 | 68 | James Carter, | Thompson's, | Elbert. |
| 11 | 4 | 121 | Judith Waters, | Royster's, | Franklin. |
| 11 | 4 | 122 | Ditha Williams, w.r.s., | Bostick's, | Twiggs. |
| 11 | 4 | 152 | Charles Cantrell, | Higginbotham's, | Rabun. |
| 11 | 4 | 176 | Edmond Knowles, | 160th, | Greene. |
| 11 | 4 | 189 | Clara Richardson, | Hill's, | Monroe. |
| 11 | 4 | 197 | John Sisson, | Liddell's, | Jackson. |
| 11 | 4 | 221 | Louisa Long, | Candler's, | Bibb. |
| 11 | 4 | 260 | Abram Reddick, | 365th, | Jasper. |
| 11 | 4 | 270 | Willis Cason, Sr., | Lester's, | Pulaski. |
| 11 | 4 | 272 | Nancy Coleman, | George's, | Appling. |
| 11 | 4 | 310 | Lewis Lanier, | 36th, | Screven. |
| 12 | 4 | 10 | Sarah Ginn, | Bowers', | Elbert. |
| 12 | 4 | 66 | Lucy Glynn, | 141st, | Greene. |
| 12 | 4 | 101 | Isaac Lindsey, Sr., | Jones', | Hall. |
| 12 | 4 | 106 | I. Cummings, w.r.s., | Garner's, | Washington. |
| 12 | 4 | 113 | Thomas Mayes, | David's, | Franklin. |
| 12 | 4 | 119 | Jacob Redwine, | Bower's, | Elbert. |

## LAND LOTTERY GRANTS. 341

| Dis. | Sec. | Lot. | Name. | District. | County. |
|---|---|---|---|---|---|
| 12 | 4 | 146 | Mary Davis, | Peterson's, | Montgomery. |
| 12 | 4 | 153 | Rachael Brooks, | Rhode's, | DeKalb. |
| 12 | 4 | 213 | Martha Singletary, | Harrison's, | Decatur. |
| 13 | 4 | 9 | Mary Myers, | 271st, | McIntosh. |
| 13 | 4 | 25 | Jane Sparks, | Stewart's, | Troup. |
| 13 | 4 | 68 | George Watts, | Mobley's, | DeKalb. |
| 13 | 4 | 84 | Nathan Dobbs, | Hamilton's, | Gwinnett. |
| 13 | 4 | 132 | John Gilbert, | 243d, | Jackson. |
| 13 | 4 | 141 | Edward Kelly, | Bush's, | Pulaski. |
| 13 | 4 | 162 | Renne Fitzpatrick, | 779th, | Heard. |
| 13 | 4 | 182 | Nancey Williams, | 177th, | Wilkes. |
| 13 | 4 | 266 | Lewis S. Nobles, | Peterson's, | Montgomery. |
| 13 | 4 | 274 | Selah Spears, w.r.s., | Hines', | Coweta. |
| 13 | 4 | 303 | John Clarke, | Collier's, | Monroe. |
| 13 | 4 | 311 | (Out) | (Out) | (Out) |
| 14 | 4 | 16 | Elizabeth Cohom, | 603d, | Taliaferro. |
| 14 | 4 | 23 | Nancy Wilkes, | Howell's, | Elbert. |
| 14 | 4 | 63 | Elizabeth Henry, | 106th, | Hancock. |
| 14 | 4 | 113 | John Harmon, Sr., | Lunceford's, | Elbert. |
| 14 | 4 | 146 | Susannah Willis, | 168th, | Wilkes. |
| 15 | 4 | 67 | Temperance Manly, w.r.s., | Crawford's, | Franklin. |
| 15 | 4 | 81 | Elizabeth Hunter, | Reid's, | Gwinnett. |
| 18 | 4 | 7 | John Spears, | Nesbit's, | Newton. |
| 18 | 4 | 12 | Elizabeth Walker, | Mason's, | Washington. |
| 18 | 4 | 36 | Mary Smith, | Newsom's, | Warren. |
| 18 | 4 | 40 | James Gilmer, Sr., | Martin's, | Hall. |
| 18 | 4 | 103 | Levi Phillips, | Higginbotham's, | Carroll, p. 408. |
| 18 | 4 | 154 | Hannah Deason, | Clinton's, | Campbell. |
| 19 | 4 | 14 | Amelia C. Mattox, | Campbell's, | Wilkes. |
| 19 | 4 | 15 | Gideon Elvington, | Folsom's, | Lowdnes. |
| 19 | 4 | 21 | Thomas Beasley, Sr., | Allen's, | Henry. |
| 19 | 4 | 73 | Rebecca Faris, | 404th, | Gwinnett. |
| 19 | 4 | 89 | Lewis Brown, | Butt's, | Monroe. |
| 19 | 4 | 91 | Joseph Brown, | Henson's, | Rabun. |
| 19 | 4 | 119 | Jane Patterson, | 466th, | Monroe. |
| 19 | 4 | 136 | Mary Ann Crawford, | Grubb's, | Columbia. |
| 19 | 4 | 139 | Sarah English, | Fleming's, | Franklin. |
| 19 | 4 | 148 | Zephanaiah Franklin, | Parham's, | Warren. |

J. A. Le CONTE.

May 31st, 1910.

Also:

| Dis. | Sec. | Lot. | Name. | District. | County. |
|---|---|---|---|---|---|
| 15 | 4 | 194 | Sarah Vickers, | 118th, | Hancock. |

## CERTIFIED LIST OF REVOLUTIONARY SOLDIERS.
### Compiled by Capt. B. F. Johnson from Lottery Lists of 1827.

[Published as Appendix B, in the Fifth Annual Aeport of the National Soci- Number 210, Fifty-seventh Congress, Second Session, pp. 326-350. List of Revolutionary Soldiers, compiled by Capt. B. F. Johnson, Chief Clerk in the office of Secretary of State, of the State of Georgia. Supplemental to the list published under Appendix E, in the Third Report of the National Society, D. A. R., to the Smithsonian Institution. This list was furnished by Mrs. Robert Emory Park, State Regent of Georgia, and Chairman of the D. A. R. Committee on Colonial and Revolutionary Records.]

### A.

Adams, Aaron, lottery 1827, Hall County.
Adams, Dancy, lottery 1827, Columbia County.
Adams, David, lottery 1827, Jasper County.
Adams, Thomas, lottery 1827, Elbert County.
Adcock, Thomas, bounty granted, Book GGG, p. 542.
Adkerson, Henry, lottery 1827, Wilkinson County.
Adkins, William, bounty granted, certified by E. Clark, Col.
Adkinson, Thomas, bounty granted, Book FFF, p. 626.
Ajon, Eli, lottery 1827, Chatham County.
Akins, James, lottery 1827, Greene County.
Akins, William, lottery 1827, Morgan County.
Akridge, Ezekiel, lottery 1827, Clark County.
Akridge, William, lottery 1827, Baldwin County.
Alberson, William, lottery 1827, Newton County.
Alexander, Isaac, lottery 1827, Elbert County.
Alexander, Thomas, Lieutenant, Commission Book, p. 228.
Allen, David, lottery 1827, Morgan County.
Allen, Joseph, lottery 1827, Elbert County.
Allen, Moses, Chaplain, "book pay rolls," certified, Robert Middleton, Col.
Allen, Philip, lottery 1827, Clark County.
Allen, Woodson, lottery 1827, Walton County.
Amison, Jesse, lottery 1827, Wilkes County.
Ammons, Jacob, lottery 1827, Madison County.
Amos, James, early lottery 1820, Hancock County.
Amos, Leary, lottery 1827, Hancock County.
Amos, Mauldin, lottery 1827, Jones County.
Andrews, Owen, lottery 1827, Gwinnett County.
Anglin, Henry, early lottery 1820, Disct. 8.
Anglin, John, lottery 1827, Madison County.
Armer, James, "book pay rolls," certified, Robert Middleton, Col.
Armor, John, lottery 1827, Greene County.

# LAND LOTTERY GRANTS. 343

Arnstorph, George, lottery 1827, Franklin County.
Arrington, William, early lottery 1820, Morgan County.
Arthur, Mathew, early lottery 1820, Franklin County.
Asabrook, Claborn, lottery 1827, Effingham County.
Ashmore, Strong, "book pay rolls," certified, Robert Middleton, Col.
Astin, Robert, lottery 1827, Greene County.
Atkinson, Joseph, Capt., "book Commission B," p. 227.
Atkinson, Robert, lottery 1827, DeKalb County.
Austin, Harris D., lottery 1827, Jefferson County.
Austin, James G., acts 1849, Forsyth County.
Austin, Michael, lottery 1827, Fayette County.

## B.

Bachelor, Cornelius, lottery 1827, Wilkinson County.
Bachlott, John, lottery 1827, Camden County.
Bagby, John, lottery 1827, Gwinnett County.
Bagley, Hermon, lottery 1827, Gwinnett County.
Bagners, Augustus, "book pay rolls," certified, Robert Middleton, Col.
Bailey, Christopher, lottery 1827, Effingham County.
Bailey, Stephen, lottery 1827, Monroe County.
Baker, Beall, lottery 1827, Hall County.
Baker, Charles, lottery 1827, Hall County.
Baker, Christopher, lottery 1827, Gwinnett County.
Baker, Dempsey, lottery 1820, Disct. 1, Hancock County.
Baker, Joshua, lottery 1827, Franklin County.
Ball, Edward, Lieutenant, "Commission B," p. 271.
Ballard, Frederick, lottery 1827, Effingham County.
Ballard, Thomas, lottery 1827, Gwinnett County.
Bandy, Lewis, lottery 1827, Morgan County.
Banks, Drury, lottery 1827, Warren County.
Banks, John, acts 1847, county unknown.
Banks, William, lottery 1827, Wilkes County.
Bankston, Abner, lottery 1827, Monroe County.
Bankston, Elijah, lottery 1827, DeKalb County.
Barber, Charles, lottery 1820, Disct. 2, Glynn County.
Barber, Stancil, lottery 1820, Disct. 11, Twiggs County.
Barker, John, lottery 1827, Twiggs County.
Barker, Joseph, lottery 1827, Crawford County
Barker, Rufus, acts 1844, Walton County.
Barkley, William, lottery 1827, Morgan County.
Barnes, William, acts 1847, Elbert County.
Barnes, Wm., lottery 1827, Jones County.
Barnett, Jesse, "book pay rolls," certified, Robert Middleton, Col.
Barnett, Robert, lottery 1827, Wilkinson County.
Barnett, Sion, lottery 1827, Jasper County.

Barnett, William, "book pay rolls," certified, Robert Middleton, Col.
Barrow, Joseph, lottery 1827, Houston County.
Barson, Isaac, lottery 1827, Jackson County.
Bass, Hardy, certified by Samuel Elbert, Book D3, p. 129.
Bass, Thomas, certified by Samuel Elbert, Book D3, p. 129.
Batson, David, lottery 1820, Disct. 2, Franklin County.
Bausworth, Jacob, lottery 1820, Disct. 17, Jackson County.
Baxter, John, acts 1834, Murray County.
Bays, Moses, lottery 1827, Henry County.
Bazemore, Thomas, lottery 1827, Jones County.
Bazer, William, lottery 1820, Disct. 16, Hancock County.
Beall, Harrison, lottery 1827, Warren County.
Beall, Thomas, "book pay rolls," certified, Robert Middleton, Col.
Beard, Robert, 1827, Henry County.
Beasley, Henry, lottery 1827, Walton County.
Beasley, John, lottery 1820, Disct. 6, Franklin County.
Beasley, William, lottery 1827, DeKalb County.
Beck, Sergeant, lottery 1827, Elbert County.
Beckham, Solomon, lottery 1827, Monroe County.
Bedell, Absalom, Major, "Commission B," p. 271.
Bedgood, John, lottery 1827, Wilkes County.
Beiser, Benjamin, Lieutenant, "Commission B," p. 274.
Bell, Archibald, "book pay rolls," certified, Robert Middleton, Col.
Bell, Benjamin, lottery 1827, Burke County.
Bellah, Samuel, lottery 1827, Morgan County.
Bennett, Daniel, lottery 1827, Habersham County.
Bennett, Micajah, acts 1843, Muscogee County.
Benson, Enoch, lottery 1827, Gwinnett County.
Bentley, James, acts 1837, Walton County.
Bentley, Jesse, lottery 1827, Walton County.
Berry, Isham, lottery 1827, Walton County.
Bethune, Peter, lottery 1827, Telfair County.
Biffle, John, lottery 1827, DeKalb County.
Bigbie, James N., acts 1847, Harris County.
Bird, Thomas, lottery 1827, Hall County.
Birdsong, John, lottery 1827, Oglethorpe County.
Bishop, Golden, lottery 1827, Newton County.
Bivins, William, lottery 1827, Wilkinson County.
Black, Samuel, lottery 1827, Oglethorpe County.
Black, Thomas, lottery 1827, Habersham County.
Blackburn, Nathan, lottery 1827, Wilkes County.
Blakely, John, lottery 1820, Disct. 18, Hancock County.
Blakely, Michael, lottery 1827, Jones County.
Blandford, Clark, lottery 1827, Wilkes County.
Blanks, James, lottery 1827, Jackson County.
Bledsoe, Benjamin, lottery 1827, Warren.
Bledsoe, Miller, lottery 1827, Oglethorpe County.

Blitch, Abraham, lottery 1827, Effingham County.
Blunt, Wm., lottery 1827, Jones County.
Blythe, Robert, lottery 1827, Habersham County.
Boen, Stephen, lottery 1827, Telfair County.
Boggs, Ezekiel, lottery 1827, Wilkinson County.
Bohan, Joseph, lottery 1827, Putnam County.
Boils, Charles, lottery 1827, Montgomery County.
Bollin, John, lottery 1827, Hall County.
Bona, Richard C., lottery 1827, Franklin County.
Bonnell, Anthony, Lieutenant, "Commission B," p. 227.
Bonnell, John, Lieutenant, "Commission B," p. 227.
Bonner, Joseph, lottery 1820, Disct. 27, Jones County.
Booker, William, lottery 1827, Wilkes County.
Boon, Jesse, lottery 1827, Greene County.
Boring, Isaac, lottery 1827, Jackson County.
Bowen, John, lottery 1827, Wilkinson County.
Bowen, Samuel, lottery 1827, Wilkes County.
Bowling, Edward, lottery 1827, Clarke County.
Boyce, Lott, certified by Samuel Elbert, Book D3, p. 129.
Boyt, Thomas, lottery 1827, Burke County.
Brack, William, Lieutenant, "Commission B," p. 275.
Bradberry, Lewis, lottery 1827, Clarke County.
Braddy, Lewis, lottery 1827, Warren County.
Bradley, John, lottery 1827, Jackson County.
Bradwell, Samuel, lottery 1827, Newton County.
Bragg, Wm., lottery 1827, Madison County.
Bramlett, Henry, lottery 1827, Elbert County.
Branch, William S., lottery 1827, Greene County.
Brand, William, lottery 1827, Walton County.
Brantley, Amos, lottery 1820, Disct. 12, Hancock County.
Brantley, William, certified by Samuel Elbert, Book D3, p. 129.
Brassell, Britton, lottery 1827, p. —, Jones County.
Brazill, Britten, lottery 1827, Jackson County.
Brewster, Hugh, lottery 1827, DeKalb County.
Bridges, Wiseman, lottery 1827, Jasper County.
Brinkley, Eley, lottery 1827, Wilkes County.
Britt, Edward, lottery 1827, Henry County.
Brittenham, Joseph, lottery 1820, Disct. 27, Warren County.
Brockman, Lewis, lottery 1827, Oglethorpe County.
Brooks, James, lottery 1827, Jasper County.
Brooks, Micajah, lottery 1827, Henry County.
Brooks, Robert, lottery 1827, Crawford County.
Brooks, William, lottery 1827, Greene County.
Brown, Ambrose, lottery 1827, Newton County.
Brown, Bond Veall, lottery 1827, Jackson County.
Brown, Dempsey, lottery 1827, Twiggs County.
Brown, Edward, lottery 1827, Baldwin County.

ROSTER OF THE REVOLUTION.

Brown, Elisha, lottery 1827, Jones County.
Brown, John, lottery 1827, Baldwin County.
Brown, John, lottery 1820, Disct. 2, Franklin County.
Brown, Larkin, lottery 1827, Richmond County.
Brown, Meredith, lottery 1827, DeKalb County.
Brown, Moses, lottery 1827, Newton County.
Brown, Stark, lottery 1820, Disct. 2, Walton County.
Brown, Uriah, lottery 1827, Baldwin County.
Bruce, William, lottery 1827, DeKalb County.
Brunifield, John, lottery 1820, Disct. 3, Elbert County.
Bryan, David, lottery 1827, Monroe County.
Bryan, James, lottery 1827, Effingham County.
Bryan, John, lottery 1827, Franklin County.
Bryant, William G., lottery 1820, Disct. 18, Putnam County.
Buchanan, James, acts 1847, Early County.
Buchannon, James P., lottery 1820, Disct. 15, Jasper County.
Buchanon, Geo. H., lottery 1827, Jasper County.
Buckles, Peter, lottery 1827, Wilkinson County.
Buckner, Benjamin, lottery 1827, Putnam County.
Bugg, John, "book pay rolls," certified, Robert Middleton, Col.
Bugg, Samuel, "book pay rolls," certified, Robert Middleton, Col.
Bugg, Sherod, "book pay rolls," certified, Robert Middleton, Col.
Bullard, James, lottery 1827, Greene County.
Bullock, Daniel, lottery 1820, Disct. 1, ———.
Bullock, Hawkins, lottery 1827, Madison County.
Bullock, Richard, lottery 1827, Bibb County.
Burgany, William, lottery 1827, Wilkes County.
Burket, Lemuel, lottery 1827, Wilkinson County.
Burkhalter, Jacob, lottery 1827, Warren County.
Burkshalter, Michael, lottery 1827, Jones County.
Burnley, Henry, lottery 1827, Columbia County.
Burwell, Daniel, Major, "Commission B," p. 271.
Bush, Levi, lottery 1827, Pulaski County.
Bush, Samuel, lottery 1827, Burke County.
Buttrell, Wm., lottery 1827, Henry County.
Butts, James, lottery 1827, Hancock County.
Bynum, Drewry, lottery 1820, Disct. 12, Warren County.
Byrd, John, lottery 1827, Hall County.

C.

Cabos, John, lottery 1827, Chatham County.
Calaway, Peter, lottery 1827, Jasper County.
Cameron, Allen, lottery 1827, DeKalb County.
Cameron, James, lottery 1827, Jasper County.
Camp, Edward, lottery 1827, Franklin County.
Camp, James, early lottery 1820, Gwinnett County.
Campbell, William, lottery 1827, Oglethorpe County.

# LAND LOTTERY GRANTS.

Candill, Benjamin, lottery 1827, Habersham County.
Candler, John, lottery 1827, McIntosh County.
Cannon, Nathaniel, lottery 1827, Wilkinson County.
Carlisle, Benjamin, lottery 1827, Columbia County.
Carlisle, Edmond, lottery 1827, Morgan County.
Carr, William, lottery 1827, Warren County.
Carr, William, lottery 1827, DeKalb County.
Carrell, John, lottery 1827, Jasper County.
Carroll, Brittain, lottery 1827, Columbia County.
Carroll, Douglas, lottery 1827, Greene County.
Carroll, Owen, lottery 1827, Laurens County.
Carson, Ephraim, lottery 1827, DeKalb County.
Carter, Charles, lottery 1827, Oglethorpe County.
Carter, Josiah.
Cartledge, Edward, "book pay rolls," certified, Robert Middleton, Col.
Casey, William, lottery 1827, Henry County.
Cash, Dorson, lottery 1827, Columbia County.
Cash, Howard, lottery 1827, Hall County.
Cash, James, lottery 1827, Franklin County.
Cash, John, lottery 1827, Jackson County.
Cason, Triplett, lottery 1827, Walton County.
Cason, William, lottery 1827, Warren County.
Catliff, Abraham, lottery 1827, Putnam County.
Caudelle, David, lottery 1827, Franklin County.
Causey, Ezekiel, lottery 1827, Jefferson County.
Cavenah, Nicholas, Captain, "book Commission B," p. 228.
Champion, John, lottery 1827, Warren County.
Chance, Simpson, lottery 1827, Jefferson County.
Chandler, John, lottery 1827, Greene County.
Chapman, Abner, lottery 1827, Jefferson County.
Chapman, Nathan, lottery 1827, Newton County.
Chappell, John, lottery 1827, Morgan County.
Chappell, John, lottery 1827, Monroe County.
Childers, Richard, lottery 1827, Wilkes County.
Childress, Richard, certified by E. Clark.
Christian, Turner, early lottery 1820, Elbert County.
Christopher, William, lottery 1827, Oglethorpe County.
Clanton, Holt, lottery 1827, Columbia County.
Clark, David, lottery 1827, Elbert County.
Clark, George, lottery 1827, Jasper County.
Clements, Clement, lottery 1827, Bibb County.
Cleveland, Jeremiah, lottery 1827, Habersham County.
Cliatt, Isaac, lottery 1827, Richmond County.
Clifton, Charles, certified by Samuel Elbert, Book D3, p. 129.
Clifton, William, certified by Samuel Elbert, Book D3, p. 129.
Clore, George, lottery 1827, Madison County.
Clower, Daniel, lottery 1827, Gwinnett County.

Cobb, Ralf, Senate Journal 1825, p. 226.
Cobbs, Thomas, lottery 1827, Columbia County.
Cochran, Mathew, lottery 1827, Monroe County.
Cockburn, George, lottery 1827, Franklin County.
Cockerel, Thomas, lottery 1827, Newton County.
Cofield, Grisham, early lottery 1820, Twiggs County.
Coil, James, lottery 1827, Madison County.
Coleman, Abner, lottery 1827, Gwinnett County.
Coleman, John, lottery 1827, Jefferson County.
Coleman, Samuel, lottery 1827, Walton County.
Collars, Mathew, lottery 1827, Lincoln County.
Colley, James, lottery 1827, Oglethorpe County.
Colley, John, lottery 1827, DeKalb County.
Collins, Joseph, lottery 1827, Twiggs County.
Colquitt, James, lottery 1827, Oglethorpe County.
Cone, Archibald, lottery 1827, Wilkes County.
Cone, John, lottery 1827, Baldwin County.
Cone, John, early lottery 1820, Baldwin County.
Congo, Benjamin, lottery 1827, Gwinnett County.
Connel, David, lottery 1827, Monroe County.
Conner, Benjamin, lottery 1827, Monroe County.
Conner, William, lottery 1827, Putnam County.
Cook, Archibald, lottery 1827, Franklin County.
Cook, Elisha, early lottery 1820, Hancock County.
Cook, James, lottery 1827, Jefferson County.
Cook, Reuben, early lottery 1820, Elbert County.
Cook, Theodosius, lottery 1827, Elbert County.
Cook, Thomas, lottery 1827, Elbert County.
Cooper, George, early lottery 1820, Wayne County.
Cooper, Henry, lottery 1827, Putnam County.
Cooper, James, lottery 1827, Madison County.
Cooper, John, lottery 1827, Wilkes County.
Cooper, John, Lieut.-Col., "book ex. council," 1783-1784, p. 151.
Cooper, Joseph, early lottery 1820, Putnam County.
Cooper, Richard, lottery 1827, Tattnall County.
Cooper, Samuel, lottery 1827, Putnam County.
Copeland, Benjamin, lottery 1827, Greene County.
Copelin, William, early lottery 1820, Gwinnett County.
Corsey, William, lottery 1827, Greene County.
Cotter, James, lottery 1827, Jefferson County.
Cousins, Adam, lottery 1827, Clarke County.
Covey, Joseph, lottery 1827, Gwinnett County.
Cowen, George, lottery 1827, Jackson County.
Cowen, James, lottery 1827, Jackson County.
Cowles, Samuel, lottery 1827, Monroe County.
Cox, John, lottery 1827, Hancock County.
Cox, Moses, lottery 1827, Wilkes County.

LAND LOTTERY GRANTS.    349

Cox, Richard, lottery 1827, Habersham County.
Cox, Thomas, lottery 1827, Greene County.
Cox, Zebulon, Lieutenant, "Commission B," p. 228.
Crabb, Asa, lottery 1827, Putnam County.
Crabtree, William, lottery 1827, Houston County.
Crawford, Jay, lottery 1827, Chatham County.
Crawford, Lemuel, lottery 1827, Clarke County.
Credelle, William, lottery 1827, Greene County.
Critington, Jonathan, lottery 1827, Rabun County.
Crittendon, Joseph, lottery 1827, Twiggs County.
Crockett, David, lottery 1827, Bibb County.
Cronan, James, lottery 1827, Habersham County.
Cronberger, Christopher, Lieutenant, "Commission B," p. 275.
Cronberger, Jacob, Lieutenant, "Commission B," p. 274.
Crouch, Shadrick, lottery 1827, Putnam County.
Cross, Stephen, lottery 1827, Burke County.
Crosson, John, lottery 1827, Lincoln County.
Crow, Isaac, lottery 1827, Clarke County.
Crow, Stephen, lottery 1827, Clarke County.
Crumbly, Thomas, lottery 1827, Habersham County.
Culbaith, Archibald, lottery 1827, Emanuel County.
Culpepper, Malakiah, lottery 1827, Morgan County.
Culver, Nathan, lottery 1827, Hancock County.
Cumming, Francis, lottery 1827, Greene County.
Cunningham, Andrew, lottery 1827, Twiggs County.
Cutts, Joseph, lottery 1827, Houston County.

D.

Dabney, Austin, acts 1848, Burke County.
Dalton, John, lottery 1827, Bibb County.
Dalton, Randolph, lottery 1827, Gwinnett County.
Dalton, Thomas, early lottery 1820, Richmond County.
Damron, Charles, early lottery 1820, Morgan County.
Daniel, Jeptha, lottery 1827, Richmond County.
Daniel, John, lottery 1827, Liberty County.
Dantignac, John, early lottery 1820, Richmond County.
Darby, Nicholas, early lottery 1820, Jackson County.
Dasher, Marion, Lieutenant, "Commission B," p. 275.
David, Isaac, lottery 1827, Madison County.
Davidson, John, lottery 1827, Jasper County.
Davie, Joseph, lottery 1827, Jones County.
Davies, Daniel, lottery 1827, Montgomery County.
Davis, Henry, lottery 1827, Gwinnett County.
Davis, Moses, Captain, "Commission B," p. 228.
Davis, Surry, lottery 1827, Habersham County.
Davis, Toliver, lottery 1827, Baldwin County.
Dawson, Charles, "book pay rolls," p. 143.

Deadwiler, Joseph, lottery 1827, Elbert County.
Dean, Charles, lottery 1827, Clarke County.
Deason, Zachariah, lottery 1827, Henry County.
Delk, Daniel, lottery 1827, Liberty County.
Dellafield, William, lottery 1827, Hall County.
Deloach, Hardy, lottery 1827, Liberty County.
Denham, Arthur, lottery 1827, Fayette County.
Dennis, Mathias, lottery 1827, Hancock County.
Denton, John, lottery 1827, Hancock County.
Dias, John, lottery 1827, Tattnall County.
Dick, James, acts 1836, Newton County.
Dicken, Richard, lottery 1827, Clarke County.
Dickerson, Zachariah, lottery 1827, Elbert County.
Dickey, Patrick, lottery 1827, Putnam County.
Dickson, Michael, Captain, certified by Samuel Jack, Col.
Dickson, John, lottery 1827, Jones County.
Dickson, Thomas, lottery 1827, Hancock County.
Dillard, James, lottery 1827, Elbert County.
Dillard, John, certified by Samuel Elbert, Book D3, p. 129.
Dillon, Thomas, lottery 1827, DeKalb County.
Dobbs, John, lottery 1827, DeKalb County.
Dobb, James, lottery 1827, Oglethorpe County.
Doles, Jesse, early lottery 1820, Baldwin County.
Donaldson, William, lottery 1827, DeKalb County.
Doster, Jonathan, lottery 1827, Wilkes County.
Doughtry, Jacob, lottery 1827, Emanuel County.
Doughtry, Joseph, lottery 1827, Screven County.
Douglas, Spencer, lottery 1827, Wilkinson County.
Dover, Francis J., lottery 1827, Habersham County.
Dowle, Thomas, Lieutenant, "Commission B," p. 273.
Downey, Joseph, lottery 1827, Gwinnett County.
Downs, John, lottery 1827, Henry County.
Doyle, Nimrod T., acts 1839.
Drake, James, lottery 1827, Telfair County.
Dubberly, John, lottery 1827, Tattnall County.
Duck, Jeremiah, "book pay rolls," certified, Robert Middleton, Col.
Duck, John, early lottery 1820, Morgan County.
Dudley, James, lottery 1827, Elbert County.
Dudley, John, early lottery 1820, Hancock County.
Dukes, Thomas, lottery 1827, Morgan County.
Duncan, Edmond, lottery 1827, Jones County.
Duncan, John, lottery 1827, Elbert County.
Duncan, John, lottery 1827, Jackson County.
Duncan, Pearson, lottery 1827, Elbert County.
Dunham, Samuel, lottery 1827, Richmond County.
Dunn, Gatewood, lottery 1827, Oglethorpe County.
Durham, Abraham, lottery 1827, Clarke County.

Durham, Jacob, lottery 1827, Irwin County.
Durouzeau, Steven, lottery 1827, Jefferson County.
Duty, Thomas, lottery 1827, DeKalb County.
Dyche, John, early lottery 1820, Jackson County.
Dye, Avery, lottery 1827, Burke County.
Dyer, Elisha, lottery 1827, Walton County.
Dykes, Jep. lottery 1827, Effingham County.
Dyson, John, lottery 1827, Wilkes County.

E.

Eagin, John, lottery 1827, Richmond County.
Earnest, George, lottery 1827, Clarke County.
Eaton, John, lottery 1827, Gwinnett County.
Ebeaheart, Jacob, lottery 1827, Oglethorpe County.
Edwards, Joseph, lottery 1827, Franklin County.
Edwards, John, lottery 1827, Monroe County.
Edwards, John, 1827, Henry County.
Edwards, John, lottery 1827, Columbia County.
Edwards, Reuben, lottery 1827, Henry County.
Edwards, Thomas, lottery 1827, Habersham County.
Edwards, William, lottery 1827, Madison County.
Eidson, Shelton, lottery 1827, Oglethorpe County.
Eidson, Thomas, lottery 1827, Wilkes County.
Elbert, John, lottery 1827, Effingham County.
Ellet, James, lottery 1827, Warren County.
Elliett, Thomas, lottery 1820, Jackson County.
Elliott, John, Lieut.-Col., "Commission B," p. 271.
Ellis, Levin, lottery 1827, Hancock County.
Ellis, Walter, lottery 1827, Jackson County.
Elsberry, Benjamin, lottery 1827, Clarke County.
Elton, Abram, lottery 1827, Wilkes County.
Embry, Joseph, lottery 1827, Oglethorpe County.
Emenson, Robert, "book pay rolls," certified by Robert Middleton, Col.
England, Charles, lottery 1827, Hancock County.
English, Parmenus, lottery 1827, Oglethorpe County.
Entrican, William, certified by John Twiggs, B. G.
Espey, John, lottery 1827, Clarke County.
Etheridge, Joel, lottery 1827, Crawford County.
Evans, James, lottery 1827, Hancock County.
Evans, Wm. D., lottery 1827, Elbert County.
Evanson, Eli, lottery 1827, Elbert County.
Everett, Archilaus, lottery 1827, Hancock County.
Ezell, Hartwell, lottery 1827, Jasper County.

F.

Faircloth, John, lottery 1827, Screven County.
Fann, Thomas, lottery 1827, Decatur County.

Faris, William, lottery 1827, Rabun County.
Farrar, Francis, lottery 1827, Clarke County.
Feagan, William, lottery 1827, Morgan County.
Fears, William, lottery 1827, Jasper County.
Felts, James, early lottery 1820, Jones County.
Ferrill, Micajah, lottery 1827, Henry County.
Finch, William, lottery 1827, Oglethorpe County.
Fincher, James, early lottery 1820, Jasper County.
Findley, John, lottery 1827, Fayette County.
Fireash, Elias, lottery 1827, Tattnall County.
Fireash, John, lottery 1827, Tattnall County.
Fitzpatrick, Pat, Lieutenant, book ex. council, 1778-1783, Dec. 6, 1779.
Fitzpatrick, William, certified by E. Clark, Col.
Flannigan, William, lottery 1827, Franklin County.
Flemmekin, David, "book pay rolls," certified by Robert Middleton, Col.
Flemmekin, Samuel, "book pay rolls," certified by Robert Middleton, Col.
Fletcher, William, lottery 1827, Telfair County.
Flint, James, Lieutenant, "Commission B," p. 273.
Florence, Thomas, lottery 1827, Lincoln County.
Flowers, Henry, lottery 1827, Tattnall County.
Fluker, John, certified by E. Clark, Col.
Fluker, William, certified by E. Clark, Col.
Foil, John, Lieutenant, "Commission B," p. 228.
Forbes, Wesley, lottery 1827, Jasper County.
Ford, Thomas, Lieutenant, "Commission B," p. 228.
Forenby, Nathan, lottery 1827, Morgan County.
Foster, Arthur, lottery 1827, Greene County.
Foster, John, lottery 1827, Putnam County.
Franklin, David, lottery 1827, DeKalb County.
Frazier, John, Lieutenant, book ex. council, 1778-1783, Dec. 6, 1789.
Freeman, Daniel, lottery 1827, Jasper County.
Fryday, Joseph, lottery 1827, Montgomery County.
Fryer, Fielding, bounty granted.
Fulcher, James, lottery 1827, Richmond County.
Fuller, William, lottery 1827, Jackson County.
Fullwood, John, lottery 1827, Laurens County.
Fulton, Thomas, lottery 1827, Twiggs County.
Fulsom, William, Lieutenant, "Commission B," p. 228.
Funderbunk, John, lottery 1827, Monroe County.
Futch, Onesimus, lottery 1827, Bryan County.

G.

Gailor, James, lottery 1827, Gwinnett County.
Gaines, Francis, lottery 1827, Elbert County.
Gaines, William, lottery 1827, Elbert County.
Gallache, James, Lieutenant, "Commission B," p. 278.
Games, George C., lottery 1827, Decatur County.

## LAND LOTTERY GRANTS.

Ganey, Bartholomew, lottery 1827, Laurens County.
Ganey, Redic, lottery 1827, Tattnall County.
Garland, John, lottery 1827, Jones County.
Garland, William, early lottery 1820, Disct. 13.
Garner, Charles, lottery 1827, Clarke County.
Garnett, Eli, "book pay rolls," certified by Robert Middleton, Col.
Garnett, John, "book pay rolls," certified by Robert Middleton, Col.
Garrison, Jedediah, lottery 1827, Franklin County.
Garrotte, Samuel, lottery 1827, Wilkes County.
Gates, Hezekiah, lottery 1827, Walton County.
Gay, Joshua, lottery 1827, DeKalb County.
Geddins, Thomas, early lottery 1820, Disct. 1.
George, Jesse, lottery 1827, Gwinnett County.
Gibbs, Herod, early lottery 1820, Disct. 13.
Gibson, Henry B., lottery 1827, Wilkes County.
Gideons, Benjamin, lottery 1827, Bulloch County.
Gilbert, Thomas, early lottery 1820, Franklin County.
Gilbert, William, lottery 1827, DeKalb County.
Gilder, Isaac, early lottery 1820, Disct. 16.
Gillees, James, lottery 1827, Henry County.
Glass, Levi, lottery 1827, Laurens County.
Glassoway, Thomas, early lottery 1820, Disct. 19.
Glaze, Reuben, lottery 1827, Oglethorpe County.
Glenn, James, lottery 1827, Jackson County.
Glover, William, lottery 1827, Franklin County.
Gober, William, lottery 1827, Newton County.
Golden, Andrew, lottery 1827, Bulloch County.
Golitely, Charles, Lieutenant, "Commission B," p. 228.
Gooch, Nathan, lottery 1827, Greene County.
Gooddown, Jacob, lottery 1827, Jefferson County.
Goodwin, James, lottery 1827, Wilkes County.
Goodwire, Sharick, lottery 1827, Jones County.
Goolsby, Elijah, Lieutenant, "Commission B," p. 277.
Goolsby, Richard, lottery 1827, Oglethorpe County.
Gordon, James, early lottery 1827, Elbert County.
Gordon, Thomas, lottery 1827, Gwinnett County.
Goslin, David, private, Book Washington, p. 17.
Goulding, Palmer, lottery 1827, Liberty County.
Goulding, Peter, Lieutenant, "Commission B," p. 271.
Grady, Arthur, lottery 1827, Houston County.
Grant, Jesse, lottery 1827, Burke County.
Grant, Joseph, lottery 1827, Hancock County.
Grantham, Nathan, lottery 1827, Telfair County.
Grantham, William, lottery 1827, Early County.
Greaves, William, lottery 1827, Burke County.
Greff, Joshua, "book pay rolls," R. Middleton, Col.
Green, Burwell, lottery 1827, Jasper County.

Green, Richard, lottery 1827, McIntosh County.
Greer, Benjamin, private, "book pay rolls," p. 143.
Greer, James, lottery 1827, Clark County.
Greer, John, "book pay rolls," Robert Middleton, Col.
Greer, John, Lieutenant, "book pay rolls," p. 143.
Greer, Thomas, "book pay rolls," Robert Middleton, Col.
Greer, William, "book pay rolls," Robert Middleton, Col.
Greiner, John Gasper, Lieutenant, "Commission B," p. 275.
Gresham, John, lottery 1827, Oglethorpe County.
Gresham, Littleberry, lottery 1827, Monroe County.
Griffin, James, lottery 1827, Irwin County.
Griffin, Joseph, lottery 1827, Monroe County.
Griffis, Charles, lottery 1827, Ware County.
Griffis, John, lottery 1827, Hancock County.
Grimmer, William, lottery 1827, Jasper County.
Grissup, James, lottery 1827, Elbert County.
Guice, Nicholas, lottery 1827, Lincoln County.
Gunn, Richard, lottery 1827, Warren County.
Gunnells, William, lottery 1827, DeKalb County.
Gunter, James, lottery 1827, Walton County.
Guthrie, John, lottery 1827, Gwinnett County.
Guthrie, William, lottery 1827, Gwinnett County.
Guttery, Francis, lottery 1827, Morgan County.
Gwynn, Richard, Captain, "Commission B," p. 275.

H.

Hackney, Robert, lottery 1827, Green County.
Hadaway, David, lottery 1827, Jones County.
Haile, James, lottery 1827, Clarke County.
Hailey, Wm., lottery 1827, Elbert County.
Hall, Dempsey, lottery 1827, Jefferson County.
Hall, Instant, lottery 1827, Laurens County.
Hall, James, Lieutenant, "Commission B," p. 220.
Hall, John, lottery 1827, Greene County.
Hamilton, Andrew, lottery 1827, Wilkes County.
Hamilton, Barker, lottery 1827, Clarke County.
Hamilton, John, lottery 1827, Hall County.
Hamilton, Stewart, lottery 1827, Montgomery County.
Hammond, Henry, lottery 1827, Warren County.
Hampton, Benjamin, early lottery 1820, Walton County.
Hamrick, Benjamin, lottery 1827, Jasper County.
Hancock, Francis, Captain, "Commission B," p. 228.
Hand, Henry, lottery 1827, Baldwin County.
Hand, Joseph, lottery 1827, Henry County.
Handley, George, Captain, "book pay rolls," p. 141.
Hanison, Joseph, lottery 1827, Wilkes County.
Hannah, James, early lottery 1820, Elbert County.

## LAND LOTTERY GRANTS.

Haralson, Jonathan, lottery 1827, Greene County.
Harbin, Alexander, lottery 1827, Butts County.
Harbin, William, early lottery 1820, Elbert County.
Harden, Henry, lottery 1827, Walton County.
Harkness, Robert, lottery 1827, Gwinnett County.
Harley, Joseph, lottery 1827, Columbia County.
Harn, John, lottery 1827, Monroe County.
Harp, Mannin, lottery 1827, Monroe County.
Harrell, Hardy, lottery 1827, Jefferson County.
Harrell, Simon, lottery 1827, Warren County.
Harris, Benjamin, early lottery 1820, Jones County.
Harris, Graves, lottery 1827, Morgan County.
Harris, Mathew, lottery 1827, Greene County.
Harris, Wm., "book pay rolls," certified by Robert Middleton, Col.
Harrison, Edward, lottery 1827, Hall County.
Harrison, Elijah W., lottery 1827, Jones County.
Hart, Benjamin, "book pay rolls," certified by Robert Middleton, Col.
Hart, Robert, lottery 1827, Jones County.
Hartsfield, Richard, lottery 1827, Oglethorpe County.
Harvey, Charles, Captain, "Commission B," p. 227.
Haskins, John, lottery 1827, Jones County.
Hatchell, Wm., lottery 1827, Oglethorpe County.
Hatcher, Thomas, lottery 1827, Twiggs County.
Hathorn, Thomas, lottery 1827, Monroe County.
Hawthorn, Wm., lottery 1827, Putnam County.
Hawthorne, John, early lottery 1820, Twiggs County.
Hawthorne, Wm., lottery 1827, Decatur County.
Hay, Isaac, lottery 1827, Wilkes County.
Hayman, Stanton, lottery 1827, Bryan County.
Haynes, Moses, lottery 1827, Elbert County.
Hays, Edward, lottery 1827, Gwinnett County.
Hays, George, lottery 1827, Jackson County.
Hays, Jonathan, lottery 1827, Franklin County.
Head, John S., lottery 1827, Gwinnett County.
Heard, John G., lottery 1827, Morgan County.
Heard, Wm., lottery 1827, DeKalb County.
Heath, Jordan, lottery 1827, Burke County.
Heaton, James, lottery 1827, Gwinnett County.
Heidt, Christian, early lottery 1820, Effingham County.
Heith, Roister, lottery 1827, Warren County.
Hemphill, Jonathan, lottery 1827, Jackson County.
Henderson, Robert, Captain, "Commission B," p. 228.
Henderson, Zachariah, Lieutenant, book ex. council, 1783-1784, p. 179.
Hendley, Jarrett, Lieutenant, "Commission B," p. 228.
Hendon, Robinson, lottery 1827, Oglethorpe County.
Hendrick, Jesse, lottery 1827, Elbert County.
Hendrick, Siah, lottery 1827, Walton County.

Hendrix, John, lottery 1827, Screven County.
Hendry, Robert, lottery 1827, Liberty County.
Herndon, Joseph, lottery 1827, Walton County.
Herrington, Ephraim, lottery 1827, Emanuel County.
Hester, David, lottery 1827, Burke County.
Hester, Zachariah, lottery 1827, Jones County.
Hicks, David, lottery 1827, Pike County.
Hicks, Samuel, "book pay rolls," certified by Robert Middleton, Col.
Higden, Daniel, lottery 1827, Hancock County.
Higgins, Reuben, lottery 1827, Gwinnett County.
Hill, Isaac, lottery 1827, Clarke County.
Hill, Mordecai, lottery 1827, Jasper County.
Hinecard, John, early lottery 1820, Clarke County.
Hines, Benjamin, ———, Jasper County.
Hines, James, lottery 1827, Jasper County.
Hines, Lewis, lottery 1827, Jackson County.
Hines, Nathaniel, lottery 1827, Greene County.
Hinsley, Thomas, early lottery 1820, Jasper County.
Hinston, Wm., lottery 1827, Glynn County.
Hobson, Mathew, "book pay rolls," certified by Robert Middleton, Col.
Hodges, Joseph, lottery 1827, Liberty County.
Hodges, Joseph, early lottery 1820, Bulloch County.
Hogg, John, "book pay rolls," certified by Robert Middleton, Col.
Holbrook, Jesse, lottery 1827, Franklin County.
Holcomb, James, lottery 1827, Franklin County.
Holcombe, James, lottery 1827, Richmond County.
Holcombe, Sherwood, lottery 1827, Habersham County.
Holder, John S., lottery 1827, Jefferson County.
Holland, Thomas, lottery 1827, Greene County.
Holley, Wm., lottery 1827, Wilkes County.
Hollinsworth, Isaac, early lottery 1820, Twiggs County.
Hollow, Henry, lottery 1827, Tattnall County.
Holloway, Lewis, certified by Samuel Elbert, Book D3, p. 129.
Holman, George, lottery 1827, Twiggs County.
Holman, Jacob, lottery 1827, Richmond County.
Holt, James, lottery 1827, Houston County.
Holt, Thomas, lottery 1827, Wilkes County.
Holt, William, early lottery 1820, Elbert County.
Hood, John, lottery 1827, Wilkes County.
Hooks, Thomas, lottery 1827, Putnam County.
Hooper, James, lottery 1827, DeKalb County.
Hopkins, Wm., "book pay rolls," certified by Robert Middleton, Col.
Hopper, Thomas, lottery 1827, Oglethorpe County.
Horn, Elisha, lottery 1827, Burke County.
Horn, Richard, early lottery 1820, McIntosh County.
Horn, Sherod, lottery 1827, Bibb County.
Horn, Wm., lottery 1827, Richmond County.

# LAND LOTTERY GRANTS.

Horsley, Valentine, lottery 1827, Monroe County.
Hough, Samuel, "book pay rolls," certified by Robert Middleton, Col.
Houston, Samuel, lottery 1827, Henry County.
Howard, Abraham, lottery 1827, Hall County.
Howard, Solomon, lottery 1827, Wilkes County.
Howard, Willis, lottery 1827, Jefferson County.
Howel, John, lottery 1827, Houston County.
Howell, Philip, "Commission B," p. 271.
Howell, Stephen, early lottery 1820, Jackson County.
Howington, Wm., lottery 1827, Madison County.
Hubbard, Bennett, lottery 1827, Oglethorpe County.
Hubbard, Elijah, lottery 1827, Telfair County.
Hubbard, Monoab, early lottery, Baldwin County.
Huckaby, Wm., lottery 1827, Oglethorpe County.
Hudgins, Ansel, lottery 1827, Newton County.
Hudler, John, lottery 1827, Bulloch County.
Hudson, David, lottery 1827, Elbert County.
Huie, James, lottery 1827, Jackson County.
Hulsey, James, lottery 1827, Hall County.
Hulsey, Jesse, lottery 1827, Hall County.
Hulsey, Jinneus, lottery 1827, Henry County.
Human, Alexander, lottery 1827, Madison County.
Hunt, Daniel, lottery 1827, Jones County.
Hunt, George, lottery 1827, Greene County.
Hunt, James, lottery 1827, Elbert County.
Hunt, Liddleton, lottery 1827, Gwinnett County.
Hunt, Turner, lottery 1827, Jasper County.
Hunter, J. W., lottery 1827, Richmond County.
Hurley, Joseph, lottery 1827, Wilkes County.
Huston, John, lottery 1827, Jasper County; S. Doc. 210—22.
Hutchinson, James, lottery 1827, Franklin County.
Hutto, Henry, lottery 1827, Laurens County.

I.

Ingram, John, lottery 1827, Hall County.
Inman, Daniel, lottery 1827, Walton County.
Inslow, Thomas, lottery 1827, Walton County.
Ivey, Ephrain, lottery 1827, Warren County.
Izely, Philip, lottery 1827, Gwinnett County.

J.

Jackson, Ebenezer, early lottery 1820, Chatham County.
Jackson, Edward, lottery 1827, Gwinnett County.
Jackson, Jeremiah, lottery 1827, Greene County.
Jackson, Moses, lottery 1827, Greene County.
Jackson, Robert, Captain, early lottery 1820, Morgan County.
Jacobs, Benjamin, lottery 1827, Upson County.

James, George, lottery 1827, Gwinnett County.
James, Stephen, lottery 1827, Putnam County.
Jameson, David, early lottery 1820, Twiggs County.
Jarvis, Elisha, lottery 1827, Morgan County.
Jenkins, James, lottery 1827, Greene County.
Jeter, Andrew, lottery 1827, Bibb County.
Jeter, Barnett, lottery 1827, Elbert County.
Jeter, Dinley, early lottery 1820, Elbert County.
Jetts, Daniel, lottery 1827, Greene County.
Jinkens, Royal, "book pay rolls," by Robert Middleton Col.
Jinkins, Berry, "book pay rolls," by Robert Middleton, Col.
Jocey, Henry, lottery 1827, Jasper County.
Johns, Ellic, lottery 1827, Burke County.
Johnson, Andrew, Captain, "Commission B," p. 229.
Johnson, Angus, lottery 1827, Monroe County.
Johnson, Bartholomew, lottery 1827, Wilkes County.
Johnson, Emanuel, lottery 1827, Richmond County.
Johnson, John, lottery 1827, Oglethorpe County.
Johnson, Joseph B., lottery 1827, Wilkes County.
Johnson, Martin, lottery 1827, Houston County.
Johnson, Willis, lottery 1827, Columbia County.
Johnston, John B., lottery 1827, Wilkes County.
Joice, John, lottery 1827, Tattnall County.
Joiner, Abraham, lottery 1827, Wilkes County.
Joiner, Jesse, lottery 1827, Laurens County.
Jones, Batt, Lieutenant, "Commission B," p. 228.
Jones, Harrison, lottery 1827, Newton County.
Jones, Isaac, lottery 1827, Telfair County.
Jones, Isham, lottery 1827, Burke County.
Jones, Josiah, lottery 1827, Dooly County.
Jones, Moses, lottery 1827, Lincoln County.
Jones, Nimrod, early lottery 1820, Columbia County.
Jones, Stephen, lottery 1827, Putnam County.
Jordan, Fountain, lottery 1827, Elbert County.
Jordan, John, certified by Samuel Elbert, Book D3, p. 129.
Jordan, John, lottery 1827, Wilkes County.
Jordan, William, lottery 1827, Warren County.
Jorden, Aven, lottery 1827, Jefferson County.
Jourdan, Edmond, lottery 1827, Oglethorpe County.
Joyce, Alexander, early lottery 1820, Hancock County.
Justice, Aaron, lottery 1827, Houston County.

K.

Kelland, James, lottery 1827, Jones County.
Kelley, Lloyd, lottery 1827, Hancock County.
Kemp, William, lottery 1827, Wilkinson County.
Kendrick, Abel, lottery 1827, Hall County.

## LAND LOTTERY GRANTS.

Kennedy, Seth, lottery 1827, Hancock County.
Kent, Daniel, lottery 1827, Oglethorpe County.
Kent, Henry, lottery 1827, Twiggs County.
Kent, Thomas W., lottery 1827, Warren County.
Kent, Sampson, lottery 1827, Oglethorpe County.
Kimbell, David, lottery 1827, Clarke County.
Kindal, William, lottery 1827, Jasper County.
Kindle, Henry, lottery 1827, Monroe County.
King, Richard, lottery 1827, Greene County.
King, Thomas, lottery 1827, Elbert County.
King, Thomas, lottery 1827, Putnam County.
King, William, lottery 1827, Elbert County.
Kitchens, Zachariah, lottery 1827, Jasper County.
Kitt, Henry, lottery 1827, Gwinnett County.
Knight, Aaron, lottery 1827, DeKalb County.
Knight, Thomas, lottery 1827, Walton County.
Knowlman, A., lottery 1827, Oglethorpe County.
Kolb, Peter, lottery 1827, Jones County.

### L.

Lacey, Noah, lottery 1827, Oglethorpe County.
Ladd, Amos, lottery 1827, Habersham County.
Lamar, John, lottery 1827, Jones County.
Lamb, Isaac, early lottery 1820, Jefferson County.
Lambert, Elisha, lottery 1827, Fayette County.
Lambert, George, lottery 1827, Putnam County.
Lambert, James, Captain, "Commission B," p. 223.
Lambert, James, lottery 1827, Burke County.
Lambert, Thomas, lottery 1827, Clarke County.
Lambert, William, lottery 1827, Jasper County.
Lampkin, Sampson, lottery 1827, Dooly County.
Lamsden, Jeremiah, lottery 1827, Jasper County.
Landers, Taprell, lottery 1827, Gwinnett County.
Landrum, Timothy, lottery 1827, Jasper County.
Lane, Abraham S., lottery 1827, Emanuel County.
Langham, William, lottery 1827, Warren County.
Langley, James, lottery 1827, Pike County.
Langley, Nathaniel, Lieutenant, "Commission B," p. 275.
Larisey, Wm., lottery 1827, Stephen County.
Larvin, John, "book pay rolls," by Robert Middleton, Col.
Lassiter, Hansell, lottery 1827, Wilkinson County.
Latta, David, lottery 1827, Hall County.
Lawless, John, lottery 1827, Oglethorpe County.
Lawrence, John, lottery 1827, Wilkes County.
Lea, William, "book pay rolls," by Robert Middleton, Col.
Leathers, Samuel, lottery 1827, Hall County.
Lee, David, lottery 1827, Bullock County.

## 360 ROSTER OF THE REVOLUTION.

Lee, John, lottery 1827, Ware County.
Lee, John, lottery 1827, Wilkes County.
Lee, Sampson, lottery 1827, Wilkes County.
Leigh, Benjamin, lottery 1827, Columbia County.
Leshley, Edmond, lottery 1827, Columbia County.
Leverett, Richard, lottery 1827, Wayne County.
Lewis, George, lottery 1827, Tattnall County.
Lewis, Joseph, lottery 1827, Hancock County.
Lewis, Judah, killed.
Lewis, Peter, lottery 1827, Henry County.
Lewis, Thomas, Lieutenant, "Commission B," p. 228.
Lindsey, James, lottery 1827, Hall County.
Lindsey, William, lottery 1827, Wilkinson County.
Liverman, Conrad, lottery 1827, Richmond County.
Locket, Soloman, lottery 1827, Warren County.
Loggins, James, lottery 1827, Hall County.
Lokey, William, lottery 1827, Williams County.
Lord, William, lottery 1827, Wilkinson County.
Love, James, lottery 1827, Walton County.
Loving, Thomas, early lottery 1820, Clarke County.
Lowe, Aquila, early lottery 1820, Twiggs County.
Lowe, Ralf, early lottery 1820, Putnam County.
Lowery, Levi, lottery 1827, Jackson County.
Lowery, Simeon, lottery 1827, Burke County.
Loyd, Benjamin, Lieutenant, "Commission B," p. 272.
Loyd, James, lottery 1827, Fayette County.
Loyd, Thomas, early lottery 1820, Hancock County.
Lucas, John, Captain, "book pay rolls," p. 144.
Lumpkin, Dickson, lottery 1827, Jones County.
Lumpkin, John, lottery 1827, Oglethorpe County.

M.

Maberry, Joel, lottery 1827, Franklin County.
Mabry, Elias, lottery 1827, Columbia County.
Mabry, Gray, lottery 1827, Morgan County.
McCall, John, early lottery 1820, Effingham County.
McCaller, James, early lottery 1820, Jackson County.
McCheer, John, Captain "Commission B," p. 272.
McClain, John, lottery 1827, Rabun County.
McClane, Ephraim, lottery 1827, Gwinnett County.
McClelland, McClain, lottery 1827, Screvens County.
McCorkle, Archibald, lottery 1827, Lincoln County.
McCullers, Wm., early lottery 1827, Morgan County.
McCullough, Jacob, early lottery 1820, Richmond County.
McCuthan, Joseph, lottery 1827, Hall County.
McDaniel, Jacob, lottery 1827, Jones County.
McDaniel, Jeremiah, lottery 1827, Habersham County.

McDerman, Joseph, lottery 1827, Madison County.
McDonald, Isam, lottery 1827, Pulaski County.
McDonald, James, lottery 1827, Bibb County.
McDowell, Robert, lottery 1827, Jackson County.
McDuff, William, lottery 1827, Henry County.
McFarland, James H., lottery 1827, Warren County.
McFarland, Robert, lottery 1827, Franklin County.
McGee, Reuben, lottery 1827, Warren County.
McGlamory, John, lottery 1827, Warren County.
McIntire, John, lottery 1827, Habersham County.
McIntosh, John, Lieutenant, "book pay rolls," p. 145.
McIntosh, William, Captain, "book pay rolls," p. 145.
McKee, Alexander, lottery 1827, Clarke County.
McKee, John, lottery 1827, Oglethorpe County.
McKee, Samuel, lottery 1827, Franklin County.
McKenzie, Samuel, lottery 1827, Monroe County.
McKenzie, William, lottery 1827, Monroe County.
McKie, Thomas, lottery 1827, Franklin County.
McKinney, Charles, lottery 1827, Jackson County.
McLain, Andrew, "book pay rolls," certified by Robert Middleton, Col.
McLain, Thomas, lottery 1827, Oglethorpe County.
McLendon, Samuel, lottery 1827, Henry County.
McLendon, Thomas, early lottery 1820, Walton County.
McLeod, Mindork, lottery 1827, Pulaski County.
McLeod, Norman, lottery 1827, Jefferson County.
McMannus, John, early lottery 1820, Richmond County.
McMichael, John, lottery 1827, Jasper County.
McMillon, Alexander, lottery 1827, Franklin County.
McNeese, James, lottery 1827, Jackson County.
McNeiley, John, Lieutenant, "Commission B," p. 229.
McWhorter, John, lottery 1827, Hancock County.
Maddon, Walter, lottery 1827, Wilkes County.
Maddox, Samuel, early lottery 1820, Hancock County.
Mahan, David, private, "book Washington warrants."
Maires, Samuel, lottery 1827, Walton County.
Malone, William, lottery 1827, Clarke County.
Mallory, John, lottery 1827, Greene County.
Mallory, Stephen, lottery 1827, Wilkes County.
Mann, William, lottery 1827, Tattnall County.
Manning, Benjamin, lottery 1827, Bibb County.
Manpin, Jesse, early lottery 1820, Elbert County.
Marlow, James, lottery 1827, Laurens County.
Marran, David, Lieutenant, "Commission B," p. 228.
Marshall, Moses, "book pay rolls," certified by Robert Middleton, Col.
Martin, David, lottery 1827, Warren County.
Martin, David, lottery 1827, Warren County.
Martin, Jesse, lottery 1827, Oglethorpe County.

Martin, William, lottery 1827, Monroe County.
Mash, Clem, Captain, book ex. council, 1778-1783, Dec. 6th, 1779.
Mash, Nathan, lottery 1827, Warren County.
Mashborn, John, lottery 1827, Gwinnett County.
Mason, Gideon, lottery 1827, Jones County.
Mason, Thomas, lottery 1827, Hancock County.
Mathews, Isaac, lottery 1827, Clarke County.
Mathews, Joel, lottery 1827, Warren County.
Mathews, Lewis, Lieutenant, "Commission B," p. 271.
Mathis, John, lottery 1827, Wilkes County.
Mattox, Charles, lottery 1827, Wilkes County.
Maxwell, James, Major, "Commission B," p. 271.
Maxwell, John, lottery 1827, Elbert County.
Meacham, Henry, lottery 1827, Baldwin County.
Meador, Jasen, lottery 1827, Jones County.
Meadows, Jacob, lottery 1827, Oglethorpe County.
Meanley, John, Lieutenant, "book pay rolls," p. 145.
Menefee, George, lottery 1827, Jackson County.
Meritt, Torrence, lottery 1827, Elbert County.
Merks, Britton, lottery 1827, Gwinnett County.
Meroney, Nathan, lottery 1827, Madison County.
Merriwether, David, lottery 1827, Clarke County.
Messer, Silas, "book pay rolls," certified by Robert Middleton, Col.
Middlebrooks, John, lottery 1827, Newton County.
Middleton, Hugh, lottery 1827, Houston County.
Middleton, John, lottery 1827, Wilkes County.
Milam, Benjamin, lottery 1827, Jasper County.
Miles, Thomas, lottery 1827, Baldwin County.
Miller, Elisha, Captain, "book pay rolls," p. 145.
Miller, John, early lottery 1820, Jackson County.
Miller, Richard, lottery 1827, Hall County.
Miller, Willis, lottery 1827, Jackson County.
Milton, John, Captain, "book pay rolls," p. 144.
Mitchell, George B., lottery 1827, Greene County.
Mitchell, Henry, lottery 1827, Jones County.
Mize, Sheppeard, lottery 1827, Putnam County.
Mobbs, Jesse, lottery 1827, Clarke County.
Monk, John, lottery 1827, Monroe County.
Monk, Silas, lottery 1827, Putnam County.
Moore, Joel, lottery 1827, Upson County.
Moore, Joseph, early lottery 1820, Jasper County.
Morel, John, Captain, book ex. council, 1778-1783, p. 105.
Moreland, Francis, lottery 1827, Jasper County.
Moreland, Robert, lottery 1827, Jasper County.
Morgan, James, lottery 1827, Richmond County.
Morris, Burwell, lottery 1827, Monroe County.
Morris, Jesse, lottery 1827, Columbia County.

## LAND LOTTERY GRANTS.

Morris, John, early lottery 1820, Clarke County.
Morris, Nathaniel, lottery 1827, Jones County.
Morris, Osten, lottery 1827, Gwinnett County.
Morris, William, early lottery 1820, Jackson County.
Morriss, Thomas, lottery 1827, Jasper County.
Morrow, Ewing, lottery 1827, Morgan County.
Mosby, Littleberry, Captain, "book pay rolls," p. 145.
Moss, Joshua, Book D3, certified by Samuel Elbert.
Mote, William, lottery 1827, Warren County.
Mott, Nathan, lottery 1827, Wilkes County.
Mullens, Malone, early lottery 1820, Hancock County.
Myrick, John, lottery 1827, Baldwin County.

### N.

Nash, John, lottery 1827, DeKalb County.
Neaves, William, early lottery 1820, Putnam County.
Neblett, Tillman, lottery 1827, Monroe County.
Neisler, John Adam, Captain, "Commission B," p. 228.
Nelson, Jeremiah, early lottery 1820, Hancock County.
Nesbit, Jeremiah, lottery 1827, DeKalb County.
New, Jacob, lottery 1827, DeKalb County.
Newingate, John, Captain, book ex. council, 1778-1783.
Newman, John, Private, book ex. council, 1778-1783, p. 228.
Newsome, John, lottery 1827, Warren County.
Niblack, Wm., lottery 1827, Columbia County.
Nichols, Julius, lottery 1827, Franklin County.
Norris, Alexander, lottery 1827, Wilkes County.
Norris, James, lottery 1827, Warren County.
Norris, John, lottery 1827, Monroe County.
Norris, William, lottery 1827, Henry County.
Norriss, William, lottery 1827, Gwinnett County.
Nunn, John, lottery 1827, Wilkinson County.
Nunnlee, James F., lottery 1827, Elbert County.

### O.

Odam, Frederick, Lieutenant, "Commission B," p. 228.
Odom, Archibald, lottery 1827, Pulaski County.
Ogden, Solomon, early lottery 1820, Baldwin County.
Oglesby, Thomas, lottery 1827, Elbert County.
Ogletree, William, lottery 1827, Monroe County.
O'Kelly, Francis, lottery 1827, Oglethorpe County.
Oliver, Barshaba, lottery 1827, Elbert County.
Oliver, Peter, lottery 1827, Elbert County.
Omans, John, lottery 1827, Camden County.
Orr, Daniel, lottery 1827, Pike County.
Osborn, Reps, lottery 1827, Henry County.
Oswald, Joseph, Captain, "Commission B," p. 271.

## P.

Paine, John, lottery 1827, Greene County.
Palmore, Elijah, lottery 1827, Greene County.
Parker, Aaron, lottery 1827, Henry County.
Parker, Richard, lottery 1827, Hancock County.
Parkerson, Levin, lottery 1827, Wilkes County.
Parr, Benjamin, lottery 1827, Clarke County.
Paschall, George, lottery 1827, Oglethorpe County.
Pate, Samuel, lottery 1820, Twiggs County.
Patmore, Wm., Private, "book Washington County warrants."
Paton, George, lottery 1827, Gwinnett County.
Patrick, William, lottery 1827, Oglethorpe County.
Patton, William, lottery 1827, Jackson County.
Paul, Robert, lottery 1827, Jones County.
Paulette, Richard, lottery 1827, Clarke County.
Payret, Jean Pierre Andres DeFau, Captain, ex. council, 1778-1783.
Peace, John, lottery 1827, Monroe County.
Peacock, Archibald, lottery 1827, Wilkes County.
Peacock, Uriah, lottery 1827, Wilkes County.
Peacock, Wm., lottery 1827, Tattnall County.
Peddy, Jeremiah, lottery 1827, Monroe County.
Penn, William, lottery 1827, Jasper County.
Penny, Edward, lottery 1820, Twiggs County.
Perkerson, Joel, lottery 1820, Jackson County.
Perkins, John, lottery 1827, Bibb County.
Perryman, Harmon, lottery 1827, Twiggs County.
Peters, Edmond, lottery 1827, Morgan County.
Peters, Jesse, lottery 1827, Walton County.
Peters, William, lottery 1820, Putnam County.
Pettis, Moses, lottery 1827, Bibb County.
Pharoah, Joshua, lottery 1827, Richmond County.
Phelps, Thomas, lottery 1827, Jasper County.
Phillips, Thomas, lottery 1827, Jackson County.
Phinisee, John, lottery 1827, Monroe County.
Pickard, John H., lottery 1827, Monroe County.
Pierce, Hugh, lottery 1827, Habersham County.
Pierce, Seth, lottery 1827, Jefferson County.
Pinson, Joseph, lottery 1827, Rabun County.
Pitts, John, lottery 1827, Telfair County.
Poe, Stephen, lottery 1827, Habersham County.
Pollard, John, lottery 1827, Jones County.
Pollett, Richard, lottery 1827, Clarke County.
Pool, Henry R., lottery 1827, Warren County.
Pool, Samuel, lottery 1827, Jackson County.
Pool, Samuel, lottery 1827, Monroe County.
Pool, Walter, lottery 1827, Newton County.
Porter, John, lottery 1827, Jasper County.

Porter, William, lottery 1827, Jasper County.
Posey, Bennett, lottery 1827, Jasper County.
Poss, Henry, lottery 1827, Walton County.
Poss, Thomas, lottery 1827, Oglethorpe County.
Postell, John, Captain, "Commission B," p. 275.
Postwood, Benjamin, lottery 1827, Jasper County.
Potter, Augustin L., lottery 1827, Jasper County.
Potts, James, lottery 1827, Jasper County.
Potts, Stephen, Captain, book grants "LLL," p. 146.
Pound, Jonathan, lottery 1827, Hall County.
Powell, Francis, lottery 1827, Wilkes County.
Powell, Seymore, lottery 1827, Newton County.
Powledge, George, lottery 1827, Effingham County.
Poythress, Wm., lottery 1827, Burke County.
Pray, Job, Captain, "book pay rolls," p. 145.
Preslem, Peter, lottery 1827, Hall County.
Presley, John, lottery 1827, Henry County.
Presley, Moses, lottery 1827, Henry County.
Price, Ephraim, lottery 1827, Greene County.
Price, Lucas, lottery 1827, Crawford County.
Prichard, Presley, lottery 1827, Putnam County.
Pridgeon, David, lottery 1827, Bullock County.
Prince, Noah, lottery 1827, Clarke County.
Proctor, Stephen, lottery 1827, Monroe County.
Prosser, Oty, lottery 1827, Wilkes County.
Pugh, Shadrack, lottery 1827, Upson County.
Pullin, John, lottery 1827, Hancock County.
Pullin, Robert, lottery 1827, Greene County.
Pullin, Thomas, lottery 1827, Laurens County.
Pullum, Robt., lottery 1827, Elbert County.
Purvis, William, lottery 1827, Emanuel County.

R.

Rachford, Joseph, lottery 1827, Jackson County.
Ragan, Brice, lottery 1827, Wilkinson County.
Ragan, Buckner, lottery 1827, Hall County.
Ragsdale, Larkin, lottery 1827, Newton County.
Rahn, Mathew, lottery 1820, Effingham County.
Railey, Charles, lottery 1827, Twiggs County.
Rainey, Isham, lottery 1827, Oglethorpe County.
Rainey, John, lottery 1820, Clarke County.
Raley, Henry, lottery 1827, Warren County.
Ramsdill, David, lottery 1827, Butts County.
Randolph, Robert, lottery 1827, Columbia County.
Ransom, Reuben, lottery 1827, Clarke County.
Rawls, William, lottery 1827, Wayne County.
Ray, Andrew, lottery 1827, Greene County.

Ray, Mark, lottery 1827, Monroe County.
Ray, Philip, lottery 1827, Oglethorpe County.
Reaves, Joseph, Lieutenant, "Commission B," p. 227.
Redd, Job, lottery 1827, Gwinnett County.
Redding, Anderson, lottery 1827, Baldwin County.
Redding, Rehum, lottery 1827, Twiggs County.
Rees, Hugh, lottery 1827, Columbia County.
Reeves, John, lottery 1827, Columbia County.
Repass, Richard, lottery 1827, Upson County.
Reynolds, Benjamin, lottery 1827, Jones County.
Reynolds, Daniel, lottery 1827, Jones County.
Reynolds, Thomas, lottery 1827, Monroe County.
Rhodes, Richard, lottery 1827, Oglethorpe County.
Rhymes, Willis, lottery 1827, Warren County.
Rice, Leonard, lottery 1827, Elbert County.
Rich, John, lottery 1827, Hall County.
Richards, John, Senate Journal, 1825, p. 226.
Richardson, John, lottery 1827, Oglethorpe County.
Ricketson, Benjm., lottery 1827, Warren County.
Ricketson, Jesse, lottery 1827, Warren County.
Riddle, John, lottery 1827, Monroe County.
Ridge, James, lottery 1820, Gwinnett County.
Riley, John, lottery 1827, Greene County.
Rivers, John, Private, "Book D3," page 129.
Rivers, Josua, Sergeant, "Book D3," page 129.
Robertson, James, lottery 1827, Wayne County.
Robertson, John, lottery 1827, Newton County.
Roberts, Aaron, lottery 1827, Franklin County.
Roberts, Graystock, lottery 1827, Burke County.
Roberts, James, Lieutenant, "Commission B," page 228.
Roberts, John, Captain, "Commission B," page 228.
Roberts, Reuben, lottery 1827, Jones County.
Roberts, Rolin, lottery 1827, Screven County.
Robertson, Fryer, lottery 1827, Clarke County.
Robertson, Thomas, lottery 1820, Jasper County.
Robison, John, lottery 1827, Jackson County.
Roddenburg, George, lottery 1827, Bullock County.
Roe, John, lottery 1827, Hancock County.
Rogers, Robert, lottery 1827, Rabun County.
Rollins, Samuel, lottery 1827, Burke County.
Rooks, John, lottery 1827, Wayne County.
Roper, John, lottery 1827, Gwinnett County.
Ross, George, lottery 1827, Jones County.
Ross, Jesse, lottery 1827, Jones County.
Rossiter, Timothy, lottery 1827, Hancock County.
Rowe, James, lottery 1827, Jones County.
Rowe, Josua, lottery 1827, Newton County.
Rowe, Shadwrick, lottery 1827, Putnam County

Roy, Isaac A., lottery 1820, Morgan County.
Royals, Jonathan, lottery 1820, Richmond County.
Royalston, John, lottery 1827, Burke County.
Rozer, Edmond, lottery 1827, Franklin County.
Rucker, John, lottery 1820, Morgan County.
Rucker, William, lottery 1827, Elbert County.
Rucks, William, lottery 1827, Gwinnett County.
Runnells, Wm., lottery 1827, Jackson County.
Russell, George, lottery 1827, Madison County
Rutherford, Claiborn, lottery 1827, Newton County.
Rutherford, James, lottery 1827, Irwin County.
Rutledge, John, lottery 1827, Gwinnett County.
Ryals, Henry, lottery 1820, McIntosh County.
Ryals, Henry, lottery 1827, McIntosh County.
Ryals, Wright, lottery 1827, Telfair County.
Rye, Joseph, lottery 1827, Pike County.

S.

Sailors, Christopher, lottery 1827, Jackson County.
Salmon, Hesekiah, lottery 1827, Richmond County.
Samples, Nathaniel, lottery 1827, Jefferson County.
Sandeford, Elemerick, lottery 1827, Wilkes County.
Sandeford, John, Col., "Commission B," p. 270.
Sanders, James, lottery 1827, Madison County.
Sanders, Thomas, lottery 1827, Upson County.
Sandidge, John, lottery 1827, Franklin County.
Sanford, Jeremiah, lottery 1827, Greene County.
Sansford, Robert, "book pay rolls," by Robert Middleton, Col.
Sapp, Henry, lottery 1820, Twiggs County.
Sapp, Levi, lottery 1827, Montgomery County.
Sapp, Shadrack, lottery 1827, Tattnall County.
Savage, Thomas, lottery 1827, Hall County.
Sawyer, John Jones, lottery 1827, Hancock County.
Schrump, Frederick, Lieutenant, "Commission B," p. 274.
Scoggin, George, lottery 1827, Jones County.
Scoggins, Benjamin, lottery 1827, Jackson County.
Scott, Patrick, lottery 1827, Madison County.
Scott, Vawn, "book pay rolls," by Robert Middleton, Col.
Screven, James, General, killed near Midway Church, Liberty County.
Screven, John, "book pay rolls," p. 143.
Scrogin, Thomas, lottery 1827, Pike County.
Scurlock, Wm., lottery 1827, Baldwin County.
Seals, William, lottery 1827, Hancock County.
Searcey, George, lottery 1827, Baldwin County.
Selman, John, lottery 1827, Franklin County.
Sevay, George, lottery 1820, Jackson County.
Sewell, Christopher, lottery 1827, Franklin County.

Sewell, Wm., lottery 1827, Franklin County.
Sharty, Edward, lottery 1820, Jones County.
Sheffield, West, lottery 1827, Wayne County.
Sheftall, Sheftall, lottery 1827, Chatham County.
Shellman, John, lottery 1827, Crawford County.
Sherrar, James, Private, Senate Journal, 1825, p. 226.
Shirling, Isom, lottery 1827, Putnam County.
Shoemack, Joseph, Lieutenant, "Commission B," p. 276.
Showers, Adam, Private, Washington warrants, p. 16.
Shurley, William, "book pay rolls," by Robert Middleton, Col.
Simmons, John, lottery 1827, Pike County.
Simmons, Philip, Private, Washington warrants, p. 16.
Simpson, John, lottery 1820, Twiggs County.
Simpson, Timothy, Book D3, by Samuel Elbert.
Sims, Jeminy, lottery 1827, Oglethorpe County.
Sims, Robert, lottery 1827, Clarke County.
Slack, John, lottery 1827, Wilkes County.
Slocumb, John C., lottery 1827, Jones County.
Smeether, Gabriel, lottery 1827, Elbert County.
Smith, Abner, lottery 1827, Jasper County.
Smith, Ezekiel, lottery 1827, Madison County.
Smith, Ezekial, lottery 1827, Richmond County.
Smith, Hardy, lottery 1827, Laurens County.
Smith, Henry, lottery 1827, Monroe County.
Smith, Job, lottery 1827, Wilkes County.
Smith, Lawrence, lottery 1827, Morgan County.
Smith, Leavin, lottery 1827, Morgan County.
Smith, Reuben, lottery 1827, Greene County.
Smith, Richard, lottery 1827, Warren County.
Smith, Robert, lottery 1827, Oglethorpe County.
Smith, William, lottery 1827, Jackson County.
Smith, William, lottery 1827, Twiggs County.
Smith, Wm., lottery 1820, Jackson County.
Snelson, Wm., lottery 1827, Wilkes County.
Snyder, Godless, lottery 1827, Effingham County.
Snyder, Jonathan, lottery 1827, Effingham County.
Soloman, Lazarus, lottery 1827, Twiggs County.
Sowel, Zadock, lottery 1827, Wilkes County.
Sparks, Jeremiah, lottery 1827, Morgan County.
Spay, David, lottery 1820, Sparks County.
Spearman, John, lottery 1827, Jasper County.
Spinks, Prestley, lottery 1827, Warren County.
Springfield, Aaron, lottery 1820, Jackson County.
Stanford, Joshua, lottery 1827, Warren County.
Stanton, John, lottery 1827, Newton County.
Stapler, Thomas, lottery 1827, Jackson County.
Stapleton, George, lottery 1827, Jefferson County.

Starling, Wm., lottery 1827, Tattnall County.
Statham, Wm., lottery 1827, Wilkinson County.
Steel, Henry, lottery 1827, Jasper County.
Stephens, Barnett, lottery 1827, Madison County.
Stephens, Burwell, lottery 1827, Jefferson County.
Stephens, James, lottery 1827, Burke County.
Stephens, Joseph, lottery 1827, Monroe County.
Stephens, Richard, lottery 1827, Twiggs County.
Stephens, Richard, lottery 1827, Twiggs County.
Stephens, Wm., Captain, "Commission B," p. 272.
Stevens, Reuben, lottery 1827, DeKalb County.
Stewart, Amos, lottery 1827, Wilkes County.
Stewart, David, Captain, "Commission B," p. 228.
Stewart, Hardy, lottery 1827, Wilkinson County.
Stewart, John, General, lottery 1827, Oglethorpe County.
Stiles, John, lottery 1820, Twiggs County.
Stovall, George, lottery 1827, Franklin County.
Stowers, Lewis, lottery 1827, Elbert County.
Strange, John, lottery 1827, Franklin County.
Stranther, James, lottery 1827, Rabun County.
Strickland, John, lottery 1827, Richmond County.
Strong, Charles, lottery 1827, Oglethorpe County.
Strong, William, lottery 1827, Jones County.
Stroud, Philip, lottery 1827, Jasper County.
Studstell, Houston, "book pay rolls," by Robert Middleton, Col.
Stugel, Nicholas, lottery 1820 Screven County.
Sturdivant, John, lottery 1827, Jasper County.
Sturdivant, John, lottery 1827, Hancock County.
Sumner, Joseph, lottery 1827, Emanuel County.
Sutton, David, lottery 1827, Ware County.
Sutton, Thomas, Lieutenant, book ex. council, 1778-1783.
Sutty, James, lottery 1827, Franklin County.
Swan, William, lottery 1827, Newton County.
Sweet, Nathan, lottery 1827, Emanuel County.

T.

Taber, Hesekiah, lottery 1827, Oglethorpe County.
Talbot, Benjamin, lottery 1820, Baldwin County.
Tallant, John, lottery 1827, Hall County.
Tanner, Meredith, Book D3, by Samuel Elbert.
Tapley, Adam, lottery 1827, Baldwin County.
Tarver, Absolem, lottery 1827, Hancock County.
Tarbutton, Joseph, lottery 1827, Hall County.
Tate, Andrew, lottery 1827, Franklin County.
Tate, Enos, lottery 1827, Elbert County.
Tate, John, Jr., lottery 1827, Franklin County.
Taunton, Henry, lottery 1827, Washington County.

Taylor, Clark, lottery 1827, Oglethorpe County.
Taylor, Dempsey, lottery 1827, Irwin County.
Taylor, Edward, lottery 1827, Warren County.
Taylor, Richard C., lottery 1827, Morgan County.
Taylor, Theophilus, lottery 1827, Habersham County.
Taylor, Wm., lottery 1827, Henry County.
Teal, Emanuel, lottery 1827, Jasper County.
Teal, Lodewick, lottery 1827, Jasper County.
Teasley, Silas, lottery 1827, Elbert County.
Terrell, James, lottery 1827, Franklin County.
Thackston, James, lottery 1827, Greene County.
Tharpe, John A., lottery 1820, Twiggs County.
Themby, Thomas, lottery 1827, Houston County.
Thigpen, Nathan, lottery 1827, Warren County.
Thomas, Archibald, lottery 1827, Laurens County.
Thomas, Caleb, lottery 1827, Tatnall County.
Thomas, Etheldred, lottery 1827, Laurens County.
Thomas, John, Colonel, "Commission B," p. 276.
Thomas, Massa, lottery 1827, Putnam County.
Thomas, Richard, lottery 1827, Monroe County.
Thombey, Thomas, lottery 1820, Twiggs County.
Thompson, Andrew, lottery 1827, Oglethorpe County.
Thompson, George, "book pay rolls," by Robert Middleton, Col.
Thompson, Moses, lottery 1827, Warren County.
Thompson, Samuel, lottery 1827, Newton County.
Thompson, William, lottery 1827, Jackson County.
Thrasher, George, lottery 1827, Habersham County.
Tidd, David, lottery 1827, Jones County.
Tiller, John, lottery 1827, Oglethorpe.
Tilley, Wm., lottery 1827, Monroe County.
Tindell, James, lottery 1827, Burke County.
Tindell, Joshua, lottery 1820, Washington County.
Toller, Lewis, lottery 1827, Henry County.
Tomlinson, Aaron, lottery 1827, Washington County.
Tomlinson, Nathaniel, lottery 1827, Putnam County.
Tondee, Charles, lottery 1827, Effingham County.
Toole, James, lottery 1827, Richmond County.
Trammell, Wm., lottery 1820, Elbert County.
Trimble, John, lottery 1827, DeKalb County.
Triplett, Wm., lottery 1827, Tattnall County.
Truitt, Pernal, lottery 1827, Wilkes County.
Tucker, Henry C., lottery 1827, Henry County.
Turner, Abisha, lottery 1827, Bullock County.
Turner, James, lottery 1827, Clarke County.
Turner, Pleasant, lottery 1827, Jackson County.
Turner, Reuben, lottery 1827, Wayne County.
Turner, Robert, lottery 1827, Habersham County.

# LAND LOTTERY GRANTS.

Turner, Samuel, lottery 1827, Hancock County.
Tweedwell, Wm., lottery 1827, Franklin County.
Twidwell, William, lottery 1820, Franklin County.
Twitty, John, Lieutenant, "Commission B," p. 228.

## U.

Umphlet, Asa, lottery 1827, Warren County.
Underwood, William, Lieutenant, "Commission B," p. 228.
Usher, Daniel, lottery 1820, Richmond County.
Ussery, John, lottery 1827, Wilkinson County.

## V.

Vanbrackle, John, lottery 1827, Bryan County.
Vaughn, Felix, lottery 1827, Franklin County.
Vaughn, Jesse, lottery 1827, Wilkinson County.
Vaughn, Wm., Book D3, by Samuel Elbert, p. 129.
Veazey, Zebulon, lottery 1827, Hancock County.
Vickery, Joseph, lottery 1827, Elbert County.
Vincent, Isaac, lottery 1827, Clarke County.
Voikle, Lewis, lottery 1827, Hancock County.

## W.

Wade, David, lottery 1827, Hancock County.
Wade, Nathaniel, lottery 1827, Habersham County.
Wadkins, Benjamin, lottery 1827, DeKalb County.
Wagnon, Daniel, lottery 1827, Greene County.
Walden, Richard, lottery 1827, Jones County.
Waldroper, James, lottery 1827, Fayette County.
Walker, James, lottery 1827, Irwin County.
Walker, Samuel, lottery 1827, Jasper County.
Wall, Henry, lottery 1827, Twiggs County.
Wall, Mial, lottery 1827, Greene County.
Waller, Elijah, lottery 1827, Warren County.
Walls, Charles, lottery 1827, Gwinnett County.
Walls, Sampson, lottery 1827, Franklin County.
Walters, Peter, lottery 1827, Franklin County.
Wandslow, John, lottery 1827, Elbert County.
Ward, Nathaniel, lottery 1827, Warren County.
Warren, George, lottery 1827, Wayne County.
Warren, Jesse, lottery 1827, Hancock County.
Warren, John, Captain, "Commission B," p. 229.
Warthen, William, lottery 1827, Warren County.
Watkins, James C., lottery 1827, Hall County.
Watkins, William, lottery 1827, Washington County.
Watley, Sherod, "book pay rolls," by Robert Middleton, Col.
Watley, Willis, "book pay rolls," by Robert Middleton, Col.
Watley, Willis, Jr., "book pay rolls," by Robert Middleton, Col.

Watley, Worten, "book pay rolls," by Robert Middleton, Col.
Watson, Ezekiel, lottery 1827, Washington County.
Watson, Magees, lottery 1827, Richmond County.
Watty, Owen, "book pay rolls," by Robert Middleton, Col.
Way, Moses, Captain, "Commission B," p. 271.
Wayne, George, lottery 1827, Jasper County.
Weatherford, James, "book pay rolls," by Robert Middleton, Col.
Weatherton, Thomas, lottery 1827, Walton County.
Webster, John, "book pay rolls," by Robert Middleton, Col.
Weeks, Charles, lottery 1827, Morgan County.
Weeks, Theophilus, lottery 1827, Camden County.
Welborn, Elias, lottery 1827, Columbia County.
Welch, Benjamin, lottery 1820, Jackson County.
Wells, Andrew Elton, Lieut.-Col., "Commission B," p. 271.
Wells, George, Colonel, "Commission B," p. 271.
Welsher, Jeremiah, lottery 1827, Jefferson County.
Welsher, Jesse, "book pay rolls," by Robert Middleton, Col.
West, Benjamin, lottery 1827, Hancock County.
West, Willis, lottery 1827, Fayette County.
Wharton, Benjamin, lottery 1827, Hall County.
Whatley, John, lottery 1820, Jones County.
Wheeler, Amos, lottery 1827, Pulaski County.
Wheeler, James, lottery 1827, Jackson County.
Wheeler, Thomas, lottery 1827, Elbert County.
Wheeler, William, lottery 1820, Twiggs County.
Whelous, Lewis, lottery 1820, Morgan County.
Whitaker, Joshua, lottery 1827, Richmond County.
White, John N., lottery 1827, Fayette County.
White, Vincent, lottery 1827, Hancock County.
Whitehead, Amos, Lieutenant, "Commission B," p. 228.
Whitfield, Lewis, lottery 1827, Burke County.
Whitington, Burrell, lottery 1827, Liberty County.
Whitten, Philip, lottery 1827, Habersham County.
Wiggins, William, lottery 1827, Warren County.
Wilbanks, Gillam, lottery 1827, Franklin County.
Wilder, Sampson, lottery 1827, Warren County.
Wilder, Willis, lottery 1820, Jones County.
Wiley, Absolem, lottery 1827, Washington County.
Wiley, William, lottery 1827, Hancock County.
Williams, Abraham, lottery 1827, Jackson County.
Williams, Anderson, lottery 1827, Effngham County.
Williams, Benjn. Z., lottery 1827, Gwinnett County.
Williams, Lewis, lottery 1827, Franklin County.
Williams, William, lottery 1827, Washington County.
Williams, Zachariah, lottery 1820, Wayne County.
Williamson, Adam, lottery 1820, Jackson County.
Williamson, John, lottery 1827, Henry County.

## LAND LOTTERY GRANTS. 373

Williamson, Richard, "book pay rolls," by Robert Middleton, Col.
Williamson, Zachariah, lottery 1827, Bibb County.
Williams, Willis, lottery 1827, Newton County.
Willingham, Jesse, lottery 1827, Madison County.
Willingham, John, lottery 1820, Columbia County.
Willis, George, lottery 1827, Wilkes County.
Willis, Joseph, lottery 1820, Effingham County.
Willy, Richard, Depy. Qr.-Master Gen'l, "book pay rolls," p. 144.
Wilson, Joshua, lottery 1827, Jasper County.
Wimberly, John, lottery 1827, Jones County.
Winbarn, Josiah, lottery 1827, Pulaski County.
Winfrey, Jesse, "book pay rolls," by Robert Middleton, Col.
Winkfield, John, lottery 1820, Elbert County.
Winslett, Samuel, lottery 1827, Greene County.
Witherington, Richard, lottery 1827, Gwinnett County.
Withight, Lewis, lottery 1827, Elbert County.
Witmoth, Wm., lottery 1827, Franklin County.
Wofford, Absolem, lottery 1827, Jackson County.
Wofford, Benjamin, lottery 1827, Habersham County.
Wolf, Andrew, lottery 1827, Wilkes County.
Womack, Abraham, lottery 1827, Monroe County.
Womack, Wm., lottery 1827, Effingham County.
Wood, Ellit, lottery 1827, Newton County.
Wood, John, lottery 1827, Wilkes County.
Wood, Thomas, lottery 1827, Clarke County.
Woodall, Joseph, lottery 1827, Oglethorpe County.
Woodcock, Wm., lottery 1827, Bullock County.
Wourd, Benjamin, "book pay rolls," by Robert Middleton, Col.
Wourd, Eldred, "book pay rolls," by Robert Middleton, Col.
Wright, Ambrose, Captain, "Commission B," p. 273.
Wright, Banego, "book pay rolls," by Robert Middleton, Col.
Wright, Elisha, lottery 1827, Jones County.
Wright, John, lottery 1820, Walton County.
Wright, Reuben, lottery 1827, Early County.
Wright, Soloman, lottery 1827, Wilkinson County.
Wyatt, John, lottery 1827, Henry County.
Willey, Thomas, lottery 1827, Effingham County.
Willy, Richard, Major, "Commission B," p. 272.

### Y.

Yancey, Lewis, lottery 1827, Jasper County.
Yarbrough, Lewis, lottery 1827, Morgan County.
Yarbrough, Wm., lottery 1827, Laurens County.
Yates, Peter, lottery 1820, Clarke County.
Yates, William, lottery 1827, Laurens County.
Young, Jacob, lottery 1827, Jefferson County.

374  ROSTER OF THE REVOLUTION.

Atlanta, Ga., March 21, 1902.
I hereby certify that the above fifty-three* pages contain a true and correct copy of names of Revolutionary soldiers, as compiled by me from the records in the office of Secretary of State.

B. F. JOHNSON.

Office of Secretary of State,
Atlanta, Ga.

I hereby certify the above fifty-three* pages contain a true and correct copy of the names of Revolutionary soldiers, as the same appears of record in this department.

Given under my hand and official seal this 17th day of October, 1902.
(Seal)                                    PHILIP COOK,
Secretary of State.

* This is the number of pages of the MS. copy from which the above list was printed.

## CERTIFIED LIST OF GEORGIA TROOPS.

Published as Appendix E, in the Third Annual Report of the National Society, D. A. R., to the Smithsonian Institution. Senate Documents, Volume 16, Number 219, Fifty-sixth Congress, Second Session, 1900-1901, pp. 347-368.

State of Georgia.
Office of Secretary of State.

I, Philip Cook, Secretary of State of the State of Georgia, do hereby certify that the attached sheets contain a true and correct copy of the names of men who served in the Revolutionary War, as compiled from the records of this department.

In testimony whereof I have hereunto set my hand and affixed the seal of my office, at the capitol, in the city of Atlanta, this 24th day of January, in the year of our Lord one thousand nine hundred and one, and of the independence of the United States of America, the one hundred and twenty-fifth.

PHILIP COOK,
Secretary of State.

### APPENDIX E.
### GEORGIA SOLDIERS OF THE LINE—REVOLUTIONARY WAR.

Copied under the direction of Mrs. William Lawson Peel, from the original papers in the office of the Secretary of State.

# CERTIFIED LIST, GEORGIA TROOPS. 375

## A.
Aaron, William, Captain.
Abbott, John.
Abercrombie, Charles.
Acord, John.
Adams, Hugh.
Adams, James.
Adams, John.
Adams, Robert.
Adams, William.
Adcock, Thomas.
Aderson, Bartlett.
Adkins, William.
Adkinson, Thomas.
Adomison, Charles.
Akins, John.
Aldridge, James.
Aldridge, James.*
Alexander, Adam, Secretary, Mate.
Alexander, Asa.
Alexander, Ayra.
Alexander, Ezekiel.
Alexander, Henry.
Alexander, Hugh.
Alexander, James.
Alexander, John L.
Alexander, Robert.
Alexander, Samuel, Captain.
Allen, Charles.
Allen, James.
Allen, John.
Allen, Moses, Captain.
Allen, Robert.
Allen, Thomas.
Allen, William.
Allison, Henry.
Allison, Henry, Lieut.
Allison, James.
Ammons, Robert.
Ammons, William.
Amos, James.
Anderson, Alex.
Anderson, Elijah.
Anderson, Henry.
Anderson, James, Lieut.
Anderson, John.
Anderson, John.*

Anderson, Jno.
Anderson, William.
Andrew, Samuel.
Andrews, Benjamin.
Andrews, Benjamin.
Andrews, George.
Andrews, John.
Angelly, Alex.
Anglin, David.
Anglin, Hy.
Anglin, Wm.
Ansley, Thomas.
Appling, Daniel.
Appling, John.
Armes, James.
Armour, Andrew.
Armstrong, Alex., Lieut.
Arrington, Wm.
Arthur, Matthew.
Ashley, Wm., Lieut.
Ashmore, John.
Ashmore, Strong.
Ashworth, Adam.
Ashworth, Arthur.
Austin, Richard, Captain.
Autrey, Alex.
Avent, Joseph.
Avera, Isaac.
Avera, William.
Averitt, Isaac.
Averitt, John.
Averitt, Thomas.
Avery, John.
Awtry, Alex., Captain.
Awtry, Alex., Private.
Awtry, Jacob.
Awtry, John, Captain.
Awtry, John.
Aycock, Richard.
Aycock, Wm.
Ayres, Abram, Captain.
Ayres, Abram.
Ayres, Daniel, Lieut.
Ayres, James.
Ayres, Thomas.
Ayres, Wm., Captain.

* Duplicated.

## B.
Babbetts, Jacob.
Bacon, John.
Bacon, Jonathan.
Bacon, Thomas.
Bagby, George.
Bagley, George.
Bags, Joseph.
Baggs, John.
Baggs, Jonathan.
Bailey, Wm.
Baillie, Robert.
Bain, Robert.
Baker, Artemas.
Baker, Artemas.
Baker, Artemas.
Baker, Dempsy.
Baker, John, Colonel.
Baker, Nathanael.
Baker, Thos.
Baker, Whitmarsh.
Baker, Wm., Major.
Baker, Wm., Major.
Baker, Wm. James.
Bakin, Sh.
Baldwin, David.
Baldwin, David.
Baldwin, Mordecai, Lieut.
Baldwin, Wm., Sergeant.
Balier, Wm., Lieut.
Ball, Sampson.
Ball, Wm.
Banks, Boling.
Banks, Reuben.
Bankston, Daniel.
Bankston, Daniel.
Bankston, Jacob.
Bankston, John.
Bankston, Lawrence.
Bansworth, Jacob.
Barber, Charles.
Barber, Chester.
Barber, George, Captain.
Barber, Gingo.
Barber, Jno.
Barber, William.
Bardine, Gilbert.
Barfield, Richard.
Barfield, Solomon.

Barkaloe, Wm.
Barker, Bryan.
Barker, Charles.
Barker, Frances.
Barker, George.
Barker, Stencil.
Barker, Wm.
Barksdale, Daniel.
Barksdale, Jeffery.
Barksdale, Richard.
Barnall, Wm.
Barnard, Jesse.
Barnard, John.
Barnard, Reuben.
Barnes, Richard B.
Barnes, Wm.
Barnes, Wm.
Barnett, Burton.
Barnett, Claiborne.
Barnett, Daniel.
Barnett, Daniel.
Barnett, Jesse.
Barnett, Joel.
Barnett, John.
Barnett, Mial.
Barnett, Nathan.
Barnett, Philip.
Barnett, Philip.
Barnette, Joshua.
Barnhart, George.
Barnwell, John.
Barrett, Thomas.
Baron, Reuben.
Baron, Samuel.
Baron, Wm., Lieut.
Barry, Wm.
Barthmore, Benjamin.
Barton, Barnett.
Barton, Richard.
Barton, Wileby, Sergeant.
Barton, Wiloby.
Barton, Willoughby.
Basnet, John.
Bass, Brantley.
Bass, Hardy.
Bass, Thomas.
Bassett, George.
Bates, John.
Batson, David.
Baughbank, Lewis.
Baxter, Jno.
Bazlewood, Rich.
Beal, Henry.
Beal, Jeremiah, Captain.
Beal, Nathan.
Beall, Arch.
Beall, Garrett.
Beall, Thos., Sergeant.
Beall, Zephaniah.
Bear, Reuben.
Beard, Edward.
Bearden, John, Sergeant.
Beasley, Jno.
Beasley, Jos.
Beason, Peter.
Beatty, Samuel.
Beatty, Samuel.
Beatty, Wm.
Beck, Simon.
Beckham, Abner.
Beckham, Abner.
Beckham, Allen.
Beckham, Samuel.
Beckham, Simon.
Beddingfield, Chas.
Beddingfield, Nathan.
Beesley, James.
Beesley, Wm.
Bell, Archibald.
Bell, Hezekiah.
Bell, Hugh.
Bell, John.
Bell, Robert.
Bellamy, Rich.
Bells, Hugh.
Bender, John.
Bender, John.
Bennefield, Robert.
Bennison, John.
Benson, John.
Bentley, Jno.
Bentley, John.
Bentley, Wm.
Benton, Robert.
Berry, John.
Berry, Rich.
Berryhill, John.
Berryhill, Samuel.
Bevill, James.
Bevill, Paul.
Bevill, Paul.
Beville, Robert.
Bird, Benj.
Bird, John.
Bird, Michael.
Bishop, Joshua.
Bitsell, Jno.
Black, Henry.
Black, Henry.
Black, John.
Black, John.
Black, Wm.
Blacksell, Thos.
Blackwell, Thomas.
Blair, Johnson.
Blakely, Benj., Sergeant.
Blakely, Benj.
Blakely, Jno.
Blanchard, Reuben.
Blanchard, Wm.
Blazer, Wm.
Blount, Jacob, Surgeon's Mate.
Blunt, Jacob, Surgeon's Mate.
Blunt, Stephen.
Bodenner, Geo.
Boderly, Wm.
Bohanon, Ben.
Boid, John.
Boloth, James.
Bond, Seny.
Benner, Jos.
Bonner, Rich.
Bonner, Wm.
Booth, Abram.
Booth, Chas.
Borneman, Benj.
Bostick, Chesly.
Bostick, Littleberry.
Bostick, Nathan.
Bowen, Ep.
Bowen, James.
Bowen, Oliver.

CERTIFIED LIST, GEORGIA TROOPS.  377

Bowen, Oliver,
Commodore.
Bowens, Joel.
Bowling, R.
Bowling, Thos. Burton.
Bowman, Jacob.
Boyce, Lott.
Boyd, Ed.
Boyd, Edward.
Boyd, John.
Boyd, Nicholas.
Boyd, Robert.
Boykin, Bruns.
Boykin, Jesse.
Boykins, Byers.
Braddock, David.
Braddock, Jno.
Braddock, John.
Bradey, Wm.,Lieut.
Bradford, Josiah.
Bradley, Abrm.
Bradley, Joshua.
Bradley, Michael.
Bradley, Rich.
Bradley, Rich.
Bradley, Rich.
Bradley, Rich.
Bradshaw, Peter.
Brady, Wm.
Brady, Wm.
Brady, Wm.
Brady, Wm., Sergeant.
Braker, Wm.
Bramfield, Jno.
Brandon, John.
Branham, Samuel.
Branham, Samuel.
Brannon, Moses.
Brannon, Thomas.
Brantley, Amos.
Brantley, Brittain.
Brantley, James.
Brantley, Thos.
Brassard, Alex.
Brassel, Samuel.
Brasswell, Jos.
Braswell, Allen.
Braswell, F.

Braswell, Ferdenan.
Braswell, Geo.
Braswell, George.
Braswell, James.
Braswell, Simpson.
Braydon, Wm.
Brazwell, Jno. Richard.
Bready, Wm.
Brevard, Geo.
Brewer, Erasmus.
Brewer, Geo.
Brewer, Moses.
Brewer, Wm.
Briants, John.
Briggs, Samuel.
Brittenham, Jos.
Brittain, Henry.
Brock, Benj.
Bronson, Ebenezer.
Brooks, Jacob.
Brooks, James.
Brooks, Jesse.
Brooks, John.
Brooks, Roger.
Brooks, Roger.
Brown, Allen.
Brown, And.
Brown, Andrew.
Brown, David.
Brown, Francis.
Brown, Fred.
Brown, James.
Brown, James.
Brown, Jno.
Brown, John.
Brown, Stark.
Brown, Thos.
Brown, Wm.
Brownen, Chas.
Brownlow, Wm.
Brownson, Nathl.
Brumley, John.
Brunson, David.
Brunson, David.
Brunson, John.
Brunson, Wm.
Bryant, Benj.
Bryant, James.

Bryant, John.
Bryant, Wm.
Bryant, William G.
Buchanan, James P.
Buck, Wm.
Buckhalter, John.
Buckhalter, Jos.
Buchalter, Michl.
Bugg, Ed.
Bugg, Ed.
Bugg, Jacob.
Bugg, Jere.
Bugg, Jere.
Bugg, John.
Bugg, Nicholas.
Bugg, Samuel.
Bugg, Samuel.
Bugg, Sherwood.
Buggs, Jona.
Bugners, Augustus.
Bullock, Daniel.
Burch, Chas.
Burch, Ed.
Burch, Ed.
Burdey, Peter.
Burges, Jos.
Burgesteiner, Danl.
Burke, Theophilus.
Burkes, David.
Burkes, James.
Burkes, Jos.
Burks, Ed.
Burks, John, Captain.
Burks, Jose.
Burley, Zach.
Burnard, Wm.
Burnett, Nathan.
Burney, Jno.
Burney, Jno., Jr.
Burney, Randall.
Burns, Andrew.
Burns, John.
Burnsides, John.
Burnsides, John.
Burt, Moody.
Burt, Moody.
Burton, Jno.
Burton, Rich.

Burton, Richard.
Burton, Thos.
Burton, Thos.
Burwell, John.
Bussey, Hezeker.
Bussey, Thos.
Busson, Jona.
Butler, Danl.
Butler, Danl.
Butler, Edmond.
Butler, Ford.
Butler, Ford.
Butler, Frances.
Butler, John.
Butler, John.
Butler, Robt.
Butler, Wm.
Butts, Solomon.
Buzer, Wm.
———
* Duplicated.

C.
Cade, Drewry.
Cade, Drury.
Cain, John.
Caldwell, James.
Caldwell, John.
Calhoun, Wm.
Calk, James, **Jr.**
Calk, James **W.**
Calson, Wm.
Camant, John.
Camant, John.
Camberger, Chestop.
Camp, Jas.
Camp, Saml., **Quartermaster,**
Camp, Sol.
Camp, Wm.
Campbell, **Drewry.**
Campbell, Wm.
Campbell, Wm.
Camps, Joseph.
Candler, Henry.
Candler, Wm., **Colonel.**
Cannon, Roger.
Cannon, **Thomas.**
Canon, D.

Cantrell, Stephen.
Canty, Zach.
Carden, Cornelius.
Carden, Cornelius.
Cargyle, John.
Carlton, Pat., Lieut.
Carlyle, John.
Carney, M.
Carney, Ousley.
Carr, Major.
Carr, Henry.
Carr, Henry.
Carr, Pat., Major.
Carroll, Wm.
Carson, Adam.
Carson, John.
Carson, John.
Carson, Jos.
Carson, Sam'l.
Carson, Thos.
Carson, Thos.
Carson, Thomas, Jr.
Carswell, Alex.
Carter, Henry.
Carter, Hepworth.
Carter, Jas.
Carter, James.
Carter, James.
Carter, Josiah.
Carter, Pat.
Cartledge, Edw.
Cartledge, Jas.
Cartledge, James.
Cartledge, James.
Cartledge, Samuel.
Carvan, Edw., Lieut.
Casey, Jno.
Casey, Wm.
Cason, Jno.
Cason, Sam'l.
Cassell, Wm.
Cassells, John.
Castello, Ed.
Caster, David.
Castleberry, Henry.
Castleberry, Jacob.
Castleberry, Jno.
Castleberry, Peter.
Catchings, Jos.

Catchings, Seymor.
Catchins, Benj.
Cathern, Wm.
Cato, Wm.
Cauley, Jacob.
Cauley, Rich.
Cauthon, Jos.
Cawthorne, Jas.
Chambers, John.
Chambless, Christopher.
Chambless, John.
Chambless, Littleton.
Chandler, Abednego.
Chandler, M.
Chaney, Emanuel.
Chaney, G.
Chapman, John, **Sergeant,**
Chapman, Wm.
Chavons, Jere.
Cheshire, John.
Chevalier, Chas. **F.**
Chidney, Thos.
Childers, David.
Childers, Thomas.
Childers, Richard.
Chiles, John.
Chipen, Jno.
Chisholm, Benj.
Chisholm, Benjamin.
Chisholm, John, **Sergeant.**
Chisholm, Thomas.
Christian, Turner.
Clark, Jno., **Sr.**
Clark, John, **Captain.**
Clark, Johnston.
Clark, Wm.
Clarke, Gibson.
Clarke, John.
Clarke, Lewis.
Clay, Abia.
Clem, John.
Clements, John, **Lieut.**
Clements, Saml.
Clements, Wm.
Clemmonds, Isaac.
Clifton, Chas.
Clifton, Wm.
Clondas, George.
Cloud, Ezekiel.

## CERTIFIED LIST, GEORGIA TROOPS. 379

Cloud, Jere.
Cloud, Jere.
Cloud, John.
Cloud, Neaugh.
Clower, Peter.
Clowers, Peter.
Coalson, Wm.
Coan, John.
Coats, Aaron.
Coats, Henry.
Coats, John.
Coats, Leslie.
Coats, Nath'l.
Cobb, Ezekiel.
Cobb, Jas.
Cobb, Jos.
Cobb, Ralph.
Cock, Caleb.
Cody, John.
Cofield, Grisham.
Cohron, Cornelius.
Cole, James.
Cole, John.
Cole, John, Sr.
Coleman, Daniel.
Coleman, F.
Coleman, James.
Colins, John.
Collins, Chas.
Collins, Cornelius, Lieut.
Collins, John.
Collins, John.
Collins, Moses.
Collins, Sol.
Collins, Steven.
Colson, Wm.
Combs, John.
Compton, Wm.
Cone, James.
Cone, Jas.
Cone, Jno.
Cone, Wm.
Cone, Wm., Jr.
Conley, Jacob.
Connally, Pat.
Connell, Jesse.
Connell, John.
Conner, Daniel.
Connor, David.

Connor, John.
Conteratt, Joseph.
Conyers, John.
Conyers, John, Captain.
Conyers, John, Jr.
Conyers, Wm.
Cook, Caleb.
Cook, Slisha.
Cook, Geo.
Cook, Isham.
Cook, John.
Cook, Rains.
Cook, Raines, Captain.
Cook, Reuben.
Cooper, Anthony.
Cooper, Geo.
Cooper, John, Lieut.-Col.
Cooper, Jos.
Coplin, Wm.
Corbin, Wm.
Cornell, Thos.
Corsea, Wm.
Coursey, David.
Cowan, Wm.
Cowns, Wm.
Cowns, Wm.
Cox, Benj.
Crabb, Sam'l.
Crain, Lewis.
Crane, Spencer.
Crawford, Anderson.
Crawford, John.
Crawford, Nathan.
Crawford, Saml.
Creswell, David.
Creswell, Sam'l, Surgeon.
Cribbs, Thos.
Crispus, James.
Croker, Wm.
Crokes, Wm.
Crook, Wm.
Crudden, Wm.
Crumley, Anthony.
Crutchfield, Jno.
Crutchfield, John.
Cruze, Thomas.
Cudington, Jno.
Culbreath, Jas.
Culbreath, Jno.

Cullars, Henry.
Cullens, Jos.
Culpepper, Jos.
Culpepper, Jos.
Cumming, Pat.
Cunningham, Jas.
Cunningham, John, Major.
Cup, Henry, Sergeant.
Cup, Michael.
Cureton, Boling.
Cureton, Rich.
Cureton, Wm.
Cureton, Wm.
Cureton, Wm., Lieut.
Cureton, Wm. J.
Curl, Henry.
Curl, John.
Curry, Jacob.
Curry, Nicolas.
Curry, Peter.
Curtis, John.
Curvey, Cary.
Cuthbert, Dan'l A., Captain.

\* Duplicated.

D.

Dabney, Asten.
Dabney, Austin.
Daley, Benj.
Dallas, John, Lieut.
Dally, Benj.
Dalton, Mathews.
Dalton, Thomas.
Dampier, Dan'l.
Daniel, Benj.
Daniel, Wm.
Danison, Chas.
Dannello, Daniel.
D'Antignac, Jno.
Darbe, Rich.
Darby, John.
Darby, John.
Darby, Nicholas.
Darcy, Joel.
Darcy, Wm.
Darden, George, Sr.
Darden, George, Jr.

## ROSTER OF THE REVOLUTION.

Darney, Benj.
Darney, James.
Darsey, James.
Dasher, Christian.
Dasher, Jno. Martin.
Daus, Ware.
Daus, Ware.
Dauthan, **Elijah**.
Davenport, Dr., Surgeon.
Davenport, Thomas, Lieut.
David, Wm.
Davies, John.
Davis, Absalom.
Davis, Benj.
Davis, Blandford.
Davis, Chas., **Sergeant**.
Davis, Chesley.
Davis, Clementine.
Davis, **David**.
Davis, Edw.
Davis, Gideon.
Davis, **Hardy**.
Davis, **Hardy**.
Davis, Jacob.
Davis, **James**.
Davis, Jenkins, **Colonel**.
Davis, **Joseph**.
Davis, Lewis.
Davis, **Meredith**.
Davis, Moses.
Davis, **Myrick**.
Davis, **Nehemiah**.
Davis, **Randolph**.
Davis, Sam'l.
Davis, Solomon.
Davis, **Valthal**.
Davis, Wiley.
Davis, Wm.
Davis, Wm.
Davison, Jos.
Dawson, Brittain.
Dawson, **David**.
Dawson, **Martin**.
Dawson, Wm.
Daw, Harry.
Day, Jos.
Day, Jos., **Captain**.
Day, Robert.
Day, Robert.
Day, Stephen.
Dean. John.
Dean, Wm.
Dean, Wm., Sergeant.
Deaton, Elizabeth.
Decks, Andrew.
DeClanchrees, Matthew, Serg.
Delaney, Dave.
Delaney, James.
DeLaplaign, E. P., Captain.
Delk, David.
Denman, Chas.
Denman, James.
Dennis, Abram.
Dennis, Isaac.
Dennis, John.
Dennis, John.
Dennis, Richmond.
Dennison, Darby.
Dannison, Dave.
Dennison, Elijah.
Denton, Chas.
Derbin, Luke.
D'Estaing, Count, Vice-Admiral.
Dethan, John.
Devaugh, John, Aide-de-Camp.
Dick, David.
Dickenson, Edwd.
Dickson, David, Captain.
Dickson, Michael, Captain.
Dickson, Nathan.
Dickson, Nathaniel.
Dickson, Wm.
Dillard, Jno.
Dillard, John.
Dickins, Lebua.
Dixon, Hugh.
Doles, Jesse.
Dollard, Anson.
Dollar, Anson.
Dollar, John, Lieut., Art.
Dolly, **Benj**.
Donelly, Cornelius.
Donely, John.
Donally, James.
Donnelly, James.
Donnelly, John.
Donoway, Wm.
Dooly, Wm.
Dorton, Thos.
Dorty, Geo., Captain.
Doss, Joel, Lieut.
Douglas, Alex.
Douglas, Geo.
Douglas, Jno.
Dovly, Hull, Lieut.
Dowday, Rich.
Dowdy, Rich.
Downs, Ambrose.
Downs, George.
Downs, Jona.
Downs, Wm.
Driver, Henry.
Ducains, John, Captain.
Duchart, John.
Duck, Jeremiah.
Duck, Jno.
Duckworth, Jacob.
Duckworth, Jeremiah.
Dudley, Jno.
Duffey, James.
Dugan, Thos., Captain
Duhart, John.
Duke, Jno. Taylor.
Dukes, Buckner.
Dukes, Henry, Captain.
Dukes, James.
Dukes, Jno. Taylor.
Dukes, Taylor.
Dukes, Wm.
Dukes, Wm., Lieut.
Dulins, Henry.
Du Maplier, Elijah.
Dunaway, John.
Duncan, James.
Dancan, James, Lieut.
Duncan, Mathew.
Duncan, Mathews.
Duncan, Thos.
Dunkin, Wm.
Dunn, Jacob.

## CERTIFIED LIST, GEORGIA TROOPS. 381

Dunn, Josiah.
Dunwoody, James.
Dyche, Jno.
Dyer, Henry.
———
* Duplicated.

E.

Eades, John.
Eady, James.
Eady, John.
Eagle, Jno.
Earley, Daniel.
Earnest, Jacob.
Earnest, Wm.
Earnest, Wm.
Easter, James.
Easton, James.
Eastwood, John.
Echols, Eph'm.
Eckles, Eph.
Edwards, Abraham.
Edwards, Peter.
Eimbeck, George.
Eimenson, Robt.
Elbert, Sam'l, Colonel.
Elleas, Wm.
Elliott, Daniel.
Elliot, Henry.
Elliot, John.
Elliot, Thomas.
Elliot, Wm.
Ellis, Jerry.
Ellis, Robert.
Ellis, Stephen.
Ellis, Walter.
Ellison, James.
Emanuel, Asa, Col.
Emanuel, David.
Emanuel, David, Capt.
Emanuel, Enos.
Embeck, M.
Embry, Jesse.
Emmett, James.
Emtrickeen, Wm.
Entechins (Enterkin), Wm.
Entriccan, Wm.

Espey, Wm.
Etons, Absolom.
Eustace, John.
Eustace, Jno. Skey, Maj.
Evans, Benj.
Evans, Benj.
Evans, Daniel.
Evans, Dan'l.
Evans, Dan'l.
Evans, David.
Evans, Jno.
Evans, Nathan, Col.
Evans, Steph.
Evans, Stephen.
Evans, Wm.
Eves, Nathaneal.
———
* Duplicated.

F.

Fain, John.
Fame, Wm.
Fane, Travis.
Fanner, Asael.
Fanner, Wm.
Fare, Jacob.
Farington, Jacob.
Farr, Benj.
Farr, John.
Farrell, Wm.
Farvin, John.
Favens, John.
Fean, Wm.
Felps (Phelps), David.
Felts, Jas.
Fenn, Zach.
Feras, Zach.
Fergason, Chas.
Ferkerson, John.
Ferrell, James.
Ferrell, Thomas.
Ferrul, Wm.
Fettler, Mathew.
Fettler, Nathl.
Few, Ignatius.
Few, Wm., Sr.
Few, Wm., Jr.
Fields, Wm.

Fincher, Jas.
Finley, James.
Finn, John.
Finshwell, Jos.
Fitzgerald, Chas.
Fitzpatrick, Pat., Lieut.
Fleming, Wm.
Flemming, Robert.
Flemming, Sam'l.
Flenneken, James.
Flennickin, David.
Flennickin, Sam'l.
Fling, John.
Flounray, Robt.
Flowers, Wm.
Fluker, John.
Fluker, Owen.
Fluker, Thos.
Fluker, Wm.
Fly, Jeremiah.
Flynn, James.
Folds, Geo.
Folsom, Benj.
Folsome, John.
Ford, John.
Ford, Joshua.
Ford, Owen.
Ford, Thomas.
Ford, Thos.
Ford, Wm.
Forgason, Chas.
Fort, Arthur.
Fort, Owen.
Fortee, Jacob.
Foster Francis.
Foster, Wm.
Fowler, Henry.
Fowler, Nathan.
Fowler, Peter.
France, Abram.
Francis, Fredk.
Franklin, David, Lieut.
Franklin, David, Lieut.
Franklin, Geo.
Franklin, Thos., Lieut.
Franklin, Wm., Sr.
Franklin, Wm., Jr.
Frazier, Alex.

Frazier, Jno., Lieut.
Frazier, John.
Frazier, John.
Frazier, Malachi.
Frederick, Thos.
Fredman, Conrad.
Freeman, Holman.
Freeman, Holman.
Freeman, John.
Freman, James.
Freman, John.
Freman, Wm.
French, James.
French, Jos.
French, Joshua.
Freyar, Humphrey.
Friels, Lewis.
Frier, John.
Fryer, Fielding.
Fugonier, Conrad.
Fukeway, Thos.
Fuller, Joshua.
Fuller, Isaac.
Fuller, Steph.
Fulsome, Lawrence.
Fulton, John.
Fulton, Sam'l.
Fuqua, Prater.
Fussell, Ezra.
Fussell, Thomas.

\* Duplicated.

G.
Gaines, Absalom.
Gaines, Bagley.
Galpin, Thomas.
Gamble, John.
Gamble, John.
Gamest, Wm.
Gamson, Jno.
Garbet, George.
Gardner, Lewis.
Gardner, Wm.
Garland, Wm.
Garmany, Sam'l.
Garnett, Eli.
Garnett, Jno.

Garrett, Jno.
Garrett, John.
Gaston, Alex., Lt.
Gaston, David, Sergt.
Gay, Joshua.
Gay, William.
Geddings, Tho.
Gedings, Frances.
Gedions, Wm.
Gent, Charles.
Gent, Wm.
German, Jno., Sr.
German, Jno., Jr.
Germany, William.
Gibbs, Hervel.
Gibbs, Rich.
Gideons, Francis, Capt.
Gideon, Wm.
Gift, Jonathan.
Gilbert, James.
Gilbert, Thomas.
Gilbert, Wm.
Gilder, Isaac.
Giles, Andrew.
Giles, Arthur.
Giles, Jno.
Giles, Robert.
Giles, Sam'l.
Giles, Sam'l.
Giles, Wm.
Gilliland, Hugh.
Gilliland, Thomas.
Gilliland, Thos.
Gilliland, Wm.
Gillons, Jas.
Girardeau, John.
Girardeau, Wm
Glampkin, John.
Glascock, Thomas, Lt.
Glascock, Thos.
Glascock, Wm
Glase, Jos.
Glaspy (Gilespie), John.
Glass, Joel.
Glass, John.
Glass, John.
Glass, Joshua.
Glassoway, Thomas.

Glover, Hardy.
Gloveyer, Step.
Godbe, Cary.
Godbe, Curry.
Godby, Wm.
Golden, Wm.
Golding, John.
Goldwire, J.
Goodall, Pleas't.
Goolsby, Jonathan.
Goolsby, Josiah.
Gordon, James.
Gordon, Jesse.
Gordon, Jesse.
Gordon, Wm.
Gorham, Jno.
Gorley, Ayres.
Gorley, James.
Goslin, David.
Gossett, Jacob.
Goultney, John.
Gouze, Henry, Lt.
Goves, Thomas.
Gragz, Thomas.
Graham, Wm.
Graham, Wm.
Grant, Capt.
Grant, Andrew.
Grant, Jno., Capt.
Grant, Peter.
Grant, Peter.
Grant, Thomas.
Grant, Wm.
Graves, Jas.
Graves, John.
Graves, John.
Graves, Rich.
Graves, Robert.
Graves, Robert, Jr.
Gray, Jacob.
Gray, Jas.
Gray, John.
Gray, Math.
Gray, R. M.
Gray, Rob.
Gray, Thomas.
Graybill, Henry.
Greasell, Elam.

CERTIFIED LIST, GEORGIA TROOPS. 383

Greazell, Clam.
Greathouse, Jacob.
Green, Benj.
Green, Henry.
Green, James.
Green, John.
Green, M. Andrew.
Green, McKeen.
Green, Sullivan.
Green, Wm.
Greene, Benj.
Greene, Benjamin.
Greene, Frederick.
Greene, Saliva.
Greene, Thomas.
Greene, Wm.
Greer, Jno., Lt.
Greer, Thos.
Greer, Wm.
Greer, Wm.
Greggs, Thos.
Griener, Philip.
Grier, Aaron.
Grier, Gilbert.
Grier, John.
Grier, Robert.
Greene, Thomas.*
Grier, Thos.
Grier, Wm.
Grierson, John.
Grierson, Robert.
Griffin, Matthew.
Griffin, Michael.
Griffin, Randal.
Griffin, Randolph.
Griffin, Sam'l.
Griffith, Sam'l.
Grimesley, Jno.
Grimsley, Adam.
Grimsley, Elijah, Sergt.
Grimsley, Jos.
Griner, Phillip.
Grizzle, Jno.
Grub, Frances.
Grubbs, Benj.
Gunnells, Daniel.
Gunnells, Jos.
Gunnells, Nicholas.

Gurnsey, Rich.
─────
* Green, Thomas.

H.

Hagan, Ed.
Hagan, Edward.
Hager, Arthur.
Haggett, John, Sergt.
Haile, George.
Haliman, Absolam.
Hall, Edward.
Halymdorf, Wm.
Hamach, Robert B.
Hamby, Dennis.
Hamilton, Thos.
Hamilton, Wm.
Hammett, Jas.
Hammett, Letha.
Hammock, Benedick.
Hammock, John.
Hammond, Abner.
Hammond, Chas.
Hammond, George.
Hampton, Benj.
Handly, Geo., Capt.
Handsard, Thos.
Hannah, James.
Hannah, Thos.
Harback, Michael.
Harbin, Wm.
Harbuck, Nicolas.
Hardy, John.
Hardy, John, Capt.
Harper, Wm.
Harrill, David.
Harrill, Joseph.
Harris, Benj.
Harris, Buckner.
Harris, David.
Harris, David.
Harris, David, Capt.
Harris, Jno.
Harris, Sam'l.
Harris, Thomas.
Harris, Walton.
Harris, Wm.
Harrison, Benjamin.

Hart, Benjamin.
Hart, John.
Hartle, Henry.
Harvey, Benj.
Harvey, Blasingame.
Harvey, Evan.
Harvey, James.
Harvey, James.
Harvey, Joel.
Harvey, Littleberry.
Harvey, Michael.
Harvey, Thomas.
Hatcher, Henry.
Hatcher, Jere.
Hatcher, John.
Hatcher, Josiah.
Hatcher, Robt.
Hatcher, Wm.
Hatchett, Archb'd, Capt.
Hawkins, James.
Hawkins, Nicholas.
Hawkins, Stephen.
Hawthorn, James.
Hawthorn, Stephen.
Hawthorne, Jno.
Haymon, Stanton.
Hays, Andrew.
Hays, Arthur, Lieut.
Heard, Barnard.
Heard, George.
Heard, Joseph.
Heard, Rich., Capt.
Heard, Stephen.
Hearthem, Wm.
Heatley, Henry.
Heatley, Robt.
Heidt, Christian J.
Henderson, Zach., Lt.
Henson, Sam'l.
Hewett, Wm.
Heyman, Stephen.
Heymond, Henry.
Hickinbotham, B.
Hickinbotham, Joseph.
Hicks, Isaac, Capt.
Hicks, John.
Hicks, Samuel.
Hill, James.

Hill, Joshua.
Hill, Richard.
Hill, Wm.
Hill, Wm.
Hillary, Christopher.
Hillary, Christopher, Lieut.
Hilliard, James.
Hines, Robert.
Hinnard, Jno.
Hinsley, Thos.
Hinton, Job.
Hobson, Mathew.
Hodge, Jno.
Hodge, Rob.
Hodge, Roger.
Hodge, Willoughby.
Hodges, Joseph.
Hoff, Samuel.
Hogg, James.
Hogg, James.
Hogg, John.
Holiday, Thomas.
Holiday, Wm.
Holliman, David.
Hollingsworth, Isaac.
Holloway, Lewis.
Holmes, John.
Holt, Beverly.
Holt, William.
Holton, Francis.
Holwell, Luther.
Hopkins, Wm.
Horn, Jesse.
Horn, Jno.
Horn, Richard.
Hornsby, Phil.
Hough, Sam'l.
Houghton, Henry.
Houghton, Thos.
House, John.
Houston, James, Surgeon.
Houston, John.
Howard, John.
Howard, John.
Howard, Julius.
Howard, Rhesa.
Howard, Wm.

Howard, Wm.
Howe, Robert.
Howe, Robert, Lieut.
Howell, Caleb.
Howell, Stephen.
Howley, Richard.
Howsley, Wm.
Hubbard, Jno.
Hubbard, Mourab.
Hubbard, Rich.
Hudson, Cuthbert.
Hudson, Nath.
Hudson, Robert.
Hudson, Sam'l.
Hudson, Wm.
Huggens, Robert.
Hughes, Nathaniel, Lieut.
Hunt, Fitzmaurice.
Hunt, Wm.
Hunter, Miles.
Huntaman, Wm.
Hutson, James, Surgeon.
———
* Duplicated.

I.
Igle, John.
Ingram, Rich.
Inman, Joshua, Capt.
Inman, Joshua, Lieut.
Inman, Shadrack, Capt.
Irelow, Levater.
Irvine, Alec.
Irvine, Wm.
Irwin, Alec.
Irwin, Hugh.
Irwin, Jared.
Irwin, Jno.
Irwin, Jno., Lawson.
Irwin, William.
Island, Absalom.
Island, Jno.

J.
Jackson, Absalom.
Jackson, Benj.
Jackson, Charles.
Jackson, Daniel.

Jackson, Drury.
Jackson, Henry.
Jackson, Isaac.
Jackson, Isaac, Col.
Jackson, James, Lieut. Co.
Jackson, Job.
Jackson, Jos.
Jackson, Michael.
Jackson, Michael.
Jackson, Peter.
Jackson, Randolph.
Jackson, Reuben.
Jackson, Robt., Capt.
Jackson, Thomas.
Jackson, Wm.
Jameson, David.
Jardine, Lewis.
Jarrett, Devereaux.
Jarrett, Robert.
Jarvis, Patrick.
Jeffries, James.
Jenkins, Arthur.
Jenkins, Benjamin.
Jenkins, Francis.
Jenkins, Michael.
Jenkins, Richard.
Jenkins, Robert.
Jenkins, Starling.
Jeter, Dudley.
Jeter, Jos.
Jinkins, Berry.
Jinkins, Royal.
John, Thomas.
Johnson, Daniel.
Johnson, Jacob.
Johnson, James.
Johnson, John.
Johnson, John, Capt.
Johnson, John H.
Johnson, John Hackner.
Johnson, Richard, Capt.
Johnson, Stephen.
Johnson, Thomas, Lieut.
Johnson, Wm., Capt.
Johnston, James.
Johnston, Jno. B.
Johnston, John.
Johnston, Wm.

# CERTIFIED LIST, GEORGIA TROOPS. 385

Johnston, Wm., Lieut.
Joiner, Benj.
Joiner, Thos.
Jones, Abraham.
Jones, Ben.
Jones, David.
Jones, Edward.
Jones, Elias.
Jones, Frederick.
Jones, Henry.
Jones, Hugh.
Jones, James.
Jones, Jesse.
Jones, Jesse.
Jones, Jno., Maj.
Jones, John.
Jones, John.
Jones, Jonathan, Capt.
Jones, Mark.
Jones, Matthew.
Jones, Michael.
Jones, Nathan.
Jones, Philip.
Jones, Robert.
Jones, Seaborn.
Jones, Simeon.
Jones, Thomas.
Jones, Wm.
Jones, Wm.
Jordan, Jacob.
Jordan, Jinsv.
Jordan John.
Jordan, Lewis.
Jordan, S.
Jordan, Sam'l.
Jordan, Wm., Lieut.
Josling, Daniel.
Jourdan, Baxton.
Jourdan, Chas.
Joyce, Alex.
Judkins, Xach.
Justice,Densey.
Justice, Isaac.

\* Duplicated.

**K.**
Kain, Henry.
Karr, Henry.
Kazey, Stephen, Jr.
Keesey, Stephen.
Keith, Sam'l.
Kell, Archibald.
Kelley, Jacob.
Kelley, Thomas.
Kelly, Edward.
Kelly, John.
Kelly, John.
Kelsey, Hugh.
Kemp, James.
Kemp, Jos.
Kemp, Thomas.
Kendall, Jeremiah.
Kendrick, Hezekiel.
Kendrick, Thomas.
Kennady, John.
Kersey, Stephen.
Ketley, Dan'l.
Kielock, Ebenezer.
Kielock, Jno.
Kilgore, Robert.
Kilgore, Jno.
Killgore, Ralph.
Kilpatrick, Thos.
Kilpatrick, Wm.
Kimborough, John, Lieut.
Kinebrew, Jacob.
King, John.
Kitchens, John.
Kitts, John.
Kneal, Patrick.

\* Duplicated.

**L.**
Lackey, Wm.
Lamar, Jas.
Lamar, Jas.
Lamar, Luke.
Lamar, Samuel.
Lamar, Thos.
Lamar, Zech.
Lamb, Abram.
Lamb, Bethial.
Lamb, Isaac.
Lamb, Thomas.
Lambeth, Wm.
Lambeth, Wm.
Lambrick (Lamback), Jno.
Lancaster, Levi.
Lancaster, Wm.
Landrum, John.
Lane, James.
Lane, Jos., Major.
Lane, Thos.
Lane, Thomas.
Lane, Wm.
Lang, John.
Langston, Samuel.
Langworthy, Ed.
Lanier, Benj.
Lanier, Clement, Capt.
Lanier, Samuel.
Lankford, Joseph.
Lankford, Moses.
Lankston, Sam'l.
Lanton, Thomas.
Laramor (Lamar), John.
Lauderdale, Jno.
Lawin, Jno.
Lawler, Jno.
Lawson, Andrew.
Lawson, Hugh.
Lawson, John.
Lawson, John, Sr.
Lawson, Roger.
Lawson, Roger, Sr.
Lawson, Thomas.
Lawson, Thompson.
Lazarus, Nicodemus.
Lea, Wm.
Leapham, Frederick, Lieut.
Leath, John.
Ledbetter, Frederick.
Ledbetter, John.
Lee, Andrew.
Lee, Joshua.
Lee, Timothy.
Lee, Timothy.
Leggett, Abner.
Leggett, John.
Lench, John.
Leslie, Jos.

386 ROSTER OF THE REVOLUTION.

Lett, Rembern.
Lett, Reuben.
Leven, Richard.
Leverett, Aaron.
Leverett, Henry.
Leverett, John.
Leverett, Robt.
Lewis, Benj.
Lewis, David, Jr.
Lewis,Evan, Surg.
Lewis, Gheza.
Lewis, Jacob.
Lewis, James.
Lewis, Joel.
Lewis, Joshua, Chaplain.
Lewis, Judah.
Lewis, Thomas.
Lewis, Wm.
Linby, Thos.
Lindow, John.
Lindsay, Dennis.
Lindsay, John, Maj.
Lineby, Wm., Lieut.
Linn, Charles.
Linn, Curtis.
Linn, John.
Linn, Thos.
Lithgrove, Andrew.
Lithgrove, Robt.
Little, Archibald.
Little, David.
Little, James.
Live, Dennis.
Livingston, Wm.
Lockhart, Benj.
Lockhart, Isaac.
Lockhart, Joel.
Locky, Thomas.
Lofton, Cornelius.
Logan, Philip.
Logan, Philip.
Long, David.
Longstreet, Daniel.
Loving, Tho.
Lowe, Aquila.
Lowe, Bev.
Lowe, Daniel.
Lowe, Geo.
Lowe, Isaac, Sr.
Lowe, Isaac, Jr.
Lowe, Jesse.
Lowe, John F.
Lowe, Jos., Maj.
Lowe, Obadiah.
Lowe, Obadiah.
Lowe, Philip, Major.
Lowe, Ralph.
Love, Wm.
Loyd, James.
Loyd, John.
Loyd, Thomas
Lucas, James.
Lucas, Jno., Capt.
Lucas, Wm.
Lunday, Theophilus.
Lunday, Thomas.
———
* Duplicated.

M.
Mabry, Reps.
McBride, Edward.
McBurnett, Daniel.
McCain, John.
McCain, John.
McCain, Thos.
McCall, John.
McCall, Thomas.
McCaller, Jas.
McCalpin, Alex.
McCalvey, Jno.
McCalvey, Wm.
McCardell,Cornelus.
McCarthy, Jno.
McCarty, Daniel.
McClendon, Isaac.
McClendon, Isaac, Sr.
McClendon, Jacob.
McClendon, Jos.
McClendon, Simeon.
McCling, Jno.
McCollough, Jacob.
McCormick, Benj.
McCormick, John.
McCormick, Jos.
McCormick, Thos.

McCoy, Dan'l.
McCullers, Wm.
McCullock, Jno.
McCullough, Pat.
McCullough, Sam'l.
McCullough, Sam'l,
 Sergt.
McCutchen, Jas.
McDonald, Hugh.
McDonald, Tekiah.
McDougal, Alex.
McDougal, Alex.
McDowell, James.
McDowell, Thos.
McDowell, Thomas, Lieut.
McDuffy, John.
McElhenry, John.
McFarland, John.
McFarland, John, Jr.
McGarry, Robt.
McGary, Ed.
McGary, Ed.
McGeary, Robert.
McGee, Hugh, Capt.
McGee, Hugh, Capt.
McGee, Lewis.
McGee, Thos.
McGee, Thos.
McGenty, Robt.
McGhee, Thos.
McGill, Jno.
McGilton, James.
McGilton, Vance.
McGruder, Merrian O.
McGruder, Zadock.
McHaney, Terry.
McIntosh, Jno., Lieut.
McIntosh, John, Colonel.
McIntosh, Lachlan,
 Lieut.
McIntosh, Lachlan,
 Maj. Gen.
McIntosh, Wm., Capt.
McKay, Jas., Capt.
McKeew, Wm.
McKenney, Henry.
McKenney, Henry.
McKenney, Jno.

## CERTIFIED LIST, GEORGIA TROOPS. 387

McKenney, Nathan.
McKinney, Travis.
McLean, Andrew.
McLean, Lewis.
McLendon, Thos.
McMannus, Jno.
McMath, Jos.
McMullen, Pat.
McMullen, Robert.
McMann, Jno.
McMurphy, Daniel.
McMurray, David.
McMurray, Wm.
McMurry, Frederick.
McMurry, Mathew.
McNabb, R.
McNail, Jesse.
McNatt, Jos.
McNatt, Sol.
McNeely, Hugh.
McNeil, Archb'd.
McNeil, Daniel.
McNeil, Michael.
McNeily, Daniel.
McNiel, ———, Col.
McNunn, John.
McOwen, Dan'l.
McRoy, James.
Maddox, John.
Maddox, Sam'l.
Maddox, Wm.
Madin, David, Lieut.
Madkins, Wm.
Maffett, Thos.
Mafield, Wm.
Mahan, David.
Mahon, Arch.
Mahon, Arch.
Mahon, Sam'l.
Maise, Joseph.
Majar, Owen.
Malone, Martin.
Maluer, Jno.
Manadee, Henry, Capt.
Manen, Drury.
Manen, John.
Manen, John, Jr.
Manhall, Abram, Chaplain.
Maning, Adrain.
Mann, John.
Mann, Jonas.
Mann, Luke.
Mannen (Manning), ———
Manning, James.
Manning, John.
Mannon, Wm.
Marberry, Wm.
Marbury, Horatio, Col.
Marbury, Leonard.
Marbury, Thos.
Marcus, Daniel.
Marcus, Elis.
Marcus, Jno.
Marlow, Wm.
Marney, Thos.
Marsh, Elijah.
Marsh, Jno.
Marsh, Nathan.
Marsh, Sol.
Marshall, Daniel.
Marshall, Jno.
Marshall, John.
Marshall, John.
Marshall, Jos.
Marshall, Levi.
Marshall, Moses.
Marshall, Nathan.
Marshall, Zach.
Martin, ———, Lieut. Col.
Martin, Barclay, Lieut.
Martin, Ed.
Martin, Ganaway.
Martin, Jacob.
Martin, James.
Martin, James.
Martin, Jno., Jr.
Martin, John, Sr.
Martin, John W.
Martin, Marshall.
Martin, Nathan.
Martin, Simon.
Martin, Wm.
Mash, Clem, Capt.
Mathews, Dan'l.
Mathews, Dan'l.
Mathews, George,
Brig. Gen.
Mathews, Isham.
Mathews, John.
Mathews, Meshack.
Mathews, Michael.
Mathews, Wm.
Mathews, Wm., Capt.
Matton, Lazarus.
Mattox, Benj.
Mattox, Jno.
Mattox, John.
Maupin, Jesse.
Maxwell, Ed.
Maxwell, James.
Maxwell, Thos.
Maxwell, Thos., Maj.
Maxwell, Thos., Capt.
May, Bailey.
May, Jos.
May, Wm.
Mayben, Mathew.
Mayborn, Wm.
Meanly, Jno., Lieut.
Meanly, John, Lieut.
Melvin, John, Capt.
Mercer, Jacob.
Mercer, James.
Mercer, Silas, Rev., Chaplain.
Merriwether, James, Capt.
Meser, Thos.
Messer, Jacob.
Messer, Silas.
Metcalf, Anthony.
Metcalf, Dunza.
Metcalf, Wm.
Meyers, Thos.
Middleton, Benedick.
Middleton, Hatton, Capt.
Middleton, Holland.
Middleton, Holland, Jr.
Middleton, Robt.
Middleton, Robt., Capt.
Middleton, Smallwood.
Middleton, Wm.
Miles, Wm.
Milledge, John.
Millen, Alex.

Millen, Charles.
Miller, Alex.
Miller, Danl.
Miller, David.
Miller, Elisha.
Miller, Elisha, Capt.
Miller, Ezekiel.
Miller, Geo.
Miller, Jesse.
Miller, Jno.
Miller, Jonathan.
Miller, Jos.
Miller, Nathaniel.
Miller, Nicholas.
Miller, Samuel.
Miller, Smith.
Miller, Wm.
Milligan, Hugh.
Mills, Wm.
Milner, John.
Milton, Jno., Capt.
Milton, Nathl.
Mims, Drury.
Mims, Jos.
Mims, Martin.
Mines, Wm.
Minnus, Fred.
Minus, John.
Mitchell, Francis.
Mitchell, Jno., Lieut.
Mitchell, John, Lieut.
Mitchell, R.
Mitchell, Thomas.
Mitchell, William.
Moak (Monk), Wm.
Moat, Daniel.
Moates, Levi.
Moates, Silas.
Moates, Wm.
Moats, Simon.
Mobley, Jno.
Mobley, John.
Mofield, Wm.
Moncrief, Josiah.
Moncrief, Sam.
Money, Jos.
Money, Pat.
Monmouth, Jos.

Montgomery, James.
Moon, George.
Moon, Jas.
Moon, Jno.
Moon, Rich.
Mooney, Jos.
Moore, Francis.
Moore, Jos.
Moore, Martin.
Moore, Samuel.
Moore, Thomas.
Moore, Wm.
Moore, Wm.
Moormes, Patrick.
Moran, Wm.
More, Mordecai.
Morel, Jno., Capt.
Morgan, Christopher.
Morgan, Jere.
Morgan, Jesse.
Morgan, Jno.
Morgan, Luke.
Morgan, Malicai.
Morgan, Philip.
Morgan, Robert.
Morgan, Step.
Morganson, Asa.
Morgin, Asa.
Moris, Jno.
Morphett (Moffatt), James.
Morphett, James.
Morphett, Thos.
Morris, James.
Morris, Reese.
Morris, Wm.
Morrison, John, Capt.
Morrison, John, Lieut.
Morton, John.
Mosby, Littleberry, Capt.
Mosby, Robert, Lieut.
Mosee, Pat.
Mosley, Jese.
Moseley, Robert.
Mosely, Benj.
Mosely, John.
Mosely, Thomas.
Mosely, Thos.

Mosely, William.
Moss, Francis.
Moss, Joshua.
Moss, Leonard.
Mott, Jos.
Mott, Uriah.
Mott, Wm.
Mott, Zach.
Mott, Zeph.
Murban, Martha.
Mullens, Malone.
Murphy, Ed.
Murphy, Miles.
Murphy, Mill.
Murphy. Willis.
Musteen, Wm.
Myers, Thos.
———
* Duplicated.

N.

Nail, Benj.
Nail, Henry.
Nail, Joseph, Capt.
Nail, Juliam.
Nail, Reuben.
Nash, Clement, Capt.
Nash, Clement, Capt.
Neaves, Wm.
Needlinger, John Gottlieb.
Neel, Thos.
Nelson, Adam.
Nelson, James.
Nelson, Jeremiah.
Nelson, John.
Nelson, Wm.
Nephew, James.
Nettles, Elisha.
Newberry, Wm.
Newell, Thomas.
Newigate, Jno., Capt.
Newman, Jno.
Newman, Joseph.
Newman, Wm.
Newsom, Sol.
Nichols, Benj.
Nicolson, Benj.
Niele, Geo.

## CERTIFIED LIST, GEORGIA TROOPS. 389

North, John.
Nowland, Philip.
Nuga, Michael.
———
* Duplicated.

### O.

Oakland, Wm.
Oates, Jeremiah.
Oates, Richard.
Obear, Josiah.
O'Bryan, James.
O'Bryant, Duncan.
Odair, Wm.
Odingchels, Chas.
Odum, Uriah.
Offutt, Ezekiel.
Offutt, Ezekiel.
Offutt, Jesse.
Offutt, John.
Offutt, Nathaniel.
Ogden, Solomon.
Oham, Wm.
Oliver, Dynowsius.
Oliver, James.
Oliver, John.
Oliver, Peter.
Ollens, Danl.
O'Neal, Axom.
O'Neal, Jno.
O'Neal, Nathan.
Oricks, James.
Osusby, Daniel.
Outlaw, Ladswick.
Owens, Ephriam.
Owens, Thos.
———
* Duplicated.

### P.

Pace, Barnard.
Pace, Thomas.
Palmer, Geo.
Palmer, John.
Palmer, Jona.
Palmer, Sol.
Pannell, Abner.
Pannell, Jos., Lieut. Col.

Pannell, Jos., Lieut. Col.
Pannell, Joseph, Lieut. Col.
Paremoore, Sol.
Paret, Wm.
Parham, Rich.
Parker, Allen.
Parker, Charles.
Parker, Daniel.
Parker, George.
Parker, James.
Parker, John, Lieut.
Parker, Jos.
Parks, Henry.
Parnell, Benj.
Parnell, Josh.
Parratt, Robert.
Parris, Peter.
Parrish, Robert.
Partin, John.
Parvill, Cader.
Paterson, Jno.
Paterson, Jno., Jr.
Paterson, Robert.
Paterson, Wm.
Patmore, Wm.
Patterson, Gideon.
Patterson, John, Sr.
Pattillo, Jno.
Patton, Thos.
Paulk, John.
Paulk, Micajah.
Paxton, Wm., Lieut.
Payne, ———, Lieut.
Payne, Saml.
Payne, Saml.
Payne, Thos., Lieut.
Payne, Wm.
Payret, Jean Pierre Andreo Defan, Capt.
Peak, John.
Peal, John.
Pearce, Jesse.
Pearce, John.
Pearce, Wm.
Pearre, Nathaniel, Lieut.
Peavry, Nathaniel, Lieut.
Peavy, Abram.

Peavy, Dial.
Peavy, John.
Peavy, Peter.
Pendall, John.
Penell, John.
Penette, Rob.
Pennington, S. R.
Pennington, Thos.
Penny, Jos.
Perkerson, Joel.
Perkins, Abram.
Perkins, Benj.
Perkins, Elijah.
Perkins, John.
Perkins, Peter.
Perkins, Richard.
Perkins, Wm.
Perry, Isaac.
Persons, Henry.
Persons, Jones.
Persons, Sam'l.
Peteete, Ben.
Peteete, Rob.
Peters, Elijah.
Peters, John.
Peters, Josiah.
Petty, Wm.
Petty, Wm.
Pew, Elijah.
Phelps, David.
Phelps, David, Sergeant.
Phelps, Samuel.
Pheny, Lackland.
Philips, David.
Philips, Joel.
Philips, Mark.
Philips, Reuben.
Philips, Samuel.
Philips, Wm.
Philips, Zach.
Phillips, Burrel.
Phillips, Dempsey.
Phillips, Hillary.
Phillips, Isham.
Phillips, Jos.
Phillips, Josiah.
Phillips, Wilder.
Pinson, Isaac.

# ROSTER OF THE REVOLUTION.

Pitman, Timothy.
Pittman, John.
Pittman, Philip.
Pittson, Wm.
Plater, Benj.
Plummer, Jos.
Plummer, Jos.
Pollett, Richard.
Porter, Benj.
Porter, John.
Porter, Thomas.
Porteus, Simon.
Potts, Jno.
Potts, Stephen, Capt.
Pounds, Reuben.
Pounds, Sam'l.
Powell, Geo.
Powell, James, Capt.
Powell, Jno.
Powell, Joshua.
Powell, Josiah.
Powell, Lewis.
Powell, Moses.
Powell, Robert.
Powell, Step.
Prather, Ed.
Prather, Samuel.
Pratt, Edw.
Pray, Job., Capt.
Prestley, David.
Prestley, David.
Price, John, Lieut.
Price, Job.
Pritchett, John.
Pruitt, Jno.
Pryor, John.
Pugh, Francis, Col.
Pugh, James.
Pugh, Jesse.
Pugh, John.
Pugh, Thos.
Pulliam, Jos.
Pulliam, Wm.
Pullone, Jos.
Putnal, Christopher.

\* Duplicated.

Q.
Quarles, Rogers.
Queen, Wm.
Querns (Kearns), John.

R.
Rae, Andrew.
Rafferty, Michl.
Ragan, Felix.
Ragan, Felix.
Ragan, John.
Ragan, John.
Ragan, Jonathan.
Ragland, Benj.
Ragling, Evan, Lieut.
Rahn, Mathew.
Raines, Robert, Capt.
Rainey, Jno.
Raior, Jamet.
Raley, Charles.
Ramling, Thos.
Ramsay, Isaac, Sr.
Ramsay, Isaac, Jr.
Ramsay, John.
Ramsay, Randal.
Ramsay, Randall.
Ramsay, Wm.
Ramsey, John.
Ramsey, John, Jr.
Ramsey, Samuel.
Rasor, Isaac.
Ratliff, James.
Ravoh, Abram.
Rawling, David.
Rawling, John W.
Rawlings, John.
Ray, Ambrose.
Ray, Berry.
Ray, Geo.
Ray, John.
Ray, Wm.
Ray, Zach.
Rayer, Ainos.
Rayfield, Isaac.
Rayne, Wm.
Rayzer, Isaac.
Rea, James, Deputy Q'mast'r.

Read, John.
Read, Wm., Dr.
Red, James.
Red, Sam'l.
Redding, George.
Redding, Rehan.
Redick, Absolom.
Reed, Samuel.
Rees, David, Judge-Advocate.
Reeves, Daniel.
Reeves, James.
Reeves, James.
Reeves, Spencer.
Reeves, Thomas.
Rench, John.
Repatoe, Wm.
Reynolds, Absalom, Fifer.
Rhodes, John.
Rice, David.
Rice, John.
Rice, Nathan.
Richards, Jacob.
Richards, Jno.
Richardson, Enos.
Richardson, Jonathan.
Richardson, Jos.
Richardson, Marmaduke.
Richardson, Walker.
Richie, John, Lieut.
Rickerson, Marmaduke.
Rickerson, Timothy.
Riddle, Wm.
Riden, Benj.
Ridge, James.
Ridgely, Fred, Surgeon's Mate.
Ridon, Jos. S.
Riggans, Darby.
Riley, Wm.
Rivers, Jarbes, Sergt.
Rivers, Jno.
Roan, James.
Roan, Tunstall.
Robard, Thos.
Roberson, Alex.
Roberson, David.
Roberson, Davie.

## CERTIFIED LIST, GEORGIA TROOPS. 391

Roberson, Samuel.
Roberson, Sylvanus.
Roberts, Amon.
Roberts, Drury.
Roberts, Francis.
Roberts, James.
Roberts, John.
Roberts, John.
Roberts, Jonas.
Robertson, Hugh, Lieut.
Robertson, John.
Robertson, Jos.
Robertson, Thomas.
Robertson, Wm.
Robertson, Zodock.
Robeson, David.
Robinson, Geo.
Rock, James.
Rodgers, Brittain.
Roe, James.
Roe, Walter.
Rogers, Burwell.
Rogers, Dread.
Rogers, Edward.
Rogers, Peleg.
Rogers, Reuben.
Rogers, Wm., Sergt.
Roquemore, Peter.
Rose, Henry.
Rose, John.
Rose, Jose.
Rose, Thomas.
Roseborn, George.
Roseboro, Wm.
Roundtree, Jesse.
Roundtree, Oliver.
Row, Walton.
Rowby, John.
Rowell, Ed.
Rowell, Howell.
Rowland, Samuel.
Rowzer, Edward.
Roy, Isaac A.
Royals, Jonathan.
Rozer, Caleb.
Rozer, Caleb.
Rozer, John.
Rucker, Jno.

Rumhey, Nathaniel.
Runn, Francis.
Runnells, Fred.
Runnells, Geo.
Runnells, Hamilton.
Runnels, Coleman,
Russell, Wm.
Rushing, Malachi.
Rushing, Mathew.
Rutherford, Samuel.
Ryals, Henry.
Ryan, John.
Ryan, James.
Ryan, Richard.
Ryan, Richard.
Ryler, Barnard.
Ryley, Jas.

\* Duplicated.

S.
Safford, Daniel.
Sallet, John.
Sallett, R.
Sallis, John.
Salsberry, Thos.
Salters, Simon.
Samford, Reuben.
Sanders, Abraham.
Sanders, Isaac.
Sanders, Jacob.
Sanders, Mark.
Sansom, Robert.
Sapp, Emanuel.
Sapp, Henry.
Sapp, John.
Satterwhile, Wm.
Savage, Loveless.
Sawyer, John.
Scott, Abrm.
Scott, Alex., Chaplain.
Scott, Benj.
Scott, Jas.
Scott, Philip.
Scott, Vason.
Scott, Wm.
Scott, Wm., Capt.
Screven, Jas., Gen'l.

Screven, Jno.
Scurry, Nicholas.
Sedmon, John.
Sedmon, John, Jr.
Sessions, Wm.
Sessums, Wm.
Settler, Daniel, Capt.
Shackleford, Jno.
Shackleford, Jos.
Shadden, David.
Shaddock, Thos.
Shadereck, Thos.
Shaffer, David.
Shamson, Thos., Sr.
Shamson, Thos., Jr.
Shannon, Owen.
Shares, Wm.
Sharp, John.
Sharp, Joshua.
Sharp, Michael.
Shartz, Edward.
Shaw, Adam.
Shaw, Daniel.
Shaw. David.
Shaw, John.
Shaw, Thomas.
Shay, David.
Sheffel, Mash.
Sheffel, Wm.
Sheffie (Sheffield), Wm.
Sheffield, John.
Sheffield, John.
Sheftall, Mardecai.
Shelby, John.
Shelton, Henry.
Shelton, Henry.
Shepherd, Benj.
Shepherd, Stephen.
Sherrar, James.
Sherrell, David.
Shick, Frank, Lieut.
Shick, Fred., Lieut.
Shields, Andrew.
Shields, Andrew.
Shields, John.
Shields, Wm.
Shower, Adam.
Shurley, William.

ROSTER OF THE REVOLUTION.

Sigman, Jno.
Sikes, Dave.
Sills, John.
Simmons, James.
Simmons, James.
Simmons, James.
Simmons, Jno.
Simmons, Malbourn.
Simmons, Philip.
Simmons, Richard.
Simmons, Stevens.
Simmons, Thomas.
Simmons, Wm.
Simmons, Wm.
Simmons, Wm., Jr.
Simpson, James.
Simpson, John.
Simpson, Sam'l.
Simpson, Timothy.
Sims, Mann.
Sims, Robert.
Sims, Wm.
Sinkfield, Wm.
Sinquefield, Sam'l.
Sitton, John.
Skinner, Isaac.
Slocomb, Elth.
Smalley, Mich'l.
Smart, Dill.
Smart, Robert.
Smith, Arthur.
Smith, Burrell.
Smith,Cornelius.
Smith, David.
Smith, Ebenezer.
Smith, Francis.
Smith, George.
Smith, Isaac.
Smith, Jacob.
Smith, James.
Smith, John.
Smith, John.
Smith, John, Jr.
Smith, Moses.
Smith, Nathan.
Smith, Nath'l.
Smith, Peyton.
Smith, Redick.

Smith, St. Sandal.
Smith, Sam'l.
Smith, Samuel.
Smith, Simeon.
Smith, Simon.
Smith, Simon.
Smith, Thos.
Smith, Thomas.
Smith, William.
Smithers, Andrew.
Snead, Dudley.
Sneads, James.
Sneads, James.
Sneed, Dudley.
Snell, David.
Snelson, James.
Snelson, Thomas, Sr.
Spencer, Wm.
Spikes, Elias.
Spikes, Nathan.
Spikes, Nathan.
Springfield, Aaron.
Spurlock, Robert.
Stafford, Samuel.
Stalling, Jas.
Stallings, Jas., Lieut.
Stallings, Ezekiel.
Stallings, Jesse.
Stallings, John.
Standford,Sam'l.
Standley, Dempsey.
Stanfard, Wm.
Stanford, John.
Stanley, Fred.
Stedman, St. James.
Stedom, Jero.
Steed, Edward.
Steed, Philip.
Stephens, Benj.
Stephens, Richard.
Stephens, Thomas.
Stevens, John.
Stewart, Chas.
Stewart, Clement.
Stewart, Daniel.
Stewart, Isaac.
Stewart, Jacob.
Stewart, James.

Stewart, Samuel.
Stewart, Wm.
Stewart, Wm.
Stickes, George.
Stiff, Wm.
Stiles, John.
Stiles, Samuel.
Stirk, Sam'l.
Stockham, Seth.
Stocks, Bender.
Stockwell, Thos.
Stokes, Samuel.
Stone, Charles.
Stone, Joshua.
Stone, Thos.
Story, Edward.
Stots, John.
Stots, Peter.
Stout, David.
Stram, James.
Strange, Eph.
Stranger, John.
Straten, Jos.
Stratt, Cornelius.
Stratt, John.
Stratt, Peter.
Stratt, Peter.
Stregel, Nicholas.
Strength, Jno.
Strickland, Sol.
String, Jno.
Stringer, John.
Stripling, Frances.
Strohaker, Rudolph.
Strong, John.
Strozier, Peter.
Stuart, John.
Stuart, John, Col.
Stuart, Robt.
Stuart, Wm.
Stubbs, Jas.
Studstell, Houston.
Studstill, Jno.
Sullivan, Owen.
Sullivan, Wm.
Summerford, Jacob, Sr.
Summerford, Jacob, Jr.
Summerlin, Dimsey.

# CERTIFIED LIST, GEORGIA TROOPS.

Summerlin, Jas.
Summerlin, James.
Summerlin, Jno.
Summerlin, R.
Summerlin, Sam'l.
Summerlin, Wm.
Summers, Dempsey.
Summers, John.
Summers, Samuel.
Sumons, Chas.
Surlock, Geo.
Sutherlin, Thos.
Suton, Philip.
Sutton, Ralph.
Suves, John.
Swain, James.
Swan, James.
Swan, John.
Sway, George.
Switzer, Leonard.
Sykes, Wm.

\* Duplicated.

T.

Talbot, Benj.
Talbott, Benj.
Talbott, John.
Tankerfield, Jno.
Tankerson, John.
Tanner, Benj.
Tanner, Joel.
Tanner, Meredith.
Tanner, Wm.
Tanneyhill, John.
Tarvin, Geo.
Tate, Andrew.
Tate, Andrew.
Tate, Rich.
Taylor, Edward.
Taylor, Henry.
Taylor, James, Capt.
Taylor, John.
Taylor, Jonah.
Taylor, Josiah.
Taylor, Josiah.
Taylor, Randolph.
Taylor, Robert, Jr.

Taylor, Thomas.
Templeton, Andrew.
Tennille, Francis, Lieut.
Terrell, Robert.
Tharpe, Jno. A.
Thayott, John.
Thomas, Allen.
Thomas, B.
Thomas, Gideon.
Thomas, Gilshot.
Thomas, Peter.
Thomas, Peter.
Thomas, Sam'l.
Thombey, Thos.
Thompson, Alex.
Thompson, Benj.
Thompson, Benj., Jr.
Thompson, David.
Thompson, Denny.
Thompson, George.
Thompson, Isham.
Thompson, Jesse.
Thompson, John.
Thompson, John, Capt.
Thompson, Jos.
Thompson, Laban.
Thompson, Peter.
Thompson, Reuben.
Thompson, Robert.
Thompson, Zachariah.
Thorn, David.
Thorn, Wm.
Thornbey, Thos.
Thornton, Samuel.
Thornton, Solomon.
Thornton, Wm.
Threadgirl, George.
Thrope, Jno. A.
Thurman, Absalom.
Thurman, Jno.
Tindall.
Tindall, Wm.
Tindall, Joshua.
Todd, Wm.
Tolar, Denny.
Tomlinson, David.
Tommeross, James.
Tommise, Jos.

Tomson, Wm., Sr.
Tomson, Wm., Sr.
Townsend, Henry.
Townsend, Thomas.
Tramell, Wm.
Trammell, Dennis.
Trammell, Wm.
Trapp, John.
Traywick, Q.
Treadwell, Wm.
Treeman, James.
Tremble, Moses.
Treutlen, Jno. A.
Truce, Benedick.
Trueman, John.
Truhantry, Henry.
Trul, John.
Tucker, George.
Tucker, Pascall.
Tucker, Robert.
Tucker, Thos., Sr.
Tucker, Thos., Jr.
Tuhantz,' Geo.
Tumer, Dennis.
Tune, Henry.
Tunis, Nicholas.
Tureman, George.
Turknett, Henry.
Turley, Wm.
Turman, Garrott.
Turner, Chas.
Turner, David.
Turner, Geo.
Turner, Henry.
Turner, John.
Turner, Peter.
Turner, Richard.
Turner, Sampson.
Turner, Samuel.
Turvisa, Nicholas.
Tweedle, John.
Twidwell, Wm.
Twiggs, Jno., Brig. Gen.
Tyner, Richard.

\* Duplicated.

## U.
Underwood, Samuel.
Upton, Ed.
Upton, Philip.
Usher, Daniel.

## V.
Vance, Patrick.
Vann, Cader.
Vann, Jas.
Van Zant, Isaac.
Vaughn, William.
Vawn, Jas.
Veazey, Jas.
Vickers, John.
Vickers, Solomon.
Vickers, Thos.

## W.
Wade, Henry.
Wade, Hezekiah, Capt.
Wade, John.
Wade, Nehemiah.
Wagner, James.
Wagnon, J. P., Lieut.
Wagnon, Jno. Peter, Lieut.
Wagnon, Thos.
Wagon, J. P., Lieut.
Wagoner, Geo.
Wagoner, Henry.
Wagoner, Wm.
Walden, Rich.
Walden, Richard.
Walden, Robt.
Walden, Willis.
Walicon, Daniel.
Walker, Edward.
Walker, Isaac, Sr.
Walker, Isaac, Jr.
Walker, Jos.
Walker, Samuel.
Walker, Sylvanus.
Walker, Sylvanus.
Walker, Wm.
Walker, Wm.
Walker, Wm., Capt.
Wall, David.

Wall, Francis.
Wall, John.
Wallace, Wm.
Wallace, Wm.
Wallace, Wm.
Waller, Benj.
Waller, Jos.
Waller, Wm.
Wallicon, Daniel.
Wallis, Absalom.
Wallis, Brittain.
Wallis, Charles.
Wallis, James.
Wallis, Jas.
Walsh, Edward.
Walsh, Patrick.
Walten, Jene.
Watley, Owen.
Watley, Sherod.
Watley, Willis.
Watley, Willis, Jr.
Watley, Worters.
Walthour, An.
Walton, Geo.
Walton, Geo., Col.
Walton, George, Capt.
Walton, Geo., Lieut.
Walton, Newell.
Walton, Robert.
Walton, William.
Ward, Benj.
Ward, Chas.
Ward, Hugh.
Ward, John.
Ward, Samuel.
Ware, Arthur.
Ware, Henry.
Ware, James.
Ware, John.
Ware, Nicholas.
Wareman, Jacob.
Warnock, Jesse.
Wasome, Jno. Palmer.
Waters, Charles.
Waters, Jas.
Waters, Rawley.
Watley, Amen.
Watley, Sherwood.

Watley, Willis.
Watley, Wootem.
Watson, Benj.
Watson, Geo.
Watson, Jacob.
Watson, John.
Watson, Leven.
Watson, Thos.
Watson, Willis.
Watts, Geo.
Watts, Jacob.
Wauden, John.
Way, Ed.
Way, John.
Way, John, Jr.
Way, Jose.
Way, Joseph.
Way, William.
Weatherford, Jas.
Weathers, Ed.
Webb, Jesse.
Webb, John.
Webb, Wm.
Webster, Abner.
Webster, Benj.
Webster, James.
Webster, Jno.
Webster, John.
Webster, Jonathan.
Webster, Thos.
Webster, Wm.
Welborn, Curtis.
Welborn, Curtis, Jr.
Welch, Benj.
Welch, Benjamin.
Welch, Caleb.
Welch, Ed., Major.
Welch, Jos.
Welch, Nicholas.
Wellbourne, David.
Wells, Benj.
Wells, Humphrey, Dr.
Wells, Jacob.
Wells, Jacob.
Wells, Jeremiah.
Wells, John.
Wells, John.
Wells, Jordan.

## CERTIFIED LIST, GEORGIA TROOPS.

Wells, Joseph.
Wells, Robert.
Welseley, Jno.
Welsher, Jere.
Welsher, Jesse.
Wereat, Jno.
Weritte, Geo.
West, Jas.
West, John.
West, Samuel.
Westbrook, Stephen.
Whare, Wm.
Whateley, Samuel.
Whateley, Walton.
Whateley, Edwin.
Whately, John.
Whately, Samuel.
Whatley, John.
Wheat, Hezekiah.
Wheat, John.
Wheeler, William.
Wheeler, William.
Wheeler, Zachariah.
Wheelis, Isham.
Whelons, Lewis.
Whilons, Lewis.
Whitaker, Samuel.
White, Demsey.
White, James, Capt.
White, James, Capt.
White, Jno., Col.
White, John.
White, John, Col.
White, Joseph.
White, Nicolas.
White, Thomas.
White, Wm.
Whitecel, John.
Whitemore, Jonathan.
Whitesides, John.
Whitt, Rich.
Whittingham, Cornelius.
Whitton, Austin.
Whitton, Philip.
Whitton, Robt.
Wiggans, John.
Wiggins, Wm.
Wikeman, John.

Wilburn, Ed.
Wilburn, Thomas.
Wilcoxson, John.
Wildair, Wm.
Wilder, Charles.
Wilder, Dred.
Wilder, Malica.
Wilder, Micajah.
Wilder, Tom.
Wilder, Willis.
Wilfred, Philip.
Wilkerson, John.
Wilkerson, Wm.
Wilkins, David.
Wilkins, Gabriel.
Wilkins, Jno.
Wilkins, William.
Willeigham, Jno.
Willey, Richard.
Williams, Burton.
Williams, Butler.
Williams, Carroll.
Williams, Chas.
Williams, Edward.
Williams, Frederick.
Williams, Geo.
Williams, Jas.
Williams, John.
Williams, John.
Williams, John.
Williams, John.
Williams, Joseph.
Williams, Joshua.
Williams, Nathl.
Williams, Saml.
Williams, Thomas.
Williams, Zach.
Williams, Zachariah.
Williamson, Adam.
Williamson, Adam.
Williamson, Chas.
Williamson, Littleton.
Williamson, Micajah.
Williamson, Micajah, Lieut. Col.
Williamson, Richard.
Williamson, Robt.
Willingham, John.

Willis, Brittain.
Willis, Joseph.
Willis, Joseph.
Willis, Joseph.
Willis, Joseph.
Willis, Mesheck.
Willis, Robert.
Willis, Robert.
Willougby, Wm.
Wilsherk, John.
Wilson, Andrew.
Wilson, David.
Wilson, Hugh.
Wilson, Jas.
Wilson, John, Capt.
Wilson, John, Lieut.
Wilson, Robert.
Wilson, Robert (Clarke).
Wilson, Robert (Lee).
Wilson, Samuel (Clarke).
Wilson, Samuel (Lee).
Windfield, John.
Winfrey, Jesse.
Winkfield, Jno.
Winn, Benj.
Winn, John.
Winn, Jos.
Winn, Peter.
Winn, Robert.
Winningham, Jno.
Wise, James.
Wise, James.
Wise, Tom.
Wise, Wm.
Wisenor, John.
Wood, Abraham.
Wood, Abraham.
Wood, Christopher.
Wood, Christopher.
Wood, Edward, Capt.
Wood, Henry.
Wood, James.
Wood, James.
Wood, James.
Wood, James, Capt.
Wood, Jas.
Wood, Joseph.
Wood, Joshua.

Wood, Richard.
Wood, Richard.
Woodruff, Joseph.
Woods, Josh.
Wood, Joshua, Jr.
Woods, Rich.
Woodworth, Thomas.
Wooten, James.
Wooten, Robt.
Wooten, Thomas.
Wooten, Thomas, Lieut.
Wormack, Jesse.
Worth, Thos.
Wourd, Benj.
Wourd, Ed.
Wourd, Eld.
Wright, Banego.
Wright, Habakkuk.
Wright, Isaac.
Wright, James.
Wright, John.
Wright, John.
Wright, Mesheck.
Wright, Shadrack, Captain.
Wright, Stephen.
Wright, William.
Wyche, Geo.
Wyche, Jno.
Wyche, Saml.
Wynn, Joshua.

———

* Duplicated.

### Y.
Yankerfield, John.
Yarbery, William.
Yarborough, Littleton.
Yarborough, Thomas.
Yates, Peter.
Yates, Peter.
York, James.
York, John.
Young, Daniel, Lieut.
Young, Edward.
Young, Isham.
Young, Jas.
Young, John, Sr.
Young, John, Jr.
Young, Jon.
Young, Wren.
Youngblood, Abraham.
Youngblood, Isaac.
Youngblood, James.
Youngblood, John, Sr.
Youngblood, John, Jr.
Youngblood, Jonathan.
Youngblood, Peter.
Younger, Wm.

———

* Duplicated.

### Z.
Zettler, Nathl.
Zinn, Jacob.

## PAID IN MONEY LIST.

Soldiers paid in money:

### B.
Barnes, Richard.
Barnes, Wm.
Bazlewood, Rich.
Bird, Benj.
Bird, John.
Brannon, Moses.
Butler, Edmond.
Butler, William.
Butts, Samuel.

### C.
Carter, James.
Clowers, Peter.

### D.
Davis, Hardy.
Douthan, Elijah.
Dulins, Henry.
Duncan, Thomas.
Duncan, Wm.

### F.
Farr, Benj.
Farr, Jno.
Ferrell, Thos.
Fowler, Henry.
Fowler, Peter.
Franklin, David, Lieut.
Franklin, Thos., Lieut.

### G.
Gauze, Henry, Lt.
Giles, Sam'l.
Gillons, Jas.

### H.
Hamilton, Wm.
Hawkins, Stephen.
Howard, John.
Howard, Wm.
Huggins, Robert.

### J.
Johnson, John.
Jones, Jesse.

### K.
Kitley, Daniel.

### L.
Lamar, James.
Linley, Thomas.
Lowe, Wm.
Loyd, James.
Loyd, John.

### M.
Masney, Thomas.

### P.
Persons, Henry.
Persons, Sam'l.
Powell, Joshua.
Pratt, Edward.
Pritchett, John.
Pritchett, Wm.

### S.
Simmerlin, Dunsey.
Simmerlin, Samuel.

CERTIFIED LIST, GEORGIA TROOPS. 397

Simmons, Wm.
Sinkfield, Wm.
Smith, Peyton.
Smith, Thomas.
Spikes, Nathan.
Spurlock, Geo.

Stockwell, Thos.
Stots, Peter.
Summerlin, Jno.
Summerlin, R.
Swan, John.
Swan, John.

W.
Wells, Jacob.
Williams, John.
Wood, James.
Worth, Thos.

## MEN WHO RECEIVED BOUNTY WARRANTS FOR REVOLUTIONARY SERVICE.

Most of these names are duplicated in Certified List No. 1 and Le Conte's lists.

A.
Adair, Bozeman.
Adams, Jno.
Akridge, Davis.
Akridge, Levy.
Allen, Robert.
Anderson, Matthew.
Anderson, Robt.
Armstrong, Alex.
Armstrong, James.
Arnold, Abraham.
Arnold, Sol.
Arnold, Solomon.
Ashurst, Wm.
Asuet, Edward.
Aycock, Richard.

B.
Bailey, George.
Bailey, Peter.
Baker, John.
Ball, John.
Barron, Jesse.
Beaseley, Harris.
Beaseley, Rich.
Bell, Zechariah.
Bennett, Reuben, Capt.
Berryhill, Merander.
Black, Lemuel.
Bledsoe, Peachy.
Boles, Henry.
Bornan, Thomas, Capt.
Bowling, Thornberry.
Bradley, John.
Bragg, Benj.

Bragg, Benj., Lieut. and Adjt.
Brand, Caswell.
Bridges, Prov.
Brockman, Bledsoe.
Brockman, Elijah.
Brockman, Elijah.
Brooks, James
Brooks, Wm.
Brown, H. Thomas.
Brown, Lemuel.
Brown, Pollard.
Browning, John.
Bruce, Daniel.
Bruce, Ward.
Bryant, Wm.
Bulloch, John.
Burges, Charles.
Burgess, Jonathan.
Burgess, Jos.
Burke, Charles.
Burkes, Ed.

C.
Carter, Thos.
Clack, James.
Clack, Wm.
Clack, Wm.
Clarke, Wm.
Cob, Caleb.
Cochran, Wm.
Colbert, Elisha.
Colley, Joseph.
Collins, James.
Colwell, Ed.

Cooper, Philip.
Cottingham, Wm.
Cowles, Wm.
Cox, Jas.
Crouch, John.
Crouch, Wm.
Culpepper, Sampson.

D.
Daggett, Wm.
Daniel, Isaac, Lieut.
Danube, John.
Davis, James.
Davis, Lewis.
Davison, Jas., Lieut
De Graffenried, John.
Diamond, John.
Dickens, Nimrod.
Dobbs, Jos., Lieut.
Dounnan, James.
Dunn, Ishmael.

E.
Early, Roderick.
Early, Wilder.
Easton, Jno.
Echols, Mitler.
Echols, Obadiah.
Edmondson, Wm.
Edwards, John.
Eiland, Isaiah.
Elder, David.
Elkins, Thos.
Elliot, Thos.
Ellis, Wm.

ROSTER OF THE REVOLUTION.

English, Henry.
Epps, Wm.
Eton, John.
Evans, Jesse, Lieut.

F.
Ferguson, Jas.
Finch, John.
Fox, James.
Franklin, Thomas.
Franklin, Wm.
Freeman, Laban.
Freeman, Roswell.
Furlow, John.

G.
Garner, Saml.
Gibson, Luke.
Ginnings, Giles.
Glascock, Lieut. Col.
Glass, Jas.
Glen, Jno.
Glenn, Wm.
Gnu, Micajah.
Gordon, Ambrose, Major.
Green, Wm.
Green, Wm., Sr.
Gresham, Wm.
Griffith, Jas.
Griggs, Geo.

H.
Haines, Robert.
Halliday, Wm.
Hammock, Jos.
Hannah, Jno.
Hanson, Wm.
Harley, Wm., Capt.
Harper, Ansel.
Harris, Edward.
Harris, Michael.
Harris, Sampson, Lieut.
Harrison, Jere.
Harrison, Olin, Lieut.
Hartsfield, Andrew.
Hatherby, Hugh.
Hendon, Isham, Capt.

Hendon, Johnson.
Hilby, Jacob.
Hill, Theophilus.
Hince, Martin.
Hinton, Wm.
Holeman, John.
Holland, Frances.
Holliday, Wm.
Hopkins, Saml.
Howard, Frances.
Hudson, Archibald.
Hudson, Ward.
Huff, John.
Huggins, Duc.
Huntsman, Michael.

I.
Ilas, John.

J.
Jackson, Jervis.
James, Wm.
Jeredeau, John.
Johnson, Abram.
Johnson, George.
Johnson, James.
Johnson, Jesse.
Johnson, Wallis.
Johnson, Wm.
Johnson, Wm.
Jones, Edward, Lieut.
Jones, Jas.
Jones, Rich.

K.
Kennan, David.

L.
Landrum, James, Capt.
Landrum, Josiah.
Landrum, Wm.
Lane, Charles.
Langford, Jas.
Law, Geo., Lieut.
Lay, Wm.
Ledbetter, Henry.
Legit, Jas.
Leigh, Ansella.

Lockett, Thos.
Longstreet, Wm.
Loyd, Moses.
Lumpkin, Wm.

M.
McCartie, Sharod.
McCirce, Rowell.
McDoreman, Bailes.
McDoreman, Bailess.
McElroy, Needham.
McElroy, Needham.
McErwin, Thos.
McKenney, Charles.
McMullen, Alex.
Martin, Matthew.
Mathews, B.
Mathews, Burwell.
Mathews, Jno.
Mathews, Rich.
Mathews, Rich.
Mathews, Thos.
Maxwell, Richard.
May, Saml.
Mays, Andrew.
Mead, Minor.
Meador, Joel.
Meador, Jonas.
Middleton, Jno.
Minis, Jas.
Mitchell, Wm.
Moffett, Gable.
Montcrief, Saml.
Moon, John.
Moore, Abednego.
Moore, Alexander.
Moore, Jas.
Moore, Martin.
Morris, Garrett.

N.
Nalls, Richard, Lieut.
Newlin, Mathias.
Nixon, Jno.
Nixon, Jos.
Norton, Jas.
Norton, Jonathan.
Norton, Wm., Lieut.

## CERTIFIED LIST, GEORGIA TROOPS. 399

### O.
Oakes, Jonathan.
O'Barre, Robt.
Olive, John.
Orr, Christopher.
Orr, John.
Owens, Thos.

### P.
Pain, Hail.
Parker, Wm.
Patrick, ———.
Patrick, Josia.
Pattison, Frederick.
Patton, Thos., Capt.
Phillips, Overton.
Pope, Jno., Capt.
Porsten, Wm.
Poss, Nicholas.
Potts, Moses, Lieut.
Pounds, John.
Powell, Jno.
Pullens, ———, Major.

### R.
Rafferty, Richard.
Rainey, Daniel.
Rainey, Jno.
Reddy, James.
Reed, Jacob.
Richards, Jeremiah.
Richardson, Allen.
Robertson, Samuel.
Rosberry, Jos.
Ross, John, Sergeant.
Runley, George.
Runnells, Green.
Ryan, ———, Major.

### S.
St. John, John.
Samuels, Joseph.
Sandell, Jno.
Sanson, Thos.
Searce, Wm.
Simmons, Jas.
Simpson, John.
Smith, John.
Smith, Samuel.
Smith, Wm.
Smith, Wm.
Smith, Wm.
Sneed, Davis.
Stallings, John, Col.
Standbanks, John.
Stephens, Wm.
Stewart, Reuben.
Stirley, Jesse.
Stone, Thompson.
Strand, Philip.
Strawn, Balson.
Strong, Robert.
Stroud, Owen.
Stroud, Sherod.
Stuman, Jno.
Sykes, Josua.

### T.
Terrell, ———.
Terrell, Jos.
Terrell, Thomas.
Terry, Alexander.
Thompson, Richard.
Thrasher, David.
Toombs, Robt.
Traywick, Spencer.
Trueall, Thomas.
Truball, John.
Tucker, Woodward.

### V.
Varner, Matthew.
Varner, Thos.

### W.
Wade, Thos.
Wallis, James.
Walton, Jno.
Wambersie, Emanuel.
Ward, Charles.
Ward, John.
Watkins, Robt.
Watkins, Thomas, Lieut.
Watson, John.
Webb, Levi.
Whelton, Robt.
Whittle, Boling.
Wiatt, John.
Wilcox, Thos.
Wilkes, Moses.
Williams, John.
Williamson, Charles, Capt.
Williamson, Peter.
Williamson, Wm.
Williford, Jas.
Willingham, Jesse.
Winn, John.
Winters, Jas.
Wood, Etheldred, Lt.
Wood, Jas.
Wood, James, Capt.
Wood, Jno.
Wooten, Richard, Lieut.
Wright, W. G.

### Y.
Young, Henry.
Young, Leonard.
Young, Stanford.

### Z.
Zoobers (Subers), Joshua.

## SOLDIERS' GRANTS LIST.

Men who received soldiers' grants:

### A.
Alford, James.
Ayers, Baker.

### B.
Ballard, Joseph.
Barclay, Jno.
Beckham, John.
Bennett, John, heirs of.
Betsall, Isaac.

Bonner, Geo.
Borland, Andrew.
Bowie, James.
Braswell, Robert.
Brigg, Wm.
Buford, Wm.
Burner, Rich.
Bush, Jno.
Bussey, Gideon.

C.
Call, Richard.
Camp, Samuel.
Carnes, Peter.
Carnes, Thomas P.
Chance, Vincent.
Chandler, Abednego.
Clark, Bolling.
Clarke, Christopher.
Cleveland, Larkin.
Collier, Edward.
Collier, James.
Connelly, John W.
Conwell, Jesse.
Cox, Zach.
Creswell, Robt.
Crosby, Wm.
Cruddy, Wm.
Curry, Robt.
Curton, B.

D.
Dalton, Thos.
Dary, Ambrose.
Debosk, Peter.
Diamond, William.
Dicks, David.
Dickson, David.
Dickson, Michael.
Dixon, Robert.
Dounaphan, Elijah.
Duck, Jeremiah.

F.
Fail, Thomas.
Fair, Peter.
Fluker, George.
Fouche, Jonas.

Fuller, Isham.

G.
Galphin, George.
Gascoign, Richard.
Gilbert, Charles.
Goode, Edward.
Goodwynn, Theod.
Gotcher, Henry.
Gray, Joshua.
Green, Daniel.
Greers, Thos.
Gresham, Archd.
Grier, Gilbert.
Guy, Wm.

H.
Hamlin, Richard.
Hammett, Wm.
Harnett, Jas.
Harper, George.
Harrington, Jno.
Harrington, Jno.
Harris, Nathan.
Harris, Sampson.
Harvey, Benj.
Haughton, Jos.
Haurst, Sammuel.
Hawkins, Abimelech.
Hay, Wm.
Headspeth, Chas.
Heatly, John.
Hicks, Ed.
Hicks, Nathl.
Hightower, William.
Hinton, Hardy.
Hobson, Briggs.
Hodges, James.
Holden, Thos.
Holliday, Ambrose.
Holly, Jonathan.
Hooper, Absolam.
Housley, Newell.
Houston, Henry.
Howell, Caleb.
Hubbard, Benj.
Huckably, Isham.
Hudson, Hall.

Humphreys, Jos.
Hunt, Fitzmaurice.
Hunt, Wm.
Hutchinson, James.

J.
Jack, John.
Jackson, Abram.
Jackson, James.
Jameson, Wm.
Johnson, Nathan.
Jones, Chas.
Jordan, Saml.

K.
Kenny, Ed.
Kenrick, James.
Kieth, John.
Kieth, Lem.
King, John.

L.
Langford, Wyatt.
Lee, Joshua.
Leonard, John.
Lewis, Wm.
Lindsay, James.
Lockhart, Rich.
Longstreet, Daniel.
Longstreet, Wm.
Lord, Wm.
Loud, John.

M.
McConnell, John.
McCracken, Wm.
McCutchin, James.
McDonald, John.
McGee, Shadrach.
Madison, James.
Martin, Jacob.
Mays, John.
Meanly, Jno.
Moore, Mordecai.
Morrison, John.

N.
Nailor, Geo.

# CERTIFIED LIST, GEORGIA TROOPS. 401

Neal, Thomas.
Nelson, Thomas.
Newman, Geo.
Niblack, William.

**O.**
Osgood, Josiah.

**P.**
Pack, John.
Parker, Daniel.
Payne, Moses.
Phillips, John.
Pickerton, John.
Pierson, John.
Pittman, Henry.
Pollard, Wm.
Pope, Wylie.
Price, Job.
Purtin, Robert.

**R.**
Reddick, Jacob.
Reese, Benj.
Reeves, Geo.
Roberts, Amon.
Robinson, John.

Russell, David.

**S.**
Sartain, Wm.
Savage, Robert.
Scarborough, Moses.
Sebech, John.
Segar, Geo.
Shaw, Wm.
Shelman, John.
Shelman, Micheal.
Shepherd, Charles.
Sherrard, Jos.
Shields, Wm.
Shuffle, John.
Simmeron, Burney.
Singleton, Robert.
Smith, John E.
Solomon, Lewis.
Spinkston, Daniel.
Stallings, Ezekiel.
Strong, Wm.
Sturgis, Andrew.

**T.**
Talbatt, Jesse.
Tarpley, Mark.

Tate, Robert.
Thurman, David.
Trimble, Moses.
Turner, Asa.

**V.**
Vining, Thomas.

**W.**
Wadsworth, Thos.
Waldon, John.
Wallis, Cammell.
Wallis, Chanet.
Wallis, Micajah.
Ward, Benj.
Warren, John.
Watts, John.
Webb, Sion.
Wheeler, Wm.
Wilborme, Wm.
Wilson, Benj.
Wise, Sherard.
Wood, Josiah.
Wyatt, Picton.

**Z.**
Zachary, Bartholomew.
Zeigler, Geo.

(See affidavit at head of list.)

## NAMES TO BE ERASED FROM LIST OF GEORGIA REVOLUTIONARY SOLDIERS PUBLISHED IN OUR THIRD REPORT, AS APPENDIX E.

The following Wilkes County names are to be erased from the main alphabetical list, the names appearing twice:

### WILKES COUNTY LIST.

Barnes, William, Private.
Brown, James, Private.
Carter, James, Private.
Clowers, Peter, Private.
Davis, Hardy, Private.
Giles, Sam, Private.
Howard, William, Private.
Johnson, John, Private.
Jones, Jesse, Private.
Lamar, Jas., Private.
Powell, Joshua, Private.
Reeves, James, Private.
Roberson, David, Private.
Simmons, William, Private.
Spikes, Nathan, Private.
Stewart, William, Private.
Strats, John, Private.
Strats, Peter, Private.
Summerlin, James, Private.
Williams, John, Private.
Wood, James, Private.

The following are to be erased because it can not be proven from the records that they were Revolutionary soldiers:

## A.
Adkins, William, Private, certified by Col. E. Clark.
Alexander, Asa, Private, certified by Col. E. Clark.
Autrey, Alexander, Captain, certified by Col. E. Clark.
Ayres, Thomas, Private, certified by Col. G. Lee.

## B.
Beckham, S'm'n, lottery 1827, Monroe County.
Bugg, Ed., Private, certified by Col. G. Lee.
Bugg, Jere., Lieutenant-Colonel, certified by John Twiggs, B. G.

## C.
Carson, Thomas, Private, certified by Col. E. Clark.
Carter, Pat., Private, certified by Col. E. Clark.
Catchings, Joseph, certified by Col. E. Clark.
Chapman, Jno., Sergeant, certified by Col. E. Clark.
Childers, David, certified by Col. Sam Elbert.
Cole, John, Jr., Private, certified by Col. E. Clark.
Crain, Lewis, Private, certified by Col. James Jackson.
Curl, Henry, Private, certified by Col. E. Clark.

## D.
Dabney, Austen, Private, certified by Col. E. Clark.
Darsey, James, Private, certified by Col. E. Clark.
Davies, John, Private, certified by John Twiggs, B. G.
Duhart, John (a).

## L.
Lackey, Thomas, Private, certified by Col. E. Clark.
Lamar, Samuel, Private, certified by John Twiggs, B. G.
Legget, John, Private, certified by Col. E. Clark.

## M.
Maddox, John, bounty granted as a soldier.
Manen, Drury, Private, certified by Col. E. Clark.

## R.
Rasor, Isaac, bounty granted.

## S.
Sapp, William (b), Private, certified by Col. Asa Emanuel.
Stripling, Frances, Private, certified by Col. E. Clark.
Summers, James (b), Private, certified by Col. E. Clark.
(a) This name appears as Duchart, John, in our third report.
(b) This name did not appear in the list as printed in our third report.

## T.
Thompson, Jos., Private, certified by Col. Greenberry Lee.
Tomlinson, David, Lieutenant, certified by Captain William Ames.

## CERTIFIED LIST, GEORGIA TROOPS. 403

Treutlen, John Adams (a); put down private, but was colonel. (See "Commission Book B," p. 277.)
Tucker, George, Private, certified by Col. E. Clark.
Tweddle, John, Private, certified by Col. E. Clark

### W.

Walker, William, Captain, certified by Col. B. Few.
Watson, Geo., Private, certified by Col. E. Clark.
White, Demsey, Private, certified by Col. James Jackson.
Wood, James, Private, certified by Lieutenant Nathaniel Pierre.

The soldiers whose names appear below served in the Indian Wars succeeding the Revolution, but were not Revolutionary soldiers. The names marked with an asterisk (*) do not appear in our third report:

### RECORD OF EXECUTIVE COUNCIL, 1790-1791, PAGE 64 (b).

*Berrihill, Merander, Lieut.
*Burke, Charles, Lieut.
*Cowles, William, Captain.
*Fox, James, Lieutenant.
Glascock, Thos., Lieut.-Col.
*Gordon, Ambroso, Major.
*Harris, James, Captain.
*Howell, John, Captain.
*Leigh, Ansoln, Lieutenant.
*Longstreet, Wm., 2d Lieut.
Low, George, Lieutenant.
*McLane, Daniel, Captain, Lieutenant.
*Pearre, James, Captain.
Stallings, James, Colonel.
*Walton, John C., Lieut.
*Wambessie, Emanuel, Lieut.
*Ward, Charles, Lieut.
*Watkins, Robert, Captain.
*Watkins, Thomas, 1st Lieut.

### RECORD OF EXECUTIVE COUNCIL, 1790-1791, PAGES 112-113 (b).

*Armstrong, James, Lieut.
*Ashurst, William, Lieut.
Aycock, Richard, Lieut.
*Bennett, Reuben, Captain.
*Black, Lemuel, Lieut.
*Bridges, Prior, Lieut.
Brooks, James, Lieut.
Brown, Thomas, Lieut.
*Culpepper, Sampson, Lieut.
*Davison, James, Lieut.
*Diamond, John, Captain.
*Doreman, James, Captain.
Dukes, William, Captain.
*Evans, Jesse, Lieutenant.
Freeman, John, Captain.
*Hannah, John, Captain.
*Harris, Sampson, Lieut.
*Hill, Theopholis, Lieut.
*Horley, William, Lieut.
*Jordan, Emanuel, Captain.
*Lane, Charles, Captain.
*Lucky, James, Captain.
*McFall, John, Lieutenant.
'McKenny, Charles, Lieut.
*Martin, Matthew, Lieut.
*Moore, Abednego, Lieut.
*Nalls, Richard, Lieut.
*Orr, Christopher, Lieut.
*Patrick, Paul, Lieut.
*Patton, Samuel, Lieut.
*Patton, Thomas, Lieut.
*Pope, John, Captain.
*Potts, Moses, Lieutenant.
*Rafferty, Richard, Lieut.
*Simmons, Asa, Lieut.
*Terrill, Thomas, Lieut.
*Thompson, James, Lieut.
*Toombs, Robert, Lieut.
*Webb, Claborn, Lieut.
*Willingham, Jesse, Capt.
*Wooten, Richard, Lieut.
Wylly, John, Lieutenant.

(a) This name, as printed in our third report, page 361, appears merely as "Treutlen, Jno. A.," without distinction of rank.

(b) These page numbers refer to pages of records in the office of the Secretary of the State, at Atlanta.

## MUSTER ROLL OF COL. JOHN STEWART REGIMENT.

Adams, John, Private.
*Akredge, Davis, Private.
*Anderson, Matthew, Priv.
*Angling, John, Private.
*Arnold, Absolem, Private.
*Arnold, Soloman, Private.
*Askedge, Levy, Private.
*Bailey, George, Private.
*Bailey, Peter, Private.
Baker, John, Private.
*Ball, John, Private.
*Beasley, Harris, Private.
*Beasley, Richard, Private.
*Bell, Zachariah, Private.
Bledsoe, Peachy, Private.
*Early, Wilder.
*Easton, John, Private.
*Echols, Miller.
*Echols, Obidah.
*Ector, Joseph.
*Edmonson, Crawford, Priv.
*Edwards, Willis, Private.
*Elder, David.
*Elkins, Thomas, Private.
*Ellis, William, Private.
*English, Henry, Private.
*Epps, William.
*Eton, John.
*Ferguson, James, Private.
*Finch, John, Private.
Franklin, William, Priv.
*Freeman, Laban, Private.
*Freeman, Roswell, Private.
*Gan, Mocajah.
*Garner, Samuel.
*Gibson, Luke, Private.
*Ginnings, Giles, Private.
*Glass, James, Private.
*Gossett, John.
Green, William.
*Green, William, Sr.
*Gresham, William, Priv.
*Griffith, James, Private.
*Hanson, William.
*Harper, Ansil.
*Harris, Robert, Private.

*Boles, Henry, Private.
*Boling, Tomberry, Private.
*Bradley, John, Private.
*Brand, Caswell.
*Briant, William, Private.
*Brockman, Bledsoe, Priv.
*Brockman, Elijah, Private.
*Brooks, William, Private.
*Brown, Lemuel, Private.
*Brown, Thomas H., Priv.
*Browning, John, Private.
*Bruce, Ward, Private.
*Bullock, John, Private.
*Burger, Charles, Private.
*Burgess, Jonathan, Priv.
Jent, Zachariah, Private.
*Jinkins, James, Private.
*Jlos, Hohn, Private.
*Johnson, Abram, Private.
*Johnson, Jesse, Private.
*Johnson, Martin, Private.
*Johnson, Wallis, Private.
Johnson, William, Private.
Jones, Edward, Private.
*Jones, Joseph, Private.
Jones, Richard, Private.
*Landrum, James, Captain.
*Landrum, Josiah, Private.
*Landrum, William, Priv.
*Landford, James, Private.
*Lay, William, Private.
*Lloyd, Moses, Private.
*Lumkin, William, Private.
*McCartin, Sharod, Private.
*McCree, Rowell, Private.
*McDorman, Bales, Private.
*McElroy, Needham, Priv.
*McEwen, Thomas, Private.
*Mathews, Burwell, Priv.
*Mathews, Richard, Priv.
*Maxwell, Richard, Private.
*May, Samuel, Private.
*Mays, Andrew, Private.
*Middleton, John, Private.
Mitchell, Thomas, Private.
Mitchell, William, Private.

*Burgess, Joseph, Private.
*Callingham, William.
*Colley, Joe, Private.
*Collins, James.
*Colwell, Edward, Private.
*Cox, Caleb.
*Crouch, John.
*Crow, Alexander.
*Dacus, Lewis, Private.
*Daggett, William.
*Daniel, Isaac, Lieutenant.
*Danube, John.
De Graffenreid, John, Priv.
*Dicking, Nimrod.
*Dunn, Ishmael, Private.
*Patrick, Josia, Private.
*Pattison, Frederick, Priv.
*Phelps, Overton, Private.
*Porter, William, Private.
*Poss, Nicholas, Private.
*Pound, John, Private.
*Powell, Johnson, Private.
Rainey, Daniel, Private.
Rainey, John, Private.
Raspberry, Joseph, Priv.
*Reed, Jacob, Private.
*Richards, Jeremiah, Priv.
*Richardson, Allen, Private.
*Robertson, Samuel, Priv.
*Runnells, Green, Private.
*St. John, John, Private.
*Sams, Joseph, Private.
*Sanson, Thomas, Private.
Simmons, James, Private.
Simpson, John, Private.
*Smith, Jobe, Private.
Smith, William, Private.
*Stancel, John, Private.
*Starley, Jesse, Private.
*Stephens, William, Priv.
*Stewart, Reuben, Private.
*Stone, Thompson, Private.
*Strawn, Balsam, Private.
Strong, John, Private.
*Strong, Robert, Private.
*Stroud, Owen, Private.

## CERTIFIED LIST, GEORGIA TROOPS. 405

*Hartsfield, Andrew, Priv.
*Helby, Jacob, Jr., Private.
*Hendon, Isham, Captain.
*Hendon, Johnson, Private.
*Hinbon, William, Private.
*Hince, Martin, Private.
*Holeman, John.
*Holland, Francis, Private.
*Hopkins, Samuel.
*Howard, Hiram, Private.
*Hudson, Archibald.
*Hudson, Ward, Private.
*Huff, John.
*Hugins, Daniel, Private.
Jackson, Charles, Private.
*James, Williamson, Priv.
*Wiat, John.
*Wilkes, Moses, Private.
*Williamson, Peter, Private.
*Williamson, William, Priv.
*Moffett, Gable, Private.
*Moore, Alexander, Private.
*Moore, James, Private.
*Moore, John, Private.
Morris, James, Private.
*Morriss, Garrett, Private.
*Nixon, John, Private.
*Nixon, Joseph, Private.
*Norton, James, Private.
*Norton, Jonathan, Private.
*Norton, William, Lieut.
*Oakes, Jonathan, Private.
*Olive, John, Private.
*Pain, Fail, Private.
*Parker, William, Private.
*Parr, William, Private.
Winn, John, Ensign.
*Wood, John.
*Wright, W. G.
*Young, Henry, Private.
*Stroud, Sharol, Private.
*Stubblefield, William, Priv.
*Telong, Joshua, Lieut.
*Terry, Alexander, Private.
*Thompson, Richard, Priv.
*Thrasher, David, Private.
*Traywick, Spencer, Priv.
*Varner, Matthew, Private.
*Varnerm, Thomas, Private.
*Wade, Thomas.
Wallis, James.
Ward, John, Private.
*Warters, James, Private.
*Watson, John, Private.
*Webb, Levi, Private.
*Whittle, Boling.
*Young, Leonard, Private.
*Young, Stanford, Private.
*Zoobes, Joshua, Private.

B. F. JOHNSON.

Office Secretary of State,
Atlanta, Ga., Oct. 17, 1902.

I hereby certify that the thirteen pages hereto contain the names of Revolutionary soldiers appearing twice in the first list of Revolutionary soldiers furnished the Atlanta and Piedmont Continental Chapters, under the direction of Mrs. William Lawson Peel.

Given under my hand and official seal this 17th October, 1902.

PHILIP COOK, Sec. of State.

## THE HARVEY LIST.

Miss Margaret B. Harvey's alphabetical list of Georgia Revolutionary Soldiers, of all ranks and names, including Continentals, Militia, Provincials, Minute Men, Rangers, Partisans, Mariners, Sons of Liberty, Independents, etc. Published as Appendix F, in the Third Annual Report of the National Society, D. A. R., to the Smithsonian Institution. Senate Documents, Volume 16, Number 219, Fifty-sixth Congress, Second Session, 1900-1901, pp. 369-393.

NOTE.—The following list contained, when presented, nearly 300 more names than are in it now. Names which were in all respects identical with some in Appendix E (see Certified List Number 1) were eliminated to save space. Many names, however, which occurred in the first list without titles have been retained here, because of the added titles which facilitate identification.

A.

Aaron, William, Private.

Adams, David, Colonel.
Adams, Edmund, Lieutenant.

Adams, Francis.
Adams, James, Jr.
Adams, Thomas, Sergeant.
Adkins, Charles, Sr.
Aikins, John.
Aitkins, James, Chaplain.
Akens, James.
Akin, James.
Akins, James (1).
Akins, James (2).
Akins, William, Sergeant.
Albritton, John.
Aldredge, William.
Alexander, ———.
Alexander, Adam, Surgeon's Mate.
Alexander, Hugh, Lieutenant.
Alexander, James, Captain.
Allen, Philip.
Allman, Philip; Son of Liberty; member of Provincial Congress.
Allread, Elias.
Allread, Elias, Sr.
Ambrose, David.
Anders, Owen.
Anderson, ———, Captain.
Anderson, ———, Lieutenant.
Anderson, Charles.
Anderson, George.
Anderson, James, Lieutenant.
Anderson, John, Lieutenant.
Anderson, John.
S. Doc. 219—24.
Andrew, ———.
Andrew, Benjamin, Sr.; Son of Liberty; member of Committee of Correspondence, Supreme Executive Council, and Provincial Congress.
Andrew, Benjamin.
Andrew, Francis,
Andrew, Isham.
Andrews, John, Lieutenant.
Andrews, Owen.
Andrews, William, Sergeant.
Anglin, Henry.
Antony, ———, Captain of Galley.
Antony, Alexander.
Antony, John.

Antrobus, Isaac, Adjutant.
Arnaud, John P.
Arnett, John.
Arnold, William.
Arthur, Franiis, Lieutenant.
Ashby, ———, Captain.
Atkin, Agrippa.
Atkinson, Joseph, Captain.
Austin, Absolom, Captain.
Austin, Richard.
Ayres, Abner, Captain.
Ayres, Abram, Captain.

B.

Barber, James.
Bacon, John, Lieutenant.
Bacon, John, Sr; member of Provincial Congress; Captain of Galley.
Bacon, Jonathan, Lieutenant.
Bacon, Joseph.
Bacon, Thomas, Lieutenant.
Bacon, William, Jr.; Son of Liberty; member of Provincial Congress.
Bagby, John.
Baggett, Joshia.
Bailey, James.
Bailey, William, Lieutenant.
Bailie, ———, Lieutenant.
Baker, ———.
Baker, Beal.
Baker, Benjamin.
Baker, Charles.
Baker, Elias.
Baker, John, Captain.
Baker, John, Private.
Baker, John, Sr., Colonel; Son of Liberty; member of Committee of Correspondence, and of Provincial Congress.
Baker, William, Private.
Baker, William, Sr., Major, Colonel; Son of Liberty; member of Provincial Congress.
Baker, William, Jr., Lieutenant; Son of Liberty; member of Provincial Congress.
Baldry, Isaac K.

## THE HARVEY LIST.

Baldwin, Abraham; Son of Liberty; Delegate to Continental Congress.
Baldwin, David, Captain
Ball, Edward, Lieutenant; member of Provincial Congress.
Ballard, Joshua.
Ballenger, John, interpreter (to Indians).
Banks, John.
Banks, Sutton; Son of Liberty; member of Committee of Correspondence.
Barber, George, Lieutenant, Captain.
Bard, John, Captain.
Bard, Peter; Son of Liberty; member of Provincial Congress.
Barker, C.
Barkley, William.
Barnard, John, Captain.
Barnard, John, Major; member of Provincial Congress.
Barnard, Robert, Lieutenant.
Barnes, Richard.
Barnett, John, Captain.
Barnett, Nat.
Barnett, Sion, Corporal.
Barnett, William, Captain.
Barnhill, Hohn.
Barnwell, ———, Major.
Barnwell, John.
Barr, James.
Barrett, Lewes.
Barron, Thomas.
Barry, Andrew.
Barton, Willoughby, Captain.
Baskin, James, Lieutenant.
Baskin, William, Captain.
Bateman, ———.
Battle, William, Lamar.
Baugh, Alexander C., Lieutenant.
Baxter, Andrew.
Baxter, John, Corporal.
Bayley, Joseph Lieutenant.
Bayly, James, Lieutenant.
Beal, Archibald.
Beale, Jeremiah, Captain.
Beale, William.
Beale, Zephaniah, Captain.

Bean, William.
Beard, Moses.
Beard, Robert.
Beasley, Amnrose.
Beasley, Richard.
Beasley, Royland.
Beasley, William.
Beckham, Samuel, Lieutenant.
Beckom, Samuel, Lieutenant.
Bedell, Absalom, Major.
Bedingfield, Charles.
Beers, Matthew.
Beezly, Burrell.
Beezly, Joseph.
Benefield, John; Son of Liberty; member of Committee of Correspondence.
Bennett, John.
Bennis, John, Captain.
Benson, Enoch.
Bentley, ———, Captain.
Bentley, ———, Lieutenant.
Benton, Joseph, Sr.
Benton, Joseph.
Beraud, ———, Captain.
Bergsterner, Daniel, Lieut.
Berk, James.
Bernard, ———, Captain.
Berrien, ———. Captain.
Berrien, John.
Berrien, John, Lieutenant, Captain, Brigade Major.
Berry, John, 1.
Berry, John, 2.
Berry, William.
Beville, George, Ensign, Surgeon's Mate.
Bickham, Abner, Captain.
Bierry, T; Son of Liberty.
Bilbo, John, Captain.
Bird, Herman.
Bird, Thompson.
Bird, William.
Birmingham, James.
Bishop, Golden.
Bishop, William.
Bivins, William.
Black, ———, Captain.

Black, David.
Black, William, Lieutenant.
Black, William, Private.
Blackshear, Edmond.
Blackshear, Edward.
Blair, James.
Bledsoe, Benjamin.
Bledsoe, Miller.
Blount, Isaac.
Blount, Jacob, Captain.
Blount, Jacob, Surgeon's Mate, Surgeon.
Blount, Stephen, Lieutenant.
Blount, Jacob, Lieutenant.
Bohan, Joseph, Captain.
Bolton, Robert.
Bond, Richard.
Bonds, Joseph.
Bonnell, Anthony, Lieutenant.
Bonnell, Daniel, Major.
Bonnell, David, Major.
Bonnell, John.
Bonner, ———, Captain.
Bonner, Henry.
Bonner, Sherwood.
Booker, Gideon, Captain.
Boon, Jesse.
Booth, Abraham.
Booth, David.
Bostick, Chesley, Captain (Bostwick).
Bostick, Littlebury, Captain.
Bosworth, Jacob.
Botsford, Edmond, Chaplain.
Bourquin, David, Francis, Major.
Bourquin, Henry.
Bourquin, Henry, Davis; Son of Liberty; member of Committee of Correspondence.
Bowen, Elijah.
Bowen, John.
Bowen, Oliver; Son of Liberty; member of Provincial Congress; Captain of Galley; Commodore.
Bowen, Samuel, Captain.
Bowen, Stephen.
Bowling, Edward, Sergeant.
Box. Philip; member of Provincial Congress; Commissary of Hospital.

Boykin, Francis, Major.
Braddock, David, Captain of Galley.
Braddock, James, Captain.
Bradford, William.
Bradley, John, Captain of Galley.
Bradley, M.
Bradley, Richard.
Bradley, William, Sergeant.
Bradwell, Thomas.
Brady, David, Hospital Chaplain.
Brady, William, Sergeant, Lieutenant.
Bragg, William.
Braidie, David, Surgeon.
Bramlett, Reuben.
Brand, William.
Branham, ———, Col.
Branham, Samuel.
Branham, Spencer.
Brantley, Amos.
Brantley, Britton.
Brasel, Bird.
Braslen, Nicholas, Lieut.
Brazil, Byrd.
Brewster, Hugh.
Brwester, Sherriff.
Briant, John, Lieutenant.
Brice, Jacob, Major.
Brisbane, Adam, Fowler; Son of Liberty; member of Provincial Congress; member of Council.
Brock, William, Lieutenant.
Brodie, David, Surgeon.
Brooke, Robert.
Brooks, George.
Brooks, Middleton.
Brooks, Robert.
Brossard, Celeron, Captain (Brusard).
Brown, ———, Lieutenant.
Brown, Ambrose.
Brown, Benjamin.
Brown, Ephraim.
Brown, Francis, Captain.
Brown, Jacob.
Brown, James, Adjutant.
Brown, James, Wagoner.
Brown, John, Mariner.
Brown, Joseph, Wagoner.
Brown, Robert.

Brown, Thomas, Lieutenant.
Brown, Uriah.
Brown, Walter.
Brownson, Nathan, Surgeon; member of Provincial Congress; Captain; capt.; Governor of Georgia.
Bruner, Benjamin, Lieutenant.
Brusard, Celerine, Captain (Brossard, De Brossard).
Bruton, James.
Bryan, Ezekiel.
Bryan, Hugh; Son of Liberty; member of Provincial Congress.
Bryan, James; Lieutenant, Captain.
Bryan, Jonathan; Son of Liberty; member of Committee of Correspondence, Supreme Executive Council, and Provincial Congress.
Bryan, Thomas.
Bryan, William; Son of Liberty; member of Provincial Congress.
Brydie, David, Lieutenant.
Bryson, ———, Lieutenant.
Bryson, James.
Bryson, John.
Buchannan, George, Sergeant.
Buchannan, James.
Bucholter, Peter.
Budd, Charles, Captain.
Buff, Michael.
Bugg, Edmond; Son of Liberty; member of General Assembly.
Bugg, Jeremiah, Lieutenant, Colonel.
Bugg, Sherwood, Captain.
Bugg, William, Lieutenant, Captain.
Bulloch, Archibald; son of Liberty; member of Provincial Congress; Colonel, Brigadier-General; Mayor of Savannah; Governor of Georgia.
Bulloch, James, Captain; member of Provincial Congress.
Bolloch, John.
Bulloch, Hawkins.
Bullough, Elias.
Bunster, William.
Burgamy, John.
Burgamy, William.
Burgess, Edward.

Burgess, Josiah.
Burnett, ———, Colonel.
Burnett, B., Captain.
Burnett, Daniel.
Burnett, Ichabod, Major.
Burnett, John, Captain.
Burney, Andrew; Son of Liberty; member of Provincial Congress.
Burnley, ———, Lieutenant.
Burnley, Henry.
Burns, Andrew; Son of Liberty; member of Provincial Congress.
Burris, John, Captain.
Burroughs, John, Major.
Burton, Thomas; Son of Liberty; member of Provincial Congress.
Bush, Prescott.
Butler, Benjamin, Lieutenant.
Butler, Elisha; Son of Liberty; member of Committee of Correspondence, and Council of Safety.
Butler, James.
Butler, Joseph; Son of Liberty; member of Provincial Congress.
Butler, Josiah.
Butler, Patrick.
Butler, Pierce (mentioned in "British Black List" as "rebel officer").
Butler, Shem; Son of Liberty; member of Assembly.
Butry, Z.
Buxton, Samuel.
Bynum, Drury.

C.

Cabos, John.
Cade, ———, Captain.
Calder, John.
Caldwell, John, Lieutenant.
Caldwell, William, Lieutenant.
Calhoun, Patrick, Ensign.
Call, Richard, Major, Surveyor-General.
Callender, Ebenezer, Surgeon's Mate.
Cameron, Alexander.
Camp, Hosea.
Camp, Samuel, Quartermaster.
Campbell, ———, Captain.
Campbell, Drury.

Campbell, George.
Campbell, Jeremiah.
Campbell, John, Ensign, Lieutenant.
Campbell, McCartin.
Candler, Henry, Major.
Cannon, Henry, Lieutenant.
Cannon, Nathaniel.
Cantley, Zachariah.
Carpenter, Soloman, Lieutenant.
Carpenter, William.
Carr, Henry, Lieutenant.
Carr, Mark, Captain.
Carr, Samuel, Captain.
Carr, William, Lieutenant.
Carraway, William, Lieutenant.
Carroll, James.
Carswell, John, Ensign.
Carter, ———, Major.
Carter, Charles.
Carter, David.
Carter, Hepworth, Captain.
Carter, Richard.
Carter, Robert.
Carter, Thomas.
Cartledge, Joseph, Major.
Cary, John.
Cash, James.
Cash, John.
Cason, William.
Catchings, Benjamin.
Catchings, Benjamin, Major.
Catchings, Meredith.
Cater, John, Surgeon.
Cavannah, Nicholas.
Cavannah, Robert, Major.
Chalfinch, Hiram, Musician.
Chambers, Peter.
Chandler, ———, Major.
Chandler, John.
Chandler, Joseph.
Chandler, Shelldeake.
Charlton, ———, Lieutenant-Colonel.
Chatfield, John.
Chook, William.
Chenault, John.
Chevalier, Charles Francis; member of Council.
Chidwell, William.
Childers, D.
Childers, Milliner.
Childers, Thomas.
Chisholm, Benjamin, Lieutenant.
Chisholm, Thomas; member of Supreme Executive Council; Captain, Lieutenant-Colonel.
Christmas, Richard.
Chunn, ———.
Claiborne, Thomas, Quartermaster-Sergeant.
Clark, Charles, Lieutenant.
Clark, Ed.
Clark, Gibson.
Clark, J. C., Lieutenant.
Clark, Jacob.
Clark, James; Son of Liberty.
Clark, John, C., Captain.
Clark, John J., Captain.
Clark, Thomas.
Clarke, Elijah, Brigadier-General.
Clarke, John, Captain, Major, Colonel.
Clarke, John F.
Clarke, John J., Captain.
Clark, William.
Clay, Joseph; member of Provincial Congress; quartermaster General, and Paymaster General; delegate to Continental Congress.
Clements, John, Lieutenant, Captain, Major, Colonel.
Cleveland, Jeremiah.
Cliffton, George.
Clifton, William, Sergeant.
Clinton, ———.
Cloud, Jeremiah.
Clowers, Daniel.
Clowers, Peter.
Cobb, Thomas, Captain.
Cochran, James, Lieutenant; member of Provincial Congress.
Cochran, Jonathan; Son of Liberty; member of Committee of Correspondence, and Provincial Congress.
Cochran, M.
Cochran, Matthew.
Cohen, Philip, Jacob.
Coile, James, Captain.

## THE HARVEY LIST.

Coile, William, Musician.
Coleman, Benjamin.
Coleman, John.
Coleman, John; Son of Liberty; member of Supreme Executive Council.
Coleman, Jonathan.
Coleman, Thomas.
Collahan, James.
Colley, John, Quartermaster-Sergeant.
Collins, J.
Collins, John.
Collins, John, Sergeant.
Collins, John, Sr., Sergeant.
Collins, Stephen.
Colomb, Peter, Lieutenant.
Colson, Jacob, Captain.
Combs, John.
Conger, Benjamin.
Connelly, James.
Connelly, Patrick, Captain.
Conner, Daniel, Lieutenant.
Conner, John.
Connolly, W. J.
Connor, John, Lieutenant.
Contey, James.
Conway, Thomas.
Conyers, John, Captain.
Conyers, John, Private.
Cook, Isham, Captain.
Cook, John, Captain.
Cook, Paris, Captain.
Cook, Ranes, Captain, Major.
Cook, Sham, Captain.
Cook, Thomas, Captain.
Cooper, ———, Captain.
Cooper, ———, Lieutenant-Colonel.
Cooper, Basil, Colonel; member of Council of Safety, and Provincial Congress.
Cooper, Benjamin.
Cooper, Richard; Son of Liberty.
Cooper, John, Major.
Cooper, William.
Cope, Charles.
Cope, Lewis.
Copeland, William.
Corbett, ———, Captain.
Corbett, Thomas; Son of Liberty.
Corker, ———.
Cortez, B., Major.
Coulder, John.
Couper, John.
Cowan, Edward, Lieutenant, Captain. (Cowen.)*
Cowen, Edward.
Cowper, Bacil (Cooper).
Cox, Abraham.
Cox, Moses.
Cox, Richard.
Cox, Thomas.
Cox, William.
Cox, Zebulon, Lieutenant.
Cox, Zebulon, Private.
Craine, Spencer.
Cramer, Christopher; Son of Liberty; member of Provincial Congress.
Crawford, Arthur, Sergeant.
Criswell, Samuel, Surgeon.
Crocker, William.
Crosby, William.
Crosson, John.
Cruddy, William.
Crumberger, Jacob, Major.
Crumby, Thomas.
Crumden, Ralph Edward, Surgeon's Mate.
Cruse, James, Colonel.
Cunningham, Ansell.
Curbow, Joseph.
Curl, Matthew.
Curry, ———.
Curry, Nicholas, Major.
Cuthbert, A.
Cuthbert, A. Daniel, Lieutenant; Son of Liberty.
Cuthbert, Alexander, Captain.
Cuthbert, Alexander D., Captain, Major.
Cuthbert, Alfred.
Cuthbert, Daniel, Lieutenant.
Cuthbert, Isaac; Son of Liberty.
Cuthbert, John A.
Cuthbert, Seth John, Captain, Major; member of Council of Safety, and Provincial Congress.
Cutts,———, Major.

Cuyler, Henry, Major.

### D.

Dalay, ———, Captain.
Damant, William, D. M. S.
Damron, Charles.
D'Angley, Paul, de la Beaune (Baron de Malves), Lieutenant.
Daniel, James.
Daniel, John, Captain.
Dantham, Elijah.
Davenport, Stephen.
Davenport, Thomas, Surgeon.
David, Agustus, Lieutenant.
Davidson, John.
Davidson, Joseph.
Davidson, William.
Davies, Edward; member of General Assembly.
Davies, Myrick; member of Supreme Executive Council; killed by Tories in a skirmish.
Davis, ———.
Davis, C., Sergeant.
Davis, Edward, Major.
Davis, Jenkins, Colonel; member of Provincial Congress.
Davis, Joel.
Davis, John (1).
Davis, John (2).
Davis, John (3).
Davis, Moses, Major.
Davis, Thomas.
Davis, Thomas L.
Davis, Tolliver.
Davis, William, Chaplain.
Davis, William, Major.
Day, Ambrose.
Debosh, Peter, Captain (Debosh, De Busk).
Default, ———, Captain.
Defatt, ———, Captain.
Defau, ———, Captain.
Defnall, David.
Defoor, ———.
DeKeyser, Lee, Captain.
De La Gall, ———, Colonel; member of Provincial Congress.
De Laplaign, Emanuel, Major.
De la Plainge, Emanuel Pierre.
De Laplaine, ———, Ensign.
De Laplaine, Peter Emanuel, Captain.
De Lisle, Bernard Roman, Major; commanded a regiment of Pennsylvania Artillery, from February 8, 1776, to November 28, 1779; afterwards served in the Georgia Continental line.
Delk, ———.
Delk, Samuel.
Dell, William G.
Demere, Raymond, Captain, Major; Member of Provincial Congress.
Dempier, ———, Sergeant.
Densler, Philip.
Depathier, ———, Lieutenant.
De Ste. Marie, ———, Captain.
Deshaver, Lewis.
Despillers, ———, Lieutenant.
Devaleile, John Duport, Chevalier, Lieutenant.
Devaliser, ———.
De Veaux, James.
De Veaux, Peter, Major, Aid de Camp; member of Provincial Congress.
Devereaux, Peter.
Dey, Joseph.
Dicken, Richard.
Dickson, David, Captain, Major, Colonel.
Dickson, Michael, Major.
Dillard, James.
Dillard, John.
Ditter, ———, Captain.
Dixon, ———, Captain.
Dixon, ———, Major.
Dixon, Walter, Lieutenant.
Dobbs, John.
Dobbs, Josiah, Lieutenant.
Dobbs, Nathan.
Doby, John.
Dollar, John, Lieutenant of Artillery, Captain, Major.
Donaldson, ———, Captain.
Donaldson, William.
Donnelly, Daniel, Lieutenant.

THE HARVEY LIST. 413

Donnelly, David, Captain.
Donnelly, James, Major.
Dooly, George, Lieutenant, Captain, Major.
Dooly, Hull, Lieutenant.
Dooly, John, Colonel; member of Supreme Executive Council.
Dooly, John, Captain.
Dooly, Thomas, Captain.
Dossey, Joel.
Doty, William, Lieutenant.
Doud, John.
Dougherty, ———, Major.
Dougherty, John.
Douglas, ———, Major.
Douglass, Thomas, Musician.
Doule, Thomas, Lieutenant.
Dowley, Thomas, Lieutenant.
Dowman, R., Captain.
Dowman, Raleigh, Captain.
Downs, Jonathan.
Dowse, Gideon.
Doyle, Nimrod, T.
Draper, James.
Drayton, Stephen; Son of Liberty; member of Provincial Congress.
Drayton, William H.; Son of Liberty.
Drew, Wilson.
Dubignon, C. P.
Dubignon, Christopher Poullain, Captain.
Du Borde, ———, Captain.
Ducin, John, Captain.
Ducoin, John, Captain.
Du Coins, John, Captain.
Du Coin, J.
Dufau, ———, Captain.
Duffell, William.
Duhart, John, Major.
Duke, Henry.
Dukes, Henry, Captain, Major.
Dumouchel, John, Lieutenant.
Duncan, James, Private.
Duncan, Joseph, Major.
Duncan, Joseph, Private.
Duncan, Matthew, Lieutenant.
Dunlap, Jonathan.
Dunlap, Joseph.

Dunlop, Joseph; Son of Liberty; member of Provincial Congress.
Dunn, ———, Captain.
Dunn, Josiah, Captain.
Dunn, Thomas.
Dunwoody, James, Surgeon.
Dupont, Josiah.
Durdan, Jacob.
Durham, Matthew, Captain.
Durkee, Nathaniel, Quartermaster.
Duval, ———, Lieutenant.
Duval, Daniel, Captain.
Dyer, Elisha.

E.

Eacholis, E.
Earley, Richard, Major.
Earnest, George.
Eastwood, Israel.
Eaton, ———, Major.
Eberhart, Jacob.
Eckles, Edward.
Edenfield, David.
Edmonston, James P.
Edwards, Adonijah.
Edwards, John.
Edwards, Reuben.
Edwards, Soloman.
Egbert, Jacob V., Surgeon's Mate.
Eidson, Shelton.
Eimbeck, George, Barrack Master.
Elbert, Samuel, Colonel, Brigadier-General; member of Council of Safety, and Provincial Congress; Governor of Georgia.
Elledge, Jacob.
Elliott, Bernard, Captain.
Elliott, Daniel.
Elliott, Gray; Son of Liberty; elected by the Georgia Assembly, as an assistant to Dr. Franklin, to plead the cause of the colonies in England.
Elliott, Henry.
Elliott, John, Lieutenant, Colonel.
Elliott, Thomas (mentioned in "British Black List" as "rebel officer").
Elliott, Thomas, Private.

Elliott, Zachariah.
Ellis, Shadrack.
Elon, Elisha, Lieutenant.
Else, Thomas, Lieutenant.
Ely, Richard.
Ely, William.
Eman, John, Lieutenant.
Emanuel, David, Captain, Colonel; member of Supreme Executive Council; Governor of Georgia.
Emanuel, Levi, Sergeant-Major.
Epposon, Thompson.
Espy, James.
Espy, John.
Espy, Thomas, Major.
Ethridge, Joel.
Eubank, George, Major.
Eustace, J.
Eustace, John.
Eustace, John Skye, Major, Aide de Camp, Adjutant-General.
Eustace, John, Major.
Evans, B.
Evans, John.
Evans, N.
Evans, William, Lieutenant.
Evans, William, Sr.; member of Assembly.
Eveleigh, Nicholas, Colonel, Deputy Adjutant-General.
Everett, John.
Ewen, William; Son of Liberty; member of Council of Safety, and Provincial Congress; Governor of Georgia.
Ewing, Thomas.

F.

Fair, Ebenezer.
Faison, William.
Fambrough, Thomas.
Fareclauth, Benjamin.
Farley, Samuel; Son of Liberty; member of Provincial Congress, and Committee of Correspondence.
Farmer, John.
Farrar, Francis.
Farrow, Jesse.
Faulks, Joseph, Captain.
Favours, John.
Fayerous, Peter, Surgeon.
Feldkeller, J., Surgeon.
Fell, Benjamin (mentioned in "British Black List" as "rebel officer").
Fell, Isaac.
Ferington, Jacob.
Fewm, Benjamin, Colonel.
Few, Ignatius, Lieutenant, Captain.
Few, William, Lieutenant, Colonel; member of Supreme Executive Council; Delegate to Continental Congress.
Fields, James, Lieutenant.
Files, Adams, J.
Finch, William.
Findley, ———.
Fineley, Thomas, Captain.
Fishbourne, Benjamin, Captain, Major; commanded, in 1777, the Fourth Regiment Pennsylvania, Continental line; removed to Savannah, Ga., in 1780; member of the Georgia Society of the Cincinatti.
Fitzgerald, George.
Fitzpatrick, Benjamin.
Fitzpatrick, John.
Fitzpatrick, Patrick, Lieutenant, Colonel.
Fitzpatrick, Richard.
Fitzpatrick, William, Lieutenant.
Flag, ———, Dr.
Flaherty, Daniel.
Flanagan, William.
Flanigan, Daniel.
Flemming, William.
Flerl, John; Son of Liberty; member of the Provincial Congress.
Flinn, William.
Flournoy, Robert, Captain.
Floyd, Charles.
Fluker, John, Sergeant.
Flinn (Flynt), John.
Folsom, William, Lieutenant.
Formby, Nathan.
Forsyth, Robert, Major.

## THE HARVEY LIST. 415

Fort, Arthur; member of the Supreme Executive Council; militia officer.
Fowlkes, ———, Captain.
Foy, Darby.
Franklin, David.
Franklin, David, Jr.
Fraser, ———, Lieutenant.
Fraser, John, Captain.
Fraser, Simon.
Frazer, John, Lieutenant.
Frazier, Elijah.
Frazier, John, Lieutenant.
Fredconer, C.
Freeman, Coldress.
Freeman, Coldrup.
Freeman, Daniel.
Freeman, Hallman, Colonel.
Freeman, Jack.
Freeman, James.
Freeman, John, Col.
Freeman, William, Captain.
Fretwell, Richard.
Frinderburk, John.
Fry, Benjamin.
Fudge, Jacob.
Fulton, John; Son of Liberty; member of Provincial Congress, and Supreme Executive Council.
Fulton, Samuel; Son of Liberty.

### G.

Gaines, William.
Galley, Richard.
Galoche, James, Lieutenant.
Galphin, George, Superintendent of Indian Affairs.
Garner, Charles.
Garner, John.
Gascoigne, Richard, Hospital Sergeant.
Gauper, John, Lieutenant.
Gay, Allen.
Germany, John; Son of Liberty; member of Provincial Congress.
Germany, Samuel; Son of Liberty; member of Provincial Congress.
Gibbons, James Martin, Lieutenant.
Gibbons, John, Vendue, Master.
Gibbons, Joseph; Son of Liberty; member of Provincial Congress.
Gibbons, William; Son of Liberty; member of Committee of Correspondence, and Provincial Congress; delegate to Continental Congress.
Gibbs, William.
Gibson, Allen.
Gibson, Churchill.
Gibson, Henry.
Gibson, John.
Gibson, Robert; Son of Liberty; member of Provincial Congress.
Gideon, Thomas, Major.
Giles, James.
Giles, Joseph, Major.
Gilmer, James, Sr.
Gilmore, James.
Gilmour, William, Lieutenant.
Gindratt, Henry, Captain.
Girardeau, John Bohun; member of Provincial Congress; Comissary-General of Issues.
Glascock, Thomas, Lieutenant, Captain, Major, Colonel, Brigadier-General.
Glascock, William; Son of Liberty; member of Council; Speaker of the Legislature.
Glasgo, William.
Glasgow, William.
Glass, ——— (1).
Glass, ——— (2).
Glass, Joseph.
Glass, Thomas, Lieutenant.
Glen, David, Lieutenant, Colonel.
Glen, John; Son of Liberty; member of Council of Safety, and Provincial Congress; Chief Justice.
Glen, Thomas.
Godby, William, Lieutenant.
Goff, Nathaniel.
Goff, Nathaniel (1).
Goffe, Daniel, Ensign.
Goggans, William.
Golding, ——— (1).
Golding, ——— (2).
Golding, Peter, Lieutenant.

Goldsmith, John.
Goldwire, James.
Golightly, Charles, Lieutenant.
Gollache, James, Lieutenant.
Goodwin, Wiley.
Goodwynn, Frederick.
Goolsby, Elijah, Lieutenant.
Goolsby, Reuben.
Gordon, Ambrose, Major.
Gordon, James, Major.
Gordon, James, Private.
Gordon, James, F.
Gordon, John.
Gordon, Nathaniel.
Goulding, Palmer.
Goulding, William.
Gouze, Henry.
Gower, Abel.
Grace, John.
Graham, John.
Graham, William, Major.
Grant,———, Captain.
Grant, Daniel.
Grant, Joseph.
Gravat, O.
Graves, Thomas.
Graves, William.
Gray, Thomas.
Greason, Abraham.
Green, ———, Captain.
Green, ———, Major.
Green, Gilbert.
Green, John, Captain.
Green, John, Lieutenant.
Green, John, R.
Green, Thomas.
Greene, Gabriel.
Greene, John, Captain; member of Provincial Congress.
Greene, William, Captain.
Gregory, Richard, Lieutenant.
Greice, John, Jr.
Gresham, Alexander.
Gresham, Archibald, Captain.
Gresham, David.
Gresham, Littlebury.
Griffin, Edward.
Griffin, James, Corporal.

Grimke, John F., Aide de Camp.
Grimke, John J.
Grimsley, Thomas.
Grinnell, William.
Grogan, Richard, Lieutenant.
Groover, Peter, Corporal and Sergeant.
Grotehouse, John.
Groves, John.
Groves, Stephens,
Groves, Stephen.
Groves, William, Sr.
Gully, Richard.
Gunn, Gabriel.
Gunn, James, Captain.
Gunnell, William.
Gunnells, Daniel, Major.
Gunter, Charles.
Guthrie, John.
Guyse, John.
Gwinnett, Button; Governor of Georgia; delegate to Continental Congress; signer of the Declaration of Independence.

H.

Habersham, James; Son of Liberty; President of Council of Safety; Governor of Georgia.
Habersham, John, Major; delegate to Continental Congress.
Habersham, Joseph, Major, Colonel; Son of Liberty; member of Provincial Congress; delegate to Continental Congress.
Haddon, William, Captain.
Hager, Arthur, Lieutenant.
Haggett, Hohn, Surgeon.
Haishey, Thomas.
Haisten, John.
Hall, Isaac; Son of Liberty.
Hall, John; Son of Liberty.
Hall, Lyman; Son of Liberty; member of Continental Congress; signer of Continental Congress; Governor of Georgia.
Haman, Alexander.
Hames, John, Sr.
Hamilton, A., Captain.

## THE HARVEY LIST.

Hamilton, Charles.
Hamilton, James, Captain.
Hamilton, John, Brigadier-General.
Hamilton, John, Sr.
Hamilton, Robert; Son of Liberty; member of Assembly.
Hamilton, Thomas, Lieutenant.
Hammond, Joshua, Lieutenant.
Hammond, Leroy, Captain.
Hammond, Samuel, Captain, Colonel.
Hampton, ———, Colonel.
Hampton, Edward, Captain.
Hampton, John.
Hampton, Wade.
Hancock, Francis, Captain.
Hancock, George, Captain.
Hancock, John, Captain.
Hand, James.
Hand, Joseph.
Handley, George, Captain; Governor of Georgia. (Hanley, Henley.)
Handley, Jerrett, Lieutenant.
Handley, Nicholas, Captain.
Hannah, Thomas.
Hannegan, James.
Haralson, Hugh.
Hardee, Thomas.
Harden, Henry.
Hardin, Henry, Lieutenant.
Hardin, William, Colonel.
Harding, ———, Captain.
Hardy, ———, Captain.
Hardy, John, Captain of Galley.
Harper, Robert, Lieutenant.
Harper, Samuel, Captain.
Harris, Benjamin.
Harris, David, Captain, Major.
Harris, Ezekiel.
Harris, Francis Henry, Captain, Lieutenant-Colonel; member of Provincial Congress, and Council of Safety.
Harris, G. L.
Harris, James.
Harris, Joseph.
Harris, Matthew.
Harris, Stephen.
Harris, Thomas, Captain.

Harrison, Robert, Wagon-master.
Harsaw, Thomas.
Hart, ———.
Hart, Benjamin.
Hart, Nancy.
Hartley, Daniel.
Harvell, James.
Harvey, Benjamin, Lieutenant.
Harvey, Blassingame, Captain.
Harvey, Charles, Captain.
Harvey, John.
Harvie, Alexander, Surgeon.
Harvie, James.
Harvie, John.
Hatchell, Archibald, Captain.
Hatcher, ———, Captain.
Hatchett, Archie, Captain.
Hatton, Josiah, Lieutenant.
Hawkins, Benjamin, Lieutenant.
Hawkins, Stephens.
Hawks, Frederick.
Haynie, William.
Hays, John.
Heard, Bernard, Major.
Heard, Jesse.
Heard, John.
Heard, Stephen, Captain; Governor of Georgia.
Hedden, ———.
Helfenstein, Jacob.
Helfenstein, Joshua.
Henderson, Richard.
Henderson, Robert, Captain.
Henderson, Robert, Private.
Hendley, George, Lieutenant.
Henshaid, Thomas.
Henshaw, Thomas.
Herd, ———, Captain.
Herman, Alexander.
Herndon, Joseph.
Hester, Robert.
Hewell, Wiatt.
Hext, ———, Lieutenant.
Heyrne, ———, Lieutenant.
Hicks, Edmond.
Hicks, Isaac, Private.
Hicks, J., Captain.
Hicks, John.

Hill, Abram.
Hill, Isaac.
Hill, James, Lieutenant.
Hill, John.
Hill, Moses.
Hill, Reuben.
Hill, William, Captain.
Hillary, C., Quartermaster, Sergeant.
Hillary, Christian, Lieutenant.
Hillery, Chris, Lieutenant.
Hillon, Chris, Lieutenant.
Hinds, John.
Hinsin, Lazarus.
Hodge, David.
Hodges, Philemon.
Hodges, William.
Hogg, James.
Holbrook, Eddy.
Holbrook, Jesse.
Holbrook, Nathan, Lieutenant.
Holiday, William, Sr.
Holland, Henry.
Holland, Hugh.
Holland, John.
Hollis, ———, Sergeant.
Holloway, James.
Holloway, Lewis, Sergeant.
Holmes, John, Captain.
Holmes, John, Chaplain.
Holmes, Robert, Captain.
Holzendorf, William; Son of Liberty; member of Supreme Executive Council.
Honea, Tobias (Honey).
Hood, Edward, Captain.
Hood, John.
Hooks, William.
Hooper, James.
Hooper, Richard B., Sergeant.
Hornby, William, Captain.
Horton, ———, Major.
Horton, Isaac.
Housley, John.
Houston, John, Private.
Houston, Samuel.
Houstoun (Houston), George; Son of Liberty; member of Provincial Congress; delegate to Continental Congress.
Houstoun (Houston), James, Surgeon.
Houstoun (Houston), John; Son of Liberty; member of Supreme Executive Council; delegate to Continental Congress; Governor of Georgia.
Hovenden, Thomas, Lieutenant, Colonel.
Howard, Soloman.
Howard, Thomas.
Howe, Robert, Lieutenant, Quartermaster.
Howell, Caleb, Lieutenant, Captain, Colonel.
Howell, Daniel, Captain.
Howell, John, Captain of Galley.
Howell, John, Private.
Howell, Miles.
Howell, Philip, Colonel; member of Provincial Congress.
Howley, Richard; Son of Liberty; delegate to Continental Congress; Governor of Georgia.
Hudson, David.
Huey, ———.
Huffman, John.
Hughes, Nathan, Lieutenant.
Hughes, William, Captain.
Hulsey, Jesse.
Hunt, John.
Hunt, Littleton.
Hunt, William.
Hunter, James, Surgeon.
Hurley, Joseph, Sergeant.
Hurt, ———.
Hutcher, ———, Captain.
Hutchins, Ed.
Hutto, Henry.

I.

Inman, Abodnego.
Inman, Jordan, Captain.
Irvine, Alexander, Lieutenant.
Irwin, Alex., Captain.
Irwin, Jared, Colonel, Brigadier-General.

Iseley, Philip.

## J.

Jack, James.
Jack, Samuel, Colonel.
Jackson, ——— (Major).
Jackson, ——— (Private).
Jackson, Charles, Ensign.
Jackson, Ebenezer, Lieutenant.
Jackson, Edward.
Jackson, Isaac, Colonel.
Jackson, James, Brigadier-General.
Jackson, Jarvis.
Jackson, John.
Jackson, Robert, Captain.
Jackson, Samuel, Lieutenant.
James, Jonathan, Lieutenant.
Jarrett, Deveaux; member of Assembly.
Jaret, ———, Captain.
Jarret, Robert, Lieutenant.
Jenkins, John, Lieutenant; member of Assembly.
Jenkins, Lewis.
Jenkins, William.
Jeter, Andrew, Captain.
Jeter, Thomas, Lieutenant.
Jiles, Samuel.
Jiles, Thomas.
Johnson, Abraham.
Johnson, Andrew, Captain.
Johnson, Hardy.
Johnson, Jonathan, Sergeant.
Johnson, Joseph.
Johnson, Laban, Lieutenant.
Johnson, Lewis.
Johnson, Stephen, Lieutenant-Colonel.
Johnson, William, Captain.
Johnston, ———, Captain.
Johnston, John, Captain.
Johnston, Stephen.
Jones, ——— (son of Noble Wimberly).
Jones, Abraham, Lieutenant-Colonel.
Jones, Abraham, Lieutenant.
Jones, Abraham, Private.
Jones, Abraham P., Second Lieutenant.
Jones, Batt, Lieutenant.
Jones, Edward, Lieutenant; member of Provincial Congress.
Jones, Harrison.
Jones, Henry, Colonel; member of Provincial Congress.
Jones, Isaac.
Jones, James; Son of Liberty; Collector of the Port of Savannah.
Jones, John (1), Captain, Major, Colonel.
Jones, John (2), Major; member of Supreme Executive Council.
Jones, John (3), Captain.
Johne, Jonathan, Private.
Jojes, Joseph, Captain.
Jones, Michael, Captain.
Jones, Moses, Aide de Camp; member of Provincial Congress.
Jones, Noble Wimberly; Son of Liberty; delegate to Continental Congress.
Jones, Soloman, Trumpet Major.
Jones, William (1), Lieutenant; member of Provincial Congress.
Jones, William (2), Private.
Jones, William (3), Private.
Jordan, Dempsey.
Jordan, Fountain.
Jordan, Matthew.
Jordan, Miles.
Jourdan, William, Lieutenant.
Jourdine, Charles, Captain.
Jourdon, John.
Judton, Paul; Son of Liberty.

## K.

Karr, Henry, Captain.
Keating, Edward.
Kehela, Christopher.
Keith, John.
Kelan, James, Corporal.
Kell, James, Captain.
Kell, John.
Kell, Robert.
Kelley, Lloyd.
Kelley, William.
Kelley, Giles.
Kemp, William, Captain.

Kendrick, John, Lieut.
Kent, Charles; Son of Liberty; member of Council.
Kerr, David.
Kerr, Henry, Captain.
Kerwell (Kernwell), William.
Key, William B.
Kidd, James H.
Kidd, William.
King, Elisah.
King, John, Lieutenant.
King, John, Private.
King, Richard.
King, Tandy.
King, Thomas; Son of Liberty.
Kirk, John.
Kitty, Daniel.
Kniel, Patrick.
Knight, Elisha.
Knox, Samuel.
Kobb, Peter.

L.

Ladson, ———, Major.
Lagardare, Isaac.
Lagram, John N.
Lain, William.
Lamar, Basil.
Lamar, John.
Lamar, Zachariah, Lieutenant, Colonel.
Lamb, William, Lieutenant.
Lambath, William, Lieutenant.
Lambert, James, Captain.
Lambert, John, Sergeant.
Lambeth, William, Lieutenant.
Lambrick, William.
Lancaster, Rowland.
Land, John.
Landeford, John, Colonel.
Landers, John.
Landrum, Thomas.
Lane, Joseph, Major.
Lane, William, Captain.
Langham, James.
Langhan, James.
Langley, John.
Langworthy, Edward; Son of Liberty; delegate to Continental Congress.
Lankford, Josiah.
Laroach, ———, Lieutenant.
Latham, Amos.
Laurence, John.
Laurens, John, Colonel.
Lavein, Peter, Lieutenant.
Law, Joseph.
Law, William.
Lawrence, John.
Lawson, Hugh, Captain.
Lawson, John, Captain of Galley, Colonel.
Lazarus, N.
Leadbitter, Drury, Colonel.
Le Conte, John Eaton; Son of Liberty.
Le Conte, Joseph; Son of Liberty.
Le Conte, William; Son of Liberty; member of Council of Safety, and Provincial Congress.
Ledbetter, George.
Ledbetter, Richard.
Ledbetter, Robert.
Le Duc, John, Quartermaster.
Lee, Burwell.
Lee, Greenbury, Colonel.
Lee, Thomas; Son of Liberty; member of Provincial Congress.
Leech, Burdett, Gunner.
Lees, ———, Captain.
Lenoir, ———, Captain.
Leopham, Frederick, Lieutenant.
Lesley, William.
Lester, Thomas.
Letham, ———, Captain.
Lett, ———, Captain.
Levay, George.
Lewis, ———; member of Supreme Executive Council; killed by the Tories in a skirmish.
Lewis, Benjamin; Son of Liberty; member of Provincial Congress.
Lewis, David; son of Liberty; member of Provincial Congress.
Lewis, Elijah, Captain.
Lewis, Evans, Captain.
Lewis, George.
Lewis, James, Lieutenant.
Lewis, James N.

# THE HARVEY LIST. 421

Lewis, John.
Lewis, Joseph.
Lewis, Josiah, Chaplain.
Lewis, Merriwether.
Lewis, Thos., Jr., Lieutenant.
Liddell, ———.
Liddell, William.
Lisle, Ephraim.
Linby, James.
Linby, William.
Lindsay, ———.
Lindsey, Dennis.
Lindsey, James.
Lindsey, John.
Line, Denis.
Linson, J.
Lintch, James.
Linville, William.
Lipham, ———, Captain.
Lipham, Frederick.
Little, James, Captain, Colonel.
Littleton, William.
Liverman, Conrad.
Livingston, William, Lieutenant.
Lloyd, Benjamin, Lieutenant.
Lloyd, Edward, Lieutenant.
Lockett, James.
Logan, Philip, Musician.
Long, Evans.
Longford, ———, Captain.
Lord, Robert, Lieutenant, Captain.
Lord, William; Son of Liberty; member of Provincial Congress.
Love, ———.
Love, John, Surgeon's Mate.
Love, Philip, Major.
Love, Thomas.
Love, William.
Lowe, Philip, Major, Lieutenant-Colonel.
Lowe, William, Lieutenant, Adjutant.
Lowery, ———.
Lowne, William, Lieutenant.
Lowry, Levi.
Lucas, John, Captain, Major.
Lumpkins, Philip.
Lynn, C.
Lynn, J.
Lyon, William.
Lyons, John, Captain.
Lyons, William.

M.

Mabry, Ralph.
McCall, Hugh, Captain.
McCall, James, Captain.
McCall, Richard.
McCance, David.
McCarthy, John, Lieutenant.
McCarty, Ebeneezer.
McCarty, John.
McCay, Charles; Son of Liberty; member of Provincial Congress.
McClelland, John; Son of Liberty.
McClelland, Samuel; Son of Liberty.
McClesky, James.
McCleur, John, Captain of Galley; member of Provincial Congress.
McClure, John, Major.
McCollins, David.
McCullough, John.
McCormack, Thomas.
McCoy, ———, Captain.
McCoy, Samuel.
McCullough, John.
McCullough, John, Sr.; Son of Liberty.
McCullough, John, Jr.
McCullough, Seth; Son of Liberty.
McCullough, William.
McCumber (Macomber), ———, Captain.
McCurdy, John.
McDade, John.
McDaniel, William, Lieutenant.
McDerment, Joseph.
McDonald, Charles; Son of Liberty.
McDonald, John.
McDonald, William, Lieutenant.
McDowell, ———, Major.
McDowell, Charles, Major.
McDowell, Robert.
McEldufy, Daniel, Captain.
McElhannon, John.
McFarland, ———, Captain.
McFarland, Andrew, Quartermaster.

McGowen, ———, Lieut.
McGowen, Joseph.
McHancy, Terry.
McIntire, John.
McIntosh, George; Son of Liberty; member of Provincial Congress.
McIntosh, John, Lieutenant, Colonel; member of Provincial Congress.
McIntosh, John, Jr., Colonel.
McIntosh, John, Moore.
McIntosh, Lachlin, Jr., Lieutenant, Captain.
McIntosh, Roderick; Son of Liberty; member of Provincial Congress.
McIntosh, William (1), Colonel; member of Provincial Congress.
McIntosh, William (2), Captain, Colonel.
McIntosh, William (3), Ensign.
McKanney, James, Lieutenant.
McKay, ———, Captain.
McKay, Charles, Ensign.
McKay, Hugh, Captain.
McKay, Rannell.
McKee, John.
MacKee, Samuel.
McKenna, James, Lieutenant.
McKenney, Charles.
McKenny, James, Lieutenant, Colonel.
McKenny, James, Lieutenant.
McKenny, John, Sr.
McKewn, Daniel, Wagoner.
Mackey, ———.
McKinne, Matthew, Surgeon.
McKinney, John, Lieutenant.
McKinney, Timothy.
McKinny, John.
McKinny, John, Sr.
McLain, John.
McLane, Thomas.
McLaughlin, John.
McLean, James.
McLean, John.
McLean, Josia.
McLendon, Isaac.
McLendon, Jacob, Sr.
McLendon, Jacob, Jr.
McMillion, John.

McMurphy, Daniel, member of General Assembly.
McMurray, Frederick.
McNeil, James.
Macomber, Matthew, Captain of Galley.
Macomeson, John.
McPherson,———.
McVickers, D.
McWicker, Daniel.
Maddock, Joseph; Son of Liberty; member of Provincial Congress.
Madison, James, Lieutenant.
Mahemson, John.
Mains, Samuel, Corporal.
Mallard, Lazarus.
Malone, Mullins.
Manaduc, Henry, Captain.
Manley, John, Lieutenant.
Mann, John; Son of Liberty; member of Committee of Correspondence.
Mann, Luke; Son of Liberty; member of Provincial Congress.
Marbury, Leonard, Captain, Colonel; member of Provincial Congress.
Marshall, Abraham, Chaplain.
Marshall, Daniel, Chaplain.
Marshall, Jesse.
Marshall, William, Sergeant.
Marten, John.
Martin, ———.
Martin, Ephraim.
Martin, James, Colonel.
Martin, John, Lieutenant, Captain, Lieutenant-Colonel; Member of Provincial Congress; Sheriff, Treasurer; Governor of Georgia.
Martin, John, Private.
Martin, Joseph.
Martin, Thomas.
Martin, William, Captain.
Mase, Joseph.
Mason, Ebenezer.
Mason, John, Sergeant-Major.
Massey, William, Colonel, Quartermaster General.
Mastein, William.

## THE HARVEY LIST.

Matthews, George, Brigadier-General; Governor of Georgia.
Matthews, Isaac.
Matthews, John, Corporal.
Matthews, Philip.
Matthews, William, Captain, Quartermaster.
Matthews, William, Private.
Maxwell, Andrew.
Maxwell, Audley.
Maxwell, Elisha.
Maxwell, James; Son of Liberty; member of Provincial Congress; Secretary of Georgia.
Maxwell, Josiah, Lieutenant.
Maxwell, Simons, Lieutenant.
Maxwell, Thomas, Surveyor-General.
Maxwell, Thomas, Jr., Colonel.
Maxwell, William, Captain of Galley; member of Provincial Congress.
Maybank, Andrew, Captain, Colonel.
Mayo, John, Sr.
Mays, Andrew.
Mays, John.
Mead, Minor.
Meador, Jason.
Meadows, John.
Meanley, John, Lieutenant, Colonel.
Meeks, Brittain.
Melton, Robert.
Melton, William, Surgeon.
Melvin, George, Captain, Brigade Major.
Menife, Willis.
Mercer, Joshua.
Mercer, Thomas.
Mercer, William.
Merriwether, ———.
Merriwether, Daniel.
Merrewether, David.
Middleton, ———.
Middleton, Charles, Captain.
Middleton, Hugh; member of Provincial Congress; (mentioned in "British Black List" as "rebel officer").
Milirous, William.
Millar (Miller), Elisha, Captain.
Millar, Nicholas, Lieutenant.

Milledge, John; Son of Liberty; Attourney-General.
Milledge, John, Jr.; member of Assembly.
Miller, John, Captain.
Miller, John, Private.
Miller, John, Jr.
Miller, Samuel; Son of Liberty; member of Supreme Executive Council; member of Assembly.
Miller, William.
Milligan, ———, Captain.
Mills, ———.
Mills, ———, Captain.
Mills, Moses.
Milner, John, Captain.
Milner, Pitt.
Milton, John, Captain.
Minis, Philip.
Minton, John.
Mitchell, Henry.
Mitchell, Reuben, Lieutenant.
Mitchell, Thomas, Lieutenant, Captain.
Mitchell, William.
Moffett, Gabriel.
Moffett, John.
Monk, John.
Montgomery, ———.
Moody, Thomas.
Moore, ———, Captain.
Moore, Andrew; Son of Liberty; member of Provincial Congress.
Moore, Francis, Major.
Moore, Isaac, Sr.
Moore, James.
Moore, Jiles; Son of Liberty.
Moore, John.
Moore, William.
Morel, John, Lieutenant, Captain; Son of Liberty; member of Committee of Correspondence, and Provincial Congress.
Morgan, Asa.
Morgan, William.
Morris, John, Captain.
Morris, Nathaniel.
Morris, Thomas, Captain.
Morris, William, Sr.

Morton, Oliver.
Morton, Thomas.
Mosby, James, Captain.
Mosby, John, Captain.
Mosby, Littleberry, Captain, Brigade Pay-master.
Mosby, Robert, Lieutenant.
Mosby, Wade.
Moseby, William.
Moseley, James.
Moseley, John, Captain.
Moseley, L.
Moseley, Littleberry, Captain.
Moseley, Robert, Lieutenant.
Moseley, Samuel.
Mosely, William.
Moxley, Benjamin.
Mullins, Malone.
Murdock, William.
Murry, Thomas, Quartermaster.
Myddleton, William.
Myers, John, Sr.
Myers, William, Lieutenant.

N.

Nailor, George, Captain.
Neal, ———, Captain.
Nealy, John.
Neely, John.
Nelson, John, from Wilkes County.
Nelson, John, from Burke County.
Nephew, ———, Captain.
Nephew, James, Captain.
Nesbit, Jeremiah.
Netherland, Benjamin, Lieutenant.
Netherland, Thomas, Lieutenant.
Neufville, John; Son of Liberty.
Newdicate, John, Captain of Galley.
Newdigate, John, Lieutenant, Captain.
Newman, Daniel.
Newnan, John.
Newson, ———, Captain.
Newson, Jones; Son of Liberty.
Nichols,———, Captain.
Nicholson, John.
Nickerson, John.
Nix, George.
Nix, James.

Nix, John.
Nolen, James.
Norman, ———, Major.
Norman, William.
Norris, William.
Norwood, George (1), Sergeant.
Norwood, George (2).
Nugan, M.
Nugard, Michael.

O.

Oakman, W., Fife Major.
Oates, ———, Lieutenant.
O'Bryan, James, Fifer.
O'Bryan, William; Son of Liberty; member of Provincial Congress; Treasurer of Georgia.
Odam (Odum), Daniel.
Odam, Fred, Lieutenant.
Odam, Seybert.
Odingsell, Benjamin, Lieutenant.
Odingsell, Charles, Captain.
Offutt, Ezekiel, Captain.
Ogier, ———, Captain.
Oliver, Dionysius.
Oliver, James, Corporal.
Oliver, John, Private.
Oliver, John, Sr., Corporal.
Oliver, Peter.
O'Neal, Axum, Lieutenant.
O'Neal, Edward.
O'Neal, Ferdinand, Captain.
Orear, Daniel.
Ornsby, Daniel, Fife Major.
Osgood, John.
Osgood, Joseph, Captain.
Osgood, Josiah.
Owen, ———, Sergeant.
Owens, Joseph.

P.

Pace, Thomas (mentioned in "British Black List" as "rebel officer").
Palmer, Joseph, Major.
Palmer, Thomas, Lieutenant.
Paltey, ———, Lieutenant.
Pannell, John, Lieutenant, Colonel.
Pannell, Joseph, Lieutenant, Colonel.

Parish, Joel, Captain.
Parke, Ezekiel Evens.
Parker, ———.
Parker, ———, Colonel.
Parker, Richard.
Parkerson, Jacob.
Parkes, Benjamin, Sr., Ensign.
Parkins, Archibald.
Parnell, Joseph, Lieutenant,Colonel.
Parr, Benjamin.
Parre, Nathaniel, Lieutenant.
Parsons, Samuel.
Paschal, George, Dragoon.
Passmore, Joseph.
Patison, Robert.
Pawlett, Richard, Lieutenant.
Paxton, William, Lieutenant.
Payne, Joseph.
Payne, Nehemiah.
Payne, Thomas, Lieutenant.
Peace, John.
Peacock, Isham.
Peacock, Uriah.
Peacock, William; Son of Liberty; member of Supreme Executive Council.
Peacock, William, Sr.
Pearce, Seth.
Pearre, Nathaniel, Captain.
Pearrie, N.
Peck, Henry.
Pendleton, Nathaniel, Major.
Penticost, William, Lieutenant.
Perkins, ———, Colonel.
Perkins, Abraham.
Perkins, Moses.
Perritt, William.
Perry, James.
Perry, Nathaniel, Lieutenant.
Peters, Jesse.
Petillo, John.
Petty, Bernard, Lieutenant.
Pharoah, Joshua, Sergeant.
Philips, George, Lieutenant.
Philips, John, Lieutenant, Captain.
Phillips, Henry, Quartermaster.
Phillips, Joel.
Phillips, John, Lieutenant, Captain.
Phillips, Joseph, Captain.
Phillips, Levi.
Phillips, Zachariah.
Phinizee, Francis.
Pickens, ———, Captain.
Pickens, John.
Pickens, Joseph, Captain.
Pierce, William, Aide de Camp.
Pierce, William; Son of Liberty; delegate to Continental Congress.
Pierey, William Chaplain.
Pierre, Nathaniel, Lieutenant.
Piggin, ———, Colonel.
Pilgrim, Michael.
Pilgrim, Thomas.
Pinder, William.
Pinkerton, John.
Pinkston, Daniel.
Pittman, James.
Pitts, James.
Platt, Ebenezer Smith.
Plummer, Joseph.
Polk, John.
Polock, Cushman.
Pool, ———.
Pool, Samuel.
Pooler, Quinton, Captain.
Pope, Burwell.
Pope, Henry.
Pope, John, Captain.
Pope, Wiley, Colonel.
Pope, William.
Porter, B., Major.
Porter, Benjamin, Major, Lieutenant, Colonel.
Porter, Oliver, Major.
Porter, Oliver, Private.
Porter, R., Lieutenant.
Porter, Robert, Lieutenant.
Porter, Thomas, Lieutenant.
Potts, John, Captain.
Potts, William.
Poullain, Anthony.
Poullain, William.
Pounds, R.
Powell, Benjamin.
Powell, Francis.
Powell, James, Captain.

Pratt, John.
Pray, Job, Captain of Galley.
Price, Charles, Lieutenant.
Price, E.
Price, William, Quartermaster-Sergeant.
Prior, John.
Pritchett, Stephen.
Pritchett, William.
Pruett, ———.
Pugh, James; Son of Liberty; member of Provincial Congress.
Pullain, ———, Major.
Pullen, Robert.
Pulliam, John, Captain.
Pullin, Robert.
Putnam, Henry.

Q.
Quarterman, John, Jr.
Quarterman, Robert.
Quarterman, Thomas.
Quarterman, William.

R.
Rabenhorst, Rev., Dr., Chaplain.
Rae, James; member of Provincial Congress; Commissary-General of Purchases.
Rae, John, Ensign, Lieutenant.
Rae, Robert, Colonel; member of Provincial Congress.
Ragland, Evan, Lieutenant.
Rahn, Jonathan, Corporal.
Raley, Charles.
Ramsay, John.
Ravot, Abraham, Major.
Rawls, Cotton.
Rawls, William.
Rawson, Elijah.
Ray, ———, Lieutenant, Colonel.
Ray, William.
Read, James.
Read, George.
Red, James, Lieutenant, Surgeon.
Redden, Scott.
Redding, Anderson.
Reed, George.
Reed, Isaac.
Reed, William, Surgeon.
Reeden, George.
Reeden, Scott.
Rees, David, Captain, Judge-Advocate.
Reeves, Joseph, Lieutenant.
Reeves, William.
Reid, Samuel.
Reid, Samuel, Captain.
Reid, William.
Reyfield, J.
Reynolds, A.
Reynolds, Benjamin.
Reynolds, Ephraim.
Reynolds, Joseph; Son of Liberty; member of Provincial Congress.
Rice, ———, Captain.
Rice, Leonard, Sergeant.
Rice, Nathan.
Richardson, ———, Colonel.
Richardson, Amos.
Rickerson, Benjamin.
Ricketson, Jesse.
Ricketson, Jordan.
Ridden, John, Scott.
Ridick, A.
Riley, James.
Rivers, John.
Rivers, John, Sergeant.
Roach, William, Lieutenant.
Roberson, David.
Roberson, Hugh.
Roberson, John.
Roberts, ———, Lieutenant, Colonel.
Roberts, ———, Major.
Roberts, Daniel, Lieutenant, Captain, Major, Lieutenant-Colonel; member of Provincial Congress.
Roberts, James, Lieutenant.
Roberts, John, Captain; member of Provincial Congress.
Roberts, Reuben.
Roberts, Richard.
Roberts, Thomas.
Robertson, ———, Lieutenant.
Robertson, James; Son of Liberty; member of Provincial Congress.
Robertson, Robert.

Robeson, ———, Lieutenant.
Robeson, David, Lieutenant, Colonel.
Robinson, A.
Robinson, Jeriah.
Robinson, John.
Robinson, John, Jr.
Roche, Matthew, Lieutenant, Adjutant.
Roche, Matthew, Jr.; member of Provincial Congress; Son of Liberty.
Roebuck, Benjamin, Lieutenant.
Rogers, ———.
Roland, John; Son of Liberty.
Roman (DeLisle), Bernard, Major.
Roper, John.
Roquemore, Peter, Captain.
Rosier, Robert.
Ross, ———, Major.
Rossiter, Thimothy W., Surgeon's Mate, Surgeon.
Routon, John.
Rowe, Joshua.
Rowell, Jesse.
Rowland, John.
Royall, John.
Rucher, William.
Rucker, William.
Rudolph, ———, Captain.
Rudolph, Michael, Captain.
Runnuls, Daniel.
Russell, James, G.
Russell, Thomas, Lieutenant.
Rutledge, William, Lieutenant.
Ryalls, William, Lieutenant.
Ryan, Daniel; Son of Liberty; member of Provincial Congress.
Rylee, James.

S.

Saffold, William.
Sallens, Peter,Jr.; Son of Liberty.
Sallette, Robert.
Salmon, Lewis.
Salter, ———, Captain.
Saltus, Samuel (mentioned in "British Black List" as "committeeman").
Sampson, Samuel.
Samson, William.
Sandiford, John.
Sanford, Jeremiah.
Sanson, William.
Sapp, Elijah.
Sarcedas, ———, Lieutenant.
Sarzedas, David, Lieutenant.
Satton, ———.
Saulberry, Thomas.
Saunders, John.
Savage, Lovelace, Chaplain.
Savage, Thomas.
Saxon, Soloman.
Saxton, Nathaniel.
Saxton, Soloman.
Scheuber, Justus H., Adjutant.
Schick, Fred, Lieutenant.
Schnider, J. Gotleib.
Schnider, John.
Schnider, Jonathan.
Schuemple, Fred, Lieutenant.
Scott, Alexander, Chaplain.
Scott, Samuel, Captain, Lieutenant, Colonel.
Scott, Thomas, Captain, Major.
Scott, William, Captain.
Scott, Private.
Screven, James, Brigadier-General; Son of Liberty; member of Provincial Congress.
Scrimger (Serimger), ———, Lieutenant.
Scruggs, Grosse.
Scurlock, William.
Serbert, John.
Segar, Samuel.
Seixas, Abraham, Lieutenant.
Seixas, William.
Sneior, Jesse, Lieutenant.
Sessions, John.
Seva, John.
Shackleford, John, Captain.
Shackleford, John, Private.
Shackleford, William.
Shad, Soloman, Lieutenant.
Shaffer, Belshazzer.
Shane, John, Sr.
Shane, John, Jr.
Shane, Richard.
Shannon, Thomas, Sr.

Shannon, Thomas, Jr.
Sharp, ―― (1).
Sharp, ―― (2).
Sharp, B. J.
Sharp, John, Captain.
Sharp, John, Private.
Share, James Boyd, Surgeon's Mate and Surgeon.
Sharpe, James D., Surgeon.
Shaw, Basil, Sergeant.
Shaw, Thomas, Jr., Surgeon.
Sheehee, John, alias John Conner.
Sheftall, Levi.
Sheftall, Mordecai, Commissary-General.
Sheftall, Sheftall, Deputy Commissary-General.
Sheftall, Sheftall, Private.
Sheldon, ――, Lieutenant.
Shellman, John, Lieutenant.
Shellman, Michael, Colonel.
Shepperd, Benjamin.
Sherd, William, Surgeon.
Sheridan, Abner.
Sherod, Joseph.
Shick, E., Lieutenant.
Shick, John, Lieutenant.
Shields, John, Major.
Shine, John.
Shirley, James.
Shirley, Joseph.
Slivers, Jonas.
Shoemack, Joseph, Lieutenant.
Shows, Adam.
Shuffield, William.
Shurr, John.
Shuttleworth, Pr.; Son of Liberty; Shuttleworth, Reu; Son of Liberty.
Sick, F.
Sillivant, ――.
Silvey, Stephen.
Simmons, William.
Simms, Abraham, Captain.
Simons, Abraham, Captain.
Simpson, Archibald.
Simpson, James.
Simpson, Robert, Lieutenant.
Sims, James.
Simson, Timothy.
Sinclair, ――, Lieutenant.
Singleton, ――, Major.
Singleton, Edmond.
Sinquefield, ――, Captain.
Sinquefield, William.
Skinner, Isaac, Captain.
Slaughter, George.
Slay, Thomas.
Slocombe, John Charles.
Smith, Alexander, Sergeant.
Smith, Andrew, Surgeon's Mate.
Smith, Austin.
Smith, Benjamin.
Smith, Burree.
Smith, Burrill, Captain.
Smith, Burwell, Major.
Smith, Charles.
Smith, Enoch.
Smith, Ezekiel.
Smith, Hardy.
Smith, Henry.
Smith, Hill.
Smith, Isaac, Sergeant.
Smith, Jesse.
Smith, John; Son of Liberty; member of Council of Safety, and Provincial Congress.
Smith, John, Private.
Smith, John Carroway, Lieutenant, Captain, Major.
Smith, Joshua, Lieutenant.
Smith, Larkin.
Smith, Leonard.
Smith, Mort.
Smith, R.
Smith, Randolph.
Smith, Randra, Captain.
Smith, Samuel, Sergeant.
Smith, Shadrach.
Smith, William, Sergeant.
Smith, William, Private.
Smyth, ――, Captain.
Snef, ――, Captain of Pioneers.
Snider, ――.
Snider, John Gotleib.
Snyder, ――.

Snyder, Jonathan.
Sodown, Jacob.
Solter, Jacob.
Sowell, Zadock.
Speake, Richard.
Spears, John.
Spears, William.
Spencer, ———, Captain.
Spencer, John.
Spencer, Samuel, Captain of Galley.
Springer, Benjamin.
Sprowl, ———, Captain.
Spurlock, George, Major.
Stacy, John; Son of Liberty; member of Committee of Correspondence.
Stafford, John.
Stallings, ———, Colonel.
Stallings, Ezekiel, Lieutenant.
Stallings, Fred, Captain.
Stallings, James, Captain.
Stanley, Shad, Lieutenant.
Staples, ———.
Stapleton, George.
Stark, John, Captain.
Statham, Zachariah.
Stedman, James, Lieutenant.
Stephens, Benjamin.
Stephens, John W.
Stephens, William, Lieutenant.
Stephens, William, Lieutenant, Captain; Attorney-General.
Stephens, John; Son of Liberty; member of Provincial Congress.
Stevens, Joseph.
Stevens, Reuben.
Stevens, Samuel; Son of Liberty; delegate from St. John's Parish, Ga., to Charleston, S. C.
Stevens, Thomas.
Stevenson, ———.
Steward, John, Captain.
Stewart, ———.
Stewart, Charles, Lieutenant.
Stewart, David, Captain.
Stewart, Fountain.
Stewart, Henry.
Stewart, James, Lieutenant.
Stewart, James, Private.
Stewart, John, Colonel.
Stewart, Matthew, Lieutenant.
Stewart, William, Sergeant.
Stiff, William.
Stiles, Joseph, Captain of Galley.
Stiles, William.
Stillwell, Jacob, Fifer.
Stirk, J., Captain.
Stirk, John, Colonel; Son of Liberty; member of Provincial Congress.
Stirk, Samuel, Major; Judge-Advocate; Secretary; Attorney-General.
St. Johns, James.
Stobe, Joseph; Son of Liberty.
Stone, Thomas; Son of Liberty; member of Supreme Executive Council.
Stone, William; Son of Liberty; member of Supreme Executive Council.
Stonecypher, John.
Stowers, Lewis.
Stregal, Nicholas.
Stripling, Francis.
Strong, Charles.
Strong, I., Quartermaster Sergeant.
Strong, J.
Strother, ———, Mr.
Strother, William D., Captain.
Stroud, Thomas.
Struther, ———, Captain.
Struthers, William.
Stuart, ———, Captain.
Stuart, Allen; Son of Liberty; member of Provincial Congress.
Stuart, John, Colonel.
Stubblefield, Jeter.
Sturdivant, Charles.
Studdath, Jared.
Sullivan, Pleasant.
Summerlin, Demsey.
Summerlin, Richard.
Summerman, Barnet.
Summers, John.
Sumner, Thomas, Captain.
Sutcliffe, John, Assistant Deputy Quartermaster-General.
Sutley, James.
Suttles, William.

Sutton, A.
Sutton, R.
Sutton, William.
Swain, William.
Swan, William.
Swan, William B.
Sway, George.
Sweatman, William.
Swinney, Richard.
Swords, James.

T.

Tait, Robert L.
Talley, Henry.
Talley, John, Dragoon.
Talliferro, ———.
Talliferro, Benjamin.
Tanner, Asa.
Tanner, Leonard.
Tanney, Michael.
Tarling, Peter, Colonel; member of Provincial Congress; Quartermaster-General.
Tate, John.
Tate, Robert L.
Tatnall, Joshia, Captain.
Taylor, ———, Captain.
Taylor, Nathan.
Taylor, Robert.
Taylor, Samuel, Major.
Taylor, Thomas, Adjutant.
Teasley, Silas.
Telfair, Edward; Son of Liberty; member of Provincial Congress; delegate to Continental Congress; Governor of Georgia.
Templeman, Andrew, Captain.
Tenn, Zechariah.
Tennell (Tannell; Tennille), Francis, Lieutenant.
Tennell, Fred, Captain.
Tennell, S.
Tenney, E.
Tenney, Ed.
Tennill, Francis, Lieutenant, Captain.
Tennill, T., Captain.
Terrell, David.
Terrell, James, Captain.
Terrell, Richard.
Terrell, William.
Tetard, Benjamin, Surgeon.
Tettler, Daniel, Captain.
Tettler, David.
Thames, Thomas.
Tharp, Charles.
Tharp, John.
Theus, Peter, Lieutenant.
Thomas, ———, Captain.
Thomas, ———, Lieutenant.
Thomas, Abraham.
Thomas, B.
Thomas, Caleb, Musician.
Thomas, Ethelred.
Thomas, John.
Thomas, William.
Thomasson, William.
Thompson, ———, Colonel.
Thompson, Benjamin.
Thompson, Frederick.
Thompson, James, Captain.
Thompson, James, Private.
Thompson, Robert, Lieutenant, Quartermaster.
Thompson, Seth.
Thompson, Sherrod.
Thornton, Presley, Corporal.
Thrasher, George.
Threadcraft, George; Son of Liberty; member of Provincial Congress.
Threadgill, Thomas, Captain.
Threadgill, William.
Tison, James.
Todd, Henry.
Tolbert, Benjamin.
Tomlinson, Aaron.
Tondee, Peter; Son of Liberty; member of Provincial Congress.
Toole, James, Lieutenant.
Torrence, John.
Trammell, William.
Treutlen, John Adam; Son of Liberty; member of Provincial Congress; Governor of Georgia.
Triplett, Francis.
Triplett, William.
Tucker, B.

## THE HARVEY LIST.

Tucker, Harbert.
Tuggle, Charles.
Tureman, Garrett.
Turmer, B.
Turner, C.
Turner, D.
Turner, David, Lieutenant, Captain.
Turner, G.
Turner, Robert.
Turner, Thomas.
Turner, William, Lieutenant.
Twidall, J.
Tyner, Benjamin.

U.

Underwood, Archibald.
Underwood, Hugh, Lieutenant.
Upchurch, Charles.
Upshaw, John.
Upton, George, Sr.
Upton, George.

V.

Valentonge, Moses.
Valotten, David Moses.
Valatton, James.
Vandegriffe, Garrett.
Venable, Abraham.
Venable, John.
Vernon, Isaac.
Vicarr, Thomas, Wagoner.
Vickers, William.
Vickory, William.

W.

Wade, Hezekiel, Captain.
Wade, Moses.
Wade, Nehemiah, Treasurer of Georgia.
Waggoner, John P.
Wagnon, John Peter, Lieutenant, Surgeon's Mate, Surgeon.
Wagnon, P. J.
Wagnon, T.
Wagnor, John P.
Wagon, J. P., Lieutenant.
Waldeburg, Jacob, Clerk of Regiment.
Waldrepe, James.

Waldroupe, James.
Walicon, Daniel, Major.
Walker, ———, Captain.
Walker, Benjamin, Captain.
Walker, Daniel, Sr.
Walker, David, Sr.
Walker, George.
Walker, John.
Walker, Sanders, Chaplain.
Walker, Thomas.
Walker, William, Captain.
Wall, William, Captain.
Wallace, John.
Wallis, Carnhill.
Walls, Charles.
Walsh, Patrick, Major.
Walters, Joseph.
Walthour, Andrew.
Walthour, Jacob; Son of Liberty; member of Provincial Congress.
Walton, George, Colonel; Son of Liberty; delegate to Continental Congress; signer of the Declaration of Independence; Governor of Georgia.
Walton, George, Jr., Lieutenant.
Walton, Jesse, Lieutenant.
Walton John, Lieutenant; member of Provincial Congress and Supreme Executive Council; Son of Liberty.
Walton, Nathaniel, Lieutenant.
Walton, Robert; Commissioner of Forfeited Estates.
Wanden (Wandin), John, Lieutenant, Surgeon, Paymaster.
Ward, John Peter, Lieutenant.
Ward, Robert, Lieutenant.
Ward, William.
Warden, J.
Warden, Samuel.
Wardlaw, William.
Ware, Edward, Sergeant.
Ware, Robert, Captain.
Warmack, Jesse, Lieutenant.
Warren, Daniel, Lieutenant.
Warren, John.
Warren, Joshia, Captain.
Warring, John, Captain.

Wash, E.
Wash, Patrick, Major.
Wash, William.
Washington, Thomas, Major.
Waters, David.
Watson, Douglass.
Watson, Sl., Lieutenant.
Wauslaw, John.
Way, Andrew.
Way, Edward.
Way, John.
Way, Moses, Lieutenant, Captain.
Way, Parmenus.
Way, Parmenus, Sr.; Son of Liberty; member of Committee of Correspondence.
Weathers, Valentine.
Webb, ———.
Webb, Austin.
Webster, B.
Welbourne, Daniel.
Weldon, John.
Welford, Lewis.
Wellborn, Elias.
Wellborn, Samuel, Major.
Wells, Andrew Elton, Lieutenant-Colonel; Son of Liberty; member of Provincial Congress.
Wells, George, Surgeon.
Wells, H., Surgeon.
Wells, Humphery; Son of Liberty; member of Supreme Executive Council.
Wells, Leonard.
Wells, M.
Welscher, Joseph, Lieutenant.
Welsh, Edward, Major.
Welsh, Samuel, Major.
Wereat, Benjamin.
Wereat, John; Son of Liberty; member of Provincial Congress; President of Supreme Executive Council; Governor of Georgia.
West, Benjamin, Sr.
West, Charles, Major.
West, Samuel, Captain.
West, Sion.
West, William.

Westbrook, Stephen, Lieutenant.
Whalen, Michael, Corporal.
Whaley, Zechariah.
Whateley, Walton.
Whateley, William.
Whatley, Daniel.
Whatley, Samuel.
Whatley, William.
Whatley, Wilson.
Wheeler, ———, Captain.
Wheeler, Charles.
Wheeler, James.
Wheelus, Abner.
Whelchel, John.
White, Edward, Captain.
White, George.
White, James, Private.
White, Jesse.
White, John, Colonel.
White, John, Private.
White, Richard.
White, Thomas, Captain.
Whitehead, Amos, Lieutenant.
Whitehead, John.
Whitemore, Howell.
Whitemore, J.
Whittaker, ———, Captain.
Whitten, Philip.
Whittington, Faddy.
Wiere, James.
Wilder, ———, Major.
Wilder, Willis, Sergeant.
Wiley, Absolem.
Wiley, R., Colonel.
Wilkinson, Benjamin.
Wilkinson, Elisha.
Willaby, W.
Williams, ———, Colonel.
Williams, ———, Drummer.
Williams, ———, Lieutenant.
Williams, Bratton (Britton).
Williams, C.
Williams, Charles, Lieutenant.
Williams, James.
Williams, John J.
Williams, Nathan.
Williams, William (1), Captain.
Williams, William (2), Private.

## THE HARVEY LIST.

Williams, William (3), Private.
Williams, William, Sr.; Son of Liberty; member of Provincial Congress.
Williamson, L.
Williamson, Micajah, Jr.
Williford, Nathan.
Willis, Francis.
Willis, Joshua.
Willis, Leonard.
Wilson, John, Lieutenant.
Wilmoth, William.
Wilson, ———.
Wilson, Agustine, Sergeant.
Wilson, Benjamin, Lieutenant.
Wilson, George.
Wilson, Goodwin, Jr.
Wilson, John, Private.
Wilson, Josiah.
Winfrey, J., Captain.
Winfrey, Jacob, Captain.
Winfrey, Jesse, Captain.
Winn, Benjamin.
Winn, John, Sr.; Son of Liberty; member of Committee of Correspondence, and Provincial Congress.
Winn, John, Major.
Winn, Joshua.
Winn, Richard, Captain.
Wise, ———, Major.
Wise, John.
Wise, Sheredy.
Witherspoon, John; Son of Liberty; member of Provincial Congress.
Witherspoon, John, Jr.; Son of Liberty.
Wofford, William, Major, Colonel.
Wolf, Andrew (1).
Wolf, Andrew (2).
Wood, ———, Surgeon's Mate.
Wood, Edward, Captain.
Wood, Elit.
Wood, J.
Wood, James, Lieutenant.
Wood, John, Paymaster.
Wood, Joseph, Major; delegate to Continental Congress.
Wood, Joseph, Jr.; Clerk of Assembly.
Wood, Joshua.
Wood, Misael.
Wood, Soloman, Captain.
Woodall, Jonathan.
Woodall, Joseph.
Woodruffe, Joseph, Major.
Woodson, William.
Woodworth, Darius.
Woolf, Andrew.
Wooten, ———, Lieutenant.
Worsham, Richard, Lieutenant.
Worth, Thomas.
Wright, ———, Major.
Wright, Ambrose; Son of Liberty; member of Provincial Congress; Commissary General.
Wright, Dionyisius.
Wright, John, Lieutenant, Captain.
Wright, John, G., Surgeon.
Wright, Nathaniel.
Wright, William, Ensign.
Wyatt, Peyton.
Wyche, George, Colonel; member of Provincial Congress; Son of Liberty.
Wylley, Richard; President of Council; Quartermaster-General.
Wylley, Thomas, Assistant Quartermaster-General.
Wynne, Peter.

### Y.

Yancey, Lewis.
Yancey, Lewis D.
Yaney, ———.
York, William.
Youmans, ———, Sergeant-Major.
Young, Edward, Captain.
Young, George.
Young, Isaac, Lieutenant; Son of Liberty; member of Provincial Congress.
Young, Jacob.
Young, James, Quartermaster-Sergeant.
Young, William; Son of Liberty; member of Council of Safety, and Provincial Congress.
Young, William, Private.

Z.

Zackery, Bartholomew, Captain.

Zittrauer, Ernest.
Zubley, David; Son of Liberty; member of Provincial Congress.

The above list has been compiled from a great number of shorter ones. No doubt it contains numerous repetitions, but these were unavoidable. Two names nearly alike may refer to the same man, but it is not always possible to determine which of two forms was the correct one, hence the spelling has not been altered in any case; but the mere fact that two names are nearly alike is not sufficient evidence that they belong to the same individual. For instance, it is known that "James Aitkin," "James Akens," and "James Akins," were three different persons.

In some instances the first name was not given. Wherever it was possible to add a title as means of identification, this has been done.

It is quite a common occurrence to find a record of two or more men bearing the same name. Names repeated and intended for different persons are marked with figures or indicated by titles.

About half the names in the foregoing list are those of officers and eminent patriots. Unfortunately, it is not always possible to find the records of private and humble heroes who risked their lives and served their country just as faithfully as their better known contemporaries. But even if these records were immediately available, and the list extended so as to include all who actually fought for freedom in Georgia during the whole Revolutionary period, there would still be an undue proportion of officers. No regiment ever included the whole number of privates called for; and, in those days of irregular warfare, it was quite common for one officer to start out upon an independent expedition with less than twenty men under him.

Companies were hurriedly formed as occasion demanded, and frequently disbanded as soon as an emergency was past.

Civil officers as well as military actually bore arms. They were obliged to do so in order to defend their homes and families. During the whole period of British occupancy the various legislative bodies fled from place to place and skirmished with English and Tories in order to keep up the form of republican government.

It is confidently believed that the foregoing list contains no doubtful names. All, except a very few, were repeated a number of times. Every list examined was largely a repetition of others, thus rendering the process of gathering new names exceedingly slow, but at the same time tending to establish the authenticity of all. In a list of ten names one might be new, but that new name was likely to come up again with twenty old ones.

The above names were gathered from the following:

McCall's History of Georgia.
Stephen's History of Georgia.
Ramsay's History of the American Revolution.
Lee's Memoirs of the War in the Southern Department of the United States.
Arthur and Carpenter's History of Georgia.
White's Statistics of Georgia.
White's Historical Collections of Georgia.

Harris's History of Georgia.
Jones's History of Georgia.
Jones's Dead Towns of Georgia.
Saffell's Revolutionary Records.
Heitman's Historical Register.
Lanman's Biographical Annals of the United States in Civil Government.
Harper's Cyclopedia of United States History.
Lossing's Field Book of the Revolution.
List of Members of the Georgia Society of the Cincinatti.
King's Mountain and It's Heroes, by Lyman C. Draper, LL.D.
The Rear Guard of the Revolution, by Edmond Kirke.
United States Pension Rolls.
List of Georgia State Officers in the Revolution, prepared by Gov. Allen D. Candler, while Secretary of State of Georgia.
History of Liberty Independent Troop, by Rev. C. C. Jones.
Force's American Archives.
Orderly Book of Generals Lee and Howe, in possession of F. B. Heitman, Washington, D. C.
The Story of Wilkes County, by Eliza A. Bowen, Washington, Ga.
Diary of George Smith, in possession of Mrs. Julia E. Smith, Savannah, Ga.
History of Medway Church, by Rev. James Stacy, Newman, Ga.
Brewers' History of Alabama.
Fairbanks' History of Florida.
History of the Families of Bellinger and DeVeaux, by Joseph Gaston Bulloch, M. D., Savannah, Ga., 1896.
Boykin's Georgia Baptists.
Campbell's Georgia Baptists.
Gilmer's Georgians.
Sherwood's Gazeteer.
Life of Jesse Mercer.
Early Settlers of North Alabama, by Mrs. W. C. Stubbs, New Orleans, La.
History of Old Cheraws, South Carolina.
History of Orangeburg, South Carolina.
Alabama Records.
Bench and Bar of Georgia, by S. F. Miller.
Salzburgers and Their Decendants, published by Strobel, Baltimore, 1855.
American State Papers (Washington, D. C.), Military Affairs.
Various unpublished manuscripts in possession of Charles Edgeworth Jones, of Augusta, Ga., and F. Apthorpe Foster, of Cambridge, Mass. Among these manuscripts are extracts from the returns of Gen. Lachlin McIntosh and Samuel Elbert, and the provision returns of the commissary, Mordecai Sheftall.
Unpublished documents in the Capitol, at Atlanta, Ga., and in the Court-house at Washington, Ga.
Lineage books of the National Society, Daughters of the American Revolution.

The foregoing list was compiled by Margaret B. Harvey, historian of Merion Chapter, Daughters of the American Revolution, Bala, Montgomery County, Pa., 1897-1900.

## GEORGIA REVOLUTIONARY PENSIONERS.

Compiled by Miss Helen M. Prescott, from the Report of the Society of War in Relation to the Pension Establishment of the United States. Senate Documents Pension Roll, First Session, 23d Congress, No. 12, Washington; printed by Duff Green, 1835.

Figures refer to pages of the Georgia list.

A.—Andrews, Wm., *Oglethorpe County, . . . . . . . . . . 7
Ambrose, David, Effingham County, . . . . . . . . . . 16
Allen, Wm., Franklin County, . . . . . . . . . . . . . 17
Arnold, William, Washington County, . . . . . . . . . 28
Anderson, Wm., *Baldwin County, . . . . . . . . . . . 30
Allen, Philip, Clarke County, . . . . . . . . . . . . 32
Arnaud, John P., Chatham County, . . . . . . . . . . 34
Adams, Thos., Elbert County, . . . . . . . . . . . . 36
Adams, James, Elbert County, . . . . . . . . . . . . 36
Aaron, Wm., Franklin County, . . . . . . . . . . . . 37
Albritton, John, Franklin County, . . . . . . . . . . 37
Akin, James, Fayette County, . . . . . . . . . . . . 39
Allred, Elias, Sr., Hall County, . . . . . . . . . . 41
Adams, Francis, Henry County, . . . . . . . . . . . . 42
Anglin, Henry, *Jackson County, . . . . . . . . . . . 45
Akins, Wm., Morgan County, . . . . . . . . . . . . . 50
Andrews, Owen, Meriwether County, . . . . . . . . . . 51
Arnett, Jno. Screven County, . . . . . . . . . . . . 55
Adkins, Chas., Sr., Upson County, . . . . . . . . . . 58
Aldredge, Wm., Wilkes County, . . . . . . . . . . . . 58

B.—Bird, Herman, Chatham County, . . . . . . . . . . . . 2
Baxter, John, Chatham County, . . . . . . . . . . . . 3
Bradley, Wm., Chatham County, . . . . . . . . . . . . 8
Brown, John, Camden County, . . . . . . . . . . . . . 14
Beale, Wm., Effingham County, . . . . . . . . . . . . 16
Brantley, Amos, Hancock County, . . . . . . . . . . . 19
Black, John, Hall County, . . . . . . . . . . . . . . 19
Bryant, Wm., Morgan County, . . . . . . . . . . . . . 22
Bragg, Wm., Madison County, . . . . . . . . . . . . . 22
Bishop, Golden, Newton County, . . . . . . . . . . . 24
Buchanan, James, Newton County, . . . . . . . . . . . 24
Bennett, John, Pulaski County, . . . . . . . . . . . 25
Bowen, Stephen, Tatnall County, . . . . . . . . . . . 27
Bohan, Joseph, Wilkes County, . . . . . . . . . . . . 28
Bynum, Drury, Warren County, . . . . . . . . . . . . 29
Brown, Uriah, Baldwin County, . . . . . . . . . . . . 30
Benton, Joseph, Sr., Butts County, . . . . . . . . . 30
Bowling, Edward, Clarke County, . . . . . . . . . . . 32
Beard, Moses, Clarke County, . . . . . . . . . . . . 32
Bowen, Samuel, Elbert County, . . . . . . . . . . . . 36

## REVOLUTIONARY PENSIONERS.

Butler, James, Elbert County, . . . . . . . . . . . . . 36
Butler, Patrick, Elbert County, . . . . . . . . . . . . 36
Brown, Ben, *Elbert County, . . . . . . . . . . . . . 37
Bond, Richard, Franklin County, . . . . . . . . . . . 37
Baber, James, Gwinnett County, . . . . . . . . . . . 40
Bagby, John, Gwinnett County, . . . . . . . . . . . . 40
Benson, Enoch, Gwinnett County, . . . . . . . . . . 40
Brewster, Hugh, Gwinnett County, . . . . . . . . . . 40
Baker, Elias, Gwinnett County, . . . . . . . . . . . . 40
Bowen, John, Gwinnett County, . . . . . . . . . . . . 40
Baker, Beal, Hall County, . . . . . . . . . . . . . . 41
Beard, Robert, Henry County, . . . . . . . . . . . . 41
Barnhill, John, Henry County, . . . . . . . . . . . . 42
Brown, Robert, Habersham County, . . . . . . . . . 42
Brazil, Byrd, Hancock County, . . . . . . . . . . . . 43
Brooks, Middleton, Jackson County, . . . . . . . . . 45
Barron, Thomas, Jackson County, . . . . . . . . . . 45
Barr, James, Jackson County, . . . . . . . . . . . . 45
Burgess, Josiah, Jasper County, . . . . . . . . . . . 46
Barnett, Sion, Jasper County, . . . . . . . . . . . . 46
Bryon, Thomas, Laurens County, . . . . . . . . . . 48
Bullock, Hawkins, Madison County, . . . . . . . . . 48
Buchanan, George, Marion County, . . . . . . . . . 49
Brooks, Robert, Marion County, . . . . . . . . . . . 49
Boon, Jesse, Morgan County, . . . . . . . . . . . . 50
Barkley, Wm., Morgan County, . . . . . . . . . . . 50
Brown, Ephraim, Muscogee County, . . . . . . . . . 50
Buff, Michael, Oglethorpe County, . . . . . . . . . . 53
Bledsoe, Millar, Oglethorpe County, . . . . . . . . . 53
Brown, Walter, Pike County, . . . . . . . . . . . . 54
Baldry, Isaac K., Tattnall County, . . . . . . . . . . 56
Bowen, Elijah, Tattnall County, . . . . . . . . . . . 56
Black, Wm., Upson County, . . . . . . . . . . . . . 58
Barrett, Lewis, Wilkes County, . . . . . . . . . . . 58
Burnley, Henry, Warren County, . . . . . . . . . . . 59
Brown, Stark, Walton County, . . . . . . . . . . . . 60
Brand, Wm., Walton County, . . . . . . . . . . . . 60
Brewster, Sheriff, Walton County, . . . . . . . . . . 60
Bosworth, Jacob, Walton County, . . . . . . . . . . 65

C.—Conners, Daniel, Clarke County, . . . . . . . . . . 3
Camp, Hosea, Campbell County, . . . . . . . . . . 4
Chalfinch, Hiram, Upson County, . . . . . . . . . . 8
Cameron, Alex, Upson County, . . . . . . . . . . . 9
Chenault, John, Columbia County, . . . . . . . . . . 13
Clark, Jacob, Camden County, . . . . . . . . . . . 14
Clark, Edward, Elbert County, . . . . . . . . . . . 15
Clower, Daniel, Gwinnett County, . . . . . . . . . . 18

## ROSTER OF THE REVOLUTION.

| | |
|---|---|
| Chatfield, John, Jasper County, | 20 |
| Crossan, John, Wilkes County, | 28 |
| Carter, Robert, Clarke County, | 32 |
| Copelan, Wm., De Kalb County, | 35 |
| Cook, John, Elbert County, | 37 |
| Cook, George, Elbert County, | 37 |
| Cheek, Wm., Franklin County, | 37 |
| Clark, Thomas, Franklin County, | 37 |
| Carter, David, Franklin County, | 37 |
| Cash, James, Franklin County, | 37 |
| Curbow, Joseph, Gwinnett County, | 40 |
| Cox, Thomas, Gwinnett County, | 40 |
| Crawford, Arthur, Hall County, | 41 |
| Carr, Wm., Hall County, | 41 |
| Coile, James, Hall County, | 41 |
| Collins, John, Sr., *Hall County, | 41 |
| Cloud, Ezekiel, Henry County, | 42 |
| Cash, John, Henry County, | 42 |
| Cook, Thomas, *Henry County, | 42 |
| Crumby, Thomas, Habersham County, | 42 |
| Clarke, William, Jefferson County, | 44 |
| Cunningham, Ansell, *Jackson County, | 45 |
| Crawford, John, Monroe County, | 49 |
| Campbell, George, Morgan County, | 50 |
| Cochran, Matthew, Morgan County, | 50 |
| Coulder, John, McIntosh County, | 52 |
| Carter, Charles, Oglethorpe County, | 53 |
| Conyers, John, Screven County, | 55 |
| Carraway, William, Upson County, | 58 |
| Combs, John, Wilkes County, | 58 |
| Cason, William, Warran County, | 59 |
| Cox, Moses, Washington County, | 60 |
| Cannon, Nathaniel, Wilkinson County, | 61 |
| Caile, William, Wilkinson County, | 65 |
| Cliffton, George, Wilkinson County, | 65 |
| D.—Dabney, Austin, Burke County, | 2 |
| Damron, Charles, Jackson County, | 6 |
| Davis, Thomas, L., Jackson County, | 9 |
| Doyle, Nimrod, T., Jackson County, | 9 |
| Duncan, James, Baldwin County, | 11 |
| Douglas, Thomas, Chatham County, | 13 |
| Durkee, Nathaniel, Chatham County, | 13 |
| Devaux, Peter, Chatham County, | 13 |
| Dillard, James, Elbert County, | 15 |
| Defnall, David, Pulaski County, | 25 |
| Davis, Talliver, Monroe County, | |
| Davidson, Joseph, Pike County, | 26 |

## REVOLUTIONARY PENSIONERS.

Dicken, Richard, Clarke County, . . . . . . . . . . . . 32
Dabbs, John, De Kalb County, . . . . . . . . . . . . 35
Donaldson, Wm., De Kalb County, . . . . . . . . . . 35
Daniel, Capt. John, Elbert County, . . . . . . . . . . 37
Davis, John, Elbert County, . . . . . . . . . . . . . 37
Dyer, Elisha, Elbert County, . . . . . . . . . . . . . 38
Darby, Richard, Fayette County, . . . . . . . . . . . 39
Davis, John, Gwinnett County, . . . . . . . . . . . . 40
Dobbs, Nathan, Gwinnett County, . . . . . . . . . . 40
Doby, John, Jasper County, . . . . . . . . . . . . . 46
Davidson, John, Jasper County, . . . . . . . . . . . 46
Durham, Matthew, Monroe County, . . . . . . . . . 49
Dunn, Thomas, Oglethorpe County, . . . . . . . . . 53
Draper, James, Warren County, . . . . . . . . . . . 59

E.—Edmondson, James P., Chatham County, . . . . . . . 2
Elliott, Thomas, Morgan County, . . . . . . . . . . 22
Espy, James, Clarke County, . . . . . . . . . . . . 32
Espy, John, Clarke County, . . . . . . . . . . . . . 32
Edwards, Solomon, Clarke County, . . . . . . . . . 32
Epposon, Thompson, Elbert County, . . . . . . . . . 38
Eastwood, Israel, Elbert County, . . . . . . . . . . 39
Edwards, Reuben, Henry County, . . . . . . . . . . 42
Eidson, Shelton, Morgan County, . . . . . . . . . . 50
Elledge, Jacob, Murray County, . . . . . . . . . . . 51
Edwards, John, Meriwether County, . . . . . . . . . 51
Earnest, George, Meriwether County, . . . . . . . . 51
Eberhart, Jacob, Oglethorpe County, . . . . . . . . 53
Evans, William, Sen., Taliaferro County, . . . . . . . 57

F.—Fry, Benjamin, Jasper County, . . . . . . . . . . . 6
Foy, Darby, Columbia County, . . . . . . . . . . . . 6
Frazier, Elijah, Putnam County, . . . . . . . . . . . 6
Farrow, Jesse, Burke County, . . . . . . . . . . . . 11
Freeman, Coldrup, Clarke County, . . . . . . . . . 14
Fitzgerald, George, Franklin County, . . . . . . . . 17
Farrar, Francis, Clarke County, . . . . . . . . . . . 32
Fluker, John, Clarke County, . . . . . . . . . . . . 33
Fleming, William, Hall County, . . . . . . . . . . . 41
Flemming, Robert, Hall County, . . . . . . . . . . 41
Flanagan, William, Hall County, . . . . . . . . . . 41
Freeman, Daniel, Jasper County, . . . . . . . . . . 46
Fincher, James, Jasper County, . . . . . . . . . . . 46
Fretwell, Richard, Newton County, . . . . . . . . . 52
Finch, William, Oglethorpe County, . . . . . . . . . 53
Fimderburk, John, Troup County, . . . . . . . . . . 56
Files, Adam J., Talbot County, . . . . . . . . . . . 57
Formby, Nathan, Walton County, . . . . . . . . . . 60

ROSTER OF THE REVOLUTION.

G.—Goolsby, Reuben, Elbert County, . . . . . . . . . . . 4
Green, John, Elbert County, . . . . . . . . . . . . . . 9
Green, Benjamin, Elbert County, . . . . . . . . . . . . 9
Green, Thomas, Elbert County, . . . . . . . . . . . . . 9
Griffin, Edward, Elbert County, . . . . . . . . . . . . 9
Green, John, R., Clarke County, . . . . . . . . . . . . 10
Goodwin, Wiley, Baldwin County, . . . . . . . . . . . . 11
Graves, William, Burke County, . . . . . . . . . . . . 11
Garner, Charles, Clarke County, . . . . . . . . . . . . 14
Gulley, Richard, Elbert County, . . . . . . . . . . . . 15
Grimsley, Thomas, Meriwether County, . . . . . . . . . 23
Gunnell, Wm., Gwinnett County, . . . . . . . . . . . . 18
Gordon, James, Oglethorpe County, . . . . . . . . . . . 24
Gay, Allan, Coweta County, . . . . . . . . . . . . . . 31
Goldsmith, John, Coweta County, . . . . . . . . . . . . 31
Gaines, William, Elbert County, . . . . . . . . . . . . 37
Groover, Peter, Elbert County, . . . . . . . . . . . . 38
Gilliland, Wm., Sen., Fayette County, . . . . . . . . . 38
Gower, Abel, Gwinnett County, . . . . . . . . . . . . . 40
Gilmore, James, Hall County, . . . . . . . . . . . . . 41
Grant, Joseph, Hancock County, . . . . . . . . . . . . 43
Gunter, Charles, Jackson County, . . . . . . . . . . . 45
Griffin, James, Irwin County, . . . . . . . . . . . . . 46
Goff, Nathaniel I., Jasper County, . . . . . . . . . . 46
Green, Thomas, Jasper County, . . . . . . . . . . . . . 46
Guice, John, Sen., Lincoln County, . . . . . . . . . . 47
Glasgo, William, Madison County, . . . . . . . . . . . 48
Groves, Stephen, Madison County, . . . . . . . . . . . 48
Gunn, Gabriel, Newton County, . . . . . . . . . . . . . 52
Gregory, Richard, Oglethorpe County, . . . . . . . . . 53
Gordon, James F., Oglethorpe County, . . . . . . . . . 53
Grace, John, Tattnall County, . . . . . . . . . . . . . 56
Gresham, Littlebury, Troup County, . . . . . . . . . . 56
Gresham, David, Troup County, . . . . . . . . . . . . . 56
Gilmore, James, Washington County, . . . . . . . . . . 60

H.—Hunt, John, Greene County, . . . . . . . . . . . . . . 5
Hannegan, James, Henry County, . . . . . . . . . . . . 5
Henderson, Richard, Upson County, . . . . . . . . . . . 8
Henshaw, Thomas, Upson County, . . . . . . . . . . . . 9
Hutto, Henry, Baker County, . . . . . . . . . . . . . . 12
Holbrook, Nathan, Chatham County, . . . . . . . . . . . 13
Hurley, David, Chatham County, . . . . . . . . . . . . 13
Hinds, John, Chatham County, . . . . . . . . . . . . . 13
Housley, John, Elbert County, . . . . . . . . . . . . . 15
Hooks, William, Emanuel County, . . . . . . . . . . . . 16
Holland, Hugh, Franklin County, . . . . . . . . . . . . 17
Holbrook, Eddy, Franklin County, . . . . . . . . . . . 17

# REVOLUTIONARY PENSIONERS. 441

Howell, Jesse, Franklin County, . . . . . . . . . . . . . 17
Hamilton, John, Hall County, . . . . . . . . . . . . . . 19
Howard, Thomas, Lincoln County, . . . . . . . . . . . . 21
Hutchins, Edward, Laurens County, . . . . . . . . . . . 21
Hicks, Isaac, Oglethorpe County, . . . . . . . . . . . . 24
Haynie, William, Pulaski County, . . . . . . . . . . . . 25
Hurley, Joseph, Wilkes County, . . . . . . . . . . . . . 28
Hicks, John, Coweta County, . . . . . . . . . . . . . . 31
Houston, John, Coweta County, . . . . . . . . . . . . . 32
Hall, Isaac, Clarke County, . . . . . . . . . . . . . . . 32
Hinson, Lazarus, Carroll County, . . . . . . . . . . . . 34
Haisley, Thomas, Carroll County, . . . . . . . . . . . . 34
Hooper, James, De Kalb County, . . . . . . . . . . . . 35
Hays, John, *De Kalb County, . . . . . . . . . . . . . . 35
Hudson, David, Elbert County, . . . . . . . . . . . . . 37
Holbrook, Jesse, Elbert County, . . . . . . . . . . . . . 38
Hooper, Richard B., Elbert County, . . . . . . . . . . . 38
Houston, Samuel, Fayette County, . . . . . . . . . . . . 39
Harris, Matthew, Greene County, . . . . . . . . . . . . 39
Haisten, Jno., Fayette County, . . . . . . . . . . . . . ..
Hunt, Littleton, Gwinnett County, . . . . . . . . . . . . 40
Harris, Stephen, Gwinnett County, . . . . . . . . . . . 40
Herring, Jesse, Gwinnett County, . . . . . . . . . . . . 40
Horton, Isaac, Gwinnett County, . . . . . . . . . . . . 40
Hames, John, Sen., Hall County, . . . . . . . . . . . . 41
Hand, Joseph, Henry County, . . . . . . . . . . . . . . 42
Haisten, John, Fayette County, . . . . . . . . . . . . . 39
Hill, John, Hancock County, . . . . . . . . . . . . . . 43
Harris, Joseph, Jackson County, . . . . . . . . . . . . 45
Henderson, Robert, Jackson County, . . . . . . . . . . . 45
Hampton, John, Jackson County, . . . . . . . . . . . . 45
Hodge, William, Madison County, . . . . . . . . . . . . 48
Human, Alexander, Madison County, . . . . . . . . . . . 48
Hawks, Frederick, Madison County, . . . . . . . . . . . 48
Hester, Robert, Morgan County, . . . . . . . . . . . . . 50
Hodges, Philemon, Muscogee County, . . . . . . . . . . 50
Hammond, Joshua, Muscogee County, . . . . . . . . . . 50
Honea, Tobias, Meriwether County, . . . . . . . . . . . 51
Hatcher, William, Meriwether County, . . . . . . . . . . 51
Hewell, Wiatt, Newton County, . . . . . . . . . . . . . 52
Holland, Henry, Tattnall County, . . . . . . . . . . . . 56
Howard, Solomon, Washington County, . . . . . . . . . 60
Hardee, Thomas, Washington County, . . . . . . . . . . 60
Herndon, Joseph, Walton County, . . . . . . . . . . . . 60
Hardin, Henry, Walton County, . . . . . . . . . . . . . 60
Harris, Benjamin, Walton County, . . . . . . . . . . . . 60

I.—Isely, Philip, Gwinnett County, . . . . . . . . . . . . 40

ROSTER OF THE REVOLUTION.

J.—Jones, Harrison, Morgan County, . . . . . . . . . . . . 7
Jones, Wm., . . . . . . . . . . . . . . . . . . . . . 6
Jordon, Miles, Columbia County, . . . . . . . . . . . . 10
Jordon, Fountain, Elbert County, . . . . . . . . . . . . 15
Jones, Thomas, Hancock County, . . . . . . . . . . . . 19
Jones, William, Jasper County, . . . . . . . . . . . . . 21
Jones, Solomon, McIntosh County, . . . . . . . . . . . 23
Jones, Abraham P., Putnam County, . . . . . . . . . . . 25
Johnson, Abraham, Wilkes County, . . . . . . . . . . . 28
Johnson, Joseph Payne, Wilkes County, . . . . . . . . . 28
Jenkins, William, Wilkinson County, . . . . . . . . . . 29
Jenkins, Lewis, Gwinnett County, . . . . . . . . . . . . 40
Johnson, Jonathan, Gwinnett County, . . . . . . . . . . 40
Jackson, Edward, Gwinnett County, . . . . . . . . . . . 40
Johnson, Hardy, Houston County, . . . . . . . . . . . . 43
Jones, Jonathan, Laurens County, . . . . . . . . . . . . 48
Jordan, Dempsey, Taliaferro County, . . . . . . . . . . 57
Jackson, William, Franklin County, . . . . . . . . . . . 59

K.—Kendrick, John, Franklin County, . . . . . . . . . . . . 9
Kerr, Henry, Franklin County, . . . . . . . . . . . . . 9
Kelly, Wm., Elbert County, . . . . . . . . . . . . . . ..
Kelan, James, Madison County, . . . . . . . . . . . . . 22
Kerr, David, Oglethorpe County, . . . . . . . . . . . . 24
Keith, John, Putnam County, . . . . . . . . . . . . . . 25
Kernell, William, Wayne County, . . . . . . . . . . . . 29
Key, William B., Elbert County, . . . . . . . . . . . . 37
Kehela, Christopher, Gwinnett County, . . . . . . . . . 40
Kelley, Lloyd, Hancock County, . . . . . . . . . . . . . 43
Knox, Samuel, Jackson County, . . . . . . . . . . . . . 45
King, John, Jackson County, . . . . . . . . . . . . . . 45
Kidd, James H., Jackson County, . . . . . . . . . . . . 45
Kolb, Peter, Jones County, . . . . . . . . . . . . . . . 47
Knight, Elisha, Meriwether County, . . . . . . . . . . . 51
Kidd, William, Oglethorpe County, . . . . . . . . . . . 51
King, Thomas, Putnam County, . . . . . . . . . . . . . 54
Kell, James, Rabun County, . . . . . . . . . . . . . . . 55
Kell, Robert, Rabun County, . . . . . . . . . . . . . . 55
King, Richard, Taliaferro County, . . . . . . . . . . . 57

L.—Lindsey, John, . . . . . . . . . . . . . . . . . . . . . 9
Lawson, Hugh, . . . . . . . . . . . . . . . . . . . . 9
Lewis, James, . . . . . . . . . . . . . . . . . . . . . 9
Lloyd, Edward, . . . . . . . . . . . . . . . . . . . . 9
Logan, Philip, Baldwin County, . . . . . . . . . . . . . 11
Latham, Amos, Glynn County, . . . . . . . . . . . . . ..
Langham, James, Upson County, . . . . . . . . . . . . 27
Love, Thomas, Washington County, . . . . . . . . . . . 28

Littleton, William, Wilkes County, . . . . . . . . . . . . . 28
Lumpkins, Philip, Burke County, . . . . . . . . . . . . 31
Lee, Burwell, Clarke County, . . . . . . . . . . . . . . 32
Lard, Robert, Clarke County, . . . . . . . . . . . . . . 32
Lambert, John, Columbia County, . . . . . . . . . . . . 33
Landers, John, De Kalb County, . . . . . . . . . . . . 37
Lockett, James, Elbert County, . . . . . . . . . . . . . 37
Leech, Burdett, Elbert County, . . . . . . . . . . . . . 38
Liddell, William, Gwinnett County, . . . . . . . . . . . 40
Lyons, William, Jefferson County, . . . . . . . . . . . . 44
Lowrey, Levi, Jackson County, . . . . . . . . . . . . . 45
Linville, William, Lincoln County, . . . . . . . . . . . 47
Lesley, William, Oglethorpe County, . . . . . . . . . . . 53
Landrum, Thomas, Oglethorpe County, . . . . . . . . . 53
Lawrence, John, Putnam County, . . . . . . . . . . . . 54
Langley, John, Troup County, . . . . . . . . . . . . . 56
Lawrence, John, . . . . . . . . . . . . . . . . . . . 65

M.—Mercer, Joshua, Greene County, . . . . . . . . . . . . 5
Morris, William, Sen., Gwinnett County, . . . . . . . . . 18
Morris, Thomas, . . . . . . . . . . . . . . . . . . . 20
McIntire, Jno., Habersham County, . . . . . . . . . . . 20
Martin, James, Jackson County, . . . . . . . . . . . . 21
Martin, John, Richmond County, . . . . . . . . . . . . 26
Morris, Thos., Jasper County, . . . . . . . . . . . . . ..
Minton, John, Wilkes County, . . . . . . . . . . . . . 28
McKinney, Timothy, Screven County, . . . . . . . . . . ..
Milirons, William, Warren County, . . . . . . . . . . . 29
Mains, Samuel, Wilkinson County, . . . . . . . . . . . 29
Murray, Thomas, Columbia County, . . . . . . . . . . 33
McDonald, Jno., Clarke County, . . . . . . . . . . . . ..
Mead, Minor, Carroll County, . . . . . . . . . . . . . 34
McDowell, Robert, De Kalb County, . . . . . . . . . . ..
Mahemson, John, *De Kalb County, . . . . . . . . . . 35
Murdock William, Elbert County, . . . . . . . . . . . 38
Mackie, Samuel, Elbert County, . . . . . . . . . . . . 38
McMillion, John, *Elbert County, . . . . . . . . . . . 38
Moseley, Samuel, Elbert County, . . . . . . . . . . . . 38
Mitchell, William, Elbert County, . . . . . . . . . . . 38
Marshall, Jesse, Elbert County, . . . . . . . . . . . . 38
Mills, Moses, Fayette County, . . . . . . . . . . . . . 39
McDade, John, Gwinnett County, . . . . . . . . . . . 40
Moore, John, Hall County, . . . . . . . . . . . . . . 41
McCleskey, James, Hall County, . . . . . . . . . . . . 41
McCance, David, Henry County, . . . . . . . . . . . . 42
Moore, Isaac, Sen., Henry County, . . . . . . . . . . . 42
Malone, Mullins, Hancock County, . . . . . . . . . . . 43
Matthews, William, *Jackson County, . . . . . . . . . . 45

ROSTER OF THE REVOLUTION.

Matthews, Isaac *Jackson County, . . . . . . . . . . . 45
Miller, William, Jackson County, . . . . . . . . . . . 45
McElahnnon, John, Jackson County, . . . . . . . . . 45
McKenney, Charles, Jackson County, . . . . . . . . . 45
Moore, James, Jasper County, . . . . . . . . . . . . 46
Morris, Nathaniel, Jones County, . . . . . . . . . . . 47
McKenney, Jno., Sr., Jones County, . . . . . . . . . ..
McCurdy, John, Madison County, . . . . . . . . . . . 48
McDerment, Joseph, Madison County, . . . . . . . . . 48
Mayo, John, Sen., Marion County, . . . . . . . . . . 49
Monk, John, Monroe County, . . . . . . . . . . . . 49
Meeks, Brittain, Meriwether County, . . . . . . . . . 51
McLain, Thomas, Newton County, . . . . . . . . . . 52
McCullers, William, Newton County, . . . . . . . . . 52
Moody, Thomas, Oglethorpe County, . . . . . . . . . 53
McLaughlin, John, Warren County, . . . . . . . . . . 59
Mathews, John, Washington County, . . . . . . . . . 60
Melton, William, Walton County, . . . . . . . . . . . 60
Miller, William, Ware County, . . . . . . . . . . . . 61

N.—Newman, John, . . . . . . . . . . . . . . . . . 9
Nealy, John, Coweta County, . . . . . . . . . . . . 31
Norwood, George, Clarke County, . . . . . . . . . . ..
Nicholson, John, Hall County, . . . . . . . . . . . . 41
Nix, James, Harris County, . . . . . . . . . . . . . 44

O.—Odum, Seybert, Chatham County, . . . . . . . . . . 2
Owens, Joseph, Columbia County, . . . . . . . . . . 13
Oliver, John, Sen., Clarke County, . . . . . . . . . . 32
Oliver, James, Pulaski County, . . . . . . . . . . . . 54
Oliver, Morton, Jones County, . . . . . . . . . . . . 47

P.—Penticost, William, Jasper County, . . . . . . . . . 6
Prior, John, Burke County, . . . . . . . . . . . . . 11
Peace, John, Monroe County, . . . . . . . . . . . . 22
Peters, Elijah, Oglethorpe County, . . . . . . . . . . 24
Paschal, George, Oglethorpe County, . . . . . . . . . 24
Pritchett, Stephen, Wilkinson County, . . . . . . . . 29
Parr, Benjamin, Clarke County, . . . . . . . . . . . 32
Phillips, Levi, Carroll County, . . . . . . . . . . . . 34
Peters, Jesse, Carroll County, . . . . . . . . . . . . 34
Patterson, Robert, DeKalb County, . . . . . . . . . . 35
Powell, Lewis, Dooly County, . . . . . . . . . . . . 36
Powell, Francis, Elbert County, . . . . . . . . . . . 37
Pullen, Robert, Greene County, . . . . . . . . . . . 39
Porter, Oliver, *Greene County, . . . . . . . . . . . 39
Payne, Nehemiah, Hall County, . . . . . . . . . . . 41
Parkes, Benjamin, Sen., Hall County, . . . . . . . . . 41

REVOLUTIONARY PENSIONERS. 445

Potts, William, Jackson County, . . . . . . . . . . . . . 45
Peck, Henry, Newton County, . . . . . . . . . . . . . . 52
Pharaoh, Joshua, Richmond County, . . . . . . . . . . 55
Peacock, Isam, Tattnall County, . . . . . . . . . . . . 56
Pool, Samuel, Upson County, . . . . . . . . . . . . . . 58
Peacock, Uriah, Washington County, . . . . . . . . . . 60
Pawlett, Richard, . . . . . . . . . . . . . . . . . . . . 65
Peters, Jesse, . . . . . . . . . . . . . . . . . . . . . . 34

R.—Ramsey, John, . . . . . . . . . . . . . . . . . . . . 9
Reynolds, Ephraim, Chatham County, . . . . . . . . . 13
Roberts, Thomas, Clarke County, . . . . . . . . . . . 14
Rowell, Jesse, . . . . . . . . . . . . . . . . . . . . . 17
Rosseter, Timothy W., Hancock County, . . . . . . . . 19
Russell, Thomas, Richmond County, . . . . . . . . . . 26
Ray, William, Franklin County, . . . . . . . . . . . . 17
Roberts, Richard, Wayne County, . . . . . . . . . . . 29
Robertson, John, Baldwin County, . . . . . . . . . . . 30
Russell, James G., Baldwin County, . . . . . . . . . . 30
Robinson, John, Sen., Coweta County, . . . . . . . . 31
Rowe, Joshua, Crawford County, . . . . . . . . . . . 35
Rahn, Jonathan, Effingham County, . . . . . . . . . . 36
Riley, James, Elbert County, . . . . . . . . . . . . . 37
Richardson, Amos, *Elbert County, . . . . . . . . . . 37
Rice, Leonard, Elbert County, . . . . . . . . . . . . . 37
Rucher, William, Elbert County, . . . . . . . . . . . . 37
Routon, John, Fayette County, . . . . . . . . . . . . . 39
Roper, John, Gwinnett County, . . . . . . . . . . . . 40
Rylee, James, Hall County, . . . . . . . . . . . . . . 41
Roberts, Reuben, Jones County, . . . . . . . . . . . . 47
Ricketson, Jesse, Warren County, . . . . . . . . . . . ..

S.—Shirley, James, Chatham County, . . . . . . . . . . 2
Seva, John, . . . . . . . . . . . . . . . . . . . . . . . 9
Shackleford, John, . . . . . . . . . . . . . . . . . . . 9
Speake, Richard, Butts County, . . . . . . . . . . . . 12
Smith, Leonard, Columbia County, . . . . . . . . . . 13
Solter, Jacob, Effingham County, . . . . . . . . . . . 16
Sutley, James, Franklin County, . . . . . . . . . . . . 17
Sessions, John, Jasper County, . . . . . . . . . . . . 20
Smith, Austin, Lincoln County, . . . . . . . . . . . . 21
Shehee, John, Lincoln County, . . . . . . . . . . . . 21
Spears, John, Newton County, . . . . . . . . . . . . . 24
Stephens, William, Putnam County, . . . . . . . . . . 25
Sweatman, William, Thomas County, . . . . . . . . . 27
Sowell, Zadock, Wilkes County, . . . . . . . . . . . . 28
Sturdivant, Charles, Warren County, . . . . . . . . . 29
Saurlock, William, Baldwin County, . . . . . . . . . . 30

## ROSTER OF THE REVOLUTION.

Stevens, Reuben, Coweta County, . . . . . . . . . . . . 31
Scott, William, Coweta County, . . . . . . . . . . . 31
Summers, John, Clarke County, . . . . . . . . . . . . . 32
Smith, John, Clarke County, . . . . . . . . . . . . . . . 32
Sudduth, Jared, Clarke County, . . . . . . . . . . . . 32
Smith, William, *Clarke County, . . . . . . . . . . . 32
Smith, Hill, Clarke County, . . . . . . . . . . . . . . . 32
Shefstall, Shefstall, Chatham County, . . . . . . . . . . 34
Smith, Samuel, Chatham County, . . . . . . . . . . . . 34
Shellman, John, Chatham County, . . . . . . . . . . . . 34
Snyder, Jonathan, Effingham County, . . . . . . . . . . 36
Slay, Thomas, De Kalb County, . . . . . . . . . . . . . . ..
Stomers, Lewis, Elbert County, . . . . . . . . . . . . . 37
Sullivan, Pleasant, Elbert County, . . . . . . . . . . . 37
Smith, Henry, Elbert County, . . . . . . . . . . . . . . 38
Smith, Jesse, Elbert County, . . . . . . . . . . . . . . 38
Smith, William, Elbert County, . . . . . . . . . . . . . 38
Spears, William, Elbert County, . . . . . . . . . . . . . 38
Stoneypker, John, Elbert County, . . . . . . . . . . . . 38
Smith, William, Elbert County, . . . . . . . . . . . . . 38
Sheridan, Abner, Elbert County, . . . . . . . . . . . . . 38
Springer, Benjamin, Fayette County, . . . . . . . . . . . 39
Slaughter, George, Greene County, . . . . . . . . . . . . 39
Shaw, John, Greene County, . . . . . . . . . . . . . . . 39
Shaw, Basil, Hall County, . . . . . . . . . . . . . . . 41
Smith, Enoch, Hall County, . . . . . . . . . . . . . . 41
Stewart, James, Heard County, . . . . . . . . . . . . 42
Swan, William, Harris County, . . . . . . . . . . . . . 42
Saxton, Solomon, Jackson County, . . . . . . . . . . . 45
Sway, George, Jackson County, . . . . . . . . . . . . . 45
Slacomb, John Charles, Jones County, . . . . . . . . . 47
Stephens, Benjamin, Laurens County, . . . . . . . . . . 48
Smith, Ezekiel, Laurens County, . . . . . . . . . . . . 48
Stewart, William, *Monroe County, . . . . . . . . . . . 49
Smith, Isaac, Monroe County, . . . . . . . . . . . . . . ..
Stephens, John W., Muscogee County, . . . . . . . . . . 50
Smith, Alexander, Meriwether County, . . . . . . . . . 51
St. Johns, James, Newton County, . . . . . . . . . . . . 52
Smith, Larkin, Oglethorpe County, . . . . . . . . . . . 53
Strong, Charles, Oglethorpe County, . . . . . . . . . . 53
Smith, Shadrach, Oglethorpe County, . . . . . . . . . . 53
Stregel, Nicholas, Screven County, . . . . . . . . . . . 55
Sharp, John, Tattnall County, . . . . . . . . . . . . . 56
Stilwell, Jacob, Troup County, . . . . . . . . . . . . . 56
Smith, Hardy, Troup County, . . . . . . . . . . . . . . 56
Silvey, Stephen, Taliaferro County, . . . . . . . . . . . 57
Swords, James, Walton County, . . . . . . . . . . . . 60

REVOLUTIONARY PENSIONERS. 447

T.—Thornton, Prisley, Clarke County, . . . . . . . . . . . . . 3
Tenney, Edward, Chatham County, . . . . . . . . . . . 13
Tison, James, Effingham County, . . . . . . . . . . . 16
Talley, John, Montgomery County, . . . . . . . . . . . 23
Talbert, Benjamin, Baldwin County, . . . . . . . . . . . 30
Terrell, William, De Kalb County, . . . . . . . . . . . 35
Teasley, Silas, Elbert County, . . . . . . . . . . . . 37
Tucker, Herbert, Elbert County, . . . . . . . . . . . 37
Thomas, William, *Elbert County, . . . . . . . . . . . 38
Tate, John, Elbert County, . . . . . . . . . . . . . 38
Thrasher, George, Gwinnett County, . . . . . . . . . . 40
Turner, Robert, Habersham County, . . . . . . . . . . 42
Townsend, Thos, Habersham County, . . . . . . . . . . . .
Tarvin, George, Houston County, . . . . . . . . . . . 43
Thompson, Benjamin, Hancock County, . . . . . . . . . 43
Taylor, Robert, Jackson County, . . . . . . . . . . . 45
Thomas, Ethelred, Laurens County, . . . . . . . . . . 48
Tait, Robert L., Madison County, . . . . . . . . . . . . .
Tuggle, Charles, Madison County, . . . . . . . . . . . 48
Thompson, James, Madison County, . . . . . . . . . . 48
Talley, Henry, Newton County, . . . . . . . . . . . . 52
Toole, James, Richmond County, . . . . . . . . . . . 55
Thompson, Frederick, Walton County, . . . . . . . . . 61
Thomas, Caleb, . . . . . . . . . . . . . . . . . 65

U.—Upson, George, Sen., Coweta County, . . . . . . . . . 31
Upshaw, John, Elbert County, . . . . . . . . . . . . 37
Upchurch, Charles, Henry County, . . . . . . . . . . 42
Underwood, Archibald, Jackson County, . . . . . . . . . 45

V.—Vickory, William, Campbell County, . . . . . . . . . . 15
Vernon, Isaac, Madison County, . . . . . . . . . . . 48
Vickers, William, Meriwether County, . . . . . . . . . 51

W.—Whateley, Samuel, Wilkes County, . . . . . . . . . . 8
White, James, . . . . . . . . . . . . . . . . . 9
Whalen, Michael, . . . . . . . . . . . . . . . . 9
Wheeler, Charles, Columbia County, . . . . . . . . . . 13
Woodworth, Darius, Camden County, . . . . . . . . . . 14
Willoughby, William, Clarke County, . . . . . . . . . . 14
Waldrepe, James, Fayette County, . . . . . . . . . . 17
Wheeler, William, Habersham County, . . . . . . . . . 20
Wiley, Absolom, Washington County, . . . . . . . . . 28
Worsham, Richard, Wilkes County, . . . . . . . . . . 28
Wade, Moses, Wilkes County, . . . . . . . . . . . . 28
Williams, William, Wilkes County, . . . . . . . . . . 28
White, Jesse, Clarke County, . . . . . . . . . . . . 32
Wright, William, Clarke County, . . . . . . . . . . . 32

ROSTER OF THE REVOLUTION.

Welborn, Elias, Columbia County, . . . . . . . . . . . 33
Wood, Ellit, De Kalb County, . . . . . . . . . . . . 35
Williford, Nathan, De Kalb County, . . . . . . . . . . 35
Ward, William, Elbert County, . . . . . . . . . . . . 37
Wanslaw, John, Elbert County, . . . . . . . . . . . . 37
Wilkinson, Elisha, Elbert County, . . . . . . . . . . . 38
Wilson, John, *Greene County, . . . . . . . . . . . . 39
Walls, Charles, Gwinnett County, . . . . . . . . . . . 40
Wardlaw, William, Gwinnett County, . . . . . . . . . . 40
Wills, Leonard, Gwinnett County, . . . . . . . . . . . 40
Welchel, John, Hall County, . . . . . . . . . . . . . 41
West, Benjamin, Sen., Hall County, . . . . . . . . . . 41
Wilmoth, William, Hall County, . . . . . . . . . . . 41
Whitmore, Howell, Hall County, . . . . . . . . . . . 41
Wood, James, Heard County, . . . . . . . . . . . . . 44
Wheeler, James, Jackson County, . . . . . . . . . . . 45
White, Joseph, Jones County, . . . . . . . . . . . . 47
Wilder, Willis, Jones County, . . . . . . . . . . . . 47
Wright, Nathaniel, Lincoln County, . . . . . . . . . . 47
Ware, Edward, Madison County, . . . . . . . . . . . 48
Warden, Samuel, Madison County, . . . . . . . . . . 48
Weathers, Valentine, Newton County, . . . . . . . . . 52
Woodall, Joseph, Oglethorpe County, . . . . . . . . . 53
Ward, Samuel, Oglethorpe County, . . . . . . . . . . 53
Walker, Daniel, Sen., Richmond County, . . . . . . . . 55
Williams, Joseph, Taliaferro County, . . . . . . . . . 57
West, John, Talbot County, . . . . . . . . . . . . . 57
Williams, William, Washington County, . . . . . . . . 60
Wilson, Augustin, Washington County, . . . . . . . . . 60
Wood, Misael, Washington County, . . . . . . . . . . 60
Wilson, George, Walton County, . . . . . . . . . . . 61
Webb, Austin, Walton County, . . . . . . . . . . . . 61
Wolf, Andrew, . . . . . . . . . . . . . . . . . . 65

Y.—Young, William, Columbia County, . . . . . . . . . . . 33
Yancy, Lewis, Jasper County, . . . . . . . . . . . . 46
York, Wm., Hall County, . . . . . . . . . . . . . . 19
*In Georgia Con. Reports on Graves.

**GEORGIA REVOLUTIONARY PENSIONERS LIVING IN OTHER STATES.**

| Name. | Where Pensioned. | Page. | Name. | Where Pensioned. | Page. |
|---|---|---|---|---|---|
| Alexander, Asa, | Alabama, | 11 | Baker, John, | Tennessee, | 22 |
| Broughton, Job, | Kentucky, | 110 | Burke, Isham, | Tennessee, | 82 |
| Bynum, John, | Tennessee, | 82 | Cochran, Thos., | Kentucky, | 67 |
| Beckham, Abner, | Louisiana, | 6 | Castleberry, Wm. M., | Kentucky, | 107 |

REVOLUTIONARY PENSIONERS. 449

| Name. | Where Pensioned. | Page. | Name. | Where Pensioned. | Page. |
|---|---|---|---|---|---|
| Childers, David, | Tennessee, | 39 | Morgan, Asa, | Alabama, | 16 |
| Coleman, John, | Tennessee, | 39 | Matthews, Wm. H., | Florida, | 3 |
| Duprey, Wm., | Kentucky, | 81 | McCormick, Ben., | Alabama, | 21 |
| Darden, Geo., | Alabama, | 24 | Netherland, Ben, Sr., | Kentucky, | 109 |
| Ebzey, William, | Tennessee, | 23 | Nail, Matthew, | Alabama, | 18 |
| Fleming, Samuel, | Alabama, | 8 | Phipps, John, | Kentucky, | 107 |
| Gent, Chas., | Tennessee, | 93 | Palmer, John, | Tennessee, | 70 |
| Garner, John, | Alabama, | 2 | Perkins, Moses, | Tennessee, | 106 |
| Garner, Jos., | Alabama, | 7 | Parrish, Robert, | Tennessee, | 112 |
| Haines, Evan, | Kentucky, | 116 | Reed, Jacob, | Kentucky, | 21 |
| Higuet, Philip, | Indiana, | 75 | Rooksburg, Jacob, | Kentucky, | 42 |
| Hooper, Jesse, | Tennessee, | 55 | Reagan, Darby, | Tennessee, | 87 |
| Johnson, James, | Kentucky, | 46 | Sack, John, | Tennessee, | 37 |
| Joiner, Jonathan, | Tennessee, | 66 | Thurman, John, | Kentucky, | 99 |
| Jackson, Samuel, | Tennessee, | 105 | Willis, Meshack, | Tennessee, | 33 |
| Lee, Joshua, | Kentucky, | 98 | Wagnon, John P. | | 40 |
| Liner, Christopher, | Tennessee, | 80 | (or Waggoner), | Tennessee, | 117 |
| Littleton, Chas., | Alabama, | 17 | Wash, John, Sr., | Missouri, | 12 |
| Morrison, Eyre, | Kentucky, | 112 | Tyner, Joshua, | Illinois, | 14 |
| McElduff, Daniel, | Tennessee, | 3 | | | |

## NORTH CAROLINA AND SOUTH CAROLINA PENSION LIST.

Pensioners in North and South Carolina, who served in Georgia:

| Name. | Where Pensioned. | Page. | Name. | Where Pensioned. | Page. |
|---|---|---|---|---|---|
| Amos Brown, | Macon Co., N. C., | 97 | Mitchell, Reuben, | N. C., | 29 |
| | | | Mabry, Reps., | N. C., | 56 |
| Bankston, Andrew, | Rutherford, N. C., | 111 | Odum, Daniel, | S. C., | 3 |
| | | | Stiles, John, | N. C., | 39 |
| Burton, Rich'd, | Edge'c, S. C., | 17 | Sardezas, David, | S. C., | 15 |
| Berry, John. | S. C., | 25 | Stewart, James, | S. C., | 15 |
| Chamberlain, John | N. C., | 54 | Southern, Gibson, | S. C., | 19 |
| Crooker, Turner, | S. C., | 4 | Taylor, John, | N. C., | 51 |
| Castleberry, Paul, | S. C., | 49 | Tearney, Gilbert, | N. C., | 54 |
| Caldwell, Wm., | S. C., | 49 | Thompson, Barthol, | N. C., | 92 |
| Dean, Julius, | S. C., | 17 | Threadgill, Thos., | N. C., | 125 |
| Fuller, Stephen, | S. C., | 24 | Turner, Geo., | S. C., | 17 |
| Fuller, Meshac, | S. C., | 25 | White, James, | N. C., | 25 |
| Guthrie, John, | N. C., | 19 | Ward, William, | N. C., | 56 |
| Girardeau, John. | S. C., | 35 | Watson, Levin, | N. C., | 60 |
| Gray, John, | S. C., | 46 | Wash, William, | S. C., | 37 |
| Hawl, Wm., | S. C., | 37 | | | |

**REVOLUTIONARY SOLDIERS DRAWING PENSIONS IN GEORGIA IN 1840.**

Reproduced from a Census of Pensions for Revolutionary or Military Services, with their names, ages, and places of residence, as returned by the Mar-

ROSTER OF THE REVOLUTION.

shals of the several Judicial Districts under the Act for Taking the Sixth Census.

Published by authority of an Act of Congress, under the direction of the Secretary of State, Washington, D. C., printed by Blair & Reeves, 1841. List alphabetically arranged by Miss Helen M. Prescott.

| Name. | County. | Page. | Name. | County. | Page. |
|---|---|---|---|---|---|
| Akins, James, | Campbell, | 90 | Bullough, Elias, | Savannah, | 77 |
| Akins, James, | Coweta, | 74 | Busn, Prescott, | Stewart, | 81 |
| Allen, James, | Burke, | 84 | Clinton, William, | Campbell, | 80 |
| Anderson, Wm., | Baldwin, | 78 | Collins, John, | Cobb, | 80 |
| Aaron, Wm., | Franklin, | 93 | Copeland, Wm., | De Kalb, | 75 |
| Anders, Owen, | Gwinnett, | 87 | Cook, John, | Elbert, | 79 |
| Anderson, James, | Hall, | 72 | Carter, David, | Elbert, | 82 |
| Allread, Elias, | Hall, | 82 | Curl, Matthew, | Emanuel, | 79 |
| Adams, Francis, | Henry, | 77 | Cash, Am., | Franklin, | 75 |
| Anglin, Henry, | Jackson, | 81 | Clarke, Thos., | Franklin, | 79 |
| Allen, Wm., | Lumpkin, | 101 | Carroll, James, | Forsyth, | 75 |
| Arnett, John, | Scriven, | 80 | Conger, Ben, | Gwinnett, | 84 |
| Bledsoe, Ben, | Campbell, | 77 | Clowers, Daniel, | Gwinnett, | 79 |
| Brewster, Hugh, | Cass, | 80 | Curbo, Joseph, | Gwinnett, | 86 |
| Baker, Chas., | Cass, | 79 | Cox, Richard, | Gilmer, | 79 |
| Bailey, James, | Crawford, | 80 | Childers, Milliner, | Hall, | 77 |
| Bunster, Wm., | Coweta, | 83 | Clark, Wm., | Hall, | 84 |
| Banks, John, | Bullock, | 34 | Cloud, Ezekiel, | Henry, | 78 |
| Brooks, Geo., | De Kalb, | 79 | Chandler, Shelldrake, | Henry, | 88 |
| Brown, Ben, | Elbert, | 77 | Cunningham, Ansel, | Jackson, | 77 |
| Brown, Henry, | Emanuel, | 70 | Cochran, M., | Morgan, | 83 |
| Baggett, Josiah, | Early, | 78 | Campbell, George, | Morgan, | 86 |
| Black, Wm., | Fayette, | 76 | Cheek, Wm., | Madison, | 89 |
| Brown, Ambrose, | Forsyth, | 83 | Calder, John, | McIntosh. | 77 |
| Bramlett, Reuben, | Gwinnett, | 75 | Christmas, Richard, | Muscogee, | 77 |
| Benson, Enoch, | Gwinnett, | 84 | Carter, Robert, | Newton, | 84 |
| Bonds, Joseph, | Hall, | 84 | Carter, Charles, | Oglethorpe, | 88 |
| Baker, Beall, | Hall, | 84 | Chalfinch, Hiram, | Upson, | 35 |
| Brasel, Bird, | Hancock, | 70 | Combs, John, | Wilkes, | 78 |
| Blount, Isaac, | Hancock, | 80 | Cox, Moses, | Washington, | 86 |
| Barnett, Sion, | Jasper, | 79 | Cason, Wm., | Warren, | 93 |
| Baker, Dempsey, | Macon, | 77 | Callahan, Josiah, | Rabun, | 81 |
| Barkly, Wm., | Morgan, | 80 | Cabos, John, | Savannah, | 94 |
| Buchanan, Geo., | Marion, | 81 | Davis, John, | Elbert, | 89 |
| Bowen, Samuel, | Meriwether, | 83 | Daniel, John, | Elbert, | 80 |
| Black, John | Meriwether, | 77 | Drew, Wilson, | Emanuel, | 75 |
| Bledso, Miller, | Oglethorpe, | 78 | Durdan, Jacob, | Emanuel, | 85 |
| Buckholter, Peter, | Randolph, | 79 | Dyer, Elisha, | Franklin, | 77 |
| Bryan, Ezekiel, | Randolph, | 75 | Davis, John, | Gwinnett, | 109 |
| Brown, John, | Randolph, | 77 | Dobs, Nathan, | Gwinnett, | 85 |

# REVOLUTIONARY PENSIONERS.

| Name. | County. | Page. | Name. | County. | Page. |
|---|---|---|---|---|---|
| Dennis, John, | Hancock, | 70 | Grant, Joseph, | Hancock, | 80 |
| Davidson, John, | Jasper, | 79 | Guyse, John, | Lincoln, | 79 |
| Davis, Toliver, | Monroe, | 84 | Grisham, David, | Pike, | 83 |
| Dunn, Thos., | Oglethorpe, | 76 | Glenn, Thos., | Stewart, | 81 |
| Doud, John, | Warren, | 85 | Harris, Ben., | Cass, | 81 |
| Draper, James, | Warren, | 89 | Hartley, Daniel, | Crawford, | 97 |
| Dillard, John, | Rabun, | 81 | Holbrook, Jesse, | Franklin, | 76 |
| Dunlap, Jonathan, | Rabun, | 81 | Horton, Isaac, | Gwinnett, | 81 |
| Davis, Thomas, | Randolph, | 85 | Harris, Stephen, | Gwinnett, | 86 |
| Darby, Richard, | Randolph, | 102 | Hunt, Littleton, | Gwinnett, | 97 |
| Edwards, Reuben, | Cass, | 82 | Herrington, Joseph, | Gwinnett, | 77 |
| Espy, John, | Clark, | 84 | Harris, Matthew, | Greene, | 88 |
| Eastwood, Israel, | Cobb, | 82 | Hulsey, Jesse, | Hall, | 81 |
| Edwards, Adonijah, | Cobb, | 73 | Hill, John, | Hancock , | 80 |
| Etheridge, Joel, | Crawford, | 77 | Howell, Mills, | Hancock, | 70 |
| Edenfield, David, | Emanuel, | 79 | Hart, Mary, | Liberty, | 72 |
| Ellis, Mary, | Gilmer, | 84 | Hames, John, | Lumpkin, | 94 |
| Earnest, George, | Meriwether, | 80 | Hill, Reuben, | Lumpkin, | 69 |
| Eberhart, Jacob, | Oglethorpe, | 83 | Haman, Alex., | Madison, | 80 |
| Evans, Wm., | Taliaferro, | 98 | Hodges, Phileman, | Muscogee, | 83 |
| Ellis, Shadrack, | Talbot, | 80 | Hewell, Wyatt, | Newton, | 84 |
| Elliott, Zach, | Stewart, | 84 | Harper, Wm., | Pike, | 88 |
| Farrar, Francis, | Clarke, | 76 | Howard, George F., | Washington, | 27 |
| Fudge, Jacob, | Crawford, | 82 | Harden, Henry, | Walton, | 89 |
| Fairclauth, Ben., | Emanuel, | 83 | Harris, Ben, | Walton, | 87 |
| Fuller, Stephen, | Franklin, | 88 | Iseley, Philip, | Gwinnett, | 91 |
| Flemming, Robert, | Franklin, | 77 | Jordan, Eliz., | Early, | 57 |
| Fain, Ebenezer, | Gilmer, | 78 | Jackson, Edward, | Gwinnett, | 86 |
| Flanagan, Wm., | Hall, | 91 | Jones, Wm., Sr., | Jasper, | 92 |
| Fleming, Wm., | Lumpkin, | 79 | Jones, Wm., | Monroe, | 45 |
| Fretwell, Richard, | Newton, | 87 | Jenkins, Lewis, | Meriwether, | 87 |
| Finch, Wm., | Oglethorpe, | 76 | Jenkins, John, Sr., | Pike, | 85 |
| Flanigan, Daniel, | Sumter, | 83 | Jenkins, Wm., | Wilkinson, | 83 |
| Gunnell, Wm. R., | Campbell, | 88 | Jackson, John, | Warren, | 85 |
| Grover, Peter, | Cobb, | 79 | Jordan, Fountain, | Troup, | 77 |
| Goodwin, Lewis, | Crawford, | 79 | Johnson, Joseph, | Troup, | 86 |
| Gay, Allen, | Coweta, | 75 | Kelley, Wm., | Elbert, | 82 |
| Gully, Richard, | Elbert, | 85 | Kell, James, | Gilmer, | 81 |
| Gains, Wm., | Elbert, | 83 | Kell, Robert, | Hall, | 89 |
| Glasgow, Wm., | Elbert, | 78 | King, John, | Jackson, | 85 |
| Gilleland, Susan, | Fayette, | 80 | Kelley, Giles, | Meriwether, | 78 |
| Gowers, Abel, | Gwinnett, | 86 | Kidd, Wm., Sr., | Oglethorpe, | 77 |
| Gatlin, Stephen, | Greene, | 54 | King, Richard, | Taliaferro, | 88 |
| Gilmer, James, Sr., | Hall, | 80 | Keith, John, | Twiggs, | 90 |
| Gunter, Chas., | Hall, | 78 | Lewis, John, | Cass, | 83 |
| Gilbert, James, | Henry, | 87 | Lagran, John U., | Forsyth, | 87 |

## ROSTER OF THE REVOLUTION.

| Name. | County. | Page. |
|---|---|---|
| Laurence, John, | Gwinnett, | 80 |
| Lowrey, Levi, | Jackson, | 76 |
| Levay, Geo., | Jackson, | 85 |
| Ledbetter, Richard, | Lumpkin, | 101 |
| Linvill, Wm., | Lincoln, | 85 |
| Love, Thos., | Washington, | 90 |
| Lile, Ephraim, | Twiggs, | 77 |
| Martin, Ephraim, | Cherokee, | 80 |
| McDowell, Robt., | Cobb, | 86 |
| Matthews, Philip, | Crawford, | 88 |
| Meadow, Jason, | Crawford, | 81 |
| McComeson, John, | De Kalb, | 84 |
| Murdock, Wm., | Franklin, | 81 |
| Mitchell, Wm., | Franklin, | 81 |
| McCoy, Sam'l, | Franklin, | 79 |
| McRight, Wm., | Gwinnett, | 21 |
| McDadde, John, | Gwinnett, | 93 |
| Moore, John, | Hall, | 83 |
| McCleskey, | Hall, | 86 |
| McCollam, Daniel, | Habersham, | 86 |
| Mullins, Malone, | Hancock, | 80 |
| Morton, Oliver, Sr., | Jones, | 77 |
| Matthews, Isaac, | Jackson, | 79 |
| Matthews, Wm., | Jackson, | 77 |
| Mayo, John, | Marion, | 81 |
| McLane, Thos., | Newton, | 80 |
| Meadows, John, | Wilkinson, | 78 |
| McLain, John, | Rabun, | 81 |
| Martin, John, | Richmond, | 103 |
| McCormick, Thos., | Taliaferro, | 90 |
| Melton, Robert, | Stewart, | 82 |
| Norwood, Geo., | Campbell, | 77 |
| Nesbit, Jeremiah, | Cobb, | 105 |
| Neely, John, | Coweta, | 83 |
| Nolen, James, | Forsyth, | 90 |
| Nicholson, John, | Hall, | 77 |
| Norris, Wm., | Harris, | 84 |
| Nix, John, | Lumpkin, | 75 |
| Newnan, Daniel, | Walker, | .. |
| Orear, Daniel, | Chattooga, | 83 |
| Oliver, John, | Clarke, | 78 |
| Parr, Ben, | Clarke, | 83 |
| Price, E., | Butts, | 79 |
| Perkins, Moses, | Dade | 77 |
| Pattisan, Robert, | Gwinnett, | 78 |
| Pullen, Robert, | Greene, | 85 |

| Name. | County. | Page. |
|---|---|---|
| Pitts, James, | Hall, | 81 |
| Pilgrim, Thos., | Habersham, | 74 |
| Pilgrim, Michael, | Lumpkin, | 86 |
| Passmore, Joseph, | Macon, | 79 |
| Peacock, Uriah, | Washington, | 88 |
| Parkerson, Jacob, | Pulaski, | 79 |
| Rowell, Jesse, | Carroll, | 87 |
| Robinson, John, Sr., | Carroll, | 88 |
| Robinson, Jeriah, | Baldwin, | 70 |
| Russell, Jas. Y., Sr., | Baldwin, | 78 |
| Roberts, Thos., | De Kalb, | 95 |
| Reeve, Wm., | De Kalb, | 84 |
| Riley, James, | Elbert, | 82 |
| Richardson, Amos, | Elbert, | 76 |
| Rice, Leonard, | Elbert, | 81 |
| Rahn, Jonathan, | Effingham, | 78 |
| Reed, Isaac, | Hall, | 87 |
| Robertson, Robert, | Hall, | 83 |
| Rossiter, Timothy, | Hancock, | 80 |
| Roberts, Reuben, | Jones, | 85 |
| Rosier, Robert, Sr., | Wilkinson, | 84 |
| Rickerson, Ben., | Warren, | 80 |
| Smith, Charles, | Cherokee, | 75 |
| Summers, John, | Cobb, | 77 |
| Stedham, Zach, | Carroll, | 89 |
| Smith, Wm., | Coweta, | 91 |
| Stowers, Lewis, Sr., | De Kalb | 76 |
| Sutton, A., | Emanuel, | 82 |
| Stonecypher, John, | Franklin, | 84 |
| Spears, Wm., | Franklin, | 95 |
| Sherdin, Abner, | Franklin, | 80 |
| Suddeth, Jared, | Fayette, | 76 |
| Smith, Enoch, | Gilmer, | 81 |
| Sloughter, George, | Greene, | 77 |
| Shurr, John, | Greene, | 77 |
| Stewart, James, | Heard, | 75 |
| Shaw, Basil, | Hall, | 92 |
| Swan, Wm. B., | Harris, | 82 |
| Shuffield, Wm., | Hancock, | 70 |
| Slocumb, John C., | Jones, | 80 |
| Spears, John, | Jasper, | 89 |
| Sodown, Jacob, | Jefferson, | 80 |
| Saxon, Soloman, | Jackson, | 73 |
| Singleton, Edmund, | Lumpkin, | 85 |
| Stone, Wm., | Murray, | .. |
| Stewart, Wm., | Monroe, | 87 |

# REVOLUTIONARY PENSIONERS.

| | | | | | |
|---|---|---|---|---|---|
| Smith, Alex., | Meriwether, | 81 | Wilson, Geo., | Clarke, | 88 |
| Strong, Chas., | Oglethorpe, | 77 | Welford, Lewis, | Camden, | 95 |
| Swords, James, | Walton, | 82 | Ward, Wm., | Elbert, | 82 |
| Story, Robert, | Walker, | 25 | Wells, Redmon, | Early, | 58 |
| Studevent, Chas., | Warren, | 80 | Waldroup, James, | Fayette, | 85 |
| Stewart, Henry, | Taliaferro, | 81 | Wells, Leonard, | Forsyth, | 84 |
| Sheftall, Sheftall, | Savannah, | 78 | Whitton, Philip, | Forsyth, | 95 |
| Smith, Ben, | Stewart, | 88 | Williams, Nathan, | Gwinnett, | 89 |
| Statham, Nathaniel, | Stewart, | 76 | West, Ben., | Hall, | 81 |
| Turner, Thos., | Crawford, | 89 | Waters, David, | Jasper, | 105 |
| Thomas, Abraham, | Burke, | 86 | White, Jesse, | Jackson, | 79 |
| Talbot, Ben., | Baldwin, | 76 | Wheeler, James, | Jackson, | 85 |
| Terrell, Wm., | De Kalb, | 84 | Whatley, Daniel, | Macon, | 87 |
| Trammel, Wm., | Elbert, | 83 | White, George, | McIntosh, | 81 |
| Thrasher, George, | Gwinnett, | 85 | Webb, John, | Newton, | 85 |
| Turner, Robert, | Habersham, | 80 | Weathers, Valentin, | Newton, | 76 |
| Thompson, Sherrod, | Jackson, | 83 | Woodall, Joseph, | Oglethorpe, | 76 |
| Tate, Robert L., | Madison, | 76 | Ward, Samuel, | Oglethorpe, | 85 |
| Tugle, Chas., | Madison, | 87 | Wise, John, | Pike, | 84 |
| Thompson, James, | Madison, | 77 | Whittington, Faddy, | Pike, | 87 |
| Terrell, Richmond, | Newton, | 80 | Williams, William, | Wilkes, | 78 |
| Tanney, Michael, | Union, | 81 | Woolf, Andrew, | Wilkes, | 88 |
| Thompson, Lustatia, | Washington, | 74 | Williams, William, | Washington, | 86 |
| Taylor, Thos., Sr., | Twiggs, | 77 | Wilson, John, | Warren, | 85 |
| Thomason, Wm., | Troup, | 92 | Williams, Edward, | Rabun, | 102 |
| Upchurch, Chas., | Henry, | 85 | Williams, Joseph, | Telfair, | 80 |
| Vandegriff, Garrett, | Habersham, | 89 | Yancy, Lewis D., | Jasper, | 78 |
| Williford, Nathan, | Cherokee, | 82 | | | |

## INVALID PENSIONERS—1849.

Revolutionary Soldiers—The following is a statement showing, respectively, the names of all the invalid pensioners paid in the State of Georgia; the town or county in which they reside; the time when their pensions commenced; the annual amount of pension received by each, distinguishing each other according to grade; with a reference to the several Acts of Congress under which such pensions are allowed; prepared in conformity with the resolution of the House of Representatives, of March 3, 1849:

**AUSTIN, JAMES G.** Private, Forsyth Co., May 5, 1849, $96; under Act of May 13, 1816.

**BAXTER, JOHN.** Corporal, Murray Co., March 23, 1834, $32; under Act of April 24, 1816.

**BANKS, JOHN.** Private, unknown, November 15, 1847, $48; military establishment.

**BARKER, RUFUS.** First lieutenant and quartermaster, Walton Co., April 22, 1844, $153; under Act of April 24, 1816.

**BIGBIE, JAMES N.** Private, Harris Co., June 11, 1847, $96; military establishment.

**BUCHANAN, JAMES.** First lieutenant, Early Co., October 3, 1847, $204; under Act of April 24, 1816.

**BARNES, WILLIAM.** Sergeant, Elbert Co., January 26, 1847, $96; military establishment.

**BENTLEY, JAMES.** Private, Walton Co., December 9, 1837, $96; under Act of April 24, 1816. (Bentley's was increased from $48 from July 13, 1841.)

**BENNETT, MICAJAH,** Sergeant, Muscogee Co., June 20, 1843, $96; under Act of April 24, 1816.

**CAMP, HOSEA.** Private, Fayette Co., February 25, 1823, $72; military establishment.

**CHALFINCH, HIRAM.** Musician, Upson Co., March 5, 1822, $64; military establishment.

**COX, ZACHARIAH.** Private, Murray Co., December 9, 1847, $64; military establishment.

**CARROLL, THOMAS W.** Private, Marion Co., December 16, 1847, $72; under Act of April 24, 1816.

**CHILDERS, JOHN.** Private, Forsyth Co., August 23, 1849, $96; under Act of April 24, 1816.

**CHEEK, JOHN.** Private, unknown, February 2, 1847, $96; under Act of April 24, 1816.

**DABNEY, AUSTIN.** Private, Burke Co., unknown, $96; unknown.

**DOYLE, NIMROD T.** Private, unknown, February 20, 1839, $48; under Act of April 25, 1808.

**DICK, JAMES.** Corporal, Newton Co., March 30, 1836, $72; under Act of April 24, 1816.

**DUNHAM, GEORGE.** Private, Chatham Co., June 26, 1848, $48; under Act of April 24, 1816.

**GREEN, JOHN.** Private, Talbot Co., October 24, 1814, $72; under Act of April 24, 1816.

**GRIFFIN, EDWARD.** Private, unknown, March 4, 1814, $34.12; under Act of March 3, 1804.

**GATLIN, STEPHEN.** Private, Green Co., January 1, 1834, $96; under Act of March 3, 1835.

**HENDERSON, RICHARD.** Private, Chambers, Ala., November 18, 1816, $96; military establishment.

## REVOLUTIONARY PENSIONERS. 455

**HANNEGAN, JAMES.** Private, unknown, July 19, 1816, $96; military establishment.

**HOWARD, GEORGE F.** Private, Washington Co., April 27, 1838, $96; under Act of April 24, 1816.

**HALCOMB, HAMPTON.** Private, Habersham Co., April 16, 1845, $48; under Act of April 24, 1816.

**HOLMES, GIDEON V.** Private, Franklin Co., October 3, 1849, $96; under Act of April 24, 1816. (Holmes' increased from $72, from January 3, 1850.)

**JONES WILLIAM.** Private, Monroe Co., May 9, 1814, $48; military establishment.

**KNIGHT, JOEL.** Private, Fayette Co., June 18, 1838, $72; under Act of April 24, 1816. (Knight's increased from $52, from October 9, 1838.)

**KILGORE, JAMES M.** Private, Jackson Co., January 20, 1845, $48; under Act of April 24, 1816.

**McRIGHT, WILLIAM.** Private, Gwinnett Co., September 23, 1837, $96; under Act of April 24, 1816.

**MONTGOMERY, BERKLEY.** Private, Floyd Co., May 4, 1840, $48; under Act of April 24, 1816.

**MASTERSON, JOHN.** Sergeant, Chatham Co., February 8, 1848, $64; military establishment.

**McLANE, WILEY.** Private, Lumpkin Co., July 3, 1849, $96; under Act of May 13, 1846.

**MABRAY, JOHN.** Private, Newton Co., December 13, 1847, $64; under Act of May 13, 1846.

**McCURDY, DAVID R.** Private, Walton Co., November 16, 1847, $72; under Act of May 13, 1846.

**NICHOLS, ISAAC B.** First sergeant, Walker Co., April 7, 1847, $48; under Act of May 13, 1846.

**ODUM, SEYBERT.** Private, Barnwell Dist., S. C., $96.

**PETERS, WILLIAM.** Private, Lowndes Co., March 30, 1846, $48.

**PRICE, WILLIAM T.** Private, Carroll Co., December 28, 1844, $64; under Act of April 24, 1816.

**RICKEY, CHARLES.** Private, Habersham Co., December 28, 1844, $64; under Act of April 24, 1816.

**ROE, JOSEPH A.** Private, Burke Co., May 4, 1848, $96; military establishment.

ROSTER OF THE REVOLUTION.

**RIDEAU, JAMES.** Private, Union Co., October 20, 1849, $96; under Act of April 24, 1816.

**SWANN, ELIJAH.** Private, Newton Co., September 7, 1839, $96; under Act of April 24, 1816.

**SULLIVAN, THOMAS.** Private, Chatham Co., October 31, 1849, $96; military establishment.

**STROUD, WILLIAM.** Private, Butler Co., March 8, 1836, $96; under Act of April 24, 1816.

**TENNILLE, WILLIAM A.** Private, Baldwin Co., January 1, 1814, $96; under Act of January 30, 1833.

**THORNTON, PRESSLEY.** Corporal, Newton Co., March 4, 1795, $48; under Act of June 7, 1785.

**TERRY, JOSEPH.** Private, Murray Co., September 24, 1837, $96; military establishment.

**TAYLOR, GEORGE.** Private, Polk Co., Tennessee, May 20, 1843, $96; under Act of April 24, 1816.

**TERRILL, RICHMOND J.** Corporal, Newton Co., November 17, 1847, $96; under Act of May 13, 1846.

**THOMPSON, WILLIAM M.** Corporal, Cass Co., April 8, 1848, $96; under Act of May 13, 1846.

**WHATLEY, SAMUEL.** Private, Wilkes Co., unknown, $96; under Act of September 29, 1789.

**WETZEL, JOHN.** Private, Cass Co., May 10, 1838, $64; military establishment.

**WILLIAMS, LEWIS.** Private, Stewart Co., May 1, 1839, $96; under Act of April 24, 1816.

**WARNOCK, JOHN P.** Sergeant, Troup Co., January 31, 1839, $48; under Act of April 24, 1816.

**WALKER, THOMAS A.** Bugler, Newton Co., July 6, 1847, $96; under Act of May 13, 1846.

**WINTERS, JOSEPH T.** Private Hall Co., July 12, 1848, $48; under Act of May 13, 1846.

**WADE, HENRY.** Private, Franklin Co., October 9, 1849, $72; under Act of April 24, 1816.

**ZAVADOOSKI, PETER.** Private, Chatham Co., April 19, 1839, $48; military establishment.

From the Report of Invalid Pensioners (House Executive Documents,

# REVOLUTIONARY SOLDIERS. 457

Thirty-first Congress, First Session), Vol. X, by Secretary Thomas Ewing, June 2, 1850.

Compliments of Margaret B. Harvey.

From "Historical Collections of the Joseph Habersham, D. A. R.," Vol. 2, pages 610 through 613.

## REVOLUTIONARY SOLDIERS MENTIONED IN WHITE'S HISTORICAL COLLECTIONS OF GEORGIA.

| | | | |
|---|---|---|---|
| James Bailey, | Crawford Co. | Wm. Morgan, | Meriwether Co. |
| Paul Bevil, | Effingham Co. | Wm. Norman, | Lincoln Co. |
| Sion Barnett, | Jasper Co. | John Nickerson, | Union Co. |
| Abraham Boothe, | Lincoln Co. | E. Price, | Butts Co. |
| Jeremish Campbell, | Jasper Co. | Arch Perkins, | Greene Co. |
| John Calder, | McIntosh Co. | Jacob Parkerson, | Putnam Co. |
| Mr. Chunn, | Meriwether Co. | Jonathan Rahn, | Effingham Co. |
| Gen. David Dickson, | Fayette Co. | Dr. Tim Rosetta, | Hancock Co. |
| Joel Etheridge, | Crawford Co. | Mr. Snider, | Effingham Co. |
| George Earnest, | Meriwether Co. | Wm. Spears, | Franklin Co. |
| Jacob Fudge, | Crawford Co. | Jas. Stewart, | Heard Co. |
| Daniel Hartley, | Crawford Co. | Jacob Sodown, | Jefferson Co. |
| Lewis Goodwin, | Crawford Co. | Mr. Chas. Strong, | Oglethorpe Co. |
| Lewis Jenkins, | Meriwether Co. | Alexander Smith, | Meriwether Co. |
| Giles Kelley, | Meriwether Co. | Thos. Turner, | Crawford Co. |
| Richard King, | Taliaferro Co. | Aaron Tomlinson, | Jefferson Co. |
| Richard Ledbetter, | Lumpkin Co. | Seth Thompson, | Meriwether Co. |
| Mr. Lowery, | Burke Co. | Wm. Thomasson, | Troup Co. |
| Wm. Lyon, | Jefferson Co. | Gen. Sol. Wood, | Jefferson Co. |
| Wm. Love, | Randolph Co. | John J. Williams, | Lumpkin Co. |
| Philip Matthews, | Crawford Co. | George White, | McIntosh Co. |
| Jason Meadow, | Crawford Co. | Abner Wheeler, | Meriwether Co. |
| Jesse Marshall, | Franklin Co. | Mr. Williams, | Rabun Co. |
| Gen. Henry Mitchell, | Hancock Co. | Mr. Yancey, | Jasper Co. |
| John Matthews, | Lincoln Co. | | |

## REVOLUTIONARY SOLDIERS IN ANDERSON'S HISTORY OF COWETA COUNTY—1880.

P. 15, John Endsley (Sr.).
16, James Aiken (Sr.).
38, John Neely.
38, William Wood.
17, O. M. Houston.
17, James Wood.
17, Abner Johnson.
37, Maj. James Wood.

P. 37, William Smith.
33, Isham Hucaby.
18, Randle Robinson.
18, Allen Gay.
19, ———— Culpepper.
19, Zedick Hudson.
29, Col. John Dickson.
42, John Thurman.

## OLD DEED BOOK LIST.

Revolutionary Soldiers whose names have been found in old deed books, by H. M. Prescott.

### WILKES CO.

BK. K. K. 112—Isham Williams, late a soldier in 3rd Ga. Regt., Com. by Col. Leonard Marbury, appoints Fr. Baldwin to receive pay, etc., 1793.
P. 113—Wm. Gordon, late soldier in S. C. Regt., Com. by Col. Neal, appoints Baldwin to collect pay, 1793.
P. 111—Wm. Strother, late soldier in 12th Va. Regt., Col. Lee's Legion of Light Dragoons, appoints Baldwin to receive pay, 1793.
P. 110—Benjamin Fry, of 14th Va., Col. Chas. Lewis, appoints Baldwin to receive pay, 1793.
P. 109—James Wright, late soldier 7th Va. Regt., Col. W. Dangerfield, appoints Baldwin to receive pay.
P. 109—John Sheke, of Pulaski's Regt., ap. to receive pay, 1793.
P. 109—Nathan Wright, of 1st Va. Regt., Col. Richard Parker.
P. 108—John Griffin (heir-at-law of his brother, Chas. Griffin), who was soldier in first detachment, Va. Levies, Com. by Col. Richard Parker, appoints Baldwin to collect pay, etc., 1793.
P. 105—Starke Brown, soldier in Va., Col. Mordecai Buckner.
P. 105—John Ross, of N. C.—in Capt. Madison's Co.
P. 105—Brian Money, of Va.

### HANCOCK CO.

2. Oct., 1785—Denza Metcalf, of Rutherford Co., N. C., sells to Wm. Washington, of Charleston, S. C., the bounty of land granted to D. M. for service in a Minute Battalion in the State of Ga.—460 Wash. Co.
Also the following R. S. sell their bounty land to Wm. Washington:
Wm. Metcalf, of Rutherford Co., N. C.
James York.
Henry Crup, of N. C.
Jacob Fortune.
Wm. Matthews, of Richmond Co.
Meshack Matthews, of Richmond Co.
Mordecai Baldwin, of Wilkes Co.
Wm. Morris.
P. 124—James Adcock & W. Eliz. 287½ a.—1785.
P. 320—Wm. Triplett to Genl. Wm. Washington, 287½ a.—1785.
P. 387—James Stewart to Gen. Wm. Washington, 287½.
P. 496— ———————————————
P. 206—George Grizzell had bounty land (see Gordon note).

### WILKES CO.

P. 104—Troops under Count Pulaski appoint Francis Baldwin to receive their pay, 1793 Thos. Wooten, Jesse Norman & Stark Brown, R. S.
P. 113—Maj. Wm. Gordon, R. S.

## LIST OF GRAVES OF DECEASED SOLDIERS MARKED BY GA. D. A. R.

Anderson, Wm., Baldwin Co. (marked by Government).
Andrews, John, Oglethorpe Co.
Axson, Samuel J. M. D., Midway, Liberty Co.
Anglin, Henry (not known).
Andrews, Wm., Oglethorpe Co.
Brooks, Micajah, five miles west Rockmart.
Bassett, George, Richmond Co.
Brannan, or Branham, two miles west Waleska.
Brown, Benj., two miles below Aberdeen.
Beckham, Major, Milledgeville.
Brack, John, Burke Co.
Cunningham, Ansel (not known).
Creswell, Daniel (Col.), Wilkes Co.
Carraway, Wm., Thomaston.
Corvan, George, Jefferson Co.
Cook, Thomas, died in Henry Co.
Carswell, Alexander, Hopeful Plantation.
Carswell, John, near Augusta.
Candler, Wm., Columbia Co.
Carswell, John Hephzibah.
Carr, Thos., McDuffie Co.
Collins, Mr., Thomson Co.
Cloud, Ezekiel, Hon., Henry Co.
Dabney, Austin (Col.), Pike Co.
Franklin, George, Rev., Davisboro, Washington Co.
Fitzpatrick, Benjamin, Morgan Co.
Hamilton, Stuart, Kibbee, Montgomery Co.
Inman, Daniel, Burke Co.
Jackson, Chas. Dungeness, (Cumberland Island).
Kendall, Henry, Capt., Upson Co.
Kendall, Jeremiah (not known).
Mitchell, Henry, Sparta.
Macomson, John, seven miles from Atlanta.
Matthews, Wm., Capt., Jackson.
Matthews, Isaac, Jackson Co.
Maxwell, Thos., Elbert Co.
Murphy, Edmund, Richmond Co.
Murphy, Nicholas, Richmond Co.
Milner, John Hamilton (marked?), Cleola (not proven).
Maffett, John (Col.).
Murphee, Edmund, Hephzibah.
Murphee, Mills, Burke Co.
McLendon, Sam'l, Henry Co.
McMullen, John, Hart Co.
Nobles, Sanders, Clinch Co.
Porter, Oliver, Newton Co.

Rowell, John, Haralson Co.
Richardson, Amos, Hart Co.
Rhodes, Matthew, Clarksville.
Robinson, Randall, Newnan.
Rucherford, John, Washington Co.
Scott, John Epps, Sparta.
Stewart, Daniel, Gen'l, Liberty Co.
Screven, James, Liberty Co.
Slaughter, Sam'l, Baldwin Co.
Stewart, Wm. Ellaville, Schley Co.
Elder, David, Oconee Co., near Elder.
Espy, James, near Athens.
Freeman, Sam'l Canton.
Fitzpatrick, Benj., Morgan Co.
Gibson, John, Fulton Co., 16 miles west Atlanta.
Garland, Mr., Upson Co.
Griffin, Charles, Clinch Co.
Gunn, Gen'l, Louisville.
Gunn, Jacob, eight miles from Milledgeville (marked).
Guest, Moses (marked), Franklin Co.
Harvey, Zepaniah, Jasper Co.
Hall, Hugh (Col.), near Sparta.
Hawkins, Benj., Crawford Co.
Hand, Henry H., Sumter Co.
Hughes, John T., Hickory Flat, near Canton.
Harves, Charles, Gordon Co.
Hays, John (marked), Decatur.
Hamilton, Jas., Lieut., Columbia Co.
Howell, Isaac, Fulton Co., near Chattahoochee.
Solomon, Lazarus, Wilkinson Co.
Stephens, Alexander, Capt. (marked), Crawfordville.
Simpson, Archibald, Wilkes Co.
Singleton, Edward, Lumpkin Co.
Smith, Wm. (nicknamed "Hellstone Smith"), Newnan
Smith, Isaac, Monroe.
Skehee, Daniel, Corporal, Washington Co.
Ternille, Francis, Lieut., Washington Co.
Thurmond, Mr., near Bishop.
Thomas, William, Oglethorpe Co.
Thorn, C. H., Major, Gwinnett Co.
Thompson, Sherwood, Jefferson.
Triplett, Wm., Major, Wilkes Co.
Wheeler, Jas. (not known).
Walker, Jas., Upson Co.
Walker, Wm., Jefferson Co.
Wilson, John, Greene Co.
White, Thos., Wrightsboro.
Wilson, John Effingham Co.

# REVOLUTIONARY GRAVES. 461

Wood (Col.), Jefferson Co.
Williams, John, Capt., removed from St. Mary's by Government to Washington, D. C., in 1908.
Ware, Jas., Madison.

## REVOLUTIONARY GRAVES: MARKED OR WELL IDENTIFIED.

Anderson, Wm., Baldwin Co., Ga.
Andrews, John, Oglethorpe Co., Ga.
Axson, Samuel, J., Dr., Liberty Co., Ga.
Andrews, Wm., Oglethorpe Co., Ga.

Bassett, George, Richmond Co., Ga.
Beckom, Samuel, Major, Beckom's Mount, near Milledgeville, Ga.
Berrien, John, Major, Colonial Cemetery, Savannah, Ga.
Bowen, Oliver, Commodore, St. Paul Churchyard, Augusta, Ga.
Brack, Benj., Brack Plantation, near Medville, Burke Co., Ga.

Brannen, or Branham, ———, Cherokee Co., near Walesca, Ga.
Brooks, Micajah, Polk Co., five miles west of Rockmart, Ga.
Brown, Benj., Two miles south of Aberdeen, Ga.
Brown, Epps, City Cemetery, Sparta, Ga.
Brown, John, City Cemetery, St. Marys, Ga.
Bryan, Jonathan, Too old for service, but a patriot, and a prisoner of war; Brampton, near south bank, Savannah River, Savannah, Ga.

Bulloch, Archibald, President of Executive Council, and ex-officio Commander-in-Chief. Supposed to be buried in Colonial Park, Savannah, in a grave marked by a cubical block of marble on which is carved the figure of a serpent.

Candler, Wm., Columbia Co., Ga.
Carr, Thomas, Fulton Place, McDuffie Co., Ga.
Carraway, Wm., Upson Co., near Thomaston, Ga.
Carswell, Alex., Burke Co., Ga.
Carswell, John, Hepzibah, Ga.
Carter, John, Capt., Supposed to be buried in churchyard of St. Paul Church, of which he was first Warden after the Revolution.

Clarke, Elijah, Colonel, Lincoln Co., Ga., on what is known as the Oliver Place, a plantation owned by Marcus A. Pharr, Washington, Ga.

Clarke, ———, Major, Near St. Marys, Ga.
Clark, John, Afterwards Governor of Georgia, and Major-General of State Troops. St. Andrew's Bay, Fla.

| | |
|---|---|
| Clay, Joseph, Colonel, | Deputy Paymaster-General. Colonial Cemetery, Savannah, Ga. |
| Cloud, Ezekiel, | Henry Co., Ga. |
| Comer, James, | Family burial ground, five miles west of Clinton, Jones Co., Ga.; aged 108 years. |
| Cornwall, Elijah, | Cornwall burying ground, near Alcovy River, two miles from Mechanicsville, Jasper Co., Ga. |
| Corvan, George, | Jefferson Co., Ga. |
| Creswell, Daniel, | Smyrna Churchyard, Wilkes Co., Ga., eight miles of Washington. |
| Cummins, Francis, Rev., | City Cemetery, Greensboro, Ga. |
| Cuthbert, Seth John, | Colonial Cemetery, Savannah, Ga. |
| Dabney, Austin, | A negro, Pike Co., Ga. |
| Elbert, Samuel, Brig.-Gen., | Chatham Co., Ga. |
| Emanuel, David, | Afterwards Governor of Georgia; Burke Co. |
| Elder, Joshua, | Oconee Co., Ga. |
| Espy, James, | Clarke Co., Ga., near Athens. |
| Farrar, Thomas, | Franklin, Ga. |
| Few, Benj., | McDuffie Co., Ga. |
| Few, Ignatius, Capt., | McDuffie Co., Ga. |
| Few, William, Colonel, | Afterwards U. S. Senator from Georgia; buried at Fish Kill, on the Hudson, State of New York. |
| Fitzpatrick, Benjamin, | Morgan Co., near Buckhead. |
| Franklin, George, Rev., | Davisboro, Washington Co |
| Flournoy, Robert, | City Cemetery, Sparta, Ga. |
| Freeman, Colquitt, | Oconee Co., Ga. |
| Freeman, John, | Oconee Co., Ga. |
| Freeman, Samuel, | Cherokee Co., Ga., near Canton. |
| Ganier, Wm., | Washington Co., Ga. |
| Garland, ———, | Upson Co., Ga. |
| Gibson, John, | Fulton Co., Ga., near Atlanta. |
| Glascock, Thomas, | Richmond Co., north of Augusta, Ga. |
| Glascock, Wm., | City Cemetery, Augusta, Ga. |
| Gordon, Ambrose, Colonel, | St. Paul Churchyard, Augusta, Ga. |
| Grant, Thomas, | Methodist Churchyard, Monticello, Jasper Co., Ga. |
| Green, Nathanael, Maj.-General, | Underneath Green's Monument, Bull St., Savannah, Ga. |
| Griffin, Charles, | Clinch Co., Ga. |
| Guest, Moses, | Franklin Co., Ga. |
| Gumm, Jacob, | Near Milledgeville, Baldwin Co., Ga. |
| Gunn, James, | Afterwards U. S. Senator; Old Town Cemetery, Louisville, Ga. |

REVOLUTIONARY GRAVES. 463

| | |
|---|---|
| Gwinnett, Button, | Signer Declaration of Independence, afterwards Governor of Georgia. Supposed to be in Colonial Cemetery, Savannah, Ga.; grave unmarked. |
| Habersham, John, | Colonial Cemetery, Savannah, Ga. |
| Habersham, Joseph, Colonel, | Colonial Cemetery, Savannah, Ga. |
| Habersham, James, Jr., | Colonial Cemetery, Savannah, Ga. |
| Hall, Hugh, | Hancock Co., near Sparta, Ga. |
| Hall, Lyman, Dr., | Signer of Declaration of Independence, afterwards Governor of Georgia. Under Monument to Signers, Greene St., Augusta, Ga. |
| Hames, John, Sr., | National Cemetery, Marietta, Ga., small granite head-stone, No. 10390. |
| Hamilton, James, Lieut., | Columbia Go., Ga. |
| Hamilton, Stuart, | Kibbee, Montgomery Co., Ga |
| Hand, Henry H., | Sumter Co., Ga. |
| Hardwick, Wm., | Washington Co., Ga. |
| Harvey, Zephaniah, | Jasper Co., Ga. |
| Harves, Charles, | Gordon Co., Ga. |
| Hawkins, Benj., | Crawford Co., Ga., near site of old Indian Agency on the Flint. |
| Hayes, John, | Town Cemetery, Decatur, Ga. |
| Heard, Stephen, | Heardmont, Elbert Co., Ga. |
| Howell, Isaac, | Fulton Co., Ga., on Chattahoochee River. |
| Hughes, John T., | Cherokee Co., Ga., near Hickory Flat. |
| Inman, Daniel, | Inman Plantation, near Medville. |
| Irwin, Jared, Gov., | Sandersville, Ga. |
| Jackson, Charles, | Carnegie burial ground, Dungeness, Cumberland Island, Ga. |
| Jackson, James, Major, | Afterwards Major-General; Congressional Cemetery, Washington, D. C. |
| Jones, Batt, | Burke Co., Ga. |
| Jones, John, Colonel, | Burke Co., Ga. |
| Jones, Noble Wymberley, Dr., | Bonaventure Cemetery, Savannah, Ga. |
| Jones, Seaborn, | St. Paul's Churchyard, Augusta, Ga. |
| Jordan, John, | Davisboro, Washington Co., Ga. |
| Kendall, Henry, Capt., | Upson Co., Ga. |
| King, ———, | Jefferson Co., Ga. |
| Lamar, John, | Jones Co., Ga., near Clinton. |
| Lee, Henry, Colonel, | "Light Horse Harry," in command of a troop of cavalry at Seige of Augusta; buried in chapel of Washington and Lee University, after removal from Dungeness, Cumberland Island, Ga. |

Lewis, John, Major, — Bartow Co., Ga.

McIntosh, Lachlan, Brig.-Gen., — Colonial Cemetery, Savannah, Ga.
McLendon, Samuel, — Henry Co., Ga.
McMullen, John, — Hart Co., Ga.
Macomson, John, — Fulton Co., Ga., seven miles from Atlanta.
Marsh, John, — Macon Co., Ga.
Martin, John, — City Cemetery, Augusta, Ga.
Mathews, George, Brig.-Gen., — Afterwards Governor of Georgia. St. Paul's churchyard, Augusta, Ga.
Matthews, Wm., Capt. — Jackson Co., Ga.
Maxwell, Thomas, — Elbert Co., Ga.
Meriwether, Thomas, — Jordan burial ground, six miles east of Monticello, Jasper Co., Ga.
Milledge, John, — Afterwards Governor of Georgia; Summerville Cemetery, Augusta, Ga.
Milner, John, — Cleola, Ga.
Mitchell, Henry, — City Cemetery, Sparta, Ga.
Morris, Wm., — Cedar Grove, DeKalb Co., Ga.
Murphree, John, — Murphree's burying ground, near Medville, Burke Co., Ga.
Murphree, Miles, — Family burying ground, fourteen miles from Waynesboro, Burke Co., Ga.

Newton, Moses, — Washington Co., Ga.
Nobles, Sanders, — Clinch Co., Ga.

Palmer, George, — Burke Co., Ga.
Penn, Wm., — Baptist Churchyard, Monticello, Jasper Co., Ga.
Phone, Daniel, — Fellowship Churchyard, near Tucker, DeKalb Co., Ga.
Porter, Oliver, — Newton Co., Ga.
Pulaski, Casimier, Count, — A Polish nobleman, killed at the Seige of Savannah, 1779. What are supposed to be his remains were re-interred under the Pulaski Monument on Bull St., Savannah, Ga., after removal from Greenwich, on Augustine Creek, the traditional place of Pulaski's burial.

Redding, Anderson, — Monroe Co., Ga.
Reid, Samuel, Capt., — of Rowan Co., North Carolina; buried in old Reid burying ground, five miles from Eatonton, Putnam Co., Ga.
Rhodes, Matthew, — Clarksville, Ga.
Richardson, Amos, — Sardis Churchyard, Hart Co., Ga.
Robinson, Randall, — Oak Hill Cemetery, Newnan, Ga.

| | |
|---|---|
| Rowell, John, | Clinch Co., Ga. |
| Rutherford, John, | On a plantation three miles west of Sandersville, Washington Co., Ga., just off the Milledgeville Road. (Marked.) |
| Sanford, Jeremiah, | City Cemetery, Greensboro, Ga. |
| Screven, James, | Midway Cemetery, Liberty Co., Ga. |
| Sheftall, Sheftall, | Deputy Commissary-General, Jewish burial ground, Guerard St., Savannah, Ga. |
| Sheftall, Mordecai, | Commissary-General, Jewish burial ground, Guerard St., Savannah, Ga. |
| Skehee, Daniel, Corporal, | Washington Co., Ga. |
| Simons Abraham, Capt., | Wilkes Co., Ga. |
| Simpson, Archibald, | Wilkes Co., Ga. |
| Singleton, Edward, | Lumpkin Co., Ga. |
| Slaughter, Samuel, | Baldwin Co., Ga. |
| Smith, Isaac, | Monroe Co., Ga. |
| Smith, Wm., "Hell Nation," | Oak Hill Cemetery, Newnan, Ga. |
| Solomon, Lazarus, | Wilkinson Co., Ga. |
| Spalding, James, | Colonial Cemetery, Savannah, Ga. |
| Sparks, John, | Washington Co., Ga. |
| Stephens Alexander, Capt., | Taliaferro Co., Ga., near Crawfordville. |
| Stewart, Daniel, | Midway Cemetery, Liberty Co., Ga. |
| Stewart, Wm., | Schley Co., Ga., near Ellaville. |
| Tattnall, Josiah, | Afterwards Governor of Georgia; Bonaventure Cemetery, Savannah, Ga. |
| Telfair, Edward, | Afterwards Governor of Georgia. Bonaventure Cemetery, Savannah, Ga. |
| Tennille, Francis, Lieut., | Washington Co., Ga. |
| Thomas, Wm., | Oglethorpe Co., Ga. |
| Thompson, Wm., | St. Paul's Churchyard, Augusta, Ga. |
| Thompson, Sherwood, | Jackson Co., Ga. |
| Thorn C. H., Major, | Gwinnett Co., Ga. |
| Thurman, David, | Oconee Co., Ga. |
| Tripplett, Francis, Maj., | Smyrna Churchyard, Washington, Ga. |
| Twiggs, John, | Twiggs burial ground, on Central Railroad, ten miles south of Augusta, Ga. |
| Walker, James, | Upson Co., Ga. |
| Walker, Wm., | Jefferson Co., Ga. |
| Walton, George, Colonel, | Signer Declaration of Independence; afterwards Governor of Georgia. Under Monument to the Signers, Greene St., Augusta, Ga. |
| Ware, Edward, Sergeant, | Madison Co., Ga., near Danielsville. |
| Wayne Anthony, Major-Gen., | Receiver surrender of Savannah from British; later a resident of Savannah. Buried in Radnor Churchyard, at Radnor, Delaware Co., Pa. |

| | |
|---|---|
| White, Edward, Major, | Colonial Cemetery, Savannah, Ga. |
| White, Thomas, | Quaker burial ground, McDuffee Co. |
| Whitley, Graner, | Fellowship Church, near Tucker, DeKalb Co., Ga. |
| Williams, John, Capt., | National Cemetery, Arlington, Va., after removal from St. Marys, Ga. |
| Williams, Joseph, | Near Jacksonville, Telfair Co., Ga. |
| Wilson, John, | Green Co., Ga. |
| Wilson, John, | Effingham Co., Ga. |
| Wood, Solomon, Col., | Jefferson Co., Ga. |
| Wylly, Richard, Colonel, | Deputy Quartermaster-General. Colonial Cemetery, Savannah, Ga. |

# INDEX

## A

Aaron, William .................................................321, 375, 405, 436, 450
Abercrombie, Charles ...................................................302, 375
Abbet, John ............................................................. 22
Abbott, John ....................................................22, 224, 225, 375
Acord, John ...................................................253-283-375
Acredge, William ....................................................... 22
Adair, Bozeman ........................................................ 397
Adams, Aaron .......................................................... 342
Adams, Benj. .......................................................... 334
Adams, Dancy .......................................................... 342
Adams, David ......................................................342-405
Adams, Edmund ........................................................ 405
Adams, Francis ...................................................406-436-450
Adams, Hugh .........................................................23-375
Adams, James .....................................................335-375-436
Adams, James, Jr. ..................................................... 406
Adams, James, Sr. ..................................................... 315
Adams, John ...................................................21-375-397-404
Adams, Martha ......................................................... 319
Adams, Robert ....................................................22-206-375
Adams, Thomas ...................................................315-342-406-436
Adams, William ........................................................ 375
Adamson, Charles ....................................................23-299
Adcock, James ........................................................250-458
Adcock, Thomas .................................................245-294-342-375
Addison, C. .......................................................... 321
Aderson, Bartlett ..................................................... 375
Adkerson, Henry ....................................................... 342
Adkins, Charles, Sr. ..............................................406-436
Adkins, William ...................................................217-342-375-402
Adkinson, Thomas ..................................................244-342-375
Adomison, Charles ..................................................... 375
Adridge, Levy ......................................................... 397
Affut, Nathaniel ...................................................... 335
Aikem, James, Sr. ..................................................... 457
Aikins, John .......................................................... 406
Aitkins, James ........................................................ 406
Ajon, Eli ............................................................. 342
Akens, James .......................................................... 406
Akin, James (or Akins) .........................................3-342-406-436-450

Akins, John ........................................................22-375
Akins, Thomas ..................................................... 320
Akins, William ...............................................342-406-436
Akredge, Davis .................................................... 404
Akridge, Davis .................................................... 397
Akridge, Ezekiel ................................................... 342
Akridge, William ................................................... 342
Alberson, William .................................................. 342
Albritton, John ..............................................320-321-406-436
Aldrage, William ................................................... 322
Aldredge, James (or Aldridge) ....................................... 22
Aldredge, William (or Aldridge) ..............................339-406-436
Aldridge, James ................................................23-375
Aldridge, William .................................................. 342
Alexander ......................................................... 406
Alexander, Adam ...............................................15-375-406
Alexander, Asa .............................................22-214-253-375-402-448
Alexander, Ayra .................................................... 375
Alexander, Ezekiel .............................................237-375
Alexander, Henry ................................................... 375
Alexander, Hugh ...............................................23-315-375-406
Alexander, Isaac ...............................................315-342
Alexander, James ..............................................22-201-251-375-406
Alexander, John .................................................... 271
Alexander, John Liston ..........................................253-375
Alexander, Mary .................................................... 315
Alexander, Matthew ................................................. 340
Alexander, Robert .............................................23-251-375
Alexander, Samuel .............................................21-202-249-258-269-278-375
Alexander, Samuel, Sr. ............................................. 21
Alexander, Susannah ................................................ 340
Alexander, Sarah ................................................... 328
Alexander, Thomas .................................................. 342
Alford, James ..................................................283-399
Alford, Lucretia ................................................... 315
Algood, John ....................................................... 319
Alison, Henry ..................................................15-201
Allen, Maj. ........................................................ 316
Allen, Benj. ....................................................... 297
Allen, Charles ..................................................... 375
Allen, David ....................................................... 342
Allen, James ..................................................234-250-252-375-450
Allen, John ...................................................238-239-375
Allen, Joseph ...................................................... **342**
Allen, Moses ..................................................15-17-342-375
Allen, Philip .................................................342-406-437
Allen, Robert .................................................214-239-263-375-397

# INDEX. 469

Allen, Thomas ............................................. 207-375
Allen, William ............................. 321-329-375-436-450
Allen, Woodson ................................................. 342
Allerton, John .................................................. 321
Allgood, John .............................................. 314-316
Allgood, Spencer ................................................ 316
Allison, Agnes .................................................. 324
Allison, Henry ................... 4-17-23-59-201-236-242-302-375
Allison, James ........................................ 22-228-237-375
Allison, Martha ................................................. 337
Allman, Philip .................................................. 406
Allred, Elias ................................................... 406
Allread, Elias, Sr. (or Allred) ............................ 406-436
Alsobrook, J., Sr. .............................................. 340
Alston, Capt. ................................................... 316
Alston, Gilly ................................................... 316
Ambrose, David .............................................. 406-436
Ames, William ................................................... 172
Amison, Jessie .................................................. 342
Ammons, Jacob ................................................... 342
Ammons, Robert ............................................... 23-375
Ammons, William .............................................. 21-375
Amos, James .................................................. 342-375
Amos, Leary ..................................................... 342
Amos, Mauldin ................................................... 342
Anders, Owen ................................................ 406-450
Anderson, Capt. ................................................. 406
Anderson, Lieutenant ............................................ 406
Anderson, Alexander ..................................... 4-21-22-200-375
Anderson, Bailey ................................................. 24
Anderson, Bartlett ............................................... 23
Anderson, Bartley ............................................... 127
Anderson, Charles ............................................ 17-406
Anderson, Elijah ............................... 127-209-225-226-375
Anderson, Elisha ............................................ 22-311
Anderson, George ................................................ 406
Anderson, Henry ...................................... 22-228-295-375
Anderson, James ....................................... 23-375-406-450
Anderson, John ...................... 21-24-250-290-301-322--375-406
Anderson, John, Lt. ............................................. 406
Anderson, Joseph ................................................ 227
Anderson, Matthew ........................................... 397-404
Anderson, Robert ................................................ 397
Anderson, Sara ................................................... 24
Anderson, Scarlett ............................................... 24
Anderson, William ............. 23-65-208-228-257-260-296-375-450-459-461
Anderson, William, Sr. .......................................... 322

# INDEX.

Andrew ................................................................ 406
Andrew, Benjamin, Jr. .................................................. 22
Andrew, Benjamin, Sr. ................................................. 406
Andrew, Francis ..................................................... 17-406
Andrew, Isham ........................................................ 406
Andrews, Benjamin ...................................... 219-300-375-406
Andrews, George .................................................... 17-375
Andrews, John .......................................... 375-406-459-461
Andrews, Joshua ....................................................... 249
Andrews, Owen .......................................... 342-406-436
Andrews, Samuel .................................................. 300-375
Andrews, William ............................................ 406-436-459-461
Angelly, Alex. ........................................................ 375
Angle, Charles ........................................................ 320
Angley, Conrad ........................................................ 327
Anglin, David .................................................. 21-249-375
Anglin, Henry .............................. 201-342-375-406-436-450-459
Anglin, John .................................................... 342-404
Anglin, William ..................................................... 22-375
Ansley, Thomas .................................................. 287-375
Anthony, David ........................................................ 336
Anthony, Mary ......................................................... 317
Antony, Capt. ......................................................... 406
Antony, Alexander ..................................................... 406
Antony, John .......................................................... 406
Antrobus, Isaac ....................................................... 406
Appling, Daniel ..................................................... 21-375
Appling, Ivell ........................................................ 322
Appling, Joel ......................................................... 322
Appling, John (or Appling) ...................................... 23-243-375
Arkins, James ......................................................... 330
Armer, James .......................................................... 342
Armes, James .......................................................... 375
Armor, John ........................................................... 342
Armour, Andrew ................................................ 296-302-375
Armstrong, Alexander ............................................. 375-397
Armstrong, James ............................................. 320-397-403
Armstrong, John ........................................................ 63
Arnand, John Peter ............................................. 339-406-436
Arnett, John .................................................. 331-406-436-450
Arnold, Abraham ....................................................... 397
Arnold, Absolem ....................................................... 404
Arnold, Charles ....................................................... 336
Arnold, Elizabeth ..................................................... 324
Arnold, James ......................................................... 322
Arnold, John .......................................................... 322
Arnold, Soloman .................................................. 397-404

Arnold, William .................................................. 406-436
Arnold, William, Sr. ................................................ 327
Arnstorph, George .................................................. 343
Arrant, Elizabeth .................................................. 328
Arrington, John .................................................... 315
Arrington, William ............................................. 343-375
Arthur, Francis ............................................ 9-15-300-406
Arthur, Matthew ................................................ 343-375
Asabrook, Claborn .................................................. 343
Asbury, Jonathan ................................................... 251
Ash, A. F. .......................................................... 322
Ash, Jane ........................................................... 322
Ash, R. R. .......................................................... 322
Ashby, Capt. ........................................................ 406
Ashley, William, Lt. ................................................ 375
Ashmore, John .................................................. 249-375
Ashmore, Strong ................................................ 343-375
Ashurst, William ............................................... 397-403
Ashworth, Adam ................................................... 23-375
Ashworth, Arthur ................................................. 23-375
Ashworth, Benj. .................................................. 21-301
Askedge, Levy ....................................................... 404
Asnet, Edward ....................................................... 397
Astin, Robert ....................................................... 343
Atkin, Agrippa ...................................................... 406
Atkins, Arnold ...................................................... 296
Atkins, Charles, Sr. ................................................ 334
Atkins, Ica, Sr. .................................................... 336
Atkinson, Joseph ............................................... 343-406
Atkinson, Robert .................................................... 343
Auldridge, Absolom .................................................. 330
Austin, Absolom, Capt. .............................................. 406
Austin, Harris D. ................................................... 343
Austin, James G. ............................................... 343-453
Austin, John, Sr. ................................................... 340
Austin, Michael ..................................................... 343
Austin, Richard ............................................... 22-375-406
Autery, John (or Autry) .............................................. 22
Autrey, Alexander ............................................ 201-375-402
Autrey, Jacob ....................................................... 201
Autrey, John ................................................. 161-201-283
Autry, Alexander .................................................... 251
Autry, John ......................................................... 283
Avent, Joseph .................................................. 210-375
Avera, Isaac .................................................... 23-375
Avera, William ...................................................... 375
Averat, John ........................................................ 202

# INDEX.

Averett, James .......... 264
Averett, John .......... 127-283-302
Averitt, Isaac .......... 375
Averitt, John .......... 375
Averitt, Thomas .......... 375
Avery, John .......... 375
Awtrey, Alexander, Jr. .......... 22
Awtry, Alexander .......... 375
Awtry, Alexander, Capt. .......... 375
Awtry, Jacob .......... 375
Awtry, John (or Autery) .......... 22-375
Axson, Samuel .......... 459
Axson, Samuel Jr., Dr. .......... 461
Aycock, Richard .......... 21-253-375-397-403
Aycock, William .......... 375
Ayres, Abner, Capt. .......... 406
Ayres, Abraham .......... 22-252-298-375-406
Ayres, Abraham, Capt. .......... 375
Ayres, Baker .......... 330-331
Ayres, Daniel .......... 23-227-375
Ayres, James .......... 250-375
Ayres, Thomas .......... 21-234-263-375-402
Ayres, William .......... 23-253-259-299-375

## B

Babbetts, Jacob .......... 375
Baber, James .......... 437
Bachelder, Nancy .......... 333
Bachelor, Cornelius .......... 343
Bachlott, John .......... 343
Bacon, John .......... 26-198-219-239-242-300-375-406
Bacon, John, Sr. .......... 406
Bacon, Jonathan .......... 25-32-375-406
Bacon, Joseph .......... 406
Bacon, Reuben .......... 292
Bacon, Thomas .......... 32-219-239-242-375-406
Bacon, William .......... 300
Bacon, William, Jr. .......... 406
Baduly, William .......... 30
Bagby, George .......... 25-219-375
Bagby, John .......... 343-406-437
Baggett, Joshia .......... 406
Baggett, Josiah .......... 450
Baggs, John .......... 41-229-375
Baggs, Jonathan .......... 375
Bagley, Herman .......... 343

## INDEX. 473

Bagners, Augustus ........................................................ 343
Bags, Joseph ............................................................ 375
Bailey, Christopher ...................................................... 343
Bailey, George ......................................................397-404
Bailey, James ..................................................406-450-457
Bailey, John ............................................................ 322
Bailey, Kesiah .......................................................... 337
Bailey, Peter .......................................................397-404
Bailey, Robert ........................................................... 24
Bailey, Stephen ......................................................... 343
Bailey, William ...............................................28-32-245-302-375-406
Bailie, Lt. ............................................................. 406
Baillie, Robert ......................................................... 375
Bain, Reuben ............................................................ 43
Bain, Robert ............................................................ 375
Baker, Dr. ..........................................................221-222
Baker, Artemus .....................................................30-42-375
Baker, Beal (or Beall)..........................................343-406-437-450
Baker, Benjamin ......................................................... 406
Baker, Charles .................................................343-406-450
Baker, Christopher ...................................................... 343
Baker, Comfort .......................................................... 320
Baker, Dempsey .................................................343-375-450
Baker, Elias .......................................................406-437
Baker, Jane ............................................................. 327
Baker, John ...........................................30-36-84-375-397-404-406-448
Baker, John, Capt. ...................................................... 406
Baker, John, Sr. ........................................................ 406
Baker, Joshua ........................................................... 343
Baker, Nathaniel .....................................................43-375
Baker, Thomas .....................................................31-33-375
Baker, Whitmarsh .....................................................42-375
Baker, William .................................................35-240-375-406
Baker, William, Jr....................................................... 406
Baker, William, Sr. ..................................................... 406
Baker, William James .................................................... 375
Bakin, Sh. .............................................................. 340
Baldasee, Isaac ......................................................406-437
Baldry, Isaac K. ........................................................ 407
Baldwin, Abraham ...............................................35-251-375-407
Baldwin, David .......................................................... 46
Baldwin, David, Sr....................................................... 458
Baldwin, Francis ................................................46-242-375-458
Baldwin, Mordecai ....................................................... 375
Baldwin, William ...................................41-44-215-230-235-241-242-375
Balier, William ......................................................... 375
Ball, Edward ...................................................300-343-407

# INDEX.

Ball, John .................................................. 25-397-404
Ball, Sampson .................................................. 46-375
Ball, William .................................................. 40-375
Ballard, Frederick .................................................. 343
Ballard, Joseph .................................................. 399
Ballard, Joshua .................................................. 407
Ballard, Thomas .................................................. 343
Ballenger, John .................................................. 407
Ballinger, John, Sr. .................................................. 313
Bamby, Randall .................................................. 127
Bandy, Lewis .................................................. 343
Banks, Boling .................................................. 375
Banks, Drury .................................................. 343
Banks, John .................................................. 343-407-450-453
Banks, Reuben .................................................. 17-41-59-252-289-375
Banks, Sutton .................................................. 407
Banks, William .................................................. 322-343
Bankston, Abner .................................................. 343
Bankston, Andrew .................................................. 449
Bankston, Daniel .................................................. 35-43-297-375
Bankston, Elijah .................................................. 35-297-343
Bankston, Jacob .................................................. 375
Bankston, John .................................................. 44-375
Bankston, Lawrence .................................................. 322-375
Bansworth, Jacob (or Bansworth) .................................................. 344-375
Barber, Charles .................................................. 343-375
Barber, Chester .................................................. 17-26-375
Barber, George .................................................. 27-35-244-248-375-407
Barber, Gingo .................................................. 375
Barber, James .................................................. 340-406
Barber, John .................................................. 375
Barber, Rhoda .................................................. 315
Barber, Stancil .................................................. 343
Barber, William .................................................. 34-375
Barclay, John .................................................. 399
Bard, John .................................................. 15-407
Bard, Peter .................................................. 407
Bardd, John .................................................. 145
Bardin, Gilbert (or Barden) .................................................. 245-375
Barfield, Richard .................................................. 253-375
Barfield, Soloman .................................................. 31-375
Barkaloe, William .................................................. 376
Barkeloe, Richard .................................................. 32-43
Barker, Bryan .................................................. 376
Barker, C. .................................................. 17-407
Barker, Charles .................................................. 376
Barker, Frances .................................................. 376

# INDEX. 475

| | |
|---|---|
| Barker, George | 376 |
| Barker, John | 343 |
| Barker, Joseph | 343 |
| Barker, Rufus | 343-453 |
| Barker, Stencil | 376 |
| Barker, William | 376 |
| Barkley, William (or Barkly) | 343-407-437-450 |
| **Barksdale, Allen** | **37** |
| Barksdale, Daniel | 376 |
| Barksdale, Jeffery | 376 |
| Barksdale, Richard | 376 |
| Barkshan, Richard | 311 |
| Barlow, William | 215 |
| Barnall, William | 376 |
| Barnard, Jesse | 24-228-376 |
| Barnard, Joel | 41 |
| Barnard, John | 376-407 |
| Barnard, John, Maj. | 407 |
| Barnard, Reuben | 376 |
| Barnard, Robert | 407 |
| Barnes, Richard | 396-407 |
| Barnes, Richard B. | 376 |
| Barnes, William | 40-343-376-396-401-454 |
| Barnett, Burton | 376 |
| Barnett, Caroline | 335 |
| Barnett, Claburn | 253 |
| Barnett, Claiborne | 376 |
| Barnett, Daniel | 26-233-376 |
| Barnett, Jesse | 343-376 |
| Barnett, Joel | 42-209-334-376 |
| Barnett, John | 27-42-233-294-376-407 |
| Barnett, Joshua (or Barnette) | 253-376 |
| Barnett, Lewis | 322 |
| Barnett, Margaret | 317 |
| Barnett, Mial | 35-376 |
| Barnett, Nathaniel (Nathan or Nat) | 28-40-233-376-407 |
| Barnett, Philip | 40-376 |
| Barnett, Robert | 343 |
| Barnett, Sion | 343-407-437-450-457 |
| Barnett, William | 42-192-209-210-245-322-344-407 |
| Barnett, William, Sr. | 322-325 |
| Barnhart, George | 376 |
| Barnhart, John | 236 |
| Barnhill, Hohn | 407 |
| Barnhill, John | 437 |
| Barnwell, Maj. | 407 |
| Barnwell, John | 340-376-407 |

# INDEX.

Barnwell, Michael .................................................... 333-334
Barnwell, Robert ........................................................ 336
Barr, Elizabeth .......................................................... 334
Barr, James ........................................................ 317-407-437
Barrett, Lewis (or Lewes) ........................................ 322-407-437
Barrett, Thomas .................................................... 251-376
Baron, Reuben ........................................................... 376
Baron, Samuel ........................................................... 376
Baron, William .......................................................... 376
Barron, Ann .............................................................. 27
Barron, Frances ......................................................... 326
Barron, Jesse ........................................................... 397
Barron, Samuel .......................................................... 27
Barron, Samuel, Jr. ..................................................... 27
Barron, Thomas .................................................... 317-407-437
Barron, William ..................................................... 42-229-298
Barrow, Joseph ......................................................... 344
Barrow, Reuben (or Reubin) ........................................ 30-35-251
Barry, Andrew .......................................................... 407
Barry, John ............................................................. 32
Barry, Mary ............................................................. 32
Barry, William ......................................................... 376
Barson, Isaac .......................................................... 344
Bartemore,.Benjamin .................................................... 205
Barthmore, Benjamin .................................................... 376
Bartley, John .......................................................... 254
Bartmore, Benjamin ..................................................... 238
Barton, Barnett ........................................................ 376
Barton, John ....................................................... 327-331
Barton, Richard ........................................................ 376
Barton, Thomas ......................................................... 316
Barton, Willoby (Willoughby or Wileby) ............... 31-32-283-307-376-407
Baskin, James .......................................................... 407
Baskin, William ........................................................ 407
Basnet, John ........................................................... 376
Bass, Brantley ......................................................... 376
Bass, Hardy ......................................................... 20-376
Bass, Thomas ..................................................... 20-344-376
Bassett, George ............................................ 28-251-376-459-461
Bateman ................................................................ 407
Bateman, Tabitha ....................................................... 335
Battery, Zachariah ..................................................... 283
Bates, John ....................................................... 36-253-376
Batson, David ..................................................... 344-376
Battle, Sarah .......................................................... 333
Battle, William Lamar .................................................. 407
Baugh, Capt. ........................................................... 318

## Index.

| | |
|---|---|
| Baugh, Alex. C. | 407 |
| Baugh, Sally | 317 |
| Baughbank, Lewis | 376 |
| Baxter, Andrew | 41-311-407 |
| Baxter, James | 311 |
| Baxter, John | 184-344-376-407-453 |
| Baxter, William | 17 |
| Bayles, Sarah | 330 |
| Bayley, Joseph | 407 |
| Bayly, James | 407 |
| Bays, Moses | 344 |
| Bazemore, Thomas | 344 |
| Bazer, William | 344 |
| Bazlewood, Richard | 376-396 |
| Beaird, George | 31 |
| Beal, Archibald (or Beall) | 24-25-32-233-292-407 |
| Beal, Henry | 376 |
| Beal, Hezekiah | 29-199 |
| Beal, James | 29 |
| Beal, Jeremiah (or Beale) | 29-376-407 |
| Beal, Nathaniel | 30-376 |
| Beal, Zephaniah | 29 |
| Beale, William | 407-436 |
| Beale, Zephaniah | 407 |
| Beall, Archibald (Beale or Beal) | 376 |
| Beall, Garrett | 32-376 |
| Beall, Harrison | 344 |
| Beall, Henry | 32 |
| Beall, Nathaniel | 338 |
| Beall, Thomas | 344-376 |
| Beall, Zephaniah | 376 |
| Bean, William | 407 |
| Bear, Reuben | 376 |
| Beard, Edmond | 41-252-295 |
| Beard, Edward | 376 |
| Beard, John | 42 |
| Beard, Moses | 326-407-436 |
| Beard, Robert | 344-407-437 |
| Bearden, Humphrey | 330 |
| Bearden, John | 376 |
| Bearfield, Richard | 25 |
| Beaseley, Harris | 397 |
| Beaseley, James | 27 |
| Beaseley, Richard | 30-397 |
| Beasley, Amnrose | 407 |
| Beasley, Burwell | 228 |
| Beasley, Harris | 404 |

# INDEX.

Beasley, Henry ......................................................... 344
Beasley, John .......................................................344-376
Beasley, Joseph ......................................................26-376
Beasley, Richard ..................................................284-404-407
Beasley, Royland ........................................................ 407
Beasley, Thomas, Sr. .................................................... 341
Beasley, William (or Beesley) .................................344-376-407
Beason, Peter ........................................................31-376
Beatty, Samuel (or Beaty) .........................................36-45-376
Beatty, William (or Beaty) ........................................40-44-376
Beazley, Joseph ........................................................ 299
Beck, Sergt. ........................................................... 344
Beck, Sary ............................................................. 316
Beck, Simon .......................................................24-217-376
Beckem, Sherwood ....................................................... 29
Beckham, Maj. .......................................................... 459
Beckham, Abner ...................................................35-298-376-448
Beckham, Allen ......................................................299-376
Beckham, John .......................................................201-399
Beckham, Samuel ..................................................44-299-376-407
Beckham, Simon ......................................................25-376-402
Beckham, Soloman .................................................44-299-344
Beckom, Samuel ......................................................407-461
Beddingfield, Charles ................................................36-376
Beddingfield, Nathaniel ..............................................36-376
Bedell, Absalom ....................................................344-407
Bedingfield, Charles ...............................................302-407
Been, Walter ........................................................... 339
Beers, Matthew ......................................................... 407
Beesly, James ........................................................27-376
Beezly, Burrell ........................................................ 407
Beezly, Joseph ......................................................... 407
Beiser, Benj. .......................................................... 344
Bell, Capt. ............................................................ 316
Bell, Archibald ....................................................344-376
Bell, Arthur ........................................................... 323
Bell, Benj. ............................................................ 344
Bell, Elizabeth ....................................................316-324
Bell, Francis .......................................................... 319
Bell, Hezekiah ......................................................... 376
Bell, Hugh .....................................................17-25-253-259-376
Bell, John ..........................................................252-376
Bell, Robert ........................................................30-376
Bell, Thomas ........................................................... 307
Bell, Zachariah .....................................................397-404
Bellah, Samuel ......................................................... 344
Bellamy, Richard .................................................32-244-304-376

## Index.

| | |
|---|---|
| Bellemy, Richard | 32-244 |
| Bellinger, John | 314 |
| Bells, Hugh | 376 |
| Bender, John | 25-43-240-297-302-376 |
| Benefield, John | 407 |
| Benfield, Richard | 42 |
| Bennefield, Robert | 376 |
| Bennett, Capt. | 320 |
| Bennett, Daniel | 344 |
| Bennett, John | 312-399-407-436 |
| Bennett, Mary | 329 |
| Bennett, Nicajah | 344-454 |
| Bennett, Rachel | 317 |
| Bennett, Reuben | 322-397-403 |
| Bennis, John | 15-17-34-407 |
| Bennison, John | 376 |
| Bensen, William, Sr. | 323 |
| Benson, Enoch | 344-407-437-450 |
| Benson, John | 376 |
| Bentley, Capt. | 407 |
| Bentley, Lieutenant | 407 |
| Bentley, James | 344-454 |
| Bentley, Jesse | 344 |
| Bentley, John | 29-44-250-252-274-376 |
| Bentley, William | 31-376 |
| Benton, Joseph | 407 |
| Benton, Joseph, Sr. | 407-436 |
| Benton, Robert | 376 |
| Benton, Richard | 131 |
| Beohom, William | 254 |
| Berand, Capt. | 407 |
| Berchell, William | 266 |
| Bergsterner, Daniel | 407 |
| Berihill, Alexander | 32 |
| Berihill, Samuel | 32 |
| Berk, James | 17-407 |
| Bernard, Capt. | 407 |
| Bernett, John | **244** |
| Berrien, Capt. | 407 |
| Berrien, John (or Berrian) | 9-15-17-45-302-407-461 |
| Berrien, John, Lt. | 407 |
| Berrihill, Andrew | 25 |
| Berry, Gideon | 298 |
| Berry, Gilson | 27 |
| Berry, Isham | 344 |
| Berry, John | 17-212-234-280-407-449 |
| Berry, Mary | 137 |
| Berry, Richard | 244-246-376 |

Berry, Samuel .................................................................. 210
Berry, William ...................................................17-29-250-284-407
Berryhill, John ................................................................. 376
Berryhill, Merander ....................................................... 397-403
Berryhill, Samuel ........................................................... 210-376
Besons, Peter .................................................................. 199
Bessett, Alex .................................................................. 219
Bethune, Peter ................................................................ 344
Betsall, Isaac ................................................................. 399
Bevill, James (or Bevil) ................................................... 32-36-376
Bevill, Paul (or Bevil) ................................................ 32-42-376-457
Beville, Robert ................................................................ 376
Beville, George ................................................................ 407
Bickham, Abner ............................................................... 27-407
Bickham, John ................................................................. 30
Bierry, T. ..................................................................... 407
Biffle, John ................................................................... 344
Bigbie, James N. ........................................................... 344-454
Bilbo, John .................................................................... 407
Binum, Drury ................................................................. 313
Bird, Benjamin ............................................................. 376-396
Bird, Herman ............................................................... 407-436
Bird, John ................................................................. 376-396
Bird, Michael ................................................................ 29-376
Bird, Thomas .................................................................. 344
Bird, Thompson ................................................................ 407
Bird, William ................................................................. 407
Birdsong, John ................................................................ 344
Birmingham, James ............................................................. 407
Bishop, Golden ........................................................... 344-407-436
Bishop, James ............................................................ 210-229-285
Bishop, Joshua .......................................................... 44-252-268-376
Bishop, Stephen ......................................................... 210-214-228
Bishop, William ....................................................... 17-253-281-287-407
Bitsell, John ................................................................. 376
Bivins, Williams ........................................................... 344-407
Black, Capt. .................................................................. 407
Black, David .................................................................. 408
Black, Edward ................................................................. 44
Black, Henry .......................................................... 28-30-228-302-376
Black, J. ..................................................................... 244
Black, John .......................................................... 31-35-40-244-376-436-450
Black, Lemuel ............................................................. 397-403
Black, Samuel ................................................................. 344
Black, Thomas ................................................................. 344
Black, William ....................................................... 43-224-376-408-437-450
Blackburn, Nathan ......................................................... 323-344

## INDEX.

Blacksell, Thomas .................................................... 46-376
Blackshear, Edmond .................................................... 408
Blackshear, Edward .................................................... 408
Blackwell, Capt. ....................................................... 316
Blackwell, Sally Chandler ............................................. 316
Blair, James .................................................. 321-325-330-408
Blair, Johnson ........................................................ 376
Blair, Samuel ......................................................... 35
Blair, Sibbiah ........................................................ 32
Blakely, Benjamin ..................................................... 376
Blakely, John ..................................................... 344-376
Blakely, Michael ...................................................... 344
Blakey, Benjamin ................................................... 25-34
Blakey, Churchel ...................................................... 323
Blalock, Eleanor ...................................................... 325
Blanchard, Reuben .................................................. 37-376
Blanchard, William ........................................ 27-239-249-260-376
Blandford, Clark ...................................................... 344
Blankenship, Capt. .................................................... 320
Blanks, James ......................................................... 344
Blayer, William ....................................................... 39
Blazer, William ....................................................... 376
Bledsoe, Benjamin ............................................... 344-408-450
Bledsoe, Miller ............................................. 344-408-437-450
Bledsoe, Peachy .................................................. 397-404
Bledsoe, William ...................................................... 323
Blitch, Abraham ....................................................... 345
Bloodworth, Samuel .................................................... 229
Blount, Benjamin ...................................................... 48
Blount, Isaac ..................................................... 408-450
Blount, Jacob .................................................. 38-40-236-253-376-408
Blount, Jacob, Capt. ............................................... 17-408
Blount, Jacob, Lieut. ................................................. 408
Blount, Stephen ................................................ 16-24-244-408
Blunt, Jacob .......................................................... 376
Blunt, Polly .......................................................... 315
Blunt, Stephen ........................................................ 376
Blunt, William ........................................................ 345
Blythe, Robert ........................................................ 345
Bobbets, Jacob ........................................................ 34
Bobough, Lewis ........................................................ 242
Bodenner, George ...................................................... 376
Boderly, William ...................................................... 376
Bodimas, George ....................................................... 31
Boen, Stephen ......................................................... 345
Boggs, Eve ........................................................ 318-334
Boggs, Ezekiel ........................................................ 345

| | |
|---|---|
| Bogs, Joseph | 29 |
| Bohan, Joseph | 345-436 |
| Bohan, Joseph, Capt. | 408 |
| Bohanon, Ben. | 376 |
| Bohannon, Lydia | 330-331 |
| Boid, John | 376 |
| Boils, Charles | 345 |
| Bolboth, Hannah | 25 |
| Bolboth, James | 25 |
| Boles, Henry | 397-404 |
| Boling, Tomberry | 404 |
| Bollin, John | 345 |
| Boloth, James | 376 |
| Bolough, Lewis | 32 |
| Bolton, Francis | 40 |
| Bolton, Mary | 327 |
| Bolton, Robert | 408 |
| Bona, Richard C. | 345 |
| Bond, George | 30-298-303 |
| Bond, Lindsey | 321 |
| Bond, Nathan | 315 |
| Bond, Nathaniel | 337 |
| Bond, Richard | 321-408-437 |
| Bond, Seny | 376 |
| Bonds, Joseph | 408-450 |
| Bondurant, Josiah | 318 |
| Bonnell, Anthony, Lieut., | 345 |
| Bonnell, Daniel | 408 |
| Bonnell, David | 243-408 |
| Bonnell, John, | 36-345-408 |
| Bonnells, Anthony | 408 |
| Bonner, Capt. | 408 |
| Bonner, George | 400 |
| Bonner, Henry | 408 |
| Bonner, Joseph | 345 |
| Bonner, Richard | 376 |
| Bonner, Robert | 228 |
| Bonner Sherwood | 408 |
| Bonner, Willian | 45-376 |
| Boooker, Gideon, | 15-17-83-96-116-253-408 |
| Booker, John, Sr., | 323 |
| Booker, William | 323-345 |
| Boon, Jesse | 345-408-437 |
| Booth, Abraham, (or Boothe) | 376-408-457 |
| Booth, Charles | 376 |
| Booth, David | 408 |
| Boring, Isaac | 345 |

## INDEX.

Boring, Phoebe .......... 318
Borland, Andrew .......... 400
Borman, Thomas .......... 397
Borneman, Benjamin .......... 376
Boseman, Ralph .......... 329
Bostick, Chesley, (or Bostwick) .......... 10-14-15-376-408
Bostick, Littleberry, (or Bostic) .......... 30-203-376-408
Bostick, Nathan .......... 43-252-376
Bostwick. Jane .......... 315
Bostwick Mary .......... 328
Boswell, David .......... 298
Boswoeth, Obediah .......... 240
Bosworth, Jacob .......... 408-437
Botsford, Edmond, .......... 408
Bourquin, David Francis .......... 408
Bourquin, Henry .......... 408
Bouquin, Henry Davis .......... 408
Boutin, John .......... 315
Bowden, James .......... 331
Bowen, Maj. .......... 317
Bowen, Elijah .......... 330-408-437
Bowen, Ep .......... 376
Bowen, James .......... 376
Bowen, Joel .......... 250
Bowen, John .......... 336-345-408-437
Bowen, Oliver, .......... 9-14-28-33-45-96-284-376-377-408-461
Bowen, Richard .......... 24
Bowen, Samuel .......... 345-408-436-450
Bowen, Samuel, Sr., .......... 323
Bowen, Stephen .......... 408-436
Bowens, Joel .......... 31-377
Bowers, James .......... 199
Bowie, James, .......... 26-311-400
Bowie, Reason, .......... 199-252
Bowie, Richard .......... 199
Bowin, Ephriam .......... 44
Bowles, Nathan .......... 317-333
Bowling, Edward .......... 345-408-436
Bowling, R., .......... 377
Bowling, Robert .......... 31
Bowling Thomas Burton, .......... 377
Bowling, Thornberry .......... 397
Bowman, Jacob .......... 377
Box, Philip .......... 408
Boyakin, Jesse (or Boykins) .......... 28
Boyce, Lott .......... 20-345-377
Boyd, Ed., .......... 377

## INDEX.

Boyd, Edward .................................................26-41-202-377
Boyd, John .......................................................26-40-377
Boyd, Nicholas, ....................................................... 377
Boyd, Nicodemus, ...................................................... 28
Boyd, Robert .....................................................26-30-377
Boykin, Boas ......................................................... 34
Boykin, Bunus ....................................................... 377
Boykin, Byus ......................................................... 46
Boykin, Francis ...........................................26-28-251-273-408
Boykin, Jesse ........................................................ 249
Boykins, Byers ...................................................... 377
Boykins, Jesse (or Boyakin) ......................................... 377
Boyle, Hannah ....................................................... 318
Boyt, Thomas ........................................................ 345
Bozeman, Ralph ...................................................... 329
Brack, Benjamin .................................................44-300-461
Brack, Eleazer, ...................................................25-254
Brack, John ......................................................... 459
Brack, Sarah ........................................................ 329
Brack, Wm. .......................................................... 345
Bradberry, Lewis .................................................... 345
Braddock, David ...............................................17-28-377-408
Braddock, James ..................................................... 408
Braddock, John .................................................17-40-377
Braddy, Lewis ....................................................... 345
Bradey, William ..................................................... 377
Bradford, Ann ....................................................... 338
Bradford, Josiah .................................................... 377
Bradford, Osiah ...................................................... 42
Bradford, William ................................................... 408
Bradie, David ........................................................ 15
Bradley, Abraham ..........................................17-28-215-253-377
Bradley, Amb ........................................................ 215
Bradley, John ..............................................345-397-404-408
Bradley, Joshua ................................................36-215-377
Bradley, M. .....................................................17-408
Bradley, Michael ................................................36-377
Bradley, Richard ............................................17-31-36-377-408
Bradley, William ............................................249-251-266-408-436
Bradley, William, Sr., ............................................... 36
Bradshaw, Peter ..................................................46-377
Bradwell, Samuel .................................................... 345
Bradwell, Thomas .................................................... 408
Brady, David ........................................................ 408
Brady, Samuel ...................................................331-336
Brady, William ..............................................30-289-377-408
Brady, William, Jr., ................................................. 34

INDEX. 485

| | |
|---|---|
| Brady, Wm., Sergt. | 377 |
| Bragg, Bejamin | 397 |
| Bragg, Benjamin, Lt., | 397 |
| Bragg, William | 345-408-436 |
| Braidie, David | 408 |
| Braidy, William | 201 |
| Braker, William | 46-377 |
| Bramfield, John | 377 |
| Bramlett, Henry | 345 |
| Bramlett, Reuben | 408-450 |
| Branan, Samuel | 25 |
| Branch, James | 332 |
| Branch, William S., | 345 |
| Brand, Caswell, | 397-404 |
| Brand, William | 345-408-437 |
| Brandon, David | 206 |
| Brandon, John | 39-43-204-377 |
| Branham, ........Col., | 408 |
| Branham, Richard | 322 |
| Branham, Samuel | 41-206-377-408 |
| Branham, Spencer | 408 |
| Branham, ....(or Branham) | 459 |
| Brannan, Thomas | 250 |
| Brannen, ........(or Branham) | 461 |
| Brannon, Michael | 330 |
| Brannon, Moses | 377-396 |
| Brannon, Thomas | 202-210-377 |
| Brantley, Amos | 314-345-377-408-436 |
| Brantley, Brittain, (or Britton) | 20-377-408 |
| Brantley, James | 377 |
| Brantley, Jeremiah | 40-244-245 |
| Brantley, Mary | 334 |
| Brantley, Thomas | 44-228-270-377 |
| Brantley, William | 345 |
| Brasel, Bird | 408-450 |
| Brasil, Ferdinand | 37 |
| Brasil, John | 30 |
| Brasley, Nicholas | 408 |
| Brassard, Alex | 377 |
| Brassell, Britton | 345 |
| Brassel, Samuel | 377 |
| Brasswell, Joseph | 377 |
| Braswell, Allen (or Allin) | 31-44-377 |
| Braswell, F., | 377 |
| Braswell, Ferdinand (or Ferdinan) | 225-377 |
| Braswell, Fred | 225-226 |
| Braswell, Frederick | 25-34-223-242 |

# INDEX.

Braswell, George ............... 28-40-377
Braswell, James ............... 24-44-377
Braswell, John ............... 225-251-260-265
Braswell, Joseph ............... 43-45
Braswell, Sampson, ............... 28-36
Braswell, Samuel ............... 257
Braswell, Samuel, Jr., ............... 34
Braswell, Simpson ............... 377
Braswell, William ............... 43
Brawner, Charles ............... 26
Bray, Barrister R., ............... 316
Bray, Thomas ............... 241-311
Braydon, William ............... 377
Brazel, Samuel ............... 31
Brazelton, Jacob, Sr., ............... 319
Brazil, Byrd ............... 408-437
Brazill, Britten ............... 345
Brazill, Sampson ............... 241
Brazwell, John Richard ............... 377
Brawner, Charles ............... 26
Bready, William ............... 377
Bresard, C. ............... 17
Brevard, George ............... 377
Brewer Benjamin ............... 301
Brewer, Erasmus ............... 39-377
Brewer, George ............... 24-244-377
Brewer, Moses ............... 27-377
Brewer, William ............... 30-377
Brewster, Hugh ............... 345-408-437-450
Brewster, Sherriff ............... 408-437
Briant, Henry ............... 26
Briant, John ............... 408
Briant, William ............... 404
Briants, John ............... 377
Brice, Jacob ............... 408
Bridges, Prior ............... 397-403
Bridges, Wiseman, ............... 345
Brigg, William ............... 400
Briggs, Samuel ............... 29-30-49-300-377
Brinkley, Eley ............... 345
Brinton, Mary ............... 324
Brisbane, Adam Fower ............... 408
Britt, Charles ............... 28-36-245-309
Britt, Edward ............... 345
Brittain, Henry ............... 34-377
Brittinham, Joseph ............... 345-377
Broadwell, Christian ............... 318-327

# INDEX.

Brock, Benjamin ............................................. 377
Brock, William ............................................... 408
Brockman, Bledsoe .......................................397-404
Brockman, Elijah ........................................397-404
Brockman, Lewis .............................................. 345
Brodie, David ................................................ 408
Bronson, Ebenezer ............................................ 377
Bronson, John Sr. ............................................. 34
Brooke, Robert ............................................... 408
Brooks, George ..........................................408-450
Brooks, Hannah ............................................... 318
Brooks, Jacob ............................................252-377
Brooks, James ...............................35-345-377-397-403
Brooks, Jesse (or Jessey) ................................41-227-377
Brooks, Joab, ................................................ 27
Brooks, John .............................................25-377
Brooks, Judith ............................................... 318
Brooks, Micajah .......................................345-459-461
Brooks, Middleton, ....................................318-408-437
Brooks, Richael .............................................. 341
Brooks, Robert ........................................331-345-408-437
Brooks, Roger .........................................35-39-300-377
Brooks, William .......................................345-397-404
Broom, Thomas, (or Broome) ............................43-245-251-293
Brossard, Celerin, (or Brusard) ........................15-30-39-408
Broughton, John .............................................. 448
Brown, Lieut. ................................................ 408
Brown, Allen ..........................45-253-302-305-311-377
Brown, Ambrose, .......................................345-408-450
Brown, Amos .................................................. 449
Brown, Andrew .........................................34-45-251-377
Brown, Ben ...........................................316-437-450
Brown, Benjamin ......................................408-459-461
Brown, Bond Veall ............................................ 345
Brown, David ..............................................58-377
Brown, Dempsey ............................................... 345
Brown, Edwards ............................................... 345
Brown, Elisha ................................................ 346
Brown, Elizabeth .........................................324-330
Brown, Ephraim .......................................203-408-437
Brown, Epps .................................................. 461
Brown, Francis .......................................17-45-377-408
Brown, Fred .................................................. 377
Brown, Frederick ..........................................27-242
Brown, H. Thomas ............................................. 397
Brown, Henry ................................................. 450
Brown, Hugh .................................................. 321

Brown, Jacob ....................................................17-408
Brown, James ...............................................42-377-401-408
Brown, James M., ..................................................... 316
Brown, Jane ........................................................ 321
Brown, Jesse ....................................................... 327
Brown, John ....................17-40-42-45-216-217-272-346-377-408-436-450-461
Brown, Joseph ..................................................341-408
Brown, Larkin ...................................................... 346
Brown, Lemuel .................................................397-404
Brown, Lewis ...................................................... 341
Brown, Loami ...................................................... 331
Brown, Mary ...................................................330-332
Brown, Meredith .................................................... 346
Brown, Mordecai .................................................... 331
Brown, Moses ...................................................... 346
Brown, Pollard ..................................................... 397
Brown, Rebecca ..................................................... 330
Brown, Robert .................................................321-408-437
Brown, Samuel ...................................................... 45
Brown, Stark ..............................................346-377-437-458
Brown, Thomas ............................15-27-28-44-250-290-377-403-409
Brown, Thomas Jr., .................................................. 29
Brown, Thomas, H., ................................................. 404
Brown, Uriah ..................................................346-409-436
Brown, Walter .................................................409-437
Brown, William ...........................................27-29-200-252-298-377
Brownen, Charles ................................................... 377
Browner, Charles ................................................... 251
Brownfield, John ................................................... 297
Browning, John ..................................................397-404
Browning, Margaret ................................................. 330
Brownlow, William .................................................. 377
Brownson, Nathan ..........................................15-17-24-28-29-37-241-252-409
Brownson, Nathaniel ................................................ 377
Bruce .........Maj. .................................................. 320
Bruce, Daniel ...................................................... 397
Bruce, Elizabeth ................................................... 324
Bruce, Ward ...................................................397-404
Bruce, William ..................................................... 346
Brumfield, John .................................................... 313
Brumley, John ...................................................... 377
Brunifield, John ................................................... 346
Brunner, Benjamin .................................................. 409
Brunson, David ..................................................26-31-377
Brunson, Ebenezer ..............................................26-203-206
Brunson, John ..................................................205-377
Brunson, Samuel, .................................................. 206

# INDEX.

Brunson, William ..................................................24-377
Brunston, William ................................................205-212
Brusard, Celerine, (Brassard, or De Brossard) ......................... 409
Bruson Frances ........................................................ 333
Bruton, James ......................................................... 409
Bruton, John .......................................................... 252
Bryan, Ann ............................................................ 336
Bryan, David .......................................................... 346
Bryan, Duncan ......................................................... 283
Bryan, Ezekiel ....................................................409-450
Bryan, Hugh ........................................................... 409
Bryan, James .....................................................15-346-409
Bryan, John ........................................................... 346
Bryan, Jonathan ..................................................409-461
Bryan, Nathan ......................................................... 323
Bryan, Thomas ......................................................... 409
Bryan, Thomas, St., ................................................... 326
Bryan, William ....................................................320-409
Bryant, Bemjamin ...................................................... 377
Bryant, Issaac ........................................................ 313
Bryant, James .....................................................28-377
Bryant, John ...........................29-35-212-213-250-284-319-377
Bryant, Patience ...................................................... 319
Bryant, William ................................................29-377-397-436
Bryant, William G .................................................346-377
Brydie, David ......................................................... 409
Bryon, Thomas ......................................................... 437
Bryson, ........Lt. ................................................... 409
Bryson, James, ....................................................... 409
Bryson, John .......................................................... 409
Buchanan, George ..............................................409-437-450
Buchanan, James ..............................................346-409-436-454
Buchanan, James P. Sr. , .............................................. 314
Buchannon, James P. ..............................................346-377
Buchannon, John ....................................................... 311
Buchannon, Mary ....................................................... 326
Buchanon, George H. ................................................... 346
Buck, William ......................................................... 377
Buckhalter, John ..................................................40-239-377
Buckhalter, Joseph .................................................... 377
Buckhalter, Joshua .................................................... 254
Buckhalter, Michael ...............................................250-377
Buckhalter, Micajah, (or Mikel) ....................................... 25
Buckhalter, William ..............................................211-250
Buckhan, Simon ........................................................ 239
Buckholter, Peter.... (or Buckhalter) .............................409-450
Buckles, Peter ........................................................ 346

## INDEX.

Buckner, Benj .................................................. 346
Buckner, Harris ............................................... 201
Budd, Charles ............................................. 15-409
Buff, Michael, ............................................. 409-437
Buford, John, Sr., ............................................. 313
Buford, William ............................................ 329-400
Bugg, Ed. ................................................... 377-402
Bugg, Edmund ............................................... 33-409
Bugg, H. ....................................................... 241
Bugg, Isaac ................................................... 219
Bugg, Jacob ........................................ 33-198-284-377
Bugg, Jere .................................................... 201
Bugg, Jeremiah ................................. 33-202-272-377-402-409
Bugg, John ................................................. 346-377
Bugg, John, Jr., ............................................... 252
Bugg, Nicholas .......................................... 33-199-377
Bugg, Samuel ............................................ 33-346-377
Bugg, Sherod .................................................. 346
Bugg, Sherwood, ..................................... 15-33-377-409
Bugg, William ............................................. 307-409
Buggs, Jona ................................................... 377
Bugners, Augustus ............................................. 377
Buice, Margaret ............................................... 338
Bullard, Ann .................................................. 316
Bullard, Daniel ............................................... 307
Bullard, James ................................................ 346
Bulloch, Archibald ........................................ 409-461
Bulloch, James ................................................ 409
Bulloch, John (or Bolloch) ............................ 397-404-409
Bullock, Daniel ........................................... 346-377
Bullock, Hawkins ...................................... 346-409-437
Bullock, Richard .............................................. 346
Bullough, Elias, .......................................... 409-450
Bunster, William .......................................... 409-450
Burch, Charles ........................................... 43-201-377
Burch, Edward ...................................... 24-38-201-331-377
Burden, Hannah ............................................... 315
Burdett, Humphrey ............................................. 323
Burdey, Peter ................................................. 377
Burdeyshaw, Peter .............................................. 35
Burford, William .............................................. 254
Burgamy, John ................................................. 409
Burgamy, William .............................................. 409
Burgany, William .............................................. 346
Burger, Charles ............................................... 404
Bugges, Charles ............................................... 397
Burges, Joseph ................................................ 377

| | |
|---|---|
| Burgess, Edward | 409 |
| Burgess, Elias | 319 |
| Burgess, Jonathan | 397-404 |
| Burgess, Joseph | 36-397-404 |
| Burgess, Joshia | 326 |
| Burgess, Josiah, | 333-409-437 |
| Burgesteiner, Daniel (or Burgsteiner) | 40-377 |
| Burk, James | 32 |
| Burk Mary | 32 |
| Burk, Theophilous | 39 |
| Burk, William | 30 |
| Burkalow, William | 43 |
| Burke, Charley (or Charles) | 250-397-403 |
| Burke, David | 284 |
| Burke, Isham | 218-286-448 |
| Burke, John | 214-228-252-292 |
| Burke, Joseph | 298 |
| Burke, Theophilus | 377 |
| Burkeloe, Richard | 301 |
| Burkes, David | 377 |
| Burkes, Ed., | 397 |
| Burkes, James | 377 |
| Burkes, Joseph | 45-377 |
| Burket, Lemuel | 346 |
| Burkett, Uriah | 399 |
| Burkhalter, Jacob | 250-346 |
| Burkhalter, Joshua, | 45 |
| Burkhalter, Micajah, (Mikel) | 25 |
| Burks Charles | 27 |
| Burks, David | 34 |
| Burks, Ed | 377 |
| Burks, Edward | 24-34 |
| Burks, John | 41-377 |
| Burks, Jose | 377 |
| Burks, Joseph | 26-323 |
| Burks, Roland, | 37 |
| Burkshalter, Michael | 346 |
| Burlamon, Benj. | 29-35 |
| Burley, Zach, | 377 |
| Burnard, William | 377 |
| Burner, Richard | 400 |
| Burnes, Andrew | 299 |
| Burnes, Susannah, Mrs. | 75 |
| Burnett, Col. | 409 |
| Burnett, Andrew | 44 |
| Burnett, B. | 409 |
| Burnett, Daniel | 409 |

Burnett, Ichabod ..... 409
Burnett, Joel ..... 334
Burnett, John ..... 17-26-36-211-250-302-409
Burnett, Joshua ..... 39
Burnett, Molly, ..... 334
Burnett, Nathan, ..... 377
Burney, Andrew ..... 409
Burney, John ..... 41-235-377
Burney, John, Jr., ..... 25-242-377
Burney, John, Sr. ..... 242
Burney, Randall, (or Randol) ..... 28-254-377
Burnley, Lt. ..... 409
Burnley, Henry ..... 346-409-437
Burnley, Samuel ..... 31-184
Burns, Andrew ..... 42-312-377-409
Burns, John, ..... 26-377
Burns, Margaret ..... 318
Burnsides, John ..... 42-251-377
Burnsides, John Sr., ..... 24
Burris, John ..... 409
Burroughs, Henry ..... 320
Burroughs, John ..... 409
Burson, Sarah, ..... 318
Burt, Moody, ..... 42-250-377
Burton, John, ..... 41-377
Burton, Richard ..... 17-35-41-209-377-378-449
Burton, Thomas ..... 31-40-378-409
Burwell, Daniel ..... 346
Burwell, John ..... 378
Bush, Daniel, Thomas ..... 322
Bush, John ..... 207-271-400
Bush, Levi ..... 307-346
Bush, Prescott ..... 409-450
Bush, Samuel ..... 346
Bush, Thomas ..... 37-42-60-72-162-322
Bussey, Gideon ..... 400
Bussey, Hezekiah (or Bussy) ..... 34-249-262-378
Bussey, Hwz, ..... 279
Bussey, Thomas ..... 34-252-276-378
Busson, Jona ..... 378
Busson, Jonathan ..... 41-298
Butler, ..........Capt. ..... 316
Butler, Benj. ..... 409
Butler, Daniel, ..... 33-44-243-244-378
Butler, Edmond, ..... 378-396
Butler, Edward ..... 45-46
Butler, Elisha ..... 409

# INDEX.    493

Butler, Ford. ....27-45-248-302-378
Butler, Frances .... 378
Butler, Hannah .... 340
Butler, James ....409-437
Butler, John ....38-378
Butler, Joseph .... 409
Butler, Josiah .... 409
Butler, Mary C. .... 329
Butler, Patrick ....316-409-437
Butler, Patrick, Sr., .... 335
Butler, Pierce .... 409
Butler, Robert, ....43-378
Butler, Shem .... 409
Butler, William ....46-378-396
Butry, Z. ....17-409
Butry, Zachariah .... 42
Butt, Esther .... 315
Buttrell, William .... 346
Butts, James .... 346
Butts, Samuel, .... 396
Butts, Solomon .... 378
Buxton, Samuel .... 409
Buzer, William .... 378
Bynum, Drewry .... 346
Bynum, Drudy ....409-436
Bynum, John .... 448
Bynum, Sugars .... 326
Byrd, John .... 346

## C

Cabaness, Henry .... 328
Cabennias, Henry .... 315
Cabos, John ....346-409-450
Cade, ........Capt. .... 409
Cade, Drewry (or Drwry) ....53-55-378
Cady, John .... 48
Cain, John (or Caine) ....257-279-378
Caison, Willis, Sr., .... 330
Calaway, Peter .... 346
Calder, John, ....409-450-457
Caldwell, George.... 57
Caldwell, James ....55-378
Caldwell, John ....15-378-409
Caldwell, William ....409-449
Calhoun, George .... 297
Calhoun, Patrick .... 409

# INDEX.

Calhoun, William ........ 378
Calk, James ........ 48-256
Calk, James, Jr., ........ 256-378
Calk, James W. ........ 378
Call, Richard ........ 136-201-205-208-216-223-242-243-252-309-400-409
Callahan, John ........ 329
Callahan, Josiah ........ 450
Callaway, Jacob ........ 323
Callender, Ebenezer ........ 409
Calson, Wilson ........ 378
Camant, John ........ 378
Camberger, Chestop ........ 378
Cameron, Alexander ........ 409-437
Cameron, Allen, ........ 346
Cameron, James ........ 346
Camp, Edward ........ 319-346
Camp, Edmond ........ 145
Camp, Hosea, ........ 409-437-454
Camp, James ........ 250-346-378
Camp, Joseph ........ 60-256
Camp, L. ........ 59
Camp, Samuel ........ 17-378-400-409
Camp, Sol. ........ 378
Camp, William (or Kemp) ........ 51-378
Campbell, ........ Capt. ........ 409
Campbell, Alexander ........ 61
Campbell, Drury ........ 59-378-409
Campbell, George ........ 410-438-450
Campbell, Gilbert ........ 48-257
Campbell, Jeremiah ........ 410-457
Campbell, John ........ 17-254-410
Campbell, McCartin ........ 410
Campbell, William ........ 48-57-239-255-280-284-346-378
Camps, Joseph ........ 378
Candill, Benjamin ........ 347
Candler, Henry ........ 57-252-256-281-297-378-410
Candler, John ........ 347
Candler, William ........ 255-276-378-461
Candler, William, Jr. ........ 50
Cane, John ........ 57
Cannon, Ann ........ 340
Cannon, Elizabeth ........ 328
Cannon, Henry ........ 410
Cannon, Mary ........ 328
Cannon, Nathaniel ........ 347-410-438
Cannon, Roger ........ 51-378
Cannon, Thomas ........ 50-240-245-246-378

# INDEX.

| | |
|---|---|
| Cannup, Thomas | 330 |
| Canon, D | 378 |
| Cantley, Zachariah | 410 |
| Cantrell, Charles | 340 |
| Cantrell, Stephen | 378 |
| Canty, Zach | 378 |
| Capeheart, John | 314 |
| Carden, Cornelius, (or Cardin) | 52-59-378 |
| Cargyle, John | 378 |
| Carithers, Robert | 329 |
| Carlisle, Benjamin | 347 |
| Carlisle, Edmond | 347 |
| Carlisle, John | 54-207 |
| Carlton, Mildred | 324 |
| Carlton, Patrick, (or Carleton) | 55-58-378 |
| Carlyle, John | 49-54-378 |
| Carnery, Ornsby, | 233 |
| Carnes John | 259-308 |
| Carnes, Peter, | 243-244-400 |
| Carnes, Rosannah | 337 |
| Carnes, Thomas | 241 |
| Carnes, Thos. P. | 400 |
| Carney, Arthur | 9-14-15 |
| Carney, M. | 378 |
| Carney, Matthew, | 54-255-299 |
| Carney, Ousley, (or Ousby) | 52-378 |
| Carpenter, ........Capt. | 315 |
| Carpenter, Soloman, | 410 |
| Carpenter, William | 410 |
| Carr, ........Maj. | 378 |
| Carr, Henry | 53-60-266-280-378-410 |
| Carr, Mark, | 410 |
| Carr, Patrick | 51-55-156-378 |
| Carr, Samuel, | 410 |
| Carr, Thomas | 307-461 |
| Carr, William | 347-410-438 |
| Carraway, William | 410-438-459-461 |
| Carrell, Elizabeth | 54 |
| Carrell, Jessey | 323 |
| Carrell, John | 347 |
| Carrell, William | 54-56 |
| Carrol, Charles | 323 |
| Carroll, Brittain | 347 |
| Carroll, Douglas, | 347 |
| Carroll, James | 410-450 |
| Carroll, John | 330 |
| Carroll, Mary | 331 |

## INDEX.

Carroll, Owen ........................................................ 347
Carroll, Thomas W. ................................................ 454
Carroll, William, ............................................. 207-378
Carruthers, Samuel ................................................ 338
Carsey, Stephen, Jr. ................................................. 53
Carson, Adam .............................................. 61-329-378
Carson, David ................................................. 58-225
Carson, Ephriam ................................................... 347
Carson, John ................................................ 56-58-378
Carson, Joseph ............................................... 49-55-378
Carson, Samuel ........................................... 56-58-208-378
Carson, Thomas ............................................ 51-254-378-402
Carson, Thomas Jr. ............................................ 56-378
Carson, Thomas Sr., .................................................. 56
Carswell, Alexander ....................................... 243-378-461
Carswell, Alexander, Sr. ............................................ 48
Carswell, John ............................................... 410-461
Carter ................. Maj. ........................................ 410
Carter, Charles, ........................................ 347-410-438-450
Carter, David, ................................. 48-127-207-321-410-438-450
Carter, Eliz ........................................................ 316
Carter, Henry ................................................. 49-378
Carter, Hepworth .......................................... 52-378-410
Carter, James ........................................ 51-340-378-396-401
Carter, John ................................................. 323-461
Carter, Josiah .............................................. 72-347-378
Carter, Lewis ...................................................... 321
Carter, Mitilda .................................................... 320
Carter, Patrick ............................................ 48-58-378-402
Carter, Richard ................................................... 410
Carter, Robert ........................................ 336-410-438-450
Carter, Thomas ............................................ 49-397-410
Carter, William ............................................... 321-323
Cartledge, Edmund .......................................... 240-245
Cartledge, Edmond, Sr. ............................................ 240
Cartledge, Edward .......................................... 347-378
Cartledge, J. Sr. ............................................... 372-332
Cartledge, James (or Cartlidge) ............ 49-50-55-57-208-240-245-246-378
Cartledge, Joseph ................................................. 410
Cartledge, Samuel ........................................... 58-255-378
Caruthers, William, (or Crudders) .................................. 48
Carven, Edw. ...................................................... 378
Carvenson, Eli .................................................... 316
Cary, John ........................................................ 410
Casey Daniel ...................................................... 314
Casey, John ....................................................... 378
Casey, William .............................................. 347-378

| | |
|---|---|
| Cash, Am | 450 |
| Cash, Dorson | 347 |
| Cash, Howard | 347 |
| Cash, James | 319-321-347-410-438 |
| Cash, John | 316-340-347-410-438 |
| Cash, Sarah | 317-335 |
| Cason, Samuel | 378 |
| Cason, Triplett | 347 |
| Cason, William | 347-410-438-450 |
| Cason, Willis, Sr., | 329-340 |
| Cassell, William | 378 |
| Cassell, John | 58-378 |
| Castello, Ed. | 378 |
| Castello, Michael | 256 |
| Caster, David | 378 |
| Castleberry, Henry (or Castelberry) | 52-206-378 |
| Castleberry, Jacob | 53-255-378 |
| Castleberry, John | 50-244-284-285-378 |
| Castleberry, Paul | 449 |
| Castleberry, Peter | 47-284-378 |
| Castleberry, Richard | 232 |
| Castleberry, William M. | 448 |
| Catchings, Benjamin | 50-199-270-299-378-410 |
| Catchings, Benjamin, Maj. | 410 |
| Catchings, James | 251 |
| Catchings, Joseph | 60-212-378-402 |
| Catchings, Meredith | 59-254-410 |
| Catchings, Seymour | 55-229-255-378 |
| Cater, John | 410 |
| Cathern, William | 378 |
| Catliff, Abraham | 347 |
| Candelle, David | 347 |
| Cato, William | 52-378 |
| Catter, James | 289 |
| Catteratz, Stephen | 62 |
| Cauley, Jacob | 378 |
| Cauley, Richard | 49-378 |
| Causey, Eliz | 315 |
| Causey, Ezekiel, | 315-347 |
| Cauthon, Joseph | 378 |
| Cavannah, Nicholas | 410 |
| Cavannah, Robert | 410 |
| Cavenah, Nicholas | 347 |
| Cawthorn, Josiah | 275 |
| Cawthorne, James | 378 |
| Chaffin, Isham | 323 |
| Chalfinch, Hiram | 410-437-450-454 |

## INDEX.

Camberlain, John .................................................... 449
Chambers, John ............................................. 52-227-378
Chambers, Martha ................................................... 328
Chambers, Peter .................................................... 410
Chambless, Christopher, (or Chambliss) ............... 54-60-127-202-378
Chambles, John (Chamblis or Chambers) ............................ 47-378
Chambless, Littleton ......................................... 50-53-378
Champion, John ..................................................... 347
Chance, Simpson .................................................... 347
Chance, Vincent .................................................... 400
Chandler, .............. Maj. ....................................... 410
Chandler, Abednego ............................................ 61-378-400
Chandler, James .................................................... 319
Chandler, John ............................................ 204-256-347-410
Chandler, Joseph ................................................... 410
Chandler, M. ....................................................... 378
Chandler, Mary ..................................................... 320
Chandler, Mordecai .................................................. 48
Chandler, Nancy .................................................... 320
Chandler, Shelldrake ........................................... 410-450
Chandler, Tabitha .................................................. 319
Chancy, Emanuel ................................................. 47-378
Chaney, G. ......................................................... 378
Chaney, Greenbury ................................................... 60
Chaplain, Joseph ................................................... 238
Chapman, Abner ..................................................... 347
Chapman, John ............................................... 50-55-378-402
Chapman, Nathan .................................................... 347
Chapman, Richard .................................................... 46
Chapman, William ............................................ 59-302-378
Chappell, John ..................................................... 347
Charlton, .............. Lt. Col. .................................. 410
Chatfield, John ................................................ 410-438
Chaves, Jeremiah ................................................... 256
Chavons, Jere ...................................................... 378
Chavos, Jeremiah .................................................... 57
Cheek, Chas. W. .................................................... 322
Cheek, John ........................................................ 454
Cheek, William ............................................. 322-410-438-450
Cheldney, William .................................................. 220
Chenault, John ................................................. 410-437
Cheney, Greenberry ................................................. 234
Cherokee, The (A Warship) ....................................... 11-13
Cheshire, John ..................................................... 378
Cheshire, Sarah .................................................... 326
Chesser, John ....................................................... 52
Chester, Easter, Sr. ............................................... 333

INDEX. 499

Chestnut, Needham ........................................................ 331
Chevalier, Charles Francis ...........................................378-410
Chicoming, Mary ......................................................... 338
Chidney, Thomas .......................................................... 378
Chidwell, William ........................................................ 410
Childers, D. ..........................................................17-410
Childers, David ...........................................17-49-198-378-402-449
Childers, Henry .......................................................... 56
Childers, John ........................................................... 454
Childers, Milliner ....................................................410-450
Childers, Richard .......................................................347-378
Childers, Thomas ...................................................17-56-59-378
Childre, Thomas .......................................................256-410
Childress, Richard ....................................................... 347
Childrey, Thomas (or Childry) .........................................53-211
Childs, Elizabeth ........................................................ 335
Childs, John ............................................................. 316
Chiles, John ............................................................. 378
Chiles, William .......................................................... 47
Chipen, John ............................................................. 378
Chisholm, ................................................................ 254
Chisholm, Benjamin ....................................................378-410
Chisholm, John .......................................................17-56-378
Chisholm, Thomas ...............................................9-14-15-47-378-410
Chissome. Benjamin ....................................................... 52
Choice, Tully, ........................................................... 329
Chrisholm, John .......................................................... 258
Christian, Turner .....................................................347-478
Christmas, Nathaniel ..................................................... 284
Christmas, Richard ....................................................410-450
Christopher, William ..................................................... 347
Chumbly, Anthony ......................................................... 204
Chunn, ................................................................... 410
Chunn, Mr. ............................................................... 457
Cimbro, William .......................................................... 50
Clack, James ............................................................. 397
Clack, William ........................................................... 397
Claiborne, Thomas ........................................................ 410
Clanton, Holt ............................................................ 347
Clark, ............Maj. ................................................... 461
Clark, Benjamin .......................................................54-60
Clark, Bolling ........................................................... 400
Clark, Charles ........................................................... 410
Clark, David ............................................................. 347
Clark, E. ................................................................ 55
Clark, Edward .........................................................410-437
Clark, Elijah .........................................................16-297

## Index

Clark, George ........... 347
Clark, J. C. ........... 410
Clark, Jacob ........... 410-437
Clark, James ........... 61-410
Clarfk, James, Sr ........... 50
Clark, John ........... 61
Clark, John, Sr. ........... 61-378
Clark, John, Capt. ........... 378
Clark, John C. ........... 410
Clark, Johnston ........... 378
Clark, Lewis ........... 50-54
Clark, Moses ........... 61
Clark, Rebecca ........... 316
Clark, Thomas ........... 320-321-410-438
Clark, William ........... 58-378-410-438-450
Clark, Charles ........... 58
Clarke, Christopher ........... 400
Clark, E. ........... 55
Clarke, Elijah (or Clark) ........... 56-57-200-226-227-240-255-262-378-410-461
Clarke, James, Sr. ........... 288
Clarke, Jane ........... 327
Clarke, John (or Clark) ........... 51-223-226-240-241-245-284-292-341-378-410-461
Clarke, John, F. ........... 410
Clark, John J. ........... 410
Clarke, John, Jr. ........... 51
Clarke, John Sebr ........... 255
Clarke, Johnson ........... 248
Clarke, Johnston ........... 243
Clarke, Lewis ........... 378
Clarke, Mary, ........... 338
Clarke, Moses ........... 241-256
Clarke, Thomas ........... 320-450
Clarke, William ........... 231-300-306-397
Clay, Abia ........... 378
Clay, Joseph ........... 15-410-462
Clayton, Stephen, Sr. ........... 326
Clem, John ........... 60-378
Clements, Clement ........... 347
Clements, Elizabeth ........... 47
Clements, John ........... 47-50-61-378-410
Clements, Samuel ........... 47-378
Clements, William ........... 50-378
Clements, William, Sr. ........... 315
Clemmonds, Isaac ........... 378
Clemmons, Henry, Sr. ........... 323
Clemmons, Isaac ........... 47
Cleveland, Abaslom ........... 319

## INDEX. 501

| | |
|---|---|
| Cleveland, Benjamin | 320 |
| Cleveland, Jeremiah | 347-410 |
| Cleveland, John | 319 |
| Cleveland, Larkin | 400 |
| Cliatt, Isaac | 347 |
| Clifton, Charles | 20-347-378 |
| Clifton, George | 410-438 |
| Clifton, William | 347-378-410 |
| Clinton, | 410 |
| Clinton, William | 450 |
| Cloud, Ezekiel | 60-231-308-378-438-450-459-462 |
| Cloud, Jere | 379 |
| Cloud, Jeremiah | 255-278-281-410 |
| Cloud, Jeremiah, Jr. | 53 |
| Cloud, Jeremiah, Sr. | 62 |
| Cloud, John | 51-243-379 |
| Cloud, Monoah | 51-243 |
| Cloud, Neough, (or Nerioula) | 51-379 |
| Cloudas, George | 52-378 |
| Clough, George | 46 |
| Clower, Daniel | 347-437-450 |
| Clower, John | 211 |
| Clower, Peter | 379 |
| Clowers, Daniel | 410 |
| Clowers, Peter | 55-379-396-401-410 |
| Coalson, William | 379 |
| Coan, John | 54-379 |
| Coan, Stephen | 243 |
| Coates, Nathaniel | 54-254-259-379 |
| Coats, Aaron | 379 |
| Coats, Henry | 49-379 |
| Coats, John | 53-220-379 |
| Coats, Lesley, (or Leslie) | 46-379 |
| Cob, Caleb | 397 |
| Cobb, ........Maj. | 241 |
| Cobb, Ezekiel | 25-47-254-273-379 |
| Cobb, James | 246-296-379 |
| Cobb, James, Sr. | 61-245 |
| Cobb, John | 298 |
| Cobb, Joseph | 49-212-213-379 |
| Cobb, Ralf | 348 |
| Cobb, Ralph | 379 |
| Cobb, Thomas | 410 |
| Cobbett, Thomas | 339 |
| Cobbs, Thomas | 348 |
| Cochran, James | 319-410 |
| Cochran, Jonathan | 410 |

## INDEX.

Cochran, M. .....................................................410-450
Cochran, Mathew ...............................................348-410-438
Cochran, Thomas ..................................................... 448
Cochran, William ................................................... 397
Cock, Caleb .......................................................49-379
Cockburn, George ................................................320-348
Cockerel, Thomas ................................................... 348
Cody, John ......................................................... 379
Cofer, Elizabeth ................................................324-347
Cofield, Grisham ................................................348-379
Cohen, Jacob ....................................................... 410
Cohen, Philip ...................................................... 410
Cohon, Elizabeth ................................................... 341
Cohron, Cornelius ...............................................51-379
Coile, James (or Coil) ..........................................348-438
Coile, James, Capt. ................................................ 410
Coile, William ..................................................411-438
Coker, Isaac ....................................................... 337
Colbert, Elisha, ................................................... 397
Colbert, Susannah .................................................. 316
Cole, James ........................................................ 379
Cole, John .......................................................53-379
Cole, John, Jr. ...............................................53-57-402
Cole, John Sr. ..................................................47-379
Cole, Joshua, ...................................................... 291
Coleman, Abner ..................................................... 348
Coleman, Benj ...................................................... 411
Coleman, Daniel ...............................................60-178-379
Coleman, Elizabeth ................................................. 332
Coleman, F. ........................................................ 379
Coleman, Harris..................................................... 51
Coleman, James ............................................53-55-256-284-379
Coleman, Jesse ..................................................327-337
Coleman, John ..............................................252-255-264-283-348-411-449
Coleman, Jonathan .................................................. 411
Coleman, Nancy ..................................................... 340
Coleman, Reuben .................................................... 22
Coleman, Samuel .................................................... 348
Coleman, Thomas .................................................... 411
Coleman, Thompson, ................................................. 323
Coleson, William ................................................... 57
Collahan, James .................................................... 411
Collars, Mathew .................................................... 348
Colley, James ...................................................... 348
Colley, Joe ........................................................ 404
Colley, John ....................................................348-411
Colley, Joseph ..................................................... 397
Collier, Edward .................................................... 400

## INDEX. 503

Collier, James ............................................. 400
Collier, William ....................................... 57-210
Collingham, William ....................................... 404
Collins, Mr. ............................................... 459
Collins, Brice ............................................. 297
Collins, C. ................................................ 17
Collins, Charles ...................................... 52-298-379
Collins, Cornelius ...................................... 15-379
Collins, Edmond ............................................ 326
Collins, J. ................................................ 411
Collins, James ...................................... 313-397-404
Collins, John .................... 17-49-59-254-298-379-411-450
Collins, John, Sergt. ...................................... 411
Collins, John, Sr. ...................................... 411-438
Collins, Joseph ...................................... 54-314-348
Collins, Moses ....................................... 54-208-284-379
Collins, Solomon ....................................... 55-379
Collins, Stephen (or Steven) ............... 17-59-60-218-379-411
Collins, William ........................................... 209
Colomb, Peter ............................................. 411
Colquitt, James ........................................... 348
Colquitt, Robert .......................................... 331
Colson, Capt. ............................................. 10
Colson, Jacob ......................................... 14-15-411
Colson, William ........................................ 47-379
Colter, John .............................................. 302
Colwell, Ed ............................................... 397
Colwell, Edward ........................................... 404
Combs, John .................... 61-323-379-411-438-450
Combs, Phillips, Sr. ...................................... 323
Comer, Hugh M. ........................................ 329-338
Comer, James .......................................... 326-462
Commins, Sarah ............................................ 326
Compton, Williams ......................................... 379
Conaway, Elizabeth ........................................ 337
Conden, John .............................................. 332
Cone, Archibald, .......................................... 348
Cone, James ........................................... 48-49-379
Cone, John ............................................ 348-379
Cone, William ................... 56-127-207-209-255-258-270-379
Cone, William, Jr. ........................................ 46
Cone, William Sr. ......................................... 46
Conger, Ben ............................................... 450
Conger, Benjamin, (or Congo) .......................... 348-411
Conley, Caleb, ............................................ 57
Conley, Jacob ............................................. 379
Connally, Patrick ...................................... 62-379
Connel, David ............................................. 348

INDEX.

Connell, Daniel ............................................. 57
Connell, Jesse ............................................ 56-379
Connell, John ........................................ 56-327-379
Connell, Thomas ......................................... 55-302
Connelly, James ......................................... 17-411
Connelly, John W. ........................................... 400
Connelly, Patrick ....................................... 284-411
Connelly, William ........................................... 208
Conner, Benjamin ........................................... 348
Conner, Daniel ........................................ 54-379-411
Conner, John ............................................ 58-411
Conner, William ............................................ 348
Conners, Daniel ............................................ 437
Connolly, W. J. ......................................... 17-411
Connon, Daniel, Sr. ......................................... 313
Connor, Daniel, ............................................. 54
Connor, David .............................................. 379
Connor, John ............................................ 379-411
Conteratt, Joseph .......................................... 379
Contey, James .............................................. 411
Conway, Thomas .......................................... 17-411
Conwell, Jesse ............................................. 400
Conyers, John ................................. 58-339-379-411-438
Conyers, John, Jr. .......................................... 379
Conyers, Margarett, Mrs. ................................. 53-242
Conyers, William ........................................ 53-379
Cook, Archibald, ........................................... 348
Cook, Caleb ................................................ 379
Cook, Deborah .............................................. 338
Cook, Eleanor .............................................. 53
Cook, Elisha ........................................... 314-348
Cook, Ferguson ............................................. 53
Cook, George .............................. 52-53-271-379-438
Cook, Isham ............................... 15-17-60-379-411
Cook, James ............................................ 315-348
Cook, James W. ......................................... 319-335
Cook, John ............................... 208-316-379-438-450
Cook, John Sr. ............................................. 239
Cook, Joshua, .............................................. 58
Cook, Lydia ............................................... 329
Cook, Mary ................................................ 316
Cook, Nathaniel ............................................ 311
Cook, Paris ............................................... 411
Cook, Ranes, (or Raines) ....................... 15-35-59-379-411
Cook, Reuben ........................................... 379-348
Cook, Sham ................................................ 411
Cook, Slisha .............................................. 379
Cook, Theodosia ............................................ 348

## INDEX.

| | |
|---|---|
| Cook, Thomas | 348-411-438-450 |
| Cooke, George | 256 |
| Cooksey, John | 334 |
| Cooper, Capt. | 411 |
| Cooper, Lt. Col. | 411 |
| Cooper, Anthony | 379 |
| Cooper, Basil | 411 |
| Cooper, Benj. | 411 |
| Cooper, George | 348-379 |
| Cooper, Henry | 348 |
| Cooper, James | 348 |
| Cooper, John | 348-379-411 |
| Cooper, John, Lt. Col | 348 |
| Cooper, John, Sr. | 323 |
| Cooper, Joseph | 348-379 |
| Cooper, Philip | 397 |
| Cooper, Richard | 348-411 |
| Cooper, Samuel | 348 |
| Cooper, William | 411 |
| Cope, Charles | 411 |
| Cope, Lewis | 411 |
| Copeland, William | 438 |
| Copeland, Benj. | 348 |
| Copeland, Martha | 328 |
| Copeland, William | 411-450 |
| Copelin, William | 348-379 |
| Coplin, William | 379 |
| Corbett, Capt. | 411 |
| Corbett, Thomas | 411 |
| Corbin, William | 17-49-213-379 |
| Corham, John | 245-304 |
| Corker, | 411 |
| Cornant, John | 52 |
| Cornell, Thomas | 379 |
| Corney, M. | 17 |
| Cornwall, Elijah | 462 |
| Correy, Robert | 175 |
| Corsea, William | 379 |
| Corsey, Stephen | 216-244 |
| Corsey, William | 348 |
| Corsia, William | 54 |
| Cortez, B. | 411 |
| Coruthers (or William Crudders) | 48 |
| Corvan, George | 459-462 |
| Corven, Edward | 17 |
| Cossins, David | 47 |
| Costell, Michael | 204 |
| Costillo, Edward | 59 |

# INDEX.

Costillo, Michael .................................................. 59
Cothorn, Josia (or Cothron) ...................................48-53
Cothorn, William .................................................. 59
Cottenhead, James ................................................ 26
Cotter, James .................................................315-348
Cotton, George, Sr. ............................................... 326
Cottingham, William ............................................... 397
Coulder, John .................................................411-438
Coup, Henry ...................................................... 60
Couper, John ..................................................... 411
Coursey, David (or Corsia) ..................................60-379-244
Courson, William .................................................. 55
Courton, William ................................................. 258
Cousins, Adam .................................................... 348
Cousins, William .................................................. 47
Covey, Joseph .................................................... 348
Covington, Thomas ................................................ 319
Cowan, Edward (or Cowen) ...................................15-171-411
Cowan, Martha .................................................... 319
Cowan, Prudence .................................................. 317
Cowan, William ................................................... 379
Cowart, Michael .................................................. 315
Cowart, Zachariah, Sr. ........................................... 338
Cowen, Edward ...............................................239-411
Cowen, George .................................................... 348
Cowen, James ..................................................... 348
Cowin, William .................................................56-308
Cowles, John ..................................................... 201
Cowles, Samuel ................................................... 348
Cowles, William ..............................................397-403
Cowns, William ................................................... 379
Cowper, Bacil, (or Cooper) ....................................... 411
Cox, Abraham ..................................................... 411
Cox, Benjamin .................................................47-379
Cox, Caleb ...................................................307-404
Cox, James ....................................................... 397
Cox, John .....................................................46-348
Cox, Moses ..............................................348-411-438-450
Cox, Richard .............................................349-411-450
Cox, Thomas ..............................................349-411-438
Cox, William ..................................................... 411
Cox, Zachariah, (or Zach) ................................308-400-454
Cox, Zebulon .................................................349-411
Cox, Zebulon, Lt. ................................................ 411
Crabb, Asa ....................................................... 349
Crabb, Samuel, (or Crab) ......................................50-379
Crabtree, William ................................................ 349
Crain, Lewis (or Crane) ..................51-230-242-270-279-379-402

| | |
|---|---|
| Craine, Spencer, (or Crane) | 54-379-411 |
| Cramer, Christopher | 411 |
| Crawford, Anderson | 56-57-379 |
| Crawford, Arthur | 411-438 |
| Crawford, Charles | 48 |
| Crawford, David | 53-154 |
| Crawford, Jay | 349 |
| Crawford, John | 53-55-205-233-256-379-438 |
| Crawford, Lemuel | 349 |
| Crowford, Lucy | 316 |
| Crawford, Mary | 330 |
| Crawford, Mary Ann | 341 |
| Crawford, Nathan | 61-379 |
| Crawford, Philips | 328 |
| Crawford, Samuel | 379 |
| Crawford, Strother | 284-287 |
| Crawford, Victor | 320 |
| Crawford, Victoria | 319-320 |
| Credelle, WWilliam | 349 |
| Creemmy, Rebecca | 330 |
| Cregg, Thomas | 248 |
| Creswell Dr. | 296 |
| Creswell, Daniel | 459-462 |
| Creswell, David | 62-254-289-379 |
| Creswell, Robert | 400 |
| Creswell, Samuel | 51-238-302-308-379 |
| Cribbs, Thomas (or Cribs) | 59-209-277-379 |
| Crider, Barbery | 320 |
| Crider, John | 320 |
| Cridington, John | 47 |
| Crispus, James | 56-256-379 |
| Criswell, Samuel | 411 |
| Critington, Jonathan | 349 |
| Crittendon, Joseph | 349 |
| Crocker, William | 411 |
| Crockett, David | 349 |
| Crockett, Samuel | 303 |
| Croford, John | 51 |
| Croker, William | 17-47-284-379 |
| Crokes, William | 379 |
| Cronan, James | 349 |
| Cronberger, Barbara | 47-56 |
| Cronberger, Christopher | 47-349 |
| Cronberger, Jacob | 56-349 |
| Cronick, Rachel | 332 |
| Croock, William | 52 |
| Crook, William | 379 |
| Crooker, Turner | 449 |

## Index.

Crosby, Urial, (or Urill) .................................................323-339
Crosby, William .................................................50-400-411
Cross, John, Sr. .................................................333
Cross, Stephen .................................................349
Crosson, John .................................................349-411-438
Crouch, John .................................................397-404
Crouch, Shadrack .................................................349
Crouch, William .................................................397
Crow, Alexander .................................................404
Crow, Isaac .................................................349
Crow, Stephen .................................................349
Crozier, John .................................................27
Crudden, William .................................................379
Cruddy, William .................................................400-411
Crumberger, Jacob .................................................411
Crumbly, Thomas .................................................349
Crumby, Thomas .................................................411-438
Crumden, Ralph Edward. .................................................411
Crumley, Anthony, (or Crumly) .................................................52-379
Crump, Mary .................................................320
Crup, Henry .................................................458
Cruse, James .................................................411
Cruse, Thomas .................................................61
Crutchfield, John .................................................57-255-286-379
Cruxe, Thomas .................................................379
Cudington, John .................................................379
Culbaith, Archibald, .................................................349
Culbertson, Celia .................................................328
Culbreath, James .................................................25-47-127-202-210-379
Culbreath, John .................................................61-127-202-244-379
Culbreath, Peter .................................................127-209-210
Cullard, Henry .................................................61
Cullars, Henry .................................................379
Cullens, Joseph .................................................379
Culpepper .................................................457
Culpepper, Joseph .................................................379
Culpepper, Joseph, Jr. .................................................60
Culpepper, Malachi .................................................240-349
Culpepper, Sampson .................................................397-403
Culver, Nancy .................................................332
Culver, Nathan .................................................349
Cummings, Francis .................................................349
Cummings, I. .................................................340
Cumming, Pat. .................................................379
Cummins, Francis .................................................462
Cunningham, Ansell (or Ancil) .................................................317-411-438-450-459
Cunningham, Andrew .................................................349
Cunningham, James .................................................49-61-379

Cunningham, John .................................................15-56-58-255-280-379
Cunningham, Nancy ....................................................... 330
Cunningham, Patrick ...................................................... 61
Cunningham, S. ........................................................... 79
Cunningham, William ..................................................... 256
Cup, Henry .............................................................. 379
Cup, Michael, ...................................................... 49-218-379
Curbo, Joseph, (or Curbow) ...................................... 411-438-450
Cureton, Boling, ......................................................58-379
Cureton, Richard ................................................... 61-210-379
Cureton, William .......................................................52-379
Cureton, William, Lt. ..................................................... 379
Cureton, William, Jr. ...................................................30-53
Cureton, Wm. J. ........................................................... 379
Curl, Henry ..........................................................48-379
Curl, John ...........................................................48-379
Curl, Matthew .......................................................411-450
Curle, Henry ............................................................ 302
Curle, John ............................................................. 256
Currey, Peter ......................................................50-57-243
Curry, .................................................................. 411
Curry, Cary .............................................................. 59
Curry, Jacob ........................................................50-379
Curry, Nicholas, (or Nicolas) ...............................55-256-379-411
Curry, Peter ..................................................295-310-323-379
Curry, Robert ........................................................... 400
Curry, William .......................................................... 311
Curtis, John .........................................................58-379
Curton, B. .............................................................. 400
Curvey, Cary ............................................................ 379
Cuthbert, A. .........................................................17-411
Cuthbert, A. Daniel .................................................215-411
Cuthbert, Alexander, .................................................... 411
Cuthbert, Alexander D. ...............................................15-411
Cuthbert Alfred ......................................................... 411
Cuthbert, Daniel ..................................................10-236-411
Cuthbert, Daniel A ...................................................... 379
Cuthbert, Isaac ......................................................... 411
Cuthbert, John A. ....................................................... 411
Cuthbert, Seth John, ................................................411-462
Cutts, ........Maj. ..................................................... 411
Cutts, Joseph ........................................................... 349
Cuyler, Henry ........................................................... 412

**D**

Dabbs, John ............................................................. 439
Dabney, Asten ........................................................... 379

# INDEX.

Dabney, Austen, (or Austin) .................. 65-349-379-402-438-545-459-462
Dacus, Lewis ........................................................ 404
Daggett, William .................................................397-404
Dalay, ............................................................. 412
Dale, Jemima ....................................................... 318
Daley, Benjamin .................................................... 379
Dallas, John ....................................................... 379
Dally, Benjamin ................................................. 66-379
Dalton, John ...:................................................337-349
Dalton, Mathews .................................................... 379
Dalton, Mathias ................................................ 68-303
Dalton, Randolph ................................................... 349
Dalton, Thomas .... ....................................303-349-379-400
Damant, William .................................................... 412
Dameron, Mary, ..................................................... 318
Dampier, Daniel ................................................46-72-379
Damron, Charles ..............................................349-412-438
Danelly, James (Daneley or Danely) ..........................28-47-68-84
D'Angley, Paul de la Beaune, (Baron de Malves) ....................... 412
Daniel, Benj. ..................................................63-258-379
Daniel, Frederick .................................................. 330
Daniel Isaac ....................................................397-404
Daniel, James ...................................................... 412
Daniel, Jeptha ..................................................... 349
Daniel, John ...........................................70-349-412-439-450
Daniel, John Sr. ................................................315-316
Daniel, Littleberry ................................................ 339
Daniel, Mary ....................................................... 331
Daniel, Sarah ...................................................... 337
Daniel, Thomas ..................................................... 311
Daniel, William ..........................................47-66-73-308-311-379
Danielly, Daniel ................................................69-254
Danielly, James ................................................65-218
Danison, Charles ................................................... 379
Dannello, Daniel ................................................... 379
Dannelly, Francis .................................................. 66
Danelly, James .................................................230-285
Dannelly, John ..................................................... 62
Dannison, Dave ..................................................... 380
Dantham, Elijah .................................................... 412
D'Antignac, John (or Dantignac) .................................349-379
Danube, John ....................................................397-404
Darbe, Richard ..................................................68-258-379
Darby, John ...................................................62-66-258-379
Darby, John, .................................................62-66-69-379
Darby Nicholas .................................................349-379
Darby, Richard .................................................439-451
Darcey, Benjamin ................................................70-258

## INDEX.

Darcey, James .................................................. 64-67-258
Darcey, Joel, ..................................................... 66
Darcey, William .................................................. 66
Darcy, Joel ...................................................308-379
Darcy, William ................................................... 379
Darden, George, (or Dardin) ........................... 71-257-303-449
Darden, George, Jr. .............................................. 379
Derden, George, Sr., ............................................71-379
Dardin, John ..................................................... 257
Darley, John ..................................................... 229
Darney, Benjamin ................................................. 380
Darney, James .................................................... 380
Darnley, James ................................................... 148
Darrys, Elizabeth ................................................ 329
Darsey, James .............................................257-380-402
Dary, Ambrose .................................................... 400
Dasher, Christian .........................................63-65-73-380
Dasher, John Martin .........................................65-73-380
Dasher, Marion ................................................... 349
Daus, Ware ....................................................... 380
Dauthan, Elijah .................................................. 380
Davenport, Dr. ................................................... 380
Davenport, Stephen .........................................17-300-412
Davenport, Thomas .....................15-17-72-258-259-380-412
David, Augustus .................................................. 412
David, Isaac ..................................................... 349
David, William .........................................64-71-205-232-380
Davidson, John ...........................................349-412-439-451
Davidson, Joseph ..........................................284-285-412-438
Davidson, William .............................................17-412
Davis, Joseph .................................................... 349
Davies, Daniel ................................................... 349
Davis, Edward ..................................................71-412
Davies, John ..................................................66-380-402
Davis, John, Sr. .................................................. 68
Davies, Myrick .................................................63-412
Davis, Sara ....................................................... 63
Davis ............................................................ 412
Davis, ........................................................... 204
Davis, Ab ........................................................ 299
Davis, Absolom ............................................66-68-257-380
Davis, Benjamin .........................................66-196-258-261-380
Davis, Blandford ..............................................67-380
Davis, Blueford, ................................................. 229
Davis, C. ......................................................18-412
Davis, C. B. ..................................................... 284
Davis, Charles ................................................67-380
Davis, Charles B. ................................................ 287

| | |
|---|---|
| Davis, Chesley, (or Chestley) | 67-285-380 |
| Davis, Chesley, Jr. | 67 |
| Davis, Clementine | 380 |
| Davis, Clementus | 66 |
| Davis, Clemtius | 257 |
| Davis, David | 65-380 |
| Davis, Edward | 380-412 |
| Davis, Gideon, | 72-308-380 |
| Davis, Hardy, | 69-380-396-401 |
| Davis, Henry | 349 |
| Davis, Isaac | 70 |
| Davis, Jacob | 71-301-380 |
| Davis, James | 56-72-285-380-397 |
| Davis, Jenkins, | 56-65-78-380-412 |
| Davis, Joel | 71-412 |
| Davis, John | 66-206-307-315-334-412-439-450 |
| Davis, John, Sr. | 64-339 |
| Davis, John, Wade, Jr. | 69 |
| Davis, Joseph | 380 |
| Davis Lewis | 66-199-237-380-397 |
| Davis, Mary | 321-337-341 |
| Davis, Mary Ann | 337 |
| Davis, Merideth, (or MMered..th) | 17-67-69-246-289-294-380 |
| Davis, Moses | 71-257-349-380-412 |
| Davis, Myrick, | 299-380 |
| Davis, Nancy | 316 |
| Davis, Nehemiah | 380 |
| Davis, Randolph | 380 |
| Davis, Russell, | 321 |
| Davis, Samuel, | 65-258-380 |
| Davis, Solomon, | 69-285-380 |
| Davis, Surry | 349 |
| Davis, Thomas | 71-412-451 |
| Davis, Thomas L. | 412-438 |
| Davis, Toliver, (or Tolliver) | 349-412-438-451 |
| Davis, Valthal (or Valthael) | 67-380 |
| Davis, Ware | 68 |
| Davis, Wiley | 67-380 |
| Davis, William | 64-220-258-323-335-342-380-412 |
| Davis, William, Maj. | 412 |
| Davis, Willis | 257 |
| Davison, James | 397-403 |
| Davison, Joseph | 62-73-380 |
| Daw, Harry, | 380 |
| Dawson, Brittain | 63-380 |
| Dawson, Charles | 349 |
| Dawson, David | 63-380 |
| Dawson, Joseph | 332 |

# INDEX.

Dawson, Martin ........................................................72-380
Dawson, William ......................................................72-380
Day, Ambrose ............................................................. 412
Day, Harry ................................................................ 70
Day, Henry ..............................................................73-257
Day, Joseph ..................................................15-18-63-73-380
Day, Joseph, Capt. ........................................................ 380
Day, Robert ...................................................18-229-232-258-380
Day, Robert, Jr. .......................................................... 66-69
Day, Robert, Sr. ........................................................... 70-71
Day, Stephen ..............................................................67-380
Deadwiler, Alice ............................................................ 327
Deadwiler, Joseph .......................................................... 350
Dean, Charles .............................................................. 349
Dean, John ......................................................66-207-266-380
Dean, Julius ............................................................... 449
Dean, Thomas .............................................................64-257
Dean William .................................................17-70-218-246-380
Dean, William, Sergt ....................................................... 380
Deason, Hannah ............................................................. 341
Deason, Zachariah .......................................................... 350
Deaton, Capt. .............................................................. 319
Deaton, Elizabeth .......................................................... 380
Debosk, Peter, Bebosh or Busk) ...................................15-18-400-412
Decks, Andrew .............................................................. 380
DeClanchrees, Mathew ....................................................... 380
DeClandeness, Matthew ....................................................... 68
DeEstang, Count ............................................................ 293
Defatt, ........Capt. ...................................................... 412
Defau, ..........Capt. ..................................................... 412
Default, ........Capt. ..................................................... 412
Defnall, David ....:................................................... 412-438
Defoor, .................................................................... 412
DeGraffenreid, John ...................................................397-404
DeKayser, Lee, ............................................................. 412
DeLaGall, Col. ............................................................. 412
Delaney, Dave .............................................................. 380
Delaney, James ............................................................. 380
Delany, Daniel ............................................................64-71
Delany, James .............................................................. 67
DeLaplaign, E. P. .......................................................... 380
DeLaplaign, Emanuel ........................................................ 412
DeLa Plaigne, Emanuel Pierre ............................................... 412
De La Plaigne, Peter Emanuel (or De Laplaine) ..........................258-412
De Laplaine Ens. .........................................................9-412
De Lisle, Bernard Roman .................................................... 412
Delk, ...................................................................... 412
Delk, Daniel ............................................................... 350

# INDEX.

Delk, David ..... 64-380
Delk, Philip ..... 306
Delk, Samuel ..... 412
Delk, William G. ..... 412
Dallafield, William ..... 350
DeLoach, Hardy ..... 350
Demere, Raymond, ..... 412
Demnon, Charles ..... 73
Dempier, Sergt. ..... 17-412
Denham, Arthur ..... 350
Denham, Charles ..... 64-215
Denman, Charles ..... 380
Denman, James ..... 380
Denmer, James ..... 326
Dennard, John ..... 316
Dennis, Capt. ..... 315
Dennis, Abraham, ..... 65-236-237-263-380
Dennis, Isaac ..... 63-257-380
Dennis, Jacob ..... 62-230
Dennis, John ..... 257-268-380-451
Dennis, John, Jr. ..... 65
Dennis, John, Sr. ..... 64
Dennis, Josiah ..... 340
Dennis, Mathias ..... 350
Dennis, R. ..... 245
Dennis, Richmond ..... 66-246-380
Dennis, William ..... 225
Dennison, D. ..... 281
Dennison, Daniel ..... 63-258-280-286
Dennison, Darby ..... 380
Dennison, Elijah ..... 298-303-380
Denny, William ..... 241
Densler, Philip ..... 412
Denson, Joseph, Sr. ..... 330
Dentham, John ..... 62
Denton, Charles ..... 380
Denton, Emily ..... 338
Denton, John ..... 350
Denton, William ..... 32
Depathier, Lt. ..... 412
Derbin, Luke ..... 380
DeRoche, Abraham ..... 73
Derracott, Rebecca, ..... 331
Deshaver, Lewis ..... 412
Despiliers, Lt. ..... 412
D'Estaing, Count ..... 222-380
De Ste, MMarie, Capt. ..... 412
Dethan, John ..... 380

INDEX. 515

| | |
|---|---|
| Devaleile, John Duport | 412 |
| Devaliser | 412 |
| Devaugh, John | 380 |
| DeVeaux, James | 412 |
| DeVeaux, Peter, (or DeVaux) | 18-63-412-438 |
| Devereaux, Peter | 412 |
| Dey, Joseph | 412 |
| Daimond, John | 397-408 |
| Diamond, William | 400 |
| Dias, John | 350 |
| Dick, Andrew | 121-233-234-235 |
| Dick, Davio | 64-380 |
| Dick, James | 350-454 |
| Dick, Susannah | 121 |
| Dicken, Richard | 350-412-439 |
| Dickens, Nimrod, | 397 |
| Dickenson, Edward | 380 |
| Dickerson, Henry | 329 |
| Dickerson, Zachariah | 350 |
| Dickey, Patrick | 350 |
| Dicking, Nimrod | 404 |
| Dickins, Lebna | 380 |
| Dicks, Andrew | 44-70 |
| Dicks, David | 70-400 |
| Dickson, David | 69-70-380-400-412-457 |
| Dickson, Hugh | 64-69 |
| Dickson, John | 70-350-457 |
| Dickson, Mary | 338 |
| Dickson, Michael, | 70-71-350-380-400-412 |
| Dickson, Nathan | 68-380 |
| Dickson, Nathaniel | 70-380 |
| Dickson, Samuel | 70 |
| Dickson, Thomas | 350 |
| Dickson, William | 70-380 |
| Dillard, James | 316-350-412-438 |
| Dillard, John | 350-380-412-451 |
| Dillard, Thomas | 350 |
| Dinkins, Gilbert | 212 |
| Dinkins, Sebree, | 72 |
| Diolendemus, Matthew | 229 |
| Ditter, Capt. | 412 |
| Dixon, Capt. | 412 |
| Dixon, Maj. | 412 |
| Dixon, David | 258 |
| Dixon, Edward, Sr. | 258 |
| Dixon, Hugh | 380 |
| Dixon, Robert | 400 |
| Dixon, Walter | 15-412 |

# INDEX.

Dobb, Nathan, (or Dobbs) .................................341-412-439-450
Dobbs, David ................................................................... 315
Dobbs, James ................................................................... 350
Dobbs, John ...............................................................350-412
Dobbs, Joseph .................................................................. 397
Dobbs, Josiah, ................................................................. 412
Dobbs, Sarah ................................................................... 333
Dobson, Henry ...........................................................328-336
Doby, John ..............................................................333-412-439
Dodd, Catherine ................................................................ 320
Dodd, William .................................................................. 320
Dodson, Henry ................................................................. 328
Doherty, Elizabeth ............................................................ 338
Doles, Elizabeth ............................................................... 332
Doles, Jesse ..............................................................350-380
Dollar, Anson (or Dollard) ................................................67-380
Dollar, John ............................................................17-176-380-412
Dollars, John ..................................................................... 68
Dolly, Benjamin ..........................................................62-70-380
Donaldson, .........Capt. ....................................................... 412
Donaldson, William ....................................................350-412-439
Donally, James .........................................................203-380
Donelly, Cornelius ........................................................... 380
Donely, John .................................................................. 380
Donnelly, Daniel .............................................................. 412
Donnelly, David ............................................................... 413
Donnelly, James .........................................................69-380-413
Donnelly, John ................................................................. 380
Donoway, William ........................................................63-380
Doolen, John ................................................................... 303
Dooley, Col. .................................................................... 178
Dooly, George, (or Dooley) ....................................15-18-71-73-229-413
Dooly, Hull ...................................................................73-413
Dooly, John .............................................................15-18-413
Dooly, John, Col. .............................................................. 413
Dooly, Thomas ..........................................................15-18-71-413
Dooly, William ..............................................................62-380
Doreman, James .............................................................. 403
Dorris, Elizabeth .............................................................. 319
Dorton, Benjamin .......................................................330-338
Dorton, Thomas .......................................................68-303-380
Dorty, George .................................................................. 380
Dose, Joel ....................................................................... 229
Doss, Joel .................................................................68-248-380
Dossey, Joel ................................................................... 413
Doster, Jonathan .........................................................323-350
Doty, William .................................................................. 413
Doud, John .................................................................413-451

Dougherty, Maj. .................................................. 413
Dougherty, John .................................................. 413
Doughtry, Jacob .................................................. 350
Doughtry, Joseph ................................................. 350
Douglas, MMaj. ................................................... 413
Douglas, Alexander ................................... 72-208-259-380
Douglas, George ...................................... 64-215-216-246-380
Douglas, James ................................................... 231
Douglas, John .......................................... 73-257-380
Douglas, M. A. ................................................... 337
Douglas, Spencer ................................................. 350
Douglas, Thomas ............................................. 413-438
Douglas, William ............................................. 66-258
Doule, Thomas .................................................... 413
Dounaphan, Elijah ................................................ 400
Dounnan, James ................................................... 397
Douthan, Elijah .................................................. 396
Dover, Frances J. ................................................ 350
Dovly, Hull ...................................................... 380
Dowd, John ....................................................... 335
Dowday, Richard .................................................. 380
Dowdy, Richard ........................................... 64-72-380
Dowle, Thomas .................................................... 350
Dowley, Thomas ................................................... 413
Dowman, R. .................................................. 18-413
Dowman, Rawleigh ................................................. 413
Dowman, Rawleigh P. .............................................. 75
Downey, Joseph ................................................... 350
Downs, Ambrose, .............................................. 323-380
Downs, Ambrose, J. ............................................... 67
Downs, George ............................................ 64-65-380
Downs, Jona ...................................................... 380
Downs, JJona ..................................................... 380
Downs, Jonathan .............................................. 65-413
Downs, William ......................................... 69-326-380
Dowse, Gideon .................................................... 413
Doyle, Nimrod, T. .................................. 350-413-438-454
Drake, James ..................................................... 350
Draper, James ............................................ 413-439-451
Draust, Russell .................................................. 321
Drayton, Stephen ................................................. 413
Drayton, William H. .............................................. 413
Drew, Wilson ................................................ 413-450
Driver, Henry .......................................... 72-246-380
Dubberly, John ................................................... 350
Dubignon, C. P. .................................................. 413
Dubignon, Christopher Poullain ................................... 413
DuBorde, ............Capt. ....................................... 413

## INDEX.

DuBose, Sarah ........................................................... 328
Ducains, John ........................................................... 380
Duchart, John ........................................................... 380
Ducin, John ..........................................................17-413
Duck, Jeremiah ..................................................350-380-400
Duck, John .......................................................350-380
Duckworth, Jacob .................................................68-284-380
Duckworth, Jeremiah ...................................................68-380
DuCoin, J. ............................................................. 413
Ducoins, John ........................................................18-413
Dudley, James .......................................................... 350
Dudley, John .....................................................350-380
Dudley, William ........................................................ 303
Dufan, Capt. ........................................................... 413
Duffell, William ....................................................... 413
Duffey, James .......................................................... 380
Duffey, John ............................................................ 72
Duffil, Lucy ........................................................... 332
Dugan, Thomas .......................................................69-380
Dugger, William, Sr. ................................................... 339
DuHart, John (or Duchart) .......................62-67-214-238-274-380-402-413
Duke, Buckner .......................................................... 257
Duke, David ............................................................ 300
Duke, Henry ............................................................ 413
Duke, James ............................................................ 358
Duke, John Taylor ..................................................200-380
Duke, John Taylor, Sr. ............................................62-200
Duke, Nancy ............................................................ 327
Duke, Taylor ........................................................... 246
Duke, William .....................................................257-273
Dukes, Buckner .......................................................65-380
Dukes, Henry .....................................................70-380-413
Dukes, James .....................................................67-380
Dukes, John Taylor, Sr. ................................................. 67
Dukes, Kesiah .....................................................324-347
Dukes, Taylor .....................................................65-303-380
Dukes, Thomas .......................................................... 350
Dukes, William ..................................................68-380-403
Dulins, Henry ....................................................380-396
Dumaplin, Elijah, (or Dumaplier) .................................72-380
Dumochel, John ......................................................... 413
Dunaway, John .......................................................... 380
Dunaway, John Sr. ....................................................... 64
Dunaway, Mary .......................................................... 339
Dunbar, James .......................................................... 228
Duncan, David .......................................................... 259
Duncan, Edmond ......................................................... 350
Duncan, James ...................................69-259-380-413-438

# INDEX. 519

Duncan, James, Lt. .................................................. 62-380
Duncan, John ...................................................... 350
Duncan, Joseph .................................................... 63-413
Duncan, Mathew, ........................................... 63-72-257-380-413
Duncan Mathews ................................................... 380
Duncan, Miles ..................................................... 302
Duncan, Pearson, .................................................. 350
Duncan, Thomas ................................................ 73-380-396
Duncan, William ................................................... 64-396
Dunham, Abraham .................................................. 350
Dunham, George ................................................... 454
Dunham, Jacob .................................................... 351
Dunham, Samuel ................................................... 350
Dunkin, William ................................................... 380
Dunlap, Jonathan ............................................... 413-451
Dunlap, Joseph ................................................... 413
Dunlop, Joseph ................................................... 413
Dunn, ....Capt. .................................................. 413
Dunn, Gatewood ................................................... 350
Dunn, Ishmael .................................................. 397-404
Dunn, Jacob ...................................................... 380
Dunn, John ....................................................... 326
Dunn, Josiah ................................................. 62-381-413
Dunn, Nehemiah ................................................... 62-67
Dunn Thomas .................................................. 413-439-451
Dunnison, Darby .................................................. 71
Dunnison, Elijah ................................................. 65
Dunsmore, James .................................................. 63
Dunwoody, James .............................................. 71-381-413
Dunwoody, Robert ................................................. 241
Dupont, Josiah ................................................... 413
Duprey, William .................................................. 449
Durban, Luke ..................................................... 69-285
Durdan, Jacob .................................................. 413-450
Durham, Isaac .................................................... 328
Durham, Luke, .................................................... 285
Durham, Matthew ............................................... 413-439
Durkee, Malinda .................................................. 320
Durkee, Nathaniel ............................................. 413-438
Durouzeaux, Eliz ................................................. 315
Durouzeaux, Stephen .......................................... 315-351
Duty, Thomas ..................................................... 350
Duval, ...........Lt. ............................................. 413
Duval, Daniel .................................................. 15-413
Dyar, Henry ...................................................... 246
Dyas, John ....................................................... 246
Dyche, John .................................................... 351-381
Dye, Avery ....................................................... 351

## INDEX.

Dye, Mary ........ 316
Dyer, Elisha, ........ 321-351-413-439-450
Dyer, Henry ........ 63-381
Dyer, Jacob C. ........ 327
Dyess, Winiford ........ 337
Dykes, Jep ........ 351
Dyson, Easther ........ 336
Dyson, John ........ 323-351

### E.

Echolis, E. (or Eachols) ........ 18-413
Eaddy, John ........ 257-259
Eades, John ........ 75-218-381
Eads, ........ 74
Eads, Mary ........ 74
Eady, James ........ 381
Eady, John ........ 75-381
Eagin, John ........ 351
Eagle, John ........ 381
Earley, Daniel ........ 381
Earley, Richard ........ 413
Early, Jeffery ........ 221
Early, Roderick ........ 397
Early, Wilder ........ 397-404
Earnest, George ........ 351-413-439-451-457
Earnest, Jacob ........ 75-220-381
Earnest, William ........ 74-76-381
Eason, Isaac ........ 323
Easter, James ........ 76-246-302-381
Easton, James ........ 381
Easton, John ........ 397-404
Eastwood, John ........ 76-381-413-439-451
Eaton, Maj. ........ 413
Eaton, John ........ 351
Eaves, Nathaniel ........ 76-259
Eberhart, Jacob ........ 7
Eberheart, Jacob (or Eberhart) ........ 351-413-439-451
Ebzey, William ........ 449
Echols, Miller ........ 404
Echols, Mitler ........ 397
Echols, Echols, Mitler ........ 397
Echols, Obadiah, (or Obidah) ........ 397
Eckles, Edward ........ 413
Eckles, Edward, Sr. ........ 323
Eckles, Ephraim, o(r Eph)) ........ 75-381
Eckles, John ........ 75
Ector, Joseph ........ 404

# INDEX.

Edenfield, David .................................................. 413-451
Edmonds, Absolem ..................................................... 73
Edmonds, W. ......................................................... 338
Edmonds, Winney .................................................. 324-347
Edmondson, Crawford ................................................. 404
Edmondson, James P. ................................................. 439
Edmondson, William .................................................. 397
Edmonston, James P. ................................................. 413
Edwards, Abraham .................................................... 381
Edwards, Adonija ................................................ 413-451
Edwards, John ............................................ 76-306-351-397-413-439
Edwards, Joseph .............................................. 217-319-351
Edwards, Peter ............................................... 237-381
Edwards, Precious E. ........................................... 324-347
Edwards, Reuben ........................................ 351-413-439-451
Edwards, Soloman ............................................ 413-439
Edwards, Thomas ..................................................... 351
Edwards, William .................................................... 351
Edwards, Willis ..................................................... 404
Egbert, Jacob V. .................................................... 413
Eidson, Shelton .............................................. 351-413-439
Eidson, Thomas ............................................... 323-351
Eigle, John .......................................................... 74
Eiland, Absolem ..................................................... 259
Eiland, Isaiah ...................................................... 397
Eiland, John ................................................. 259-262
Eimbeck, George ............................................. 18-381-413
Eimenson, Robert .................................................... 381
Elbert, Maj. ........................................................ 268
Elbert, John ........................................................ 351
Elbert, S. ........................................................... 20
Elbert, Samuel, Gen. ........................... 9-15-18-76-216-301-381-413-462
Elder, David ................................................ 397-404-460
Elder, Joshua ............................................... 338-462
Elkins, Thomas .............................................. 397-404
Elleas, William ..................................................... 381
Elledge, Jacob .............................................. 413-439
Ellet, James ........................................................ 351
Elliett, Thomas ..................................................... 351
Elliot, Daniel, (or Elliott) .................................. 18-380
Elliot, Henry ....................................................... 381
Elliot, John (or Elliott) ........................................... 381
Elliot, Thomas ................................................ 381-397
Elliot, William ..................................................... 381
Elliott, Bernard, ................................................... 413
Elliott, Daniel ............................................... 74-76-413
Elliott, Elizabeth .................................................... 74

## Index.

Elliott, Gray .......... 413
Elliott, Henry .......... 75-76-413
Elliott, John .......... 75-351-413
Elliott, Thomas .......... 413-439
Elliott, Wm. Jr. .......... 75
Elliott, William Sr. .......... 76
Eliott, Zachariah .......... 414-451
Ellis, Henry .......... 193
Ellis, Jerry .......... 381
Ellis, Leivine .......... 351
Ellis, Mary .......... 451
Ellis, Robt. .......... 18-74-259-381
Ellis, Shadrack .......... 331-414-451
Ellis, Stephen .......... 77-259-381
Ellis, Walter .......... 351-381
Ellis, William .......... 76-397-404
Ellison, J. W. .......... 81
Ellison, James .......... 76-381
Elmonds, Absolem .......... 76
Elon, Elisha, (or Eton) .......... 414
Elrod, Samuel, Sr. .......... 330
Elsberry, Benj. .......... 351
Else, Thomas .......... 414
Elton, Abram, .......... 351
Elton, Anthony M. .......... 317-333
Elumbley, Anthony .......... 203
Elvington, Gideon .......... 341
Ely, Richard .......... 414
Ely, William .......... 414
Eman, John .......... 9-414
Emanuel, Amos .......... 75
Emanuel, Asa .......... 74-214-239-249-381
Emanuel, David .......... 74-214-301-306-381-414-462
Emanuel, David, Capt. .......... 381
Emanuel, Enos .......... 381
Emanuel, Levi .......... 73-75-414
Embeck, M. .......... 381
Embrick, George .......... 75
Embricken, William .......... 76
Embry, Jesse, (or Jessey) .......... 76-306-307-381
Embry, Joseph, .......... 351
Emenson, Robert .......... 351
Emmett, James .......... 76-381
Emtrickeen, William .......... 381
Endsley, John, (Sr.) .......... 457
England, Charles .......... 351
England, Margaret .......... 331

# INDEX. 523

English, Henry .................................................... 398-404
English, Parmenus ................................................ 351
English, Sarah ..................................................... 341
Enlo, John ......................................................... 315
Entechins, William (or Enterkin) ................................. 381
Entichens, Wiliam .................................................. 76
Entrican, William, (or Entriccan) ............................... 351-381
Epperson, John .................................................... 321
Epperson, Mary .................................................... 321
Epperson, Thomas .................................................. 327
Epperson, Thompson ............... (or Epperson) ........... 321-418-439
Epps, William ..................................................... 398-404
Espey, John ........................................................ 351
Espey, Thomas ...................................................... 75
Epsy, James ........................................................ 338
Espy, James ................................................ 414-439-460-462
Espey, William .................................................... 75-381
Espy, John .................................................. 414-439-451
Espy, Thomas ...................................................... 414
Estar, George ..................................................... 323
Estes, Isabella, .................................................. 326
Etheridge, Joel ........................................... 351-414-451-457
Eton, Elisha, ..................................................... 414
Eton, John ........................................................ 398-404
Etons, Absolom .................................................... 381
Eubanks, George ................................................. 339-414
Eubanks, Susannah ................................................ 335
Eustace, J. ..................................................... 18-414
Eustace, John ................................................... 381-414
Eustace, John, Maj. .............................................. 414
Eustace, John, J. Key ............................................. 75
Eustace, Jno., S. .................................................. 15
Eustace, Jno, Skey, (or Skye) ................................... 381-414
Evans, B. ...................................................... 18-414
Evans, Benj. ............................................... 73-74-303-381
Evans, Daniel ..................... 73-74-77-198-199-237-267-381
Evans, David ................................................... 74-381
Evans, James .................................................... 26-351
Evans, Jane ....................................................... 327
Evans, Jesse .................................................... 398-403
Evans, John, ................................................ 18-76-381-414
Evans, N. ....................................................... 18-414
Evans, Nathan ..................................................... 381
Evans, Stephen ........................... 75-246-248-259-295-381
Evans, Thomas ..................................................... 323
Evans, William ............................... 73-74-381-414-451
Evans, William, Sen. ........................................... 414-439

INDEX.

Evans, William D. ... 351
Evanson, Eli. ... 351
Evant, Eliz. ... 316
Eveleigh, Nicholas ... 414
Everett, Archalaus ... 351
Everett, John ... 414
Eves, Nathaniel ... 73-381
Ewen, William ... 414
Ewing, Samuel ... 336
Ewing, Thomas ... 414
Ezell, Hartwell, ... 351

## F

Fail, Thomas ... 400
Fair, Ebenzer ... 414
Fain, John ... 381
Faine, William ... 381
Fair, Ebenzer ... 411
Fair, Jacob ... 385
Fair, Peter ... 400
Fairclauth, Ben, (or Fareclauth) ... 414-451
Faircloth, John ... 351
Faison, William ... 414
Fambrough, Thomas ... 414
Fane, Travis ... 381
Fann, John ... 78
Fann, Thomas ... 351
Fanner, Asael ... 381
Fanner, William ... 82-217-381
Fannin, A. B. ... 19
Fare, Jacob ... 77-381
Farechild, Elizabeth ... 328
Farington, Jacob ... 381
Faris, Rebecca ... 341
Faris, WWilliam ... 352
Farley, Robt. M. ... 320
Farley, Samuel ... 414
Farmer, Asael ... 81-82
Farmer, John ... 414
Farqua, Thomas ... 210
Farr, Benj. ... 381-396
Farr, John ... 381-396
Farrar, Francis ... 352-414-439-451
Farrar, Thomas ... 462
Farrell, John ... 173
Farrell, William ... 77-82-242-381

## INDEX.

| | |
|---|---|
| Farrill, Richard | 269 |
| Farrish, Robert | 303 |
| Farrow, Jesse | 414-439 |
| Farvin, John | 381 |
| Fason, William | 327 |
| Faulks, Joseph | 414 |
| Favens, John | 381 |
| Favours, John | 79-80-414 |
| Fayerous, Peter | 414 |
| Faylor, Henry | 265 |
| Feagan, William | 352 |
| Fean, William | 381 |
| Fears, William | 352 |
| Feldkeller, J. | 414 |
| Fell, Benj. | 414 |
| Fell, Isaac | 414 |
| **Felp, David** | 78 |
| Felps, David, (or Phelips) | 381 |
| Felps, John | 287 |
| Felter, Nathaniel | 78 |
| Felts, James | 352-381 |
| Fenn, John | 82-260-285-290-293 |
| Fenn, Travis | 80-210 |
| Fenn, William | 80-82-243-246 |
| Fenn, Zachariah | 77-228-285-381 |
| Fequa, Prater | 80-299-382 |
| Feras, Zach. | 381 |
| Fergason, Charles, (or Ferguson) | 78-381 |
| Ferguson, James | 398-404 |
| Ferington, Jacob | 414 |
| Ferkerson, John | 77-381 |
| Ferrell, James | 81-381 |
| Ferrel, Thomas | 381-396 |
| Ferrell, Micajah | 352 |
| Ferrill, William, (or Ferrul) | 81-381 |
| Ferrin, George | 213 |
| Ferrington, Jacob | 79 |
| Fettler, Mathew | 78-381 |
| Fettler, Nathaniel | 381 |
| Few, Benjamin | 78-79-234-260-263-276-298-299-303-311-462 |
| Few, Ignatius, | 10-15-79-223-230-232-244-247-260-278-303-310-381-414-462 |
| Few, Ignatius, Col. | 244 |
| Few, William, Jr. | 381 |
| Few, William, Sr. | 381 |
| Few, William | 78-227-236-246-292-381-414-462 |
| Fewn, Benjamin | 414 |
| Fields, William | 219 |

# INDEX.

Fields, James ................................................. 414
Fields, Lewis ................................................. 81
Fields, William ......................................... 79-303-381
Files, Adams, J. ........................................... 414-439
Fimderburk, John ............................................ 439
Finch, John ............................................. 398-404
Finch, William ...................................... 352-414-439-451
Fincher, James ........................................ 352-381-439
Fincher, Jemina ............................................ 340
Finchwell, Joseph (or Finshwell) ..................... 79-260-381
Findley, ................................................... 414
Findley, James ............................................. 199
Findley, John .............................................. 352
Findley, Morris ............................................ 267
Fineley, Thomas ............................................ 414
Finley, James ........................................... 77-381
Finn, John ................................................. 381
Fireash, Elias ............................................. 352
Fireash, John .............................................. 352
Fishbourne, Benjamin ....................................... 414
Fitts, Mary ................................................ 327
Fitzgerald, Charles ..................................... 81-381
Fitzgerald, George ...................................... 414-439
Fitzpatrick, Benjamin, ............................ 414-459-460-462
Fitzpatrick, John .......................................... 414
Fitzpatrick, Patrick, ............................ 15-352-381-414
Fitzpatrick, Renne, (or Rene) .......................... 304-341
Fitzpatrick, Richard ....................................... 414
Fitzpatrick, William ................................ 304-352-414
Fireash, Elias ............................................. 352
Flag, Dr. .................................................. 414
Flaherty, Daniel ........................................... 414
Flanagan, William ................................ 339-352-414-439-451
Flanigan, Daniel ....................................... 414-451
Flanigan, Polly, ........................................... 317
Flannigan, William, ........................................ 319
Fleming, G. M. ............................................. 321
Fleming, James ............................................. 80
Fleming, L. M. ............................................. 322
Fleming Margaret ........................................... 316
Fleming,, Martha ........................................... 332
Fleming, R. ................................................ 249
Fleming, Robert .................................... 8-260-274-321
Fleming, Samuel ......................................... 81-449
Fleming, William ................... 81-258-259-381-414-439-451
Flemmekin, David, (or Flemmickin) ...................... 352-381
Flemmekin, Samuel, (or Flemmikin) ...................... 352-381

## INDEX. 527

Flemming, Robert .................................................381-439-451
Flemming, Samuel ........................................................ 381
Flenneken, James ......................................................82-381
Flerl, John ............................................................... 414
Fletcher, William ........................................................ 352
Fling, John ..........................................................216-381
Flinn, John (or Flynt) ................................................... 414
Flinn, William ........................................................... 414
Flint, James ............................................................. 352
Flood, Jane .............................................................. 339
Florence, Thomas ......................................................... 352
Flournoy, Robert (or Flounray) .............................285-381-414-462
Flowers, Henry ........................................................... 352
Flowers, William ......................................................80-381
Floyd, Charles ........................................................... 414
Floyd, Penmon ............................................................. 82
Fluker, George ........................................................... 400
Fluker, John ...............................................83-259-352-381-414-439
Fluker, Owen .........................................................80-259-381
Fluker, Thomas ........................................................... 381
Fluker, William ......................................................231-352-381
Flukeway, Thomas .......................................................... 82
Fly, Jeremiah ..........................................................82-381
Flynn, James ...........................................................79-381
Flynn, John ............................................................... 79
Flynt, Sarah, .........................................................324-347
Foil, John ............................................................... 352
Fold, George ............................................................. 323
Folds, George ............................................................ 381
Folds, George, Sr. ........................................................ 81
Folsom Benjamin ........................................................79-381
Folsom, Easter ............................................................ 79
Folsom, William .......................................................... 414
Folsome, John ............................................................ 381
Fontaine, James ........................................................... 65
Forbes, Wesley, .......................................................... 352
Ford, John ............................................................80-82-381
Ford, John, Jr. .......................................................80-82-297
Ford, Joshua, .......................................................791203-381
Ford, Mary, .............................................................. 316
Ford, Owen, ...........................................................77-381
Ford, Thomas .......................................................301-352-381
Ford, Thomas, Jr. ......................................................... 83
Ford, William ......................................................78-245-246-381
Forenby, Nathan .......................................................... 352
Forgason, Charles ........................................................ 381
Formby, Nathan .......................................................414-439

# INDEX.

Forsyth, Robert .................................................... 414
Fort, Arthur ................................................77-199-238-381-415
Fort, Eliz ........................................................ 315
Fort, Owen, ................................................77-198-381
Fortee, Jacob ..................................................... 381
Fortune, Jacob ...............................................285-358
Foster, Arthur .................................................... 352
Foster, Francis .............................................77-82-381
Foster, John ...................................................... 352
Foster, Panolope .................................................. 82
Foster, William ........................................77-88-81-82-260-381
Fouche, Jonas ..................................................... 400
Fould, George ...............................................265-276
Fould, James ...................................................... 332
Foulder, George ................................................... 264
Foulds, George ...............................................82-285
Fountain, J. ...................................................... 249
Fountain, James ................................................... 309
Fountain, Jourdan ................................................. 316
Fountain, Sarah ................................................... 315
Fowler, George Sr. ................................................ 315
Fowler, Henry ...............................................381-396
Fowler, Martha .................................................... 339
Fowler, Nathan ..............................................78-285-381
Fowler, Peter ...............................................381-396
Fowlkes, .........Capt. ............................................ 415
Fox, James ..................................................398-403
Fox, Willmouth .................................................... 340
Fox, Dabby ..................................................415-439
Francis, Abraham .................................................. 81
Francis, Abraham .................................................. 81
Francis, Frederick .........................................77-78-249-262-381
Franklin, David .............................................352-381-396-415
Franklin, David, Jr. .............................................. 415
Franklin, G. ...................................................... 246
Franklin, George ...........................................83-93-294-381-459-462
Franklin, Thomas ............................................381-396-398
Franklin, William ...........................................229-398-404
Franklin, Wiliam, Jr. .............................................80-381
Franklin, William Sr. .............................................83-381
Rranklin, Zephanaiah .............................................. 341
Fraser, Lt. ....................................................... 415
Fraser, John .................................................16-415
Fraser, Simon, .................................................... 415
Frasser, Malachiah ................................................ 83
Frazer, Andrew .................................................... 80
Frazer, Barbany ................................................... 221

# INDEX. 529

| | |
|---|---|
| Frazer, John | 18-79-415 |
| Frazer, Mary | 221 |
| Frazer, Penelope | 221 |
| Frazer, Reuben | 70 |
| Frazier, Alex | 81-381 |
| Frazier, Dyer | 80 |
| Frazier, Elijah | 415-439 |
| Frazier, John | 80-189-352-382-415 |
| Frazier, Malachi | 381 |
| Frazier, Malakiah | 215 |
| Fredconer, C. | 18-415 |
| Frederick, Thomas | 83-207-208-274-382 |
| Fredman, Conrad | 382 |
| Fredonia, Conrad | 83-78 |
| Freeman, Coldress | 415 |
| Freeman, Coldrup | 415-439 |
| Freeman, Colquitt | 462 |
| Freeman, Daniel | 352-415-439 |
| Freeman, Elizabeth | 327 |
| Freeman, H. | 303 |
| Freeman, Hallman, | 415 |
| Freeman, Holman | 77-245-382 |
| Freeman, Jack | 415 |
| Freeman, James | 81-303-311-393-415 |
| Freeman, John | 78-80-81-211-240-246-303-382-403-415-462 |
| Freeman, Joshua | 206 |
| Freeman, Laban | 398-404 |
| Freeman, Roswell | 398-404 |
| Freeman, Samuel | 460-462 |
| Freeman, Sarah | 324-347 |
| Freeman, William | 59-81-211-415 |
| Freil, John | 228-382 |
| Freman, James | 382 |
| Freman, John | 382 |
| Freman, William | 382 |
| French, James | 78-382 |
| French, Joseph | 382 |
| French, Joshua | 382 |
| Fretwell, Richard | 415-439-451 |
| Frewn, Zacheus | 76 |
| Freyar, Humphrey | 81-382 |
| Frice, John | 270 |
| Frie, John | 269 |
| Friels, Lewis | 230-382 |
| Frier, John | 79-382 |
| Frigonier, Conrad | 82 |
| Frinderburk, John | 415 |

# INDEX.

Fry, Benjamin .................................................... 415-439-458
Fryar, Fielding ......................................................... 236
Fryar, Zach ............................................................ 304
Fryday, Joseph ........................................................ 352
Fryer, Fielding .................................................... 352-382
Fudge, Jacob ..................................................... 415-451-457
Fugonier, Conrad ...................................................... 382
Fukeway, Thomas ...................................................... 382
Fuldher, James ........................................................ 352
Fuller, Cooper, B. .................................................... 321
Fuller, Diantha ....................................................... 322
Fuller, Elizabeth ..................................................... 335
Fuller, George W. ..................................................... 321
Fuller, Hugh .......................................................... 322
Fuller, Isaac ..................................................... 82-83-382
Fuller, Isham ......................................................... 400
Fuller, John ..................................................... 206-246-259
Fuller, John, Sr. ...................................................... 80
Fuller, Joshua .................................................... 82-259-382
Fuller, Kesiah ........................................................ 340
Fuller, Meshac ........................................................ 449
Fuller, Nancy ......................................................... 318
Fuller, Stephen .......................................... 79-246-321-382-449-451
Fuller, William ....................................................... 352
Fullwood, John ........................................................ 352
Fulsom, William ....................................................... 352
Fulsome, Lawrence, (or Laurence) .................................. 78-382
Fulson, John ........................................................... 77
Fulton, John ...................................................... 40-382-415
Fulton, Samuel ................................................... 238-382-415
Fulton, Samuel, Jr. ................................................ 79-82
Fulton, Samuel, Sr. ................................................... 78
Fulton, Thomas ........................................................ 352
Funderbunk, John ...................................................... 352
Fuqua, Prater .................................................... 80-299-382
Fuqua, Thomas ..................................................... 83-246
Furlow, John .......................................................... 398
Furlow, William ................................................... 83-217
Fussell, Ezra .................................................... 82-260-382
Fussell, Thomas ................................................... 77-382
Futch, Onesimus ....................................................... 352

## G

Gadden, Mary, ( Gaddens or Gaddis) ................................ 319-320
Gaddis, Mary .......................................................... 320

# INDEX. 531

| | |
|---|---|
| Gailor, James | 352 |
| Gaines, Absalom | 90-382 |
| Gaines, Bagley | 86-382 |
| Gaines, Bagley, | 80-382 |
| Gaines, William | 316-352-415-440-451 |
| Gaines, Francis | 352 |
| Gaines, Wiliam | 316-352-415-440-451 |
| Gainer, William | 462 |
| Gaison, Wiloughby | 337 |
| Galaspy, John | 84193 |
| Gallache, James | 352 |
| Galley, Richard | 415 |
| Gilliland, Thomas | 382 |
| Gilliland, Wiliam | 382 |
| Gillons, James | 382-396 |
| Galoche, James | 415 |
| Galphin, George | 235-285-400-415 |
| Galphin, George | 235-285-400-415 |
| Galphine, John | 233-235 |
| Galphin, Thomas | 91-214-220-382 |
| Gamade, Charity | 340 |
| Gamble, John | 84-85-261-382 |
| Gambol, John | 231-285 |
| Games, Ann | 332 |
| Games, George C. | 352 |
| Gamest, William | 87-382 |
| Gammill, Jane | 330 |
| Gamson, John | 382 |
| Gan, Mocajah | 404 |
| Ganes, Frances | 316 |
| Ganey, Bartholomew | 353 |
| Ganey, Redic | 353 |
| Ganier, Wiliam | 462 |
| Garbet, George | 84 382 |
| Gardiner, William | 83 |
| Gardner, Lewis | 88-92-260-382 |
| Gardner William | 232-260-382 |
| Garland, | 462 |
| Garland Mr. | 460 |
| Garland, John | 353 |
| Garland, William | 353-382 |
| Garmany, Samuel | 382 |
| Garner, Charles | 353-415-440 |
| Garner, George | 320 |
| Garner, John | 415-449 |
| Garner, Joseph | 449 |
| Garner, Martha | 319 |

# INDEX.

| | |
|---|---|
| Garner, Samuel | 398-404 |
| Garner, Thomas | 327 |
| Garnett, Eli | 88-353-382 |
| Garnett, John | 353-382 |
| Garr, Catherine | 334 |
| Garrard, Anthony | 323 |
| Garrett, John | 91-247-261-275-286-382 |
| Garrison, Jedediah | 353 |
| Garrotte, Samuel | 353 |
| Garvin, Rebecca | 315 |
| Gascoign Richard, (or Gascoigne) | 400-415 |
| Gaston, Alexander (or Alex,) | 91-261-382 |
| Gaston, David | 86-382 |
| Gates, Charles, Sr. | 328-335 |
| Gates, Hezekiah | 353 |
| Garland | 462 |
| Garland | 460 |
| Gatlin, Stephen | 451-454 |
| Gauper, John | 415 |
| Gauze, Henry | 396 |
| Gay, Allen | 84-415-440-451-457 |
| Gay, Joshua | 84-353-382 |
| Gay, William | 90-304-382 |
| Gean, Sherod | 317 |
| Gean, Shroomas | 352-382 |
| Geddins, Thomas | 353-382 |
| Gedeon, Wiliam | 88 |
| Gedings, Frances | 382 |
| Gedions, William | 382 |
| Gent, Charles | 86-90-382-449 |
| Gent, William | 353 |
| Gent, William | 86-92-382 |
| George, Isaac | 353 |
| German, John Jr. | 88-382 |
| German, John Sr. | 382 |
| German, John | 86-205-233-415 |
| Germany, Samuel | 91-208-415 |
| Germany, Wiliam | 233-234-261-382 |
| Germany, William, Jr. | 85 |
| Germany, William, Sr. | 85 |
| Getmany, John | 232 |
| German, John | 91-208-415 |
| Gibbons, James Martin | 415 |
| Gibbons, John Vendue | 415 |
| Gibbons, Joseph | 415 |
| Gibbons, William | 415 |
| Gibbons, William, Sr. | 247 |

# INDEX. 533

Gibbs, Cornelius ........................................................ 336
Gibbs, Herod ........................................................... 353
Gibbs, Hervel .......................................................... 382
Gibbs, Richard ..................................................... 86-382
Gibbs, William ............................................. 18-259-267-415
Gibson, Allen .......................................................... 415
Gibson, Churchill ...................................................... 415
Gibson, Henry ......................................................... 415
Gibson, Henry, B. ................................................. 323-353
Gibson, John .................................... 88-323-415-460-462
Gibson, Luke ....................................................... 398-404
Gibson, Robert ........................................................ 415
Gibson, William .................................................... 243-253
Giddens, William ....................................................... 87
Gideon, Francis, (or Gideons) .................................. 87-296-382
Gideon, Thomas ........................................................ 415
Gideon, William ........................................................ 382
Gideons, Benj. ......................................................... 353
Gideons, Elizabeth ........................................... 324-329-347
Gideons, William ....................................................... 85
Gift, Jonathan .................................................... 83-85-382
Gilbert, Charles ....................................................... 400
Gilbert, James ............................................... 61-84-382-451
Gilbert, John ..................................................... 336-341
Gilbert, Thomas ................................................ 314-353-382
Gilbert, William ............................................. 84-314-353-382
Gilder, Isaac ..................................................... 353-382
Giles, Andrew ......................................................... 382
Giles, Arthur ..................................................... 89-382
Giles, Celia .......................................................... 340
Giles, James .......................................................... 415
Giles, John ........................................................ 87-382
Giles, Joseph ......................................................... 415
Giles, Robert ...................................................... 92-382
Giles, Samuel .............................................. 89-382-396-401
Giles, William .................................................. 86-249-382
Gill, John ............................................................ 143
Gilland, Thomas ........................................................ 90
Gilliland, William .................................................... 382
Gilleland, Susan ...................................................... 451
Gillers, James ........................................................ 353
Gillett, Elijah ....................................................... 207
Gilliland, Hugh .................................................... 85-382
Gilliland, Thomas .................................................. 87-260
Gilliland, William .......................................... 88-260-440
Gilmer, James, Sr. .......................................... 341-415-451
Gilmore, James .............................................. 334-415-440

| | |
|---|---|
| Gilmour, William | 415 |
| Gilton, James | 252 |
| Gindratt, Henry | 415 |
| Ginkins, Robert | 88 |
| Ginn, Sarah | 340 |
| Ginnings, Giles | 398-404 |
| Girardeau, John | 84-382-449 |
| Girrardeau, John, Bohm | 415 |
| Giradeau, William | 84-382 |
| Girtman, Cath | 315 |
| Givins, John | 206 |
| Glimpins, John | 91-261-382 |
| Glascock, | 292-398 |
| Glascock, Thomas | 215-229-286-382-403-415-462 |
| Glascock, William | 91-200-248-382-415-462 |
| Glase, Joseph | 382 |
| Glasgo, William | 415 |
| Glasgow, William (or Glasgo) | 415-440-451 |
| Glasby, John, (or Gilespie) | 382 |
| Glass, | 415 |
| Glass, James | 398-404 |
| Glass, Joel | 90-261-382 |
| Glass, John | 89-261-382 |
| Glass, Joseph | 88-415 |
| Glass, Joshua | 90-382 |
| Glass, Levi | 353 |
| Glass, Thomas | 415 |
| Glassoway, Thomas | 353-382 |
| Glaze, Reuben | 353 |
| Glazier, Sarah | 338 |
| Glen, David | 415 |
| Glen, John | 398-415 |
| Glenn, Andrew | 320 |
| Glenn, Ann | 336 |
| Glenn, Elizabeth | 318-336 |
| Glenn, James | 353 |
| Glenn, Thomas | 331-337-415-451 |
| Glenn, William | 398 |
| Glover, Andrew | 92 |
| Glover, Hardy | 382 |
| Glover, Sarah | 92 |
| Glover, William | 320-321-353 |
| Gloveyer, Stephen | 88-127-382 |
| Glynn, Lucy | 340 |
| Gnu, Micajah | 398 |
| Gober, William | 353 |
| Gober, William, Sr. | 317 |

## Index.

Godbe, Cary .................................................. 88-382
Godbe, Curry ..................................................... 382
Godbe, Cary .................................................. 89-382
Godby, William ............................... 84-87-285-382-415
Goff, Nathaniel I. .......................................... 415-440
Goffe, Daniel ..................................................... 415
Goggans, William ................................................ 415
Golden, Andrew .................................................. 353
Golden, Elender ................................................. 338
Golden, Francis B. .............................................. 328
Golden, John ..................................................... 249
Golden, William ............................................ 88-90-382
Golding, ......................................................... 415
Golding John .................................................. 91-382
Golding, Peter ................................................... 415
Goldsbery, Jonathan .............................................. 87
Goldsmith, John ............................................. 416-440
Golwire, J. ....................................................... 382
Goldwire, James ............................................. 84-85-416
Goldwire, John .................................................... 85
Golightly, Charles ............................................... 416
Golighty, S. ..................................................... 338
Golitely, Charles ................................................ 353
Gollache, James .................................................. 416
Golson, John ..................................................... 235
Goober, William .................................................. 285
Gooch, Nathan .................................................... 353
Goodall, Park ..................................................... 46
Goodall, Pleasant ......................... 89-243-255-300-382
Gooddown, Jacob .................................................. 353
Goode, Edward .................................................... 400
Goodman, Lewis .............................................. 328-333
Goodson, William .................................................. 86
Goodwin, James ................................................... 353
Goodwin, Lewis .............................................. 451-457
Goodwin, Wiley .............................................. 416-440
Goodwire, Sharick ................................................ 353
Goodwyn, Theodore ................................................ 301
Goodwynn, Frederick .............................................. 416
Goodwynn, Theod .................................................. 400
Goolsby, Elijah, (or Elijach) ............................... 353-416
Goolsby, Isaiah ................................................... 91
Goolsby, Jonathan ................................................ 382
Goolsby, Joshia .................................................. 382
Goolsby, Mary .................................................... 327
Goolsby, Reuben ............................................. 416-440
Goolsby, Richard ................................................. 353

## INDEX.

Goore, Thomas, Sr. ........................................................ 314
Golden, Jesse ........................................................... 87-88
Gordon, Ambrose ............................................. 398-403-416-462
Gordon, Andrew .......................................................... 252
Gordon, James ............................................... 353-382-416-440
Gordon, James, Maj. .................................................... 416
Gordon, James F. .................................................... 416-440
Gordon, Jesse .......................................................... 382
Gordon, John ............................................... 221-247-416
Gordon, Nancy .......................................................... 334
Gordon, Nathaniel ...................................................... 416
Gordon, Thomas ......................................................... 353
Gordon, William .................................................... 382-458
Gordon, William, Maj. .................................................. 458
Gore, Thomas ............................................................ 91
Gorham, John ..................................................... 89-240-382
Gorley, Ayers ..................................................... 91-382
Gorley, James ..................................................... 92-382
Goslin, David ................................................... 353-382
Gossett, Jacob ................................................... 92-382
Gossett, John .......................................................... 404
Gotcher, Henry ......................................................... 400
Goulding, Palmer ................................................. 353-416
Goulding, Peter ........................................................ 353
Goulding, William ...................................................... 416
Goulsby, Jonathan ............................................... 261-270
Goultney, John ......................................................... 382
Gluze, Henry .................................................... 382-416
Goves, Thomas .......................................................... 382
Gower, Abel ................................................. 339-416-440-451
Grace, John ................................................. 340-416-440
Graddy, Mary ........................................................... 320
Grady, Arthur .......................................................... 353
Grady, Mary ............................................................ 327
Gragz, Thomas ..................................................... 88-382
Graham, John ........................................................... 416
Graham, William ............................................... 83-84-382-416
Grant, Capt. ....................................................... 382-416
Grant, Andrew ..................................................... 92-297-382
Grant, Daniel .......................................................... 416
Grant, Jesse ........................................................... 353
Grant, John ........................................................ 87-382
Grant, Joseph ............................................... 313-353-416-440-451
Grant, Peter ................................................. 85-90-261-382
Grant, Thomas ................................................. 88-382-462
Grant, William ................................................... 86-382
Grantham, Nathan ....................................................... 353

## INDEX.

| | |
|---|---|
| Grantham, William | 353 |
| Gravat, O. | 18-416 |
| Gravat, Odediah | 83 |
| Graves, James | 87-382 |
| Graves, John | 86-89-300-323-382 |
| Graves, Richard | 33-83-89-237-260-382 |
| Graves, Robert | 92-214-231-382 |
| Graves, Robert, Jr. | 89-382 |
| Graves, Robert, Sr. | 92 |
| Graves, Thomas | 33-87-89-416 |
| Graves, William | 87-225-226-416-440 |
| Gray, Diana | 336 |
| Gray, Isaac | 319 |
| Gray, Jacob | 90-221-382 |
| Gray, James | 91-243-286-327-382 |
| Gray, John | 87-226-382-449 |
| Gray, Josheph | 400 |
| Gray, Mathew | 86 |
| Gray, Matthias | 301-382 |
| Gray, R. M. | 382 |
| Gray, Rob | 382 |
| Gray, Robert | 84 |
| Gray, Susannah | 316-331 |
| Gray, Thomas | 81-258-382-416 |
| Greasell, Elam | |
| Greasell, Elam (or Greasel) | 84-284-382 |
| Greasell, George | 270 |
| Greason, Abraham | 416 |
| Greaves, William | 207-353 |
| Greazell, Elam | 383 |
| Greathouse, Jacob | 383 |
| Green, Capt. | 181-416 |
| Green, Maj. | 416 |
| Green, Andrew M. | 92 |
| Green, Ben | 315 |
| Green, Benj. | 315 |
| Green, Benj. | 86-92-383-440 |
| Green, Bery | 243 |
| Green, Burwell, | 353 |
| Green, aDniel | 400 |
| Green, Frederick | 86 |
| Green, Gilbert | 416 |
| Green, Henry | 87-383 |
| Green, Isaac | 89 |
| Green, James | 33-85-91-382 |
| Green, John | 10-14-15-91-92-126-205-301-385-416-440-454 |
| Green, John, Capt. | 92-416 |

538　INDEX.

Green, John R. .................................................... 416-440
Green, M. Andrew ..................................................... 383
Green, McKeen .............................................. 89-212  383
Green, Nathaniel ..................................................... 462
Green, Phil .......................................................... 233
Green, Richard ....................................................... 354
Green, Saliva .................................................... 86-383..
Green, Sullivan ................................................... 85-383
Green, Thomas ............................................. 86-261-416-440
Green, Thomas, Jr. ................................................... 89
Green, Will ...................................................... 204-205
Green, William ......................... 89-92-198-206-274-383-398-404
Green, William, Sr. ............................................. 398-404
Greene, Benjamin ........................................... 256-261-383
Greene, Daniel ....................................................... 339
Greene, Forrest ...................................................... 313
Greene, Frederick .................................................... 383
Greene, Gabriel ...................................................... 416
Greene, Isaac ........................................................ 286
Greene, James ........................................................ 218
Greene, John ......................................................... 416
Greene, Thomas ....................................................... 383
Greene, William ............................................ 236-383-416
Greer, Araon ......................................................... 279
Greer, Benjamin ...................................................... 354
Greer, David ..................................................... 299-304
Greer, Gilbert ........................................................ 91
Greer, James ......................................................... 354
Greer, John ................................................... 90-354-383
Greer, Robert ..................................................... 90-314
Greer, Thomas ............................................. 217-260-354-383
Greer, William ............................................. 286-354-383
Greers, Thomas ................................................... 383-400
Greeson, John ......................................................... 88
Greff, Joshua ........................................................ 353
Greggs, Thomas .................................................... 85-383
Gregory, Richard .......................................... 325-416-440
Griece, John, Sr. .................................................... 416
Greiner, John Jasper ................................................. 354
Gresham, Alexander ................................................... 416
Gresham, Archivald ............................................... 400-416
Gresham, David .................................................. 416-440
Gresham, John ........................................................ 354
Gresham, Littlebury ........................................ 354-416-440
Gresham, Wiliam .................................................. 398-404
Grey, James ........................................................... 90

## INDEX. 539

| | |
|---|---|
| Grey, John | 90 |
| Grey, Robert, M. | 84 |
| Grey, Thomas | 261 |
| Grezel, George | 231 |
| Griener, Philip | 383 |
| Grier, Aaron | 86-260-383 |
| Grier, Gilbert | 383-400 |
| Grier, John | 383 |
| Grier, Robert | 85-260-383 |
| Grier, Thomas | 88-92 |
| Grier, William | 85-383 |
| Grierson, John | 383 |
| Grierson, Robert | 383 |
| Griffin, Charles | 354-458-460-462 |
| Griffin, Edward | 416-440-454 |
| Griffin, James | 354-416-440 |
| Griffin, John | 458 |
| Griffin, Joseph | 328-354 |
| Griffin, Matthew | 85-234-383 |
| Griffin, Michael | 83-383 |
| Griffin, Randall | 90-383 |
| Griffin, Randolph | 90-383 |
| Griffin, Samuel | 90-261-383 |
| Griffis, John | 354 |
| Griffith, James | 398-404 |
| Griffith, Samuel | 84-383 |
| Griggs, George | 398 |
| Grimesley, John | 383 |
| Grimke, John F. | 416 |
| Grimke, John J. | 416 |
| Grimmer, William | 354 |
| Grimsby, Adam | 84 |
| Grimsey, Richard | 84 |
| Grimsley, Adam | 383 |
| Grimsley, Elijah | 88-383 |
| Grimsley, John | 87-260 |
| Grimsley, Joseph | 88-383 |
| Grimsley, Thomas | 416-440 |
| Griner, Philip | 84-90-206-261-383 |
| Grinnell, William | 416 |
| Grirsly, James | 266 |
| Grisham, David | 451 |
| Grissam, Sally | 338 |
| Grissap, James | 316 |
| Grisson, Arch | 304 |
| Grissup, James | 354 |
| Grizzelle, John (or Grizzell) | 458 |

# INDEX.

Grizzell, George ........................................................90-383
Grizzard, Susannah ................................................... 333
Grogan, Richard ...................................................... 416
Groover, Jacob ....................................................... 321
Groover, Peter ............................................321-416-440-451
Grotehouse, Jacob .................................................... 87
Grotehouse, Jacob, Jr. ............................................... 87
Grotehouse, John ..................................................... 416
Groves, John ......................................................... 416
Groves, Stephen ..................................................416-440
Groves, William, Sr. ................................................. 416
Grub, Frances ........................................................ 383
Grubbs, Benjamin .................................................91-383
Grubs, Francis ....................................................... 88
Grumbles, George .................................................329-336
Gualtney, John ....................................................... 85
Guest, Moses .............................................320-321-460-462
Guice, John, Sr. ..................................................... 440
Guice, Nicholas ...................................................... 354
Guise, John .......................................................... 327
Guise, Peter ......................................................... 337
Gulley, Richard ..................................................416-440-451
Gumm, Jacob .......................................................... 462
Gunn, General ........................................................ 460
Gunn, Gabriel ....................................................416-440
Gunn, Jacob .......................................................... 460
Gunn, James .......................................................... 462
Gunn, James, Capt. ................................................... 416
Gunn, Richard ........................................................ 354
Gunnell, William .................................................416-440
Gunnell, William R. .................................................. 451
Gunnells, Daniel .................................................86-383-416
Gunnells, Joseph .................................................91-383
Gunnells, Nicholas ...............................................90-383
Gunnells, William .................................................... 354
Gunnold, M. .......................................................... 298
Gunter Charles ...................................................416-440-451
Gunter, James ........................................................ 354
Gurnsey, Richard ..................................................... 383
Gustavous, Micajah ................................................... 207
Guthrie, John ....................................................354-416-449
Guthrie, William ..................................................... 354
Guttery, Francis ..................................................... 354
Guy, William ......................................................... 400
Guyse, John ......................................................416-451
Gwaltnery, John ...................................................... 84
Gwinn, Transilvania .................................................. 315

# INDEX.

Gwinnett, Button, .................................................. 416-463
Gwynn, Richard ..................................................... 354

## H.

Habersham, George .................................................. 332
Habersham, James .................................................. 28-416
Habersham, James, Jr. .............................................. 463
Habersham, John ........................................... 9-18-75-416-463
Habersham, Joseph ............................................... 9-15-463
Hackney, Robert .................................................... 354
Hadaway, David ..................................................... 354
Hadden, William ................................................... 95-262
Hadden, Mary ....................................................... 315
Haddon, William .................................................. 231-416
Hagan, Ed. ....................................................... 282-383
Hagan, Edward (or Gagan) .......................... 98-229-231-232-383
Hagan, James ....................................................... 232
Hager, Arthur .................................................... 383-416
Haggett, Hohn ...................................................... 416
Haggett, John ...................................................... 383
Haile, George ...................................................... 383
Haile, James ....................................................... 354
Hailey, William .................................................. 315-354
Haines, Evan ....................................................... 449
Haines, Robert ..................................................... 398
Haishey, Thomas .................................................... 416
Haisley, Thomas .................................................... 441
Haisten, John .................................................... 416-441
Halbrooks, Edy. .................................................... 334
Halcomb, Hampton, .................................................. 455
Hale, George ....................................................... 94
Haliman, Absolam ................................................... 383
Hall, Ann, Mrs. .................................................... 315
Hall, Dempsey ...................................................... 354
Hall, Dempsey, Sr. ................................................. 315
Hall, Ed. .......................................................... 242
Hall, Edward ............................................. 232-291-293-383
Hall, George, ............................................... 242-264-276
Hall, Hugh ....................................................... 460-463
Hall, Hudson, Sr. .................................................. 315
Hall, Instant ...................................................... 354
Hall, Isaac .................................................. 334-416-441
Hall, James ........................................................ 354
Hall, John ....................................................... 354-416
Hall, L. ........................................................... 65
Hall, Lyman, Dr. ................................................. 415-463
Hall, Wm. G. ....................................................... 333

Halliday, William .................................................. 98-398
Halwell, Luther ...................................................... 95
Halymdorf, William ................................................. 383
Ham, William .................................................... 333-337
Hamach, Robert B. ................................................. 383
Haman, Alexander .............................................. 416-451
Hamby, Dennis ..................................................... 383
Hamel, Daniel ....................................................... 95
Hames, John ....................................................... 451
Hames, John, Sr. (or Haines) .......................... 335-416-441-463
Hamilton, A. ...................................................... 416
Hamilton, Andrew .............................................. 323-354
Hamilton, Barker .................................................. 354
Hamilton, C. ...................................................... 333
Hamilton, Charles ................................................. 417
Hamilton, George .................................................. 323
Hamilton, James .......................................... 417-460-463
Hamilton John ............................................. 354-417-441
Hamilton, John Sr. ................................................ 417
Hamilton, Robert .................................................. 417
Hamilton, Stewart, (or Stuart) ................................ 354-463
Hamilton, Stuart .................................................. 459
Hamilton, Thomas ....j................................. 16-96-262-383-417
Hamilton, William .......................................... 287-383-396
Hamlin, Richard ................................................... 400
Hammet, James ................................................ 200-383
Hammet, John ..................................................... 333
Hammet, Setha, (or Sitha) ..................................... 264-383
Hammet, William ................................................... 400
Hammiten, William ................................................. 257
Hammock, Benedict, (or Benedick) ............................. 228-383
Hammock, John ................................................. 286-383
Hammock, Joseph .................................................. 398
Hammock, Robert .................................................... 98
Hammock, William .................................................. 200
Hammond, Col. ..................................................... 100
Hammond, Abner ................................................ 98-383
Hammond, Charles .............................................. 94-383
Hammond, George ............................................... 98-383
Hammond, Henry ................................................... 354
Hammond, Joshua .................................................. 441
Hammond, Joshua, Lt. .............................................. 417
Hammond, Leroy .................................................... 417
Hammond, Samuel ................................................... 417
Hammons, John ..................................................... 323
Hampton, —— Col. ................................................ 417
Hampton, Benjamin ............................................ 354-383
Hampton, Edward ................................................... 417

## INDEX.

Hampton, John .................................................33-94-97-417-441
Hampton, Wade ..................................................... 417
Hamrick, Benjamin .................................................. 354
Hancock, ........................................................... 354
Hancock, Francis ................................................... 417
Hancock, Isam ...................................................... 328
Hancock, Isham ..................................................... 331
Hancock, John .................................................15-417
Hancock, William ................................................... 323
Hand, Henry ........................................................ 354
Hand, Henry H. ................................................460-463
Hand, James ........................................................ 417
Hand, Joseph ................................................354-417-441
Handley, —— Maj. ..........................................185-258
Handley, George, (or Handly) ..........15-78-85-106-109-263-279-354-383
Handley, Jerrett, .................................................. 417
Handley, Nicholas .................................................. 417
Handsard, Thomas ................................................... 383
Handshaw, Thomas ................................................... 94
Handy, Nathaniel ................................................... 327
Haney, Elizabeth ................................................... 338
Hanison, Joseph .................................................... 354
Hannah, James .................................................354-383
Hannah, John ..................................................398-403
Hannah, Thomas ...........................................95-263-383-417
Hannegan, James ..........................................417-440-455
Hanry, George ...................................................... 317
Hansard, Janet ..................................................... 316
Hanson, Samuel ..................................................... 94
Hanson, William ...............................................398-404
Haralson, Hugh ..................................................... 417
Haralsol, Jonathan ................................................. 355
Harback, Michael ................................................... 383
Harbin, Alexander .................................................. 355
Harbin, William ...............................................355-383
Harbrick, Michael .................................................. 262
Harbrick, Nicholas (or Nicholas) ..............................263-383
Hardee, Thomas, ................................................417-441
Hardeman, Rooks, ................................................... 314
Harden, Henry. (or Hardin) ...............................355-417-441-451
Hardin, William .................................................... 417
Harding, —— Capt. .............................................. 417
Hardwick, William .................................................. 463
Hardy, —— Capt. ................................................ 417
Hardy, John ...................................................95-383-417
Hardy, John, —— Capt. ........................................96-383
Hargis, James ...................................................... 304
Harkins, Thomas .................................................... 237

# INDEX.

Harkness, Robert ....................................................... 355
Harley, Joseph ......................................................... 355
Harley, William ........................................................ 398
Harmon, John. Sr. ...................................................... 341
Harn, John ............................................................. 355
Harnett, James ......................................................... 400
Harp, Mannin ........................................................... 355
Harper, Ansel, (or Ansil) ..........................................398-404
Harper, George .................................................264-336-400
Harper, John ......................................................323-340
Harper, Joseph ......................................................... 262
Harper, Joyce .......................................................... 319
Harper, Mary ........................................................... 337
Harper, Richard ........................................................ 319
Harper, Robert ..................................................97-264-289-417
Harper, Samuel, Capt. .............................................97-417
Harper, William ...................................................264-383-451
Harper, William M. ..................................................... 335
Harrell, Ethelred, Sr. ................................................. 331
Harrell, Hardy ......................................................... 355
Harrell, Simon. ........................................................ 355
Harrill, David ......................................................... 383
Harrill Joseph ......................................................... 383
Harriman, John ......................................................... 280
Harrington, John ..................................................255-286-400
Harrington, Thomas ..................................................... 262
Harris, Absolom ........................................................  49
Harris, Benjamin ..................................230-355-383-417-441-451
Harris, Buckner ...................................................93-383
Harris, Calra .......................................................... 331
Harris David ....................................................93-263-383-417
Harris, David, Capt. ................................................... 383
Harris, Edward ......................................................... 398
Harris, Ezekiel ...................................................323-417
Harris, Francis ........................................................  14
Harris, Francis Henry ..............................................9-417
Harris, G. L. .....................................................18-417
Harris, Graves ......................................................... 355
Harris, James .....................................................199-403-417
Harris, Jesse .......................................................... 201
Harris, Joel ........................................................... 213
Harris, John ...................................................93-310-337-383
Harris, John, Sr. ...................................................... 316
Harris, Lavina ......................................................... 329
Harris, Mathew ......................................................... 355
Harris, Michael ...................................................398-417-441-451
Harris, Nathan ....................................................264-400
Harris, Rebecca ........................................................ 316

# INDEX. 545

Harris, Robert ........ 404
Harris, Sampson ........ 398-400-403
Harris, Samuel ........ 93-383
Harris, Stephen ........ 417-441-451
Harris, Thomas ........ 304-383-417
Harris, Tyre Glenn ........ 93-203-204-263
Harris, Walter ........ 201
Harris, Walton ........ 283-383
Harris, William ........ 355-383
Harrison, Ben ........ 221
Harrison, Benjamin ........ 221-319-320-383
Harrison, Edward ........ 355
Harrison, Elijah ........ 355
Harrison, Gilbert ........ 300
Harrison, James ........ 199
Harrison, Jere ........ 398
Harrison, Joseph ........ 317-323-417-441
Harrison, Olin ........ 398
Harrison, Robt. ........ 417
Harrison, Thomas ........ 221
Harrup, Arthur ........ 328
Harsaw, Thomas ........ 18-417
Hart ........ 417
Hart, Benjamin ........ 355-383-417
Hart, George ........ 232-233
Hart, John ........ 95-383
Hart, Mary ........ 451
Hart, Nancy ........ 417
Hart, Robert ........ 355
Hartle, Henry ........ 263-270-383
Hartley, Daniel ........ 417-451-457
Hartley, Henry ........ 255
Hartsfield, Andrew ........ 398-405
Hartsfield, Richard ........ 355
Hartshorn, Thomas ........ 252-263
Harvell, James ........ 417
Harves, Charles ........ 460-463
Harvey, B. ........ 219
Harvey, Benjamin ........ 16-383-400
Harvey, Blasingame ........ 94-219-383-417
Harvey, Charles ........ 226-227-232-355-417
Harvey, Elizabeth ........ 320
Harvey, Evan ........ 216-383
Harvey, J. H. ........ 256
Harvey, James ........ 383
Harvey, James Hill ........ 96-219
Harvey, Joel ........ 96-261-383
Harvey, John ........ 98-262-264-265-275-314-417

## Index.

Harvey, Littleberry ................................................. 98-248-383
Harvey, Michael .................................................. 263-265-383
Harvey, Richard ........................................................ 225
Harvey, Sarah ...................................................... 326-330
Harvey, Thomas ....................................................... 263-383
Harvey, Ursula ......................................................... 326
Harvey, Zephaniah .................................................. 460-463
Harvie, Alexander ...................................................... 417
Harvie, James .......................................................... 47
Harvie, John ........................................................... 417
Harvill, Joseph ......................................................... 96
Has, John .............................................................. 398
Haskins, John .......................................................... 355
Hatchell, William ....................................................... 355
Hatcher, —— Capt. .................................................... 417
Hatcher, Archibald ............................................ 96-201-272-417
Hatcher, Henry ............................................... 96-263-264-383
Hatcher, Jeremiah, (or Jere) .................................. 98-280-305-383
Hatcher, John ...................................................... 95-262-383
Hatcher, Joseph ........................................................ 97
Hatcher, Josiah .................................................... 96-336-383
Hatcher, Robert .................................................... 96-231-383
Hatcher, Thomas ........................................................ 355
Hatcher, Valentine ..................................................... 304
Hatcher, William ................................................... 94-383-441
Hatchett, Archie, (or Archibald) ................................... 383-417
Hatherby, Hugh ......................................................... 398
Hathorn, Thomas ........................................................ 355
Hatton, Josiah ......................................................... 417
Haughton, Joseph ....................................................... 400
Haughton, Joshua ....................................................... 311
Haurst, Samuel ......................................................... 400
Hawkins, Abimelech ................................................. 304-400
Hawkins, Benjamin ............................................ 16-417-460-463
Hawkins, James ................................................... 95-98-240-383
Hawkins, Nicholas ................................................ 95-96-98-383
Hawkins, Stephen .................................................. 383-396-417
Hawkins, Thomas ........................................................ 95
Hawks, Frederick ................................................... 417-441
Hawl, William .......................................................... 449
Hawley, Richard ........................................................ 93
Hawthorn, James ........................................................ 383
Hawthorn, Stephen ................................................... 97-383
Hawthorn, William, (or Hawthorne) ................................... 355
Hawthorne, John .................................................... 355-383
Hay, Isaac ............................................................. 355
Hay, William .................................................. 304-310-400
Hayes, Andrew ..................................................... 265-286

## INDEX. 547

Hayes, Arthur .................................................. 15
Hayes, John .............................................. 335-463
Hayman, Henry ............................................. 98-339
Hayman, Stanton, (or Heyman) .................... 98-231-355-383
Hayman, Stephen ..................................... 231-257-329
Haynes, Arthur ................................................ 18
Haynes, Moses ............................................... 355
Haynie, George .............................................. 339
Haynie, William ......................................... 417-441
Hays, Andrew ................................................ 383
Hays, Arthur ................................................ 383
Hays, Edward ................................................ 355
Hays, George ................................................ 355
Hays, John ........................................... 417-441-460
Hays, Jonathan .............................................. 355
Head, John S. ............................................... 355
Head, Sarah ................................................. 328
Headspeth, Charles .......................................... 400
Heard, —— Capt. ............................................. 50
Heard, B. ................................................... 218
Heard, Bernard, (or Barnard) ..................... 98-286-290-383-417
Heard, Elizaebth ........................................ 316-318
Heard, Elizabeth A. ..................................... 324-347
Heard, George ............................................... 383
Heard, Jesse ................................................ 417
Heard, John .......................................... 200-287-417
Heard, John Sr. ............................................. 263
Heard, John G. .............................................. 355
Heard, Joseph ............................................... 383
Heard, Richard .......................................... 93-95-383
Heard, Stephen ..................................... 93-262-383-417-463
Heard, William .............................................. 355
Hearthem, William ........................................... 383
Heath, Jordan ............................................... 355
Heatley, Robert ....................................... 249-383-400
Heatly, Henry ............................................ 94-383
Heaton, Jordan .............................................. 355
Heaton, James ............................................... 355
Hedden, ..................................................... 417
Heidt, Christian ............................................ 355
Heidt, Christian, J. ........................................ 383
Heith, Roister .............................................. 355
Helby, Jacob, Jr. ........................................... 405
Helfenstein, Jacob .......................................... 417
Helfenstein, Joshua ......................................... 417
Helmes, John ................................................ 323
Hemp, Jonathan ............................................... 46
Hemphill, Esther ............................................ 318

Hemphill, Jonathan ..................................................... 355
Henderson, John G. ..................................................... 318
Henderson, Richard ........................................32-417-440-454
Henderson, Robert .....................................317-330-355-417-441
Henderson, —— Capt. ................................................ 417
Henderson, Robert, —— Sr. .......................................... 335
Henderson, Zachariah ............................................?11-355-383
Hendley, George ...................................................18-417
Hendley, Jarrett ...................................................... 355
Hendon, Isham ....................................................398-405
Hendon, Johnson ..................................................398-405
Hendon, Robinson ..................................................... 355
Hendrick, Jesse ...................................................... 355
Hendrick, John ....................................................... 328
Hendrick, Siah ....................................................... 355
Hendricks, Elias ..................................................... 331
Hendricks, H. ........................................................ 249
Hendrix, John ........................................................ 356
Hendry, Ann .......................................................... 340
Hendry, Robert ....................................................... 356
Henley, George ....................................................... 9
Henry, Elizabeth .................................................320-341
Henshaid, Thomas ..................................................... 417
Henshaw, Thomas ..................................................417-440
Henson, Samuel ....................................................96-383
Herd, —— Capt. ..................................................... 417
Herd, George ......................................................... 96
Herd, Joseph ......................................................... 98
Hereat, John ......................................................... 97
Herman, Alexander .................................................... 417
Hernby, Dennis ....................................................... 98
Herndon, Frances ..................................................... 336
Herndon, Joseph ..............................................356-417-441
Herring, Jesse ....................................................... 441
Herrington, Ephraim .................................................. 356
Herrington, Joseph ................................................... 451
Hertshorn, William ................................................... 237
Hester, David ........................................................ 356
Hester, Diana ........................................................ 336
Hester, Robert ...................................................417-441
Hester, Zachariah .................................................... 356
Hewell, Susannah ..................................................... 329
Hewell, Wiatt, (or Wyatt) ....................................340-417-441
Heweitt, William, (or Hewett) ................................263-264-383
Hext, —— Lt. ....................................................... 417
Heyman, Stephen ...................................................96-383
Heyme —— Lt. ....................................................... 417
Heymond, Henry ....................................................... 383

INDEX. 549

Hickinbotham, B. .................................................. 383
Hickinbotham, Burros .............................................. 127
Hickinbotham, Joseph .............................................. 383
Kickman, John ..................................................... 339
Hicks, Bugg ....................................................... 215
Hicks, David ...................................................... 356
Hicks, Ed. ........................................................ 400
Hicks, Edmond ..................................................... 417
Hicks, Isaac ..........................................94-112-383-417-441
Hicks, J. ......................................................18-417
Hicks, John ...........................................95-205-383-417-441
Hicks, Nathaniel, (or Nathan) .........................209-269-300-400
Hicks, Samuel .............................................207-266-356-383
Higden, Daniel .................................................... 356
Higginbotham, Burroughs ........................................... 209
Higginbotham, Jacob ............................................... 315
Higginbotham, Jean ................................................ 333
Higgins, Jackson .................................................. 243
Higgins, Reuben ................................................... 356
Higgs, John ....................................................... 337
Higgs, Thomas, —— Sr. ............................................. 33?
Highsmith, Sarah .................................................. 338
Hightower, William ................................................ 400
Highet, Philip .................................................... 449
Hilby, Jacob ...................................................... 398
Hill, Abram ....................................................... 418
Hill, Edward ..................................................241-286
Hill, Isaac ...................................................356-418
Hill, James ................................................96-264-383-418
Hill, John ....................................203-210-249-264-313-418-441-451
Hill, Joshua .............................................96-263-264-384
Hill, Mordecai .................................................... 356
Hill, Moses ...............................................257-262-418
Hill, Reuben ..................................................418-451
Hill, Richard .............................................219-308-384
Hill, Theopilus ...........................................398-403
Hill, Thomas ...................................................... 210
Hill, William .....................................95-97-231-267-284287384-418
Hillary, C. ...................................................18-418
Hillary, Christian ................................................ 418
Hillary, Cristopher, (or Chris) ...........................15-95-384-418
Hillary, Christopher, Lt. ......................................... 384
Hilley, Thomas, Sr. ............................................... 315
Hilliard, James ...............................................264-384
Hillon, Chris ..................................................... 418
Hinbon, William ................................................... 405
Hince, Martin .................................................398-405
Hinds, John ...................................................418-440

# INDEX.

Hinds, Martha .................................................. 328
Hinecard, John ................................................ 356
Hines, Benjamin ............................................... 356
Hines, James .................................................. 356
Hines, John ................................................... 335
Hines, Nancy ............................................. 318-340
Hines, Lewis .................................................. 356
Hines, Nathaniel .............................................. 356
Hines, Robert ................................................. 384
Hinnard, John ................................................. 384
Hinsin, Lararus ............................................... 418
Hinsley, Thomas .......................................... 356-384
Hinson, Lazarus ........................................... 333441
Hinston, William .............................................. 356
Hinton, Hardy ............................................ 393-400
Hinton, Job .............................................. 231-384
Hinton, Pester ................................................ 336
Hinton, Peter ................................................. 316
Hinton, William ............................................... 398
Hix, John ..................................................... 206
Hobbs, John ................................................... 274
Hobbs, Margery ................................................ 337
Hobgood, William .............................................. 319
Hobson, Briggs ................................................ 400
Hobson, Mathew ........................................... 356-384
Hodge, David .................................................. 418
Hodge, Jacob .................................................. 233
Hodge, John ................................................... 93
Hodge, Robert ......................................... 93-94-217-384
Hodge, Roger ............................................... 93-384
Hodge, William ................................................ 441
Hodge, Willoughby ......................................... 95-384
Hodges, J. .................................................... 321
Hodges, James ......................................... 244-384-400
Hodges, Joseph ........................................... 356-384
Hodges, Philemon, (or Phileman) ...................... 332-418-441-451
Hodges, Thomas ................................................ 321
Hodges, William ............................................... 418
Hoff, Samuel .................................................. 384
Hogg, James ..................... 43-218-258-261-262-264-278-286-384-418
Hogg, John ................................................ 356-384
Hogg, William ............................................. 127-262
Hoggett, John ................................................. 96
Holbrook, Berrian ............................................. 322
Holbrook, Charity ............................................. 322
Holbrook, Eddy ........................................... 418-440
Holbrook, Hannah .............................................. 339

# INDEX.

| | |
|---|---|
| Holbrook, Jesse | 321-356-418-441-451 |
| Holbrook, Nathan | 418-440 |
| Hilcomb, James | 356 |
| Holcomb, Moses | 328 |
| Holcombe, Sherwood | 356 |
| Holden, Thomas | 400 |
| Holder, John S. | 315-356 |
| Holeman, John | 398-405 |
| Holiday, Capt. | 318 |
| Holiday, Thomas | 384 |
| Holiday, William | 334-418 |
| Holland, Francis, | 398-405 |
| Holland, Henry | 416-441 |
| Holland, Jacob | 221 |
| Holland, John | 418 |
| Holland, Thomas | 356 |
| Holley, William | 356 |
| Holiday, Ambrose | 97-304-307-400 |
| Holliday, Ayers | 263 |
| Holliday, William | 332-398 |
| Holliman, Absolem | 95 |
| Holliman, David | 204-384 |
| Holliman, Mark, | 203-204-206 |
| Holliman, Richard | 203 |
| Holliman, Robert | 214 |
| Holliman, Samuel, (or Sam) | 211-331 |
| Hollinger, Titus | 204-205-233-238 |
| Hollinger, William | 203 |
| Hollingshead, John | 302 |
| Hollingsworth, Isaac | 314-356-384 |
| Hollingsworth, John | 247 |
| Hollis, Sergt. | 418 |
| Holloman, Levicey | 337 |
| Hollow, Henry | 356 |
| Holloway, James | 418 |
| Holloway, Lewis | 20-356-384-418 |
| Holly, Jonathan | 400 |
| Holman, George | 356 |
| Holman, Jacob | 356 |
| Holmes, David | 243 |
| Holmes, Gideon V. | 455 |
| Holmes, John | 10-201-239-384-418 |
| Holmes, John, Capt. | 418 |
| Holmes, Robert | 208-418 |
| Holmes, Thomas | 321-334 |
| Holt, Beverly | 94-384 |
| Holt, James | 356 |

552 INDEX.

Holt, Reuben ............ 97
Holt, Thomas ............ 356
Holt, William ............ 356-384
Holton, Francis ............ 127-210-284-384
Holtzendorf, William (or Holzendorf) ............ 95-418
Holwell, Luther ............ 384
Honea, Tobias, (or Honey) ............ 418-441
Hood, Edward ............ 418
Hood, John ............ 323-356-418
Hoof, Samuel ............ 263-280
Hooks, Thomas ............ 356
Hooks, William ............ 418-440
Hooper, Absolam ............ 400
Hooper, James ............ 356-418-441
Hooper, Jesse ............ 449
Hooper, Richard ............ 332
Hooper, Richard B. ............ 321-418-441
Hooper, William ............ 246
Hopkins, Isaac ............ 323-336
Hopkins, Lambert, (or Lambert) ............ 217-286-287
Hopkins, Samuel ............ 398-405
Hopkins, William ............ 356-384
Hopper, Thomas ............ 356
Horley, William ............ 403
Horn, Dorcas ............ 340
Horn, Elisha ............ 356
Horn, Jacob ............ 248
Horn, Jesse, (or Horne) ............ 248-264-275-384
Horn, John ............ 221-384
Horn, Richard ............ 356-384
Horn, Sherod ............ 356
Horn, William ............ 356
Hornby, Philip ............ 233-235
Hornby, William ............ 15-418
Hornsby, Philip ............ 96-384
Horsley, Valentine ............ 357
Horton, ............ 415-418
Horton, H. ............ 273
Horton, Hugh ............ 277
Horton, Isaac ............ 326-418-441-451
Horton, Sarah K. ............ 319
Hough, Samuel ............ 357-384
Houghton, Henry ............ 384
Houghton, Thomas ............ 384
Houghton, William ............ 311
House, John ............ 97-384
House, Lawrence ............ 208

# INDEX.

| | |
|---|---|
| Houseley, Weldon | 250 |
| Housley, John | 418-440 |
| Houslly, Newell | 400 |
| Housley, Weldon | 262 |
| Houston, James | 215-236-242-253-267-384 |
| Houston, James | 21-5236-242-253-267-384 |
| Houston, John | 60-236-262-384-441 |
| Houston, O. M. | 457 |
| Houston, Patrick | 193 |
| Houston, Samuel | 357-418-414 |
| Houston, William | 236-262 |
| Houstoun, George, (or Houston) | 418 |
| Houstoun, Gov. | 97 |
| Houstoun, James, (or Houston) | 15-18-93-418 |
| Houstoun, John, (or Houston) | 418 |
| Houton, John | 52 |
| Hovenden, Thomas | 418 |
| Howard, Abraham | 357 |
| Howard, Benj. | 232 |
| Howard, Francis | 398 |
| Howard, George F. | 451-455 |
| Howard, Hiram | 405 |
| Howard, John | 384-396 |
| Howard, Julius | 249-384 |
| Howard, R. | 273 |
| Howard, Rhesa | 263-384 |
| Howard, Soloman | 357-418-441 |
| Howard, Thomas | 418-441 |
| Howard, William | 94-384-396-401 |
| Howard, Willis | 357 |
| Howe, Robert | 15-216-384-418 |
| Howe, Robert, Lt. | 384 |
| Howel, John | 357 |
| Howell, Caleb | 9-15-94-241-384-400-418 |
| Howell, Daniel | 243-306-418 |
| Howell, David | 263-274 |
| Howell, Isaac | 460-463 |
| Howell, Jesse | 441 |
| Howell, John | 403-418 |
| Howell, John, Capt. | 418 |
| Howell, Miles | 418 |
| Howell, Mills, | 451 |
| Howell, Nathaniel | 262-264 |
| Howell, Philip | 357-418 |
| Howell, Samuel | 220 |
| Howell, Stephen, | 357-384 |
| Howell, Thomas | 306-335 |

## INDEX.

Howell, William ............ 306
Howington, William ............ 357
Howley, Richard ............ 63-384-418
Howsley, William ............ 94-384
Hubbard, Benjamin ............ 248-400
Hubbard, Bennet ............ 357
Hubbard, Elijah ............ 357
Hubbard, Elizabeth ............ 333
Hubbard, Jacob ............ 94-248-296
Hubbard, John ............ 95-97-221-248-384
Hubbard, Monaob ............ 357
Hubbard, Mourab ............ 384
Hubbard, Rich ............ 384
Hubbardm, Susannah ............ 337
Huckaby, Isham, or Hucaby) ............ 400-457
Huckaby, Philip ............ 323
Huckaby, William ............ 357
Hudgens, William ............ 323
Hudgins, Ansel ............ 357
Hudler, John ............ 357
Hudson, Archibald, ............ 398-405
Hudson, Cuthbert ............ 221-384
Hudson, David ............ 357-418-441
Hudson, Eliz ............ 316
Hudson, Hall ............ 400
Hudson, James ............ 93-216-286
Hudson, John ............ 339
Hudson, Joseph ............ 98-248
Hudson, Molly ............ 316
Hudson, Nathaniel, (or Nath) ............ 95-205-206-384
Hudson, Robert ............ 97-203-204-232-384
Hudson, Samuel ............ 95-98-249-384
Hudson, Ward ............ 398-405
Hudson, William ............ 384
Hudson, Zedick ............ 457
Hudspeth, Charles ............ 286
Heuy, ............ 418
Huey, Henry ............ 336
Huff, John ............ 398-405
Huff, Mathew ............ 323
Huffman, John ............ 418
Hugelly, Alexander ............ 220
Hughes, Nathaniel ............ 94
Huggens, Robert ............ 384
Huggins, Duc ............ 398
Huggins, Robert ............ 396
Hugh, Nich ............ 232

# INDEX.

| | |
|---|---|
| Hughes, John, T. | 460-463 |
| Hughts, Nathaniel, (or Nathan) | 15-97-384-418 |
| Hughts, Nicholas (or Hughs) | 211-211-236 |
| Hughes, William | 323-418 |
| Hughs, N. | 18 |
| Hughton, Elizabeth | 338 |
| Hugins, Daniel | 405 |
| Huie, James | 357 |
| Hukenbottom, Joseph | 228 |
| Huling, James | 323 |
| Hulsey, James | 357 |
| Hulsey, Jesse | 357-418-451 |
| Hulsey, Jinneus | 357 |
| Human, Alexander | 357-441 |
| Humphreys, Joseph | 400 |
| Hunt, Daniel | 357 |
| Hunt, Fitzmurice | 97-299-384-400 |
| Hunt, George | 357 |
| Hunt, James | 315-357 |
| Hunt, John. | 418-440 |
| Hunt, Liddleton, (or Littleton) | 357-418-441-451 |
| Hunt, Moses | 316 |
| Hunt, Turner | 357 |
| Hunt, William | 96-225-384-400-418 |
| Hunt, William, Jr. | 304 |
| Hunter, Elizabeth | 341 |
| Hunter, James | 4ˈ8 |
| Hunter, J. W. | 357 |
| Hunter, Miles | 218-384 |
| Hunter, Moses | 329 |
| Huntsman, MMichael | 398 |
| Huntsman, William | 97-384 |
| Hurley, David | 440 |
| Hurley, Joseph | 323-357-418-441 |
| Hurt, | 418 |
| Huskey, Rebecca | 324-347 |
| Huston, John | 357 |
| Hutcher, Capt. | 418 |
| Hutcherson, James | 320 |
| Hutchins, Edward | 418-441 |
| Hutchinson, James | 357-400 |
| Hutson, James | 384 |
| Hutson, Joseph | 97 |
| Hutto, Henry | 357-418-440 |
| Hynes, Robert | 286-288 |

## I

Igle, John ........................................................... 99-384
Inger, John ......................................................... 314
Ingram, John ....................................................... 314
Ingram, Richard .................................................. 99-384
Inlow, Sevastin ................................................... 99-304
Inman, Abednego .................................................. 418
Inman, Daniel .............................................. 357-459-463
  rdan ............................................................... 418
Inman, Joseph ...................................................... ⁿ2
Inman, Joshua, ........................................... 999-180-234-384
Inman, Joshua, Lt. ................................................ 384
Inman, Shadrack ............................................... 99-265-384
Inslow, Thomas .................................................... 357
Irelow, Levater .................................................... 384
Irvin, Alexander ................................................... 226
Irvin, H. ........................................................... 225
Irvin, Hugh ........................................................ 213
Irvin, Jared .................................................. 212-259
Irvin, John Lawson, ............................................... 213
Irvin, William .................................................... 212
Irvine, Alec ....................................................... 384
Irwin, Alexander ............................................... 99-418
Irvin, Alexander ................................................... 418
Irvine, William .................................................... 384
Irwin, Alec ........................................................ 384
Irwin, Hugh .................................................... 99-384
Irwin, Jared ............................................ 99-301-384-418-463
Irwin, John .................................................... 99-384
Irwin, John Lawson ............................................. 99-384
Irwin, William ................................................. 99-384
Iseley, Philip ............................................ 419-441-451
Island, Absolem ............................................. 99-207-384
Island, John ............................................ 99-235-252-384
Ivey, Ephrain ...................................................... 357
Izely, Philip ...................................................... 357

## J.

Jack James ......................................................... 419
Jack John ..................................................... 304-400
Jack, Margaret ..................................................... 316
Jack, Samuel ..................................... 16-100-206--266-280-287--291-419
Jackett, Simon ..................................................... 299
Jackson ............................................................ 419
Jackson, Col. ...................................................... 65

# INDEX.

Jackson, Maj. .......................................................... 419
Jackson, Abram ........................................................ 400
Jackson, Absolom ............................................... 103-258-384
Jackson, Benjamin ..................................................... 384
Jackson, Charles ........................................ 384-405-419-459-463
Jackson, Daniel ................................................... 103-384
Jackson, Drury .................................................... 103-384
Jackson, Eben, Sr. .................................................... 327
Jackson, Ebenezer ............................................... 357-419
Jackson, Edward ........................................... 357-419-442-451
Jackson, Henry .................................................... 103-384
Jackson, Isaac ................................................ 103-265-384
Jackson, Isaac, Col ........................................... 103-384-419
Jackson, James ........................... 15-104-234-384-400-419-463
Jackson, Jarvis, ...................................................... 419
Jackson, Jeremiah ..................................................... 357
Jackson, Jervis ...................................................... 398
Jackson, Job ................................................... 103-265-384
Jackson, John ................................................. 265-419-451
Jackson, Joseph ................................................... 104-384
Jackson, Mary ........................................................ 334
Jackson, Michael (or Machael( .................................... 145-384
Jackson, Moses ....................................................... 357
Jackson, Peter ................................................ 263-265-384
Jackson, Randall, (or Randal) ..................................... 262-263
Jackson, Randolph ............................................... 265-384
Jackson, Reuben ......................................... 104-200-273-384
Jackson, Robert .............................................. 357-384-419
Jackson, Samuel .................................................. 419-449
Jackson, Thomas ............................................. 100-287-384
Jackson, Timothy ..................................................... 275
Jackson, William ...................................... 103-106-200-249-384-442
Jacobs, Benjamin ..................................................... 357
James, Benjamin ...................................................... 298
James, George ........................................................ 358
James, Jonathan ...................................................... 419
James, Stephen ....................................................... 358
James, William ....................................................... 398
James, Williamson .................................................... 405
Jameson, David ................................................... 358-384
Jameson, William ................................................. 219-400
Jameson, William C. .................................................. 219
Jardine, Lewis ....................................................... 384
Jaret, Capt. ..................................................... 15-419
Jarrett, Devereaux ........................................... 248-384-419
Jarrett, Robert, (or Jarrett) ............. 100-105-222-265-282-384-419
Jarvell, Richard ..................................................... 314

| INDEX. | |
|---|---|
| Jarvis, Elisha | 358 |
| Jarvis, Nicholas, | 99-213 |
| Jarvis, Pat | 213-276-384 |
| Jefferson, James | 100-219 |
| Jeffries, James | 384 |
| Jenkins, Arthur | 104-266-384 |
| Jenkins, Benjamin | 100-252-254-278-307-384 |
| Jenkins, Francis | 384 |
| Jenkins, Francis, Jr. | 105 |
| Jenkins, James | 358 |
| Jenkins, John | 9-419 |
| Jenkins, John, Sr. | 451 |
| Jenkins, Lewis | 333-339-419-442-451-457 |
| Jenkins, Michael | 384 |
| Jenkins, Richard | 105-230-231-384 |
| Jenkins, Robert | 105-304-384 |
| Jenkins, Rosanna, | 329 |
| Jenkins, Starling, (or Sterling) | 105-323-384 |
| Jenkins, William | 419-442-451 |
| Jennings, Robert | 334 |
| Jent, Zachariah | 404 |
| Jeredeau, John | 398 |
| Jernigan, Mary | 339 |
| Jester, Levi | 328 |
| Jeter, Andrew | 358-419 |
| Jeter, Barnett | 358 |
| Jeter, Dinley | 358 |
| Jeter, Dudley | 384 |
| Jeter, Jo. | 215 |
| Jeter, Joseph | 105-216-246-284 |
| Jeter, Thomas | 419 |
| Jetts, Daniel | 358 |
| Jiles, Samuel | 419 |
| Jiles, Thomas | 419 |
| Jinkins, Berry, (or Jinkens) | 358-384 |
| Jinkins, James | 404 |
| Jinkins, Royal | 358-384 |
| Jlos, Horn | 404 |
| Jocey, Henry | 358 |
| Johne, Jonathan | 419-442 |
| John, Thomas | 384 |
| Johns, Ellic | 358 |
| Johns, John | 323 |
| Johnson, Abner | 457 |
| Johnson, Abraham | 323-398-404-419-442 |
| Johnson, Andrew | 358-419 |
| Johnson, Angus | 358 |

## Index. 559

Johnson, Bartholomew .................................................323-358
Johnson, Daniel ...................................................... 384
Johnson, Emanuel ..................................................... 358
Johnson, George ..................................................298-398
Johnson, Hardy ................................................329-419-442
Johnson, Henry ....................................................... 104
Johnson, Jacob ...................................................313-384
Johnson, James ......................................104-105-204-384-398-449
Johnson, Jesse ...............................................318-328-398-404
Johnson, John ...........................................104-358-384-396-401
Johnson, John Capt. .................................................. 384
Johnson, John H. ..................................................... 384
Johnson, John Hackner ................................................ 384
Johnson, John Hatcher ................................................ 104
Johnson, Jonathan ................................................419-442
Johnson, Joseph ..................................................419-451
Johnson, Joseph B. ...............................................323-358
Johnson, Jos. P. ...................................................... 323
Johnson, Joseph Payne ................................................ 442
Johnson, Laban ....................................................... 419
Johnson, Lewis ....................................................... 419
Johnson, Martha W. ................................................... 333
Johnson, Martin ..................................................358-404
Johnson, Nathan ...................................................... 400
Johnson, Richard .............................................100-301-384
Johnson, Rosannah .................................................... 339
Johnson, Sarah ....................................................... 336
Johnson, Stephen .................................................104-105-384-419
Johnson, Thomas .............................................104-105-202--209-384
Johnson, Wallis ..................................................398-404
Johnson, William ..............................15-46-105-384-398-404-419
Johnson, Willis ...................................................... 358
Johnston, Capt ....................................................... 419
Johnston, Caleb ...................................................... 265
Johnston, Daniel ..................................................... 266
Johnston Jacob ...................................................104-106
Johnston, James ..................................................315-384
Johnston, Jesse ...................................................... 222
Johnston, John .............................................265-289-304-384-419
Johnston, John B. ................................................313-358-384
Johnston, John H. .................................................... 248
Johnston, Mary ....................................................... 315
Johnston, Richard ................................................104-305
Johnston, Stephen .................................................... 419
Johnston, Thomas .................................................209-228
Johnston, William ...................18-205-219-248--265-273-283-287-297-384-385
Johnstone, William ................................................... 104

## INDEX.

Toice, John .................................................................. 358
Joiner, Abraham ........................................................ 358
Joiner, Assalom ......................................................... 328
Joiner, Benjamin ............................................. 104-213-339-385
Joiner, Jesse ............................................................ 358
Joiner, Jonathan ....................................................... 449
Joiner, Sarah ........................................................... 100
Joiner, Thomas .................................................. 100-104-385
Jojes, Joseph ........................................................... 419
Jonathan, John .......................................................... 222
Jones, (son of Noble Winberly) ......................................... 419
Jones, A. ................................................................ 221
Jones, Abraham ................................................. 100-102-385-419
Jones, Abraham, Lt. Col. ................................................ 419
Jones, Abraham P. .............................................. 102-419-442
Jones, Alithea Anderson ........................................ 221-244-247
Jones, Ambrose .......................................................... 202
Jones, Batt ..................................................... 297-358-419-463
Jones, Benj. .................................................... 220-249-385
Jones, Benjamin, Jr. .................................................... 103
Jones, Benjamin, Sr. .................................................... 103
Jones, Charles .......................................................... 400
Jones, David ................................................... 103-219-228-385
Jones, Edward .............................................. 103-385-398-404-419
Jones, Elias ......................................................... 266-385
Jones, Fanny ............................................................ 316
Jones, Fred ............................................................. 239
Jones, Frederick .............................................. 103-265-385
Jones, Gabriel .......................................................... 328
Jones, Harrison, ............................................... 358-419.442
Jones, Henry ................................................... 106-385-419
Jones, Hugh ...................................................... 103-385
Jones, Isaac .................................................... 358-419
Jones, Isham ............................................................ 358
Jones, James ..................................... 102-221-236-247-297-385-397-398-419
Jones, Jesse ..................................... 102-227-265-275-280-308-385-396-401
Jones, John ....................................... 103-199-211-236-261-265-385-419-463
Jones, John, Maj. ............................................... 385-419
Jones, Jonathan ............................................ 103-236-265-385
Jones, Joseph ........................................................... 404
Jones, Josiah ........................................................... 358
Jones, Mark ............................................................. 385
Jones, Mary ............................................................. 336
Jones, Mathew ..................................................... 102-385
Jones, Michael ................................................ 102-385-419
Jones, Moses ..................................................... 358-419
Jones, Nancy ............................................................ 340

INDEX. 561

Jones, Nathan .................................................102-236-265-385
Jones, Nimrod ........................................................ 358
Jones, Noble Wymberly, Dr. ..........................................419-463
Jones, Peter ......................................................... 102
Jones, Philip .............................................102-243-265-297-385
Jones, Reuben ........................................................ 70
Jones, Richard ....................................................398-404
Jones, Robert ...................................................102-230-385
Jones, Seaborn ...............................100-102-105-204-206-221-385-463
Jones, Simeon .................................................102-220-385
Jones, Simon ......................................................... 220
Jones, Solomon ....................................................419-442
Jones, Stephen ....................................................... 358
Jones, Thomas ...............................................248-287-385-442
Jones, William ............198-199-242-266-284-287-289-305-316-385-419-442-451-455
Jones, William, Sr. .................................................334-451
Jordan, Abner ........................................................ 320
Jordan, Aven ......................................................... 358
Jordan, Benjamin ..................................................... 332
Jordan, Charles, Sr. .................................................. 334
Jordan, Dempsey ............................................105-305-419-442
Jordan, Eliz ......................................................... 451
Jordan, Emanuel ...................................................... 403
Jordan, Fountain ............................................358-419-442-451
Jordan, Jacob ...................................................99-100-385
Jordan, Jinsv ........................................................ 385
Jordan, Job .......................................................... 337
Jordan, John .................................................20-358-385-463
Jordan, Lewis ....................................................287-385
Jordan, Mattburn ..................................................... 320
Jordan, Matthew ...................................................... 419
Jordan, Miles .....................................................419-442
Jordan, S. ........................................................... 385
Jordan, Samue .................................................99-385-400
Jordan, Starling ..................................................... 105
Jordan, W. ........................................................... 332
Jordan, William ............................................15-18-335-358-385
Josling, Daniel ..................................................105-385
Jourdan, Baxton ...................................................... 385
Jourdan, Charles ..................................................... 385
Jourdan, Edmond ...................................................... 358
Jourdan, Elizabeth ................................................... 331
Jourdan, William ..................................................... 419
Jourdine, Charles .................................................... 419
**Jourdon, John** ..................................................... 419
Joyce, Alexander .................................................358-385
Judkins, Xach ........................................................ 385

# INDEX.

Judton, Paul ........................................................ 419
Justice, Aaron ...................................................... 358
Justice, Dempsey ............................................ 105-209
Justice, Densey .................................................... 385
Justice, Isaac ................................................. 265-385

## K.

Kair, Henry ........................................................ 234
Kar, Henry ......................................................... 43
Karr, Henry ............................................... 107-385-419
Kasey, Stephen, Jr. (or Kazey) ............................. 106-385
Keating, Edward ............................................... 54-419
Keelock, Ebenezer ................................................ 108
Keen, Elizabeth ................................................... 326
Keesey, Stephen ................................................... 385
Kehela, Christopher ......................................... 419-442
Keiloch, John ..................................................... 108
Keith, David ...................................................... 107
Keith, John ............................................... 419-442-451
Keith, Samuel ..................................................... 385
Keith, Samuel, Jr. ................................................ 108
Keith, Samuel, Sr. ................................................ 107
Kelan, James ............................................... 419-442
Kell, Archibald, ............................................. 240-385
Kell, James ............................................... 419-442-451
Kell, John ................................................... 204-419
Kell, Robert .............................................. 419-442-451
Kelland, James .................................................... 358
Kelley, Giles ............................................ 419-451-457
Kelley, Jacob ..................................................... 385
Kelley, John .............................................. 106-107-323
Kelley, Lloyd ............................................ 358-419-442
Kelley, Thomas ........................................... 106-279-385
Kelley, William (or Kelly) ...................... 107-108-419-442-451
Kellum, George ............................................... 323-339
Kelly, David ...................................................... 213
Kelly, Edward ........................................ 106-213-341-385
Kelly, Jacob ................................................ 106-305
Kelly, James ...................................................... 198
Kelly, John ........................................... 299-302-305-385
Kelly, Thomas ............................................... 218-232
Kelly, William ........................................ 213-264-266-298-315
Kelly, William Sr. ........................................... 266-275
Kelsey, Hugh .............................................. 107-385
Kelsey, Thomas ................................................... 107
Kemp, James ...................................................... 385

| | |
|---|---|
| Kemp, Jonathan | 26 |
| Kemp, Joseph | 287-385 |
| Kemp, Joseph, Jr. | 107 |
| Kemp, Thomas | 107-239-385 |
| Kemp, William | 265-266-287-358-419 |
| Kendall, Eliz. P. | 339 |
| Kendall, Henry | 459-463 |
| Kendall, James Key | 325 |
| Kendall, Jeremiah | 108-200-385-459 |
| Kendall, John | 290 |
| Kendrick, Abel | 358 |
| Kendrick, Hezekiah | 106-396-305-385 |
| Kendrick, John | 106-420-442 |
| Kendrick, Nathaniel | 106-266 |
| Kendrick, Thomas | 385 |
| Kenedy, John | 107 |
| Kennady, John | 385 |
| Kennan, David | 398 |
| Kennedy, John | 108-287-305 |
| Kennedy, Seth | 359 |
| Kenny, Ed. | 400 |
| Kenrick, James | 400 |
| Kent, Charles | 420 |
| Kent, Daniel | 358 |
| Kent, Henry | 358 |
| Kent, John | 313-339 |
| Kent, Peter | 323 |
| Kent, Sampson | 359 |
| Kent, Thomas W. | 358 |
| Kerlin, Eliz | 316 |
| Kernell, William | 442 |
| Kerr, David | 420-442 |
| Kerr, Henry | 420-442 |
| Kersey, Stephen | 108-385 |
| Kerwel, William (or Kernwell) | 420 |
| Kerzy, Stephen, Jr. | 108 |
| Keslerson, Nancy | 337 |
| Ketley, Daniel | 385 |
| Key, William B. | 316-420-442 |
| Kidd, James H. | 420-442 |
| Kidd, William | 420-442 |
| Kidd, William, Sr. | 451 |
| Kielock, Ebenezer | 385 |
| Kielock, John | 385 |
| Kieth, John | 256-400 |
| Kieth, Lem | 400 |
| Kilgore, James M. | 455 |

# INDEX.

Kilgore, John .................................................. 107-205-266-385
Kilgore, Ralph .................................................. 107-225-385
Kilgore, Ralph, Sr. .................................................. 107
Kilgore, Robert .................................................. 108-231-385
Kilgore, Robert, Sr. .................................................. 108
Kilgore, William .................................................. 107-266
Killcreast, Robert .................................................. 43
Kilpatrick, Thomas .................................................. 106-107-287-385
Kilpatrick, William .................................................. 385
Kimbell, David .................................................. 359
Kimble, Charles .................................................. 297
Kimbo, John .................................................. 273
Kimbrey, John .................................................. 50
Kimbrough .................................................. 235
Kimbrough, John .................................................. 108-214-385
Kimbrough, William .................................................. 214-286
Kimbrough, William, Jr .................................................. 107
Kimbrough, William, Sr. .................................................. 107
Kindal, William .................................................. 359
Kindle, Henry .................................................. 359
Kinebrew, Jacob .................................................. 385
King, .................................................. 463
King, Elisah .................................................. 420
King, Joel .................................................. 108
King, John .................................................. 18-106-216-295-305-318-337-385-400-420-442-451
King, John, Lt. .................................................. 420
King, Mary .................................................. 338
King, Richard .................................................. 359-420-442-451-457
King, Richard, Sr. .................................................. 323
King, Tandy .................................................. 420
King, Thomas .................................................. 322-359-420-442
King, William .................................................. 328-359
Kinnebrew, Jacob .................................................. 106-295
Kirk, John .................................................. 420
Kirkham, Joseph .................................................. 108-287
Kirkland, Joseph .................................................. 287
Kirklin, Mary .................................................. 336
Kitchens, John .................................................. 385
Kitchens, Zachariah .................................................. 359
Kitley, Daniel .................................................. 396
Kitt, Henry .................................................. 359
Kitts, John .................................................. 107-385
Kitty, Daniel .................................................. 420
Kneal, Henry .................................................. 213
Kneal, Patrick, (or Kneel) .................................................. 107-213-385
Knell, Patrick .................................................. 18
Kniel, Patrick .................................................. 420

INDEX. 565

Knight, Aaron ......... 359
Knight, Betahny ......... 336
Knight, Elisha ......... 420-442
Knight, Joel ......... 455
Knight, Thomas ......... 359
Knowles, Edmond ......... 340
Knowlman, A. ......... 359
Knox, Samuel ......... 420-442
Kunckles, Benjamin ......... 279
Kolb, Peter (or Kobb) ......... 359-420-442
Kupert, John ......... 238

## L.

Lacey, Noah ......... 359
Lackey, Thomas ......... 109-113-402
Lackey, William ......... 113-385
Lacy, John ......... 297
Lacy, Sarah ......... 329
Ladd, Amos ......... 359
Ladson, Maj. ......... 420
Lagardare, Isaac ......... 420
Lagran, John U., (or N.) ......... 420-451
Lain, William ......... 420
Lamar, Basil ......... 112-222-420
Lamar, Benjamin ......... 112
Lamar, Duke ......... 112
Lamar, James ......... 385-396-401
Lamar, Joel ......... 112
Lamar, John ......... 229-307-359-420-463
Lamar, Luke ......... 385
Lamar, Philip ......... 43
Lamar, Samuel ......... 112-237-385-402
Lamar, Thomas ......... 112-268-277-288-305-385
Lamar, William ......... 112-237
Lamar, Z. ......... 309
Lamar, Zachariah ......... 112-254-308-420
Lamar, Zech ......... 385
Lamb, Abraham ......... 121-204-267-385
Lamb, Bethial ......... 216-385
Lamb, Isaac ......... 359-385
Lamb, Thomas ......... 385
Lamb, William ......... 420
Lambath, William ......... 420
Lambert, Elisha ......... 359
Lambert, George ......... 359
Lambert, James ......... 28-359-420

## Index.

Lambert, John ..........420-443
Lambert, Sarah ..........318-328
Lambert, Thomas ..........359
Lambert, William ..........115-359
Lambeth, James ..........301
Lambeth, William ..........114-385-420
Lambreech, John ..........115
Lambrick, John, (or Lamback) ..........385
Lambrick, William ..........18-420
Lampkin, Sampson ..........359
Lamsden, Jeremiah ..........359
Lancaster, Levi ..........109-385
Lancaster, Rowland ..........18-154-222-224-420
Lancaster, William ..........18-109-300-385
Land, John ..........267-420
Landeford, John ..........420
Landers, Abram ..........257-266
Landers, Jacob ..........199-212
Landers, John ..........420-443
Landers, Taprell, ..........359
Landford, James ..........404
Landrum, James ..........398-404
Landrum, John ..........114-323-328-385
Landrum, Josiah ..........398-404
Landrum, Thomas ..........420-443
Landrum, Timothy ..........359
Landrum, William ..........398-404
Landrum, Zachariah ..........414
Lane, Abraham, S. ..........359
Lane, Charles ..........398-403
Lane, James ..........18-109-385
Lane, Joseph ..........15-18-114-385-420
Lane, Thomas ..........109-385
Lane, William ..........109-385-420
Lang, John ..........277-385
Langford, James ..........398
Langford, Joseph ..........263-264-267
Langford, Joshia ..........267
Langford, Moses ..........267
Langford, Wyatt, ..........400
Langham, James ..........420-442
Langham, William ..........359
Langley, James ..........359
Langley, John ..........420-443
Langley, Nathaniel ..........359
Langston, Samuel ..........109-115-234-385
Langsworthy, Ed. ..........385

# INDEX. 567

| | |
|---|---|
| Langsworthy, Edward | 420 |
| Lanier, Benjamin | 111-385 |
| Lanier, Clement | 111-306-385 |
| Laniel, Lemuel | 109 |
| Lanier, Lewis | 340 |
| Lanier, Samuel | 385 |
| Lankford, John | 113 |
| Lankford, Jonathan | 113 |
| Lankford, Joseph | 113-385 |
| Lankford, Josiah | 18-420 |
| Lankford, Moses | 18-113-385 |
| Lankford, Parish | 115 |
| Lankston, Samuel | 385 |
| Lansford, Elizabeth | 335 |
| Lantern, Thomas, (or Lanton) | 114-385 |
| Lard, Robert | 443 |
| Lard, William | 336 |
| Laremore, John (Laramor, Laramore or Lamar) | 113-214-235-285 |
| Larinia, W. | 321 |
| Larisey, William | 359 |
| Larkey, William | 114 |
| Laroach, Lt. | 420 |
| Larvin, John | 359 |
| Lasbee, Elizabeth (or Laseby) | 320 |
| Lasley, Thomas | 323 |
| Lassiter, Hansell | 359 |
| Latham, Amos | 420-442 |
| Latta, David | 359 |
| Lauderdale, John, (or Lauderdeal) | 113-240-385 |
| Laurns, John | 420 |
| Lavein, Peter | 420 |
| Law, George | 111-241-398 |
| Law, William | 420 |
| Lawin, John | 385 |
| Lawler, John | 385 |
| Lawless, Agnes | 327 |
| Lawless John | 359 |
| Lawrence, John | 337-359-420-443-452 |
| Lawson, Andrew | 110-267-385 |
| Lawson, Hugh | 40-41-46-47-48-109-110-385-120-442 |
| Lawson, John | 110-241-385-420 |
| Lawson, John, Jr. | 110 |
| Lawson, John, Sr. | 323-385-387 |
| Lawson, Martha | 331 |
| Lawson, Roger | 110-267-301-385 |
| Lawson, Roger, Jr. | 110-111 |
| Lawson, Roger, Sr. | 385 |

## INDEX.

Lawson, Thomas .................................................. 110-267-385
Lawson, Thompson ..................................................... 110-385
Lay, ,Capt. ............................................................... 318
Lay, William ..................................................... 398-404
Lazarus, N. ............................................................. 18-420
Lazarus, Nicholas ............................................... 108-305
Lazarus, Nicodemus ................................................... 385
Lea, Wiliam ..................................................... 359-385
Leach, Burdett ......................................................... 338
Leadbitter, Drury ...................................................... 420
Leak, Judith ........................................................... 321
Leansley, Thomas ...................................................... 338
Leapham, Abraham ............................................ 268-273-277
Leapham, Frederick ............................................... 115-385
Leapham, Moses ................................................... 217-272
Leath John ........................................................ 112-385
Leathers, Samuel ...................................................... 359
LeConte, Guillaume ..................................................... 74
Le Conte, James A. ..................................................... 74
LeConte, John .......................................................... 74
LeConte, John Eton .................................................... 420
LeConte, J. N. Dr. ..................................................... 74
LeConte, Joseph .................................................... 74-420
Leconte, William ................................................... 74-420
LeConte, William L. .................................................. 6-74
Ledbetter, Drury ...................................................... 242
Ledbetter, Frederick ......................................... 108-288-385
Ledbetter, George ..................................................... 420
Ledbetter, Henry ...................................................... 398
Ledbetter, John ........................... 113-115-237-267-288-290-385
Ledbetter, Lewis ...................................................... 242
Ledbetter, Richard ........................................... 420-452-457
Ledbetter, Robert ..................................................... 420
LeDuc. John ........................................................... 420
Lee, Andrew ....................................................... 113-385
Lee, Burwell ...................................................... 420-443
Lee, David ............................................................ 359
Lee, Greenbury ........................................................ 420
Lee, Henry ............................................................ 463
Lee, John ......................................................... 307-360
Lee, Joshua .................................................. 226-385-400-449
Lee, M. ............................................................... 320
Lee, Margaret ..................................................... 324-347
Lee, Sampson, ......................................................... 360
Lee, Thomas ........................................................... 420
Lee, Timothy ...................................................... 113-385
Lee, William .......................................................... 307

## INDEX.

| | |
|---|---|
| Leech, Burdett | 420-443 |
| Lees, Capt. | 420 |
| Leggett, Abner (or Legett) | 112-114-201-237-385 |
| Leggett, John (or Legett) | 108-114-237-267-305-385-402 |
| Legit, James | 398 |
| LeGrand, John M. | 331 |
| Leigh, Ansella, | 398 |
| Leigh, Ansoln | 403 |
| Leigh, Benjamin | 360 |
| Leitch, David | 222 |
| Lench, John | 385 |
| Lenoir, Capt. | 420 |
| Leonard, Elijah | 109-267 |
| Leonard, John | 400 |
| Leopham, Frederick | 420 |
| Lepham, Moses | 212 |
| Leshley, Edmond | 260 |
| Lesley, James | 256 |
| Lesley, William | 337-338-420-443 |
| Leslie, Joseph | 114-230-385 |
| Lester, Thomas | 18-259-267-420 |
| Letham, Capt. | 420 |
| Lett, Capt. | 420 |
| Lett, Hannah | 108 |
| Lett, James | 108 |
| Lett, Rembern | 386 |
| Lett, Reuben | 113-232-234-306-386 |
| Levar, Mary | 330 |
| Levay, George | 420-452 |
| Leven, Richard | 115-383 |
| Leverett, Aaron | 109-110-386 |
| Leverett, Cealey | 330 |
| Leverett, Henry | 110-199-386 |
| Leverett, John | 110-267-386 |
| Leverett, Richard | 360 |
| Leverett, Robert | 110-386 |
| Levins, Richard | 114-305 |
| Lewis | 420 |
| Lewis, Benjamin | 110-111-298-386-420 |
| Lewis, Benjamin Thomas | 110 |
| Lewis, Catherine | 328 |
| Lewis, Celia | 339 |
| Lewis, David | 111-298-420 |
| Lewis, David, Jr. | 111-386 |
| Lewis, Elizer | 111 |
| Lewis, Elijah | 219-242-306-420 |
| Lewis, Evan | 15-111-306-386-420 |

Lewis, George .................................................... 360-420
Lewis, Gheza ..................................................... 386
Lewis, Jacob .................................................... 111-301-386
Lewis, James ................................................ 111-386-420-442
Lewis, James N. .................................................. 420
Lewis, Joel .................................................. 111-214-305-306-386
Lewis, John .................................................... 225-421-451
Lewis, Jonathan Rees ............................................. 110
Lewis, Joseph .................................................. 242-360-421
Lewis, Josiah .................................................. 110-421
Lewis, Joshua .................................................... 386
Lewis, Judah .................................................... 360-386
Lewis, Kesiah .................................................... 111
Lewis, Merriwether ............................................... 421
Lewis, Nancy ..................................................... 326
Lewis, Nathaniel ................................................. 336
Lewis, Peter ..................................................... 360
Lewis, Susannah .................................................. 110
Lewis, Susannah, Jr. ............................................. 110
Lewis, Thomas .................................................. 111-205-206-260-286
Lewis, Thomas, Jr. .............................................. 111-421
Lewis, Thomas Sr. ................................................ 111
Lewis, William ................................................... 386-400
Lewis, William, Jr. .............................................. 306
Lewis, William, Sr. .............................................. 306
Liddell, .......................................................... 421
Liddell, Capt. .................................................... 318
Liddell, Sheppard ................................................. 319
Liddell, William ................................................. 421-443
Lile, Ephraim .................................................... 452
Liles, Ephraim ................................................... 330
Liles, Henry ..................................................... 24
Linby, James ..................................................... 421
Linby, Thomas .................................................... 386
Linby, William ................................................... 421
Linch, John ...................................................... 115
Linden, Joseph ................................................... 114
Linden, Mary ..................................................... 114
Lindon, Joseph ................................................... 312
Lindow, John ..................................................... 386
Lindsay, ......................................................... 421
Lindsay, Dennis ............................................ 108-112-114-267-275-386-421
Lindsay, James ................................................... 305-400
Lindsey, Isaac, Sr. .............................................. 340
Lindsey, Jacob, Sr. .............................................. 323
Lindsey, James ................................................... 360-421
Lindsey, John ................................................ 114-323-386-431-442

INDEX. 571

| | |
|---|---|
| Lindsey, William | 360 |
| Line, Denis | 421 |
| Lineby, William | 386 |
| Liner, Christopher | 449 |
| Linn, Curtis | 112-113-266-267-386 |
| Linn, curtis | 102-113-266 |
| Linn, John | 109-112-215-266-267-272-301-386 |
| Linn, Curtis | 112-113-266-267-386 |
| Linn, Sally, | 334 |
| Linn, Thomas | 295-386 |
| Linley, Thomas | 396 |
| Linson, J. | 18-421 |
| Linteh, J. | 18 |
| Lintch, James | 421 |
| Linton, John | 109 |
| Linvill, William, (or Linville) | 421-443-452 |
| Lions, William | 315 |
| Lipham, Capt. | 421 |
| Lipham, Frederick | 421 |
| Lisle Ephraim | 421 |
| Lisle, Romande | 16 |
| Lithgoe, Andrew, (or Lithgowe) | 268-306 |
| Lithgoe, Robert | 267 |
| Lithgrove, Andrew | 386 |
| Lithgrove, Robert | 386 |
| Little, Archibald | 109-386 |
| Little, David | 112-386 |
| Little, James | 113-248-294-296-386-421 |
| Little, William | 113-421-443 |
| Little, Wm. Sr. | 329 |
| Littleton, Charles | 449 |
| Litton, John | 338 |
| Live, Dennis | 386 |
| Liverman, Conrad | 360-421 |
| Livingston, William | 113-386-421 |
| Lloyd, Benjamin | 421 |
| Lloyd, Edward | 421-442 |
| Lloyd, Mary | 335 |
| Lloyd, Moses | 404 |
| Locket, Soloman | 360 |
| Lockett, James | 421-443 |
| Lockett, Thomas | 398 |
| Lockhart, Benjamin | 229-386 |
| Lockhart, Charlotte | 332 |
| Lockhart, Isaac | 114-226-386 |
| Lockhart, James | 315-333 |
| Lockhart, Joel | 386 |

Lockhart, Polly ........................................................ 324-347
Lockhart, Richard ..................................................... 305-400
Locky, Thomas ........................................................... 386
Loftin, Cornelius, (or Lofton) ........................................ 113-386
Logan, Philip .............................................. 115-288-386-421-442
Loggins, James ............................................................ 360
Lokey, William ............................................................. 360
Long, David ............................................................ 112-386
Long Evans ................................................................. 421
Long, Henry ............................................................ 217-224
Long, John ................................................................. 114
Long, Louisa ............................................................... 340
Long, Martha ............................................................... 334
Long, Michael .............................................................. 303
Long, Nicholas ............................................................. 289
Long, Robert ........................................................... 113-230
Longbridge, Susanna ........................................................ 320
Longford, Capt. ............................................................ 421
Longstreet, Daniel .................................................... 306-386-400
Longstreet, William ................................................... 398-400-403
Lord, Robert ............................................................... 421
Lord, William ...................................................... 306-317-360-400-421
Lorn, Thomas ............................................................... 115
Loud, John ................................................................. 400
Love, ..................................................................... 421
Love, James ................................................................ 360
Love, John ................................................................. 421
Love, Philip ............................................................... 421
Love, Thomas .......................................................... 421-442-452
Love, William ......................................................... 386-421-457
Lovejoy, Jemina ............................................................ 326
Loving, Thomas ........................................................ 360-386
Low, P. ..................................................................... 18
Lowe, Aquila .......................................................... 360-386
Lowe, Beverly .......................................................... 111-386
Lowe, Daniel, (or Low) ................................................ 109-268-386
Lowe, George, (or Low) ................................................. 386-403
Lowe, Isaac ....................................................... 110-111-243-284-288
Lowe, Isaac, Jr. ........................................................... 386
Lowe, Isaac, Sr. ....................................................... 110-386
Lowe, Jesse ................................................................ 386
Lowe, John ......................................................... 111-226-234-306
Lowe, John F. .............................................................. 386
Lowe, John, Tolson ......................................................... 239
Lowe, Joseph ............................................................... 386
Lowe, Obediah, (or Obadiah) ........................................... 111-127-386

# Index.

Lowe, Philip ................................................. 15-57-109-386-421
Lowe, Ralph ................................................. 360-386
Lowe, William ............................................... 396-421
Lowery ...................................................... 421
Lowery, Mr. ................................................. 457
Lowery, Levi ................................................ 360
Lowery, Simeon .............................................. 360
Lowne, William .............................................. 15-421
Lowns, William .............................................. 79
Lowrey, Levi ................................................ 443-452
Lowry, Levi ................................................. 421
Loyd, Benjamin .............................................. 360
Loyd, James ................................................. 360-386-396
Loyd, John .................................................. 386-396
Loyd, Moses ................................................. 398
Loyd, Thomas ................................................ 360-386
Lucas, J. ................................................... 18
Lucas, James ................................................ 109-386
Lucas, John ................................................. 15-360-386-421
Lucas, Mary ................................................. 337
Lucas, William .............................................. 114-297-386
Luker, Luraney .............................................. 331
Lumpkin, Dickson ............................................ 360
Lumpkin, George ............................................. 28-297
Lumpkin, John ............................................... 360
Lumpkin, Philip ............................................. 421-443
Lumpkin, William ............................................ 398-404
Lunday, Theophilus .......................................... 112-386
Lunday, Thomas .............................................. 386
Lundy, Theophilus ........................................... 114
Lunn, C. .................................................... 18-421
Lynch, Isaac ................................................ 317
Lynch, John ................................................. 213
Lynn, J. .................................................... 18-421
Lynn, John .................................................. 216
Lynn, Thomas ................................................ 110
Lyon, William ............................................... 421-457
Lyons, John ................................................. 15-421
Lyons, William .............................................. 421-443
Lytton, John ................................................ 237

## Mc

McAlphin, Alexander ......................................... 269
McBride, Edward ............................................. 18-133-386
McBurnett, Daniel ........................................... 134-308-386
McCain, John ................................................ 386

## Index.

McCain, Thomas .................................................128-240-296-386
McCall, Maj. ............................................................................... 299
McCall, Hugh ........................................................................... 421
McCall, James .......................................................................... 421
McCall, John ........................................................................360-386
McCall, Richard ....................................................................18-421
McCall, Thomas .....................................134-207-209-308-335-386
McCaller, James ..................................................................360-386
McCalphin, Alexander ...........................................................119-386
McCalvey, John ....................................................................129-386
McCalvey, William .................................................................... 386
McCance, David .................................................................421-443
McCardell, Cornelius ............................................................129-245-386
McCarry, Edward ..................................................................... 249
McCartey, Daniel ..................................................................129-133
McCartey, John ....................................................................... 133
McCartey, Daniel ..................................................................129-133
McCarthy, John ..................................................................133-289-386-421
McCarthy, John Drum ............................................................... 289
McCartie, John ........................................................................ 276
McCartie, Sherod .................................................................... 398
McCartin, Sharod .................................................................... 404
McCarty, Daniel ...................................................................... 386
McCarty, Ebenezer ................................................................... 421
McCarty, John ........................................................................ 421
McCay, Charles ....................................................................... 421
McCay, James ......................................................................... 119
McCelvey, Wm. ....................................................................... 134
McCheer, John ........................................................................ 360
McCibben, Margarette .............................................................. 336
McCirce, Rowell ...................................................................... 398
McClain, John .....................................................................334-360
McClain, Mary ........................................................................ 333
McClain, Nicholas ................................................................... 129
McClane, Ephraim ................................................................... 360
McCelland, John ...................................................................... 421
McCelland, McClain ................................................................. 360
McClelland, Samuel ................................................................. 421
McClendon, Isaac ...............................................................122-269-386
McClendon, Isaac, Sr. ............................................................... 386
McClendon, Jacob ................................................................119-386
McClendon, Joseph .................................................................. 386
McClendon, Samuel ................................................................. 119
McClendon, Simeon ................................................................. 386
McClendon, Travis ................................................................... 133
McCeskey, ............................................................................. 452
McCleskey, James ................................................................421-443

INDEX.   575

McCleur, John .................................................. 421
McCling, John .................................................. 386
McCloud, Norman ............................................... 315
McClung, John .................................................. 116
McClure, John .................................................. 421
McClure, Sampson ............................................... 128
McCollan, Daniel ............................................... 452
McCollins, David ............................................... 421
McCollouch, Samuel ............................................. 203
McCollough, Jacob .............................................. 386
McCollum, Daniel ............................................... 332
McCollum, Margaret ............................................. 329
McComeson, John ................................................ 452
McConery, Katherine ............................................ 315
McConnell, John ................................................ 400
McCordell, Cornelius ........................................... 240
McCorkle, Archibald ............................................ 360
McCormack,, Thomas ............................................. 421
McCormick, Benjamin ..............................133-214-335-270-386-449
McConnicly, John ..........................................133-386
McCormick, Joseph .........................................134-386
McCormick, Thomas .................................134-269-323-386-452
McCourney, Angus, Sr. .......................................... 315
McCowen, Daniel ...........................................128-295
McCoy, Capt. ................................................... 421
McCoy, Daniel .............................................294-386
McCoy, James, ................................................. 127
McCoy, Samuel .............................................421-452
McCracken, William ............................................. 400
McCree, Roswell ................................................ 404
McCullers, William ....................................360-380-444
McColloch, Patrick, ............................................ 270
McColloch, Samuel .....................................121-203-295
McCulloch, John ................................................ 386
McCullough, Jacob .............................................. 360
McCullough, John ..........................................128-421
McCullough, John, Jr. .......................................... 421
McCullough, John, Sr. .......................................... 421
McCullough, Patrick, ......................................128-386
McCullough, Samuel ........................................128-386
McCullough, Samuel-Sergt. ...................................... 386
McCullough, Seth ............................................... 421
McCullough, William ............................................ 421
McCumber, Capt, (or Macomber) .................................. 421
McCurdy, David R. .............................................. 455
McCurdy, John .............................................421-444
McCutchen, James, (or McCutchin) ..........................386-400

INDEX.

McCutchen, Jane ..................................................... 330
McCutchins, Joseph ................................................. 246
McCuthan, Joseph ............................................... 295-360
McDade, John, (or McDodde) ........................... 339-421-443-452
McDaniel, Daniel .................................................... 318
McDaniel, Elizabeth ................................................. 339
McDaniel, Jacob .................................................... 360
McDaniel, Jeremiah ................................................. 360
McDaniel, Tokiah ................................................... 127
McDaniel, William .................................................. 421
McDerman, Joseph .................................................. 361
McDerment, Joseph .............................................. 421-444
McDonald, Charles .................................................. 421
McDonald, Hugh ................................................ 127-386
McDonald, Isam .................................................... 361
McDonald, James ................................................... 361
McDonald, John .................................... 308-317-338-400-421-443
McDonald, Tekiah ................................................... 386
McDonald, William ............................................... 15-421
McDoreman, Bailes (McDorman) ................................ 398-404
McDoreman, Bailes, ................................................ 398
McDougal, Alexander ........................................... 128-386
McDouglas, Alexander .............................................. 208
McDowell, Maj. ..................................................... 421
McDowell, Charles .................................................. 421
McDowell, James ........................................... 18-116-134-386
McDowell, Robert ......................................... 361-421-443-452
McDowell, Thomas ........................... 85-128-216-217-266-288-386
McDuff, William .................................................... 361
McDuffy, John .................................................. 134-386
McElduff, Daniel ................................................... 449
McEldufy, Daniel ................................................... 421
McElhannon, John .................................................. 444
McElhenry, John .................................................... 386
McElroy, Needham .............................................. 398-404
McErwin, Thomas ................................................... 398
McEwen, Thomas ................................................... 404
McFail, Judith ..................................................... 339
McFall, John ....................................................... 403
McFarland, Capt. ................................................... 421
McFarland, Andrew ................................................. 421
McFarland, James ......................... 93-212-236-279-280-285
McFarland, James H. ................................................ 361
McFarland, John ..................................... 211-221-213-273-386
McFarland, John, Jr. ............................................ 117-386
McFarland, Robert ............................................. 320-361
McField, William ................................................... 127

# INDEX. 577

McGamery, John ................................................................. 314
McGarr, Cuen ................................................................... 270
McGarr, Owen ................................................................... 275
McGarry, Robt. .......................................................123-269-386
McGary, Ed. .................................................................... 386
McGary, Edward ............................................................128-134
McGeary, Robert ............................................................128-386
McGee, Hugh .................................................................133-386
McGee, Lewis ................................................................133-386
McGee, Reuben .................................................................. 361
McGee, Shadroch ................................................................ 400
McGee, Thomas ..............................................................133-386
McGhee, Thomas ................................................................ 118
McGeehee, Thomas ............................................................... 270
McGeehee, William .............................................................. 274
McGehee, Lewis ................................................................. 232
McGehee, Thomas ................................................................ 230
McGehee, William ............................................................... 232
McGenty, Robert ............................................................128-386
McGetton, Vance ................................................................ 216
McGill, John ...............................................................127-386
McGhee, Thomas ............................................................118-386
McGilton, James ...................................18-120-234-266-269-386
McGilton, Vance ........................................................18-120-386
McGinnis, ——— Capt. ........................................................... 317
McGlamory, John ................................................................ 361
McGowen, ——— Lt. .............................................................. 422
McGowen, Joseph ................................................................ 422
McGoy, Ann ..................................................................... 335
McGree, Thomas ................................................................. 242
McGregor, Alexander ............................................................ 215
MMcGruder, Merrian O. .......................................................... 386
McGruder, Ninian Offitt ........................................................ 288
McGruder, William .............................................................. 326
McGruder, Zadock .........................................................117-271-386
McGuire, Anderson .............................................................. 315
McHaney, Terry, (or McHancy) .........................................18-116-386-422
McHarland, James ...........................................................265-268
McIlhenny, John ................................................................ 122
McIntire, John ...........................................................361-422443
McIntosh, Gen .................................................................. 286
McIntosh, George ............................................................... 422
McIntosh, John ..................................9-14-18-215-361-386-422
McIntosh, John, Col. ........................................................... 386
McIntosh, John Moore ........................................................... 442
McIntosh, Lachlan .............9-11-13-15-18-121-208-215-216-268-300-386-464
McIntosh, Lachlan, Maj. ....................................................268-386

# INDEX.

McIntosh, Lachlin, Jr. ...121-422
McIntosh, Roderick ... 422
McIntosh, William ...10-15-18-268-361-386-422
McIntosh, William, Col. ... 422
McKanney, James ... 422
McKay, ———Capt. ... 422
McKay, Charles ... 422
McKay, Hugh ... 422
McKay, James ...271-386
McKay, Rannell, ... 422
McKee, Alexander ... 361
McKee, Jesse ... 207
McKee, John ...361-422
McKee, Samuel ... 361
McKeen, Green ... 205
McKeen, William ... 119
McKeew, William ... 386
McKenna, James ... 422
McKenney, Charles ...398-403-422-444
McKenney, James ... 422
McKenney, James, Lt. Col. ... 422
McKenney, John ...128-386-422
McKenney, John, Sr. ...422-444
McKenzie, Samuel ... 361
McKenzie, William ... 361
McKewn, Daniel ... 422
McKey, James ... 207
McKie, Thomas ... 361
McKinne ... 15
McKenne, Matthew ... 422
McKinney, Charles ... 361
McKinney, Henry ...128-134-208-386
McKinney, Matthew ...117-128-208
McKinney, Nathan ...128-387
McKinney, Thomas ... 128
McKinney, Timothy ...422-443
McKinney, Travis ...128-387
McKinney, William ...117-128
McKinney, William M. ... 288
McKoy, Daniel ...119-296
McLain, Andrew ... 361
McLain, James ... 127
McLain, John ...117-127-241-422-452
McLain, Lewis ... 117
McLane, Daniel ... 403
McLane, Thomas ...361-422-444-452
McLane, Wiley ... 455

McLaughlin, John ................................................. 422-444
McLaughlin, Peter ................................................... 323
McLean, Andrew ..................................................... 387
McLean, James ...................................................... 422
McLean, John .................................................... 270-422
McLean, Josia ...................................................... 422
McLean, Lewis ................................................... 296-387
McLendon, Dennis ................................................... 296
McLendon, Isaac .................................................... 422
McLendon, Jacob .................................................... 288
McLendon, Jacob, Jr. ............................................... 422
McLendon, Jacob, Sr. ............................................... 422
McLendon, Samuel ........................................... 361-459-464
McLendon, Thomas ............................................... 361-387
McLeod, Mindork .................................................... 361
McLeod, Norman ..................................................... 361
McMann, John ....................................................... 387
McMann, Mathew ..................................................... 134
McMannus, John ................................................. 361-387
McMath, Joe ........................................................ 220
McMath, Joseph ................................................. 219-387
McMatt, Joseph ..................................................... 134
McMichael, John .................................................... 361
McMillan, John, (McMullen or McMillions) .............. 320-321-422-443-459-464
McMillan, John K. (or McMullions) .............................. 334-335
McMinn, James ...................................................... 263
McMinn, Jane ....................................................... 326
McMullen, Alex. (or McMillon) .................................. 361-398
McMullen, Pat .................................................. 134-387
McMullen, Robert ............................................... 200-387
McMullen, Rolen .................................................... 123
McMunn, John ................................................... 123-227
McMurphy, Dal. ...................................................... 58
McMurphy, Daniel ......................................... 132-271-387-422
McMurran, David .................................................... 334
McMurray, David ................................................ 134-387
McMurray, Frederick ................................................ 422
McMurray, William .................................................. 387
McMurray, John ..................................................... 127
McMurry, Frederick ............................................. 116-387
McMurry, Mathew .................................................... 387
McMurry, William ............................................... 117-134
McNabb, R. ......................................................... 387
McNabb, Robert ..................................................... 123
McNail, Jesse ...................................................... 387
McNair, Daniel ............................................. 127-202-269
McNatt, Joseph ..................................................... 387

580 INDEX.

McNatt, Solomon, .................................................127-387
McNeely, Daniel ...................................................120-230
McNeely, Elinor .......................................................... 310
McNeely, Hugh ........................................................... 387
McNeely, Mary ............................................................ 319
McNeese, James .......................................................... 361
McNeil, Archibald ................................................127-209-387
McNeil, ——Col. ........................................................... 387
McNeil, Daniel ............................................127-209-210-270-387
McNeil, Daniel, Jr. ..................................................127-269
McNeil, Daniel, Sr. ...................................................... 127
McNeil, David ............................................................ 202
McNeil, Duncan ........................................................... 127
McNeil, James ................................................53-120-127-422
McNeil, Jesse ..................................................124-127-202
McNeil, Michael ..............................................120-127-209-387
McNeiley, John ........................................................... 361
McNeill, Jesse ........................................................... 340
McNeilly, Hugh ........................................................... 231
McNeily, Daniel .......................................................... 387
McNelly, Daniel .......................................................... 133
McNelly, Hugh ............................................................ 133
McNunn, John ............................................................. 387
McNutt, Alex ............................................................. 308
McOwen, Daniel ........................................................... 387
McPherson ................................................................ 422
McQueen, John .......................................................242-305-307
McRae, Mary .............................................................. 338
McRight, William .....................................................452-455
McRoy, James ............................................................. 387
McVickers, D. ..........................................................18-422
McVickers, John .......................................................... 329
McWhorter, John .......................................................... 361
McWhorter, Margaret ...................................................... 332
McWickers, Daniel ........................................................ 422

M

Maban, Matthew ........................................................... 126
Maberry, Joel ............................................................ 360
Mabray, John ............................................................. 455
Mabrey, Joel, Sr. ........................................................ 320
Mabry, Elias ............................................................. 360
Mabry, Gray .............................................................. 360
Mabry, Ralph ..........................................................18-421
Mabry, Reps ......................................................123-386-449
Mackee, Samuel ........................................................... 422

INDEX.                                                      581

| | |
|---|---|
| Mackey, | 422 |
| Mackie, Samuel | 321-443 |
| MMacklin, Jane | 325-347 |
| Macomber, Matthew | 422 |
| Macomeson, John | 422 |
| Macomson, John | 459-464 |
| Madden, David | 236 |
| Madock, Joseph | 422 |
| Maddon, Walter | 361 |
| Maddox, John | 124-127-387-402 |
| Maddox, McNeil | 124 |
| Maddox, Peavy | 124 |
| Maddox, Samuel | 361-387 |
| Maddox, Walter | 323 |
| Maddox, William | 124-127-207-210-323-387 |
| Maden, David | 124 |
| Madin, David | 387 |
| Madison, James | 400-422 |
| Madkins, William | 132-387 |
| Maffett, John | 459 |
| Maffett, Thomas | 387 |
| Mafield, William | 387 |
| Magar, Owen | 132 |
| Magbee, Rachel | 329 |
| Magee, Elizabeth | 333 |
| Magie, Hugh | 29-186 |
| Maginty, John | 328-333 |
| Magruder, Ninian | 54 |
| Magruder, Ninian Ofiot, (See McGruder) | 117 |
| Mahan, Archibald | 124 |
| Mahan, David | 361-387 |
| Mahan, Samuel | 124 |
| Mahemson, John | 422-443 |
| Mahon, Arch | 387 |
| Mahon, Samuel | 387 |
| Mainer, John | 132 |
| Mains, Samuel | 422-443 |
| Maires, Samuel | 361 |
| Maise, John | 306 |
| Maise, Joseph | 118-387 |
| Majar, Owen | 387 |
| Mallard, Lazarus | 126-422 |
| Malone, Mullins | 422-443 |
| Mallory, John | 361 |
| Mallory, Mary | 325-347 |
| Mallory, Stephen | 361 |
| Malner, John | 387 |

Malone, Martin, .................................................... 387
Malone, William ................................................. 361
Manadee, Henry .................................................. 387
Manadue, Henry (or Manadoc) ..............................129-225-422
Manen, Drury ................................................387-402
Manen, John ...................................................... 387
Manen, John, Jr. .................................................. 387
Mangum, Hoxwell ................................................. 333
Manhall, Abram .................................................. 387
Manley, John ..................................................15-422
Manley, Temple ................................................... 320
Manly, Temperance ............................................... 341
Mann, John ...........................................121-126-202-238-267-387-422
Mann, Jonas ...................................................... 387
Mann, Judith ..................................................... 316
Mann, Luke ............................................70-121-387-422
Mann, William ................................................... 361
Mannen, (or Manning) ............................................ 387
Mannen, Drury .................................................. 118-123
Mannen, James .................................................... 117
Mannen, John ................................................117-268
Mannen, Joseph ................................................... 118
Manners, Isaac ................................................... 207
Manning, Adam (or Manning) ...................................218-268
Manning, Benjamin ................................................ 361
Manning, James ................................................... 387
Manning, John .................................................... 387
Manning, Robert ..............................................124-226
Mannon, James (or Manon) ....................................298-308
Mannon, John, Jr. ................................................. 123
Mannon, William ..............................................123-387
Mappin, Mary ..................................................... 332
Marberry, William ................................................ 387
Marbury, .....................................................70-239-29£
Marbury, H. ..................................................221-240
Marbury, Horatio .............................................124-222-387
Marbury, Jo. ..................................................... 286
Marbury, L. ....................................................... 18
Marbury, Leonard .........................................73-221-222-241-387-422
Marbury, Leonard, Sr. .........................................122-124
Marbury, Thomas ............................................124-222-233-289-387
Marbury, William ................................................ 295
Marcus, Daniel ................................................... 387
Marcus, Elias ..................................................... 308
Marcus, Ellis, (or Elis) .......................................119-387
Marcus, John ..............................................119-288-291-387
Marganton, Asa. .................................................. 198

# INDEX.

Marlow, James ................................................. 361
Marlow, William (or Marler) .......................... 250-271-387
Marney, Thomas ............................................. 387
Marran, David ................................................ 361
Marsh, Clement .............................................. 254
Marsh, Elijah ................................................. 387
Marsh, John ............................................ 120-387-461
Marsh, Nathan ............................................ 120-387
Marsh, Sol. ................................................... 387
Marshall, Abraham ....................... 84-123-213-215-271-422
Marshall, Daniel ...................................... 270-387-422
Marshall, Jesse ........................................ 321-422-443-457
Marshall, John ........................................ 121-123-225-226-387
Marshall, Joseph ...................................... 271-283-387
Marshall, Levi .............................................. 289-387
Marshall, Matthew ......................................... 121-227
Marshall, Moses ............................................ 361-387
Marshall, Nathan ........................................... 387
Marshall, Soloman .......................................... 121-202
Marshall Thomas ............................................ 247
Marshall, William ........................................... 422
Marshall, Zacheus .......................................... 270-387
Martin .......................................................... 422
Martin, Lt. Col. ............................................... 387
Martin, Alexander ........................................... 340
Martin, Andrew .............................................. 398
Martin, Austin ............................................... 125
Martin, Barclay .............................................. 387
Martin, Bartlett ..................................... 134-242-265
Martin, Betty ................................................. 126
Martin, Cornelius ............................................ 125
Martin, David ................................................. 361
Martin, Ed. ................................................... 387
Martin, Edmond .............................................. 125
Martin, Elizabeth ............................................ 126
Martin, Ephraim ......................................... 422-452
Martin Ganaway ....................................... 125-323-387
Martin, Jacob ..................................... 125-306-307-387-400
Martin, James .................... 81-125-203-204-271-387-422-443
Martin, Jesse ................................................. 361
Martin, John .............. 10-15-126-185-203-230-231-422-443-452-464
Martin, John, Lt. Col. ...................................... 422
Martin, John, Jr. ...................................... 125-271-387
Martin, Jno. W. .............................................. 387
Martin, Joseph ............................................... 422
Martin, Macajah ............................................. 321
Martin, Marshall ......................................... 126-387

# INDEX.

Martin, Matthew .................................................... 126-403
Martin, Medience ..................................................... 318
Martin, Meloan ....................................................... 271
Martin, Nathan ....................................................... 387
Martin, Robert ....................................................... 126
Martin, Simon ..................................................... 126-387
Martin, Thomas ....................................................... 422
Martin, William .................................... 122-126-274-362-387-422
Mase, Joseph ...................................................... 18-422
Mash, Clem ....................................................... 362-387
Mash, Nathan ......................................................... 362
Mash, Thomas ......................................................... 132
Mashborn, John ....................................................... 362
Masney, Thomas ....................................................... 396
Mason, Ebenezer ...................................................... 422
Mason, Gideon ........................................................ 362
Mason, John .......................................................... 422
Mason, Thomas ;....................................................... 362
Massey, Alston, S. ................................................... 338
Massey, William .................................................. 122-422
Mastein, William .................................................. 18-422
Masterson, John ...................................................... 455
Mathews, B. .......................................................... 398
Mathews, Burwell ................................................. 398-404
Mathews, Daniel ...................................................... 124
Mathews, Daniel, Jr. ................................................. 124
Mathews, George ................................................ 18-51-387
Mathews, Isham................................... 122-124-296-362-387-459
Matthews, James, Sr. ................................................. 323
Mathews, Joel ........................................................ 362
Mathews, John ............................................ 125-387-398-444
Mathews, Lewis ....................................................... 362
Mathews, Meshack ................................................. 125-387
Mathews, Michael ..................................................... 387
Mathews, Rebecca ................................................. 325-347
Mathews, Reuben ...................................................... 125
Mathews, Richard ................................................. 398-404
Mathews, Thomas ...................................................... 398
Mathews, William ............................... 15-18-122-125-317-387-464
Mathews, William, Capt. .............................................. 387
Mathews, William H. .................................................. 449
Mathis, John ......................................................... 362
Matthews, Daniel ................................................. 296-387
Matthews, Elizabeth .............................................. 320-329
Matthews, George ....................................... 30-122-265-423-464
Matthews, Isaac ........................................ 240-423-444-452
Matthews, James .................................................. 125-270

INDEX. 585

Matthews, John .................................................. 238-239-423-457
Matthews, Mesheck ................................................ 232-289-458
Matthews, Moses ........................................................ 270
Matthews, Oliver ....................................................... 307
Matthews, Philip ................................................... 423-452-457
Matthews, William ........ 204-232-233-234-240-271-289-296-325-423-443-452-458-459
Matthews, William, Capt. ................................................ 423
Matthews, Winnefred .................................................. 325-347
Matton, Lazarus ........................................................ 387
Mattox, Amelia C. ...................................................... 341
Mattox, Benjamin ................................................... 124-387
Mattox, Charles ..................................................... 323-362
Mattox, John .................................................... 121-124-335-387
Maupin, Jesse ..................................................... 316-361-387
Maxwell, Andrew ....................................................... 423
Maxwell, Audley ........................................................ 423
Maxwell, Bazil ......................................................... 154
Maxwell, Ed. .......................................................... 387
Maxwell, Edward ....................................................... 123
Maxwell, Elisha ........................................................ 423
Maxwell, George .................................................... 216-300
Maxwell, James .................................................. 123-300-362-387-423
Maxwell, John ...................................................... 315-362
Maxwell, Joseph ........................................................ 216
Maxwell, Josiah ................................................. 15-18-120-123-269-423
Maxwell, Richard ................................................... 398-404
Maxwell, Simons ....................................................... 423
Maxwell, Thomas ............................................. 120-123-242-387-423-459-464
Maxwell, Thomas, Capt. ................................................. 387
Maxwell, Thomas, Maj. .................................................. 387
Maxwell, Thomas, Jr. ................................................... 423
Maxwell, Thomas, Sr. ................................................... 315
Maxwell, William ....................................................... 423
May, Bailey ......................................................... 118-387
May, John .......................................................... 270-295
May, Joseph ........................................................ 132-387
May, Moses ............................................................ 126
May, Samuel ........................................................ 398-404
May, William, ................................................. 118-126-224-259-387
Maybank, Andrew ....................................................... 423
Mayben, Mathew ........................................................ 387
Mayborn, William (or Mayben) ....................................... 126-387
Mayes, Thomas ......................................................... 340
Maynard, Elizabeth .................................................... 319
Mayo, John ............................................................ 452
Mayo, John, Sr. .................................................... 423-444
Mayo, William ......................................................... 235

Mays, Andrew ..................................................398-404
Mays, John ........................................................223-400-423
Meacham, Henry ................................................... 362
Mead, Minor, (or Miner) ....................................332-398-423-443
Meador, Jason, (or Meadow) ....................................362-423-452
Meador, Joel .......................................................... 398
Meador, Jonas ........................................................ 398
Meadows, Jacob ...................................................... 362
Meadows, Jason ...................................................... 457
Meadows, John ....................................................423-452
Meanly, J. ............................................................ 18
Meanly, John, (or Meanley) ..............................289-362-387-400-423
Meeks, Brittain ....................................................423-444
Meers, Samuel ........................................................ 219
Mellone, Martin ...................................................... 116
Meloy, Andrew ........................................................ 323
Melton, John .......................................................... 185
Melton, Robert ....................................................423-452
Melton, William ...................................................423-444
Melvin, George ................................................15-18-117-423
Melvin, John .......................................................... 387
Menefee, George ...................................................... 362
Menifer, Willis ....................................................... 423
Mercer, Asa .......................................................... 269
Mercer, Jacob ..............................................117-129-314-387
Mercer James ......................................................117-387
Mercer, Joshua ....................................................423-443
Mercer, Silas ..................................................129-308-387
Mercer, Thomas ....................................................... 423
Mercer, William ...................................................... 423
Merder, Asa .......................................................... 265
Meritt, Torrence ..................................................... 362
Merks, Britton ....................................................... 362
Moroney, Nathan ...................................................... 362
Merritt, Barbara ..................................................... 327
Merriwether .......................................................... 423
Merriwether, Daniel .................................................. 423
Merriwether, David ................................................362-423
Merriwether, James ................................................... 387
Merriwether, Thomas ............................................330-464
Mercer, Thomas ....................................................... 423
Messer, Jacob ........................................................ 387
Messer, Silas .....................................................362-387
Messer, Thomas ................................................117-298-387
Metcalf, Anthony ..............................................129-200-292-387
Metcalf, Danza, (or Denza, or Dunza) ..................124-130-201-289-387-458
Metcalf, William ...............................................129-288-387-458
Metts, Frederick ..................................................... 330

Meyers, Thomas .................................................... 132-387
Middlebrook, Milly ............................................... 333
Middlebrooks, John ............................................. 362
Middleton .......................................................... 423
Middleton, Benedick ............................................ 121-387
Middleton, Charles ............................................. 151-123
Middleton, Hatton .............................................. 132-387
Middleton, Holland ............................................. 164-288-387
M'ddleton, Holland, Jr. ....................................... 122-387
Middleton, Holland, Sr. ....................................... 121
Middleton, Hugh ................................................. 362-423
Middleton, John .................................................. 362-398-404
Middleton, R. ....................................................... 250
Middleton, Robert ............................................... 271-387
Middleton, Robert, Capt. ..................................... 387
Middleton, Smallwood ........................................ 387
Middleton, William ............................................. 132-296-387
Mikell, James ..................................................... 328-334
Milam, Benjamin ................................................ 362
Miles, Thomas ..................................................... 362
Miles, William ..................................................... 387
Milican, Hugh ..................................................... 122
Milirous, William ................................................ 423-443
Millar, F. ............................................................ 18
Millar, Elisha, (or Miller) .................................... 423
Millar, Nicholas .................................................. 16-423
Milledge, John .................................................... 122-387-423-464
Milledge, John, Jr. ............................................... 423
Millen, Alex ........................................................ 387
Millen, Charles ................................................... 388
Miller, Capt. ....................................................... 317
Miller, Alexander ................................................ 115-388
Miller, Charles .................................................... 116
Miller, Daniel ...................................................... 131-388
Miller, David ...................................................... 116-388
Miller, Elish ....................................................... 15-131-388
Miller, Elisha ..................................................... 74-362-388
Miller, Ezekiel .................................................... 116-288-388
Miller, George .................................................... 116-388
Miller, Jesse ....................................................... 116-303-338-388
Miller, John ........................................................ 362-388-423
Miller, John, Capt. .............................................. 423
Miller, John, Jr. ................................................... 423
Miller, Jonathan .................................................. 388
Miller, Joseph .................................................... 131-388
Miller, Joshua .................................................... 116-227-296
Miller, Lewis ...................................................... 323

## INDEX.

Miller, Lucretia ... 329
Miller, Mary ... 115
Miller, Moses ... 116-234-295
Miller, Nathaniel ... 116-333-388
Miller, Nicholas ... 115-220-388
Miller, Richard ... 362
Miller, Samuel ... 115-116-388-423
Miller, Smith ... 145-388
Miller, William ... 116-388-423-444
Miller, Willis ... 362
Millican, Thomas ... 328
Milligan, Capt. ... 423
Milligan, Hugh ... 388
Mills ... 423
Mills, Capt. ... 423
Mills, John ... 202
Mills, Moses ... 315-423-443
Mills, William ... 116-388
Milner, John ... 131-235-280-388-423-464
Milner, John Hamilton ... 459
Milner, Pitt ... 423
Milton, J. ... 18
Milton, John ... 9-15-268-362-388-423
Milton, Nathaniel ... 122-388
Mimms, Drury (or Minus) ... 117-226
Mimms, John ... 132-271
Mimms, Shadrack ... 270
Mimms, William (or Mims) ... 117-268-275
Mims, Drury ... 289-388
Mims, Frederick ... 118
Mims, Joseph ... 117-388
Mims, Martin ... 388
Mines, William ... 388
Minis, James ... 398
Minis, Philip ... 423
Minnus, Fred ... 388
Minus, John ... 388
Minton, John ... 423-443
Mitchell, Capt. ... 319
Mitchell, Maj. ... 318
Mitchell, Charles ... 269
Mitchell, David ... 129
Mitchell, Eleanor ... 322
Mitchell, Francis ... 308-388
Mitchell, George B. ... 362
Mitchell, Henry ... 362-423-457-459-464
Mitchell, J. ... 18

## INDEX. 589

| | |
|---|---|
| Mitchell, John | 15-121-129-270-388 |
| Mitchell, R. | 388 |
| Mitchell, Reuben | 423-449 |
| Mitchell, Robert | 121-122-129-218-219-240-331 |
| Mitchell, Sarah | 320 |
| Mitchell, Thomas | 15-70-127-130-388-404-433 |
| Mitchell, Wm. | 18-130-121-211-232-270-296-319-320-321-322-329-388-398-404-423-443-452 |
| Mitchell, William, Jr. | 322 |
| Mitchell, Willian, Sr. | 329 |
| Mitcher, David | 335 |
| Mize, Sheppeard | 362 |
| Mizell, Charles | 306 |
| Moak, William, (or Monk) | 388 |
| Moat, Daniel (or Moats) | 118-388 |
| Moates, Levi, (or Moats) | 118-271-388 |
| Moates, Silas | 130-207-208-388 |
| Moates, Simon, (or Moats) | 118-206-207-208-388 |
| Moates, William | 118-206-207-388 |
| Mobbs, Jesse | 362 |
| Mobley, John | 117-388 |
| Mocock, Henry | 132 |
| Moffett, Gable | 398-405 |
| Moffett, Gabriel | 423 |
| Moffett, John | 423 |
| Moffett, Thomas | 130 |
| Mofield, William | 388 |
| Moncrief, Mathew | 323 |
| Moncrief, Mary | 117 |
| Moncrief, Joshia | 388 |
| Moncrief, Sam | 388 |
| Moncrief, Sampson | 117 |
| Moncrief, Samuel | 398 |
| Money, Brain | 458 |
| Money, Joseph | 122-388 |
| Money, Pat | 388 |
| Monk, John | 362-423-444 |
| Monk, Silas | 362 |
| Monk, Susannah | 332 |
| Monmouth, Joseph | 388 |
| Monroe, David, Sr. | 335 |
| Montaigut, David | 193 |
| Montgomery | 423 |
| Montgomery, Ann | 315 |
| Montgomery, Berkley | 455 |
| Montgomery, David | 323 |
| Montgomery, James | 132-388 |
| Moody, Anna | 327 |

| | |
|---|---|
| Moody, Thomas | 423-444 |
| Moon, George | 388 |
| Moon, James | 388 |
| Moon, John | 35-388-398 |
| Moon, Richard | 388 |
| Moon, Samuel | 268-274 |
| Mooney, Joe | 218 |
| Mooney, Jos | 388 |
| Moore, Capt. | 423 |
| Moore, Abenego | 398-403 |
| Moore, Alexander | 130-260-289-398-405 |
| Moore, Andrew | 423 |
| Moore, Francis | 15-18-235-268-423 |
| Moore, George | 117 |
| Moore, Isaac | 328 |
| Moore, Isaac, Sr. | 423-443 |
| Moore, James | 120-229-398-423-405-444 |
| Moore, Jiles | 423 |
| Moore, Joel | 362 |
| Moore, John | 130-269-323-331-337-343-405-423-443-462 |
| Moore, Jonas | 271 |
| Moore, Joseph | 362 |
| Moore, Martin | 130-338-398 |
| Moore, Mordecia | 117-307-400 |
| Moore, Richard | 130-237 |
| Moore, Sarah | 317 |
| Moore, Samuel | 388 |
| Moore, Thomas | 118-120-388 |
| Moore, William | 130-240-270-301-388-423 |
| Moormes, Patrick | 388 |
| Mophett, Mary | 332 |
| Morgan, Asa | 449 |
| Moran, William | 118-388 |
| Morce, Alexander | 239 |
| More, Mordecia | 388 |
| Morel, John | 362-388-423 |
| Moreland, Francis | 362 |
| Moreland, Robert | 362 |
| Moreman, Thomas | 323 |
| Moremouth, Joseph | 132 |
| Morgan, Asa | 119-388-423 |
| Morgan, Christopher | 119-131-388 |
| Morgan, Elizabeth | 119 |
| Morgan, Isham | 308 |
| Morgan, James | 362 |
| Morgan, Jere | 388 |
| Morgan, Jeremiah | 119-131 |

## INDEX.

Morgan, Jesse .................................................131-199-218-388
Morgan, John ..............................................119-131-271-296-388
Morgan, Luke .........................................................131-388
Morgan, Malaciah ................................................131-269-388
Morgan, Philip ..................................................119-271-388
Morgan, Robert .......................................................118-388
Morgan, Step .........................................................131-388
Morgan, William ..................................119-131-261-270-275-423-457
Morganson, Asa ............................................................ 388
Moris, John ............................................................... 388
Morphett, James, (or Moffatt) ...................................122-130-388
Morphett, Thomas ................................................131-308-388
Morris, Burwell ........................................................... 362
Morris, Celia ............................................................. 326
Morris, Garrett, (or Morriss) ............................................. 398
Morris, James ..................................................130-388-405
Morris, Jesse ............................................................. 362
Morris, John ...................................................288-337-362-423
Morris, Nathaniel ..............................................363-423-444
Morris, Osten ............................................................. 363
Morris, Patrick .....................................................122-130
Morris, Reese .....................................................123-130-388
Morris, Thomas ...................................................15-68-423-443
Morris, William .........................................130-288-363-388-458-464
Morris, William, Sr. ..............................................314-423-443
Morrison, Alexander ....................................................... 317
Morrison, Eyre ............................................................ 449
Morrison, J. .............................................................. 18
Morrison, John ...........................9-15-28-53-121-132-296-298-300-388
Morriss, Thomas ........................................................... 363
Morrow, Ann ............................................................... 339
Morrow, Ewing ............................................................. 363
Morton, John (or Morten) ........................................131-388
Morton, Oliver ............................................................ 424
Morton, Oliver, Sr. ....................................................... 452
Morton, Thomas ............................................................ 424
Mosby, James .............................................................. 424
Mosby, John ............................................................... 424
Mosby, Littleberry, (or Litt. ...............................73-242-360-388-423
Mosby, Robert .................................................119-253-388-424
Mosby, Wade ............................................................... 424
Mose, William ............................................................. 215
Moseby, William ......................................................229-424
Mosee, Pat ................................................................ 388
Moseley, Capt. ............................................................ 259
Moseley, Benjamin (or Mosely or Mosley) ....................119-120-269-388
Moseley, James ............................................................ 424

## Index.

Moseley Jesse .................................................................. 120
Moseley, John (or Mosely) .................................15-119-388-424
Moseley, L. ..................................................................... 18-424
Moseley, Littleberry (or Mosely) ..................................15-253-424
Moseley, Robert (or Mosely) ..............................18-242-269-388-424
Moseley, Samuel ..............................................................329-424-443
Moseley, Thomas (or Mosely) .............................215-268-270-388
Moseley, Thomas, Jr. ........................................................... 124
Moseley, William (or Mosely) ..............................120-132-388-424
Mosely, Wm. H. .................................................................. 132
Mosley, Jese ....................................................................... 388
Moss, Francis ..................................................................... 388
Moss, James ....................................................................... 130
Moss, Joshua ..............................................................19-363-388
Moss, Leonard ............................................................116-270-388
Moss, Martha D. ................................................................. 315
Moss, William .................................................................222-296
Mote, William .................................................................... 363
Mott, Joseph (or Motte) ..............................................131-288-388
Mott, Nathan ..................................................................... 363
Mott, Uriah .................................................................131-388
Mott, William (or Motte) ..............................131-268-294-296-388
Mott, Zach ........................................................................ 388
Mott, Zephania ............................................................131-215-388
Moxley, Benjamin ............................................................... 424
Moxley, Thomas .................................................................. 299
Muckelhannon, John ............................................................ 318
Mullens, Malone, (or Mullins) ..............................363-388-424-452
Murban, Martha .................................................................. 388
Murdock, Thomas H. ............................................................ 321
Murdock, William .......................................................321-424-443-452
Murphey, Francis ................................................................ 323
Murphey, Morris ................................................................. 315
Murphy, Daniel ................................................................... 256
Murphy, Ed. ....................................................................... 388
Murphy, Edward ...........................................................117-122-229
Murphy, John (or Murphree) .........................................323-464
Murphy, Martha ............................................................325-326-347
Murphy, Miles .................................................................... 388
Murphy, Mill ...................................................................... 388
Murjhy, Mills, (or Murphree, Murjhee, or Murphrey) .............132-240-459-464
Murphy, Nicholas ................................................................ 459
Murphy, Willis .................................................................... 388
Murry, Nancy ..................................................................... 315
Murry, Thomas (or Murray) .........................................335-424-443
Murs, Samuel ..................................................................... 219
Musteen, William ..........................................................116-388

INDEX. 593

Mydleton, William ..................................................... 424
Myers, John, Sr. ...................................................... 424
Myers, Mary .......................................................... 341
Myers, Thomas ....................................................117-388
Myers, William ....................................................... 424
Myhand, James, Sr. ................................................... 313
Myrick, John ......................................................... 363

**N.**

Nail, Benjamin ....................................................135-388
Nail, Henry .......................................................135-388
Nail, Joseph .............................................13-33-135-212-310-388
Nail, Julian .................................................33-308-388
Nail, Matthew ........................................................ 449
Nail, Reuben ............................................135-214-231-335-388
Nail, Matthew ........................................................ 449
Nailor, George ...................................................400-424
Nails, Henry ......................................................... 212
Nails, Reuben ........................................................ 228
Naish, Francis ....................................................... 316
Nalls, Richard ....................................................398-403
Napier, Col. ......................................................... 254
Napp, Mary ........................................................... 335
Nash, Clem ........................................................... 312
Nash, Clement ...........................................15-18-134-289-388
Nash, John ........................................................... 363
Nash, Mary .......................................................134-329
Naylor, Josiah ....................................................... 121
Neal, Capt ........................................................... 424
Neal, R. A. R. ....................................................... 322
Neal, Thomas ......................................................... 401
Neaves, William ..................................................363-388
Neblett, Tillman ..................................................... 363
Needlinger, John, Gottlieb ........................................... 388
Neal, Thomas (or Neil) ...........................................272-388
Neely, John .....................................................424-452-457
Neidlinger, Godleib .................................................. 157
Neidlinger, John Godleib ............................................. 135
Neilly, John ......................................................... 135
Neisler, John Adam ................................................... 363
Nelly, John .......................................................... 294
Nelms, Nancy .....................................................325-347
Nelson, Adam ......................................................... 388
Nelson, James ....................................................135-388
Nelson, Jeremiah .................................................314-363-388
Nelson, John, ...............................................135-323-388-424

# Index.

Nelson, Thomas ..................................................... 307-401
Nelson, William ................................................... 135-388
Nephew, Capt. ......................................................... 424
Nephew, James ............................................... 135-388-424
Nesbit, Jeremiah .............................................. 363-424-452
Nesler, Adam ......................................................... 135
Netherland, Ben, Sr. .................................................. 449
Netherland, Benj. .................................................... 424
Netherland, Thomas ................................................ 15-424
Nettles, Elisha ............................................... 135-136-388
Neufville, John ...................................................... 424
Nevel, Thomas ........................................................ 135
New, Jacob ........................................................... 363
Newberry, Nancy ...................................................... 316
Newberry, William ................................................ 203-388
Newby, Samuel ........................................................ 320
Newdicate, John ...................................................... 424
Newdigate, John ................................................. 15-18-424
Newell, Thomas ....................................................... 388
Newgate, John (or Newigate) ...................................... 289-388
Newingate, John ...................................................... 363
Newlin, Matthias ..................................................... 398
Newman, Daniel ................................................... 424-452
Newman, George ....................................................... 401
Newman, John .................................................. 135-289-363-388
Newman, Joseph ....................................................... 388
Newman, Thomas ....................................................... 339
Newman, William .................................................. 136-388
Newman, John ..................................................... 424-444
Newman, John .......................................................... 19
Newsom, Sol. ......................................................... 388
Newsome, John ........................................................ 363
Newsom, Capt. ........................................................ 424
Newsome, Solomon ..................................................... 135
Newson, Jonēs ........................................................ 424
Newson, Nancy ........................................................ 333
Newton, Moses .................................................... 315-464
Niblack, William ................................................. 363-401
Nicholas, Ben ........................................................ 218
Nichols, Capt. ....................................................... 424
Nichols, Beniamjn ............................................... 258-289-388
Nichols, Isaac B. .................................................... 455
Nichols, Julius ...................................................... 363
Nichols, Mary ........................................................ 335
Nichols, William ..................................................... 293
Nicholson, Benj. (or Nicolson) ................................... 135-388
Nicholson, John ................................................ 424-444-452
Nickerson, John .................................................. 424-457

INDEX. 595

Nickson, Archibald ............ 135
Niels, George ............ 199-388
Night, Richard ............ 256
Nisbet, Eugenius A. ............ 74
Nisbet, James ............ 74
Nisbet, John ............ 74
Nisbet, Sarah A. ............ 74
Nix George ............ 19-134-424
Nix, James ............ 424-444
Nix, John ............ 424-452
Nix, John Sr. ............ 332
Nix, Rebecker ............ 329
Nixon, John ............ 398-405
Nixon, Joseph ............ 398-405
Nobles, Lewis S. ............ 338-341
Nobles, Sanders ............ 459-464
Noland, Philip ............ 272
Nolen, James ............ 424-452
Norman, Maj. ............ 424
Norman, Jesse ............ 458
Norman, John, Sr. ............ 323-339
Norman, William ............ 424-457
Norris, Alexander ............ 323-363
Norris, James ............ 363
Norris, John ............ 363
Norris, William (or Norriss) ............ 363-424-452
North, John ............ 289-389
Norton, James ............ 398-405
Norton, Jonathan ............ 398-405
Norton, William ............ 398-405
Norwood, George ............ 424-444-452
Norwood, Richard ............ 135-299
Nowland, Philip ............ 389
Nuga, Michael ............ 389
Nugan, M. ............ 19-424
Nugan, Michael ............ 136-222
Nugard, Michael ............ 18-424
Nunn, John ............ 363
Nunnalee, James F. ............ 316
Nunnelly, Margaret ............ 325-347
Nunnlee, James F. ............ 363

O

Oakes, Jonathan ............ 399-405
Oakland, William ............ 389
Oakman, William ............ 136-137
Oakman, W. ............ 19-424
Oates, Lt. ............ 424

## Index.

Oates, Jere ......................................................... 175
Oates, Jeremiah ................................................. 136-389
Oates, Richard ................................................. 136-389
Oates, Richard W. ............................................... 331
O'Barn, Wm. ....................................................... 136
O'Barre, Robert .................................................. 399
Obear, Josiah ..................................................... 389
O'Bryan, James ........................................ 19-136-272-389-424
O'Bryan, William ................................................. 424
O'Bryant, Duncan ............................................... 136-389
Odair, William .................................................. 136-389
Odam, Daniel (or Odum) .......................................... 424
Odam, Frederick ............................................... 363-424
Odam, Seybeit .................................................... 424
Odam, Uriah ...................................................... 136
Odingchels, Charles .............................................. 389
Odingfield, Chas ................................................. 136
Odingsell, Benjamin ........................................... 15-424
Odingsell, Charles ...................................... 203-204-290-424
Odinsell, Benj. ..................................................... 9
Odinsell, Charles ................................................. 203
Odom, Archibald .................................................. 363
Odum, Daniel ..................................................... 449
Odum, Seybert ................................................. 444-455
Odum, Uriah ...................................................... 389
Offutt, Ezekiel ................... 224-228-286-290-293-296-309-389-424
Offutt, Jesse .................................................. 136-389
Offutt, John .............................................. 136-137-293-389
Offutt, Nathaniel .............................................. 136-389
Ogden, Solomon ................................................ 363-389
Ogier, Capt. ...................................................... 424
Oglesby, Thomas .................................................. 363
Ogletree, John .................................................... 274
Ogletree, William ................................................ 363
Oham, William .................................................... 389
O'Hearn, Josiah (or O'Hern) ................................. 136-137-238
O'Kelly, Francis .................................................. 363
Oldham, Uriah .................................................... 272
Olive, John ............................................. 200-399-405-424-452
Oliver, Dynowsius ............................................ 389-424
Oliver, Jackson ................................................... 321
Oliver, James .......................................... 137-389-424-444
Oliver, Jane ...................................................... 330
Oliver, John .................................................. 137-389
Oliver, John, Sr. .............................................. 424-444
Oliver, Morton ................................................... 444
Oliver, Peter ........................................... 137-363-389-424
Ollens, Daniel .................................................... 389

## INDEX.

Omans, John ............................................................ 363
O'Neal, (Axom-Caxam or Asum,) ............................137-214-389-424
O'Neal, Edward ........................................................ 424
O'Neal, Ferdinand ..................................................... 424
O'Neal, John, (or O'Neil) .......................................137-204-389
O'Neal, Nathan ........................................................ 389
O'Neal, Nathaniel ..................................................... 137
O'Neal, John .......................................................... 293
Orear, Daniel .....................................................424-452
Oricks, James ......................................................... 389
Oriner, Philips ....................................................... 206
Ornsby, Daniel ...................................................19-137-424
Ornsby, Isabel ........................................................ 137
Orr, Capt. ............................................................ 317
Orr, Christopher .............................................246-323-399-403
Orr, John ............................................................. 399
Orr, Nancy ............................................................ 317
Orrick, James ......................................................... 290
Osborn, Reps .......................................................... 363
Osgood, John .......................................................... 424
OsGood, Joshia ........................................................ 307
Osgood, Josiah ...................................................241-401-424
Osusby, Daniel ........................................................ 389
Oswald, Joshua ........................................................ 363
Outlaw, Edward ........................................................ 137
Outlaw, James ......................................................... 137
Outlaw, Ladswick ...................................................... 389
Outlaw, Leudovick ..................................................... 137
Owen, Sergt. .......................................................... 424
Owens, Barsheba ....................................................... 316
Owens, Ephraim ....................................................137-389
Owens, John, Sr. ...................................................... 323
Owens, Joseph .....................................................424-444
Owens, Robert ....................................................137-258-272
Owens, Thomas ....................................................137-389-399

### P

Pace, Bernard ....................................................146-295-389
Pace, Thomas .................................................144-145-215-389-424
Pack, John ............................................................ 401
Pain, Fail ............................................................ 405
Pain, Hail ............................................................ 399
Pain, Samuel .....................................................203-204-232
Paine, John ........................................................... 364
Paine, Samuel ......................................................... 139
Paine, Samuel, Sr. ................................................142-145
Paine, Winefred ....................................................... 338
Palmer, George ...................................................138-389-464

## Index.

Palmer, Jona ............................................................. 389
Palmer, Jonathan ....................................................... 290
Palmer, John ...................................138-229-241-274-293-389-449
Palmer, Joseph ......................................................... 424
Palmer, Soloman ...............................................138-252-274-389
Palmer, Thomas ......................................................... 424
Palmer, William ........................................................ 338
Palmore, Elijah ........................................................ 364
Paltey, Lt. ............................................................ 424
Pannell, Abner ......................................................... 389
Pannell, John .......................................................... 424
Pannell, Joseph (or Pannill) ..............................75-138-260-274-389-424
Paremoore, Sol ......................................................... 389
Paret, William ......................................................... 389
Parham, Richard ...................................................19-144-389
Paris Jane ............................................................. 335
Paris, Peter ........................................................... 145
Parish, Elizabeth ...................................................... 337
Parish, Joel ........................................................... 425
Parish, Robert ......................................................... 146
Park, Henry ............................................................ 321
Park, Mary ............................................................. 315
Park, Phebe ............................................................ 339
Park, Ezekiel Evans .................................................... 425
Parker ................................................................. 425
Parker, Col. ........................................................... 425
Parker, Aaron .......................................................... 364
Parker, Allen .....................................................138-389
Parker, Charles ........................................................ 389
Parker, Daniel .....................................................389-401
Parker, Daniel, Sr. .................................................... 332
Parker, George ....................................................138-389
Parker, James .....................................................138-389
Parker, John ..............................................138-139-202-278-389
Parker, Joseph ....................................................138-389
Parker, Richard ...................................................364-425
Parker, William ...............................................138-399-405
Parkerson, Jacob ..............................................425-452-457
Parkerson, Levin ..................................................323-364
Parkes, Benjamin, Sr. .........................................425-444
Parkins, Archibald ..................................................... 425
Parks, Charles, Jr. .................................................... 139
Parks, Charles, Sr. .................................................... 139
Parks, Henry ......................................................309-321-389
Parks, John .......................................................139-229
Parnell, Capt. ......................................................... 110
Parnell, Lt. Col. ...................................................... 19
Parnell, Benjamin ...................................................... 389

# INDEX.

Parnell, Joseph ............................................................. 425
Parnell, Josh ............................................................... 389
Parr, Benjamin ............................................... 364-425-444-452
Parr, William .............................................................. 405
Parratt, Robert ............................................................ 389
Parre, Nathaniel ........................................................... 425
Parris, Peter .............................................................. 389
Parrish, Robert ........................................................ 389-449
Parsons, Samuel ............................................................ 425
Patillo, James ............................................................. 138
Patillo, John .............................................................. 138
Partin, John ....................................................... 146-302-389
Parton, John ............................................................... 309
Parvil, Cader .............................................................. 389
Paschall, George .................................................... 364-425-444
Paschall, Mary ......................................................... 325-347
Passmore, Joseph ....................................................... 425-452
Pate, Cloey ................................................................ 315
Pate, Samuel ............................................................... 364
Paterson, John (or Patterson) ....................................... 145-389
Paterson, John Jr. (or Patterson) ................................... 145-389
Paterson, Robert (or Patterson) ............................... 263-274-389-444
Paterson, William (or Patterson) .................................... 145-389
Patillo, John .............................................................. 266
Patison, Robert ............................................................ 425
Patmore, William ...................................................... 364-389
Paton, George .............................................................. 364
Patrick, .................................................................. 399
Patrick, David ......................................................... 326-338
Patrick, John A. ....................................................... 319-320
Patrick, Josia ......................................................... 399-404
Patrick, Paul .............................................................. 403
Patrick, William ....................................................... 333-364
Patterson, George .......................................................... 200
Patterson, Gideon .................................................. 200-274-389
Patterson, Jane ............................................................ 341
Patterson, Mary ............................................................ 315
Patterson, Mary Ann ........................................................ 317
Pattillo, John ............................................................. 389
Pattison, Frederick .................................................... 399-404
Pattison, Gideon ........................................................... 144
Pattison, Robert ....................................................... 214-452
Patton, Samuel ............................................................. 403
Patton, Thomas ..................................... 138-294-389-399-403
Patton, William ........................................1............... 364
Pattilo, John .............................................................. 389
Paul, Robert ............................................................... 364
Paulette, Richard (or Pawlett) ................................. 364-425-445
Paulk, John ................................................................ 389

Paulk, Micajah .................................................. 138-142-389
Paxton, William ........................................ 19-139-273-389-425
Payne, Lt. ............................................................. 389
Payne, Joseph ....................................................... 425
Payne, M. H. ......................................................... 319
Payne, Moses ........................................................ 401
Payne, Nehemiah ................................................ 425-444
Payne, Samuel ............................................... 294-296-389
Payne, Samuel, Jr. ................................................... 145
Payne, Thomas ............................. 15-19-222-242-274-280-309-425
Payne, William ............................................ 139-264-273-389
Payret, Jean Pierre Andreo Defau ............................... 364-389
Peace, John ................................................. 364-425-444
Peacock, Amy ....................................................... 337
Peacock, Archibald .................................................. 364
Peacock, Isam ....................................................... 445
Peacock, Isham ...................................................... 425
Peacock, Uriah ............................................ 364-425-445-452
Peacock, William ............................................... 364-425
Peacock, William, Sr. ............................................... 425
Peak, John ................................................... 139-273-389
Peal, John .............................................. 138-144-230-231-389
Pearce, Jesse ....................................................... 389
Pearce, John .................................................. 139-389
Pearce, Joshua, Jr. .................................................. 241
Pearce, Nathaniel .......................................... 109-216-272
Pearce, Seth ........................................................ 425
Pearce, William ............................................... 139-389
Pearre, James ....................................................... 403
Pearre, Nathaniel ............................................ 97-389-425
Pearre, N. ........................................................ 19-425
Pearry, John .................................................. 234-250
Peavey, Nathaniel ................................................... 389
Peavie, Nat. ........................................................ 184
Peavie, Nathaniel ................................................. 41-76
Peavy, Abram .................................................. 139-389
Peavy, Dial (or Dyal) ...................................... 139-290-327-389
Peavy, John ................................................... 139-389
Peavy, Joseph ....................................................... 139
Peavy, Peter .................................................. 139-389
Peck, Henry .................................................. 425-445
Peddy, Jeremiah ..................................................... 364
Pendall, John ................................................. 140-389
Pendergrass, Margarett ............................................. 318
Pendleton, Nathaniel ................................................ 425
Pendleton, Soloman ........................................... 219-233
Pennell, John ....................................................... 389
Penette, Rob. ....................................................... 389

| | |
|---|---|
| Penington, Stephen | 139 |
| Penn, William | 364-464 |
| Pennington, Neddy | 330 |
| Pennington, S. R. | 389 |
| Pennington, Thomas | 139-210-389 |
| Penny, Edward | 364 |
| Penny, Joseph | 389 |
| Pentecost, William (or Penticost) | 318-328-425-444 |
| Perkerson, Joel | 364-489 |
| Perkins, Col. | 425 |
| Perkins, Abraham | 140-273-389-425 |
| Perkins, Archibald | 337-457 |
| Perkins, Benjamin | 140-389 |
| Perkins, Elijah | 389 |
| Perkins, Elisha | 140 |
| Perkins, John | 140-234-273-323-364-389 |
| Perkins, Moses | 425-449-452 |
| Perkins, Peter | 140-273-281-389 |
| Perkins, Richard | 140-389 |
| Perkins, William | 226-389 |
| Perre, Nathaniel | 15 |
| Perrett, John, (or Perritt) | 272 |
| Perrett, Robert (or Perrit) | 142-146-148-205-272 |
| Perritt, William | 140-235-276-425 |
| Perry, Isaac | 139-273-389 |
| Perry, James | 425 |
| Perry, Joshua | 30 |
| Perry, N. | 269 |
| Perry, Nathaniel | 425 |
| Perry, Peter | 277 |
| Perryman, Harmon | 364 |
| Persett, John | 144 |
| Persons, Henry | 389-396 |
| Persons, Jones | 144-298-389 |
| Persons, Samuel | 389-396 |
| Peteet, Richard | 323 |
| Peteete, Ben. | 389 |
| Peteete, Rob. | 389 |
| Petere, Berieman | 145 |
| Peters, Edmond | 364 |
| Peters, Elijah | 144-389-444 |
| Peters, Jesse | 364-425-444-445 |
| Peters, John | 140-389 |
| Peters, Josiah | 140-389 |
| Peters, William | 364-455 |
| Petrie, Dyall | 274 |
| Petillo, John | 19-425 |

# INDEX.

Pettis, Moses .......... 364
Pttite, Benj. .......... 140
Petty, Bernard .......... 425
Petty, William .......... 140-389
Pettyjohn, Elizabeth .......... 318
Pevey, Peter .......... 274
Pew, Elijah .......... 144-389
Powell, Josiah .......... 272
Pharoah, Joshua .......... 364-425-444
Pharr, Edward .......... 122-317
Phelps, David .......... 140-201-389
Phelps, David, Sergt. .......... 140-389
Phelps, Overton, .......... 404
Phelps, Samuel .......... 389
Phelps, Thomas .......... 364
Pheny, Lackland .......... 389
Philips, Burrel .......... 140-389
Philips, David .......... 389
Philips, Dempsey .......... 140-389
Philips, George .......... 425
Philips, Hillary .......... 141-389
Philips, Joel .......... 389
Philips, John .......... 425
Philips, Mark .......... 389
Philips, Reuben .......... 389
Philips, Samuel .......... 389
Philips, William .......... 389
Philips, Zach, .......... 389
Philips, Benj. .......... 329-331
Phillips, Casander .......... 141
Phillips, Henry .......... 425
Phillips, Isaac .......... 290
Phillips, Isham .......... 141-273-290-389
Phillips, Joel .......... 141-272-425
Phillips, Joel, Jr. .......... 141
Phillips, Joel, Sr. .......... 141
Phillips, John .......... 141-272-401-425
Phillips, Josh .......... 141-273-389
Phillips, Joseph .......... 141-389-425
Phillips, Josiah .......... 141-273-389
Phillips, Levi .......... 341-425-444
Phillips, Mark .......... 141-218
Phillips, Mary .......... 339
Phillips, Overton .......... 399
Phillips, Reuben .......... 141
Phillips, Samuel .......... 142
Phillips, Thomas .......... 364

## INDEX. 603

Phillips, Wilder ........................................................ 389
Phillips, William ............................................. 141-142-199-290
Phillips, Wm, Sr. ....................................................... 141
Phillips, Zachariah ......................................... 142-199-267-425
Phillpot, Warren ....................................................... 309
Phiney, L. ............................................................... 19
Phiney, Lachlan ..................................................... 145-146
Phinisee, John ......................................................... 364
Phinizee, Francis ...................................................... 425
Phinney, Larkin ....................................................... 274
Phipps, John .......................................................... 449
Phone, Daniel ......................................................... 464
Pickard, John H. ...................................................... 364
Pickens, Capt. ........................................................ 425
Pickens, Joseph ....................................................... 425
Pickerton, John ....................................................... 401
Pierce, Abraham ....................................................... 293
Pierce, Hugh .......................................................... 364
Pierce, Seth ...................................................... 315-364
Pierce, William ....................................................... 425
Piercy, Wililam ....................................................... 425
Pierre, Nathaniel ................................................. 150-425
Pierson, John ......................................................... 401
Pigget, Susanna ....................................................... 347
Piggin, Col. .......................................................... 425
Piggot, Susanna ....................................................... 325
Pilgrim, James ........................................................ 452
Pilgrim, Michael .................................................. 425-452
Pilgrim, Thomas ................................................... 425-452
Pinder, William ....................................................... 425
Pinkerton, John ....................................................... 425
Pinkston, Daniel ...................................................... 425
Pinson, Isaac ................................................. 142-263-273-389
Pinson, Joseph ........................................................ 364
Pinson, Moses ......................................................... 328
Pinson, William ............................................... 146-309-310
Pitman, John ................................................. 140-142-146-253
Pitman, Henry ......................................................... 401
Pittman, James ........................................................ 425
Pittman, John ................................................... 248-293-390
Pittman, Philip (or Pitman) ..................................... 142-273-390
Pittman, Timothy, (or Pitman) ............................... 145-198-287-390
Pitts, James ..................................................... 425-452
Pitts, John ........................................................... 364
Pittson, William ...................................................... 390
Plaigne, D. E. L. ...................................................... 19
Plater, Benjamin ...................................................... 390

## INDEX.

Platt, Ebenezer Smith ..................... 425
Platten, Benj. ..................... 146
Pledger, Thomas ..................... 329
Plummer, Joseph (or Plumer) ..................... 121-142-390-425
Poe, Stephen ..................... 364
Polk, John ..................... 144-425
Pollard, John ..................... 364
Pollard, Robert ..................... 219-220-146-219-220
Pollard, Thomas ..................... 323
Pollard, William ..................... 401
Pollett, Richard ..................... 364-390
Pollock, Jesse ..................... 339
Polock, Cushman ..................... 425
Pool, ..................... 425
Pool, Dicey ..................... 334
Pool, Dudley ..................... 323
Pool, Elizabeth ..................... 325-347
Pool, Henry R. ..................... 364
Pool, Samuel ..................... 364-425-445
Pool, Walter ..................... 364
Pool, William ..................... 323
Pooler, Quinton ..................... 425
Pope, Burrell, (or Burwell) ..................... 211-425
Pope, Henry ..................... 425
Pope, John ..................... 323-399-403-425
Pope, Wiley, (or Wylie) ..................... 401-425
Pope, William ..................... 257-404-425
Pope, Willis ..................... 273-276
Porsten, William ..................... 399
Portens, Simon ..................... 390
Porter, B. ..................... 19-425
Porter, Benj ..................... 15-142-259-271-390-425
Porter, Elizabeth ..................... 336
Porter, John ..................... 143-364-390
Porter, Josiah ..................... 143
Porter, Oliver ..................... 425-444-459-464
Porter, R. ..................... 19-425
Porter, Robert ..................... 15-425
Porter, T. ..................... 19
Porter, Thomas ..................... 15-143-323-390-425
Porter, William ..................... 365
Porterre, Simon ..................... 145
Posey, Bennett ..................... 365
Poss, Christopher ..................... 323
Poss, Henry ..................... 365
Poss, Nicholas ..................... 399-404
Poss, Thomas ..................... 365

## INDEX. 605

Postell, John .................................................................. 365
Postwood, Benjamin ......................................................... 365
Potter, Augustin L. .......................................................... 365
Potts, James .................................................................. 365
Potts, John ...............................................142-148-232-274-331-333-390-425
Potts, Moses ...........................................................................399-403
Potts, Stephen .................................................................222-365-390
Potts, William ..................................................................317-425-445
Poullain, Anthony ............................................................. 425
Poullain, William ............................................................. 425
Pound, John ................................................................... 404
Pound, Jonathan .............................................................. 365
Pounds, John .................................................................. 399
Pounds, R. .....................................................................19-425
Pounds, Reuben ...............................................................144-273-390
Pounds, Samuel ...............................................................144-390
Powell, Ann D. ................................................................. 315
Powell, Benj. ...................................................................143-425
Powell, Cader ..................................................................143-273
Powell, Francis ................................................................365-425-444
Powell, George ................................................................143-251-254-273-390
Powell, J. ....................................................................... 19
Powell, James .................................................................15-143-390-425
Powell, John ...................................................................390-399
Powell, Johnson ............................................................... 404
Powell, Joshia, (or Joshua) ..................................................282-390
Powell, Joshua ................................................................143-396-401
Powell, Josiah ................................................................. 390
Powell, Lewis ..................................................................143-207-210-272-390-444
Powell, Moses .................................................................143-213-390
Powell, Robert ................................................................. 390
Powell, Seymore ............................................................... 365
Powell, Step ................................................................... 390
Powledge, George ............................................................. 365
Poythress, William ............................................................ 365
Prather, Daniel ................................................................ 143
Prather, Ed. ....................................................................143-226-390
Prather, Samuel ............................................................... 390
Pratt, Edward ..................................................................390-396
Pratt, John ..................................................................... 426
Pray, Job .......................................................................19-365-390-426
Preslem, Peter ................................................................. 365
Presley, John .................................................................. 365
Presley, Moses ................................................................. 365
Presnell, William .............................................................. 313
Prestley, David ................................................................ 390
Price, Charles ................................................................. 426

# Index.

Price, E. ..........426-452-457
Price, Epheaim ..........365
Price, Job ..........146-390-401
Price, John ..........143-390
Price, Lucas ..........365
Price, William ..........426
Price, Wm. T. ..........455
Prichard, Presley ..........365
Prickett, Israel ..........320
Pridgeon, David ..........365
Prince, John ..........328
Prince, Noah ..........365
Pritchett, John ..........390-396
Pritchet, Stephen ..........426-444
Pritchett, William ..........396-426
Prior, John ..........426-444
Proctor, Biddy ..........331
Proctor, Stephen ..........365
Proctor, William ..........323
Prosser, Oty ..........365
Pruett ..........426
Pruitt, John ..........390
Pruitt, Peny ..........330
Pryor, John ..........390
Pugh, Elijah ..........203
Pugh, Francis ..........114-108-215-267-390
Pugh, James ..........216-260-390-426
Pugh James, Jr. ..........272-274
Pugh, Jesse ..........211-390
Pugh, John ..........236-390
Pugh, Shadrack ..........365
Pugh, Thomas ..........390
Pulaski, Casimer, Count ..........464
Pullain, Maj ..........426
Pullen, Joseph, Sr. ..........323
Pullen Robert ..........426-444-452
Pullens, Maj. ..........399
Pulliam, Ben ..........319
Pulliam, Benj. ..........309
Pulliam, James ..........144
Pulliam, Jane ..........320
Pulliam, John ..........426
Pulliam, Joseph ..........292-390
Pulliam, Robert ..........292
Pulliam, S. ..........293
Pulliam, William ..........138-144-223-245-292-293-298-320-390
Pullin, John ..........365

| | |
|---|---|
| Pullin, Robert | 365-426 |
| Pullin, Thomas | 365 |
| Pullium | 145 |
| Pullone, Joseph | 390 |
| Pullum, Robert | 315-365 |
| Purtin, Robert | 401 |
| Purvis, William | 365 |
| Pusley, David | 145 |
| Patnal, Christopher | 140-390 |
| Putnam, Henry | 426 |

## Q

| | |
|---|---|
| Quarles, Peter | 146 |
| Quarles, Rogers | 146-390 |
| Quarterman, John, Jr. | 426 |
| Quarterman, Robert | 426 |
| Quarterman, Thomas | 426 |
| Quarterman, William | 426 |
| Queen, John | 146 |
| Queen, William | 146-293-390 |
| Querns, John (or Kearns) | 214-390 |

## R

| | |
|---|---|
| Rabenhorst, Rev. Dr. | 426 |
| Rachford, Joseph | 365 |
| Rae, Andrew | 390 |
| Rae, James | 148-152-426 |
| Rae, James & Co. | 301 |
| Rae, John | 9-14-426 |
| Rae, Robert | 15-19-426 |
| Rae, Samuel | 268 |
| Rafferty, Michael | 154-214-390 |
| Rafferty, Richard | 399-403 |
| Ragan, Brice | 365 |
| Ragan, Buckner | 365 |
| Ragan, Felix | 147-390 |
| Ragan, James | 270 |
| Ragan, John | 146-234-235-261-270390 |
| Ragan, Jonathan | 146-390 |
| Ragan, M. | 235 |
| Ragland, Benjamin | 147-390 |
| Ragland, Evan | 147-390-426 |
| Ragland, William | 328 |
| Ragsdale, Larkin | 365 |
| Rahn, Jonathan | 426-445-452-457 |

| | |
|---|---|
| Rahn, Mathew | 365-390 |
| Railey, Charles | 365 |
| Rainey, Daniel | 399-404 |
| Raines, Edmond | 326 |
| Raines, Robert | 390 |
| Rainey, Isham | 365 |
| Rainey, John | 365-390-399-404 |
| Raior, Jamet | 390 |
| Raley, Charles | 390-426 |
| Raley, Henry | 365 |
| Ramling, Thomas | 390 |
| Ramsay, Isaac Jr. | 147-390 |
| Ramsay, Isaac, Sr. | 147-390 |
| Ramsay, John | 275-390 |
| Ramsay, Randall | 390 |
| Ramsay, Randolph | 275 |
| Ramsay, William | 390 |
| Ramsdill, David | 365 |
| Ramsey, Isaac | 227 |
| Ramsey, John, (or Ramsey) | 275-390-426-445 |
| Ramsey, John, Jr. | 147-390 |
| Ramsey, John, Sr. | 147 |
| Ramsey, Randal | 207 |
| Ramsey, Randal, Jr. | 147 |
| Ramsey, Randolph | 275 |
| Ramsey, Samuel | 127-202-390 |
| Ramsey, Samuel, Jr. | 147 |
| Ramsey, Thomas | 147-262-275 |
| Ramsey, Thomas, Jr. | 147 |
| Ramsey, William | 127-147-202-209 |
| Randolph, Capt. | 241 |
| Randolph, Dorothy | 325-333-347 |
| Randolph, Robert | 365 |
| Raney, William | 154 |
| Rann, Francis | 146 |
| Ransom, Reuben | 365 |
| Rapatoe, William | 390 |
| Raspberry, Joseph | 404 |
| Rasor, Isaac | 153-390-402 |
| Ratchford, Joseph | 156 |
| Ratliff, James | 155-390 |
| Ravah, Abraham | 154-390-426 |
| Ravatt, Abraham | 292 |
| Rawling, David | 390 |
| Rawling, John W. | 390 |
| Rawlings, John | 390 |
| Rawls, Cotton | 426 |

| | |
|---|---|
| Rawls, Sally | 319 |
| Rawls, William | 365-426 |
| Rawson, Elijah | 426 |
| Ray, Lt. Col. | 426 |
| Ray, Ambrose | 148-390 |
| Ray, Andrew | 365 |
| Ray, Benj. | 147 |
| Ray, Berry | 390 |
| Ray, George | 147-390 |
| Ray, Jane | 332 |
| Ray, John | 148-323-390 |
| Ray, John, Sr. | 327 |
| Ray, Mark | 366 |
| Ray, Philip | 366 |
| Ray, William | 148-279-290-390-426-445 |
| Ray, Zach | 390 |
| Ray, Zachariah | 148 |
| Rayer, Ainos | 390 |
| Rayfield, Isaac | 390 |
| Rayfield, Spencer | 253-254 |
| Rayne, William | 390 |
| Rayzer, Isaac (or Razor) | 202-204-390 |
| Rea, James | 390 |
| Read, George | 426 |
| Read, James | 426 |
| Read, John | 148-275-390 |
| Read, William | 19-111-149-390 |
| Reagan, Darby | 449 |
| Reaves, Joseph | 366 |
| Reaves, Lucy | 320 |
| Red, James | 268-274-390-426 |
| Red, Samuel | 238-390 |
| Redd, Job | 365 |
| Redden, Scott | 426 |
| Reddick, Abram | 340 |
| Reddick, Jacob | 401 |
| Redding, Anderson | 366-426-464 |
| Redding, George | 148-243-390 |
| Redding, Rehan (or Rehun) | 366-390 |
| Reddick, Absolom | 390 |
| Reddy, James | 399 |
| Reddix, Absolom | 154-275 |
| Redwine, Jacob | 340 |
| Reed, George | 426 |
| Reed, Isaac | 426-452 |
| Reed, Jacob | 399-404-449 |
| Reed, James | 148-271 |

Reed, Joseph ... 326
Reed, Samuel ... 149-390
Reed, William ... 426
Reeden, George ... 426
Reeden, Scott ... 426
Rees, David ... 15-390-426
Rees, Hugh ... 366
Rees, Joel ... 62
Reese, Benj. ... 401
Reese, David ... 104-166
Reese, Silva ... 332
Reeves, David ... 148-390
Reeves, George ... 401
Reeves, James ... 149-390-401
Reeves, John ... 366
Reeves, Joseph ... 426
Reeves, Spencer ... 149-260-290-390
Reeves, Thomas ... 149-390
Reeves, William (or Reeve) ... 426-452
Reid, Alexander ... 319
Rench, John ... 154-285-390
Reid, Samuel ... 426-464
Reid, William ... 300-426
Rendroe, Stephen H. ... 327
Repass, Richard ... 366
Resseto, William ... 154
Reyfield, Isaac ... 154
Reyfield, J. ... 19-426
Reynolds, A. ... 19-426
Reynolds, Absalom ... 151-390
Reynolds, Ann ... 318
Reynolds, Benjamin ... 366-426
Reynolds, Coleman ... 151
Reynolds, Daniel ... 366
Reynolds, Ephraim ... 426-445
Reynolds, George ... 151
Reynolds, John ... 193
Reynolds, Joseph ... 426
Reynolds, Thomas ... 366
Rhan, Jonathan ... 335
Rhodes, John ... 149-390
Rhodes, Mathew ... 460-464
Rhodes, Richard ... 366
Rhymes, Willis ... 366
Rice, Capt. ... 426
Rice, David ... 153-390
Rice, Edward ... 309

## INDEX. 611

Rice, John ..................................................152-202-205-390
Rice, Leonard .................................................366-426-445-452
Rice, Nathan .....................................................152-390-426
Rice, John ........................................................... 366
Richards, Jacob ....................................................154-390
Richards, Jeremiah .................................................399-404
Richards, John .....................................................366-390
Richardson, Col. ...................................................... 426
Richardson, Allen ..................................................399-404
Richardson, Amos ..........................315-332-425-445-452-560-464
Richardson, Clara .................................................... 340
Richardson, Elizabeth ................................................ 336
Richardson, Enos ....................................................148-390
Richardson, Jesse .................................................... 331
Richardson, John ..................................................... 366
Richardson, Jonathan ................................................. 390
Richardson, Joseph ........................................148-207-266-390
Richardson, Marmaduke ...............................................148-390
Richardson, Timothy .................................................. 148
Richardson, Walker .........................................221-222-248-390
Richie, John ........................................................149-390
Rickerson, Ben ....................................................... 452
Rickerson, Benj ...................................................... 426
Rickerson, Marmaduke ................................................. 390
Rickerson, Timothy ................................................... 390
Rickertson, Benj ..................................................... 366
Ricketson, Jesse ................................................366-426-445
Ricketson, Jordan .................................................... 425
Ricketson, Marmaduke ................................................. 217
Ricketson, Timothy ................................................... 214
Rickey, Charles ...................................................... 455
Rickey, John ......................................................... 241
Ridden, John Scott ................................................... 426
Riddle, John ......................................................... 366
Riddle, William .....................................................148-390
Ridean, James ........................................................ 456
Riden, Capt. ......................................................... 317
Riden, Benjamin ...................................................... 390
Riden, Joseph Scott .................................................. 277
Rider, Benj .......................................................... 153
Rider, Joseph, S. .................................................... 153
Ridick, A. ........................................................... 426
Ridge, James ........................................................366-390
Ridgely, Fred ........................................................ 390
Ridgley, Frederick ................................................... 15
Riding, George ....................................................... 152
Ridley, John, Sr. .................................................... 323

## INDEX.

Ridon, Joseph S. .................................................... 390
Riggans, Darby .................................................. 148-390
Riley, James ............................................ 316-426-445-452
Riley, John ......................................................... 366
Riley, Joseph ....................................................... 153
Riley, William ................................................. 153-390
Rivers, Jarbes ...................................................... 390
Rivers, Joel ................................................... 313-314
Rivers, John ............................................ 20-366-390-426
Rivers, John, Sergt. ................................................ 426
Rivers, Joshua ..................................................... 366
Roach, Samuel ...................................................... 327
Roach, William .................................................. 15-426
Roan, James ..................................................... 148-390
Roan, Tunstall .................................................. 148-390
Robard, Thomas .................................................. 154-390
Roberson, Alex .................................................. 150-390
Roberson, David ............................................ 390-401-426
Roberson, David, Jr. ............................................... 150
Roberson, George ................................................... 150
Roberson, Hugh ..................................................... 426
Roberson, John ..................................................... 426
Roberson, Samuel ................................................ 150-391
Roberson, Sylvanus .............................................. 150-391
Roberts, Lt. Col. .................................................. 426
Roberts, Maj. ...................................................... 426
Roberts, Aaron .................................................. 319-366
Roberts, Amon ................................................... 391-401
Roberts, Daniel .................................................... 426
Roberts, Drury ..................................................... 391
Roberts, Elizabeth ................................................. 327
Roberts, Francis ................................................ 152-391
Roberts, Graystock ................................................. 366
Roberts, James ........................................ 152-203-366-391-426
Roberts, John ................... 152-199-206-211-250-275-330-366-391-426
Roberts, Jonas ............................................ 152-274-391
Roberts, Reuben ......................................... 366-426-445-452
Roberts, Richard ............................................... 420-445
Roberts, Rolin ..................................................... 366
Roberts, Thomas ......................................... 152-274-426-445-452
Robertson, Lt. ..................................................... 426
Robertson, Archibald ............................................... 150
Robertson, D. ...................................................... 211
Robertson, David ................................................... 257
Robertson, Fyer .................................................... 366
Robertson, Hugh .................................................... 391
Robertson, James ............................................... 366-426

# INDEX. 613

Robertson, Jo ............................................................... 203
Robertson, John .........................................150-366-391-445-452
Robertson, Jonathan ...................................................... 275
Robertson, Joseph ................................................150-203-391
Robertson, Robert ........................................................ 426
Robertson, Samuel ................................................... 399-404
Robertson, Thomas .................................................... 366-391
Robertson, William .................................................. **150-391**
Robertson, Zodock .................................................... 150-391
Robeson, Lt. ............................................................... 427
Robeson, David ....................................................... 391-427
Robinson, A. ........................................................... 19-427
Robinson, David .......................................................... 150
Robinson, George ......................................................... 391
Robinson, Jeriah ......................................................... 427
Robinson, John ....................................................... 401-427
Robinson, John, Jr. ...................................................... 427
Robinson, John, Sr. .................................................. 445-452
Robinson, Polly .......................................................... 337
Robinson, Randall, (or Randle) .................................. 457-460-464
Robinson, Sarah .......................................................... 317
Robison, John ............................................................ 366
Roche, Matthew ....................................................... 97-427
Roche, Matthew, Jr. ..................................................... 427
Rock, James .......................................................... 151-391
Roddenbury, George ...................................................... 366
Rodgers, Brittain ........................................................ 391
Roe, Andrew ............................................................. 275
Roe, James ........................................................... 152-391
Roe, John ................................................................ 366
Roe, Joseph A. ........................................................... 455
Roe, Walter .......................................................... 152-391
Roebrick, Benjamin ....................................................... 427
Rogan, Felix ............................................................. 150
Rogers .................................................................. 427
Rogers, Brittain ..................................................... 149-237
Rogers, Burwell ...................................................... 238-391
Rogers, Burwick ...................................................... 236-237
Rogers, Dread ..................................................... 149-279-391
Rogers, Drury ........................................................ 149-275
Rogers, Drury, Jr. ....................................................... 149
Rogers, Edward ..................................................... 149-266-391
Rogers, Jeremiah ......................................................... 149
Rogers, John ................................................. 149-150-252-287-303
Rogers, Mary ............................................................. 150
Rogers, Peleg ........................................................ 149-391
Rogers, Peter ............................................................ 295

Rogers, Reuben .................................................... 150-391
Rogers, Robert ....................................................... 366
Rogers, William .................................................... 150-264
Roland, John ......................................................... 427
Rolling, David ....................................................... 151
Rolling, John ........................................................ 151
Rolling, John, Jr. ................................................... 151
Rollins, Samuel ...................................................... 366
Roman, Bernard, (De Lisle) ........................................... 427
Rooks, John .......................................................... 366
Rooks, Mary .......................................................... 337
Rooksburg, Jacob ..................................................... 449
Roper, John ...................................................... 366-427-445
Roquemire, James ..................................................... 275
Roquemore, James ..................................................... 151
Roquemore, Peter ............................................. 151-275-391-427
Rosberry, Joseph ..................................................... 399
Rosborough, William .................................................. 294
Rose, Henry ...................................................... 151-391
Rose, John ....................................................... 152-294-391
Rose, Jose ........................................................... 391
Rose, Thomas ......................................................... 391
Rose, William ........................................................ 152
Roseborn, George ..................................................... 391
Roseboro, William, (or Roseborough) .............................. 151-391
Roseborough, George .............................................. 151-214
Roseseau, Peter ...................................................... 223
Rosetta, Tim, Dr. .................................................... 457
Rosier, Robert ....................................................... 427
Rosier, Robert, Sr. .................................................. 452
Ross, Maj. ........................................................... 427
Ross, Ann ............................................................ 144
Ross, George ......................................................... 366
Ross, Jesse .......................................................... 366
Ross, John ..................................................... 151-399-458
Ross, Mary ........................................................... 333
Ross, Thomas ......................................................... 151
Ross, Thomas, Sr. .................................................... 151
Ross, William ........................................................ 144
Rosseter, Timothy W. ................................................. 445
Rossiter, Timothy ................................................ 366-452
Rossiter, Timothy W. ................................................. 427
Rountree, Abner ...................................................... 153
Rountree, Job ........................................................ 153
Roundtree, Oliver .................................................... 391
Roundtree, Jesse ..................................................... 391
Routon, John ..................................................... 427-445

## INDEX. 615

Row, Walton ............................................................. 391
Rowby, John ............................................................ 391
Rowe, James ............................................................ 366
Rowe, Joshua (or Josua) .....................................366-427-445
Rowe, Shadwrick ....................................................... 366
Rowell, Edward ...........................................153-198-274-284-391
Rowel,l Howell ...............................................153-198-274-391
Rowell, Jesse ..................................................319-427-445-452
Rowell, John ........................................................460-465
Rowland, George ....................................................... 256
Rowland, John ......................................................153-427
Rowland, Samuel ....................................................153-391
Rowley, John ........................................................... 154
Rowzer, Edward ........................................................ 391
Roy, Isaac A. ......................................................367-391
Royal, Elizabeth ...................................................316-317
Royals, Jonathan ...................................................367-391
Royalston, John ........................................................ 367
Rozer, Amos ............................................................ 153
Rozer, Caleb .......................................................153-391
Rozer, Edmond .......................................................... 367
Rozer, Edward .......................................................... 153
Rozer, John ........................................................153-391
Rozer, Shadrack ........................................................ 153
Rucherford, John ....................................................... 460
Rucker, John .................................................316-367-391-427
Rucker, T. W. E. ....................................................... 322
Rucker, William ...............................................315-367-427-445
Rucks, William ......................................................... 367
Ruddell, Lee Ann ..................................................325-338-347
Rudolph, Capt. ......................................................... 427
Rudolph, Elizabeth ..................................................... 338
Rudolph, Michael ....................................................... 427
Rumbley, Nathaniel ..................................................... 290
Rumhey, Nathaniel ...................................................... 391
Rumsey, Richard ........................................................ 315
Runley, George ......................................................... 399
Runn, Francis .......................................................... 391
Runnells, Frederick, (or Rumals) ..................................151-275-391
Runnells, Daniel ....................................................... 427
Runnells, George ...................................................290-391
Runnells, Green ....................................................399-404
Runnells, Hamilton, (or Rumals) .......................................151-391
Runnells, William ...................................................... 367
Runnells, Coleman ...................................................... 391
Runnels, Richard ....................................................... 395
Runnels, Sallie ....................................................325-347

Sunnels, Sarah T. .................................................... 325-347
Ruroy, James ......................................................... 155
Rusheon, Specey ...................................................... 333
Rushing, Malachi .................................................. 153-391
Rushing, Matthew .............................................. 154-204-391
Rushing, Sarah ....................................................... 336
Russell, David ....................................................... 401
Russell, George ...................................................... 367
Russell, Jacob ....................................................... 219
Russell, James G. ................................................ 427-445
Russell, James Y. Sr. ................................................ 452
Russell, Joel ........................................................ 219
Russell, Thomas .................................................. 427-445
Russell, William .................................................. 154-391
Rutherford, Claiborn ................................................. 367
Rutherford, James .................................................... 367
Rutherford, John .............................................. 27-72-338-465
Rutherford, Mary ..................................................... 326
Rutherford, Samuel ................................................... 391
Rutherford, Samuel, Jr. .............................................. 154
Rutledge, John ....................................................... 367
Rutledge, William .................................................... 427
Ryals, Henry ..................................................... 367-391
Ryals, William ....................................................... 427
Ryals, Wright ........................................................ 367
Ryan, Maj. ........................................................... 399
Ryan, Daniel ......................................................... 427
Ryan, James ................................................... 154-262-275-391
Ryan, John ....................................................... 154-391
Ryan, Joseph ......................................................... 297
Ryan, Obedience ...................................................... 317
Ryan, Richard ................................................. 154-274-391
Rye, Elizabeth ....................................................... 328
Rye, Joseph .......................................................... 367
Rylee, James, Sr. ................................................ 326-331
Ryler, Barnard (or Ryley) ........................................ 153-391
Ryley, James (or Rylee) .......................................... 391-427-445
Ryley, Joseph ........................................................ 275

S

Sack, John ........................................................... 449
Saffold, Daniel ...................................................... 156
Saffold, William ..................................................... 427
Safford, Daniel .................................................. 295-391
Sager, Ann ........................................................... 331
Sailors, Christopher ................................................. 367

| | |
|---|---|
| St. John, James | 429-446 |
| St. John, James, Sr. | 330 |
| St, John, John | 399-404 |
| Salis, John | 127 |
| Sallens, Peter, Jr. | 427 |
| Sallet, John | 391 |
| Sallett, R. | 391 |
| Sallette, Robert (or Sallet) | 167-293-427 |
| Sallis, John | 391 |
| Salmon, Hesekia | 367 |
| Salmon, Lewis | 427 |
| Salsberry, Thomas | 165-391 |
| Salter, Capt. | 427 |
| Salter, Simon | 155-211 |
| Saltus, Samuel | 427 |
| Saltus, Simon | 391 |
| Samford, Reuben | 391 |
| Sammons, Nancy | 315 |
| Samples, Nathaniel | 367 |
| Sampson, Samuel | 19-427 |
| Sams, Joseph | 404 |
| Samson, William | 427 |
| Samuels, Joseph | 399 |
| Sandeford, Elmerick, (or Kelmerick) | 323-367 |
| Sandeford, John | 367 |
| Sandell, John | 399 |
| Sanders, Abraham | 155-391 |
| Sanders, David | 314 |
| Sanders, Isaac | 391 |
| Sanders, Jacob | 155-391 |
| Sanders, James | 367 |
| Sanders, Jesse | 256 |
| Sanders, John | 331 |
| Sanders, Joshua | 155-234-235-278-281 |
| Sanders, Mark | 155-235-391 |
| Sanders, Simon | 155 |
| Sanders, Thomas | 367 |
| Sandiford, John | 427 |
| Sandige, John, (or Sandiges) | 320-367 |
| Sandridge, Claborn | 315-326 |
| Sanford, Jeremiah | 367-427-465 |
| Sanford, Jesse | 311 |
| Sansford, Robert | 367 |
| Sansom, Robert | 391 |
| Sanson, James | 266 |
| Sanson, Thomas | 399-404 |
| Sanson, William | 427 |

## Index.

Sapp, D. .......... 301
Sapp, Dill .......... 155-270-278
Sapp, Elijah (or Eliger) .......... 121-155-427
Sapp, Emanuel .......... 121-155-234-391
Sapp, Henry .......... 367-391
Sapp, John .......... 121-234-278-307-391
Sapp, Levi .......... 367
Sapp, Philip .......... 301
Sapp, Shadrack .......... 367
Sapp, William .......... 121-155-277-278-309-402
Sapp, William, Jr. .......... 155
Sappington, John .......... 323-327-329
Sarcedas, Lt. .......... 427
Sardezas, David .......... 449
Sartain, William .......... 401
Sarzedas, David .......... 15-427
Satterwhite, WWilliam .......... 155-203-204-232-391
Satton, .......... 427
Saulberry, Thomas .......... 19-427
Saunders, John .......... 427
Saurlock, William .......... 445
Savage, Lovelace .......... 155-391-427
Savage, Robert .......... 401
Savage, Thomas .......... 367-427
Sawyer, John .......... 156-391
Sawyer, John James .......... 367
Saxon, Eliz. M. .......... 316
Saxon, Soloman, (or Saxton) .......... 319-427-446-452
Saxton, Nathaniel .......... 427
Scarborough, Moses .......... 401
Scheuber, Justus H. .......... 427
Schick, Fred .......... 427
Schnider, J. Gotleib .......... 427
Schnider, John .......... 427
Schnider, Jonathan .......... 427
Schuemple, Fred .......... 427
Schrump, Frederick .......... 367
Scoggin, George .......... 367
Scoggins, Benjamin .......... 367
Scott .......... 427
Scott, Abraham .......... 156-290-391
Scott, Alexander .......... 156-223-295-391-427
Scott, Allen .......... 288
Scott, Ben .......... 211
Scott, Benj .......... 156-262-275-391
Scott, Cornelius .......... 156-238-239
Scott, Frances .......... 335

| | |
|---|---|
| Scott, James | 391 |
| Scott, John | 326 |
| Scott, John, Jr. | 156 |
| Scott, John, Sr. | 156 |
| Scott, John Epps | 460 |
| Scott, Joseph | 156-290 |
| Scott, Mary | 315-320 |
| Scott, Patrick | 367 |
| Scott, Peter | 156-276 |
| Scott, Philip | 156-391 |
| Scott, Samuel | 59-427 |
| Scott, Thomas | 15-93-246-293-427 |
| Scott, Vason | 391 |
| Scott, Vawn | 367 |
| Scott, William | 19-156-220-334-391-427-446 |
| Scott, William, Capt. | 156-391 |
| Scott, William, Jr. | 156 |
| Screven, James | 15-19-367-391-427-465 |
| Screven, John | 367-391-460 |
| Scrimger, Lt. (or Seringer | 427 |
| Scrogin, Thomas | 367 |
| Scruggs, Grosse | 427 |
| Scurlock, William | 367-427 |
| Scurry, Nicholas | 289-391 |
| Seabert, John | 301 |
| Seal, Anthony | 339 |
| Seals, Elizabeth | 316 |
| Seals, William | 367 |
| Seaman, John | 295 |
| Searce, William | 399 |
| Searcy, George | 367 |
| Sebech, John | 401 |
| Sedmon, John | 391 |
| Sedmon, John, Sr. | 391 |
| Segar, George | 298-401 |
| Segar, Samuel | 301-427 |
| Seixas, Abraham | 15-427 |
| Seixas, William | 427 |
| Sellers, Soloman | 333 |
| Sells, John | 159 |
| Selman, John | 367 |
| Selman, William | 334 |
| Serbert, John | 427 |
| Sessions, John | 427-445 |
| Sessions, William | 391 |
| Sessoms, William | 156 |
| Sessoms, William, Jr. | 156 |

## Index.

Sesson, John .................................................. 318
Sessums, William ................................. 19-309-391
Sessums, William, Sr. .................................... 218
Setger, Jacob ................................................ 319
Sett, Samuel ................................................. 336
Settler, Daniel ......................................... 157-391
Setzer, Jacob ............................................... 330
Seva, John ............................................. 427-445
Sevay, George .............................................. 367
Sewell, Christopher ....................................... 367
Sewell, Joshua ............................................. 320
Sewell, William ............................................ 368
Shackelford, Maj. .................................... 319-320
Shackleford, Edmond ...................................... 337
Shackleford, John ............................. 157-391-427-445
Shackleford, Joseph ....................................... 391
Shackleford, Judith ....................................... 318
Shackleford, William ...................................... 427
Shad, Soloman .............................................. 427
Shadden, David ............................................. 391
Shaddock, Thomas (or Shaddocks) ............ 159-199-218-391
Shadereck, Thomas ......................................... 391
Shaffer, Belshazzer ....................................... 427
Shaffer, David ...................................... 158-200-391
Shaggs, Tabitha ............................................ 316
Shamson, Thomas, Sr. ..................................... 391
Shamson, Thomas, Jr. ..................................... 391
Shane, John, Sr. ........................................... 427
Shane, John, Jr. ............................................ 427
Shane, Richard ............................................. 427
Shank, John ................................................ 323
Shannon, John ........................................ 228-294
Shannon, Owen ........................................ 294-391
Shannon, Thomas ..................................... 155-158
Shannon, Thomas, Jr. ..................................... 428
Shannon, Thomas, Sr. ................................ 158-427
Share, James Boyd ......................................... 428
Shares, William ............................................ 391
Sharp ........................................................ 428
Sharp, Abrilla .............................................. 317
Sharp, B. J. ............................................. 19-428
Sharp, James D. ............................................ 428
Sharp, John .............................. 217-285-391-428-446
Sharp, John, Capt. ......................................... 428
Sharp, Joshua (or Sharpe) ............... 157-217-272-291-391
Sharpe, Michael ......................... 157-217-272-291-391
Sharpe, James Boyd ........................................ 157

## INDEX. 621

Sharpe, J. Z. ............................................................ 159
Sharpe, John ....................................................... 276-290
Sharpe, John, Sr. ................................................. 157-291
Sharty, Edward ........................................................ 368
Shartz, Edward ........................................................ 391
Shaw, Adam ................................................. 158-268-277-391
Shaw, Basil .................................................. 428-446-452
Shaw, Daniel ......................................................... 391
Shaw, David ............................................. 157-213-326-391-392
Shaw, John ................................................ 223-294-391-446
Shaw, Thomas ............................................. 158-262-263-277-391
Shaw, Thomas, Sargt. ................................................. 158
Shaw, Thomas, Jr. ................................................. 158-428
Shaw, Thomas, Sr. ..................................................... 157
Shaw, William ..................................................... 263-401
Shay, David .......................................................... 391
Sheck, Frederick ..................................................... 157
Sheehee, John, (alias John Comoer) ............................... 428-445
Sheffel, John ........................................................ 158
Sheffel, Mark .................................................... 157-160
Sheffel, Mash ........................................................ 391
Sheffel, William (or Sheffle) ................................. 158-291-391
Sheffie, William, (or Sheffield) ..................................... 391
Sheffield, John ........................................... 167-266-276-278-391
Sheffield, West ...................................................... 368
Sheftall, C. G. ....................................................... 15
Sheftall, Levi ....................................................... 428
Sheftall, M. ......................................................... 19
Sheftall, Mordecai ....................................... 158-278-391-428-465
Sheftall, S. ......................................................... 19
Sheftall, Sheftall, ......................................... 15-368-428-446-453-465
Sheke, John ......................................................... 458
Shelby, John ........................................................ 391
Sheldon, Lt. ......................................................... 428
Shellman, John ............................................... 368-401-428-446
Shelman, Michael ................................................ 401-428
Shelton, Henry ............................................... 158-276-391
Shephard, Samuel ..................................................... 336
Shepherd, Benjamin (or Shepperd) ................................ 391-428
Shepherd, Charles .................................................... 401
Shepherd, James ...................................................... 222
Shepherd, Stephen .................................................... 158
Sheppard, Maj. ....................................................... 279
Sherd, William ....................................................... 428
Sherdin, Abner (or Sheridan) ............................. 321-428-446-452
Sherod, Joseph (or Sherrard) ..................................... 401-428
Sherrell, David .................................................. 158-391

| | |
|---|---|
| Sherrer, James (or Sherrar) | 323-368-391 |
| Shick, E. | 15-428 |
| Shick, Frank | 391 |
| Shick, Frederick | 160-391 |
| Shick, John | 428 |
| Shields, Andrew | 19-157-198-391 |
| Shields, John | 157-391-428 |
| Shields, Margaret | 157 |
| Shields, William | 157-308-391-401 |
| Shields, William, Jr. | 157 |
| Shiffel, Mark | 208 |
| Shine, John | 428 |
| Shirley, James | 428-445 |
| Shirley, John | 160 |
| Shirley, Joseph | 428 |
| Shirling, Isom | 368 |
| Shoawe, Thomas, Jr. | 202 |
| Shoemack, Joseph | 368-428 |
| Shoemaker, Catherine | 325-347 |
| Shone, Adam | 213 |
| Shower, Adam (or Showers) | 368-391 |
| Shows, Adam | 428 |
| Shuffield, William | 428-452 |
| Shuffle, John | 401 |
| Shurden, Abner | 321 |
| Shurley, William | 368-391 |
| Shurr, John | 428-452 |
| Shuttleworth, Pr. | 428 |
| Shuttleworth, Reu. | 428 |
| Sick, F. | 19-428 |
| Sidman, John, Sr. | 160 |
| Sigman, John | 160-392 |
| Sikes, Dave | 392 |
| Sikes, William | 225 |
| Sillivant | 428 |
| Sills, John | 392 |
| Silvey, Stephen | 428-446 |
| Simmerlin, Dunsey | 396 |
| Simmerlin, Samuel | 396 |
| Simmeron, Burney | 401 |
| Simmons, Asa | 403 |
| Simmons, Charles | 158-233-234 |
| Simmons, J. | 239 |
| Simmons, James | 158-159-281-392-399-404 |
| Simmons, John | 277-368-392 |
| Simmons, J. M. | 218 |
| Simmons, Malbourne | 159-392 |

## INDEX. 623

Simmons, Philip .................................................. 368-392
Simmons, Richard ............................................ 159-326-392
Simmons, Sarah ...................................................... 326
Simmons, Sterns ............................................. 159-235-290
Simmons, Stevens .................................................... 392
Simmons, Thomas ............................................. 159-337-392
Simmons, William ...................................... 294-392-397-401-428
Simmons, William, Jr. ........................................... 159-392
Simmons, William, Sr. ............................................... 159
Simmonson, Isaac .................................................... 220
Simms, Abraham ..................................................... 428
Simms, James (or Sims) ......................................... 233-428
Simms, Mann (or Sims) ......................................... 159-211-392
Simms, Robert (or Sims) ....................................... 159-368-392
Simms, William (or Sims) ...................................... 159-307-392
Simons, Abraham ............................................. 323-428-465
Simmons, Benj. ...................................................... 165
Simpson, Archibald ........................................... 428-460-465
Simpson, Hester ................................................. 325-347
Simpson, James ........................................ 127-159-209-392-428
Simpson, John ............................................. 368-392-399-404
Simpson, Lucy ................................................... 325-347
Simpson, Robert .................................................. 15-428
Simpson, Samuel ............................................. 159-277-392
Simpson, Timothy (or Simson) .............................. 20-368-392-428
Sims, Anne Jane ..................................................... 320
Simms, Jeminy ....................................................... 368
Sinar, Peril ......................................................... 327
Sinclair Lt. ........................................................ 428
Singletary, Martha .................................................. 341
Singleton, Edmond (or Edmund) ................................... 428-452
Singleton, Maj. ..................................................... 428
Sindleton, Edward .............................................. 460-465
Singleton, Robert ................................................... 401
Sinquefield, Capt. .................................................. 428
Sinquefield, Aaron .................................................. 211
Sinquefield, James .................................................. 160
Sinquefield, Samuel (or Sinkfield) ............................ 160-303-392
Sinquefield, Samuel, Jr. ............................................ 160
Sinquefield, William (or Sinkfield) ............................. 397-428
Siocumb, Seth ....................................................... 165
Sisson, John ........................................................ 340
Sitton, John .................................................. 160-227-392
Sitton, Sarah ....................................................... 160
Sizemore, William .............................................. 159-226
Skehee, Daniel ................................................ 460-465
Skinner, Isaac .......................................... 127-160-202-392-428

## Index

Skinner, Urith ......................................................... 337
Slack, John ............................................................ 368
Slatin, George ......................................................... 327
Slaton, George ......................................................... 318
Slatter, Elvilah ....................................................... 333
Slaughter, George (or Sloughter) ...............................428-446-452
Slaughter, Samuel .............................................460-465
Slay, Thomas .................................................332-428-446
Sleeker, George ........................................................ 160
Slivers, Jonas ......................................................... 428
Slocomb, Elth .......................................................... 392
Slocomb, John C. ....................................................... 368
Slocumb, John Charles, (or Clocombe) ..........................428-446-452
Smalley, Michael .............................................255-277-392
Smallwood, Middleton ................................................... 240
Smart, Dill ............................................................ 392
Smart, Robert ................................................160-162-276-392
Smethers, Gabriel (or Smeether) ................................316-368
Smith, Abner ........................................................... 368
Smith, Alexander ..............................................428-446-453-457
Smith, Andrew .................................................160-428
Smith, Annie ........................................................... 322
Smith, Arthur .................................................160-309-392
Smith, Austin .................................................428-445
Smith, Ben ............................................................. 453
Smith, Benj ..................................................336-428
Smith, Burree .......................................................... 428
Smith, Burrell, (or Burrill) ..................................161-392-428
Smith, Burwell ......................................................... 428
Smith, Charles ...............................................428-452
Smith, Colesby ......................................................... 332
Smith, Corneliue .............................................160-276-277-392
Smith, David .................................................160-236
Smith, Ebenezer ..............................................160-392
Smith, Enoch .................................................428-446-452
Smith, Ezekiel ...............................................368-428-446
Smith, Francis ...............................................161-392
Smith, Gabriel ......................................................... 319
Smith, George ................................................161-392
Smith, Hardy .................................................368-428-446
Smith Hezikiah ......................................................... 321
Smith, Hill ..................................................428-446
Smith, Isaac .................................................392-428-446-460-465
Smith, Isam ............................................................ 321
Smith, Israel .......................................................... 161
Smith, Ivey ............................................................ 330
Smith, Jacob .................................................161-392

Smith, James ..................................................161-339-392
Smith, James F. ...................................................... 325
Smith, Jesse .........................................319-321-322-427-428-446
Smith, Jo. ........................................................... 278
Smith, John ...........................161-245-307-309-323-392-399-428-446
Smith, John, Jr. ...................................................... 392
Smith, John Carroway ................................................ 428
Smith, John E. ....................................................... 401
Smith, John, Sr. ..................................................161-313
Smith, Job (or Jobe) ...............................................368-404
Smith, Joseph .....................................................276-289
Smith, Joshua ....................................................... 428
Smith, Joshua, Sr. ................................................... 326
Smith, Keese, Sr. .................................................... 334
Smith, Larkin .....................................................428-446
Smith, Larkin, Sr. .................................................... 332
Smith, Lawrence ..................................................... 368
Smith, Leavin ....................................................... 368
Smith, Leonard ...................................................428-445
Smith, Mary ......................................................332-341
Smith, Mort ......................................................... 428
Smith, Moses ....................................................161-392
Smith, Nathan ...................................................161-392
Smith, Nathaniel ............................................161-210-392
Smith, Peter ........................................................ 297
Smith, Peyton ....................................................392-397
Smith, R. ..........................................................19-428
Smith, Randolph ...............................................15-162-428
Smith, Randra ...................................................... 428
Smith, Reddick ..................................................162-392
Smith, Reuben ...................................................... 368
Smith, Richard ...................................................... 368
Smith, Robert ....................................................... 368
Smith, Robert, Sr. ................................................333-338
Smith, St. Sandall ................................................... 392
Smith, Samuel .......................................162-328-392-399-428-446
Smith, Sarah ........................................................ 328
Smith, Shadrach ..................................................428-446
Smith, Simeon ...................................................... 392
Smith, Simon ................................................162-230-321-392
Smith, Susan ........................................................ 328
Smith, Thomas ...............................................162-227-392-397
Smith, Thomas, Jr. ................................................162-276
Smith, William .........214-215-291-314-319-368-392-399-404-428-446-452-457-460-465
Smithers, Andrew .................................................... 392
Smyth, Capt. ........................................................ 428

# INDEX.

Sneed, Davis ............................................................ 399
Sneed, Dudley (or Snead) ........................................159-278-392
Snef, Capt ............................................................. 428
Snell, David .......................................................160-392
Snelling, Rebecca ....................................................... 316
Snelson, James ..................................................159-392-393
Snelson, Thomas ............................................159-199-207-294
Snelson, Thomas, Sr. ................................................... 392
Snelson, William ....................................................... 368
Snelson, William, Sr. .................................................. 323
Snider, ................................................................ 428
Snider, Mr. ............................................................ 457
Snider, Christian ...................................................... 323
Snider, John Gotleib ................................................... 428
Snow, Mark ............................................................. 313
Snyder ................................................................. 428
Snyder, Godless ........................................................ 368
Snyder, Jonathan ...............................................368-429-446
Sodown, Jacob .................................................429-452-457
Solomon, Lazarus ..............................................368-460-465
Solomon, Lewis ......................................................... 401
Solter, Jacob .....................................................429-445
Southern, Gibson ....................................................... 449
Southerland, Daniel .................................................... 321
Southerland, Samuel .................................................... 321
Sowel, Zadock, (or Zadok) .................................323-368-429-445-
Spalding, James ........................................................ 465
Sparks, Jane ........................................................... 341
Sparks, Jeremiah ....................................................... 368
Sparks, John ........................................................... 465
Spray, David ........................................................... 368
Speak, Richard, Sr. ..............................................334-337
Speake, Richard ..................................................429-445
Spearman, John ......................................................... 368
Spears, John ..............................................341-429-445-452
Spears, Selah .......................................................... 341
Spears, William .......................................321-331-429-446-452-457
Speller, Martha ...................................................325-347
Spencer, Capt. ......................................................... 429
Spencer, John .......................................................... 429
Spencer, Samuel ........................................................ 429
Spencer, William ..................................................163-392
Spikes, Elias .....................................................163-392
Spikes, Josiah ......................................................... 163
Spikes, Nathan ............................................166-392-397-401
Spinks, Prestley ....................................................... 368

# INDEX. 627

Spinkston, Daniel .................................................... 401
Spivy, Mary ........................................................... 315
Spradling, James ..................................................... 162
Springer, Amee ....................................................... 334
Springer, Benj ...................................................429-446
Springer, John ....................................................... 323
Springfield, Aaron ...............................................368-392
Sprowl, Capt. ........................................................ 429
Spurlock, George ................................................397-429
Spurlock, Mary ....................................................... 162
Spurlock, Robert ..............................................162-278-392
Stacy, John .......................................................... 429
Stafford, John ....................................................... 429
Stafford, Samuel ..........................................163-216-223-294-392
Stall, John .......................................................... 165
Stall, Peter ......................................................... 165
Stallings, Col ....................................................... 429
Stallings, Ezekiel ................................16-163-165-291-392-401-429
Stallings, Frederick .......................................163-164-165-429
Stallings, Hannah .................................................... 163
Stallings, James .................................15-164-166-291-392-403-429
Stallings, Jesse ...............................................163-277-392
Stallings, John ...............................................163-166-392-399
Stallings, Mary ...................................................... 163
Stamper, Mary ........................................................ 337
Stamps, Powell ....................................................... 235
Stancel, John ........................................................ 404
Standbanks, John ..................................................... 399
Stanford, John ...............................................164-224-294-392
Standford, Joshua .................................................... 368
Standford, Samuel .................................................... 392
Standford, William ...............................................163-392
Stanley, Dempsey (or Standley) ...................................164-392
Stanley, Fred ........................................................ 392
Stanley, Shadrack ................................................165-429
Stanton, John ........................................................ 368
Stapler, John ........................................................ 163
Stapler, Ruth ........................................................ 317
Stapler, Thomas ...................................................... 368
Staples .............................................................. 429
Stapleton, George ................................................368-429
Stark, John .......................................................... 429
Starley, Jesse ....................................................... 404
Starling, William .................................................... 369
Starrell, James ...................................................... 332
Statens, Joseph ...................................................... 277
Statham, Nathaniel ................................................... 453

## INDEX.

Statham, William ..... 369
Statham, Zachariah ..... 429
Staten, Joel ..... 230
Statten, Joseph ..... 163
Steadman ..... 15
Stedham, Zach ..... 452
Stedman, James ..... 166-167-429
Stedman, John ..... 163
Stedman, St. James ..... 392
Stedom, Jero ..... 392
Steed, Edward ..... 165-392
Steed, Philip ..... 165-287-392
Steel, Henry ..... 369
Stennie, Bradley ..... 254
Stephens, Alexander ..... 460-465
Stephens, Barnett ..... 369
Stephens, Benjamin ..... 163-392-429-446
Stephens, Burwell ..... 369
Stephens, James ..... 369
Stephens, John ..... 163-204-277-429
Stephens, John W. ..... 429
Stephens, Joseph ..... 369
Stephens, Richard ..... 369-392
Stephens, Thomas ..... 163-392
Stephens, William ..... 369-399-404-429-445
Sterk, Samuel ..... 287
Stevens, John ..... 163-165 392
Stevens, Joseph ..... 429
Stevens, Reuben ..... 369-429-446
Stevens, Samuel ..... 429
Stevens, Thomas ..... 429
Stevenson ..... 429
Steward, I. ..... 264
Steward, John ..... 429
Stewart ..... 429
Stewart, Amos ..... 323-369
Stewart, Charles ..... 166-222-392-429
Stewart, Clement ..... 209-392
Stewart, Daniel ..... 392-460-465
Stewart, David ..... 369-429
Stewart, Fountain ..... 429
Stewart, Hardy ..... 369
Stewart, Henry ..... 429-453
Stewart, Isaac ..... 164-276-392
Stewart, Jacob ..... 291-392
Stewart, James ..... 163-164-166-392-429-446-449-452-457-458
Stewart, James, Sr. ..... 164

## INDEX.

Stewart, Jane ....................................................... 331
Stewart, John ........................................16-50-164-166-167-222-369-404-429
Stephens, John W. .................................................. 446
Stewart Matthew .................................................... 429
Stewart, Reuben .................................................399-404
Stewart, Robert .................................................... 167
Stewart, Samuel .................................................... 392
Stewart, Tabithy ................................................... 331
Stewart, William ...........................392-401-429-446-452-460-465
Sticken, George .................................................... 293
Stickes, George .................................................... 392
Stiff, William .............................................19-164-277-392-429
Stiles, John .................................................369-382-449
Stiles, Joseph ..................................................... 429
Stiles, Samuel ..................................................... 392
Stiles, Wiliam ..................................................... 429
Stillwell, Jacob, (or Stilwell) ...........................331-429-446
Stirk, J. .......................................................176-429
Stirk, John ........................................................ 429
Stirk, Samuel .............................................166-291-392-429
Stirley, Jesse ..................................................... 399
Stoat, David ....................................................... 164
Stobe, Joseph ...................................................... 429
Stockham, Seth .................................................166-392
Stockley, Jonathan ................................................. 327
Stocks, Bender ..................................................... 392
Stocks, Bentley, (or Stokes) ..................................165-200
Stockwell, Thomas .............................................392-397
Stokes, Bentley .................................................... 200
Stokes, Samuel ..................................................... 392
Stomers, Lewis ..................................................... 446
Stone, Charles .................................................160-225-392
Stone, Henry ....................................................... 330
Stone, Joshua ..................................................165-392
Stone, Thomas ..............................................28-166-392-429
Stone, Thompson .................................................399-404
Stone, William .................................................336-429-452
Stonecypher, Ben ................................................... 322
Stonecypher, John .........................................320-321-322-429-446-452
Stoneham, Jane ..................................................... 317
Story, Edward .................................................. 276-392
Story, Robert ...................................................... 453
Stots, John ........................................................ 392
Stots, Peter ....................................................392-397
Stout, David ....................................................307-392
Stovall, George ................................................320-369
Stovall, George, Sr. ............................................... 320

# INDEX.

Stovall, William A. .................................................. 320
Stowers, Lewis ................................................. 369-429
Stowers, Lewis, Sr. ............................................ 315-452
Strad, Priscilla .................................................... 335
Stradford, Samuel ................................................... 156
Stram, James ................................................... 164-392
Strand, Philip ...................................................... 399
Strange, Eph ....................................................... 392
Strange, John ...................................................... 369
Stranger, John ..................................................... 392
Straten, Joseph .................................................... 392
Strats, John ....................................................... 401
Strats, Peter ...................................................... 401
Stratt, Cornelius .................................................. 392
Stratt, John ....................................................... 392
Stratt, Peter ...................................................... 392
Strauther, James ................................................... 369
Strawn, Balson ................................................. 399-404
Stregel, Nicholas ............................................ 392-429-446
Strength, John ............................................... 165-276-392
Strickland, John ................................................... 369
Strickland, Sol .................................................... 392
String, John ....................................................... 392
Stringer, Celia .................................................... 339
Stringer, John ................................................ 164-309-392
Stripling, Francis, (or Stripplung) ................... 164-166-392-402-429
Strohacker, Randolph ........................................... 164-265
Strohaker, Rudolph, (or Strohecker) ............................ 239-392
Strong, Charles ..................................... 369-429-446-453-457
Strong, I. ......................................................... 429
Strong, J. ......................................................... 429
Strong, John ................................................. 164-166-298-392-404
Strong, Robert ................................................. 399-404
Strong, William ............................................... 369-401
Strother, Mr. ...................................................... 429
Strother, William .................................................. 458
Strother, William, D. .............................................. 429
Stroud, Owen ................................................... 399-404
Stroud, Philip ..................................................... 369
Stroud, Sharol ..................................................... 405
Stroud, Sherod ..................................................... 399
Stroud, Sherwood ................................................... 338
Stroud, Thomas ..................................................... 429
Stroud, William .................................................... 456
Strozier, Peter ........................................ 164-166-309-323-392
Struther, Capt. .................................................... 429
Struthers, Wililiam ................................................ 429

## INDEX. 631

| | |
|---|---|
| Stuart, Capt. | 429 |
| Stuart, Allen | 429 |
| Stuart, Charles | 209-276 |
| Stuart, Clement | 166-293 |
| Stuart, James | 276-292 |
| Stuart, John | 276-392-429 |
| Stuart, John, Col. | 392 |
| Stuart, Robert | 392 |
| Stuart, Samuel | 167 |
| Stuart, William | 164-392 |
| Stubbefield, Jeter | 429 |
| Stubblefield, Wiliam | 405 |
| Stubbs, James | 293-392 |
| Studdath, Jared | 429 |
| Studevent, Charles | 453 |
| Studman, James | 19 |
| Studstell, Houston | 369-392 |
| Studstill, John | 164-392 |
| Stugel, Nicholas | 369 |
| Stuman, John | 399 |
| Sturdivant, Charles | 429-445 |
| Sturdivant, John | 369 |
| Sturgeon, William | 255 |
| Sturgis, Andrew | 223-401 |
| Sudduth, Jared | 446-452 |
| Sullavan, Owen, Sr. | 167 |
| Sullivan, Owen | 392 |
| Sullivan, Pleasant | 429-446 |
| Sullivan, Thomas | 456 |
| Sullivan, Wiliam | 167-200-277-392 |
| Sumner, Joseph | 369 |
| Sumner, Thomas | 429 |
| Summerford, Jacob | 156-167-246-294 |
| Summerford, Jacob, Jr. | 165-392 |
| Summerford, Jacob, Sr. | 392 |
| Summerford, Richard | 167 |
| Summerlin, Demsey, (or Dimsey) | 392-429 |
| Summerlin, James | 167-393-401 |
| Summerlin, John | 392-397 |
| Summerlin, R. | 392-397 |
| Summerlin, Richard | 429 |
| Summerlin, Samuel | 392 |
| Summerlin, William | 167-295-393 |
| Summerman, Barnett | 429 |
| Summers, Dempsey | 167-393 |
| Summers, James | 402 |
| Summers, John | 167-393-429-446-452 |

Summers, Samuel ................................................. 167-393
Sumons, Charles ..................................................... 393
Sunday, Abram ....................................................... 243
Sunday, Theophilus ................................................. 242
Sures, John .......................................................... 294
Surlock, George ..................................................... 393
Sutcliffe, John ...................................................... 429
Sutherlin, Thomas .................................................. 393
Sutley, James ................................................... 429-445
Suttles, William ................................................. 335-429
Sutton, A. ....................................................... 430-452
Sutton, David ....................................................... 369
Sutton, Philip (or Suton) .................................. 277-281-393
Sutton, R. ........................................................ 19-430
Sutton, Ralph .................................................. 309-393
Sutton, Sarah ....................................................... 333
Sutton, Thomas ..................................................... 369
Sutton, William .................................................... 430
Sutty, James ........................................................ 369
Suves, John ......................................................... 393
Swain, James ................................................... 293-393
Swain, William ..................................................... 430
Swan, James ........................................................ 393
Swan, John ..................................................... 393-397
Swan, William .............................................. 369-430-446
Swan, William B. ............................................. 430-452
Swann, Elijah ....................................................... 456
Swanson, Wiliam ..................................................... 66
Sway, George ................................................. 393-430-446
Sweatman, William ............................................. 430-455
Sweet, Nathan ...................................................... 369
Swinney, Richard ................................................... 430
Switzer, Leonard .............................................. 210-393
Swords, James ............................................ 332-430-446-453
Sykes, Joshua ...................................................... 399
Sykes, William ..................................................... 393

## T

Taber, Hesekiah .................................................... 369
Tabor, Capt. ....................................................... 320
Tabor, Elizabeth ................................................... 326
Tabor, John ........................................................ 320
Tabot, Benj ........................................................ 369
Tait, Robert, L. .............................................. 430-447
Talbot, Ben ........................................................ 453
Talbot, Benj (or Falbert) ..................................... 447-493

# INDEX.

Talbot, Elizabeth .................................................. 327
Talbot, Jesse, (or Talbott) ........................................ 401
Talbot, John, (or Talbott) ............................... 302-309-393
Taliaberro, Benj ............................................. 295-324
Taliferro, Eliza A. ............................................... 338
Tallant, John ..................................................... 369
Talley, Henry ............................................... 430-447
Talley, John ................................................ 430-447
Talliferro, ....................................................... 430
Talliferro, Benj .................................................. 430
Tammons, Zipporah ................................................ 330
Tankerfield, John ............................................ 168-393
Tankersley, John ............................................. 262-286
Tankerson, John .................................................. 393
Tanner, Asa ....................................................... 430
Tanner, Benjamin .................................................. 393
Tanner, Elizabeth ................................................ 301
Tanner, Joel ............................................... 168-291-393
Tanner, Leonard .................................................. 430
Tanner, Meredith ........................................... 20-369-393
Tanner, Thomas ................................................... 335
Tanner, William .............................................. 223-393
Tanney, Michael ............................................. 430-453
Tanneyhill, John (or Tannyhill) .............................. 167-393
Tannyhill, James ................................................. 285
Tapley, Adam ..................................................... 369
Tapley, Joel ..................................................... 307
Tapley, Mark ..................................................... 307
Tarbutton, Joseph ................................................ 369
Tarling, Peter .............................................. 300-430
Tarpley, Mark .................................................... 401
Tarver, Absolem .................................................. 369
Tarvin, George ............................................. 168-393-447
Tate, Capt. ...................................................... 316
Tate, Andrew ................................................ 369-393
Tate, Eliz .................................................. 316-320
Tate, Enos ....................................................... 369
Tate, Enos, Sr. .................................................. 316
Tate, John ................................................. 321-340-447
Tate, John Jr. ................................................... 369
Tate, John, Sr. .................................................. 320
Tate, Richard ............................................... 168-393
Tate, Robert ..................................................... 401
Tate, Robert L. ............................................. 430-453
Tatnall, Joshua .................................................. 430
Tattnall, Josiah ................................................. 465
Tatum, Jesse ..................................................... 316

## INDEX.

Taunton, Henry ....... 369
Taylor, Capt. ....... 430
Taylor, Clark ....... 370
Taylor, Dempsey ....... 370
Taylor, Edmond ....... 168
Taylor, Edward ....... 370-393
Taylor, George ....... 456
Taylor, Henry ....... 168-239-393
Taylor, James ....... 168-393
Taylor, John ....... 168-201-284-393-449
Taylor, Jonah ....... 393
Taylor, Joseph Grove ....... 244-311
Taylor, Josiah ....... 168-233-393
Taylor, Nathan ....... 430
Taylor, Randoljh ....... 168-393
Taylor, Richard C. ....... 370
Taylor, Robert ....... 168-212-430-447
Taylor, Robert Jr. ....... 168-393
Taylor, Samuel ....... 430
Taylor, Theophilus ....... 370
Taylor, Thomas ....... 168-203-256-393-430
Taylor, Thomas Sr. ....... 453
Taylor, William ....... 370
Teal, Emanuel ....... 370
Teal, Lodewick ....... 370
Tearney, Gilbert ....... 449
Teasley, Sarah ....... 315
Teasley, Silas ....... 315-370-430-447
Tedder, William ....... 335
Telfair, Edward ....... 83-223-224-247-278-281-430-465
Telly, Lazarus ....... 335
Telong, Joshua ....... 405
Temple, Andrew ....... 171
Templeman, Andrew ....... 430
Templeton, A. ....... 19
Templeton, Andrew ....... 15-393
Tenn, Zechariah ....... 430
Tennell, Francis (Tannell, or Tennille) ....... 15-26-279-393-430-465
Tennell, Fred ....... 430
Tennell, S. ....... 19-430
Tenney, E. ....... 430
Tenney, Edward ....... 430-447
Tennill, Francis ....... 430
Tennill, T. ....... 19-430
Tennille, William A. ....... 455
Ternkille, Francis ....... 460
Terondel, Daniel ....... 168

| | |
|---|---|
| Terondet, Daniel | 223 |
| Terrell, | 399 |
| Terrell, David | 430 |
| Terrell, James | 370 |
| Terrell, Joseph | 399-430 |
| Terrell, Levisa | 315 |
| Terrell, Richard | 430 |
| Terrell, Richmond | 453 |
| Terrell, Robert | 393 |
| Terrell, Simon | 321 |
| Terrell, Thomas | 399 |
| Terrell, William, (or Terrill) | 281-332-430-447-453 |
| Terrill, Joseph | 316 |
| Terrill, Peter | 274 |
| Terrill, Richmond J. | 456 |
| Terrill, Thomas | 403 |
| Terry, Alexander | 399-405 |
| Terry, Hannah | 327 |
| Terry, Joseph | 456 |
| Tetard, Benjamin | 430 |
| Tettler, Daniel | 430 |
| Tettler, David | 430 |
| Thackston, James | 370 |
| Thames, Thomas | 430 |
| Tharp, Charles | 430 |
| Tharp, John | 430 |
| Tharpe, John A. | 370-393 |
| Tharpe, Joseph | 257 |
| Thaygott, John (or Thegott) | 168-393 |
| Themby, Thomas | 370 |
| Theus, Peter | 430 |
| Thigpen, Nathan | 370 |
| Thomas Capt. | 430 |
| Thomas, Lt. | 430 |
| Thomas, Abraham | 430-453 |
| Thomas, Agnes | 322 |
| Thomas, Allen | 169-393 |
| Thomas, Archibald | 370 |
| Thomas, B. | 19-393-430 |
| Thomas, Benj | 169-170 |
| Thomas, Caleb | 370-430-447 |
| Thomas, Connell | 240 |
| Thomas, Ethelred | 370-330-447 |
| Thomas, Gideon | 169-393 |
| Thomas, Gilshot | 170-393 |
| Thomas, James | 170-172-251-278-282-297 |
| Thomas, Jesse | 319 |

Thomas, Joel ........................................................... 322
Thomas, Joel T. ........................................................ 322
Thomas, John ................................................326-370-430
Thomas, Massa ......................................................... 370
Thomas, Nancy ......................................................... 321
Thomas, Peter .....................................................170-393
Thomas, Richard ....................................................... 370
Thomas, Samuel ...............................................169-307-393
Thomas, Susan ......................................................... 306
Thomas, William ......................................248-321-430-447-460-465
Thomason, William (or Thomasson) ............................430-453-457
Thombey, Thomas .................................................370-393
Thompson, Col. ........................................................ 430
Thompson, Alex ........................................................ 393
Thompson, Andrew ..................................................... 370
Thompson, Barthol ..................................................... 449
Thompson, Benjamin .........................169-236-278-291-339-393-430-447
Thompson, Benjamin, Jr. ............................................... 393
Thompson, David ....................................................... 393
Thompson, Denny ....................................................... 393
Thompson, Drury ....................................................... 169
Thompson, Frederick .............................................338-430-447
Thompson, George .................................................270-393
Thompson, Isham .................................................169-223-393
Thompson, James .........................170-171-223-246-306-403-430-447-453
Thompson, Jesse ..............................169-171-230-231-257-393
Thompson, John ...............................................169-170-315-393
Thompson, John, Capt. ................................................. 393
Thompson, Joseph .................................................393-402
Thompson, Joshua .................................................171-238
Thompson, Laban ...............................................169-121-238-393
Thompson, Lustatia .................................................... 453
Thompson, Mary ........................................................ 319
Thompson, Moses ....................................................... 370
Thompson, Peter ...............................................169-170-393
Thompson, Reuben .................................................170-393
Thompson, Richard ............................................248-399-405
Thompson, Robert ............................................170-238-309-393-430
Thompson, Samuel .................................................105-370
Thompson, Sarah ....................................................... 315
Thompson, Seth ...............................................333-430-457
Thompson, Sherod (or Sherwood) .....................317-430-453-460-465
Thompson, Will ........................................................ 202
Thompson, William  170-171-205-218-221-223-279-281-290-295-305-314-315-330-333-370
 ........................................................................ 465
Thompson, William M. .................................................. 456
Thompson, Zachariah ..............................................170-393

## INDEX.

Thorn, C. H. Maj. .................................................. 460-465
Thorn, David ............................................ 170-171-216-220-393
Thorn, William .................................................. 168-171-393
Thornbey, Thomas ..................................................... 393
Thornton, Dozier ..................................................... 316
Thornton, John ....................................................... 263
Thornton, Presley, (or Prisley) ................................ 430-447-456
Thornton, Samuel ............................................... 169-278-393
Thornton, Soloman .......................................... 169-239-275-393
Thornton, William ...................................... 168-170-299-310-393
Thorp, John .......................................................... 168
Thrasher, David ................................................... 399-405
Thrasher, George ............................................ 370-430-447-453
Threadcraft, George .................................................. 430
Threadgill, F. ........................................................ 19
Threadgill, George ................................................... 171
Threadgill, Thomas .......................................... 15-171-430-449
Threadgill, William ............................................... 19-430
Threadgirl, George ................................................... 383
Thrope, John A. ...................................................... 393
Thrower, Sarah ....................................................... 329
Thurman, Absolom ............................................... 171-279-393
Thurman, David ................................................... 401-465
Thurman, John ............................................. 171-309-393-449-457
Thurmond, Mr. ........................................................ 460
Thurmond, Mary ....................................................... 318
Tidd, David .......................................................... 370
Tierce, Brandeth ..................................................... 219
Tillary, John, Sr. ................................................... 332
Tiller, John ......................................................... 370
Tilley, William ...................................................... 370
Tindall, John .................................................... 171-223
Tindall, William ................................................. 171-393
Tindall, Joshua ...................................................... 393
Tindell, James ....................................................... 370
Tindell, Joshua ...................................................... 370
Tine, Henry .......................................................... 171
Tinney, Ed. R. ....................................................... 313
Tison, James .................................................. 313-430-447
Todd, Henry .......................................................... 430
Todd, William .................................................... 171-393
Tolar, Dempsey ....................................................... 171
Tolar, Denny ......................................................... 393
Tolbert, Benjamin .................................................... 430
Toller, John ......................................................... 305
Toller, Lewis ........................................................ 370
Tomalson, William .................................................... 335

Tomkins, William ... 172
Tomlinson, Aaron ... 370-430-457
Tomlinson, David ... 172-393-402
Tomlinson, M. W. ... 336
Tomlinson, Nathaniel ... 370
Tomme, Joseph ... 172
Tommeross, James ... 393
Tommise, Joseph ... 393
Tomson, William, Sr. ... 393
Tondee, Charles ... 370
Tondee, Peter ... 430
Tool, Jane ... 330
Toole, James ... 370-430-447
Toombs, Robert ... 399-403
Torrence, John ... 172-223-430
Towns, John ... 172-223
Townsend, Henry ... 172-252-278-393
Towsend, Thomas ... 172-279-393-447
Trainum, Elizabeth ... 335
Trammell, Dennis ... 172-393
Trammell, Peter ... 324
Trammell, William (or Trammel) ... 370-393-430-453
Trapp, John ... 172-278-393
Trapp, Joseph ... 172-174-223
Travilian, Thomas ... 46
Travis, Berry ... 309
Travis, Francis ... 172-278
Trawick, Q. ... 393
Traywick, Spencer ... 399-405
Treadwell, William ... 393
Tredwell, Stephen ... 326
Tremble, Moses ... 393
Treutlen, John Adams ... 393-403-430
Trimble, John ... 370
Trimble, Moses ... 172-212-310-401
Trimble, Virginia ... 74
Triplett, Francis (Tripplett) ... 430-465
Triplett, William ... 324-370-430-458-460
Troy, John ... 173-223-278-293
Truball, John ... 399
Truce, Benedick ... 393
Trueall, Thomas ... 399
Trueman, Garrett ... 172-212
Trueman, George ... 174
Trueman, James ... 172
Trueman, John ... 172-212-393
Truhantry, Henry ... 393
Truitt, Perual ... 324-370

## INDEX. 639

Truitt, Henry ......... 321
Trul, John ......... 393
Tubett, John ......... 332
Tucker, Capt ......... 315
Tucker, Allen ......... 335
Tucker, B. ......... 430
Tucker, George ......... 173-393-403
Tucker, Godfrey ......... 316
Tucker, Henry C. ......... 370
Tucker, Herbert ......... 431-447
Tucker, P. ......... 19
Tucker, Pascall ......... 174-393
Tucker, Robert ......... 174-278-333-393
Tucker, Thomas ......... 210-278
Turker, Thomas, Jr. ......... 174-393
Tucker, Thomas, Sr. ......... 174-393
Tucker, Woodward ......... 399
Tuggle, Charles, (or Tugle) ......... 431-447-453
Tuhantz, George ......... 393
Tulley, Henry, Sr. ......... 335
Tully, William ......... 174
Tumer, Dennis ......... 393
Tune, Henry ......... 393
Tunis, Nehemiah ......... 167-278
Tunnis, Nicholas ......... 393
Tureman, Garrett ......... 431
Tureman, George ......... 310-393
Tureman, John ......... 310
Turk, Theo ......... 276
Turke, Margaret ......... 334
Turkinett, George ......... 174
Turknett, Henry (or Turkinett) ......... 174-279-393
Turley, William ......... 393
Turman, Garrott, ......... 393
Turner, Abisha ......... 370
Turner, Asa ......... 401
Turner, B. ......... 19-401
Turner, C. ......... 19-431
Turner, Charles ......... 173-393
Turner, D. ......... 19-431
Turner, David ......... 15-173-393-431
Turner, Dennis ......... 173
Turner, G. ......... 19-431
Turner, George ......... 173-393-447-449
Turner, Henry ......... 173-298-393
Turner, James ......... 370
Turner, John ......... 173-325-330-393
Turner, Nehemiah ......... 173

# INDEX.

Turner, Peter ....................................................... 173-393
Turner, Pleasant ..................................................... 370
Turner, Reuben ...................................................... 370
Turner, Richard ..................................................... 393
Turner, Robert .............................................. 370-431-453
Turner, Robert K. .................................................... 321
Turner Sampson .................................................. 173-393
Turner, Samuel .................................................. 371-393
Turner, Thomas .............................................. 431-453-457
Turner, Thomas, Jr .................................................. 173
Turner, Thomas, Sr. .................................................. 173
Turner, William ..................................................... 431
Turvisa, Nicholas ................................................... 393
Tweddle, John ................................................... 171-403
Tweddle, John ....................................................... 223
Tweedle, John ................................................... 172-393
Twidall, J. ........................................................ 19-431
Twidwell, William ............................................... 371-393
Twiggs, John .................................................. 174-393-465
Twitty, John ........................................................ 371
Twitty, Sally ....................................................... 338
Tyler, Elizabeth .................................................... 333
Tyner, Benjamin .................................................... 431
Tyner, Joshua ...................................................... 449
Tyner, Richard .................................................. 173-393

## U

Umphlet, Asa ....................................................... 371
Underwood, Ann ..................................................... 315
Unlerwood, Archibald .......................................... 317-431-447
Underwood, Hugh .................................................... 431
Underwood, Samuel ............................................. 174-205-394
Underwood, Wayneford ............................................... 316
Underwoood, William ................................................ 371
Upchurch, Charles ............................................. 431-447-453
Upshaw, John .................................................. 431-447
Upson, George, Sen .................................................. 447
Upton, Edward ............................................ 174-223-293-303-394
Upton, George ...................................................... 431
Upton, George, Sr. .................................................. 431
Upton, Philip .................................................. 174-393
Usery, Thomas ...................................................... 333
Usher, Daniel ................................................... 371-393
Ussery, John ....................................................... 371

## V

| | |
|---|---|
| Valentonge, Moses | 431 |
| Valotten, David Moses | 431 |
| Valloten, James | 431 |
| Valsey, Joseph, Sr. | 315 |
| Vandbracle, John | 371 |
| Vance, Patrick | 174-262-394 |
| Vandegriff, Garrett, (or Vandegriffe) | 431-453 |
| Vann, Cader | 174-394 |
| Van, Edward | 291 |
| Vann, James | 175-394 |
| Van, Zant Isaac | 175-394 |
| Varnadore, Henry | 326 |
| Varner, George | 334 |
| Varner, Matthew (or Matthews) | 399-405 |
| Varner, Matthew, Sr. | 304 |
| Varner Thomas | 399 |
| Vernerm, Thomas | 405 |
| Vaughn, Felix | 371 |
| Vaughn, Jesse | 371 |
| Vaughn, William | 20-371-394 |
| Vawn, James | 394 |
| Veazey, Jacob | 175 |
| Veasey, James | 175-393 |
| Veazey, William | 68 |
| Veazey, Zebulon | 371 |
| Venable, Abraham | 431 |
| Venable John | 431 |
| Verdel, John A. | 316 |
| Verdin, Winny, | 339 |
| Vernon, Isaac | 431-447 |
| Vernon, Patsey | 329-334 |
| Vicarr, Thomas | 431 |
| Vickers, John | 394 |
| Vickers, Sarah | 341 |
| Vickers, Solomon | 19-66-175-394 |
| Vickers, Thomas | 175-260-279-394 |
| Vickers, William | 330-431-447 |
| Vickery, Joseph | 371 |
| Vickory, William | 431-447 |
| Vincent, Isaac | 371 |
| Vining, Thomas | 401 |
| Visage, Elizabeth | 333 |
| Voikle, Lewis | 371 |

## W

| | |
|---|---|
| Wade, Ann | 322 |
| Wade, David | 371 |

| | |
|---|---|
| Wade, Henry | 394-456 |
| Wade, Hezkiah | 176-394-431 |
| Wade, John | 176-322-394 |
| Wade, Moses | 325-431-447 |
| Wade, Nathaniel | 176-290-293-371 |
| Wad, Nathaniel | 176-290-293-371 |
| Wade, Nehemiah | 176-186-208-394-431 |
| Wade, Thomas | 322-399-405 |
| Wadkins, Benjamin | 371 |
| Wadsworth, James | 331 |
| Wadsworth, Thomas | 401 |
| Waggoner, John P. | 431 |
| WWaggoner, William | 324 |
| Wagner, George | 231-291 |
| Wagner, James | 291-394 |
| Wagnon, Daniel | 371 |
| Wagnon, John Michael | 177 |
| Wagnon, J. P. | 15-178-394-431 |
| Wagnon, John Peter, (or Waggoner) | 181-394-431-449 |
| Wagnon, J. W. | 49 |
| Wagnon, P. J. | 19-431 |
| Wagnon, T. | 19-431 |
| Wagnon, Thomas | 177-178-292-394 |
| Wagnon, William | 177 |
| Wagnor, John P. | 431 |
| Wagoner, George | 282-394 |
| Wagoner, Henry | 190-281-394 |
| Wagoner, James | 282 |
| Wagoner, William | 394 |
| Wagonon, George | 177 |
| Wainwright, George | 183-227 |
| Waits, Samuel | 334 |
| Waldeburg, Jacob | 431 |
| Walden, Richard | 371-394 |
| Walden, Robert | 179-394 |
| Walden, Willis | 394 |
| Waldon, John | 401 |
| Waldrepe, James | 431-447 |
| Waldroper, James | 371 |
| Waldroup, James, (or Waldroupe) | 431-453 |
| Walicon, Daniel | 394-431 |
| Walker, Capt. | 431 |
| Walker, Benjamin | 178-431 |
| Walker, Daniel, Sr. | 431-448 |
| Walker, David | 178-281 |
| Walker, David, Sr. | 431 |
| Walker, Edward | 178-394 |
| Walker, Elisha | 178 |

INDEX. 643

Walker, Elizabeth .................................................... 341
Walker, George ..........................................?............ 431
Walker, Isaac ....................................................... 178
Walker, Isaac, Jr. .................................................. 394
Walker, Isaac, Sr. .................................................. 394
Walker, James ............................................... 371-460-465
Walker, James, Sr. .................................................. 334
Walker, Jesse ....................................................... 241
Walker, John ............................................... 178-307-431
Walker, Joseph ........................................ 178-278-281-394
Walker, Samuel ................................................ 371-394
Walker, Sanders ............... 64-50-53-54-57-178-235-256-258-273-276-280-282
Walker, William ........... 52-64-178-179-224-235-241-267-310-394-403-431-460-465
Walker, Sylvanus ............................................... 178-394
Walker, Thomas ................................................. 178-431
Walker, Thomas A. ................................................... 456
Walker, William, Capt. ......................................... 179-394
Walker, William, Sr. ................................................ 179
Wall, Arthur ........................................................ 179
Wall, David .................................................... 179-394
Wall, Francis .................................................. 186-394
Wall, Henry ......................................................... 371
Wall, John ................................................ 179-282-289-394
Wall, Wial .......................................................... 371
Wall, William ....................................................... 431
Wallace, James ...................................................... 310
Wallace, John ....................................................... 431
Wallace, William ................... 177-187-204-205-218-232-233-256-265-282-394
Waller, Benjamin ............................................... 187-394
Waller, Elijah ...................................................... 371
Waller, Jeremiah .................................................... 187
Waller, Joseph ................................................. 310-394
Waller, Samuel ...................................................... 185
Waller, William ..................................................... 394
Walley, Elijah ...................................................... 320
Wallicon, Daniel .................................................... 394
Wallis, Absalom ............................................... 177-186-394
Wallis, Brittain .................................................... 394
Wallis, Cammell ..................................................... 401
Wallis, Carnhill .................................................... 431
Wallis, Chanet ...................................................... 401
Wallis, Charles ................................................ 187-394
Wallis, James ............................................. 187-394-399-405
Wallis, Jane ........................................................ 318
Wallis, Micajah .................................................... 4401
Walls, Charles ............................................. 371-431-448
Walls, Sampson ................................................ 320-371
Walsh Edward .................................................. 187-394

644    INDEX.

Walsh, Patrick ................................................. 187-394-431
Walten, Jane ....................................................... 394
Walter, Joseph ..................................................... 187
Walters, Capt. ..................................................... 319
Walters, Elijah ................................................... 319
Walters, Joseph ................................................... 431
Walters, Peter .................................................... 371
Walthour, An ...................................................... 394
Walthour, Andrew ............................................121-186-431
Walthour, Jacob ................................................... 431
Walton, Ge. ....................................................... 217
Walton, George ................10-15-19-84-178-186-203-224-304-310-394-431-465
Walton, George, Capt. ............................................. 394
Walton, George Col. ............................................... 394
Walton, George, Jr. ..........................................186-431
WWalton, George, Jr. .........................................186-431
Walton, Jesse ...............................................15-19-224-431
Walton, John ...................................................399-431
Walton, John C. ................................................... 403
Walton, Joshia .................................................... 333
Walton, Josiah .................................................... 337
Walton, Nathaniel .............................................19-431
Walton, Newell ...................................186-266-280-287-394
Walton, Peter ..................................................... 320
Walton, Robert .......................186-224-291-293-297-309-394
Walton, William ..............................................224-310-394
Wambersie, Emanuel, (or Wambessie) ............................399-403
Wanden, John, (or Wandin) .....................................394-431
Wandslow, John .................................................... 371
Wanslaw, John .................................................432-448
Ward, Benjamin ...................................187-243-394-401
Word, Bryan, (or Bryant) .......................................224-243
Ward, Charles ...................................187-243-299-394-399-403
Ward, David ....................................................... 306
Ward, Elizabeth .............................................307-333-335
Ward, Hugh ....................................................187-394
Ward, Jane ........................................................ 335
Ward, John ......................................186-187-307-394-399-405
Ward, John Peter .................................................. 431
Ward, Joseph ...................................................... 243
Ward, Nathaniel ................................................... 371
Ward, R. A. ....................................................... 322
Ward, Robert ..................................................15-431
Ward, Samuel ...................................................... 394
Ward, William ...................................431-448-449-453
Warden, J. ....................................................19-431
Warden, John ...................................................... 187
Warden, Samuel ........................186-310-325-431-448-453

| | |
|---|---|
| Warlaw, William | 431-448 |
| Wardman, Jacob | 185 |
| Ware, Arthur | 394 |
| Ware, Edward | 431-448-465 |
| Ware, Henry | 394 |
| Ware, Henry, Jr. | 189 |
| Ware, Henry Sr. | 189 |
| Ware, James | 189-394-461 |
| Ware, John | 189-215-246-394 |
| Ware, Nicholas | 189-282-394 |
| Ware, Robert | 187-431 |
| Ware, William | 189 |
| Wareman, Jacob | 394 |
| Warmack, Jesse | 431 |
| Warner, Cath | 315 |
| Warnock, Jesse | 186-394 |
| Warnock, John P. | 456 |
| Warren, Benj. | 306 |
| Warren, Daniel | 431 |
| Warren, Elias | 300 |
| Warren, George | 371 |
| Warren, Jeremiah | 186 |
| Warren, Jesse | 371 |
| Warren, John | 300-371-401-431 |
| Warren, Joshia | 431 |
| Warren, Mary | 328 |
| Warring, John | 431 |
| Warters, James | 405 |
| Warthen, William | 371 |
| Wash, E. | 19-432 |
| Wash, John Sr. | 449 |
| Wash, Patrick | 19-432 |
| Wash, William | 19-214-224-258-305-432-449 |
| Washington, Sen. | 11-13 |
| Washington, Thomas | 15-432 |
| Washington, William | 458 |
| Wasome, John Palmer (or Wasone) | 186-394 |
| Waters, Charles | 179-280-394 |
| Waters, Clement | 336 |
| Waters, David | 432-453 |
| Waters, James | 187-394 |
| Waters, Judith | 340 |
| Waters, Rawley | 186-394 |
| Watkins, James C. | 371 |
| Watkins, M. S. | 336 |
| Watkins, Robert | 399-403 |
| Watkins, Thomas | 399-403 |
| Watkins, William | 371 |

Watley, Amen ........................................................... 394
Watley, Owen ........................................................... 394
Watley, Shewood (or Sherod) ....................................... 371-394
Watley, Willis ........................................................ 371-394
Watley, Willis, Jr. .................................................. 371-394
Watley, Wooten (or Worten) ......................................... 372-394
Watley, Worthers ...................................................... 394
Watson, Benj ....................................................... 187-394
Watson, Douglass ..................................................... 432
Watson, Elevin ....................................................... 188
Watson, Elizabeth .................................................. 94-114
Watson, Ezekiel ...................................................... 372
Watson, George ................................................. 187-394-403
Watson, Isam ................................................. 329-334-529
Watson, Jacob .................................................... 188-394
Watson, John ............................................. 188-394-399-405
Watson, Joshua ....................................................... 315
Watson, Leven, (or Levin) ........................................ 394-449
Watson, Magers ....................................................... 372
Watson, Peter .................................................... 198-301
Watson, Sl. .......................................................... 432
Watson, Thomas ............................................... 188-227-394
Watson, Willis ................................................ 224-295-394
Watts, George ................................................ 187-341-394
Watts, Jacob .................................................... 187-394
Watts, John .......................................................... 401
Watty, Owen .......................................................... 372
Way, Andrew .......................................................... 432
Way, Edward ................................................... 188-394-432
Way, John ........................................................ 394-432
Way, John, Jr. ............................................... 188-224-394
Way, John, Sr. .................................................. 188-217
Way, Jose ............................................................ 394
Way, Joseph ..................................................... 188-394
Way, Moses ....................................................... 372-432
Way, Parmenus ........................................................ 432
Way, Parmenus, Sr. ................................................... 432
Way, Thomas .......................................................... 188
Way, William .................................................... 188-394
Wayne, Anthony ....................................................... 465
Wayne, George ........................................................ 372
Weatherford, James ............................................... 372-394
Weathers, Edward ............................................ 176-282-394
Weathers, Valentine ......................................... 432-448-453
Weatherton, Thomas ................................................... 372
Weaver, Mary ......................................................... 332
Webb, ................................................................ 432
Webb, Austin, ............................................ 222-224-432-448

## INDEX.

Webb, Claiborne, (or Claiborn) .................................. 313-403
Webb, Jesse ............................................. 176-234-245-295-394
Webb, John ......................................... 19-176-224-244-394-453
Webb, Levi ...................................................... 399-405
Webb, Rachel ........................................................ 318
Webb, Sion .......................................................... 401
Webb, William ............................................. 177-224-394
Webster, Abner ...................................... 176-281-324-344-394
Webster, B. ...................................................... 19-432
Webster, Benj ................................................... 176-394
Webster, James ..................................................... 394
Webster, John .............................................. 176-372-394
Webster, Jonathan .............................................. 176-394
Webster, Peter ..................................................... 176
Wbster, Samuel ................................................. 176-292
Webster, Thomas ...................................... 19-176-280-394
Webster, William ............................................. 176-235-394
Weeks, Charles ..................................................... 372
Weeks, Theophilus ................................................. 372
Welborn, Curtis ................................................ 304-394
Welborn, Curtis, Jr. ........................................... 177-394
Welborn, David ..................................................... 176
Welborn, Edward .................................................... 176
Welborn, Elias ................................................. 372-448
Welborne, Thomas ............................................. 176-311
Welbourne, Daniel .................................................. 432
Welch, Benjamin .......................................... 235-288-372-394
Welch, Caleb .................................................. 177-315-395
Welch, Ed. ......................................................... 394
Welch, Joseph ...................................................... 394
Welch, Joshua .................................................. 178-280
Welch, Joshua, Sergt. .............................................. 178
Welch, Mary, Mrs. .................................................. 178
Welch, Nicholas .............................................. 177-178-394
Welch, William ..................................................... 253
Welchel, John ...................................................... 446
Welcher, Jere ...................................................... 315
Welcher, Jeremiah .................................................. 226
Welcher, John .................................................. 178-215
Welcher, Jordan ................................................ 178-310
Welcher, William ................................................... 281
Weldon, John ....................................................... 432
Welden, Andrew ..................................................... 177
Welford, Lewis ................................................ 432-453
Wellborn, Samuel ................................................... 432
Wellborn, Elias .................................................... 432
Wellborn, Thomas ................................................... 261
Wellborne, David ................................................... 394

## INDEX.

Wells, Abigail, Mrs. ... 175
Wells, Andrew ... 175
Wells, Andrew Elton ... 372-432
Wells, Benjamin ... 175-227-258-394
Wells, Benjamin, Jr. ... 279-281
Wells, George ... 372-432
Wells, H. ... 432
Wells, Humphrey ... 175-394-432
Wells, Isaac ... 214
Wells, Jacob ... 175-394-397
Wells, Jeremiah ... 372-394
Wells, John ... 175-394
Wells, Jordan (or Jourdan) ... 174-179-394
Wells, Joseph ... 175-281-394
Wells, Leonard ... 432-453
Wells, M. ... 19-432
Wells, Masheck ... 175
Wells, Redmon ... 453
Wells, Robert ... 175-394
Welscher, Joseph ... 432
Welseley, John ... 395
Welsh, Edward ... 432
Welsh, Joshua ... 227
Welsh, Samuel ... 432
Welsher, Jere ... 394
Welsher, Jesse ... 372-395
Wence, Mary ... 340
Werber, Peter ... 208
Wereat, Benjamin ... 432
Wereat, John ... 169-186-395-432
Weritte, George ... 395
Wesson, Sarah ... 339
West, Ben ... 372-453
West, Benj, Sr. ... 432-448
West, Charles ... 432
West, James ... 177-291-395
West, John ... 177-332-395-448
West, Samuel ... 177-310-395-432
West, Samuel, Maj. ... 177
West, Sion ... 432
West, William ... 291-432
West, Willis ... 372
Westbrook, John ... 224-326
Westbrook, Stephen ... 177-212-310-395-432
Wetherclift, Thomas ... 219
Wetter, William ... 333
Wetzel, John ... 456
Whalen, Michael ... 432-447

INDEX. 649

Whaley, Zachariah ................................................. 432
Whare, William ................................................... 395
Wharton, Benj. ................................................... 372
Whateley, Edwin .................................................. 385
Whatley, Daniel ................................................432-453
Whatley, Edward .................................................. 190
Whatley, John, (or Whately) ...........................279-280-372-395
Whatley, Michael ..........................................188-279-280
Whatley, Richard ................................................. 188
Whatley, Richard, Sr. ............................................ 188
Whatley, Samuel, (Whateley or Whately) .....188-218-235-324-395-432-447-456
Whatley, Walton (or Whateley) ............................188-395-432
Whatley, Wharton ................................................. 279
Whatley, William, (or Whateley) ............................235-432
Whatley, Wilson .................................................. 432
Whealer, Thomas, Sr. ............................................. 316
Wheat, Hezekiah .............................................188-395
Wheat, John ..................................................189-395
Wheeler, Capt. ................................................... 432
Wheeler, Abner ................................................... 457
Wheeler, Amos .................................................... 372
Wheeler, Charles .............................................432-447
Wheeler, Freeman ................................................. 320
Wheeler, James ......................................372-432-448-453-460
Wheeler, Mary ................................................320-326
Wheeler, Richard ................................................. 320
Wheeler, Susanna ................................................. 327
Wheeler, Thomas .................................................. 372
Wheeler, William .....................................372-395-401-447
Wheeler, Zachariah ...................................189-215-279-395
Wheelis, Isham ................................................... 395
Wheelis, John .................................................... 283
Wheelus, Abner ................................................... 432
Whelchel, John ................................................... 432
Whelons, Lewis ...............................................372-395
Whelton, Robert .................................................. 399
Where, William .......................................189-199-206
Whiggam, John .................................................... 183
Whiggams, John ................................................... 201
Whilons, Lewis ................................................... 395
Whitaker, Daniel ................................................. 258
Whitaker, John ................................................... 190
Whitaker, Joshua ................................................. 372
Whitaker, Samuel .....................................190-280-395
Whitby, Thomas ...............................................189-216
White, Dempsey ...............................................189-395-403
White, Edward ................................................432-466
White, George ........................................302-432-453-457

White, James ............................................. 189-395-432-447-449
White, Jesse ..................................................... 432-447-453
White, John .............................. 15-19-189-250-261-267-280-395-432
White, John, Col. ......................................................... 19
White, John M. .......................................................... 316
White, John N. .......................................................... 372
White, Joseph ..................................................... 189-395-448
White, Mary ......................................................... 320-321
White, Nicholas ..................................................... 189-395
White, Richard ........................................................... 432
White, Thomas ................................. 190-241-316-395-432-460-466
White, Cincent .......................................................... 372
White, Will ............................................................. 202
White, William .......................................................... 395
White, William, Sr. ...................................................... 315
White, Zacharah ......................................................... 326
Whitecel, John .......................................................... 395
Whitehead, Amos ..................................................... 372-432
Whitehead, John ......................................................... 432
Whitemore, Howell ....................................................... 432
Whitemore, J. ........................................................ 19-432
Whitemore, Jonathan ..................................................... 395
Whiteside, John ................................................ 190-260-282-395
Whitefield, Lewis ....................................................... 372
Whiticel, John, Dr. ..................................................... 190
Whitington, Burrell ..................................................... 372
Whitley, Graner ......................................................... 466
Whitlock, Mary ...................................................... 325-347
Whitlow, Thomas ......................................................... 320
Whitmore, Howell ........................................................ 448
Whitmore, Humphrey ...................................................... 189
Whitmore, Jonathan ...................................................... 189
Whitset, John ........................................................... 190
Whitt, Rich ........................................................ 189-395
Whittaker, Capt. ........................................................ 432
Whittaker, Samuel ....................................................... 288
Whitten, Austin ......................................................... 280
Whitten, Philip ..................................................... 372-432
Whittington, Cornelius .............................................. 190-395
Whittington, Faddy .................................................. 432-453
Whittle, Boling ..................................................... 399-405
Whitton, Austin ..................................................... 190-395
Whitton, Philip ................................................. 190-395-453
Whitton, Robert ..................................................... 190-395
Wiatt, John ......................................................... 399-405
Wicker, Dr. ............................................................. 241
Wickman, John ........................................................... 179
Wideman, Adam ........................................................... 179

| | |
|---|---|
| Wiere, James | 432 |
| Wiggins, John, (or Wiggans) | 201-395 |
| Wiggins, William | 183-237-372-395 |
| Wiggins, Willam, Jr. | 183 |
| Wiggane, William, Sr. | 183 |
| Wikeman, John | 395 |
| Wilbank, Gillam | 320-372 |
| Wilborne, William | 401 |
| Wilburn, Ed | 395 |
| Wilburn, Thomas | 395 |
| Wilcason, John | 182-184 |
| Wilcher, Elizabeth | 329 |
| Wilcher, Jeremiah | 179 |
| Wilcox, Thomas | 399 |
| Wilcoxson, John | 395 |
| Wild, Charles | 281 |
| Wildair, William | 395 |
| Wilder, Maj. | 432 |
| Wilder, Cha:les | 395 |
| Wilder, Dred | 181-395 |
| Wilder, Malachi, (or Malica) | 181-310-395 |
| Wilder, Micajah | 395 |
| Wilder, Sampson | 181-282-372 |
| Wilder, Tom | 395 |
| Wilder, William | 181-267-273-281-283 |
| Wilder, Willis | 372-395-432-448 |
| Wilds, Charles | 190-198 |
| Wiley, Absolem | 372-432-447 |
| Wiley, Jane | 329 |
| Wiley, R. | 432 |
| Wiley, William | 372 |
| Wilfred, Philip, (or Wilford) | 180-395 |
| Wilhite, Lewisi | 326 |
| Wilie, William | 205 |
| Wilkerson, John | 184-395 |
| Wilkerson, William | 395 |
| Wilkes, Moses | 399-405 |
| Wilkes, Nancy | 341 |
| Wilkes, Richard | 115 |
| Wilkes, Ruth | 78 |
| Wilkins, David | 182-395 |
| Wilkins, Gabriel | 182-282-395 |
| Wilkins, John | 173-182-316-395 |
| Wilkins, William | 182-262-279-395 |
| Wilkinson, Benjamin | 432 |
| Wilkinson, Elisha | 432-448 |
| Wilkinson John | 95 |
| Wilkinson, William | 184 |

Wilkinson, Elisha ..................................................... 319
Willaby, W. ........................................................19-432
Willeby, John ........................................................ 313
Willeby, William ..................................................... 181
Willey, Richard ...................................................... 395
Wiley, Sol. .......................................................... 228
Wiley, Thomas ....................................................... 373
Williams, Lt. ........................................................ 432
Williams, Col. ....................................................... 432
Williams, Mr. ........................................................ 457
Williams, Abraham .................................................... 372
Williams, Benj. Z. ................................................... 372
Williams, Bratton, (or Britton) ...................................... 432
Williams, Burton .................................................180-395
Williams, Butler .................................................180-395
Williams, C. .......................................................19-432
Williams, Carroll ................................................180-395
Williams, Charles ...............................180-202-225-260-281-395-432
Williams, Ditha ...................................................... 340
Williams, Edward .....................................180-281-287-305-395-453
Williams, Frederick ..............................................180-395
Williams, George .............................................180-279-282-395
Williams, Henry ...................................................... 305
Williams, Isham ...................................................... 458
Williams, James ..............................................180-217-395-432
Williams, Joe ........................................................ 204
Williams, John .......180-181-218-220-253-277-280-297-324-332-395-399-401-461-466
Williams, John J. ................................................432-457
Williams, Joseph .................................................181-395
Williams, Joshua .................................................181-395
Williams, Levi ....................................................... 320
Williams, Lewis ..................................................372-456
Williams, Littleton .................................................. 181
Williams, Lucy ....................................................... 317
Williams, Maddox ..................................................... 178
Williams, Mary ....................................................... 332
Williams, Nancy ...................................................... 341
Williams, Nathan .................................................432-453
Williams, Nathl ..................................................181-395
Williams, Rebecca .................................................... 335
Williams, Robert ..................................................... 181
Williams, Samuel .................................................181-395
Williams, Soloman .................................................... 339
Williams, Thomas .................................................181-395
Williams, Thomas, Jr. ................................................ 181
Williams, William ......................................324--372-432-433-447-448-453
Williams, William, Sr. ............................................... 433
Williams, Zachariah ..............................................372-395

| | |
|---|---|
| Williamson, Adam | 372-395 |
| Williamson, Charles | 183-235-395-399 |
| Williamson, George | 183 |
| Williamson, John | 372 |
| Williamson, L. | 19-433 |
| Williamson, Littleton | 20-183-292-395 |
| Williamson, M. | 79-98-200 |
| Williamson, Micajah | 217-282-395 |
| Williamson, Micajah, Lt. Col. | 182-395 |
| Williamson, Micajah, Jr. | 183-433 |
| Williamson, Nancy | 327 |
| Williamson, Peter | 399-405 |
| Williamson, Richard | 373-395 |
| Williamson, Robert | 234-395 |
| Williamson, William | 399-405 |
| Williamson, Zachariah | 373 |
| Willie, Richard (or Willis) | 180-205 |
| Willie, Robert | 180 |
| Willie, Sarah, (or Willis) | 180 |
| Willie, William, (or Willis) | 180-205 |
| Williford, James | 399 |
| Williford, Nathan | 433-448-453 |
| Willingham, Jane | 329 |
| Willingham, Jesse | 373-399-403 |
| Willingham, John | 373-395 |
| Willis, Brittain | 179-280-395 |
| Willis, Francis | 373-395 |
| Willis, George | 291-373 |
| Willis, George, Sr. | 324 |
| Willis, Isaiah | 179-279 |
| Willis, James, (or Willie) | 180 |
| Willis, Joseph | 179-373-395 |
| Willis, Joshua | 433 |
| Willis, Leonard | 329-433 |
| Willis, Mesheck | 395-449 |
| Willis, Patty, (or Willie) | 180 |
| Willis, Robert | 395 |
| Willis, Susannah | 341 |
| Willis, William | 203-373 |
| Willmott, William | 320 |
| Willoughby, Unity | 330 |
| Willoughby, William, (or Wiloughby) | 395-447 |
| Wills, Leonard | 329-448 |
| Willy, R. Col. | 85 |
| Willy, Richard | 373 |
| Willy, Richard, Maj. | 373 |
| Wilmoth, William | 433-448 |
| Wilsherk, John | 395 |

Wilson ............................................................................ 433
Wilson, Andrew ....................................................181-395
Wilson, Ann ........................................................... 336
Wilson, Augustin ................................................433-448
Wilson, Benjamin ................................................401-433
Wilson, David ....................................................181-395
Wilson, George ..............................................335-433-448-453
Wilson, Goodwin, Jr. ................................................ 433
Wilson, H. ........................................................... 305
Wilson, Hugh ..................................................181-311-395
Wilson, James ................................................182-302-320-395
Wilson, John ............................182-213-280-395-433-448-453-460-466
Wilson, John, Lt. ..........................................182-395-433
Wilson, John, Sr. .................................................... 337
Wilson, Joshua ...................................................... 373
Wilson, Josiah ....................................................... 433
Wilson, Levin ....................................................... 208
Wilson, Perry ....................................................... 37
Wilson, Rebecca ..................................................... 331
Wilson, Robert ................................................182-395
Wilson, Samuel ....................182-198-212-228-232-279-281-292-325-395
Wilson, William ................................................318-337
Wimberly, John ...................................................... 373
Winbard, Josiah ..................................................... 373
Windfield, John ..................................................... 395
Windham, Lucy ...................................................... 326
Winfrey, J. ......................................................19-433
Winfrey, Jacob ...................................................... 280
Winfrey, Jesse ..............................................15-373-395-433
Wingfield, John, (or Winkfield) ..........................221-310-373-395
Wingate, Mary ...................................................... 332
Winn, Benj ...................................................183-395-433
Winn, John ..............................................183-395-388-405-433
Winn. John, Sr. ..................................................... 433
Winn, Joseph .................................................183-241-395
Winn, Joshua .................................................184-295-433
Winn, Peter ..................................................183-395
Winn, Richard ....................................................... 433
Winn, Robert ..................................................183-395
Winningham, Abney .................................................. 182
Winningham, John ..............................................182-395
Winskett, Samuel .................................................... 282
Winslett, Samuel .................................................... 373
Winters, Fred ....................................................... 238
Winters, James ...................................................... 399
Winters, Joseph T. .................................................. 456
Wise, Maj. .......................................................... 433
Wise, James ..................................................183-395
Wise, John ...................................................433-453

## INDEX.

Wise, Joseph .................................................. 184-224
Wise, Sherard ...................................................... 401
Wise, Sheredy ..................................................... 433
Wise, Tom ......................................................... 395
Wise, William ................................................. 184-395
Wiseman, Joseph .................................................. 233
Wisener, John (or Wisenor) ............................ 182-223-294-395
Witherington, Richard ............................................. 373
Witherspoon, Capt. ................................................ 319
Witherspoon, John ................................................. 433
Witherspoon, John, Jr. ............................................ 433
Withight, Lewis ................................................... 373
Witmoth, William .................................................. 373
Wofford, Absolem .................................................. 373
Wofford, Benjamin ................................................. 373
Wolecon, Daniel, Jr. .............................................. 184
Wofford, William .................................................. 433
Wolf, Andrew ................................................ 373-433-448
Wolfe, Andrew, Sr. ................................................ 324
Wolicon, Daniel, Sr. .............................................. 179
Womack, Abraham ................................................... 373
Womack, Jesse ................................................. 184-291
Womack, William ................................................... 373
Womley, John ...................................................... 316
Wood .......................................................... 15-433
Wool, Col. ........................................................ 461
Wood, Abraham ................................................. 184-395
Wood, Christopher ............................................. 184-395
Wood, Edward ................................................. 292-395-433
Wood, Elit, (or Ellitt) ..................................... 373-433-448
Wood, Etheldred ................................................... 399
Wood, Henry ............................................... 184-251-282-395
Wood, J. ....................................................... 19-433
Wood, J. Jr. ....................................................... 45
Wood, James ............. 19-184-239-292-337-395-397-399-401-403-433-448-457
Wood, James, Corporal ............................................. 184
Wood, James, Maj. ................................................. 457
Wood, John ................................... 310-324 373-399-405-433
Wood, Jonathan .................................................... 281
Wood, Joseph .................................................. 395-433
Wood, Joseph, Jr. ................................................. 433
Wood, Joshua ................................................. 184-395-433
Wood, Josiah ...................................................... 401
Wood, Misael .................................................. 433-448
Wood, Richard ................................................. 310-396
Wood, Sol. ........................................................ 457
Wood, Solomon ................................................. 433-466
Wood, Thomas ...................................................... 373

## INDEX.

Wood, William .................................................. 185-457
Wood, William, Sr. .................................................. 316
Woodall, Jonathan .................................................. 433
Woodall, Joseph .................................................. 373-433 448-453
Woodcock, William .................................................. 373
Woodroof, Richard .................................................. 324-333
Woodruff, James .................................................. 265
Woodruff, Joseph .................................................. 185-235-396-433
Woods, Joseph .................................................. 185
Woods, Josh .................................................. 396
Woods, Joshua .................................................. 127-202
Woods, Joshua, Jr. .................................................. 184
Woods, Joshua, Sr. .................................................. 184
Woods, Nathaniel .................................................. 279
Woods, Richard .................................................. 185-396
Woodson, William .................................................. 433
Woodsworth, Darius .................................................. 433-447
Woodsworth, Thomas .................................................. 185-396
Woolbright, Jacob .................................................. 324
Woolf, Andrew .................................................. 433-453
Wooten, —— Lt. .................................................. 433
Wooten, Jamse .................................................. 238-280-282-396
Wooten, Nathaniel .................................................. 206
Wooten, Richard .................................................. 399-403
Wooten, Robert .................................................. 185-396
Wooten, Thomas .................................................. 185-237-238-281-282-396-458
Wooten, Thomas, Lt. .................................................. 185
Wormack, Jesse .................................................. 396
Worsham, Mary .................................................. 333
Worsham, Richard .................................................. 433-447
Worth, Thomas .................................................. 396-397-433
Wourd, Benjamin .................................................. 373-396
Wourd, Ed. .................................................. 396
Wourd, Eld .................................................. 396
Wourd, Eldred .................................................. 373
Wright, —— Maj. .................................................. 433
Wright, Abendago .................................................. 185-262-275
Wright, Ambrose .................................................. 373-433
Wright, Amis .................................................. 331
Wright, Banego .................................................. 373-396
Wright, Dionyisius .................................................. 433
Wright, Elisha .................................................. 373
Wright, Francis .................................................. 318
Wright, Habakuk .................................................. 281-396
Wright, Habank .................................................. 185
Wright, Isaac .................................................. 396
Wright, Isaiah .................................................. 185-279-288

Wright, James .................................................. 185-193-260-396-458
Wright, John ............................... 185-241-280-314-324-327-373-396-433
Wright, John C. ........................................................ 433
Wright, Meshack ..................................................... 185-396
Wright, Nathan ......................................................... 458
Wright, Nathaniel ................................................... 433-448
Wright, Rebecca ........................................................ 318
Wright, Reuben ......................................................... 373
Wright, S. Capt. ........................................................ 19
Wright, Shadrack ..................................................... 10-15
Wright, Soloman ....................................................... 373
Wright, Stephen ....................................................... 396
Wright, Susan ......................................................... 337
Wright, W. G. ......................................................... 399-405
Wright, William .......................................... 102-281-396-433-447
Wyatt, John ........................................................... 373
Wyatt, Peyton ......................................................... 244-433
Wyatt, Picton ......................................................... 401
Wyche, Batt ........................................................... 186
Wyche, George ........................................... 186-242-279-290-396-433
Wyche, John ........................................................... 396
Wych, Samuel ......................................................... 186-396
Wylley, Richard, (or Wyley) ........................................... 15-433
Wylley, Thomas ........................................................ 433
Wylly, John ........................................................... 403
Wylly, Richard ........................................................ 466
Wynn, Joshua .......................................................... 396
Wynne, Peter .......................................................... 433

# Y

Yancey ................................................................ 433
Yancey, Mr. ........................................................... 457
Yancey, Lewis ......................................................... 373-433-448
Yancey, Lewis D. ...................................................... 433-453
Yankerfield, John ..................................................... 282-396
Yarbery, William ...................................................... 396
Yarborough, James ..................................................... 190-212
Yarborough, Littleton ................................................. 191-396
Yarborough, Thomas .................................................... 191-396
Yarborough, William ................................................... 191
Yarbrough, Lewis ...................................................... 373
Yarbrough, Richard .................................................... 333
Yarbrough, Thomas ..................................................... 292
Yarbrough, William .................................................... 373
Yates, Peter .......................................................... 373-396
Yates, Susannah ....................................................... 338
Yates, William ........................................................ 373

Yoes, Katherine .................................................... 315
York, James (or Yorke) ........................... 191-275-283-396-458
York, John ........................................................ 191-396
York, Nancy ....................................................... 317
York, William .............................................. 320-433-448
Youmans .......................................................... 433
Young, Daniel, Mrs. ............................................... 21
Young, Daniel ............................... 191-200-257-281-283-292-396
Young, Edward ........................ 16-191-232-233-253-274-283-396-433
Young, George .................................................... 433
Young, George, Sr. ............................................... 335
Young, Henry ................................................ 399-405
Young, Isaac ..................................................... 433
Young, Isham ........................................ 192-299-311-396
Young, Jacob ................................................ 373-433
Young, James ........................................ 192-288-396-433
Young, John ...................................................... 232
Young, John, Jr. ...................................... 192-232-396
Young, John Sr. ........................................... 192-396
Young, Jon ....................................................... 396
Young, Leonard .............................................. 399-405
Young, Rhoda ..................................................... 320
Young, Standford ............................................ 399-405
Young, William ........................... 191-218-282-293-310-433-448
Young, Wren ...................................................... 396
Youngblood, Abraham ........................................ 192-396
Youngblood, Isac ............................................ 192-396
Youngblood, James ...................................... 192-271-283-396
Youngblood, John ........................................ 192-239-299
Youngblood, John, Jr. ............................................ 396
Youngblood, John, Sr. ............................................ 396
Youngblood, Jonathan ....................................... 192-396
Youngblood, Peter .................................... 192-228-283-396
Young, Ed. ....................................................... 265
Younge, John ..................................................... 219
Younger, William ................................................. 396

Z

Zachary, Bartholomew (or Balholomew) ........................... 401-434
Zachary, James ................................................... 192
Zavadooski, Peter ................................................ 456
Zeigler, George .................................................. 401
Zettler, Nathaniel .......................................... 192-396
Zinn, Henry ...................................................... 332
Zinn, Jacob ............................................... 192-210-396
Zittraner, Ernest ................................................ 434
Zoobers, Joshua, (or Suber) ................................. 399-405
Zubley, David .................................................... 434

www.ingramcontent.com/pod-product-compliance
Lightning Source LLC
Chambersburg PA
CBHW070904300426
44113CB00008B/934